CRIMINAL LAW

ASPEN CASEBOOK SERIES

CRIMINAL LAW
Case Studies & Controversies

Third Edition

Paul H. Robinson
Colin S. Diver Professor of Law
University of Pennsylvania

Wolters Kluwer
Law & Business

Published by Wolters Kluwer Law & Business in New York.

Wolters Kluwer Law & Business serves customers worldwide with CCH,
Aspen Publishers, and Kluwer Law International products.
(www.wolterskluwerlb.com)

To contact Customer Service, e-mail customer.service@wolterskluwer.com,
call 1-800-234-1660, fax 1-800-901-9075, or mail correspondence to:

Wolters Kluwer Law & Business
Attn: Order Department
PO Box 990
Frederick, MD 21705

Printed in the United States of America.

1 2 3 4 5 6 7 8 9 0

ISBN 978-1-4548-0702-5

Library of Congress Cataloging-in-Publication Data

Robinson, Paul H., 1948-
  Criminal law : case studies & controversies / Paul H. Robinson. — 3rd ed.
    p. cm.
  Includes bibliographical references and index.
  ISBN-13: 978-1-4548-0702-5 (casebound : alk. paper)
  ISBN-10: 1-4548-0702-4 (alk. paper)
  1. Criminal law—United States. 2. Criminal law—United States—Cases. I. Title.

  KF9219.R597 2012
  345.73—dc23

                              2011047469

SFI label applies to the text stock.

About Wolters Kluwer Law & Business

Wolters Kluwer Law & Business is a leading global provider of intelligent information and digital solutions for legal and business professionals in key specialty areas, and respected educational resources for professors and law students. Wolters Kluwer Law & Business connects legal and business professionals as well as those in the education market with timely, specialized authoritative content and information-enabled solutions to support success through productivity, accuracy and mobility.

Serving customers worldwide, Wolters Kluwer Law & Business products include those under the Aspen Publishers, CCH, Kluwer Law International, Loislaw, Best Case, ftwilliam.com and MediRegs family of products.

CCH products have been a trusted resource since 1913, and are highly regarded resources for legal, securities, antitrust and trade regulation, government contracting, banking, pension, payroll, employment and labor, and healthcare reimbursement and compliance professionals.

Aspen Publishers products provide essential information to attorneys, business professionals and law students. Written by preeminent authorities, the product line offers analytical and practical information in a range of specialty practice areas from securities law and intellectual property to mergers and acquisitions and pension/benefits. Aspen's trusted legal education resources provide professors and students with high-quality, up-to-date and effective resources for successful instruction and study in all areas of the law.

Kluwer Law International products provide the global business community with reliable international legal information in English. Legal practitioners, corporate counsel and business executives around the world rely on Kluwer Law journals, looseleafs, books, and electronic products for comprehensive information in many areas of international legal practice.

Loislaw is a comprehensive online legal research product providing legal content to law firm practitioners of various specializations. Loislaw provides attorneys with the ability to quickly and efficiently find the necessary legal information they need, when and where they need it, by facilitating access to primary law as well as state-specific law, records, forms and treatises.

Best Case Solutions is the leading bankruptcy software product to the bankruptcy industry. It provides software and workflow tools to flawlessly streamline petition preparation and the electronic filing process, while timely incorporating ever-changing court requirements.

ftwilliam.com offers employee benefits professionals the highest quality plan documents (retirement, welfare and non-qualified) and government forms (5500/PBGC, 1099 and IRS) software at highly competitive prices.

MediRegs products provide integrated health care compliance content and software solutions for professionals in healthcare, higher education and life sciences, including professionals in accounting, law and consulting.

Wolters Kluwer Law & Business, a division of Wolters Kluwer, is headquartered in New York. Wolters Kluwer is a market-leading global information services company focused on professionals.

To Sarah, Sam, Mandy, Mac, Harry, and Atticus

Summary of Contents

Contents

Table of Problem Cases

Preface

Criminal law is different from your other first year courses in several ways, and *Criminal Law: Case Studies & Controversies, Third Edition* is correspondingly different from typical law school coursebooks.

The most obvious special feature of criminal law is its form. The "legality principle," as it is called, which prefers prior written liability rules, applies primarily to criminal rather than civil law for reasons discussed in Section 2. Since the 1960s, two-thirds of the states have adopted comprehensive modern criminal codes. To the extent that court opinions continue to play a role in criminal law, it is most often to interpret ambiguous provisions of codes rather than to make or alter the liability rules as earlier courts commonly did. For these reasons, criminal law typically is the course by which statutory reading and interpretation are taught in the first year of law school.

A second unique feature of criminal law arises from the fact that even laypersons have deeply felt intuitions of justice. A criminal law that seeks to influence conduct must at least take account of these feelings when setting its rules and planning its influence. To ensure that the course addresses this aspect of criminal law, the coursebook includes a series of case studies, each of which gives not only the abstract details that judges and lawyers might find important but also tells the full story of the case leading up to the offense in a way that is likely to trigger people's intuitions of justice.

A final feature of modern criminal law is its tendency toward conceptual cohesiveness and theoretical consistency. Modern American criminal codes are typically built on several interacting base principles. Understanding those underlying principles and how they are expressed through criminal law doctrine is necessary for effective lawyering in criminal law more than in many other areas of law. Accordingly, the coursebook examines not only the doctrinal rules and their major variations but also the underlying principles that drive them.

Section Template. The sections of the coursebook commonly follow a template of sorts:

Principal Case. The coursebook gives two or three pages of factual detail about the people and events leading up to the offense. (A "liability scale" at the conclusion of each case asks you to provide your own intuitive judgement about what punishment, if any, the offender deserves. The scale is aimed at putting your own analytic wheels in motion.)

The Law. The relevant statutes as they existed in the jurisdiction at the time of the offense are then presented. Where the criminal code is incomplete, as is often the case in non-modern code jurisdictions, the statutes are supplemented with one-paragraph summaries of the controlling cases that provide the legal rule missing from the statutes. Criminal law is constitutionally within the power of the states rather than the federal government. There are 52 American criminal codes. The coursebook's Principal Cases are drawn from a wide number of jurisdictions, including Alaska, Arizona, California, Georgia, Indiana, Kansas, Kentucky, Maine, Maryland, Massachusetts, Michigan, Mississippi, Nevada, New York, Tennessee, Texas, Washington, Wisconsin, Wyoming, and the federal system, as well as Israel. By the end of the course you will have a familiarity with the standard American criminal law rule as well as its major variations.

Overview Notes. Following the Principal Case and its relevant law is a treatise-like presentation of the law in that subject area, and its underlying theory. These Notes are meant to present the basics as efficiently as possible.[1] They put the Principal Case's legal rules into the larger legal picture. The Notes often will begin with a Hypothetical that will then be analyzed throughout the following text. It is worth mastering, not just reading, the Notes, for they will be central in your studying for the course.

Core Case Opinion. The treatise-like Notes commonly are a more efficient means of conveying information than reading a collection of cases, typical in other coursebooks, but cases remain important even in criminal law. And case reading remains an important lawyering skill. Each Section contains a Core Case Opinion that has special historical, theoretical, or doctrinal significance in the subject area.

Problem Cases. Following the Overview Notes and Core Case Opinion are a series of Problem Cases by which you can check your comprehension of the Overview material and that your instructor may use as a vehicle to raise additional issues. If you develop confidence in your liability analysis of all the Principal, Hypothetical, and Problem cases, you will have mastered the central elements of the course. These cases are numbered consecutively throughout the coursebook to make it easy for you to keep track of them.

Discussion Issue. Each Section ends with a Discussion Issue, usually the most important controversy in the topic area. Excerpts from the legal literature discussing each side of the issue appear in Appendix A.

Appendix A: Discussion Materials & Advanced Issues—In addition to the Discussion Issue Materials, Appendix A contains materials, such as Notes and Problem Cases, on a variety of advanced issues that your instructor may wish to cover.

Appendix B: Model Penal Code—This appendix reproduces Parts I and II of the Model Penal Code, which serves as the foundation for the majority of American criminal codes and therefore is a useful point of comparison to the statutes appearing after each Principal Case. Have a great time with these materials! Criminal law is a wonderful and special subject that has the potential to tell us much about law, our society, and ourselves.

Paul H. Robinson

December 2011

---

1. The paragraph headings in the Notes Section signal the paragraph's importance in relation to other paragraphs. In descending order of superiority the heading formats are: **HEADING, Heading,** *Heading,* Heading.

Acknowledgments

This Third Edition was made possible by the contributions of many people, in particular the research assistance of Melissa Krain of the University of Pennsylvania Law School Class of 2013. I also thank again the many people who helped in obtaining facts and documents about the stories reported here, as detailed in previous editions.* Special thanks also go to Michael Cahill, my co-author on the new Second Edition of my general treatise, Criminal Law (Aspen 2012), from which much of the Overview material contained herein has been taken.

Thanks are also in order for permission to reprint the following books and articles:

Adlestein, Alan L., Conflict of the Criminal Statute of Limitations with Lesser Offenses at Trial, 37 William & Mary Law Review, 199 (1995). Copyright 2000 by the *William and Mary Law Review.*

Ager, Susan, The Incident, Detroit Free Press Magazine 17 (March 22, 1992). Reprinted by permission of Detroit Free Press in the format Textbook via Copyright Clearance Center.

Amar, Akhil Reed, Fourth Amendment First Principles, 107 Harvard Law Review 757 (1994). Reprinted by permission of Harvard Law Review in format Textbook via Copyright Clearance Center.

American Law Institute, Model Penal Code Sections 1.01-251.4, Commentary for Sections 1.06, 2.02, 2.04, 2.06, 210.2, 210.3, 210.5, 2.13, 3.04, 3.06, 3.09(2), 5.01, and5.03. Copyright 1985 by the American Law Institute. Reprinted with permission.

Andenaes, Johannes, The General Preventive Effects of Punishment, 114 University of Pennsylvania Law Review 949, 981-983 (1966). Reprinted with permission of University of Pennsylvania Law Review in the format Textbook via Copyright Clearance Center.

Ashworth, Andrew, A New Form of Corporate Liability? Principles of Criminal Law 86-88 (Oxford Univ. Press 1991). Reprinted by permission.

Ashworth, Andrew, Criminal Attempts and the Role of Resulting Harm under the Code and in the Common Law, 19 Rutgers Law Journal 725, 750-753 (1988). Copyright © 1988, Rutgers Law Journal. Reprinted with permission.

Ashworth, Andrew J., Defences of General Application: The Law Commission's Report No. 83: (3) Entrapment, [1978] Criminal Law Review 137-138. Reprinted by permission.

---

* N.B. — The facts recounted in the principle case stories are true as best as we can determine from our research of court documents, newspaper articles, personal interviews, and other available sources. In places, we have added what we think are reasonable speculations about a person's motivation or state of mind as it appears from the person's conduct and circumstances.

Bedau, Hugo A., Arguments For and Against Capital Punishment, Encyclopedia of Crime and Justice 138-141 (S. Kadish ed., 1983). Reprinted by permission of the author.

Bedau, Hugo A., Innocence and the Death Penalty, The Death Penalty in America: Current Controversies 344, 345, 350-359 (H. Bedau ed., Oxford Univ. Press 1997). Reprinted by permission.

Bell, Jeannine, Behind This Mortal Bone: The (In)Effectiveness of Torture, Indiana Law Review (2008). Reprinted by permission of the author and Indiana Law Review.

Bryden, David P., Redefining Rape, 3 Buffalo Criminal Law Review 317, 373-385 (2000). Reprinted by permission of University of California Press Journals.

Callahan, Lisa, et al., Insanity Defense Reform in the United States—Post-Hinckley, 11 Mental and Physical Disability Law Reporter 54-60 (1987). Reprinted by permission of Mental and Physical Disability Law Reporter in format Textbook via Copyright Clearance Center.

Coffee, John, Corporate Criminal Responsibility, 1 Encyclopedia of Crime and Justice 253, 256-261 (S. Kadish ed., Oxford Univ. Press 1983). Reprinted by permission of the author.

Crocker, Lawrence, Justice in Criminal Liability: Decriminalizing Harmless Attempts, 53 Ohio State Law Journal 1057, 1069-1072 (1992). Originally published in 53 Ohio St. Law Journal 1057, 1069-1072 (1972). Reprinted by permission of the author.

Crump, David & Susan Waite Crump, In Defense of Felony Murder, 8 Harvard Journal of Law and Public Policy 359, 362-364, 367-371 (1985). Reprinted by permission of Harvard Journal of Law & Public Policy in format Textbook via Copyright Clearance Center.

Delgado, Richard, Ascription of Criminal States of Mind: Toward a Defense Theory for the Coercively Persuaded ("Brainwashed") Defendant, 63 Minnesota Law Review 1, 1-11 (1978). Reprinted by permission of Minnesota Law Review.

Dershowitz, Alan, Should the Ticking Bomb Terrorist Be Tortured?, Why Terrorism Works: Understanding the Threat, Responding to the Challenge (Yale Univ. Press 2002). Copyright 2002 Alan M. Dershowitz. Reprinted by permission of Yale Univ. Press.

Dressler, Joshua, Professor Delgado's "Brainwashing" Defense: Courting a Determinist Legal System, 63 Minnesota Law Review 335, 335-336, 339-340, 351-360 (1979). Reprinted with permission of Minnesota Law Review.

Dressler, Joshua, Some Brief Thoughts (Mostly Negative) About "Bad Samaritan" Laws, 40 Santa Clara Law Review 971-975, 980-988 (2000). Reprinted by permission.

Dressler, Joshua, Where We Have Been, and Where We Might be Going: Some Cautionary Reflections on Rape Law Reform, 46 Cleveland State Law Review 409, 430-439 (1998). Reprinted by permission.

English, Jodie, The Light Between Twilight and Dusk: Federal Criminal Law and the Volitional Insanity Defense, 40 Hastings Law Journal 1, 45-52 (1988). Reprinted with permission of the Hastings Law Journal.

Epps, Garrett, Any Which Way But Loose: Interpretive Strategies and Attitudes Toward Violence in the Evolution of the Anglo-American "Retreat Rule," 55 Law and Contemporary Problems 303-305, 327-331 (1992). Reprinted by permission of the author.

Erb, Todd D., A Case for Strengthening School District Jurisdiction to Punish Off-Campus Incidents of Cyberbullying, 40 Arizona State Law Journal 257 (2008). Reprinted by permission of the author.

Estrich, Susan, Rape, 95 Yale Law Journal 1087, 1096-1097, 1098-1101, 1102-1105 (1986). Reprinted by permission of Yale Law Journal.

Fischel, Daniel R. and Alan O. Sykes, Corporate Crime, 25 Journal of Legal Studies 320 (1996). Reprinted by permission of The University of Chicago Press.

Fletcher, George P., A Crime of Self Defense: Bernhard Goetz and the Law on Trial 64-67 (Free Press 1988). Reprinted by permission.

Fletcher, George P., Arguments for Strict Liability: Mistakes of Law, Rethinking Criminal Law 731-736 (Oxford Univ. Press 1978). Reprinted by permission.

Fletcher, George P., The Theory of Criminal Negligence: A Comparative Analysis, 119 University of Pennsylvania Law Review 401, 426-427, 429-430, 433-434 (1971). Reprinted by permission of University of Pennsylvania Law Review in the format Textbook via Copyright Clearance Center.

Friedman, Lawrence, In Defense of Corporate Criminal Liability, 23 Harvard Journal of Law & Public Policy 833 (1999-2000). Reprinted by permission of Harvard Journal of Law & Public Policy in format Textbook via Copyright Clearance Center.

Gellman, Susan, Hate Crime Laws Are Thought Crime Laws, 1992/1993 Annual Survey of American Law 509, 509-513, 518-520, 528-531. Reprinted by permission of New York University.

Gordon, Margaret T., & Stephanie Riger, The Female Fear: The Social Cost of Rape 2, 26-28, 32-36 (Univ. of Illinois Press 1991). Reprinted by permission.

Gorsuch, Neil M., The Right to Assisted Suicide and Euthanasia, 23 Harvard Journal of Law & Public Policy 599 (2000). Reprinted by permission of Harvard Journal of Law & Public Policy in format Textbook via Copyright Clearance Center.

Hardaway, Robert M. et al., The Right to Die and the Ninth Amendment: Compassion and Dying After Glucksberg and Vacco, 7 George Mason Law Review 313 (1999). Reprinted by permission of George Mason Law Review.

Hart, H.L.A., Punishment and Responsibility 153-154 (1968). Reprinted with permission of Clarendon Press (imprint of Oxford University Press).

Harvard Law Review, Developments in the Law: Criminal Conspiracy, 72 Harvard Law Review 920, 922-925 (1959). Reprinted by permission of Harvard Law Review in format Textbook via Copyright Clearance Center.

Henderson, Lynne N., Review Essay: What Makes Rape a Crime? Review of Estrich, Real Rape, 3 Berkeley Woman's Law Journal 193, 211-219 (1987-88). Reprinted by permission of Berkeley Woman's Law Journal in the format Textbook via Copyright Clearance Center.

Jacobs, James B., & Kimberly Potter, Hate Crime Laws, Hate Crimes: Criminal Law & Identity Politics 29-44 (Oxford Univ. Press 1998). Reprinted by permission.

Kahan, Dan M., Ignorance of the Law Is an Excuse — But Only for the Virtuous, 96 Michigan Law Review 127, 131, 133, 141-142 (1997). Reprinted by permission of the author.

Keiter, Mitchell, Just Say No Excuse: The Rise and Fall of the Intoxication Defense, 87 Journal of Criminal Law and Criminology 482, 482-483, 518-519 (1997). Reprinted with permission of the Journal of Criminal Law and Criminology.

LaFave, Wayne R., Rape — Overview; Act and Mental State Substantive Criminal Law §7.18 (2d ed. 2003). Reprinted by permission of West, a Thomson Reuters Business.

LaFave, Wayne, Jerold Israel & Nancy King, An Overview of the Criminal Justice Process: The Steps in the Process, Criminal Procedure §1.3 (3d ed. 2000). Reprinted with permission of West, a Thomson Reuters Business.

La Fond, John Q., The Case for Liberalizing the Use of Deadly Force in Self-Defense, 6 University of Puget Sound Law Review 237, 237-238, 274-284 (1983). Reprinted by permission.

Lawrence, Frederick M. Reprinted by permission of the publisher from Punishing Hate: Bias Crimes Under American Law by Frederick M. Lawrence, pp 58-63, 161-163, 167-169, Cambridge, Mass.: Harvard University Press, Copyright © 1999 by the President and Fellows of Harvard College.

Levenson, Laurie L., Good Faith Defenses: Reshaping Strict Liability Crimes, 78 Cornell Law Review 401, 419-427 (1993). Reprinted by permission.

Levin, Michael, The Case for Torture, Newsweek (1982). From Newsweek June 7, 1982 © 1982 The Newsweek/Daily Beast company LLC. All rights reserved. Used by permission and protected by the Copyright Laws of the United States. The printing, copying, redistribution, or retransmission of the Material without express written permission is prohibited.

Levmore, Saul & Ariel Porat, Bargaining with Double Jeopardy, Journal of Legal Studies (2011). Reprinted by permission of The University of Chicago Press.

Luban, David, Liberalism, Torture, and the Ticking Bomb, 91 Virginia Law Review 1425 (October 2005). Reprinted by permission of Virginia Law Review in the format Textbook via Copyright Clearance Center.

Luna, Erik, In Support of Restorative Justice, Criminal Law Conversations 586-595 (Oxford Univ. Press 2009). Reprinted by permission.

Lynch, Jennifer, Identity Theft in Cyberspace: Crime Control Methods and Their Effectiveness in Combating Phishing Attacks, 20 Berkeley Technology Law Journal 259 (2005). Reprinted by permission of Berkeley Technology Law Journal in the format Textbook via Copyright Clearance Center.

MacKinnon, Catharine, A Rally Against Rape, Feminism Unmodified 81-83 (1987). Reprinted by permission of the author.

McCurdy, Jessica L., Computer Crimes, 47 American Criminal Law Review 287 (Spring 2010). Reprinted by permission of the author and the American Criminal Law Review.

Moore, Michael S., The Independent Moral Significance of Wrongdoing, 5 Journal of Contemporary Legal Issues 237, 253-258 (1994). Reprinted by permission of Journal of Contemporary Legal Issues.

Morse, Stephen J., Fear of Danger, Flight From Culpability, 4 Psychology, Public Policy, and the Law 250, 253-256 (1998). Reprinted by permission of the American Psychological Association.

New York Times, 37 Who Saw Murder Didn't Call Police. From the New York Times, March 27, 1964 © 1964 The New York Times. All rights reserved. Used by permission and protected by the Copyright Laws of the United States. The printing, copying, redistribution, or retransmission of the Material without express written permission is prohibited.

Parker, Lori J., Validity, Constructions, and Application of Federal Enactments Proscribing Obscenity and Child Pornography or Access Thereto on the Internet, 7 American Law Reports Federal 2d 1 (2005). Reprinted with permission from A.L.R., © 2005-2011 Thomson Reuters.

Pillsbury, Samuel H., Crimes of Indifference, 49 Rutgers Law Review 105-106, 150-151 (1996). Reprinted by permission.

Remick, Lani Anne, Read Her Lips: An Argument for a Verbal Consent Standard in Rape, 141 University of Pennsylvania Law Review 1103-1105 (1993). Reprinted with permission of University of Pennsylvania Law Review in format Textbook via Copyright Clearance Center.

Rudstein, David S., Retrying the Acquitted in England, Part I: The Exception to the Rule Against Double Jeopardy for "New and Compelling Evidence," 8 San Diego International Law Journal 387 (2007). Reprinted by permission of San Diego International Law Journal.

Sayre, Francis B., Criminal Attempts, 41 Harvard Law Review 821, 845-847 (1928). Reprinted with permission of the Harvard Law Review.

Schulhofer, Stephen J., Rape: Legal Aspects, Encyclopedia of Crime and Justice 1306-1309 (2d ed., Cengage 2002). From *Encyclopedia of Crime & Justice*, 2E. © 2001 Gale, a part of Cengage Learning, Inc. Reproduced by permission. www.cengage.com/permissions

Seidman, Louis Michael, The Supreme Court, Entrapment, and Our Criminal Justice Dilemma, 5 The Supreme Court Review 111, 127-133, 135-137, 139-142, 145-146 (1981). Reprinted by permission of The University of Chicago Press.

Simpson, Gerry J., Didactic and Dissident Histories in War Crimes Trials, 60 Albany Law Review 801, 801-803, 804, 814-819 (1997). Reprinted by permission.

Steiker, Carol S., Second Thoughts about First Principles, 107 Harvard Law Review 820 (1994). Reprinted by permission of Harvard Law Review in format Textbook via Copyright Clearance Center.

Sunstein, Cass R., Why They Hate Us: The Role of Social Dynamics, 25 Harvard Journal of Law & Public Policy 429, 429-433, 439-440 (2002). Reprinted by permission of Harvard Journal of Law & Public Policy in format Textbook via Copyright Clearance Center.

Tennenbaum, Abraham N., The Influence of the Garner Decision on Police Use of Deadly Force, 85 Journal of Criminal Law & Criminology 241-242, 257-260 (1994). Reprinted with permission of the Journal of Criminal Law & Criminology.

van den Haag, Ernest, Punishing Criminals 219-220 (1975). Reprinted with permission of Perseus Books Group in the format Textbook via Copyright Clearance Center.

von Hirsch, Andrew, Incapacitation in Principled Sentencing 101-108 (von Hirsch & Ashworth eds., 1992). Reprinted by permission of the author.

Wechsler, Herbert & Jerome Michael, The Rationale of the Law of Homicide, 37 Columbia Law Review 701, 736 (1937). Reprinted with permission of Columbia Law Review in the format Textbook via Copyright Clearance Center.

Weisberg, Robert, Deregulating Death, The Supreme Court Review 303, 386-387 (1983). Reprinted by permission of The University of Chicago Press.

White, Thomas W., Reliance on Apparent Authority as a Defense to Criminal Prosecutions, 77 Columbia Law Review 775, 779, 801 (1977). Reprinted with permission of Columbia Law Review in the format Textbook via Copyright Clearance Center.

Williams, Gregory Howard, Controlling the Use of Non Deadly Force: Policy and Practice, 10 Harvard BlackLetter Law Journal 79, 79-80, 82-93, 95-96, 102-104 (1993). Reprinted by permission of Harvard BlackLetter Law Journal in the format Textbook via Copyright Clearance Center.

Wilson, James Q., Thinking About Crime 145-158 (Vintage rev. ed. 1983). Reprinted by permission of Vintage in the format Textbook via Copyright Clearance Center.

Yeager, Daniel B., A Radical Community of Aid: A Rejoinder to Opponents of Affirmative Duties to Help Strangers, 71 Washington University Law Quarterly 1-8, 13-38 (1993). Reprinted by permission.

Thanks are also in order for permission to reprint the following photographs and illustrations:

Cash case, Iverson on surveillance tape. Photograph. Reproduced with permission of the Las Vegas Sun.

Cash case, Primadonna Resort. Photograph. Reproduced with permission of Frank Reynolds, www.vegasgallery.com

Cash case, surveillance tape of Strohmeyer. Photograph. Reproduced with permission of the Las Vegas Sun.

Davidson case, Christopher Wilson. Photograph. Kansas State Collegian. Reproduced with permission of James Hurla.

Davidson case, Davidsons' home with 6-foot fence. Photograph. Kansas State Collegian. Reproduced with permission of James Hurla.

Davidson case, Guard Dog Training Center. Photograph. Reproduced with permission.

Davidson case, neighbors visiting site of mauling. Photograph. Kansas State Collegian. Reproduced with permission of James Hurla.

DeLorean case, DA's evidence. Photograph. Reproduced with permission of Associated Press.

Delorean case, DeLorean at bankruptcy conference. Photograph. Bettmann/CORBIS. Reproduced with permission of Corbis.

DeLorean case, DeLorean seated inside car. Photograph. © Hulton-Deutsch Collection/CORBIS. Reproduced with permission of Corbis.

DeLorean case, John DeLorean in his Manhattan office. Photograph. Reproduced with permission of Anthony Howarth.

Ford Motor Company case, accident scene. Photograph. Reproduced with permission from Reckless Homicide, And Books.

Ford Motor Company case, Donna Ulrich. Photograph. Reproduced with permission from Reckless Homicide, And Books.

Ford Motor Company case, Henry Ford II announcing restructuring. Photograph. Bettmann/CORBIS. Reproduced with permission of Corbis.

Ford Motor Company case, Judy Ulrich. Photograph. Reproduced with permission from Reckless Homicide, And Books.

Ford Motor Company case, Lyn Ulrich. Photograph. Reproduced with permission from Reckless Homicide, And Books.

Ford Motor Company case, 1973 Ford Pinto. Photograph provided by fordpinto.com. Reproduced with permission of fordpinto.com.

Ford Motor Company case, Prosecutor Mike Consentino. Photograph. Reproduced with permission from Reckless Homicide, And Books.

Ford Motor Company case, van and Pinto. Photograph. Reproduced with permission from Reckless Homicide, And Books.

Garnett case, Frazier's house. Photograph. Reproduced with permission of Catherine McAlpine.

Goetz case, Bernhard Goetz at his home. Photograph. Bettmann/CORBIS. Reproduced with permission of Corbis.

Goldstein case, Andrew Goldstein escorted by police. Photograph. AP Photo/Marty Lederhandler. Reproduced with permission of Associated Press.

Gounagias case, Camas Mill, circa 1918. Postcard. Reproduced with permission of the Camas-Washougat Historical Society.

Hearst case, closet where Hearst was held. San Francisco Examiner, Bob McLeod. Reproduced with permission of the San Francisco Examiner.

Hearst case, Hearst posing before an SLA banner. Bettmann/CORBIS. Reproduced with permission of Corbis.

Hearst case, Hibernia Bank. Photograph. Reproduced with permission of Associated Press.

Hearst case, lines of people at the food giveaway. Photograph. Reproduced with permission of United Press International.

Hearst case, Patricia Hearst and Steven Weed's apartment. Photograph. San Francisco Examiner, Florence Fang. Reproduced with permission of the San Francisco Examiner.

Hearst case, Patty Hearst in the Hibernia Bank. Photograph. Reproduced with permission of Associated Press.

Hearst case, Steven Weed. Photograph. San Francisco Examiner, Florence Fang. Reproduced with permission of the San Francisco Examiner.

Hearst case, William Randolph Hearst. Photograph. Reproduced with permission of Associated Press.

Hymon case, Edward Garner. Photograph. Reproduced with permission of NCJRS.

Hymon case, Officer Elton Hymon. Photograph. Reproduced with permission of NCJRS.

Ignatow case, Mary Ann Shore testifying in court. Photograph by Michael Hayman, © Courier-Journal Reproduced with permission of Courier-Journal.

Israeli General Security Service case, Dr. Yehuda Hiss. Photograph. Jonathan Bloom, Jerusalem Post. Reproduced with permission of Tom Rose.

Israeli General Security Service case, Fatma Harizat holding a photo of her son. Photograph. AP Photo/Nasser Shiyoukhi. Reproduced with permission of Associated Press.

Israeli General Security Service case, methods of interrogation. Illustrations. Reproduced with permission of David Gerstein.

Ivy case, Leroy Ivy. Photograph. Reproduced with permission of the Northeast Mississippi Daily Journal.

Jackson case, 1976 Lincoln Continental. Photograph. Reproduced with permission of Earle K. Gould. Web site photograph courtesy of Delaware Auto Consultant, Owner, W. H. Gilbert, www.DelawareAutoConsultantLLC.com.

Jahnke case, Richard John Jahnke, Jr., circa 1984. Photograph. Reproduced with permission of Associated Press.

King case, Berry and King. Photograph. Greg Smith/CORBIS. Reproduced with permission of Corbis.

King case, Byrd's funeral. Photograph. Beaumont Enterprises/Sygma/Corbis. Reproduced with permission of Corbis.

King case, Huff Creek Road. Photograph. Greg Smith/CORBIS. Reproduced with permission of Corbis.

King case, James Byrd, Jr. Photograph. AP/Byrd Family Photo. Reproduced with permission of Associated Press.

King case, John William King, circa 1999. Photograph. Beaumont Enterprises/ Sygma/Corbis. Reproduced with permission of Corbis.

King case, King's tattoos. Photograph. © Mike Stewart/Sygma/Corbis. Reproduced with permission of Corbis.

King case, Lawrence Russell Brewer. Photograph. AP Photo/College Station Eagle, Butch Ireland. Reproduced with permission of Associated Press.

King case, Shawn Berry. Photograph. AP Photo/David J. Phillip. Reproduced with permission of Associated Press.

Laseter case, downtown Fairbanks. Photograph. Joel W. Rogers/CORBIS. Reproduced with permission of Corbis.

Law case, Blessed Sacrament Parish in Saugus, Massachusetts. Photograph. Reproduced with permission of Itia and Menachem Roth.

Law case, Cardinal Bernard Law speaking in Boston. Photograph. Bettmann/ CORBIS. Reproduced with permission of Corbis.

Law case, chapel at Pontifical College Josephinium. Photograph. The Columbus Dispatch Copyright 2002 by MCCLATCHY-TRIBUNE REGIONAL NEWS. Reproduced with permission of MCCLATCHY-TRIBUNE REGIONAL NEWS in the format Textbook via Copyright Clearance Center.

Law case, John Geoghan. Photograph. AP Photo/Michael Dwyer. Reproduced with permission of Associated Press.

Law case, Patrick McSorley. Photograph. Reuters/CORBIS. Reproduced with permission of Corbis.

Law case, St. Paul's Church. Photograph. Reprinted with permission of James F. Rafferty.

Marsh case, investigators colleting bodies. Photograph. Reuters/CORBIS. Reproduced with permission of Corbis.

Marsh case, police en route to the crematory. Photograph. Reuters/CORBIS. Reproduced with permission of Corbis.

Marsh case, women yelling at Marsh outside the courthouse. Photograph. Reuters/ CORBIS. Reproduced with permission of Corbis.

Mitchell case, Todd Mitchell at his trial. Photograph. Reproduced with permission of Kenosha News.

Olson case, Soliah at SLA rally. Photograph. Reproduced with permission of Associated Press.

Olson case, Soliah's arrest photo. Photograph. AP Photo/St. Paul Police Dept. Reproduced with permission of Associated Press.

Olson case, St. Paul, Minnesota, home. Photograph. Andy King/Sygma/Corbis. Reproduced with permission of Corbis.

Rahman case, Egyptian President Hosni Mubarak. Photograph. Reproduced with permission of the Egyptian Press and Information Office.

Rahman case, Mohammed Salameh. Photograph. Reuters/CORBIS. Reproduced with permission of Corbis.

Rahman case, Ramzi Yousef. Photograph. Jeffrey Markowitz/Sygma/Corbis. Reproduced with permission of Corbis.

Rahman case, Sheik Rahman. Photograph. Reuters/CORBIS. Reproduced with permission of Corbis.

Rahman case, Sheik Rahman surrendering to the F.B.I. Photograph. Les Stone/Sygma/Corbis. Reproduced with permission of Corbis.

Rahman case, World Trade Center. Photograph. Reproduced with permission of Craig Nevill-Manning.

Weaver case, Jordan Weaver. Photograph. Richard Miller, Indianapolis Star. Reproduced with permission.

CRIMINAL LAW

BACKGROUND MATERIALS

Overview of the Criminal Justice Process
Overview of Proving Crimes

Overview of the Criminal Justice Process: The Steps in the Process

Wayne LaFave, Jerold Israel & Nancy King,
Criminal Procedure § 1.3 (3d ed. 2000)

The overview presented in this section follows the sequence of the procedure in a typical felony case. . . .

(c) Step 1: The Reported Crime. Descriptions of the sequence of events in the criminal justice process commonly start with the commission of a crime. Our focus, however, is on the major steps taken in the administration of the process. From that perspective, the starting point ordinarily is the event that brings to the attention of the police the possible commission of a crime, for that event commonly triggers those series of administrative steps that may lead to the eventual enforcement of the criminal law against the offender. Quantitatively, there is a vast difference between the number of instances in which crimes are committed and the number in which the commission of a crime is brought to the attention of the police. The best available studies indicate that substantially less than half of all crimes are brought to the attention of the police.

Police may learn about crimes that have been committed from reports of citizens (usually victims), discovery in the field (usually observation on patrol), or from investigative and intelligence work. Where the police conclude that a crime may well have been committed, it will be recorded as a "reported crime" or "known offense." This record-keeping function has no legal significance with respect to further police action; police are not required to investigate further because a crime is recorded as a "known offense" and they are not prevented from seeking to obtain information where they do not have knowledge of an offense.

The long standing tradition of police departments, however, is to devote the vast bulk of their investigative efforts to solving "known offenses" and to at least initially attempt to investigate the vast majority of such offenses. Accordingly, the distribution of "known offenses" provides a fairly accurate general picture of the types of crimes that are investigated (albeit sometimes minimally) by police. The dominant offenses among the reported crimes are those involving the taking or destruction of property (likely to approximate 50%), offenses relating to the use of alcohol or drugs, and assaults of various types. The most serious violent offenses (e.g., robbery, rape, aggravated assault, and homicide) are likely to constitute as a group no more than 7% of all reported crimes.

(d) Step 2: Prearrest Investigation. Various distinctions are used in grouping prearrest investigatory procedures, but the most common are the agency involved (distinguishing primarily between the investigative activities of the police and the prosecutor) and the focus of the procedure (distinguishing primarily between activities aimed at solving past crimes and activities aimed at anticipated crimes). Those distinctions create three basic groups of prearrest investigative procedures: (1) police procedures that are aimed at solving specific past crimes known to the police (commonly described as "reactive" procedures), (2) police procedures that are aimed at anticipated ongoing and future criminal activity (commonly described as "proactive" procedures), and (3) prosecutorial and other non-police investigations conducted primarily through the use of subpoena authority. . . .

(e) Step 3: Arrest. Once a police officer has obtained sufficient information to justify arresting a suspect (i.e., probable cause to believe the person has committed a crime), the arrest ordinarily becomes the next step in the criminal justice process. The term "arrest" is defined differently for different purposes. We refer here only to the act of taking a person into custody for the purpose of charging him with a crime (the standard commonly used in collecting statistics on the reporting of arrest statistics). This involves the detention of the suspect (by force if necessary) for the purpose of first transporting him to a police facility and then requesting that charges be filed against him. As an alternative to such a "full custody" arrest, many jurisdictions authorize the officer in some situations to briefly detain the suspect and then release him upon issuance of an official document (commonly titled a "citation," "notice to appear" or "appearance ticket") which directs the suspect to appear in court on a set date to respond to the charge specified in the document. This release-on-citation alternative commonly is authorized only for minor offenses, with the choice between the release procedure and the custodial arrest then lying in the discretion of the individual officer. In many localities, the standard practice is to use the citation alternative, rather than the arrest, for a wide range of minor offenses (including such offenses as disorderly conduct, vandalism, and petty shoplifting). In others, police generally prefer arrests and largely confine their regular use of the citation alternative to a few minor offenses, primarily regulatory in character. Where citations regularly are used for even a handful of the more common minor offenses, the number of citations issued can readily equal a quarter or a third of the total number of misdemeanor arrests.

Where there is no immediate need to arrest a suspect, an officer may seek to obtain an arrest warrant (a court order authorizing the arrest) prior to taking the person into custody. Arrest warrants in most jurisdictions are issued by magistrates. To obtain a warrant, the police must establish, to the satisfaction of the magistrate, that there exists probable cause to believe that the prospective arrestee committed the crime for which he will be arrested. The showing of probable cause may be made by affidavits or live testimony of either the investigating officer or a witness (usually the victim). Where a warrant is issued, it ordinarily will authorize the arrest to be made by any police officer in the state, not simply the officer seeking the warrant.

Arrests also can be made without a warrant, and that is the predominant practice in all localities. Of course, in a large percentage of all arrests (including, for example, "on scene" arrests), the police officer will make the arrest immediately after he has obtained probable cause for believing the person committed a crime. Yet, even where the investigating officer, after establishing probable cause, expects a lapse of a day or more before making an arrest, the common practice in most jurisdictions is not to use that opportunity to obtain an arrest warrant. Officers here will seek to obtain a warrant, rather than rely on a warrantless arrest, only where the special setting makes a warrant legally necessary or otherwise advantageous. The most common of those settings are: (1) cases in which the offender is located in another jurisdiction (as a warrant is needed to utilize procedures for having the person arrested by officers of another state and later extradited); (2) cases in which the person cannot be found and his name therefore will be entered into the computerized state or local law enforcement information network as someone who is subject to an arrest on the basis of an outstanding warrant; (3) cases in which there will probably be a need to enter into a dwelling without consent in order to make the arrest (a situation that requires a warrant); (4) cases in which the offense was a misdemeanor not committed in the officer's presence (a situation requiring a warrant in some states); and (5) cases in which the police have sought the advice of the prosecutor before deciding to proceed (where the prosecutor responds affirmatively, a complaint typically will be filed immediately, with a warrant then obtained prior to the arrest).

As noted in subsection (d), many offenses that come to the attention of the police cannot be solved. Hence, the number of arrests made will be substantially less than the number of offenses recorded as a known offense. The proportion of known offenses that are "cleared" by an arrest varies substantially with the nature of the crime. For those eight "Index" offenses on which national data is collected by the F.B.I., the overall clearance rate is roughly 21%, ranging from a high of 65% for homicide to a low of 13% for burglary.

The vast majority of arrests (60–80%) will be for misdemeanors, with more arrests made for driving-under-the-influence than for any other offense. Among felony arrests, property offenses will account for roughly a third, and drug offenses for 25–30%, and crimes of violence for another 25%. A substantial percentage of all of the persons arrested (e.g., 10–20%) will be juveniles, with that percentage varying considerably with the offense. Ordinarily, juvenile arrestees will be separated from adult arrestees shortly after they are taken into custody, and will be processed through the juvenile justice system, although some will later be returned to the regular criminal justice process and be prosecuted as adults. From this point on, we will assume the arrestee is an adult or a juvenile treated as an adult.

(f) Step 4: Booking. Immediately after making an arrest, the arresting officer usually will search the arrestee's person and remove any weapons, contraband, or evidence relating to a crime. If the arrested person was driving a vehicle, the officer may also search the passenger compartment of the vehicle for the same items. The arrestee will then be taken, either by the arresting officer or other officers called to the scene, to the police station, a centrally located jail, or some similar "holding" facility. It is at this facility that the arrestee will be taken through a process known as "booking." Initially, the arrestee's name, the time of his arrival, and the offense for which he was arrested are noted in the police "blotter" or "log." This is strictly a clerical procedure, and it does not control whether the arrestee will be charged or what charge might be brought. As part of the booking process, the arrestee also will be photographed and fingerprinted.

Once the booking process is completed, the arrestee ordinarily will be allowed to make at least one telephone call. In many jurisdictions, an arrestee booked on a minor misdemeanor will be given the opportunity to obtain his immediate release by posting what is described as "stationhouse bail." This involves posting a specified amount of cash, as prescribed for the particular offense in a judicially approved bail schedule, and agreeing to appear in court on a specified date. Persons arrested for more serious offenses and those eligible to post stationhouse bail but lacking the resources will remain at the holding facility until presented before a magistrate (see step 9). Ordinarily they will be placed in a "lockup," which usually is some kind of cell. Before entering the lockup, they will be subjected to another search, more thorough than that conducted at the point of arrest. This search is designed primarily to inventory the arrestee's personal belongings and to prevent the introduction of contraband into the lockup.

(g) Step 5: Post-Arrest Investigation. The initial post-arrest investigation by the police consists of the search of the person (and possibly the interior of the automobile) as discussed above. The extent of any further post-arrest investigation will vary with the fact situation. In some cases, such as where the arrestee was caught "red-handed," there will be little left to be done. In others, police will utilize many of the same kinds of investigative procedures as are used before arrest (e.g., interviewing witnesses, searching the suspect's home, and viewing the scene of the crime). Post-arrest investigation does offer one important investigative source, however, that ordinarily is not available prior to the arrest—the person of the arrestee. Thus, the police may seek to obtain an eyewitness identification of the arrestee by placing him in a lineup, having the witness view him individually (a "showup"), or taking his picture and showing it to the witness (usually with the photographs of several other persons in a "photographic lineup"). They may also require the arrestee to provide handwriting or hair samples that can be compared with evidence the police have found at the scene of the crime. The arrest similarly facilitates questioning the arrestee at length about either the crime for which he was arrested or other crimes thought to be related (although warnings must be given prior to the custodial interrogation).

Although we do not have precise data on the use of these post-arrest procedures involving the arrestee, the best available estimates indicate they are not utilized in the vast majority of cases. In most communities, they are used almost exclusively in the investigation of felony cases and even then their use is tied to need and likelihood of success. Eyewitness identification, for example, is not sought where there were no eyewitnesses, where an eyewitness was well acquainted with the arrestee, or where the officer observed the crime and immediately thereafter made the arrest. Police more frequently seek to engage felony arrestees in sustained interrogation, but a substantial portion of those arrestees are either never questioned or simply given warnings and asked if they desire to make a statement.

   (h) Step 6: The Decision to Charge. The initial decision to charge a suspect with the commission of a crime ordinarily comes with the decision of a police officer to arrest the suspect. That decision will subsequently be reviewed, first by the police and then by the prosecutor. As discussed in subsection (k), the arrestee must be brought before a magistrate within a relatively short period (typically 24 or 48 hours), and prior to that point, the charges against the arrestee must be filed with the magistrate. It is during this period that the police will review the arresting officer's initial decision to charge. The prosecutor's review of the decision to charge often occurs during this same period, but prosecutorial review is, in any event, an ongoing process. Whether or not the initial filing of charges comes after review of the prosecutor, the filed charges remain subject to reconsideration by the prosecutor up to and through the trial.

   The decision to charge a person with a crime thus may be seen as having four components: (1) the decision of the investigating officer to arrest and charge; (2) the police review of that decision prior to filing charges; (3) prosecutorial review prior to filing; and (4) ongoing prosecutorial review after the filing. The first component has already been noted in step (3) (the arrest), and we consider here the remaining three. The third component, prosecutorial post-filing screening, is treated here, rather than at the later points in the process where it occurs chronologically, because of its close relationship to the pre-filing screening of the prosecutor.

   Pre-Filing Police Screening. Sometime between the booking of the arrestee and the point at which the arrestee is to be taken before the magistrate, there will be an internal police review of a warrantless arrest. Ordinarily that occurs shortly after the booking, when the arresting officer prepares an arrest report to be given to his or her supervisor. The supervisor may approve the bringing of charges at the level recommended in the police report, raise or reduce the level of the recommended charges, or decide against bringing charges. A decision not to bring charges ordinarily will be based on the supervisor's conclusion either that the evidence is insufficient to charge or that the offense can more appropriately be handled by a "stationhouse adjustment" (e.g., in the case of a fight among acquaintances, a warning and lecture may be deemed sufficient). If the supervising officer decides against prosecution, the arrestee will be released from the lockup on the officer's direction (with some departments following the practice of seeking prosecutor approval before releasing felony arrestees). Studies that track the ultimate disposition of arrests have typically been limited to felony arrests. They report police decisions to release arrestees and forego prosecution in the range of 4% to 10%. Since police are more likely to utilize stationhouse adjustments for misdemeanor arrests, the percentage of misdemeanor arrestees released by the police without charging is likely to be somewhat higher.

Pre-Filing Prosecutor Screening. Prosecutors' offices vary substantially in their approach to pre-filing review of the decision to charge. In many jurisdictions, all arrests, both for misdemeanors and felonies, will be screened, and no charges will be filed except upon approval of the prosecutor. In many others, however, particularly in urban districts, police often file charges on their own initiative for at least some types of offenses. Typically, prosecutors here will screen the vast majority of the felony charges, but there will be districts in which prosecutors review only the most serious felony charges before they are filed. In those districts, the initial prosecutorial screening of most felony charges occurs sometime between the first appearance and the preliminary hearing or grand jury review (see steps 9 and 10 infra). Prosecutors are more likely to permit police to file misdemeanor charges without advance prosecutorial screening. When that occurs, prosecutors may not review a misdemeanor charge until it is scheduled for trial (and thus may never screen those charges that result in a guilty plea at the first appearance). . . .

A prosecutorial decision not to proceed commonly is described as a "rejection," "declination" or "no-paper" decision. The leading statistical studies on pre-charge prosecutor review have sorted out six major grounds for that decision. These are: (1) insufficient evidence; (2) witness difficulties (e.g., where the victim was acquainted with the offender and does not desire to proceed, the victim fears reprisal and is reluctant to pursue prosecution, or the victim cannot be located); (3) due process problems (e.g., critical evidence was obtained illegally and will not be admissible at trial); (4) adequate disposition will be provided by other criminal proceedings (e.g., prosecution by another jurisdiction, probation revocation, or prosecution for another offense); (5) the "interests of justice"; and (6) anticipated use of a diversion program. Among these factors, the two most frequently cited are the first two (evidence insufficiency and witness difficulty); while rejections based on the "interest of justice" attract the greatest attention, they are far less significant statistically.

As one might expect from the differences among prosecutors' offices in the proportion of arrests reviewed pre-filing, the differences in the depth of such review, and the subjective nature of many of the grounds for declining prosecution, studies reveal considerable variation from one community to another in the impact of pre-filing prosecutorial screening. Thus, a study of 13 urban prosecutorial districts found that the percentage of felony arrests that did not result in charges ranged from a low of 0% (in a jurisdiction which apparently did no pre-filing screening) to a high of 38%. Even higher rates of pre-filing rejections have been reported for other urban districts. On the other hand, the most comprehensive study, covering all districts within six states, found a prefiling prosecutorial rejection rate of only 11%, reflecting perhaps, fewer rejections influenced by case-load pressures where the sample includes both urban and rural districts. Within the individual district, the rejection rate is likely to show considerable variation across the range of felony offenses, with the rate of rejections for some felony offenses being as much as twice that for others. . . .

Post-Filing Prosecutorial Screening. Post-filing prosecutorial review of the charging decision is inherent in the many post-filing procedures that require the prosecutor to review the facts of the case. If the prosecutor should determine that the charge is not justified, a dismissal can be obtained through a nolle prosequi motion (noting the prosecutor's desire to relinquish prosecution), which ordinarily will be granted in a perfunctory fashion by the court. Similarly, if the prosecutor considers the charge to be too high, a motion can be entered to reduce the charges. In deciding whether to make such motions, the prosecutor will look to basically the same grounds that might justify a pre-filing rejection or reduction of the charge recommended by the police. Even where a charge was carefully screened and approved prior to filing, post-filing review can readily lead to a contrary conclusion as circumstances change (e.g., evidence becomes unavailable) or the prosecutor learns more about the facts of the case. Of course, where the charge was not previously screened or was screened only on a skimpy arrest report, post-filing review is even more likely to lead to a decision to drop or reduce the charges.

Although post-filing review is an ongoing process, the most critical point, particularly where there has been no pre-filing review, is the first instance at which the prosecutor must carefully review the facts of the case. In felony cases, that will usually come in the preparation of the case for the preliminary hearing or grand jury review (see steps 10 and 11), although it may even come before that. Accordingly, dismissals and reductions based on post-filing prosecutorial screening of the charging decision are most likely to come before the felony case reaches the general trial court, but even after that point, changed circumstances or additional information can lead to a significant portion of the post-filing dismissals occurring at the trial court level.

Available statistics make it difficult to measure the precise impact of post-filing prosecutorial screening. In categorizing the disposition of felony charges by both magistrate and general trial courts, many states use a single category of dismissal that includes both dismissals on a prosecutor's nolle prosequi motion and dismissals by the court on a challenge to the charge by the defense. Only a small group of states keep separate statistics on dismissals on the motion of the prosecutor. These states attribute to such dismissals a range of 19% to 37% of all final dispositions of felony cases. That range is consistent with a study of adjudication outcomes for felony defendants in the nation's 75 largest counties, which found an average rate of disposition of felony defendants by dismissals (of all types) of 26% (varying for offense groupings from a low of 20% for drug offenses to a high of 37% for violent offenses).

Of course, the prosecutorial-screening dismissal rate for felony charges builds upon the earlier pre-filing screening which determined the number of felony arrests that were converted into felony charges. Two jurisdictions may have identical dismissal rates, but their dismissal numbers, and the significance of that rate, will be quite different if one reduced its number of charges by 20% through pre-filing screening and the other reduced its number by only 2%. Thus, to evaluate the true impact of dismissals upon prosecutorial screening, they are best judged by reference to the disposition of felony arrests. The studies that measure dismissals in this fashion have shown that, as a general rule, the higher the percentage of arrests rejected in pre-filing screening, the lower the percentage of arrests as to which charges once filed are subsequently dismissed (although the jurisdiction with more extensive initial screening is likely to have an even higher dismissal rate measured by reference to charge dispositions). In other words, the greater the number of felony arrests rejected, the smaller the number of felony charges that will be dismissed on post-filing screening. A similar pattern is indicated for charge reductions, as jurisdictions with limited pre-filing screening tend to be more active in post-filing reductions of felonies to misdemeanors.

What is the end product of the combined pre-filing screening by police and prosecutor and post-filing screening by the prosecutor? The best source on that question is a series of studies on the attrition of felony arrests. A 1988 study, using a dozen urban prosecutorial districts, found that those districts screened out of the criminal justice system from 31% to 46% of all felony arrests, with a jurisdictional mean of 39%. When diversions were added, no jurisdiction removed from prosecution less than 33% of their felony arrests, all but three removed in excess of 40%, and one removed 50%. A 1992 study, drawing information from 11 states, provides data suggesting removal by screening (including diversion) fell in the range of 31–36% for those states as a group. California provides arrest-disposition data over the longest period, dating back to 1975. The California data show the potential for a substantial variation over a period of years in the proportion of felony arrests removed from the process through police and prosecutorial screening. While the California removal rate for 1994 was no higher than 32.5%, it had been close to 50% in 1975. A study of convictions as compared to felony arrests over a six year period in the nation's 75 largest counties suggests that substantial variations are possible over even a shorter period of time. . . .

(i) Step 7: Filing the Complaint. Assuming that the pre-charge screening results in a decision to prosecute, the next step is the filing of charges with the magistrate court. Typically, the initial charging instrument will be called a "complaint." In misdemeanor cases, which are triable before the magistrate court, the complaint will serve as the charging instrument throughout the proceedings. In felony cases, on the other hand, the complaint serves to set forth the charges only before the magistrate court; an information or indictment will replace the complaint as the charging instrument when the case reaches the general trial court.

For most offenses, the complaint will be a fairly brief document. Its basic function is to set forth concisely the allegation that the accused, at a particular time and place, committed specified acts constituting a violation of a particular criminal statute. The complaint will be signed by a "complainant," a person who swears under oath that he or she believes the factual allegations of the complaint to be true. The complainant usually will be either the victim or the investigating officer. When an officer-complainant did not observe the offense being committed, but relied on information received from the victim or other witnesses, the officer ordinarily will note that the allegations in the complaint are based on "information and belief."

With the filing of the complaint, the person accused in the complaint will have become a "defendant" in a criminal proceeding. The formal charge initiates a judicial record keeping procedure that puts his case on the docket and follows it through to its termination. Ordinarily that termination will come in a dismissal, a conviction, or an acquittal. However, some cases will either be transferred to an "inactive" docket, or dismissed with the prosecution specifically given authority to later reinstate the charge. These are the cases in which the defendant is "unavailable"—usually because he has absconded, but occasionally because he is incarcerated elsewhere or is outside the jurisdiction. The portion of the docket handled in this fashion depends in part on how long a state is willing to wait for the apprehension of a defendant before the charge against him will be "written off" as a disposition. In some jurisdictions, that portion will exceed 10%, while in others, it may not even amount to 1%. For misdemeanors, the portion tends to be somewhat larger; more cases were initiated by summons rather than arrest, and more arrestees obtained their pretrial release (commonly without posting bond or other financial security), so there tends to be a higher percentage of "no shows."

Just as the mix of offenses for which arrests were made differed from the mix of offenses known to police, the mix of offenses charged by complaint will differ from the mix of those arrest offenses. The differences here will not be nearly so striking as between arrests and known-offenses, but the pre-filing decisions by police and prosecutor—Including juvenile arrestees transferred to juvenile court, arrestees not charged, arrestees placed in diversion programs, and the reduction of charges—make the mix of offenses charged somewhat different than the mix of arrest offenses. Most significant will be the reduced proportion of felonies. While felony arrests might account for 20–40% of all arrests in a particular jurisdiction, felony complaints are likely to constitute only 10–20% of all complaints. Among felony complaints, the mix of offenses by general category is similar to that for arrests. Property offenses are likely to account for slightly over a third of the complaints, drug offenses for roughly 30%, and crimes of violence for roughly 25%. Within these general categories, however, there will be some shifts, as arrests for particular offenses (e.g., motor vehicle theft in the property category) are more likely to result in a decision not to prosecute or in a reduction of the offense when the charge is brought.

(j) Step 8: Magistrate Review of the Arrest. Following the filing of the complaint and prior to or at the start of the first appearance (see step 9), the magistrate must undertake what is often described as the "Gerstein review." As prescribed by the Supreme Court's decision in Gerstein v. Pugh, if the accused was arrested without a warrant and remains in custody, the magistrate must determine that there exists probable cause for the continued detention of the arrestee for the offense charged in the complaint. This ordinarily is an ex parte determination, similar to that made in the issuance of an arrest warrant and relying on the same sources of information. Where the arrest was made pursuant to a warrant, the judicial probable cause determination has already been made and a Gerstein review is not required. If the magistrate finds that probable cause has not been established, he will direct the prosecution to promptly produce more information or release the arrested person. Such instances are exceedingly rare, however.

(k) Step 9: The First Appearance. Once the complaint is filed, the case is before the magistrate court, and the accused must appear before the court within a specified period. This appearance of the accused is usually described as the "first appearance," although the terminology varies, with jurisdictions also using "preliminary appearance," "initial presentment," "preliminary arraignment," "arraignment on the warrant," and "arraignment on the complaint." The timing of the first appearance varies with the custodial status of the accused. Where the accused was not taken into custody, but was released on issuance of a citation, there is likely to be a gap of at least several days between the issuance of the citation and the first appearance date as specified in the citation. The same is

often true also of the first appearance set for the arrestee who gained his release by posting stationhouse bail.

Almost all felony arrestees and many misdemeanor arrestees will have been held in custody following their arrest, however, and here the time span between the arrest and the first appearance is much shorter. All jurisdictions require that an arrestee held in custody be brought before the magistrate court in a fairly prompt fashion. Ordinarily, the time consumed in booking, transportation, limited post-arrest investigation, reviewing the decision to charge, and preparing and filing the complaint makes it unlikely that the arrestee will be presented before the magistrate until at least several hours after his arrest. Thus, if the magistrate court does not have an evening session, a person arrested in the afternoon or evening will not be presented before the magistrate until the next day. Many jurisdictions do not allow much longer detention than this, as they impose a 24 hour limit on pre-appearance detention, requiring both the filing of the complaint and the presentation of the detained arrestee within that period. Others, desiring to limit weekend sessions of the court, allow up to 48 hours of pre-appearance detention.

The first appearance often is a quite brief proceeding. Initially, the magistrate will make certain that the person before him is the person named in the complaint. The magistrate then will inform the defendant of the charge in the complaint and will note various rights that the defendant may have in further proceedings. The range of rights mentioned will vary from one jurisdiction to another. Commonly, the magistrate will inform the defendant of his right to remain silent and warn him that anything he says in court or to the police may be used against him at trial. Further advice as to rights may depend upon whether the defendant is charged with a felony or misdemeanor. In felony cases, the magistrate will advise the defendant of the next step in the process, the preliminary hearing, and will set a date for that hearing unless the defendant desires to waive it. If the defendant is charged with a misdemeanor, he will not be entitled to a preliminary hearing or a subsequent grand jury review (see steps 10 and 11).

At least where the defendant is not represented by counsel at the first appearance, the magistrate will inform the defendant of his right to be represented by retained counsel, and, if indigent, his right to court appointed counsel. The scope of the right to appointed counsel may vary with the level of the offense. In some jurisdictions, appointed counsel will not be available for defendants who are charged with low-level misdemeanors if they will not be sentenced to incarceration if convicted. Where there is a right to appointed counsel, which will be the case in all jurisdictions for indigent defendants charged with felonies and serious misdemeanors, the magistrate usually will have the responsibility for at least initiating the appointment process. This involves first determining that the defendant is indigent and that he desires the assistance of counsel. The magistrate then will either directly appoint counsel or notify a judge in charge of appointments that an appointment should be made. . . .

One of the most important first-appearance functions of the magistrate is to set bail (i.e., the conditions under which the defendant can obtain his release from custody pending the final disposition of the charges against him). In many misdemeanor cases, there will be no need to set bail. The defendant will already have been released on the police issuance of a citation or on the posting of station-house bail or the defendant will enter a guilty plea at the first appearance and be promptly sentenced. However, a bail determination ordinarily must be made in all felony and serious misdemeanor cases and in a substantial portion of the lesser misdemeanor cases.

At one time, bail was limited almost entirely to the posting of cash or a secured bond purchased from a professional bondsman. Today, those are only two of several alternatives available to the magistrate. Others are: (1) release upon a promise to appear (release on "personal recognizance"); (2) release on making a personal promise to forfeit a specified dollar amount upon a failure to appear (an "unsecured" personal bond); (3) release upon the imposition of one or more nonfinancial conditions (e.g., restrictions on defendant's associations or travel); and (4) the posting with the court of a percentage of the bail forfeiture amount (commonly 10%), which will be returned to the defendant if he appears as scheduled. In a few states, the 10% alternative has basically replaced the secured bond, resulting in the elimination of professional bondsmen.

In general, the magistrate is directed to impose such bail conditions as appear reasonably needed to assure that the defendant will make court appearances as scheduled throughout the proceedings. In making that determination, the magistrate looks to a variety of factors that might indicate a likelihood of flight (e.g., severity of possible punishment if convicted). Most jurisdictions also direct the magistrate to consider community safety in setting bail conditions, and approximately half of our fifty-two jurisdictions authorize preventive detention—a procedure under which the magistrate orders that the accused be detained because no bail condition will provide satisfactory assurance against his commission of an offense posing danger to the community.

In misdemeanor cases, magistrates most commonly utilize release on personal recognizance or personal bonds, and even where a secured bond is required, the amount is sufficiently low so that only a small percentage of defendants fail to gain their release. As a result, studies that cover both misdemeanor and felony arrestees report overall release rates of 85% or higher, with the vast majority of defendants released on nonfinancial conditions. However, when felony defendants alone are considered, the picture changes dramatically, especially for the more serious felony offenses. Thus, a study of the nation's 75 largest counties found that 37% of all felony defendants were detained until the final disposition of their charges, and that percentage rose to 50% or above for those charged with murder, rape, and robbery. As for the defendants who were released, more were released on non-financial conditions than on financial conditions. However, for the group released, a non-appearance rate of 25% and a rearrest rate of 14% for new offenses led to revocation of bail for a significant number. Also, at the end of a year, 8% of those released were unapprehended fugitives.

(l) Step 10: Preliminary Hearing. Following the first appearance, the next scheduled step in a felony case ordinarily is the preliminary hearing (sometimes called a preliminary "examination"). All but a few of our fifty-two jurisdictions grant the felony defendant a right to a preliminary hearing, to be held within a specified period (typically, within a week or two if the defendant does not gain pretrial release and within a few weeks if released). This hardly means, however, that the preliminary hearing will be held in almost all or even most cases. Initially, as mentioned previously, the critical stage for post-arrest prosecutorial screening

of charges is in the period prior to the scheduled preliminary hearing, and a prosecution can readily dismiss 15–30% of the felony cases before the scheduled hearing (the high percentage coming in those jurisdictions in which there is little or no pre-filing screening). Where the charges are not dismissed, two additional decisions—one by the prosecutor and one by the defense—can sharply reduce the number of preliminary hearings.

In almost all jurisdictions, if the prosecutor obtains a grand jury indictment prior to the scheduled preliminary hearing, the preliminary hearing will not be held, as the grand jury's finding of probable cause has rendered irrelevant any contrary finding that the magistrate might make at the preliminary hearing. Prosecutorial bypassing of the preliminary hearing by immediately obtaining a grand jury indictment is most likely to occur in those twenty jurisdictions that require prosecution by indictment (see step 11 infra). In some of these jurisdictions, prosecutors make such frequent use of the bypass option as to preclude preliminary hearings in 50–80% of the felony cases that reach the felony trial court. In many others, however, the bypass procedure is used sparingly, precluding no more than 10% of the potential preliminary hearings. Such sparing use (or no use) of the bypass procedure also tends to be the norm in jurisdictions that ordinarily prosecute by information (see step 12), although an occasional prosecutor in an information state may prefer grand jury indictments and bypass the preliminary hearing as a regular practice.

Finally, where the preliminary hearing is made available to the defendant, there nonetheless may not be a preliminary hearing because the defendant prefers to waive the hearing and move directly to the trial court. That is often the strategy employed where the defendant intends to plead guilty. Thus, a number of jurisdictions report a waiver rate exceeding 50%, although there also are jurisdictions in which defendants ask for the hearing in the vast majority of cases.

Where the preliminary hearing is held, it will provide, like grand jury review, a screening of the decision to charge by a neutral body. In the preliminary hearing, that neutral body is the magistrate, who must determine whether, on the evidence presented, there is probable cause to believe that defendant committed the crime charged. Ordinarily, the magistrate will already have determined that probable cause exists as part of the ex parte screening of the complaint (see step 8). The preliminary hearing, however, provides screening in an adversary proceeding in which both sides are represented by counsel. Jurisdictions vary in the evidentiary rules applicable to the preliminary hearing, but most require that the parties rely primarily on live witnesses rather than affidavits. Typically, the prosecution will present its key witnesses and the defense will limit its response to the cross-examination of those witnesses. The defendant has the right to present his own evidence at the hearing, but traditional defense strategy advises against subjecting defense witnesses to prosecution cross-examination in any pretrial proceeding.

If the magistrate concludes that the evidence presented establishes probable cause, he will "bind the case over" to the next stage in the proceedings. In an indictment jurisdiction (see step 11), the case is bound over to the grand jury, and in a jurisdiction that permits the direct filing of an information (see step 12), the case is bound over directly to the general trial court. If the magistrate finds that the probable cause supports only a misdemeanor charge, he will reject the felony charge and allow the prosecutor to substitute the lower charge, which will then be set for trial in the magistrate court. If the magistrate finds that the prosecution's evidence does not support any charge, he will order that the defendant be released. The rate of dismissals at the preliminary hearing quite naturally varies with the degree of previous screening exercised by the prosecutor. In a jurisdiction with fairly extensive screening, the percentage of dismissals is likely to fall in the range of 5–10% of the cases heard. However, other jurisdictions (usually those in which hearings are more sparingly utilized) report a much higher dismissal rate. In either type of jurisdiction, the preliminary hearing dismissal is likely to account for the disposition of less than 5% of all felony complaints.

(m) *Step 11: Grand Jury Review.* Although almost all fifty-two jurisdictions still have provisions authorizing grand jury screening of felony charges, such screening is mandatory only in those jurisdictions requiring felony prosecutions to be instituted by an indictment, a charging instrument issued by the grand jury. In a majority of the states, the prosecution is now allowed to proceed either by grand jury indictment or by information at its option. Because prosecutors in these states most often choose to prosecute by information, the states providing this option commonly are referred to as "information" states. Eighteen states, the federal system, and the District of Columbia currently require grand jury indictments for all felony prosecutions. These jurisdictions commonly are described as "indictment" jurisdictions. Four additional states are "limited indictment" jurisdictions, requiring prosecution by indictment only for their most severely punished offenses (capital, life imprisonment, or both).

Indictment and limited indictment jurisdictions commonly make prosecution by indictment an absolute mandate only for capital offenses. As to other offenses, the defendant may waive the right to be proceeded against by indictment, thereby allowing the prosecution to proceed by information. As in the case of preliminary hearing, defendants may prefer to waive when intending to plead guilty. Waiver rates vary from one jurisdiction to another but waivers are likely to be made by at least 10% of all felony defendants. Where a potential charge is brought to the grand jury for its possible issuance of an indictment, the grand jury is in no way bound by any prior ruling at a preliminary hearing on that charge. The grand jury may indict even though the magistrate dismissed the charge at the preliminary hearing, and may refuse to indict even though the magistrate bound over to the grand jury.

The grand jury is composed of a group of private citizens who are selected to review cases presented over a term that may range from one to several months. Traditionally the grand jury consisted of 23 persons with the favorable vote of a majority needed to indict. Today, many states use a somewhat smaller grand jury (e.g., 12) and some require more than a simple majority to indict. As in the case of the magistrate at the preliminary hearing, the primary function of the grand jury is to determine whether there is sufficient evidence to justify a trial on the charge sought by the prosecution. The grand jury, however, participates in a screening process quite different from the preliminary hearing. It meets in a closed session and hears only the evidence presented by the prosecution. The defendant has no right to offer his own evidence or to be present during grand jury proceedings. If a majority of the grand jurors conclude that the prosecution's evidence is sufficient, the grand jury will issue the indictment requested by the prosecutor. The indictment will set forth a brief description of the offense charged, and the grand jury's approval of that charge will be indicated by its designation of the indictment as a "true bill." If the grand jury majority refuses to approve a proposed indictment, the charges against the defendant will be dismissed. In indictment jurisdictions, grand juries typically refuse to indict in less than 10% of the cases presented before them.

(n) Step 12: The Filing of the Indictment or Information. If an indictment is issued, it will be filed with the general trial court and will replace the complaint as the accusatory instrument in the case. Where grand jury review either is not required or has been waived, an information will be filed with the trial court. Like the indictment, the information is a charging instrument which replaces the complaint, but it is issued by the prosecutor rather than the grand jury. In most information states, the charge in the information must be supported by a preliminary hearing bindover (unless the preliminary hearing was waived).

(o) Step 13: Arraignment on the Information or Indictment. After the indictment or information has been filed, the defendant is arraigned—i.e., he is brought before the trial court, informed of the charges against him, and asked to enter a plea of guilty, not guilty, or, as is permitted under some circumstances, nolo contendere. In the end, most of those felony defendants whose cases reach the trial court will plead guilty. At the arraignment, however, they are likely to enter a plea of not guilty. Where there has not been a preliminary hearing, defense counsel probably will not be fully apprised of the strength of the prosecution's case at this point in the proceedings. Also, in most jurisdictions, guilty pleas in felony cases are the product of plea negotiations with the prosecution, and in many places, that process does not start until after the arraignment. When the defendant enters a plea of not guilty at the arraignment, the judge will set a trial date, but the expectation generally is that the trial will not be held.

Between the arraignment and the scheduled trial date, three possible dispositions can result in the termination of the case without trial. Although there will have been extensive prosecutorial screening by this point, changed circumstances and new information typically will lead to dismissals on a prosecutor's nolle prosequi motion in roughly 5–15% of the cases. A smaller percentage of the informations or indictments will be dismissed on motion of the defense, as discussed in step 14. The vast majority of the dispositions without trial will be the product of guilty pleas.

Guilty pleas in felony cases commonly will be entered in response to a plea agreement under which the prosecution offers certain concessions in return for the defendant's entry of the plea. Those concessions may take the form of a reduction of the charges (sometimes to a misdemeanor and sometimes to a lesser felony charge), a dismissal of related charges where the defendant faces multiple charges, a recommendation on sentence, or a specific sentence (when agreed to by the trial court). Prosecutors' offices vary in the concessions they offer and their willingness to bargain over concessions (as opposed to presenting a take-it-or-leave-it offer). Prosecutors also vary as to the types of cases in which they will offer concessions, with some generally refusing to do so on the most serious charges. Indeed, there are jurisdictions in which prosecutors will not plea bargain, although defendants here may still find an inducement to plead guilty in a general policy of trial judges to give favorable weight in sentencing to the defendant's willingness to plead guilty.

Although the guilty plea remains the primary mode of disposition for felony indictments and informations in all jurisdictions, considerable variation exists in the percentage of defendants who enter guilty pleas. Most jurisdictions appear to fall within the range of 60–85%. Of course when dismissals and other dispositions are excluded, and only guilty pleas and trials are compared, the rate of guilty pleas is much higher. Thus, a leading study of 14 communities found a median ratio of 11 pleas for every trial, with one jurisdiction having as many as 37 pleas for each trial. . . .

(p) Step 14: Pretrial Motions. In most jurisdictions, a broad range of objections must be raised by a pretrial motion. Those motions commonly present challenges to the institution of the prosecution (e.g., claims regarding the grand jury indictment process), attacks upon the sufficiency of the charging instrument, requests for disclosure of evidence within the government's possession that has not been made available through discovery, and requests for the suppression of evidence allegedly obtained through a constitutional violation. While some pretrial motions are made only by defendants who intend to go to trial, other motions (e.g., discovery) may benefit as well defendants who expect in the end to plead guilty. Nevertheless, pretrial motions are likely to be made in only a small portion of the felony cases that reach the trial court. Their use does vary considerably, however, with the nature of the case. In narcotics cases, for example, motions to suppress are quite common. In the typical forgery case, on the other, pretrial motions of any type are quite rare.

As a group, pretrial motions are unlikely to result in the dismissal of more than 5% of the felony cases before the trial court, and quite often will produce a dismissal rate of less than 2.5%. The pretrial motion most likely to produce a dismissal is the motion to suppress. Quite frequently, if the defendant gains suppression of unconstitutionally obtained evidence, there will be insufficient remaining evidence to continue with the prosecution. In misdemeanor cases before the magistrate court, motions tend to be made only in cases slated for trial and even there, they are uncommon. Thus, the percentage of cases dismissed on the basis of a successful defense motion probably will fall below two percent.

(q) Step 15: The Trial. Assuming that there has not been a dismissal and the defendant has not entered a guilty plea (or a nolle contendere plea), the next step in the criminal process is the trial. In most respects, the criminal trial resembles the civil trial. There are, however, several distinguishing features that are either unique to criminal trials or of special importance in such trials. These include (1) the presumption of defendant's innocence, (2) the requirement of proof beyond a reasonable doubt, (3) the right of the defendant not to take the stand, (4) the exclusion of evidence obtained by the state in an illegal manner, and (5) the more frequent use of incriminating statements of defendants. In most jurisdictions, the misdemeanor trial will be almost indistinguishable from a felony trial. In some jurisdictions, however, misdemeanor trials tend to be less formal, with rules of evidence applied in a rather loose fashion.

As noted previously, most felony and misdemeanor cases are likely to be disposed of either by a guilty plea or by a dismissal. Typically, only 4% to 8%

of all felony complaints are resolved by a trial. Because a substantial portion of felony complaints are likely to be resolved at the magistrate level, the percentage of trials will be somewhat higher for the disposition of the smaller group of felony informations or indictments filed in the general trial court, but even so, that percentage will not ordinarily exceed 15%—although there are some exceptional jurisdictions in which the percentage is over 30%. For misdemeanor cases resolved at the magistrate level (including both cases originally filed as misdemeanors and felony complaints reduced to misdemeanors) the percentage of trials is likely to fall in the range of 3% to 7% on a statewide basis. However, individual judicial districts, particularly in urban areas, not uncommonly have trials in less than 1% of their misdemeanor dispositions—although, as with felonies, there also are very unusual districts in which the trial rate is in the neighborhood of 20–30%.

The median time frame from the arrest of the defendant to the start of the felony trial can exceed a year in judicial districts with slow moving dockets, but for most judicial districts, it is likely to fall within the range of 5–8 months. The median will be influenced, in particular, by the mix of jury and bench trials, as the time frame tends to be considerably longer for jury trials. While most jurisdictions have speedy trials requirements that impose time limits of 6 months or less, there are various excludable time periods (for factors such as witness unavailability and the processing of motions) which commonly extend the time limit by at least a few months.

The trial itself tends to be relatively short. Misdemeanor trials typically last less than a day. Felony jury trials are somewhat longer, but most will be completed within 2–3 days. One variable will be the local practice governing voir dire (the questioning of prospective jurors, either by judge or counsel), as some jurisdictions tend to spend considerably more time on jury selection than others. Another will be the type of case, as certain types of offense (e.g., complex white collar offenses and capital homicide cases) produce trials substantially longer than the typical felony. In general trials to the bench are considerably shorter, and unlikely to last more than a day.

In all fifty-two jurisdictions, the defendant will have a right to a jury trial for all felony offenses and for misdemeanors punishable by more than 6 months imprisonment. Most states also provide a jury trial for lesser misdemeanors as well (although that right may exist only through the opportunity to seek a trial de novo in the general trial court after an initial bench trial before the magistrate court). Juries traditionally were composed of 12 persons, but most states now utilize 6 person juries in misdemeanor cases and several use the smaller juries in non-capital felony cases as well. Of course, the right to a jury trial can be waived, and in most jurisdictions, a significant number of defendants will waive the jury in favor of a bench trial. Over the country as a whole, roughly 70% of all felony trials are tried to a jury, but in various individual judicial districts, as well as some states, bench trials actually outnumber jury trials. In misdemeanor cases, in contrast, bench trials typically predominate (often accounting for 95% or more of all trials), even in jurisdictions that extend the defendant's jury trial right to all misdemeanors. In all but a few jurisdictions, the jury verdict in both misdemeanor and felony cases, whether for acquittal or conviction, must be unanimous. Where the jurors cannot agree, no verdict is entered and the case may be retried. For most communities, such "hung juries" occur in only a very small percentage of all jury trials (e.g., 3–6%, but there are large urban districts in which juries cannot reach a verdict in as many as 10–15% of all jury trials).

Whether a criminal case is tried to the bench or the jury, the odds favor conviction over acquittal. A fairly typical ratio for felony charges will be 3 convictions for every acquittal. That ratio may vary significantly, however, with the nature of the offense. In some jurisdictions, the rate of conviction at trial tends to be substantially lower (though still well above 50%) for some crimes (e.g., rape and murder) than for others (e.g., drug trafficking).

With the end of the trial stage, the criminal justice process will have produced a disposition as to all persons who originally entered the process through an arrest or the issuance of citation. As for those who were arrested on felony charges, only one out of a hundred will have had the case against him carried through to a trial that resulted in an acquittal.

A much larger portion of the felony arrestees, anywhere from 30–50%, also will not have been convicted, but the dispositions in their favor will have come before the filing of the complaint, through pre-charge police and prosecutor screening, or before the trial, either through nolle prosequi motions or judicial and grand jury screening procedures. Because of the high percentage of cases disposed of through these procedures, as well as the high percentage of convictions obtained through guilty pleas, the median time from arrest to final adjudication (including sentencing for those convicted) is much shorter for the total body of arrests than is the time from arrest to trial. Indeed, more than half of all arrests are likely to have reached a final adjudication within 100 days.

Of the 50–70% of the felony arrestees who will have been convicted, many will not have been convicted of felonies. Depending upon the plea negotiation practices followed in the particular jurisdiction, anywhere from 10–30% of those felony arrestees convicted are likely to be convicted of misdemeanors. The mix of offenses for which felony convictions are obtained will differ somewhat from the mix of felony offenses first charged by complaint. The most significant difference by general category will be in the "violent crime" grouping. Because those offenses as a group are less likely to produce convictions (although one of the offenses in that group—murder—has one of the highest conviction rates), they experience a substantial reduction (to roughly 18% from 25%) in their portion of felony convictions as compared to their portion of felony complaints. The other major categories retain their relative positions, with property offenses slightly ahead of drug offenses in their respective proportions of all felony convictions. Within categories, the portions for individual offenses tend to be altered here and there as one or two offenses in the category will produce comparatively a much lower rate on convictions or a higher percentage of convictions that are for misdemeanors rather than felonies.

(r) Step 16: Sentencing. Following conviction, the next step in the process is the determination of the sentence. In all but a few jurisdictions (which allow for jury sentencing, even apart from capital punishment), the sentence determination is the function of the court. Basically three different types of sentences may be used: financial sanctions (e.g., fines, restitution orders); some form of release into the community (e.g., probation, unsupervised release, house arrest); and incarceration in a jail (for lesser sentences) or prison (for longer sentences). The

process applied in determining the sentence is shaped in considerable part by the sentencing options made available to the court by the legislature. For a particular offense, the court may have no choice. The legislature may have prescribed that conviction automatically carries with it a certain sentence and there is nothing left for the court to do except impose that sentence. Most frequently, however, legislative narrowing of options on a particular offense does not go beyond eliminating the community release option (by requiring incarceration) and setting maximums (and sometimes mandatory minimums) for incarceration and financial sanctions.

The sentence of incarceration for a felony offense probably presents the widest diversity of approach to judicial sentencing authority. Initially, jurisdictions divide on the use of determinate and indeterminate sentences. In states utilizing indeterminate sentences, the sentencing structure calls for a maximum and minimum term of imprisonment, with the parole board determining the actual release date within the span set by the two terms. The legislature always sets the outer limit for the maximum term, but beyond that point, division of sentencing authority between the court and the legislature varies with the jurisdiction and the offense. Possibilities include: judicial authority to set both the maximum term (within the legislatively prescribed outer-limit) and the minimum term; judicial authority to set only the minimum (with the maximum and sometimes a mandatory minimum prescribed by the legislature); and judicial authority to set only a maximum within the prescribed outer-limit (with the minimum then set by law as certain percentage of the judicially set maximum).

The federal system and roughly a dozen states largely utilize determinate sentences. Those jurisdictions have eliminated for all or most offenses the discretionary release authority of the parole board. The sentence imposed by the court sets a fixed term which the prisoner will serve (subject to gaining earlier release through credits earned for "good time"). In all determinate sentencing jurisdictions, as in all indeterminate sentencing jurisdictions, the legislature sets the maximum sentence possible. In a few, the legislature sets a presumptive prison term (or narrow range of terms) which the sentencing judge is directed to use for the typical offense of a particular character (e.g., burglary), absent a finding of specific aggravating or mitigating factors calling for upward and downward adjustments. Typically, however, the setting of the specific sentence within the maximum is left either to unfettered judicial discretion or to judicial discretion operating within the restraints of guidelines formulated by a sentencing commission.

A second major division in felony sentencing structures relates to the use of legislatively mandated penalties. The legislature may mandate a specific penalty, as where it specifies that conviction for a specific crime automatically carries a sentence of life imprisonment. More frequently, however, the mandatory penalty consists of a mandated sentence of at least a certain term of incarceration. The judge in an indeterminate sentencing jurisdiction then must set a minimum term at least equal to the mandatory penalty and the judge in a determinate sentencing jurisdiction must set a fixed term at least equal to the mandatory penalty. All fifty-two jurisdictions make some use of mandatory penalties, but there is substantial variation in the frequency of their use. Some jurisdictions use mandatory penalties for a wide range of offenses and wide range of special circumstances (e.g., recidivist offenders, offenders who utilized weapons) and some use them in connection with offenses that account for only a small portion of a court's docket (e.g., murder). Where mandatory sentences are widely available (and utilized by prosecutors in their charging decisions), a significant portion of judicial sentencing in felony cases will follow automatically from those mandates.

Insofar as the legislature leaves the judge authority to choose, a third major division is found in felony sentencing structures. Most states do not seek to direct the trial court in its choice of a sentence that would fit within statutorily prescribed limits, but the federal system and a growing number of states are relying on sentencing guidelines promulgated by a sentencing commission to channel the exercise of such discretion. Those guidelines serve to establish a presumptively correct sentence of incarceration for a particular offense in accordance with the circumstances of the offense and the criminal history of the offender. Where the jurisdiction utilizes determinate sentences, the guideline presumption sets the fixed sentence; where the jurisdiction uses indeterminate sentences, the guideline ordinarily sets the minimum sentence. Typically, the guidelines also specify where a sentence other than incarceration would be appropriate, although they do not direct that such a sentence be used. In some states, the guidelines are "voluntary," and the court is free to disregard them. In most guideline jurisdictions, however, the court can depart from the guidelines only if it finds good reason to do so. Jurisdictions vary in their toleration of "departures" from the guidelines, but even where most lenient in this regard, a substantial majority of the sentences (e.g., in excess of 80%) are likely to fit within the guidelines.

The process utilized in felony sentencing varies to some extent according to whether judicial discretion is broad or is channeled or limited by guideline or legislative reference to specific sentencing circumstances. In all jurisdictions, the process is designed to obtain for the court information beyond that which will have come to its attention in the course of trial or in the acceptance of a guilty plea. The primary vehicle here is the presentence report prepared by the probation department, although the prosecution and defense commonly will be allowed to present additional information and to challenge the information contained in the presentence report. The presentation of this information is not subject to the rules governing the presentation of information at trial. The rules of evidence do not apply, and neither the prosecution nor the defense has a right to call witnesses or to cross-examine the sources of adverse information presented in the presentence report or in any additional documentation presented by the opposing side. However, where the sentencing authority of the judge is restricted by guidelines or legislatively set presumptive sentences that require findings of fact as to specific factors, the sentencing process tends to be more formal. Here, the court often will find it necessary to hold an evidentiary hearing and utilize trial-type procedures if the presence of a critical factor is controverted. . . .

Sentences that are not automatically mandated, at least as to felony convictions and serious misdemeanor convictions, will be geared to a wide range of factors in addition to the basic elements of the crime of conviction. In choosing among allowable alternatives, the judge may consider, and often under guidelines will be required to consider, such factors as aggravating and mitigating circumstances relating to the particular offense, past criminal convictions, criminal behavior that did not result in a conviction, and the defendant's acceptance of responsibility. The end result is that it became very difficult without close analysis of individual cases to compare sentences even where convictions were for the same offense. Nonetheless, some general patterns emerge by reference to the level of the offense for which the sentence is imposed. . . .

As for felony convictions, the level of the offense and prior criminal history are the keys to the choice between incarceration and non-incarceration and the location of the incarceration. Defendants convicted of low level felony offenses more often than not receive a sentence of incarceration, but a substantial portion (e.g., 30–45%) will receive a sentence of non-incarceration (most often including probation). Among defendants sentenced to incarceration for such offenses, a majority tend to be sentenced to prison, but a substantial minority (35–45%) are sentenced to jail, receiving terms less than a year. Where the defendant convicted of such a felony has one or more prior felony convictions, however, there will be a substantial drop in the percentage receiving a sentence of nonincarceration and a substantial increase in those sentenced to prison rather than to jail. For more serious felonies which do not involve violence, such as burglary and drug trafficking, the proportion of defendants sentenced to prison terms is likely to approach or exceed 50%, with the remainder about equally divided between jail sentences (often combined with probation) and straight probation. Serious violent crimes, such as murder, rape, and robbery, have the highest rate of prison sentences, ranging from above 90% for the murder category (which includes non-negligent manslaughter) to close to 70% for the rape category (which includes forcible rapes and attempted forcible rapes).

Although the length of the prison sentence set by the court has quite different significance in different sentencing structures, nationwide sentence lengths are usually assessed by reference to the maximum term that can be served under the court's sentence. Under this standard, in 1992, the nationwide mean prison sentence was 164 months for persons convicted in state courts of rape, 117 months for persons convicted of robbery, 76 months for persons convicted of burglary, 53 months for persons convicted of larceny, and 55 months for persons convicted of drug possession. Since most of those terms merely set the maximum length in an indeterminate sentencing structure, the more important measurement is the minimum term that determines when the individual becomes eligible for parole. Moreover, many jurisdictions provide for extensive "good time credits" that will reduce that minimum term or the fixed term of a determinate sentence. As a result, prisoners nationwide tend to serve between 40% and 60% of the mean maximum sentence, with the percentage varying with the nature of the offense. Thus, while the mean term for rape is 164 months, the mean time actually served is likely to be in the range of 91 months, and while the mean term for larceny is 53 months, the mean time actually to be served will be about 17 months.

   (s) *Step 17: Appeals.* For criminal cases disposed of in the general trial court, the initial appeal is to the intermediate appellate court. If the state has no intermediate appellate court, then the initial and final appeal within the state system is to the state's court of last resort. Initial appeals in cases disposed of by the magistrate court will be to the general trial court. In some jurisdictions, the appeal procedure from a conviction in the magistrate court is a trial de novo before the general trial court, rather than that court exercising appellate review of the lower court record.

Although all convicted defendants are entitled to appeal their convictions, appeals are taken predominantly by convicted defendants who were sentenced to imprisonment on a felony conviction. Imprisoned defendants convicted pursuant to a guilty plea are included in this group, but they account for only a narrow slice of all appeals. Though the trial court's acceptance of a guilty plea may be challenged on appeal, such appellate challenges are limited to exceptional cases, so that appeals by guilty plea defendants tend to be sentencing challenges, which usually are significant only in jurisdictions that use sentencing guidelines or legislatively mandated presumptive sentences. In those jurisdictions, challenges to the sentence can constitute a substantial portion (e.g., 15–30%) of all appeals.

Appeals challenging the conviction itself come primarily from imprisoned defendants who are seeking review of a trial conviction. Indeed, in some jurisdictions, as many as 90% of the defendants who were convicted after trial and sentenced to prison will appeal their convictions. Even with almost automatic appeal by this group, however, the total number of appeals to the intermediate appeals court is likely to amount to less than 10% of all convictions entered by the state's general trial court. Of course, where the jurisdiction provides for extensive appellate review of sentencing, the overall percentage of appeals is likely to be somewhat higher. Appeals from misdemeanor convictions before the magistrate courts, on the other hand, can very well amount to less than 1% of the number of convictions entered in the magistrate courts.

Appeals challenging convictions raise a wide range of issues, usually relating to some action or inaction of the trial judge. The court's admission of evidence challenged as unconstitutionally obtained stands out in several jurisdictions as by far the most frequently raised appellate objection, but in others, that objection is raised no more frequently than several other claims, such as the alleged insufficiency of the evidence and incompetency of counsel. Defense success on appeal varies with the particular appellate court. Among the federal Courts of Appeals, for example, for criminal appeals terminated on the merits in 1990, the percentage of reversals ranged from a high of 15% in the District of Columbia Circuit to a low of 7.4% in the First Circuit, with an overall rate of 10.4% for all circuits. State intermediate appellate courts commonly have a reversal rate on defense appeals of right in the 5–10% range, although those rates will be somewhat higher when reversals in part are included. Courts of last resort, with discretionary jurisdiction, may have a substantially higher rate of reversals than the intermediate appellate courts in the same state.

(t) Step 18: Postconviction Remedies. After the appellate process is exhausted, imprisoned defendants may be able to use postconviction remedies to challenge their convictions on limited grounds. In particular, federal postconviction remedies are available to state as well as federal prisoners to challenge their convictions in the federal courts on most constitutional grounds. The federal district courts currently receive roughly 18,000 such postconviction applications. Relief is granted on less than 3 percent of these petitions, however, and the relief often is limited to requiring a further hearing. In the state system, annual postconviction challenges typically fall below 5% of all felony filings.

● OVERVIEW OF PROVING CRIMES

Model Penal Code Section 1.12
(Official Draft 1962)

Section 1.12. Proof Beyond a Reasonable Doubt; Affirmative Defenses; Burden of Proving Fact When Not an Element of an Offense; Presumptions

(1) No person may be convicted of an offense unless each element of such offense is proved beyond a reasonable doubt. In the absence of such proof, the innocence of the defendant is assumed.

(2) Subsection (1) of this Section does not:

(a) require the disproof of an affirmative defense unless and until there is evidence supporting such defense; or

(b) apply to any defense which the Code or another statute plainly requires the defendant to prove by a preponderance of evidence.

(3) A ground of defense is affirmative, within the meaning of Subsection (2) (a) of this Section, when:

(a) it arises under a section of the Code which so provides; or

(b) it relates to an offense defined by a statute other than the Code and such statute so provides; or

(c) it involves a matter of excuse or justification peculiarly within the knowledge of the defendant on which he can fairly be required to adduce supporting evidence.

(4) When the application of the Code depends upon the finding of a fact which is not an element of an offense, unless the Code otherwise provides:

(a) the burden of proving the fact is on the prosecution or defendant, depending on whose interest or contention will be furthered if the finding should be made; and

(b) the fact must be proved to the satisfaction of the Court or jury, as the case may be.

(5) When the Code establishes a presumption with respect to any fact which is an element of an offense, it has the following consequences:

(a) when there is evidence of the facts which give rise to the presumption, the issue of the existence of the presumed fact must be submitted to the jury, unless the Court is satisfied that the evidence as a whole clearly negatives the presumed fact; and

(b) when the issue of the existence of the presumed fact is submitted to the jury, the Court shall charge that while the presumed fact must, on all the evidence, be proved beyond a reasonable doubt, the law declares that the jury may regard the facts giving rise to the presumption as sufficient evidence of the presumed fact.

(6) A presumption not established by the Code or inconsistent with it has the consequences otherwise accorded it by law.

Notes

Each jurisdiction sets rules for establishing which party in a criminal case has the burden of proving which issues. In addition, the federal Constitution has been interpreted to impose some restrictions on how a state may allocate these evidentiary burdens, also known as burdens of proof. Three distinct burdens of proof are involved: the burden of pleading; the burden of production; and the burden of persuasion.

Burden of Pleading   The party that has the *burden of pleading* on an issue, also known as the *burden of going forward*, has the obligation to raise the issue. Little evidence is required. The state has the burden of pleading on all elements of the offense, but the defendant frequently has the burden of pleading for issues of defense, even if such defenses operate by negating an offense element. For example, the defendant may have the burden of raising the issue of his mental illness even if its claimed effect is to show he lacked the culpability element required for liability. If the defendant does not raise the claim of mental illness in a timely and proper fashion, he may be unable to offer evidence to support that claim, even if such evidence would be relevant to the issue of culpability.

Burden of Production   Once all applicable burdens of pleading have been satisfied, the *burden of production* establishes the amount of evidence that a party must present on an issue to get that issue to the jury (or factfinding judge, in a bench trial). The prosecution has the burden of production for all elements of the offense, including issues raised by the defendant that suggest the absence of a required element. Thus, if the defendant offers an alibi or claims a mistake or mental illness negating an offense element, the prosecution nonetheless must establish that, notwithstanding the evidence of alibi, mistake, or mental illness, sufficient evidence exists to satisfy its burden of production for all offense elements. The defendant may bear the burden of production, however, for issues of defense other than those relating to offense elements.

Failure to Satisfy Burden of Production   If the prosecution fails to meet its burden of production on any offense element, the trial judge enters a verdict of acquittal. If the prosecution has the burden of production to disprove a defense and fails to meet that burden, the jury will be instructed on the defense. (Of course, if the prosecution also has the burden of persuasion to disprove the defense, the court may simply enter a judgement of acquittal, on the theory that if the prosecution cannot meet its burden of production, it would be unable to meet its more demanding burden of persuasion.) If the defense has the burden of production on a defense issue and fails to meet that burden, the jury will not be instructed to consider that defense.

Burden of Production vs. Pleading   The burden of production must be distinguished from the burden of pleading, discussed above. The burden of pleading simply imposes an obligation on the burdened party to raise the issue, but merely raising an issue is not enough to get it before the factfinder. The burden of production imposes a standard of evidence that must be met for the burdened party to succeed in having the issue presented to (or, for a few issues, withheld from) the jury. The burden of pleading is simply the first step in the evidentiary battle. The defense may meet its burden of pleading for a defense, yet if it fails to back up its claim with any evidence, or if the prosecution introduces contrary evidence that discredits the defense's initial claim, the defense will not satisfy its burden of production, and the claimed defense will not be presented to the jury.

Evidence Required to Satisfy Burden of Production   The amount of evidence required to satisfy a burden of production typically is stated in vague terms and may vary from jurisdiction to jurisdiction. Such tests generally appear in statutes or court rules of procedure, and so they do not have constitutional status. However, the Supreme Court has provided what is in effect a constitutional minimum standard for the prosecution's burden of production, by elaborating a rule for reviewing the sufficiency of evidence to support a conviction.[1] In *Jackson v. Virginia*, the Court held that a conviction must be reversed if the evidence presented at the trial, taken in the light most favorable to the prosecution, could not lead any rational trier of fact to find proof of guilt beyond a reasonable doubt. If the prosecution's evidence does not satisfy this standard, meaning that any resulting conviction will be reversed as a violation of due process, it would seem to follow that a trial court should not give the case to the jury in the first place, but should simply enter a judgement of acquittal—that is, the court should find that the prosecution has failed to meet its burden of production.

Model Penal Code's Burden of Production   In civil practice, each party carries the burden of production for those issues from which the party will benefit. Thus, the defendant typically has the burden of production for all defenses. This tends to be true in criminal trials as well, but many jurisdictions follow the Model Penal Code in allocating the burden of production on many defense issues to the prosecution, even though that is not constitutionally required. Where this occurs, the prosecution must introduce sufficient evidence to *disprove* the defense. Where the burden is not met, the trial court will not let the case go to the jury and will, instead, enter a judgement of acquittal. Under the Model Penal Code, the defendant bears the burden of production only for defenses that are denoted *affirmative defenses*. "Disproof of an affirmative defense [by the state is not required] *unless*

---

1. Jackson v. Virginia, 443 U.S. 307 (1979) (defendant, convicted of first degree murder, challenged jury finding of premeditation beyond reasonable doubt).

and until there is evidence supporting such defense."[2] Note that no set amount of evidence is required of the defendant, but "evidence" presumably means something more than an unsubstantiated claim.[3] The Code also provides:

> A ground of defense is affirmative when:
>
>   (a) it arises under a section of the Code which so provides; or
>
>   (b) it relates to an offense defined by a statute other than the Code and such statute so provides; or
>
>   (c) it involves a matter of excuse or justification peculiarly within the knowledge of the defendant on which he can fairly be required to adduce supporting evidence.[4]

General defenses labeled as "affirmative" in the Model Penal Code include the involuntary-intoxication excuse, duress, military orders, all justification defenses, insanity, and renunciation.[5]

Burden of Persuasion   Once the case reaches the jury, the burden of persuasion tells the jury (or other factfinder) which party needs to convince them of its position on any given issue, and how firmly convinced they must be. The default position is that, for any given issue, the jury should find for the party without the burden; the burdened party wins the issue only if its evidence sufficiently persuades the jury to find otherwise. The prosecution has the burden of persuasion for all offense elements, and its burden is heavy: the jury must be convinced that all elements have been shown *beyond a reasonable doubt*. If a reasonable doubt remains as to even a single element—even if the jury thinks the element is "probably" satisfied, that is, more likely to be true than not—the jury is obliged to acquit the defendant. The prosecution may also have the burden of persuasion for some defenses; for example, it is common to allocate the burden to the prosecution for justification defenses, so that the prosecution must persuade the jury beyond a reasonable doubt that the defendant was *not* justified. For other defenses—such as, commonly, insanity—the defendant may have the burden of persuasion (limitations on allocating this burden to the defendant are discussed below). When the defendant bears the burden of persuasion, it is typically less strict than the beyond-a-reasonable-doubt standard, requiring instead proof by a *preponderance* of the evidence (that is, more likely then not), or by *clear and convincing* evidence. (The clear-and-convincing standard is meant to be easier to satisfy than the reasonable-doubt standard, but juries might not apply the two standards accordingly—there is some evidence that laypeople, who are potential jurors, think the clear-and-convincing standard requires *more* proof, not less.)

Burden of Persuasion vs. Production   Note that the burden of persuasion is distinct from the burden of production. The burden of production imposes a legal standard, assessed by the court, whereas the burden of persuasion is assessed by the factfinder (typically a jury). The burden of production usually demands only a conclusion that *some* rational factfinder could *potentially* find in favor of

---

2. Model Penal Code § 1.12(2)(a) (emphasis added).

3. The commentary states the drafters' preference for leaving the requisite amount of evidence vague in the code. They "thought it the wiser course to leave this question to the courts." Model Penal Code § 1.12 comment 3 at 193 (1985).

4. Model Penal Code § 1.12(3).

5. Model Penal Code §§ 2.08(4), 2.09(1), 2.10, 3.01, 4.03(1), 5.01(3), 5.02(3), 5.03(6). Specific offenses also contain affirmative defenses.

the burdened party, not that such a finding is required, or even likely. Satisfying the burden of production will get the case to the jury, but says nothing about what the jury will do with it—the jury's decision is governed by the burden of persuasion. Note also that the burdens of production and persuasion may fall on different parties for the same issue. For example, as noted above, the defendant typically has the burden of production (and pleading) for justification defense, but the prosecution typically has the burden of persuasion to disprove such defenses. The defense must introduce sufficient evidence for the defense to be presented to the jury, but having done so, the prosecution is charged with convincing the jury that the justification claim should fail.

Constitutional Restrictions in Allocating Burden of Persuasion   The federal Constitution limits the issues on which the defendant may be given the burden of persuasion. *In re Winship* held that the prosecution must prove beyond a reasonable doubt "every fact necessary to constitute the crime with which [the defendant] is charged."[6] In *Mullaney v. Wilbur*, this was held to include *disproving* the defendant's claim of provocation; under the Maine murder statute, provocation was seen as inconsistent with the required element of malice aforethought, so that the presence of provocation would mean a killing did not constitute murder.[7] In *Patterson v. New York*, however, the Court held that the state need not carry the burden of persuasion on disproving the defendant's claim of extreme emotional disturbance.[8] A modern, expanded form of the provocation mitigation, New York's "extreme emotional disturbance" doctrine was defined not as something that negated a required offense element, but rather as providing an independent doctrine of mitigation; the rule's effect was not to exclude such killings from the category of murder, but to treat them as a subcategory of murder entitled to mitigated punishment. Earlier cases held, and *Patterson* confirmed, that the burden of persuasion also may be constitutionally allocated to the defendant for a defense of insanity.[9] Aside from these, the Court has not fully clarified the criteria to be used in assessing whether an issue is sufficiently like an offense element to require the prosecution to carry the burden of persuasion on it, or whether it is sufficiently like the defense of insanity or the mitigation of extreme emotional disturbance to allow allocation to the defendant.

Model Penal Code's Burden of Persuasion   The Model Penal Code, as noted above, allocates the burden of persuasion to the prosecution on most issues, including defenses, even though such allocation is not constitutionally required. The Code provides:

> No person may be convicted of an offense unless each element of such offense is proved beyond a reasonable doubt. In the absence of such proof, the innocence of the defendant is assumed.[10]

The code then defines "element of an offense" very broadly to include the absence of most general defenses:

---

6. 397 U.S. 358, 364 (1970) (in juvenile delinquency proceeding for 12-year-old charged with stealing, child entitled, as matter of due process, to have case against him proven beyond reasonable doubt).

7. 421 U.S. 684 (1975).

8. 432 U.S. 197 (1977).

9. Leland v. Oregon, 343 U.S. 790 (1952); Rivera v. Delaware, 429 U.S. 877 (1976); Patterson, 432 U.S. at 204.

10. Model Penal Code § 1.12(1).

"element of an offense" means (i) such conduct or (ii) such attendant circumstances or (iii) such a result of conduct as

(a) is included in the description of the forbidden conduct in the definition of the offense; or

(b) establishes the required kind of culpability; or

(c) negatives an excuse or justification for such conduct; or

(d) negatives a defense under the statute of limitations; or

(e) establishes jurisdiction or venue[.][11]

The only exception to the prosecution's burden of persuasion is "any defense which the Code or another statute plainly requires the defendant to prove by a preponderance of evidence."[12] The Code allocates the burden of persuasion to the defendant for, among other things, the general mistake-of-law defense for unavailable law and reliance on official misstatement; the due diligence defense to liability of an organization; and entrapment.[13] For the few facts that do not fall under the Code's broad meaning of the phrase "element of an offense," the allocation of the burden of persuasion is governed as follows:

When the application of the Code depends upon the finding of a fact which is not an element of an offense, unless the Code otherwise provides:

(a) the burden of proving the fact is on the prosecution or defendant, depending on whose interest or contention will be furthered if the finding should be made; and

(b) the fact must be proved to the satisfaction of the Court or jury, as the case may be.[14]

Most states do not follow the Model Penal Code on these issues. Most define "elements of an offense" in a more common-sense way to include just the elements of the offense definition, and are more likely to put the burden of persuasion for a general defense on the defendant.

Mandatory Presumptions The law has sometimes established *presumptions* that allow, or even require, a jury to conclude one thing based on proof of something else. For example, murder requires proof of an intention to kill, but the jury might be instructed that "the law presumes that a person intends the ordinary consequences of his voluntary acts." Yet the effect of such a presumption— essentially telling the jury that its default position should be to conclude the defendant had the required intent—may be similar to shifting the burden of persuasion to the defendant, for it effectively requires the defendant to convince the jury that she did *not* have that intent. This kind of *de facto* burden-shifting subverts the usual constitutional requirement (imposed in *Winship*, as noted above) that the prosecution must prove all elements, such as intention to kill, beyond a reasonable doubt. For this reason, such a presumption was held unconstitutional in *Sandstrom v. Montana*.[15] These presumptions are called *mandatory* presumptions because they *direct*, or might be interpreted by a jury as directing, the jury to find the presumed fact if the other fact is proved.

---

11. Model Penal Code § 1.13(9).
12. Model Penal Code § 1.12(2)(b).
13. Model Penal Code §§ 2.04(4), 2.07(5), 2.13(2).
14. Model Penal Code § 1.12(4).
15. 442 U.S. 510 (1979).

Permissive Inferences Only mandatory presumptions have been held unconstitutional. It is acceptable to instruct a jury that the law *allows,* but does not require, it to find one fact (the "presumed fact") based on proof of another fact (the "proved fact"). Such a rule commonly is called a *permissive inference.* Thus, a jury may be instructed that it is permitted to find that a prohibited weapon in a vehicle was possessed by the person in the vehicle. Under such a permissive inference, proof that a gun and a person were both in a car at the same time suffices, as a matter of law, for the jury to conclude that the person possessed the gun—though the jury may also conclude otherwise, even if it agrees that both the person and the gun were in the car. Permissible inferences are constitutional, however, only if in practice the existence of the presumed fact follows, more likely than not, from the proved fact. It is likely that a person in a car containing a weapon possesses that weapon; but it is not, for example, more likely than not that a person who bumps someone into the street from a crowded crosswalk, causing him to be struck and killed, intended to kill that person.

Multiple Functions of Permissive Inferences Permissive inferences may serve either or both of two different evidentiary purposes: (1) the proved fact may satisfy, or help satisfy, a party's burden of *production* as to the presumed fact; and (2) the proved fact may entitle the jury to find the burden of *persuasion* is satisfied as to the presumed fact. For example, the Model Penal Code provides:

> When the Code establishes a presumption with respect to any fact which is an element of an offense, it has the following consequences:
>
> (a) when there is evidence of the facts which give rise to the presumption, the issue of the existence of the presumed fact must be submitted to the jury, unless the Court is satisfied that the evidence as a whole clearly negatives the presumed fact; and
>
> (b) when the issue of the existence of the presumed fact is submitted to the jury, the Court shall charge that while the presumed fact must, on all the evidence, be proved beyond a reasonable doubt, the law declares that the jury may regard the facts giving rise to the presumption as sufficient evidence of the presumed fact.[16]

Subsection (a) addresses the consequences for purposes of the burden of production, subsection (b) for the burden of persuasion. The Code uses the term "presumption," but the effect of its rules is to create a permissive inference, making its scheme constitutional even under the Supreme Court cases decided years after the Code was drafted (and probably influenced by the Model Code's provisions).

Evidentiary Burdens for Sentencing Guidelines As discussed earlier, a number of jurisdictions have adopted sentencing guidelines that create rules to determine an acceptable range of liability for offenders given their particular offense. Typically the guidelines identify various factors—such as prior criminal history, expressions of remorse, and so on—for judges to consider in deciding where in the range the punishment should fall, or even whether to go outside the usual default range (to *depart* upward or downward, in the usual language). A series of Supreme Court cases have addressed the relation between sentencing guidelines and the Sixth Amendment right to a jury trial. In one case, *United*

---

16. Model Penal Code § 1.12(5)&(6).

States v. Booker,[17] the Supreme Court ruled that if a guideline scheme imposes mandatory rules, such that finding certain facts *requires* the judge to aggravate or reduce an offender's sentence, any fact necessary to enhance an offender's sentence beyond the default sentencing range (that is, beyond the maximum authorized by the facts required to convict the defendant in the first place) is subject to the rules set out in *Winship*: the prosecution must prove any such fact to a jury beyond a reasonable doubt.

Example of Application of Winship *Rules to Sentencing*   Suppose, for example, that a defendant is convicted of a drug offense whose elements require selling an illegal drug in an amount exceeding 50 grams. The jury's vote to convict establishes that the jury has found, beyond a reasonable doubt, that the defendant sold at least 50 grams of the drug. But it does not establish that the jury concluded anything about whether the defendant sold *more* than 50 grams; the defendant might have sold much more, but the jury was not required to determine that. Suppose that selling 50 grams would lead to a guidelines sentence of 21 to 27 months in prison, but the prosecution wants to have the defendant sentenced under the guideline for selling 600 grams, which would lead to a sentence of 63 to 78 months in prison. Prior to *Booker,* the prosecution could obtain a sentence in the higher range by convincing the sentencing judge, by a preponderance of the evidence, that the defendant sold 600 grams. After *Booker,* in any mandatory guidelines scheme, the prosecution would be required to convince a jury, beyond a reasonable doubt, that the defendant sold 600 grams (or whatever minimum quantity would support the sentencing range being pursued).

Guidelines as Advisory, Rather than Mandatory   After holding that the existing federal guidelines system was unconstitutional, because it allowed sentencing enhancements based on facts proved to a judge by a preponderance of evidence instead of to a jury beyond a reasonable doubt, the *Booker* court fashioned a remedy that would make the guidelines constitutional: it held that the guidelines would henceforth be advisory, rather than mandatory. Accordingly, sentencing judges are now free to depart from the recommended guideline ranges, subject to appellate review of their sentences for "reasonableness" in light of the facts of the case and the overall purposes of the guidelines.

---

17. 543 U.S. 220 (2005).

INTRODUCTORY MATERIALS

The Nature of Criminal Law and Its Structure

How is criminal law different from other kinds of law? How are the sources and the form of criminal law different from that of other kinds of law? How are criminal cases analyzed under modern criminal codes? These are the questions addressed in this Section. Fundamental to the study of criminal law is an understanding of the distinct function of criminal law that distinguishes it from civil law. While the behavior that each seeks to condemn or punish may often overlap, the following section attempts to highlight the important differences between the two and to illustrate the manner in which criminal law assigns liability for an actor's actions. In the following hypothetical, consider the differences between civil and criminal law in the matters of consent, justification, requisite level of culpability, and the extent of the offense harm or evil.

● OVERVIEW OF THE NATURE OF CRIMINAL LAW

Hypothetical: Fear, Pain, and Bubble Gum (#1)

Ike has decided to join ZBT fraternity. During "hell week" the aspiring "pledges" are on call at all times to provide labor, entertainment, or anything else that a current ZBT brother might desire. School policy prevents skipping classes during hell week. This rule is a godsend for the pledges: Classes provide the only opportunity to sleep. With the altered function of classes, books are unnecessary. Instead, pledges carry hardwood pledge paddles and the favorite candy of each brother.

After a very restful hour of thermodynamics, Ike meets Brother Constin. "Cherry bubble gum, pledge."

Ike's mouth drops, and his heart stops. "Aaaah . . . I thought you liked strawberry, Mr. Constin."

"You have five minutes to compensate for your incompetence, pledge."

Ike scrambles. He spots Ed Begley, another ZBT pledge, 100 yards away.

"Ed, have you got cherry bubble gum for Constin?"

Ed's eyebrows pop up. "I thought he liked strawberry."

Ike bolts for the local convenience store, with Ed close behind. He spots cherry in the bubble gum box—but the moment sours as they realize that neither has any money. Ike grabs two pieces and heads for the door. "I'll be back later to pay for this," he shouts over his shoulder to the shopkeeper, who is unimpressed and shouts back, "Come back here! You can't take that without paying for it."

Ed explains their situation to the shopkeeper. After some discussion, the shopkeeper lets Ed have two pieces free, but notes that he still considers Ike a thief. Ed dashes out the front and around the back of the store. He thinks he can make up for lost time by taking a shortcut that he knows. But as he squeezes between two cars parked in the alley behind the store, he loses his footing. As he falls, he cuts his leg badly and becomes wedged between the two cars. His struggle only wedges him tighter and his cries for help go unheard. He feels himself getting faint from loss of blood and decides that he must break the window of one of the cars to get maneuvering room to extricate himself. After smashing the window, he manages to free himself and limps back into the store, where the owner calls an ambulance and puts a tourniquet on his bleeding leg.

Meanwhile, Ike is wondering what happened to Ed; he concludes that Ed may be having second thoughts about pledging ZBT. Brother Constin is waiting at the edge of campus. "That was six minutes, pledge." By Ike's watch, it has been only four minutes, but he decides protesting would not be useful. Brother Constin pronounces sentence. "Three whacks." Ike hands Brother Constin his paddle and bends to receive three stinging strikes. Ike expects that, like many of the current brothers of ZBT, he will emerge from hell week with permanent scars. For now he responds, "Thank you, sir, you have helped me in my quest to reach the perfection of brotherhood."

"You are welcome," Constin replies, handing back the paddle. While hazing is technically unlawful, it has been generally ignored in the past. But the incident at the convenience store, in particular, draws the university's ire, and the fraternity's pledge privileges are suspended for a year. To show its concern for lawless conduct during pledge week, the university supports both civil claims and criminal charges against Brother Constin for assault, against Ike for theft of the bubble gum, and against Ed for damage to the car. The civil assault claims against Constin are dismissed on the ground that Ike consented, he knew the effects of the paddling he was consenting to, and he is an adult who can make an informed decision to consent to the injury. In the civil action for taking the gum without permission, Ike concedes his liability and pays the minor damages sought by the store owner. Ed similarly concedes and compensates the car owner.

What criminal liability, if any, should ensue for Constin, Ike, and Ed? Consider Brother Constin's liability for assaulting Ike, Ike's liability for theft, and Ed's liability for damaging the car.

Model Penal Code
(Official Draft 1962)

Section 2.02. General Requirements of Culpability

(1) Minimum Requirements of Culpability. Except as provided in Section 2.05, a person is not guilty of an offense unless he acted purposely, knowingly, recklessly or negligently, as the law may require, with respect to each material element of the offense. . . .

(3) Culpability Required Unless Otherwise Provided. When the culpability sufficient to establish a material element of an offense is not prescribed by law, such element is established if a person acts purposely, knowingly or recklessly with respect thereto. . . .

Section 2.11. Consent

(1) In General. The consent of the victim to conduct charged to constitute an offense or to the result thereof is a defense if such consent negatives an element of the offense or precludes the infliction of the harm or evil sought to be prevented by the law defining the offense.

(2) Consent to Bodily Injury. When conduct is charged to constitute an offense because it causes or threatens bodily injury, consent to such conduct or to the infliction of such injury is a defense if:

    (a) the bodily injury consented to or threatened by the conduct consented to is not serious; or

    (b) the conduct and the injury are reasonably foreseeable hazards of joint participation in a lawful athletic contest or competitive sport or other concerted activity not forbidden by law; or

    (c) the consent establishes a justification for the conduct under Article 3 of the Code.

(3) Ineffective Consent. Unless otherwise provided by the Code or by the law defining the offense, assent does not constitute consent if:

    (a) it is given by a person who is legally incompetent to authorize the conduct charged to constitute the offense; or

    (b) it is given by a person who by reason of youth, mental disease or defect or intoxication is manifestly unable or known by the actor to be unable to make a reasonable judgment as to the nature or harmfulness of the conduct charged to constitute the offense; or

    (c) it is given by a person whose improvident consent is sought to be prevented by the law defining the offense; or

    (d) it is induced by force, duress or deception of a kind sought to be prevented by the law defining the offense.

Section 2.12. De Minimis Infractions

The Court shall dismiss a prosecution if, having regard to the nature of the conduct charged to constitute an offense and the nature of the attendant circumstances, it finds that the defendant's conduct:

(1) was within a customary license or tolerance, neither expressly negatived by the person whose interest was infringed nor inconsistent with the purpose of the law defining the offense; or

(2) did not actually cause or threaten the harm or evil sought to be prevented by the law defining the offense or did so only to an extent too trivial to warrant the condemnation of conviction; or

(3) presents such other extenuations that it cannot reasonably be regarded as envisaged by the legislature in forbidding the offense. The Court shall not dismiss a prosecution under Subsection (3) of this Section without filing a written statement of its reasons.

Section 3.02. Justification Generally: Choice of Evils

(1) Conduct which the actor believes to be necessary to avoid a harm or evil to himself or to another is justifiable, provided that:

(a) the harm or evil sought to be avoided by such conduct is greater than that sought to be prevented by the law defining the offense charged; and

(b) neither the Code nor other law defining the offense provides exceptions or defenses dealing with the specific situation involved; and

(c) a legislative purpose to exclude the justification claimed does not otherwise plainly appear.

(2) When the actor was reckless or negligent in bringing about the situation requiring a choice of harms or evils or in appraising the necessity for his conduct, the justification afforded by this Section is unavailable in a prosecution for any offense for which recklessness or negligence, as the case may be, suffices to establish culpability.

Notes

Criminal-Civil Similarities and Overlaps
    Government as Complainant in Civil, as Well as Criminal Cases
General Difference: Criminal Law Focuses on Moral Blame
Specific Examples Reflecting General Distinction
    Culpability Requirement
    Crimes vs. Violations
    Malum In Se vs. Malum Prohibitum
        Malum Prohibitum Category Is Controversial, But Ever Expanding
    Consent as Defense to Civil Liability
    Role of Consent for Criminal Law
    Justification and Excuse Defenses
    De Minimis Defense
    Only Moral Wrongdoing Merits "Condemnation as Criminal"

Criminal-Civil Similarities and Overlaps   Criminal law often does not have unique or exclusive authority over the conduct it punishes. Often, conduct violates both criminal and civil law. For example, striking another person without her consent may be both a crime and a tort. Nor is criminal law unique in the deprivations that it imposes. Civil commitment, tort law, and a variety of other civil measures can deprive a person of his or her liberty, put restrictions on what a person can do, and compel the payment of money.

Government as Complainant in Civil, as Well as Criminal Cases   Criminal cases do typically have procedural characteristics different from civil cases. For example, crimes are prosecuted by the state rather than by the victim, while civil cases often have a private "plaintiff" who brings the action. On the other hand, state prosecution is not unique to criminal actions. Many legal claims the state pursues against its citizens—including claims whose impact on the defendant can be quite harsh—are characterized as civil claims, such as when the state seeks to remove a mother's custody over her child, to have an undocumented alien deported, to have a person's property condemned or forfeited, or to demand payment of taxes.

If criminal law is not unique with respect to the parties involved, the subject matter of the claim, or the forms or remedy or relief it imposes, what makes it distinctive? Its existence as a separate body of law must have an explanation apart from its prohibitions, deprivations, or procedures.

order

General Difference: Criminal Law Focuses on Moral Blame   The conventional wisdom holds that criminal liability generally reflects moral blameworthiness deserving condemnation and punishment, whereas civil liability does not. Crimes are thought to comprise behavior "which, if duly proven to have taken place, will incur a formal and solemn pronouncement of the moral condemnation of the community."[1] Another way of expressing this distinction is to say that criminal liability imposes *punishment*—that is, it causes people to experience some pain or hardship as a penalty for some wrong they have committed. Although civil liability may also lead to hardship or deprivation, it typically does so for the sake of providing compensation, promoting public welfare, or some other goal, rather than to make the defendant experience punishment and its attendant moral censure.

Specific Examples Reflecting General Distinction   The specific ways in which civil and criminal law differ tend to support this sense that the distinctive quality of criminal law is its focus on moral blameworthiness. Various substantive and procedural rules peculiar to criminal law ensure that its reach is limited to cases where an offender has committed a moral wrong.

Culpability Requirement   Characteristic of criminal law is a requirement that the actor's state of mind reflect *culpability*—a blameworthy attitude or disposition—as to the offense elements. Bringing about a prohibited harm or evil is not itself sufficient for criminal liability; for example, one who causes harm purely by accident lacks culpability and therefore merits no punishment. Generally, the criminal law demands at least *recklessness* as to every offense element. That is, an actor must have some personal awareness of the facts that make his or her conduct wrongful. Still higher culpability levels, such as *knowledge* or *purpose*, commonly are required as to one or more offense elements. Liability based on lower degrees of culpability—such as criminal *negligence*, where an actor is blameworthy for lacking (rather than possessing) an awareness of what she is doing, or *strict liability* where no culpability is required at all—is less frequent and more controversial. Strict liability may even be limited to mere "violations,"[2] which are distinguished from "crimes." Civil liability, in contrast, frequently requires no culpable state of mind. When culpability is required, commonly only negligence need be shown,

---

1. Henry M. Hart, The Aims of the Criminal Law, 23 Law & Contemp. Probs. 401, 405 (1958).
2. Model Penal Code § 2.05(2).

and even then, the civil negligence standard may be less demanding than the criminal standard.

Crimes vs. Violations   As just noted, many criminal codes distinguish "crimes" from mere "violations," which do not reflect the same moral gravity as crimes. In the words of the influential Model Penal Code, a violation "does not constitute a crime and conviction of a violation shall not give rise to any disability or legal disadvantage based on conviction of a criminal offense."[3] Thus, illegal parking, motor vehicle violations, and other such prohibitions—which often do not require culpability, and which typically address morally trivial misconduct—generally are not "crimes," even though they are enforced by the same officers who enforce the criminal law.

Malum In Se vs. Malum Prohibitum   In keeping with the understanding that criminal law exists to punish and prevent harmful or wrongful conduct, criminal offenses have traditionally focused on behavior that is considered, to use the traditional Latin phrase, *malum in se*: bad in itself. Such conduct violates some pre-legal moral or social norm; in criminalizing the conduct, the criminal law is merely reflecting and cementing that independent norm. Yet criminal law has also long recognized offenses punishing conduct viewed as *malum prohibitum,* or "bad because it is prohibited"—not wrongful by its nature, but only because the law says it is. *Malum prohibitum* offenses can be entirely justified and sensible, as where the law is solving a coordination problem to define shared conventions whose violation, once they are established, can cause genuine disruption and harm. For example, there is nothing inherently wrong with driving on the left side of the road: People in many countries do it all the time and properly so. Yet once the law decrees that people should drive only on the right side of the road, driving on the left side of the road undermines social order on the roadways (even where it does not endanger others, as it often will). Many regulatory schemes would struggle or collapse if they could not punish those who refuse to play by their rules: There would be little reason to pay taxes, or to get a license before driving or hunting or practicing medicine, if the law could not penalize failure to do so.

Malum Prohibitum Category Is Controversial, but Ever Expanding   Even so, offenses falling in the *malum prohibitum* category are sometimes thought to need special justification. The state should not employ the criminal sanction lightly, and often civil, rather than criminal, regulatory enforcement will be a satisfactory means of ensuring compliance with the law. It is therefore troubling that many jurisdictions have greatly expanded the number and severity of *malum prohibitum* offenses over time. According to one estimate, there are now an astounding 300,000 or so federal "crimes," many of which extend criminalization beyond even the domain of traditional *malum prohibitum* offenses, imposing criminal sanctions solely for the sake of giving regulators greater leverage in enforcing all manner of legal requirements. Yet this proliferation of regulatory crimes may be counterproductive, for by imposing criminal liability in cases lacking moral blameworthiness, the practice dilutes the condemnatory meaning of criminal liability, thereby damaging its moral force—the very trait criminalization efforts seek to exploit. Moreover, criminalization of such minor conduct does not effectively access more severe sanctions, for regulatory offenses are unlikely to generate a

---

3. Model Penal Code § 1.04(5).

prison sentence and usually lead to a fine or restitution, which could as easily be made available as civil and not criminal sanctions.

Consent as Defense to Civil Liability   The significance of consent also differs in the criminal and civil contexts. Consent generally provides a complete defense to a civil action; a plaintiff typically has no right to recover for a harm to which he or she consented. This is why Brother Constin, in the "Fear, Pain, and Bubble Gum" hypothetical above, was able to successfully defend the civil suit for assault. In contrast, consent provides a defense to a criminal charge only if it *vitiates the harm or evil of the offense*. That is, consent is a defense to criminal liability only if the presence of consent means that there no longer is a harm. Again looking at the "Bubble Gum" hypothetical, the shopkeeper's permission to take the bubble gum without paying for it means that Ed's taking is not theft.

Role of Consent for Criminal Law   For many criminal offenses, however, consent is not a defense. For example, criminal assault occurs if one "purposely, knowingly, or recklessly causes bodily injury to another."[4] The criminal law generally does not allow a defense to assault (or homicide) based on the victim's consent to bodily injury. Criminal conduct is generally seen as a harm against the community, not just the individual victim (if there even is one). While it may be an individual who suffers the immediate injury, it is the breach of the society's rules of conduct prohibiting the act that serves to justify punishment. If the law prohibits the conduct without exception, it is not within any individual's power to revoke the law's prohibition. The law may give a person the authority to consent to minor injury, just as it gives people the authority to give away their property, as the shopkeeper gave Ed free bubble gum. But causing more than minor injury is an offense, even if the victim consents.[5]

Justification and Excuse Defenses   Even if an actor has the required culpable state of mind for the offense, criminal liability is barred if the actor's conduct is *justified* because it avoids a greater societal harm. The law grants such an actor a justification defense. Thus, Ed will have a justification defense to breaking the car window, as he was acting to avoid the greater harm of being rendered unconscious, trapped between the cars. Even if the actor is not justified, criminal liability also is barred if the surrounding circumstances or conditions render the person blameless for committing what would otherwise be an offense. For example, the law does not blame one who is insane or who commits the offense because coerced to do so by another, but rather gives such actors an *excuse* defense. Criminal codes recognize a wide range of justification and excuse defenses.[6]

Civil liability, such as tort, typically recognizes neither justification nor excuse defenses. If you tie your ship to a dock in a storm in order to save the ship and those aboard, you will have a justification defense to criminal liability but none-theless may be liable to the owner in tort for any damage you cause the dock.

---

4. Model Penal Code § 211.1(1)(a).

5. Model Penal Code § 2.11 permits a consent defense to causing bodily injury (assault, under § 211.1(1)(a)) but not to causing *serious* bodily injury (aggravated assault, under § 211.1(2)(a)). Whether Constin's paddling of the pledges, with its expected permanent scarring, constitutes serious bodily injury, depends upon whether a jury would find that it satisfies the definition of serious bodily injury, set out in § 210.0(3), which includes injury that "causes serious, permanent disfigurement."

6. See, e.g., Model Penal Code §§ 3.02 (lesser evils); 3.07 (law enforcement authority); 4.01 (insanity); 4.10 (immaturity); 2.08(4) (involuntary intoxication); 2.09 (duress).

Similarly, an insane person may gain an insanity defense to criminal liability, but the person (or his guardian) nonetheless must compensate the victims of any harm he causes. The difference logically follows from the difference in the criteria for and purposes of criminal and civil liability. Criminal liability seeks to punish serious moral blameworthiness of the actor, while civil liability seeks to compensate victims with a focus on considerations such as the fair or efficient allocation of loss.

De Minimis *Defense*   Another point of contrast is found in the fact that criminal law addresses only harms of a sufficient seriousness. Where a defendant causes only trivial harm, civil law may allow liability with nominal damages, but such cases typically do not support criminal liability. For example, the Model Penal Code grants a defense for *de minimis,* or trivial, infractions, even where they violate the literal terms of a criminal prohibition: "The Court shall dismiss a prosecution if . . . it finds that the defendant's conduct . . . did not actually cause or threaten the harm or evil sought to be prevented by the law defining the offense or did so only to an extent *too trivial to warrant the condemnation of conviction. . . .*"[7] Consider the person who leaves a restaurant with an apple from a buffet, after paying for the buffet, but in violation of the establishment's rule against removal of food. The conduct violates the terms of the theft prohibition—taking property of another without consent— yet one might conclude, as a court did, that such a violation is too trivial to merit the community condemnation associated with a criminal conviction. At civil law, in contrast, the extent of the harm is important to assessment of the amount of the award, but generally does not affect liability. Thus, in the "Bubble Gum" hypothetical, the shopkeeper will not recover much in a tort claim against Ike for stealing his gum, but he does have a right to compensation from Ike for the extent of his injury.

Only Moral Wrongdoing Merits "Condemnation as Criminal"   Aspects of civil law may recognize some doctrines similar to these; the requirement of conscious culpability, rejection of consent as a general defense, and recognition of defenses for justification, excuse, and *de minimis* violations, but criminal law is distinct in its reliance on such a collection of doctrines. This is just as one would expect, given criminal law's defining feature. Taken together, these doctrines serve "to safeguard conduct that is without fault from condemnation as criminal,"[8] and it is this moral condemnation that distinguishes criminal law from all other law.

● OVERVIEW OF THE SOURCES OF CRIMINAL LAW

Notes

Modern American Criminal Law Is Statutory
"Common Law" as Judge-Made Rules or a Specific Historical Period
    Current Role of Common Law

---

7. Model Penal Code § 2.12(2) (emphasis added).
8. Model Penal Code § 1.02(1)(c).

Two centuries ago in England, criminal law was not written down in one place and was not created by legislative enactment. Rather, the law of crimes was part of the "common law," developing and finding expression in judicial opinions. The American colonies adopted this common law of England as it existed at the time of their independence. The most popular treatise at that historical moment, Blackstone's *Commentaries on the Laws of England*, became a highly influential work in America, not because of anything particularly distinguished about its four volumes, but rather because its popularity coincided with American independence. Volume 4 of Blackstone's treatise provided a useful summary of then-existing English common law crimes.[9] American courts then took on the traditional English judicial role of further refining and developing the law, so that over time American criminal law became distinct from that inherited common law and also from the independently developing contemporary law of England. Indeed, the courts of each American state developed their own rules, though they shared the family resemblance of their English common law lineage.

Modern American Criminal Law is Statutory Today, courts generally no longer make criminal law. That function has been taken over by the legislatures. Nearly every state has a criminal code—a relatively comprehensive statutory enactment—as its primary source of criminal law. Courts interpret the code, but generally have no authority to create new crimes or to change the definitions of existing crimes. (The shift from judge-made to legislatively enacted criminal law is rooted chiefly in the rationales for what is called the *legality principle*.) Yet even today, the power of courts to interpret criminal statutes can have significant effect.

"Common Law" as Judge-Made Rules or a Specific Historical Period When lawyers speak of "common law," they may mean either (1) the law as it existed during the common law period in England, or (2) law that is derived from a process of judicial development. The intended meaning frequently is evident from the context. For example, the "common law *process*" typically refers to the process of judicial law making, whether or not it occurred during the common law *period*. "*The* common law rule" usually refers to the legal rule that existed in England during the eighteenth century. On the other hand, a minority of states continue to rely upon judicially modified variations of the original common law rule. Such rules may also be referred to as "common law" rules, because they developed in the courts, even if they are significantly different from the rule described by Blackstone.

Current Role of Common Law While no state continues to permit judges to create crimes, the common law (in both senses) continues to be important for several reasons. Some state criminal codes incorporate common law offenses by name, without defining them. Under these so-called *reception* statutes, judicial decisions must be relied on to determine the elements of a criminal offense. In addition, because some statutes simply codify the previously existing common

---

9. William Blackstone, Commentaries on the Laws of England (1803, reprinted 1969).

law doctrine, ambiguous code language that calls for an examination of the drafters' intent may require review of the cases in which the doctrine was developed. Similarly, the common law cases may be consulted because they tend to explain the rationale behind a rule if the legislative history of the rule does not. An attorney seeking to persuade a court of the wisdom, or folly, of the policy behind a particular interpretation of a statute may look to common law cases to establish and explain the policy.

Modern Criminal Code Reform While there were some heroic efforts, little criminal code reform occurred in the United States before the 1960s.[10] Most states had moved to reliance on statutes instead of judicial law making, but state "codes" at the time were not comprehensive and uniform sets of rules, but collections of ad hoc statutory enactments, each enactment triggered by a crime or a crime problem that gained public interest. The greatest catalyst of modern American criminal law codification has been the Model Penal Code, promulgated by the American Law Institute. Starting even before its formal adoption in 1962, the Model Penal Code—which we will also call the "MPC" or simply "the Code"—has served as just that, a model code; to date, it has provided a basis for wholesale replacement of existing criminal codes in almost three-quarters of the states. Some states have adopted the Code with only minor revision, while others, especially those that adopted it early, tended to redraft their existing doctrine, borrowing only pieces of the Model Penal Code language but most of its style and form.

The Model Penal Code The American Law Institute (or "ALI"), which drafted the Code, is a nongovernmental, broad-based, highly regarded group of lawyers, judges, professors, and others who undertake research and drafting projects designed to make American law more rational, sensible, and effective. The ALI's Restatements of the Law have been influential in bringing clarity and uniformity to many fields. When the ALI decided to undertake a criminal law project in 1953, it concluded that the criminal law of the various states had become too disparate to permit a "restatement" and, in any case, the existing law was seen as too unsound and ill-considered to merit restating. What was needed instead was a model criminal code. After nine years of work and a series of Tentative Drafts, the ALI approved an Official Draft in 1962. The original commentary, which was contained in the various Tentative Drafts, was consolidated, revised, and republished with the 1962 text in 1980 and 1985 as a seven-volume set.

Federal Criminal Code Reform Of the one-quarter of American jurisdictions that have not yet adopted a modern criminal code, the federal system is the most unfortunate example of frustrated reform. Congress has been engaged in on-again, off-again efforts to reform the federal criminal code since 1966. During that time, several modern code bills passed the Senate but did not pass the House. Criminal code reform is always difficult because it touches highly political issues, but the lack of a modern federal criminal code is a matter of some embarrassment in a country whose states, many believe, lead the world in enlightened criminal law codification. The form of the present federal criminal code is not significantly different from the unsystematic alphabetical listing of offenses typical of the original American codes in the 1800s.

---

10. See Sanford H. Kadish, *Codifiers of the Criminal Law: Wechsler's Predecessors*, 78 COLUM. L. REV. 1098 (1978) (describing statutory reform efforts of Edward Livingston and David Dudley Field in Louisiana and New York, respectively).

Format of Modern Codes   As noted previously, modern criminal codes are typically comprised of two major, interrelated sections: a *general part* that contains general provisions, and a *special part* containing the definitions of specific offenses. The general part contains provisions that explain how to understand and interpret the various offenses in the special part. For example, the general part defines culpability requirements employed in the definition of specific crimes. In addition, the general part includes such things as the rules concerning omission liability, complicity, and voluntary intoxication; general defenses such as self-defense, insanity, and time limitations; and a collection of definitions for commonly used terms. In the special part of a code, offenses are defined, organized into conceptually related groups, and consolidated and revised to avoid overlaps and gaps. A significant practical effect of reform is that code sections are no longer to be read in isolation. To fully understand each offense definition in the special part, several general part provisions must be consulted. The largely successful goal of modern criminal code reform is to generate a code that provides clarity in defining a sophisticated and rational set of rules for distributing liability and punishment.

Modern Sentencing Reform   For a long time after the power to criminalize was taken from judges and given to legislatures, judges retained their broad traditional authority to determine the punishment an individual offender would receive: that is, the sentence. In the last generation, however, there has been another shift of power away from ad hoc judicial decision making in individual cases and toward clear *ex ante* rules governing sentencing. Accordingly, these rules, usually known as *sentencing guidelines,* provide another important contemporary source of criminal law.

● OVERVIEW OF THE OPERATIONAL STRUCTURE OF CRIMINAL LAW

Now that the function and sources of criminal law are apparent, how does criminal law operate? Consider the following hypothetical in terms of how to comprehensively evaluate criminal liability for a particular act. What does one need to know about the actor's intentions, the circumstances under which the act was committed, and the nature of the act itself to assign the appropriate liability? In particular, examine the Model Penal Code and reflect on how the codification of criminal law affects the liability analyses. Note the interaction discussed above between the General Part and Special Part of the Code and the need to reference several different sections in order to obtain a full picture of the criminal liability likely to be imposed.

Hypothetical: Fear of the Daggers (#2)

Box lives next door to the Golden Daggers' clubhouse. On this morning, as Box is walking by on his way home from his night shift at the Tower Grill, two gang members grab him and drag him inside. "I hear you're friendly with Bet Peppe," one spits, with his face an inch from Box's.

"No, not really," Box says, shaking. "I used to see her around, hanging with you guys. I'm not really a friend of hers."

The man responds, "Then you won't mind doing me a favor. You'll cut her face for me." Box isn't thrilled about the idea. He says nothing. "Look, it's either your face or hers," the man says as he sticks a knife in Box's face an inch below his eye.

"Okay. Okay. I'll do it." — *Duress*

The Dagger stares, "If I don't see cuts on her face tomorrow, we'll be looking for you."

Duress

Culpability

Voluntary Intoxication

Box goes to his apartment and pours himself a drink, spilling much of it because his hands are shaking. Yes, he is scared of those guys, he admits to himself. Hurting Bet would be a bad thing, but what's the alternative, especially if the Daggers find out that he and Bet have been dating?

After several more hours of anxious drinking, Box gets a butcher knife from the kitchen and heads for Bet's, bottle in hand. By the time he gets there, he is staggering badly and barely coherent. Bet opens the door. "Hi Box." Box lurches forward, stumbling into the back of the sofa. "What's wrong with you?"

Shows Intoxication Level

Box does not respond. He staggers around the apartment, knocking over furniture. "This is your own fault," he screams at her, and babbles on about blood, knives, and eyes. When he has worked himself into a frenzy, he pulls his knife and begins flailing at everything around him: curtains, lamps, pictures on the wall. Bet gets caught by several of his swings and is badly cut. She runs from the apartment, screaming for the police. Box also runs. He takes the subway to his brother's place on the other side of town, where he spends the night.

After reflecting on his situation, Box decides not to return to his apartment, but rather to take a job in a small town in the southern part of the state. Unaware that Box has left town, Bet does not disclose his identity to the police for fear of reprisals by Box. Bet's shoulder heals but a cut to her hand has permanently damaged the muscles. She is no longer able to write with that hand and becomes increasingly bitter about the episode.

Statute of Limitations

Several years later Box returns to town. Bet chances to see him on the subway one day and, after much stewing, decides to report him to the police. His arrest comes three years after the incident.

Is Box liable for aggravated assault? Which different elements need to be established in order for Box to be found criminally liable? What defenses could be asserted and what offense element(s) does each negate, if any? The following overview section will guide you through the elements of Box's offense and explain the function and application of each, providing an introduction to analyzing a case using a modern criminal code.

Notes

Offense Elements
    General vs. Special Part of Code
    Objective and Culpability Offense Elements
    Example: Elements of Aggravated Assault
Doctrines of Imputation
    Imputing Objective Elements

Offense Elements   Let us use the "Fear of the Daggers" hypothetical to examine how the rules of criminal law operate. Each rule typically does one of three things. First, a rule may define what constitutes an *offense*. Second, a rule may define the conditions under which an actor will be held liable even though he does *not* satisfy the elements of an offense; such a rule may be called a doctrine of *imputation*. Third, a rule may define the conditions under which an actor will be acquitted even though he satisfies the elements of an offense; such a rule commonly is termed a *defense*. The interaction of these three types of rules in the analysis of criminal cases might be summarized as the following flowchart illustrates.

General vs. Special Part of Code   Modern criminal codes are divided into a *general part* and a *special part*. The general rules governing the definition of the

Figure 1 **Operational Structure of Criminal Law's Liability Decision**

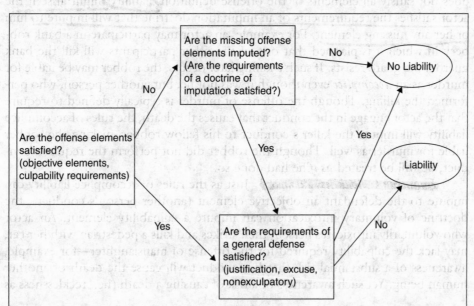

offenses, together with the doctrines of imputation and defense, make up the general part of a code and typically apply to many or all specific offenses. The definitions of specific offenses make up what is called the special part of a criminal code.

Objective and Culpability Offense Elements   The definition of an offense typically consists of *objective elements*, which describe the physical behavior the offense requires, and *culpability elements*, which describe the offender's subjective awareness or attitude toward that behavior. Thus, the objective elements of murder might require that an actor engage in *conduct* that causes the *death* of *another human being*. The culpability elements might require that the actor *know* the nature of his conduct, that it will cause a death, and that the death caused is that of a human being. The culpability requirements may be different for different objective elements of the same offense. A jurisdiction might, for example, require that an actor *know* the nature of his conduct and that it will cause a death, but only require that the actor be *reckless* as to whether the death is that of a human being.

Example: Elements of Aggravated Assault   For example, aggravated assault might be defined to require, as objective elements, that an actor engage in conduct that causes serious bodily injury to another person.[11] In the "Fear of the Daggers" hypothetical, Box has done that. The offense also might require, as culpability elements, that the actor be at least reckless as to causing such injury at the time of his conduct. It is unclear that Box satisfies this requirement. Recklessness as to causing an injury requires that the actor be aware of a risk that his conduct will cause such injury. Because of his grossly intoxicated state, it may well be that, at the time he cut Bet, Box was simply flailing madly at the world around him with no awareness that he might cut Bet with his swings. If he were sober, he certainly would realize the potential effect of such knife swinging, but he is not sober. If Box is not aware of this risk of harm to Bet at the time of his flailing, he does not satisfy the requirements of the offense definition of aggravated assault. Yet he nonetheless may be liable for the offense.

Doctrines of Imputation   *Imputing Objective Elements*   Even if an actor does not satisfy all elements of the offense definition, liability might arise if the actor satisfies the requirements of an imputation doctrine that will impute to him or her any missing element. For example, an actor may participate in a bank robbery in which it is planned that one of the other participants will kill the bank guard if the guard resists. If such a killing later occurs, the robber may be liable for murder as an *accomplice* even though it was not he, but another person, who performed the killing. Though the offense of murder is typically defined to require that the actor engage in the conduct that causes the death, the rules of accomplice liability will impute the killer's conduct to his fellow robber, making the robber liable for murder as well. Though the robber did not perform the required conduct, he will be treated *as if* he had done so.

Imputing Culpability Elements   Just as the rules of accomplice liability can impute to the defendant an objective element (another person's conduct), the doctrine of voluntary intoxication can impute a culpability element. An actor who voluntarily intoxicates herself, then strikes and kills a pedestrian with her car, may lack the culpability required for the offense of manslaughter—for example, awareness of a substantial risk that her conduct will cause the death of another human being. Yet such awareness of a risk of causing a death (i.e., recklessness as

---

11. Model Penal Code § 211.1(2).

to causing death) may be imputed to the actor under the doctrine of voluntary intoxication. That is, because of her voluntary intoxication, she may be treated *as if* she satisfies the required element of recklessness as to causing death, and therefore may be convicted of manslaughter. Looking at the "Fear of the Daggers" scenario, this doctrine might apply to Box. Because his intoxication was voluntary, recklessness as to causing serious bodily injury, required for aggravated assault liability, may be imputed to him.[12]

Doctrines of Defense   Where an actor satisfies all of the elements of an offense, actually or through imputation, he nonetheless may be acquitted of the offense if he satisfies the conditions of a defense. In the "Fear of the Daggers" hypothetical, Box has several claims of defense that he might make, although some are more promising than others. He might claim that his conduct was *justified* by his need to protect himself from the Golden Daggers. He might claim that he should be *excused* because the Daggers coerced him into doing what he did. Or, he might claim the *nonexculpatory defense* that the period of limitation has run.

Failure-of-Proof Defenses   Some doctrines that are called *defenses* are nothing more than the absence of a required offense element. When I take your umbrella believing it to be my own, I may claim a *mistake defense.* Yet my defense derives not from a special defense doctrine about mistake as to ownership but rather derives from the elements of the theft offense. The definition of theft includes a requirement that the actor know that the property taken is owned by another person. If I mistakenly believe that the umbrella I take is my own, I do not satisfy that required element of knowledge. Such a mistake defense is called a *failure-of-proof defense* because it derives from the inability of the state to prove a required element. If Box were to claim, as suggested earlier, that he did not have the required recklessness as to causing serious bodily injury to Bet, he would be asserting such a failure-of-proof defense, claiming that the prosecution could not prove all of the elements of the offense. In casual usage, such claims are called "defenses," but they are simply another way of talking about the requirements of the offense definition itself.

Offense-Modification Defenses   Some defenses are indeed independent of the offense elements, but concern criminalization issues closely related to the definition of the offense, refining or qualifying the definition of a particular offense or group of offenses. Voluntary renunciation, for example, can provide a defense to inchoate offenses like attempt or conspiracy. But this "defense" is really just helping to refine the definition of these inchoate offenses: It makes clear that they include only unrenounced criminal plans. Similarly, consent is recognized as a defense to some kinds of assault. Where it applies, the consent defense helps to define what we mean by the offense of assault: It applies to minor injury only when the victim did not consent to that injury. Indeed, assault frequently is defined as an *unconsented-to* touching. That is, the absence of consent sometimes is included as an element of the offense. As this illustrates, the difference between failure of proof defenses and offense modification defenses is one of form more than substance. An *offense-modification defense* can as easily be drafted as a *negative element* of the offense itself.

Criminalization Defenses vs. General Defenses   Because both failure-of-proof and offense-modification defenses serve to refine the offense definition—and therefore are called *criminalization defenses*—they tend to apply to a single offense or

---

12. Model Penal Code § 2.08(2).

group of offenses. Justifications, excuses, and nonexculpatory defenses, by contrast, are not linked to any particular offense; they theoretically apply to all offenses and therefore are called *general defenses*. The recognition of each general defense rests upon reasons extraneous to the criminalization goals and policies of any particular offense. Where a criminalization defense applies, the defendant has committed no criminal wrong at all; general defenses, on the other hand, prevent criminal liability *despite* the occurrence of a legally recognized harm or evil. The special conditions establishing the general defense suggest that the violator should not be punished, even though he may have engaged in generally wrongful conduct.

Justification Defenses   Sometimes conduct otherwise amounting to an offense is tolerated, or even encouraged, because it is considered to be *justified* under the circumstances. For example, injuring another person constitutes assault and generally is prohibited, yet it is justified if done in self-defense against an aggressor to protect one's life. Burning another's farm is arson, yet it is tolerated and even encouraged if it creates a firebreak that saves a town from a raging forest fire. Providing a justification defense in such cases is not meant to lessen the general prohibitions against assault and arson, but only to recognize that the harm or evil of even such serious offenses as these can be outweighed by a greater good where the special justifying circumstances obtain.

Justification for Box?   Considering the "Fear of the Daggers" hypothetical, Box might claim a justification defense, arguing that the cuts to Bet were a less serious harm than the injury he was likely to suffer at the hands of the Daggers. His conduct is not likely to be deemed justified, however. The defensive force justifications may authorize use of force against aggressors, but Bet is an innocent person.[13] Justification defenses also typically require that no other, less harmful means of avoiding the harm is available.[14] In Box's case, cutting Bet was not the least harmful means of avoiding the harm: Box could have reported the incident to police, gone into hiding as he did, or both.

Excuse Defenses   Even if an actor's conduct is harmful or evil in itself and is not justified by special circumstances, the actor may nonetheless receive an *excuse* defense on the ground that she is not blameworthy for her actions. It may not be appropriate to assign blame to one who is insane, involuntarily intoxicated, or immature, or who acts involuntarily, under duress, or under a reasonable mistake of law or mistake as to a justification. We may feel that such an actor in such a situation could not reasonably have been expected to remain law-abiding. The excuse defenses are designed to exculpate such blameless offenders.

Excuse for Box?   Returning to the hypothetical, Box might claim an excuse of some sort. Because his intoxication was voluntary, it cannot form the basis for an excuse.[15] He might do better to claim a duress defense based on the coercion from the Daggers. Many states, however, deny duress as a defense for offenses of violence against another person. Additionally, where it is not expressly barred for crimes of violence, as in the Model Penal Code, a duress defense is available only where a person of reasonable firmness would have been unable to resist the coercion to commit the offense.[16] It seems unlikely that a jury could be persuaded that, faced with threats

---

13. Model Penal Code § 3.04.
14. See, e.g., Model Penal Code § 3.02.
15. Model Penal Code § 2.08(4).
16. Model Penal Code § 2.09.

like those from the Daggers, a person of reasonable firmness would be coerced to slash Bet the way Box did. In other words, a jury is likely to find that, despite the Daggers' threats, Box is blameworthy and ought to be held liable for his offense.

Nonexculpatory Defenses Even blameworthy actors may be acquitted if they satisfy the requirements of a *nonexculpatory defense*. Such defenses are disfavored yet recognized because they each further an important societal interest, judged to be more important than punishing the offender at hand.

Diplomatic immunity, for example, is allowed to shield blameworthy criminal offenders because by recognizing such a defense we protect our diplomats abroad, and this in turn allows the establishment of diplomatic relations among nations. Nonexculpatory defenses may seem similar to justifications in that they are grounded in some overriding societal benefit, but note that the benefit here flows not from the actor's offense conduct itself, as is the case with justifications, but rather from the decision to forgo punishing that conduct, despite the undesirability of the conduct and the actor's blameworthiness.

Nonexculpatory Defense for Box? Looking again to the hypothetical, Box may claim a nonexculpatory defense in the statute of limitation.[17] The passage of three years, during which he has been in the jurisdiction, may well bar his prosecution for the offense. The defense is not based on any lack of harm or blame; both are present here. Rather, a limitation period is said to avoid a counterproductive preoccupation with the past. At some point, the argument goes, society is better off letting go of the past and moving ahead to deal with the problems and challenges of today. In many jurisdictions, if the arrest warrant for Box is issued more than three years after the assault, prosecution will be barred.

Criminal Law's Conceptual Structure

Three Types of Rules for Assigning Liability This, then, is the three-part *operational structure* of criminal law in making a liability decision: requirements of offense definitions, doctrines of imputation, and general defenses, with the interrelation among them as described in Figure 1 above. But while criminal law doctrines technically operate in this way, a more meaningful way to describe their interrelation is to capture the different roles that the doctrines play. That *conceptual structure*, as it might be called, can be summarized this way:

Figure 1A Conceptual structure of criminal law

	Offense Requirements		General Defenses
Prohibited and Authorized Conduct	*Objective offense elements*—defining the prohibitions	*Doctrines of imputation*	*Justification defenses*—describing general justifying exceptions to the prohibitions
Requirements for Punishing Violations	*Culpability offense elements*—setting the standard culpability requirements for blameworthiness in violating a prohibition		*Excuse defenses*—describing special conditions under which an unjustified (and even culpable) violation of a prohibition may nonetheless be excused

---

17. Model Penal Code § 1.06. ← *Statute of limitation*

This somewhat oversimplified summary is filled out at the end of Section 5 with a more detailed account of how different kinds of doctrines perform different functions within criminal law's conceptual structure.

Liability Assignment vs. Sentencing   All of these criminal law doctrines—offense definitions, doctrines of imputation, and general defenses—serve only to assign criminal liability. Such liability suggests that some punishment is appropriate, but does not specify with precision *how much* punishment is appropriate for a given offense. Each offense will have a general classification, or grade (for example, third-degree felony or first-degree misdemeanor) that will establish a range of possible punishments. The amount and nature of the punishment a specific offender receives for a specific offense is limited by the offense's grade; however, it is specifically determined during the sentencing process, in which the sentencing judge frequently has discretion to select the exact amount (and, perhaps, form) of liability from within the limits set by the offense grade. In that sense, the criminal law, for all its intricacy and for all the resources devoted to its adjudication of an individual case, has a limited effect in determining the ultimate sanction. It has the important role of determining *who* shall be punished, but it leaves to the sentencing process much of the determination of *how much* or *what kind* of punishment will be imposed. (The extent to which the final amount of punishment is controlled by the sentencing process, rather than the criminal code, will depend largely on the number of offense grades the code recognizes and the relative breadth or narrowness of the punishment range available within each grade.)

Criminal Law Principles in Sentencing   This state of affairs may seem peculiar. The criminal law is drafted with great care to make the assignment of liability a matter of rules rather than discretion. This commitment to the articulation of liability rules, called the principle of legality, has always been a foundation of Anglo-American criminal law. Yet the thoroughly articulated criminal law has a limited effect in determining the punishment imposed. Instead, the highly discretionary sentencing process determines the punishment. If unguided discretion is carefully avoided in the liability-assignment process, why is it tolerated in sentencing? In part because of legality concerns, the trend in modern sentencing systems is toward more articulated sentencing rules. As one might expect, these articulations typically draw upon and extend principles of criminal law. Thus, while the rules of liability assignment are only a stop on the way to determining punishment, the principles behind those rules are likely to play an increasingly larger role in the formulation of sentencing rules and guidelines.

Practical Importance of Criminal Law Theory   The articulation of sentencing rules is but one example of the value of understanding the principles behind criminal law and not just its rules. The effective advocate and the informed judge are at their best when they understand the theory of the rules and why the doctrine is the way it is. Only then can they interpret code provisions to give them proper effect or criticize interpretations that would frustrate the purpose of a provision. In addition, lawyers inevitably play a large role in the law-making process in which criminal codes are drafted and enacted. Therefore, a rational, effective, and just criminal law depends on an informed bar. The structure for criminal law described above is an example of a conceptualization that can have significant practical value. Lawyers and judges, not just academics, benefit from a sense of this larger conceptual framework of criminal law, for it is through such a structure that they can appreciate the role that each doctrine plays within the larger whole.

The Legality Principle

The widespread codification of criminal law in the 1960s and 1970s, discussed in the previous Section, makes American criminal law primarily a statutory creature. Why should this be so? What prompted the enactment of these comprehensive criminal codes? The answer lies in what is called the *legality principle,* a concept that expresses interests and values with special application to criminal law.

◆ THE CASE OF RAY BRENT MARSH (#3)

Noble, Georgia, is a small unincorporated cluster of houses and businesses off Highway 27, about 20 miles outside Chattanooga. Though people tend to live here for decades, they are not as close as they might be in the typical small town. "We come here and we stay here, but a lot of people don't know who their neighbors are," explains the owner of a video store in town, who has been living there for 47 years. "It's a place where you don't need to worry about what's in your backyard."

One prominent family in town is the Marsh family, descendants of Willie Marsh, who in the nineteenth century was the first African-American child in Walker County. In a county that is almost 94 percent white, the Marshes have become one of the more prominent families in town. Members of the family served in both World Wars and in Vietnam. During World War I, one of the Marshes got into the lumber business. Many of his 13 children (9 of them boys) worked in the mill, where their father hired whites and blacks. His motto, passed down through the family, was "you don't look up, you don't look down; you look 'em straight in the eye." Several generations of Marshes are buried in the family graveyard a few blocks from the Tri-State Crematory, a family business started by Tommy Ray Marsh in 1982.

Tommy Ray had been a postal worker, but he also worked digging septic tanks. In the mid-1970s, a family friend, William J. Willis, Sr., who now runs Willis Funeral Home, called Tommy Ray because he needed a grave digger. Realizing the business potential, Tommy Ray started his own burial vault. After a decade of digging graves, he bought a $20,000 cremation unit from Industrial Equipment & Engineering in Apopka, Florida, and opened Tri-State Crematory. Local newspapers reported that it was the first minority-owned crematory in the country.

When he started the business, cremations were rare in that part of Georgia, but starting in the late 1980s they have become increasingly common, partly because they are less expensive than the alternatives. Tommy Ray's family now owns and rents out a fair amount of land in Noble.

In 1996, Tommy Ray has a stroke, which confines him to a wheelchair. His son Ray Brent Marsh now runs his father's cremation business. Like the rest of his family, Ray Marsh is well regarded in the community. He was a star sprinter at LaFayette High School, co-captain of the football team, and a linebacker at the University of Tennessee at Chattanooga. He is the treasurer at New Home Missionary Baptist Church, which his family helped start 93 years earlier. His mother sings in the choir. He and his wife Venessa recently had a baby girl. Like his parents, Marsh lives on the crematory grounds.

More than 30 funeral homes in the area use Tri-State Crematory, which is the only independent crematory. The Marshes charge as little as $250, while other similar companies tend to start at $600 per cremation. The Marshes have never needed to advertise. One funeral director who did business with them noted that there wasn't really any paperwork or tracking system and that the business, which operated out of a shed, seemed unprofessional. However, with low prices and no obvious problems, the Marshes' business flourishes.

Indeed, "professionalism" in the cremation industry is not necessarily a priority in Georgia, which left the industry completely unregulated until 1990. Even when regulation began, there were only two inspectors. Recently, Georgia's Funeral Service Board has been trying to close down Tri-State. After an investigation that resulted in charges of operating without a state license, Marsh was granted exemption from some of the newer regulations, such as that requiring that a funeral director run the facilities; the Marshes argued that their daughter needed time to get certified as a funeral director. When the two-year exemption ended, the Board tried again to enforce the regulations and close the business. Marsh lobbied State Representative Mike Snow for another exemption, but Snow refused. The Marshes' attorney successfully argued, however, that the Marshes' facility did not fall within the regulatory definition of *crematory*, defined as a place where cremations are done that is run by a funeral director and "open to the public."

Revised regulations are proposed for the industry, but language to close the loophole that the Marshes exploited have not been added in the final draft. The Board eventually gives up, thinking that the Marshes will get tired of the business and close it down after a short time, or that people won't want to do business with an unlicensed crematory. "We felt he would be out of our hair in a short while," James Neal, a member of Georgia's Funeral Services Board, would later say.

Despite the Board's opinion of it, the Tri-State remains busy. For the most part, funeral directors are happy to let Marsh continue his father's business. They know that there is sometimes abuse in the industry and that they should visit facilities or make unannounced inspections, but they never do because Tri-State offers such prompt service, and the family has a good reputation. The Marshes have never had any trouble with the law; the only run-in arose when Tommy Ray received a citation for letting his son Ray drive without a license in 1988. Although in the past few years Ray's parents and sister have broken regulations by signing papers as if they were licensed funeral directors, people have either not noticed or not cared.

The community mainly tries to ignore the crematory tucked into the corner of their county. Neighbors don't go down to the nearby woods much. "We didn't like to be over there [because of] the fact that they were supposed to be burning bodies," explains Jessica Johnson, 22, a neighbor and niece of Ray Marsh.

After running the business for a year, Marsh has been having financial problems with the crematory. In 1997 a vault company filed suit against Marsh for nonpayment of about $2,000. In August, the cremation machine stops working. Marsh orders a $152 starter motor part for the crematorium. For the past thirteen years, the family has declined service visits from the equipment company, so the service representatives are not surprised when Marsh says that no one needs to come to install the new part.

After receiving the part, Marsh determines that he cannot fix the machine. Given the financial pressures on him, he decides nonetheless to keep accepting bodies for cremation but starts hiding bodies in the grove behind the crematory. He does not abuse them. He simply dumps them on the property in whatever condition he gets them. The grove is already littered with dryers, broken chairs, and a house trailer. There are six rusty cars abandoned there, stuffed with rusted tools and other trash. Among the debris, hundreds of corpses start piling up. The corpse of a baby is stuffed in a box in the back of a rusty hearse. Dozens of bodies are stacked like cordwood in sheds or half-buried around the grove.

While Marsh lives among the bodies, he acts as if everything is normal. Unlike the smoke that can carry the smell of a crematory, the localized smell of a body takes just two weeks to stop, so it isn't very surprising that the neighbors haven't noticed what has been going on. For each new customer, Marsh continues to be prompt in arriving to pick up the body, the transit permit, the family's authorization, and the $200 check. He always insists on doing pickups and returning the "ashes" himself, often returning the next day. But in fact, Marsh often delivers a box of cement chips and limestone rather than cremated remains.

Marsh continues to be disorganized with his paperwork. He lets notices, papers, and bills, often unopened, pile up in the office and tucks them into corners and around his home. Still, from the outside things seem normal, though the locals later comment that they have not seen any smoke in a long time. In fact, although Marsh seems to exhibit no concern for the bodies once he has them, in some ways he has become more careful about the industry regulations. In the fall of 2001, Neva Mason calls him to arrange service for her father-in-law. Marsh explains that even though her family had arranged the cremation and burial directly with Tri-State when her mother died a few years before, the rules have changed and she now must go through a funeral home. She does so and calls him later to make sure that Marsh received her father-in-law's body. Marsh tells her that he is taking care of him. Marsh adds Mason's body to the piles rotting in the grove.

In November 2001, the Atlanta office of the EPA receives an anonymous call reporting that someone has seen "body parts" on Tri-State's property. The EPA turns the tip over to the sheriff's office, which briefly investigates, but as the investigators have no search warrant, they leave after a cursory look that fails to reveal anything.

By the beginning of 2002, Marsh has hidden bodies all over the property. His indifference may be rooted in depression or some other psychological disorder; a former F.B.I. profiler comments later that Marsh's behavior is like those who have a hoarding obsessive-compulsive disorder. He hoards all his papers and stacks all the bodies, perhaps hoping to deal with them later. He doesn't make decisions about what to do about the problem, and as it gets harder to decide, everything just piles up in a disordered and haphazard fashion.

By now, the result looks like something out of a Stephen King novel. After five years, some of the bodies look like they have been there for decades and now seem almost skeletal. Others, once quasi-buried and embalmed, are now half disinterred, possibly to make them easier to stack later. Some are dumped still dressed in formal wear; others are wrapped in hospital sheets and wearing toe tags. More than 20 bodies are stuffed into a single cement vault that is designed to hold one coffin. Four other vaults are just as full. Some cremated remains are mixed among the bodies. In all, there are more than 340 bodies in the grove. The bodies now outnumber Noble's living population.

In February 2002, the Atlanta EPA gets another call. This time officials come to town to investigate. The next morning, February 15, a woman walking a dog finds a human skull, spurring a full investigation. As the first bodies are discovered, the county population is horrified. Soon Dr. Kris Sperry, the state's chief medical examiner, is obliged to call in the Federal Disaster Mortuary Team, the group usually called when a cemetery is disrupted by a natural disaster. Dr. Sperry has performed more than 5,000 autopsies and viewed more than 30,000 bodies but is not prepared for what he sees around the crematory. He is most horrified by the lack of reverence for the dead. During the first week of the recovery effort, he has nightmares.

By Saturday, February 16, the governor has declared "the Walker County incident" a state of emergency, making state funds available for the recovery efforts. He meets with a hundred families who dealt with Tri-State and agrees to pay the cost of identifying bodies to give the families closure. He vows to use the full powers of the State to investigate and prosecute. The sheriff says the Marshes are "good folks. I don't know what went wrong."

The Marshes turn over their company records and generally cooperate with the authorities. The legislative loophole that protected Tri-State is quickly closed, and other states begin to review their licensing schemes.

On Sunday, a prayer service is held, while county employees comb the woods for bodies. Meanwhile, Marsh's sister puts up her house as a bond for $25,000 bail, and Marsh is released. His mother goes to church and reports that he is doing nicely. She refuses to talk about the case. "I don't have anything to say about the charges, if that's what they are. I'm just surrounding myself in the Lord and the people who support me."

After the investigators clear away the bodies in plain view, they find the bodies stacked in the concrete burial vaults. Seeing the other vaults around the property, the crew stops trying to estimate numbers. At this point in the investigation, only 16 bodies have been identified. Investigators set up a makeshift morgue on the site to process the bodies and help the families identify them. People are asked to bring in photographs. Meanwhile, the Georgia Bureau of Investigation (GBI) urges people

Figure 2 **Police en route to the crematory**   (Reuters/Corbis)

Figure 3 **Investigators collecting bodies in the woods on February 20, 2002**

(Reuters/Corbis)

Figure 4 **Investigators collecting bodies in the woods on February 20, 2002**   (AP)

to bring in the remains they were given so they can be checked. At the Walker State Community Center, people line up holding "ashes" of loved ones received from Tri-State. Many turn out to be just dirt and cement chips.

On Thursday, February 21, underwater cameras spot a torso and skull in the lake behind the crematory. They begin to test the water for contamination, to see if it is safe for divers. Local residents are warned not to drink tap water.

By February 24, almost 300 bodies have been found. Investigators don't know when it will end. The families are devastated. Some tell GBI director Buddy Nix that their loved ones had asked to be cremated because "they were frightfully afraid of being buried or frightfully afraid of insects." When Pat Higdon's husband died of lung cancer, she couldn't afford a burial, so she chose to cremate him. "He looked like a corpse for two months before he died. He just laid there with his mouth open and his eyes open," she says. "I can't bear to think he still looks like that, only he's lying in a shed or a creek somewhere." Ellen West, on learning that the body of her mother, author Emmy Govan West, was among those discarded at the crematory, says, "When they called me and told me, it was worse news than her dying. I couldn't function." The Cash family moves the urn of Mrs. Cash's mother, Norma, from its prominent place at the end table in their front room. "The urn they gave us is nothing," says Mr. Cash. "If it is somebody, it is not my somebody. We put it in the garage."

The funeral directors who trusted the Marshes are also reeling. One director sent more than 100 bodies there, including his brother Clyde. He says, "I don't sleep. It's a bad deal." He has tried to comfort the families, who have told him they are praying for him and aren't blaming him. Other funeral homes have had civil suits brought against them.

On Tuesday morning, February 25, Marsh's bail is set at $100,000. By that afternoon, 102 more charges of theft by deception are brought against him,

(MPC 223.3)

requiring another bond hearing before he goes anywhere. The GBI tells a family member that there have been 260 threats against Marsh and his family. The prosecution is concerned for his safety if Marsh were to be released.

The last body on land is found on February 26. The next Monday, March 4, agents start draining the three-acre lake, which is eight feet deep at its deepest point. The potentially contaminated water is carted away in tankers to keep it from affecting the local water supply. Eventually, using flat-bottomed boats, investigators probe the few feet of water that remain. No more bodies are found. Georgia has had to add $8.5 million to the state budget to cover the expenses of the excavation.

The excavation and search finishes on March 6, 2002. Investigators determine that over the course of more than 5 years, Marsh dumped 339 bodies on his property.

Figure 5 **Women yelling at Marsh outside the courthouse**
(Reuters/Corbis)

1. Relying only upon your own intuitions of justice, what liability and punishment, if any, does Ray Brent Marsh deserve **for his offensive treatment of the dead bodies?*** (Assume that any fraud charges—based upon his taking payment for services not performed—have been dropped pursuant to a civil settlement.)

N	0	1	2	3	4	5	6	7	8	9	10	11
☐	☐	☐	☐	☐	☐	☐	☒	☐	☐	☐	☐	☐
no liability	liability but no punishment	1 day	2 wks	2 mo	6 mo	1 yr	3 yrs	7 yrs	15 yrs	30 yrs	life imprison-ment	death

---

*N.B.—Throughout this coursebook, you will be asked to give your views of the liability and punishment deserved, if any, by the defendant in the principal case. Accept all the facts in the narrative to be true—don't second guess them—and assume all relevant facts are given—don't read in new facts. In making your judgment, ignore what you know or think you know about criminal law. Also ignore utilitarian crime control considerations. Indicate simply what your own intuitive sense of justice tells you is the criminal liability and punishment deserved, if any, by the defendant. There are no right or wrong answers. If you decide that some punishment is deserved, you are asked to give a sentence of imprisonment that reflects the appropriate amount of punishment. In some cases, you may think punishment would best be imposed through a sentence other than imprisonment, such as supervised probation, fine, or community service. For the purposes of this question, translate any such non-imprisonment sentence into a term of imprisonment of the same punishment "bite." (This makes it possible to compare the amount of punishment imposed by different persons.) This process of your forming your own independent intuition about what the defendant deserves in the case is important. Without doing so, it will be difficult for you to evaluate the legal rules that in practice determine the outcome of the case. Also, as we will see in Section 3, concerning punishment theory, a community's shared intuitions of justice can have an important influence on the effectiveness of a criminal law rule.

2. What "justice" arguments could defense counsel make on the defendant's behalf?[†] *Mental Illness*

3. What "justice" arguments could the prosecution make against the defendant? *Wanton Disregard for treatment of corpses*

4. What liability, if any, for Marsh under the then-existing statutes? Prepare a list of all criminal code subsections in the order in which you rely upon them in your analysis.

5. What liability, if any, under the Model Penal Code? Prepare a list of all criminal code subsections in the order in which you rely upon them in your analysis.

▪ THE LAW

Code of Georgia Annotated
(2002)

Title 16. Crimes and Offenses

Chapter 1. General Provisions

Section 16-1-4. Code Governs Crimes

No conduct constitutes a crime unless it is described as a crime in this title or in another statute of this state. However, this Code section does not affect the power of a court to punish for contempt or to employ any sanction authorized by law for the enforcement of an order, civil judgment, or decree.

Title 31. Health

Chapter 21. Dead Bodies
Article 3. Offenses

Section 31-21-44.1. Abuse of a Dead Body

(a)(1) A person commits the offense of abuse of a dead body if, prior to interment and except as otherwise authorized by law, such person willfully defaces a dead body while the dead body is lying in state or is prepared for burial, showing, or cremation whether in a funeral establishment, place of worship, home, or other facility for lying in state or at a grave site. The lawful presence of the offender at a place where the dead body is abused shall not be a defense to a prosecution under this Code section.

(2) A person who is providing care to another person, other than in a hospital, either on a permanent or temporary basis, shall, upon the death of such person while in such person's care, be required to notify a local

[handwritten margin notes: men reas — what desitr mean GA? limited to a particular place]

[†]In other words, articulate the intuitions of justice of this sort that guided the judgment you made on the liability scale in Question 1.

law enforcement agency or coroner or a relative of such deceased person within six hours of the discovery of the death of such person. Any person who intentionally violates the provisions of this paragraph shall commit the offense of abuse of a dead body.

(b) Any person who violates subsection (a) of this Code section shall be guilty of a felony and shall be punished by imprisonment for not less than one nor more than three years.

Glover v. State
272 Ga. 639, 533 S.E.2d 374 (2000)

The defendant was originally sentenced to 30 years for child molestation, with 7 years to be served in prison and the remaining balance to be served on probation. While on probation, he violates its terms and has his probation revoked. The probation violation statute authorizes the court to "revoke the balance of probation or not more than two years in confinement." The lower court seeks to revoke the balance of his probation and to sentence him to an additional 10 years but, depending upon how the statute is interpreted, the court might be authorized to impose only an additional two years imprisonment. The Georgia Supreme Court bars the additional 10 year term, holding that the interpretation of penal statutes is to be guided by the rule of strict construction, which requires adopting the interpretation most favorable to the defendant.

State v. Bradbury
136 Me. 347, 9 A.2d 657 (1939)

Where a defendant disposed of his recently deceased sister by burning her in their home's furnace, he was guilty of a common law offense of abuse of corpse. "[A]ny disposal of a dead body which is contrary to common decency is an offense at common law."

Model Penal Code
(Official Draft 1962)

Section 1.05. All Offenses Defined by Statute; Application of General Provisions of the Code

(1) No conduct constitutes an offense unless it is a crime or violation under this Code or another statute of this State.

(2) The provisions of Part I of the Code are applicable to offenses defined by other statutes, unless the Code otherwise provides.

(3) This Section does not affect the power of a court to punish for contempt or to employ any sanction authorized by law for the enforcement of an order or a civil judgment or decree.

Section 250.10.   Abuse of Corpse

Except as authorized by law, a person who treats a corpse in a way that he knows would outrage ordinary family sensibilities commits a misdemeanor.

Did he knowingly do it
mental illness

● OVERVIEW OF THE LEGALITY PRINCIPLE

Notes*

The Doctrines
    Prohibition Against Vagueness
        Vague vs. Ambiguous
    Rule of Lenity: Resolve Ambiguity in Favor of Defendant
    Ban on Ex Post Facto Laws
The Rationales
    Procedural Fairness
    Promoting Effective Deterrence and Avoiding Improper Overdeterrence
    Promoting Democracy: Criminalization as a Legislative Function
    Rationales Focus on Conduct Rules, Not Adjudication Rules
    Adjudication Concerns: Avoiding Disparity and Abuse of Discretion
Countervailing Interests
    Fostering Inflexibility and Unresponsiveness
    Promoting Technicalities
    Precision as Imperfect Proxy for Normative Judgments
    Principle of Analogy
Legality in Context
    Legality in Liability vs. Sentencing
        Difficulty in Justifying Disparate Respect for Legality Concerns
    Legality and Function
        Legality in Rule Articulation vs. Adjudication

THE DOCTRINES

Prohibition Against Vagueness   The *vagueness* prohibition is rooted in the Due Process Clauses of the Fifth and Fourteenth Amendments to the Constitution. The doctrine requires that a statute give "sufficient warning that men may conform their conduct so as to avoid that which is forbidden."[1] It has been used to invalidate so-called *vagrancy* statutes, which commonly provided for the arrest and conviction of persons such as "rogues and vagabonds, . . . common night walkers, . . . wanton and lascivious persons, . . . common railers and brawlers, . . . habitual loafers, [and] disorderly persons[.]"[2] As the Supreme Court has explained, such a provision "fail[s] to give a person of ordinary intelligence fair notice that his

---

*N.B.— Remember that the formatting of paragraph titles signal descending superiority of paragraphs as follows: **Heading,** **heading,** *heading,* heading.

1. Rose v. Locke, 423 U.S. 48, 50 (1975) (statutory phrase "crime against nature" gave adequate notice that forced cunnilingus was prohibited).

2. Jacksonville, Florida Ordinance Code § 26-57, invalidated in *Papachristou, infra.*

contemplated conduct is forbidden by statute."[3] Similarly, a common law offense that is incorporated into a code by reference, without a definition of its elements, is likely to be void for vagueness. Thus, when a prosecution sought to obtain a conviction for the common law offense of being a "common scold," relying on a statute that sought to criminalize all conduct that was indictable at common law, the state court explained, "One can scarcely conceive of anything more vague or indefinite. To know the criminal risks he might run, the average citizen would be obliged to carry a pocket edition of Blackstone with him."[4]

Vague vs. Ambiguous However, a statute is not unconstitutionally vague merely because one of its elements calls for a matter of judgment or is subject to multiple interpretations. An offense provision is *vague* if it does not adequately define the prohibited conduct. If a provision defines the conduct with some specificity, yet is subject to two or more interpretations, then it is termed *ambiguous,* which is not necessarily unconstitutional. In *People v. Nunez,* the prisoner injured a guard during an escape while awaiting transport to a state prison to serve a life sentence.[5] He was charged with an offense that punishes assault by a "person undergoing a life sentence in a state prison." Must the person physically be "in a state prison," or is it enough that he is a person who is undergoing "a life sentence in a state prison"? Do we give the word "undergoing" a physical or legal meaning? There is nothing vague about the prohibited conduct, but the provision is ambiguous because it is subject to either of two interpretations.

Rule of Lenity: Resolve Ambiguity in Favor of Defendant Two of the doctrines that instantiate the legality principle were noted earlier: Modern American criminal law abolishes common law crimes and prohibits the judicial creation of new offenses. In 1962, the English House of Lords (which, among other things, serves the function of our Supreme Court) approved prosecution of a common law offense of "conspiracy to corrupt public morals."[6] American jurisdictions typically would bar prosecution for such an offense because it has not been legislatively enacted (and is also probably too vague). In addition, the legality principle is embodied in the constitutional prohibition against vague statutes, the rule requiring strict construction of penal statutes (also known as the rule of lenity), and the constitutional prohibition against *ex post facto* laws. When faced with an ambiguity, the law traditionally applies a special rule for interpreting criminal statutes. The *rule of strict construction* directs that an ambiguity in a penal statute must be resolved against the state and in favor of the defendant. Because it supports lenient treatment, it also is called the *rule of lenity.* In *Nunez,* the rule of lenity would hold that the statutes should be given the narrower interpretation, to require that the prisoner be physically located "in a state prison" at the time of the offense. Note that the rule of lenity is a doctrine of statutory interpretation, not a constitutional requirement, so courts are free to abandon it, and legislatures may supersede it by statute. (The modern trend is to ameliorate the strictness of the rule of lenity by statutorily replacing it with a *rule of fair import.*)

---

3. Papachristou v. City of Jacksonville, 405 U.S. 156, 162 (1972), quoting United States v. Harris, 347 U.S. 612, 617 (1954).

4. State v. Palendrano, 293 A.2d 747 (N.J. Super. Law Div. 1972).

5. 208 Cal. Rptr. 450, 451 (Cal. App. 1984).

6. Shaw v. Director of Public Prosecutions, [1962] A.C. 220 (H.L.).

Ban on Ex Post Facto Laws   One final aspect of the legality principle is embodied in the constitutional prohibition against *ex post facto* laws.[7] This has been interpreted to invalidate laws that criminalize previously lawful behavior, and laws that aggravate the punishment for a crime to a level greater than when the crime was committed or apply a harsher penalty than when the crime was committed. For example, the prohibition bars liability for past use of a drug that is now prohibited, but was not at the time it was used. It similarly would bar application of a statute that changes an offense's punishment from life imprisonment or death to a mandatory death penalty, where the offense is committed before the statutory change.

THE RATIONALES

The basis for the legality principle does not lie in the actor's blamelessness, but rather in non-blameworthiness rationales. While not all of the rationales may apply in all situations, the rationales most commonly offered in support of the legality principle include the following.

Procedural Fairness   Fairness requires that an actor have at least an opportunity to determine what the criminal law prohibits, rather than being subjected to criminal liability after the fact for conduct that was not illegal at the time. Actual notice is not required for liability, however; it is enough that the prohibition has been lawfully enacted and has taken effect prior to the actor's conduct. By the same token, legality-based defenses will apply even where an actor thinks, or knows, that the law does seek to prohibit or punish her conduct. For example, an actor who knows the legislature is in the process of enacting a new crime may still engage in the relevant conduct until the crime is enacted and takes effect, and an actor who believes a criminal statute was intended to cover his conduct may still invoke the rule of lenity. The concern of the legality principle is procedural fairness, not blamelessness.

Promoting Effective Deterrence and Avoiding Improper Overdeterrence   Effective deterrence requires that the prohibited conduct be clearly defined. Citizens cannot conform their behavior to the law's commands if the law does not exist, or cannot be understood. For vague prohibitions, a reverse effect also can occur: Persons may refrain from engaging in lawful, and perhaps even desirable, conduct that they mistakenly assume, or fear, is included within the prohibition. For example, a vague prohibition may have the effect of chilling the exercise of constitutional rights, such as the rights to free speech or free assembly.

Promoting Democracy: Criminalization as a Legislative Function   In a democracy, the legislature, which is the most representative branch of government, is generally thought to be the proper body to exercise the criminalization decision. This rationale directly supports the prohibition of judicial creation of offenses and the abolition of common law (that is, judicially created) offenses. In less obvious ways, it also supports the invalidation of vague statutes, because vague statutes are *de facto* delegations of criminalization authority to the courts. Courts applying and interpreting vague prohibitions are left to provide the specificity the legislature has not.

---

7. U.S. Const. art. I, § 9, cl. 3 ("No bill of attainder or *ex post facto* law shall be passed"); U.S. Const. art I, § 10, cl. 1 ("No State shall . . . pass any bill of attainder, [or] *ex post facto* law . . . ").

Rationales Focus on Conduct Rules, Not Adjudication Rules All of the rationales noted so far—procedural fairness, effective deterrence, the danger of overdeterrence, and preserving the criminalization function for the legislature—concern the rule articulation function of the criminal law, that is, its obligation to communicate the governing rules of conduct to all members of society. The rationales reflect our preference for how that rule articulation function ought to be performed: The legislature should set the rules, and the formulations should be calculated to give adequate notice in order to deter effectively and properly and to condemn a violation fairly. But the criminal law also serves an adjudication function, and there are rationales for the legality principle associated with that function as well.

Adjudication Concerns: Avoiding Disparity and Abuse of Discretion Consistent treatment of similar cases is possible only with a sufficiently clear and precise definition of an offense, one that does not call for discretionary judgments. Individual discretion inevitably generates disparity based on the inherent differences among decision makers, even if they are all acting in good faith. Worse, the exercise of discretion also can allow the operation of malevolent influences of racism, sexism, and the like. An unclear prohibition, therefore, can create a potential for abuse of discretion by police officers, prosecutors, and others with decision-making authority. In *Papachristou v. City of Jacksonville*, for example, police officers arrested "mixed" (black and white) couples and charged them with a variety of vague offenses, such as "vagrancy," "loitering," and "disorderly loitering on street." The Court reversed the convictions and invalidated the relevant statutes, finding that their vagueness encouraged arbitrary convictions as well as arbitrary arrests.[8]

COUNTERVAILING INTERESTS

Unfortunately, the virtues of the legality principle create their own vices. While precise prior written rules make liability decisions more predictable and uniform, such rules also tend to leave decision makers less able to adapt the law as needed to deal with new or unusual problems, create the potential for criminal law adjudication to be caught up in technicalities that undercut the moral credibility of the law, and make it more difficult for the law to incorporate the normative judgments of the community.

Fostering Inflexibility and Unresponsiveness Fixed rules can leave the criminal law unable to punish new forms of criminal conduct. A precise listing of what constitutes a prohibited weapon, for example, may serve legality interests well, but may disallow the conviction and punishment of persons who develop new, "creative" weapons. The fact is the legislature may not be able to keep up with what one court called "the malicious ingenuity of mankind."[9] Precise prior written rules also make it difficult for the law to account for unusual offenses, common offenses committed in unusual contexts, and the infinite combinations of factors that may be relevant in determining liability and its degree.

Promoting Technicalities The constraints dictated by the legality principle burden courts even in simple, commonplace cases. Precision tends to spawn technicalities that frustrate effective justice. For example, in the *Nunez* case,

---

8. 405 U.S. 156, 162 (1972).
9. Commonwealth v. Taylor, 5 Binn. 277, 281 (Pa. 1812).

discussed previously, the court read the statute literally and held that it did not apply to the defendant because, although he assaulted someone while he was sentenced to serve a life sentence in state prison, he was at the time of the assault still physically located in county jail.[10] While the statute was subsequently amended to more explicitly cover such cases,[11] many would regard the result as a frustration of the legislature's will as to defendant Nunez. Legality also frequently makes proving guilt more difficult and costly.

Precision as Imperfect Proxy for Normative Judgments   Another effect of the precision demanded by the legality principle is its tendency to exclude moral judgments, which typically cannot be expressed in precise language, in favor of objective descriptions of observable behavior, which might be over or underinclusive in capturing the relevant underlying harm or wrong. The more intricate the rules, the greater the predictability and consistency, but also the greater the possibility that some cases will give results inconsistent with the community's moral assessment. The call for a normative judgment is sometimes codified, as with a *de minimis* defense for conduct "too trivial to warrant the condemnation of conviction" or the causation requirement that the result be "not too remote or accidental." But such codification only makes clear that the vagueness is intended; it does not avoid the vagueness challenge. Finally, because fixed rules can accommodate only a limited degree of factual detail, they tend to group meaningfully different cases into a single factual category and treat them as if they were identical.

Principle of Analogy   Many of these difficulties of precise written rules can be avoided by affording discretion to decision makers. Discretion to expand the definition or interpretation of an offense to include conduct analogous to that expressly prohibited is sometimes described as application of the *principle of analogy*. In *Lewis v. Commonwealth*, for example, the prosecutor sought to uphold the defendant's conviction for riotous and disorderly conduct on a bus, arguing that even though the statute (enacted before buses were invented) referred only to disorderly conduct on a "railroad or street passenger railway," it could logically be assumed that the legislature wanted the same statute to apply to all similar forms of transportation. A principle of analogy would allow such an expansion of the literal language of the statute to allow it to be applied to disorderly conduct on a bus. (The *Lewis* court, however, applied the legality principle and reversed the conviction.) The difficulty with a principle of analogy is that it may be used to extend liability without prior notice in situations more serious and less analogous than the streetcar-bus dispute in *Lewis*. For this reason, American criminal law commonly frowns on the analogy principle.

LEGALITY IN CONTEXT

Legality in Liability vs. Sentencing   Given the competing interests of legality and discretion, one might expect the legal system to strike a balance between the two. This is essentially what occurs in the rules governing the interpretation of criminal statutes. But in other respects, current practice creates a dichotomy rather than a compromise. In assessing whether to impose liability, and what general grade of liability to impose, the criminal law follows fixed and specific rules that allow little discretion; the legality principle is well respected. But

---

10. Nunez, 208 Cal. Rptr. 450, 452 (Cal. App. 1984).
11. Cal. Penal Code § 4500 (amendment effective January 1, 1987).

in the determination of an offender's specific sentence, it has long been common to have few or no rules and broad judicial discretion.

Difficulty in Justifying Disparate Respect for Legality Concerns   It is unclear whether this dramatic difference is justifiable. Determination of liability and grade is, after all, only the first of two necessary steps in the distribution of criminal liability; imposing a specific punishment is an equally important step. As the traditional statement of the legality principle provides, "no *crime* without law, no *punishment* without law." The rationales that support precise written rules to govern the assignment of liability apply as well to criminal sentencing. There is little reason to insist that decision makers strictly adhere to legality when they determine whether a particular offender is liable for a Grade C felony or a Grade A misdemeanor, for example, if there is then nearly complete discretion to give the same sentence for either grade of the offense. If the distribution of punishment is to be discretionary at the sentencing stage, society has benefited little from the strict adherence to legality at the liability-assignment stage. It is in part for this reason that the recent wave of sentencing reform has introduced articulated rules and significantly reduced sentencing discretion.

Legality and Function   One can distinguish, on grounds other than liability versus sentencing, instances where the legality interests operate differently. Different legality rationales apply to different criminal law functions. The fair notice and deterrence rationales apply primarily to the criminal law's rule-articulation function—defining and announcing the rules of conduct—and to the doctrines that serve that function. The uniformity and abuse-of-discretion rationales, on the other hand, apply primarily to the adjudication functions of liability assignment and grading, and to the doctrines that serve them. This suggests differential application of the legality principle depending on the function of the doctrine to which it is applied.

Legality in Rule Articulation vs. Adjudication   The rationales of the legality principle would have the rules of conduct formulated to maximize procedural fairness and effective deterrence and to minimize over-deterrence of protected activities. For example, objective and simple criteria might be much preferred in the rules of conduct, for these are directed to the general public, who have no special training or background and who must apply the rules in the course of their everyday lives. On the other hand, the rationales of the legality principle would have the doctrines of adjudication—those that assess the minimum conditions of liability and set the range of punishment—formulated to maximize uniformity in application to similar cases and to minimize the potential for abuse of discretion. Here, a high degree of specificity might be desirable even if it creates a degree of complexity that would be unreasonable to expect the public to master. The special training of decision makers and the more contemplative pace of the adjudication process means that greater complexity can be tolerated.

Calder v. Bull

Supreme Court of the United States
3 U.S. (3 Dall.) 386, 1 L. Ed. 648 (1798)

All the restrictions contained in the constitution of the United States on the power of the state legislatures, were provided in favor of the authority of the federal government. The prohibition against their making any ex post facto laws was introduced for greater caution, and very probably arose from the knowledge that the parliament of Great Britain claimed and exercised a power to pass such laws, under the denomination of bills of attainder, or bills of pains and penalties; the first inflicting capital, and the other less punishment. These acts were legislative judgments; and an exercise of judicial power. Sometimes, they respected the crime, by declaring acts to be treason, which were not treason, when committed; at other times, they violated the rules of evidence (to supply a deficiency of legal proof) by admitting one witness, when the existing law required two; by receiving evidence without oath; or the oath of the wife against the husband; or other testimony, which the courts of justice would not admit; at other times, they inflicted punishments, where the party was not, by law, liable to any punishment; and in other cases, they inflicted greater punishment, than the law annexed to the offence. The ground for the exercise of such legislative power was this, that the safety of the kingdom depended on the death, or other punishment, of the offender: as if traitors, when discovered, could be so formidable, or the government so insecure? With very few exceptions, the advocates of such laws were stimulated by ambition, or personal resentment and vindictive malice. To prevent such and similar acts of violence and injustice, I believe, the federal and state legislatures were prohibited from passing any bill of attainder, or any ex post facto law.

The constitution of the United States, article I., section 9, prohibits the legislature of the United States from passing any ex post facto law; and, in §10, lays several restrictions on the authority of the legislatures of the several states; and, among them, "that no state shall pass any ex post facto law." . . .

I will state what laws I consider ex post facto laws, within the words and the intent of the prohibition. 1st. Every law that makes an action done before the passing of the law, and which was innocent when done, criminal; and punishes such action. 2d. Every law that aggravates a crime, or makes it greater than it was, when committed. 3d. Every law that changes the punishment, and inflicts a greater punishment, than the law annexed to the crime, when committed. 4th. Every law that alters the legal rules of evidence, and receives less, or different testimony, than the law required at the time of the commission of the offence, in order to convict the offender. All these, and similar laws, are manifestly unjust and oppressive. . . . But I do not consider any law ex post facto, within the prohibition, that mollifies the rigor of the criminal law: but only those that create or aggravate the crime; or increase the punishment, or change the rules of evidence, for the purpose of conviction. . . .

[The Court concludes that the prohibition against ex post facto laws applies only to criminal laws and has no effect with respect to civil laws.]

▲ PROBLEMS

The Human Puppet Master (#4)

Baker is a tough lady. Practically running a farm on her own is difficult work and not overwhelmingly profitable. In order to make ends meet, she and her husband take in welfare paupers, housing them, feeding them, and caring for them on the farm. In exchange, Baker and her husband are paid a monthly stipend by the state Public Welfare Office for each lodger they have kept during that month. The state check arrives on the first of the month, made out to the boarder, who signs it over to Baker as payment for the previous month. On April 2nd one spring, a boarder dies without first signing over her check for March. Baker tries to have the check cashed without a signature, explaining the situation, but the state decides that it will not pay. Baker is upset but continues to board people at the farm.

Ed White is an elderly homeless man with a failing kidney. He asks to be sent to Baker's farm after hearing that she cares for people in exchange for welfare payments. Baker cares for him, treating the open sores that cover his body, preparing him three meals a day, and buying him medicines for his various conditions.

Late in November, White suffers a stroke and dies. Remembering her failure to get paid previously, Baker does not report White's death, but rather props his corpse up in a chair and goes through her usual routine of bringing him food and seeming to care for him. She regularly repositions and moves his corpse to avoid suspicion. As the old man rarely moved or spoke to begin with, and typically smelled bad, no one notices that he has passed away. On the morning of December 2nd, Baker signs White's welfare check, which has just arrived, and cashes it. That night, she sends for the undertaker. The medical examiner swiftly determines that the corpse has been decomposing for at least a week.

Baker is liable for welfare fraud but the authorities are more concerned about her liability for her mishandling of White's corpse. Is she criminally liable for it? The state has adopted a statutory provision allowing for the prosecution of common law crimes.

What liability for Baker, if any, under the Model Penal Code? Prepare a list of all criminal code subsections in the order in which you rely upon them in your analysis. How does the Code treat prosecution of common law crimes? What is the Code's rationale?

Is a Fetus Less Human Than Human? (#5)

Keeler is recently divorced and none too happy about the matter. He has difficulty letting go of his now ex-wife, Theresa, and is frequently jealous. He is especially angry when he hears that she is eight months pregnant with another man's child only five months after their divorce. Theresa, now living with the father-to-be, has custody on alternate weekends of the two daughters she had with Keeler. After dropping them off at Keeler's at the end of a weekend, she gets in her car and heads down the road toward her new house. Keeler himself is on his way home to meet his daughters. Spotting Theresa's car, he swerves to block the road and forces her to pull over. He is calm but menacing, telling Theresa that if what he hears about her pregnancy is true she should keep away from both him and their daughters.

Theresa does not reply. She is not particularly worried as he opens her car door and helps her out. However, when Keeler sees her in her obviously pregnant state, he becomes violent. He tells her she obviously is pregnant and shouts, "I'm going to stomp it out of you." Theresa faints as Keeler knees her hard in the abdomen. When she comes to, Keeler has left. She feels severe pains and, after returning to her house, calls for medical help. When she is rushed to the hospital, it is determined that the fetus she is carrying has suffered a fractured skull. A Cesarean section is performed, and the baby is delivered stillborn. A pathologist determines that the death of the fetus was likely immediate and caused solely by the force applied to the mother's abdomen. At 35 weeks, the fetus would have had a 96 percent chance of survival outside of the womb. California's Penal Code defines *murder* as the unlawful and malicious killing of a human being. The Code gives no definition of what constitutes a "human being."

What liability for Keeler for homicide, if any, under then-exiting California law? If the court concludes that there is liability, would Keeler have a constitutional challenge?

What homicide liability for Keeler, if any, under the Model Penal Code? Prepare a list of all criminal code subsections in the order in which you rely upon them in your analysis.

Gangsters Can't Stop (#6)

Morales is standing on a sidewalk with a group of his friends. He is in an area of the city known for gang activities, and police who regularly monitor gangs have identified him as a gang member. In response to rising gang violence and drug offenses, the city has made it a crime for anyone reasonably suspected of being a "criminal street gang member" to "loiter" with other gang members or persons in any public place. *Loitering* is defined by the Council's act as "remain[ing] in any one place with no apparent purpose." The Council believes this measure to be necessary as gang members are able to spot police and curtail any illegal acts while they are observed, only to start up again as soon as the police presence is gone. In order to be convicted, a person must be first ordered by a member of the police department's Gang Crime Section to disperse and must fail to disperse. As Morales and his friends pass time, a Gang Crime Section officer orders them to disperse. Morales refuses to leave.

What liability for Morales, if any, under the Council's anti-gang measure? If he is found to be in violation, would he have a constitutional challenge? What liability for Morales, if any, under the Model Penal Code? Prepare a list of all criminal code subsections in the order in which you rely upon them in your analysis.

● OVERVIEW OF STATUTORY INTERPRETATION

Notes

Vagueness, Ambiguity, and Conflict
Difficulty of Determining Legislative Intent
Plain-Meaning Rule
    Drafting Errors and Implied Exceptions to Plain-Meaning Rule
Rules for Resolving Ambiguities
    Canons of Statutory Construction
    Going Beyond Statutory Language to Consider Legislative History

Vagueness, Ambiguity, and Conflict   Because words are not perfect representations of ideas and because unanticipated situations inevitably arise, criminal statutes, like all other statutes, frequently are unclear. As previously noted, *vague* language may invalidate a statute as unconstitutional. If a statute's language is *ambiguous*—that is, if it is subject to two or more meanings—a court will be required to interpret the statute, to decide which of the possible meanings should be adopted. Interpretation problems also may arise where two or more statutes give conflicting rules, in which case the court must determine which of the two statutes is controlling.

Difficulty of Determining Legislative Intent   In such situations, courts are not free to choose the interpretation that they think results in the best rule or result. Recall that a central rationale of the legality principle is to reserve the criminalization decision to the legislative branch. It follows that a court's role in interpreting a criminal statute is to determine and follow the legislature's intent, rather than to assert its own substantive judgment. Unfortunately, the legislature frequently will not have addressed, or even thought about, the issues giving rise to an ambiguity. Any effort to assess what the legislature *would have* thought about the issue may be complete speculation. Further, the average person bound by the law may be able to find the legal provision itself, but has little access to or familiarity with legislative history or other indications of the legislature's intent, so deference to intent can undercut fair notice.

Plain-Meaning Rule   To reaffirm the limited judicial role in applying statutes and avoid the difficult inquiry into legislative intent unless a definite ambiguity exists, courts interpreting statutes follow a *plain-meaning rule*. Courts are simply to follow the statute, and eschew any inquiry beyond its four corners, "[w]here the language is plain and admits of no more than one meaning."[12] A court is bound to apply a statute's plain meaning even if it disagrees strongly with the wisdom of the policy the statute's language advances.

Drafting Errors and Implied Exceptions to Plain-Meaning Rule   On the other hand, it is said that a court need not mindlessly follow the literal language of a statute that clearly does not represent the legislative intent. A court may take note of an obvious drafting or typographical error, even if the bill as enacted by the legislature contained the error. A court may recognize logically implied exceptions. But in each case, the court must conclude that *the legislature* would see the statute as obviously containing a drafting error or implied exception. Further, the conclusion that the legislature would want to correct the obviously mistaken language cannot come simply from the fact that *the court* strongly believes the language as written reflects a bad policy.

---

12. Caminetti v. United States, 242 U.S. 470, 485 (1917).

Rules for Resolving Ambiguities   Where a statute's meaning is not plain and multiple interpretations are possible, courts have recognized three sorts of rules to guide them in resolving the ambiguity: (1) rules for interpreting the language within a statute; (2) rules directing where a court may look outside of the statutory language; and (3) in criminal cases, a special rule setting the standard of interpretation, usually either the *rule of strict construction* or the *rule of fair import.*

Canons of Statutory Construction   Over time, courts have developed some general rules (or as they are sometimes called, *canons*) of *statutory construction*—that is, rules about how a court should *construe* a provision's meaning—to guide judicial interpretation of statutes. At least five rules have been recognized for interpreting ambiguous language on the face of a statute:

> *Different language implies a different meaning.* Where a document uses different language in different parts, there is a presumption that the legislature intended different meanings by the different language. For example, if a statute referred to "causing injury" in one place and to "causing harm" in another, the different terms would be presumed to mean different things.
>
> *A catch-all phrase is limited by the common factor of the items in the list.* Where a list of things ends in a catch-all phrase, such as "or other . . . ," the phrase must be interpreted to be limited to the theme or common factor of the specific entries in the list. This is called the rule of *ejusdem generis.* For example, if a statute refers to "dogs, cats, or other such animals," the interpretation of "other such animals" should be guided by whatever category is suggested by "dogs" and "cats."
>
> *The expression of one thing excludes other things.* Where a statute sets forth a list, for example, other things that are not listed are by implication excluded. This is the rule of *expressio unius; exclusio alterius.* For example, if a statute specifically refers only to apples and oranges, it does not apply to other fruit, even if it might seem sensible to apply the same rule to other fruit.
>
> *The special controls the general.* Two statutes may each apply to the same fact situation and may generate different results. Where this occurs, the rules of construction provide that the more specific statute has priority over the more general. For example, if the Fruit Control Act and the Orange Control Act conflict in a case involving an orange, the Orange Control Act would take priority.
>
> *The later controls the earlier.* Where two statutes enacted at different times conflict, the rules of construction give priority to the later enactment over the earlier.

Going Beyond Statutory Language to Consider Legislative History   If a conflict or ambiguity remains unresolved after applying these rules to the language on the face of a statute, a court may look beyond the literal language of the statute. Legislatures sometimes keep records, even transcripts, of their deliberations, and sometimes even the deliberations of their committees. The United States Congress is particularly good in this regard. (Some state legislatures are particularly bad.) These records of the *legislative history* of a statute may be examined to see whether they reveal the interpretation intended by the legislature. Where the statute was borrowed from another jurisdiction, the legislative history of that jurisdiction may be enlightening, although not as persuasive as that of the home jurisdiction. In this regard, the extensive Model Penal Code commentaries are particularly important and influential. The Code's provisions have been widely adopted, and its commentaries provide what is sometimes the only source of legislative history for many state code provisions. Finally, an authoritative interpretation of a statute sometimes may be available from an agency or official empowered by the legislature to issue such interpretations.

Special Status of Criminal Statutes   Because they are held to a higher standard of precision and clarity than civil statutes, criminal statutes are subject to special rules of statutory interpretation. One might argue that, if the rules of construction described above must be brought to bear to determine the proper interpretation of a criminal statute, the goals of the legality principle already have been frustrated. Only lawyers and judges are likely to know these rules for interpreting ambiguous language, or to have access to legislative history and authoritative agency interpretations. Thus, while the general rules for statutory construction described above are adequate for civil statutes, they sometimes are ignored in favor of a special rule for criminal statutes, the rule of strict construction.

Rule of Strict Construction   Under the rule of strict construction, also known as the *rule of lenity,* "ambiguity concerning the ambit of criminal statutes should be resolved in favor of lenity,"[13] that is, in favor of showing lenience and sparing the defendant. This rule suggests that while the terms of a prohibition are to be strictly construed, the same does not apply to the terms of a defense. In this respect the "rule of strict construction" label is potentially misleading, and the "rule of lenity" is preferable.

Strengths and Weaknesses of Rule of Lenity   Given that the rule of lenity (strict construction) is one aspect of the legality principle, it should be no surprise that it shares the virtues and vices of the principle. Most important, it furthers the interest of fair notice by barring application of an offense provision against a defendant if, under one interpretation of the provision, the defendant's conduct is not in violation. The rule also serves to preserve the legislature's exclusive criminalization authority, preventing courts from expanding an offense by adopting a broad interpretation of its language. On the other hand, the rule may frustrate a legislature's obvious intent as to a potentially important issue and risks bringing the criminal justice system into disrepute, as a game governed by technicalities having little relation to fairness or justice.

Rule of Fair Import   Because of the dangers of the rule of strict construction, and in recognition of modern codes' greater attention to clarity and precision, most current codes abrogate the rule of strict construction and adopt instead a *rule of fair import.*

> The rule of the common law, that penal statutes are to be strictly construed, has no application to this Code. All its provisions are to be construed according to the fair import of their terms, with a view to effect its objects and to promote justice.[14]

The fair import rule gives courts the authority to interpret statutes in a way that does not frustrate the legislative purpose, yet by relying upon the "fair import" or most sensible reading of the terms, the rule seeks to ensure that some reasonable notice of the offense is possible. In that sense, the rule of fair import attempts a compromise between the virtues of legality and its countervailing interests.

---

13. See, e.g., Bell v. United States, 349 U.S. 81, 83 (1955).
14. Cal. Penal Code § 4.

Possible Practical Equivalence of Two Interpretive Rules Despite appearances, it is unclear just how different the two rules are in application. An appearance of difference may come from the tendency to overestimate how literally and strongly judges apply the rule of lenity. If the rule of lenity were applied literally, it would require no exercise of discretion: Courts would have to adopt whichever of the offered interpretations is most favorable to the defendant. But courts rarely apply the rule in mindless disregard for its intended meaning and purposes. First, the rule of strict construction applies only if there is an ambiguity, and it is for the court to decide whether an ambiguity exists in the first place. An absurd and farfetched interpretation may simply be ignored by a court as not raising an ambiguity.

Further, the rule of lenity has been tempered with the exception that a statute is "not to be construed so strictly as to defeat the obvious intention of the legislature"[15] or "to override common sense."[16] Nor is it necessary that a statute be given its narrowest possible meaning or a "forced, narrow or overstrict construction."[17] Indeed, even in jurisdictions that employ the rule of lenity, a common method is to apply lenity only after all efforts to ascertain the statute's meaning—such as canons of construction and legislative history—have been exhausted, leaving ineradicable ambiguity. In other words, in practice, courts exercise considerable discretion in determining whether a "legitimate" ambiguity exists and in choosing among interpretations, even under the apparently mechanical rule of lenity.

Practical Significance of Lenity vs. Fair Import Perhaps the interpretive rules do retain a significant difference in application, if a fair import rule is more likely to induce a court to follow legislative intent that conflicts with the most obvious literal reading. That is, judges will be more hesitant to deviate from a strict reading under a rule of strict construction that does not appear to permit such deviation. But the accuracy of such a conjecture is difficult to assess. The primary difference between the tests may be the *admission* that judicial discretion is at work under fair import, and the apparent denial of such discretion under the rule of lenity.

Defense For Conduct Not Envisaged by Legislative Prohibition In addition to explicitly adopting a rule of fair import, a number of modern codes follow the lead of the Model Penal Code in providing a defense for what it calls "*de minimis* infractions."[18] In reality, the provision has a broader effect than simply providing a defense for trivial harms, such as taking a piece of bubble gum. It directs a court to exempt from liability conduct that, for any of a variety of reasons, the legislature did not mean for the offense to cover. It calls on a judge to dismiss a prosecution if the defendant's conduct did not cause or threaten "the harm or evil sought to be prevented by the law defining the offense" or if it occurred under such conditions that "it cannot reasonably be regarded as envisaged by the legislature in forbidding the offense."[19] The provision explicitly directs the court to do what the rules of construction are designed to achieve: to dismiss

---

15. United States v. Wiltberger, 5 Wheat. 76, 95 (U.S.1820).
16. United States v. Brown, 333 U.S. 18, 25-26 (1948).
17. State v. Carter, 570 P.2d 1218, 1221 (Wash. 1977).
18. See, e.g., N.J. Stat. 2C:2-11; 18 Pa. Cons. Stat. § 312.
19. See Model Penal Code § 2.12.

a prosecution if, in the judge's view, the legislature did not intend for the case at hand to be punished by conviction for the offense charged. For the sake of clarity, these two distinct aspects of the "*de minimis*" defense might best be divided into a defense for trivial harms and a separate defense for "conduct not envisioned by the offense."

Inevitable Tension in Addressing Statutory Ambiguity In the end, none of these rules of construction gives a clear or easy answer to the range of ambiguities that can arise. The absence of clear rules with clean results may be inevitable. In one sense, ambiguities in statutes create an unresolvable conflict among interests that are each important to us; they are the points of tension within the legality principle, and between that principle and the principle of analogy. We prefer to apply statutes as they read, for this is the best way to assure fair notice. We also prefer to interpret statutes to give rational results consistent with the legislative intent. But, in reality, applying a statute as written can give irrational results contrary to the legislative intent. We prefer that the legislature, rather than judges, make the criminalization decisions. Yet, if a statute is ambiguous, we must either turn to judges to fix it or suffer frustration of the legislative purpose. There is no obvious means of resolving the conflict among these interests: rational and effective adjudication of cases, fair notice, and preservation of the legislative criminalization power. The conflict would not arise if every statute were perfectly clear and could anticipate every possible form of violation, but even if legislative drafting is perfect, language is not. There seems little alternative other than to have judges continue to balance the competing interests as each case arises.

▲ PROBLEMS

Marsh Continued . . . (#7)

Reconsider the case of Ray Brent Marsh, appearing at the beginning of this section, under the following statute:

> Abuse of corpse. A person commits a misdemeanor if, knowing others would be offended by his conduct, he dismembers, disfigures, injures, or otherwise abuses any corpse, or he disturbs a buried corpse in any way.

What liability for Marsh under this statute, if any, for his treatment of the dead bodies?

Is a Judge a Member of His Family? (#8)

Gray is a man who often feels persecuted. As is his right, he files a number of civil complaints against people he feels have wronged him. However, instead of receiving the satisfaction he seeks, two of his complaints are dismissed by the federal judge before whom they are brought. Gray now feels mistreated by the judge as well, but seeks recourse in a more aggressive manner. He writes the judge a letter, stating none too subtly, "I am going to kill you." To ensure that his displeasure is known, he signs his name at the bottom of the letter. Upon his arrest, he admits that the reason he wrote the letter was to retaliate for the adverse outcomes in these cases. He also insists that he still intends to carry out the threat.

At the time of Gray's threat, the only relevant federal laws are these. 18 U.S.C. 1114 provides in part:

> Whoever kills or attempts to kill any judge of the United States . . . shall be punished as provided under Sections 1111 and 1112 of this title, except that any such person who is found guilty of attempted murder shall be imprisoned for not more than twenty years.

18 U.S.C 115(a) provides in part:

> Whoever assaults, kidnaps, or murders, or attempts to kidnap or murder, or threatens to assault, kidnap or murder a member of the immediate family of a United States official, judge or law enforcement officer while he is engaged in or on account of the performance of his official duties, shall be punished as provided in subsection (b).

Is Gray liable under federal law for threatening the federal judge? Explain your conclusion.

✳ DISCUSSION ISSUE

Should the Criminal Law Recognize an Exception to the Legality Principle When the Crime Is Serious?

Materials presenting each side of this Discussion Issue appear in the Advanced Materials for Section 2 in Appendix A.

Theories of Punishment

Having a criminal justice system that imposes punishment can be justified on a variety of grounds; it can give offenders the punishment they deserve, it can deter future violations, it can take control over dangerous persons to rehabilitate or incapacitate them. Once it is decided to have a criminal justice system, as all civilized societies have, there arises the question of how to distribute liability and punishment within that system. That is the central question in criminal law, an examination of which is begun in this Section.

◆ THE CASE OF SARA JANE OLSON (#9)

Sarah Jane Olson, then Kathleen Soliah ("Kathy"), is born in 1947 into a comfortable middle-class family in Fargo, North Dakota. While still a young child, her family moves to Palmdale, California, a desert town an hour northeast of Los Angeles, where her father teaches high school English and her mother stays home with the children. The family is close-knit and active, often camping in the mountains and going to the beach together. As a child, Kathy is involved in everything—Girl Scouts, the Rainbows, Sunday school. In high school, her upbeat and energetic personality makes her the president of the Pep Club, while still graduating with honors. She attends the University of California at Santa Barbara and falls in love with an economics graduate student, James Kilgore.

In 1971, Kathy and James move to San Francisco, where they become involved with groups in the counterculture movement. It is a time of social upheaval—many are even pushing for revolution. One group of particular notoriety is the Symbionese Liberation Army (SLA), which is led by a career criminal and composed of mostly white, college-educated twenty-somethings who have aligned themselves with society's "oppressed." They commit acts of murder, kidnaping, and robbery in an effort to topple the "establishment." The SLA is both well organized and disciplined, and has become well versed in surveillance, security, field operations, explosives, and political indoctrination techniques. Their motto is, "Death to the fascist insect that preys upon the life of the people." Kathy is not a full-fledged revolutionary, but she believes strongly in the movement for social equality and has friends who are intimately involved in more radical politics.

While working as an actress, Kathy meets Angela Atwood, a fellow actress and New Jersey native. Atwood is a graduate of the University of Indiana, where she majored in speech and earned honors in theater. They become close friends and take waitressing jobs together at the same San Francisco cocktail lounge to make ends meet. They are fired, however, when they start a campaign to unionize employees in response to being forced to wear revealing outfits. Because they share a similar political orientation, Atwood, a member of the SLA, introduces Kathy to her comrades. By this time, the SLA is connected to both the murder of the Oakland schools' superintendent and the kidnapping of heiress Patty Hearst. Kathy claims her ties to the SLA are only through Atwood. Atwood then disappears. When Kathy returns to San Francisco from vacationing in Mexico, she learns that Atwood was one of six SLA members who were killed during a shootout with more than 400 police on May 17, 1974. Kathy organizes a public

Figure 6 **Soliah at SLA rally in Berkeley, 1974**
(AP)

memorial service for June 2 in Berkeley's Ho Chi Minh Park and, distraught over her friend's death, takes the stage. Introducing herself as a close friend of Angela, Kathy calls her "a truly revolutionary woman" who was murdered by "500 pigs." She ends her speech with a pledge to the surviving SLA members, "Tania [Patty Hearst's alias], Emily, and Bill, your message—you have made your message clear. Keep fighting. We are with you. I am with you."

A few days after the memorial service, SLA member Emily Harris approaches Kathy at the bookstore where she works and pleads for help. The surviving SLA revolutionaries are on the run from the police and need food, new identities, and a hideout. Kathy helps by renting them cars and apartments under false names, creating aliases from the names of dead infants, and giving the revolutionaries money from time to time. She also becomes an SLA spokeswoman, attempting to explain its philosophy to the underground press in the Bay Area.

A little more than a year after Atwood's death, on August 20, 1975, Kathy accompanies a solidly built white male, approximately six feet tall with short, blond hair, to Larsen Supply Company in Southgate, CA. The man purchases pipe fittings—two 3-inch by 12-inch galvanized nipples and one 3-inch galvanized cap, paying $16.53 in cash.

The next day, Officer James J. Bryan of the Los Angeles Police Department, Hollywood Division, and his partner, John David Hall, are on patrol duty. Around 11:15 p.m., they park their car in the parking lot of the International House of Pancakes at 7006 Sunset Boulevard, go inside, and have something to eat. The officers exit the restaurant around midnight and resume their patrol. About thirty minutes later, Bryan and Hall return to the IHOP in response to a request from another patrol unit to help block traffic on Sunset Blvd. Subsequently, they receive a robbery call and move their car to Sunset and LeBrea. They then receive information that police still at IHOP found a pipe bomb in the parking space where they had parked earlier that night. Bryan and Hall hurriedly check underneath their car and find a U-shaped magnet attached to a length of fishing line and a wooden wedge on the frame of the car. That same day, an identical pipe bomb is found underneath a police car parked near the Hollenbeck Police Station in Los Angeles. Both bombs were linked to the supplies that Kathy and the unidentified white male had bought two days earlier.

On September 18, 1975, between 9 and 10 a.m., F.B.I. Agent Frank R. Doyle, Jr., while surveilling an apartment at 288 Precita in San Francisco, observes Kathy leaving the SLA safehouse with her sister, Josephine Soliah, and brother, Steven Soliah. Around 1 or 2 p.m., Doyle observes Bill and Emily Harris exiting the apartment. The Harrises are arrested shortly thereafter and the apartment is searched. In the apartment that Kathy had just exited, the F.B.I. finds numerous weapons, a standing carbine, knapsacks, gas masks, Browning Hi-Power publications (including "Carbines" and "The Browning Hi-Power Pistols"), blank checks, and bomb-making materials (wiring, knife switches, batteries, endpipe caps, pipe nipples, a wooden wedge, blasting caps with wires attached, magnets, epoxy, fishing line, clothespins, black tape, nails, plastic garbage bags). The F.B.I. identifies the fingerprints of Kathleen Soliah on gun manuals and weapons in the apartment, along with the fingerprints of Patricia Hearst, James Kilgore, Emily Harris, Wendy Yoshimura, Steven Soliah, William Harris, Josephine Soliah, and Bonnie Wilder. F.B.I. explosives expert Frederick T. Smith, Jr., also matches the

Figure 7 **Weapons and SLA literature found in safehouse**
(Los Angeles Police Department)

bomb-making materials found in the apartment to the bomb components found in the IHOP parking space and underneath the police car driven by Officers Bryan and Hall.

On February 18, 1976, a grand jury is convened to inquire into Kathy's participation in a conspiracy with William and Emily Harris to murder the police officers during their shoot-out, to possess destructive devices, and to place bombs under police cars. Three days of testimony followed, during which 26 witnesses testify and numerous exhibits are presented showing Kathy's intimate involvement in the SLA plans to murder the police officers. Kathy Soliah is indicted on February 26, 1976, for one count of Conspiracy to Commit Murder, two counts of Possession of a Destructive Device in a Specified Area for the two pipe bombs, and two counts of Possession of a Destructive Device with Intent to Commit Murder. An arrest warrant is issued for her that day.

Before she can be arrested, Kathy flees to Minnesota and takes the last name Olson because it is common, the first name Sara from a Bob Dylan song, and her sister's name, Jane, as her middle name.

She soon begins dating a young, socially conscious doctor named Fred Peterson. They join a local anti-apartheid group and work with African refugees in Minneapolis. In 1980, they marry and a few years later, after having their first child, Emily, move to rural Zimbabwe, where Peterson sets up a free clinic and Olson teaches English. Olson gives

Figure 8 **F.B.I. Identification Order, June 20, 1978**
(F.B.I.)

birth to their second daughter, Sophia, while still in Zimbabwe. They return to Minnesota in 1982 and have their third daughter, Leila, in 1987. Olson stays at home to raise the children. She remains an active volunteer in political causes, and her home becomes a gathering place for "the larger peace and justice community in the Twin Cities." She also involves herself in the Twin Cities' theater scene, winning praise from the local press for many of her performances.

Figure 9 **St. Paul, Minnesota, home, June 1999**
(King Andy/Corbis)

Olson maintains limited contact with her parents, who are often visited by F.B.I. agents searching for their daughter. In a February 1984 interview with detectives from the Los Angeles Police Department's Criminal Conspiracy Section, they indicate that their daughter no longer lives in California, has assumed a new identity, and is married with children.

In 1989, Kathleen secretly attempts to surrender through her attorney, but the negotiations fail because of the government's unwillingness to grant her blanket immunity on all charges. In 1999, L.A.P.D. detective Tom King, whose father, Mervin, had been in charge of the deadly 1974 shoot-out with the SLA, decides to reopen the case. In June, Olson is on her way to teach a citizenship class to immigrants in suburban St. Paul when a swarm of police, acting on a tip from a viewer who saw her photograph during a broadcast of "America's Most Wanted," surround her minivan and take her into custody pursuant to the still outstanding 1976 warrant.

Olson insists that she is innocent and hires famed anti-establishment lawyer J. Tony Serra, known for defending members of the Black Panthers, Hells Angels, and New World Liberation Front, as well as a professional fire-eater. Within days, nearly 250 friends, many putting their homes up as collateral, raise $1 million for her bail. Many friends also form a defense committee and publish a fund-raising cookbook of Olson's favorite recipes titled, "Serving Time: America's Most Wanted Recipes." It features provocative imagery that includes allusions to SLA symbols and Olson mocking the trial proceeding by posing with a picture frame around her face. Olson demands a plea agreement with no jail time, but the district attorney refuses.

Figure 10 **Olson in community theater production of** *Great Expectations*, **1997**
(Act One/Corbis Sygma)

Figure 11 **Olson cookbook**
(Sara Olson Defense Fund Committee)

At trial, Olson maintains her innocence, claiming she was motivated by compassion for her friends, whom she believed would be killed by police if ever found. "Though it seems misguided now, I thought that giving [Emily Harris] money [in support of the SLA] would help save their lives and I thought that was an honorable and Christian thing to do." She also attributes her actions in part to the turmoil of the era. "Like many who participated in the activities of the 1960s and 1970s to bring about change in our country, to make it what I thought would be a better country, I have, for many years, realized that my zeal led to some bad decisions."

1. Relying only on your own intuitions of justice, what liability and punishment, if any, does Sara Jane Olson deserve?

N	0	1	2	3	4	5	6	7	8	9	10	11
☐	☐	☐	☐	☐	☐	☐	☐	☐	☐	☐	☐	☐
no liability	liability but no punishment	1 day	2 wks	2 mo	6 mo	1 yr	3 yrs	7 yrs	15 yrs	30 yrs	life imprison- ment	death

2. What "justice" arguments could defense counsel make on the defendant's behalf?

3. What "justice" arguments could the prosecution make against the defendant?

4. What liability, if any, for Olson under the then-existing statutes? Prepare a list of all criminal code subsections in the order in which you rely upon them in your analysis.

5. What liability, if any, under the Model Penal Code? Prepare a list of all criminal code subsections in the order in which you rely upon them in your analysis.

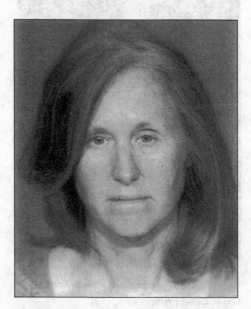

Figure 12 **Arrest photo, June 1999**
(AP)

▪ THE LAW

Deering's California Penal Code Annotated
(1975)

Title 7. Of Crimes Against Public Justice
Chapter 8. Conspiracy

Section 182. Definition; Punishment; Venue

If two or more persons conspire:

(1) To commit a crime.

(2) Falsely and maliciously to indict another for any crime, or to procure another to be charged or arrested for any crime.

(3) Falsely to move or maintain any suit, action or proceeding.

(4) To cheat and defraud any person of any property, by any means which are in themselves criminal, or to obtain money or property by false pretenses or by false promises with fraudulent intent not to perform such promises.

(5) To commit an act injurious to the public health, to public morals, or to pervert or obstruct justice, or the due administration of the laws.

(6) To commit any crime against the person of the President or Vice President of the United States, the governor of any state or territory, any United States justice or judge, or the secretary of any of the executive departments of the United States.

They are punishable as follows:

When they conspire to commit any crime against the person of any official specified in subdivision (6), they are guilty of a felony and are punishable by imprisonment in the state prison for not less than 10 years.

When they conspire to commit any other felony, they shall be punishable in the same manner and to the same extent as is provided for the punishment of the said felony. If the felony is one for which different punishments are prescribed for different degrees, the jury or court which finds the defendant guilty thereof shall determine the degree of the felony defendant conspired to commit. If the degree is not determined, the punishment for conspiracy to commit such felony shall be that prescribed for the lesser degree, except in the case of conspiracy to commit murder, in which case the punishment shall be that prescribed for murder in the first degree.

If the felony is conspiracy to commit two or more felonies which have different punishments and the commission of such felonies constitute but one offense of conspiracy, the penalty shall be that prescribed for the felony which has the greater maximum term.

When they conspire to do an act described in subdivision 4 of this section, they shall be punishable by imprisonment in the county jail for not more than 1 year, or by a fine not exceeding five thousand dollars ($5,000), or both.

When they conspire to do any of the other acts described in this section they shall be punishable by imprisonment in the county jail for not more than one year, or in the state prison for not more than three years, or by a fine not exceeding five thousand dollars ($5,000) or both.

All cases of conspiracy may be prosecuted and tried in the superior court of any county in which any overt act tending to effect such conspiracy shall be done.

Section 183. Non-Criminal Conspiracies; No Criminal Punishment

No other conspiracies punishable criminally. No conspiracies, other than those enumerated in the preceding section, are punishable criminally.

Section 184. Overt Act; Venue

No agreement amounts to a conspiracy, unless some act, besides such agreement, be done within this state to effect the object thereof, by one or more of the parties to such agreement and the trial of cases of conspiracy may be had in any county in which any such act be done.

Title 8. Of Crimes Against the Person

Chapter 1 Homicide

Section 187. Murder Defined

(a) Murder is the unlawful killing of a human being, or a fetus, with malice aforethought.

(b) This section shall not apply to any person who commits an act that results in the death of a fetus if any of the following apply:

(1) The act complied with the Therapeutic Abortion Act, Chapter 11 (commencing with Section 25950) of Division 20 of the Health and Safety Code.

(2) The act was committed by a holder of a physician's and surgeon's certificate, as defined in the Business and Professions Code, in a case where, to a medical certainty, the result of childbirth would be death of the mother of the fetus or where her death from childbirth, although not medically certain, would be substantially certain or more likely than not.

(3) The act was solicited, aided, abetted, or consented to by the mother of the fetus.

(c) Subdivision (b) shall not be construed to prohibit the prosecution of any person under any other provision of law.

Section 188. Malice, Express Malice, and Implied Malice Defined

Such malice may be express or implied. It is express when there is manifested a deliberate intention unlawfully to take away the life of a fellow creature. It is implied, when no considerable provocation appears, or when the circumstances attending the killing show an abandoned malignant heart.

Section 189. Murder; Degrees

All murder which is perpetrated by means of a destructive device or explosive, poison, lying in wait, torture, or by any other kind of willful, deliberate, and premeditated killing, or which is committed in the perpetration of, or attempt to perpetrate, arson, rape, robbery, burglary, mayhem, or any act punishable under Section 288, is murder of the first degree; and all other kinds of murders are of the second degree.

As used in this section, "destructive device" shall mean any destructive device as defined in Section 12301, and "explosive" shall mean any explosive as defined in Section 12000 of the Health and Safety Code.

Section 190. Murder, Punishment, Discretion of Jury

Every person guilty of murder in the first degree shall suffer death, confinement in the state prison for life without the possibility of parole, or confinement in the state prison for a term of 25 years to life. . . .

Every person guilty of murder in the second degree shall suffer confinement in the state prison for a term of 15 years to life.

The provisions of Article 2.5 (commencing with Section 2930) of Chapter 7 of Title 1 of Part 3 of the Penal Code shall apply to reduce any minimum term of 25 years to 15 years in a state prison imposed pursuant to this section, but such a person shall not otherwise be released on parole prior to such time.

Title 2. Control of Deadly Weapons
Chapter 2.5

Section 12303.2 Possession of a Destructive Device

Every person who recklessly or maliciously has in his possession any destructive device or any explosive on a public street or highway, in or near any theater, hall, school, college, church, hotel, other public building, or private habitation, in, on, or near any aircraft, railway passenger train, car, cable road or cable car, vessel engaged in carrying passengers for hire, or other public place ordinarily passed by human beings is guilty of a felony, and shall be punishable by imprisonment in the state prison for a period of not less than five years.

Section 12308 Attempted Explosion of a Destructive Device with Intent to Murder

Every person who explodes, ignites, or attempts to explode or ignite any destructive device or any explosive with intent to commit murder is guilty of a felony, and shall be punished by imprisonment in the state prison for a period of not less than 10 years.

Model Penal Code
(Official Draft 1962)

Section 1.02. Purposes; Principles of Construction.

(1) The general purposes of the provisions governing the definition of offenses are:

(a) to forbid and prevent conduct that unjustifiably and inexcusably inflicts or threatens substantial harm to individual or public interests;

(b) to subject to public control persons whose conduct indicates that they are disposed to commit crimes;

(c) to safeguard conduct that is without fault from condemnation as criminal;

(d) to give fair warning of the nature of the conduct declared to constitute an offense;

(e) to differentiate on reasonable grounds between serious and minor offenses.

(2) The general purposes of the provisions governing the sentencing and treatment of offenders are:

(a) to prevent the commission of offenses;

(b) to promote the correction and rehabilitation of offenders;

(c) to safeguard offenders against excessive, disproportionate or arbitrary punishment;

(d) to give fair warning of the nature of the sentences that may be imposed on conviction of an offense;

(e) to differentiate among offenders with a view to a just individualization in their treatment;

(f) to define, coordinate and harmonize the powers, duties and functions of the courts and of administrative officers and agencies responsible for dealing with offenders;

(g) to advance the use of generally accepted scientific methods and knowledge in the sentencing and treatment of offenders;

(h) to integrate responsibility for the administration of the correctional system in a State Department of Correction [or other single department or agency].

(3) The provisions of the Code shall be construed according to the fair import of their terms but when the language is susceptible of differing constructions it shall be interpreted to further the general purposes stated in this Section and the special purposes of the particular provision involved. The discretionary powers conferred by the Code shall be exercised in accordance with the criteria stated in the Code and, insofar as such criteria are not decisive, to further the general purposes stated in this Section.

American Law Institute, Model Penal Code Amendment
(Adopted May 16, 2007)

Section 1.02(2). Purposes . . .

(2) The general purposes of the provisions on sentencing, applicable to all official actors in the sentencing system, are:

    (a) in decisions affecting the sentencing of individual offenders:

        (i) to render sentences in all cases within a range of severity proportionate to the gravity of offenses, the harms done to crime victims, and the blameworthiness of offenders;

        (ii) when reasonably feasible, to achieve offender rehabilitation, general deterrence, incapacitation of dangerous offenders, restoration of crime victims and communities, and reintegration of offenders into the law-abiding community, provided these goals are pursued within the boundaries of proportionality in subsection (a)(i); and

        (iii) to render sentences no more severe than necessary to achieve the applicable purposes in subsections (a)(I) and (a)(ii); . . .

● OVERVIEW OF THEORIES OF PUNISHMENT

Hypothetical: Daughters' Mustard (#10)

Devon receives a call from the doctor who has been caring for her mother and her sister, Erie, back home. The doctor asks Devon to return home as soon as possible, explaining that the effects of Erie's mental illness have become more severe and have made her difficult to handle. The doctor strongly recommends civil commitment. Mother has been painfully ill for several years and as a result has been unable to care for troubled Erie. Devon takes the first train home. She is met at the station by Fina, her other sister, who also was called by the doctor. Devon considers Fina deceitful and untrustworthy. She believes Fina's primary interest in the family is in trying to inherit as much as possible from her mother's sizeable fortune.

Soon after they arrive at the house, it becomes apparent why Erie's condition has worsened. Mother is in constant pain, unabated by the massive doses of painkillers prescribed by the doctor. She is frequently screaming and crying, asking to be killed. Devon feels that it is her mother's condition, rather than Erie's, that presents the emergency. The nurse who cares for both Mother and Erie reveals that Erie currently believes that her screaming Mother is actually a wild dog who will kill her if she does not kill it first. The nurse explains that disturbed Erie has tried to poison Mother several times, but to date has given her harmless substances—peanut butter, chicken bones—that she thinks might kill a dog.

After a week at the house, Devon can no longer bear her mother's suffering. She concludes that Mother's death would be a blessing. Erie's constant mumblings indicate that she next intends to poison Mother with the "yellow poison," by which she apparently means the hot mustard in the refrigerator. Devon throws out the mustard and substitutes a jar laced with arsenic. Erie feeds it to Mother, and Mother dies within hours. Both Devon and Erie are taken into custody after investigators piece together what happened. To Devon's surprise, Fina also is taken into custody. It turns out that, in order to inherit her share of the estate more quickly, Fina came up with the same mustard-substitution plan. When Devon threw away the mustard jar in the refrigerator, she was throwing away a jar that Fina had laced with arsenic.

What liability should ensue for each daughter, if any, under each of the alternative principles discussed below for distributing liability and punishment—general deterrence, special deterrence, rehabilitation, incapacitation, just deserts—if each, in turn, were considered the sole distributive principle?

Notes

INTRODUCTION

Separating Rhetoric from Substance   Political debates over incarceration policies often feature appeals to different methods of treating offenders. However, the labels political figures use for these methods or justifications are often substantially different from the principles whose name they share. It is therefore important, when reading this section, to distinguish the substance of the theories discussed below from political rhetoric that may misappropriate or distort the meaning of those theories.

Justifying Punishment   Criminal law's defining feature is that it imposes punishment: It deliberately inflicts hardship on people as a response to their wrongdoing. Recognizing this central trait of criminal law gives rise to the initial question of whether state-sanctioned punishment is necessary or desirable. Indeed, many movements, both religious and secular, have advocated a world without punishment. Yet every known organized society has a system for the imposition of punishment for a violation of important social rules. Should it be so? What justifies a society in intentionally imposing suffering on one of its members? The typical justifications generally fit within two major, competing accounts of the rationale of punishment: *retributive* and *utilitarian.*

Retributive Justification   The retributive justification of punishment is based on the moral principle that wrongdoers deserve punishment. On this account, achieving retributive justice is inherently good or valuable, so that imposing deserved punishment requires no further justification (such as a showing that punishment will lead to some other beneficial consequence). A striking illustration of this theory is Kant's argument that an island society ought to execute its convicted murderers before disbanding, even if no one would be present to be threatened by them.[1] While retributive justifications are not concerned with preventing future crimes, they may have that effect by generating legal rules that resonate with the moral values of the governed population, enhancing the criminal law's own moral force and thereby promoting respect for its authority.

Utilitarian Justification   The alternative justification, often described as a utilitarian view, is *consequentialist* in nature. According to this account, punishment is justified because (and to the extent that) it creates beneficial consequences— sometimes described as producing *utility* or promoting social welfare. The most commonly advanced utilitarian benefit of punishment is the prevention of future crime. Utilitarian punishment schemes often seek to prevent crime through various mechanisms: by deterring it with the threat of official sanction; by rehabilitating a potential offender to remove the inclination to commit an offense; or by incapacitating a dangerous offender as by physically restraining the person from committing an offense.

Agreement: Punishment Is Justified   Both of these theories, retributivist and utilitarian, support an affirmative answer to the question, "Should we punish?" Each theory supports the creation of some system by which wrongdoers are punished. The criminal law, however, is also interested in other questions: Who should be punished? And how much?

Disagreement: How to Distribute Punishment   Answering those questions— determining not only whether to punish, but how to *distribute* punishment—is more complex. There are any number of principles by which one could distribute punishment, for each justifying purpose could be translated into several different distributive principles. For example, even if it were agreed that punishment is generally justified by utilitarian considerations, there might be disagreement about whether to distribute punishment so as to maximize deterrence of future crimes or rehabilitation of past offenders.

---

1. Immanuel Kant, The Metaphysical Elements of Justice 102 (J. Ladd trans. 1965).

Each principle following a different distributive criterion—one giving people the punishment they deserve, another giving the punishment that will most efficiently deter, still another giving the punishment that will most effectively incapacitate, and so forth—would, of course, generate a distribution of punishment different from the other principles. The central foundational issue for criminal law theory and policy is to determine which distributive principle, or combination of distributive principles, should be preferred. In order to understand the significance of the choice of a distributive principle, we will examine the most commonly suggested principles: deterrence (general and special), incapacitation, rehabilitation, and desert (deontological and empirical).

ALTERNATIVE DISTRIBUTIVE PRINCIPLES AND THEIR BASES

Let us first consider the specific criterion that would govern different distributive principles, then review the strengths and weaknesses of each principle, in order to lay the foundation for attempting to judge which distributive principle or combination should be preferred.[2]

General and Special Deterrence Tie Punishment to Offense Seriousness One might set the distribution of punishment so as to most efficiently deter future offenses. Aiming to deter other potential offenders is called *general deterrence*; aiming to deter the offender at hand is *special deterrence*. In both cases, the objective is to make a would-be offender perceive the "costs" of committing crime as outweighing its benefits. Both of these distributive principles will be likely to make the amount of punishment proportional to the seriousness of the offense, all other things being equal.

Need to Maintain Prospect of Additional Punishment for Additional Crimes This *proportionality* principle, as it is sometimes called, exists partly because a deterrent distributive principle must avoid threatening the maximum punishment. It may seem as if a deterrence-based scheme would frequently impose the harshest sentence allowed, to maximize the potential cost of committing a crime and thereby discourage would-be offenders as much as possible. Yet if an offender thinks he is already subject to the maximum punishment (if he is caught), then it becomes almost impossible to deter any further criminal activity on his part. For example, if attempted murder is punishable by death, then the actor who has failed in an attempt to murder someone might as well try again, because the penalty for what he has already done is no greater than if he goes on to complete the murder successfully. Such an actor will avoid further crimes only to the extent those crimes make it more likely he will be caught (and convicted).

Practical Considerations: Cost, Probability of Capture Further, deterrence theorists are not interested in spending money for no good reason. Punishment imposes costs on the state as well as on the person punished; accordingly, the punishment should be set just high enough to maximize deterrence (or, more precisely, to achieve the efficient rate of deterrence), but no higher. Normal rules of efficiency would suggest investing more punishment dollars to deter more serious offenses. Similarly, both general and special deterrence would increase punishment for offenses with low capture rates. Deterrence depends on an offender's

---

2. For a fuller discussion of the various distributive principles of criminal law presented below, see Paul H. Robinson, Distributive Principles of Criminal Law ch. 3-8, 12-17 (2008).

consideration of the "costs" of punishment, and those costs depend on both the *amount* of punishment and the *likelihood* of punishment. To hold the deterrence level constant, a reduction in the probability of punishment must be offset by an increase in the amount of punishment imposed on those who are caught. Thus for offenses whose detection or enforcement rates are lower than average, the amount of punishment threatened must be correspondingly higher in order to maintain the overall deterrent threat.

Punishing One Crime Can Also Deter Different Crimes Punishment of one kind of offense can have a positive deterrent effect, in terms of both general and special deterrence, for other offenses as well. Thus, punishment for homicide will discourage both the offender and others from committing other homicides in similar situations, but also may provide some general reminder about the existence and enforcement of criminal law sanctions and therefore help deter other crimes in general. The closer the contemplated offense to the conduct punished, all other things being equal, the more likely the punishment will have a deterrent effect. Punishment for homicide, for example, is likely to have a greater deterrent effect on assaults than on tax evasion.

Differences between General and Special Deterrence In other respects, however, general deterrence and special deterrence may rely on different factors. For example, general deterrence would impose greater punishment in cases receiving greater media coverage. The broad reach of the message sent by punishment in these cases would give a greater general-deterrent payoff for the punishment-cost investment. Special deterrence has little reason to care about the degree of media coverage, as its target audience is only the offender at hand.

For another example, general deterrence would not support excuses like the insanity defense, while special deterrence would. Persons who do not or cannot take account of the consequences of a violation cannot be deterred by the threat of sanctions. Thus, considering the "Daughters' Mustard" hypothetical, punishing (or threatening to punish) Erie serves no purpose in terms of deterring Erie herself, as she is incapable of understanding the sanction or why it is being applied. However, punishing Erie can deter others. Indeed, punishing people who, like Erie, are incapable of appreciating the nature of their conduct may send a strong message to other, able-minded people that the law allows nobody to escape liability. Therefore it may serve as a general deterrent to punish Erie for her crime despite her insanity. The failure to punish such an actor can undermine the effectiveness of the prohibition against killing, for it might suggest to potential offenders the possibility that they can kill, and be caught, yet not be punished.

Incapacitation of the Dangerous The most direct means of preventing future offenses is through *incapacitation* of persons likely to commit such offenses. Incapacitation may occur via imprisonment, execution, or any other restraint or impairment that prevents a subsequent offense. For example, castrating a potential rapist or cutting off the hand of a potential pickpocket could prevent an offense.

Punishment Distributed According to Future Dangerousness, Not Past Offense If the dangerousness of two people is the same, the degree of punishment justified under a rationale based purely on incapacitation would be the same. Thus, looking at the "Daughters' Mustard" hypothetical, under a distributive principle of incapacitation, Fina's attempt would generally be punished the same as Devon's completed offense. Both sisters may be judged equally dangerous, even though only Devon's actions actually killed their mother. In fact, under an incapacitation principle, punishment would not even need to wait until after the commission of an offense; a reliable prediction of future criminality would provide adequate justification. Indeed, if the circumstances stimulating the offense are unique or even rare, incapacitation is a persuasive justification for punishment *only* before the offense occurs. For example, if Devon was brought to the point of killing only because of her special love for her mother, and if there is no danger that she will develop such love for another person similarly in pain, then there is no danger that Devon will kill again and thus no incapacitative justification for sanctioning her. The same may be true for Fina if she will not have another opportunity to realize financial gain through the hastened death of another. Indeed it is Erie who, because of her mental illness, is the most likely to cause injury or death to another; thus she provides the strongest case for incapacitative sanction.

Rehabilitation   Rehabilitating or reforming an offender is another means by which future offenses can be avoided. *Rehabilitation* takes away the offender's desire or need to engage in criminal conduct. Medical treatment, psychological counseling, and education and training programs are the most common forms of rehabilitation. However, anything that is designed to minimize the actor's wish to commit future crimes, other than intimidation by a deterrent threat, typically is included under the label of rehabilitation. Rehabilitation regimes frequently are seen as making the actor a "better" or more law-abiding person. Nothing in this crime-prevention mechanism, however, requires that the potential offender agree with or approve of the changes that are made to him. Effectiveness of this mechanism requires the ability to accurately identify people who need rehabilitation (that is, people in danger of committing an offense in the future), the ability to find treatment regimes that will rehabilitate, and the ability to determine when a person under treatment is rehabilitated. As with incapacitation, the effectiveness of rehabilitation does not require that punishment, or treatment, wait until after the potential offender has committed an offense.

Deontological Desert   An alternative to these utilitarian distributive principles is *retribution* or "just desert," which, as noted above, bases punishment on the theory that punishing wrongdoers is a desirable end in itself. Under a distributive principle following a *deontological* notion of desert, the sole criterion for punishment is the actor's moral blameworthiness, as dictated by general moral principles. A person receives punishment if and only if the person is blameworthy, and the amount of punishment corresponds to the degree of blameworthiness— no more, no less. The degree of an offender's blameworthiness, in turn, depends upon both the seriousness of the violation and the extent of the actor's accountability for it, as the governing moral principles dictate. Under such a desert theory (and also under an empirical desert theory, as discussed below), Erie in the "Daughters' Mustard" hypothetical would have no liability if her mental illness was seen as rendering her morally blameless for her conduct, as is likely the case. Similarly, Devon may be held less blameworthy than someone, like Fina, who would kill her mother for personal gain.

Empirical Desert   Social science research suggests that average people, no matter their training or level of education, hold strong—and commonly similar—intuitive views in judging a person's blameworthiness for wrongdoing.

Indeed, the studies suggest an astounding level of agreement across demographics regarding the relative blameworthiness of different offenders, at least with respect to the core of wrongdoing, including offenses involving physical aggression and the taking of property. Thus, one could adopt a distributive principle of desert based on the community's shared intuitions of desert, rather than abstract philosophical notions of desert. This might be termed *empirical desert* to distinguish it from the deontological theory of desert, for the two can be different. For example, while moral philosophers disagree as to whether moral blameworthiness varies based on whether resulting harm occurs—for example, whether attempted murder should be punished the same as murder where the failure to cause death had nothing to do with the actor—lay persons almost universally see resulting harm as important to assessing blameworthiness and would punish attempted murder less than murder. Thus, for example, Fina in the "Daughters' Mustard" hypothetical seems clearly blameworthy, but because her conduct did not actually cause her mother's death, a scheme tracking empirical desert would give her less punishment than an actor with the same culpable state of mind who did cause the death.

Desert as a Relative Rather Than Absolute Judgment   Though people often disagree as to the *absolute* amount of punishment a given offense deserves, they commonly share a sense of the *relative* blameworthiness of different offenders. Accordingly, once a society establishes the end point of its punishment continuum, as all societies must do—be it the death penalty, life imprisonment, or 15 years' imprisonment—then each offender's blameworthiness relative to other offenders will place that offender at a specific point on the punishment continuum and thereby produce a specific sentence. If the continuum endpoint were changed, the punishment amounts for each offender along the continuum also would change. Therefore, while it might seem as if there is no stable, identifiable agreement on the relative blameworthiness of different offenders, research into the matter suggests that the agreement is simply masked by failure to agree on the severity of punishment generally, but is quite strong as to the degree of punishment different offenders merit as compared to each other.

Conflicts Among Distributive Principles   Because each of these alternative distributive principles—general deterrence, special deterrence, rehabilitation, incapacitation, deontological desert, and empirical desert—relies upon a different distributive criterion, they will inevitably conflict with one another. Deterrence as a distributive principle might justify punishment of an innocent or insane person if the deterrent benefit of punishment was greater than the cost of the punishment, a result that would offend both forms of desert. Less dramatic but more likely is a deterrence principle's infliction of punishment according to the extent of media coverage or the offense's capture rate, results similarly inconsistent with desert. Incapacitation and rehabilitation have a similar potential for conflict with desert and with deterrence. Even if an offender's crime is minor, a long term of imprisonment might be justified under an incapacitation or rehabilitation theory if the offender is seen as likely to commit another offense in the future. Indeed, at the extreme, distributive principles based upon incapacitation or rehabilitation would not require commission of an offense. If reliable predictive judgments could be made as to an offender's future dangerousness, a criminal justice system under these distributive principles could "convict" an "offender" who has not yet committed an offense, but is predicted to do so, and "punish" him in order to incapacitate or rehabilitate him.

Alternative Justification: Restorative Justice Restorative processes include a wide variety of mechanisms, such as sentencing circles and victim-offender remediation that can be quite valuable in bringing victims and offenders together.[3] Such processes provide something that nothing else in the traditional criminal justice system can. For offenders, the processes can provide a better understanding of the real impact of their offenses and can put a human face on the victim. They also can give offenders an important insight into the norms they violated: During the process they see people whom they know and respect openly expressing disapproval of the conduct. The potential influence of this kind of social interaction should not be underestimated.

Restorative processes also have a special benefit for victims. Consider the case of an elderly woman who had her house burglarized by a neighborhood youth.[4] The emotional cost to her was devastating. She was afraid to go out, yet afraid when she stayed in. The incident turned into a generalized fear of everything around her. As part of the offender's reparations, the youth agreed to do some house chores for her and, by design, came to know her better, and she him. That contact let her better understand what had happened and how and, with that understanding, her generalized fear faded. However, restorative processes do not always align with community opinions on justice and desert and can thus be problematic. The prospect of applying restorative processes is expanded upon further in the Discussion Materials in the Appendix of this Section.

● OVERVIEW OF CONSTRUCTING A DISTRIBUTIVE PRINCIPLE

Notes

Evaluating the Alternative Distributive Principles
    General Deterrence Potential for Efficient Crime Control
        Conditions Required for General Deterrence May Often Be Lacking
    Special Deterrence Shares Possible Limitations of General Deterrence
    Rehabilitation: Possibly Valuable Beyond Its Crime-Control Effect
        Limited Crime-Control Value of Rehabilitation
        Rehabilitation as Complementary or Subsidiary Principle
    Incapacitation: Direct Control, Not Just Influencing Offender Choices
        Concerns about Fairness, Accuracy, Cost
        Incapacitation as Basis for Detention, but Not Punishment Per Se

---

3. See, e.g., Leena Kurki, *Restorative and Community Justice in the United States*, 27 Crime & Just. 235, 280-281 (2000) (explaining that sentencing circles involve victim, offender, key community members, that they are also open to the public, and that the agreements reached in the circles are either recommendations for the judge or the final sentence).

4. See Kathy Elton & Michelle M. Roybal, *Restoration, A Component of Justice,* 2003 Utah L. Rev. 43, 53 n.57 (2003) (citing Mark S. Umbreit with Robert B. Coates & Boris Kalanj, Victim Meets Offender: The Impact of Restorative Justice and Mediation 160 (1994)).

EVALUATING THE ALTERNATIVE DISTRIBUTIVE PRINCIPLES

The "Daughter's Mustard" hypothetical, above, demonstrates the conflict among different distributive principles. Depending on which principle is selected, each daughter may receive anywhere from no punishment to the maximum allowed. The existence of such discrepancies illustrates both the importance of selecting a distributive principle and the implications of choosing one over another, or choosing a hybrid. With this in mind, consider the strengths and weaknesses of each.[5]

General Deterrence Potential for Efficient Crime Control Under the right conditions, a distributive principle of general deterrence can avoid future crime. Indeed, it has the potential for enormous efficiency. For the cost of punishing just the offender at hand, it can deter thousands, or millions, of others who hear about the case and heed its warning.

Conditions Required for General Deterrence May Often Be Lacking On the other hand, general deterrence may be effective in only a limited number of instances, since three prerequisites must be satisfied for it to work.[6] First, a deterrence-based rule can deter only if the intended targets are aware of the rule, directly or indirectly. However, evidence suggests that this is rarely the case. For example, a primary justification for the felony-murder rule—treating even accidental killings during a felony as murder—is its presumed deterrent effect on potential felons. But few felons are likely to know whether their jurisdiction has such a rule, much less its specific terms. Second, even if the target audience knows of the deterrence-based rule, effective deterrence requires that the targets have the capacity and inclination to rationally calculate what is in their best interest. Yet the

---

5. For a fuller discussion of the strengths and weaknesses of various distributive principles, see Paul H. Robinson, Distributive Principles of Criminal Law ch. 3, 6, 7, 10, 11 (2008).

6. See generally Paul H. Robinson & John M. Darley, *The Role of Deterrence in the Formulation of Criminal Law Rules: At Its Worst When Doing Its Best*, 91 GEO. L.J. 949 (2003); Paul H. Robinson & John M. Darley, *Does Criminal Law Deter? A Behavioural Science Investigation*, 24 OXFORD J. LEGAL STUD. 173 (2004).

evidence again suggests that this is not the case. Potential offenders as a group are less inclined than most people to think carefully about the future consequences of their conduct, and they are more likely to be under the distorting influence of drugs, alcohol, or mental illness. Third, even if a person knows of the deterrence-based rule, and can and does make rational calculations about his conduct, the rule will deter only if the person concludes that the costs of committing the offense exceed its anticipated benefits. Yet a variety of factors, such as the low punishment rates for many offenses and the tendency of people to discount the significance of future punishment, commonly lead potential offenders to conclude that the perceived benefits of committing a crime outweigh its perceived costs. There are also ethical objections to the project of general deterrence. Obviously, a deterrent scheme pays no regard to what an offender deserves in any moral sense. A general ethical objection is that deterrence treats the person being punished as a mere instrument by which to influence the conduct of others.

Special Deterrence Shares Possible Limitations of General Deterrence Under the right conditions, a special-deterrence distributive principle can avoid future crime by the offender at hand, although it lacks a general-deterrence system's potential for enormous efficiency. Moreover, as with general deterrence, special deterrence will not work without its prerequisite conditions—knowledge of the deterrence-based rule, the capacity and inclination to rationally calculate one's best interest, and a perception that the costs of crime exceed its benefits—which, again, commonly do not exist. Finally, as with general deterrence, a distributive principle of special deterrence seems destined to distribute punishment in ways that conflict with both deontological and empirical desert.

Rehabilitation: Possibly Valuable Beyond Its Crime-Control Effect Rehabilitation, if successful, can avoid crime by the offender at hand. Further, rehabilitation may have value beyond its effect in avoiding crime. It may bring personal fulfillment to the person, as well as a better life to the person's family and friends. Indeed, some people may see rehabilitation as having a deontological component—as being a value in itself that ought to be pursued even if it does not produce specific beneficial consequences such as less crime.

Limited Crime-Control Value of Rehabilitation On the other hand, a rehabilitation-oriented distributive principle seems to have only limited potential to generate crime-control benefits. It can only have an effect on the offender at hand; it does not share general deterrence's potential to reach many others. More importantly, the success rate of rehabilitation programs is typically quite modest and commonly limited to a narrow range of offenders and offenses. Finally, a rehabilitation-oriented distributive principle, like the other utilitarian distributive principles discussed above, is destined to distribute liability and punishment in ways that conflict with both deontological and empirical desert. If rehabilitation is possible at all, minor offenses may require long terms of rehabilitation, and serious offenses may require short terms. Finally, forcibly changing a person's nature may raise ethical questions about the state intruding upon personal autonomy.

Rehabilitation as Complementary or Subsidiary Principle Employing rehabilitation as the sole distributive principle would be problematic, for it would mean that if a person could not be rehabilitated, which would commonly be the case, the criminal justice system would have no basis for taking custody or control. It would make more sense to combine rehabilitation with another distributive principle, such as incapacitation, so that if a person could not be rehabilitated, the criminal-justice system could still subject the person to incapacitation for as long as he remained dangerous. Perhaps more importantly, the rehabilitation objective can often be advanced even if rehabilitation does not serve as a distributive principle at all. That is, the correctional system might adopt a governing policy of pursuing every opportunity to rehabilitate amenable offenders during whatever sentence is determined by some *other* distributive principles. Such a commitment to rehabilitation does not rely on rehabilitation as a distributive principle, for it does not use the rehabilitation goal as a basis for determining who is punished or how much.

Incapacitation: Direct Control, Not Just Influencing Offender Choices
While there are serious concerns about the crime-control effectiveness of the utilitarian distributive principles discussed above—general deterrence, special deterrence, and rehabilitation—no similar doubts exist for incapacitation as a distributive principle. Unlike deterrence, for example, the effectiveness of this crime-prevention mechanism does not depend on effective communication of the threatened sanction to potential offenders or on the potential offenders' calculations of a cost-benefit analysis in governing their conduct. On the other hand, incapacitation can have a crime-control effect only on the offender at hand. Like special deterrence and rehabilitation, it lacks the enormous potential for efficiency that general deterrence has in influencing a multitude of potential offenders.

Concerns About Fairness, Accuracy, Cost The weaknesses of incapacitation as a distributive principle reside primarily in the costs and fairness of its administration. For incapacitation to be effective as a distributive principle, one must be able to identify dangerous persons before they act, preferably with a minimum of "false positives" (people who are predicted to commit offenses and therefore incapacitated, yet who in fact would not have committed offenses even if left free). The behavioral sciences presently have only a limited ability to make such predictions accurately. This is especially true where the criminal justice system uses rough approximations of future dangerousness, such as prior criminal record, as it typically does. A high false-positive rate means a large amount of wasted resources as well as serious and unjustified intrusions on the personal liberty of detainees. Further, like the other utilitarian distributive principles described above, incapacitation as a distributive principle will distribute liability and punishment in ways that conflict with empirical and deontological desert.

Incapacitation as Basis for Detention, but Not Punishment Per Se The greatest argument against incapacitation as a distributive principle for criminal liability and punishment may be that its purposes can be as effectively, and perhaps more effectively and fairly, achieved using a civil system of preventive detention instead.[7] Civil commitment is currently used for people who are dangerous because they are mentally ill, have a contagious disease, or have a drug dependency. The civil-commitment approach would enable the system to distinguish between punishment, which is based on a person's past misconduct, and preventive detention, which is based on a person's potential for future misconduct. Accordingly, the civil-commitment component of the system would properly seek to impose as

---

7. See generally Paul H. Robinson, *Punishing Dangerousness: Cloaking Preventive Detention as Criminal Justice*, 114 HARV. L. REV. 1429 (2001).

little restraint as is needed to achieve the incapacitative goal, rather than seeking to impose any unnecessary pain or suffering on those who are detained.

Deontological Desert Can Maintain Law's Moral Standards   The obvious strength of deontological desert is that it "does justice" by imposing punishment consistent with moral desert. Deontological desert principles also hold out the potential to impose a transcendent, principled counterweight against mere reliance on existing community norms, as the empirical desert principle requires.[8] There is the danger that moral philosophy may directly or tacitly rely on shared intuitions of justice in its methodology, and therefore may construct principles of justice unfortunately biased toward rules consistent with people's shared intuitions of justice. But an awareness of this danger among moral philosophers may help avoid the difficulty.

Practical Impossibility   The central weakness of deontological desert as a distributive principle is the practical impossibility of its implementation. Moral philosophers disagree among themselves about many central issues important to assessing desert, such as the significance, if any, to be given resulting harm. How are such disagreements to be resolved? How are policymakers and other officials, who are not philosophers, to judge which philosophical camp to prefer over others?

Inattention to Crime-Control Issues   Another obvious weakness of deontological desert as a distributive principle is that it fails to prevent avoidable crimes. It would distribute liability and punishment in ways that ignore the crime control opportunities of all the utilitarian distributive principles, including that of empirical desert. Deontological desert, recall, does not concern itself with building the criminal law's moral credibility with the community. Indeed, it can produce rules that seriously conflict with empirical desert—rules that would seriously undermine the criminal law's moral credibility if adopted. For example, as noted above, laypersons nearly universally believe that resulting harm is important in assessing blameworthiness (such that, for example, attempted murder should be punished less than murder), but many moral philosophers urge a conflicting view (punishing attempted murder the same as murder), and thereby would undermine the criminal law's moral credibility with the community.

Empirical Desert: Retributive Means to Promote Utilitarian Ends   Empirical desert may be an attractive distributive principle not only because it avoids the failure of the traditional utilitarian schemes to "do justice," and imposes punishment according to moral desert, but also because of its crime-control potential. While there is often the perception that desert punishment schemes exist in irresolvable conflict with utilitarian ones, there may be good utilitarian reasons for adopting desert as a distributive principle—at least this empirical form of desert.

Avoiding Disrespect That Arises When Citizens See System as Unjust   The effective operation of the criminal justice system depends on the cooperation, or at least acquiescence, of those involved in it: offenders, judges, jurors, witnesses, prosecutors, police, and others. To the extent people see the system as unjust—as in conflict with their own intuitions of justice—that acquiescence and cooperation is likely to fade and be replaced with subversion and resistance. Jurors may

---

8. Paul H. Robinson, *The Role of Moral Philosophers in the Competition Between Deontological and Empirical Desert*, 48 Wm. & Mary L. Rev. 1831 (2007).

disregard their jury instructions. Police officers, prosecutors, and judges may make up their own rules. Witnesses may lose an incentive to offer their information or testimony. Offenders may be inspired to fight the adjudication and correctional processes rather than submitting to their authority.

Avoiding Vigilantism   Problems can arise from perceptions of injustice in both directions: either imposition of undeserved punishment or failure to impose punishment that is deserved. Historically, vigilante groups have often sprung up in newly settled areas in which laws were not being enforced because there was no police presence. Vigilante action has also arisen when citizens perceive that the police or other elements of the criminal justice system are failing in their responsibilities to protect innocent citizens from wrongdoing. Vigilantism may be the most dramatic reaction to perceived failures of justice, but lower-level subversion and resistance may be more common.

Harnessing Power and Efficiency of Stigmatization   Some of the system's power to control conduct derives from its potential to stigmatize violators. For some potential offenders this is a more powerful, yet essentially cost-free, control mechanism, and can have effect even in the absence of official conviction and punishment. The domestic abuser or habitually drunk driver may suffer stigmatization among family and friends, even if never arrested. Yet the criminal law's ability to stigmatize certain conduct depends on its having moral credibility with the community. That is, for commission of conduct deemed criminal to trigger stigmatization, the law must have earned a reputation for accurately assessing what does and does not deserve moral condemnation. Liability and punishment rules that conflict with a community's shared intuitions of justice undermine this reputation; rules that track community views reinforce it.

Gaining Compliance in Borderline Cases   Criminal law may also effect compliance with its commands through another mechanism. If criminal law earns a reputation as a reliable statement of what the community perceives as condemnable, people are more likely to defer to its commands as morally authoritative and as appropriate to follow. This is particularly powerful in borderline cases where the propriety of certain conduct is unsettled or ambiguous. The importance of this role should not be underestimated; in a society with the complex interdependencies characteristic of ours, an apparently harmless action can have destructive consequences. When conduct is criminalized, a citizen should respect the law even though he or she does not immediately intuit why that conduct is banned. Such deference will be facilitated if citizens are disposed to believe that the law is an accurate guide to appropriate prudential and moral behavior.

Having a Role in Shaping Societal Norms   Perhaps the greatest potential utility of an empirical desert distribution comes through a more subtle but possibly more influential form. As has been hinted above, the real power to gain compliance with society's rules of conduct often lies not in the threat of official criminal sanction, but in the influence of the intertwined forces of social and individual moral control. The networks of interpersonal relationships in which people find themselves, the social norms and prohibitions shared among those relationships and transmitted through those social networks, and the internalized representations of those norms and moral precepts control people's conduct. The law interacts with and informs these social and personal forces. Criminal law, in particular, plays a central role in creating and maintaining the social consensus necessary for sustaining moral norms. In fact, in a society as diverse as ours, the criminal law may be the only societywide mechanism that transcends cultural and ethnic differences. Thus, the criminal law's most important real-world effect may be its ability to assist in the building, shaping, and maintaining of these norms and moral principles. Greater moral credibility gives the criminal law greater influence in the public conversation by which societal norms are shaped and reinforced. A society's ability to change norms—such as those regarding domestic violence, drunk driving, or date rape—is at its greatest when it has criminal law as a tool in its arsenal to shape people's views on the condemnability of the conduct at issue.

Utilitarian Crime-Control Power of Empirical Desert   The extent of the criminal law's effectiveness in all these respects—in bringing the power of stigmatization to bear; in avoiding resistance and subversion to a system perceived as unjust; in gaining compliance in borderline cases through deference to its moral authority; and in facilitating, communicating, and maintaining societal consensus on what is and is not condemnable—is to a great extent dependent on the degree to which the criminal law has gained moral credibility in the minds of the citizens it governs. Thus, the criminal law's moral credibility is essential to effective crime control, and is enhanced if the distribution of criminal liability is perceived as "doing justice"—that is, if it assigns liability and punishment in ways that the community perceives as consistent with its shared intuitions of justice. Conversely, the system's moral credibility, and therefore its crime-control effectiveness, is undermined by a distribution of liability that conflicts with community perceptions of just desert.

Empirical Desert Versus General Deterrence Strategy   An empirical-desert proponent might point out that an empirical-desert distribution of punishment will itself provide some level of general deterrence. Greater deterrence than this can be achieved only by deviating from community notions of justice, that is, by doing what the community sees as injustice or a failure of justice. And such deviations create special problems for deterrence—not only in terms of sacrificing the principle of desert, but in terms of achieving deterrence itself. Empirical studies suggest that people tend to assume that criminal law commands whatever morality requires: In other words, they believe the criminal law tracks the dictates of empirical desert. As a result, effectively communicating a rule that deviates from desert requires a special campaign to tell people that the rule is different than they assume. And, as noted above, it is such deviations from desert that run the risk of undermining the criminal law's moral credibility, breeding disrespect for the law.

Concerns with Empirical Desert's Dependence on Existing Norms   The central weakness of the empirical desert as a distributive principle is its potential to do injustice that is not apparent to the present community. The community's shared views of justice may simply be wrong. Consider the lessons of slaveholding Southerners before the Civil War and the treatment of Jews in prewar Germany. Only a transcendent notion of justice, derived independently from principles of right and good—that is, deontological desert—can assure that the law accords with moral principles. Accordingly, from a retributive perspective, empirical desert might sometimes seem a poor proxy for, or even a subversion of, a scheme based on a proper moral conception of desert.

Concerns with Possible Sacrifice of Optimal Crime Control   Utilitarians might also object to empirical desert to the extent such a principle might pass up even a great crime-control opportunity—perhaps an instance where the prerequisites to effective general deterrence really did exist—if such required a deviation from empirical desert. This may not happen often, but it seems likely that some opportunities will arise where the crime-control benefits from deviating from empirical desert will be so great as to exceed the crime-control cost of undermining the criminal law's moral credibility.

Efforts to Construct Hybrid Distributive Principle It might seem desirable to construct a hybrid distributive principle that would combine the strengths of one or more individual principles while avoiding their weaknesses. An early attempt at this may be seen in Model Penal Code Section 1.02, which lists a variety of distributive principles and urges judges to try to advance them all. But because different distributive principles suggest different liability rules and different sentences, the failure to articulate any relationship or prioritization among the alternative distributive principles means that the Model Penal Code section in fact provides little guidance. Worse, it creates a facade behind which judges can seem to make principled decisions when in fact they are exercising unguided discretion. To provide real guidance, a hybrid distributive principle must fully articulate the relation between the underlying principles it seeks to synthesize. That is, when different principles suggest different results, the hybrid distributive principle must tell the decision maker which principle to follow.[9] Is it possible to construct a genuine hybrid principle?

Difficulty of Combining Deontological and Utilitarian Principles Because deontological retribution and the utilitarian distributive principles focus on different goals—doing justice versus preventing crime—it can be difficult to construct a hybrid principle that gives voice to both. It is easier to develop a hybrid principle that combines two or more utilitarian distributive principles, for they at least share a common objective: crime reduction. One obvious possible hybrid utilitarian strategy is to adopt a policy of case-by-case decision making, choosing among different specific utilitarian distributive principles in individual cases based on which will generate the greatest crime-control benefit (relative to its cost) in a given situation.

Revision to MPC § 1.02 The American Law Institute's recent proposed revision to Model Penal Code Section 1.02 sets desert as the primary distributive principle and allows reliance upon deterrence, rehabilitation, and incapacitation to the extent that (1) they are shown to be effective, and (2) they do not conflict with desert. The amendment is certainly an advance over the 1962 formulation, which failed to define any relationship among conflicting distributive principles.

Concern That Revision Ignores Nondesert Principles The amendment's apparent integration of alternative principles may be more apparent than real, however. Its ultimate effect may be essentially the adoption of desert as the governing distributive principle. Some supporters of the amendment assumed that desert considerations suggest only a reasonably broad range of punishment, rather than a specific amount, thus leaving room for nondesert principles to guide selection within the broader range. But as noted above, judgments about offenders' relative desert reveal considerable sophistication and precision. The nuance of

---

9. Paul H. Robinson, *Hybrid Principles for the Distribution of Criminal Sanctions*, 82 Nw. U. L. Rev. 19, 19-22, 28-35 (1987).

these relative blameworthiness judgments, combined with a finite punishment continuum, means that only a fairly narrow range of punishments will satisfy the need to punish the offender based on his proper ordinal ranking relative to other offenders.

Defining "Fudge Range" for Nondesert Principles   On the other hand, one could construct a hybrid distributive principle that used the specific desert sentence as a midpoint to a "fudge range" within which deterrence, rehabilitation, and incapacitation are allowed to operate, under the theory that deviations from desert within the "fudge range" are not as likely to be as noticed or, if noticed, are not likely to be seen as so objectionable as to seriously undermine the criminal law's moral credibility.[10]

Crime Reduction through Other Mechanisms   While distributive principles are important, they are not the only means, or even necessarily the most efficient means, of reducing crime. Changes in procedural rules, or in the allocation of criminal justice resources, often can reduce crime more effectively than manipulating the principles for the distribution of liability and punishment. For example, relaxing rules that limit police in their ability to search and seize could make law enforcement more effective. (Of course, it would do so at a cost to important privacy interests and limitations on governmental power.) Indeed, it may be that reforms entirely outside the criminal justice system would do more to reduce crime than would criminal justice reform. Education and training programs, drug treatment programs, and income redistribution programs, to name an obvious few, all may have the potential to reduce crime. Still further, it may be that non-governmental institutions, such as churches, social groups, extended families, and social reform movements, have as great or greater potential for reducing crime than anything the government can do. Therefore it would be a mistake to rely on principles for the distribution of criminal liability and punishment as the only means by which crime can be controlled. Accordingly, to the extent that interests other than crime control are at stake in selecting a distributive principle—such as adhering to the principle of desert-based punishment, or rehabilitating offenders for its own sake—policymakers might consider whether the criminal system should pursue those interests, and try to achieve crime-control goals through other mechanisms.

▲ PROBLEMS

Sara Jane Olson—Revisited (#11)

What liability for Sara Jane Olson, if any, would be imposed under each of the alternative principles discussed above for distributing liability and punishment—general deterrence, special deterrence, rehabilitation, incapacitation,

---

10. See, e.g., Paul H. Robinson, Distributive Principles of Criminal Law 240-260 (2008); Paul H. Robinson, *The A.L.I.'s Proposed Distributive Principle of "Limiting Retributivism": Does It Mean in Practice Anything Other Than Pure Desert?*, 7 Buff. Crim. L. Rev. 3 (2004).

empirical desert, deontological desert—if each, in turn, were relied on as the sole distributive principle?

Stopping Desertions in a Time of War (#12)

In August of 1944, two and a half years after the United States entered the Second World War, Private Eddie Slovik is assigned to a rifle unit fighting in France. Slovik arrives prior to the liberation of Paris, with Nazi forces still in control of much of France. The fighting is intense. The Axis powers have launched major counter-offensives in response to Allied gains, putting nearly all of their remaining resources into a last push to conquer Europe. Military leaders in the United States are unsure if they can successfully repel the offensive. Of particular concern is the record number of drafted soldiers that are now deserting as a result of increasing intensification of fighting. Many of the new draftees had successfully avoided the draft during the first years of the war. The increase in desertions is putting the Allied forces at risk of having insufficient and demoralized troops at a crucial juncture in the war. Military officials fear that allowing desertion to go unpunished will mean that some of the most important, but also the most dangerous, military actions will fail as more soldiers choose not to fight in the face of the higher mortality rates.

Private Slovik is one of the deserters. A slight, frail man, he initially avoids being drafted when he is classified as unfit for service owing to a long history of minor criminal convictions, starting at age 12. However, after spending nearly four years in prison, Slovik has straightened out. He married Antoinette Wisniewski and is gainfully employed. Shortly after his first wedding anniversary, he is reclassified as fit for duty and is drafted into the army. He reports for training in January 1944 and is sent to France that August. En route to his unit, he becomes separated from his detachment under enemy fire. Terrified by the experience, he spends six weeks at the rear of the line with a non-combat Canadian unit. When he finally reports for duty with his Infantry Regiment on October 7, he informs his commander that he is too frightened to serve in a rifle company and requests to be reassigned to non-combat duty. He also states his intention to run away if assigned to a combat unit and asks if that would be considered desertion. He is told that it would, and his request for reassignment is denied. On October 9, Slovik hands in a letter informing his superiors of his intention to desert if sent into combat. He is given the opportunity to recant and is made aware of the consequences of desertion, but he refuses to report for combat duty. He is then taken into custody, where a judge advocate offers him another opportunity to avoid a court martial by rejoining his unit. Slovik refuses and asks for his court martial, which he is given.

What arguments can you make in favor of serious punishment, even the death penalty, for Slovik? What arguments can you make for giving him little or no punishment?

Air Conditioning Fraud as Strike Three (#13)

William J. Rummel is a con man, but not an especially ambitious one. He has trouble holding down a job and occasionally makes up for his lack of income with minor larceny and fraud. In addition to a string of misdemeanor offenses, he is convicted of two felonies, one in 1964 for using a company credit card without authorization to buy himself two new tires and another in 1969 for forging a check. Having the company pay for his tires saves Rummel $80 and the phony check nets him $28.36. However, the two convictions cost him over four years of jail time.

In 1973, undeterred by his previous convictions and unaware of Texas' stern view of recidivist criminals, Rummel enters Captain Hook's Lounge in San Antonio and seizes a golden opportunity to swindle the owner. On a hot August day, the bar's air conditioner is malfunctioning. Rummel offers to fix the unit and, with the owner's consent, conducts a brief inspection. He tells the owner that the compressor is broken and that he can replace it for $120.75. The owner writes him a check and Rummel cashes it, never to return again. The owner does not take kindly to this type of treatment and files a complaint with the police. Because Rummel has used his real name, he is not hard to track down. Rummel has a growing reputation in San Antonio for passing bad checks, and the prosecutor charges him with felony theft, for obtaining more than $50 by false pretense. Under then-existing Texas law, a third felony conviction automatically triggers a life sentence as a frequent recidivist offender. Rummel is 30 years old.

What liability for Rummel, if any, under the Model Penal Code for obtaining $120.75 (roughly $560 dollars in present value) by false pretense? What additional penalty for Rummel, if any, should be added in light of his prior criminal record? What would justify the imposition of an additional penalty? What arguments could be made against additional punishment because of his prior record?

✳ DISCUSSION ISSUES

What Are the Strengths and Weaknesses of Deterrence as a Principle for Distributing Criminal Liability and Punishment?

What Are the Strengths and Weaknesses of a Principle for Distributing Criminal Liability and Punishment that Would Optimize Rehabilitation and, Failing that, Incapacitate Dangerous Persons?

What Are the Strengths and Weaknesses of Desert as a Principle for Distributing Criminal Liability and Punishment?

What Are the Strengths and Weaknesses of Using "Restorative" Processes, Rather Than Traditional Criminal Justice Adjudication?

Materials presenting each side of these Discussion Issues appear in the Advanced Materials for Section 3 in Appendix A.

PART II

OFFENSE REQUIREMENTS

This coursebook is structured around the operational distinctions described in Section 1: offense definitions, doctrines of imputation, and general defenses. This Part takes up the first of these, the definition of offenses. Offense definitions commonly contain both objective elements—which include conduct, circumstance, or result elements—and culpability requirements. It is the latter that are most problematic and of greatest interest, and are the subjects of the two Sections in this Part.

The particular requirements of offenses of special interest are examined in Part III, concerning homicide, Part IV, concerning inchoate offenses (such as attempt and conspiracy), and Part VII, concerning offenses of current reform attention or modern relevance, specifically rape, hate crimes, corporate criminality, and computer crime.

Culpability Requirements

Perhaps the central distinguishing feature of criminal law is its requirement that the offender not only brought about some harm or evil but that he or she have some personal culpability as to the offense conduct. What "culpability" should be required, exactly, and why?

◆ THE CASE OF THOMAS FUNGWE (#14)

It is Wednesday, July 14, 1999, in Southfield, Michigan, one of Detroit's quiet northern suburbs. Thomas V. Fungwe is an assistant professor in the Department of Nutrition and Food Science at Wayne State University in downtown Detroit. He studies the effects that diet and certain enzymes have on cholesterol regulation.

He is part of a team that investigates major contributors to excessive morbidity within specific communities.

Fungwe is forty-seven years old and lives with his thirty-seven-year-old wife, Florence. They are viewed as friendly, good neighbors. Their youngest son, Thorence, is five months old, and is usually the center of attention. The Fungwes are loving parents, and talk about their children constantly.

Figure 13 **Wayne State University College of Science**
(Wayne State University)

On this morning, Fungwe loads his children into the family's Chevy Venture minivan. His plan is to drop off his sons before going to teach summer session classes, which have just begun. First, he heads to his older sons' day camp, where he drops off the two boys. He then stops on Woodward Avenue to get gas, then parks his car in the faculty school parking lot on Putnam near Warren and Cass and makes his way to his campus office.

Fungwe does not yet realize it, but he has left his youngest son, five-month-old Thorence, trapped in the locked car. It is a typical summer day. The temperature will rise to 88 degrees by three in the afternoon, but

Figure 14 **Thomas V. Fungwe**
(Wayne State University)

it feels much worse with the high humidity. Generally, infants cannot manage heat stress well because they do not have effective mechanisms to cool themselves.

Locked in the Chevy Venture with the windows closed, Thorence soon feels uncomfortable and begins to cry. After an hour or so, the temperature continues to rise and he begins screaming. Soon he is beyond screaming. He begins having seizures, and his jaw starts to clamp shut. He finally passes out.

A passerby notices that he is motionless with his eyes rolled back. Someone calls the university police to report an abandoned baby. Thorence has now been in the van for almost five hours.

Meanwhile, Mrs. Fungwe picks up her older sons at day camp and goes to day care to pick up Thorence. When she finds that he is not there, she calls her husband.

As soon as his wife calls, Fungwe realizes what he has done. He runs out of his office and over to his car, just as a crowd is gathering around. The university police soon arrive. Thorence is pale and unconscious. Fungwe screams in anguish, "I killed my baby! I killed my baby!"

Thorence is rushed to the Michigan Children's Hospital and found to have a severe case of hyperthermia. The doctors try to resuscitate him but because his jaw is locked tightly, they have difficulty intubating him. He dies soon after reaching the hospital.

A Detroit Police Department spokesman later reports that the baby's body temperature was at least 108 degrees. The doctors are sure Thorence's temperature was higher than that, but "the thermometer would go no higher."

1. Relying only on your own intuitions of justice, what liability and punishment, if any, does Thomas Fungwe deserve?

Figure 15 **1998 Chevrolet Venture**

N	0	1	2	3	4	5	6	7	8	9	10	11
☐	☐	☐	☐	☐	☐	☐	☐	☐	☐	☐	☐	☐
no liability	liability but no punishment	1 day	2 wks	2 mo	6 mo	1 yr	3 yrs	7 yrs	15 yrs	30 yrs	life imprison-ment	death

2. What "justice" arguments could defense counsel make on the defendant's behalf?

3. What "justice" arguments could the prosecution make against the defendant?

4. What liability, if any, for Fungwe under the then-existing statutes? Prepare a list of all criminal code subsections and cases in the order in which you rely upon them in your analysis.

5. What liability, if any, under the Model Penal Code? Prepare a list of all criminal code subsections in the order in which you rely upon them in your analysis.

▪ THE LAW

Michigan Statutes Annotated
(1999)

Title 28. Crimes, Part Two. Substantive Criminal

Chapter 286a. Law Penal Code
Chapter XLV. Homicide

Section 28.548. First-Degree Murder; Penalty; Definitions.

Sec. 316. (1) A person who commits any of the following is guilty of first degree murder and shall be punished by imprisonment for life:

(a) Murder perpetrated by means of poison, lying in wait, or any other willful, deliberate, and premeditated killing.

(b) Murder committed in the perpetration of, or attempt to perpetrate, arson, criminal sexual conduct in the first, second, or third degree, child abuse in the first degree, a major controlled substance offense, robbery, carjacking, breaking and entering of a dwelling, home invasion in the first or second degree, larceny of any kind, extortion, or kidnapping.

(c) A murder of a peace officer or a corrections officer committed while the peace officer or corrections officer is lawfully engaged in the performance of any of his or her duties as a peace officer or corrections officer, knowing that the peace officer or corrections officer is a peace officer or corrections officer engaged in the performance of his or her duty as a peace officer or corrections officer.

(2) As used in this section:

(a) "Arson" means a felony violation of chapter X.

(b) "Corrections officer" means any of the following:

(i) A prison or jail guard or other prison or jail personnel.

(ii) Any of the personnel of a boot camp, special alternative incarceration unit, or other minimum security correctional facility.

(iii) A parole or probation officer.

(c) "Major controlled substance offense" means any of the following:

(i) A violation of section 7401(2)(a)(i) to (iii) of the public health code, MCL 333.7401.

(ii) A violation of section 7403(2)(a)(i) to (iii) of the public health code, MCL 333.7403.

(iii) A conspiracy to commit an offense listed in subparagraph (i) or (ii).

(d) "Peace officer" means any of the following:

(i) A police or conservation officer of this state or a political subdivision of this state.

(ii) A police or conservation officer of the United States.

(iii) A police or conservation officer of another state or a political subdivision of another state.

Section 28.549. Murder; Second Degree.

Sec. 317. All other kinds of murder shall be murder of the second [2nd] degree, and shall be punished by imprisonment in the state prison for life, or any term of years, in the discretion of the court trying the same.

Section 28.553. Manslaughter; Penalties.

Sec. 321. Any person who shall commit the crime of manslaughter shall be guilty of a felony punishable by imprisonment in the state prison, not more than fifteen [15] years or by fine of not more than seven thousand five hundred [7,500] dollars, or both, at the discretion of the court.

Section 28.556. Negligent Homicide; Penalty

Sec. 324. Any person who, by the operation of any vehicle upon any highway or upon any other property, public or private, at an immoderate rate of speed or in a careless, reckless or negligent manner, but not wilfully or wantonly, shall cause the death of another, shall be guilty of a misdemeanor, punishable by imprisonment in the state prison not more than 2 years or by a fine of not more than $2,000.00, or by both such fine and imprisonment.

Section 28.557. Negligent Homicide; Inclusion in Manslaughter; Verdict of Guilty.

Sec. 325. The crime of negligent homicide shall be deemed to be included within every crime of manslaughter charge to have been committed in the operation of any vehicle, and in any case where a defendant is charged with manslaughter committed in the operation of any vehicle, if the jury shall find the defendant not guilty of the crime of manslaughter, it may render a verdict of guilty of negligent homicide.

Section 28.330. Exposing Child with Intent to Injure or Abandon.

Sec. 135. Any father or mother of a child under the age of six [6] years, or any other person who shall expose such child in any street, field, house or other place, with intent to injure or wholly to abandon it, shall be guilty of felony, punishable by imprisonment in the state prison not more than ten [10] years.

Section 28.331(2). Definitions; Child Abuse.

Sec. 136b. (1) As used in this section:

(a) "Child" means a person who is less than 18 years of age and is not emancipated by operation of law as provided in section 4 of MCL 722.4.

(b) "Cruel" means brutal, inhuman, sadistic, or that which torments.

(c) "Omission" means a willful failure to provide the food, clothing, or shelter necessary for a child's welfare or the willful abandonment of a child.

(d) "Person" means a child's parent or guardian or any other person who cares for, has custody of, or has authority over a child regardless of the length of time that a child is cared for, in the custody of, or subject to the authority of that person.

(e) "Physical harm" means any injury to a child's physical condition.

(f) "Serious physical harm" means any physical injury to a child that seriously impairs the child's health or physical well-being, including, but not limited to, brain damage, a skull or bone fracture, subdural hemorrhage or hematoma, dislocation, sprain, internal injury, poisoning, burn or scald, or severe cut.

(g) "Serious mental harm" means an injury to a child's mental condition or welfare that is not necessarily permanent but results in visibly demonstrable manifestations of a substantial disorder of thought or mood which significantly impairs judgment, behavior, capacity to recognize reality, or ability to cope with the ordinary demands of life.

(2) A person is guilty of child abuse in the first degree if the person knowingly or intentionally causes serious physical or serious mental harm to a child. Child abuse in the first degree is a felony punishable by imprisonment for not more than 15 years.

(3) A person is guilty of child abuse in the second degree if any of the following apply:

Yes (a) The person's omission causes serious physical harm or serious mental harm to a child or if the person's reckless act causes serious physical harm to a child.

No (b) The person knowingly or intentionally commits an act likely to cause serious physical or mental harm to a child regardless of whether harm results.

No (c) The person knowingly or intentionally commits an act that is cruel to a child regardless of whether harm results.

(4) Child abuse in the second degree is a felony punishable by imprisonment for not more than 4 years.

No (5) A person is guilty of child abuse in the third degree if the person knowingly or intentionally causes physical harm to a child. Child abuse in the third degree is a misdemeanor punishable by imprisonment for not more than 2 years.

Yes (6) A person is guilty of child abuse in the fourth degree if the person's omission or reckless act causes physical harm to a child. Child abuse in the fourth degree is a misdemeanor punishable by imprisonment for not more than 1 year.

(7) This section does not prohibit a parent or guardian, or other person permitted by law or authorized by the parent or guardian, from taking steps to reasonably discipline a child, including the use of reasonable force.

People v. Richardson
293 N.W.2d 332 (Mich. 1980)

Defendant was convicted of first-degree murder, and appealed on the contention that the jury was not instructed on the definition of involuntary manslaughter, a crime for which his evidence provided support. The court held the judge's refusal to instruct on the lesser crimes to be in error, and noted that Michigan's "manslaughter statute does not define that offense [involuntary manslaughter], but instead incorporates the common-law definition."

People v. Ryczek
194 N.W. 609 (Mich. 1923)

Defendant was convicted of involuntary manslaughter for colliding with a boy pushing his baby sister in a cart, which resulted in the baby's death. The court affirmed his conviction and applied the common law definition that involuntary manslaughter is "the killing of another without malice and unintentionally, but in doing some unlawful act not amounting to a felony nor naturally tending to cause death or great bodily harm, or in negligently doing some act lawful in itself, or by the negligent omission to perform a legal duty. . . . [Here, the defendant] while doing a lawful act in driving his automobile, . . . did it in such a negligent manner that it amounted to gross negligence on his part." The court found that if the "defendant [had] given the most casual glance ahead of him, he would have observed the children approaching." Consequently, the jury was "well within their province in finding that such conduct was gross negligence," deserving of conviction.

People v. Clark
556 N.W.2d 820 (Mich. 1996)

Defendant was convicted of involuntary manslaughter for the death of her four-year-old son. She was suspected of child abuse. The court adopted the common law definition of the crime, and added that "[t]he kind of negligence required for manslaughter is . . . often described as . . . 'gross negligence,' [for which] three elements must be satisfied. . . . These elements are: (1) Knowledge of a situation requiring the exercise of ordinary care and diligence to avert injury to another. (2) Ability to avoid the resulting harm by ordinary care and diligence in the use of the means at hand. (3) The omission to use such care and diligence to avert the threatened danger when to the ordinary mind it must be apparent that the result is likely to prove disastrous to another."

People v. Clark
431 N.W.2d 88 (Mich. App. 1988)

Defendant was convicted of negligent homicide after he drove his semi-trailer truck through a red light and struck an oncoming car. The court stated that "the crime of negligent homicide is the killing of a person through an act of ordinary negligence, an act which is otherwise noncriminal, which becomes criminal because the victim dies."

People v. Traughber
439 N.W.2d 231 (Mich. 1989)

Defendant was convicted of negligent homicide for causing a fatal crash when he swerved into another lane of traffic. On appeal, the defendant challenged the jury instructions as prejudicial by requiring more than a reasonable standard of care. The court held the trial judge's instructions were correct, and stated that "[t]here is no question that the applicable standard of care in negligent homicide cases is that of a reasonable person. [Criminal Jury Instructions 16:5:02(1) states: 'For negligent homicide the prosecution must prove beyond a reasonable doubt that the defendant was guilty of ordinary negligence.' This instruction goes on to explain that '[o]rdinary negligence is defined as want of reasonable care; that is, failing to do what an ordinarily sensible person would have done under the conditions and circumstances then existing. . . . ' Criminal Jury Instructions 16:5:02(4)." However, the court reversed the conviction because the defendant had reacted to an emergency situation in a manner that was not contrary that of a reasonably prudent man under similar circumstances.

Model Penal Code
(Official Draft 1962)

Section 1.13. General Definitions

In this Code, unless a different meaning plainly is required: . . .

(9) "element of an offense" means (i) such conduct or (ii) such attendant circumstances or (iii) such a result of conduct as

    (a) is included in the description of the forbidden conduct in the definition of the offense; or

    (b) establishes the required kind of culpability; or

    (c) negatives an excuse or justification for such conduct; or

    (d) negatives a defense under the statute of limitations; or

    (e) establishes jurisdiction or venue;

(10) "material element of an offense" means an element that does not relate exclusively to the statute of limitations, jurisdiction, venue or to any other matter similarly unconnected with (i) the harm or evil, incident to conduct, sought to be prevented by the law defining the offense, or (ii) the existence of a justification or excuse for such conduct; . . .

Section 2.02. General Requirements of Culpability

(1) Minimum Requirements of Culpability. Except as provided in Section 2.05, a person is not guilty of an offense unless he acted purposely, knowingly, recklessly or negligently, as the law may require, with respect to each material element of the offense.

(2) Kinds of Culpability Defined.

    (a) Purposely. A person acts purposely with respect to a material element of an offense when:

        (i) if the element involves the nature of his conduct or a result thereof, it is his conscious object to engage in conduct of that nature or to cause such a result; and

        (ii) if the element involves the attendant circumstances, he is aware of the existence of such circumstances or he believes or hopes that they exist.

    (b) Knowingly. A person acts knowingly with respect to a material element of an offense when:

        (i) if the element involves the nature of his conduct or the attendant circumstances, he is aware that his conduct is of that nature or that such circumstances exist; and

        (ii) if the element involves a result of his conduct, he is aware that it is practically certain that his conduct will cause such a result.

    (c) Recklessly. A person acts recklessly with respect to a material element of an offense when he consciously disregards a substantial and unjustifiable risk that the material element exists or will result from his conduct. The risk must be of such a nature and degree that, considering the nature and purpose of the actor's conduct and the circumstances known to him, its disregard involves a gross deviation from the standard of conduct that a law-abiding person would observe in the actor's situation.

(d) Negligently. A person acts negligently with respect to a material element of an offense when he should be aware of a substantial and unjustifiable risk that the material element exists or will result from his conduct. The risk must be of such a nature and degree that the actor's failure to perceive it, considering the nature and purpose of his conduct and the circumstances known to him, involves a gross deviation from the standard of care that a reasonable person would observe in the actor's situation.

(3) Culpability Required Unless Otherwise Provided. When the culpability sufficient to establish a material element of an offense is not prescribed by law, such element is established if a person acts purposely, knowingly or recklessly with respect thereto.

(4) Prescribed Culpability Requirement Applies to All Material Elements. When the law defining an offense prescribes the kind of culpability that is sufficient for the commission of an offense, without distinguishing among the material elements thereof, such provision shall apply to all the material elements of the offense, unless a contrary purpose plainly appears.

(5) Substitutes for Negligence, Recklessness and Knowledge. When the law provides that negligence suffices to establish an element of an offense, such element also is established if a person acts purposely, knowingly or recklessly. When recklessness suffices to establish an element, such element also is established if a person acts purposely or knowingly. When acting knowingly suffices to establish an element, such element also is established if a person acts purposely.

(6) Requirement of Purpose Satisfied if Purpose Is Conditional. When a particular purpose is an element of an offense, the element is established although such purpose is conditional, unless the condition negatives the harm or evil sought to be prevented by the law defining the offense.

(7) Requirement of Knowledge Satisfied by Knowledge of High Probability. When knowledge of the existence of a particular fact is an element of an offense, such knowledge is established if a person is aware of a high probability of its existence, unless he actually believes that it does not exist.

(8) Requirement of Wilfulness Satisfied by Acting Knowingly. A requirement that an offense be committed wilfully is satisfied if a person acts knowingly with respect to the material elements of the offense, unless a purpose to impose further requirements appears.

(9) Culpability as to Illegality of Conduct. Neither knowledge nor recklessness or negligence as to whether conduct constitutes an offense or as to the existence, meaning or application of the law determining the elements of an offense is an element of such offense, unless the definition of the offense or the Code so provides.

(10) Culpability as Determinant of Grade of Offense. When the grade or degree of an offense depends on whether the offense is committed purposely, knowingly, recklessly or negligently, its grade or degree shall be the lowest for which the determinative kind of culpability is established with respect to any material element of the offense.

◆ THE CASE OF RAYMOND LENNARD GARNETT (#15)

Raymond Lennard Garnett is a 20-year-old man living in Silver Spring, Maryland, a Washington, D.C., suburb. Garnett is average height (5' 8") and weight, but is legally mentally retarded, with an I.Q. of 52. (The Supreme Court has held that an I.Q. of 70 or lower qualifies as mentally retarded.) Garnett reads at about a third-grade level, and his math skills put him on a fifth-grade level. He attended special education classes but recently left school for a short time when the other students teased him so mercilessly that he became too scared to return to class. He was home-schooled for a time but eventually returned to public school. He cannot complete many of the required tasks, because he does not understand the vocational assignments. He is often confused and sometimes gets lost. He does not pass any of the state's graduation tests and so receives only a certificate of attendance rather than a diploma. He presently interacts with others and processes things much as an 11- or 12-year-old would.

In November of 1990, two of Garnett's friends introduce him to Erica Frazier. They both tell Garnett that Erica is 16 years old, a fact later confirmed by her friends. In reality, Erica is only 13. Garnett is surprised that she is interested in talking to him. He likes her and enjoys spending time with someone who does not make fun of him. Erica and Garnett talk on the phone off and on over the next several months. On the evening of February 28, 1991, Garnett is stranded. He needs a ride home and notices that Erica's house is nearby. He approaches her house on Liberty Heights Lane at about 9 p.m. Erica opens her bedroom window and invites him in. She tells him to get a ladder and to climb up to her window so as not to disturb her parents. He enters her room and the two sit and talk for a while. One thing leads to another and they eventually end up having consensual sex. Afterwards, Garnett and Erica lay for hours talking. Finally, at 4:30 a.m., Garnett leaves.

Eight and a half months after their encounter, on November 19, 1991, Erica gives birth to a baby girl at Shady Grove Adventist Hospital. Her mother, Brenda Freeman, had not been aware of the pregnancy. Erica exp-lains that Garnett had visited once and that it was her only sexual experience. The next day, Ms. Freeman contacts the Youth Division of the police to report the rape of her daughter. Garnett is subsequently arrested for statutory rape after being determined to be the biological father.

Figure 16 **Frazier's house, number 19306**
(Catherine McAlpine)

1. Relying only on your own intuitions of justice, what liability and punishment, if any, does Raymond Lennard Garnett deserve?

N	0	1	2	3	4	5	6	7	8	9	10	11
☐	☐	☐	☐	☐	☐	☐	☐	☐	☐	☐	☐	☐
no liability	liability but no punishment	1 day	2 wks	2 mo	6 mo	1 yr	3 yrs	7 yrs	15 yrs	30 yrs	life imprison-ment	death

2. What "justice" arguments could defense counsel make on the defendant's behalf?

[handwritten: Sec. 463 2nd dg. rape]

3. What "justice" arguments could the prosecution make against the defendant?

4. What liability, if any, for Garnett under the then-existing statutes? Prepare a list of all criminal code subsections and cases in the order in which you rely upon them in your analysis.

[handwritten: Sec. 464C 4th deg sex. offense]

5. What liability, if any, under the Model Penal Code? Prepare a list of all criminal code subsections in the order in which you rely upon them in your analysis.

[handwritten: strict liability = failure to meet the standards of a reasonable person]

■ THE LAW

Annotated Code of Maryland
(1990)

Article 27. Crimes and Punishments

I. Sexual Offenses

Section 461. Definitions

(a) In general.—In this subheading, the following words have the meanings indicated.

(b) Mentally defective.— "Mentally defective" means (1) a victim who suffers from mental retardation, or (2) a victim who suffers from a mental disorder, either of which temporarily or permanently renders the victim substantially incapable of appraising the nature of his or her conduct, or resisting the act of vaginal intercourse, a sexual act, or sexual contact, or of communicating unwillingness to submit to the act of vaginal intercourse, a sexual act, or sexual contact.

(c) Mentally incapacitated.— "Mentally incapacitated" means a victim who, due to the influence of a drug, narcotic or intoxicating substance, or due to any act committed upon the victim without the victim's consent or awareness, is rendered substantially incapable of either appraising the nature of his or her conduct, or resisting the act of vaginal intercourse, a sexual act, or sexual contact.

(d) Physically helpless.— "Physically helpless" means (1) a victim who is unconscious; or (2) a victim who does not consent to an act of vaginal intercourse, a sexual act, or sexual contact, and is physically unable to resist an act of vaginal intercourse, a sexual act, or sexual contact or communicate unwillingness to submit to an act of vaginal intercourse, a sexual act, or sexual contact.

(e) Sexual act.— "Sexual act" means cunnilingus, fellatio, analingus, or anal intercourse, but does not include vaginal intercourse. Emission of semen is not required. Penetration, however slight, is evidence of anal intercourse. Sexual act also means the penetration, however slight, by any object into the genital or anal opening of another person's body if the penetration can be reasonably construed as being for the purposes of sexual arousal or gratification or for abuse of either party and if the penetration is not for accepted medical purposes.

(f) Sexual contact.— "Sexual contact" as used in §§464B and 464C, means the intentional touching of any part of the victim's or actor's anal or genital areas or other intimate parts for the purposes of sexual arousal or gratification or for abuse of either party and includes the penetration, however slight, by any part of a person's body, other than the penis, mouth, or tongue, into the genital or anal opening of another person's body if that penetration can be reasonably construed as being for the purposes of sexual arousal or gratification or for abuse of either party. It does not include acts commonly expressive of familial or friendly affection, or acts for accepted medical purposes.

(g) Vaginal intercourse.— "Vaginal intercourse" has its ordinary meaning of genital copulation. Penetration, however slight, is evidence of vaginal intercourse. Emission of semen is not required.

Section 461A. Admissibility of Evidence in Rape Cases

(a) Evidence relating to victim's chastity.—Evidence relating to a victim's reputation for chastity and opinion evidence relating to a victim's chastity are not admissible in any prosecution for commission of a rape or sexual offense in the first or second degree. Evidence of specific instances of the victim's prior sexual conduct may be admitted only if the judge finds the evidence is relevant and is material to a fact in issue in the case and that its inflammatory or prejudicial nature does not outweigh its probative value, and if the evidence is:

(1) Evidence of the victim's past sexual conduct with the defendant; or

(2) Evidence of specific instances of sexual activity showing the source or origin of semen, pregnancy, disease, or trauma; or

(3) Evidence which supports a claim that the victim has an ulterior motive in accusing the defendant of the crime; or

(4) Evidence offered for the purpose of impeachment when the prosecutor puts the victim's prior sexual conduct in issue.

(b) In camera hearing.—Any evidence described in subsection (a) of this section may not be referred to in any statements to a jury nor introduced at trial without the court holding a prior in camera hearing to determine the admissibility of the evidence. If new information is discovered during the course of the trial that may make the evidence described in subsection (a) admissible, the court may order an in camera hearing to determine the admissibility of the proposed evidence under subsection (a).

Section 461B. Instructions

In any criminal prosecution for rape, attempted rape, assault with intent to commit a rape, assault with intent to commit a sexual offense, or any other sexual offense, the jury may not be instructed:

(1) To examine with caution the testimony of the prosecuting witness, solely because of the nature of the charge;

(2) That the charge is easily made or difficult to disprove, solely because of the nature of the charge; or

(3) As to any other similar instruction, solely because of the nature of the charge.

Section 462. First Degree Rape

(a) What constitutes.—A person is guilty of rape in the first degree if the person engages in vaginal intercourse with another person by force or threat of force against the will and without the consent of the other person and:

(1) Employs or displays a dangerous or deadly weapon or an article which the other person reasonably concludes is a dangerous or deadly weapon; or

(2) Inflicts suffocation, strangulation, disfigurement, or serious physical injury upon the other person or upon anyone else in the course of committing the offense; or

(3) Threatens or places the victim in fear that the victim or any person known to the victim will be imminently subjected to death, suffocation, strangulation, disfigurement, serious physical injury, or kidnaping; or

(4) The person commits the offense aided and abetted by one or more other persons; or

(5) The person commits the offense in connection with the breaking and entering of a dwelling house.

(b) Penalty.—Any person violating the provisions of this section is guilty of a felony and upon conviction is subject to imprisonment for no more than the period of his natural life.

Section 463. Second Degree Rape

(a) What constitutes.—A person is guilty of rape in the second degree if the person engages in vaginal intercourse with another person:

(1) By force or threat of force against the will and without the consent of the other person; or

(2) Who is mentally defective, mentally incapacitated, or physically helpless, and the person performing the act knows or should reasonably know the other person is mentally defective, mentally incapacitated, or physically helpless; or

(3) Who is under 14 years of age and the person performing the act is at least four years older than the victim.

(b) Penalty.—Any person violating the provisions of this section is guilty of a felony and upon conviction is subject to imprisonment for a period of not more than 20 years.

Section 464. First Degree Sexual Offense

(a) What constitutes.—A person is guilty of a sexual offense in the first degree if the person engages in a sexual act:

(1) With another person by force or threat of force against the will and without the consent of the other person, and:

(i) Employs or displays a dangerous or deadly weapon or an article which the other person reasonably concludes is a dangerous or deadly weapon; or

(ii) Inflicts suffocation, strangulation, disfigurement, or serious physical injury upon the other person or upon anyone else in the course of committing the offense; or

(iii) Threatens or places the victim in fear that the victim or any person known to the victim will be imminently subjected to death, suffocation, strangulation, disfigurement, serious physical injury, or kidnaping; or

(iv) The person commits the offense aided and abetted by one or more other persons; or

(v) The person commits the offense in connection with the breaking and entering of a dwelling house.

(b) Penalty.—Any person violating the provisions of this section is guilty of a felony and upon conviction is subject to imprisonment for no more than the period of his natural life.

Section 464A. Second Degree Sexual Offense

(a) What constitutes.—A person is guilty of a sexual offense in the second degree if the person engages in a sexual act with another person:

(1) By force or threat of force against the will and without the consent of the other person; or

(2) Who is mentally defective, mentally incapacitated, or physically helpless, and the person performing the act knows or should reasonably know the other person is mentally defective, mentally incapacitated, or physically helpless; or

(3) Under 14 years of age and the person performing the sexual act is four or more years older than the victim.

(b) Penalty.—Any person violating the provisions of this section is guilty of a felony and upon conviction is subject to imprisonment for a period of not more than 20 years.

Section 464B. Third Degree Sexual Offense

(a) What constitutes.—A person is guilty of a sexual offense in the third degree if the person engages in sexual contact:

(1) With another person against the will and without the consent of the other person, and:

(i) Employs or displays a dangerous or deadly weapon or an article which the other person reasonably concludes is a dangerous or deadly weapon; or

(ii) Inflicts suffocation, strangulation, disfigurement or serious physical injury upon the other person or upon anyone else in the course of committing that offense; or

(iii) Threatens or places the victim in fear that the victim or any person known to the victim will be imminently subjected to death, suffocation, strangulation, disfigurement, serious physical injury, or kidnaping; or

(iv) Commits the offense aided and abetted by one or more other persons; or

(2) With another person who is mentally defective, mentally incapacitated, or physically helpless, and the person knows or should reasonably know the other person is mentally defective, mentally incapacitated, or physically helpless; or

(3) With another person who is under 14 years of age and the person performing the sexual contact is four or more years older than the victim.

(b) Penalty.—Any person violating the provisions of this section is guilty of a felony and upon conviction is subject to imprisonment for a period of not more than 10 years.

Section 464C. Fourth Degree Sexual Offense

(a) What constitutes.—A person is guilty of a sexual offense in the fourth degree if the person engages:

(1) In sexual contact with another person against the will and without the consent of the other person; or

(2) In a sexual act with another person who is 14 or 15 years of age and the person performing the sexual act is four or more years older than the other person; or

(3) In vaginal intercourse with another person who is 14 or 15 years of age and the person performing the act is four or more years older than the other person.

(b) Penalty.—Any person violating the provisions of this section is guilty of a misdemeanor and upon conviction is subject to imprisonment for a period of not more than one year, or a fine of not more than $ 1,000, or both fine and imprisonment.

Eggleston v. State

241 A.2d 433, 434 (Md. Spec. App. 1968)

Defendant was charged with statutory rape. On appeal, he argued that the statute's language describing the crime as "feloniously" committed meant that a specific intent was required. However, the court rejected his argument, and held that the state's statutory rape provision did not permit a mens rea requirement and the term "feloniously" was merely a description used to classify the offense. The court applied the "generally accepted state of the law as set out in Wharton's Criminal Law, [which] fail[ed] to vindicate appellant's proposition: 'It is no defense that the defendant did not know that the female was under the statutory age of consent. It is immaterial that the defendant in good faith believed that the female was above the prohibited age; that his belief, though erroneous, was reasonable; or that the defendant had been misled by the appearance or statements of the female. The defendant acts at his peril that the female may in fact be under the age of consent. The fact that the defendant cannot assert as a defense his bona fide belief in the victim's age does not make unconstitutional the statutes under consideration.'"

Michael M. v. Superior Court of Sonoma County
450 U.S. 464, 465 (1981)

The defendant was convicted of statutory rape under the California Penal Code §261.5. He appealed his conviction on the grounds that the statute violated the Equal Protection Clause of the Fourteenth Amendment by defining unlawful sexual intercourse as "an act of sexual intercourse accomplished with a female not the wife of the perpetrator, where the female is under the age of 18 years." Thus, the statute made men alone criminally liable. However, the Court overturned the California Supreme Court's ruling and upheld the statute as not being invidious, and instead found it "realistically reflect[ed] the fact that the sexes are not similarly situated in certain circumstances." The Court recognized the state's interest in making the crime of statutory rape a strict liability offense, and held that California's interest of preventing teenage pregnancy to be a valid interest.

● **OVERVIEW OF CULPABILITY REQUIREMENTS**

Hypothetical: Babies and Ditches (#16)

Geets and Carrie find Anver intolerable. He struts about their country club, being pompous beyond belief, expecting that he will be elected the next president. They concoct a practical joke to bring him down to earth. A winding road leading down the hill from the club runs by a playground. They plan to buy a baby carriage and two lifelike dolls and to place them in the middle of the road near the playground. As Anver comes around the turn, he will be surprised by the carriage. If he pulls his precious Jaguar off the road into the high grass, he may get stuck in the soft ground. If he fails to pull off, he will blast through the carriage and the "babies." Either way, Geets and Carrie will have a tale to tell, either about Anver's humorous slide or his apparent indifference to killing babies. Either one will serve Carrie's purpose.

Geets has a slightly different goal in playing the practical joke: to kill Anver. While he jokes with Carrie about what a buffoon Anver is, the truth is Anver is likely to be elected the next president, a position that Geets covets for himself. He knows that the tall grass adjacent to the stretch of road by the playground hides a drainage ditch. If Anver swerves to miss the baby carriage and slides off the road in the direction of the ditch, he may get injured and possibly even killed. Geets sees the chances of successfully killing Anver through this scheme as something less than 10% but he is hoping for the best. Carrie is unaware that their joke creates any risk of killing Anver.

The next day is perfect for the scheme, overcast with a light rain. Geets and Carrie put the carriage and dolls in the road just before Anver is scheduled to leave the club. Without telling Carrie about the ditch, Geets selects the location that he thinks maximizes the chance that Anver will slide into it. Anver's car approaches, swerves before hitting the carriage, hits the ditch, and sends Anver through the windshield. When he sees Anver's serious injuries, Geets has second thoughts about whether his scheme was such a good idea. He feels bad about Anver's injuries and hopes he will survive. Unfortunately, Anver dies two days later from injuries sustained in the accident. Are Geets and Carrie liable for homicide? If so, for which homicide offense?

does not change culpability

Notes

HISTORY

The requirement of culpability distinguishes the criminal law from other bodies of law. Without *mens rea*, the common law expression, there is little justification for condemning or punishing an actor. An actor's conduct may be harmful; the victim may have a claim in tort; and fairness and utility both may suggest that the actor rather than the victim should bear the loss for the injury. But without culpability in the actor, causing the injury may be seen as lacking sufficient blameworthiness to deserve the condemnation and reprobation of criminal conviction.

Early Notions of Culpability   The law did not always require culpability of an actor. Early Germanic tribes, it is suggested, imposed liability upon the causing of an injury, without regard to culpability. But this was during a period before tort law and criminal law were divided. It seems likely that as the distinction between tort and crime appeared—that is, as the function of compensating victims became distinguished from the function of imposing punishment—the requirement of culpability took on increasing importance. Early notions of *mens rea* requirements are seen in *Regina v. Prince*.[1] The defendant had taken an underage girl "out of the possession" of her father, reasonably believing she was over the age of consent. That the defendant's conduct was generally immoral was sufficient for Lord Bramwell to find that the defendant had the *mens rea* necessary for the crime. Lord Brett, on the other hand, would require that Prince at least have intended to do something (anything) that was criminal, not just immoral. A somewhat more demanding requirement is expressed in *Regina. v. Faulkner*.[2] In the process of stealing rum from the hold of a ship, Faulkner accidentally set the ship afire, destroying it. Lords Fitzgerald and Palles conclude that the *mens rea* requirement means that Faulkner must have at least intended to do something criminal that might reasonably have been expected to have led to the actual harm caused and charged. Thus, Faulkner should not be liable for the offense of burning a ship when he intended only to steal rum from it, and by that conduct could not reasonably have foreseen its destruction.

From One *Mens Rea* to Multiple Categories   This last shift in the notion of *mens rea* meant not only a dramatic increase in the demand of the requirement, but also a significant qualitative change. No longer did there exist a single, undifferentiated *mens rea* requirement for all offenses—the intention to do something immoral or, later, something criminal. Now different offenses might have different *mens rea* requirements: The *mens rea* required for the offense of burning a ship was different from the *mens rea* required for theft. Now an actor had to intend to do something that might reasonably be expected to lead to the harm of the particular offense. As some have expressed it, there was no longer a *mens rea* for criminal liability but rather *mentes reae*.[3]

Confusion in Common Law Categories of "Specific Intent" and "General Intent" The Common Law focused on two varieties of *mentes reae* in particular: As the law developed, most offenses came to be understood as requiring either *specific intent* or *general intent*. Unfortunately, the meanings of these terms, and the distinction between them, were difficult to pin down. Even more unfortunately, the obscurity and confusion did not diminish, and may even have increased, over time; the terms became more familiar, but their content was no less fuzzy. Perhaps worst of all, this confusion was not merely an intellectual shortcoming but had serious legal consequences, as the Common Law also developed rules and defenses that applied differently to specific-intent versus general-intent crimes. The term *specific intent* sometimes seemed to contemplate that, beyond having the (general) intent to perform certain conduct, the actor must have some further purpose or design in mind when doing so: For example, "assault with intent to kill," or trespass "with intent to commit a felony" (the definition of burglary). At other times "specific intent" seemed to suggest an intent to do a particular thing in a particular way, such as an intent to kill a particular person or steal a particular object, as opposed to "general intent" to act on an unknown or undetermined victim or thing. Sometimes "general intent" seemed to capture an overall capacity for wrongdoing, whereas "specific intent" demanded a particular decision to engage in a wrongful act.

---

1. 13 Cox's Crim. Cases 138 (1875).
2. 13 Cox's Crim. Cases 550 (1877).
3. Francis Bowes Sayre, The Present Significance of Mens Rea in the Criminal Law, Harv. Legal Essays 399, 404 (1934).

Other Common Law Mens Rea Categories   Specific intent and general intent were not the only *mentes reae* recognized at Common Law. Instead of, or in addition to, requiring specific or general intent, a number of Common Law offenses required that the relevant conduct must be performed "maliciously," "fraudulently," "feloniously," "wantonly," and the like. In contrast to the concepts of specific and general intent, which suggest a focus on the actor's psychology (his goals, perceptions, beliefs, and so on), many of these terms suggest a normative assessment of the actor's conduct—a focus on so-called *objective fault* (the blameworthiness of the activity per se) rather than *subjective fault* (the blameworthiness of the actor).

From Offense Analysis to Element Analysis   Even after recognizing more than one category of *mens rea*, the Common Law retained a sense that the required *mens rea* (or *mentes reae*) applied in a general way to the offense as a whole. The Model Penal Code further refines the understanding of how culpability should apply, requiring culpability "with respect to each material element of the offense."[4] In what may be described as a shift from *offense analysis* to *element analysis*,[5] the Model Penal Code emphatically rejected the notion of having one overall "umbrella" culpability requirement for an offense (a notion that was poorly understood and inconsistently employed even at Common Law). The Code instead adopted the position that culpability requirements should apply to individual elements of offenses. One consequence of this shift is that under the Code, and other modern criminal codes, the required level of culpability may be different for different elements of the same offense.

Element Analysis as Comprehensive   This element analysis approach provides, for the first time, a comprehensive statement of the culpability required for an offense. The early conceptions of *mens rea* were not simply undemanding; they were hopelessly vague and incomplete. They failed to tell courts enough about the required culpability for an offense to enable the courts to resolve the cases that commonly arose. These vague conceptualizations left it for courts to fill in the culpability requirements as the cases arose. Element analysis permits legislatures to reclaim from the courts the authority to define the conditions of criminal liability and, for the first time, to provide a comprehensive statement of the culpability required for an offense.

Misconceptions That Permitted Offense Analysis   The shift to element analysis did not come from a determination by the Model Penal Code drafters to change the traditional offense requirements. Rather, the drafters believed that element analysis was necessary to describe accurately an offense's culpability requirements, even requirements that had been recognized during the Common Law period. That is, Common Law lawyers and judges were wrong to think that their offense-analysis view of offense culpability requirements was adequate to describe the culpability that the Common Law required. Their misconception stemmed in part from their conceptualization of an independent "law of mistake," which they saw as supplementing the culpability requirements of an offense definition. Thus, an actor might satisfy the requirements of theft, yet have a defense if the "law of mistake" allowed

---

4. Model Penal Code § 2.02(1).
5. See generally Paul H. Robinson & Jane A. Grall, *Element Analysis in Defining Criminal Liability: The Model Penal Code and Beyond*, 35 STAN. L. REV. 681 (1983).

a defense in the situation. The Model Penal Code drafters, in contrast, recognized that a mistake defense and a culpability requirement are one and the same: They are simply two ways of describing the same thing. Thus, the Model Code provides that mistake gives a defense if it negates an offense culpability requirement.[6]

CULPABILITY UNDER MODERN CRIMINAL CODES

Aside from their insight into the relation between mistake defenses and culpability requirements, the Code drafters' greatest contribution in this area is their use of a limited number of carefully defined culpability terms. In place of the plethora of common law terms—wantonly, heedlessly, maliciously, and so on—the Code defines four levels of culpability: purposely, knowingly, recklessly, and negligently. Ideally, all offenses are defined by designating one of these four levels of culpability as to each objective element. If the objective elements of an offense require that an actor take the property of another, the culpability elements might require, for example, that the actor know that he is taking property and that he be at least reckless as to it being someone else's property. Modern codes give detailed definitions of each of the four culpability levels. (The Code's culpability levels are defined slightly differently as to each of the kinds of objective elements of an offense—conduct, circumstance, and result. For this discussion, let us focus on the definition of culpability as to causing a result).

Purpose   Under the Code, a person acts "purposely" with respect to a result if his or her conscious object is to cause such a result.[7] Notice that, while the criminal law generally treats an actor's motive as irrelevant, the requirement of "purpose" is a requirement that the actor have a particular motive for acting, such as to cause a particular result. This is a demanding requirement that often is difficult to prove. The offense of indecent exposure, for example, requires more than showing that the actor "flashed" another, knowing that it would alarm the person; it must be proven that the conduct was motivated by a desire to gain sexual gratification or arousal by the conduct. Doing it just to annoy or alarm the victim would not satisfy the offense's special purpose requirement.

Knowledge   A person acts "purposely" as to a result if it is his conscious object to cause the result. A person acts "knowingly" with respect to a result if it is not his conscious object, yet he is practically certain that the conduct will cause that result.[8] The anti-war activist who sets a bomb to destroy the draft board offices may be practically certain that the bomb will kill the night watchman yet wish that the watchman would go on a coffee break so that he will not be killed. The essence of the narrow distinction between these two culpability levels is the presence or absence of a *positive desire* to cause the result; purpose requires a culpability beyond the knowledge of a result's near certainty. In the broader sense, this distinction divides the vague notion of "callousness" from the more offensive "maliciousness" or "viciousness." The latter two may simply be aggressively ruthless forms of the former.

Recklessness   A person acts "knowingly" with respect to a result if she is nearly certain that her conduct will cause the result. If she is aware only of a

---

6. See Model Penal Code § 2.04(1).
7. Model Penal Code § 2.02(2)(a)(i).
8. Model Penal Code § 2.02(2)(b)(ii).

substantial risk, she acts "recklessly" with respect to the result.[9] The narrow distinction between knowledge and recklessness lies in the *degree of risk*—"practically certain" versus "substantial risk"—of which the actor is aware. The distinction between recklessness (and lower levels of culpability) and the two higher levels of culpability (purposely and knowingly) is that we tend to scold a reckless actor for being "careless," while we condemn an offender who falls within one of the higher culpability categories for "intentional" conduct.

Negligence A person acts "recklessly" with respect to a result if she consciously disregards a substantial risk that her conduct will cause the result; she acts only "negligently" if she is unaware of the substantial risk but should have perceived it.[10] Whereas recklessness focuses on whether the actor was aware of a substantial risk, negligence asks whether she should have been aware of the risk, even though she was not aware of it.

Faultless (Strict) Liability Finally, liability occasionally is imposed for activities without requiring culpability. Liability imposed in this manner is termed *strict* or *absolute* liability. The narrow distinction between negligence and strict liability focuses on whether the defendant's unawareness of the risk is a *failure to meet the standard of the reasonable person* in the actor's situation. Faultless liability is unconcerned with whether or not a reasonable person would have acted similarly. The broader distinction between the four categories of culpability, on the one hand, and faultlessness, on the other, is the distinction between a blameworthy and a blameless actor. Theoretical objections to strict liability understandably stem from a reluctance to punish conduct that is not unreasonable. However, as the Supreme Court has noted,[11] in areas such as statutory rape, there may be an important interest to protect that can only or best be accomplished through strict liability.

APPLICATION OF A MODERN CULPABILITY SCHEME

The Model Penal Code definitions of culpability levels provide precision in determining whether or not an actor is blameworthy to an extent that justifies some form of criminal law sanction. And while the fine distinctions between purpose, knowledge, recklessness, and negligence can prove difficult to apply with absolute certainty, differentiating between small, but significant, variations in the actor's culpable state is widely viewed as an essential element of establishing the moral credibility of the law. Thus, it is important to understand not only the culpability levels in a general sense, but how they function and the details of their operation.

Purpose as Independent of Likelihood While knowing and reckless culpability focus on the likelihood of causing the result—"practically certain" versus "substantial risk"—purposeful culpability pays no regard to the likelihood of the result. Geets believes that his chance of killing Anver is slight, but causing death is Geets's conscious object. This characteristic of the purpose requirement reflects an instinct that *trying* to cause the harm, whatever the likelihood, is more condemnable than acting with the belief that the harm will result without desiring it.

9. Model Penal Code § 2.02(2)(c).
10. Model Penal Code § 2.02(2)(d).
11. See Michael M. v. Sonoma County Superior Court, 450 U.S. 464 (1981).

The practical effect of this is that reckless conduct, as manifested in risk taking, can be elevated to purposeful conduct if the actor hopes that the risk will come to fruition. Even if Geets and Carrie had been aware of the same degree of risk, Geets's desire for Anver's death gives him a higher culpability level than Carrie. This characteristic of purpose also illustrates how specially demanding it is. A requirement of a particular belief is something a jury might logically deduce from other facts: The actor "must have known" the certainty or the risk of harm if he knew this fact or that. A purpose requirement requires the jury to determine an actor's objective or goal, a somewhat more complex psychological state. To find this, a jury may have to dig deeper into the actor's psyche, his general desires and motivations, to reach a conclusion. If a jury is conscientious in adhering to the proof-beyond-a-reasonable-doubt standard constitutionally required for offense elements, this may be a difficult conclusion to reach.

"Willful Blindness"   Most common law courts and modern codes make clear that an actor's deliberate blindness to a fact does not protect him from being treated as "knowing" that fact. For example, one who drives across the border in a car with a secret compartment but carefully avoids actually knowing that marijuana is hidden in the secret compartment can be held liable for knowingly transporting marijuana if it can be shown that "his ignorance in this regard was solely and entirely the result of his having made a conscious purpose to disregard the nature of that which was in the vehicle, with a conscious purpose to avoid learning the truth."[12] The Model Penal Code resolves the problem of willful blindness in a slightly different way. Section 2.02(7) provides:

> Requirement of Knowledge Satisfied by Knowledge of High Probability. When knowledge of the existence of a particular fact is an element of an offense, such knowledge is established if a person is aware of a high probability of its existence, unless he actually believes that it does not exist.

Thus, the smuggler is held to "know" of the marijuana if he is aware of a high probability that it is there. (Note that this standard requires something less than the "practically certain" standard that the Code uses when defining "knowingly" as to causing a result.[13])

Recklessness vs. Negligence   The narrow distinction between recklessness and negligence lies in the actor's *awareness of risk*. If it never occurred to Carrie that their little joke might create a risk of death to Anver, she cannot be held reckless as to the death, because she was never aware than death might occur and thus could not consciously disregard such risk. The distinction between negligence and the three higher levels of culpability is one of the most critical to criminal law. A person who acts purposely, knowingly, or recklessly is aware of the circumstances that make his or her conduct criminal or is aware that harmful consequences may result and is therefore both blameworthy and deterrable. A defendant who acts negligently, in contrast, is unaware of the circumstances or consequences and therefore, some writers argue, is neither blameworthy nor deterrable. While writers disagree over whether negligence ought to be adequate to support criminal liability, it is agreed that negligence represents a lower level of culpability than,

---

12. United States v. Jewell, 532 F.2d 697 (9th Cir. 1976).
13. Compare Model Penal Code § 2.02(7) to § 2.02(2)(b)(ii).

and is qualitatively different from, recklessness, in that the negligent actor fails to recognize, rather than consciously disregards, the risk. For this reason, recklessness is considered the norm for criminal culpability, while negligence is punished only in exceptional circumstances, as when a death is caused.

Negligence as Normative Assessment A person who fails to appreciate the risk that her conduct will cause a result is "negligent" as to the result if the failure "involves a gross deviation from the standard of care that a reasonable person would observe in the actor's situation."[14] Thus, unless she grossly deviates from the standard of care that a reasonable person would observe, she is not negligent and, at least in the eyes of the criminal law, is without cognizable fault. If Carrie was not aware of the risk of death created by their joke, should she have been? Would a reasonable person in her situation have been aware that a risk of death existed? Was her failure to perceive the risk a gross deviation from the attentiveness to the possibility of risk that the reasonable person in her situation would have had? These are the issues that the jury would consider in assessing whether she is negligent. They are not factual but normative issues. The jury is asked to judge whether her failure to perceive the risk was, under the circumstances, a blameworthy failure.

Negligence and Omissions One might think that "negligence" has something to do with omissions because of the common usage of the term; one "neglects" to act. Older cases sometimes suggested or assumed such a connection, but it has long since been agreed that "negligence," when used to refer to a level of culpability, can apply as easily to a commission as to an omission. With regard to Carrie, for example, the issue is whether she was negligent as to causing Anver's death in her *conduct* in putting the carriage and dolls in the road. The crux of negligent culpability is the failure to perceive a risk of which one should be aware, a risk from either an act or an omission to perform a legal duty. It is equally clear that one can have any level of culpability as to an omission, not just negligence. Where a parent *fails* to obtain needed medical care for a child and as a result the child dies, the actor may have been purposeful, knowing, reckless, negligent, or faultless as to allowing the resulting death. The parent may have failed to get medical care because she desired to cause the child's death; or, she may not have desired to cause the death, but she may have been practically certain that her omission to get care would result in the death; or, she may have been aware only of a substantial risk that her omission would result in death; or, she may have been unaware of a substantial risk but should have been aware (the reasonable person would have been aware); or, she may have been unaware and a reasonable person similarly would have been unaware. Generally, culpability requirements apply to omissions in the same way that they apply to commissions.

Concurrence Requirement When an offense definition requires a particular level of culpability as to a particular element, it means that the required culpability as to the element must exist at the time of the conduct constituting the offense. This *concurrence requirement,* as it is called, reflects the law's interest in judging the culpability of the act rather than the general character of the actor. The required concurrence between act and culpability is implicit in the Model Penal Code culpability definitions discussed above. In *State v. Hopple*, for example, Hopple took possession of a neighbor's sheep in order to protect his land

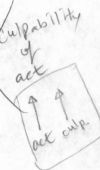

---

14. Model Penal Code § 2.02(2)(d).

from their unauthorized trampling of his cattle feed. Without the neighbor's permission, he subsequently attempted to sell the sheep.[15] Citing the "concurrence requirement," the court held that if the defendant had formed his intention to deprive the owner permanently of the sheep only after gaining possession, there was no concurrence between the taking and the intent to deprive permanently, as is required for theft. (Hopple might be liable nonetheless for an offense other than theft, such as unlawful "conversion" of another's property.) Note that the concurrence requirement applies to the time of the offense conduct, not to the time of the result. It is neither necessary nor sufficient that the culpability exists at the later time of the result of the conduct. Changing one's mind after setting a bomb does not bar liability for deaths caused by the blast, even if the intent to kill no longer exists at the time the bomb explodes or the victims die.[16] Thus it does not change Geets's culpability of purposely causing Anver's death that, at the time of Anver's death, Geets genuinely hopes that Anver will live.

Subverting Concurrence Requirement In *Thabo Meli and Others v. The Queen*, the defendants struck the victim over the head, intending to kill him.[17] They believed they were successful and rolled his body off a cliff to make the killing appear to be an accident. The victim, however, was alive after the beating but died later when they rolled him off the cliff. Strict application of the concurrence requirement would find liability for attempted murder for the beating and would find reckless or negligent homicide for rolling the body off the cliff (assuming it is reckless or negligent as to causing death to treat apparently dead bodies in this manner). However, the court chose to treat the two events as one "transaction" and, therefore, affirmed the conviction for murder.

Dangers of "Transaction" Analysis Even if one finds the result in *Thabo Meli* to be intuitively appealing, such "transaction" analysis has the potential to undermine the concurrence requirement's purpose. There seems little to distinguish the events in *Thabo Meli* from many other instances of related but distinct acts. Would it matter if the attackers went home after their deed and only happened upon the apparently dead body two days later, then thought it prudent to shove it off the cliff? Would this still be one transaction? What if the victim had recovered from his injuries during the intervening two days and, on this occasion, was simply lying in a drunken stupor when found, mistaken for a dead body, and tossed over the cliff? If a transaction approach were to be taken, as in *Thabo Meli*, it is unclear how the law is to define the bounds of such an analysis.

Model Penal Code Section 2.02 Commentary
Applying Culpability Requirements
Official Draft and Revised Comments 244-247, 250-251 (1985)

[Model Penal Code §2.02, the subject of this official commentary, is reproduced above at the end of the *Garnett* case Law Section.]

---

15. 357 P.2d 656 (Idaho 1960).

16. See People v. Claborn, 224 Cal. App. 2d 38, 36 Cal. Rptr. 132 (1964) (defendant's conviction for assault with automobile affirmed despite existence of 21 feet of skid marks leading up to victim's vehicle that defendant argued indicated change of intent at last moment).

17. [1954] 1 W.L.R. 228, 1 ALL E.R. 373.

§2.02
§(3)

5. *Offense Silent as to Culpability*. Subsection (3) provides that unless the kind of culpability sufficient to establish a material element of an offense has been prescribed by law, it is established if a person acted purposely, knowingly or recklessly with respect thereto. This accepts as the basic norm what usually is regarded as the common law position. More importantly, it represents the most convenient norm for drafting purposes. When purpose or knowledge is required, it is conventional to be explicit. And since negligence is an exceptional basis of liability, it should be excluded as a basis unless explicitly prescribed.

Some recent revisions and proposals have substantially similar provisions.

6. *Ambiguous Culpability Requirements*. Subsection (4) seeks to assist in the resolution of a common ambiguity in penal legislation, the statement of a particular culpability requirement in the definition of an offense in such a way that it is unclear whether the requirement applies to all the elements of the offense or only to the element that it immediately introduces. The draftsmen of the Wisconsin revision posed the problem in these terms: "When, for example, a statute says that it is unlawful to 'wilfully, maliciously, or wantonly destroy, remove, throw down or injure any [property] upon the land of another,' do the words denoting the requirement of intent apply only to the doing of the damage or do they also modify the phrase 'upon the land of another,' thus requiring knowledge or belief that the property is located upon land which belongs to another?" The Model Penal Code agrees with their view that these "problems can and should be taken care of in the definition of criminal intent."

The Code proceeds in the view that if a particular kind of culpability has been articulated at all by the legislature as sufficient with respect to any element of the offense, the assumption is that it was meant to apply to all material elements. Hence this construction is required, unless a "contrary purpose plainly appear." When a distinction is intended, as it often is, proper drafting ought to make it clear.

Two examples may help to clarify the intended scope of the provision and to illustrate its relationship with Subsection 3. False imprisonment is defined by Section 212.3 of the Model Code to include one who "knowingly restrains another unlawfully so as to interfere substantially with his liberty." Plainly, the word "knowingly" is intended to modify the restraint, so that the actor must, in order to be convicted under this section, know that he is restraining his victim. The question whether "knowingly" also qualifies the unlawful character of the restraint is not clearly answered by the definition of the offense, but is answered in the affirmative by the subsection under discussion.

To be contrasted with this illustration is the case of burglary, as defined in Section 221.1. The offense includes one who "enters a building . . . with purpose to commit a crime therein . . . ." The grading provisions make burglary a felony of the second degree if the offense is perpetrated "in the dwelling of another at night." Since an actor must have a "purpose" to commit a crime within a building, the definition of the offense might be thought ambiguous as to what culpability level applies to elements like "dwelling house" and "night." Must the actor know that he is entering a dwelling house in order to be convicted of a second degree felony, or is some lesser culpability level sufficient?

Section 2.02(3) should control elements of this character, and therefore recklessness should suffice in the absence of special provision to the contrary.

Subsection (4) does not produce a contrary result, since it is designed to apply, as noted above, only to offenses where a particular culpability requirement is stated in such a way as to make it unclear whether the requirement applies to all of the material elements of an offense or only to the material element it introduces. In the burglary illustration, the phrase "with purpose to commit a crime therein" plainly does not make purpose the required level of culpability with respect to all material elements of the offense.

Most of the recently enacted and proposed revisions are in substantial agreement with the Model Code's formulation in this subsection.

7. Substitutes for Prescribed Culpability Levels. Subsection (5) establishes that when negligence suffices for liability, *a fortiori* purpose, knowledge or recklessness are sufficient; that purpose and knowledge similarly are sufficient for recklessness; and that purpose is sufficient for knowledge. Thus it is only necessary to articulate the minimal basis of liability in drafting specific offenses for the more serious bases to be implied. Many recent revisions and proposals contain similar provisions.

8. Conditional Purposes. Subsection (6) provides that a requirement of purpose is satisfied when purpose is conditional, unless the condition negatives the harm or evil sought to be prevented by the law defining the offense. Thus, it is no less a burglary if the defendant's purpose was to steal only if no one was at home or if he found the object he sought. The condition does not negative the evil that the law defining burglary is designed to control, irrespective of whether the condition is fulfilled or fails. But it would not be an assault with the intent to rape, if the defendant's purpose was to accomplish the sexual relation only if the mature victim consented; the condition negatives the evil with which the law has been framed to deal. If his purpose was to overcome her will *if* she resisted, he would of course be guilty of the crime. This is believed to be a statement and rationalization of the present law. Some recent revisions contain similar language. . . .

11. Culpability as to Illegality of Conduct. Subsection (9) states the conventional position that knowledge of the existence, meaning or application of the law determining the elements of an offense is not an element of that offense, except in the unusual situations where the law defining the offense or the Code so provides.

It should be noted that the general principle that ignorance or mistake of law is no excuse is greatly overstated; it has no application, for example, when the circumstances made material by the definition of the offense include a legal element. Thus it is immaterial in theft, when claim of right is adduced in defense, that the claim involves a legal judgment as to the right of property. Claim of right is a defense because the property must belong to someone else for the theft to occur and the defendant must have culpable awareness of that fact. Insofar as this point is involved, there is no need to state a special principle; the legal element involved is simply an aspect of the attendant circumstances, with respect to which knowledge, recklessness or negligence, as the case may be, is required for culpability by Subsections (1) and (3). The law involved is not the law defining the offense; it is some other legal rule that characterizes the attendant circumstances that are material to the offense.

The proper arena for the principle that ignorance or mistake of law does not afford an excuse is thus with respect to the particular law that sets forth the definition of the crime in question. It is knowledge of *that* law that is normally not a part of the crime, and it is ignorance or mistake as to *that* law that is denied defensive significance by this subsection of the Code and by the traditional common law approach to the issue.

It needs to be recognized, however, that there may be special cases where knowledge of the law defining the offense should be part of the culpability requirement for its commission, i.e., where a belief that one's conduct is not a violation of the law or, at least, such a belief based on reasonable grounds, ought to engender a defense. Such a result might be brought about directly by the definition of the crime, e.g., by explicitly requiring awareness of a regulation, violation of which is denominated as an offense. It also may be brought about by a general provision in the Code indicating circumstances in which mistakes about the law defining an offense will constitute a defense. In either case, the result is exceptional and arises only when the governing law "so provides."

Many recent revisions and proposals have provisions similar to Subsection (9) in their definitions of culpability. . . .

Morissette v. United States
Supreme Court of the United States
342 U.S. 246 (1952)

JACKSON, J.

[Without hiding what he was doing, Morissette took spent bomb casings that had been lying around on Air Force practice bombing ranges for years. He flattened out the rusted casings and openly sold them at the city junk market, making a profit of $84. He was convicted under 18 USC §641, which made it an offense to "knowingly convert" government property.[18] It was clear that the defendant knew that what he took and sold were Air Force bomb casings. He claimed that he honestly believed that they had been abandoned and that he was therefore not committing an offense by taking them. The trial judge did not allow this as a defense and specifically instructed the jury that "[t]he question on intent is whether or not he intended to take the property." The court of appeals affirmed the conviction, ruling that, while the crime of stealing traditionally required intent to take another's property without claim of right, the crime of knowing conversion did not include an element of criminal intent because none was expressly provided in the statute. In other words, the court assumed that Congress intended the phrase "knowingly convert" to have its conventional tort law meaning, requiring only an intentional exercise of dominion over property that in fact is not one's own. The Supreme Court reversed, holding that to be liable for unlawful conversion it must be proven that the defendant had knowledge of the facts that made the conversion wrongful. In other words, it required that the defendant know that the property had not been abandoned by the owner.]

The contention that an injury can amount to a crime only when inflicted by intention is no provincial or transient notion. It is as universal and persistent in

---

18. 18 U.S.C. §641 reads, in part: "Whoever embezzles, steals, purloins, or knowingly converts to his use or the use of another, or without authority, sells . . . any . . . thing of value of the United States . . . shall be fined not more than $10,000 or imprisoned not more than ten years, or both; but if the value of such property does not exceed the sum of $100, he shall be fined not more than $1,000 or imprisoned not more than one year, or both."

mature systems of law as belief in freedom of the human will and a consequent ability and duty of the normal individual to choose between good and evil. A relation between some mental element and punishment for a harmful act is almost as instinctive as the child's familiar exculpatory 'But I didn't mean to,' and has afforded the rational basis for a tardy and unfinished substitution of deterrence and reformation in place of retaliation and vengeance as the motivation for public prosecution. . . .

Crime, as a compound concept, generally constituted only from concurrence of an evil-meaning mind with an evil-doing hand, was congenial to an intense individualism and took deep and early root in American soil. As the state codified the common law of crimes, even if their enactments were silent on the subject, their courts assumed that the omission did not signify disapproval of the principle but merely recognized that intent was so inherent in the idea of the offense that it required no statutory affirmation. . . .

However, the *Balint* and *Behrman* offenses belong to a category of another character, with very different antecedents and origins. The crimes there involved depend on no mental element but consist only of forbidden acts or omissions. This, while not expressed by the Court, is made clear from examination of a century-old but accelerating tendency, discernible both here and in England, to call into existence new duties and crimes which disregard any ingredient of intent. The industrial revolution multiplied the number of workmen exposed to injury from increasingly powerful and complex mechanisms, driven by freshly discovered sources of energy, requiring higher precautions by employers. Traffic of velocities, volumes and varieties unheard of came to subject the wayfarer to intolerable casualty risks if owners and drivers were not to observe new cares and uniformities of conduct. Congestion of cities and crowding of quarters called for health and welfare regulations undreamed of in simpler times. Wide distribution of goods became an instrument of wide distribution of harm when those who dispersed food, drink, drugs, and even securities, did not comply with reasonable standards of quality, integrity, disclosure and care. Such dangers have engendered increasingly numerous and detailed regulations which heighten the duties of those in control of particular industries, trades, properties or activities that affect public health, safety or welfare.

While many of these duties are sanctioned by a more strict civil liability, lawmakers, whether wisely or not, have sought to make such regulations more effective by invoking criminal sanctions to be applied by the familiar technique of criminal prosecutions and convictions. This has confronted the courts with a multitude of prosecutions, based on statutes or administrative regulations, for what have been aptly called "public welfare offenses." . . . Many of these offenses are not in the nature of positive aggressions or invasions, with which the common law so often dealt, but are in the nature of neglect where the law requires care, or inaction where it imposes a duty. Many violations of such regulations result in no direct or immediate injury to person or property but merely create the danger or probability of it which the law seeks to minimize. While such offenses do not threaten the security of the state in the manner of treason, they may be regarded as offenses against its authority, for their occurrence impairs the efficiency of controls deemed essential to the social order as presently constituted. In this respect, whatever the intent of the violator, the injury is the same, and the consequences are injurious or not according to fortuity. Hence, legislation applicable to such offenses, as a matter of policy, does not specify intent as a necessary element. The accused, if he does not will the violation, usually is in a position to prevent it with no more care than society might reasonably expect and no more exertion than it might reasonably exact from one who assumed his responsibilities. Also, penalties commonly are relatively small, and conviction does not grave damage to an offender's reputation. Under such considerations, courts have turned to construing statutes and regulations which make no mention of intent as dispensing with it and holding that the guilty act alone makes out the crime. This has not, however, been without expressions of misgiving. . . .

After the turn of the Century . . . New York enacted numerous and novel regulations of tenement houses, sanctioned by money penalties. Landlords contended that a guilty intent was essential to establish a violation. Judge Cardozo wrote the answer:

> The defendant asks us to test the meaning of this statute by standards applicable to statutes that govern infamous crimes. The analogy, however, is deceptive. The element of conscious wrongdoing, the guilty mind accompanying the guilty act, is associated with the concept of crimes that are punished as infamous. . . . Even there it is not an invariable element. . . . But in the prosecution of minor offenses there is a wider range of practice and of power. Prosecutions for petty penalties have always constituted in our law a class by themselves . . . That is true, though the prosecution is criminal in form.

Tenement House Department of City of New York v. McDevitt, 1915, 215 N.Y. 160, 168, 109 N.E. 88, 90 (1915) . . .

Thus, for diverse but reconcilable reasons, state courts converged on the same result, discontinuing inquiry into intent in a limited class of offenses against such statutory regulations.

Before long, similar questions growing out of federal legislation reached this Court. Its judgments were in harmony with this consensus of state judicial opinion, the existence of which may have led the Court to overlook the need for full exposition of their rationale in the context of federal law. . . .

Neither this Court nor, so far as we are aware, any other has undertaken to delineate a precise line or set forth comprehensive criteria for distinguishing between crimes that require a mental element and crimes that do not. We attempt no closed definition, for the law on the subject is neither settled nor static. The conclusion reached in the *Balint* and *Behrman* cases has our approval and adherence for the circumstances to which it was there applied. A quite different question here is whether we will expand the doctrine of crimes without intent to include those charged here.

Stealing, larceny, and its variants and equivalents, were among the earliest offenses known to the law that existed before legislation; they are invasions of rights of property which stir a sense of insecurity in the whole community and arouse public demand for retribution, the penalty is high and, when a sufficient amount is involved, the infamy is that of a felony, which, says Maitland, is " . . . as bad a word as you can give to man or thing." State courts of last resort, on whom fall the heaviest burden of interpreting criminal law in this country, have consistently retained the requirement of intent in larceny-type offenses. If any state has deviated, the exception has neither been called to our attention nor disclosed by our research.

Congress, therefore, omitted any express prescription of criminal intent from the enactment before us in the light of an unbroken course of judicial decision in all constituent states of the Union holding intent inherent in this class of offense, even when not expressed in a statute. Congressional silence as to mental elements in an Act merely adopting into federal statutory law a concept of crime already so well defined in common law and statutory interpretation by the states may warrant quite contrary inferences than the same silence in creating an offense new to general law, for whose definition the courts have no guidance except the Act. Because the offenses before this Court in the *Balint* and *Behrman* cases were of this latter class, we cannot accept them as authority for eliminating intent from offenses incorporated from the common law.

The Government asks us by a feat of construction radically to change the weights and balances in the scales of justice. The purpose and obvious effect of doing away with the requirement of a guilty intent is to ease the prosecution's path to conviction, to strip the defendant of such benefit as he derived at common law from innocence of evil purpose, and to circumscribe the freedom heretofore allowed juries. Such a manifest impairment of the immunities of the individual should not be extended to common-law crimes on judicial initiative. . . .

We hold that mere omission from §641 of any mention of intent will not be construed as eliminating that element from the crimes denounced. . . .

Of course, the jury, considering Morissette's awareness that these casings were on government property, his failure to seek any permission for their removal and his self-interest as a witness, might have disbelieved his profession of innocent intent and concluded that his assertion of a belief that the casings were abandoned was an afterthought. Had the jury convicted on proper instructions it would be the end of the matter. But juries are not bound by what seems inescapable logic to judges. They might have concluded that the heaps of spent casings left in the hinterland to rust away presented an appearance of unwanted and abandoned junk, and that lack of any conscious deprivation of property or intentional injury was indicated by Morissette's good character, the openness of the taking, crushing and transporting of the casings, and the candor with which it was all admitted. They might have refused to brand Morissette as a thief. Had they done so, that too would have been the end of the matter.

Reversed.

▲ PROBLEMS

A Vegan Death (#17)

Joseph and Lamoy Andressohn are committed vegans. They refuse to eat meat or any animal products, including dairy foods, believing that by doing so they will lead healthier lives. Joseph and Lamoy are also parents of five children, including baby Woyah and her four siblings ages four to nine. All of their children are raised as vegans. Like her older sister, Woyah is breastfed for three months before being switched to a formula of wheat grass mixed with almond and coconut juice. At six months, Woyah weighs just seven pounds, less than half of the average for a baby her age and only a few ounces more than when she was born. Her older siblings weigh, on average, less than 97 percent of children their age.

Woyah, however, is different from her siblings. She is diagnosed at birth with DiGeorge Syndrome. The syndrome, characterized by a missing chromosome, exhibits different symptoms in different people, but is commonly associated with recurring infections and heart abnormalities. One night Woyah is having difficulty breathing. Her parents call 911, but Woyah is unresponsive when paramedics arrive. Woyah dies at the hospital, and the cause of death is determined to be malnutrition.

What liability for Joseph and Lamoy, if any, under the Model Penal Code in the death of baby Woyah? What level of culpability, if any, do the parents have toward causing Woyah's death? Prepare a list of all criminal code subsections in the order in which you rely upon them in your analysis.

Cut! (#18)

California

John Landis is a big-time Hollywood director. Having several blockbusters to his credit, he is highly sought after, directing major motion pictures for major studios. He is having some minor problems with his latest film, however. With all the regulations about when he can use which actors, he is falling behind schedule and is slightly over budget. Neither of these seriously imperils the project, which is slated to be a major release, but he is doing what he can to make up for lost time and prevent further setbacks. In particular, he is trying to expeditiously get through the filming of his final scene. His vision is clear: A Vietnamese village is attacked, and the main character, played by Victor Morrow, saves two children, fleeing as a helicopter fires on them. It is a technically difficult scene to film and the helicopter pilot expresses some hesitation about Landis' plan to use real explosives and live ammunition in the destruction of the village. However, Landis wants everything to be as realistic as possible, and it is not unusual to use live rounds in filming similar scenes.

To achieve the maximum verisimilitude, Landis decides to shoot the scene outdoors at night, and to use real children rather than midgets or dolls. Chosen to play the children are Renee and My-Can, both young children of immigrant families. Landis knows that under California law, the children are not allowed to work at night without special permission and that he is supposed to have a social worker or teacher present who can stop filming if the children are in physical or moral danger. However, rather than apply for a permit to film at night, he ignores the rule. He is an experienced director and does not think that the scene will be dangerous, merely "tricky." The parents of the children are present but are not aware of the regulations that are being ignored.

Prior to filming the climactic scene, Landis' assistants question the presence of children in a shot using live explosives and ammunition, but ultimately everyone agrees to proceed. In the course of filming the scene, Landis instructs the helicopter pilot to fly lower, altering the rehearsed route for the helicopter. A pyrotechnics operator, believing the helicopter to be safely out of range, triggers an explosive. The helicopter is, however, directly overhead. The explosion engulfs the tail of the helicopter and the pilot loses control. As the craft goes down, Morrow and My-Can are decapitated by its blades and Renee is crushed underneath.

What liability for Landis, if any, under the Model Penal Code for the deaths of Morrow, My-Can, and Renee? Prepare a list of all Code subsections in the order that you rely upon them in your analysis.

The Weight of Authority (#19)

Betty Mentry's eight-year old son, Stephen, has a bad habit of stealing and has been caught by police on several occasions. Mentry, an electronics worker who has been determined to possess below-average intelligence, punishes her son to get him to change his ways but in vain. He repeatedly fails to respond to punishment and continues stealing. Frustrated, yet determined to change her son's behavior, Mentry follows police advice to take her son to counseling. She brings him to the Alum Rock Communications Center in San Jose, which is a state-funded counseling service. There she speaks with center counselor Jorge Sousa, who insists on using a technique developed in the 1960s by Dr. Milton H. Erickson of New York. The technique consists of sitting on the child, literally, to make him understand who is in charge. When Mentry objects to using such an aggressive form of punishment, Sousa threatens to advise the courts to remove Stephen from her custody if she refuses to follow his advice. Sousa assures her that no harm will come to the boy.

Mentry is a 200-pound woman. The first time she uses the technique, she sits her full weight on her son for eight hours. She eats in front of him, talks on the phone, and acts like she is having a fun time while sitting on Stephen. The boy yells, screams, curses, and struggles to get free. Mentry, following the counselor's advice, ignores her son's tantrum, hoping that Stephen will get the message that she is in charge. She uses the technique on three other occasions. On the next two occasions, she sits on him for a half hour and for one and a half hours, respectively. The last time Mentry sits on him, however, Stephen complains, "I can't breathe." Mentry stays on top of her son for two hours before she notices he has stopped breathing. Stephen dies nine days later from his injuries.

Is Ms. Mentry liable for a homicide offense under the Model Penal Code? If so, which offense? Prepare a list of all criminal code subsections in the order in which you rely upon them in your analysis.

Buying Weight (#20)

Robert Ryan and David Hopkins are friends who also have a professional relationship. Ryan likes to purchase hallucinogenic mushrooms, controlled substances; Hopkins, who knows where to order them, acts as a middleman. Needless to say, the State of New York frowns upon such dealings. After a recent request from Ryan, Hopkins calls his supplier and asks for the "usual shipment." It arrives several days later, but the Federal Express delivery man is actually an investigator, and Hopkins is arrested as soon as he signs for the package. Friendship being a fleeting thing, he agrees to set up Ryan in exchange for lenient treatment. He phones Ryan to let him know that the package has arrived, indicating the presence of a "shitload of mushrooms in there." He later refers to the weight of the package as two pounds. Ryan acknowledges this information and they arrange to meet. After taking the package, Ryan is arrested.

Tests reveal that the package of mushrooms contained 932.8 grams of mushrooms (a shade over two pounds) and that a 140 gram sample of the mushrooms contained 796 milligrams of the hallucinogenic agent psilocybin. While Ryan partakes in the product, he is not a psycho-pharmacologist and is unaware of the precise proportion of psychedelic alkaloids present in the mushrooms he had planned to purchase. Thus, he is blissfully ignorant of the exact quantity of psilocybin in his possession. The New York Code is based on the Model Penal Code, but whereas the Model Code does not contain drug offenses, New York's does. Penal Law §220.18(5) makes it a felony to "knowingly and unlawfully possess . . . six hundred twenty-five milligrams of a hallucinogen." Lesser drug amounts are punished as a lesser offense.

Is Ryan liable under §220.18(5)? (Assume the Model Penal Code is in effect together with the New York drug offense code quoted above.) Prepare a list of all criminal code subsections in the order in which you rely upon them in your analysis.

Rough Play (#21)

Like many Canadians, Jimmy Boni grew up playing hockey. He was the star player of his youth team but his dreams of playing in the NHL never materialized. However, as a dual Italian citizen, he finds work playing professionally for a northern Italian team, where the level of competition is significantly lower. What Italian players lack in skill, they make up for in physicality, and the league is renowned for its rough play. Boni, by contrast, plays more of a finesse game, utilizing his superior speed and puck-handling and generally avoiding fights.

However, Boni is not above the usual hockey retribution. During a game against his club's main rival, he is punched in the face by Schrott, the opposing team's largest and most intimidating player. In retaliation, Boni slashes his stick across Schrott's chest, which he knows to be the most padded area of the opposing player. The slash is illegal, as was the punch, but it is an accepted practice in hockey to use such a maneuver to send a message that one is willing to fight back. The slash is meant to cause minor, temporary pain, so Boni is surprised when Schrott immediately falls motionless to the ice. Boni assumes Schrott is simply trying to draw a penalty, and even Schrott's own teammates are unconcerned. Schrott has a history of epilepsy, and at worse his teammates believe he is having an episode, as he has had before in practice. However, this is no epileptic fit. Schrott has suffered a cardiac arrest, and by the time he is taken off the ice he is already dead. It is later determined that Schrott's aorta (the major blood vessel of the heart) was narrower than normal, a congenital defect that may have been the cause of his epilepsy. As a result of Schrott's condition, Boni's slash triggered a massive, fatal heart attack.

What liability, if any, for Boni under the Model Penal Code, for striking Schrott? Prepare a list of all criminal code subsections in the order in which you rely upon them in your analysis.

✳ DISCUSSION ISSUES

What Is the Minimum Culpability, If Any, That Should Be Required for Criminal Liability?

Should a Person's Negligence (and Recklessness) Be Judged Against an Objective or an Individualized Standard?

Materials presenting each side of these Discussion Issues appear in the Advanced Materials for Section 4 in Appendix A.

Culpability and Mistake

The previous section described the meaning and use of offense culpability requirements. How are these related to mistake defenses? When will an offender's mistake provide a defense?

◆ THE CASE OF THOMAS LASETER (#22)

Fairbanks, Alaska is located in the heart of Alaska and is the hub town connecting Anchorage to Canada, which then leads to the only road passage to the continental United States. Athabascans have been living in this area for thousands of years, but when gold was discovered in the area in 1902, it suddenly boomed with new people and got a court, a jail, a post office, and electricity. With the construction of the Alcan Highway (connecting Alaska to Canada to the United States) and the even more dramatic oil boom, Fairbanks got another boost. By 1982, it had the second largest population in Alaska.

Fairbanks is a land of extremes. It goes from bright, scorching 20-hour days in the summer, when highs hit the mid-90s, to snowy, frigid winters with lows reaching −70° (without factoring in the wind chill) and a mere 4 hours of pale light. The large variations in climate affect the personality, culture, and lifestyle

Figure 17 **Downtown Fairbanks**
(Joel Rogers/Corbis)

of the region. As a result of these extremes and other factors, Fairbanks has a large drug and alcohol problem. It also has high incidences of domestic violence, incest, and property crimes. In winter, many people become depressed from the weather, lack of daylight, and isolation, and turn to drugs and alcohol for release. There are also great disparities in lifestyle and wealth. More than 10 percent of Fairbanks's population lives below the poverty line. Of the 30,000 residents, more than 200 families still lack plumbing. More than a third of the adults are not in the workforce.

Fairbanks also serves as a hub for people coming in from surrounding villages. Mixed in with the savvy city people are people who have what is called "village innocence." These differences lead to strong rural-urban cultural tensions.

The tensions are further accentuated by the military's presence in Fairbanks. As with many city-military base interactions, there are often striking differences between the two cultures. Many of the people in Fairbanks were born and raised there, often having never been farther than 50 miles out of town. They have their own understandings for how people should behave. The people brought in by the military are from many different regions, none quite like Fairbanks. They are typically far from home and from everything familiar to them. Faced with the cultural differences on top of adjusting to the peculiar climate, many military personnel become homesick and depressed. Some try to fit in with the local culture, venturing into town for drinks, dates, and conversation.

Figure 18 **U.S. Army Fort Wainwright**
(William Gossweiler/U.S. Army Alaska)

On the evening of April 18, 1982, just as there is a glimmer of hope that spring will come (even though snow will be on the ground until early June),

Thomas Laseter leaves the Fort Wainwright Army base and heads into downtown Fairbanks. He is about 6 feet 1 inch tall, weighs 215 pounds, and is a 21-year-old career soldier. He has to work the next morning but decides nonetheless to go to the French Quarter, a local bar on the strip. He is not necessarily trying to pick up a girl; he just wants to have some fun. When he gets to the bar, he notices a woman with long dark hair drinking beer and playing pool. L. P. is a 23-year-old Fairbanks native. She has a boyfriend, Bill, but he has been working up north for about two weeks, so tonight she is out with a girlfriend. After she is finished with three or four games, Laseter walks over and asks L. P. if she would be willing to play one round with him. She agrees. They play and talk, and Laseter buys her four or five drinks. He notices that she looks as if she might be pregnant and asks her about it. She says she is not, although in reality she is more than five months along. Laseter can tell that she is, but drops the subject. The French Quarter is winding down, and Laseter is interested in going to another bar. L. P. is still pretty sober. She declines his invitation to go to the Stampede, a bar just down the street. The Quarter closes at 2 a.m.

Later, both Laseter and L. P. somehow separately end up at the Stampede. When he sees her there he sits down next to her at the bar. They talk until early in the morning, discussing, among other things, her boyfriend and her pregnancy. They keep chatting, and he buys her another four or five drinks. At this point, Laseter has consumed about 15 beers and L. P. has had about 12. They listen to the jukebox until the bartender shuts things down.

By now, L. P. is tired and a little drunk. She has a history of problems with alcohol and sometimes suffers from blackouts. She begins to fade in and out. Meanwhile, Laseter notices that it is getting late. He also realizes that if he is going to give L. P. a ride and still make it to work on time, he needs to get going. He offers her a ride, but she says she wants to stay. He tells her he is leaving and heads out to the parking lot. As he is unlocking his car door, he sees her walking past the passenger side on the way to her friend's house. Again, he asks her if she would like a ride. His car is filthy, but this time she accepts.

Laseter is pretty drunk and still not very familiar with the layout of Fairbanks. He tells L. P. she will have to give him directions. She explains where to go but then falls asleep (or passes out). Laseter ends up in an area of town that is far from where he thinks he should be. L. P. wakes up frightened and confused, and tells him to turn around. He says he will, but then she passes out and he turns down the wrong street. At one point she wakes up as the car is starting to slow down at a stop sign. She seems scared and starts fumbling with the door handle and tries to get out. Laseter reaches over, grabs her arm, and pulls her back into the car. He keeps driving and she passes out again. It is now about five in the morning and Laseter feels completely lost. He starts to shake L. P. to try to wake her up. The car hits some ice and slides into Bradford Gustin's fence.

Laseter gets out and gives Gustin his name and license plate number and explains that he is taking his date home. Gustin can tell Laseter has been drinking, but decides he is sober enough to drive. Gustin sees L. P. sitting up in the front seat. Laseter returns to the car and starts to drive down the road but does not get very far before getting stuck in a huge mud slick as he turns down an alley. Laseter gets out and tries to rock and push the car out of the hole but cannot.

He asks Bill Hoople, who is passing by on his way to work, for assistance. Hoople cannot help and suggests that Laseter wait for a tow truck. Hearing it will be at least half an hour until a truck arrives, Laseter returns to the car. He shakes L. P., attempting to wake her up. He does not think she knows where she is. After waiting a little, he leans in and starts to kiss her. To Laseter, L. P. still seems out of it and does not say anything, but she seems to respond. Thinking that she is enjoying herself, Laseter keeps kissing her and starts taking their clothes off. He pulls down her pants and underwear, but before he gets any further he ejaculates. Embarrassed, he quickly puts his clothes back on and climbs out of the car to try to find someone to help him get his car out of the hole. He soon finds a man who offers him a tow with a rope. Meanwhile, L. P., still tired and disoriented, is now extremely upset. She works her way out of the car and, stumbling a little, pounds on the door of a nearby apartment building. By the time Laseter returns, she is gone. The woman who lets her in later reports that L. P. seems badly shaken and says that a man raped her. The next thing L. P. remembers is a doctor examining her.

The police arrive as Laseter is hooking up the tow strap to his car. He is arrested and charged with sexual assault.

1. Relying only upon your own intuitions of justice, what liability and punishment, if any, does Thomas Laseter deserve?

N	0	1	2	3	4	5	6	7	8	9	10	11
☐	☐	☐	☐	☐	☐	☐	☐	☐	☐	☐	☐	☐
no liability	liability but no punishment	1 day	2 wks	2 mo	6 mo	1 yr	3 yrs	7 yrs	15 yrs	30 yrs	life imprison-ment	death

2. What "justice" arguments could defense counsel make on the defendant's behalf?

3. What "justice" arguments could the prosecution make against the defendant?

4. What liability, if any, for Laseter under the then-existing statutes? Prepare a list of all criminal code subsections in the order in which you rely upon them in your analysis.

5. What liability, if any, under the Model Penal Code? Prepare a list of all criminal code subsections in the order in which you rely upon them in your analysis.

6. *Jury Instructions*. The defense in *Laseter* proposed two instructions, which read:

> "Without Consent." In order to find the defendant guilty of sexual assault in the first degree, you must find that he was subjectively aware that [L. P.] did not consent to sexual penetration. If from all the evidence you have a reasonable doubt as to the question whether the defendant believed that [L. P.] consented to sexual penetration, you must give the defendant the benefit of that doubt and find him not guilty.

> "Recklessly." With respect to the circumstance of consent, a person acts recklessly with respect to a circumstance described by the law when he is aware of and consciously disregards a substantial and unjustifiable risk that the circumstance exists. The risk must be of such a nature and such a degree that disregard of it constitutes a gross deviation from the standard

of conduct that a reasonable person would observe in the situation. A person who is unaware of a risk of which he would have been aware had he not been intoxicated acts recklessly with respect to that risk.

The state objected to both instructions, and would have the court substitute the following instruction as to "reasonable belief."

> If from all the evidence you find that the defendant had a reasonable belief that L. P. consented to sexual penetration, you shall find the defendant not guilty as to the crime of sexual assault in the first degree. If the defendant's belief as to L. P.'s consent was induced by his state of intoxication, you shall find it is not a reasonable belief.

Given the Alaska statutes below, which, if either, of these proposed instructions should the court have given?

■ THE LAW

Alaska Statutes
(1982)

Article 4. Sexual Offenses

Section 11.41.410. Sexual Assault in the First Degree.

(a) A person commits the crime of sexual assault in the first degree if,

(1) being any age, he engages in sexual penetration with another person without the consent of that person;

(2) being of any age, he attempts to engage in sexual penetration with another person without the consent of that person and causes serious physical injury to that person;

(3) being 16 years or older, he engages in sexual penetration with another person under 13 years of age or aids, induces, causes or encourages a person under 13 years of age to engage in sexual penetration with another person; or

(4) being 18 years of age or older, he engages in sexual penetration with another person who is under 18 years of age and who

(A) is entrusted to his care by authority of law; or

(B) is his son or daughter, whether adopted, illegitimate, or stepchild.

(b) Sexual assault in the first degree is a class A felony.

Section 11.41.420. Sexual Assault in the Second Degree.

(a) A person commits the crime of sexual assault in the second degree if he coerces another person to engage in sexual contact by the express or implied threat of imminent death, imminent physical injury, or imminent kidnapping to

[handwritten margin notes: Legislative to limit by requiring evidence victim was resisting and as a result suffered injuries physical manifestation of struggle]

be inflicted on anyone or by causing physical injury to any person, regardless of whether the victim resists.

(b) Sexual assault in the second degree is a class B felony.

Section 11.41.430. Sexual Assault in the Third Degree.

(a) A person commits the crime of sexual assault in the third degree if he engages in sexual penetration with a person who he knows

(1) is suffering from a mental disorder or defect which rendered him incapable of appraising the nature of the conduct under the circumstances in which a person who is capable of appraising the nature of the conduct would not engage in sexual penetration; or

(2) is incapacitated.

(b) Sexual assault in the third degree is a class C felony.

Section 11.41.445. General Provisions

(a) In a prosecution under secs. 410-440 of this chapter, it is an affirmative defense that, at the time of the alleged offense, the victim was the legal spouse of the defendant unless

(1) the spouses were living apart; or

(2) the defendant caused physical injury to the victim.

(b) In the prosecution under secs. 410-440 of this chapter, whenever a provision of law defining an offense depends upon a victim's being under a certain age, it is an affirmative defense that, at the time of the alleged offense, the defendant reasonably believed the victim to be that age or older, unless the victim was under 13 years of age at the time of the alleged offense.

Section 11.41.470. Definitions

For purposes of secs. 410-470 of this chapter, unless the context requires otherwise,

(1) "incapacitated" means that a person is temporarily incapable of appraising the nature of his conduct and is physically unable to express unwillingness to act;

(2) "victim" means the person alleged to have been subject to sexual assault in any degree or sexual abuse of a minor;

(3) "without consent" means that the person

(A) with or without resisting, is coerced by the use of force against a person or property, or by the express or implied threat of imminent death, imminent physical injury, or imminent kidnapping to be inflicted on anyone; or

(B) is incapacitated as a result of an act of the defendant.

Article 3 Kidnapping and Custodial Interference

Section 11.41.300. Kidnapping

(a) A person commits the crime of kidnapping if

(1) he restrains another person with intent to

(A) hold him for ransom, reward, or other payment;

(B) use him as a shield or hostage;

(C) inflict physical injury upon him or sexually assault him or place him or a third person in apprehension that any person will be subjected to serious physical injury or sexually assault;

(D) interfere with the performance of a governmental or political function;

(E) facilitate the commission of a felony or flight after commission of a felony; or

(2) he restrains another person

(A) by secreting and holding him in a place where he is not likely to be found; or

(B) under circumstances which expose him to a substantial risk of serious injury.

(b) In prosecution under (a)(2)(A) of this section, it is an affirmative defense that

(1) the defendant was a relative of the victim;

(2) the victim was a child under 18 years of age or an incompetent person; and

(3) the primary intent of the defendant was to assume custody of the victim.

(c) Except as provided in (d) of this section, kidnapping is an unclassified felony and is punishable as provided in AS 12.55.

(d) In a prosecution for kidnapping, it is an affirmative defense which reduces the crime to a class A felony that the defendant voluntarily caused the release of the victim alive in a safe place before arrest, or within 24 hours after arrest, without having engaged in conduct described in sec. 410(a)(1) or (2) or 420 of this chapter.

Section 11.41.370. Definitions.

In secs. 300-370 of this chapter, unless the context requires otherwise, . . .

(2) "relative" means a parent, stepparent, ancestor, descendant, sibling, uncle, or aunt, including a relative of the same degree through marriage or adoption. . . .

(3) "restrain" means to restrict a person's movements unlawfully and without consent, so as to interfere substantially with his liberty by moving him from one place to another or by confining him either in the place where the restriction commences or in a place to which he has been moved; a restraint is "without consent" if it is accomplished

(A) by acquiescence of the victim, if the victim is under 16 years of age or is an incompetent person and his lawful custodian has not acquiesced in the movement or confinement; or

(B) by force, threat, or deception.

Chapter 31. Attempt and Solicitation

Section 11.31.100. Attempt

(a) A person is guilty of an attempt to commit a crime if, with intent to commit a crime, he engages in conduct which constitutes a substantial step toward the commission of that crime.

(b) In a prosecution under this section, it is not a defense that it was factually or legally impossible to commit the crime which was the object of the attempt if the conduct engaged in by the defendant would be a crime had the circumstances been as he believed them to be.

(c) In a prosecution under this section, it is an affirmative defense that the defendant, under circumstances manifesting a voluntary and complete renunciation of his criminal intent, prevented the commission of the attempted crime.

(d) An attempt is a

(1) class A felony if the crime attempted is murder in any degree or kidnapping;

(2) class B felony if the crime attempted is a class A felony;

(3) class C felony if the crime attempted is a class B felony;

(4) class A misdemeanor if the crime attempted is a class C felony;

(5) class B misdemeanor if the crime attempted is a class A or class B misdemeanor.

Section 11.31.140. Multiple Convictions Barred

(a) It is not a defense to a prosecution under sec. 100 [attempt] or 110 [solicitation] of this chapter that the crime that is the object of the attempt or solicitation was actually committed pursuant to the attempt or solicitation.

(b) A person may not be convicted of more than one crime defined by sec. 100 or 110 of this chapter for conduct designed to commit or culminate in commission of the same crime.

(c) A person may not be convicted on the basis of the same course of conduct of both (1) a crime defined by sec. 100 or 110 of this chapter; and (2) the crime that is the object of the attempt or solicitation.

(d) This section does not bar inclusion of multiple counts in a single indictment or information charging commission of a crime defined by sec. 100 or 110 of this chapter and commission of the crime that is the object of the attempt of solicitation.

Section 11.31.150. Substantive Crimes Involving Attempt or Solicitation.

Notwithstanding sec. 140(d) of this chapter,

(1) a person may not be charged under sec. 100 of this chapter if the crime allegedly attempted by the defendant is defined in such a way that an

attempt to engage in the proscribed conduct constitutes commission of the crime itself; . . .

Section 11.81.610. Construction of Statutes with Respect to Culpability

(a) . . .

(b) Except as provided in AS 11.81.600(b), if a provision of law defining an offense does not prescribe a culpable mental state, the culpable mental state that must be proved with respect to

(1) conduct is "knowingly"; and

(2) a circumstance or a result is "recklessly."

(c) When a provision of law provides that criminal negligence suffices to establish an element of an offense, that element is also established if a person acts intentionally, knowingly, or recklessly. If acting recklessly suffices to establish an element, that element also is established if a person acts intentionally or knowingly. If acting knowingly suffices to establish an element, that element is also established if a person acts intentionally.

Section 11.81.620. Effect of Ignorance or Mistake upon Liability

(a) Knowledge, recklessness, or criminal negligence as to whether conduct constitutes an offense, or knowledge, recklessness, or criminal negligence as to the existence, meaning, or application of the provision of law defining an offense, is not an element of an offense unless the provision clearly so provides. Use of the phrase "intent to commit a crime," "intent to promote or facilitate the commission of a crime," or like terminology in a provision of law does not require that the defendant act with a culpable mental state as to the criminality of the conduct that is the object of the defendant's intent.

(b) A person is not relieved of criminal liability for conduct because the person engages in the conduct under a mistaken belief of fact, unless

(1) the factual mistake is a reasonable one that negates the culpable mental state required for the commission of the offense;

(2) the provision of law defining the offense or a related provision of law expressly provides that the factual mistake constitutes a defense or exemption; or

(3) the factual mistake is a reasonable one that supports a defense of justification as provided in AS 11.81.320-11.81.430.

Section 11.81.630. Intoxication as a Defense

Voluntary intoxication is not a defense to prosecution for an offense, but evidence that the defendant was intoxicated may be offered whenever it is relevant to negate an element of the offense that requires that the defendant intentionally cause a result.

Section 11.81.900. Definitions

(a) For purposes of this title, unless the context requires otherwise,

(1) a person acts "intentionally" with respect to a result described by a provision of law defining an offense when his conscious objective is to cause that result;

(2) a person acts "knowingly" with respect to conduct or to a circumstance described by a provision of law defining an offense when he is aware that his conduct is of that nature or that the circumstance exists; when knowledge of the existence of a particular fact is an element of an offense, that knowledge is established if a person is aware of a substantial probability of its existence, unless he actually believes it does not exist; a person who is unaware of conduct or a circumstance of which he would have been aware had he not been intoxicated acts knowingly with respect to that conduct or circumstance;

(3) a person acts "recklessly" with response to a result or to a circumstance described by provision of law defining an offense when he is aware of and consciously disregards a substantial and unjustifiable risk that the result will occur or that the circumstance exists; the risk must be of such a nature and degree that disregard of it constitutes a gross deviation from the standard of conduct that a reasonable person would observe in the situation; a person who is unaware of a risk of which he would have been aware had he not been intoxicated acts recklessly with respect to that risk;

(4) a person acts with "criminal negligence" with respect to a result or to a circumstance described by a provision of law defining an offense when he fails to perceive a substantial and unjustifiable risk that the result will occur or that the circumstance exists; the risk must be of such a nature and degree that the failure to perceive constitutes a gross deviation from the standard of care that a reasonable person would observe in the situation;

(b) As used in this title, unless otherwise specified or unless the context requires otherwise,

(1) "affirmative defense" means that

(A) some evidence must be admitted which places in issue the defense; and

(B) the defendant has the burden of establishing the defense by a preponderance of the evidence; . . .

(5) "conduct" means an act or omission and its accompanying mental state; . . .

(9) "crime" means an offense for which a sentence of imprisonment is authorized: a crime is either a felony or a misdemeanor;

(10) "culpable mental state" means "intentionally," "knowingly," "recklessly," and with "criminal negligence," as those terms are defined in (a) of this section; . . .

(15) "defense," other than an affirmative defense, means that

(A) some evidence must be admitted which places in issue the defense; and

(B) the state then has the burden of disproving the existence of the defense beyond a reasonable doubt; . . .

(19) "felony" means a crime for which a sentence of imprisonment for a term of more than one year is authorized; . . .

(22) "force" means any bodily impact, restraint, or confinement or the threat of imminent bodily impact, restraint, or confinement; force includes deadly and nondeadly force;

(23) "government" means the United States, and state of any municipality or other political subdivision within the United States or its territories; any department, agency, or subdivision of any of the foregoing; any agency carrying out the functions of government; or any corporation or agency formed under interstate compact or international treaty; . . .

(25) "includes" means "includes but is not limited to";

(26) "incompetent person" means a person who is impaired by reason of mental illness or mental deficiency to the extent that he lacks sufficient understanding or capacity to make or communicate decisions concerning his person;

(27) "intoxicated" means intoxicated from the use of a drug or alcohol;

(28) "law" includes statutes and regulations; . . .

(31) "misdemeanor" means a crime for which a sentence of imprisonment for a term of more than one year may not be imposed; . . .

(33) "offense" means conduct for which a sentence of imprisonment or fine is authorized; an offense is either a crime or a violation; . . .

(39) "person" means a natural person and, when appropriate, an organization, government, or governmental instrumentality;

(40) "physical injury" means physical pain or an impairment of physical condition; . . .

(44) "property" means any article, substance, or thing of value, including money, tangible and intangible personal property, real property, a credit card, choses-in-action, and evidence of debt or of contract, a commodity of a public utility such as gas, electricity, steam, or water constitutes property but the supplying of such commodity to premises from an outside source by means of wires, pipes, conduits, or other equipment is considered a rendition of a service rather than a sale of delivery of property; . . .

(48) a "renunciation" is not "voluntary and complete" if it is substantially motivated, in whole or in part, by

(A) a belief that circumstances exist which increase the probability of detection or apprehension of the defendant or another participant in the criminal enterprise, or which render more difficult the accomplishment of the criminal purpose; or

(B) a decision to postpone the criminal conduct until another time or to transfer the criminal effort to another victim on another but similar objective;

(49) "serious physical injury" means physical injury which creates a substantial risk of death or which causes serious and protracted disfigurement, protracted impairment of health, or protracted loss or impairment of the function of a body member or bodily organ, or physical injury which unlawfully terminates a pregnancy;

(50) "services" includes labor, professional services, transportation, telephone or other communications service, entertainment, the supplying

of food, lodging, or other accommodations in hotels, restaurants, or elsewhere, admission to exhibitions, and the supplying of equipment for use;

(51) "sexual contact" means

(A) the intentional touching, directly or through clothing, by the defendant of the victim's genitals, anus, or female breast; or

(B) the defendant's intentionally causing the victim to touch, directly or through clothing, the defendant's or victim's genitals, anus or female breast;

(52) "sexual penetration" means genital intercourse, cunnilingus, fellatio, anal intercourse, or an intrusion, however slight, of an object or any part of a person's body into the genital or anal opening of another person's body; each party to any of the acts defined as "sexual penetration" is considered to be engaged in sexual penetration; . . .

(54) "threat" means a menace, however communicated, to engage in conduct described in (1)-(7) of AS 11.41.520(a) but under (1) of that subsection includes all threat to inflict physical injury on anyone.

Model Penal Code
(Official Draft 1962)

Section 2.04. Ignorance or Mistake

(1) Ignorance or mistake as to a matter of fact or law is a defense if:

(a) the ignorance or mistake negatives the purpose, knowledge, belief, recklessness or negligence required to establish a material element of the offense; or

(b) the law provides that the state of mind established by such ignorance or mistake constitutes a defense.

(2) Although ignorance or mistake would otherwise afford a defense to the offense charged, the defense is not available if the defendant would be guilty of another offense had the situation been as he supposed. In such case, however, the ignorance or mistake of the defendant shall reduce the grade and degree of the offense of which he may be convicted to those of the offense of which he would be guilty had the situation been as he supposed.

(3) A belief that conduct does not legally constitute an offense is a defense to a prosecution for that offense based upon such conduct when:

(a) the statute or other enactment defining the offense is not known to the actor and has not been published or otherwise reasonably made available prior to the conduct alleged; or

(b) he acts in reasonable reliance upon an official statement of the law, afterward determined to be invalid or erroneous, contained in (i) a statute or other enactment; (ii) a judicial decision, opinion or judgment; (iii) an administrative order or grant of permission; or (iv) an official interpretation of the public officer or body charged by law with responsibility for the interpretation, administration or enforcement of the law defining the offense.

(4) The defendant must prove a defense arising under Subsection (3) of this Section by a preponderance of evidence.

● OVERVIEW OF MISTAKE DEFENSES

Notes

Mistakes and Culpability
    Mistakes vs. Accidents
    General Mistake Defenses
    Exculpatory Mistakes vs. Inculpatory Mistakes
    Mistake at Common Law
        Mistake and General vs. Specific Intent Offenses
    Categories of Exculpatory Mistake
    Rule of Logical Relevance
        Negating Recklessness
        Negating Negligence
        Mistake and Strict Liability
    Common Law: "Reasonable" and "Unreasonable" Mistake Distinction
        Negligent and Reckless Mistakes
        Ambiguity of "Unreasonable" Mistake
        Summary: Culpability Requirements and Mistake Defenses
Mistakes of Law
    Common Law's Rejection of Mistake of Law Defense
    Mistake of Law in Modern Codes
    Mistake of Law Negating Element
    Mixed Fact-Law Mistake
    Mistake as to Criminality of Conduct

MISTAKES AND CULPABILITY

When leaving a restaurant, you take the wrong umbrella from the coatroom by mistake. While you may satisfy the objective elements of theft (an unlicensed taking of another's property), your mistake (mistaken belief that the umbrella you take is your own) means that you do not have the culpable state of mind required for theft; you do not intend to take "property of another." Mistakes that provide a defense in this way, by negating a culpability requirement, are the topic of this section.

Mistakes vs. Accidents Your mistake in taking another's umbrella concerns what is called a "circumstance" element—the ownership of the umbrella. One can also make mistakes as to result elements. Under common language usage, we call these "accidents." While you were *mistaken* as to whose umbrella you took, you *accidentally* drop it under a street-sweeping machine (that is, you claim you have no culpability as to the result of property destruction).

General Mistake Defenses You have just finished reading in the newspaper about a diplomat who is stabbed in the leg with a poison-tipped umbrella. A suspicious-looking man carrying an umbrella at your bus stop looks exactly like the man in the newspaper picture who is sought in the diplomat's death. Just as he seems to be about to stab the distinguished-looking woman in front of him in line, you strike him over the head with your umbrella in an effort to protect her. It turns out that your imagination has been a bit overactive. The "suspect" is entirely innocent; no attack was imminent. Your mistaken belief in an imminent umbrella attack does not negate a culpability element of assault; you *did* intend to hit the suspected attacker without consent. Nonetheless, you may have a defense if your mistake satisfies the conditions of a general defense, such as mistaken defense of another, one of the mistakes as to justification defenses. A mistake also may provide a general defense if you commit an offense but are unaware that your conduct is criminal, because you relied upon an official misstatement of law or because the law you violated was not made reasonably available. Again, such ignorance or mistake of law does not negate an offense element.

Exculpatory Mistakes vs. Inculpatory Mistakes   Mistaken umbrella thefts and mistaken killings are both instances of an actor mistakenly believing that his conduct is not an offense. The reverse type of mistakes also are possible: An actor may believe that he *is* committing an offense when, because of a mistake, he really is not. A downpour starts just as you are leaving the restaurant. Because you lost your umbrella last week, you steal someone else's from the coatroom. When you get outside you find that the umbrella you have "stolen" is your own, apparently "lost" in the coatroom the week before. You satisfy the culpability elements of theft (you have the intention to take the property of another), but you do not satisfy the objective elements (you did not take the property of another). Such instances of mistaken belief that one *is* committing an offense commonly are punished in modern codes as an impossible *attempt* to commit an offense.

Mistake at Common Law   With this general orientation to the various roles of mistake, let us turn to a closer examination of mistake negating a circumstance element of an offense. The Common Law did not recognize a defense of mistake negating an offense element. Rather than seeing mistake defenses as logical corollaries of culpability requirements, courts conceived of mistake defenses as independent doctrines. Thus, while each offense had a culpability requirement—a specific intent or a general intent, or strict liability—a court nonetheless would commonly analyze the public policy arguments for and against recognizing a particular kind of mistake defense and announce an appropriate rule.[1] This was done even by courts that eagerly confirmed that the legality principle forbade the judicial creation or redefinition of offenses. In the courts' view, mistakes concerned independent matters of exculpation and, therefore, like other *defenses,* could be created and refined by the courts. They did not see that the definition of a mistake defense necessarily had the effect of defining the offense culpability that would be adequate for liability.

Mistake and General vs. Specific Intent Offenses   In time, some courts saw a connection between mistake defenses and culpability requirements. A general principle developed in these courts that defined the mistake defense in terms of the culpability requirements of the offense: An honest mistake provided a defense to a specific intent offense; only a reasonable mistake provided a defense to a general intent offense; no mistake could provide a defense to an offense of strict liability. (Note the "offense analysis," as opposed to "element analysis," basis

---

1. See, e.g., Regina v. Prince, 13 Cox's Crim. Cases 138 (1875).

of the rule; it assumes each offense has a single culpability requirement.) While courts felt free to deviate from this general rule, ad hoc, it nonetheless was of central importance to the development of the modern view. At the very least, the principle recognized some logical connection between culpability requirements and mistake defenses.

CATEGORIES OF EXCULPATORY MISTAKE

Rule of Logical Relevance Model Penal Code Section 2.04(1)(a) states the modern view:

> Ignorance or mistake as to a matter of fact or law is a defense if the ignorance or mistake negatives the purpose, knowledge, belief, recklessness or negligence required to establish a material element of the offense. . . .

In other words, a mistake is a defense if it negates a required culpability element. This is sometimes called the "rule of logical relevance"; mistake evidence is relevant if it is logically related to an offense culpability requirement. While the principle is simple, its application sometimes is difficult because it is not always easy to determine the culpability requirements of an offense. Nonetheless, determination of an offense's culpability elements is the only means in a modern code by which one can determine the kind of mistake, if any, that will provide a defense.

Negating Recklessness Where recklessness is required, the defendant will have a defense if his mistake is reasonable or only negligent. In *Laseter v. State*,[2] for example, a general provision similar to Model Penal Code Section 2.02(3) read in a requirement of "recklessness" as to lack of consent in a rape.[3] The defendant claimed that he believed the victim consented. The jury was instructed that to qualify as a defense, the defendant's mistake as to the victim's consent had to be reasonable. But if recklessness as to lack of consent is required, either a reasonable (non-negligent) *or a negligent mistake* should provide a defense; either would show the absence of the required recklessness. If the mistake were a negligent one, then by definition Laseter would not have been aware of his mistake (even if he should have been) and thus could not have consciously disregarded a substantial risk that he was mistaken. The instruction given, requiring a reasonable mistake, gave too narrow a mistake defense. Laseter's conviction was reversed. (The defendant had requested an instruction that would have required the state to show that the defendant "was subjectively aware" that the victim did not consent, but this could have been misinterpreted as requiring knowledge as to lack of consent, and therefore would have given too broad a mistake defense.)

Negating Negligence Where negligence is required, a reasonable (or non-negligent) mistake will provide a defense. In *State v. Elton*,[4] for example, a general provision was used to read in "negligence" as to the age of the underage partner in statutory rape. The trial court excluded the defendant's proffered evidence that his mistake as to age was reasonable. The reasonableness (non-negligence) of his belief would have negated the negligence as to age required for liability. The conviction was reversed.

---

2. 684 P.2d 139 (Alaska Ct. App. 1984).
3. See Alaska Stat. § 11.81.610(b).
4. 680 P.2d 727 (Utah 1984).

Mistake and Strict Liability   Where no culpability is required, no mistake, even a reasonable (non-negligent) mistake, will provide a defense. In a Pennsylvania statutory rape case, *Commonwealth v. Robinson*,[5] for example, a special code provision imposed strict liability as to age for certain sex offenses. The court held that the special provision preempted application of a general provision, which would have required at least negligence as to age.[6] Thus, even a reasonable mistake as to age was no defense. The larger point here is that the culpability required by the offense definition, whatever it may be, determines the kind of mistakes that will provide a defense.

Common Law: "Reasonable"—"Unreasonable" Mistake Distinction   A carryover from the Common Law period is our tendency to speak of "reasonable" and "unreasonable" mistakes. This terminology was adequate when an honest, albeit "unreasonable," mistake provided a defense to a specific intent offense, but only a "reasonable" mistake provided a defense to a general intent offense. However, with the advent of modern culpability rules, including the provision that mistake is a defense when it negates a required culpability element, the terms "reasonable" and "unreasonable" became inadequate to recognize the relevant distinctions. A "reasonable" mistake can be accurately translated into modern code terms as a "non-negligent" mistake. But an "unreasonable" mistake has an ambiguous meaning in modern terms. A mistake might be unreasonable either because it is a negligent mistake or because it is a reckless mistake, and the difference can be significant.

Negligent and Reckless Mistakes   In modern codes, a *negligent mistake* occurs when an actor is unaware of a substantial risk that the required circumstance exists and a reasonable person would have been aware—for example, it never occurs to him that the umbrella he takes is not his own, but a reasonable person would be aware of this possibility. A *reckless mistake* occurs when an actor is aware of a substantial risk that the required circumstance exists—for example, he is aware of a substantial risk that the umbrella might not be his, although he thinks it probably is. A reckless mistake will provide a defense only when the offense requires purpose or knowledge as to the circumstance. By contrast, a negligent mistake will provide a defense whenever purpose, knowledge, or recklessness is required.

Ambiguity of "Unreasonable" Mistake   The ambiguity of the term *unreasonable mistake* in including both negligent and reckless mistakes is particularly problematic because it makes it impossible to describe the kind of mistake that will provide a defense in the most common situation: where recklessness is required. Recall that recklessness typically is the minimum culpability required and is the culpability read in by Model Penal Code Section 2.02(3) whenever the required culpability is not stated. Where recklessness is required, a negligent mistake will provide a defense, but a reckless mistake will not. Thus, the distinction between reckless and negligent mistakes describes the borderline of criminality, but the term *unreasonable mistake* includes both kinds of mistakes and makes it impossible accurately to describe the borderline. To give a defense for an "unreasonable" mistake is improperly to give a defense to a reckless mistake (recklessness satisfies the required culpability); to deny a defense for an "unreasonable" mistake

---

5. 399 A.2d 1084 (Pa. Super. 1979), aff'd, 438 A.2d 964 (981).
6. Model Penal Code § 213.6(1).

is to improperly deny a defense for a negligent mistake (negligence falls short of the required culpability of recklessness). A better course is to avoid use of the term *unreasonable mistake* and to use the more specific terms *reckless mistake* and *negligent mistake*.

Summary: Culpability Requirements and Mistake Defenses The relation between culpability requirements and mistake defenses, in Model Penal Code culpability terms and in the common law terms of *reasonable* and *unreasonable*, may be summarized as follows:

Chart: Translation Between Culpability Requirements and Mistake Defenses

Culpability requirement	Using MPC culpability terms, negated by:	Using common law reasonable—unreasonable terms, negated by:
"purposely"	any mistake	any mistake
"knowingly"	any mistake (i.e., reckless, negligent, or faultless)	any mistake (i.e., reasonable or unreasonable)
"recklessly"	a negligent or faultless mistake	an unreasonable (in the sense of a "negligent"[7]) or a reasonable mistake
"negligently"	a faultless mistake	a reasonable mistake
none (strict liability)	no negation (not even faultless mistake)	no negation (not even reasonable mistake)

MISTAKES OF LAW

Common Law's Rejection of Mistake of Law Defense At Common Law, mistake or ignorance as to a matter of fact might have provided a defense, as described above, but mistake or ignorance as to a matter of law did not. All persons were presumed by the law to know the law. In *State v. Woods*,[8] for example, the defendant was charged with violation of Vermont's "Blanket Act," which, among other things, punished "a woman [if she is found in bed together] *with another woman's husband* . . . under circumstances affording presumption of an illicit intention."[9] Defendant Woods had married a man from Vermont after the man's divorce in Reno, Nevada. However, the Reno divorce, and thus her own marriage to the man, was invalid. She contended that her honest belief in the validity of the Reno divorce and of her subsequent marriage provided a defense. The court held, however, that even if her belief were reasonable it could not be a defense because it was "a mistake of law rather than a mistake of fact," citing the maxim "*Ignorantia legis non excusat*" (ignorance of the law does not excuse) and "the corresponding presumption that everyone is conclusively presumed to know the law."[10] Any other rule, it was feared, would encourage people to remain

---

7. Importantly, however, note that there was no defense under the Common Law for an "unreasonable," in the sense of a "reckless," mistake. It is this point at which the reasonable-unreasonable terminology breaks down in its translation to modern culpability terms. This is a particularly serious problem given that "recklessness" is the norm—the most common culpability required as to circumstance elements.

8. 179 A. 1 (Vt. 1935).

9. Vt. Pub. L. § 8602 (1933) (emphasis added).

10. *Woods*, 179 A. at 356-357.

ignorant of the law and, in any case, was thought to allow defendants to raise frivolous yet hard-to-disprove claims in every case.

Mistake of Law in Modern Codes   The concern to avoid a flood of mistake-of-law claims might have been justified at a time when "the law of mistake" was seen as independent of an offense's defined culpability requirements. Presumably, it was within the power of the court to recognize a defense for any mistake in any case. Under modern codes, however, where the potential for a mistake defense is defined, and therefore limited, by the requirements of the legislature's offense definition, no such danger exists. A mistake of law provides a defense under modern codes *if it negates a required culpability element.* In practice, this does not frequently occur because most circumstance elements concern factual rather than legal matters.

Mistake of Law Negating Element   In the *Woods* case described above, one circumstance element of the offense requires that the defendant be in bed with "another woman's husband." Therefore, under normal rules of modern codes, some culpability is required as to the partner being "another woman's husband." (Recklessness would be read in by Model Penal Code Section 2.02(3).) A reasonable belief in the validity of the man's divorce and remarriage would mean lack of culpability as to the man being "another woman's husband" and would provide a defense.

Mixed Fact-Law Mistake   In some common law cases, Woods's mistake might have been called a factual mistake as to a legal matter, sometimes called a "mixed fact/law mistake."[11] Whether the man in *Woods* is single or married might be described as a fact, but admittedly it is an issue that depends upon legal matters; marriage and divorce are legal concepts. Many circumstance elements of offenses are in some part legal concepts, such as ownership of property, privilege to enter, and status as a fiduciary. Under modern codes, however, the fact-law distinction is irrelevant and such categorization issues are avoided. Any mistake, fact or law, will provide a defense if it negates an offense element.

Mistake as to Criminality of Conduct   An actor frequently may wish to claim a mistake as to whether the offense conduct was in fact a crime. That is, while the actor knew the circumstances that in fact constitute the offense— for example, he knew he was entering the United States and he knew he possessed certain vegetables—the actor may claim that he or she did not realize such conduct constituted an offense under the Customs laws. The same principle— mistake of law or fact is a defense if it negates an element—can work to provide a defense for a mistake as to whether one's conduct is criminal. This application of the defense is rarer, however, because culpability as to the unlawfulness of one's conduct is rarely an element of an offense. Model Penal Code Section 2.02(9) expressly provides that such culpability as to the criminality of one's conduct is never to be "read in" or assumed to be an element; it must be explicitly provided by the offense definition.[12] Nevertheless, some offense definitions do explicitly or implicitly require culpability as to the criminality of the conduct. In *People v. Weiss,* for example, the defendants "arrested" one Paul H. Wendel, believing him to be the kidnapper of the Lindbergh baby.[13] He was not. Defendants were charged with kidnapping: "A person who wilfully seizes, confines, [etc. another],

---

11. See Glanville Williams, Criminal Law: The General Part 334 (1961).
12. Model Penal Code § 2.02(9).
13. 12 N.E.2d 514 (N.Y. 1938).

with intent to cause him, *without authority of law*, to be . . . in any way held . . . against his will . . . is guilty of kidnapping."[14] Defendants claimed that they had been deputized by the New Jersey Secret Service, or so they believed, and therefore believed they had authority for the "arrest." On appeal, the court held that their mistaken belief that their conduct was lawful provided a defense because the statute required that they intend to act "without authority of law." Their conviction was reversed. Indeed, the Supreme Court has held that a "wilfully" requirement in federal criminal statutes often should be interpreted to require proof of a "voluntary, intentional violation of a known legal duty."[15]

People v. Olsen

Supreme Court of California
36 Cal. 3d 638, 685 P.2d 52 (1984)

BIRD, C. J.

[Shawn M., 13 years and 10 months old at that time, was sleeping in her family's camper trailer parked in the driveway in front of the house, while her family had visiting guests. On her third night in the trailer, Olsen and Garcia entered the trailer to engage in sexual intercourse with Shawn. Michael M., Shawn's father, entered the trailer while Olsen was having intercourse with Shawn. Garcia stabbed Michael M. as he and Olsen fled. At trial, there was conflicting testimony as to whether the intercourse was consensual. Olsen and Garcia denying Shawn's claims that they forced her to have intercourse. Shawn admitted, however, to lying to Olsen and Garcia, claiming that she was 16 years old and even conceding that she looked as if she were at least 16.]

At the conclusion of the trial, the court found Garcia and appellant guilty of violating section 288, subdivision (a).[16] In reaching its decision, the court rejected defense counsel's argument that a good faith belief as to the age of the victim was a defense to the section 288 charge. Appellant was sentenced to the lower term of three years in state prison. This appeal followed. . . .

Twenty years ago, this court in People v. Hernandez [61 Cal. 2d 529, 393 P.2d 673 (1964)], overruled established precedent, and held that an accused's good faith, reasonable belief that a victim was 18 years or more of age was a defense to a charge of statutory rape.[17] . . .

One Court of Appeal has declined to apply *Hernandez* in an analogous context. In People v. Lopez (1969) 271 Cal. App.2d 754, 77 Cal. Rptr. 59, the court refused to recognize a reasonable mistake of age defense to a charge of offering or furnishing marijuana to a minor. The court noted that the act of furnishing marijuana is criminal regardless of the age of the recipient and that furnishing

---

14. *Weiss*, 12 N.E.2d at 514 (emphasis added).

15. See, e.g., Cheek v. United States, 498 U.S. 192 (1991).

16. Garcia was also found guilty of assault with a deadly weapon with infliction of great bodily injury. Both Garcia and appellant were found not guilty of burglary, forcible rape, and lewd or lascivious acts upon a child under the age of 14 by use of force.

17. One commentator believes that *Hernandez* marked a clear break from the "universally accepted view of the courts in this country." (Annot., *Mistake or Lack of Information as to Victim's Age as Defense to Statutory Rape* (1966) 8 A.L.R.3d 1100, 1102-1105, and cases cited.) The view that mistake of age is not a defense to a charge of statutory rape still prevails in the overwhelming majority of jurisdictions.

marijuana to a minor simply yields a greater punishment than when the substance is furnished to an adult. "[A] mistake of fact relating only to the gravity of an offense will not shield a deliberate offender from the full consequences of the wrong actually committed." (Ibid.)

. . . There exists a strong public policy to protect children of tender years. [S]ection 288 was enacted for that very purpose. Furthermore, even the *Hernandez* court recognized this important policy when it made clear that it did not contemplate applying the mistake of age defense in cases where the victim is of "tender years." . . .

This conclusion is supported by the Legislature's enactment of section 1203.066. Subdivision (a)(3) of that statute renders certain individuals convicted of lewd or lascivious conduct who "honestly and reasonably believed the victim was 14 years old or older" eligible for probation. The Legislature's enactment of section 1203.066, subdivision (a)(3) . . . strongly indicates that the Legislature did not intend such a defense to a section 288 charge. To recognize such a defense would render section 1203.066, subdivision (a)(3) a nullity, since the question of probation for individuals who had entertained an honest and reasonable belief in the victim's age would never arise.

Other legislative provisions also support the holding that a reasonable mistake of age is not a defense to a section 288 charge. Time and again, the Legislature has recognized that persons under 14 years of age are in need of special protection. . . .

The Legislature has also determined that persons who commit sexual offenses on children under the age of 14 should be punished more severely than those who commit such offenses on children under the age of 18. . . .

It is significant that a violation of section 288 carries a much harsher penalty than does unlawful sexual intercourse (§ 261.5), the crime involved in *Hernandez*. Section 261.5 carries a maximum punishment of one year in the county jail or three years in state prison, while section 288 carries a maximum penalty of eight years in state prison. The different penalties for these two offenses further support the view that there exists a strong public policy to protect children under 14. . . .

The legislative purpose of section 288 would not be served by recognizing a defense of reasonable mistake of age. . . . Accordingly, the judgment of conviction is affirmed.

GRODIN, J., Concurring and Dissenting.

I agree that the enactment of Penal Code section 1203.066, which renders eligible for probation persons convicted of lewd or lascivious conduct who "honestly and reasonably believed the victim was 14 years old or older" is persuasive evidence that in the eyes of the Legislature such a belief is not a defense to the crime.[18] What troubles me is the notion that a person who acted with such belief,

---

18. "I do not agree that legislative intent to eliminate good faith mistake of fact as a defense can be inferred from the imposition of relatively higher penalties for that crime. On the contrary, as this court has stated in connection with the crime of bigamy: 'The severe penalty imposed . . . the serious loss of reputation conviction entails, the infrequency of the offense, and the fact that it has been regarded . . . as a crime involving moral turpitude, make it extremely unlikely that the Legislature meant to include the morally innocent to make sure the guilty did not escape.'" (People v. Vogel (1956) 46 Cal. 2d 798, 804, 299 P.2d 850).

and is not otherwise shown to be guilty of any criminal conduct,[19] may not only be convicted but be sentenced to prison notwithstanding his eligibility for probation when it appears that his belief did not accord with reality. To me, that smacks of cruel or unusual punishment.

. . . I recognize . . . that our legal system includes certain "strict liability" crimes, but generally these are confined to the so-called "regulatory" or "public welfare" offenses. . . . (Morissette v. United States (1952) 342 U.S. 246). Moreover, with respect to such crimes, "*The accused, if he does not will the violation, usually is in a position to prevent it with no more care than society might reasonably expect . . . from one who assumed his responsibilities. Also, penalties commonly are relatively small, and conviction does no grave damage to an offender's reputation.*" (Id., at p. 256, italics added.)

. . . No doubt the standard of what is reasonable must be set relatively high in order to accomplish the legislative objective of protecting persons under 14 years of age against certain conduct. Perhaps it is not enough that a person "looks" to be more than 14; perhaps there is a duty of reasonable inquiry besides. At some point, however, the belief becomes reasonable by any legitimate standard, so that one would say the defendant is acting in a way which is no different from the way our society would expect a reasonable, careful, and law-abiding citizen to act.

At that point, it seems to me, the imposition of criminal sanctions, particularly imprisonment, simply cannot be tolerated in a civilized society. . . .

▲ PROBLEMS

Stomach, Kidney, Whatever (#23)

Alida Lamour is an elderly woman suffering from a litany of health problems. She is diabetic, blind, shows signs of dementia, and has end-stage renal disease. As a result of her failing kidneys, she has been undergoing dialysis and has a catheter in place for that purpose. The catheter is meant to allow blood to be drawn from Lamour so that toxins can be filtered out by the dialysis machine in lieu of her kidneys. While she is certainly not well, she is not in imminent danger of dying, and is stable enough to be transferred from a medical center to a nursing home. When she arrives at the home, Dr. Einaugler is the physician on call. Her medical charts are, unfortunately, not transferred with her, and Einaugler, without the aid of any medical history, mistakes the dialysis catheter for a feeding tube. He therefore orders nurses to pump nutritional solution into the catheter.

---

19. The People suggest that defendant was at least guilty of "sexual intercourse accomplished with a female not the wife of the perpetrator, where the female is under the age of 18 years." Defendant was neither charged nor convicted of that offense, however, and it is by no means clear from the record that he had sexual intercourse with the victim.

Einaugler's mistake is discovered by the nurses 36 hours later, when Lamour's condition deteriorates. The excess fluids that have built up in her abdomen are quickly removed, and though she is vomiting and having problems breathing, her condition stabilizes. The nurses call Einaugler at 6:00 a.m. about the mistake. Einaugler, in turn, consults with a physician at the hospital, who advises that Lamour be transferred to the hospital's emergency room. However, as her condition is again stable, Einaugler decides that she is not an emergency. He waits ten hours, during which time he checks her condition another two times. That evening, however, her condition begins to deteriorate, and Einaugler finally decides to have Lamour transferred to the ER. By this time, the hospital's dialysis team is no longer available, and Lamour is unable to receive dialysis until two days later, putting her life in danger.

Leaving aside tort liability for medical malpractice, what criminal liability for Dr. Einaugler, if any, under the Model Penal Code? Prepare a list of all criminal code subsections in the order in which you rely upon them in your analysis.

Life-Saving Necrophilia (#24)

Nino is an 18-year-old Romanian living in Bucharest, the capital city. After a fight with her boyfriend, she decides to medicate her problems away. She takes a good quantity of sleeping pills, chasing them with many drinks. As a result, she collapses and is taken to the hospital, where physicians make repeated unsuccessful efforts to revive her. She is declared dead and her body is sent to a morgue.

Giorgi, a morgue attendant, has also had a few drinks. When Nino's body is brought in, Giorgi finds it attractive. During a break in work, he decides to have intercourse with the body, thinking that no one will ever find out about it. He is greatly shocked when during the intercourse the supposedly dead Nino wakes up. Apparently Giorgi's intercourse succeeds in reviving Nino where the doctors had failed.

What liability for Giorgi, if any, under the Model Penal Code? Prepare a list of all criminal code subsections in the order in which you rely upon them in your analysis.

✳ DISCUSSION ISSUE

What Kind of Mistake as to Consent, If Any, Should Be Permitted to Provide a Defense to Rape?

Materials presenting each side of this Discussion Issue appear in the Advanced Materials for Section 5 in Appendix A.

OVERVIEW OF THE FUNCTIONS OF CRIMINAL LAW DOCTRINE

Notes

Criminal law doctrines integrate three important functions, each of which is necessary for criminal law to operate: rule articulation; liability assignment; and liability grading. *Rule articulation* informs everyone, before they act, what behavior is allowed and what is not; *liability assignment* determines, after the fact, whether a particular person who has engaged in prohibited behavior will be punished as a criminal offender; and *liability grading* determines how much punishment such an offender should receive. These functions will be discussed in greater detail below, but consider the following situation and what questions arise for assessing possible criminal liability.

Hypothetical: Your Basement Burglar

You are awakened by an unfamiliar sound from the basement garage of your row house. As you sit up in bed, the handgun in your hall closet comes to mind. Then you remember Earl Miller, a neighbor down the block who shot and killed a night burglar in his garage last year. The prosecutor said Earl had no right to kill the burglar. Earl's attorney claimed that Earl did in fact have the right and that even if he didn't—although she was sure he did—Earl honestly and reasonably believed he had the right. Earl was tried and acquitted. You aren't sure what that means for you. Can you or can't you lawfully shoot a burglar in your basement garage?

You grab your gun from the hall closet and head down to the first floor. The light switch is at the top of the basement stairs. You open the door quietly, flip the switch, and draw back into the dark hall. The sound of steps is followed by the shattering of glass, a muffled scream then silence. On descending the stairs, you find the intruder standing by the back door. You quickly aim, squeeze . . . shoot! After recovering from the recoil of the handgun you realize that you missed the intruder. You are about to squeeze off another round, but it occurs to you that the intruder is motionless. A closer look shows him to be unconscious, hanging from the back door with his arm through the door's broken window. Blood is pouring from a cut in his neck.

You believe you can stop the bleeding by applying pressure, but you don't really want to help the man. After all, you think, he might have intended to steal from you. And on top of that, the gushing blood and mess make you wince. Should you help him? Must you? You aren't sure. You remember a newspaper story about a motorist who stood and watched another motorist bleed to death after their cars collided. The prosecutor claimed that the motorist could have and should have stopped the bleeding, but he stood and watched . . . which is exactly what you are doing now. The motorist's attorney claimed that he had no legal duty to act and, in any case, was dazed from the accident and unable to think clearly. The man was tried and acquitted. What does that mean for you? If you can, must you help the intruder? Will you be a criminal if you just stand and do nothing?

You wish you weren't thinking so clearly. Perhaps it would have been better if you had just fallen down the stairs and been dazed. Not a good time to be making jokes, you conclude.

Would it have been legal for you to shoot the burglar in your basement? Are you criminally liable for not helping?

INTRODUCTION: THREE FUNCTIONS

Criminal law rules serve three primary functions. As you read this subsection and the following ones, recalling the burglar hypothetical above and ask yourself which function each question in the hypothetical addresses and how the law's rules help resolve those questions.

Rule Articulation First, criminal law must define the conduct that it prohibits (or requires). The rules of conduct provide direction to the members of the community as to the conduct they must avoid (or must perform) upon pain of criminal sanction. This may be termed the *rule articulation* function of criminal law.

Assigning Liability   Once a violation of the rules of conduct occurs, the criminal law must take on another role, deciding whether the violation is sufficiently blameworthy to merit criminal liability. Many instances of prohibited conduct are accidental, involuntary, coerced, or otherwise blameless, and criminal law must have rules to ensure that its sanctions are imposed only on violators who merit punishment. This second function, setting the minimum conditions for *assigning liability*, is part of the adjudication process. It assesses *ex post* whether an actor who has violated a rule of conduct ought to be held criminally liable for that violation.

Liability Grading   Finally, where liability is imposed, criminal law must assess the relative seriousness of the violation and the blameworthiness of the offender to determine how much punishment is appropriate. While the first, liability-assigning step in the adjudication process expresses a binary yes-or-no decision as to whether *any* punishment is appropriate, this second step, the *grading* function, expresses a judgment of degree.[20]

Functions Cut Across Doctrinal Distinctions   These three functions (rule articulation, liability assignment, and grading) are the primary functions of criminal law doctrine, but the current doctrinal structure in American criminal law (offense definitions, defenses, and imputation rules), does a poor job of tracking these functions. For example, some elements of offenses may articulate conduct rules while other elements express liability-assignment or grading rules. Nor are the different functions precisely captured by the traditional distinctions between types of offense elements: *actus reus* and *mens rea*, or objective and culpability elements. Similarly, some defenses serve one function while other defenses serve other functions. To give a sense of which doctrines serve which functions requires a review of most aspects of the doctrine.

DOCTRINES OF RULE ARTICULATION

The conduct rules of the rule-articulation doctrines state both prohibitions and requirements. For example, a theft offense might define a specific form of prohibited conduct as follows: No person shall take, exercise control over, or transfer property of another without consent of the owner.

Presumably, your basement burglar was in the process of violating this prohibition, as well as one that prohibits trespass, or entry without consent. These prohibitions describe prohibited conduct in terms of the surrounding circumstances in which it occurs: One's act of taking must involve "property of another" and occur "without consent of the owner." The same act (of possessing or exerting control over property) would be perfectly acceptable in other circumstances (if it were one's own property, or if the owner gave permission to use it). Other offenses define prohibited conduct in terms of harmful or wrongful results that the conduct risks: No person shall engage in conduct that creates a risk of death to another person. Thus, much of the criminal law's rule-articulation function is performed by the conduct and circumstance elements of offense definition.

---

20. For a general discussion, see Paul H. Robinson, *A Functional Analysis of Criminal Law*, 88 Nw. U. L. Rev. 857 (1994); Paul H. Robinson, *Rules of Conduct and Principles of Adjudication*, 57 U. Chi. L. Rev. 729 (1990).

Duties and Omissions   The law not only prohibits some conduct, but also affirmatively requires other conduct, imposing rules such as:

- All legal custodians of a child must protect the child's health and safety.
- All persons over the age of 18 must register with the Selective Service System.

You may have a similar legal duty to save the life of the helpless bleeding burglar. The law creates many duties and punishes the failure to perform them. The law's statement of legal duties, then, serves part of the law's rule-articulation function.

Secondary Prohibitions   In addition to these "primary violations" are what may be called "secondary violations." Secondary violations are not independent prohibitions, but rather prohibitions defined by reference to the primary rules. Not only are persons bound to avoid conduct that would be a primary prohibition, but also:

- No person shall engage in conduct that assists another person in conduct that would be a violation of the rules of conduct.
- No person shall engage in conduct that constitutes a substantial step toward a violation of the rules of conduct.

Thus, additional aspects of the criminal law's rule-articulation function are performed by the conduct and circumstance elements of such secondary prohibitions as complicity and inchoate offenses.

Rule Articulation via Culpability Elements   Not all rule-articulation doctrines are objective elements, like conduct and circumstance elements. Some culpability elements also serve to define rules of conduct. That is, culpability elements can be necessary elements in describing the conduct that the criminal law prohibits. For example, in the general attempt offense, the conduct and circumstance elements of the offense provide some statement of the prohibition, but these objective elements, standing alone, do not fully define the prohibited conduct. The requirement that the conduct constitute a "substantial step toward commission of an offense," which is common in modern attempt definitions,[21] is inadequate in itself to define the prohibited conduct. As a purely objective matter, some conduct that constitutes a "substantial step toward commission of an offense" may in fact be entirely innocent and acceptable conduct. Your shooting a target in your basement may not be an offense. However, such conduct becomes unacceptable and a societal harm when accompanied by an intention to violate the substantive rules of conduct. That is, the same conduct (shooting) becomes potentially criminal if accompanied by an intention to shoot another person, rather than to simply shoot at a target. Similarly, lighting one's pipe is not a violation of the rules of conduct, unless it is a step in a plan to ignite a neighbor's haystack. Thus, to describe the minimum requirements of prohibited conduct, the definition of a criminal attempt must include a state of mind requirement: the intention to engage in conduct that would constitute a rule violation.

---

21. See Model Penal Code § 5.01(1)(c).

Rule Articulation via Offense Modifications Also serving the rule-articulation function are miscellaneous doctrines outside of offense definitions. Recall that these doctrines, such as the consent defense, further modify or refine the conduct rules. For example, while the rules prohibit conduct that risks causing bodily harm, they also provide an exception to the prohibition where the victim consents to a risk of minor injury or where the risk arises from participation in a lawful sporting event.[22]

Justification Defenses Taken together, these rule-articulation doctrines give a complete account of what a person must not do or must do in order to obey the criminal law. They are not, however, a complete statement of the rules of conduct. The law recognizes that in some instances a greater harm can be avoided, or a greater good can be achieved, by allowing a person to violate a prohibition. Burning another person's property is a violation, but it is tolerated (even encouraged) if the burning acts as a firebreak to save a town. Striking another person without consent is a violation, but is to be tolerated if done by a police officer when necessary to overcome resistance to a lawful arrest. These doctrines of justification define permissions rather than prohibitions; they tell persons when they are permitted to violate a rule of conduct.[23] Looking at the "Basement Burglar" hypothetical, while your attempt to shoot another person normally would be illegal, it may be justified if it serves to protect yourself and your family from an unlawful attack.

Confusion in Rules of Conduct The rules of lawful conduct frequently are unclear even to actors who are intelligent, thoughtful, and informed. May you lawfully shoot the intruding burglar? Does the law require that you aid the helpless burglar? In the "Basement Burglar" hypothetical, the actor knows the disposition of a recently litigated case closely analogous to each dilemma confronted, and seeks to use those cases as guides to what conduct is legal, yet remains unable to discern the applicable legal rules. Such uncertainty is not uncommon in our current system. Frequently, neither existing statements of the law nor our process of public adjudication effectively communicates the rules that define lawful conduct. Unfortunately, current criminal law doctrine does a poor job at one of its most important functions: Telling people what they can, must, and must not do, under threat of criminal sanction.

Need for Clear Rules Our condemnation and punishment of criminal law violators, as distinguished from civil violators, rests on an assumption that a criminal violation entails some consciousness of wrongdoing, or at least a gross deviation from a clearly defined standard of conduct. But how can such an assumption be sustained if the demands of the law are unclear? How can we condemn and punish violations of the rules of conduct if the rules are not, and cannot reasonably be, known by the general public? One also may wonder how effective the criminal law can be in deterring criminal conduct if the law's demands are unclear.

---

22. See, e.g., Model Penal Code § 2.11.

23. For a further discussion of the doctrines of justification and their relation to the doctrines of criminalization, see Paul H. Robinson, Rules of Conduct and Principles of Adjudication, 57 U. CHI. L. REV. 729, 740-742 (1990).

DOCTRINES OF LIABILITY

The liability function of criminal law doctrine arises from the special condemnatory nature of criminal law, which leads the law to shun punishment of inadvertent or unavoidable violations. If the actor's conduct is blameless, liability ought not to be imposed, even though the actor may have violated the terms of the rules of conduct.[24] The moral base of the criminal law is such that only violations of sufficient seriousness, committed with sufficient blameworthiness, will justify the condemnation that attends criminal liability.

Offense Culpability Element   To ensure this minimum level of blameworthiness, the law requires proof of an actor's culpability as to each of an offense's conduct rules.[25] Thus, in the "Basement Burglar" scenario, the "burglar" has committed burglary only if he knew he was entering another's house without permission. If, because all of the row houses are identical and he just moved in next door, he had entered your garage honestly believing it to be his own, his trespass might be a violation of the rules of conduct, but might lack the culpability required to support criminal liability. Generally, the law requires at least recklessness as to each such objective element. Thus, an actor must be aware of a substantial risk that his conduct may (for example) cause another's death, or obstruct a highway.[26]

Culpability Offense Modifications   Some of the requirements for ensuring an actor's blameworthiness appear outside the offense definition. Recall that the *de minimis* defense bars liability if the actor's conduct, though amounting to a violation of the rules, was "too trivial to warrant the condemnation of conviction."[27] The renunciation defense similarly refines the blameworthiness requirements for inchoate offenses. (Voluntary renunciation of one's criminal project undercuts the blame that otherwise would apply to one's intention to violate the conduct rules.)

Voluntariness Doctrines   In addition, the minimum requirements of blameworthiness are set by such doctrines as the voluntariness requirement in commission offenses, the capacity requirement for omission liability, and the requirement in possession offenses that the actor know of the possession for a period of time sufficient to terminate possession. These requirements are designed to ensure that the actor could have avoided the violation, for only then should the actor be blamed for not avoiding it. Thus, the motorist who fails to help an accident victim might be acquitted if his dazed condition made it impossible for him to help.

Excuse Defenses   The general excuse defenses—such as insanity, immaturity, involuntary intoxication, and duress—serve a function analogous to the voluntariness doctrines noted above. While most actors have the capacity to follow the rules, in the unusual case an actor may suffer a disability—insanity, immaturity, intoxication, or coercion—and its effects may be such that he or she cannot

---

24. "The general purposes of the provisions governing the definition of offenses are: . . . to safeguard conduct that is without fault from condemnation as criminal." Model Penal Code § 1.02.

25. See Model Penal Code § 2.02(1).

26. See Model Penal Code § 210.3 (defining manslaughter as criminal homicide committed recklessly); § 250.7(1) (defining violation for recklessly rendering highway impassable).

27.   Model Penal Code § 2.12(2).

reasonably be expected to avoid violating the conduct rules. The mistake excuses also are of this category, but their excusing conditions operate in a different way.

Similarity in Function of Culpability Requirements and Excuses Offense definitions' culpability requirements, noted above, serve a purpose similar to these voluntariness and excuse doctrines, although they function in a slightly different way. We assume that most conduct is voluntary, most omitted conduct was possible, and most possession knowing. It is the unusual case, frequently where the actor suffers some disability, where an assumption of voluntariness, capacity to act, or knowledge of possession is not warranted. In contrast, it is common that an actor may be unaware of some characteristic or circumstance of his or her conduct—that is, it is common that an actor may lack the culpability an offense definition requires. People frequently make mistakes and inadvertently create risks. Culpability requirements are designed to exclude these common, blameless violations.

DOCTRINES OF GRADING

The rules of conduct and doctrines of liability provide the starting point for the grading function. The rule-articulation doctrines contain many of the most important factors in assessing the degree of punishment an actor deserves, for they define the harm or evil of the offense. Assessing the relative seriousness of an offense requires (among other things) an assessment of the relative value of the full range of interests protected by the criminal law: protecting against injury, property damage, fraud, sexual predation, and so on. How should we assess the relative gravity of offenses against these different interests? Criminal law theorists have only recently attempted to formulate principles for determining the relative seriousness of violations.

Culpability Level In addition to the harm or evil of an offense, an actor's deserved punishment will depend on his other level of culpability. Culpability greater than the minimum required for liability frequently increases the actor's deserved punishment. Purposely causing a death is more culpable than recklessly doing so, which is more culpable than negligently doing so. Thus, culpability elements that require more than the minimum needed to establish criminal liability serve the grading function by distinguishing the case of greater culpability from the case of minimum culpability.

Result and Causation Requirements Result elements and causation requirements also serve a grading function. Most codes have a provision like the Model Penal Code's attempt offense, which provides in part:

> A person is guilty of an attempt to commit a crime if . . .
> when causing a particular result is an element of the crime, [he] does or omits
> to do anything with the purpose of causing or with the belief that it will cause
> such result without further conduct on his part . . . .[28]

---

28. Model Penal Code § 5.01(1)(b).

Thus, where the offense requires a result that does not occur (or does occur but is not attributable to the actor because of the absence of an adequate causal connection), the actor will still be liable for an attempt to commit the offense—and typically, an attempt will receive less punishment than the offense itself would.

Result vs. Conduct and Circumstances   Note that result elements are objective elements, like conduct and circumstance elements, but they are not necessary to define the prohibited conduct. The criminal law prohibits conduct, not the conduct's results, for the law can only influence conduct. The law may claim to prohibit a particular result, but what it means by that is to direct actors not to engage in conduct that would bring about (or risk bringing about) that result. An actual resulting harm may make the violation more serious—most people would argue that it does—but the fortuity of whether the result actually occurs does not alter the nature of the conduct that constitutes the violation. The conduct remains objectionable notwithstanding the happenstance that the result does not occur. In the "Basement Burglar" hypothetical, wounding or killing the person in your basement might elevate your potential liability, but even if you miss, the act of firing the shot may subject you to liability (assuming you have no general defense). Result elements, then, are like many culpability elements in this regard; they serve the grading function of aggravating the actor's liability. The causation requirement, which defines the relation between an actor's conduct and a result that will give rise to an actor's accountability for the result, similarly serves the grading function rather than the rule-articulation function. Like the requirement of a result, the causation rules determine when an actor is more blameworthy, and thus when the actor's liability is to be aggravated.

Special Grading Doctrines   Special grading provisions also are recognized for specific offenses or categories of offenses, including both doctrines of aggravation (such as the doctrines of felony murder and abandoned and malignant heart murder) and doctrines of mitigation (such as the doctrines of provocation and extreme emotional disturbance). These rules appear as offense elements, but their effect is to grade rather than to establish liability; they increase or decrease an actor's punishment by generating liability for a greater or lesser offense. Other special grading

Flow Chart of Functions of Criminal Law

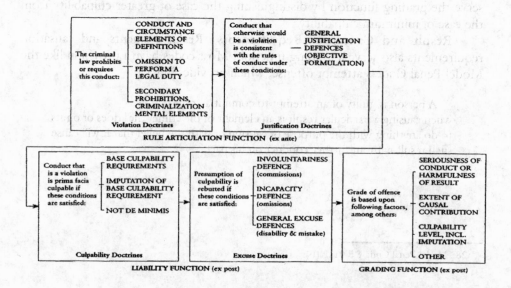

provisions are explicitly defined as grading provisions and vary the degree of liability within the same offense definition. For example, a theft provision might grade the offense differently based on the value of the property taken. In other words, like the rule articulation and liability functions, the grading function of criminal law doctrine is implemented through doctrines of many different sorts.

DISTINGUISHING BETWEEN FUNCTIONS

The various doctrines and their functional interrelation might be simply summarized this way:

Cumulative Nature of Functions The previous discussion refers to doctrines as if each doctrine serves exclusively one function or another. In fact, the interrelation of the doctrines is slightly more complex than this. A complete description of the minimum requirements for liability requires reference not only to the doctrines serving the liability function, but also to the doctrines serving the rule-articulation function. In other words, one prerequisite of liability is violation of the rules of conduct. Similarly, the criminal law's grading function cannot be performed by reference to the doctrines of grading alone. The doctrines of liability are part of the grading function because they define the requirements for minimum grade. The doctrines serving different functions might best be thought of as having cumulative or serial roles as the law's inquiry moves from rule articulation to liability to grading, or represented in the graphic below.

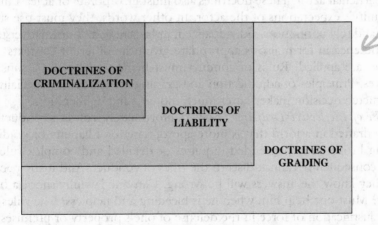

Failure to Distinguish between Functions Current criminal law sometimes does poorly in its three primary functions, in part because its doctrines often fail to distinguish the functions. For example, the criminal law frequently fails to communicate clear rules of conduct because it fails to appreciate the different demands of its communicative and adjudicative functions. The failure of its communicative function derives in part from the ambiguity inherent in case dispositions involving either acquittals or dismissals, for example. Looking to the "Basement Burglar" hypothetical, does the acquittal of the neighbor who shot the burglar mean that shooting burglars is lawful—that such a shooting is permitted by the rules of conduct? Or does the acquittal mean that such killing is *not* permitted but that the neighbor's mistake on the issue, given the difficult circumstances, was not blameworthy? Similarly, does the acquittal of a motorist who lets an accident victim bleed to death mean that there is no legal duty to help the victim? Or, given his dazed condition and his decreased abilities, does the acquittal mean that he cannot be fairly blamed for his failure to perform what was his duty?

Danger of Undercutting Rules of Conduct   The general "not guilty" acquittal does not tell us whether (1) the defendant's conduct was not a violation of the rules of conduct, or (2) it was a violation of the rules of conduct, but a blameless one. Thus, each adjudication of acquittal serves only to blur the rule of conduct rather than to reinforce it. Only a system that distinguishes a no-violation-of-the-rules-of-conduct acquittal from a blameless-violation acquittal can avoid the ambiguity, and resurrect the educational value of our public adjudication system.

Making Formulations Sensitive to Function   The failure to distinguish between these kinds of functions—communicating rules of conduct (the rule articulation function), and adjudicating a violation of those rules (the liability and grading functions)—also creates another kind of difficulty: The doctrines may be ineffectively formulated to serve their function. For example, rules of conduct need to communicate a legal standard that can be understood, remembered, and applied by the general public. To be most effective, the rules of conduct should be simple, based on objective criteria with easily communicable and comprehensible standards. The doctrines embodying the liability and grading functions, on the other hand, must take account of the complex and varied situational factors relevant to an actor's blameworthiness, as well as the capacities and characteristics of the particular actor. These doctrines also must incorporate or at least mirror the community's expectations of the actor. In other words, they must use subjective criteria and rely upon more individualized, judgmental, and normative standards. The difference in form also is appropriate given the different contexts in which the rules are applied. Rules of conduct must be applied by all persons in their daily lives. Principles of adjudication and grading are applied by specially trained or instructed decision makers after much thought and deliberation.

Use of Ineffective Drafting Form   Unfortunately, rules of conduct are frequently drafted in a form that is more appropriate for a liability or grading rule, entailing broad and open-ended inquiries or detailed and complex rules. Many people consequently cannot discern the rules of conduct. And many people who think they know the answers will be wrong. Can one lawfully shoot a basement burglar? Must one help him when he is bleeding and helpless? The rules governing the justification of force in the defense of one's property or premises and the rules defining one's affirmative duties to act are notoriously complex.[29] In other instances, principles of adjudication are drafted in a form that may be appropriate for a rule of conduct, which may be a form that does not accommodate the complex and multifaceted analyses needed to accurately determine an actor's blameworthiness.

---

29. The lawfulness of your use of force against the burglar might require use of Model Penal Code §§ 3.04, 3.05, and 3.06, perhaps part of 3.07, each of which runs for more than a page of detail.

PART III

HOMICIDE AND RELATED ISSUES

To give us a point of reference in our discussion of offense requirements, let us examine the details of one particular offense: homicide. It is a useful illustration because, as the most serious offense, it is particularly nuanced and well-developed and raises many, if not most, of the issues that can arise in the definition of offenses. For these same reasons, however, it is a unique offense, and it would be wrong to assume that it is typical of other offense definitions.

Homicide grading schemes focus primarily on culpability level. In modern terms, this means grading the offense according to whether the defendant purposely or knowingly (murder), recklessly (manslaughter), or negligently (negligent homicide) caused the death. In other words, the grading schemes rely upon the definitions and distinctions already closely examined in Sections 4 and 5. However, most homicide schemes also recognize some exceptions to this pegging of homicide liability to culpability level; they create exceptions in both directions: aggravating reckless killings to murder, discussed in Section 6, and mitigating purposeful killings to manslaughter, the subject of Section 8.

Homicide: Doctrines of Aggravation

◆ THE CASE OF SABINE DAVIDSON (#25)

Sabine Davidson, a 26-year-old German citizen, lives with her husband, Jeffrey, 40, in Geary County, Kansas, a small community in the northeastern part of the state. They have three children, including Vicky, who is eight, and Ashley, who is two. For several years Mrs. Davidson has been buying and training dogs. She started with German shepherds and, in 1995, began purchasing rottweilers. At one point they had so many dogs and litters of puppies that one of their neighbors complained that they were unlawfully operating a kennel.

Her dogs are not well-behaved. One nipped the calf of a neighbor's three-year-old daughter.

Figure 19 **Sabine Davidson, circa 1998**
(CourtTV.com)

173

Figure 20 **Attack dog training**
(Guard Dog Training Center)

Mrs. Davidson laughs when told of it. One of the puppies tried to bite Ashley. Mr. Davidson threw it against a wall.

Ms. Bernardi, who has sold Mrs. Davidson three dogs, has begun insisting that in subsequent sales the dogs be socialized and trained in basic obedience. Bernardi also adds as a condition to further sales that the dogs not be allowed to run free. She has seen some of Davidson's dogs get out of their yard. The Davidsons install a six-foot chain-link fence with a stirrup latch on the gate. Because the dogs still seem to get out quite often, they also discuss chaining them but never begin to do so. Ms. Bernardi finally insists that they put a padlock through the gate latch to keep it horizontal, hoping it will stop the escapes.

Davidson has been trying to train her dogs in Schutzhund, "protection dog" training, a German dog sport that teaches the dogs tracking, obedience, retrieving, and protection. Part of the protection training teaches the dog to attack an "agitator" and hang on, even when being hit, until the handler gives the command to let go. Experts say that once this training begins, dogs should be socialized extensively to humans and kenneled individually to keep them from developing pack behavior. The violence training makes it more important to use discipline to ensure that their natural "prey" drive does not overwhelm the control of the owner. Davidson has experience in the matter: <u>She once had to put down one of her German</u> shepherds that was beyond control.

Her early attempts to train the dogs at one of the local dog clubs are not very successful. She attends meetings in Topeka for Schutzhund training for one of her dogs but is eventually ejected for treating her dogs irresponsibly. At an Oklahoma Schutzhund club, the training director comments that her handling of her dogs is "very, very poor." Another Schutzhund club official says "with a better dog, she'd be dangerous." Her application for the Schutzhund club in Salina is rejected because she does not get along well with club members and because her dogs are badly trained and dirty. She buys a video about "Bite Training Puppies" to try to train them herself. Experts say that such training can be dangerous unless combined with effective obedience training.

[handwritten margin notes: What did Davidson plan to do with the dogs? Any indicator she was able to sell dogs if she was so awful at training them?]

Figure 19 **Davidsons' home with 6-foot fence**
(Craig Hacker, Kansas State Collegian)

The dogs still sometimes escape from their enclosure and roam the neighborhood. In June 1996, at an intersection near the Davidsons' house, a Kansas patrol trooper, Officer Van Buren, is in his front yard when he hears dogs barking. Three rottweilers have formed a semicircle around two children, remaining in the same formation as the children try to move away. When Van Buren runs toward them with a pistol and baseball bat, they run off toward the Davidsons' house. He rings

Figure 22 **An angry rottweiler**
(Antons Video Productions)

their doorbell to no avail. His call to the Davidsons finds their phone disconnected. After his wife calls the sheriff, an officer stops by the Davidsons' house but is unable to get in touch with them. The officer leaves her business card but does not follow up further.

By April 1997, Sabine Davidson has four large rottweilers. The largest, a young male named Chance, is close to 80 pounds. Her dogs regularly fight each other inside the fence. A woman who often gives Mr. Davidson a ride to work has seen the dogs since they were puppies. She has grown so afraid of the dogs that she now stays in her car when she drives to the house. While she is waiting for Mr. Davidson, the dogs bark, growl, and sometimes get out and jump on her car. Mrs. Davidson explains that they are just playing.

Many neighbors feel terrorized by the rottweilers, who have a tendency to get agitated and bark aggressively whenever someone bikes or walks by the fence. The children in the neighborhood bike past the Davidsons' yard quickly because the dogs jump and bark and seem as though they may attack. Mrs. Davidson is not sympathetic because she claims that some of the children, like the Wilson boys, who live a few houses away, tease the dogs when they come by her property.

On the morning of April 24, Mrs. Davidson lets the dogs out into the enclosure at 6:30 a.m. Still tired, she takes a sleeping pill and goes back to sleep on the living room couch. The rottweilers soon escape. Apparently, the dirt is loose around the post to which the latch hooks. The dogs push the post and cause the latch to slip off.

Fifteen minutes later, a neighbor, Mary Smith, sees the three dogs sitting in a nearby yard. By 7 a.m., they have a neighbor's dog cornered on a porch. When the scared dog's owner comes out to see what is going on, the dogs start to advance on him. He goes back inside for his gun. When the owner returns, he sees the dogs run off, and by the time he gets dressed and follows them, it looks as though they are back in the fenced enclosure.

Figure 23 **Christopher Wilson, circa 1997**
<FGS>(Kansas State Collegian)

But ten minutes later, the dogs race into the garage of another neighbor, Learie Thompson, just as he opens the door to go to work. They circle his pickup truck. He jumps up on his truck to avoid them. He knows the dogs are Mrs. Davidson's because he complained to the sheriff last year when the dogs were in his yard. His wife hears him yelling and activates the automatic door. Startled by the noise, the dogs run off. A few minutes later, three rottweilers are seen crossing and recrossing the highway that runs by the Davidsons' subdivision.

A few minutes away, Violet Wilson sets off for the Fort Riley PX to shop. Her husband, Brian, is an army sergeant first class with the 1st Battalion 41st Infantry at Fort Riley, and is now stationed in Bosnia. She drops off her 11-year-old son, Chris, and 8-year-old son, Tramel, at the bus stop about a block from the Davidson's house. The bus stop is at the same intersection where Officer Van Buren had found the dogs menacing children the year before.

While waiting for their bus, the boys see the dogs coming at them. Panicked, they climb up the nearest tree as fast as they can. The dogs circle, barking wildly. After a few minutes, the biggest dog leaves, and the other two follow. Soon the boys cannot see them anymore. Tramel wants to stay up in the tree until their school bus arrives, but Chris wants to go and see where the dogs went. Leaving his brother in the tree, Chris climbs down and starts to look around the near-by ravine. Then, in the distance, he sees the dogs circling back toward him. He starts running.

At that moment, the school bus approaches. As the bus slows down at the stop, the dogs catch Chris on the slope of the ravine. The bus driver, Kathy Roberge, does not see Tramel or Chris at first, but notices the boys' backpacks and musical instruments lying abandoned under the tree. As soon as Tramel sees the bus pull up, he climbs down from the tree and runs toward it. He gets on, out of breath, and tries to tell the bus driver what happened. She hears something incomprehensible about Chris and dogs. She waits a few minutes, then moves the bus around to signal Chris that he needs to hurry. From her side mirror she can now see three dogs fighting in the ravine. The 17 children on the bus look over, curious. One says, "It looks like they have a rag doll." The driver realizes, horrified, that the pack of dogs have caught Chris in the ravine. She slams down on the horn to try to distract them and calls 911 on her radio. While they wait for the police, the driver tries to distract the children from the sight of the continuing attack. Another passing driver also calls 911 when he sees what is happening.

Chris is severely mauled by the dogs. The largest dog, Chance, tears Chris's carotid artery, and with a second bite breaks Chris' neck. The dogs' jaws engulf Chris's neck; their back teeth leave marks. The dogs sever Chris's jugular vein, his esophagus, and crush his spinal cord. Bones are shattered. He dies within minutes of the attack, all within sight of the school bus. The attack continues for almost ten minutes. (The county sheriff, Bill Deppish, later reports that Chris had no blood in him when the deputy got to him. He tells reporters it is the worst incident he has witnessed in 27 years of law enforcement.)

Figure 24 **Neighbors visiting site of mauling, April 1997**
(Craig Hacker, Kansas State Collegian)

As the neighbors gather near the scene to comfort each other, David Morrison, the deputy sheriff, arrives. The dogs advance on him as he moves toward the ravine. He shouts and gestures, but they continue to advance. As the lead dog gets closer, Morrison can see blood in its jaws and on its legs. When it is 15 feet away, the officer shoots. The other two dogs scatter as another officer shoots at them, hitting one of them. As Deputy Shumate arrives, he is told that a wounded dog is running toward the Davidsons. He heads in the direction of their house and shoots the dog. A Kansas highway patrol sharpshooter kills the third dog. At the Davidson house, Deputy Shumate notices a fourth dog, Dunja, in a carrier. She strains wildly to get out and attack him. He can tell that the dog has been attack-trained. When the dog control officer later comes to take custody of the remaining dog, he tells Mrs. Davidson of the dog's aggressive behavior toward the officer. She laughs.

Deputy Shumate tells the Davidsons that their dogs attacked children and mauled one to death. Sabine Davidson says, "The dead one should be one of the Wilson boys," explaining that they waited at the nearby bus stop and sometimes teased the dogs.

1. Relying only upon your own intuitions of justice, what liability and punishment, if any, does Sabine Davidson deserve?

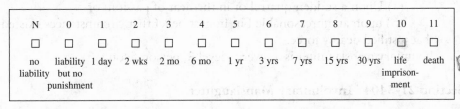

N	0	1	2	3	4	5	6	7	8	9	10	11
☐	☐	☐	☐	☐	☐	☐	☐	☐	☐	☐	☐	☐
no liability	liability but no punishment	1 day	2 wks	2 mo	6 mo	1 yr	3 yrs	7 yrs	15 yrs	30 yrs	life imprisonment	death

2. What "justice" arguments could defense counsel make on the defendant's behalf?

3. What "justice" arguments could the prosecution make against the defendant?

4. What liability, if any, for Davidson under the then-existing statutes? Prepare a list of all criminal code subsections in the order in which you rely upon them in your analysis.

5. What liability, if any, under the Model Penal Code? Prepare a list of all criminal code subsections in the order in which you rely upon them in your analysis.

■ THE LAW

Kansas Statutes Annotated
(1997)

Chapter 21. Crimes and Punishments

Section 21-3401. Murder in the First Degree.

Murder in the first degree is the killing of a human being committed:

(a) Intentionally and with premeditation; or

(b) in the commission of, attempt to commit, or flight from an inherently dangerous felony as defined in K.S.A. 21-3436 and amendments thereto.

Murder in the first degree is an off-grid person felony.

Section 21-3402. Murder in the Second Degree.

Murder in the second degree is the killing of a human being committed:

(a) Intentionally; or

(b) unintentionally but recklessly under circumstances manifesting extreme indifference to the value of human life.

Murder in the second degree as described in subsection (a) is an off-grid person felony.

Murder in the second degree as described in subsection (b) is a severity level 2, person felony.

Section 21-3403. Voluntary Manslaughter.

Voluntary manslaughter is the intentional killing of a human being committed:

(a) Upon a sudden quarrel or in the heat of passion; or

(b) upon an unreasonable but honest belief that circumstances existed that justified deadly force. . . .

Voluntary manslaughter is a severity level 3, person felony.

Section 21-3404. Involuntary Manslaughter.

Involuntary manslaughter is the unintentional killing of a human being committed:

(a) Recklessly;

(b) in the commission of, or attempt to commit, or flight from any felony, other than an inherently dangerous felony as defined in K.S.A. 21-3436 and amendments thereto, that is enacted for the protection of human life or safety or a misdemeanor that is enacted for the protection of human life or safety, including acts described in K.S.A. 8-1566 and 8-1568 and amendments thereto but excluding the acts described in K.S.A. 8-1567 and amendments thereto; or

(c) during the commission of a lawful act in an unlawful manner. Involuntary manslaughter is a severity level 5, person felony.

Section 21-3436. Inherently Dangerous Felony; Definition.

(a) Any of the following felonies shall be deemed an inherently dangerous felony whether or not such felony is so distinct from the homicide alleged to be a violation of subsection (b) of K.S.A. 21-3401 and amendments thereto as not to be an ingredient of the homicide alleged to be a violation of subsection (b) of K.S.A. 21-3401 and amendments thereto:

(1) Kidnapping . . .;

(2) aggravated . . .;

(3) robbery . . .;

(4) aggravated robbery . . .;

(5) rape . . .;

(6) aggravated criminal sodomy . . .;

(7) abuse of a child . . .;

(8) felony theft . . .;

(9) burglary . . .;

(10) aggravated burglary . . .;

(11) arson . . .;

(12) aggravated arson . . .;

(13) treason . . .;

(14) any felony offense as provided in K.S.A. 65-4127a, 65-4127b or 65-4159 or K.S.A. 1995 Supp. 65-4160 through 65-4164 and amendments thereto; and

(15) any felony offense as provided in K.S.A. 21-4219 and amendments thereto.

(b) Any of the following felonies shall be deemed an inherently dangerous felony only when such felony is so distinct from the homicide alleged to be a violation of subsection (b) of K.S.A. 21-3401 and amendments thereto as to not be an ingredient of the homicide alleged to be a violation of subsection (b) of K.S.A. 21-3401 and amendments thereto:

(1) Murder in the first degree, as defined in subsection (a) of K.S.A. 21-3401 and amendments thereto;

(2) murder in the second degree, as defined in subsection (a) of K.S.A. 21-3402 and amendments thereto;

(3) voluntary manslaughter, as defined in subsection (a) of K.S.A. 21-3403 and amendments thereto;

(4) aggravated assault . . .;

(5) aggravated assault of a law enforcement officer . . .;

(6) aggravated battery . . .; and

(7) aggravated battery against a law enforcement officer. . . .

(c) This section shall be part of and supplemental to the Kansas criminal code.

Section 21-3608. Endangering a Child.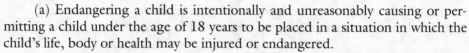

(a) Endangering a child is intentionally and unreasonably causing or permitting a child under the age of 18 years to be placed in a situation in which the child's life, body or health may be injured or endangered.

(b) Nothing in this section shall be construed to mean a child is endangered for the sole reason the child's parent or guardian, in good faith, selects and depends upon spiritual means alone through prayer, in accordance with the tenets and practice of a recognized church or religious denomination, for the treatment or cure of disease or remedial care of such child.

(c) Endangering a child is a class A person misdemeanor.

Section 21-3609. Abuse of a Child.

Abuse of a child is intentionally torturing, cruelly beating, shaking which results in great bodily harm or inflicting cruel and inhuman corporal punishment upon any child under the age of 18 years.

Abuse of a child is a severity level 5, person felony.

Section 21-3201. Criminal Intent.

(a) Except as otherwise provided, a criminal intent is an essential element of every crime defined by this code. Criminal intent may be established by proof that the conduct of the accused person was intentional or reckless. Proof of intentional conduct shall be required to establish criminal intent, unless the statute defining the crime expressly provides that the prohibited act is criminal if done in a reckless manner.

(b) Intentional conduct is conduct that is purposeful and willful and not accidental. As used in this code, the terms "knowing," "willful," "purposeful," and "on purpose" are included within the term "intentional."

(c) Reckless conduct is conduct done under circumstances that show a realization of the imminence of danger to the person of another and a conscious and unjustifiable disregard of that danger. The terms "gross negligence," "culpable negligence," "wanton negligence" and "wantonness" are included within the term "recklessness" as used in this code.

Section 21-3202. Criminal Intent; Exclusions.

(1) Proof of criminal intent does not require proof of knowledge of the existence or constitutionality of the statute under which the accused is prosecuted, or the scope or meaning of the terms used in that statute.

(2) Proof of criminal intent does not require proof that the accused had knowledge of the age of a minor, even though age is a material element of the crime with which he is charged.

Section 21-3204. Guilt Without Criminal Intent, When.

A person may be guilty of an offense without having criminal intent if the crime is a misdemeanor, cigarette or tobacco infraction or traffic infraction and the statute defining the offense clearly indicates a legislative purpose to impose absolute liability for the conduct described.

Section 21-3107. Multiple Prosecutions for Same Act.

(1) When the same conduct of a defendant may establish the commission of more than one crime under the laws of this state, the defendant may be prosecuted for each of such crimes. Each of such crimes may be alleged as a separate count in a single complaint, information or indictment.

(2) Upon prosecution for a crime, the defendant may be convicted of either the crime charged or an included crime, but not both. An included crime may be any of the following:

(a) A lesser degree of the same crime;

(b) an attempt to commit the crime charged;

(c) an attempt to commit a lesser degree of the crime charged; or

(d) a crime necessarily proved if the crime charged were proved.

(3) In cases where the crime charged may include some lesser crime, it is the duty of the trial court to instruct the jury, not only as to the crime charged but as to all lesser crimes of which the accused might be found guilty under the information or indictment and upon the evidence adduced. If the defendant objects to the giving of the instructions, the defendant shall be considered to have waived objection to any error in the failure to give them, and the failure shall not be a basis for reversal of the case on appeal.

(4) Whenever charges are filed against a person, accusing the person of a crime which includes another crime of which the person has been convicted, the conviction of the included crime shall not bar prosecution or conviction of the crime charged if the crime charged was not consummated at the time of conviction of the included crime, but the conviction of the included crime shall be annulled upon the filing of such charges. Evidence of the person's plea or any admission or statement made by the person in connection therewith in any of the proceedings which resulted in the person's conviction of the included crime shall not be admissible at the trial of the crime charged. If the person is convicted of the crime charged, or of an included crime, the person so convicted shall receive credit against any prison sentence imposed or fine to be paid for the period of confinement actually served or the amount of any fine actually paid under the sentence imposed for the annulled conviction.

Section 21-3110. Definitions.

The following definitions shall apply when the words and phrases defined are used in this code, except when a particular context clearly requires a different meaning.

(1) "Act" includes a failure or omission to take action.

(2) "Another" means a person or persons as defined in this code other than the person whose act is claimed to be criminal.

(3) "Conduct" means an act or a series of acts, and the accompanying mental state.

(4) "Conviction" includes a judgment of guilt entered upon a plea of guilty. . . .

(14) "Person" means an individual, public or private corporation, government, partnership, or unincorporated association. . . .

(17) "Prosecution" means all legal proceedings by which a person's liability for a crime is determined. . . .

(22) "State" or "this state" means the state of Kansas and all land and water in respect to which the state of Kansas has either exclusive or concurrent jurisdiction, and the air space above such land and water. "Other state" means any state or territory of the United States, the District of Columbia and the Commonwealth of Puerto Rico.

Section 21-4703. Definitions [for the Kansas Sentencing Guidelines].

As used in this act: . . .

(f) "departure" means a sentence which is inconsistent with the presumptive sentence for an offender;

(g) "dispositional departure" means a sentence which is inconsistent with the presumptive sentence by imposing a nonprison sanction when the presumptive sentence is prison or prison when the presumptive sentence is nonimprisonment; . . .

(i) "durational departure" means a sentence which is inconsistent with the presumptive sentence as to term of imprisonment, or term of nonimprisonment; . . .

(q) "presumptive sentence" means the sentence provided in a grid block for an offender classified in that grid block by the combined effect of the crime severity ranking of the current crime of conviction and the offender's criminal history; . . .

Section 21-4719. Same; Limitations.

. . .

(c) When a sentencing judge imposes a prison term as a dispositional departure: . . .

(2) the term of imprisonment shall not exceed the maximum duration of the presumptive imprisonment term listed within the sentencing grid. Any sentence inconsistent with the provisions of this section shall constitute an additional departure and shall require substantial and compelling reasons independent of the reasons given for the dispositional departure.

The Kansas Sentencing Commission Desk Reference Manual

15, 19-25, 33-38 (1997)

Chapter I: The Basics of the Sentencing Guidelines

Sentencing Guidelines.

The Kansas Sentencing Guidelines Act became effective July 1, 1993. Two grids, which portray the sentencing range for drug crimes and nondrug crime, were developed for use as a tool in sentencing. The sentencing guidelines grids provide practitioners in the criminal justice system with an overview of presumptive felony sentences. The determination of a felony sentence is based on two factors: the current crime of conviction and the offender's prior criminal history. The sentence contained in the grid box at the juncture of the severity level of the crime of conviction and the offender's criminal history category is the presumed sentence. . . .

Grid Boxes.

Each grid box has three numbers, which represent months of imprisonment. The three numbers provide the judge with a range for sentencing. The judge has discretion to sentence at any place within the range. The middle number in the grid box is the standard number and is intended to be the appropriate sentence for typical cases. The upper and lower numbers should be used for cases involving aggravating or mitigating factors insufficient to warrant a departure. The court may increase the sentence up to double the duration within the grid box, lower the duration to any extent, or impose a dispositional departure when aggravating or mitigating circumstances exist which are substantial and compelling. . . .

Chapter III: Crime Severity Levels

General Rules for Determining Severity Levels.

The severity levels range from level 1 to level 10 on the nondrug grid. Level 1 is used to categorize the most severe crimes, and the level 10 is used to categorize the least severe crimes. Crimes listed within each level are considered to be relatively equal in severity.

The crime severity scale contained in the sentencing guidelines grid for drug crimes consists of 4 levels of crimes. Crimes listed within each level are also considered to be relatively equal in severity. Level 1 crimes are the most severe crimes and level 4 crimes are the least severe crimes. . . .

The sentencing judge will designate the appropriate severity level if it is not provided by statute. The following provisions shall be applicable with regard to ranking offenses according to the crime severity scale:

1. When considering an unranked offense in relation to the crime severity scale, the sentencing judge should refer to comparable offenses on the crime severity scale;

2. Except for off-grid felony crimes, which are classified as person felonies, any felony crimes omitted from the crime severity scale shall be considered nonperson felonies;

3. All unclassified felonies shall be scored as level 10 nonperson crimes; . . .

. . . The severity level designation of each felony crime is included in the statutory definition of the crime.

Some crimes include a broad range of conduct. In such circumstances, there may be a different severity level designated for violations of different subsections of the statute. These felonies are listed in Appendix B [of the Manual]. . . .

Chapter IV: Criminal History

Criminal History Rules.

The horizontal axis, or top of the grid represents the criminal history categories. There are nine categories used to designate prior criminal history. Category A is used to categorize offenders having three (3) or more prior felony convictions designated as person crimes. Category I is used to categorize offenders having either no criminal record or a single conviction or juvenile adjudication for a misdemeanor. The criminal history categories classify an offender's criminal history in a quantitative as well as a qualitative manner. The categories between A and I reflect cumulative criminal history with an emphasis on whether prior convictions were for person crimes or nonperson crimes. Generally, person crimes are weighted more heavily than nonperson crimes. Within limits, prior convictions for person crimes will result in a harsher sentence for the current crime of conviction.

The criminal history scale is represented in an abbreviated form on the horizontal axis of the sentencing guidelines grid for nondrug crimes and the sentencing guidelines grid for drug crimes. The relative severity of each criminal history category decreases from left to right on the grids, with criminal history category A being the most serious classification and criminal history category I being the least serious classification.

Category	Descriptive Criminal History
A	The offender's criminal history includes three or more adult convictions or juvenile adjudications, in any combination, for person felonies.
B	The offender's criminal history includes two adult convictions or juvenile adjudications, in any combination, for person felonies.
C	The offender's criminal history includes one adult conviction or juvenile adjudication for a person felony, and one or more adult convictions or juvenile adjudications for nonperson felonies.
D	The offender's criminal history includes one adult conviction or juvenile adjudication for a person felony, but no adult conviction or juvenile adjudication for a nonperson felony.
E	The offender's criminal history includes three or more adult convictions or juvenile adjudications for nonperson felonies, but no adult conviction or juvenile adjudication for a person felony.
F	The offender's criminal history includes two adult convictions or juvenile adjudications for nonperson felonies, but no adult conviction or juvenile adjudication for a person felony.
G	The offender's criminal history includes one adult conviction or juvenile adjudication for a nonperson felony, but no adult conviction or juvenile adjudication for a person felony.
H	The offender's criminal history includes two or more adult convictions or juvenile adjudications for nonperson and/or select misdemeanors, and no more than two adult convictions or juvenile adjudications for person misdemeanors, but no adult conviction or juvenile adjudication for either a person or nonperson felony.
I	The offender's criminal history includes no prior record; or, one adult conviction or juvenile adjudication for a person, nonperson, or select misdemeanor, but no adult convictions or juvenile adjudications for either a person or nonperson felony.

Table 6.1 **1997 Sentencing Range—Nondrug Offenses**   *most serious* → *least serious*

Category →	A	B	C	D	E	F	G	H	I
Severity Level ↓	3+ Person Felonies	2 Person Felonies	1 Person Nonperson Felonies	1 Person Felony	3+ Nonperson Felonies	2 Nonperson Felonies	1 Nonperson Felony	2+ Misdemeanor	1 Misdemeanor No Record
I	816 776 740	772 732 692	356 340 322	334 316 300	308 292 276	282 268 254	254 244 230	232 220 208	206 194 184
II	616 584 552	576 548 520	270 256 242	250 238 226	230 218 206	210 200 198	192 182 172	172 164 154	154 146 136
III	206 194 184	190 180 172	89 85 80	83 78 74	77 73 68	69 66 62	64 60 57	59 55 51	51 49 46
IV	172 162 154	162 154 144	75 71 68	69 66 62	64 60 57	59 56 52	52 50 47	48 45 42	43 41 38
V	136 130 122	128 120 114	60 57 53	55 52 50	51 49 46	47 44 41	43 41 38	38 36 34	34 32 31
VI	46 43 40	41 39 37	38 36 34	36 34 32	32 30 28	29 27 25	26 24 22	21 20 19	19 18 17
VII	34 32 30	31 29 27	29 27 25	26 24 22	23 21 19	19 18 17	17 16 15	14 13 12	13 12 11
VIII	23 21 19	20 19 18	19 18 17	17 16 15	15 14 13	13 12 11	11 10 9	11 10 9	9 8 7
IX	17 16 15	15 14 13	13 12 11	13 12 11	11 10 9	10 9 8	9 8 7	8 7 6	7 6 5
X	13 12 11	12 11 10	11 10 9	10 9 8	9 8 7	8 7 6	7 6 5	7 6 5	7 6 5

Recommended probation terms are:
36 months for felonies classified in Severity Levels 1-5
24 months for felonies classified in Severity Levels 6-10

Postrelease terms are:
For felonies committed on or after 4/20/95
36 months for felonies classified in Severity Levels 1-6
24 months for felonies classified in Severity Level 7-10
For felonies committed before 4/20/95
24 months for felonies classified in Severity Levels 1-6
12 months for felonies classified in Severity Levels 7-10

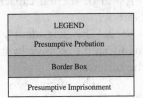

LEGEND

Presumptive Probation

Border Box

Presumptive Imprisonment

Chapter VI: Sentencing

Departure Factors.

Either party may file a motion seeking a departure, or the court may depart on its own motion. Any party filing a motion to depart must state the type of departure sought and the reasons relied upon. The parties are entitled to notice that the court is considering a departure, stating the type of departure intended by the court, and the reasons and factors relied upon. Both the prosecution and defense shall have a reasonable time to prepare for a departure hearing, and the court shall transmit to both parties copies of the presentence investigation report prior to the hearing. . . .

Mitigating Factors.

. . . The following nonexclusive list of statutorily enumerated mitigating factors may be considered in determining whether substantial and compelling reasons for downward or dispositional departure exists:

1. The victim was an aggressor or participant in the criminal conduct associated with the crime of conviction.

2. The offender played a minor or passive role in the crime or participated under circumstances of duress or compulsion. This factor is not sufficient as a complete defense.

3. The offender, because of physical or mental impairment, lacked substantial capacity for judgment when the offense was committed. The voluntary use of intoxicants, drugs or alcohol does not fall within the purview of this factor.

4. The defendant, or the defendant's children, suffered a continuing pattern of physical or sexual abuse by the victim of the offense and the offense is a response to that abuse.

5. The degree of harm or loss attributed to the current crime of conviction was significantly less than typical for such an offense.

Aggravating Factors.

. . . The following nonexclusive list of aggravating factors may be considered in determining whether substantial and compelling reasons for departure exist:

1. The victim was particularly vulnerable due to age, infirmity, or reduced physical or mental capacity that was known or should have been known to the offender.

2. The defendant's conduct during the commission of the current offense manifested excessive brutality to the victim in a manner not normally present in the offense.

3. The offense was motivated entirely or in part by the race, color, religion, ethnicity, national origin or sexual orientation of the victim.

4. The offense involved a fiduciary relationship which existed between the defendant and the victim.

5. The defendant, 18 or more years of age, employed, hired, used, persuaded, induced, enticed, or coerced any individual under 16 years of age to commit or assist in avoiding detection or apprehension for commission of any person felony or any attempt, conspiracy or solicitation to commit any person felony regardless of whether the defendant knew the age of the individual under 16 years of age.

6. The defendant is a predatory sex offender convicted of a crime of extreme sexual violence [as defined by this section].

Model Penal Code
(Official Draft 1962)

Section 210.1. Criminal Homicide.

(1) A person is guilty of criminal homicide if he purposely, knowingly, recklessly or negligently causes the death of another human being.

(2) Criminal homicide is murder, manslaughter or negligent homicide.

Section 210.2. Murder.

(1) Except as provided in Section 210.3(1)(b), criminal homicide constitutes murder when:

(a) it is committed purposely or knowingly; or

(b) it is committed recklessly under circumstances manifesting extreme indifference to the value of human life. Such recklessness and indifference are presumed if the actor is engaged or is an accomplice in the commission of, or an attempt to commit, or flight after committing or attempting to commit robbery, rape or deviate sexual intercourse by force or threat of force, arson, burglary, kidnapping or felonious escape.

(2) Murder is a felony of the first degree [but a person convicted of murder may be sentenced to death, as provided in Section 210.6].

Section 210.3. Manslaughter.

(1) Criminal homicide constitutes manslaughter when:

(a) it is committed recklessly; or

(b) a homicide which would otherwise be murder is committed under the influence of extreme mental or emotional disturbance for which there is reasonable explanation or excuse. The reasonableness of such explanation or excuse shall be determined from the viewpoint of a person in the actor's situation under the circumstances as he believes them to be.

(2) Manslaughter is a felony of the second degree.

Section 210.4. Negligent Homicide.

(1) Criminal homicide constitutes negligent homicide when it is committed negligently.

(2) Negligent homicide is a felony of the third degree.

Section 1.12. . . . Presumptions.

. . . (5) When the Code establishes a presumption with respect to any fact which is an element of an offense, it has the following consequences:

(a) when there is evidence of the facts which give rise to the presumption, the issue of the existence of the presumed fact must be submitted to the jury, unless the Court is satisfied that the evidence as a whole clearly negatives the presumed fact; and

(b) when the issue of the existence of the presumed fact is submitted to the jury, the Court shall charge that while the presumed fact must, on all the evidence, be proved beyond a reasonable doubt, the law declares that the jury may regard the facts giving rise to the presumption as sufficient evidence of the presumed fact.

(6) A presumption not established by the Code or inconsistent with it has the consequences otherwise accorded it by law.

● OVERVIEW OF HOMICIDE AGGRAVATIONS

Notes on Reckless Murder

Reckless and Negligent Homicide
    Culpably Creating and Taking Risks of Death
    Taking Account of Actor's Purpose, Knowledge, and "Situation"

Aggravation to Murder Where Killing Shows "Depraved Heart"
Modern Aggravation Based on "Extreme Indifference to Value of Human Life"
    Is "Extreme Indifference" a Matter of Conduct or Character?
    Extreme Indifference Used as Form of Intent
    Presumption of Indifference as Substitute for Felony Murder

An unintentional killing may constitute any of a number of grades of homicide: murder (through aggravation), manslaughter, or negligent homicide.

Reckless and Negligent Homicide As the paradigm for murder is an intentional (or, under modern culpability schemes, knowing) killing, the paradigm for manslaughter—at least, the category often described as *involuntary manslaughter*—is a reckless killing. The Model Penal Code provides that "criminal homicide constitutes manslaughter when it is committed recklessly,"[1] which means manslaughter requires a killing where the actor consciously disregards a substantial and unjustifiable risk as to causing death.[2] The same culpability of recklessness presumably applies also to whether the victim is a human being. Some modern codes simply label this offense as *reckless homicide*.[3] Where an actor is not consciously aware of a substantial risk that he will cause another person's death, but should have been aware of such a risk, he is negligent as to causing the death, and is liable for negligent homicide. At common law, "grossly" negligent homicide would fall within the category of involuntary manslaughter, though the common law understanding of gross negligence may be closer to the modern concept of recklessness. A few current codes also fail to distinguish reckless from negligent killings, continuing to treat both as involuntary manslaughter.[4] A few codes do not authorize liability for negligent homicide at all.[5]

Culpably Creating and Taking Risks of Death Both reckless and negligent homicide punish risk creation or risk taking as to death: The actor's conduct (or omission to perform a legal duty) must create the risk and the actor must be reckless or negligent, respectively, toward that risk. For each offense, the nature of the risk must be such that:

> considering the nature and purpose of the actor's conduct and the circumstances known to him, [the actor's disregard/failure to perceive the risk] involves a gross deviation from the standard of conduct that a [law-abiding/reasonable[6]] person would observe in the actor's situation.[7]

In other words, the ultimate determination of whether the risk taking is sufficiently culpable is left to the jury's judgment about whether the actor's disregard of, or failure to perceive, the risk is a gross deviation from its sense of reasonable conduct. This standard can be partially individualized to take account

---

1. Model Penal Code § 210.3(1)(a).

2. This language tracks Model Penal Code § 2.02(2)(c).

3. See, e.g., Ind. Code § 35-42-1-5; Ohio Rev. Code § 2903.041; Tenn. Code § 39-13-215.

4. See, e.g., Cal. Penal Code § 192(2); Fla. Stat. Ann. § 782.07; Ga. Code Ann. § 16-5-3.

5. See, e.g., 720 Ill. Ann. Stat. 5/9-3; Ind. Stat. Ann. § 35-42-1-5.

6. The Model Panel Code's general culpability provision, § 2.02, requires for recklessness that the "law-abiding" person "consciously disregard" the risk, § 2.02(2)(c), while it requires for negligence that the "reasonable" person "fail to perceive the risk," § 2.02(2)(d), under circumstances reflecting this "gross deviation."

7. Model Penal Code §§ 2.02(2)(c) & (d).

of the actor's purpose, the circumstances known to the actor, and the actor's "situation."

Taking Account of Actor's Purpose, Knowledge, and "Situation" The effect of partially individualizing the reasonableness standard is illustrated by *People v. Mentry*.[8] A family counselor had advised defendant to sit on her son as a means of imposing discipline, even if the son objected. When the son protested that he could not breathe, the defendant ignored him, and as a result, the son died from asphyxiation. The defendant's slightly subnormal intelligence, together with her legitimate purpose, led to an acquittal at trial, although a purely objective reasonableness standard would call for her conviction. Taking account of the actor's purpose and situation can also increase the chance of liability, as another case, *People v. Cruciani*, illustrates. The defendant helped his girlfriend to inject herself with an illegal drug.[9] He was found guilty of reckless homicide after the injection caused her death. No doubt his criminal purpose of helping her take illegal drugs increased the likelihood that the jury would judge his conduct to be a gross deviation from the standard of care of a law-abiding person. If he had helped her create a risk of the same magnitude by injecting a lawfully prescribed drug in an emergency, his conduct might well have been judged not to be a gross deviation from the standard of conduct of a law-abiding person.

Aggravation to Murder Where Killing Shows "Depraved Heart" Homicide doctrine typically deviates from the paradigm of reckless killings as manslaughter to aggravate a reckless killing to murder in circumstances judged to be egregious. At Common Law, this doctrine of aggravation was called *depraved heart* murder (or *abandoned and malignant* heart, or mind, or some other combination of these adjectives).[10] Both the contours of the category, and the basis for recognizing the aggravation, were often left somewhat unclear, relying perhaps on a more intuitive overall assessment of blame. In *Commonwealth v. Malone*,[11] for example, the 17-year-old defendant shot his friend while they played "Russian roulette" sitting on stools at a lunch counter. Despite the killing's unintentional nature, the court affirms the defendant's conviction for murder because it reflects "a wicked disposition evidenced by the intentional doing of an uncalled-for act in callous disregard of its likely harmful effect on others."[12] Accurate or not, the court's characterization of the crime—"wicked," "uncalled-for," "callous"— merely asserts its conclusion rather than explaining it.

Modern Aggravation Based on "Extreme Indifference to Value of Human Life" Modern codes carry forward the aggravation of some reckless homicides to murder, but provide different criteria, focusing instead on the actor's "depraved indifference"[13] or "extreme indifference to the value of human life."[14] This formulation is somewhat more precise, asking the jury to consider the defendant's recognition of the gravity of taking another person's life, as compared to

---

8. Case No. 84637 (Santa Clara County Super. Ct.) 44.

9. 327 N.E.2d 803 (N.Y. 1975).

10. See Okla. Stat. Ann. tit. 21, § 701.8 ("depraved mind"); Cal. Penal Code § 188 ("abandoned and malignant heart").

11. Commonwealth v. Malone, 47 A.2d 445, 447 (Pa. 1946).

12. Id. at 449.

13. See, e.g., N.Y. Penal Law § 125.25(2).

14. Model Penal Code § 210.2(1)(b).

the common law's request that the jury assess whether the actor generally has a "wicked disposition." In the *Malone* case, for example, the jury would focus on whether the defendant insufficiently valued the life of his friend, as opposed to whether he did value the life of his friend but insufficiently contemplated the possible consequences of what he was doing.

Is "Extreme Indifference" a Matter of Conduct, or Character? Often the modern formulation asks whether the killing was performed "under circumstances manifesting" extreme indifference. Does this mean that the focus is on the objective conduct and situation, rather than the defendant's subjective disposition? The preference for looking at the "circumstances," rather than the particular defendant's actual attitude on the issue, may reflect a desire to stay out of the business of assessing overall character, to avoid a review of the defendant's entire biography to see what it suggests about her views on the value of human life. Rather, the inquiry should be limited in focus to the circumstances of the defendant's conduct causing the death, though the ultimate concern is to gauge what these say about the defendant's view of the value of human life.

Extreme Indifference Used as Form of Intent In England and in several American jurisdictions, murder does not require intent to cause death, but only intent to cause serious injury. This reflects a view that, where a resulting death occurs, the difference between the two intentions is not sufficient to distinguish murder from manslaughter. (Presumably an intention to cause serious bodily injury generally reflects at least recklessness as to causing death, and thus would support manslaughter liability if it were not defined to be murder.) In practice, the extreme-indifference form of murder is sometimes used for a similar purpose. In *State v. Draves*,[15] for example, the defendant attempted to steal the victim's motorcycle. When the victim resisted, the defendant stabbed him several times. While the defendant may not have intended to cause death, a jury might conclude that his intention was not too far from the intent to kill and that his blameworthiness in the situation is analogous to that of one who does intend to kill. Draves was held liable for extreme-indifference murder.

Presumption of Indifference as Substitute for Felony Murder Cases like *Draves* also illustrate the potential application of the Model Penal Code's proposal for a substitute for felony murder. Recklessly causing a death while attempting to commit rape, robbery, or any of a variety of other serious offenses against the person, the argument goes, shows an extreme indifference to the value of human life. Thus, the Model Penal Code rebuttably presumes both recklessness as to causing the death and extreme indifference if the death is caused during, or while fleeing from, commission or attempted commission of such a felony.[16] This is as close as the Code comes to having a felony murder rule, which traditionally punishes as murder any killing during a felony, even a nonculpable killing.

Hypothetical: Visiting a Witness (#26)

Quince and Ray have made a good living as loan sharks, lending money at exorbitant rates. One of their customers, Constello, has fallen behind in his

---

15. 524 P.2d 1225 (Or. App. 1974).
16. Model Penal Code § 210.2(1)(b).

payments and, rather than struggle further to keep up, he has gone to the police. On his testimony, Quince and Ray have been indicted for usury and are scheduled for trial next month. Quince and Ray think that Constello can be persuaded not to testify if he is given a sufficient bribe. They decide to go see him, agreeing that they will remain polite and go unarmed.

[margin note: Both agreed to go unarmed But Q brings a gun (thinks not loaded)]

When they arrive, Constello is less than warm. He orders them to leave. "You guys are in big trouble. I hope you get locked up."

Quince is incredulous. "Watch it, meat. Any more mouth and I'll punch your face in."

But Constello is undeterred. "You'll be in jail before long, Quince Boy."

Quince blows up, "I can hurt you right now. Is that what you want?" He pulls a gun from his coat and waves it in Constello's face.

Ray recoils, "We agreed—no threats and no guns."

[margin note: Negligent unintended?]

Quince leans over to Ray and whispers, "It's not loaded." But, at that moment, the gun goes off, and Constello drops to the floor, dead. Both men stare in disbelief, and then flee.

Both are captured within the week. The prosecutors have sufficient evidence to convict both of witness tampering, a third-degree felony if force or bribery is used. Quince also can be convicted of making terroristic threats, also a third-degree felony.

[margin note: Felony murder Jurisdiction, may be liable for murder]

For what homicide offense, if any, is each liable?

[margin note: Depending on Jurisdiction may be liable for murder]

Notes on Felony Murder

Felony Murder Law
    Murder Liability on Killer and Co-Felons for Killings During Felony
    Limitations to Offset Absence of Culpability Requirement
        Limiting Rule to Inherently Dangerous Felonies
    "Merger" Rule Prevents Use of Underlying Assault as Predicate Felony
    Limitations on Rule's Complicity Aspect
    Offsetting Potentially Harsh Effects of Rule with Affirmative Defense
    MPC Replaces Felony Murder with Presumption of Extreme Indifference
    Continuing Popularity of Felony Murder Rule
  Felony Murder: Underlying Rationales
  Causal Theory
  Equivalency Theory
    Variation Equating *Cumulative* Culpability with Murder Culpability
  Evidentiary Theory
  Deterrence Theory
  Different Rationales Support Different Limitations
  Some Limitations Are Supported by Multiple Rationales
  Variations or Modifications Reveal Underlying Rationale
  Compensating for Inadequacies of Graded Homicide

FELONY MURDER LAW
Murder Liability on Killer and Co-Felons for Killings During Felony

The traditional felony murder rule has two components. First, it imposes murder liability for any death caused, even if entirely accidentally, in the course of the attempt, commission, or flight from a felony. Thus, in the "Visiting a Witness" hypothetical, Quince's killing of Constello would be murder although it was an accident.

[margin note: #1 caused death → murder liability]

#2

accomplices = accomplices in murder

Second, the traditional felony murder rule holds accomplices in the felony to be accomplices in the murder, whether or not they aided the killing specifically, and even if the killing was performed by a nonfelon (such as the felony's victim, or a responding police officer). Thus, Ray, an accomplice to the witness tampering, becomes an accomplice to Quince's murder as well. The common law's *misdemeanor manslaughter* rule has a similar effect, aggravating even an accidental killing to manslaughter if caused in the course of a misdemeanor.[17] Most jurisdictions require for both rules that the killing be in furtherance of the underlying offense—known as the *predicate felony*—or in flight therefrom.[18] Jurisdictions have limited these expansive liability rules over time.

Limitations to Offset Absence of Culpability Requirement Nearly every jurisdiction limits the first aspect of the felony murder rule, imposing murder liability on the killer without proof of the usual culpability, in one or more of the following ways. The killing frequently must be a "probable consequence of the unlawful act."[19] A similar limitation requires that the predicate felony be a *malum in se* offense, an offense evil in and of itself, not a mere *malum prohibitum* offense. Under this variation, causing a death while hunting without permission would not be misdemeanor manslaughter.[20] Also frequently excluded are instances where the predicate felony is an offense of strict liability. Thus, causing a death by distributing a drug in violation of the Health and Safety Code, where the pharmacist is found "morally entirely innocent" because of "a reasonable mistake" or "unavoidable accident," is not misdemeanor manslaughter.[21]

Limiting Rule to Inherently Dangerous Felonies In the same vein, many jurisdictions require that the predicate felony must be inherently dangerous for felony murder liability to arise. (A number of states do this by specifying particular crimes that may serve as predicates to felony murder.) Under this rule, a killing while committing extortion was held not to be felony murder.[22] Some courts assess the dangerousness of the felony in the abstract, that is, by examining the statutory elements, rather than the actual context of the offense at hand, to determine its dangerousness.[23] Under this approach, extortion may be judged a nondangerous felony, even though it sometimes may be committed in a dangerous way.[24] Other courts assess the dangerousness of the felony by examining the actual circumstances of the offense. Thus, while the statutory elements of unlawful possession of a weapon by a convicted felon do not require violence of any sort, the offense may give rise to liability for felony murder if the commission of the offense in the

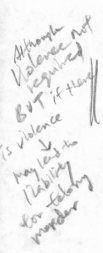

Limiting felony murder rule

Although violence not required BUT if there is violence → may lead to liability for felony murder

17. Some states retain a misdemeanor-manslaughter rule, either explicitly by statute or using common law principles. See, e.g., Bell v. State, 172 P.3d 622 (Okla. App. 2007) (affirming conviction for misdemeanor-manslaughter, under 21 Okla. Stat. Ann. § 711(1), with "driving while impaired" as predicate misdemeanor).

18. Thus, killing a pedestrian after deciding to return a previously stolen car is not felony murder. See State v. Diebold, 277 P. 394 (Wash. 1929).

19. *Diebold*, 277 P. at 396.

20. See State v. Horton, 51 S.E. 945 (N.C. 1905).

21. See People v. Stuart, 302 P.2d 5 (Cal. 1956).

22. See Commonwealth v. Matchett, 436 N.E.2d 400 (Mass. 1982).

23. See, e.g., People v. Phillips, 414 P.2d 353 (Cal. 1966) (defendant induced parents to forgo legitimate cancer treatment for child in favor of his fraudulent treatment, for which he charged $700, resulting in child's death from nontreatment; felony murder conviction reversed because grand theft not an inherently dangerous felony in abstract).

24. *Matchett*, 436 N.E.2d at 410.

particular occasion involves violence. In the "Visiting a Witness" hypothetical, if Quince is charged with felony murder using his terroristic threats as the predicate felony, threats may well be judged dangerous in the abstract and also on the facts of the case. Ray, however, is not an accomplice to the terroristic threats because he lacks the required culpability as to this offense. Ray can be charged with felony murder only if witness tampering is used as the predicate felony. Whether this is judged to be a dangerous felony may depend on whether the jurisdiction looks to dangerousness in the abstract or on the facts of the particular case. Witness tampering through bribery does not necessarily involve violence, but it did here (though Ray did not expect that it would).

"Merger" Rule Prevents Use of Underlying Assault as Predicate Felony   Many jurisdictions also adopt a *merger rule* that bars conviction for felony murder if the predicate offense is simply causing the injury that results in death. Thus, a defendant who assaults another is not liable for felony murder if the assault victim dies; the assault is not "independent" of the killing. A felony murder charge cannot be "based upon a felony which is an integral part of the homicide."[25] It is thought that any other rule would aggravate most acts causing another's death to murder under the felony murder rule, because most acts resulting in another's death involve injurious conduct, and this conduct is itself likely to be a felony. Thus, to allow felonies that are not independent of the killing to trigger felony murder would undercut the traditional grading of homicides according to an actor's culpability as to causing the victim's death, effectively collapsing the grades into the single category of murder. In the "Visiting a Witness" hypothetical, a court might find that Quince's terroristic threats, which occasioned the killing, are not sufficiently independent of the killing to support felony murder, but this would not be a traditional application of the merger rule.

Limitations on Rule's Complicity Aspect   In addition to the limitations on the aggravating-culpability aspect of the felony murder rule, many jurisdictions limit the complicity aspect of felony murder. Some bar liability where an innocent party, responding to the felony attempt, kills another innocent person.[26] Some bar liability where the person killed by the felon is one of the co-felons, rather than an innocent victim. Not surprisingly, many also bar liability in the overlapping situation where an innocent person, responding to an attack, kills one of the felons. For each of these situations, however, some other jurisdictions would impose felony murder liability. Thus, in some jurisdictions, if Quince's accidental shooting in the "Visiting a Witness" hypothetical had killed co-felon Ray rather than Constello, he nonetheless could be liable for felony murder. Indeed, if Quince had accidentally killed himself, Ray could be liable for felony murder in these jurisdictions. These wide-ranging disagreements about the proper formulation of the doctrine hint that its underlying rationale may be a bit murky.

Offsetting Potentially Harsh Effects of Rule with Affirmative Defense   Some jurisdictions define felony murder broadly, but then limit the effect of the rule by providing an affirmative defense to defendants who satisfy a relatively detailed list of conditions, going to both the aggravation-of-culpability and the

---

25. People v. Ireland, 450 P.2d 580, 590 (Cal. 1969).

26. See e.g., Commonwealth ex rel. Smith v. Myers, 261 A.2d 550 (Pa. 1970) (conviction reversed where unclear whether officer trying to thwart robbery of supermarket was killed by fleeing felon or by another officer).

complicity aspects of the rule. Typically, the defendant must show that he did not commit, assist, or request the homicidal act, was not armed, had no reason to believe an accomplice was armed, and had no reason to believe that an accomplice might do something to cause death. Each of the conditions excludes a possible basis for the accomplice's blameworthiness for the killing. The effect of such an affirmative defense is to change the irrebuttable presumption of murder liability into a rebuttable presumption, which allows an accomplice to rebut the presumption of blameworthiness. In the "Visiting a Witness" hypothetical, Ray might qualify for such an affirmative defense, but Quince, because he committed the homicidal act, would remain liable for felony murder. (The accidental nature of the killing itself is not enough to qualify for the affirmative defense.)

MPC Replaces Felony Murder with Presumption of Extreme Indifference   The Model Penal Code does not have a felony murder rule, but creates a legal presumption, where a killing occurs in the course of one of several specified serious felonies, of the recklessness and extreme indifference to the value of human life required for reckless murder.[27] The Code's presumption is of only modest help to prosecutors, however; it serves only to satisfy the prosecutor's burden of production. That is, it enables the state to get its case to the jury, but as to the ultimate burden of persuasion, the jury is still instructed that the prosecution must prove, beyond a reasonable doubt, both the required recklessness and extreme indifference.[28] As to the jury, the effect of the presumption is merely an instruction that they *may*, but need not, regard the fact that the killing occurred in the course of the felony as sufficient evidence of recklessness and extreme indifference. Neither witness tampering nor terroristic threats are on the Model Penal Code's list of qualifying felonies, so not even the Code's weak permissive inference of reckless murder would apply to Quince or Ray in the "Visiting a Witness" hypothetical.

Continuing Popularity of Felony Murder Rule   One might conclude from this review of the state of the felony murder rule that it is an archaic doctrine that is slowly but surely passing from the legal landscape by being limited into extinction. Many commentators wish this were the case, but in fact the rule continues to survive and, perhaps because it has been limited in application, shows little sign of dying. Despite the great success of the Model Penal Code as a model for state codifications, more often than not, these codifications reinsert felony murder into what is otherwise an adoption of the Code's homicide scheme. Only five American states have abolished felony murder.[29] The resilience and continuing popularity of the rule, despite vehement criticism, deserves some exploration. What is the reason for the rule's continued vitality? What inspires states to keep the rule when they shift to the Model Penal Code's formulation of other homicide doctrines? Empirical studies suggest that the rule reflects (albeit perhaps in an

---

27. Model Penal Code § 210.2(1)(b).

28. See Model Penal Code § 1.12(5).

29. See David Crump & Susan Waite Crump, *In Defense of the Felony Murder Doctrine*, 8 HARV. J.L. & PUB. POL'Y 359, 360 n. 4-5 (1985) (stating that four states—Hawaii, Kentucky, New Hampshire, and Ohio—have repealed the felony murder rule by statute, and one, Michigan, has judicially abrogated the common law rule).

imperfect way) the lay view of the appropriate liability in such situations.[30] How might one explain why people feel this way? The following subsection addresses these questions.

FELONY MURDER: UNDERLYING RATIONALES

Felony murder is essentially a codified form of imputation: It uses participation in the predicate felony as a basis for imputing the culpability usually required for murder, or as a basis for imposing accomplice liability for murder, or both. The propriety of a doctrine of imputation is the strength of its rationale for treating an actor as if she has an offense element that she does not in fact have. Four kinds of explanations might be offered to support the felony murder rule, and each of these rationales suggests a different set of limitations on it. The explanations are often inconsistent with one another, suggesting that jurisdictions must pick between them. Because a rationale may support one formulation of (or limitation on) the rule but be inconsistent with another, the particular limitations that a given jurisdiction adopts may reveal the rationale on which the jurisdiction relies. Taken separately, each rationale explains one or more of the common limitations. Taken together, they may explain why the felony murder rule remains so popular.

Causal Theory A causal rationale for felony murder argues that the defendant should be held responsible for the death as a predictable outgrowth of the felony he tried to commit. The actor undertook the felony, thus causing the conditions that, in turn, caused the death. That his culpability existed at an earlier time—at the time of choosing to commit the underlying offense—rather than at the time of the killing does not alter the actor's blameworthiness. The causal rationale allows the actor's culpability toward death at the earlier time (when creating the underlying conditions) as a substitute for culpability at a later time (when the act directly causing the death occurred), which the concurrence requirement would typically demand for murder liability. Under this rationale, however, the felony murder rule should apply only where the predicate felony involves an inherent risk to human life, for otherwise the logic of the rationale does not apply. In the "Visiting a Witness" hypothetical, Quince's decision to go to the meeting armed, and his subsequent waving of his gun at Constello, might support felony murder under this theory. Quince made a choice to engage in risky conduct that created conditions with the potential to result in death, even if the shot that directly caused the death was purely accidental. It would be difficult to justify application of the rule to Ray, however, since he had a more remote connection to creating the conditions that ultimately caused the death.

Equivalency Theory A second, equivalency rationale holds that while the offender who commits felony murder does not possess the same culpability (toward death) as the typical murderer, the culpability she does possess (toward the predicate felony) is morally equivalent to the typical murderer's culpability. In Commonwealth v. Matchett,[31] for example, the defendant was hired to drive another person from Boston to Pittsfield to collect a gambling debt. An altercation

---

30. See Paul H. Robinson & John M. Darley, Justice, Liability & Blame: Community Views and the Criminal Law 169-181 (1995) (reporting study suggesting lay notions of justice mirror a "felony-manslaughter" rule).

31. 436 N.E.2d 400 (Mass. 1982).

ensued during which the defendant shot the debtor. The Supreme Judicial Court of Massachusetts described the felony murder rule as one of "constructive malice," based "on the theory that the intent to commit the felony is equivalent to the malice aforethought required for murder."[32] Accordingly, the court concluded that the theory was tenable only if the underlying felony was one that exhibited a "conscious disregard for human life, hardness of heart, cruelty, recklessness of consequences and a mind regardless of social duty."

Variation Equating Cumulative Culpability with Murder Culpability A slightly different version of the equivalency rationale suggests that, while the defendant did not have the culpability for murder, his blameworthiness for the underlying offense and the killing *together* are equivalent to the culpability for murder. As one court explains, the law "superadds the intent to kill to the original intent to commit the felony."[33] This rationale would insist on such limitations as a merger rule, since the blameworthiness for the underlying offense is subsumed within that for felony murder, and hence no longer provides an independent quantum of blameworthiness to support liability for a separate offense. More broadly, the cumulative-blameworthiness rationale would require a predicate felony involving culpability that, when added to the offender's reduced culpability for the killing, would be equivalent to depraved-indifference murder. Under this theory, in the "Visiting a Witness" hypothetical, Quince's combined blameworthiness for the terroristic threats and the reckless (negligent?) killing (and for the witness tampering?) arguably may add up to a blameworthiness equivalent to that required for reckless murder, but one could disagree about this. Ray has no blameworthiness to add to that for witness tampering, so felony murder liability would not seem justified for him under this theory.

Evidentiary Theory A third theory argues that imputation of culpability for murder in the felony murder setting makes sense because the defendant probably had the culpability for murder (of the depraved-indifference kind, for example), but it may be difficult to prove that culpability beyond a reasonable doubt, so the imputation rule facilitates imposition of the appropriate degree of punishment. As the Model Penal Code commentary explains,

> The fact that the actor was engaged in a crime of the kind that is included in the usual first-degree felony murder enumeration or was an accomplice in such crime . . . will frequently justify a finding [of extreme indifference to the value of human life, as required for reckless murder]. Indeed, the probability that such a finding will be justified seems high enough to warrant the presumption of extreme indifference that Subsection (1)(b) creates.[34]

While the Code makes the presumption rebuttable, the traditional rule does not. This evidentiary theory reveals a utilitarian bent: The need to convict such violators of murder outweighs the danger of imposing greater liability than deserved on some violators as a result of the reduced evidentiary requirements. Applying the rationale to the hypothetical, the presumption of recklessness and depraved indifference arguably may be appropriate for Quince; it seems misguided and inaccurate for Ray.

---

32. Id. at 409-410.
33. People v. Cabaltero, 87 P.2d 364, 368 (Cal. App. 1939).
34. Model Penal Code § 210.2 comment at 39 (1985).

Deterrence Theory The final rationale for felony murder liability strikes an even more strident crime-prevention chord. Unlike the other rationales, which seek to find some culpability-related basis for imposing liability, this rationale concedes that the felony murder offender does not have the requisite culpability (or its moral equivalent), but asserts that liability is appropriate nonetheless, based on the significant deterrent value in threatening felons with severe sanctions if a death occurs. This threat will make them more careful to avoid deaths when engaged in criminal activity—a time when the danger of accidental injury is great, and when comparably greater care is needed to avoid causing a death.

> [I]f experience shows, or is deemed by the law maker to show, that somehow or other deaths which the evidence makes accidental happen disproportionately often in connection with other felonies, or with resistance to officers, or if on any other ground of policy it is deemed desirable to make special efforts for the prevention of such deaths, the law maker may consistently treat acts which, under the known circumstances, are felonious . . . as having a sufficiently dangerous tendency to be put under a special ban. The law may, therefore, throw on the actor the peril, not only of the consequences foreseen by him, but also of consequences which, although not predicted by common experience, the legislator apprehends.[35]

The rule also is desirable, it is argued, because it has the collateral effect of providing an additional deterrent to felonies generally, especially to dangerous felonies. Applying the rationale to the hypothetical, felony murder liability for both Quince and Ray may be justified. If the efficacy of deterrence is accepted, even Ray's liability may serve as an incentive to future felons to take all possible precautions to avoid an accidental killing, and to make absolutely sure that their accomplices do the same.

Different Rationales Support Different Limitations The differences among these four rationales may help explain why some jurisdictions adopt certain limitations on felony murder, while other jurisdictions do not. For example, the merger rule is critical under a cumulative-blameworthiness equivalency theory, to be sure that there exists an independent offense with which the culpability for the killing can be accumulated. There is little need for a merger rule under a causal theory, however, and the rule seems contrary to a deterrence rationale. (Dangerous assaults, for example, are instances where there is the greatest need to motivate an actor to be careful not to cause death.) The same is true of the rule—mandated by the federal Constitution—that prevents conviction for the predicate felony if the actor is convicted of felony murder.[36] Such a rule is necessary to avoid double-counting under a cumulative equivalency theory, but it has no obvious rationale under the other theories. As another example, under a causal theory, felony murder may be appropriate for killings by an innocent person resisting the felony. By undertaking the felony, the felon instigates such resistance and the

---

35. Oliver Wendell Holmes, The Common Law 49 (1881).

36. See, e.g., Harris v. Oklahoma, 433 U.S. 682 (1977) ("When, as here, conviction of a greater crime, murder, cannot be had without conviction of the lesser crime, robbery with firearms, the Double Jeopardy Clause bars prosecution for the lesser crime after conviction of the greater one."). Note that his rule is different from the merger rule. Merger permits conviction for the predicate felony, but bars conviction for felony murder. This rule permits conviction for felony murder, but bars an additional conviction for the predicate felony.

possibility of a resulting death; the death would not have occurred but for the actor's felony. Under a deterrence rationale, however, the propriety and need for such liability is less clear. It is felons, not victims, whom the rule seeks to make more careful during the commission of a felony.

Some Limitations Are Supported by Multiple Rationales   Some limitations seem consistent with many, if not most, of the rationales. The common limitation of the rule's application to cases involving an inherently dangerous predicate felony is supported by most of the rationales. An inherently dangerous felony provides the most suitable degree of blameworthiness for an equivalency theory, provides evidence of culpability as to causing death under a causal or evidentiary theory, and focuses the deterrent threat on the cases where deterrence is most needed. Similarly, the requirement that the killing be in furtherance of the felony is appropriate under most theories. Applying the rule to killings outside this limitation would not serve the intended deterrent function and would provide little basis for using the culpability of the underlying felony to impute the culpability for reckless murder.

Variations or Modifications Reveal Underlying Rationale   A jurisdiction's rationale for felony murder sometimes becomes explicit when the doctrine is modified. Thus, the Model Penal Code's substitute for the rule—a presumption of the recklessness and indifference required for reckless murder—suggests that the drafters embraced the evidentiary theory and, while watering down the effect of the doctrine, sought to make its rationale explicit. In a slightly different way, the California Supreme Court reveals its support for a causal rationale in fashioning a substitute for the expansion of felony murder. After rejecting an extension of the felony murder rule to killings of a co-felon by an innocent party,[37] the court imposes direct liability for depraved-indifference murder in another case involving similar facts, *Taylor v. Superior Court*.[38] The court reasons that, by committing the felony, the felons provoked a gun battle that resulted in the death, and by such provocation, showed a "wanton disregard for human life" and "a base, anti-social motive."[39] This was held an adequate basis for the jury to find the culpability normally required for standard murder. While refusing to extend the felony murder rule itself as far as a causal theory might take it—making felons per se accountable for all killings, including killings of co-felons by innocents—the court left open the possibility of imposing murder liability in specific cases based on a theory of causal accountability for another (innocent) person's lethal conduct, so long as the jury was willing to conclude that the offenders satisfied the usual culpability requirements.

Compensating for Inadequacies of Graded Homicide   Taylor's shift from reliance on felony murder to explicit adoption of a causal theory for murder liability illustrates one basis of criticism of the felony murder rule. The concern is that even if the rule's results are generally appropriate, the rule is undesirable because it compensates for, and thus conceals and helps perpetuate, underlying weaknesses in the traditional doctrines governing graded homicide. Under this view, felony murder remains popular only because the normal doctrines governing homicide

---

37. See People v. Washington, 402 P.2d 130 (Cal. 1965).
38. 477 P.2d 131 (Cal. 1970).
39. Id. at 134.

liability are too restrictive. The rule should and will fade away, this view predicts, if and when the standard rules of graded homicide are modified to incorporate its useful aspects. Perhaps a scheme along the lines of the Model Penal Code's presumption of recklessness and indifference—which softens but does not entirely obviate the need to prove culpability—if expanded to be available for more of the cases that the felony murder rule now covers, might escape the deserved criticisms of critics, yet be as popular as the existing felony murder rule.

Mayes v. People
Supreme Court of Illinois
106 Ill. 306, 46 Am. Rep. 698 (1883)

Mr. Justice SCHOLFIELD delivered the opinion of the Court:

Plaintiff in error, by the judgment of the court below, was convicted of the crime of murder, and sentenced to the penitentiary for the term of his natural life. . . .

It is contended the facts proved do not constitute murder. They are, briefly, these: The deceased was the wife of plaintiff in error, and came to her death by burning, resulting from plaintiff in error throwing a beer glass against a lighted oil lamp which she was carrying, and thereby breaking the lamp and scattering the burning oil over her person. Plaintiff in error came into the room where his wife, his mother-in-law and his young daughter were seated around a table engaged in domestic labors, about nine o'clock at night. He had been at a saloon near by, and was, to some extent, intoxicated,—not, however, to the degree of unconsciousness, for he testifies to a consciousness and recollection of all that occurred. When he sat down, the deceased, noticing that one side of his face was dirty, asked him if he had fallen down. He replied that it was none of her business. She then directed the daughter to procure water for him with which to wash his face, which being done, he washed his face, and he then directed the daughter to procure him a clean beer glass, which she did. He had brought some beer with him from the saloon, and he then proceeded to fill the glass with the beer and handed it to the deceased. She took a sup of it, and then offered it to her mother, who declined tasting it. The deceased then brought plaintiff in error his supper, but he declined eating it, and was about to throw a loaf of bread at the deceased when she took it from his hands and returned it to the cupboard. After this, having sat quietly for a few minutes, he asked for arsenic. No reply was made to this request, and thereupon he commenced cursing, and concluded by saying that he would either kill deceased or she should kill him. He wanted a fire made, but deceased told him it was bed time and they did not need any fire. He then picked up a tin quart measure and threw it at the daughter. Thereupon deceased started, with an oil lamp in her hand, toward a bed-room door, directing the daughter to go to bed, and as the deceased and daughter were advancing toward the bed-room door, he picked up the beer glass, which is described as being a large beer glass, with a handle on one side, and threw it with violence at the deceased. It struck the lamp in her hand and broke it, scattering the burning oil over her person and igniting her clothes. Plaintiff in error made no effort to extinguish the flames, but seems to have caught hold of the deceased, temporarily, by her arms. This occurred on Monday night, and on Saturday of that week she died of the wounds caused by this burning.

The plaintiff in error claims that he was only intending to pitch the beer glass out of doors—that he did not design hitting the deceased, and that the striking of the lamp was therefore purely an accident. In this he is positively contradicted by his daughter and mother-in-law, the only witnesses of the tragedy besides himself. He says, to give plausibility to his story, that the door leading into the yard was open, and that deceased and daughter had to pass between him and that door in going to the bed-room, and that deceased was near the edge of the door and moving across the door when he pitched the glass. They both say this door was closed, and that he threw the glass. The language of his mother-in-law, in regard to the throwing, is: "He threw at her with vengeance a heavy tumbler;" and his daughter's language is: "He picked up a tumbler and threw it with such force that it struck the lamp." We can not say the jury erred in believing the mother-in-law and daughter, and disbelieving plaintiff in error.

. . .The plaintiff in error asked the court to instruct the jury, "that to constitute a murder there is required a union of act and intent, and the jury must believe, beyond a reasonable doubt, both that the weapon used was thrown with the intent to inflict bodily injury upon the person of Kate Mayes, and if they have a reasonable doubt as to whether his intent was to strike his wife or not, the jury should give the prisoner the benefit of such doubt, and acquit him." The court refused to give this as asked, but modified it by adding: "Unless the jury further believe, from the evidence, beyond a reasonable doubt, that all the circumstances of the killing of Kate Mayes, (if the evidence shows that she was killed by defendant,) shows an abandoned and malignant heart on the part of the defendant," and then gave it. Plaintiff in error then also asked the court to instruct the jury as follows:

"The court instructs the jury, for the defendant, that intention to commit a crime is one of the especial ingredients of an offence, and the People are bound to show, beyond a reasonable doubt, that the defendant threw the glass in question at the deceased with the intention to do her bodily injury, and if you believe, from the evidence, that there is a reasonable doubt as to the defendant having thrown said glass with intent to do her bodily injury, the jury will give the defendant the benefit of said doubt, and acquit the defendant."

This, also, the court refused to give as asked, but modified it by adding: "Unless all the circumstances of the killing of Mrs. Mayes (if she is shown, beyond a reasonable doubt, to have been killed by defendant,) show an abandoned and malignant heart on the part of the defendant," and then gave it. Exceptions were taken to the rulings in these modifications, so the question whether they were erroneous is properly before us.

We perceive no objection to these rulings. Malice is an indispensable element to the crime of murder. But our statute, repeating the common law rule, says: "Malice shall be implied when no considerable provocation appears, or when all the circumstances of the killing show an abandoned and malignant heart." (Rev. Stat. 1874, p. 374, sec. 140.) And hence it is said: "When an action, unlawful in itself, is done with deliberation, and with intention of mischief or great bodily harm to particulars, or of mischief indiscriminately, fall where it may, and death ensue, against or beside the original intention of the party, it will be murder."

(Wharton on Homicide, 45.) And as illustrative of the principle, the author says: "Thus, if a person, breaking in an unruly horse, willfully ride him among a crowd of persons, the probable danger being great and apparent, and death ensue from the viciousness of the animal, it is murder. . . .So, if a man mischievously throw from a roof into a crowded street, where passengers are constantly passing and repassing, a heavy piece of timber, calculated to produce death on such as it might fall, and death ensue, the offence is murder at common law. And upon the same principle, if a man, knowing that people are passing along the street, throw a stone likely to do injury, or shoot over a house or wall with intent to do hurt to people, and one is thereby slain, it is murder on account of previous malice, though not directed against any particular individual. It is no excuse that the party was bent upon mischief generally." To like effect is, also, 1 Russell on Crimes, (7th Am. ed.) 540, *541; 1 Wharton on Crim. Law, (7th ed.) sec. 712b. So, here, it was utterly immaterial whether plaintiff in error intended the glass should strike his wife, his mother-in-law, or his child, or whether he had any specific intent, but acted solely from general malicious recklessness, disregarding any and all consequences. It is sufficient that he manifested a reckless, murderous disposition,—in the language of the old books, "A heart void of social duty, and fatally bent on mischief." A strong man who will violently throw a tin quart measure at his daughter—a tender child—or a heavy beer glass in a direction that he must know will probably cause it to hit his wife, sufficiently manifests malice in general to render his act murderous when death is the consequence of it. He may have intended some other result, but he is responsible for the actual result. Where the act is, in itself, lawful, or, even if unlawful, not dangerous in its character, the rule is different. In cases like the present, the presumption is the mind assented to what the hand did, with all the consequences resulting therefrom, because it is apparent he was willing that any result might be produced, at whatever of harm to others. In the other case, the result is accidental, and, therefore, not presumed to have been within the contemplation of the party, and so not to have received the assent of his mind.

The classic formulation of the felony murder doctrine declares that one is guilty of murder if a death results from conduct during the commission or attempted commission of any felony. Some courts have made no effort to qualify the application of this doctrine, and a number of earlier English writers also articulated an unqualified rule. At the time the Model Code was drafted, a number of American legislatures, moreover, perpetuated the original statement of the rule by statute. As thus conceived, the rule operated to impose liability for murder based on the culpability required for the underlying felony without separate proof of any culpability with regard to the death. The homicide, as distinct from the underlying felony, was thus an offense of strict liability. This rule may have made sense under the conception of *mens rea* as something approaching a general criminal disposition rather than as a specific attitude of the defendant towards each element of a specific offense. Furthermore, it was hard to claim that the doctrine worked injustice in an age that recognized only a few felonies and that punished each as a capital offense.

In modern times, however, legislatures have created a wide range of statutory felonies. Many of these crimes concern relatively minor misconduct not inherently dangerous to life and carry maximum penalties far less severe than those authorized for murder. Application of the ancient rigor of the felony murder rule to such crimes will yield startling results. For example, a seller of liquor in violation of a statutory felony becomes a murderer if his purchaser falls asleep on the way home and dies of exposure. And a person who communicates disease during felonious sexual intercourse is guilty of murder if his partner subsequently dies of the infection.

The prospect of such consequences has led to a demand for limitations on the felony murder rule. American legislatures had responded to these demands at the time the Model Code was drafted primarily by dividing felony-homicides into two or more grades or by lowering the degree of murder for felony homicide. Only Ohio had abandoned the rule completely.

In addition, the courts had imposed restrictions, both overt and covert, on the reach of the felony murder doctrine. . . .

These limitations confine the scope of the felony murder rule, but they do not resolve its essential illogic. This doctrine aside, the criminal law does not predicate liability simply on conduct causing the death of another. Punishment for homicide obtains only when the deed is done with a state of mind that makes it reprehensible as well as unfortunate. Murder is invariably punished as a heinous offense and is the principal crime for which the death penalty is authorized. Sanctions of such gravity demand justification, and their imposition must be premised on the confluence of conduct and culpability. Thus, under the Model Code, as at common law, murder occurs if a person kills purposely, knowingly, or with extreme recklessness. Lesser culpability yields lesser liability, and a person who inadvertently kills another under circumstances not amounting to negligence is guilty of no crime at all. The felony murder rule contradicts this scheme. It bases conviction of murder not on any proven culpability with respect to homicide but on liability for another crime. The underlying felony carries its own penalty and the additional punishment for murder is therefore gratuitous—gratuitous, at least, in terms of what must have been proved at trial in a court of law.

It is true, of course, that the felony murder rule is often invoked where liability for murder exists on another ground. One who kills in the course of armed robbery is almost certainly guilty of murder in the form of intentional or extremely reckless homicide without any need of special doctrine. Similarly, a man who burns another's house will scarcely be heard to complain that he lacks the culpability for murder if the blaze kills a sleeping occupant. For the vast majority of cases it is probably true that homicide occurring during the commission or attempted commission of a felony is murder independent of the felony murder rule. At bottom, continued adherence to the doctrine may rest on assessments of this sort.

The problem is that criminal liability attaches to individuals, not generalities. It is a weak rejoinder to a complaint of unjust conviction to say that for most persons in the defendant's situation the result would have been appropriate. To be sure, limiting the rule to specified felonies increases the probability that conviction in a particular case will be warranted. Criminal punishment should be premised, however, on something more than a probability of guilt. Requiring that the defendant's conduct in committing the underlying felony create a foreseeable risk to human life is a roundabout way of limiting felony murder to cases of negligent homicide. This is a worthwhile reform, for it effectively excludes extreme applications of the rule to instances in which the actor would not otherwise be guilty of any homicide offense. Yet murder and negligent homicide are not interchangeable; they carry vastly different sanctions. Punishment for the greater offense, on proof that should suffice only for conviction of the lesser, works within reduced compass the same essential violence to the general principles of criminal liability as does the unqualified rule.

▲ PROBLEMS

An Exxon Kidnap Gone Bad (#27)

Arthur and Irene Seale come from humble beginnings. Arthur, the son of a police officer, joins the New Jersey police force but leaves after sustaining an injury in the line of duty. Leaving law enforcement turns out to be a boon for the couple as Arthur is able to parlay his police experience into a relatively lucrative job with Exxon Corporation, serving as a security official. While Arthur is at Exxon he develops the company's policy for responding to the kidnapping of top executives. Exxon's dealings in oil-rich but politically unstable nations has placed executives at risk before, including one incident where the company paid more than $15 million to secure the release of an executive taken hostage in South America. For his work, Arthur is given a six-figure salary. He and his wife spend lavishly and are known for their expensive lifestyle.

The Seales' prosperity, however, is short-lived. Arthur leaves the company following a dispute with management, after which he and his wife take part in a number of failed business ventures and get-rich-quick schemes. They end up living with Arthur's parents in a retirement community, where, despite having almost no income, they continue their free-spending ways, amassing nearly $1 million in debt. On the brink of financial collapse, the Seales devise a plan to become financially secure for the rest of their lives. Arthur decides to use his knowledge of Exxon security procedures to kidnap and hold for ransom Sidney Reso, president of Exxon International. They stake out Reso's home in order to follow his routine, and set their plan. A few days later, as Reso is out getting his morning paper, they kidnap him at gunpoint. While the Seales had not planned on using their guns, intent only to collect the ransom and eventually release Reso, they accidently shoot Reso during the initial kidnapping. The Seales do not believe the wound to be fatal, since it went straight through his arm. As per their plan, they throw a gagged and handcuffed Reso into a wooden box and place the box in a storage locker while they negotiate the ransom. The box has air holes cut out for ventilation, but the storage locker is sealed and temperatures inside reach over 100 degrees. The Seales contact the F.B.I., pretending to be environmentalists angry at Exxon, and demand $18.5 million. In the mean time, Reso begins suffering from his wound, lack of air, and the sweltering heat from being trapped in the storage box. He is given only water and a piece of orange for food, as well as acetaminophen (a common pain reliever) and sleeping pills for his wound. Five days after the kidnapping, Reso dies from a heart attack and dehydration. The

Seales bury Reso in a state park and continue with their ransom demands. They are soon apprehended by the F.B.I.

What liability for the Seales, if any, under the Model Penal Code? Prepare a list of all criminal code subsections in the order in which you rely upon them in your analysis.

Are the Seales liable under the traditional felony murder rule?

Fleeing as Murder (#28)

Sean McCarty is a 17-year old known to the police as a drug dealer and gang member. He also has a nine-month-old son with his girlfriend and is taking classes towards his GED. In order to support his new family, he has been working at the airport in a less-than-lucrative position. He has no car, but arranges to rent one from an acquaintance in exchange for a dime bag of cocaine. McCarty does not return the car as planned; instead he unsuccessfully tries to sell it. He is driving back home when he notices that a police car is following him. Officer Laura in the patrol car decides that McCarty is driving erratically and turns on his flashers to pull McCarty over.

McCarty tries to flee, driving 55 mph through a 25 mph zone. Laura stays close behind and McCarty decides he is better off on foot. He turns into an alley, jumps out of the car and starts to run. Laura gets out as well and chases after him, radioing back that he is engaged in a foot pursuit. Officer Brogden is in the area and has responded to the initial car pursuit. He is driving to the area when the dispatcher informs him that Laura is now pursuing McCarty on foot. Brogden sees the fleeing McCarty run across the street ahead of him. He radios his location to the dispatcher and applies his brakes. He then feels a thump and his front wheel leaves the ground. He has just hit Officer Laura, who was running behind McCarty. Laura had slipped and, rather than be thrown onto the hood of Brogden's squad car, he is pulled underneath and dragged approximately 100 feet before Brogden comes to a complete stop. Officer Laura is killed in the accident. McCarty, meanwhile, unaware of what has happened, continues to run. He is picked up a few days later after police trace him through the stolen car. He claims that he had not intended to hurt anyone, but had run because he was afraid of arrest.

What liability for McCarty, if any, under the Model Penal Code? Prepare a list of all criminal code subsections in the order in which you rely upon them in your analysis.

Is McCarty liable under the traditional felony murder rule?

A Robbers' Dispute (#29)

C. Cabaltero, Delmacio Dasalla, and Pedro Ancheta are laborers employed together on a small California farm. They are paid regularly but are dissatisfied with the amount they receive and the poor working conditions. Approached by other workers about a plot to rob the farm on the next payday, they eagerly join in. The plan is for Dasalla to enter the barn where their employer hands out the workers' salaries and rob him of the payroll at gunpoint. Ancheta is to stand guard outside, while Cabaltero is to wait in a getaway car parked near the barn.

The robbery begins smoothly, as Dasalla collects nearly $1,300 in the holdup. However, as he prepares to leave, he hears gunshots from outside. Cabaltero, anxious to play a more active role in the robbery, has left the car to join Dasalla in the barn. Ancheta, seeking to keep the plan simple, has, in turn, fired two warning shots at Cabaltero. Dasalla runs out of the barn, screaming at Ancheta for his intervention. As the argument becomes more violent, Dasalla fatally shoots Ancheta. Dasalla gets in the car with Cabaltero and the money. Both are soon apprehended, along with their other conspirators.

Is Cabaltero liable for Dasalla's killing of Ancheta under the traditional felony murder rule?

What liability for Cabaltero, if any, under the Model Penal Code? Prepare a list of all criminal code subsections in the order in which you rely upon them in your analysis.

Killing Your Co-Felon Through a Gun Battle with Police (#30)

James Redline and Erbor Worseck's plan to hold up the Midway Restaurant goes well at the beginning. They enter the restaurant brandishing guns, rob several patrons, and even manage to disarm the two police officers who happen to be dining there. However, by the time they are through, more police are outside waiting for them. They decide to use the disarmed officers as hostages and to create a diversion. Redline runs out of the restaurant and shouts to the waiting police, "The man you want is in there," pointing to the restaurant. He then immediately opens fire with a .45 caliber revolver, shooting at one of the officers who is about 20 feet away. Redline's first shot misses. The police return fire at Redline. Worseck, hearing the shots, follows Redline out with a hostage, as Redline instructed, and uses the hostage as a human shield. Worseck fires at the police officers as he attempts to escape. When the smoke clears, two police officers are seriously wounded, Redline is injured, and Worseck is dead from a shot fired by one of the officers.

Under the traditional felony murder rule, is Redline liable for the police killing of Worseck?

What liability for Redline, if any, under the Model Penal Code? Prepare a list of all criminal code subsections in the order in which you rely upon them in your analysis.

✳ **DISCUSSION ISSUE**

Should the Criminal Law Recognize a Felony Murder Rule?

Materials presenting each side of this Discussion Issue appear in the Advanced Materials for Section 6 in Appendix A.

Death Penalty

SELL

The death penalty is the most severe punishment that criminal law can impose. The debate surrounding its use has a long and distinguished history. The central policy considerations are addressed in the Discussion Materials in the Appendix. If the death penalty is authorized, as it is in two-thirds of the states, the central questions for substantive criminal law become: For what kinds of offenses should the penalty be available and how is it to be determined whether it should be imposed in a given case?

◆ THE CASE OF WILLIAM KING (#31)

Approximately 7,500 people live in the east Texas town of Jasper—a population almost equally divided between blacks and whites. As with many towns in the "New South," Jasper's race relations record is mixed. Several prominent political and civic leaders are African Americans, including the mayor, and the local country club admits African-American members. Nonetheless, racial epithets are still heard, and racial tensions clearly exist. For example, although the recent hanging death of a prominent African-American high school athlete who had been dating a white girl was ruled a suicide, some Jasper residents believe it was a lynching. For the most part, however, racism in Jasper lives on only in words and resentment; there have been few acts of violence in recent years.

Figure 26 **James Byrd, Jr., 1997**
(AP/Byrd Family)

James Byrd, Jr., is the third of eight children born to James, Sr., a dry cleaner, and Stella, a homemaker. James, Jr., was an excellent student, graduating from high school in 1967, which was the final year of school segregation in Jasper. He does not follow his two older sisters to college and instead remains in Jasper to marry Thelma Adams, with whom he has three children, Renee, Ross, and Jamie. James leads a colorful life; sometimes selling vacuum cleaners door to door, in and out of jail on forgery and theft charges. He is noted for his musical talent, playing the piano and singing spirituals and hymns—his favorite is "Walk with Me, Lord."

Around the time James and Thelma are starting their family, Shawn Berry is born in Jasper. His mother divorces twice while he is very young and Berry experiences further trauma as a teenager when, having grown close to his mother's second husband, the man commits suicide by shooting himself in the chest with a shotgun. Berry is then raised by his paternal grandparents until they too divorce. Berry drops out of high school and becomes friends with John William ("Bill") King.

King, born in 1975, is adopted as an infant by a working-class family from Jasper. He is the youngest of four children in his adoptive family; his adoptive father, Ronald King, describes Bill as "the most loved boy I knew." King grows up in an integrated neighborhood; his father has several black friends, and one of King's own closest childhood friends is black. Although King was diagnosed once as manic depressive, friends describe him as a low-key and unassuming child.

King's adoptive mother dies when he is 15. In 1992, at the age of 17, he drops out of high school. Soon afterwards, he is arrested for burglary and placed on probation. A few months later, he and Berry are convicted of burglarizing a jukebox warehouse and receive ten-year prison sentences.

They catch a break and are sent instead to a 90-day "boot camp" that is supposed to scare them away from a life of crime. The program seems to work for Berry, who returns to Jasper and settles into a normal life, first working at a tire dealership in exchange for a room in the boss's trailer home. He then moves on to a job at the local movie theater, where he meets future girlfriend Christie Marcontell, a local beauty who has twice been chosen to represent her region in the Miss Texas pageant. The two begin a relationship and she gives birth to their son, Montana, in 1997. Christie describes Shawn as a loving and attentive father: "Montana slept with his daddy the first three weeks of his life." Shawn and Christie set an August 1998 wedding date.

Unfortunately, "boot camp" seems to have little effect on Bill King, who violates his parole and is sent to Beto I, a maximum security prison near Houston in 1995. On his first day in prison, King is "pretty badly beaten" and raped by black inmates, who make up the prison majority. King is approximately 5' 7" and weighs only 140 pounds

Figure 27 **Berry and King, June 1998**
(Greg Smith/Corbis Saba)

at the time. Like at many prisons, Beto I has gangs that can make life easier for their members and, conversely, more difficult for enemies. King becomes immersed in a "thriving subculture" of racist hate groups and rises in the ranks to be known as an "exalted cyclops" of the Confederate Knights of America, a white supremacist gang. King is paroled in July 1997 and returns to Jasper a changed man. "When he came back, he was a person I'd never seen," said Shawn Berry's brother, Louis Berry. Once an avid guitar player in a rock band, King now spends all his time advocating his new racist beliefs. Among his many tattoos are a woodpecker (a term used in prison for whites) in a Ku Klux Klansman's uniform making an obscene gesture; a "patch" incorporating "KKK," a swastika, and the words "Aryan Pride;" and a black man with a noose around his neck hanging from a tree, of which he often remarks, "See my little n_____r hanging from a tree." He entered prison a Baptist and leaves a believer in Odinism, a pagan creed that is popu-

Figure 28 **John William King, circa 1999** (R. Jaap/Beaumont Enterprises/Corbis Sygma)

lar among neo-Nazi groups. Friend Louis Berry maintains, "we always thought all that hatred Bill had would kind of wear down and go away." In the fall of 1997, Bill begins dating Kylie Greeney, a local 17-year-old, who soon becomes pregnant with their child. Kylie concedes that Bill does not like Jews and most black people but she does not consider him a racist, claiming, "[H]e did have some black friends." In May 1998, Shawn Berry moves into King's apartment, along with Russell Brewer, King's former cellmate from Beto I, who returns to Jasper after his own prison stay.

Lawrence Russell Brewer, Jr., is older than Shawn Berry and Bill King and has his own criminal tendencies. He was convicted of burglary and sentenced to 15 years for drug possession in 1989. He is released in 1991 but violated parole in 1994 and was sent back to prison, where he too joined the Confederate Knights of America. There he met and befriended King. Oddly, Brewer is married to a Hispanic woman and, while in prison, he hides the fact of his marriage and their son from fellow gang members because he is afraid they will hurt him.

King and Brewer sleep late on Saturday, June 6, 1998, and then drive to a nearby town to hang out with Berry and drink beer. When King and Brewer arrive, Berry is having a heavy-metal jam session with some friends, one of whom is black. King gets angry that Berry has a black man over and refuses to come inside, saying he does not like black people.

Berry tells him to leave, so he and Brewer take off. Later that night, King and Brewer go to the Twin Cinemas to meet up with Berry. While they are at the theater, Christie Marcontell comes by, trying to patch up an argument with Berry. Berry tells her he is going to go home and go to bed early, but instead he, King, and Brewer drive around trying to find a party. They are unsuccessful and end up drinking beer and driving the country roads.

Figure 29 **Shawn Berry, 1999** (AP)

Figure 30 **Lawrence Russell Brewer, 1999**
(AP)

On that same afternoon, James Byrd attends a bridal shower for his niece where he plays with his one-year-old granddaughter and sees his sisters. His sisters give him a present after the shower and drop him off at a friend's house around 6 p.m. Byrd bids his sisters farewell, "I love ya'll both. I'll be all right from here on." Later that evening, Byrd goes to a party near the public housing development where he lives and around 1:30 a.m., unable to find a ride, sets out to walk home on Martin Luther King Boulevard. Byrd walks quite a bit because he cannot afford a car. He has acquired the nickname "Toe" because he walks with a limp due to a childhood accident in which he lost a toe.

While driving down Martin Luther King Boulevard, King, Berry, and Brewer come upon Byrd walking home. Berry recognizes Byrd because they had once shared a parole officer and offers him a ride over King's objections that they should not pick up a "f_____g n_____r." Berry stops the truck and Byrd gets in the back, with the three white men in the cab. The four men stop at a convenience store then drive off with King at the wheel.

King drives out of town to a secluded area and stops the truck in a clearing. He and Brewer drag Byrd from the back. They beat him viciously until he loses consciousness. Once he regains consciousness, they tie a chain used to haul lumber around Byrd's ankles and, with Berry driving, drag Byrd behind the truck for two to three miles. Byrd experiences intense burning pain as his flesh is torn off by the pavement, down to the bone in places. Byrd tries to relieve the pain by rolling from side to side, shifting one exposed part of his body for another, and struggles to keep his head off the ground. He manages to stay alive until the truck passes over a large drainage culvert and his body hits it with such force that his head and right arm are ripped away from his body. Berry finally stops the truck in front of an African American church on Huff Creek Road. They leave what remains of Byrd's mangled torso in the road in front of the church.

Almost all of Byrd's anterior ribs are fractured, and he suffers "massive brush burn abrasions" over most of his body. Both testicles are missing and gravel is inside the scrotal sac. Byrd's knees and part of his feet are "ground down" and his left cheek is ground down to the jawbone, his buttocks down to the sacrum and lower spine. Some of his toes are missing, others fractured, and large lacerations expose muscle up and down his legs. However, though separated from the rest of his body, his brain and skull are intact, suggesting, horrifically, that he maintained consciousness while being dragged. Byrd's heart was probably still beating when his body hit the culvert.

The next morning, June 7, police receive a phone call leading them to the church, where they find Byrd's torso with the remains of pants and underwear gathered around his ankles. "A trail of smeared blood and drag marks" lead from the torso down the road a mile and a half, where police find his head, neck, and right arm by a culvert. The gruesome trail continues another mile and a half down Huff Creek Road and onto a dirt logging road. At the end of the logging road police discover an area of matted-down grass where Byrd was beaten. The police mark the road where he was dragged with 81 orange spray-painted circles, designating his bodily remains and personal effects strewn along the way: "dentures," "keys," "head." Police can identify him only by his fingerprints. His sister Mylinda wonders, "What was going through his mind? What was he thinking while they were doing this to him?" The police also find a trail of personal effects of the suspects strewn down the road and at the fight scene: a wrench inscribed with the name "Berry," a cigarette lighter engraved with the words "Possum" (Bill King's nickname) and "KKK," three cigarette butts, a can of "fix-a-flat," a compact disc, a woman's watch, a can of black spray paint, a pack of Marlboro Lights, and beer bottles.

The wrench found at the murder scene makes Shawn Berry a suspect. The day after the murder, police spot his truck, notice that it has expired tags, and use that as an excuse to pull him over. They discover a set of tools matching the wrench found at the fight scene and bring him to the station for questioning. He says he was with King and Brewer on the night of the murder and that he knew James Byrd but offers nothing more. King and Brewer get word that

Figure 31 **Huff Creek Road in Jasper, Texas, where Byrd's body was found, June 12, 1998**

(Greg Smith/Corbis Saba)

Berry is in custody and worry that he will implicate them. The police put the apartment under surveillance, and when King and Brewer emerge at 2 a.m. Sunday for a trip to the Wal-Mart across the street, police ask the pair if they will come to the station. They agree and are taken in the squad car because neither King nor Brewer has a car of his own. During questioning, King appears smug and admits that on the night in question the three were driving around together looking for a party and picked up James Byrd, but claims that the last time he saw "Mr. Byrd" was when Berry drove off with Byrd after having dropped him and Brewer off at his apartment. Sheriff Rowles then asks King if they can search his apartment, to which he replies, "I've got nothing to hide; go ahead and search," and signs a voluntary consent-to-search form. By this time, it is almost 4 a.m. Berry has been in the interrogation room for many hours and is losing his composure. Sheriff Rowles tells him that King and Brewer have been arrested and warns him that prison time will be much harder for him because he has never been there before. Rowles gives him an out: "Tell us what you know, and I will make sure the federal prosecutors I call down here come to your cell first. Otherwise, I may just start with King and Brewer, and there's no telling what they are going to say." Berry breaks down in tears and writes a statement confessing to the murder of James Byrd and detailing King's and Brewer's involvement. Soon thereafter, Rowles is on his way to a meeting with an F.B.I. hate crimes unit in Beaumont.

Figure 32 **King's tattoos, photograph released by DA's Office**

(Corbis Sygma)

As news of the crime spreads, the people of Jasper are stunned and wonder how something so horrifying could happen in their town. Community meetings are held to discuss race relations—whites feel pangs of guilt; blacks are scared. Local African-American leaders struggle to prevent a violent response from angry black citizens. On Tuesday morning, two days after the body is found, yellow ribbons expressing solidarity begin appearing all over town. Thousands send cards and flowers expressing their sympathy and horror—so many that they cannot fit into the 300-seat Greater New Bethel Baptist Church for the funeral. National African-American leaders, including Jesse Jackson, U.S. Transportation Secretary Rodney Slater, Rep. Maxine Waters, and NAACP President Kweisi Mfume attend the funeral. President Clinton calls to express his condolences, and Chicago Bull and Texas native Dennis Rodman pays for the funeral and gives Byrd's family $25,000. Fight promoter Don King gives Byrd's children $100,000 to be put toward their education expenses.

Meanwhile, the three offenders do not attempt to hide the evidence. When police search the apartment, they find their bloody clothing. DNA analysis shows that the blood matches Byrd's DNA. DNA analysis also is performed on the cigarette butts found at the fight scene and along the logging road, revealing matches with the DNA of all three defendants. Further testing reveals that blood spatters underneath Berry's truck and on several of its tires match Byrd's DNA. The day after his arrest, Berry leads police and F.B.I. agents to the murder weapon buried in the woods behind his friend, Tommy Faulk's, trailer. He guides them to a piece of plywood and kicks it up, revealing a large hole and, inside, the 24-foot logging chain used to drag Byrd. The chain matches the rust imprint of a chain in the bed of Berry's truck. It does not take long for a grand jury to indict King, Brewer, and Berry for the capital murder of James Byrd.

While in jail awaiting trial, Bill King sends a letter to Russell Brewer celebrating the murder: "Reguardless [sic] of the outcome of this, we have made history

and shall die proudly remembered if need be. Much Arayan Love, Respect, and Honor, my brother in arms. Sieg Heil, Possum." Unbeknownst to King and Brewer, jailers intercept many notes passed between them in which they all but admit to the murder. The notes are admitted at trial, and defense attorneys call them "the most damning evidence against their clients."

Bill King, Russell Brewer, and Shawn Berry are convicted of capital murder.

Should King be executed for his crime?

Figure 33 **Byrd's funeral, Jasper, Texas**

(Beaumont Enterprise/Corbis Sygma)

1. Relying only upon your own intuitions of justice, what liability and punishment, if any, does Bill King deserve?

N	0	1	2	3	4	5	6	7	8	9	10	11
☐	☐	☐	☐	☐	☐	☐	☐	☐	☐	☐	☐	☒
no liability	liability but no punishment	1 day	2 wks	2 mo	6 mo	1 yr	3 yrs	7 yrs	15 yrs	30 yrs	life imprison- ment	death

2. What "justice" arguments could defense counsel make on the defendant's behalf?

3. What "justice" arguments could the prosecution make against the defendant?

4. What liability, if any, for King under the then-existing statutes? Prepare a list of each criminal code subsection in the order that you rely upon it in your analysis.

5. What liability, if any, under the Model Penal Code? Prepare a list of each criminal code subsection in the order that you rely upon it in your analysis.

■ THE LAW

Texas Penal Code
(1998)

Title 5. Offenses Against the Person

Chapter 19. Criminal Homicide

Section 19.01. Types of Criminal Homicide

(a) A person commits criminal homicide if he intentionally, knowingly, recklessly, or with criminal negligence causes the death of an individual.

(b) Criminal homicide is murder, capital murder, manslaughter, or criminally negligent homicide.

Section 19.02. Murder

(a) In this section:

(1) "Adequate cause" means cause that would commonly produce a degree of anger, rage, resentment, or terror in a person of ordinary temper, sufficient to render the mind incapable of cool reflection.

(2) "Sudden passion" means passion directly caused by and arising out of provocation by the individual killed or another acting with the person killed which passion arises at the time of the offense and is not solely the result of former provocation.

(b) A person commits an offense if he:

(1) intentionally or knowingly causes the death of an individual;

(2) intends to cause serious bodily injury and commits an act clearly dangerous to human life that causes the death of an individual; or

(3) commits or attempts to commit a felony, other than manslaughter, and in the course of and in furtherance of the commission or attempt, or in immediate

flight from the commission or attempt, he commits or attempts to commit an act clearly dangerous to human life that causes the death of an individual.

(c) Except as provided by Subsection (d), an offense under this section is a felony of the first degree.

(d) At the punishment stage of a trial, the defendant may raise the issue as to whether he caused the death under the immediate influence of sudden passion arising from an adequate cause. If the defendant proves the issue in the affirmative by a preponderance of the evidence, the offense is a felony of the second degree.

Section 19.03. Capital Murder

(a) A person commits an offense if he commits murder as defined under Section 19.02(b)(1) and:

(1) the person murders a peace officer or fireman who is acting in the lawful discharge of an official duty and who the person knows is a peace officer or fireman;

(2) the person intentionally commits the murder in the course of committing or attempting to commit kidnapping, burglary, robbery, aggravated sexual assault, arson, or obstruction or retaliation;

(3) the person commits the murder for remuneration or the promise of remuneration or employs another to commit the murder for remuneration or the promise of remuneration;

(4) the person commits the murder while escaping or attempting to escape from a penal institution;

(5) the person, while incarcerated in a penal institution, murders another:

(A) who is employed in the operation of the penal institution; or

(B) with the intent to establish, maintain, or participate in a combination or in the profits of a combination;

(6) the person:

(A) while incarcerated for an offense under this section or Section 19.02, murders another; or

(B) while serving a sentence of life imprisonment or a term of 99 years for an offense under Section 20.04, 22.021, or 29.03, murders another;

(7) the person murders more than one person:

(A) during the same criminal transaction; or

(B) during different criminal transactions but the murders are committed pursuant to the same scheme or course of conduct; or

(8) the person murders an individual under six years of age.

(b) An offense under this section is a capital felony.

(c) If the jury or, when authorized by law, the judge does not find beyond a reasonable doubt that the defendant is guilty of an offense under this section, he may be convicted of murder or of any other lesser included offense.

Chapter 20. Kidnapping and Unlawful Restraint

Section 20.01. Definitions

In this chapter:

(1) "Restrain" means to restrict a person's movements without consent, so as to interfere substantially with his liberty, by moving him from one place to another or by confining him. Restraint is "without consent" if it is accomplished by:

(A) force, intimidation, or deception; or

(B) any means, including acquiescence of the victim, if he is a child less than 14 years of age or an incompetent person and the parent, guardian, or person or institution acting in loco parentis has not acquiesced in the movement or confinement.

(2) "Abduct" means to restrain a person with intent to prevent his liberation by:

(A) secreting or holding him in a place where he is not likely to be found; or

(B) using or threatening to use deadly force.

(3) "Relative" means a parent or stepparent, ancestor, sibling, or uncle or aunt, including an adoptive relative of the same degree through marriage or adoption.

Section 20.03. Kidnapping

(a) A person commits an offense if he intentionally or knowingly abducts another person.

(b) It is an affirmative defense to prosecution under this section that:

(1) the abduction was not coupled with intent to use or to threaten to use deadly force;

(2) the actor was a relative of the person abducted; and

(3) the actor's sole intent was to assume lawful control of the victim.

(c) An offense under this section is a felony of the third degree.

Section 20.04. Aggravated Kidnapping

(a) A person commits an offense if he intentionally or knowingly abducts another person with the intent to:

(1) hold him for ransom or reward;

(2) use him as a shield or hostage;

(3) facilitate the commission of a felony or the flight after the attempt or commission of a felony;

(4) inflict bodily injury on him or violate or abuse him sexually;

(5) terrorize him or a third person; or

(6) interfere with the performance of any governmental or political function.

(b) A person commits an offense if the person intentionally or knowingly abducts another person and uses or exhibits a deadly weapon during the commission of the offense.

(c) Except as provided by Subsection (d), an offense under this section is a felony of the first degree.

(d) At the punishment stage of a trial, the defendant may raise the issue as to whether he voluntarily released the victim in a safe place. If the defendant proves the issue in the affirmative by a preponderance of the evidence, the offense is a felony of the second degree.

Title 2. General Principles of Criminal Responsibility

Chapter 6. Culpability Generally

Section 6.03. Definitions of Culpable Mental States

(a) A person acts intentionally, or with intent, with respect to the nature of his conduct or to a result of his conduct when it is his conscious objective or desire to engage in the conduct or cause the result.

(b) A person acts knowingly, or with knowledge, with respect to the nature of his conduct or to circumstances surrounding his conduct when he is aware of the nature of his conduct or that the circumstances exist. A person acts knowingly, or with knowledge, with respect to a result of his conduct when he is aware that his conduct is reasonably certain to cause the result.

Chapter 7. Criminal Responsibility for Conduct of Another
Subchapter A. Complicity

Section 7.01. Parties to Offenses

(a) A person is criminally responsible as a party to an offense if the offense is committed by his own conduct, by the conduct of another for which he is criminally responsible, or by both.

(b) Each party to an offense may be charged with commission of the offense.

(c) All traditional distinctions between accomplices and principals are abolished by this section, and each party to an offense may be charged and convicted without alleging that he acted as a principal or accomplice.

Section 7.02. Criminal Responsibility for Conduct of Another

(a) A person is criminally responsible for an offense committed by the conduct of another if:

(1) acting with the kind of culpability required for the offense, he causes or aids an innocent or nonresponsible person to engage in conduct prohibited by the definition of the offense;

(2) acting with intent to promote or assist the commission of the offense, he solicits, encourages, directs, aids, or attempts to aid the other person to commit the offense; or

(3) having a legal duty to prevent commission of the offense and acting with intent to promote or assist its commission, he fails to make a reasonable effort to prevent commission of the offense.

(b) If, in the attempt to carry out a conspiracy to commit one felony, another felony is committed by one of the conspirators, all conspirators are guilty of the felony actually committed, though having no intent to commit it, if the offense was committed in furtherance of the unlawful purpose and was one that should have been anticipated as a result of the carrying out of the conspiracy.

Section 7.03. Defenses Excluded

In a prosecution in which an actor's criminal responsibility is based on the conduct of another, the actor may be convicted on proof of commission of the offense and that he was a party to its commission, and it is no defense:

(1) that the actor belongs to a class of persons that by definition of the offense is legally incapable of committing the offense in an individual capacity; or

(2) that the person for whose conduct the actor is criminally responsible has been acquitted, has not been prosecuted or convicted, has been convicted of a different offense or of a different type or class of offense, or is immune from prosecution.

Title 1. Introductory Provisions

Chapter 1. General Provisions

Section 1.02. Objectives of Code

The general purposes of this code are to establish a system of prohibitions, penalties, and correctional measures to deal with conduct that unjustifiably and inexcusably causes or threatens harm to those individual or public interests for which state protection is appropriate. To this end, the provisions of this code are intended, and shall be construed, to achieve the following objectives:

(1) to insure the public safety through:

(A) the deterrent influence of the penalties hereinafter provided;

(B) the rehabilitation of those convicted of violations of this code; and

(C) such punishment as may be necessary to prevent likely recurrence of criminal behavior;

(2) by definition and grading of offenses to give fair warning of what is prohibited and of the consequences of violation;

(3) to prescribe penalties that are proportionate to the seriousness of offenses and that permit recognition of differences in rehabilitation possibilities among individual offenders;

(4) to safeguard conduct that is without guilt from condemnation as criminal;

(5) to guide and limit the exercise of official discretion in law enforcement to prevent arbitrary or oppressive treatment of persons suspected, accused, or convicted of offenses; and

(6) to define the scope of state interest in law enforcement against specific offenses and to systematize the exercise of state criminal jurisdiction.

Model Penal Code
(Official Draft 1962)

Section 210.6. Sentence of Death for Murder; Further Proceedings to Determine Sentence.

(1) Death Sentence Excluded. When a defendant is found guilty of murder, the Court shall impose sentence for a felony of the first degree if it is satisfied that:

(a) none of the aggravating circumstances enumerated in Subsection (3) of this Section was established by the evidence at the trial or will be established if further proceedings are initiated under Subsection (2) of this Section; or

(b) substantial mitigating circumstances, established by the evidence at the trial, call for leniency; or

(c) the defendant, with the consent of the prosecuting attorney and the approval of the Court, pleaded guilty to murder as a felony of the first degree; or

(d) the defendant was under 18 years of age at the time of the commission of the crime; or

(e) the defendant's physical or mental condition calls for leniency; or

(f) although the evidence suffices to sustain the verdict, it does not foreclose all doubt respecting the defendant's guilt.

(2) Determination by Court or by Court and Jury. Unless the Court imposes sentence under Subsection (1) of this Section, it shall conduct a separate proceeding to determine whether the defendant should be sentenced for a felony of the first degree or sentenced to death. The proceeding shall be conducted before the Court alone if the defendant was convicted by a Court sitting without a jury or upon his plea of guilty or if the prosecuting attorney and the defendant waive a jury with respect to sentence. In other cases it shall be conducted before the Court sitting with the jury which determined the defendant's guilt or, if the Court for good cause shown discharges that jury, with a new jury empaneled for the purpose.

In the proceeding, evidence may be presented as to any matter that the Court deems relevant to sentence, including but not limited to the nature and circumstances of the crime, the defendant's character, background, history, mental and physical condition and any of the aggravating or mitigating circumstances enumerated in Subsections (3) and (4) of this Section. Any such evidence, not legally privileged, which the Court deems to have probative force, may be received, regardless of its admissibility under the exclusionary rules of evidence, provided that the defendant's counsel is accorded a fair opportunity to rebut such evidence. The prosecuting attorney and the defendant or his counsel shall be permitted to present argument for or against sentence of death.

The determination whether sentence of death shall be imposed shall be in the discretion of the Court, except that when the proceeding is conducted before the Court sitting with a jury, the Court shall not impose sentence of death unless it submits to the jury the issue whether the defendant should be sentenced to death or to imprisonment and the jury returns a verdict that the sentence should be death. If the jury is unable to reach a unanimous verdict, the Court shall dismiss the jury and impose sentence for a felony of the first degree.

The Court, in exercising its discretion as to sentence, and the jury, in determining upon its verdict, shall take into account the aggravating and mitigating circumstances enumerated in Subsections (3) and (4) and any other facts that it deems relevant, but it shall not impose or recommend sentence of death unless it finds one of the aggravating circumstances enumerated in Subsection (3) and further finds that there are no mitigating circumstances sufficiently substantial to call for leniency. When the issue is submitted to the jury, the Court shall so instruct and also shall inform the jury of the nature of the sentence of imprisonment that may be imposed, including its implication with respect to possible release upon parole, if the jury verdict is against sentence of death. . . .

(3) Aggravating Circumstances.

(a) The murder was committed by a convict under sentence of imprisonment.

(b) The defendant was previously convicted of another murder or of a felony involving the use or threat of violence to the person.

(c) At the time the murder was committed the defendant also committed another murder.

(d) The defendant knowingly created a great risk of death to many persons.

(e) The murder was committed while the defendant was engaged or was an accomplice in the commission of, or an attempt to commit, or flight after committing or attempting to commit robbery, rape or deviate sexual intercourse by force or threat of force, arson, burglary or kidnapping.

(f) The murder was committed for the purpose of avoiding or preventing a lawful arrest or effecting an escape from lawful custody.

(g) The murder was committed for pecuniary gain.

(h) The murder was especially heinous, atrocious or cruel, manifesting exceptional depravity.

(4) Mitigating Circumstances.

(a) The defendant has no significant history of prior criminal activity.

(b) The murder was committed while the defendant was under the influence of extreme mental or emotional disturbance.

(c) The victim was a participant in the defendant's homicidal conduct or consented to the homicidal act.

(d) The murder was committed under circumstances which the defendant believed to provide a moral justification or extenuation for his conduct.

(e) The defendant was an accomplice in a murder committed by another person and his participation in the homicidal act was relatively minor.

(f) The defendant acted under duress or under the domination of another person.

(g) At the time of the murder, the capacity of the defendant to appreciate the criminality [wrongfulness] of his conduct or to conform his conduct to the requirements of law was impaired as a result of mental disease or defect or intoxication.

(h) The youth of the defendant at the time of the crime.

● OVERVIEW OF THE DEATH PENALTY

Notes

Death Penalty
    Concern with Racial Bias in Administering Death Penalty

Death Penalty   The Supreme Court has held that the death penalty is not per se cruel and unusual,[1] though the Court has invalidated its application to specific categories of offenders such as juveniles,[2] the mentally retarded,[3] and those who are incompetent at the time they are to be executed[4] (and, has invalidated capital punishment where disproportionate to the underlying crime). Capital punishment also may be imposed in a way that is unconstitutional for due process or other reasons. The Court addressed the proper process for administrating capital punishment in *Gregg v. Georgia*, (a portion of the decision is presented below) in which they upheld as constitutional a scheme replacing the one the Court had invalidated four years earlier (in *Furman v. Georgia*[5]). The Georgia statute approved in *Gregg* is one of several common formulations, providing a list of aggravating factors and requiring the jury to find at least one of these factors before recommending death.

---

1. Gregg v. Georgia, 428 U.S. 153 (1976).
2. Roper v. Simmons, 543 U.S. 551 (2005).
3. Atkins v. Virginia, 536 U.S. 304 (2002).
4. Panetti v. Quarterman, 551 U.S. 930 (2007).
5. 408 U.S. 238 (1972). In *Furman*, a 5–4 majority of the Supreme Court held that the death penalty in that case violated the prohibition against cruel and unusual punishment. Two of the justices in the majority thought all forms of capital punishment were unconstitutional; three based their decision on the discretionary nature of the penalty's administration. Within 4 years, at least 35 states had revised their death penalty statutes to meet the challenges offered by *Furman*, and one such scheme was upheld in *Gregg*.

Concern with Racial Bias in Administering Death Penalty   One concern driving *Furman*'s earlier rejection of Georgia's death penalty scheme was the potential for racial discrimination in administration of the penalty. In *McCleskey v. Kemp*,[6] the Court was presented with a statistical study suggesting that, while there may not be a greater likelihood that a black *defendant* will be given the death penalty than a white defendant in the same circumstances, the race of the *victim* might make a difference: Murders involving white victims led to the death penalty much more often than murders with black victims. A majority of the Court concluded, however, that nothing in the study showed that McCleskey, a black man who had killed a white man, had been the subject of discrimination that would make his death sentence a violation of either the Equal Protection or Cruel and Unusual Punishment Clauses.

Currently, 34 states, the federal government, and the United States Military allow for the imposition of the death penalty for certain crimes. The tables below, compiled by the United States Department of Justice, demonstrate that nearly all such sentences follow from convictions for murder. *Gregg v. Georgia*, excerpted below, sets out constitutionally mandated rules for how to determine whether a sentence of death may be imposed in a given case. (The opinion owes much to the Model Penal Code, from which it adopted the idea of a system of aggravating and mitigation factors.) The dissent in *Gregg* notes that there is no conclusive evidence that imposing the death penalty aids in either deterring crime or adequately serves retributivist goals. The question of whether or not the death penalty should be available as a punishment option is the focus of the Discussion Issue at the conclusion of this Section.

Gregg v. Georgia
Supreme Court of the United States
428 U.S. 153 (1976)

Judgment of the Court, and opinion of Mr. Justice STEWART, Mr. Justice POWELL, and Mr. Justice STEVENS, announced by Mr. Justice STEWART. . . .

We address initially the basic contention that the punishment of death for the crime of murder is, under all circumstances, "cruel and unusual" in violation of the Eighth and Fourteenth Amendments of the Constitution. . . . We now hold that the punishment of death does not invariably violate the Constitution. . . .

It is clear from the . . . precedents that the Eighth Amendment has not been regarded as a static concept. As Mr. Chief Justice Warren said, in an oft-quoted phrase, "[t]he Amendment must draw its meaning from the evolving standards of decency that mark the progress of a maturing society." Trop v. Dulles, 356 U.S. 86, 101 (1958). Thus, an assessment of contemporary values concerning the infliction of a challenged sanction is relevant to the application of the Eighth Amendment. . . .

But our cases also make clear that public perceptions of standards of decency with respect to criminal sanctions are not conclusive. A penalty also must accord with "the dignity of man," which is the "basic concept underlying the Eighth Amendment." Trop v. Dulles, supra, 356 U.S., at 100. This means, at least, that the punishment not be "excessive." . . . [T]he inquiry into "excessiveness" has two aspects. First, the punishment must not involve the unnecessary and wanton infliction of pain. Second, the punishment must not be grossly out of proportion to the severity of the crime.

Of course, the requirements of the Eighth Amendment must be applied with an awareness of the limited role to be played by the courts. . . . [W]hile we have an obligation to insure that constitutional bounds are not overreached, we may not act as judges as we might as legislators. . . .

---

6. 481 U.S. 279 (1987).

Therefore, in assessing a punishment selected by a democratically elected legislature against the constitutional measure, we presume its validity. We may not require the legislature to select the least severe penalty possible so long as the penalty selected is not cruelly inhumane or disproportionate to the crime involved. And a heavy burden rests on those who would attack the judgment of the representatives of the people.

. . . We now consider specifically whether the sentence of death for the crime of murder is a Per se violation of the Eighth and Fourteenth Amendments to the Constitution. We note first that history and precedent strongly support a negative answer to this question. . . . It is apparent from the text of the Constitution itself that the existence of capital punishment was accepted by the Framers. . . . For nearly two centuries, this Court, repeatedly and often expressly, has recognized that capital punishment is not invalid Per se. . . .

Four years ago, the petitioners in *Furman* and its companion cases predicated their argument primarily upon the asserted proposition that standards of decency had evolved to the point where capital punishment no longer could be tolerated. . . . The petitioners in the capital cases before the Court today renew the "standards of decency" argument, but developments during the four years since *Furman* have undercut substantially the assumptions upon which their argument rested. Despite the continuing debate, dating back to the 19th century, over the morality and utility of capital punishment, it is now evident that a large proportion of American society continues to regard it as an appropriate and necessary criminal sanction. The legislatures of at least 35 States have enacted new statutes that provide for the death penalty for at least some crimes that result in the death of another person. . . . [T]he relative infrequency of jury verdicts imposing the death sentence does not indicate rejection of capital punishment Per se. Rather, the reluctance of juries in many cases to impose the sentence may well reflect the humane feeling that this most irrevocable of sanctions should be reserved for a small number of extreme cases.

As we have seen, however, the Eighth Amendment demands more than that a challenged punishment be acceptable to contemporary society. The Court also must ask whether it comports with the basic concept of human dignity at the core of the Amendment. Although we cannot "invalidate a category of penalties because we deem less severe penalties adequate to serve the ends of penology," the sanction imposed cannot be so totally without penological justification that it results in the gratuitous infliction of suffering.

The death penalty is said to serve two principal social purposes: retribution and deterrence of capital crimes by prospective offenders.

In part, capital punishment is an expression of society's moral outrage at particularly offensive conduct. This function may be unappealing to many, but it is essential in an ordered society that asks its citizens to rely on legal processes rather than self-help to vindicate their wrongs. "The instinct for retribution is part of the nature of man, and channeling that instinct in the administration of criminal justice serves an important purpose in promoting the stability of a society governed by law. When people begin to believe that organized society is unwilling or unable to impose upon criminal offenders the punishment they 'deserve,' then there are sown the seeds of anarchy of self-help, vigilante justice, and lynch law." Furman v. Georgia, 408 U.S., at 308 (Stewart, J., concurring). . . .

Statistical attempts to evaluate the worth of the death penalty as a deterrent to crimes by potential offenders have occasioned a great deal of debate. The results simply have been inconclusive. . . . The value of capital punishment as a deterrent of crime is a complex factual issue the resolution of which properly rests with the legislatures, which can evaluate the results of statistical studies in terms of their own local conditions and with a flexibility of approach that is not available to the courts.

Finally, we must consider whether the punishment of death is disproportionate in relation to the crime for which it is imposed. There is no question that death as a punishment is unique in its severity and irrevocability. . . . But we are concerned here only with the imposition of capital punishment for the crime of murder, and when a life has been taken deliberately by the offender, we cannot say that the punishment is invariably disproportionate to the crime. It is an extreme sanction, suitable to the most extreme of crimes.

We hold that the death penalty is not a form of punishment that may never be imposed . . . regardless of the procedure followed in reaching the decision to impose it. . . . Because of the uniqueness of the death penalty, *Furman* held that it could not be imposed under sentencing procedures that created a substantial risk that it would be inflicted in an arbitrary and capricious manner. . . .

Jury sentencing has been considered desirable in capital cases in order "to maintain a link between contemporary community values and the penal system a link without which the determination of punishment could hardly reflect 'the evolving standards of decency that mark the progress of a maturing society.' "But it creates special problems. Much of the information that is relevant to the sentencing decision may have no relevance to the question of guilt, or may even be extremely prejudicial to a fair determination of that question. This problem, however, is scarcely insurmountable. Those who have studied the question suggest that a bifurcated procedure, one in which the question of sentence is not considered until the determination of guilt has been made, is . . . likely to ensure elimination of the constitutional deficiencies identified in *Furman*.

But the provision of relevant information under fair procedural rules is not alone sufficient to guarantee that the information will be properly used. . . . Since the members of a jury will have had little, if any, previous experience in sentencing, they are unlikely to be skilled in dealing with the information they are given. . . . It seems clear, however, that the problem will be alleviated if the jury is given guidance regarding the factors about the crime and the defendant that the State, representing organized society, deems particularly relevant to the sentencing decision. . . .

While some have suggested that standards to guide a capital jury's sentencing deliberations are impossible to formulate, the fact is that such standards have been developed. When the drafters of the Model Penal Code faced this problem, they concluded "that it is within the realm of possibility to point to the main circumstances of aggravation and of mitigation that should be weighed and *weighed against each other* when they are presented in a concrete case." ALI, Model Penal Code §201.6, Comment 3, p. 71 (Tent. Draft No. 9, 1959) (emphasis in original). While such standards are by necessity somewhat general, they do provide guidance to the sentencing authority and thereby reduce the likelihood that it will impose a sentence that fairly can be called capricious or arbitrary. . . .

In summary, the concerns expressed in *Furman* that the penalty of death not be imposed in an arbitrary or capricious manner can be met by a carefully drafted statute that ensures that the sentencing authority is given adequate information and guidance. As a general proposition these concerns are best met by a system that provides for a bifurcated proceeding at which the sentencing authority is apprised of the information relevant to the imposition of sentence and provided with standards to guide its use of the information. . . .

We now turn to consideration of the constitutionality of Georgia's capital-sentencing procedures. In the wake of *Furman*, Georgia amended its capital punishment statute, but chose not to narrow the scope of its murder provisions. See Part II, Supra. Thus, now as before *Furman*, in Georgia "[a] person commits murder when he unlawfully and with malice aforethought, either express or implied, causes the death of another human being." Ga. Code Ann., §26–1101(a) (1972).

Georgia did act, however, to narrow the class of murderers subject to capital punishment by specifying 10 statutory aggravating circumstances, one of which must be found by the jury to exist beyond a reasonable doubt before a death sentence can ever be imposed.[7] In addition, the jury is authorized to consider any other appropriate aggravating or mitigating circumstances. The jury is not required to find any mitigating circumstance in order to make a recommendation of mercy that is binding on the trial court, but it must find a Statutory aggravating circumstance before recommending a sentence of death. . . .

On their face these procedures seem to satisfy the concerns of *Furman*. No longer should there be "no meaningful basis for distinguishing the few cases in which [the death penalty] is imposed from the many cases in which it is not."

The petitioner contends, however, that the changes in the Georgia sentencing procedures are only cosmetic, that the arbitrariness and capriciousness condemned by *Furman* continue to exist. . . . First, the petitioner focuses on the opportunities for discretionary action that are inherent in the processing of any murder case

---

7. The statute provides in part:

"(a) The death penalty may be imposed for the offenses of aircraft hijacking or treason, in any case.

"(b) In all cases of other offenses for which the death penalty may be authorized, the judge shall consider, or he shall include in his instructions to the jury for it to consider, any mitigating circumstances or aggravating circumstances otherwise authorized by law and any of the following statutory aggravating circumstances which may be supported by the evidence:

"(1) The offense of murder, rape, armed robbery, or kidnapping was committed by a person with a prior record of conviction for a capital felony, or the offense of murder was committed by a person who has a substantial history of serious assaultive criminal convictions.

"(2) The offense of murder, rape, armed robbery, or kidnapping was committed while the offender was engaged in the commission of another capital felony, or aggravated battery, or the offense of murder was committed while the offender was engaged in the commission of burglary or arson in the first degree.

"(3) The offender by his act of murder, armed robbery, or kidnapping knowingly created a great risk of death to more than one person in a public place by means of a weapon or device which would normally be hazardous to the lives of more than one person.

"(4) The offender committed the offense of murder for himself or another, for the purpose of receiving money or any other thing of monetary value.

"(5) The murder of a judicial officer, former judicial officer, district attorney or solicitor or former district attorney or solicitor during or because of the exercise of his official duty.

"(6) The offender caused or directed another to commit murder or committed murder as an agent or employee of another person.

"(7) The offense of murder, rape, armed robbery, or kidnapping was outrageously or wantonly vile, horrible or inhuman in that it involved torture, depravity of mind, or an aggravated battery to the victim.

"(8) The offense of murder was committed against any peace officer, corrections employee or fireman while engaged in the performance of his official duties.

"(9) The offense of murder was committed by a person in, or who has escaped from, the lawful custody of a peace officer or place of lawful confinement.

"(10) The murder was committed for the purpose of avoiding, interfering with, or preventing a lawful arrest or custody in a place of lawful confinement, of himself or another.

"(c) The statutory instructions as determined by the trial judge to be warranted by the evidence shall be given in charge and in writing to the jury for its deliberation. The jury, if its verdict be a recommendation of death, shall designate in writing, signed by the foreman of the jury, the aggravating circumstance or circumstances which it found beyond a reasonable doubt. In non-jury cases the judge shall make such designation. Except in cases of treason or aircraft hijacking, unless at least one of the statutory aggravating circumstances enumerated in section 27–2534.1(b) is so found, the death penalty shall not be imposed." §27–2534.1 (Supp. 1975).

under Georgia law. He notes that the state prosecutor has unfettered authority to select those persons whom he wishes to prosecute for a capital offense and to plea bargain with them. Further, at the trial the jury may choose to convict a defendant of a lesser included offense rather than find him guilty of a crime punishable by death, even if the evidence would support a capital verdict. And finally, a defendant who is convicted and sentenced to die may have his sentence commuted by the Governor of the State and the Georgia Board of Pardons and Paroles.

The existence of these discretionary stages is not determinative of the issues before us. At each of these stages an actor in the criminal justice system makes a decision which may remove a defendant from consideration as a candidate for the death penalty. *Furman*, in contrast, dealt with the decision to impose the death sentence on a specific individual who had been convicted of a capital offense. Nothing in any of our cases suggests that the decision to afford an individual defendant mercy violates the Constitution. *Furman* held only that, in order to minimize the risk that the death penalty would be imposed on a capriciously selected group of offenders, the decision to impose it had to be guided by standards so that the sentencing authority would focus on the particularized circumstances of the crime and the defendant. . . .

For the reasons expressed in this opinion, we hold that the statutory system under which Gregg was sentenced to death does not violate the Constitution. Accordingly, the judgment of the Georgia Supreme Court is affirmed. . . .

Mr. Justice WHITE, with whom THE CHIEF JUSTICE and Mr. Justice REHNQUIST join, concurring in the judgment. [Omitted]

Justice MARSHALL, dissenting. . . .

I would be less than candid if I did not acknowledge that . . . developments [following *Furman*] have a significant bearing on a realistic assessment of the moral acceptability of the death penalty to the American people. But if the constitutionality of the death penalty turns, as I have urged, on the opinion of an informed citizenry, then even the enactment of new death statutes cannot be viewed as conclusive. In *Furman*, I observed that the American people are largely unaware of the information critical to a judgment on the morality of the death penalty, and concluded that if they were better informed they would consider it shocking, unjust, and unacceptable. . . .

The two purposes that sustain the death penalty as nonexcessive in the Court's view are general deterrence and retribution. . . . The evidence I reviewed in *Furman* remains convincing, in my view, that "capital punishment is not necessary as a deterrent to crime in our society."

The other principal purpose said to be served by the death penalty is retribution. The notion that retribution. . . . As my Brother BRENNAN stated in *Furman*, "[t]here is no evidence whatever that utilization of imprisonment rather than death encourages private blood feuds and other disorders." It simply defies belief to suggest that the death penalty is necessary to prevent the American people from taking the law into their own hands. . . .

Sourcebook of Criminal Justice Statistics

(2000); online at http://www.albany.edu/sourcebook/

The accompanying statistics give an overview of the use of the death penalty in the United States. The debate over this controversial practice is the subject of the Discussion Issue, below.

Table 7.1 **Prisoners under sentence of death**

By demographic characteristics, prior felony conviction history, and legal status, United States, on Dec. 31, 1996-2000[a]

	Percent of prisoners				
	1996	1997	1998	1999	2000
Sex					
Male	98.5%	98.7%	98.6%	98.6%	98.5%
Female	1.5	1.3	1.4	1.4	1.5
Race					
White	56.5	56.3	55.2	55.2	55.4
Black	41.9	42.2	43.0	42.9	42.7
Other	1.6	1.6	1.7	1.8	1.9
Hispanic origin					
Hispanic	8.8	9.2	10.0	10.2	10.6
Non-Hispanic	91.2	90.8	90.0	89.8	89.4
Age[b]					
17 years and younger	(c)	0	0	0	0
18 to 19 years	0.5	0.4	0.4	0.5	0.3
20 to 24 years	8.7	8.2	7.7	7.1	6.6
25 to 29 years	14.9	14.9	15.0	14.6	13.6
30 to 34 years	18.5	17.3	16.9	16.8	17.1
35 to 39 years	21.8	21.8	20.6	20.0	19.1
40 to 44 years	14.9	15.6	16.7	17.0	18.2
45 to 49 years	10.6	10.6	10.2	10.5	10.9
50 to 54 years	5.7	6.5	7.5	7.9	8.0
55 to 59 years	2.5	2.6	2.9	3.2	3.5
60 years and older	1.8	1.9	2.1	2.3	2.7
Education					
Grade 8 or less	14.4	14.2	14.3	13.9	14.4
Grades 9 to 11	37.5	37.6	37.6	37.7	37.3
High school graduate/GED	37.8	38.0	38.0	38.2	38.2
Any college	10.2	10.1	10.1	10.1	10.1
Marital status					
Married	24.9	24.5	24.0	22.9	22.6
Divorced or separated	21.3	21.3	20.8	21.2	21.0
Widowed	2.7	2.6	2.7	2.8	2.8
Never married	51.1	51.5	52.5	53.0	53.6
Prior felony conviction history					
Prior felony conviction	65.7	65.3	65.0	64.1	64.0
No prior felony conviction	34.3	34.7	35.0	35.9	36.0
Prior homicide conviction history					
Prior homicide conviction	8.6	8.6	8.6	8.4	8.1
No prior homicide conviction	91.4	91.4	91.4	91.6	91.9
Legal status at time of capital offense					
Charges pending	7.3	7.6	7.2	7.4	7.1
Probation	10.0	10.1	9.9	10.0	10.1
Parole	20.0	19.5	18.1	17.9	17.6
Prison escapee	1.4	1.3	1.3	1.3	1.2
Incarcerated	2.4	2.6	2.9	2.8	2.7
Other status	1.1	1.0	0.9	0.7	0.6
None	57.7	58.0	59.7	60.0	60.6

Note: Thirty-eight States and the Federal Government had death penalty statutes in effect at yearend 1996-2000. Percents are based on those cases for which data were reported. The U.S. military also has a death penalty provision, but the Bureau of Justice Statistics does not collect data for persons under military death sentence.

[a]Percents may not add to 100 because of rounding.
[b]The youngest person under sentence of death in 1996 was a black male in Nevada born in May 1979 and sentenced to death in June 1996; in 1997, a black male in Alabama born in November 1979 and sentenced to death in October 1997; in 1998, a black male in Alabama born in July 1980 and sentenced to death in December 1998; in 1999, a black male in Texas born in December 1981 and sentenced to death in November 1999; in 2000, a white male in Arizona born in April 1982 and sentenced to death in October 2000. The oldest person under sentence of death during the years 1996 to 2000 was a white male in Arizona born in September 1915 and sentenced to death in June 1983.

[c]Less than 0.1%.

Source: U.S. Department of Justice, Bureau of Justice Statistics, *Capital Punishment 1996*, Bulletin NCJ-167031, p. 8, Table 7; p. 9; p. 10, Table 9; *1997*, Bulletin NCJ-172881, p. 8, Table 7; p. 9; p. 10, Table 9; *1998*, Bulletin NCJ 179012, p. 8, Table 7; p. 9; p. 10, Table 9; *1999*, Bulletin NCJ 184795, p. 8, Table 7; p. 9; p. 10, Table 9; *2000*, Bulletin NCJ 190598, p. 8, Table 7; p. 9; p. 10, Table 9 (Washington, DC: U.S. Department of Justice). Table adapted by SOURCEBOOK staff.

Table 7.2 **Arrests**

By offense charged, age group, and race, United States, 2000

(9,017 agencies; 2000 estimated population 182,090,101)

Offense charged	Total arrests					Percent[a]				
	Total	White	Black	American Indian or Alaskan Native	Asian or Pacific Islander	Total	White	Black	American Indian or Alaskan Native	Asian or Pacific Islander
Total	9,068,977	6,324,006	2,528,368	112,192	104,411	100.0%	69.7%	27.9%	1.2%	1.2%
Murder and nonnegligent manslaughter	8,683	4,231	4,238	87	127	100.0	48.7	48.8	1.0	1.5
Forcible rape	17,859	11,381	6,089	197	192	100.0	63.7	34.1	1.1	1.1
Robbery	72,149	31,921	38,897	445	886	100.0	44.2	53.9	0.6	1.2
Aggravated assault	315,729	200,634	107,494	3,542	4,059	100.0	63.5	34.0	1.1	1.3
Burglary	188,726	131,049	53,573	1,787	2,317	100.0	69.4	28.4	0.9	1.2
Larceny-theft	779,166	519,671	236,801	9,916	12,778	100.0	66.7	30.4	1.3	1.6
Motor vehicle theft	98,318	54,490	40,886	1,099	1,843	100.0	55.4	41.6	1.1	1.9
Arson	10,634	8,121	2,305	99	109	100.0	76.4	21.7	0.9	1.0
Violent crime[b]	414,420	248,167	156,718	4,271	5,264	100.0	59.9	37.8	1.0	1.3
Property crime[c]	1,076,844	713,331	333,565	12,901	17,047	100.0	66.2	31.0	1.2	1.6
Total Crime Index[d]	1,491,264	961,498	490,283	17,172	22,311	100.0	64.5	32.9	1.2	1.5
Other assaults	855,536	564,571	269,736	11,695	9,534	100.0	66.0	31.5	1.4	1.1
Forgery and counterfeiting	70,828	48,197	21,227	421	983	100.0	68.0	30.0	0.6	1.4
Fraud	211,984	142,684	66,672	1,173	1,455	100.0	67.3	31.5	0.6	0.7
Embezzlement	12,539	7,975	4,281	51	232	100.0	63.6	34.1	0.4	1.9
Stolen property; buying, receiving, possessing	78,429	46,233	30,690	579	927	100.0	58.9	39.1	0.7	1.2
Vandalism	184,010	139,662	39,779	2,573	1,996	100.0	75.9	21.6	1.4	1.1
Weapons; carrying, possessing, etc.	104,996	64,410	38,596	776	1,214	100.0	61.3	36.8	0.7	1.2
Prostitution and commercialized vice	61,347	35,567	24,222	514	1,044	100.0	58.0	39.5	0.8	1.7
Sex offenses (except forcible rape and prostitution)	60,936	45,317	14,149	668	802	100.0	74.4	23.2	1.1	1.3
Drug abuse violations	1,039,086	667,485	358,571	5,547	7,483	100.0	64.2	34.5	0.5	0.7
Gambling	7,149	2,195	4,607	29	318	100.0	30.7	64.4	0.4	4.4
Offenses against family and children	90,502	61,212	26,805	931	1,554	100.0	67.6	29.6	1.0	1.7
Driving under the influence	900,089	793,696	86,194	11,855	8,344	100.0	88.2	9.6	1.3	0.9
Liquor laws	433,637	371,186	46,107	13,091	3,253	100.0	85.6	10.6	3.0	0.8
Drunkenness	421,859	357,283	57,806	4,633	2,137	100.0	84.7	13.7	1.1	0.5
Disorderly conduct	419,408	273,884	136,573	6,030	2,921	100.0	65.3	32.6	1.4	0.7
Vagrancy	21,967	11,772	9,524	562	109	100.0	53.6	43.4	2.6	0.5
All other offenses (except traffic)	2,400,906	1,579,231	758,669	31,441	31,565	100.0	65.8	31.6	1.3	1.3
Suspicion	3,675	2,535	1,086	11	43	100.0	69.0	29.6	0.3	1.2
Curfew and loitering law violations	105,563	76,233	26,065	1,165	2,100	100.0	72.2	24.7	1.1	2.0
Runaways	93,267	71,180	16,726	1,275	4,086	100.0	76.3	17.9	1.4	4.4

Table 7.3 **Prisoners executed under civil authority**
By race and offense, United States, 1930-97
(- represents zero)

	Total				White				Black				Other			
	Total	Murder	Rape	Other offenses[a]	Total	Murder	Rape	Other offenses	Total	Murder	Rape	Other offenses	Total	Murder	Rape	Other offenses
1997	74	74	-	-	45	45	-	-	27	27	-	-	2	2	-	-
1996	45	45	-	-	31	31	-	-	14	14	-	-	-	-	-	-
1995	56	56	-	-	33	33	-	-	22	22	-	-	1	1	-	-
1994	31	31	-	-	20	20	-	-	11	11	-	-	-	-	-	-
1993	38	38	-	-	23	23	-	-	14	14	-	-	1	1	-	-
1992	31	31	-	-	19	19	-	-	11	11	-	-	1	1	-	-
1991	14	14	-	-	7	7	-	-	7	7	-	-	-	-	-	-
1990	23	23	-	-	16	16	-	-	7	7	-	-	-	-	-	-
1989	16	16	-	-	8	8	-	-	8	8	-	-	-	-	-	-
1988	11	11	-	-	6	6	-	-	5	5	-	-	-	-	-	-
1987	25	25	-	-	13	13	-	-	12	12	-	-	-	-	-	-
1986	18	18	-	-	11	11	-	-	7	7	-	-	-	-	-	-
1985	18	18	-	-	11	11	-	-	7	7	-	-	-	-	-	-
1984	21	21	-	-	13	13	-	-	8	8	-	-	-	-	-	-
1983	5	5	-	-	4	4	-	-	1	1	-	-	-	-	-	-
1982	2	2	-	-	1	1	-	-	1	1	-	-	-	-	-	-
1981	1	1	-	-	1	1	-	-	-	-	-	-	-	-	-	-
1980	-	-	-	-	-	-	-	-	-	-	-	-	-	-	-	-
1979	2	2	-	-	2	2	-	-	-	-	-	-	-	-	-	-
1978	-	-	-	-	-	-	-	-	-	-	-	-	-	-	-	-
1977[b]	1	1	-	-	1	1	-	-	-	-	-	-	-	-	-	-
1967	2	2	-	-	1	1	-	-	1	1	-	-	-	-	-	-
1966	1	1	-	-	1	1	-	-	-	-	-	-	-	-	-	-
1965	7	7	-	-	6	6	-	-	1	1	-	-	-	-	-	-
1964	15	9	6	-	8	5	3	-	7	4	3	-	-	-	-	-
1963	21	18	2	1	13	12	-	1	8	6	2	-	-	-	-	-
1962	47	41	4	2	28	26	2	-	19	15	2	2	-	-	-	-
1961	42	33	8	1	20	18	1	1	22	15	7	-	-	-	-	-
1960	56	44	8	4	21	18	-	3	35	26	8	1	-	-	-	-
1959	49	41	8	-	16	15	1	-	33	26	7	-	-	-	-	-
1958	49	41	7	1	20	20	-	-	28	20	7	1	1	1	-	-
1957	65	54	10	1	34	32	2	-	31	22	8	1	-	-	-	-
1956	65	52	12	1	21	20	-	1	43	31	12	-	1	1	-	-
1955	76	65	7	4	44	41	1	2	32	24	6	2	-	-	-	-
1954	81	71	9	1	38	37	1	-	42	33	8	1	1	1	-	-
1953	62	51	7	4	30	25	1	4	31	25	6	-	1	1	-	-
1952	83	71	12	-	36	35	1	-	47	36	11	-	-	-	-	-
1951	105	87	17	1	57	55	2	-	47	31	15	1	1	1	-	-
1950	82	68	13	1	40	36	4	-	42	32	9	1	-	-	-	-
1949	119	107	10	2	50	49	-	1	67	56	10	1	2	2	-	-
1948	119	95	22	2	35	32	1	2	82	61	21	-	2	2	-	-
1947	153	129	23	1	42	40	2	-	111	89	21	1	-	-	-	-
1946	131	107	22	2	46	45	-	1	84	61	22	1	1	1	-	-
1945	117	90	26	1	41	37	4	-	75	52	22	1	1	1	-	-
1944	120	96	24	-	47	45	2	-	70	48	22	-	3	3	-	-
1943	131	118	13	-	54	54	-	-	74	63	11	-	3	1	2	-
1942	147	115	25	7	67	57	4	6	80	58	21	1	-	-	-	-
1941	123	102	20	1	59	55	4	-	63	46	16	1	1	1	-	-
1940	124	105	15	4	49	44	2	3	75	61	13	1	-	-	-	-
1939	160	145	12	3	80	79	-	1	77	63	12	2	3	3	-	-
1938	190	154	25	11	96	89	1	6	92	63	24	5	2	2	-	-
1937	147	133	13	1	69	67	2	-	74	62	11	1	4	4	-	-
1936	195	181	10	4	92	86	2	4	101	93	8	-	2	2	-	-
1935	199	184	13	2	119	115	2	2	77	66	11	-	3	3	-	-
1934	168	154	14	-	65	64	1	-	102	89	13	-	1	1	-	-
1933	160	151	7	2	77	75	1	1	81	74	6	1	2	2	-	-
1932	140	128	10	2	62	62	-	-	75	63	10	2	3	3	-	-
1931	153	137	15	1	77	76	1	-	72	57	14	1	4	4	-	-
1930	155	147	6	2	90	90	-	-	65	57	6	2	-	-	-	-
1930-97	4,291	3,666	455	70	2,016	1,929	48	39	2,228	1,792	405	31	47	45	2	-

[a]Includes 25 executed for armed robbery, 20 for kidnaping, 11 for burglary, 6 for sabotage, 6 for aggravated assault, and 2 for espionage.

[b]There were no executions from 1968 through 1976.

Source: U.S. Department of Justice, Bureau of Justice Statistics, *Correctional Populations in the United States, 1997*, NCJ 177613 (Washington, DC: U.S. Department of Justice, 2000), Table 7.26. Table adapted by SOURCEBOOK staff.

Table 7.4 **Reported reasons for favoring the death penalty for persons convicted of murder**
United States, 2001

Question: "Why do you favor the death penalty for persons convicted of murder?"

Reason for favoring	
An eye for an eye/they took a life/fits the crime	48%
Save taxpayers money/cost associated with prison	20
Deterrent for potential crimes/set an example	10
They deserve it	6
Support/believe in death penalty	6
Depends on the type of crime they commit	6
They will repeat their crime/keep them from repeating it	6
Biblical reasons	3
Relieves prison overcrowding	2
If there's no doubt the person committed the crime	2
Life sentences don't always mean life in prison	2
Don't believe they can be rehabilitated	2
Serve justice	1
Fair punishment	1
Would help/benefit families of victims	1
Other	3
No opinion	1

Note: This question was asked only of the respondents who answered
"yes, in favor" to the question presented in table [2.64].

Source: The Gallup Organization, Inc., *The Gallup Poll* [Online]. Available:
http://www.gallup.com/poll/releases/pr010302.asp [Mar. 2, 2001]. Table adapted by
SOURCEBOOK staff. Reprinted by permission.

▲ PROBLEMS

If the death penalty is ever to be available, there is widespread acceptance that it ought to be in cases of aggravated first-degree murder. For what other offenses ought it be available, if any, and how would one determine this question? Recall the Slovik Problem Case (#12) in Section 3, of desertion in time of war. Should the death penalty be available for such an offense? Should it be available in the three Problem cases below?

What effect, if any, do the distributive principles discussed in Section 3 have in this question? Might one come to different conclusions about when to apply the death penalty depending on the distributive principle being relied upon: deterrence, incapacitation, or desert?

Drunk Driving as Capital Murder (#32)

Thomas Richard Jones has a history of drug and alcohol abuse. Starting at age 15, he has been abusing drugs, drinking excessively, and getting into trouble. As he grows older, his problems only increase. Often, he combines his drug and alcohol use with driving, endangering the lives of others as well as his own. He is twice convicted of driving while impaired and recently forced a police car off the road while driving drunk. Fortunately the officer was not injured, but Jones faces criminal charges over the incident. With his impending trial looming, Jones resorts all the more to narcotics, guzzling plenty of beer along with them. Against his mother's pleading, Jones gets behind the wheel following another of his drug and alcohol binges. He rear-ends a car stopped at a red light, then speeds off on the wrong side of the road, striking another car head-on.

The car he hits is carrying six female Wake Forest students, who are going to get a snack during a late-night study break. While Jones is able to walk away from the accident, four of the women need to be hospitalized; and two, Maia Witzl and Julie Hansen, eventually die. They are each 19 years old.

Fed up with Jones's drunk driving recidivism, the prosecutor pursues a felony-murder charge, elevating what would normally be reckless homicide to murder, on the grounds that Jones used a deadly weapon (his car) to cause the death. Convicted of first-degree murder, the prosecutor seeks the death penalty in sentencing in order to publicize the tough stance taken on drunk driving.

Under the Model Penal Code, would Jones qualify for the death penalty? Prepare a list of all criminal code subsections in the order in which you rely upon them in your analysis.

What arguments can you make for and against the death penalty in this case?

Child Rape and the Death Penalty (#33)

Patrick Kennedy is recently married. Along with his new wife, he now also has an eight-year-old stepdaughter and four-year-old stepson. His wife goes to work early, so Kennedy is in charge of getting the children ready for school before he too goes to work. One morning, however, he calls his office to say that he cannot come in. His boss is worried because Kennedy sounds frantic and asks him how to remove blood stains from a carpet. Kennedy explains that his stepdaughter has "just become a young lady" and hangs up to call a professional carpet cleaner. He arranges for the cleaners to come to the house, but before they arrive Kennedy calls 911 and reports that his stepdaughter has been raped. He tells the 911 operator that he heard screams from outside while he helped his stepson get ready for school and found his stepdaughter lying in the front yard and bleeding.

However, when the police arrive, they notice that there is little blood in the yard and a trail of blood leading from the house. Entering the house to investigate, they find a trail of blood leading up the stairs, where they find Kennedy and his stepdaughter. She is wrapped in a blanket and bleeding profusely. At first, Kennedy answers for her when the police ask her questions. He insists on being present during her questioning. While she initially corroborates his story, claiming that she was raped by two teenagers, her description does not match the physical evidence. She later confides to a family member that her stepfather is the rapist. Taken to the hospital, her injuries are found to be extensive. As a result of the rape, she requires surgery to repair several internal organs.

Under the Model Penal Code, would Kennedy qualify for imposition of the death penalty? Prepare a list of all criminal code subsections in the order in which you rely upon them in your analysis.

What arguments can you make for and against the death penalty in this case?

The Original Nuclear Proliferation (#34)

Julius and Ethel Rosenberg are self-professed communists living in the United States at the dawn of the Cold War. They met as members of the Young Communist League, when Julius had been the president of the group. In 1942, they join the American Communist Party but drop out a year later when Julius finds work as a civilian engineer with the United States Army Signal Corps. However, the Rosenbergs have not abandoned their communist ideology. In fact, with Julius's new access to military intelligence, they go to work as spies for the Soviet Union, disclosing United States military secrets. Eventually, Julius's past involvement with communist politics is discovered, and he is discharged from the army. However, the Rosenbergs are still valuable spies.

Ethel's brother, Sergeant David Greenglass, is a machinist working on America's top secret "Manhattan Project," which is exploring how to build an atomic bomb. The Rosenbergs approach Greenglass about obtaining information about the project for them, and, sharing their communist sympathies, Greenglass agrees. The Rosenbergs are soon providing their Soviet contact with American and British nuclear secrets. In 1949, only four years after the United States developed the atomic bomb, the Soviet Union shocks the world with their first successful nuclear test. A year later, a Soviet spy is apprehended. It is the Rosenbergs' contact, and they are soon identified as the source of information that allowed the Soviets to make such rapid progress. The Rosenbergs are tried for espionage and are both found guilty. Under the Espionage Act, they are eligible for the death penalty.

What arguments can you make for and against the death penalty in this case?

While the Soviet Union never used a nuclear device against the United States, such a possibility did exist. In a modern context, should a person found guilty of providing nuclear technology to a terrorist organization be subject to the death penalty? Why or why not?

✳ DISCUSSION ISSUE

Should Capital Punishment Be Allowed?

Materials presenting each side of this Discussion Issue appear in the Advanced Materials for Section 7 in Appendix A.

Homicide: Doctrines of Mitigation

Just as unintentional killings can sometimes be aggravated to murder, intentional killings can sometimes be mitigated to manslaughter. The common law doctrine of provocation can so mitigate, as can mental illness short of insanity. These older doctrines are carried forward in broader form in modern codes as the doctrine of extreme mental or emotional disturbance. The point is to identify those cases in which the circumstances of the killing, while still deserving of serious punishment, are meaningfully different from cases of killings where no such mitigation is present. That is, the doctrines of mitigation serve as much to reinforce the greater condemnation deserved by non-mitigation cases as to reduce the condemnation in mitigation cases.

◆ THE CASE OF JOHN GOUNAGIAS (#35)

Like many Greek immigrants living in Camas, Washington, John Gounagias and Dionisios Grounas work at the local paper mill. They also room together and frequent a local coffeehouse, a popular gathering place for the Greek community.

Figure 38 **Postcard of the Camas Mill, circa 1918**
(Camas-Washougal Historical Society)

On April 18, 1914, the day before Greek Easter, Gounagias and two friends *? probs not* are leafing through a Greek magazine when they come across an ad for a .32-caliber revolver and other miscellaneous articles. Gounagias thinks he sees a bargain and orders the gun.

The next day, on Greek Easter, both Gounagias and Grounas are at home. Gounagias is drinking beer and becomes extremely drunk, almost to the point of passing out. The two men get into an argument, during which Grounas insults Gounagias and his wife, who is still living in Greece. Later, when Gounagias is lying helplessly on the floor in a semiconscious state, Grounas forcibly sodomizes him and leaves the house. After recovering his senses, Gounagias gathers his things and moves out, relocating to another house nearby. The following day, he happens upon Grounas and confronts him. Grounas just laughs, "You're all right. It did not hurt you." Gounagias pleads with him not to tell their countrymen in order to avoid the humiliation that he knows it would bring. Grounas ignores his request and Gounagias is tortured by his countrymen with lewd gestures and remarks when he goes into town during the days following the event. Under the constant and brutal ridicule, Gounagias develops severe, debilitating headaches.

About two weeks later, the revolver Gounagias ordered arrives. He buys ammunition for it and stores it in a slit in the underside of his mattress. Meanwhile, his countrymen, encouraged by Grounas, continue to taunt him about Gounagias being sodomized. A week after receiving the gun, Gounagias wakes up with such an excruciating headache that he cannot go to work. He tries to distract himself by going to the billiards hall, visiting the coffeehouse, and playing cards with the local baker. As the afternoon wears on, though, he becomes so depressed that he goes to the river intending to commit suicide, but balks. He then visits some friends. Afterward, Gounagias meets a man from the old country and invites him back to his house, where they converse for quite some time. Around 11 p.m. he decides to return to the coffeehouse but is barely inside before a group of rowdy Greeks publicly taunt him again about being sodomized. Gounagias finally snaps. He rushes out, enraged and full of vengeance, wishing to kill Grounas. Quickly returning home, he retrieves his new gun, loads it, and runs up the hill to Grounas' house. Gounagias lights a match to find his way through Grounas's dark home, and discovers Grounas asleep in bed. Without hesitating, Gounagias shoots him in the head, firing five shots, emptying the revolver. He returns home, removing the empty shells on the way, and puts the gun back inside the mattress. He is arrested shortly after he gets into bed.

1. Relying only upon your own intuitions of justice, what liability and punishment, if any, does John Gounagias deserve?

Symptoms of Post traumatic stress disorder

N	0	1	2	3	4	5	6	7	8	9	10	11
☐	☐	☐	☐	☐	☐	☐	☐	☐	☒	☐	☐	☐
no	liability	1 day	2 wks	2 mo	6 mo	1 yr	3 yrs	7 yrs	15 yrs	30 yrs	life	death
liability	but no										imprison-	
	punishment										ment	

2. What "justice" arguments could defense counsel make on the defendant's behalf?

3. What "justice" arguments could the prosecution make against the defendant?

4. What liability, if any, for Gounagias under the then-existing statutes? Prepare a list of all criminal code subsections and cases in the order in which you rely upon them in your analysis.

5. What liability, if any, under the Model Penal Code? Prepare a list of all criminal code subsections in the order in which you rely upon them in your analysis.

▪ THE LAW

Annotated Codes and Statutes of Washington
(1914)

Crimes and Punishments, Title XIV

Section 2390 Homicide—Defined and Classified

Homicide is the killing of a human being by the act, procurement or omission of another and is either (1) murder, (2) manslaughter, (3) excusable homicide or (4) justifiable homicide.

Section 2392 Murder in the First Degree

The killing of a human being, unless it is excusable or justifiable, is murder in the first degree when committed either—

(Handwritten margin notes: Took place over 3 weeks, must have thought about it, thought blamed Gounagias, can't remove Gounagias from humiliating experience, when snaps, goes directly to Gounagias' house)

(1) With a premeditated design to effect the death of the person killed, or of another; or

(2) By an act imminently dangerous to others and evincing a depraved mind, regardless of human life, without a premeditated design to effect the death of any individual; or

(3) Without a design to effect death, be a person engaged in the commission of, or in an attempt to commit, or in withdrawing from the scene of a robbery, rape, burglary, larceny or arson in the first degree; or

(4) By maliciously interfering or tampering with or obstructing any switch, frog, rail, roadbed, sleeper, viaduct, bridge, trestle, culvert, embankment, structure, or appliance pertaining to or connected with any railway, or any engine, motor or car of such railway.

Murder in the first degree shall be punishable by death or by imprisonment in the state penitentiary for life, in the discretion of the court.

Section 2393 Murder in the Second Degree

The killing of a human being, unless it is excusable or justifiable, is murder in the second degree when—

(1) Committed with the design to effect the death of the person killed or of another, but without premeditation; or

(2) When perpetrated by a person engaged in the commission of, or in an attempt to commit, or in withdrawing from the scene of, a felony other than those enumerated in section 2392.

Murder in the second degree shall be punished by imprisonment in the state penitentiary for not less than three years.

Section 2395 Manslaughter

In any case other than those specified in sections 2392, 2393 and 2394 [dueling], homicide, not being excusable or justifiable, is manslaughter.

Manslaughter is punishable by imprisonment in the state penitentiary for not more than twenty years, or by imprisonment in the county jail for not more than one year, or by a fine of not more than one thousand dollars, or by both fine and imprisonment.

Section 2404 Homicide, When Excusable

Homicide is excusable when committed by accident or misfortune in doing any lawful act by lawful means, with ordinary caution and without any unlawful intent.

Section 2405 Justifiable Homicide by Public Officer

Homicide is justifiable when committed by a public officer, or person acting under his command and in his aid, in the following cases:

(1) In obedience to the judgment of a competent court.

(2) When necessary to overcome actual resistance to the execution of the legal process, mandate or order of a court or officer, or in the discharge of a legal duty.

(3) When necessary in retaking an escaped or rescued prisoner who has been committed, arrested for, or convicted of a felony; or in arresting a person who has committed a felony and is fleeing from justice; or in attempting, by lawful ways or means, to apprehend a person for a felony actually committed; or in lawfully suppressing a riot or preserving the peace.

Section 2406 Homicide by Other Person, When Justifiable

Homicide is also justifiable when committed either—

(1) In the lawful defense of the slayer, or his or her husband, wife, parent, child, brother or sister, or any other person in his presence or company, when there is reasonable ground to apprehend a design on the part of the person slain to commit a felony or to do some great personal injury to the slayer or to any such person, and there is imminent danger of such design being accomplished; or

(2) In the actual resistance of an attempt to commit a felony upon the slayer, in his presence, or upon or in a dwelling, or other place of abode, in which he is.

Section 2299 Common Law to Supplement Statute

The provisions of the common law relating to the commission of crime and the punishment thereof, in so far as not inconsistent with the institutions and statutes of this state, shall supplement all penal statutes of this state and all persons offending against the same shall be tried in the superior courts of the state.

Procedure in Criminal Actions, Title XIII

Section 2173 "Criminally Insane," Defined—Mental Irresponsibility

Any person who shall have committed a crime while insane, or in a condition of mental irresponsibility, and in whom such an insanity or mental irresponsibility continues to exist, shall be deemed criminally insane within the meaning of this act. No condition of mind induced by the voluntary act of a person charged with a crime shall be deemed mental irresponsibility within the meaning of this act.

Maher v. People
10 Mich. 212, 81 Am. Dec. 781 (1862)

The defendant appealed his conviction for assault with intent to murder another man, Patrick Hunt. During his trial, the defendant offered mitigating evidence to show that he was provoked by Hunt's adultery with the defendant's wife within half an hour of the assault, and consequently, his charges should be reduced to manslaughter. The defendant testified that he saw Hunt and his wife go into the woods together, which caused him to believe they were having an affair, and saw them return from the woods soon after. Additionally, he learned from a third party that they had been in the woods the day before. He followed Hunt into a bar in a state of excitement and assaulted him. The trial judge excluded this evidence, but the state supreme court reversed his judgment and remanded for a new trial because the evidence was admissible to show the defendant's nature and intent when committing the act. The supreme court held that in "determining whether the provocation is sufficient or reasonable, ordinary human nature, or the average of men recognized as men of fair average mind and disposition, should be taken as the standard." Further, it held that the question of adequate and reasonable provocation is generally a question for the jury, and "if [the jury] should find such provocation from the facts proved, and should further find that it did produce that effect in the particular instance, and that the homicide was the result of such provocation, it would give it the character of manslaughter."

Model Penal Code
(Official Draft 1962)

Section 210.2. Murder

(1) Except as provided in Section 210.3(1)(b), criminal homicide constitutes murder when:

(a) it is committed purposely or knowingly; or

(b) it is committed recklessly under circumstances manifesting extreme indifference to the value of human life. Such recklessness and indifference are presumed if the actor is engaged or is an accomplice in the commission of, or an attempt to commit, or flight after committing or attempting to commit robbery, rape or deviate sexual intercourse by force or threat of force, arson, burglary, kidnapping or felonious escape.

(2) Murder is a felony of the first degree [but a person convicted of murder may be sentenced to death, as provided in Section 210.6].

Section 210.3. Manslaughter

(1) Criminal homicide constitutes manslaughter when:

(a) it is committed recklessly; or

(b) a homicide which would otherwise be murder is committed under the influence of extreme mental or emotional disturbance for which there is reasonable explanation or excuse. The reasonableness of such explanation or excuse shall be determined from the viewpoint of a person in the actor's situation under the circumstances as he believes them to be.

(2) Manslaughter is a felony of the second degree.

● OVERVIEW OF HOMICIDE MITIGATIONS

Notes

Common Law "Provocation" Mitigation
   Limited to "Heat of Passion" Cases, Where Killer Lacked Time to "Cool Off"
   Limited to Killing of Provocateur, and Often to Specific Provoking Situations
   Difficulties with Common Law Test, Including Its View of "Reasonableness"
Broader Modern "Extreme Emotional Disturbance" Mitigation
   Modern Mitigation Abandons Common Law Restrictions
Modern Rules Partially Individualize "Reasonableness" Standard
   Difficulties in Individualizing Standard
"Diminished Capacity" as Basis for MItigation
   Modern Rules for Mental Illness Negating Culpability Element
   Mental Illness Negating Offense Element—Survey

Common Law "Provocation" Mitigation A common exception to the paradigm of an intentional killing as murder is found in the common law doctrine of provocation, under which intentional killings would be mitigated from murder to the lesser crime of *manslaughter*—specifically, what is known as *voluntary manslaughter*—if the killer was "provoked" into committing the crime. The mitigation reflected the position that passion frequently obscures reason and, in some limited way, renders the provoked intentional killer less blameworthy than the unprovoked intentional killer.

Limited to "Heat of Passion" Cases, Where Killer Lacked Time to "Cool Off" In its common law form, the mitigation has very demanding standards. Typically, the provocation must be "reasonable," in the sense that a reasonable person would have been similarly provoked:

> The doctrine of mitigation is briefly this: That if the act of killing, though intentional, be committed under the influence of sudden, intense anger, or heat of blood, obscuring the reason, produced by an adequate or reasonable provocation, and before sufficient time has elapsed for the blood to cool and reason to reassert itself, so that the killing is the result of temporary excitement rather than of wickedness of heart or innate recklessness of disposition, then the law, recognizing the standard of human conduct as that of the ordinary or average man, regards the offense so committed as of less heinous character than premeditated or deliberate murder. Measured as it must be by the conduct of the average man, what constitutes adequate cause is incapable of exact definition . . . [1]

One significant aspect of the rule above is the requirement that the actor must not have had time to "cool off." He loses the mitigation if sufficient time has passed for "the blood to cool and reason to reassert itself." The manslaughter mitigation is thus often described as covering killings that occur in the *heat of passion*. In the *Gounagias* case, for example, it seems unlikely that Gounagias would qualify for a common law provocation mitigation, because three weeks is likely to be judged adequate time for the reasonable person to cool off.

Limited to Killing of Provocateur, and Often to Specific Provoking Situations The common law doctrine has several additional specific limitations. For one, the person killed must be the person who created the provocation. Early forms of the mitigation also required the provoking incident to have occurred in the presence of the defendant. Finally, only certain common types of provoking situations would typically make the mitigation available: "extreme assault or battery upon the defendant; mutual combat; defendant's illegal arrest; injury or serious abuse of a close relative of the defendant's; on the sudden discovery of a spouse's adultery."[2] Even where the mitigation is not explicitly limited to specific types of provoking situations, certain events are often held inadequate, as a matter of law, to support the mitigation. For example, it was common to hold that "mere words" are insufficient to support a mitigation,[3] even if the words described an incident (such as adultery, or harm to a relative) that would itself count as sufficient provocation if the defendant had witnessed it personally. These rules hint that, notwithstanding its asserted focus on the actor's state of mind, the common law mitigation may have approached provocation as a partial justification of sorts,

---

1. State v. Gounagias, 53 P. 9, 11-12 (Wash. 1915).
2. Girouard v. State, 583 A.2d 718 (Md. App. 1991).
3. See, e.g., People v. Murback, 30 P. 608 (Cal. 1883).

where the objective circumstances of the killing are such as to reduce its overall harmfulness or wrongfulness.

Difficulties with Common Law Test, Including Its View of "Reasonableness" It may seem unrealistic or inappropriate for the provocation mitigation to apply a purely objective test, at least if the test seems to ask whether a reasonable person would have acted the same as the defendant. If the defendant's killing satisfies such a test—if a reasonable person would have acted the same way in the situation—shouldn't the defendant be held blameless? It is likely more accurate to say that the common law mitigation means to assess whether the actor's conduct is *reasonable* only in the sense that it is *understandable.* In other words, the mitigation is meant to cover cases where the killing remains condemnable, but the conditions of the killing suggest that the actor is noticeably less blameworthy than one who kills without such provocation. Yet the restrictions of the common law doctrine fail to make a full assessment of the actor's blameworthiness and may make the mitigation unavailable for many actors whose killings seem considerably less blameworthy than typical murders. The *Gounagias* case may be an example of such a case. It seems difficult to deny that Gounagias seems noticeably less blameworthy under these circumstances than if he had shot Grounas without the provocation of the earlier rape.

Broader Modern "Extreme Emotional Disturbance" Mitigation   Modern codes, following the Model Penal Code, give a broader mitigation than the common law provocation doctrine. The Code's manslaughter mitigation applies where:

> murder is committed under the influence of extreme mental or emotional disturbance for which there is reasonable explanation or excuse. The reasonableness of such explanation or excuse shall be determined from the viewpoint of a person in the actor's situation under the circumstances as he believes them to be.

This formulation of the mitigation has two components. First, the killing must have been committed "under the influence of extreme mental or emotional disturbance." A defendant will not be eligible for the mitigation if she did not personally suffer such a disturbance or if it did not drive or dictate her act, even if the circumstances would have created such a disturbance in most other people and would have driven them to violence. Second, there must be a "reasonable explanation or excuse" for the disturbance. No mitigation is available if the disturbance has no reasonable basis or is peculiar to the actor.

Modern Mitigation Abandons Common Law Restrictions   The Model Penal Code broadens the common law mitigation in several important respects. Unlike the common law rules, it does not explicitly require, or exclude, particular situations; there are no conditions that are inadequate as a matter of law to provide a mitigation. It also drops the common law rule barring the mitigation if the killing occurs some period of time after the provoking event. In other words, the Code postulates that an actor's emotional disturbance does not necessarily decrease with time; indeed, it might increase.[4] Further, nothing in the Code's mitigation limits it to cases where the actor kills the source of the provocation, as the common

---

4. Model Penal Code § 210.3 comment at 48 (Tent. Draft No. 9, 1959).

law does. The Code's position is that if the actor's killing is less blameworthy by virtue of the influencing conditions, then such reduced blameworthiness exists no matter who is killed. Indeed, the Code does not even require a provocation as such; the relevant "disturbance" may arise from any source so long as it satisfies the rule's requirements. The underlying theory of this version of the mitigation does not appear to be one related to a possible partial justification. (Defensive force defenses, for example, may justify force against an aggressor but not against anyone else.) The mitigation's basis, rather, is more akin to excuse defenses, which look to the actor rather than the objective circumstances and apply regardless of the identity of the offense's victim.

Modern Rules Partially Individualize "Reasonableness" Standard The Model Penal Code mitigation uses a "reasonableness" standard, as the common law doctrine does, but instead of adopting a purely objective understanding of reasonableness, modern rules partially individualize the standard through the requirement that the reasonableness of the explanation or excuse is to be determined "under the circumstances as [the actor] believes them to be" and "from the viewpoint of a person in the actor's situation." These two phrases provide significant opportunities for a court, or jury, to take account of the particular characteristics of the defendant and the specific conditions in which the defendant acted. (Recall that the same two phrases are used in the Code's definitions of recklessness and negligence.[5]) The Code's drafters intended the second phrase—in particular "in the actor's *situation*"—to permit a trial judge great leeway in partially individualizing the reasonable-person standard.[6]

Difficulties in Individualizing Standard The most difficult aspect in applying the modern "extreme emotional disturbance" formulation of the manslaughter mitigation is determining which characteristics of the defendant should be used in judging the reasonableness of the defendant's conduct. Clearly such things as an actor's age may be relevant in assessing the reasonableness of his disturbance. But, presumably, a defendant's certifiably bad temper would not be a basis for lowering our expectations of him with respect to engaging in violent behavior. He is not to be judged against the standard of the "reasonable bad-tempered person," for having an improperly short fuse might be exactly what makes his behavior seem unreasonable and blameworthy. To individualize the objective standard fully would turn it into a purely subjective standard, which would give mitigations where the community would see no reduced blameworthiness. More difficult to deal with are factors like having a genetic predisposition toward violent reaction when provoked. If true, should it alter the standard by which he is judged? We

---

5. Model Penal Code § 2.02(2)(c)&(d).

6. As the Model Penal Code commentary explains:

There is an inevitable ambiguity in "situation." If the actor were blind or if he had just suffered a blow or experienced a heart attack, these would certainly be facts to be considered in a judgment involving criminal liability, as they would be under traditional law. But the heredity, intelligence or temperament of the actor would not be held material in judging negligence, and could not be without depriving the criterion of all its objectivity. The code is not intended to displace discriminations of this kind, but rather to leave the issue to the courts.

Model Penal Code § 2.02 comment 4 at 242 (1985). See also id. at n.27 (noting that a similar problem exists with recklessness, and that discriminations similar to those required by the negligence standard must be made).

are inclined to believe that people can, and must, control their tempers, but the claim of genetic predisposition clouds the issue by making it seem that the actor may lack full control over his ability to do this. Unfortunately, criminal law theory has yet to develop a principle that will distinguish those characteristics that are properly included from those that are properly excluded when individualizing the reasonable-person standard. The Model Penal Code leaves the issue to the ad hoc determination of the trial judge.[7] (The analogous problem of how to individualize an objective standard arises under the standard modern definitions of negligence and recklessness.)

"Diminished Capacity" as Basis for Mitigation   Another doctrine that can reduce the degree of an intentional killing from murder to manslaughter, or to an even lesser offense, is the doctrine frequently called *diminished capacity* or *diminished responsibility*. These labels are misleading because they suggest a kind of partial insanity defense, giving a mitigation where an actor suffers a degree of mental illness short of that required for a full insanity defense. The Code's extreme *mental* disturbance mitigation, described above, operates roughly in this way: An extreme mental disturbance may mitigate murder to manslaughter, even though the actor fully intended to cause the death. The diminished-capacity claim, in contrast, applies when an actor's mental illness *negates a culpable state of mind* required for the offense charged.

Accordingly, it is not a doctrine of mitigation at all, but rather a claim that the defendant simply does not satisfy the elements of murder. In other words, it is a simple absent-element defense, like an actor's mistake negating an element. Depending on whether the offense charged has lesser included offenses with lower culpability requirements, and depending on the actual effect of an actor's mental illness in negating the culpability elements of the different offenses, the doctrine may provide only a slight mitigation or it may amount to a complete defense. The real purpose of the doctrine of diminished capacity at common law was to *prevent* an actor from using evidence of mental illness to negate a required culpable state of mind. Such practice continues to exist in some jurisdictions today, but it is hopefully diminishing.

Modern Rules for Mental Illness Negating Culpability Element   Model Penal Code Section 4.02(1) states the modern form of the mitigation:

> Evidence that the defendant suffered from a mental disease or defect is admissible whenever it is relevant to prove that the defendant did or did not have a state of mind which is an element of the offense.

Unlike the insanity defense, the actor's general mental capacity or incapacity is not the issue.[8] Impaired ability to control one's conduct, in particular, is not relevant here, because only cognitive dysfunctions can negate an offense's required culpable state of mind. Such is the nature of the requirements of purpose, knowledge, recklessness, and negligence.[9] The ultimate issue remains the same as in all prosecutions: Did the actor have the culpable state of mind required by the offense definition? If, because of mental illness, she did not, she has a "defense"

---

7. See Model Penal Code § 210.3 comment at 63 (1980).
8. Compare Model Penal Code § 4.02(1) to § 4.01(1).
9. See Model Penal Code § 2.02(2).

to that offense, although she may be liable for a lesser offense if she satisfies its culpability requirements.

Mental Illness Negating Offense Element—Survey American jurisdictions take a variety of positions on the admission of mental disease or defect evidence that negates a required offense mental element. About 40 percent of the jurisdictions, typically those with modern criminal codes, admit any evidence of mental disease or defect that is relevant to negate any culpable state of mind offense element.[10] Another 30 percent allow such evidence to be admitted but purport to limit such admission to negating only a "specific intent"[11]—a concept that has little meaning in modern codes—or, even more restrictively, to negate only the malice or premeditation requirements in murder prosecutions.[12] The final 30 percent purport to exclude the admission of mental illness evidence to negate any offense element.[13] While some of these efforts have been held unconstitutional,[14] the Supreme

---

10. See Alaska Stat. § 12.47.020 (Michie 2002); Ark. Code Ann. § 5-2-303 (Michie 2002); State v. Burge, 487 A.2d 532 (Conn. 1985); Colo. Rev. Stat. Ann. § 18-1-803 (West 2003); Haw. Rev. Stat. Ann. § 704-401 (Michie 2002); Idaho Code § 18-207 (Michie 2002); Robinson v. Commonwealth, 569 S.W.2d 183 (Ky. Ct. App. 1978); Me. Rev. Stat. Ann. tit. 17-A, § 38 (West 2003); Hoey v. State, 536 A.2d 622 (Md. 1988); Mo. Ann. Stat. § 552.030 (West 2002); Mont. Code Ann. § 46-14-102 (2002); Finger v. State, 27 P.3d 66 (Nev. 2001) (finding abolition of insanity defense unconstitutional and holding that evidence not meeting legal insanity standard may be admitted at trial to negate an offense element); Novosel v. Helgemoe, 384 A.2d 124 (N.H. 1978) (applying only in bifurcated trials); N.J. Stat. Ann. § 2C: 4-2 (West 2002); Or. Rev. Stat. § 161-300 (2001); State v. Perry, 13 S.W.3d 724 (Tenn. Crim. App. 1999); 2003 Utah Laws Ch. 11 (making minor revisions to Utah Code Ann. § 76-2-305 (2002)); State v. Smith, 396 A.2d 126 (Vt. 1978); United States v. Pohlot, 827 F.2d 889 (3d Cir. 1987) (holding that in codifying an insanity excuse, 18 U.S.C.A. §17 (West 2003), Congress abolished defenses of "diminished capacity" and "partial responsibility" but did not intend to preclude admission of psychiatric evidence relevant to negate an element of the offense).

11. Cal. Penal Code § 28 (West 2003); Veverka v. Cash, 318 N.W.2d 447 (Iowa 1982); State v. Dargatz, 614 P.2d 430 (Kan. 1980); People v. Atkins, 325 N.W.2d 38 (Mich. Ct. App. 1982); People v. Segal, 444 N.Y.S.2d 588 (N.Y. 1981); Commonwealth v. Walzack, 360 A.2d 914 (Pa. 1976); State v. Correra, 430 A.2d 1251 (R.I. 1981); State v. Huber, 356 N.W.2d 468 (S.D. 1984); State v. Bottrell, 14 P.3d 164 (Wash. App. 2000).

12. People v. Leppert, 434 N.E.2d 21 (Ill. App. Ct. 1982) (considering defendant's claim that, due to mental defect, he lacked the requisite intent to attempt murder); Commonwealth v. Baldwin, 686 N.E.2d 1001 (Mass. 1997); Washington v. State, 85 N.W.2d 509 (Neb. 1957); State v. Beach, 699 P.2d 115 (N.M. 1985); State v. Shank, 367 S.E.2d 639 (N.C. 1988); LeVasseur v. Commonwealth, 304 S.E.2d 202 (Va. 1979).

13. Barnett v. State, 540 So. 2d 810 (Ala. Crim. App. 1988); State v. Schantz, 403 P.2d 521 (Ariz. 1965); Bates v. State, 386 A.2d 1139 (Del. 1978); Bethea v. United States, 365 A.2d 64 (D.C. 1976); Zamora v. State, 361 So. 2d 776 (Fla. Dist. Ct. App. 1978); Hudson v. State, 319 S.E.2d 28 (Ga. Ct. App. 1984); Brown v. State, 448 N.E.2d 10 (Ind. 1983); State v. Murray, 375 So. 2d 80 (La. 1979); State v. Bouwman, 328 N.W.2d 703 (Minn. 1982); Garcia v. State, 828 So. 2d 1279 (Miss. Ct. App. 2002); State v. Wilcox, 438 N.E.2d 523 (Ohio 1982); Gresham v. State, 489 P.2d 1355 (Okla. Crim. App. 1971); Gill v. State, 552 S.E.2d 26 (S.C. 2001); Warner v. State, 944 S.W.2d 812 (Tex. App. 1997); State v. Flint, 96 S.E.2d 677 (W. Va. 1957) (providing statement against diminished capacity defense, which has since been questioned but not overruled, in State v. Simmon, 309 S.E.2d 89 (W. Va. 1983)); Muench v. Israel, 715 F.2d 1124 (7th Cir. 1983) (finding that Wisconsin may constitutionally reject the diminished capacity defense and refuse to admit evidence proving defendant's inability to form requisite intent); Price v. State, 807 P.2d 909 (Wyo. 1991). To date, North Dakota courts have not explicitly spoken to this issue—their position remains unclear.

14. See, e.g., Hendershott v. People, 653 P.2d 385 (Colo. 1982) (finding unconstitutional Colorado statute that barred evidence of mental illness to negate *mens rea* requirement for nonspecific intent crimes), and Finger v. State, supra (holding Nevada statute unconstitutional); but see Muench v. Israel, supra (rejecting a constitutional challenge to Wisconsin's practice of excluding evidence of mental illness relevant to a mens rea requirement).

Court's recent decision in *Clark v. Arizona* held that states are not required to allow admission of evidence of mental illness.[15]

United States v. Brawner
United States Court of Appeals for the District of Columbia Circuit
153 U.S. App. D.C. 1, 471 F.2d 969 (D.C. Cir. 1972)

LEVENTHAL, Circuit Judge:

The principal issues raised on this appeal from a conviction for second degree murder and carrying a dangerous weapon relate to appellant's defense of insanity. After the case was argued to a division of the court, the court sua sponte ordered rehearing en banc. We identified our intention to reconsider the appropriate standard for the insanity defense. . . .

THE TRIAL RECORD

Passing by various minor disagreements among the witnesses, the record permits us to reconstruct the events of September 8, 1967, as follows: After a morning and afternoon of wine-drinking, appellant Archie W. Brawner, Jr. and his uncle Aaron Ross, went to a party at the home of three acquaintances. During the evening, several fights broke out. In one of them, Brawner's jaw was injured when he was struck or pushed to the ground. The time of the fight was approximately 10:30 p.m. After the fight, Brawner left the party. He told Mr. Ross that some boys had jumped him. Mr. Ross testified that Brawner "looked like he was out of his mind." Other witnesses who saw him after the fight testified that Brawner's mouth was bleeding and that his speech was unclear (but the same witness added, "I heard every word he said"); that he was staggering and angry; and that he pounded on a mailbox with his fist. One witness testified that Brawner said, "[I'm] going to get my boys" and come back, and that "someone is going to die tonight."

Half an hour later, at about eleven p.m., Brawner was on his way back to the party with a gun. One witness testified that Brawner said he was going up there to kill his attackers or be killed.

Upon his arrival at the address, Brawner fired a shot into the ground and entered the building. He proceeded to the apartment where the party was in progress and fired five shots through the closed metal hallway door. Two of the shots struck Billy Ford, killing him. Brawner was arrested a few minutes later, several blocks away. The arresting officer testified that Brawner appeared normal, and did not appear to be drunk, that he spoke clearly, and had no odor of alcohol about him.

After the Government had presented the evidence of its non-expert witnesses, the trial judge ruled that there was insufficient evidence on "deliberation" to go to the jury: accordingly, a verdict of acquittal was directed on first degree murder.

The expert witnesses, called by both defense and prosecution, all agreed that Brawner was suffering from an abnormality of a psychiatric or neurological nature. The medical labels were variously given as "epileptic personality disorder,"

---

15. Clark v. Arizona, 548 U.S. 735 (2006).

"psychologic brain syndrome associated with a convulsive disorder," "personality disorder associated with epilepsy," or, more simply, "an explosive personality." There was no disagreement that the epileptic condition would be exacerbated by alcohol, leading to more frequent episodes and episodes of greater intensity, and would also be exacerbated by a physical blow to the head. The experts agreed that epilepsy per se is not a mental disease or defect, but a neurological disease which is often associated with a mental disease or defect. They further agreed that Brawner had a mental, as well as a neurological, disease. . . .

Mental condition, though insufficient to exonerate, may be relevant to specific mental element of certain crimes or degrees of crime.

Our decision [holds] that expert testimony as to a defendant's abnormal mental condition may be received and considered, as tending to show, in a responsible way, that defendant did not have the specific mental state required for a particular crime or degree of crime—even though he was aware that his act was wrongful and was able to control it, and hence was not entitled to complete exoneration.

Some of the cases following this doctrine use the term "diminished responsibility," but we prefer the example of the cases that avoid this term, for its convenience is outweighed by its confusion: Our doctrine has nothing to do with "diminishing" responsibility of a defendant because of his impaired mental condition, but rather with determining whether the defendant had the mental state that must be proved as to all defendants.

Procedurally, the issue of abnormal mental condition negativing a person's intent may arise in different ways: For example, the defendant may offer evidence of mental condition not qualifying as mental disease under *McDonald*. Or he may tender evidence that qualifies under *McDonald*, yet the jury may conclude from all the evidence that defendant has knowledge and control capacity sufficient for responsibility under the ALI rule.

The issue often arises with respect to mental condition tendered as negativing the element of premeditation in a charge of first degree premeditated murder. As we noted in Austin v. United States, 127 U.S. App. D.C. 180, 382 F.2d 129 (1967), when the legislature modified the common law crime of murder so as to establish degrees, murder in the first degree was reserved for intentional homicide done deliberately and with premeditation, and homicide that is intentional but "impulsive," not done after "reflection and meditation," was made murder only in the second degree.

An offense like deliberated and premeditated murder requires a specific intent that cannot be satisfied merely by showing that defendant failed to conform to an objective standard. This is plainly established by the defense of voluntary intoxication. In Hopt v. Utah, 104 U.S. 631, 634, 26 L. Ed. 873 (1881), the Court, after stating the familiar rule that voluntary intoxication is no excuse for crime, said:

> [W]hen a statute establishing different degrees of murder requires deliberate premeditation in order to constitute murder in the first degree, the question of whether the accused is in such a condition of mind, by reason of drunkenness or otherwise, as to be capable of deliberate premeditation, necessarily becomes a material subject of consideration by the jury. . . .

Neither logic nor justice can tolerate a jurisprudence that defines the elements of an offense as requiring a mental state such that one defendant can properly argue that his voluntary drunkenness removed his capacity to form the specific intent but another defendant is inhibited from a submission of his contention that an abnormal mental condition, for which he was in no way responsible, negated his capacity to form a particular specific intent, even though the condition did not exonerate him from all criminal responsibility.

In Fisher v. United States, 80 U.S. App. D.C. 96, 149 F.2d 28 (1946), the court upheld the trial court's refusal to instruct the jury that on issues of premeditation and deliberation "it should consider the entire personality of the defendant, his mental, nervous, emotional and physical characteristics as developed by the evidence in the case." Justice Arnold's abbreviated opinion was evidently premised on two factors: (1) that the instruction confused the issue of insanity with the issue of deliberation; (2) that "To give an instruction like the above is to tell the jury they are at liberty to acquit one who commits a brutal crime because he has the abnormal tendencies of persons capable of such crimes." . . .

. . . [W]e deem it appropriate to change the rule of Fisher on a prospective basis, and to accept the approach which . . . has been adopted by the overwhelming majority of courts that have recently faced the question. We are convinced by the analysis set forth in the recent opinions of the highest courts of California, Colorado, New Jersey, Iowa, Ohio, Idaho, Connecticut, Nebraska, New Mexico and Nevada. They have joined the states that spoke out before Fisher—New York, Rhode Island, Utah, Wisconsin and Wyoming.

The pertinent reasoning was succinctly stated by the Colorado Supreme Court as follows:

> The question to be determined is not whether defendant was insane, but whether the homicidal act was committed with deliberation and premeditation. The evidence offered as to insanity may or may not be relevant to that issue. . . . "A claim of insanity cannot be used for the purpose of reducing a crime of murder in the first degree to murder in the second degree or from murder to manslaughter. If the perpetrator is responsible at all in this respect, he is responsible in the same degree as a sane man; and if he is not responsible at all, he is entitled to an acquittal in both degrees. However, . . . *evidence of the condition of the mind* of the accused at the time of the crime, together with the surrounding circumstances, may be introduced, not for the purpose of establishing insanity, but to prove that the situation was such that a specific intent was not entertained—that is, *to show absence of any deliberate or premeditated design.*" (Emphasis in original.)

On the other side of the coin, very few jurisdictions which have recently considered this question have held to the contrary position.

Intervening developments within our own jurisdiction underscore the soundness of a doctrine for consideration of abnormal mental condition on the issue of specific intent. In the *Fisher* opinion of 1946, the court was concerned lest such a doctrine "tell the jury that they are at liberty to acquit one who commits a brutal crime because he has the abnormal tendencies of persons capable of such crimes." That a man's abnormal mental condition short of legal insanity may be material as negativing premeditation and deliberation does not set him "at liberty" but reduces the degree of the criminal homicide. . . .

There has also been a material legislative development since . . . *Fisher*. . . . In 1964, after extensive hearings, Congress enacted the Hospitalization of the Mentally Ill Act, which provides civil commitment for the "mentally ill" who are dangerous to themselves or others. . . . These statutory provisions provide a shield against danger from persons with abnormal mental condition. . . .

Our rule permits the introduction of expert testimony as to abnormal condition if it is relevant to negative, or establish, the specific mental condition that is an element of the crime. The receipt of this expert testimony to negative the mental condition of specific intent requires careful administration by the trial judge. Where the proof is not offered in the first instance as evidence of exonerating mental disease or defect within the ALI rule the judge may, and ordinarily would, require counsel first to make a proffer of the proof to be adduced outside the presence of the jury. The judge will then determine whether the testimony is grounded in sufficient scientific support to warrant use in the courtroom, and whether it would aid the jury in reaching a decision on the ultimate issues.

The case is remanded for further consideration by the District Court in accordance with this opinion.

So ordered.

▲ PROBLEMS

The Vigilante Mother (#36)

Ellie Nesler has been an emotional wreck ever since her seven-year-old son told her that he had been molested by Daniel Mark Driver. Driver was previously convicted of felony child molestation almost five years earlier, but was released after five months in prison. Despite her concerns over the effect on her son's mental health, Nesler allows the authorities to question her son. Driver is apprehended for abusing Nesler's son and several other children. Nesler's son, now 11 years old, is called to testify against Driver, but must struggle to keep his composure on the stand as he recounts the abuse he suffered. The experience is so disturbing that during recesses he cannot stop vomiting. His emotional distress is affecting his testimony. The mother of another alleged victim tells Nesler that Driver is likely to go free.

Compounding Nesler's frustration is the fact that Driver does not seem to be taking the case seriously. As he sits in the witness box, he seems to smile at her with a little smirk. For Nesler, Driver's smirking is the last straw. At the next recess, she leaves the courtroom, returning a few moments later with a .25-caliber pistol hidden in her pocket. At point-blank range she shoots Driver five times in the head and neck, killing him instantly. She drops the gun as deputies advance on her, and she surrenders without incident. After Nesler is arrested, her sister explains, "[s]he wouldn't have done it if he didn't have that cocky look." (A psychologist later testifies that Driver was emotionally disturbed and that when he was under stress he had a tendency to smile as a nervous reflex that he could not control.)

What liability for Nesler, if any, under the Model Penal Code? Prepare a list of all criminal code subsections in the order in which you rely upon them in your analysis.

What liability, if any, at common law?

A Mercy Killing as His Last Act (#37)

Vernal "Bob" Ohlrich and his wife, Phyllis, have been happily married for 54 years. Their four children lead successful lives, and Bob and Phyllis are enjoying their retirement. However, while they enjoy traveling together and spending time with friends from church, the Ohlrichs are not without their share of problems. Phyllis was diagnosed with cancer earlier in life and nearly died during the corrective surgery. She also has had numerous other medical problems throughout their marriage. During her many illnesses, Bob has remained by her side to care for her. Recently, however, Phyllis has taken a turn for the worse. Her cancer has returned and she now has two malignant tumors. Her physicians estimate that she has only a 25 percent chance of surviving.

It turns out that even this grim prognosis is overly optimistic. Chemotherapy fails and Phyllis's condition worsens dramatically. She is no longer given any chance of survival and is in constant pain as she simply waits to die. Bob helps as much as he is able, but cannot care for her in her weakened state. His visits to the hospital are agonizing, as he cannot bear to see Phyllis in pain as the cancer ravages her body. He eventually decides that the best thing he can do for his wife is to help her out of her misery by ending her life. Unable to imagine life without her, he also plans to commit suicide after he has killed her. He writes a detailed note to his four children, explaining what he is going to do and how he would like his belongings to be disposed of. He includes two checks for his and Phyllis' funerals.

When he gets to the hospital and finds that her condition has again worsened, he returns to his car and retrieves a .22-caliber semi-automatic handgun. He shuts the door of his wife's hospital room and says, "Honey, I love you. I'm coming right with you." Bob shoots Phyllis once in the head, killing her instantly. Following through with his plan, Bob then turns the gun on himself. However, the gun jams and Bob is unable to fix it. He turns himself in to hospital security, who have come to investigate the gunshot that killed Phyllis.

What liability for Bob Ohlrich, if any, under the Model Penal Code? Prepare a list of all criminal code subsections in the order in which you rely upon them in your analysis. For a discussion on assisted suicide, refer to the readings in Appendix for this Section.

What liability, if any, at common law?

Escaping the Aliens (#38)

Eric Clark was a typical teenager until mental illness began to take over his life. Formerly a good student and varsity running back, he has become withdrawn, giving up sports and rarely studying. He also begins to exhibit odd behaviors; he refuses to drink tap water, saying he is worried about lead poisoning. He grows moody as well, exploding one minute and breaking down in tears the next. As the year 2000 approaches, Clark drops out of school and spends almost $1,700 of his parents' money to purchase Y2K survival gear. After 2000 passes, he returns to school, but he continues to act in an unusual manner. He starts referring to his parents as "aliens" and often exclaims "they're after me." His conduct becomes increasingly bizarre. Clark sets up a fishing line with beads and wind chimes throughout his home as an alarm system for alien invasions. He starts to keep a bird in his car to warn him of airborne poison.

Some time later, Clark becomes frantic because he thinks an alien attack has started. He steals his older brother's keys and speeds off in his truck. He is trying to escape the aliens who he believes are chasing him. He begins to circle the neighborhood, blaring loud music in an attempt to keep the aliens away. Clark thinks that his town is inhabited by "aliens" (particularly aliens disguised as government agents). After neighbors call the police to report the excessive noise he is making, Clark is pulled over by an officer. Believing the policeman to be an alien (not a human being), Clark fatally shoots the officer. Clark is later diagnosed with paranoid schizophrenia, a subtype of schizophrenia characterized by delusions and hallucinations.

Does Clark satisfy the elements of the offense definition for murder under the Model Penal Code? What liability for Clark, if any? Prepare a list of all criminal code subsections in the order in which you rely upon them in your analysis.

✳ DISCUSSION ISSUES

Should One Have the Right to End One's Own Life? If so, Should Others Be Able to Help if Necessary?

Materials presenting each side of this Discussion Issue appear in the Advanced Materials for Section 8 in Appendix A.

Causation

The extent of an offender's liability can be dramatically different depending on whether he or she is held to be causally accountable for a result prohibited by an offense. Homicide is the most obvious example; the difference between murder and attempted murder can be the difference between the death penalty or a moderate term of imprisonment. When is an offender causally accountable for a result? Why should such a causal connection matter?

◆ THE CASE OF JOE PAUL GOVAN (#39)

It is April 5, 1980, in Phoenix, Arizona. For the past three years, Joe Paul Govan and his girlfriend, Sharon Keeble, have lived together. Sharon has three children: Kimberly, 13; Jimmy, 12; and Christian, 3. Both Govan and Keeble own guns. Govan is 5 foot, 9 inches and weighs 160 pounds.

In the afternoon they have their guns out, cleaning them. As usual, they are arguing. Unwilling to continue fighting, Govan steps out to get some air. While

Figure 39 **Crime scene, stairs leading up to porch and blood streaks along balcony on left**
(Superior Court of Arizona)

he is out, Kimberly tells her mother that Govan was "messing" with her; she says that he kissed her on the neck. "Flipping out," Sharon immediately starts yelling at Govan as he returns. This time, however, yelling is not enough. She loads her gun and shoots at him but misses, as Govan quickly leaves. Sharon tells Kimberly that she was only trying to scare Govan. She has Kimberly take the other children to their friend Carrie Gray's apartment. (The children call her "Mama Carrie.")

Later that day, Govan and Sharon meet at Carrie Gray's apartment. Before long, they are outside the apartment again arguing loudly, this time over Sharon's attempt to call the police to report Govan's "messing around." Govan is desperately trying to convince her not to call. Finally, frustrated and angry, Govan turns to walk away. However, soon after starting down the stairs, he notices Sharon following behind him in pursuit. He takes his gun out of his pocket and says, "Well, I'll stop this." Without stopping to aim, as if just to scare her, he shoots in Sharon's direction. A minute later, after hearing Kimberly yell, he realizes in horror that his shot has actually hit her. Govan panics and flees.

The bullet has hit the left side of Keeble's neck. She is rushed to a Phoenix hospital, where doctors perform a tracheotomy to help her breathe, a procedure that requires inserting a tube into her throat. It is a medical necessity in this instance but, unfortunately, is likely to increase her susceptibility to future respiratory problems.

On May 1, 1980, authorities charge Govan with aggravated assault. Despite the charge, Govan visits Sharon frequently in the hospital. He expresses his remorse for the incident and wishes to care for her and help her recover. The continual courting works and they are eventually married.

Ten months later, on March 11, 1981, the assault charge is dropped without prejudice.

The incident has left Sharon a quadriplegic; she is unable to perform even the most basic activities to care for herself, and requires constant assistance, including keeping her trachea tube clear. For several months, Govan tries to care for Sharon, but by year's end he feels obliged

Figure 40 **Crime scene, close-up of porch and blood**
(Superior Court of Arizona)

to place her in a convalescent home. Unhappy with
the change, Sharon arranges
to move to California, where
her parents have her admitted
to the University of California
at Irvine Medical Center. She
subsequently annuls her marriage to Govan. After a year in
treatment, Sharon is able to
leave the hospital and move
into an apartment with a nursing assistant to care for her.

Figure 41 **Sharon Keeble after partially recovering from the shooting**
(Superior Court of Arizona)

Sharon realizes that her
life is not over. She begins taking classes at Coastline Community College with hopes of
becoming a counselor. Even her doctor, Dr. Edward Weir, notices that she is generally upbeat and excited about her studies. Nonetheless, Sharon is never free of the
physical ailments connected with her quadriplegia; her trachea tube continues to be
bothersome, and she is frustrated with the efforts it takes to stay healthy.

In January 1985, Sharon develops pneumonia. After allowing it to go
untreated for several weeks, her condition becomes quite serious. She finally seeks
medical care and is admitted to the hospital on January 24 but dies the next day.
Her doctor concludes that she died of "aspiration pneumonia due to tracheotomy
problems due to the quadriplegia."

On May 13, 1985, Govan is charged with second-degree murder for Sharon's
death based on the shooting five years earlier.

1. *Assuming the earlier assault has already been fully dealt with,* relying only
upon your intuitions of justice, what *additional* liability and punishment, if any,
does Joe Paul Govan deserve *because of Keeble's subsequent death?*

N	0	1	2	3	4	5	6	7	8	9	10	11
⊗	▨	☐	☐	☐	☐	☐	☐	☐	☐	☐	☐	☐
no liability	liability but no punishment	1 day	2 wks	2 mo	6 mo	1 yr	3 yrs	7 yrs	15 yrs	30 yrs	life imprison- ment	death

2. What "justice" arguments could defense counsel make on the defendant's
behalf?

3. What "justice" arguments could the prosecution make against the defendant?

4. Would Govan be causally accountable for Keeble's death under the following causation provision?

Section 203. Causal Relationship Between Conduct and Result

(1) Conduct is the cause of a result if:

(a) the conduct is an antecedent but for which the result in question
would not have occurred; and

(b) the result is not too remote or accidental in its manner of occurrence, and not too dependent upon another's volitional act, to have a just
bearing on the actor's liability or on the gravity of his offense; and

(c) the relationship between the conduct and result satisfies any additional
causal requirements imposed by the Code or by the law defining the offense.

(2) Concurrent Causes. Where the conduct of two or more persons each
causally contributes to a result and each alone would have been sufficient to cause
the result, the requirement of Subsection (1) of this section is satisfied as to both
persons.[1]

5. If there had been no death, what liability, if any, would be imposed under the
then-existing statutes? After the death, what liability, if any? Prepare a list of all criminal code subsections in the order in which you rely upon them in your analysis.

6. If there had been no death, what liability, if any, would be imposed under the
Model Penal Code? After the death, what liability, if any? Prepare a list of all criminal code subsections in the order in which you rely upon them in your analysis.

▪ THE LAW

In applying these statutes to the Govan case, take into account the fact that,
several years after the shooting but before being charged for the homicide resulting from it, Govan is convicted of third-degree burglary, a felony, and serves two
years in prison for it.

Arizona Revised Statutes
(1980)

Title 13. Criminal Code

Chapter 11. Homicide

Section 13-1101. Definitions

In this chapter, unless the context otherwise requires:

1. "Premeditation" means that the defendant acts with either the
intention or the knowledge that he will kill another human being, when
such intention or knowledge precedes the killing by a length of time to permit reflection. An act is not done with premeditation if it is the instant effect
of a sudden quarrel or heat of passion.

2. "Homicide" means first degree murder, second degree murder,
manslaughter or negligent homicide.

3. "Person" means a human being.

4. "Adequate provocation" means conduct or circumstances sufficient
to deprive a reasonable person of self-control.

---

1. Illinois Proposed Criminal Code § 203; see also Rhode Island Proposed Criminal Code § 11A-2-2;
Kentucky Proposed Criminal Code § 501.203.

Section 13-1102. Negligent Homicide; Classification

A. A person commits negligent homicide if with criminal negligence such person causes the death of another person.

B. Negligent homicide is a class 4 felony.

Section 13-1103. Manslaughter; Classification

A. A person commits manslaughter by:

1. Recklessly causing the death of another person; or

2. Committing second degree murder as defined in Section 13-1104, subsection A upon a sudden quarrel or heat of passion resulting from adequate provocation by the victim; or

3. Intentionally aiding another to commit suicide; or

4. Committing second degree murder as defined in Section 13-1104, subsection A, paragraph 3, while being coerced to do so by the use or threatened immediate use of unlawful deadly physical force upon such person or third person which a reasonable person in his situation would have been unable to resist.

B. Manslaughter is a class 3 felony.

Section 13-1104. Second Degree Murder; Classification

A. A person commits second degree murder if without premeditation:

1. Such person intentionally causes the death of another person; or

2. Knowing that his conduct will cause the death or serious physical injury, such person causes the death of another person; or

3. Under circumstances manifesting extreme indifference to human life, such person recklessly engages in conduct which creates a grave risk of death and thereby causes the death of another person.

B. Second degree murder is a class 2 felony.

Section 13-1105. First Degree Murder; Classification

A. A person commits first degree murder if:

1. Knowing that his conduct will cause death, such person causes the death of another with premeditation; or

2. Acting either alone or with one or more other persons such person commits or attempts to commit sexual assault . . . , child molestation . . . , narcotics offenses . . . , kidnapping . . . , burglary . . . , arson of an occupied structure . . . , robbery . . . , escape . . . , and in the course of and in furtherance of such offense or immediate flight from such offense, such person or another person causes the death of any person.

B. Homicide, as defined in paragraph 2 of subsection A of this section, requires no specific mental state other than what is required for the commission of any of the enumerated felonies.

C. First degree murder is a class 1 felony and is punishable by death or life imprisonment as provided by Section 13-703.

Title 13. Criminal Code

Chapter 12. Assault and Related Offenses

Section 13-1201. Endangerment; Classification

A. A person commits endangerment by recklessly endangering another person with a substantial risk of imminent death or physical injury.

B. Endangerment involving a substantial risk of imminent death is a class 6 felony. In all other cases, it is a class 1 misdemeanor.

Section 13-1203. Assault; Classification

A. A person commits assault by:

1. Intentionally, knowingly or recklessly causing any physical injury to another person; or

2. Intentionally placing another person in reasonable apprehension of imminent physical injury; or

3. Knowingly touching another person with the intent to injure, insult or provoke such person.

B. Assault committed intentionally or knowingly pursuant to subsection A, paragraph 1 is a class 1 misdemeanor. Assault committed recklessly pursuant to subsection A, paragraph 1 or assault pursuant to subsection A, paragraph 2 is a class 2 misdemeanor. Assault committed pursuant to subsection A, paragraph 3 is a class 3 misdemeanor.

Section 13-1204. Aggravated Assault

A. A person commits aggravated assault if such person commits assault as defined in Section 13-1203 under any of the following circumstances:

1. If such person causes serious physical injury to another.

2. If such person uses a deadly weapon or dangerous instrument.

3. If such person commits the assault after entering the private home of another person with the intent to commit the assault. . . .

B. Aggravated assault pursuant to subsection A, paragraph 1 or 2 of this section is a class 3 felony. Aggravated assault pursuant to subsection A, paragraphs 3, 4, 5, 6, 7 or 8 of this section is a class 6 felony.

Section 13-1001. [Attempt] Classifications . . .

C. Attempt is a:

1. Class 2 felony if the offense attempted is a class 1 felony.

2. Class 3 felony if the offense attempted is a class 2 felony.

3. Class 4 felony if the offense attempted is a class 3 felony.

4. Class 5 felony if the offense attempted is a class 4 felony.

5. Class 6 felony if the offense attempted is a class 5 felony.

6. Class 1 misdemeanor if the offense attempted is a class 6 felony.

7. Class 2 misdemeanor if the offense attempted is a class 1 misdemeanor.

8. Class 3 misdemeanor if the offense attempted is a class 2 misdemeanor.

9. Petty offense if the offense attempted is a class 3 misdemeanor or petty offense.

Section 13-604. Dangerous and Repetitive Offenders; Definitions

A. . . .

B. Except as provided in subsection G of this section, a person who is at least eighteen years of age or who has been tried as an adult and who stands convicted of a class 2 or 3 felony, whether a completed or preparatory offense and who has previously been convicted of any felony shall be sentenced to imprisonment for not less than the sentence and not more than three times the sentence authorized by §13-701 for the offense for which the person currently stands convicted. . . .

G. Upon a first conviction of a class 2 or 3 felony involving use or exhibition of a deadly weapon or dangerous instrument or upon conviction of a class 2 or 3 felony when the intentional or knowing infliction of serious physical injury upon another has occurred, the defendant shall be sentenced to imprisonment for not less than the sentence and not more than three times the sentence authorized in §13-701 for the offense for which the person currently stands convicted. . . .

Section 13-701. Sentence of Imprisonment for Felony; Presentence Report

A. A sentence of imprisonment for a felony shall be a definite term of years and the person sentenced, unless otherwise provided by law, shall be committed to the custody of the state department of corrections.

B. No prisoner may be transferred to the custody of the state department of corrections without a certified copy of the judgment and sentence, signed by the sentencing judge, and a copy of a recent presentence investigation report unless the court has waived preparation of the report.

C. Except as provided in §13-604 the term of imprisonment for a felony shall be determined as follows for a first offense:

1. For a class 2 felony, seven years.
2. For a class 3 felony, five years.
3. For a class 4 felony, four years.
4. For a class 5 felony, two years.
5. For a class 6 felony, one and one-half years.

Section 13-702. Sentencing

A. Sentences provided in § 13-701 for a first conviction of a class 4, 5, or 6 felony, except those felonies involving a use or exhibition of a deadly weapon or dangerous instrument or when the intentional or knowing infliction of serious physical injury upon another has occurred, may be increased by the court up to twenty-five per cent or may be reduced by the court up to fifty per cent of the sentence prescribed for said offense. Such reduction or increase shall be based on the aggravating and mitigating circumstances contained in subsections D and E of this section.

B. Sentences provided in § 13-701 for a first conviction of a class 2 or 3 felony, except those felonies involving a use or exhibition of a deadly weapon or dangerous instrument or when the intentional or knowing infliction of serious physical injury upon another has occurred, may be increased by the court up to one hundred per cent or may be reduced by the court up to twenty-five per cent of the sentence prescribed for the said offense. Such reduction or increase shall be based on aggravating and mitigating circumstances contained in subsections D and E of this section. . . .

D. For the purpose of determining the sentence pursuant to subsections A and B of this section, the court shall consider the following aggravating circumstances:

> 1. Infliction or threatened infliction of serious physical injury.
> 2. Use, threatened use or possession of a deadly weapon or dangerous instrument during the commission of the crime. . . .
> 9. Any other factors which the court may deem appropriate to the ends of justice.

E. For the purpose of determining the sentence pursuant to subsections A and B of this section, the court shall consider the following mitigating circumstances: . . .

> 3. The defendant was under unusual or substantial duress, although not such as to constitute a defense to prosecution. . . .
> 5. Any other factors which the court may deem appropriate to the ends of justice.

In determining what sentence to impose, the court shall take into account the amount of aggravating circumstances and whether the amount of mitigating circumstances is sufficiently substantial to call for the lesser term. . . .

Section 13-707. Sentence of Imprisonment for Misdemeanor

A sentence of imprisonment for a misdemeanor shall be for a definite term to be served other than a place within custody of the state department of corrections. The court shall fix the term of imprisonment within the following maximum limitations:

> 1. For a class 1 misdemeanor, six months.
> 2. For a class 2 misdemeanor, four months.
> 3. For a class 3 misdemeanor, thirty days.

Section 13-101. Purposes

It is declared that the public policy of this state and the general purposes of the provisions of this title are:

> 1. To proscribe conduct that unjustifiably and inexcusably causes or threatens substantial harm to individual or public interests;
> 2. To give fair warning of the nature of the conduct proscribed and of the sentences authorized upon conviction;

3. To define the act or omission and the accompanying mental state which constitute each offense and limit the condemnation of conduct as criminal when it does not fall within the purposes set forth;

4. To differentiate on reasonable grounds between serious and minor offenses and to prescribe proportionate penalties for each;

5. To insure the public safety by preventing the commission of offenses through the deterrent influence of the sentences authorized; and

6. To impose just and deserved punishment on those whose conduct threatens the public peace.

Section 13-103. Abolition of Common Law Offenses

All common law offenses are hereby abolished. No conduct or omission constitutes an offense unless it is an offense under this title or under another statute or ordinance.

Section 13-104. Rule of Construction

The general rule that a penal statute is to be strictly construed does not apply to this title, but the provisions herein must be construed according to the fair meaning of their terms to promote justice and effect the objects of the law, including the purposes stated in §13-101.

Section 13-105. Definitions

In this title, unless the context otherwise requires:

1. "Act" means a bodily movement.

2. "Benefit" means an act of value or advantage, present or prospective.

3. "Conduct" means an act or omission and its accompanying culpable state.

4. "Crime" means a misdemeanor or a felony.

5. "Culpable mental state" means intentionally, knowingly, recklessly or with criminal negligence as those are thusly defined:

(a) "Intentionally" or "with the intent to" means, with respect to a result or to conduct described by a statute defining an offense, that a person's objective is to cause that result or to engage in that conduct.

(b) "Knowingly" means, with respect to conduct or to a circumstance described by a statute defining an offense, that a person is aware or believes that his or her conduct is of that nature or that the circumstance exists.

(c) "Recklessly" means, with respect to a result or to a circumstance described by a statute defining an offense, that a person is aware of and consciously disregards a substantial and unjustifiable risk that the result will occur or that the circumstance exists. The risk must be of such nature and degree that disregard of such risk constitutes a gross deviation from the standard of conduct that a reasonable person would observe in the situation. A person who creates such a risk but is unaware of such risk solely by reason of voluntary intoxication also acts recklessly with respect to such risk.

(d) "Criminal negligence" means, with respect to a result or to a circumstance described by a statute defining an offense, that a person fails to perceive a substantial and unjustifiable risk that the result will occur or that the circumstance exists. The risk must be of such nature and degree that the failure to perceive it constitutes a gross deviation from the standard of care that a reasonable person would observe in the situation. . . .

7. "Dangerous instrument" means anything that under the circumstance in which it is used, attempted to be used or threatened to be used is readily capable of causing death or serious physical injury.

8. "Deadly physical force" means force which is used with the purpose of causing death or serious physical injury or in the manner of its use or intended use is capable of creating a substantial risk of causing death or serious physical injury.

9. "Deadly weapon" means anything designed for lethal use. The term includes a firearm. . . .

11. "Felony" means an offense for which a sentence to a term of imprisonment to the custody of the department of corrections is authorized by any law of this state. . . .

15. "Intoxication" means any mental or physical incapacity resulting from the use of drugs, toxic vapors, or intoxicating liquors.

16. "Misdemeanor" means an offense for which a sentence to a term of imprisonment other than to the custody of the department of corrections is authorized by any law of this state.

17. "Narcotic drug" means narcotic drugs as defined by Section 36-1001.

18. "Offense" means conduct for which a sentence to a term of imprisonment or of a fine is provided by any law of this state or by any law, regulation or ordinance of a political subsection of this state.

19. "Omission" means the failure to perform an act as to which a duty of performance is imposed by law. . . .

22. "Petty offense" means an offense for which a sentence of a fine only is authorized by law.

23. "Physical force" means the impairment of physical condition. . . .

27. "Property" means anything of value, tangible or intangible. . . .

29. "Serious physical injury" includes physical injury which created a reasonable risk of death, or which causes serious and permanent disfigurement, or serious impairment of health or loss or protracted impairment of the function of any bodily organ or limb.

30. "Unlawful" means contrary to law or, where the context so requires, not permitted by law. . . .

32. "Voluntary act" means a bodily movement performed consciously and as a result of effort and determination.

33. "Voluntary intoxication" means intoxication caused by the knowing use of drugs, toxic vapors or intoxicating liquors by the defendant, the tendency of which to cause intoxication the defendant knows or ought to know, unless the defendant introduces them pursuant to medical advice or under duress as would afford a defense to an offense.

Title 13. Criminal Code

Chapter 2. General Principles of Criminal Liability

Section 13-201. Requirements for Criminal Liability

The minimum requirement for criminal liability is the performance by a person of conduct which includes a voluntary act or the omission to perform a duty imposed by law which the person is physically capable of performing.

Section 13-203. Causal Relationship Between Conduct and Result; Relationship to Mental Culpability

A. Conduct is the cause of a result when both of the following exist:
    1. But for the conduct the result in question would not have occurred.
    2. The relationship between the conduct and result satisfies any additional causal requirements imposed by the statute defining the offense.

B. If intentionally causing a particular result is an element of an offense, and the actual result is not within the intention or contemplation of the person, that element is established if:
    1. The actual result differs from that intended or contemplated only in the respect that a different person or different property is injured or affected or that the injury or harm intended or contemplated would have been more serious or extensive than that caused; or
    2. The actual result involves similar injury or harm as that intended or contemplated and occurs in a manner which the person knows or should know is rendered substantially more probable by such person's conduct.

C. If recklessly or negligently causing a particular result is an element of an offense, and the actual result is not within the risk of which the person is aware or in the case of criminal negligence, of which the person should be aware, that element is established if:
    1. The actual result differs from the probable result only in the respect that a different person or different property is injured or affected or that the injury or harm intended or contemplated would have been more serious or extensive than that caused; or
    2. The actual result involves similar injury or harm as the probable result and occurs in a manner which the person knows or should know is rendered substantially more probable by such person's conduct.

Model Penal Code
(Official Draft 1962)

Section 2.03. Causal Relationship Between Conduct and Result; Divergence Between Result Designed or Contemplated and Actual Result or Between Probable and Actual Result

(1) Conduct is the cause of a result when:
    (a) it is an antecedent but for which the result in question would not have occurred; and

(b) the relationship between the conduct and result satisfies any additional causal requirements imposed by the Code or by the law defining the offense.

(2) When purposely or knowingly causing a particular result is an element of an offense, the element is not established if the actual result is not within the purpose or the contemplation of the actor unless:

(a) the actual result differs from that designed or contemplated, as the case may be, only in the respect that a different person or different property is injured or affected or that the injury or harm designed or contemplated would have been more serious or more extensive than that caused; or

(b) the actual result involves the same kind of injury or harm as that designed or contemplated and is not too remote or accidental in its occurrence to have a [just] bearing on the actor's liability or on the gravity of his offense.

(3) When recklessly or negligently causing a particular result is an element of an offense, the element is not established if the actual result is not within the risk of which the actor is aware or, in the case of negligence, of which he should be aware unless:

(a) the actual result differs from the probable result only in the respect that a different person or different property is injured or affected or that the probable injury or harm would have been more serious or more extensive than that caused; or

(b) the actual result involves the same kind of injury or harm as the probable result and is not too remote or accidental in its occurrence to have a [just] bearing on the actor's liability or on the gravity of his offense.

(4) When causing a particular result is a material element of an offense for which absolute liability is imposed by law, the element is not established unless the actual result is a probable consequence of the actor's conduct.

Section 5.05. Grading of Criminal Attempt, Solicitation and Conspiracy; Mitigation in Cases of Lesser Danger; Multiple Convictions Barred

(1) Grading. Except as otherwise provided in this Section, attempt, solicitation and conspiracy are crimes of the same grade and degree as the most serious offense which is attempted or solicited or is an object of the conspiracy. An attempt, solicitation or conspiracy to commit a [capital crime or a] felony of the first degree is a felony of the second degree.

(2) Mitigation. If the particular conduct charged to constitute a criminal attempt, solicitation or conspiracy is so inherently unlikely to result or culminate in the commission of a crime that neither such conduct nor the actor presents a public danger warranting the grading of such offense under this Section, the Court shall exercise its power under Section 6.12 to enter judgment and impose sentence for a crime of lower grade or degree or, in extreme cases, may dismiss the prosecution.

(3) Multiple Convictions. A person may not be convicted of more than one offense defined by this Article for conduct designed to commit or to culminate in the commission of the same crime.

● OVERVIEW OF CAUSATION

Whenever an offense definition includes a result element—as, for example, homicide requires a resulting death—a causation requirement also is implied. That is, it must not only be shown that the prohibited result occurred, but also that the actor's conduct caused that result. This required relationship between the actor's conduct and the result derives from our notions of causal accountability. A result ought to affect an actor's liability only if the actor is responsible for it, and responsibility demands some causal connection. Causation doctrine provides the rules that determine how much of a causal connection is required to hold an actor legally accountable for the occurrence of some harm.

Hypothetical: Manny the Master (#40)

An informant in the police department reports that Prosecutor Baylor is being investigated for taking bribes to forgo prosecutions. Kenny "The Hat," the local underworld boss, suspects that if Baylor is arrested he will reveal all to the authorities. Kenny decides to have Baylor killed. To be sure that the job gets done, he gives contracts to both Squeeze and Manny. Squeeze, who is somewhat brighter and more experienced than her competitor Manny, arranges to poison Prosecutor Baylor at the corner hotdog stand where he frequently eats. Manny is tailing Baylor looking for an opportunity. When he sees Squeeze at the hotdog stand, he suspects he has been outdone. Squeeze glides over with a smile. "He ate enough to kill an elephant," she tells Manny. "He'll be dead in 45 minutes. Better luck next time."

Manny is not giving up so easily. He scurries after Baylor, who has finished his hotdog and is headed down to the subway. Manny spots Baylor at the edge of the platform and positions himself several feet behind him in the crowd. As the train approaches, he pushes another waiting passenger into Baylor, so that Baylor will be pushed in front of the train and be killed instantly. But as Manny pushes, the crowd surges due to an influx of people from a local bar closing early, and his push sends the wrong person off the platform. His push is also much too early. The fallen passenger scrambles back onto the platform before the train arrives. Manny turns to leave, angry and humiliated. Maybe he should go to computer school, he thinks, recalling an ad he saw on a matchbook cover. Screams from the track make him turn. People are milling about, peering under the train. He learns from others that a man straining to see the fallen passenger leaned out too far and was hit by the oncoming train. He presses forward to see the dead man. Could he be so lucky? They pull Prosecutor Baylor from under the train. Manny turns and heads for the exit, full of himself. Squeeze won't be making fun of him today.

Manny (and Squeeze, and Kenny "The Hat") intended that Prosecutor Baylor be killed and acted upon that intention. Liability for at least attempted murder, then, seems clear. But is Manny criminally liable for causing the death, thus liable for murder? Is Squeeze? Is Kenny "The Hat"?

Notes

REQUIREMENTS OF CAUSATION: FACTUAL AND PROXIMATE CAUSE

Current doctrine typically contains two independent requirements to establish a causal connection between an actor's conduct and a result. First, the conduct must be a factual, or "but for," cause of the result, meaning that if the actor's conduct had not occurred, the result in question also would not have occurred. Second, the conduct must be a "legal," or "proximate," cause of the result, meaning that it must relate to the result in a sufficiently strong way: As a common formulation puts it, the resulting harm must not be "too remote or accidental in its occurrence to have a [just] bearing on the actor's liability or on the gravity of his offense."[2] Some states also add to this the requirement that the resulting harm "not be too . . . dependent on another's volitional act."[3]

Factual ("But-For") Cause: Scientific Inquiry Conduct is a factual cause of a result if the result would not have occurred but for the conduct (hence the term *but-for causation*). In other words, the conduct is a factual cause if it was necessary for the result to occur. The factual-cause inquiry is essentially scientific, though also hypothetical. It asks what the world would have been like if the actor had not performed her conduct. Specifically, would the result still have occurred when it did? If not, then the actor's conduct was necessary for the result—it was a "but for" cause. In the "Manny the Master" hypothetical above, Manny's conduct is a necessary cause of Baylor's death. Because Baylor died from the fall and would have died then whether he had been poisoned or not, Squeeze's poisoning is *not* a but-for cause of Baylor's death (unless the poisoning, or her telling Manny about it, induced Manny to formulate his platform-push plan in an effort to kill Baylor right away, in which case it would be a but-for cause).

Alternative Sufficient-Cause Test This *necessary*-cause test is not the only possible formulation of the factual-cause requirement. Criticisms of some results of

---

2. Model Penal Code § 2.03(2)(b), (3)(b).
3. See, e.g., N.J. Stat. Ann. § 2C:2-3.

the necessary-cause test—such as Squeeze's escape from causal accountability for Baylor's death—may lead one to examine whether other formulations, such as a *sufficient*-cause test, might be preferable. A sufficient-cause test similarly presents a scientific and hypothetical inquiry, but a different inquiry: Would the actor's conduct have been enough, by itself, to cause the result?

Proximate (Legal) Cause: Normative Inquiry In contrast to the scientific inquiry of the factual-cause requirement, the proximate (legal) cause requirement presents an essentially normative inquiry. Deciding whether a result is "too remote or accidental in its occurrence" or "too dependent on another's volitional act" calls for an exercise of evaluative judgment. The inquiry cannot be resolved by examining the facts more closely or having a more advanced understanding of the science of cause and effect. To hold that an act proximately caused a harm is to say that it seems fair, or just, to hold the actor responsible for that harm, and the fairness of imposing accountability cannot be measured scientifically.

Proximity Examples Some examples may help illustrate the concept. Consider a common hypothetical used to illustrate a failure to satisfy the proximate cause test: The actor who shoots at, but misses, his intended victim, who flees to escape the attack and four blocks later is struck and killed by a falling piano that has broken loose from its rope as it is being hoisted to a third-floor apartment. The actor's shot is a but-for cause of the death; the deceased would not have been under the piano at the moment it fell *but for* the shot that caused him to flee. But many people would judge the actor's missed shot to be too remote from the ultimate cause (the falling piano) for the shooter to be held accountable as the legal cause of death.

Compare this, however, to *People v. Acosta*, in which the jury concluded, and a majority of the appellate court agreed, that the defendant's conduct in trying to elude chasing police proximately caused the collision of two police helicopters.[4] Acosta was convicted of murder for the death of three officers in the crash, even though it appeared that the unusual crash occurred because one of the pilots flew recklessly and in violation of FAA regulations. Consider also *People v. Arzon*, in which the defendant's murder conviction was upheld on a finding that his setting fire to a couch proximately caused the death of a fireman, who, while trying to escape the fire set by the defendant, was enveloped in dense smoke from *another* arson fire of independent origin.[5]

Foreseeability as Factor in Determining Proximate Cause Although the proximate cause inquiry involves case-by-case evaluation, it is possible to offer some generalizations about what is likely to be held to constitute a proximate cause. For example, the foreseeability of the result following from the actor's conduct is a highly influential factor in determinations of proximate cause. Considering the "Manny the Master" hypothetical again, if Baylor had died from Squeeze's poisoning, there would be little dispute that the poisoning proximately caused the death— even if the death had not occurred until a week, or a month, after the act—because the tendency of poison to cause death is quite obvious. But jurors also look to other factors aside from foreseeability. Did Manny foresee Baylor's death when he did his pushing? Yes, but not quite in the way that Baylor's death

4. 284 Cal. Rptr. 117 (1991).
5. 92 Misc. 2d 739, 401 N.Y.S.2d 156 (1978).

came about. The foreseeability of the general manner in which the result came about is relevant to jurors, but not every aspect of the way in which the result occurs need be foreseen. Imagine that Squeeze expects (and most doctors would expect) that her poison will kill Baylor by slowly interfering with his respiratory system. She is not likely to be judged less causally accountable if, instead, her poison induces uncontrollable vomiting and Baylor dies of extreme dehydration.

Vagueness in the Proximate Cause Standard   As is apparent from the usual statutory language, the standard for proximate cause is somewhat vague, in part because the judgment called for is complex and case-specific. One might try to provide additional guidance by giving a decision maker particular examples of what the law holds to be, or not to be, "too remote" and "too dependent on another's volitional act" for liability to be proper. But it seems likely that "remoteness" and "dependence" are not judgments that can be conceived of as part of a single continuum, along which a single point marks the boundary of "too remote" or "too dependent." Instead, the judgments appear to depend on the interaction of complex factors.[6] Perhaps criminal law theorists will someday be able to articulate a standard with some greater guidance than is now available, but the project is an ambitious one. At present, the best we can do is to identify certain general factors that seem highly relevant: the degree of "remoteness," the extent to which the result seems "accidental," the degree of dependence on "another's volitional act." We also can help the decision maker by making explicit, as the Model Penal Code does, that the inquiry is a normative one, and that the decision maker should not look for a scientific solution, but rather ought to rely on his or her own intuitive judgment of what should and should not "have a [just] bearing on the actor's liability or on the gravity of his offense."[7]

CAUSING ANOTHER PERSON TO CAUSE A RESULT

A special yet common case of causation arises when one actor causes another to cause the prohibited result, as with the informant and Kenny and Manny in the hypothetical above. Establishing causal accountability in the first of two serial causes (i.e., the cause of something that, in turn, causes the result) frequently is troublesome. The potential for a remoteness problem appears in part because the presence of the second actor seems to remove the first actor further from the result. That is, an additional link exists in the causal chain between the first actor and the result. The remoteness problem is further exacerbated by the fact that the intermediate link is a human agent, capable of independent volitional conduct. Typically one person's action cannot determine another's action in the same way that acting on a physical object might determine a subsequent event. Where an engineer pushes the accelerator, causing the train to hit a person on the tracks, we can reliably predict the physical chain of events that necessarily follow from the act of pushing the accelerator. Kenny, in contrast, can only provide motivation to Manny. The issue is not just one of foreseeability or predictability. While Manny might in this instance be as predictable as the effect of pushing the accelerator, the fact remains that it is within Manny's ability to choose not to follow Kenny's

---

6. See Paul H. Robinson, *Legality and Discretion in the Distribution of Criminal Sanctions*, 25 HARV. J. LEGIS. 395 (1988).

7. Model Penal Code § 2.03(2)(b) & (3)(b).

wishes. Obviously, no such possibility of volitional choice exists with the accelerator. And this possibility for independent action has a significant effect on the assessment of causal accountability under the proximate cause test.

Intervening Actor's Volitional Act Breaks Chain   In *Commonwealth v. Root*, the defendant was drag racing with another, who was killed when his car hit an oncoming truck as he was trying to pass the defendant.[8] The court found that while the defendant's conduct may have been a factual (necessary) cause of the death—the deceased would not have crashed but for the defendant's drag racing with him—the defendant's conduct was not a proximate, legal cause because the deceased had voluntarily chosen to engage in the conduct that caused his own death. In *People v. Campbell*, the defendant was drinking with another man with whom he was angry. He encouraged the man to kill himself. When the man responded that he had no weapon, defendant offered to sell him his weapon, and subsequently gave the man his gun. The man shot himself. The defendant's conviction for murder was reversed for lack of proximate cause.[9]

Influencing Intervening Actor's Exercise of Volition   An intervening actor's potential to act independently does not itself insulate the first actor from causal accountability for the result. The potential for independence must be sufficiently realized. In *State v. Lassiter*, for example, the defendant pimp was brutally beating one of his prostitutes when she jumped from an eleventh-floor window to escape his attack.[10] While she chose to jump, the prostitute's choice was so highly influenced (coerced) by the defendant that it was close to no choice. Similarly, in *Stephenson v. State*, the defendant abducted and repeatedly performed sexual perversions, including inflicting bite wounds, on a woman who then secretly took poison because she was "distracted with the pain and shame so inflicted on her." The woman eventually received medical treatment but died of an infection. Defendant was held liable for second-degree murder.[11]

Continuum of Volition   In some cases, the intervening actor's potential for volitional conduct is altogether illusory. In *People v. Kibbe*, for example, the defendants robbed the victim and left him drunk and partially undressed on a dark, snowy rural road. Approximately 20-30 minutes later, a motorist struck and killed the victim.[12] Under the circumstances, one might conclude that the motorist was exercising little or no independent choice when he hit the victim. The court concluded that the defendants' conduct had caused the death despite the presence of a human agent in the causal chain. In *Lassiter*, noted above, the prostitute's decision to jump may be more akin to the lack of choice by the motorist in *Kibbe* than to the free choice exercised by the deceased drag racer in *Root*. Root's drag racing may have tempted his opponent, but it did not compel the lethal conduct in the way that Lassiter's beating compelled the prostitute to jump. The point is that there is a continuum of voluntariness, and in each case the decision maker must determine whether the intervening actor's choice reaches that point on the continuum that extinguishes the primary actor's causal accountability for the result.

---

8. 170 A.2d 310, 310-11 (Pa. 1961).
9. 335 N.W.2d 27 (Mich. App. 1983).
10. 484 A.2d 13, 15-16 (N.J. Super. App. Div. 1984).
11. 179 N.E. 633 (Ind. 1932).
12. 321 N.E.2d 773 (N.Y. 1974).

Causing Another's Crime as Form of Complicity To avoid such causation difficulties of the intervening actor where one actor induces another to commit an offense, most jurisdictions treat such conduct either as a form of complicity or as a special form of liability for causing crime by an innocent, depending on the status of the person induced to commit the offense.[13]

Commonwealth v. Root

Supreme Court of Pennsylvania
403 Pa. 571, 170 A.2d 310 (1961)

CHARLES ALVIN JONES, Chief Justice.

The appellant was found guilty of involuntary manslaughter for the death of his competitor in the course of an automobile race between them on a highway. . . . On appeal from the judgment of sentence entered on the jury's verdict, the Superior Court affirmed. We granted allocatur because of the important question present as to whether the defendant's unlawful and reckless conduct was a sufficiently direct cause of the death to warrant his being charged with criminal homicide.

The testimony . . . discloses that, on the night of the fatal accident, the defendant accepted the deceased's challenge to engage in an automobile race; that the racing took place on a rural three-lane highway; that the night was clear and dry, and the traffic was light; that the speed limit on the highway was 50 miles per hour; that, immediately prior to the accident, the two automobiles were being operated at varying speeds of from 70 to 90 miles per hour; that the accident occurred in a no-passing zone on the approach to a bridge where the highway narrowed to two directionally-opposite lanes; that, at the time of the accident, the defendant was in the lead and was proceeding in his right hand lane of travel; that the deceased, in an attempt to pass the defendant's automobile, when a truck was closely approaching from the opposite direction, swerved his car to the left, crossed the highway's white dividing line and drove his automobile on the wrong side of the highway head-on into the oncoming truck with resultant fatal effect to himself.

This evidence would of course amply support a conviction of the defendant for speeding, reckless driving and, perhaps, other violations of The Vehicle Code. . . . In any event, unlawful or reckless conduct is only one ingredient of the crime of involuntary manslaughter. Another essential and distinctly separate element of the crime is that the unlawful or reckless conduct charged to the defendant was the *direct* cause of the death in issue. The first ingredient is obviously present in this case but, just as plainly, the second is not.

While precedent is to be found for application of the tort law concept of "proximate cause" in fixing responsibility for criminal homicide, the want of any rational basis for its use in determining criminal liability can no longer be properly disregarded. When proximate cause was first borrowed from the field of tort law and applied to homicide prosecutions in Pennsylvania, the concept connoted a much more direct causal relation in producing the alleged culpable result than it does today. Proximate cause, as an essential element of a tort founded

---

13. See, e.g., Model Penal Code § 2.06(2)(a)&(3)(a)(ii).

in negligence, has undergone in recent times, and is still undergoing, a marked extension. More specifically, this area of civil law has been progressively liberalized in favor of claims for damages for personal injuries to which careless conduct of others can in some way be associated. To persist in applying the tort liability concept of proximate cause to prosecutions for criminal homicide after the marked expansion of *civil* liability of defendants in tort actions for negligence would be to extend possible *criminal* liability to persons chargeable with unlawful or reckless conduct in circumstances not generally considered to present the likelihood of a resultant death. . . .

The instant case is one of first impression in this State; and our research has not disclosed a single instance where a district attorney has ever before attempted to prosecute for involuntary manslaughter on facts similar to those established by the record now before us. The closest case, factually, would seem to be Commonwealth v. Levin, 135 A.2d 764 (1957), which affirmed the defendant's conviction of involuntary manslaughter. In the *Levin* case two cars were racing on the streets of Philadelphia at speeds estimated at from 85 to 95 miles per hour. The defendant's car, in the left hand lane, was racing alongside of the car in which the deceased was a passenger when the defendant turned his automobile sharply to the right in front of the other car thereby causing the driver of the latter car to lose control and smash into a tree, the passenger being thrown to the road and killed as a result of the impact. It is readily apparent that the elements of causation in the *Levin* case were fundamentally different from those in the present case. Levin's act of cutting his automobile sharply in front of the car in which the deceased was riding directly forced that car off of the road and into the tree. The defendant's reckless and unlawful maneuver was the direct cause of the crucial fatality. In the instant case, the defendant's conduct was not even remotely comparable. Here, the action of the deceased driver in recklessly and suicidally swerving his car to the left lane of a 2-lane highway into the path of an oncoming truck was not forced upon him by any act of the defendant; it was done by the deceased and by him alone, who thus directly brought about his own demise. The *Levin* case was properly decided but it cannot, by any ratiocination, be utilized to justify a conviction in the present case.

Legal theory which makes guilt or innocence of criminal homicide depend upon such accidental and fortuitous circumstances as are now embraced by modern tort law's encompassing concept of proximate cause is too harsh to be just. A few illustrations should suffice to so demonstrate.

In Mautino v. Piercedale Supply Co., 12 A.2d 51 (1940),—a civil action for damages—we held that where a man sold a cartridge to a person under 16 years of age in violation of a State statute and the recipient subsequently procured a gun from which he fired the cartridge injuring someone, the injury was proximately caused by the act of the man who sold the cartridge to the underage person. If proximate cause were the test for criminal liability and the injury to the plaintiff in the *Mautino* case had been fatal, the man who sold the bullet to the underage person (even though the boy had the appearance of an adult) would have been guilty of involuntary manslaughter, for his unlawful act would, according to the tort law standard, have been the proximate cause of the death.

In Schelin v. Goldberg, 146 A.2d 648 (1958), it was held that the plaintiff, who was injured in a fight, could recover in tort against the defendants, the owners of a taproom who prior to the fight had unlawfully served the plaintiff drinks while he was in a visibly intoxicated condition, the unlawful action of the defendants being held to be the proximate cause of the plaintiff's injuries. Here, again, if proximate cause were the test for criminal liability and the plaintiff had been fatally injured in the fight, the taproom owners would have been guilty of involuntary manslaughter, for their unlawful act would have been no less the proximate cause of death.

In Marchl v. Dowling & Company, 41 A.2d 427 (1945), it was held that where a truck driver had double parked his truck and the minor plaintiff was struck by a passing car when she walked around the double parked truck, the truck driver's employer was held liable in tort for the plaintiff's injuries on the ground that the truck driver's act of double parking, which violated both a State statute and a city ordinance, was the proximate cause of the plaintiff's injuries. Here, also, if proximate cause were the test for criminal liability and the plaintiff's injuries had been fatal, the truck driver would have been guilty of involuntary manslaughter since his unlawful act would have been the proximate cause of the death for which his employer was held liable in damages under respondeat superior. To be guilty of involuntary manslaughter for double parking would, of course, be unthinkable, yet if proximate cause were to determine criminal liability, such a result would indeed be a possibility.

Even if the tort liability concept of proximate cause were to be deemed applicable, the defendant's conviction of involuntary manslaughter in the instant case could not be sustained under the evidence. The operative effect of a supervening cause would have to be taken into consideration. But, the trial judge refused the defendant's point for charge to such effect and erroneously instructed the jury that "negligence or want of care on the part of [the deceased] is no defense to the criminal responsibility of the defendant . . . . "

Under the uncontradicted evidence in this case, the conduct of the defendant was not the proximate cause of the decedent's death as a matter of law. . . .

In [Johnson v. Angretti, 364 Pa. 602, 73 A.2d 666 (1950)], while Angretti was driving his truck eastward along a highway, a bus, traveling in the same direction in front of him, stopped to take on a passenger. Angretti swerved his truck to the left into the lane of oncoming traffic in an attempt to pass the bus but collided with a tractor-trailer driven by the plaintiff's decedent, who was killed as a result of the collision. In affirming the entry of judgment n. o. v. in favor of the defendant bus company, we held that any negligence on the part of the bus driver, in suddenly bringing his bus to a halt in order to pick up a passenger, was not a proximate cause of the death of the plaintiff's decedent since the accident "was due entirely to the intervening and superseding negligence of Angretti in allowing his truck to pass over into the pathway of the westbound tractor-trailer . . . . "

In the case now before us, the deceased was aware of the dangerous condition created by the defendant's reckless conduct in driving his automobile at an excessive rate of speed along the highway but, despite such knowledge, he recklessly chose to swerve his car to the left and into the path of an oncoming truck, thereby bringing about the head-on collision which caused his own death.

To summarize, the tort liability concept of proximate cause has no proper place in prosecutions for criminal homicide and more direct causal connection is required for conviction. In the instant case, the defendant's reckless conduct was not a sufficiently direct cause of the competing driver's death to make him criminally liable therefor. . . .

EAGEN, Justice (dissenting).

The opinion of the learned Chief Justice admits, under the uncontradicted facts, that the defendant, at the time of the fatal accident involved, was engaged in an unlawful and reckless course of conduct. Racing an automobile at 90 miles per hour, trying to prevent another automobile going in the same direction from passing him, in a no-passing zone on a two-lane public highway, is certainly all of that. Admittedly also, there can be more than one direct cause of an unlawful death. To me, this is self-evident. But, says the majority opinion, the defendant's recklessness was not a direct cause of the death. With this, I cannot agree.

If the defendant did not engage in the unlawful race and so operate his automobile in such a reckless manner, this accident would never have occurred. He helped create the dangerous event. He was a vital part of it. The victim's acts were a natural reaction to the stimulus of the situation. The race, the attempt to pass the other car and forge ahead, the reckless speed, all of these factors the defendant himself helped create. He was part and parcel of them. That the victim's response was normal under the circumstances, that his reaction should have been expected and was clearly foreseeable, is to me beyond argument. That the defendant's recklessness was a substantial factor is obvious. All of this, in my opinion, makes his unlawful conduct a direct cause of the resulting collision. . . .

The majority opinion states, "Legal theory which makes guilt or innocence of criminal homicide depend upon such *accidental and fortuitous circumstances* as are now embraced by modern tort law's encompassing concept . . . is too harsh to be just." If the resulting death had been dependent upon "accidental and fortuitous circumstances" or, as the majority also say, "in circumstances not generally considered to present the likelihood of a resultant death," we would agree that the defendant is not criminally responsible. However, acts should be judged by their tendency under the known circumstances, not by the actual intent which accompanies their performance. Every day of the year, we read that some teenagers, or young adults, somewhere in this country, have been killed or have killed others, while racing their automobiles. Hair-raising, death-defying, law-breaking rides, which encompass "racing" are the rule rather than the exception, and endanger not only the participants, but also every motorist and passenger on the road. To call such resulting accidents "accidental and fortuitous," or unlikely to result in death, is to ignore the cold and harsh reality of everyday occurrences. . . .

While the victim's foolhardiness in this case contributed to his own death, he was not the only one responsible and it is not he alone with whom we are concerned. It is the people of the Commonwealth who are harmed by the kind of conduct the defendant pursued. Their interests must be kept in mind.

I, therefore, dissent and would accordingly affirm the judgment of conviction.

▲ PROBLEMS

Two Killers, One Killing (#41)

Luman Smith and Joseph Wood are in a fight over a horse. Wood, Luman's father-in-law, claims Luman has no right to use his daughter's horse. Luman says the horse is his, not Wood's daughter's, and that he can do as he wishes. Underlying the fight is the fact that Luman's marriage to Wood's daughter Alma is not going terribly well. She has already moved out once, but Luman, unable to run the farm on his own, persuaded her to come back in exchange for signing over most of his property into her name. The horse was not part of the property transferred, but Wood stubbornly persists. When he pulls a gun on Luman, the fight turns decidedly violent. As Luman struggles for the gun, Wood shoots him in the abdomen, inflicting a fatal wound.

However, Luman does not die immediately. His wound is indeed fatal, but it will take about a week before he will finally succumb, according to the then-current medical wisdom. Meanwhile, Alma has heard the gunshot and comes out of the house to investigate with her own gun drawn. Leaving the barn, mortally wounded, Luman sees the gun and grabs for it. Alma refuses to relinquish the gun. She shoots Luman, this time in the chest, a wound from which he soon dies. Wood and Alma go back to work on the farm.

Is Wood causally accountable for the death of Luman? Is Alma? Distinguish between factual and proximate causation in your analysis. If causal accountability exists, what liability, if any, under Model Penal Code?

Pulling Out His Own Tubes (#42)

Benjamin Hamilton and John Slye both love to play pool. They often meet in the local pool hall, throwing back pints of beer and engaging in fervent banter. One night, however, the drinking is accompanied by arguing, which gets out of hand. Hamilton and Slye come to blows. After they are asked to leave the pool hall, they continue their fight outside. Eventually, Hamilton gets the better of Slye, knocking him down during the fight. He does not stop there, but rather explodes into a fit of rage, kicking Slye in the head as he lies on the ground and even jumping on Slye's face. Slye begins to bleed profusely from his face and is taken to the hospital in a state of shock.

At the hospital, Slye is given a blood transfusion and doctors begin clearing his airways. They insert tubes into his nasal passages and trachea in order to keep him from choking on his own blood. When Slye is moved to a hospital room, he has to be tied to his bed, as his doctors fear that he is still confused from the trauma to his head. They worry that without restraints he will remove the tubes that are keeping him alive. Nurses fasten handcuffs to him so that he will not disturb the tubes. Later in the evening, the doctors decide that Slye has calmed down enough to remove the restraints and allow him to rest more comfortably. The next morning, however, Slye has a convulsion and immediately thereafter yanks the tubes out of his nose and mouth with his hands. Less than an hour later, he dies from asphyxiation.

Is Hamilton causally accountable for the death of Slye? Distinguish between factual and proximate causation in your analysis. If causation exists, for which homicide offense, if any, would Hamilton be liable under the Model Penal Code?

A Patriotic Suicide (#43)

In 1913, Colonel Alfred Redl is a star in Austria-Hungary's counterespionage bureau, rising in rank to the chief of the General Staff of the Prague Army Corps and mentioned as a candidate to become Minister of War. In his current position he is responsible for keeping military plans safe. However, Redl is also a spy for Russia, Austria-Hungary's main enemy. As Austria-Hungary prepares for war against Russia, Redl is selling his knowledge of their military's mobilization plans, endangering hundreds of thousands of Austrian lives.

Unbeknownst to Redl, the Austrian Secret Service has caught on to him. He is followed from the post office one day as he attempts to pick up what the authorities have flagged as a suspicious package. When Redl realizes he is being tailed by his own subordinates, he tries to lose them by switching cabs and even making a break on foot. He shreds some of the documents he has just received in the hopes that his pursuers will stop to retrieve the information. However, despite his efforts, he is soon captured.

As Redl is a high-ranking official, Urbanski von Ostromiesc, the head of the Secret Service, is immediately notified of the situation. He hopes to avoid a scandal over the enormous security breach that would come from a public trial because it would damage both military and civilian morale on the eve of war. He directs Redl to kill himself. After admitting that he became a spy because the Russians had blackmailed him, Redl agrees to die for his country as a form of amends. He requests a handgun from one of the Secret Service officers so that he can commit suicide. The officer obliges, and Redl fatally shoots himself on the spot.

Is von Ostromiesc causally accountable for the death of Redl? Distinguish between factual and proximate causation in your analysis. If causation exists, for which homicide offense, if any, would von Ostromiesc be liable under the Model Penal Code?

[handwritten margin notes: Yes — factual causation — providing gun to commit act — No — Proximate causation — Redl has a choice to make use of gun or not]

A Jump to Escape, and Drown (#44)

Deletha Word, 33, is struggling to get through school. She dreams of completing her degree and owning her own business. To finish all her coursework and keep up with her daily life, she occasionally resorts to using PCP for energy. Unfortunately, along with energy comes irrational behavior. One night, she is out at an impromptu party on an island park after dark. The park is known as a place for young people to gather, and particularly to show off their cars along "the Strip," a road running through the park. Word drinks, smokes pot, and ingests PCP. Her behavior becomes erratic, including dancing naked on top of cars. Around midnight, her dog, which she has brought to the park, runs underneath a car that is slowly passing along the Strip. Word jumps in front of the car, slamming her hands onto the hood to get the driver to stop. The driver,

Martell Welch, backs up and the dog runs out. But he is not happy about the way Word has treated his car. Welch is a car aficionado and takes these things seriously. He steps out and confronts her, but his friends calm him down and they leave.

Several hours later, Word is herself ready to leave. She gets in her car and drives down the strip toward home. In her intoxicated state, her driving leaves something to be desired and she sideswipes another car, causing moderate damage. Rather than stop, she drives away. As it turns out, the car she has hit is Welch's. Perhaps still in an aggressive state from the earlier episode, he follows Word. His pursuit does not last long because there is a traffic jam on the bridge connecting the park to the city. Seeing that she is stuck, and fearful of the person following her, Word attempts to pull a U-turn. However, when she backs up, she smashes into Welch's car again, breaking a headlight and denting the hood. Having had enough, Welch gets out of his car, drags Word out of hers and begins to beat her. Welch stands 6 feet 4 inches tall, weighs 240 pounds, and is a former high school football star. Word is 4 feet 11 inches tall and weighs around 115 pounds. After being punched and having her head smashed against her car, she manages to escape from Welch's grasp.

By now a crowd has gathered, but they are egging on the fight rather than trying to help Word. Welch grabs her again, and this time solicits offers from the crowd for "a go" with Word. She again breaks free as someone offers Welch $10. Although she does not swim well, she sees her only escape as jumping off the bridge, so she gets near the edge and hangs off. She warns Welch she will jump if he approaches, but he approaches nonetheless. She jumps.

Though she falls 24 feet, she is able to stay afloat in the water below. The water is about 20 feet deep in the middle and Word is in the process of maneuvering herself safely to the shore when two men, arriving late to the scene on the bridge, dive in to rescue her. Word thinks that the men are coming to further assault her and swims away from her would-be rescuers, disappearing into the river. Her body is found later that morning. The cause of death is drowning. (The injuries she sustained on the bridge turned out to have been minor—bruises and a small abrasion. The coroner indicates that they alone would not have caused any incapacitation.)

Is Welch causally accountable for the death of Word? Distinguish between factual and proximate causation in your analysis. If causation exists, for which homicide offense, if any, would Welch be liable under the Model Penal Code?

▲ HOMICIDE REVIEW PROBLEM

This Part of the coursebook has examined the various facets of liability for homicide offenses as well as causation requirements. Recalling elements from each of the previous Sections, consider the following case reported by Dr. Don Harper Mills, President of the American Academy of Forensic Sciences at the Academy's annual meeting.

Can You Be Your Own Intervening Actor? (#45)

Ronald Opus is part of a rich but highly dysfunctional family. He has learned that his mother is about to cut off his financial support. He contemplates his alternatives but finds none that will save him from a life of misery, as he sees it, other than to dispose of her. He hatches a plan that makes use of his father's habit of menacing his wife with an unloaded shotgun. Ronald figures if he secretly loads the gun, his father will eventually "accidentally" shoot his mother. He buys bullets and loads the gun while his father is out, but, unfortunately for Ronald, his parents enter a rare period of domestic tranquility.

Son loads gun

Ronald cannot muster the nerve to kill his mother directly, and with his plan failed he becomes despondent. He writes a suicide note confessing to his failed plan and stating his desire to die. He then proceeds to the rooftop of the apartment building in which he and his parents live. He sits on the ledge for a long while, contemplating all that has gone wrong in his life.

While Ronald is preparing to end his life, his plan is actually starting to work. His parents have begun arguing again and his father is waving the now-loaded shotgun at his mother, completely unaware that he could actually kill her with it. Perhaps if Ronald could hear them fighting Ronald would refrain from jumping, but on the rooftop he stays true to his suicide plan. He eases himself over the ledge and begins a 20-story free fall. Just as he jumps, his parents' argument comes to a head. His father, as is his habit, pulls the trigger of his gun for emphasis. He is shocked when it actually fires; the recoil sends him sprawling to the floor. Fortunately for Ronald's mother, he was not paying much attention to his aim. The shot misses and goes through the living-room window, which Ronald is falling past at that exact moment. The bullet strikes Ronald in the chest, piercing his heart and killing him instantly. A second or so later, his corpse lands softly in a safety net extending out from the eighth floor. As it turns out, construction on the building was planned for later that week and the net had been placed to ensure the workers' safety. Had he not been shot, Ronald would have landed harmlessly in the net.

jumps off rooftop, attempted suicide

father pulls trigger unaware gun is loaded

No mens rea element

← *Would have survived if not shot*

Using your knowledge of homicide offenses and causal accountability, what liability under the Model Penal Code for Ronald's father for Ronald's death?

If Ronald had survived the shot, what liability for Ronald, if any?

⚹ Actual causation No proximate cause, harm unforeseeable

⚹ DISCUSSION ISSUE

Should Resulting Harm Be Relevant to Criminal Liability?
Should a Completed Offense Be Punished More than an Unsuccessful Attempt?

Materials presenting each side of this Discussion Issue appear in the Advanced Materials for Section 9 in Appendix A.

PART IV

INCHOATE LIABILITY

The previous Section, concerning causation, introduces the notion that the occurrence of results can make a difference to criminal liability. The causation requirements ensure that a defendant's liability and punishment are increased because of resulting harm only if the results are sufficiently causally attributable to the defendant. This Part continues the inquiry into the significance of results. Although there is some controversy regarding the issue, in most American jurisdictions a person who unsuccessfully attempts murder might be as dangerous (or as much in need of deterrence and rehabilitation) as an identical person who succeeds in the killing, but the successful murderer is nonetheless assigned greater liability and punishment than the attempter. Why should this be so?

Inchoate liability also presents issues beyond the grading effect of resulting harm. Most important, it represents the criminal law's minimum requirements for liability. The criminal law commonly punishes mere risk creation as well as "evil" conduct, such as cheating, incest between adults, or gambling. It should be no surprise, then, to find that the criminal law punishes inchoate offenses—that is, incomplete or unsuccessful offenses. Actors who plan or attempt offenses may well be blameworthy and dangerous and in need of deterrence and rehabilitation.

While punishing inchoate offenses is consistent with the idea of liability in the absence of harmful results, such offenses go further: to impose liability even in the absence of the prohibited offense conduct. One can be liable for attempted cheating, attempted incest, or attempted gambling. It is enough for inchoate liability that the person in some way *sought* to commit an offense. In that sense, inchoate offenses are unique; they define the borderline of criminal conduct—the minimum that one can do to be criminally liable.

It is in part this role of defining the borderline of criminal liability that makes inchoate offenses so important and so interesting. Deciding the minimum requirements for liability forces hard decisions, and the choices a society makes reveals much about its views on the nature of criminal liability generally. Principles and dilemmas that are part of the criminal liability landscape in many other areas come into sharp focus in this Part. If criminal liability does not require completed offense conduct, what does it require? If an intention to commit an offense is the gravamen of inchoate offenses, why require any act at all? It is in the definition of this liability borderline that the rationales underlying the criminal law's purposes and principles are revealed.

Attempt Liability

Where liability for a substantive offense fails because of lack of a prohibited result or of a causal accountability for it, the offender nonetheless may be liable for an attempt. Indeed, attempt liability may attach even if the person never completes the required offense conduct. On the other hand, not every thought of committing an offense is itself a crime. The criminal law requires that the thought first mature into action. Why should this be? And exactly how much action is required to make conduct a criminal attempt?

◆ THE CASE OF ROBERT JACKSON (#46)

It is Thursday, June 10, 1976, in Brooklyn, New York. Vanessa Hodges is again explaining her plan to the enthusiastic Martin Allen, whom she met through her friend Rea Longhorne. Hodges has decided Allen trustworthy enough to be included in her plot to rob the Manufacturers Hanover Trust Company Bank, on the corner of Flushing and Washington Avenues, in Brooklyn. The plan is simple: Arrive at the bank around 7:30 a.m. Monday morning, when the weekend deposits are still there, and make an entrance just as the manager is opening the

Figure 42 **1976 Lincoln Continental**
(Earle K. Gould)

door. Allen quickly agrees to the plan and tells Hodges that he has a shotgun and a .38-caliber pistol they can use, if necessary.

On Monday morning, Allen meets Hodges at about 7:30 a.m. Robert Jackson, the third member of their team, then picks them up in Longhorne's brown Lincoln Continental. On the back seat is a red and black plaid suitcase containing their supplies—a sawed-off shotgun, shells, handcuffs, and some face masks.

They reach the bank a bit late, at a little past 8:00 a.m. and the place seems busy. The manager has already opened the door, so they cannot force their way in with him as planned. Discouraged, the three decide to have some breakfast at a nearby restaurant and discuss whether to proceed. After about an hour, they elect to return to the bank to take another look. After getting out to assess the situation, Allen and Hodges decide it is too risky to make an attempt now. They also decide they need another person because the night deposit bags are bigger and more bulky than Hodges had anticipated.

They drive to Coney Island to look for William Scott as the potential fourth member of their team. After hearing the plan, Scott immediately signs on. Allen stops to get the sawed-off shotgun, and they head back to the bank. By the time they are there, however, it is well past noon, and the bank is even busier. Scott goes into the bank to assess the situation more closely. Trying to act casual, he pretends to be filling out a credit card application. Outside, Jackson covers the car's license plate with a fake one.

Inside, Scott observes that the tellers have begun to process the weekend deposits. He carefully notes that the lone surveillance camera is located over the door and hurries back to the team. After he describes the layout, the group recognizes that they have missed their chance for the day. They agree to try again next Monday, June 21, at 7:30 a.m. sharp.

They head back to Coney Island. Hodges has decided that the facemask material they have is not right, and they buy some stockings to wear as masks. They also buy gloves for all members.

That Friday, June 18, the police arrest Hodges on an unrelated robbery charge. She tells them of the plan to rob the Flushing Avenue bank and to watch for a brown car with a cardboard license plate and three black men inside. The

Figure 43 **Chase Bank in Brooklyn, formerly the Manufacturers Hanover Trust Company**
(Michael Cahill)

agents ask her to confirm the plan, so she calls Allen on Saturday to ask if he is still in. He tells her that he "is ready." Just to be sure, Hodges calls again on Sunday to finalize the details. At that time, Allen tells her he knows of her arrest and now thinks the bank job is a bad idea because the F.B.I. might be watching. Hodges suggests that they should proceed without her.

Monday, June 21, is a sunny, clear day. The F.B.I. begin their surveillance at 7:00 a.m. Ten agents are stationed around the bank—in the building across the street, in cars along the same block, and in a nearby parking lot. At a little past 7:00 a.m., they spot a brown Lincoln Continental approaching the bank from the west. The three men are driving cautiously and pass the bank. Circling around, they park one block south of the bank, in front of a fire hydrant on Washington Avenue. Scott, wearing a denim hat, gets out and starts walking toward the bank. He walks past the bank on Washington, buys a cup of coffee, and then returns to the corner in front of the bank. He stands there for a few minutes, sipping his coffee and surveying the situation before rejoining the men in the car. The car pulls out, makes a left turn and drives west, then makes a U-turn and stops a little west of the bank, on Flushing. After sitting for some time, they drive east toward the bank, continue two blocks past, then turn right and pull over. Jackson, wearing a maroon leisure suit, gets out, removes the front license plate, and throws it on the floor of the car.

Turning around, they drive back toward the bank and pull over near the hydrant on Washington again. They sit, debating what to do for almost thirty minutes. It is about 8:15 a.m. when they finally pull out again and drive east, away from the bank, having decided not to rob it. As they pass one of the F.B.I. cars, one of the men does a quick double take. The agents know they have been spotted. The Lincoln turns south onto Grand. Two blocks later, the F.B.I. agents pull the three men over and arrest them. After having the defendants step out of their car, the arresting officers open the suitcase they find in the back. It contains two loaded shotguns—one is 24 inches cut down to a 14-inch barrel, the other is 27 inches cut down to a 15-inch barrel—and six additional rounds of ammunition, along with mask, a navy watch cap, and a nickel-plate toy revolver.

1. Relying only on your intuitions of justice, what liability and punishment, if any, does Robert Jackson deserve?

N	0	1	2	3	4	5	6	7	8	9	10	11
☒	☐	☐	☐	☐	☐	☐	☐	☐	☐	☐	☐	☐
no liability	liability but no punishment	1 day	2 wks	2 mo	6 mo	1 yr	3 yrs	7 yrs	15 yrs	30 yrs	life imprison- ment	death

2. What "justice" arguments could defense counsel make on the defendant's behalf?

3. What "justice" arguments could the prosecution make against the defendant?

4. What liability, if any, for Jackson under the then-existing statutes? Prepare a list of all criminal code subsections or case in the order in which you rely upon them in your analysis.

5. What liability, if any, under the Model Penal Code? Prepare a list of all criminal code subsections in the order in which you rely upon them in your analysis.

■ THE LAW

United States Code
(1976)

Title 18. Part I. Crimes
Chapter 103. Robbery and Burglary

Section 2113. Bank Robbery and Incidental Crimes

(a) Whoever, by force and violence, or by intimidation, takes, or attempts to take, from the person or presence of another any property or money or any other thing of value belonging to, or in the care, custody, control, management, or possession of, any bank, credit union, or any savings and loan association; or

Whoever enters or attempts to enter any bank, credit union, or any savings and loan association, or any building used in whole or in part as a bank, credit union, or as a savings and loan association, with intent to commit in such bank, credit union, or loan association, or building, or part thereof, so used, any felony affecting such bank, credit union, or such savings and loan association and in violation of any statute of the United States, or any larceny—

Shall be fined not more than $5,000 or imprisoned not more than twenty years, or both.

(b) Whoever takes and carries away, with intent to steal or purloin, any property or money or any other thing of value exceeding $100 belonging to, or in the care, custody, management, or possession of any bank, credit union, or any savings and loan association, shall be fined not more than $5,000 or imprisoned not more than ten years, or both; or

Whoever takes and carries away, with intent to steal or purloin, any property or money or any other thing of value not exceeding $100 belonging to, or in the care, custody, management, or possession of any bank, credit union, or any savings and loan association, shall be fined not more than $1,000 or imprisoned not more than one year, or both.

(c) Whoever receives, possesses, conceals, stores, barters, sells, or disposes of, any property or money or other thing knowing the same to have been taken from a bank, credit union, or any savings and loan association, in violation of subsection (b) of this section shall be subject to the punishment by said subsection (b) for the taker.

(d) Whoever, in committing, or in attempting to commit, any offense defined in subsections (a) and (b) of this section, assaults any person, or puts in jeopardy the life of any person by the use of a dangerous weapon or device, shall be fined not more than $10,000 or imprisoned not more than twenty-five years, or both.

(e) Whoever, in committing any offense defined in this section, or in avoiding or attempting to avoid apprehension for the commission of such offense, or in freeing himself or attempting to free himself from arrest or confinement for such offense, kills any person, or forces any person to accompany him without the consent of such person, shall be imprisoned not less than ten years, or punished by death if the verdict of the jury shall so direct.

(f) As used in this section the term "bank" means any member of the Federal Reserve System, and any bank, banking association, trust company, savings bank, or other banking institution organized or operating under the laws of the United States, and any bank the deposits of which are insured by the Federal Deposit Insurance Corporation.

(g) As used in this section the term "savings and loan association" means any federal savings and loan association and any "insured institution" as defined in section 401 of the National Housing Act, as amended, and any "Federal credit union" as defined in section 2 of the Federal Credit Union Act.

(h) As used in this section the term "credit union" means any federal credit union and any State-chartered credit union the accounts of which are insured by the Administrator of the National Credit Union Administration.

Part I. Crimes

Chapter 19. Conspiracy

Section 371. Conspiracy to Commit Offense or to Defraud United States

If two or more persons conspire either to commit any offense against the United States, or to defraud the United States, or any agency thereof in any manner or for any purpose, and one or more of such persons do any act to effect the object of the conspiracy, each shall be fined not more than $10,000 or imprisoned not more than five years, or both. If, however, the offense, the commission of which is the object of the conspiracy, is a misdemeanor only, the punishment for such conspiracy shall not exceed the maximum punishment provided for such misdemeanor.

misdemeanor

Title 26

Subtitle E. Alcohol, Tobacco and Certain Other Excise Taxes

Chapter 53. Machine Guns, Destructive Devices and Certain Other Firearms
Subchapter C. Prohibited Acts

Section 5861. Prohibited Acts

It shall be unlawful for any person—

(a) to engage in business as a manufacturer or importer or, or dealer in, firearms without having paid the special (occupational) tax required by section 5801 for his business or having registered as required by section 5802; or

(b) to receive or possess a firearm transferred to him in violation of the provisions of this chapter; or

(c) to receive or possess a firearm made in violation of the provisions of this chapter; or

(d) to receive or possess a firearm which is not registered to him in the National Firearms Registration and Transfer Record; or

(e) to transfer a firearm in violation of the provisions of this chapter; or

(f) to make a firearm in violation of the provisions of this chapter; or

___ (g) to obliterate, remove, change, or alter the serial number or other identification of a firearm required by this chapter; or

___ (h) to receive or possess a firearm having the serial number or other identification required by this chapter obliterated, removed, changed, or altered; or

___ (i) to receive or possess a firearm which is not identified by a serial number as required by this chapter; or

(j) to transport, deliver, or receive any firearm in interstate commerce which has been registered as required by this chapter; or

(k) to receive or possess a firearm which has been imported or brought into the United States in violation of section 5844; or

(l) to make, or cause the making of, a false entry on any application, return, or record required by this chapter, knowing such entry to be false.

United States v. Mandujano
499 F.2d 370 (5th Cir. 1974)

Defendant appealed his conviction for attempted distribution of heroin. He had procured an ounce of heroin from a third party for an undercover narcotics agent. The Court affirmed his conviction, and defined the extent of action necessary to establish an attempt as "conduct which constitutes a substantial step toward commission of the crime." This substantial step must be "strongly corroborative of the firmness of the defendant's criminal intent. . . . [O]mission or possession, as well as positive acts, may in certain cases provide a basis for liability." The Court contrasted a substantial step, which would constitute an attempt, with mere preparation, which would not. The culpability required for an attempt was "the kind of culpability otherwise required for the commission of the crime which he is charged with attempting."

Model Penal Code
(Official Draft 1962)

Section 5.01. Criminal Attempt

(1) Definition of Attempt. A person is guilty of an attempt to commit a crime if, acting with the kind of culpability otherwise required for commission of the crime, he:

(a) purposely engages in conduct which would constitute the crime if the attendant circumstances were as he believes them to be; or

(b) when causing a particular result is an element of the crime, does or omits to do anything with the purpose of causing or with the belief that it will cause such result without further conduct on his part; or

(c) purposely does or omits to do anything which, under the circumstances as he believes them to be, is an act or omission constituting a substantial step in a course of conduct planned to culminate in his commission of the crime.

(2) Conduct Which May Be Held Substantial Step Under Subsection (1)(c). Conduct shall not be held to constitute a substantial step under Subsection (1)(c) of this Section unless it is strongly corroborative of the actor's criminal purpose. Without negativing the sufficiency of other conduct, the following, if strongly corroborative of the actor's criminal purpose, shall not be held insufficient as a matter of law:

(a) lying in wait, searching for or following the contemplated victim of the crime;

(b) enticing or seeking to entice the contemplated victim of the crime to go to the place contemplated for its commission;

(c) reconnoitering the place contemplated for the commission of the crime;

(d) unlawful entry of a structure, vehicle or enclosure in which it is contemplated that the crime will be committed;

(e) possession of materials to be employed in the commission of the crime, which are specially designed for such unlawful use or which can serve no lawful purpose of the actor under the circumstances;

(f) possession, collection or fabrication of materials to be employed in the commission of the crime, at or near the place contemplated for its commission, where such possession, collection or fabrication serves no lawful purpose of the actor under the circumstances;

(g) soliciting an innocent agent to engage in conduct constituting an element of the crime.

(3) Conduct Designed to Aid Another in Commission of a Crime. A person who engages in conduct designed to aid another to commit a crime which would establish his complicity under Section 2.06 if the crime were committed by such other person, is guilty of an attempt to commit the crime, although the crime is not committed or attempted by such other person.

(4) Renunciation of Criminal Purpose. When the actor's conduct would otherwise constitute an attempt under Subsection (1)(b) or (1)(c) of this Section, it is an affirmative defense that he abandoned his effort to commit the crime or otherwise prevented its commission, under circumstances manifesting a complete and voluntary renunciation of his criminal purpose. The establishment of such defense does not, however, affect the liability of an accomplice who did not join in such abandonment or prevention. Within the meaning of this Article, renunciation of criminal purpose is not voluntary if it is motivated, in whole or in part, by circumstances, not present or apparent at the inception of the actor's course of conduct, which increase the probability of detection or apprehension or which make more difficult the accomplishment of the criminal purpose. Renunciation is not complete if it is motivated by a decision to postpone the criminal conduct

until a more advantageous time or to transfer the criminal effort to another but similar objective or victim.]

Section 5.05. Grading of Criminal Attempt, Solicitation and Conspiracy; Mitigation in Cases of Lesser Danger; Multiple Convictions Barred

(1) Grading. Except as otherwise provided in this Section, attempt, solicitation and conspiracy are crimes of the same grade and degree as the most serious offense which is attempted or solicited or is an object of the conspiracy. An attempt, solicitation or conspiracy to commit a [capital crime or a] felony of the first degree is a felony of the second degree.

(2) Mitigation. If the particular conduct charged to constitute a criminal attempt, solicitation or conspiracy is so inherently unlikely to result or culminate in the commission of a crime that neither such conduct nor the actor presents a public danger warranting the grading of such offense under this Section, the Court shall exercise its power under Section 6.12 to enter judgment and impose sentence for a crime of lower grade or degree or, in extreme cases, may dismiss the prosecution.

(3) Multiple Convictions. A person may not be convicted of more than one offense defined by this Article for conduct designed to commit or to culminate in the commission of the same crime.

● OVERVIEW OF ATTEMPT LIABILITY

Hypothetical: A Plan to Kill (#47)

Quaxito Xinchesi has had enough of the President's unfair trade policies toward his homeland. To save the hundreds of people who are suffering under the poor economic conditions there, he decides to kill the President. The Vice President is on record as supporting a change in policy that Xinchesi prefers.

Xinchesi knows several patriots who feel as he does and he believes they would be willing to help if asked. He works out a plan to assassinate the President as he leaves his hotel after a local speech scheduled for next week. Xinchesi studies the layout each day as he passes it on his way to work, and he decides that for the plot to be successful, one of his friends must feign an attack from the opposite direction to divert Secret Service attention. Before he is able to raise the issue with his friends, or to collect any of the needed material, his nosy house cleaner finds his notes about his plan and reports him to the police. The evidence of his intention is overwhelming. He is charged with attempted murder.

Xinchesi's defense counsel does not deny Xinchesi's intention, but argues that Xinchesi has done nothing toward actual commission of the offense and therefore cannot be held liable for an attempt. Is counsel correct?

Notes

OBJECTIVE REQUIREMENTS OF ATTEMPT

Attempt Versus Mere Preparation   At some point in the chain of events from entertaining initial thoughts of committing an offense to completing that offense, an actor's conduct becomes criminal. That point typically is described as the point at which *mere preparation* becomes a *criminal attempt*. Defining the border between preparation and attempt is an important part of criminal law, for it demarcates both when an actor becomes criminally liable and when authorities lawfully may intervene. Unlike other offenses, even after this point is reached and all the elements of attempt (or another general inchoate offense) are satisfied, an actor may escape liability if he or she satisfies the rules for renouncing the attempt. Absent such renunciation, the failure to complete an offense only avoids liability for the full offense; it does not relieve the actor from liability for the attempt.

"Complete" and "Incomplete" Attempts   In some cases, often called "complete" attempts, the actor has performed *all* the conduct required for the offense, but the offense has not occurred because some required circumstance or result is absent. Examples would include an attempted murder where the would-be assassin fires the gun but misses the target (conduct complete, but result of death is missing) or an attempted distribution of drugs where the transaction takes place, but the item sold proves to be talcum powder rather than cocaine (conduct complete, but circumstance of controlled substance is missing). The real challenges in defining attempts arise in cases of "incomplete" attempts, where the actor has performed some conduct in the direction of the offense, but must still perform additional conduct for the offense to occur. Courts typically have adopted one of three types of test for distinguishing an (incomplete) attempt from mere preparation: One of various *proximity* tests, the *unequivocality* test, or the *substantial-step* test. (Note that although the tests are conceptually distinct, their overlap, and

imprecision, is such that for many specific cases fact finders may reach similar results under any of the tests.)

Proximity Tests   Prevalent at common law were various *proximity* tests: the physical proximity doctrine,[1] the dangerous proximity doctrine,[2] the indispensable-element approach,[3] and the probable-desistance test.[4] The common characteristic of these tests is that they each define the minimum attempt conduct in terms of the actor's closeness (or proximity) to commission of the substantive offense. Under any of these tests, preparation will not ripen into an attempt until the crime is about to occur, or the actor's efforts toward it are nearly complete. Applying these tests to the "Plan to Kill" hypothetical, it is unlikely that Xinchesi has reached the point that any of the proximity tests would require. The contemplated offense is a week or so off, and Xinchesi has not collected any of the people or materials needed to carry it out.

Proximity Tests Reflect Objectivist View of Criminality   One may argue, however, that the proximity tests take too restrictive a view. In the "Plan to Kill" hypothetical, for example, Xinchesi does seem to present some danger: He is apparently willing to commit a very serious offense, and is not simply daydreaming, but has engaged in conduct toward his goal (reconnaissance, making notes, etc.) that suggests a willingness to act on his intention. What, then, could be the reason for *not* imposing attempt liability on Xinchesi? The rules for attempt can reflect deeper general orientations toward criminal law, and some writers say that the proximity tests for attempt reveal an *objectivist* view of criminality in general.[5] According to this view, the gravamen of an offense is its harm or evil, tangible or intangible, and only this—rather than a mere possibility, or subjective culpability without harm—merits criminal sanction. The objectivist would not go so far as to require the actual occurrence of the offense before making liability possible; no society could survive without the authority to intervene to prevent offenses. But where liability is to be imposed in the absence of the offense's harm or evil, the objectivist view requires that the actor actually have come close to committing the offense. Some proximity tests explicitly require a real present danger that the offense will be committed.

Unequivocality (*Res Ipsa Loquitur*) Test   A second approach is to impose an *unequivocality* test, also known as the *res ipsa loquitur* test (Latin for "the thing speaks for itself"). This approach focuses not on how close the actor actually comes to committing the substantive offense, but rather on whether the conduct offers clear evidence of the actor's criminal intent. Of course, regardless of which *conduct* test applies, attempt liability also requires proof (beyond a reasonable doubt) of *culpability*: the actor's intention to commit the substantive offense. The *res ipsa* conduct test goes further, however: It requires not only proof of intent, but demands that the actor's conduct, standing alone, provide such proof. Holding aside any other facts demonstrating the actor's criminal objective, his external behavior must "speak for itself" so that an outside observer of that behavior could draw only one unequivocal conclusion, namely, that the actor is in the process of

1. See, e.g., People v. Werner, 105 P.2d 927 (Cal. 1940).
2. See, e.g., Commonwealth v. Peaslee, 59 N.E. 55, 57 (Mass. 1901).
3. See, e.g., Model Penal Code § 5.01 comment at 38–48 (Tent. Draft No. 10, 1960).
4. See, e.g., State v. Schwarzbach, 86 A. 423 (N.J. Ct. Err. & App. 1913).
5. See George P. Fletcher, Rethinking Criminal Law 135–144 (1978).

committing the offense. In many cases, this test is even more demanding than a proximity test, for even conduct in close proximity to a complete offense may not unequivocally manifest an actor's intent. Lighting one's pipe next to a neighbor's haystack is equivocal as to intention, although it may be the last act in a plan to set the haystack on fire (and other evidence might clearly demonstrate the existence of such a plan). Considering the "Plan to Kill" hypothetical, nothing in Xinchesi's public conduct displays his intention to commit the offense: He examined the planned scene of crime on his normal trips to and from work, and his incriminating planning notes are hidden in his room. Should he be liable under this test? It may depend on the reason for having a test like this. If the actor's intention to commit the offense is clear from other sources, why require that his external conduct in particular must manifest that intention?

Unequivocality Test Rationale of Assuring Clear Proof of Intent Two explanations might be offered for an unequivocality requirement. First, unlike a substantive offense where some harm or evil arises, attempt liability depends almost exclusively on the actor's intention to commit the offense. Otherwise innocent conduct—that is, conduct that does *not* give rise to any criminalized harm or evil—may become a criminal attempt by virtue of an actor's culpable state of mind. Given this heavy reliance on state of mind, it is imperative that the actor's intention be clear; hence the *res ipsa* test requirement that the conduct manifest the intention. But this explanation for the *res ipsa* test is ultimately unpersuasive. Demanding clear proof of the actor's intention is a valid goal, but the *res ipsa* test is not the only, or best, means of achieving that goal. More reliable evidence of intent frequently exists independently of the attempt conduct. As in the "Plan to Kill" hypothetical, a diary or an overheard discussion planning the offense may conclusively confirm an actor's criminal intention though her conduct has been, and will continue to be, ambiguous on its face. By its terms, the *res ipsa* test will bar attempt liability, even if evidence of culpability is overwhelming, if that evidence does not appear in the actor's conduct.

Unequivocality Test Rationale of Demanding "Manifest Criminality" An alternative rationale for the *res ipsa loquitur* test is the view that attempts are punishable not because they come close to completing the offense, as the proximity tests suggest, but rather because they create anxiety and disruption in society by openly displaying the actor's disregard for law and the interests it protects. This view has been called the *manifest criminality* view, and it seems naturally to support an unequivocality test, under which only behavior that clearly and publicly flouts the law is criminal.[6] The manifest-criminality account of criminal law seems persuasive in certain limited contexts, such as the early system of blood feuds,[7] where a tribe member's manifest intent to harm a rival tribe might provoke a preemptive attack. If the central goal of law at that point was to avoid reprisals or ongoing (and escalating) series of attacks and counterattacks, then it would need to intervene if, and only if, a would-be aggressor's harmful intent had been revealed and was known to the would-be victim, prompting a feud. Certainly conduct that manifests a

---

6. See Fletcher at 471–472.

7. For more on blood feuds, see William Ian Miller, Bloodtaking and Peacemaking: Feud, Law, and Society in Saga Iceland (1990).

criminal intention disrupts society even today, but it is unclear why these are the *only* situations in which attempt liability is appropriate.

Substantial-Step Test Examines What Actor Has Done, Not What Remains to Be Done   The Model Penal Code's requirement that an actor take a "substantial step" toward commission of the offense illustrates a third kind of conduct test for attempt.[8] Rather than focusing on *how close to the end* of the chain of activity the actor has come, this approach focuses on *how far from the beginning* of the chain the actor has gone. Many jurisdictions now adopt the substantial-step test, and others adopt a similar approach. This approach makes the substantial-step and similar tests easier to satisfy than the other tests, marking the boundary between preparation and attempt at an earlier point. An actor may have taken a substantial step toward the crime, but still have a number of other steps to go, and thus may not yet be in proximity to its commission. The Code gives seven illustrations of conduct that "shall not be held insufficient as a matter of law" to constitute a substantial step (the list is not meant to be exhaustive):

> (a) lying in wait, searching for or following the contemplated victim of the crime;
>
> (b) enticing or seeking to entice the contemplated victim of the crime to go to the place contemplated for its commission;
>
> (c) reconnoitering the place contemplated for the commission of the crime;
>
> (d) unlawful entry of a structure, vehicle or enclosure in which it is contemplated that the crime will be committed;
>
> (e) possession of materials to be employed in the commission of the crime, which are specially designed for such unlawful use or which can serve no lawful purpose of the actor under the circumstances;
>
> (f) possession, collection or fabrication of materials to be employed in the commission of the crime, at or near the place contemplated for its commission, where such possession, collection or fabrication serves no lawful purpose of the actor under the circumstances;
>
> (g) soliciting an innocent agent to engage in conduct constituting an element of the crime.[9]

Note that most of these examples of conduct, without more, would likely fail a proximity or *res ipsa* test. In the "Plan to Kill" hypothetical, Xinchesi's examinations of the hotel probably satisfy example (c), reconnoitering.

Conduct Must Be "Strongly Corroborative of Criminal Purpose"   The Code's "substantial step" test requires in addition that the actor's conduct must be "strongly corroborative of [his] criminal purpose."[10] This rule resembles, but is weaker than, the *res ipsa* test.[11] Under the Code, the actor's "criminal purpose" need not be shown exclusively, or unequivocally, by his or her conduct. The actor's

---

8. Model Penal Code § 5.01(1)(c).

9. Model Penal Code § 5.01(2)(a)-(g).

10. Model Penal Code § 5.01(2).

11. As the Code's commentary states:

The requirement of proving a substantial step generally will prove less of a hurdle for the prosecution than the *res ipsa loquitur* approach, which requires that the actor's conduct itself have manifested the criminal purpose. . . . Under the Model Code formulation, the two purposes to be served by the *res ipsa loquitur* test are, to a large extent, treated separately. Firmness of criminal purpose is intended to be shown by requiring a substantial step, while problems of proof are dealt with by the

conduct must corroborate, or give added assurance of, his or her intent, but that intent may be proved using other evidence. This requirement is appropriate given that the substantial-step test's relatively relaxed conduct standard increases the importance of requiring strong proof of intent. In the "Plan to Kill" hypothetical, Xinchesi's conduct may satisfy the corroboration requirement. He has reconnoitered the place contemplated for the offense, and has also made planning notes. The reconnaissance alone may not demonstrate his criminal purpose, especially given the way it was done (on his way to and from work), but it may be taken to corroborate the stronger evidence of intent that the notes provide.

Substantial-Step Test Reflects Subjectivist View of Criminality The substantial-step test reflects a shift in the justification for attempt liability, away from a focus on objective proximity to the offense and toward a focus on subjective intent to commit an offense. An actual danger of commission is not required. Indeed, the Model Penal Code imposes attempt liability even if commission of the offense is literally impossible (because, for example, the "illegal drugs" purchased are really powdered sugar). The justification for attempt liability under the Code is, instead, the actor's intention to break the law and demonstrated willingness to act on that intention, as shown by the externalization of intent in conduct. Persons who possess culpability as to a criminal harm or evil, and also act on that culpability, are both blameworthy and dangerous, and are therefore appropriate subjects of criminal sanction. Note that this justification reflects a different, *subjectivist* view of the basis and minimum requirements of criminal liability, focusing primarily on culpability rather than harm or the immediate prospect of harm.

CULPABILITY REQUIREMENTS OF ATTEMPT

Otherwise lawful conduct may become a criminal attempt by virtue of the attempter's culpable state of mind. Entering a bank itself may be lawful, but it becomes criminal if it is done with the purpose to rob the bank. Driving another person to a remote cabin itself may be lawful, but it becomes criminal if it is done with the intention forcibly to detain the person and demand a ransom. This potential for one's intention to make innocent conduct criminal highlights the central importance of culpability in assessing attempt liability and shows the need for requirements that will ensure proof of that culpability. There is some confusion, however, over just what culpability should be required for attempt liability.

Common Law Required "Specific Intent" for Attempt At Common Law, attempt was said to be a "specific intent offense,"[12] requiring a higher level of culpability than a "general intent" offense, for which the actor's intention could be assumed from his conduct. As discussed previously, criminal law has had some difficulty in determining exactly what is meant by "specific intent" and "general intent." The two concepts are consistent with the Common Law's handling of culpability, under which the standard "offense analysis" treated each offense as having a single culpability requirement, and those requirements generally were vague and malleable. But when translated into a modern "element analysis" context,

---

requirement of corroboration—although under the reasoning previously expressed, the latter will also tend to establish firmness of purpose.

Model Penal Code § 5.01 comment at 330 (1985).

12. People v. Trinkle, 369 N.E. 2d 892 (Ill. 1977).

which requires a specifically defined culpability as to each offense element, the Common Law's concepts create confusion. The "specific intent" requirement of attempt typically is taken to require some sort of *purpose* to commit the object offense. But, one may ask, purpose as to what in particular?

Does Purpose Requirement Apply to Some, or All, Elements? Does the special "purpose" requirement in attempt require simply a purpose to engage in the *conduct* constituting the substantive offense; or does it (also) require a purpose to cause any *result* required by the substantive offense; or does it require that the actor be "purposeful" as to *every element* of the offense? Under the second and, even more, the third interpretation, the rules governing attempt liability would likely elevate the culpability requirements for some elements above what the substantive offense itself requires: The attempt would require purpose as to all elements, even if the substantive offense did not. The holding in *People v. Trinkle* illustrates this view. After being refused further service, the resentful defendant fired a shot into a tavern, wounding a patron within. The jurisdiction's murder offense requires only that the actor "knows that [his] acts create a strong probability of death or great bodily harm,"[13] and the attempt statute explicitly defines attempted murder to require this same culpability.[14] Yet the court reverses the conviction, applying the common law rule that "attempt is a specific intent offense" and interpreting that rule to require not only that the actor intend to engage in the conduct constituting the substantive offense, but also that the actor intend the prohibited result and the required circumstances of the substantive offense.

Effect of Elevating Culpability to Require Purpose as to All Elements Such elevation of culpability requirements, demanding purpose as to all elements for attempt even if the substantive offense requires less, has a fairly dramatic effect. For example, the offense of statutory rape frequently requires little or no culpability as to the victim's age: Negligence or even strict liability might apply. But if the intercourse is frustrated at the last moment, would prosecution for *attempted* statutory rape[15] require not only that the actor intended to have intercourse, but that he *intended* that the victim be underage? If the attempt rules elevate all culpability elements to require purpose, the answer is yes. Similarly, where the offense has a result element—as with murder in *Trinkle*—elevation to purpose means that there is no attempt liability even if the actor *knew* (was practically certain) that his conduct would cause the result (death); attempt liability is available only if causing death was the actor's "conscious object."[16] Many people would argue that these are inappropriate results, and that the liability rules for attempt should not depart so widely from the rules governing the substantive offense.

Model Penal Code: Three Rules for Different Types of Attempt Consider how the Model Penal Code attempt provision, section 5.01, deals with the elevation issue. The section provides for attempt liability under any of three subsections. Subsection (1)(a) is designed to govern so-called impossible attempt cases, where the offense conduct is complete, and liability for the substantive offense would be imposed, except that a required *circumstance* is absent (for

---

13. 720 Ill. Comp. Stat. 5/9–1(a)(2).

14. Trinkle, 369 N.E.2d at 890.

15. See, e.g., State v. Davis, 229 A.2d 842 (N.H. 1967) (defendant convicted of attempted rape of "woman child under the age of 16 years," N.H. Rev. Stat. Ann. § 585:16).

16. Model Penal Code § 2.02(2)(a)(i).

example, the white powder purchased is not a controlled drug, as was expected). Subsection (1)(b) is intended to govern cases where the offense conduct is complete, but a required *result* does not occur (for example, a "shoot and miss" case). Subsection (1)(c) governs the cases of interrupted or incomplete *conduct* toward the substantive offense. (This last subsection, addressing "incomplete" attempts, is the one that must draw a line between attempt and "mere preparation"; the Code defines attempt as a "substantial step" toward the offense.)

Language of Code Leaves Culpability Requirements Unclear The provision might be interpreted as reflecting the common law view that attempt is a specific intent offense, and imposing a similar elevation of culpability requirements. It imposes liability, in section 5.01(1)(a) and (1)(c), respectively, only if the actor "*purposely* engages in conduct which would constitute the crime" or "*purposely* does or omits to do anything which [is] a substantial step" toward the crime. Section 5.01(1)(b) requires only that the actor act "with the purpose of causing *or with the belief*" that his conduct will cause the prohibited result, thus seeming to require a lower culpability than the other subsections, requiring only *knowing* rather than *purposeful* conduct. Yet the structure of the provision leaves the culpability requirements somewhat ambiguous. The introductory language of section 5.01(1), which precedes and applies to all of the three subsections, requires the actor to be "acting with the kind of culpability otherwise required for commission of the crime." That phrase alone would suggest that attempt liability requires *no* elevation of the normal culpability requirements of the substantive offense, but the requirements in the specific subsections might suggest that *all* elements are elevated.

Analogy to Ambiguity of Code's Complicity Provision The issue here—what is meant by the *purposeful* and *knowing* requirements that appear in the subsections of section 5.01(1)—is similar to one that arises in the context of complicity, discussed previously, where Model Penal Code section 2.06(3)(a) requires that an accomplice have "the purpose of promoting or facilitating the commission of the offense." In that context, it is unclear whether the "purpose" requirement demands (1) purpose as to *assisting the perpetrator's conduct* constituting the offense, or (also) (2) purpose as to *all elements of the offense* (including the circumstances and results of the perpetrator's offense conduct). The attempt provision presents this same ambiguity between a narrow interpretation (conduct only) and a broad interpretation (all elements) of "purposeful conduct." And as with complicity, the narrow interpretation appears to be the more sound position.

Reading "Purpose" Language to Cover Conduct, but Not Circumstances or Results? The narrow interpretation of the "purpose" requirement would require a showing that it was the actor's purpose to engage in all of the *conduct* required to constitute the substantive offense. That is, it must be proven beyond a reasonable doubt that she had made it her conscious object, her intention, to perform the conduct constituting the offense (including any conduct she had not yet performed). However, it need not be shown that the actor was purposeful as to every *circumstance* and *result* of the substantive offense. As the introductory language of § 5.01(1) indicates, the substantive offense's culpability requirements as to these elements will suffice. Under this interpretation, attempted murder would not require purpose as to causing death; rather, knowledge (i.e., being "practically certain"[17]) that one's conduct would cause death would suffice (assuming it would also suffice for the completed offense of murder).

No Elevation as to Circumstances Elements   As noted, under the narrow interpretation of the attempt subsections' "purpose" language, the culpability required as to a circumstance is the same as that required for the substantive offense. For example, the actor who is interrupted before he can complete a statutory rape would be liable for attempted statutory rape although he did not desire, or know, that his partner was underage. To take another example, in *State v. Galan*,[18] the defendant was charged with attempted trafficking in stolen property. The substantive offense required only recklessness as to the property being stolen, but the defendant claimed that the indictment was defective because "an attempt . . . requires a specific intent which is incompatible with a reckless state of mind."[19] The governing attempt statute was similar to the Model Penal Code provision (except for the substitution of the term *intentionally* for *purposely*, a common lexical alteration). The court concluded:

> A common sense reading of the provision leads to the conclusion that the words *intentionally engages in conduct* refers [sic], in this case, to the actions that make up trafficking like buying property . . . and that the words *acting with the kind of culpability otherwise required for the commission of an offense* requires [sic] only that the acts be accompanied by a reckless state of mind as to the circumstances attending the status of the property. A contrary conclusion would mean that the words *acting with the kind of culpability otherwise required for the commission of an offense* are superfluous.[20]

The court goes on to quote the Model Penal Code commentary, which confirms that, in the drafters' view, the actor's "purpose" need not encompass all the circumstance elements of the substantive offense. As to these circumstances, it is sufficient that the actor has the culpability required by the substantive offense.[21] This is the accepted view under modern statutes.

State v. Maestas
Supreme Court of Utah 652 P.2d 903
(Utah 1982)

HALL, Chief Justice:

The state appeals from an order by the trial court dismissing a charge of attempted murder against defendant in spite of a jury verdict finding him guilty. The state seeks reinstatement of the jury verdict.

---

17. Model Penal Code § 2.02(2)(b)(ii).

18. 658 P.2d 243 (Ariz. App. 1982).

19. *Galan*, at 244.

20. *Galan*, at 244–245 (emphasis in original). Additional language from the opinion, deleted from the passage quoted, suggests that "intentionally engages in conduct" might also require proof that the actor intended to resell the property. This might well be required by the substantive offense of trafficking, but it is hard to see how such a requirement be drawn from the "engages in conduct" language.

21. "[W]ith respect to the circumstances under which a crime must be committed, the culpability otherwise required for commission of the crime is also applicable to the attempt." Model Penal Code § 5.01 explanatory note at 297 (1985).

On February 20, 1980, defendant allegedly robbed a bank and attempted to escape in a black van. As defendant drove south on State Street at about 650 South, he passed Sergeant Cecil Throckmorton of the Salt Lake City Police Department, who had stationed his car on the island in the center of the street and was standing beside the car awaiting defendant's approach. As defendant's van passed him, Sergeant Throckmorton fired a shot with his shotgun into the front of the van in an unsuccessful attempt to disable it. A few seconds later, as he drove away from Sergeant Throckmorton, defendant allegedly leaned out of the van window holding a 38-caliber revolver and fired it at the officer. Defendant drove several blocks further before crashing into a parked car, at which time he was apprehended by other police officers.

Defendant was charged with attempted first degree murder. At the conclusion of his trial, he filed a motion to dismiss, which the court denied. The jury then deliberated, returning a verdict of guilty. On the date set for defendant's sentencing, he renewed his motion to dismiss. The court granted defendant's motion on the ground that "specific intent to kill could not properly be inferred from the evidence."

U.C.A., 1953, 76–5-202(1) describes the elements of first degree murder:

> Criminal homicide constitutes murder in the first degree if the actor *intentionally or knowingly* causes the death of another under any of the following circumstances: . . .
>
> (d) The homicide was committed while the actor was engaged in the commission of, or an attempt to commit, or flight after committing or attempting to commit, aggravated robbery, robbery, rape, forcible arson, aggravated burglary, burglary, aggravated kidnapping or kidnapping.
>
> (e) The homicide was committed for the purpose of avoiding or preventing an arrest by a peace officer acting under color of legal authority or for the purpose of effecting an escape from lawful custody. [Emphasis added.]

Thus, in order to find defendant guilty of attempted first degree murder, the jury was required to determine beyond a reasonable doubt that he "intentionally or knowingly" attempted to kill Sergeant Throckmorton under one of the circumstances listed above.

Defendant founds his argument for dismissal on the theory that the crime of attempted murder requires a stronger showing of intent than does the crime of murder itself. This theory derives from the common law rule that intent is a necessary element of every "attempt" crime even where the corresponding completed crime does not require intent as an element. As an example, defendant cites cases which discuss the common law rule that there is no crime of "attempted felony murder" because of the fact that felony murder requires no specific intent to kill, while an "attempt" crime must always consist of an intent to commit the corresponding completed crime accompanied by a substantial step toward realization of that crime. Defendant then attempts to carry this rule one step further by asserting that the crime of attempted first degree murder with which he is charged requires a "specific intent" beyond that which would have been required in order to prove first degree murder itself if an actual death had occurred. Defendant does not argue that the evidence concerning intent would have failed to support a first degree murder conviction in the event of actual death, but rather that such evidence fell short of establishing the stronger "specific intent" allegedly required for the crime of attempted first degree murder.

Defendant's argument ignores the fact that common law definitions of criminal behavior have no application in this jurisdiction. The criminal code of this state explicitly abolishes all common law crimes and our legislature has expressed its intention that its statutes be construed liberally even when they conflict with the common law. U.C.A., 1953, 76–4-101(1) defines the crime of "attempt" as follows:

> For purposes of this part a person is guilty of an attempt to commit a crime if, acting *with the kind of culpability otherwise required for the commission of the offense,* he engages in conduct constituting a substantial step toward commission of the offense. [Emphasis added.]

The above statute makes it clear that regardless of any requirements which the common law may impose concerning "attempt" crimes, Utah law requires only "the kind of culpability otherwise required for the commission of the [completed] offense." Thus, there can be no difference between the intent required as an element of the crime of attempted first degree murder and that required for first degree murder itself. . . .

. . . Because substantial evidence supported the jury's guilty verdict, the trial court erred in interfering with the jury's exercise of its fact-finding role. We order that the verdict be reinstated.

Reversed.

▲ PROBLEMS

Second Thoughts on a Holiday Breakout (#48)

George McCloskey is serving a one-to-three-year prison term for larceny. He is unhappy about being away from his family and works hard while in prison to earn points for good behavior. On Christmas Eve during his first year, McCloskey requests a Christmas furlough, hoping to celebrate with his family. His request is denied, and December 25th goes unmarked. McCloskey becomes extraordinarily upset, so much so that on the day after Christmas he plans to escape from prison. During his overnight shift in the boiler room, McCloskey sets out for the recreation area of the prison with a bag packed full of civilian clothes. He scales the wall to the prison yard, cutting the barbed wire. However, once inside the prison yard, he has second thoughts. He is overcome by the shame he would cause his family by breaking out of prison and is afraid of the further consequences. With just the final prison wall between him and at least temporary freedom, McCloskey turns around and returns to work.

Unbeknownst to him, during his half-executed escape he has already set off an alarm, which sounds only in the prison office. When McCloskey cut the barbed wire fence, the guard on duty in the office immediately radioed two other guards in the area in an effort to catch McCloskey in the act. However, by the time they arrive on the scene, McCloskey is already back at work in the boiler room. After his shift is over, McCloskey voluntarily approaches the guard supervisor and confesses to his planned escape and his subsequent decision not to follow through.

What liability for McCloskey, if any, under the Model Penal Code? Prepare a list of all criminal code subsections in the order in which you rely on them in your analysis.

No Risk, No Foul? (#49)

Elmo Scatena owns and operates a service station in Pennsylvania near the Susquehanna River. Scatena and his sons agree to allow chemicals to be discharged into a borehole at the back of their property. These chemicals are generally not properly treated, and the dumping is done without the necessary legal permits. The Scatenas are aware that the chemicals may leak from the borehole and create a potentially catastrophic situation, either by combining with underground gases and exploding or by contaminating the public water supply. However, they hope their backdoor operation will go unnoticed.

Assume inspectors catch the Scatenas just as they are about to dump the chemicals in the borehole. Because no dumping has yet occurred and there is not yet an actual risk of catastrophe, the defendants cannot be convicted of a violation of Model Penal Code §220.2(2) (risking catastrophe). Can the Scatenas be convicted of attempted risking catastrophe under the Model Penal Code?

Would the answer be the same if the Model Penal Code followed the position of the *Maestas* decision, above?

Killing with AIDS (#50)

Dwight Smallwood has been diagnosed as HIV-positive. He is able to resume his normal life, but his health care provider makes it clear to him that he must start practicing "safe sex," including always using a condom, or else he poses a serious risk of infecting another person. While HIV is not always transmitted in cases of unprotected sex with an uninfected partner, studies show the risk of seroconversion to be substantial, a serious concern given the gravity of contracting the virus. HIV is known to attack the human immune system and despite available treatments that enable HIV-positive individuals to live longer, healthier lives than previously possible, there is no cure, and the disease is eventually fatal. Smallwood, who claims only to have one sexual partner, promises to always use a condom so as not to transmit HIV.

Two years later, Smallwood and an accomplice rob a woman at gunpoint. They then force her into a grove of trees where they each take turns raping her while the other holds a gun to her head. Smallwood does not wear a condom during the rape. Two days later, Smallwood and his accomplice strike again, robbing another woman and again raping her. As in the first incident, Smallwood does not wear a condom. After yet another almost identical rape, Smallwood is finally apprehended.

Is Smallwood liable for any form of attempted homicide under the Model Penal Code?

Would the liability be the same if the Model Penal Code followed the *Maestas* decision, excerpted above?

✸ DISCUSSION ISSUE

What Conduct Toward an Offense Should Be Sufficient to Constitute a Criminal Attempt?

Materials presenting each side of this Discussion Issue appear in the Advanced Materials for Section 10 in Appendix A.

Impossibility

It is sometimes the case that the situation itself makes it impossible for a person to complete the offense contemplated. Should this impossibility of commission affect the person's liability for attempt? If so, how and why? If the underlying theory of attempt liability is coming close to causing a harm, such impossibility may undercut the offense's rationale. If the underlying theory is a manifested intention to break the law, then such impossibility may not be relevant. In other words, the impossibility cases force the underlying theory of attempt out into the open.

◆ THE CASE OF JOHN HENRY IVY (#51)

It is July 1988 in the Lee County seat of Tupelo, Mississippi, a town of 28,000 that prides itself on being the birthplace of Elvis. John Henry Ivy is a 25-year-old from Oxford, Mississippi, a small town about 60 miles west of Tupelo. He now stands before Judge Thomas Gardner III awaiting sentencing for his latest armed robbery. This time he held up a gas station and made off with about $500. A hearty man, John Henry loves cracking jokes and generally does not take life too seriously. He is a little worried about his sentencing, however, because

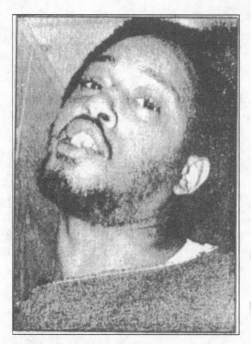

Figure 44 Leroy Ivy, 1989
(Northeast Mississippi Daily Journal)

he has previous convictions for selling cocaine and for armed robbery, meaning he might get the maximum penalty. Doing him no favors, Judge Gardner sentences him to 40 years in the state penitentiary.

A few months later, John Henry calls his half-brother, Leroy Ivy, from state prison. Leroy Ivy, 33, is more quiet and serious than his half-brother and, unlike him, has not had legal troubles except for a few minor scrapes in his youth. Like his ten other siblings, he lives in Oxford. John Henry is calling Leroy today to set up a three-way conference call between themselves and Emma Gates, Judge Gardner's housekeeper. His purpose for the call is to arrange a meeting between Leroy and Ms. Gates, so John Henry can buy some personal items that belong to Judge Gardner, such as an old picture and a hairbrush with some of the judge's hair still in the bristles. Although slightly puzzled, Leroy does what his brother asks.

During the conference call, the brothers explain to Ms. Gates the items they want. They offer several hundred dollars for them. Gates refuses at first, but they continue to press her.

The items requested are commonly used in voodoo rituals. John Henry, who sincerely believes that voodoo has the power to kill the person who is targeted, plans to send the items to a shaman contact in New Orleans, which is the center of the nation's voodoo activity. The items will then be sent to a voodoo priestess in Jamaica, who will use them to put a death hex on Judge Gardner.

John Henry is familiar with voodoo practices from people in town and from other inmates. Although belief in voodoo is not particularly common in Mississippi, there is a community of those who believe in the West African religion, which combines aspects of Catholicism with worship of some African gods. Local law enforcement officials in Oxford say they have not heard of anyone practicing voodoo there, although a few locals remember friends who bought voodoo gambling charms or who were hexed by an ex-wife. A University of Mississippi anthropologist estimates that there are about forty voodoo priests in Mississippi, and believes its practice is gathering support. For example, a local department store expects to sell about twenty-one tons of voodoo supplies, including candles, roots, and powder.

After hearing the request for a photo and hair, Ms. Gates immediately recognizes their possible use in a voodoo ritual. Fearful of what they might be planning, she tells the judge about the call. Not a believer in voodoo, Judge Gardner dismisses the death hex as a toothless threat. However, the housekeeper is frightened by the episode, and details of the plot are soon relayed to the authorities.

A team from the Mississippi Highway Patrol, headed by 22-year-old Jerry Butler (he calls himself "Jailhouse Jerry"), is formed to investigate and set up a sting operation to catch the brothers. Ms. Gates arranges to meet with Leroy at the J.C. Penney store on Main St. in Tupelo on October 14. The sheriff's office tapes a phone call between her and the Ivy brothers. The men have bargained a price of $500 for the items. The police intend to use an officer in disguise to meet Leroy instead of Ms. Gates.

On October 14, Leroy drives to Tupelo to complete the purchase. At the appointed time, he exchanges a suitcase containing the money for a photograph and a lock of hair (which was taken from a detective on the case). After photographing the transaction, undercover officers from the Highway Patrol arrest Leroy. They later learn that the suitcase contained only $100; Leroy makes no attempt to explain why he is $400 short.

Both men are charged with planning "feloniously and with malice aforethought to kill and murder Judge Gardner."

1. Relying only on your own intuitions of justice, what liability and punishment, if any, does John Henry Ivy deserve?

Figure 44 **Judge Gardner**
(Lee County Court)

N	0	1	2	3	4	5	6	7	8	9	10	11
☐	☐	☐	☐	☐	☐	☐	☐	☐	☐	☐	☐	☐
no liability	liability but no punishment	1 day	2 wks	2 mo	6 mo	1 yr	3 yrs	7 yrs	15 yrs	30 yrs	life imprison- ment	death

2. What "justice" arguments could defense counsel make on the defendant's behalf? *Attempt cannot be Applied as the crime charged even if carried out would not have produced a crime in any scenario*

3. What "justice" arguments could the prosecution make against the defendant? *The intent was to kill. The actions taken even if impossible were a substantial step toward a crime*

4. What liability, if any, for John Henry Ivy under the then-existing statutes? Prepare a list of all criminal code or case subsections in the order in which you rely upon them in your analysis.

5. What liability, if any, under the Model Penal Code? Prepare a list of all criminal code subsections in the order in which you rely upon them in your analysis.

▪ THE LAW

Mississippi Code Annotated
(1988)

Section 97-3-19. Homicide; Murder Defined; Capital Murder

(1) The killing of a human being without the authority of law by any means or in any manner shall be murder in the following cases:

(a) When done with deliberate design to effect the death of the person killed, or of any human being;

(b) When done in the commission of an act eminently dangerous to others and evincing a depraved heart, regardless of human life, although without any premeditated design to effect the death of any particular individual;

(c) When done without any design to effect death by any person engaged in the commission of any felony other than rape, kidnapping, burglary, arson, robbery, sexual battery, unnatural intercourse with any child under the age of twelve (12), or nonconsensual unnatural intercourse with mankind, or felonious abuse and/or battery of a child in violation of subsection (2) of Section 97-5-39, or in any attempt to commit such felonies.

(2) The killing of a human being without the authority of law by any means or in any manner shall be capital murder in the following cases:

(a) Murder which is perpetrated by killing a peace officer or fireman while such officer or fireman is acting in his official capacity or by reason of an act performed in his official capacity, and with knowledge that the victim was a peace officer or fireman. For purposes of this paragraph, the term "peace officer" means sheriffs of counties and their deputies, constables, marshals, and policemen of cities and towns, game wardens, parole officers, a judge, prosecuting attorney or any other court official, agents of the Alcoholic Beverage Control Division of the State Tax Commission, agents of the Bureau of Narcotics, personnel of the Mississippi Highway Patrol, and the superintendent and his deputies, guards, officers and other employees of the Mississippi State Penitentiary;

(b) Murder which is perpetrated by a person who is under sentence of life imprisonment;

(c) Murder which is perpetrated by use or detonation of a bomb or explosive device;

(d) Murder which is perpetrated by any person who has been offered or has received anything of value for committing the murder, and all parties to such a murder, are guilty as principals;

(e) When done with or without any design to effect death, by any person engaged in the commission of the crime of rape, burglary, kidnapping, arson, robbery, sexual battery, unnatural intercourse with any child under the age of twelve (12), or nonconsensual unnatural intercourse with mankind, or in any attempt to commit such felonies;

(f) When done with or without any design to effect death, by any person engaged in the commission of the crime of felonious abuse and/or battery of a child in violation of subsection (2) of Section 97-5-39, or in any attempt to commit such felony;

(g) Murder which is perpetrated by the killing of any elected official of a county, municipal, state or federal government with knowledge that the victim was such public official.

Section 1-3-4. Capital Case, Capital Offense, Capital Crime, and Capital Murder

The terms "capital case," "capital cases," "capital offense," "capital offenses," and "capital crime" when used in any statute shall denote criminal cases, offenses and crimes punishable by death or imprisonment for life in the state penitentiary. The term "capital murder" when used in any statute shall denote criminal cases, offenses and crimes punishable by death, or imprisonment for life in the state penitentiary.

Section 97-1-7. Attempt to Commit Offense; Punishment

Every person who shall design and endeavor to commit an offense, and shall do any overt act toward the commission thereof, but shall fail therein, or shall be prevented from committing the same, on conviction thereof, shall, where no provision is made by law for the punishment of such offense, be punished as follows: If the offense attempted to be committed be capital, such offense shall be punished by imprisonment in the penitentiary not exceeding ten years; if the offense attempted be punishable by imprisonment in the penitentiary, or by fine and imprisonment in the county jail, then the attempt to commit such offense shall be punished for a period or for an amount not greater than is prescribed for the actual commission of the offense so attempted.

Section 97-1-9. Attempt to Commit Offense;
No Conviction if Offense Completed

A person shall not be convicted of an assault with intent to commit a crime, or of any other attempt to commit an offense, when it shall appear that the crime intended or the offense attempted was perpetrated by such person at the time of such assault or in pursuance of such attempt.

Section 97-1-1. Conspiracy

If two (2) or more persons conspire either:
    (a) To commit a crime; or
    (b) Falsely and maliciously to indict another for a crime, or to procure to be complained of or arrested for a crime; or
    (c) Falsely to institute or maintain an action or suit of any kind; or
    (d) To cheat and defraud another out of property by any means which are in themselves criminal, or which, if executed, would amount to a cheat, or to obtain money or any other property or thing by false pretense; or
    (e) To prevent another from exercising a lawful trade or calling, or doing any other lawful act, by force, threats, intimidation, or by interfering or threatening to interfere with tools, implements, or property belonging to or used by another, or with the use of employment thereof; or
    (f) To commit any act injurious to the public health, to public morals, trade or commerce, or for the perversion or obstruction of justice, or of the due administration of the laws; or
    (g) To overthrow or violate the laws of this state through force, violence, threats, intimidation, or otherwise; or
    (h) To accomplish any unlawful purpose, or a lawful purpose by any unlawful means;

such persons, and each of them, shall be guilty of a felony and upon conviction may be punished by a fine of not more than five thousand dollars ($5,000.00) or by imprisonment for not more than five (5) years, or by both.

Provided, that where the crime conspired to be committed is capital murder . . . , the offense shall be punishable by a fine of not more than five hundred thousand dollars ($ 500,000.00) or by imprisonment for not more than twenty (20) years, or by both.

Provided, that where the crime conspired to be committed is a misdemeanor, then upon conviction said crime shall be punished as a misdemeanor as provided by law.

William Stokes v. State of Mississippi
92 Miss. 415, 46 So. 627, 1908 Miss. LEXIS 245 (1908)

Will Stokes and Cora Lane, who were having an affair, hired Shorty Robertson to kill Lane's husband, Wallace Lane, for the proceeds of life insurance policies. They promised Robertson $1,000 and agreed that he would lay in wait for the husband on a particular night at a particular place to surprise the husband as he returned from a lodge meeting. But Robertson reported his conversations to the police, who planned to hide themselves at the appointed place and time. The agreed-upon night was rainy. Robertson went to Lane's house, where he found Stokes, and together they went to the planned location. Stokes produced a loaded gun and showed Robertson where he should wait. As Stokes was handing the gun to Robertson, the police intervened and arrested him. No money ever changed hands. In fact, the husband did not plan on taking his usual route home that night. Stokes was convicted of attempt to murder Wallace Lane. He appealed on the basis that the facts did not constitute an attempt.

. . . All the authorities hold, that, in order to constitute an attempt, the act attempted must be a possibility; and counsel for appellant argue from this that the appellant could not have committed this crime at the time he was arrested, because Lane was not even there, and therefore, they say, no conviction could be had. It was no fault of Stokes that the crime was not committed. He had the gun, and the testimony warrants the conclusion that it had been taken for the purpose of killing Lane. It only became impossible by reason of the extraneous circumstance that Lane did not go that way, and, further, that defendant was arrested and prevented from committing the murder. [The impossibility defense] has application only to a case where it is inherently impossible to commit the crime. It has no application to a case where it becomes impossible for the crime to be committed, either by outside interference or because of miscalculation as to a supposed opportunity to commit the crime which fails to materialize; in short, it has no application to the case when the impossibility grows out of extraneous facts not within the control of the party. . . .

. . . [T]he defendant's conviction of attempt to kill and murder Wallace Lane is affirmed.

Model Penal Code
(Official Draft 1962)

Section 5.01. Criminal Attempt

(1) Definition of Attempt. A person is guilty of an attempt to commit a crime if, acting with the kind of culpability otherwise required for commission of the crime, he:

(a) purposely engages in conduct which would constitute the crime if the attendant circumstances were as he believes them to be; or

(b) when causing a particular result is an element of the crime, does or omits to do anything with the purpose of causing or with the belief that it will cause such result without further conduct on his part; or

(c) purposely does or omits to do anything which, under the circumstances as he believes them to be, is an act or omission constituting a substantial step in a course of conduct planned to culminate in his commission of the crime. . . .

Section 5.05. . . . ; Mitigation in Cases of Lesser Danger; . . .

(1) . . .

(2) Mitigation. If the particular conduct charged to constitute a criminal attempt, solicitation or conspiracy is so inherently unlikely to result or culminate in the commission of a crime that neither such conduct nor the actor presents a public danger warranting the grading of such offense under this Section, the Court shall exercise its power under Section 6.12 to enter judgment and impose sentence for a crime of lower grade or degree or, in extreme cases, may dismiss the prosecution. . . .

● OVERVIEW OF IMPOSSIBILITY

Hypothetical: The Smuggler's Deceit (#52)

Watson and So are surprised and pleased to find each other on the same flight from Panama to London. They are classmates from reform school and spend the flight trading years' worth of stories, most of which concern their criminal exploits during and since school. After an hour of catching up, the conversation turns to their current activities.

To neither one's surprise, each is on the flight to smuggle something into England. It is 1974, and Watson is smuggling in sugar concentrate, a profitable business because of England's current sugar shortage. So compliments Watson on his plan and explains, with some pride, that his trip is part of a just-developing drug-smuggling business operating with the unofficial help of certain Panamanian officials.

Watson is deflated by the conversation. As was always the case in school, So has the better scheme and stands to make over 20 times as much for smuggling in a shipment of the same size. But Watson has become somewhat craftier since his school days and, when So gets up to go to the bathroom, Watson switches their cases, which are similar in appearance. So does not notice until they are in line at customs. Instead of being angry with Watson, however, he just laughs.

Apparently having second thoughts about drug-smuggling, which he knows carries high penalties, Watson moves forward in the customs line without bringing his bag with him. So, who is further back in the same line, speaks up helpfully, "Don't forget your bag, sir." Each man is stopped by the customs officers and taken with his bag for questioning. Each is at first cagey, but when things look bad, each turns the other in to ingratiate himself to the authorities; then, under further questioning, each also confesses his own wrongdoing. Their accounts are somewhat different, however, for So was really on the plane to smuggle sugar also, and had only made up the story about the drugs to impress Watson. Additionally, it turns out that smuggling sugar is not in fact a crime (although it was widely thought to be at the time).[1]

What liability for Watson and for So, if any, under the Model Penal Code? Would either's liability change if the Model Penal Code adopted the common law impossibility doctrines?

Notes

Theoretical Importance of Impossibility Debate
Classic Distinction between Legal and Factual Impossibility
Difficulty in Applying Distinction
    Modern Element Analysis May Help Define Distinction
    Categorization Depends on Facts and Offense Structure
    Distinction Can Be Defined, but Seems Hard to Justify
MPC Rejects Factual-Legal Distinction and Denies Impossibility Defense
Imaginary Offenses: Crime Exists Only in Actor's Mind
    Some Support for Punishing, but Legality Principle Prohibits
    Attempt Statute Probably Meant to Exclude Imaginary Offenses
Inherently Unlikely Attempt

Conduct toward a criminal offense may fail to result in that offense for any number of reasons. The planned offense may be frustrated by the intervention of authorities, by the resistance of the intended victim or others, by facts or circumstances making it impossible to commit the crime as planned, or by the voluntary desistance of those who had undertaken the offense. Where intervention or resistance causes the offense to fail, the actor will still be held liable, though for an inchoate offense rather than the object offense. Where impossibility or desistance prevent the offense's occurrence, on the other hand, the actor may obtain a complete defense in some jurisdictions, so that not even inchoate liability will arise. This section examines the impossibility defense; much of the discussion will focus on it in the context of attempt, where the issues are clearest and most common, but the principles apply equally to conspiracy and solicitation.

Theoretical Importance of Impossibility Debate Impossibility is of special theoretical interest because to determine whether, or how, impossibility should affect liability, it is necessary to clarify precisely why attempts are punished. If the rationale for attempt liability is the danger of completion—that is, the risk that the harm or evil of the offense will come to pass—then the impossibility of completing the offense would seem to undercut the rationale, making a defense appropriate for impossible attempts. If, on the other hand, the rationale

---

1. "Travellers trying to beat Britain's sugar shortage are smuggling more and more of it into [that] country. They do not know that importing sugar is legal. A woman filled a shoebox with sugar and wrapped it like a gift, with fancy ribbons and bright paper. Another woman had sugar in a can marked 'face powder.'" N.Y. Herald Tribune, Oct. 22, 1974, reprinted in Glanville Williams, Textbook of Criminal Law 398 (1978).

for attempt liability relates to the actor's culpability and his demonstrated willingness to carry out a criminal intention, then the impossibility of the offense's completion (assuming the actor is unaware of the impossibility) does not undercut the rationale for liability, and no defense is warranted.

Classic Distinction between Legal and Factual Impossibility Impossibility at Common Law was divided into two categories: Legal and factual. *Legal impossibility,* which gave rise to a complete defense to attempt liability at common law, involved cases where, even if the defendant were to do everything she wanted to do, her conduct still would not constitute a crime. A person who buys a white powder believing it to be cocaine cannot be convicted of a drug offense if the powder turns out to be talc. At common law, she cannot be convicted of attempt either: The conduct she sought to perform (and did perform), buying the white powder, is not a crime. *Factual impossibility,* in contrast, arose where the actor's intended conduct was a crime but the actor could not complete the intended conduct or could not bring about the contemplated result. For example, an actor who shoots into an empty bed or tries to pick an empty pocket is trying to engage in criminal conduct, but is unable to do so. Factual impossibility was not a defense at common law. In the "Smugglers' Deceit" hypothetical, both Watson's conduct and So's conduct, even if completed as planned, would not have been criminal. Both have only sugar, and bringing sugar into England is not a crime. Hence, both attempts would seem to be instances of legal impossibility, for which the common law (and some states currently) would give a complete defense.

Difficulty in Applying Distinction The distinction between legal and factual impossibility has been criticized as being difficult to apply and as generating results that are difficult to rationalize. Consider, for example, the actor who lights the fuse on what he mistakenly believes are dynamite sticks. The completed conduct—lighting a fuse leading to harmless wooden sticks—is not a substantive offense, thus one might conclude that the conduct constitutes a legally impossible attempt (for which there is a defense). Yet, in another sense, the case seems to be one of factual impossibility. The actor is seeking to create an explosion, which would be criminal—so how is lighting an ineffective fuse different from picking an empty pocket? Similarly, how is shooting a deer while believing hunting is out of season (said to be legal impossibility) different from shooting at a bed believing that it contains the intended victim (said to be factual impossibility)?

Modern Element Analysis May Help Define Distinction In fact, there may be a way to make some sense of this distinction. Remember that the absence of some objective element is what makes the conduct an attempt, rather than a completed offense. It is not surprising that, before the more sophisticated analysis of individual offense elements came into being with the drafting of modern codes, the legal-factual impossibility distinction seemed somewhat unpredictable, and its basis was hard to articulate. Using modern element analysis, however, the categorization of most impossibility cases can be predicted by the nature of the missing objective element: whether it is a conduct, circumstance, or result element. Where the missing offense element is a conduct or result element, the case is more likely to be characterized as one of factual impossibility. Where the pocket is empty, the would-be thief cannot "take" (conduct) property, as required by theft. The actor cannot cause death (result) where the victim is not in the bed or the gun is not loaded. Where the missing offense element is a circumstance, the case is more likely to be characterized as legal impossibility. Cases involving absence of a circumstance arise when the white powder is not a controlled substance, the deer is not shot out of season, and the intended recipient of the bribe is not a public servant or juror—all of which were treated as involving legal impossibility.

Categorization Depends on Facts and Offense Structure   This test for distinguishing factual and legal impossibility requires careful reference to the elements of the offense charged. In many instances, failed attempts cannot be judged factually or legally impossible in the abstract, but must be judged according to the particular conduct and, importantly, according to the definition of the particular offense charged. Under the element-analysis approach, if an offense prohibited "killing a deer out of season," then killing a deer during the hunting season, but thinking it was out of season, would be a legally impossible attempt (missing circumstance of "out of season"); and killing a different animal out of (deer) season, thinking it was a deer, would also be a legally impossible attempt (missing circumstance of "deer"); but shooting a stuffed deer out of (deer) season, thinking it was a live deer, would be a factually impossible attempt (missing result of "killing," i.e., causing death). On the other hand, if the offense were defined as "shooting a live deer" rather than "killing a deer," the last case would involve a legally impossible attempt (missing circumstance of "[a]live," but conduct of "shooting" satisfied, and no result element required). Under this analysis, in the "Smugglers' Deceit" hypothetical, because Watson believes that he is smuggling drugs when in fact he is bringing in sugar, he cannot be held liable for the substantive offense of smuggling drugs because of the missing circumstance element, drugs. His attempt is one of legal impossibility, so he may have a defense to attempt liability also, depending on the rule in the jurisdiction.

Distinction Can Be Defined, but Seems Hard to Justify   While the legal-factual impossibility distinction feasibly *can* be applied, the more important issue is whether the distinction *should* be applied. Why impose attempt liability where an actor's attempt fails because he or she cannot perform the required conduct or cause the required result, yet impose no liability at all where the actor engages in the required conduct, yet the attempt fails because, unknown to him, a required circumstance does not exist? In at least some respects, the common law position seems counterintuitive, or even to reverse the proper distribution of liability. Where the actor has completed his or her conduct (and has culpability as to the circumstances, though they are not actually present), we are sure of the actor's willingness to carry the criminal intention to completion. Where the actor cannot complete the required conduct or cause the required result, we may not be quite as sure that he or she would have completed the conduct or caused the result if it had been possible. In fact, modern renunciation rules follow those intuitions to generate the reversed distribution from the (element-analysis gloss on the) common law impossibility rules: Granting a defense where the conduct is incomplete, but imposing liability where the conduct is (thought to be) complete yet the offense fails for lack of a required circumstance.[2]

---

2. For example, Model Penal Code § 5.01(4) denies a renunciation defense for an attempt under § 5.01(1)(a), which imposes liability for an actor who has "engaged in conduct which would constitute the crime if the attendant circumstances were as he believes them to be[.]" One might argue that where the actor engages in all of the conduct required, but where the result does not occur, as in the case under § 5.01(1)(b), he or she also should be excluded from the renunciation defense. The Code permits the

MPC Rejects Factual-Legal Distinction and Denies Impossibility Defense Sharing the position that the common law distinction is hard to justify, the Model Penal Code abandons that distinction and denies a defense for impossibility, whether legal or factual. Section 5.01(1) holds an actor liable for attempt if he:

> (a) . . . engages in conduct which would constitute the crime *if the attendant circumstances were as he believes them to be*; or
>
> (b) . . . does or omits to do anything . . . *with the belief* that it will cause [a criminal result]; or
>
> (c) . . . does or omits to do anything which, *under the circumstances as he believes them to be*, is an act or omission constituting a substantial step [toward the offense].

The statute does not mention the terms *factual impossibility* or *legal impossibility* because, under the Code's approach, the distinction is not relevant. The actor will be held liable for an attempt to commit the offense he believed he was committing, without regard to whether or why commission of the offense is impossible. Under this approach, in the "Smugglers' Deceit" hypothetical, Watson will be liable for attempted drug-smuggling (at least if his conduct of switching the bags and moving forward in line amounts to a "substantial step"). He believes So's bag contains drugs and he is seeking to bring those drugs into the country; thus, under the circumstances as he believes them to be, he has attempted the offense.

Imaginary Offenses: Crime Exists Only in Actor's Mind Even modern codes, like the Model Penal Code, that reject the traditional defense for legal impossibility may provide a defense (or mitigation) for two particular forms of "impossibility": *Imaginary offenses* and *inherently unlikely attempts*. *Imaginary offenses* arise when no applicable offense prohibits what the actor does, or intends—in other words, the actor makes no mistake about the conduct or situation, but makes a mistake about the *law* governing that conduct, thinking it is a crime when it is not. The foreign tourist who takes a picture of an American military base may honestly believe that he is committing an offense because such an act is illegal in his native country. However, if there is no such crime in this country, then his offense is an imaginary one.

Some Support for Punishing, but Legality Principle Prohibits Under one interpretation of Model Penal Code section 5.01(1)(a), the military-base photographer might still seem to satisfy the requirements for attempt: "[I]f the attendant circumstances were as he believes them to be" (if taking pictures of a military installation were a crime), he would then have "engage[d] in conduct which would constitute the crime." One might also argue that such liability is appropriate, as the photographer has shown his intention to violate the law and his willingness to carry out that intention. Yet such liability is generally disallowed,[3] primarily because of the demands of the legality principle. That principle, and the legal doctrines implementing it, require a prior, written, specific statement

---

defense for this person, however, because of its overriding commitment to crime control. It wishes to provide an incentive to stop more than it wishes to do justice.

3. See, e.g., Commonwealth v. Henley, 474 A.2d 1115 (Pa. 1984) ("[A]n intent to commit an act which is not characterized as a crime by the laws of the subject jurisdiction can not be the basis of a criminal charge and conviction, even though the actor believes or misapprehends the intended act to be proscribed by the criminal laws," but "in all other cases, the actor should be held responsible for his conduct").

of a prohibition before its violation can be punished. In the case of an imaginary offense, no such prohibition exists.

Attempt Statute Probably Meant to Exclude Imaginary Offenses   Imaginary offenses may also fall outside the Model Penal Code's impossibility language—"if the attendant circumstances were as he believes them to be"—if that language is read to refer to "the attendant circumstances" that *the offense definition makes relevant*, but not to the "circumstance" of the offense's existence. In other words, liability arises where the circumstances the actor believes to exist are those that the relevant offense requires as elements. But the law's own existence is not a circumstance element: Only the circumstances described within the offense definition are relevant to determining liability, and general rules also make clear that culpability as to the criminality of one's offense typically is not required for liability.[4] Under this view, in the "Smugglers' Deceit" hypothetical, So cannot be held liable for "attempted sugar smuggling" merely because he thinks that smuggling sugar is a crime; no such offense exists, so it can neither be committed nor attempted.

Inherently Unlikely Attempt   A second possible "impossibility" defense even under some modern codes is that for an *inherently unlikely attempt*, as provided in the Model Penal Code:

> If the particular conduct charged to constitute a criminal attempt, solicitation or conspiracy is so inherently unlikely to result or culminate in the commission of a crime that neither such conduct nor the actor presents a public danger warranting the grading of such offense under this Section, the Court shall exercise its power . . . to enter judgment and impose sentence for a crime of lower grade or degree or, in extreme cases, may dismiss the prosecution.[5]

Under this provision, the actor who tries to kill using a method that poses no objective risk of success—such as by sticking pins in a voodoo doll—and who is judged not to be dangerous (that is, not likely to try a more effective method), might get a defense (or a mitigation) to the charge of attempted murder. One traditional example of this kind of case is the defendant who shakes his fist at a rain cloud, believing he can thereby destroy the world. (But, as this example suggests, where the actor's mistaken belief departs too far from reality, an insanity defense also may be available.) Many Model Penal Code-based criminal codes do not follow the Code in adopting this defense, for reasons discussed immediately below.

People v. Rollino
Supreme Court of New York, Criminal Term, Queens County
37 Misc. 2d 14, 233 N.Y.S. 2d 580 (1962)

J. IRWIN SHAPIRO, Justice.

At the conclusion of his trial without a jury, under an indictment charging him with Grand Larceny, Second Degree, defendant has moved for its dismissal and thereby revived the question whether a would-be thief can be guilty of either a consummated or an attempted larceny when the coveted property is turned over to him with the knowledge and consent of the owner, by one of its agents,

---

4. See Model Penal Code § 2.02(9).
5. Model Penal Code § 5.05(2).

by pre-arrangement with the police, in order to supply a basis for the miscreant's criminal prosecution. . . .

. . . [T]he question of "impossibility" was raised for the first time in *Regina v. McPherson*, Dears. & B. 197, 201 (1857), when Baron Bramwell said:

> . . . The argument that a man putting his hand into an empty pocket might be convicted of an attempt to steal, appeared to me at first plausible; but suppose a man, believing a block of wood to be a man who was his deadly enemy, struck it a blow intending to murder, could he be convicted of attempting to murder the man he took it to be?

Subsequently, in *Regina v. Collins*, 9 Cox C.C. 497, 169 Eng. Rep. 1477 (1864) the court expressly held that attempted larceny was not made out by proof that the defendant pickpocket actually inserted his hand into the victim's empty pocket with intent to steal, Chief Justice Cockburn declaring:

> We think that an attempt to commit a felony can only be made out when, if no interruption had taken place, the attempt could have been carried out successfully, and the felony completed of the attempt to commit which the party is charged.

This very broad language, encompassing as it did all forms of "impossibility," was subsequently rejected by the English courts and it was held that the inability of the pickpocket to steal from an empty pocket did not preclude his conviction of an attempted larceny. Regina v. Ring, 17 Cox C.C. 491, 66 L.T.(N.S.) 300 (1892). The determination in that case, generally speaking, represents the existing state of the law in the United States.

In this country it is generally held that a defendant may be charged with an attempt where the crime was not completed because of "physical or factual impossibility" whereas a "legal impossibility" in the completion of the crime precludes prosecution for an attempt.

What is a "legal impossibility" as distinguished from a "physical or factual impossibility" has over a long period of time perplexed our courts and has resulted in many irreconcilable decisions and much philosophical discussion by legal scholars in numerous articles and papers in law school publications and by text-writers.

The reason for the "impossibility" of completing the substantive crime ordinarily falls into one of two categories: (1) where the act if completed would not be criminal, a situation which is usually described as a "legal impossibility" and (2) where the basic or substantive crime is impossible of completion, simply because of some physical or factual condition unknown to the defendant, a situation which is usually described as a "factual impossibility."

The authorities in the various States and the text-writers are in general agreement that where there is a "legal impossibility" of completing the substantive crime, the accused cannot be successfully charged with an attempt, whereas in those cases in which the "factual impossibility" situation is involved, the accused may be convicted of an attempt. Detailed discussion of the subject is unnecessary to make it clear that it is frequently most difficult to compartmentalize a particular set of facts as coming within one of the categories rather than the other. Examples of the so-called "legal impossibility" situations are:

(a) A person accepting goods which he believes to have been stolen, but which were not in fact stolen goods, is not guilty of an attempt to receive stolen goods. (People v. Jaffe, 185 N.Y. 497, 78 N.E. 169, 9 L.R.A., N.S., 263).

(b) It is not an attempt to commit subornation of perjury where the false testimony solicited, if given, would have been immaterial to the case at hand and hence not perjurious.

(c) An accused who offers a bribe to a person believed to be a juror, but who is not a juror, is not guilty of an attempt to bribe a juror.

(d) An official who contracts a debt which is unauthorized and a nullity, but which he believes to be valid, is not guilty of an attempt to illegally contract a valid debt.

(e) A hunter who shoots a stuffed deer believing it to be alive is not guilty of an attempt to shoot a deer out of season.

(f) [An attempt to unlawfully buy what one mistakenly believes is a controlled drug is an instance of legal impossibility.][6]*

Examples of cases in which *attempt* convictions have been sustained on the theory that all that prevented the consummation of the completed crime was a "factual impossibility" are:

(a) The picking of an empty pocket.

(b) An attempt to steal from an empty receptacle or an empty house.

(c) Where defendant shoots into the intended victim's bed, believing he is there, when in fact he is elsewhere.

(d) Where the defendant erroneously believing that the gun is loaded points it at his wife's head and pulls the trigger.

(e) Where the woman upon whom the abortion operation is performed is not in fact pregnant. . . .

The foregoing lines of demarcation laid down in the cases and by text writers as to when an attempt may and may not be successfully charged has been roundly criticized. Thus in Hall, General Principles of Criminal Law, the writer says:

> . . . There are no degrees of impossibility and no sound basis for distinguishing among the conditions necessary for commission of the intended harm.

And we find Judge Thurman W. Arnold saying, with regard to the artificiality of the distinctions attempted to be made, the following:

> The distinctions . . . are ingenious, but . . . they lead us either to absurd results or else to no results.

In an exhaustive and extremely well considered opinion on this subject in *United States v. Thomas and McClellan*, we find the United States Court of Military Appeals dealing with this subject and saying:

> The lack of logic between some of the holdings; the inherent difficulty in assigning a given set of facts to a proper classification; the criticism of existing positions in this area; and, most importantly, the denial of true and substantial justice by these artificial holdings have led, quite naturally, to proposals for reform in the civilian legal concepts of criminal attempts.

---

6. * Editor's Note.—See, e.g., United States v. Everett, 700 F.2d 900 (1983); People v. Rosencrants, 89 Misc. 2d 721, 392 N.Y.S.2d 808 (1977).

. . . Some Courts have by "heroic efforts" taken what I consider to be a progressive and more modern view on the subject than is permitted by the decisional law in this State. Thus, California has now abandoned the *People v. Jaffe* rationale that "a person accepting goods which he believes to have been stolen, but which was not in fact stolen goods, is not guilty of an attempt to receive stolen goods and imposes liability for the attempt."

Returning now from the discussion of "attempts" to the facts in this case. . . .

Having determined that the defendant in this case may not be found guilty of the completed act of larceny because the drugs were not in fact taken from the owner without its consent, the next question is whether, under such circumstances, he may be found guilty of an attempt to commit larceny.

The answer would seem to be "no" for the very fact that prevents a conviction for the completed crime of larceny also precludes a conviction of an attempted larceny. "[I]n the present case, the act, which it was doubtless the intent of the defendant to commit would not have been a crime if it had been consummated" (People v. Jaffe, 185 N.Y. 497, 500, 78 N.E. 169) and "an unsuccessful attempt to do that which is not a crime, when effectuated, cannot be held to be an attempt to commit the crime specified." When the owner's agent offered the drugs to Rollino, to entrap him, defendant "succeeded in what he attempted, but what he did was not criminal." Since the completed act did not and could not as a *matter of law* constitute a larceny it is *legally impossible* for defendant to be guilty of an attempted larceny.

The *Jaffe* [case] has been the subject of analytic discussion and much criticism . . . , but that rule of law has never been modified or overruled in this state and it must, accordingly, be accepted and enforced by this Court.

The defendant's moral guilt is unquestionable. He intended to commit the crime of grand larceny and did everything that he could to implement and effectuate his criminal purpose and intent. That he cannot be adjudged legally guilty is due entirely to the existing state of the decisional and statutory law on the subject [in New York]. Clearly a modification of the law in this regard, to make it less favorable to criminal elements, is called for but this Court may only adjudicate; it may not legislate.

In this connection, attention is called to the proposal of The American Law Institute for the adoption of a "Model Penal Code" which in Article 5.01 defines "Criminal Attempts."

Tentative Draft No. 10 of the Model Penal Code makes obvious the reason and necessity for the adoption of the proposed Article 5.01 when it says:

> . . . It should suffice, therefore, to indicate at this stage what we deem to be the major results of the draft. They are:
>
> (a) to extend the criminality of attempts by sweeping aside the defense of impossibility (including the distinction between so-called factual and legal impossibility) and by drawing the line between attempt and non-criminal preparation further away from the final act; the crime becomes essentially one of criminal purpose implemented by an overt act strongly corroborative of such purpose; . . . .

The motion to dismiss the indictment is granted since an element essential to defendant's legal guilt of either a larceny or an attempted larceny of the kind here charged is entirely lacking.

▲ PROBLEMS

Lethal Spitting (#53)

Gregory Smith is neither particularly healthy nor particularly law-abiding. He pleads guilty to several offenses and is sentenced to three five-year terms, to be served concurrently. He is HIV-positive, which has developed into full-blown AIDS. At this time, there is limited understanding of how HIV is transmitted. It is commonly believed that the disease can be readily transmitted through human saliva. There are also widespread, anecdotal stories of transmission through biting. It is believed that infection with HIV amounts to a "death sentence," as the mortality rate is close to 100 percent.

While in the medical ward of the jail, Smith begins acting disruptive, kicking his cell door, banging on the walls and repeatedly pressing the medical alarm button located in his cell. When officers attempt to subdue him, he threatens to bite them and spit on them in order to infect them with HIV, saying, "I'll take you out you mother-[expletive]." He is eventually taken to a hospital after complaining of back pain and while there continuously threatens in a similar vein the two guards accompanying him, explicitly stating that he intends to bite them to give them AIDS. On his way from the hospital to the squad car at the end of his hospital stay, Smith tries to break free. He and the two guards fall to the ground, and during the ensuing scuffle, Smith bites Officer Waddington, breaking through the officer's gloves and puncturing the skin.

It is later determined that there are no blood injuries in Smith's mouth, thus Waddington could only have been infected through saliva. In light of modern medical knowledge, it would have been impossible for Smith to have transmitted HIV to Waddington in the manner he contemplated.

What liability, if any, for Smith for attempted murder under the Model Penal Code? Prepare a list of all criminal code subsections in the order in which you rely upon them in your analysis.

Would Smith's liability change if the Model Penal Code followed the common law position on impossibility?

An Impossible Rape (#54)

Roger Thomas is a 19-year-old Naval Airman recently transferred to a new town. He has been married for ten months and his wife is pregnant. He is out at a bar with two Navy friends, Dennis McClellan and Robert Abruzzese, when they meet Caryl Laverne Alvis, a young mother who has left her husband and 24-month-old child at home for a rare night out. She is dancing with McClellan when she suddenly slumps into him and falls to the ground. No one is very much concerned, because passing out is a regular occurrence at the bar. Someone says she might be having a fit. Thomas puts his wallet in the corner of her mouth to ensure she doesn't swallow her tongue. The three men then decide to take her home, and place her in the back of McClellan's car. En route, McClellan suggests they pull over and have sex with her. After initial hesitation, Thomas agrees that he will if the other two will. They all agree and take Alvis to a remote location. She is still unconscious. After Thomas and McClellan have intercourse with her, they drive back to town. Alvis has still not regained consciousness, and the men decide she needs medical attention. They call the police. When the officer arrives he can find no pulse. An autopsy reveals that Alvis died of a major heart attack caused by an inflammation of the muscular walls of the heart. Alvis was dead the moment she collapsed on the dance floor.

Would Thomas be liable for attempted rape under the Model Penal Code? Prepare a list of all criminal code subsections in the order in which you rely upon them in your analysis.

Would Thomas' liability change if the Model Penal Code followed the common law position on impossibility?

In re "The Nose . . . " (#55)

Dear Ann Landers:

I'm a 31-year-old bachelor, college-educated, church-going, and normal in every way, except one: I love the smell of women's feet.

There is no fragrance more exciting than the sweet bouquet of an unshod feminine foot, provided it is not abnormally sweaty or just out of a tennis shoe. I have sniffed the toes of dozens of ladies and could identify any of them blindfolded.

Usually women I have dated a few times don't mind. Some even find this kinkiness amusing. Lately, however, my patience is waning and I don't care to go through the formality of getting to know a woman well before I take off her shoe and savor the heavenly aroma.

Some of these women are stunned, grossed out, and afraid that I am trying to undress them. I have been called "a nut," and the evening has ended abruptly.

Questions: Could I be accused of attempted rape for suddenly taking off a woman's shoe? Am I the only man in the world who has this bizarre preference? Am I crazy? Please rush your reply.

The Nose Knows in Arizona

Assume "The Nose" took a job in a women's shoe store in order to gratify his sexual desire by smelling women's feet. Could he be held liable for sexual assault under Model Penal Code Section 213.4, below? Could "The Nose" be held liable for attempted sexual assault?

A person who subjects another not his spouse to any sexual contact is guilty of sexual assault, a misdemeanor, if:

(1) he knows that the contact is offensive to the other person; or . . .

(3) he knows that the other person is unaware that a sexual act is being committed. . . .

Sexual contact is any touching of the sexual or other intimate parts of the person of another for the purpose of arousing or gratifying sexual desire of either party.

✳ DISCUSSION ISSUE

If It Is Impossible for a Person to Commit the Offense Attempted, Should the Attempt Nonetheless Constitute a Crime? In Other Words, Should a Potential for Actual Commission Be Required, or Is a Subjective Belief in the Potential for Commission Enough?

Materials presenting each side of this Discussion Issue appear in the Advanced Materials for Section 11 in Appendix A.

Conspiracy

As attempt punishes conduct toward an offense, conspiracy punishes a specific kind of such conduct: an agreement with another that one of those agreeing will commit the offense. While this is just another form of inchoate conduct, albeit a very preliminary form, it is of special interest as conspiracy has often been transformed into a different, and controversial, offense. This is so in part because conspiracy also represents a form of criminality arising from group conduct.

◆ THE CASE OF SHEIK OMAR ABDEL RAHMAN (#56)

Sheik Omar Abdel Rahman comes to the United States in 1990. He is an elderly blind cleric, sick with diabetes and other age-related health problems. He views the United States as Islam's main oppressor and thinks that America is helping Israel gain power in the Middle East because it is under the control of the "Jewish lobby." Rahman comes to the United States nonetheless because he considers his homeland of Egypt to be little better. He is particularly dissatisfied with then-

Figure 46 **Sheik Rahman, February 20, 1993**
(Reuters Newsmedia Inc./Corbis)

President Hosni Mubarak, who he views as another oppressor of Islam. Because of this oppression, Rahman believes that the Qur'an authorizes a jihad, or holy war, against the two countries.

In 1989, before Rahman arrives, his followers had already started organizing into small cells in New York City. They maintain contact with Rahman while he is still in Egypt, providing updates about their training and overall plans. The followers record their conversations with the Sheik and distribute them as inspirational propaganda to other cells in New York. By the time Rahman arrives in 1990 (after dropping his two sons off in Afghanistan to train in Osama bin Laden's Al Qaeda camps), several cells are fully operational.

Rahman is careful to avoid direct involvement with the particulars of any operation, but instead provides only general comment. For example, both before and after his arrival, Rahman issues fatwas, which are religious opinions on the holiness of an act, condoning the proposed plans from the cells as furthering the jihad against the United States and Egypt. Meanwhile, the F.B.I. has been conducting surveillance against several of his followers and has photos of them firing AK-47s at a public range on Long Island, as well as recordings of their conversations with Rahman.

In 1990, an F.B.I. informant, Emad Salem, makes contact with Rahman's New York City group. He meets with Rahman and is successful in gaining the Sheik's immediate trust. A few days later, Salem accompanies Rahman to a conference in Detroit. En route, Salem attempts to further prove his loyalty by describing how he fought in the Egyptian

Figure 47 **Sheik Rahman with Emad Salem, May 1993**
(Elatab Said/Corbis-Sygma)

military against Israel in 1973. Rahman is unimpressed, however, explaining to Salem that paid service does not count as jihad. Rahman suggests that a true act of jihad would be to assassinate the "loyal dog to the Americans"—Egyptian President Mubarak.

Salem continues to ingratiate himself with Rahman's group, including cultivating a friendship with another of Rahman's confidantes, El-Gabrowny. Eventually, El-Gabrowny invites Salem for dinner but turns up the television before talking because he is suspicious of eavesdropping equipment. He regales Salem with talk of bombings and jihad, which will become the usual topic of conversation during the course of their relationship.

In July, Salem breaks with the F.B.I. and, shortly thereafter, withdraws as the New York group's paramilitary leader by leaving for Spain to allegedly sort out a jewelry deal. By late 1992, however, the group resumes paramilitary training under a new leader, Siddig Ali, who also reports regularly to Rahman.

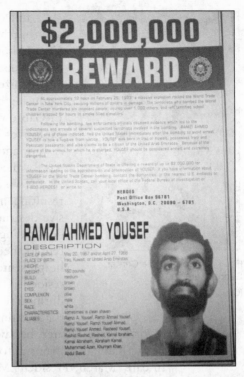

Figure 48 **Ramzi Yousef, 1995**
(Jeffrey Markowitz/Corbis-Sygma)

Meanwhile, Hampton-El, another Rahman follower, tries purchasing guns and detonators from Garret Wilson. He also says he wants "train[ing] in commando tactics," including training techniques and bomb identification. Contemporaneously, Ramzi Yousef, who is later convicted for his involvement in the 1993 World Trade Center bombing, arrives in the United States. (When passing through the I.N.S. entry gate, Yousef shows multiple pieces of identification for different identities, but immigration officials, while suspicious, are unable to detain him because the airport holding cells are full. They order him to appear in court, but he never shows, and the I.N.S takes no further action.)

In early 1993, Rahman attends a conference in Brooklyn. He tells the attendees that he supports a violent jihad and that the Qur'an condones terrorist acts if directed toward Islam's enemies, foremost of which are the United States and its allies.

Figure 49 **Mohammed Salameh, circa 1993**
(Reuters Newsmedia Inc./Corbis)

Figure 50 **World Trade Center, September 1999**

(Craig Nevill-Manning)

In New York, Yousef joins Mohammed Salameh, and together they develop plans to attack the World Trade Center buildings. They continue to advise Rahman of their plans. After a month of careful planning, the details are finalized. On February 24, 1993, Salameh rents a van using a fake New York license that lists his name and El-Gabrowny's address. They will use the van to deliver the explosives into the World Trade Center. Simultaneously, Ayyad, another follower, arranges to purchase hydrogen gas for the bomb's construction.

Two days later, the World Trade Center is bombed, resulting in six deaths, thousands of injured, and massive destruction. Authorities arrest Salameh after he tries demanding his deposit back from the place where he rented the van to carry the bomb. Using the fake license he presented as a lead, the police search El-Gabrowny's residence. They arrest him after he tries to assault them during the search. Yousef also is eventually caught. While transporting him by helicopter, passing the twin towers of the World Trade Center, he says, "Next time we will take them both down." Meanwhile, Rahman remains untouched.

In early March, President Mubarak schedules a visit to New York, which Rahman's followers see as a perfect opportunity to kill him. Needing funding for the operation, Ali, the training leader, contacts a man in the United Arab Emirates, and asserts that Rahman will vouch for him. When Mubarak cancels his visit, the plan fades into the background.

The following month, Ali proposes an attack on the United Nations building. Rahman approves of the proposed attack as jihad. By now, Salem has made amends with the F.B.I. and has reestablished his connections with Rahman's group. Ali allows Salem to speak with Rahman about the proposed attack, but emphasizes that he must be careful because of surveillance. Ali instructs Salem to "phrase statements in a broad and general manner in order to assure that Rahman [is] insulated from active involvement in the plot."

Figure 51 **United Nations Headquarters in New York City**

(Daniel E. Beards)

Salem meets with Rahman in May and reaffirms his loyalty to him. When Salem tells Ali of the meeting, Ali informs him that Rahman has approved of the United Nations bombing plan by issuing an official fatwa, the issuance of which allows them to enjoy God's blessing to employ unlawful violence.

Ali and Salem then discuss plans to bomb the Lincoln and Holland tunnels. They draft the plan on cardboard (later found in the safe house Rahman's group unknowingly rented from the F.B.I.) and decide that the attack requires three explosions spaced five minutes apart. They laugh at the thought of thousands of surprised commuters drowning on their way home. Ali and Amir drive to the tunnels, the United Nations building, and the Federal building to observe the targets and check traffic patterns. During one reconnaissance trip, Amir suggests that they bomb Manhattan's diamond district, which is known for its large Jewish population, saying this would be like bombing Israel itself.

Figure 52 **Former Egyptian President Hosni Mubarak** (Egyptian Press and Information Office)

In June, the group meets to finalize the plan and to decide what additional preparations are necessary. Hampton-El says that he will find detonators. Saleh, another member of the group, agrees to buy military equipment. They purchase timers for the bombs in Chinatown and buy stolen cars to use as a delivery vehicle and getaway car. To refine the plan, they meet with an engineer to discuss the plan's overall feasibility and determine where the tunnels' weak points are located.

On June 17, Rahman holds a press conference announcing that the United States will pay a tremendous price for supporting President Mubarak. Three days later, the group buys 55-gallon steel drums to hold the fuel for the explosions. They fill some of the drums at a gas station owned by Saleh. Even though Saleh has arranged for them not to pay for the fuel, his employee, Bal-Habri, makes out a receipt, which includes the license plate number of the van they are driving. The next day, they return to fill the remaining drums, but this time they chide Bal-Habri when he begins to write the plate number on the receipt. Elsewhere, Ali and Salem purchase the bombs' other principal component, fertilizer. About this time, Rahman, anticipating their success, tells followers that the bombing will "move Duane Street to Reade Street."

On the evening of June 23, Amir and Fadil bring the fuel to the safe house, and the operational group briefly meets to review the plan. After returning from prayers at a mosque, they begin mixing the fuel and fertilizer for the bombs while also watching a video shot by Ali earlier in the day of the tunnels they plan to destroy.

Meanwhile, in Yonkers, the F.B.I. arrests Saleh. He denies selling the fuel but says that Salem demanded it twice. He later calls an employee from prison and instructs him to tell Bal-Habri to burn the receipts. At 2:00 a.m., the F.B.I. raids the safe house, arrests the group, and seizes the fuel, fertilizer, and Ali's cardboard diagram illustrating the plan. Rahman is arrested shortly thereafter.

Figure 53 **Sheik Rahman surrendering to the F.B.I., July 1993** (Les Stone/Corbis)

1. Relying only upon your own intuitions of justice, what liability and punishment, if any, does Sheik Rahman deserve?

N	0	1	2	3	4	5	6	7	8	9	10	11
☐	☐	☐	☐	☐	☐	☐	☐	☐	☐	☐	☒	☐
no liability	liability but no punishment	1 day	2 wks	2 mo	6 mo	1 yr	3 yrs	7 yrs	15 yrs	30 yrs	life imprison-ment	death

2. What "justice" arguments could defense counsel make on the defendant's behalf?

3. What "justice" arguments could the prosecution make against the defendant?

4. What liability, if any, for Sheik Rahman under the then-existing statutes? Prepare a list of all criminal code subsections and cases in the order that you rely on them in your analysis.

5. What liability, if any, under the Model Penal Code? Prepare a list of all criminal code subsections in the order that you rely on them in your analysis.

■ THE LAW

United States Code
Title 18 (1993)

Part I. Crimes

Chapter 115. Treason, Sedition, and Subversive Activities

Section 2384. Seditious Conspiracy

If two or more persons *who* in any State or Territory, or in any place subject to the jurisdiction of the United States *where* conspire to overthrow, put down, or to destroy by force the Government of the United States, or to levy war against them, or to oppose by force the authority thereof, or by force to prevent, hinder, or delay the execution of any law of the United States, or by force to seize, take, or possess any property of the United States contrary to the authority thereof, they shall each be fined not more than $ 20,000 or imprisoned not more than twenty years, or both.

Section 2385. Advocating Overthrow of Government

Whoever knowingly or willfully advocates, abets, advises, or teaches the duty, necessity, desirability, or propriety of overthrowing or destroying the government of the United States or the government of any State, Territory, District or

Possession thereof, or the government of any political subdivision therein, by force or violence, or by the assassination of any officer of any such government; or

Whoever, with intent to cause the overthrow or destruction of any such government, prints, publishes, edits, issues, circulates, sells, distributes, or publicly displays any written or printed matter advocating, advising, or teaching the duty, necessity, desirability, or propriety of overthrowing or destroying any government in the United States by force or violence, or attempts to do so; or

Whoever organizes or helps or attempts to organize any society, group, or assembly of persons who teach, advocate, or encourage the overthrow or destruction of any such government by force or violence; or becomes or is a member of, or affiliates with, any such society, group, or assembly of persons, knowing the purposes thereof—

Shall be fined not more than $ 20,000 or imprisoned not more than twenty years, or both, and shall be ineligible for employment by the United States or any department or agency thereof, for the five years next following his conviction.

If two or more persons conspire to commit any offense named in this section, each shall be fined not more than $ 20,000 or imprisoned not more than twenty years, or both, and shall be ineligible for employment by the United States or any department or agency thereof, for the five years next following his conviction.

As used in this section, the terms "organizes" and "organize", with respect to any society, group, or assembly of persons, include the recruiting of new members, the forming of new units, and the regrouping or expansion of existing clubs, classes, and other units of such society, group, or assembly of persons.

Section 2389. Recruiting for Service Against United States

Whoever recruits soldiers or sailors within the United States, or in any place subject to the jurisdiction thereof, to engage in armed hostility against the same; or

Whoever opens within the United States, or in any place subject to the jurisdiction thereof, a recruiting station for the enlistment of such soldiers or sailors to serve in any manner in armed hostility against the United States—

Shall be fined not more than $ 1,000 or imprisoned not more than five years, or both.

Section 2390. Enlistment to Serve Against United States

Whoever enlists or is engaged within the United States or in any place subject to the jurisdiction thereof, with intent to serve in armed hostility against the United States, shall be fined $ 100 or imprisoned not more than three years, or both.

Chapter 19. Conspiracy

Section 371. Conspiracy to Commit Offense or to Defraud United States

If two or more persons conspire either to commit any offense against the United States, or to defraud the United States, or any agency thereof in any manner or for any purpose, and one or more of such persons do any act to effect the object of the conspiracy, each shall be fined not more than $ 10,000 or imprisoned not more than five years, or both.

If, however, the offense, the commission of which is the object of the conspiracy, is a misdemeanor only, the punishment for such conspiracy shall not exceed the maximum punishment provided for such misdemeanor.

Section 373.   Solicitation to Commit a Crime of Violence

(a) Whoever, with intent that another person engage in conduct constituting a felony that has as an element the use, attempted use, or threatened use of physical force against property or against the person of another in violation of the laws of the United States, and under circumstances strongly corroborative of that intent, solicits, commands, induces, or otherwise endeavors to persuade such other person to engage in such conduct, shall be imprisoned not more than one-half the maximum term of imprisonment or fined not more than one-half of the maximum fine prescribed for the punishment of the crime solicited, or both; or if the crime solicited is punishable by death, shall be imprisoned for not more than twenty years.

(b) It is an affirmative defense to a prosecution under this section that, under circumstances manifesting a voluntary and complete renunciation of his criminal intent, the defendant prevented the commission of the crime solicited. A renunciation is not "voluntary and complete" if it is motivated in whole or in part by a decision to postpone the commission of the crime until another time or to substitute another victim or another but similar objective. If the defendant raises the affirmative defense at trial, the defendant has the burden of proving the defense by a preponderance of the evidence.

(c) It is not a defense to a prosecution under this section that the person solicited could not be convicted of the crime because he lacked the state of mind required for its commission, because he was incompetent or irresponsible, or because he is immune from prosecution or is not subject to prosecution.

Chapter 40. Importation, Manufacture, Distribution and Storage of Explosive Materials

Section 842.   Unlawful Acts

(a) It shall be unlawful for any person—

(1) to engage in the business of importing, manufacturing, or dealing in explosive materials without a license issued under this chapter;

(2) knowingly to withhold information or to make any false or fictitious oral or written statement or to furnish or exhibit any false, fictitious, or misrepresented identification, intended or likely to deceive for the purpose of obtaining explosive materials, or a license, permit, exemption, or relief from disability under the provisions of this chapter; and

(3) other than a licensee or permittee knowingly—

(A) to transport, ship, cause to be transported, or receive in interstate or foreign commerce any explosive materials, except that a person who lawfully purchases explosive materials from a licensee in a State contiguous to the State in which the purchaser resides may ship, transport, or cause to be transported such explosive materials to the State in which he resides and may receive such explosive materials in the State in which he resides, if such transportation, shipment, or receipt is permitted by the law of the State in which he resides; or

(B) to distribute explosive materials to any person (other than a licensee or permittee) who the distributor knows or has reasonable cause to believe does not reside in the State in which the distributor resides.

(b) It shall be unlawful for any licensee knowingly to distribute any explosive materials to any person except—

(1) a licensee;

(2) a permittee; or

(3) a resident of the State where distribution is made and in which the licensee is licensed to do business or a State contiguous thereto if permitted by the law of the State of the purchaser's residence.

(c) It shall be unlawful for any licensee to distribute explosive materials to any person who the licensee has reason to believe intends to transport such explosive materials into a State where the purchase, possession, or use of explosive materials is prohibited or which does not permit its residents to transport or ship explosive materials into it or to receive explosive materials in it.

(d) It shall be unlawful for any licensee knowingly to distribute explosive materials to any individual who:

(1) is under twenty-one years of age;

(2) has been convicted in any court of a crime punishable by imprisonment for a term exceeding one year;

(3) is under indictment for a crime punishable by imprisonment for a term exceeding one year;

(4) is a fugitive from justice;

(5) is an unlawful user of or addicted to any controlled substance (as defined in section 102 of the Controlled Substances Act (21 U.S.C. 802)); or

(6) has been adjudicated a mental defective.

(e) It shall be unlawful for any licensee knowingly to distribute any explosive materials to any person in any State where the purchase, possession, or use by such person of such explosive materials would be in violation of any State law or any published ordinance applicable at the place of distribution.

(f) It shall be unlawful for any licensee or permittee willfully to manufacture, import, purchase, distribute, or receive explosive materials without making such records as the Secretary may by regulation require, including, but not limited to, a statement of intended use, the name, date, place of birth, social security number or taxpayer identification number, and place of residence of any natural person to whom explosive materials are distributed. If explosive materials are distributed to a corporation or other business entity, such records shall include the identity and principal and local places of business and the name, date, place of birth, and place of residence of the natural person acting as agent of the corporation or other business entity in arranging the distribution.

(g) It shall be unlawful for any licensee or permittee knowingly to make any false entry in any record which he is required to keep pursuant to this section or regulations promulgated under section 847 of this title [18 U.S.C.S. §847].

(h) It shall be unlawful for any person to receive, conceal, transport, ship, store, barter, sell, or dispose of any explosive materials knowing or having reasonable cause to believe that such explosive materials were stolen.

(i) It shall be unlawful for any person—

(1) who is under indictment for, or who has been convicted in any court of, a crime punishable by imprisonment for a term exceeding one year;

(2) who is a fugitive from justice;

(3) who is an unlawful user of or addicted to any controlled substance (as defined in section 102 of the Controlled Substances Act (21 U.S.C. 802)); or

(4) who has been adjudicated as a mental defective or who has been committed to a mental institution;

to ship or transport any explosive in interstate or foreign commerce or to receive any explosive which has been shipped or transported in interstate or foreign commerce.

(j) It shall be unlawful for any person to store any explosive material in a manner not in conformity with regulations promulgated by the Secretary. In promulgating such regulations, the Secretary shall take into consideration the class, type, and quantity of explosive materials to be stored, as well as the standards of safety and security recognized in the explosives industry.

(k) It shall be unlawful for any person who has knowledge of the theft or loss of any explosive materials from his stock, to fail to report such theft or loss within twenty-four hours of discovery thereof, to the Secretary and to appropriate local authorities.

Section 844. Penalties

(a) Any person who violates subsections (a) through (i) of section 842 of this chapter [18 U.S.C.S. §842(a) through (i)] shall be fined not more than $10,000 or imprisoned not more than ten years, or both.

(b) Any person who violates any other provision of section 842 of this chapter [18 U.S.C.S. §842] shall be fined not more than $ 1,000 or imprisoned not more than one year, or both.

(c) Any explosive materials involved or used or intended to be used in any violation of the provisions of this chapter or any other rule or regulation promulgated thereunder or any violation of any criminal law of the United States shall be subject to seizure and forfeiture, and all provisions of the Internal Revenue Code of 1954 [26 U.S.C.S. §§1 et seq.] relating to the seizure, forfeiture, and disposition of firearms, as defined in section 5845(a) of that Code [26 U.S.C.S. §5845(a)], shall, so far as applicable, extend to seizures and forfeitures under the provisions of this chapter [18 U.S.C.S. §§841 et seq.].

(d) Whoever transports or receives, or attempts to transport or receive, in interstate or foreign commerce any explosive with the knowledge or intent that it will be used to kill, injure, or intimidate any individual or unlawfully to damage or destroy any building, vehicle, or other real or personal property, shall be imprisoned for not more than ten years, or fined not more than $ 10,000, or both; and if personal injury results to any person, including any public safety officer performing duties as a direct or proximate result of conduct prohibited by this subsection, shall be imprisoned for not more than twenty years or fined not more than $ 20,000, or both; and if death results to any person, including any public safety officer performing duties as a direct or proximate result of conduct prohibited by this subsection, shall be subject to imprisonment for any term of years, or to the death penalty or to life imprisonment as provided in section 34 of this title [18 U.S.C.S. §34].

(e) Whoever, through the use of the mail, telephone, telegraph, or other instrument of commerce, willfully makes any threat, or maliciously conveys false information knowing the same to be false, concerning an attempt or alleged attempt being made, or to be made, to kill, injure, or intimidate any individual or unlawfully to damage or destroy any building, vehicle, or other real or personal property by means of fire or an explosive shall be imprisoned for not more than five years or fined not more than $ 5,000, or both.

(f) Whoever maliciously damages, or destroys, or attempts to damage or destroy, by means of fire or an explosive, any building, vehicle, or other personal or real property in whole or in part owned, possessed, or used by, or leased to, the United States, any department or agency thereof, or any institution or organization receiving Federal financial assistance shall be imprisoned for not more than ten years, or fined not more than $ 10,000, or both; and if personal injury results to any person, including any public safety officer performing duties as a direct or proximate result of conduct prohibited by this subsection, shall be imprisoned for not more than twenty years, or fined not more than $ 20,000, or both; and if death results to any person, including any public safety officer performing duties as a direct or proximate result of conduct prohibited by this subsection, shall be subject to imprisonment for any term of years, or to the death penalty or to life imprisonment as provided in section 34 of this title [18 U.S.C.S. §34].

(g)(1) Except as provided in paragraph (2), whoever possesses an explosive in an airport that is subject to the regulatory authority of the Federal Aviation Administration, or in any building in whole or in part owned, possessed, or used by, or leased to, the United States or any department or agency thereof, except with the written consent of the agency, department, or other person responsible for the management of such building or airport, shall be imprisoned for not more than five years, or fined under this title, or both.

(2) The provisions of this subsection shall not be applicable to—

(A) the possession of ammunition (as that term is defined in regulations issued pursuant to this chapter [18 U.S.C.S. §§841 et seq.]) in an airport that is subject to the regulatory authority of the Federal Aviation Administration if such ammunition is either in checked baggage or in a closed container; or

(B) the possession of an explosive in an airport if the packaging and transportation of such explosive is exempt from, or subject to and in accordance with, regulations of the Research and Special Projects Administration for the handling of hazardous materials pursuant to the Hazardous Materials Transportation Act (49 App. U.S.C. 1801, et seq.).

(h) Whoever—

(1) uses fire or an explosive to commit any felony which may be prosecuted in a court of the United States, or

(2) carries an explosive during the commission of any felony which may be prosecuted in a court of the United States, including a felony which provides for an enhanced punishment if committed by the use of a deadly or dangerous weapon or device shall, in addition to the punishment provided for such felony, be sentenced to imprisonment for five years. In the case of a second or subsequent conviction under this subsection, such person shall be sentenced to imprisonment for ten years. Notwithstanding any other provision of law, the court shall not place on probation or suspend the sentence of any person convicted of a violation of this subsection, nor shall the term of imprisonment imposed under this subsection run concurrently with any other term of imprisonment including that imposed for the felony in which the explosive was used or carried.

(i) Whoever maliciously damages or destroys, or attempts to damage or destroy, by means of fire or an explosive, any building, vehicle, or other real or personal property used in interstate or foreign commerce or in any activity affecting interstate or foreign commerce shall be imprisoned for not more than ten years or fined not more than $ 10,000, or both; and if personal injury results to any person, including any public safety officer performing duties as a direct or proximate result of conduct prohibited by this subsection, shall be imprisoned for not more than twenty years or fined not more than $ 20,000, or both; and if death results to any person, including any public safety officer performing duties as a direct or proximate result of conduct prohibited by this subsection, shall also be subject to imprisonment for any term of years, or to the death penalty or to life imprisonment as provided in section 34 of this title [18 U.S.C.S. §34].

(j) For the purposes of subsections (d), (e), (f), (g), (h), and (i) of this section, the term "explosive" means gunpowders, powders used for blasting, all forms of high explosives, blasting materials, fuzes (other than electric circuit breakers), detonators, and other detonating agents, smokeless powders, other explosive or incendiary devices within the meaning of paragraph (5) of section 232 of this title [18 U.S.C.S. §232(5)], and any chemical compounds, mechanical mixture, or device that contains any oxidizing and combustible units, or other ingredients, in such proportions, quantities, or packing that ignition by fire, by friction, by concussion, by percussion, or by detonation of the compound, mixture, or device or any part thereof may cause an explosion.

Chapter 51. Homicide

Section 1111. Murder

(a) Murder is the unlawful killing of a human being with malice aforethought. Every murder perpetrated by poison, lying in wait, or any other kind of willful, deliberate, malicious, and premeditated killing; or committed in the perpetration of, or attempt to perpetrate, any arson, escape, murder, kidnaping, treason, espionage, sabotage, aggravated sexual abuse or sexual abuse burglary, or robbery; or perpetrated from a premeditated design unlawfully and maliciously to effect the death of any human being other than him who is killed, is murder in the first degree. Any other murder is murder in the second degree.

(b) Within the special maritime and territorial jurisdiction of the United States, Whoever is guilty of murder in the first degree, shall suffer death unless the jury qualifies its verdict by adding thereto "without capital punishment", in which event he shall be sentenced to imprisonment for life; Whoever is guilty of murder in the second degree, shall be imprisoned for any term of years or for life.

Section 1112. Manslaughter

(a) Manslaughter is the unlawful killing of a human being without malice. It is of two kinds:

Voluntary—Upon a sudden quarrel or heat of passion.

Involuntary—In the commission of an unlawful act not amounting to a felony, or in the commission in an unlawful manner, or without due caution and circumspection, of a lawful act which might produce death.

(b) Within the special maritime and territorial jurisdiction of the United States,

Whoever is guilty of voluntary manslaughter, shall be imprisoned not more than ten years;

Whoever is guilty of involuntary manslaughter, shall be fined not more than $ 1,000 or imprisoned not more than three years, or both.

Section 1113. Attempt to Commit Murder or Manslaughter

Except as provided in section 113 of this title, whoever, within the special maritime and territorial jurisdiction of the United States, attempts to commit murder or manslaughter, shall, for an attempt to commit murder be imprisoned not more than twenty years or fined under this title, or both, and for an attempt to commit manslaughter be imprisoned not more than three years or fined under this title, or both.

Section 1116. Murder or Manslaughter of Foreign Officials, Official Guests, or Internationally Protected Persons

(a) Whoever kills or attempts to kill a foreign official, official guest, or internationally protected person shall be punished as provided under sections 1111, 1112, and 1113 of this title [18 U.S.C.S. §§1111-1113], except that any such person who is found guilty of murder in the first degree shall be sentenced to imprisonment for life, and any such person who is found guilty of attempted murder shall be imprisoned for not more than twenty years.

(b) For the purposes of this section:

(1) "Family" includes (a) a spouse, parent, brother or sister, child, or person to whom the foreign official or internationally protected person stands in loco parentis, or (b) any other person living in his household and related to the foreign official or internationally protected person by blood or marriage.

(2) "Foreign government" means the government of a foreign country, irrespective of recognition by the United States.

(3) "Foreign official" means—

(A) a Chief of State or the political equivalent, President, Vice President, Prime Minister, Ambassador, Foreign Minister, or other officer of Cabinet rank or above of a foreign government or the chief executive officer of an international organization, or any person who has previously served in such capacity, and any member of his family, while in the United States; and

(B) any person of a foreign nationality who is duly notified to the United States as an officer or employee of a foreign government or international organization, and who is in the United States on official business, and any member of his family whose presence in the United States is in connection with the presence of such officer or employee.

(4) "Internationally protected person" means—

(A) a Chief of State or the political equivalent, head of government, or Foreign Minister whenever such person is in a country other than his own and any member of his family accompanying him; or

(B) any other representative, officer, employee, or agent of the United States Government, a foreign government, or international organization who at the time and place concerned is entitled pursuant to international law to special protection against attack upon his person, freedom, or dignity, and any member of his family then forming part of his household.

(5) "International organization" means a public international organization designated as such pursuant to section 1 of the International Organizations Immunities Act (22 U.S.C. 288) [22 U.S.C.S. §288] or a public organization created pursuant to treaty or other agreement under international law as an instrument through or by which two or more foreign governments engage in some aspect of their conduct of international affairs.

(6) "Official guest" means a citizen or national of a foreign country present in the United States as an official guest of the Government of the United States pursuant to designation as such by the Secretary of State.

(c) If the victim of an offense under subsection (a) is an internationally protected person, the United States may exercise jurisdiction over the offense if the alleged offender is present within the United States, irrespective of the place where the offense was committed or the nationality of the victim or the alleged offender. As used in this subsection, the United States includes all areas under the jurisdiction of the United States including any of the places within the provisions of sections 5 and 7 of this title [18 U.S.C.S. §§5 and 7] and section 101(38) of the Federal Aviation Act of 1958, as amended (49 U.S.C. 1301(38)) [49 U.S.C.S. Appx. §1301(38)].

(d) In the course of enforcement of this section and any other sections prohibiting a conspiracy or attempt to violate this section, the Attorney General may request assistance from any Federal, State, or local agency, including the Army, Navy, and Air Force, any statute, rule, or regulation to the contrary notwithstanding.

Section 1117. Conspiracy to Murder

If two or more persons conspire to violate section 1111, 1114, or 1116 of this title [18 U.S.C.S. §§1111, 1114, or 1116], and one or more of such persons do any overt act to effect the object of the conspiracy, each shall be punished by imprisonment for any term of years or for life.

Yates v. United States

354 U.S. 298, 1 L. Ed. 2d 1356, 77 S. Ct. 1064 (1957)

The Smith Act (18 U.S.C.S. §2385) is aimed at the advocacy and teaching of concrete action for the forcible overthrow of the government, and not of principles divorced from action. In determining whether the advocacy of the forcible overthrow of government was directed to action to that end, and hence punishable under the Smith Act, or was merely advocacy of abstract doctrines, and hence not punishable under the Act, the essential distinction is that those to whom the advocacy is addressed must be urged to do something, now or in the future, rather than merely to believe in something.

Scales v. United States

260 F.2d 21 (4th Cir. 1958)

In a prosecution under "membership clause" of 18 U.S.C. §2385, the trial judge must determine not only the relevancy and sufficiency of evidence as whole, as in the ordinary case, but must also determine whether the facts proved constituted such a clear and present danger to the state as to overcome the prohibitions of constitutional amendments and to justify conviction under 18 U.S.C. §2385.

United States v. Sinclair

321 F. Supp. 1074, 1079 (E.D. Mich. 1971)

"In this turbulent time of unrest, it is often difficult for the established and contented members of our society to tolerate, mush less try to understand, the contemporary challenges to our existing form of government. If democracy as we know it, and as our forefathers established it, is to stand, then 'attempts of domestic organizations to attack and subvert the existing structure of the Government' (see affidavit of Attorney General), cannot be, in and of themselves, a crime. Such attempts become criminal only where it can be shown that the activity was/is carried on through unlawful means, such as the invasion of the rights of others by use of force or violence."

Pinkerton v. United States

328 U.S. 640, 66 S. Ct. 1180, 90 L. Ed. 1489 (1946)

While the defendant was in jail, he was indicted for conspiring with his brother to evade taxes and for specific tax evasions. The jury was instructed that the defendant could be convicted of the substantive offenses if they found he had been engaged in a conspiracy and the specific offenses were in furtherance of the conspiracy. The Supreme Court affirmed, essentially holding that direct partici-pation in the substantive offenses was not necessary for substantive liability, and that being a co-conspirator was sufficient for liability for a substantive offense in furtherance of the conspiracy.

United States v. Falcone

311 U.S. 205, 210, 61 S. Ct. 204, 207, 85 L. Ed. 128, 132 (1940)

The defendants sold sugar, yeast, and cans, with the knowledge that the materials would be used in illicit distilling operations, but without the knowl-edge that the buyers were parties to a conspiracy. The Court held that they could not be convicted as participants to the conspiracy, and that "[t]he gist of the offense of conspiracy as defined by [the federal statute] is agreement among the conspirators to commit an offense attended by an act of one or more of the conspirators to effect the object of the conspiracy." Here, the defendants were suppliers to an illicit distiller, and furthered the goal of the conspiracy, but they had not entered into an agreement. Thus, while they knew of the illicit use at the time they aided, that in itself was not enough to make them members of the conspiracy.

United States v. Feola

420 U.S. 671, 687, 95 S. Ct. 1255, 1265, 43 L. Ed. 2d 541, 554 (1975)

Defendants were convicted for having assaulted federal officers in the per-formance of their official duties, and for conspiring to commit that offense. The defendants appealed, arguing that, unlike the requirements of the substantive crime, a conspiracy charge required the government to prove their actual knowl-edge of the victim's official identity. The Court rejected this argument, and held that "[a] natural reading of these words would be that since one can violate a criminal statute simply by engaging in the forbidden conduct, a conspiracy to commit that offense is nothing more than an agreement to engage in the pro-hibited conduct. Then where, as here, the substantive statute does not require that an assailant know the official status of his victim, there is nothing on the face of the conspiracy statute that would seem to require that those agreeing to the assault have a greater degree of knowledge."

Model Penal Code

(Official Draft 1962)

Section 5.03. Criminal Conspiracy

(1) Definition of Conspiracy. A person is guilty of conspiracy with another person or persons to commit a crime if with the purpose of promoting or facilitat-ing its commission he:

(a) agrees with such other person or persons that they or one or more of them will engage in conduct which constitutes such crime or an attempt or solicitation to commit such crime; or

(b) agrees to aid such other person or persons in the planning or commission of such crime or of an attempt or solicitation to commit such crime.

(2) Scope of Conspiratorial Relationship. If a person guilty of conspiracy, as defined by Subsection (1) of this Section, knows that a person with whom he conspires to commit a crime has conspired with another person or persons to commit the same crime, he is guilty of conspiring with such other person or persons, whether or not he knows their identity, to commit such crime.

(3) Conspiracy With Multiple Criminal Objectives. If a person conspires to commit a number of crimes, he is guilty of only one conspiracy so long as such multiple crimes are the object of the same agreement or continuous conspiratorial relationship.

(4) Joinder and Venue in Conspiracy Prosecutions.

(a) Subject to the provisions of paragraph (b) of this Subsection, two or more persons charged with criminal conspiracy may be prosecuted jointly if:

(i) they are charged with conspiring with one another; or

(ii) the conspiracies alleged, whether they have the same or different parties, are so related that they constitute different aspects of a scheme of organized criminal conduct.

(b) In any joint prosecution under paragraph (a) of this Subsection:

(i) no defendant shall be charged with a conspiracy in any county [parish or district] other than one in which he entered into such conspiracy or in which an overt act pursuant to such conspiracy was done by him or by a person with whom he conspired; and

(ii) neither the liability of any defendant nor the admissibility against him of evidence of acts or declarations of another shall be enlarged by such joinder; and

(iii) the Court shall order a severance or take a special verdict as to any defendant who so requests, if it deems it necessary or appropriate to promote the fair determination of his guilt or innocence, and shall take any other proper measures to protect the fairness of the trial.

(5) Overt Act. No person may be convicted of conspiracy to commit a crime, other than a felony of the first or second degree, unless an overt act in pursuance of such conspiracy is alleged and proved to have been done by him or by a person with whom he conspired.

(6) Renunciation of Criminal Purpose. It is an affirmative defense that the actor, after conspiring to commit a crime, thwarted the success of the conspiracy, under circumstances manifesting a complete and voluntary renunciation of his criminal purpose.

(7) Duration of Conspiracy. For purposes of Section 1.06(4):

(a) conspiracy is a continuing course of conduct which terminates when the crime or crimes which are its object are committed or the agreement that they be committed is abandoned by the defendant and by those with whom he conspired; and

(b) such abandonment is presumed if neither the defendant nor anyone with whom he conspired does any overt act in pursuance of the conspiracy during the applicable period of limitation; and

(c) if an individual abandons the agreement, the conspiracy is terminated as to him only if and when he advises those with whom he conspired of his abandonment or he informs the law enforcement authorities of the existence of the conspiracy and of his participation therein.

Section 1.07. Method of Prosecution When Conduct Constitutes More Than One Offense

(1) Prosecution for Multiple Offenses; Limitation on Convictions. When the same conduct of a defendant may establish the commission of more than one offense, the defendant may be prosecuted for each such offense. He may not, however, be convicted of more than one offense if:

(a) one offense is included in the other, as defined in Subsection (4) of this Section; or

(b) one offense consists only of a conspiracy or other form of preparation to commit the other; or

(c) inconsistent findings of fact are required to establish the commission of the offenses; or

(d) the offenses differ only in that one is defined to prohibit a designated kind of conduct generally and the other to prohibit a specific instance of such conduct; or

(e) the offense is defined as a continuing course of conduct and the defendant's course of conduct was uninterrupted, unless the law provides that specific periods of such conduct constitute separate offenses....

(4) Conviction of Included Offense Permitted. A defendant may be convicted of an offense included in an offense charged in the indictment [or the information]. An offense is so included when:

(a) it is established by proof of the same or less than all the facts required to establish the commission of the offense charged; or

(b) it consists of an attempt or solicitation to commit the offense charged or to commit an offense otherwise included therein; or

(c) it differs from the offense charged only in the respect that a less serious injury or risk of injury to the same person, property or public interest or a lesser kind of culpability suffices to establish its commission....

Section 5.05.   ... ; Multiple Convictions Barred. ...

(3) Multiple Convictions. A person may not be convicted of more than one offense defined by this Article for conduct designed to commit or to culminate in the commission of the same crime.

● OVERVIEW OF CONSPIRACY

Notes

Introduction: Three Roles of Conspiracy

The offense of *conspiracy*, which addresses multiparty agreements or plans to engage in criminal activity, may serve any of three distinct roles, and sometimes more than one of those roles at once. First, conspiracy is an inchoate offense that enables punishment of preparatory conduct; in this respect, it operates in a way analogous to attempt. Second, conspiracy may be viewed not only as involving preliminary conduct toward some harm, but as a harm in itself, or at least as a factor aggravating the seriousness of the object offense because of the additional dangers inherent in group criminal activity. Finally, prosecutors frequently charge conspiracy not for the liability that it generates, either as an inchoate offense or as an aggravation for group criminality, but rather for the procedural advantages that it gives. Lack of clarity about which of these is, or should be, the primary role of conspiracy accounts for much of the confusion surrounding the offense.

Conspiracy as Inchoate Offense The Model Penal Code, and the state codes following its lead, treat conspiracy only as an inchoate offense. Its placement in Article 5 of the Code, "Inchoate Crimes," formally signals this treatment, but other provisions confirm the role. For example, the Code's renunciation defense, a defense that is unavailable for substantive offenses, applies to conspiracy.[1] The Code also bars conviction for both conspiracy and the substantive offense that is its object (the so-called *target* or *object* offense),[2] just as liability for an attempt would be subsumed into liability for its target offense. The Code also bars conviction for

---

1. See Model Penal Code § 5.03(6).
2. See Model Penal Code § 1.07(1)(b).

both conspiracy and another inchoate offense toward the same crime, again suggesting that the drafters see conspiracy only as punishing inchoate conduct.[3]

Theory Underlying View of Conspiracy as Inchoate   The underlying theory of conspiracy as an inchoate offense is similar to that for attempt: It punishes an actor who intends that an offense be committed and externally manifests her willingness to carry out that intention. The agreement with another to commit an offense—the gist of conspiracy—is an externalization of what, until then, may have been simply a thought of the actor. The act of agreeing suggests that the actor has moved beyond mere fantasizing, and also provides some evidentiary confirmation of the actor's criminal intention. (The law frequently demands further confirmation by requiring proof of an overt act advancing the conspiracy.) The agreement with another to commit an offense often gives a more reliable, unambiguous indication of an actor's blameworthiness and dangerousness than does the "substantial step" toward commission required for attempt liability. In addition, conspiracy has the advantage of commonly allowing earlier law enforcement intervention than attempt's substantial-step requirement allows. Thus, as an inchoate offense, conspiracy often is better than attempt not only at reliably identifying blameworthy offenders, but also at increasing the chances of crime prevention.

Conspiracy as Aggravation for Group Criminality   Alternatively, conspiracy has been viewed,

> "as a curb to the immoderate power to do mischief which is gained by a combination of the means." Conspiracy as an offense recognizes increased public harm by group action. It seeks to strike at the special dangers incident to group activity.[4]

From this perspective, conspiracy serves as a substantive offense, capturing the increased danger and harm that attends group criminality. There is little reason to provide a renunciation defense for this version of conspiracy, as renunciation generally is not a defense where an offense's substantive harm or evil has already occurred (in this instance, the formation of a group for a criminal purpose). Also, under this view, where the conspiracy's target offense does occur, there is no impropriety in convicting an offender for both that offense and conspiracy to commit it, as some states allow,[5] for the latter conviction provides aggravated liability to reflect the aggravated harm of a group offense.

Wharton's Rule: No Added Liability Where Object Is by Nature a Group Crime   Under the aggravation-for-group-criminality view of conspiracy, however, it would not be appropriate to allow conviction for both conspiracy and the target offense if the target offense itself necessarily involved the conduct of multiple actors. That is, what has traditionally been called *Wharton's Rule*, after the treatise writer who proposed it, bars conviction for both conspiracy and the target offense for target offenses that are defined to involve a group, since conviction for the target offense would already take into account the harm of group criminality and adding conspiracy liability would improperly "double-count" that

---

3. See Model Penal Code § 5.05(3).

4. Archbold v. State, 397 N.E.2d 1071, 1073 (Ind. App. 1979) (quoting 15A C.J.S. Conspiracy § 36 at 729 (1967)).

5. See, e.g., N.Y. Jur. 2d, Crim Law § 3604 nn.86-93.

harm.[6] For example, if the offense of unlawful restraint of trade requires at least two persons to fix prices, Wharton's Rule will bar conspiracy liability where the two offenders are convicted of price fixing. The Wharton's Rule rationale does not apply, however, if the actor is not convicted of the target offense. Thus, if the two only got so far as to agree to fix prices, and are not liable for the completed offense, they *can* be held liable for conspiracy to fix prices. In other words, even jurisdictions that treat conspiracy as an aggravation for group criminality will also use it as an inchoate offense, to punish preliminary conduct toward another, uncompleted offense.

Collateral Effects of Conspiracy Prosecution   A third role of conspiracy is found in certain collateral consequences of charging it. These effects, including unique procedural features of conspiracy prosecutions, typically benefit the state more than the defendant and make charging conspiracy attractive to prosecutors. For example, the Sixth Amendment and many state constitutions require that a defendant be tried in the district where the crime is committed. In conspiracy prosecutions, this is interpreted to allow prosecution in any district where an overt act is performed by any one of the conspirators. Especially in larger conspiracies, this gives the prosecution considerable choice in selecting a district in which to bring the prosecution. Additionally, though hearsay generally is not admissible in a criminal prosecution, an exception is made for statements made by a conspirator during, or in furtherance of, the conspiracy. Such hearsay statements are admissible against all coconspirators. Thus, larger and longer conspiracies allow more statements by co-conspirators to be admissible against the entire group of conspirators.

Joint Trial of Conspiracy Defendants   Another procedural distinction is that, while a defendant generally is entitled to request a trial separate from other offenders, defendants charged in a single conspiracy may be tried together. Such joint trials provide judicial and prosecutorial economy, but they also have the potential to disadvantage defendants in several ways. Defendants may be required to share peremptory challenges of jurors, meaning that each defendant may have fewer to use than if tried alone. Each defendant may find it more difficult to get the jury to focus on the particular facts and circumstances of that defendant's situation. Also of concern is the tendency of juries to apply damaging evidence to all defendants, unless a defendant can affirmatively explain why it is inapplicable to him or her—in short, the danger of guilt by association.

Pinkerton *Doctrine: Conspiracy as Complicity*   One additional collateral effect of conspiracy is the practice in some jurisdictions that allows conspiracy to be treated as a sort of automatic basis of complicity liability. The *Pinkerton* doctrine, as this frequently is called, holds a conspirator liable as an accomplice for any offenses committed by other conspirators in furtherance of the conspiracy.[7] There is no requirement that the other conspirators satisfy the culpability requirements of the offense committed, or even that they be aware of it at all; only the conspirator committing the offense need satisfy the elements of the offense. This potential of the rule to hold an actor liable for crimes of another beyond those

---

6. The Model Penal Code explicitly adopts Wharton's Rule in § 5.04(2), incorporating by reference § 2.06(6)(b), which provides a defense to complicity if the accomplice's conduct "is inevitably incident" to commission of the offense. See Model Penal Code § 5.04(2).

7. See Pinkerton v. United States, 328 U.S. 640 (1946).

agreed to, and beyond the bounds of normal complicity liability, has led to criticism of *Pinkerton*. The federal system continues to follow *Pinkerton*, but modern codes do not. Rather, they allow accomplice liability where an actor "*agrees . . . to aid such other person in planning or committing [an offense],*"[8] and upon proof of the normal culpability requirements of complicity, including "the purpose of promoting or facilitating the commission of the offense [charged]."[9]

OBJECTIVE REQUIREMENTS

Agreement Requirement   Conspiracy typically requires an agreement between two or more people that one, or some, or all of them will commit a crime. The agreement need not involve an overt declaration: Speaking, writing, or nodding can signal agreement, but one also can agree through silence where, under the circumstances or custom, silence is meant to indicate positive agreement. A mutual understanding, even if tacit, shows an agreement. One can become a conspirator by agreeing with a person whom one knows to be a member of a conspiracy with others. There is no special requirement that the actor's conduct corroborate his or her intent, as there is for attempt liability. The agreement to commit an offense is taken as adequate proof of the actor's criminal intention.

Bilateral Agreement   At Common Law, and still in some jurisdictions, the agreement requirement requires actual agreement on both sides, a genuine "meeting of the minds." Thus, for an actor to be liable for conspiracy, *the other conspirator* must actually be agreeing, not just pretending to agree. An actor who "conspires" with an undercover police agent, for example, gets a defense under this so-called *bilateral agreement* requirement, because the officer does not in fact share his intention to commit the offense. Where an actor conspires with another, true conspirator in addition to the undercover agent, however, conspiracy liability does arise, for a real criminal agreement does exist in such a case.

Unilateral Agreement   Modern criminal codes have generally adopted a *unilateral* agreement requirement, which permits conspiracy liability as long as *the actor* agrees with another person—whether or not the other person is actually agreeing back. In such a case, the actor has demonstrated a criminal intention. That the other seeming conspirator in fact is an undercover police officer does not undercut the blameworthiness and dangerousness demonstrated by the actor's intention to have the offense committed.[10]

Agreement Rules and Objectivist vs. Subjectivist Views of Criminality   The difference between a bilateral and a unilateral agreement requirement is consistent with the difference between the objectivist and subjectivist views of criminality. Just as an objectivist view of criminality rejects liability for a legally impossible attempt because the actor never really comes close to committing an offense, so too would such a view reject liability for an apparent agreement that never in fact exists. If there is no real agreement, there is no actual danger that the substantive offense will be committed. Only from a subjectivist view of criminality would

---

8. Model Penal Code § 2.06(3)(a)(ii).

9. Model Penal Code § 2.06(3)(a).

10. See, e.g., People v. Schwimmer, 411 N.Y.S.2d 922 (N.Y. App. 1978), aff'd, 394 N.E.2d 288 (N.Y. 1979) (where defendant conspired with two undercover police officers to steal diamonds owned by City of New York, court ruled legislature had adopted unilateral agreement requirement; therefore, defendant's agreement itself was sufficient).

liability be justified for a unilateral agreement, based on the actor's own *belief* that he is agreeing to the commission of an offense (or that he is engaging in the aggravated harm of group criminality).

Overt Act   Perhaps because conspiracy's agreement requirement is so slim, liability for conspiracy also typically requires an *overt act* by one of the conspirators in furtherance of the agreement.[11] Even this requirement is not very demanding, however: Any overt act by *any* conspirator will suffice to support liability for *all* conspirators (so long as the agreement and culpability requirements are also satisfied for each conspirator). The overt-act requirement furthers many of the purposes for which the criminal law has an act requirement. An overt act helps confirm the actor's intention and the actor's willingness to carry through with his intention (to have the agreement carried out). The Model Penal Code drops the overt-act requirement for conspiracies to commit a first- or second-degree felony, presumably on the theory that agreements to commit such serious offenses carry their own indicia of blameworthiness and dangerousness.[12]

CULPABILITY REQUIREMENTS

The culpability requirements for conspiracy follow a now-familiar pattern. As with attempt, the Common Law viewed conspiracy as a specific-intent offense. Modern criminal codes might be interpreted as following this view, to some extent, in that they require the actor to have "the purpose of promoting or facilitating [the] commission" of the offense.[13] As in the analysis of the attempt requirements, the issue is: What is the meaning, and extent, of this *purpose* requirement?

Common Law Required Purpose as to All Elements   A broad interpretation, adopting the apparent common law position, would take "purpose" to mean that the actor must be purposeful not only as to the conduct—making the agreement and performing the conduct that would constitute the offense—but also as to all circumstance and result elements of the object offense, no matter what culpability normally is required by the substantive offense definition. Under this broad purpose requirement, there can be no liability for conspiracy to commit an offense that requires less than purpose as to a result or circumstance element—no offense of "conspiracy to commit reckless homicide" or "conspiracy to commit statutory rape," for example. (Or, more accurately, such offenses could exist, but they would require proof of purpose as to all elements, so that conspiracy to commit statutory rape would require the conspirators to have purpose as to the age of the victim.) *State v. Beccia* provides an example of this view.[14] In *Beccia*, the owner of the Night Owl Café Club was convicted of conspiracy to commit third-degree arson, which requires recklessly damaging or destroying a building by intentionally starting a fire. Beccia agreed with another that one of them would intentionally start a fire, being aware of a substantial risk that the fire would destroy or damage the building. The court reversed the conviction, holding that, because "conspiracy is a specific intent crime," it must be shown that the conspirators "intended to bring about the elements of the conspired offense. ... Since conspir-

---

11. See, e.g., Model Penal Code § 5.03(5).
12. Model Penal Code § 5.03 comment at 452-455 (1985).
13. Model Penal Code § 5.03(1).
14. 505 A.2d 683 (Conn. 1986).

ators cannot agree to accomplish a result recklessly when that result is an essential element of the crime, they cannot conspire to commit this particular crime."[15]

Modern Codes Continue to Require Purpose as to Result The conspiracy rules of most modern codes retain the purpose requirement for result elements. For example, the Model Penal Code drafters explicitly require purpose as to result elements of the target offense, such as the requirement of damage or destruction in *Beccia*. No matter what culpability as to a result is required to commit the target offense, conspiracy liability requires a purpose to cause the result. (Accordingly, the Code rule, if applied in *Beccia*, would generate the same outcome: no purpose as to result, so no liability.) The drafters explain:

> While this result may seem unduly restrictive from the viewpoint of the completed crime, it is necessitated by the extremely preparatory behavior that may be involved in conspiracy.[16]

The elevation of the culpability requirement to the highest level, purpose, is seen as necessary to counterbalance conspiracy's minimal conduct requirement. The commentary distinguishes conspiracy, where the conduct may be very preliminary, from attempt and from complicity in a completed offense, which require more substantial conduct. As the conduct progresses, the commentary notes, the culpability requirement is elevated less. Complete-conduct attempt liability can be based not only on purpose as to a required result, but also knowledge.[17] Once the offense conduct is complete and the result occurs, there is no elevation of culpability: The elements of the target offense govern.[18]

Required Culpability as to Circumstance Left Unclear While nothing on the face of the Code's conspiracy provision would suggest that its purpose requirement should apply differently to a circumstance element than to a result element, the commentary claims different treatment of the two. Regarding culpability as to a circumstance element, the drafters explain:

> The conspiracy provision in the code does not attempt to solve the problem [of culpability as to a circumstance] by explicit formulation, nor have the recent legislative revisions. Here, as in the section on complicity, it was believed that the matter is best left to judicial resolution as cases that present the question may arise, and that the formulations proposed afford sufficient flexibility for satisfactory decision.[19]

This approach to code drafting seems questionable in terms of the requirements, and the spirit, of the legality principle, as it asks the courts to determine the rules for conspiracy liability *ex post* instead of legislatively defining the offense's elements *ex ante*. It is also unclear how or why a court should be expected to give different treatment to circumstance and result elements if the statute's language gives no hint that such differential treatment is proper. There is no apparent statutory ambiguity that would authorize a court to examine the legislative history or official commentary, thus little opportunity for courts to engage in the kind of

---

15. Id. at 685 (emphasis and internal quotations removed).
16. Model Penal Code § 5.03 comment at 408 (1985).
17. Model Penal Code § 5.01(1)(b).
18. Model Penal Code § 2.06(4).
19. Model Penal Code § 5.03 comment at 413 (1985).

lawmaking that the Model Penal Code drafters contemplate. If a court gives the same treatment to both result and circumstance elements, it can either give a narrow interpretation to the purpose requirement—having it elevate neither result nor circumstance elements—or a broad interpretation—requiring purpose as to both result and circumstance elements. The latter would bar conspiracy liability for any offense where the conspirator is less than purposeful as to all circumstance elements, such as the elements of consent or age in sexual offenses.

State v. Hardison
New Jersey Supreme Court
99 N.J. 379, 492 A.2d 1009 (1985)

The opinion of the Court was delivered by O'HERN, J.

This appeal concerns the circumstances under which a conviction for a criminal conspiracy and a completed offense that was an object of the conspiracy will merge. Specifically, the appeal concerns *N.J.S.A.* 2C:1-8a(2), which provides that a defendant may not be convicted of more than one offense if "one offense consists only of a conspiracy or other form of preparation to commit the other." We hold that if the conspiracy proven has criminal objectives other than the substantive offense proven, the offenses will not merge. In this case the conviction does not establish that the conspiracy embraced criminal objectives in addition to the offense proven. Hence, we affirm the judgment below that merged the conviction of conspiracy with the completed offense.

I

[The case arises from two incidents, commencing on the evening of November 19, 1980. At approximately 11:30 p.m., four men entered the Lincoln Café in New Brunswick. After about twenty minutes, when the crowd had thinned out, one of the defendants pulled out a gun, pointed the gun at the bartender and forced him to lie face down behind the bar. Two of the men herded the two remaining patrons, a man and a woman, into the bathroom. The four cleaned out the cash register and took the bartender's watch and the woman's purse. All three victims were then locked in the men's room with a cigarette machine in front of the door. The four fled in a red and white Cadillac.

Soon afterwards, Hardison and Jackson entered the Edison Motor Lodge and asked the night manager about the price of a room. They went out, came back in with a gun, and robbed him at gunpoint of the motel's property. One of the defendants threatened to kill him; the other brutally assaulted him with brass knuckles, shattering his teeth. Having been told of both robberies and a description of the car involved in the first robbery, police began to follow the defendant's car. The car fled at high speed. The chase ended when the car ran into a cement divider.]

The four were charged with conspiracy to commit robbery, four counts of robbery of the three people in the tavern and the night manager at the motel, possession of a gun for an unlawful purpose, aggravated assault of the night manager; and Hardison was charged with possession of brass knuckles for an unlawful purpose. The trial of two co-defendants was severed. Hardison and Jackson went to trial together.

The jury acquitted these two defendants of the robbery of the Lincoln Café, but convicted them on all other charges. Each was sentenced to an aggregate term of twenty years with five years of parole ineligibility. Separate and consecutive sentences were imposed on the conspiracy and robbery counts. On appeal, the Appellate Division, in two separate opinions, affirmed on all issues but merger, concluding that because the illegal agreement included robbery and the jury found defendants guilty of the motel robbery within the ambit of the conspiracy, the convictions for both the conspiracy and the robbery were barred. It also ruled that the convictions of unlawful possession of a handgun and robbery should be merged. Both the State and the defendants petitioned for review. We granted the State's petition for certification, limited solely to the issue of whether the conviction for conspiracy to commit robbery should have merged with that of armed robbery. The defendants' cross-petitions were denied, We now affirm.

II

The law of conspiracy serves two independent values. First is the protection of society from the danger of concerted criminal activity. The second aspect is that conspiracy is an inchoate crime. "This is to say, that, although the law generally makes criminal only antisocial conduct, at some point in the continuum between preparation and consummation, the likelihood of a commission of an act is sufficiently great and the criminal intent sufficiently well formed to justify the intervention of the criminal law." *United States v. Feola*, 420 *U.S.* 671, 694 (1975) (citing Note, "Developments in the Law-Criminal Conspiracy," 72 *Harv. L. Rev.* 920, 923-925 (1959)). Thus, the law of conspiracy identifies the agreement to engage in a criminal venture as an event of sufficient threat to social order, therefore permitting the imposition of criminal sanctions for the agreement alone, regardless of whether the crime agreed upon actually is committed.

In New Jersey, as elsewhere, prior to the adoption of the 1979 Code of Criminal Justice, *N.J.S.A.* 2C:1-1 to 2C:98-4 (the Code), the law traditionally considered conspiracy and the completed substantive offense to be separate crimes. Accordingly, the conspiracy to commit an offense and the subsequent commission of that crime normally did not merge.

The reason for the rule was the common law's deep distrust for criminal combinations. The group activity was seen as posing a "greater potential threat" to the public than individual crime.

For two or more to confederate and combine together to commit or cause to be committed a breach of the criminal laws is an offense of the gravest character, sometimes quite outweighing, in injury to the public, the mere commission of the contemplated crime.

Deeply rooted in the fear of criminal political conspiracy, the substantive crime of conspiracy became superimposed on offenses having no such political motivation. The crime took on a life of its own. At common law, and under some statutes, the combination could be a criminal conspiracy even if it contemplated only acts that were not crimes at all when perpetrated by an individual, or by many acting severally, or could result in a conspirator being found guilty not only of the conspiracy but of a completed offense even when the accused did not participate in the substantive offense.

In addition to its substantive overlay, the crime had distinct procedural advantages including the ability to use the statements of a co-conspirator made during and in furtherance of a conspiracy, the ability to try co-conspirators jointly, flexibility in the selection and place of trial, and finally, the ability to establish the existence of such an agreement through circumstantial evidence.

In this setting, there was perceived a danger of punishment for mere criminal intent with juries unable to separate individual guilt from guilt by association. The drafters of the American Law Institute's 1962 Model Penal Code undertook the "difficult task of achieving an appropriate balance between the desire to afford adequate opportunity for early law enforcement efforts and the obligation to safeguard" individual rights.

The drafters of the New Jersey Criminal Code substantially adopted the approach of the Model Penal Code. They undertook, in the words of the drafters, to "meet or mitigate these objections and...then go on to develop a basic framework for the development of a law of conspiracy." II *New Jersey Criminal Law Revision Commission: Commentary* p. 126 (1971) (hereinafter cited as *Code Commentary*). Our Code recognizes the dual conception of the offense (1) to reach further back into preparatory criminal conduct than attempt, and nip the crime before its inception, and (2) to provide additional means of facilitating prosecutions, striking against the special dangers of group criminal activity. It balances it with fairness thus:

> The [Code] embraces this conception in some part but rejects it in another. When a conspiracy is declared criminal because its object is a crime, we think it is entirely meaningless to say that the preliminary combination is more dangerous than the forbidden consummation; the measure of its danger is the risk of such a culmination. On the other hand, the combination may and often does have criminal objectives that transcend any particular offenses that have been committed in pursuance of its goals.

The Code's resolution then is to permit cumulative sentences when the combination has criminal objectives beyond any particular offense committed in pursuance of its goals. Unlike the common-law distinction between the grades of an offense that treats a conspiracy as a misdemeanor and the substantive crime as a felony, the Code grades the conspiracy by the nature of the offense contemplated. *See N.J.S.A.* 2C:5-4. Thus, a conspiracy to commit robbery would be graded, for purposes of punishment, as a robbery, and would carry the same sentence as provided in *N.J.S.A.* 2C:15-1b. Since, under the Code, the conspiracy is punished in the same degree as the substantive offense, when the preliminary agreement does not go beyond the consummation, double conviction and sentence is barred by *N.J.S.A.* 2C:1-8a(2).

The Code takes the view that in this sense conspiracy is similar to attempt, which is a lesser-included offense of the completed offense. A conviction of the completed offense will adequately deal with the conduct. The Code's drafters were equally explicit that "[t]his is not true, however, where the conspiracy has as its objective engaging in a course of criminal conduct since that involves a distinct danger in addition to that involved in the actual commission of any specific offense." *Code Commentary* at 18-19. The Code recognizes the grave dangers that organized criminal activity poses to society. *See N.J.S.A.* 2C:5-2g (conspiracy conviction of leader of organized criminal activity does not merge with crime constituting racketeering activity under *N.J.S.A.* 2C:41-1). Therefore, the limitation of the Code is confined to the situation in which the completed offense was the sole criminal objective of the conspiracy. "There may be conviction of both a conspiracy and a completed offense committed pursuant to that conspiracy if the prosecution shows that the objective of the conspiracy was the commission of additional offenses." *Code Commentary* at 19.

III

Turning to the record before us, we must determine whether the judgment of conviction establishes that the conspiracy had additional criminal objectives other than the completed offense. For purposes of analysis, we shall view the indictment as charging two robberies—one at the Lincoln Café and another at the Edison Motor Lodge—and a conspiracy. The jury acquitted the defendants of the incident at the Lincoln Café, but convicted them of robbery and assault at the Motor Lodge and of conspiracy. The question comes down to this: Does the jury verdict establish that Hardison and Jackson conspired to commit the Lincoln Café Robbery?

[The court reviews the jury instructions and the special jury verdicts.]

The trial court, in denying [Jackson's motion to set aside the verdict of conspiracy for insufficient evidence], concluded that it was satisfied "the facts are such that a reasonable jury on a case could have found and as in fact I find they did here, determine at the very least that there was a conspiracy as to the Edison robbery." The same logic would appear to apply to Hardison.

Based upon this record, we cannot conclude that the judgments establish that the preparatory conduct proven had other or further criminal objectives than the completed robbery. Hence, the Appellate Division correctly ordered that the convictions should be merged....

[S]ince we are satisfied that the conviction did not establish such multiple purposes, the judgment of the Appellate Division is affirmed.

▲ PROBLEMS

Arranging a Birthday Party Fight, or a Killing? (#57)

Bennie Bridges and Andy Strickland are among the 50 or so guests attending a mutual friend's sixteenth birthday party. While in the basement of their friend's house, Bridges and Strickland get into an argument, which ends when a heated Bridges storms out of the party, yelling about his imminent return with his "boys." Good to his word, Bridges goes off to recruit his friends Bing and Rolle to return to the party with him and confront Strickland. On their way to the party, the trio stops at Bing's house to pick up guns. Bridges wants to fight Strickland alone and figures that with the guns, Bing and Rolle can keep Strickland's friends from joining the fight.

When they return to the party, Bridges and Strickland resume their argument, with Bridges yelling that he wants to fight someone. One of Strickland's friends steps up to fight, and he and Bridges go outside to brawl. Bing and Rolle stand by with their guns concealed as a crowd gathers to watch the fight. As the fight escalates, Bridges is hit in the face by someone in the crowd. Immediately, Bing and Rolle draw their guns, firing several shots into the air, and then several more shots into the crowd. While not aiming at anyone in particular, they hit two people, one of whom dies. Realizing they have just killed someone, Bing and Rolle flee with Bridges, but all three are apprehended.

What homicide liability, if any, for Bing and Rolle under the Model Penal Code? Is Bridges liable for conspiracy to commit murder under the Model Penal Code? For what other offenses, if any, might Bridges be liable under the Code? Prepare a list of all criminal code subsections in the order in which you rely on them in your analysis.

Is Bridges liable for conspiracy to commit homicide at common law?

Truck Driver or Drug Smuggler? (#58)

The DEA is cracking down on marijuana smugglers by using undercover agents to break up drug rings. Agent Martinez has just become aware of a drug import plan involving 110,000 pounds of marijuana. Posing as a member of the team, Martinez is able to gather information on the smugglers and their plan to fly the drugs into Miami. The agent accompanies one of the conspirators to the airport, hoping to meet the mastermind behind the operation, Genaro Cruz, and arrest him.

Cruz, who owns the farm where the marijuana was grown, spent the previous night at his friend Manuel Alvarez's house. In the morning, Alvarez drives Cruz to the airport to meet with Martinez and others to finalize their smuggling plans. When they meet Martinez, Cruz tells him that Alvarez will be at the offloading location with his truck to help transport the drugs. While Alvarez knows of the illegal operation, his role is only to provide labor and the truck. He does not take part in the planning or details of transporting the drugs. Martinez, to confirm the extent of Alvarez's involvement in the scheme, strikes up a conversation with him about the plan. Alvarez smiles and talks in a way that makes clear that he knows what the cargo is. Martinez then springs the DEA sting, arresting Alvarez as well as Cruz.

Assume that Alvarez is prosecuted in a state that follows the Model Penal Code that has an offense making it illegal to "purposefully bring into the state what one knows may be a controlled substance." Would Alvarez be liable under the Code for conspiracy to commit this offense? Prepare a list of all criminal code subsections in the order in which you rely on them in your analysis.

Call-Girl Phone Service (#59)

Louis Lauria's telephone answering service is very popular with a group of local professionals. Sex workers use his phone service to set up meetings with their clients. Lauria knows that some of his clients are engaged in an illegal trade and keeps a record of those clients he knows to be sex workers. However, unless the police ask him about any specific name, Lauria never reports any of his clients to the authorities or turns over any records. Indeed, Lauria doesn't pay much attention to the police until his company comes under investigation.

Stella Weeks, an undercover officer, approaches Lauria about opening up an account with his answering service. She states clearly that she needs the service to make money from "tricks." Lauria tells Weeks that his business is "taking messages," but also makes clear that as long as her bill is paid, he doesn't mind that her profession is illegal. After opening the account, she tells Lauria repeatedly that she has missed calls from his service, resulting in lost customers. Lauria assures her that he will improve the system and talks to his employees about her situation. Soon thereafter, three of the sex workers using Lauria's service are arrested, as is Lauria.

Under the Model Penal Code, is Lauria liable for conspiracy to commit prostitution? Prepare a list of all criminal code subsections in the order in which you rely on them in your analysis.

No Risk, No Foul?—Revisited (#49)

Reconsider the facts of Problem Case "No Risk, No Foul?" (#49) in Section 10.

Recall that, assuming the Scatenas were caught just before they dump the chemicals, in fact no risk has yet been created, hence they have not committed the substantive offense of risking catastrophe. Can the Scatenas be held liable for conspiracy to risk catastrophe under the Model Penal Code? Prepare a list of all criminal code subsections in the order in which you rely on them in your analysis.

✳ DISCUSSION ISSUE

In Addition to Using Conspiracy as an Inchoate Offense, Should the Law Also Recognize It as a Substantive Offense in Order to Aggravate Punishment for Group Criminality?

Materials presenting each side of this Discussion Issue appear in the Advanced Materials for Section 12 in Appendix A.

V

DOCTRINES OF IMPUTATION

Part II of this coursebook described how offenses are defined. Typically, an actor is liable for an offense if and only if she satisfies the elements of an offense definition. There exist two kinds of exceptions to this paradigm of equivalency between satisfying an offense definition and exposure to criminal liability. An actor may be *liable* for an offense even though she does not satisfy all offense elements if a rule or doctrine *imputes* the missing element. A second, and reverse, exception is found in general defenses, in which an actor *escapes liability* even though she *does* satisfy the elements of an offense, if she satisfies the conditions of a *general defense*. General defenses are the subject of Part VI. This Part examines doctrines of imputation—voluntary intoxication, complicity, and omission liability.

Notes on Imputation Generally

Criticisms of Imputation
Imputation as a Common and Accepted Basis of Liability
Imputation Rules Could Be Written into Offenses
Criminalization via Imputation as Legislative Prerogative
Imputation Rules Merit Scrutiny
Doctrines Imputing Culpability Elements
Doctrines Imputing Objective Elements
Doctrines Imputing Both Objective and Culpability Elements

Criticisms of Imputation Some writers have suggested that it is illogical and immoral to impose criminal liability if all elements of the offense are not satisfied. In *Director of Public Prosecutions v. Majewski*,[1] for example, the defendant argued against imputation of culpability based on his intoxication, relying on a passage from Lord Hailsham in *Director of Prosecutions v. Morgan*:

---

1. [1976] 2 All E.R. 142.

[O]nce it be accepted that an intent of whatever description is an ingredient essential to the guilt of the accused I cannot myself see that any other direction [than requiring proof of the intent] can be logically acceptable. Otherwise a jury would in effect be told to find an intent where none existed or where none was proved to have existed. I cannot myself reconcile it with my conscience to sanction as part of the English law what I regard as logical impossibility, and, if there were any authority which, if accepted, would compel me to do so, I would feel constrained to declare that it was not to be followed.[2]

Imputation as Common and Accepted Basis of Liability   However, just as the law commonly recognizes many general defenses, which exculpate an actor even though he satisfies the elements of an offense, so too are many doctrines of imputation common and well established. For example, if an actor helps or causes another person to commit a crime, the actor may be liable for that crime even though he did not perform the criminal conduct himself. The conduct of the other person is imputed to him under rules governing complicity or causing crime by an innocent. Similarly, the law commonly imputes a requisite culpable state of mind to an actor if she would have had the culpable state of mind but for her voluntary intoxication. Under each of these doctrines, there is no suggestion that the actor in fact satisfies the required offense element. Rather, the special conditions required by the doctrine of imputation are said to justify treating the actor *as if* he satisfies the imputed element.

Imputation Rules Could Be Written into Offenses   A legislature conceivably could include inculpatory (and exculpatory) exceptions to the offense paradigm within the offense definition. For example, Tennessee defines the offense of arson to include not only setting the fire, but also assisting another in doing so.[3] More typically, however, doctrines of imputation like complicity are drafted in a form independent of offense definitions, a form that applies to all offenses. This approach offers drafting efficiency as well as conceptual clarity and consistent application. Like the general defenses, which are separate and apart from any offense definition, the rules of imputation represent principles of liability independent of any single offense. Also like general defenses, most of the doctrines of imputation, at least theoretically, can be applied to any offense. Some doctrines of imputation may tend to apply most frequently to certain recurring situations—for example, the "transferred intent" rule applies most commonly in bad-aim murder cases—but this is a factual happenstance rather than a theoretical limitation of the principle.

Criminalization via Imputation as Legislative Prerogative   Imputation may well be questionable in some or even many cases. Yet criticism and skepticism should be directed not at the general mechanism of imputation, as in the *Majewski* opinion, but rather at specific imputation rules or applications of those rules. It is clearly within the legislature's authority to alter or expand the scope of criminal offenses, so even if imputation rules did not exist, the legislature could always achieve the same result by redefining offenses (along the lines of the Tennessee arson offense, for example). The legislative decision to define the scope of criminal

---

2. Morgan, [1975] 2 All E.R. 347 at 360, quoted in Majewski, [1976] 2 All E.R. at 166.

3. "Any person who willfully and maliciously sets fire to or burns, causes to be burned, *or who aids, counsels or procures* the burning of any house . . . shall be guilty of arson . . . . " Tenn. Code Ann. § 39-3-202 (emphasis added).

liability by adopting a general imputation rule, rather than by directly revising the elements of one or more offenses, is more a matter of form than substance—at least, so long as the imputation rule imposes the same evidentiary and other procedural burdens on the prosecution that an offense element would.

Imputation Rules Merit Scrutiny Of course, as with offenses themselves, one might accept that the legislature has authority but still question whether the legislature has exercised its authority well. For some imputation rules, the special conditions required for imputation may be a poor substitute for the usual offense requirements; that is, satisfying the imputation rule might not seem to be truly equivalent to satisfying the missing offense element itself. Defenses—which are also exceptions to the offense paradigm, but have the reverse effect of imputation, in that they benefit the defendant—typically are supported by articulable, rational explanations. Can one articulate sound theoretical and practical reasons to support each inculpating exception of imputation? Many of the imputation rules discussed in this Part have a sound justification. For some, however, the rationale for the imputation seems weak or unpersuasive. The crucial issue in each instance is this: Do the special conditions of the doctrine justify treating the actor as if he or she satisfies the missing offense element?

Doctrines Imputing Culpability Elements American criminal law permits the imputation of both objective and culpability elements of an offense. As to culpability, the law often must adopt rules allowing one form of culpability to substitute for another. The doctrine of "transferred intent" imputes the required culpability to an actor who intends to harm one person but who actually harms another. In such a case, the culpability that the actor possesses—intent to cause a death—equivalent to the culpability the offense requires, so imputation seems quite intuitive. In other cases, however, the actor commits one offense while having culpability as to an entirely different offense. In such situations imputation may be accomplished through "substituted culpability." The actor's culpability for the offense she *thought* she was committing becomes the basis for imputing the culpability required for the offense actually committed. Thus, the actor who commits statutory rape but who, because of his mistake as to the true identity of his partner, believes he is instead committing incest, can nonetheless be held liable for statutory rape: Culpability he lacks (as to his partner being underage) is imputed to him by substituting or "transferring" the culpability he does have (as to committing incest). Perhaps the most common rules imputing culpability relate to voluntary intoxication. In such cases, the intoxicated actor—because of the intoxication itself—may not have the required culpability at the moment he acts. Even so, the law may treat the actor as if he was reckless as to the risk he was in fact creating via his conduct if he would have been aware of the risk had he been sober. Another doctrine of imputation is apparent in those cases where courts permit suspension of the requirement of concurrence between act and intent: An actor's earlier intention to commit an act that the actor believes is the offense, but is not, is relied upon to impute the required intention during the later conduct that actually constitutes the offense. Finally, a variety of statutory and judicial presumptions effectively impute culpability elements, upon proof of a logically related fact.

Doctrines Imputing Objective Elements The most obvious and common instances of imputing objective elements are found in the rules governing complicity.[4] But complicity is only one of several doctrines that impose liability even though the defendant does not satisfy the objective elements of an offense. Where an actor exercises control over an innocent or irresponsible person, the latter's satisfaction of the objective elements of an offense may be imputed to the former as an instance of causing an innocent's crime. Similarly, various statutory and judicial presumptions permit the imposition of liability even though the evidence adduced at trial would not establish the objective elements of the offense. On occasion, the doctrines of "substituted objective elements" and "transferred *actus reus*" are used to impute a missing objective element and thereby hold an actor liable for the offense the actor intended to commit but, because of mistake, did not commit. Under this doctrine, for example, using the hypothetical above, the actor who commits statutory rape, but believes he is instead committing incest, would be held liable for incest—that is, the offense he thought he was committing—and the missing objective elements would be imputed to him. (Modern codes more frequently adopt the "substituted culpability" doctrine noted above, which imputes missing culpability requirements rather than missing conduct, so that the actor would be held liable for statutory rape, not incest.) Finally, the rules imposing liability for an actor's omissions, even when the offense charged is defined only in terms of affirmative conduct, also may be viewed as instances of imputed conduct.

Doctrines Imputing Both Objective and Culpability Elements   Other rules impute both objective and culpability elements. If, for example, A and B conspire to rob a bank together and B purposely kills a guard, both the killing and the purposeful culpability as to killing may be imputed to A under the federal *Pinkerton* doctrine for co-conspirators. The "natural and probable consequence" rule, part of the common law's complicity doctrine and still codified in several jurisdictions,[5] analogously expands the liability of accomplices. Under this rule, "an accessory is liable for any criminal act which in the ordinary course of things was the natural or probable consequence of the crime that he advised or commanded, although such consequence may not have been intended by him."[6] Even without statutory authority, courts have employed the natural and probable consequence rule to impute both mental and objective elements. The Model Penal Code's complicity provision and those patterned after it, however, reject the natural and probable consequence rule, and impose liability for a confederate's offense only when the normal complicity requirements are met.[7] Similarly, the complicity aspect of the felony-murder rule imputes both objective and culpability elements to the accomplice. Finally, vicarious liability, and its special subclass governing the liability of officials of organizations, can impute offense elements to an actor because of his relationship to another. This, however, is not an exhaustive list of the criminal law's instances of imputation; a few others are discussed in the following subsection regarding doctrines of "codified imputation."

---

4. See, e.g., Model Penal Code § 2.06(3).
5. See Wis. Stat. Ann. § 939.05(2)(c).
6. 22 C.J.S. Criminal Law § 92.
7. See Model Penal Code § 2.06(3).

Voluntary Intoxication

The effects of drugs or alcohol can block formation of a culpable mental state required by an offense definition, such as the awareness of risk required for recklessness. While this effect might normally bar criminal liability for an offense, the law takes account of an offender's role in voluntarily bringing about the effect by imputing a culpable mental state to the offender, usually recklessness, if the offender would have been aware of the risk had she been sober. Do the special conditions that trigger imputation under the voluntary intoxication rules justify the culpability imputed?

◆ THE CASE OF JORDAN WEAVER (#60)

It is late in the afternoon in Indianapolis on April 2, 1991, when Jordan Weaver takes two "triple-dipped" paper blotter "hits" of a particularly potent batch of lysergic acid diethylamide (LSD or "acid"). Toxicologists report that LSD can produce extremely disorienting effects. A "bad trip," or acute psychotic reaction to the drug, may cause irrational random violence and paranoia. During this "trip," Weaver will later report effects far beyond anything that he has previously experienced.

Later in the day, Weaver's girlfriend of 15 months, seventeen-year-old Wendy Waldman, picks him up to go out to eat. The two have planned a "special night" together at Renee's Restaurant because Wendy is leaving for a spring break trip to Florida.

Their relationship has been a stormy one, a type of "fatal attraction" affair. Friends and family question why the two stay together given that they have such dissimilar interests. Wendy's parents have tried to forbid her from seeing Jordan, but she continues to be drawn to his "exciting" personality. She is a serious student, deeply involved with her family, and "morally" disapproves of drug use and excessive drinking. In stark contrast, Weaver dropped out of high school during his junior year and is the product of a broken home. After they divorced, his parents both moved to Texas, in August 1990, so Weaver now lives with his twenty-year-old sister, her husband, and their two young children. He has a long history of substance abuse, he was first drunk at age 12, started smoking marijuana at 13, began taking hits of LSD at 15, and has experimented with a number of other drugs, including peyote, opium, and cocaine, as well as "huffing" gasoline. In the last two years, he has "dropped acid" at least 15 times.

Chill bro

Before leaving for the restaurant, Weaver tells Wendy that he is tripping hard and is unsure about going out because he usually tries to "keep the trip under control" by remaining in a secluded space with close friends. However, when Wendy insists on going out, Weaver relents and accompanies her. Wendy later says that Weaver was "not acting like himself." At the restaurant, Weaver seems only loosely connected to the reality around him. He cannot read the menu. Weaver ends up handing the waitress some money before they have ordered anything and gets up to leave. Wendy makes up a story to explain the strange behavior. Outside, Weaver begins to say bizarre things—asking Wendy if he is dead and telling her he is Jesus Christ.

no duh

They end up going back to his sister's apartment. There he sees the walls breathing and closing in on him, objects floating in midair, and "tracers" of light following behind moving objects. He is also shocked to see his sister's face melting. Wendy arranges to meet some friends—Kris Hettle, Tracie Glanzman, Jessica Godley, and Kurt Steigerwald—at Broad Ripple Park. At the park, Weaver's behavior becomes even more erratic; he now seems entirely in another world. He becomes fearful because his whole body has gone numb. He claims that "a slimy mold is crawling around" in his brain and that something is eating

Figure 54 **Jordan Weaver**
(Richard Miller, Indianapolis Star)

through his stomach. The group decides to take him to the deserted Alverna Retreat Center, a former Franciscan monastery, located on Indianapolis' quiet north side. Kurt later observes that "It didn't seem to me like he had any idea of what was going on."

At the Center, Weaver becomes increasingly agitated. He won't sit down on a blanket on the ground. Weaver begins biting Wendy's hand and fingers, although it is not clear what it is that he thinks he is doing. Wendy tries to calm Weaver by offering to have sex with him, but he instead begins wrestling with Kurt and licking his neck. Kris intervenes but the episode escalates into violence as Weaver frantically escapes, hitting Kurt in the eye in the process. Weaver is now completely out of control and spasms into constant, random violence. He then gets into Kurt's car and seizes Jessica by the throat. When she resists, Weaver begins strangling and shouting at her. Kurt and Kris grab a tire iron from the trunk and hit Weaver twice, but the blows have no effect. They then throw a blanket over him and choke him, eventually getting him off Jessica. They try to put him in the car trunk but are unsuccessful. They briefly consider running him down with the car.

EVERYBODY needs Jesus

Weaver begins to attack Wendy, lifting her up and hurling her headfirst into the pavement. While she is lying on the ground, he begins slamming her head and face into the concrete. He then pulls her head up by the hair and repeatedly punches her face, then kicks her limp body. At the end of the beating, Wendy's face is a "bloody pulp," with no distinguishable features—her nose is smashed in, her jaw is shattered, her ears are "inside her head," she is missing five teeth, her chin is partially torn off, her eyes are swollen shut, many of her facial bones are broken, and her brain is bruised. The state trooper who finds her will have to clear teeth and blood from her throat so she can breathe.

The others have vainly been trying to distract Weaver, who seems impervious to all assaults: Indeed, he is oblivious to them. They finally drive away to get help. When they leave, Wendy is comatose, lying facedown in a pool of blood.

At some point, Weaver gets into Wendy's car, which he perceives to be a spaceship, and drives off. However, in his impaired state, he quickly hits a tree and rolls the car over on its side. He thinks that with the crash of his spaceship he is out of air. Rather than using a door, he breaks through the car's "force

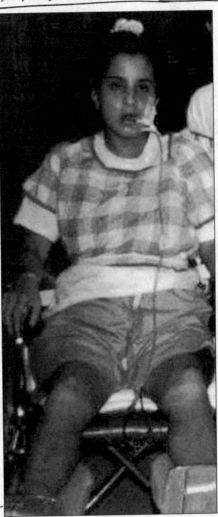

Figure 55 **Wendy Waldman three weeks after beating**
(Marion County Superior Court)

Figure 56 **Wendy Waldman's car after Weaver's wreck**
(Marion County Superior Court Records)

Figure 57 **Michael Blickman after his altercation with Weaver**

(Marion County Superior Court Records)

field"—the windshield—to escape, and begins wandering into Indianapolis's Far Northside neighborhood, perhaps the quietest in the city. In the 8100 block of Round Hill Court, for reasons connected only to Weaver's own realty, he crashes through the kitchen bay window of Barbara and Michael Blickman. *holla*

Michael, an attorney, races into the kitchen upon hearing the glass shatter and confronts Weaver, freshly bloodied by the glass. Fearing for his family's safety, Blickman smashes Weaver with a chair and then tries to wrestle him out of the house. During the scuffle, which lasts several minutes, Weaver is thrusting his hand into Blickman's mouth. Blickman bites it, drawing blood. His wife, who has been screaming throughout the melee, beats Weaver with the leg of a broken chair. Mrs. Blickman later comments that Weaver had a "crazy look in his eye."

A neighbor calls the sheriff's department. Shortly after, Blickman and others finally manage to drag Weaver into the driveway where five deputies are able subdue him. As he struggles with the officers, Weaver screams.

1. Relying only on your own intuitions of justice, what liability and punishment, if any, does Jordan Weaver deserve for his assault on Wendy?

2. What "justice" arguments could defense counsel make on the defendant's behalf?

N	0	1	2	3	4	5	6	7	8	9	10	11
☐	☐	☐	☐	☐	☐	☐	☐	☐	☐	☐	☒	☐
no liability	liability but no punishment	1 day	2 wks	2 mo	6 mo	1 yr	3 yrs	7 yrs	15 yrs	30 yrs	life imprison-ment	death

3. What "justice" arguments could the prosecution make against the defendant?

4. What liability, if any, for Weaver under the then-existing statutes? Prepare a list of all criminal code subsections and cases in the order in which you rely upon them in your analysis.

5. What liability, if any, under the Model Penal Code? Prepare a list of all criminal code subsections in the order in which you rely upon them in your analysis.

■ THE LAW

West's Annotated Indiana Codes
(1991)

Title 35. Criminal Law and Procedure

Article 42. Offenses Against the Person
Chapter 1. Homicide

Section 35-42-1-1. Murder

A person who:

(1) knowingly or intentionally kills another human being; [or]

(2) kills another human being while committing or attempting to commit arson, burglary, child molesting, consumer product tampering, criminal deviate conduct, kidnaping, rape, robbery; . . .
commits murder, a felony.

Section 35-42-1-5. Reckless Homicide

A person who recklessly kills another human being commits reckless homicide, a Class C felony.

Section 35-42-1-4. Involuntary Manslaughter

A person who kills another human being while committing or attempting to commit:

(1) a Class C or Class D felony that inherently poses a risk of serious bodily injury

(2) a Class A misdemeanor that inherently poses a risk of serious bodily injury; or

(3) battery;
commits involuntary manslaughter, a Class C felony. However, if the killing results from the operation of a vehicle, the offense is a Class D felony.

Chapter 2. Battery and Related Offenses

Section 35-42-2-1.   Battery

(a) A person who knowingly or intentionally touches another person in a rude, insolent, or angry manner commits battery, a Class B misdemeanor. However, the offense is:

(1) a Class A misdemeanor if it results in bodily injury to any other person, or if it is committed against a law enforcement officer or against a person summoned and directed by the officer while the officer is engaged in the execution of his official duty;

(2) a Class D felony if it results in bodily injury to:

(A) a law enforcement officer or a person summoned and directed by a law enforcement officer while the officer is engaged in the execution of his official duty;

(B) a person less than thirteen (13) years of age and is committed by a person at least eighteen (18) years of age;

(C) a person of any age who is mentally or physically disabled and is committed by a person having the care of the mentally or physically disabled person, whether the care is assumed voluntarily or because of a legal obligation;

(D) the other person and the person who commits the battery was previously convicted of a battery in which the victim was the other person;

(E) an endangered adult (as defined by IC 35-46-1-1); or

(F) an employee of the department of correction while the employee is engaged in the execution of the employee's official duty; and

(3) a Class C felony if it results in serious bodily injury to any other person or if it is committed by means of a deadly weapon.

Section 35-42-2-2. Criminal Recklessness; . . .

(a) A person who recklessly, knowingly, or intentionally performs an act that creates a substantial risk of bodily injury to another person commits criminal recklessness, a Class B misdemeanor.

However, the offense is a:

(1) Class A misdemeanor if the conduct includes the use of a vehicle; or

(2) Class D felony if it is committed while armed with a deadly weapon.

(b) A person who recklessly, knowingly, or intentionally inflicts serious bodily injury on another person; or commits criminal recklessness, a Class D felony. However, the offense is a Class C felony if committed by means of a deadly weapon.

Article 41. General Substantive Provisions
Chapter 1. Jurisdiction; Definitions

Section 35-41-1-4. "Bodily Injury" Defined

"Bodily injury" means any impairment of physical condition, including physical pain.

Section 35-41-2-2. Culpability

(a) A person engages in conduct "intentionally" if, when he engages in the conduct, it is his conscious objective to do so.

(b) A person engages in conduct "knowingly" if, when he engages in the conduct, he is aware of a high probability that he is doing so.

(c) A person engages in conduct "recklessly" if he engages in the conduct in plain, conscious, and unjustifiable disregard of harm that might result and the disregard involves a substantial deviation from acceptable standards of conduct.

(d) Unless the statute defining the offense provides otherwise, if a kind of culpability is required for commission of an offense, it is required with respect to every material element of the prohibited conduct.

Chapter 3. Defenses Relating to Culpability

Section 35-41-3-5. Intoxication

(a) It is a defense that the person who engaged in the prohibited conduct did so while he was intoxicated, if the intoxication resulted from the introduction of a substance into his body:
    (1) without his consent; or
    (2) when he did not know that the substance might cause intoxication.

(b) Voluntary intoxication is a defense only to the extent that it negates an element of an offense referred to by the phrase "with intent to" or "with an intention to."

Chapter 5. Offenses of General Applicability

Section 35-41-5-1. Attempt

(a) A person attempts to commit a crime when, acting with the culpability required for commission of the crime, he engages in conduct that constitutes a substantial step toward commission of the crime. An attempt to commit a crime is a felony or misdemeanor of the same class as the crime attempted. However, an attempt to commit murder is a Class A felony.

(b) It is no defense that, because of a misapprehension of the circumstances, it would have been impossible for the accused person to commit the crime attempted.

Rhodes v. State
181 Ind. App. 265, 391 N.E.2d 666 (Ind. Ct. App. 1979)

Indiana's attempt law, based on §35-41-5-1, does not permit an offense of "attempted reckless homicide." Citing Model Penal Code commentary, the Court ruled that, despite the attempt statute's language that only "the culpability required for the commission of the offense" is required, a "specific intent" must be proven, since the very definition of attempt is "to try."

Terry v. State of Indiana
465 N.E.2d 1085 (Ind. 1984)

Section 35-41-3-5(b) violates the state constitution and is therefore invalid, since "the attempt by the legislature to remove [voluntary intoxication as a defense] goes against [the] firmly ingrained principle [that] intoxication may be offered to negate capacity to formulate intent. . . . Any factor which serves as a denial of the existence of mens rea must be considered by a trier of fact before a guilty finding is entered." But the Court goes on to uphold the conviction, holding: "The potential of this defense should not be confused with the reality of the situation. It is difficult to envision a finding of not guilty by reason of intoxication when the acts committed require a significant degree of physical or intellectual skills. As a general proposition, a defendant should not be relieved of responsibility when he was able to devise a plan, operate equipment, instruct the behavior of others or carry out acts requiring physical skill."

Model Penal Code
(Official Draft 1962)

Section 2.08. Intoxication

(1) Except as provided in Subsection (4) of this Section, intoxication of the actor is not a defense unless it negatives an element of the offense.

(2) When recklessness establishes an element of the offense, if the actor, due to self-induced intoxication, is unaware of a risk of which he would have been aware had he been sober, such unawareness is immaterial.

(3) Intoxication does not, in itself, constitute mental disease within the meaning of Section 4.01.

(4) Intoxication which (a) is not self-induced or (b) is pathological is an affirmative defense if by reason of such intoxication the actor at the time of his conduct lacks substantial capacity either to appreciate its criminality [wrongfulness] or to conform his conduct to the requirements of law.

(5) Definitions. In this Section unless a different meaning plainly is required:

(a) "intoxication" means a disturbance of mental or physical capacities resulting from the introduction of substances into the body;

(b) "self-induced intoxication" means intoxication caused by substances which the actor knowingly introduces into his body, the tendency of which to cause intoxication he knows or ought to know, unless he introduces them pursuant to medical advice or under such circumstances as would afford a defense to a charge of crime;

(c) "pathological intoxication" means intoxication grossly excessive in degree, given the amount of the intoxicant, to which the actor does not know he is susceptible.

● OVERVIEW OF VOLUNTARY INTOXICATION

Hypothetical: Food for Thought (#61)

Sharon and Buff have become very close as they have struggled together through their first year of law school. Buff is particularly appreciative of Sharon's support because Buff's husband, Peter, is so unsupportive. Buff is somewhat understanding about her husband's complaints. She knows she has been moody and, during the past exam week, even verbally and emotionally abusive. Sharon is less understanding. She thinks Peter is a worthless, whining leech who is taking gross advantage of her friend. She repeatedly urges Buff to "Kill the pig!" only half in jest.

After their last exam, Sharon suggests that they stop at a local club for a few drinks to celebrate and unwind. Sharon's real plan is to get roaring drunk. She wants to kill Peter and knows that when she gets drunk she becomes increasingly violent toward people she does not like. She assumes that, while intoxicated, her conversation with Buff will turn to Peter and that he will become the focus of her drunken rage. In such a drunken state she knows she will not hesitate to kill him, but has learned from her criminal law outline that she will not be responsible for the killing because, if she is sufficiently intoxicated, she will not at the time be acting consciously. Sharon does not tell Buff of her plan.   *MPC 2.08 (1) + (2)?*

At the club, Sharon orders two Bloody Marys. Buff orders a glass of white wine. Sharon wants Buff to help her in the killing and figures that white wine won't do the trick, so she adds a few pills to both of their drinks, telling Buff that the pills will give the drinks more zap: "It'll really make us fly." Buff is hesitant. She generally doesn't drink, but she reminds herself that she has just finished a tough year and she deserves to celebrate. She sips her glass of wine while Sharon has three more Bloody Marys (with additive) in quick succession. Both women are now grossly intoxicated and barely coherent.

A friend of Buff's sees them at the club, falling out of their chairs, and insists on taking Buff home. Sharon goes along. When they arrive, they stagger from the friend's car and sprawl on Buff's front yard. Buff discovers that they are lying on her law books, apparently thrown from the upstairs window by a disgusted Peter, who is angry at her exam week abuse. "My books!"

"The pig!" Sharon responds. They stagger into the house, rip pages from the books, and stuff them in sleeping Peter's mouth. Both break into a chant of "Eat, pig, eat."

The next morning, Sharon and Buff awake in bed with Peter's body. Neither woman remembers anything after the first drink at the club. Peter is found to have died of asphyxiation. From witnesses, the police piece together the events, including Sharon's plan to kill Peter by making herself grossly intoxicated.

What should be the extent of Sharon's and Buff's liability, if any? What will be their liability, if any, under the Model Penal Code?   *No more law school*

Notes

Intoxication Negating Element: Involuntary versus Voluntary   If an actor becomes intoxicated involuntarily—for example, if it occurs against her will or without her knowing it—and, as a result, she lacks the culpable state of mind required for an offense, the actor will have a defense, much as when ignorance or mistake negates a required culpability element.[8] If the intoxication is voluntary, however, the actor may be criminally liable despite the absence of the usually required culpability. Under the Model Penal Code, for example, recklessness as to an offense element may be imputed to an actor whose voluntary intoxication prevents her from recognizing a risk she would have recognized if sober.[9]

Situations Where Intoxication is Involuntary   The case law typically recognizes four grounds upon which intoxication may be found involuntary: coerced intoxication; pathological intoxication; intoxication by innocent mistake; and unexpected intoxication resulting from the ingestion of a medically prescribed drug. Under the Model Penal Code and the many modern codes following its lead, intoxication is involuntary if it is not "self-induced" or if it is "pathological." These definitions appear to include all four of the categories recognized by the case law as well as several others:

> "self-induced intoxication" means intoxication caused by substances which the actor knowingly introduces into his body, the tendency of which to cause intoxication he knows or ought to know, unless he introduces them pursuant to medical advice or under such circumstances as would afford a defense to a charge of crime.[10]

This sets a negligence standard as to becoming intoxicated: Intoxication is self-induced if the actor "knows or *ought to know*" the substance's tendency to intoxicate. Sharon intends to become intoxicated. Buff is probably at least negligent as to the tendency of her drink to intoxicate. That is, even if Buff is in fact unaware of a substantial risk that the drink would have intoxicating effects, a reasonable person in her position would have been aware of such a risk.

Law's Treatment of Voluntary Intoxication   Under the common law rule, voluntary intoxication was permitted as a defense to a specific-intent offense but not to a general-intent offense. Unsurprisingly, because of the frequent difficulty in distinguishing specific-intent offenses from general-intent offenses, that approach was problematic. The Model Penal Code's treatment of voluntary intoxication is a somewhat more refined version of the common law's approach, based on the modern element analysis rather than offense-based approach to culpability. Section 2.08 provides:

> (1) Except as provided [by the general excuse of involuntary intoxication], intoxication of the actor is not a defense unless it negatives an element of the offense.
>
> (2) When recklessness establishes an element of the offense, if the actor, due to self-induced intoxication, is unaware of a risk of which he would have been aware had he been sober, such unawareness is immaterial.

---

8. See Model Penal Code § 2.08(1).
9. Model Penal Code § 2.08(2).
10. Model Penal Code § 2.08(5)(b).

The first subsection confirms that, even if the intoxication is voluntary, it is permitted to provide a defense if it demonstrates an actor's lack of the requisite purpose or knowledge as to an element. The second subsection, however, prevents an actor from using self-induced intoxication to demonstrate a lack of recklessness, even if the intoxication does in fact negate the actor's potential recklessness. Even if the actor's self-induced intoxication removes her subjective awareness of a risk such awareness and recklessness are imputed to the actor, so long as such awareness would have existed had the actor been sober.

Problematic Compromise between Safety and Desert Both the traditional common law and the Model Penal Code approaches create a legal fiction—that the defendant has a certain culpable state of mind that in fact he does not have. These rules attempt to structure a compromise between, on the one hand, the desire for some liability to protect society—and to punish the actor's culpability in bringing about his intoxicated state—and, on the other, the belief that a voluntarily intoxicated offender may be less culpable than an unintoxicated actor who commits the offense. The idea is that a defense to intent and knowledge requirements, coupled with a rule imputing recklessness, will lead to some liability (i.e., for an offense requiring recklessness), but not the fullest possible liability (i.e., for an offense requiring intent or knowledge as to the same harm), for the intoxicated offender. Unfortunately, the compromise frequently fails to achieve the desired result. The offense requiring purpose or knowledge (or specific intent), for which a defense is given, commonly does not have an included lesser offense of recklessness (or general intent) for which liability can be imposed. Homicide offenses are structured this way, but other offenses generally are not. When voluntary intoxication negates the intent required for attempted rape, for example, the defendant may escape all liability, since an attempt charge cannot be based on recklessness. On the other hand, for a *completed* rape that requires only recklessness, imputation based on voluntary intoxication leads to full liability, so no mitigation is provided to distinguish the intoxicated actor unaware of the victim's lack of consent from the rapist who is not intoxicated and is aware of the lack of consent.[11]

Alternative Proposal: Fixed Mitigation The current law's poor performance in reaching the desired compromise—imposing some liability, to protect the public and to punish the actor's blameworthiness in becoming intoxicated, yet less liability than for an unintoxicated offender, to reflect less relative blameworthiness—may suggest that an alternative approach deserves consideration. The doctrine could better ensure some, but reduced, liability in all cases if it used the grading mechanism seen for most inchoate offenses: Providing a standard mitigation reduction of one grade. Thus, where the actor lacks the culpability required for an offense because of voluntary intoxication, he would always be liable for an offense, but an offense of one grade less than if he were sober. However, even this proposal may be criticized as "rough justice": The voluntarily intoxicated actor may have much less blameworthiness than that normally associated even with this reduced grade of liability—or, in some cases, much more.

---

11. See, e.g., United States v. Short, 4 U.S.C.M.A. 437, 446, 16 C.M.R. 11, 20 (1954) (J. Brosman, concurring in part, dissenting in part) (if drunken American soldier achieved intercourse with unwilling Japanese girl, drunkenness is no defense because would not negative mens rea of rape; if drunkenness caused soldier to mistake Japanese girl for consenting prostitute, could negative intent to rape and give defense to offense of assault with intent to rape).

Criticism of Imputation   The more strenuous attacks on current law's voluntary intoxication doctrine are against its fundamental operation as an instance of imputation, not its awkward performance in attempting a rough compromise between liability levels. Treating an actor as if she has a culpable state of mind that in fact she does not have is said to be both illogical and unethical. As noted previously, such treatment is said to be inconsistent with the general principles of criminal liability and unfair to the defendant. In *Director of Public Prosecutions v. Majewski*,[12] excerpted below, the House of Lords concedes these claims, but argues that public policy concerns require them to maintain the current unprincipled rule. In rejecting the defendant's claim that his voluntary intoxication ought to be allowed to negate all culpable states of mind, even general intent (or recklessness), the Lords reason that allowing a defense for voluntary intoxication would endanger the community by frustrating the prosecution of offenses perpetrated by drug users. The danger from drug-induced or drug-assisted offenses, the court points out, is growing and requires sterner sanctions, not lighter ones. Indeed, some jurisdictions have taken such public policy arguments to their logical conclusion and have adopted a rule that would bar voluntary intoxication from negating nearly any culpable state of mind.[13] In *State v. Stasio*, for example, the court concludes that voluntary intoxication should be permitted only to negate the deliberation and premeditation required for first-degree murder, but not the intent required for any other offense. The court's conclusion is based in part on the difficulty of the general-intent/specific-intent distinction, but primarily on the need to ensure public safety. The *Stasio* court specifically rejects the Model Penal Code approach that the dissent urges (and that the state later adopted by statute).[14]

Misguided Concerns with General Process of Imputation   Though the *Majewski* court's concerns are real, the court concedes too much when it describes the process of substituting intoxication for the typically required culpability as somehow inherently illogical and unfair. The court fails to see that the law frequently treats an actor *as if* he satisfies an offense element that, in fact, he does not satisfy. As noted in the introduction to this Part, such imputation of missing offense elements occurs in a wide variety of doctrines, such as complicity and omission liability, and requires no general apology.

Concerns with Specific Imputation Rule for Intoxication   At the same time, specific doctrines of imputation—including the doctrine of voluntary intoxication—should be criticized if they have inadequate justification for the particular imputation that they provide. There seems to be general agreement that the conditions required by the doctrines of complicity and omission liability, and others as well, adequately justify the imputation of required conduct. For voluntary intoxication, in contrast, it is not clear that the actor's culpability in becoming intoxicated justifies the imputation of recklessness (or general intent) as to all manner of offense elements—for example, recklessness as to causing death in manslaughter.

---

12. [1976] 2 All E.R. 142.

13. See Ga. Code Ann. § 16-3-4(c); Del. Code Ann. tit. 11, § 421; Mont. Code Ann. § 45-2-203; Okla. Stat. Ann. tit. 21, § 153; 18 Pa. Cons. Stat. Ann. § 308.

14. 396 A.2d 1129, 1132-35 (N.J. 1979). *Stasio* was effectively overruled when the new New Jersey Criminal Code took effect. The Code had been enacted and was awaiting its effective date at the time *Stasio* was decided.

Negligent Intoxication as Inadequate to Impute Recklessness   The most common rationale for imputing recklessness in cases of voluntary intoxication is that the act of intoxicating oneself reflects culpability, and that act leads to the actor's later misconduct while intoxicated. However, imputing recklessness on this ground has been noted as troubling for several reasons. The imputation of recklessness under the Model Penal Code, and of greater culpability under many other codes, is triggered by a definition of "voluntariness" in becoming intoxicated that requires only negligence. As noted above, under the Model Penal Code, intoxication is "self-induced" if the actor "knows or *ought to know*" the tendency of the substance to intoxicate. Therefore, the Code may use intoxication to impute recklessness when the actor was merely negligent in becoming intoxicated. This may be the case for Buff, who despite being only negligent as to becoming intoxicated, may have recklessness imputed for the death of Peter. In contrast, Sharon, who became intoxicated for the purpose of killing Peter, may also have recklessness imputed if, because of her intoxication, she lacked the requisite purpose at the time of the commission of the offense.

Culpability as to Intoxication Inadequate to Impute Offense Culpability   A second and potentially more serious weakness in the justification for imputing recklessness concerns the object of the culpability. The notion that a person risks all manner of resulting harm when she voluntarily becomes intoxicated is common, but obviously incorrect. Becoming intoxicated in itself is not an offense, or is at most a minor offense and only when done in public. It therefore seems difficult to use a person's culpability as to becoming intoxicated as the grounds for imputing the required culpability as to causing a death. Buff's culpability as to becoming intoxicated is far from the equivalent of being reckless as to causing another's death, and this would be so even if she were reckless as to becoming intoxicated, not just negligent. (Notice that the doctrine, at the same time, seems to understate Sharon's blameworthiness. She will have the same recklessness imputed to her as Buff, even though it was her purpose to get intoxicated, and that purpose was motivated by the further purpose of killing while in such a state.[15])

Mitchell Keiter, Just Say No Excuse: The Rise and Fall of the Intoxication Defense

87 Journal of Criminal Law and Criminology 482, 482-483, 518-519 (1997)

On perhaps no other legal issue have courts so widely differed, or so often changed their views, as that of the legal responsibility of intoxicated offenders. The question contrasts the individual's right to avoid punishment for the unintended consequences of his acts with what then-New Hampshire Supreme Court Justice David Souter described as the individual's "responsibility . . . to stay sober if his intoxication will jeopardize the lives and safety of others." The issue presents the choice of whether the magnitude of an offense should be measured from the objective perspective of the community or the subjective perspective of the offender.

---

15. Sharon, however, might be charged with murder for her grand scheme, if her liability is based on her earlier conduct of getting intoxicated, rather than her later conduct of stuffing pages in Peter's mouth. On that theory of liability, the issue might then become whether the act of becoming intoxicated suffices as a legal cause of the subsequent killing.

Prompted by myriad changes in social, political, medical and legal philosophies, nineteenth and early twentieth century courts greatly expanded the exculpatory effect of intoxication. Beginning in the 1980s and 1990s, however, the pendulum began to swing back toward a policy of accountability for acts committed while intoxicated. Throughout this process, the issue has been highlighted by the competing positions of courts and legislatures. For example, in 1994 both the California and Canada Supreme Courts issued decisions which protected or expanded a defendant's right to introduce evidence of his intoxication. Both decisions sparked public outrage, and were in effect reversed by new statutes in 1995.

The United States Supreme Court's decision in *Montana v. Egelhoff* will likely have a profound effect on the debate surrounding the intoxication defense. The Court upheld a Montana statute which holds intoxicated offenders fully responsible for the consequences of acts they commit while intoxicated. While the plurality, concurring, and various dissenting opinions reflected differing perspectives, none found it would be unconstitutional for a state to equate a severe state of intoxication with the requisite mens rea for any crime. The Court's approval will likely influence other states to adopt a full responsibility policy. . . .

Appendix

The following states do not admit intoxication evidence as a defense to any crime: Arizona, Arkansas, Delaware, Georgia, Hawaii, Mississippi, Missouri, Montana, South Carolina, Texas.

The following states admit intoxication evidence as a defense only to first degree murder: Pennsylvania, Virginia.

The following states admit intoxication evidence as a defense only to crimes requiring purpose: Alaska, Colorado.

The following states follow the Model Penal Code and admit intoxication evidence as a defense only to crimes requiring purpose or knowledge: Alabama, Connecticut, Kentucky, Maine, New Hampshire, New Jersey, New York, North Dakota, Oregon, Tennessee, Utah, Wisconsin.

The following states admit intoxication as a defense only to crimes requiring a "specific intent": California, Florida, Idaho, Illinois, Iowa, Kansas, Louisiana, Maryland, Massachusetts, Michigan, Minnesota, Nebraska, Nevada, New Mexico, North Carolina Oklahoma, Rhode Island, South Dakota, Vermont, West Virginia, Wyoming.

The following states admit intoxication as a defense to all crimes requiring purpose, knowledge or recklessness: Ohio, Washington.

The following state admits intoxication evidence as a defense to any crime: Indiana.

Director of Public Prosecutions v. Majewski
House of Lords
(1976) 62 Cr. App. R. 262

[Each of seven Law Lords prepared an address and each reached the same conclusion. Only the address of Lord Edmund-Davies is reproduced here.]

Lord Edmund-Davies. My Lords, during a brawl in a public house the appellant attacked the landlord and two others, injuring all three of them. When the police arrived, he assaulted the officer who arrested him. Another officer was struck by the appellant when he was being driven to the police station. The next morning in his cell he attacked a police inspector. As a result, he was indicted at the Chelmsford Crown Court on four counts of occasioning actual bodily harm and on three counts of assaulting a police constable in the execution of his duty. The appellant testified that he had no recollection of the greater part of what had transpired after he entered the public house, and that during the preceding 48 hours he had taken a substantial quantity of drugs and had ordered one drink at the public house. There was adduced a statement from a doctor who saw him the following morning and evidence by another doctor as to the possible effect of the ingestion of such drink and drugs as the appellant had spoken of. During the course of legal submissions, the attention of the learned judge was drawn to the short report of *Bolton v. Crawley* in which the Court of Appeal held that on a charge of assault occasioning actual bodily harm the consumption of drink or drugs was irrelevant to criminal responsibility. Accordingly, after telling the jury that an assault 'means some blow, not something which is purely accidental', the judge directed them that—

> . . . the fact that [the appellant] may have taken drink and drugs is irrelevant, provided that you are satisfied that the state which he was in was a result of those drink and drugs [*sic*] or a combination of both was self-induced. . . .

The jury convicted on six of the seven counts and the convictions were upheld by the Court of Appeal, who, however, granted leave to appeal, certifying that the following point of law of general importance was involved:

> Whether a defendant may properly be convicted of assault notwithstanding that, by reason of his self-induced intoxication, he did not intend to do the act alleged to constitute the assault.

. . . The argument advanced on behalf of the appellant can be summarized in the following propositions: (i) Save in relation to offenses of strict responsibility, no man is guilty of a crime unless he has a guilty mind. (ii) A person who, though not insane, commits what would in ordinary circumstances be a crime when he is in such a mental state (whether it be called 'automatism' or by any other name) that he does not know what he is doing, lacks a guilty mind and is therefore not criminally culpable for his actions. (iii) Such freedom from culpability exists regardless of (a) whether the offence charged is one involving a "specific" (or "ulterior") intent or one involving only a "general" (or "basic") intent; and (b) whether the automatism was due to causes beyond the control of the person charged or was self-induced by the voluntary taking of drink or drugs. (iv) Assaults being crimes involving a guilty mind, a man who in a state of automatism unlawfully assaults another must be treated as free from all blame and is accordingly entitled to be wholly acquitted: the certified question therefore demands a negative answer. (v) Not only is it logically and ethically indefensible to convict such a man of assault; it also constitutes a contravention of §8 of the Criminal Justice Act 1967. (vi) There accordingly having been a fatal misdirection the appeal should be allowed.

The basic submission of the Crown, on the other hand, may be far more shortly stated thus: a rule of law has been established that self-induced intoxication can provide a defence only to offenses requiring an "ulterior" intent, and is therefore irrelevant to offenses of "basic" intent such as assaults; the direction given was accordingly right, the certified question must be answered in the affirmative, and the appeal should be dismissed. . . .

If logic is to be the sole guide, . . . a man can never be regarded as committing an assault unless he is conscious of what he is doing. Whatever be the reason for its absence, if he in fact lacks such consciousness he cannot be said to act either intentionally or recklessly. It is submitted on the appellant's behalf that he was at all material times in a condition of "non-insane automatism resulting from pathological intoxication." In *Bratty v. Attorney General for Northern Ireland* Lord Kilmuir LC acceptably defined "automatism" as—

> the state of a person who, though capable of action, "is not conscious of what he is doing. . . . It means unconscious involuntary action, and it is a defence because the mind does not go with what is being done."

In strict logic it may be that a physical action performed in such a state ought never to be punished as a criminal assault, no matter how grievous the injury thereby inflicted on the person attacked.

Then is it the case that a man is always to be absolved by the criminal law from the consequences of acts performed when in a state of automatism, regardless of how that state was brought about? The law is certainly clear and commendable in relation to cases where the actor is wholly free from fault in relation to the onset of such a mental state.

But a markedly different attitude has long been taken in respect of a state of automatism brought about by the *voluntary* act of the person charged with a crime.

. . . [T]he established law then was and is now that self-induced intoxication, however gross, cannot excuse crimes of basic intent such as that giving rise to this appeal.

Of recent years there has been increasing academic criticism of this virtually uniform judicial attitude. Such criticism is understandable, being based on what is advanced as the logical necessity of acquitting an accused who acted without mens rea, whatever be the reason for its absence. Thus Professor Glanville Williams comments: 'There is no reason why drunkenness should not negative a battery, if it tends to show that the accused did not intend to hit anyone.' The contrary view applied in our courts certainly presents problems. . . .

The criticism by the academics of the law presently administered in this country is of a two-fold nature: (1) It is illogical and therefore inconsistent with legal principle to treat a person who of his own volition has taken drink or drugs any differently from a man suffering from some bodily or mental disorder of the kind earlier mentioned or whose beverage had, without his connivance, been 'laced' with intoxicants. (2) It is unethical to convict a man of a crime requiring a guilty state of mind when, *ex hypothesi*, he lacked it. I seek to say something about each of these two criticisms.

(1) *Illogicality*

The appellant's counsel places strong reliance on a passage in the speech of Lord Hailsham of St. Marylebone in *Director of Public Prosecutions v. Morgan* in which, alluding to criminal intent, he said:

. . . once it be accepted that an intent of whatever description is an ingredient essential to the guilt of the accused I cannot myself see that any other direction can be logically acceptable. Otherwise a jury would in effect be told to find an intent where none existed or where none was proved to have existed. I cannot myself reconcile it with my conscience to sanction as part of the English law what I regard as logical impossibility, and, if there were any authority which, if accepted, would compel me to do so, I would feel constrained to declare that it was not to be followed.

Well, I have respectfully to say that were such an attitude rigorously adopted and applied, it would involve the drastic revision of much of our established law. Many would say that this would not be a bad thing, but it is well to realize clearly that such would be the consequence, for the criminal law is unfortunately riddled with illogicalities.

So we find the Court of Appeal decision in *R v. Lipman* criticized because Widgery LJ justified the conviction for manslaughter on the basis of death being caused by what was described as the unlawful act of the accused in stuffing bed-clothes down his companion's throat under the delusion (induced by the drugs he had taken) that he was dealing with snakes. . . . The undeviating application of logic leads inexorably to the conclusion that a man behaving even as Lipman unquestionably did must be completely discharged from all criminal liability for the dreadful consequences of his conduct. It was, as I recall, submissions of this startling character which led my noble and learned friend, Lord Simon of Glaisdale, to comment trenchantly to appellant's counsel: "It is all right to say 'Let justice be done though the heavens fall.' But you ask us to say 'Let logic be done even though public order be threatened,' which is something very different."

If such be the inescapable result of the strict application of logic in this branch of the law, it is indeed not surprising that illogicality has long reigned, and the prospect of its dethronement must be regarded as alarming.

(2) *Lack of ethics*

It is sometimes said in such cases as the present that it is morally wrong to convict of a crime involving a certain state of mind even where it be established that the charge is based on a man's behavior when he lacked that guilty mind. Rightly or wrongly, Coke was not of that view, for although he asserted that "*Actus non facit reum nisi mens sit rea*"* he also said that, so far from gross intoxi-cation excusing crime, it aggravated the culpability.

Your Lordships are presently concerned with a publichouse brawl, which is said to have been due to the ingestion of drugs rather than drink. Such a plea is becoming much more common, and those acting judicially or who have other-wise acquired any knowledge of addiction are familiar with such parlance of the drug scene as "going on a trip" or "blowing the mind," the avowed intention of the taker of hallucinatory drugs being to lose contact with reality. Irrationality is in truth the very essence of drug-induced phantasies.

Illogical though the present law may be, it represents a compromise between the imposition of liability on inebriates in complete disregard of their condition (on the alleged ground that it was brought on voluntarily), and the total exculpation

---

*Editor's Note—"An act does not make [the doer of it] guilty, unless the mind be guilty."

required by the defendant's actual state of mind at the time he committed the harm in issue. It is at this point pertinent to pause to consider why legal systems exist. The universal object of a system of law is obvious—the establishment and maintenance of order. . . . The relevant quotations on the purpose of law are endless and they serve to explain (if, indeed, any explanation be necessary) the sense of outrage which would naturally be felt not only by the victims of such attacks as are alleged against the appellant—and still more against Lipman—were he to go scot free. And a law which permitted this would surely deserve and earn the contempt of most people. But not, it seems, of the joint authors of Smith and Hogan, who in the third edition of their valuable book write:

> While a policy of not allowing a man to escape the consequence of his voluntary drunkenness is understandable, it is submitted that the principle that a man should not be held liable for an act over which he has no control is more important and should prevail.

They add that this is not to say that such a man should in all cases escape criminal liability but that, if he is to be held liable, it should be for the voluntary act of taking the drink or drug. Such a suggestion is far from new. Thus, it appears from Hale's Pleas of the Crown that some lawyers of his day thought that the formal cause of punishment ought to be the drink and not the crime committed under its influence. Edwards expressed concern in 1965 over the possible existence of this gateway to exemption from criminal responsibility and stressed the need for urgent attention to the provision of new statutory powers under which the courts may place such offenders on probation or commit them, as the case may require, to a hospital capable of treating them for the underlying cause of their propensity to automatism. Glanville Williams anticipated in 1961 the Butler Report on Mentally Abnormal Offenders by recommending the creation of an offence of being drunk and dangerous and the committee itself proposed that a new offence of 'dangerous intoxication' be punishable on indictment for one year for a first offence or for three years on a second or subsequent offence.

Such recommendations for law reform may receive Parliamentary consideration hereafter but this House is presently concerned with the law as it is. The merciful relaxation of the old rule that drunkenness was no defence appears to have worked reasonably well for 150 years. As to the complaint that it is unethical to punish a man for a crime when his physical behavior was not controlled by a conscious mind, I have long regarded as a convincing theory in support of penal liability for harms committed by voluntary inebriates, the view of Austin, who argued that a person who voluntarily became intoxicated is to be regarded as acting recklessly, for he made himself dangerous in disregard of public safety.

But, to my way of thinking, the nearest approach to a satisfactory refutation of charges of lack of both logic and ethics in punishing the most drunken man for actions which, were he sober, would call for his criminal conviction is that of Stroud, who wrote:

> [D]runkenness is not incompatible with *mens rea*, in the sense of ordinary culpable intentionality, because mere recklessness is sufficient to satisfy the definition of *mens rea*, and drunkenness is itself an act of recklessness. The law therefore establishes a conclusive presumption against the admission of proof of intoxication for the purpose of disproving *mens rea* in ordinary

crimes. Where this presumption applies, it does not make "drunkenness itself" a crime, but the drunkenness is itself an integral part of the crime, as forming, together with the other unlawful conduct charged against the defendant, a complex act of criminal recklessness.

This explanation affords at once a justification of the rule of law, and a reason for its inapplicability when drunkenness is pleaded by way of showing absence of full intent, or of some exceptional form of mens rea essential to a particular crime, according to its definition.

Reverting to the same topic immediately after the decision in *Beard*, Stroud added:

> . . . His drunkenness can constitute a defence only in those exceptional cases where some additional mental element, of a more heinous and mischievous description than ordinary mens rea, is required by the definition of the crime charged against him, and is shown to have been lacking in consequence of his drunken condition.

Professor Glanville Williams would probably condemn such an approach as savoring of "judge-made fiction." While generally sharing his dislike of such fictions, in my judgment little can properly be made out of the criticisms that a law which demands the conviction of such persons who behave as the appellant did is both illogical and unethical. It may be that Parliament should look at it, and devise a new way of dealing with drunken or drugged offenders. But, until it does, the continued application of the existing law is far better calculated to preserve order than the recommendation that he and all who act similarly should leave the dock as free men. . . .

For these reasons, I concur in holding that Yes is the proper answer to the certified question and that, there having been no misdirection, the appeal should be dismissed.

▲ PROBLEMS

Poker Interrupted (#62)

Joseph McKinney and four friends are enjoying a game of cards, playing on a makeshift card table in a vacant lot. In the same lot, Michele Cameron is drinking with friends from a quart bottle of wine she has brought. The bottle is passed around numerous times, and Cameron takes a number of swigs. After a while, she wanders over to the card game. She does not know the players, but has taken a dislike to something about the game. When she approaches the card table she is abusive and threatening. The players assume she is drunk and move their game to a different part of the lot. Cameron follows and in a violent outburst overturns the table. The players right the table and again resume their game as Cameron wanders off. She returns, however, with a broken bottle and attacks McKinney. As he fights Cameron off, she cuts his hand with the bottle. The cut requires 36 stitches, and the physician informs him that his hand will never fully recover.

What liability for Cameron, if any, under the Model Penal Code? Prepare a list of all criminal code subsections in the order in which you rely on them in your analysis.

What result in this case if there were no special rule regarding voluntary intoxication?

Blacked Out Drunk, Murderer (#63)

James Egelhoff heads to the mountains to camp out and pick mushrooms. As is his habit, he brings his gun along with him. While there, he meets Robert Pavola and John Christenson, who are also collecting mushrooms. The three quickly become friends and continue their foraging together. At the end of the day, they head into town and sell the mushrooms. With the profits burning a hole in their pockets, they spend the evening drinking in bars and partying. Later in the evening, Egelhoff, Pavola, and Christenson take their binge drinking on the road. They pile into Christenson's station wagon and buy more beer at a convenience store. They then continue to drink at various locations as they drive around town. Eventually, Egelhoff ends up in the backseat in a drunken stupor.

He is not the only one of the group who is intoxicated. Indeed, all of the drinking has taken a toll on Christenson's driving, and the police receive several calls about a possible drunk driver. When they arrive to investigate, they find the car sitting in a ditch off the side of the road. Egelhoff is lying on the backseat screaming obscenities at no one in particular. Pavola and Christenson are lying in the front of the car, each dead from a single bullet wound to the back of the head.

Egelhoff has no recollection of how the deaths of Pavola and Christenson occurred. However, on the floor of the car, near the brake pedal, is Egelhoff's .38 caliber handgun. There are four rounds left in the chamber and two casings on the floor. Tests find gunpowder residue on Egelhoff's hands. Further tests find Egelhoff's blood-alcohol content (BAC) to be .36% one hour after the police find him. A BAC of over .20% typically causes memory loss and unconsciousness, while a BAC of over .30% is considered to place a person at risk of death from alcohol poisoning.

What liability for Egelhoff, if any, under the Model Penal Code? Prepare a list of all criminal code subsections in the order in which you rely on them in your analysis.

What result in this case if there were no special rule regarding voluntary intoxication?

✳ DISCUSSION ISSUE

What Level of Culpable Mental State, if Any, Should Be Imputed When It Is Absent Because the Offender Voluntarily Intoxicated Himself?

Materials presenting each side of this Discussion Issue appear in the Advanced Materials for Section 13 in Appendix A.

▲ PROBLEM

Escaping the Aliens—Revisited (#38)

Recall the "Escaping the Aliens" Problem Case (#38) from Section 8 (Homicide Mitigations). In that case, Clark's impairment was due to mental illness; there was no issue of intoxication, voluntary or otherwise. However, the liability rule in that jurisdiction, Arizona, barred the introduction of evidence of mental illness to negate any offense element. (The practice was approved as constitutional by the United States Supreme Court in *Arizona v. Clark.*)

Reconsider that Problem Case in light of the understanding of imputation that you have from this Section. Under the Arizona rule, what level of culpability does such a rule impute? Do the conditions that trigger the imputation—being mentally ill—justify the imputation that the Arizona rule permits?

Complicity

Offense definitions typically require certain conduct. But, when offenders act in a group, only one member of the group may satisfy the offense conduct requirement. The law takes account of the contribution of the accomplices in assisting the perpetrator by imputing that conduct to all of the accomplices. What exactly are the requirements for complicity liability, and do they justify such imputation?

◆ THE CASE OF CARDINAL BERNARD LAW (#64)

Ordained in 1962, Father John Geoghan begins sexually abusing children at his first parish, Blessed Sacrament, in Saugus, a working-class community outside Boston. Among his victims are four young boys from the same family, as Geoghan preys primarily on children with troubled home lives. In 1967, when more allegations of abuse surface, Geoghan's superiors transfer him to St. Paul's

Figure 58 **Blessed Sacrament Parish in Saugus, Massachusetts**

(Itia Roth)

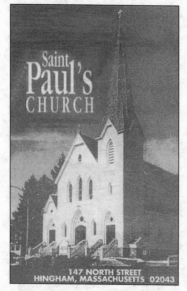

Figure 59 **St. Paul's Church, Hingham, Massachusetts**

(St. Paul's Church)

in Hingham, a southern suburb of Boston. At St. Paul's, another family accuses him of abuse. This time the parish priest assures them that "It will never happen again. He will never be a priest again."

Notwithstanding these assurances, the archdiocese again transfers Geoghan to another parish. In his new assignment, St. Andrews, in Boston's Forest Hills community, he supervises altar boys and a Boy Scout troop. In 1974, he lures a boy into the rectory and fondles him. A few days later, Geoghan attempts to do so again but is interrupted when another priest enters yelling, "Jack, we told you not to do this up here. . . . Are you nuts?" He does not stop, however, and over the next two years molests all seven of Maryette Dussourd's boys. When she learns what is happening, Dussourd contacts a pastor in a nearby parish, Reverend Thomas. He confronts Geoghan, who then confesses, saying simply, "Yes, that's all true." Reverend Thomas immediately contacts the archdiocese, where Bishop Daily, an administrator, relieves Geoghan of his duties and sends him home. The archdiocese also prepares a memorandum marked "personal and confidential," that notes the frequency and extent of Geoghan's abuse. Finally, Reverend Thomas informs Dussourd about Geoghan's confession but urges her not to publicize the story.

In 1980 and 1981, the archdiocese places Geoghan on sick leave. He lives at home with his sister in West Roxbury. During this period, he also undergoes church-mandated treatment, consisting of psychotherapy and psychoanalysis, with respectively, Dr. Mullins, his longtime physician and friend, and Dr. Brennan, a psychiatrist. Neither have specialized training in the treatment of sex offenders. The archdiocese eventually permits Geoghan to return to work based on the doctors' conclusion that "he [is] able to resume priestly duties."

In February 1982, the archdiocese assigns Geoghan to St. Brendan's in Dorchester, a diverse working-class neighborhood, without informing the parish priest, Father Lane, about his history. Geoghan again works with children, including supervising first communions.

On August 16, 1982, Margaret Gallant, the Dussourd children's aunt, writes Cardinal Medeiros, asking why the archdiocese fails to deal with Geoghan. Specifically, she writes, "As you know, our family had a conference with Bishop Daly [sic] over two weeks ago. Since that priest is still in his parish, it appears that no action has been taken." Cardinal Medeiros quickly replies, in a letter dated August 20, thanking Gallant for her "candid expression of opinion concerning

ah my god

the priest . . . who has caused hardship to your family and most especially to several of the boys." He reassures her that the archdiocese is working to find the "most Christian way to deal with the problem with him and at the same time remove any source of scandal for the sake of the faithful."

That same month, Cardinal Medeiros informs Geoghan that funds have been provided to enable him to study in Rome. The Cardinal writes, "It is my hope that the three months will provide [the] renewal of mind, body and spirit that will enable you to return to parish work refreshed and strengthened in the Lord." Upon returning, Geoghan claims that he no longer is attracted to children and rejoins St. Brendan.

Bernard Francis Law follows his graduation from St. Joseph's Seminary in St. Benedict, Louisiana, with six years of rigorous study at Pontifical College Josephinum in Worthington, Ohio. Ordained a priest in 1961, he is initially assigned to St. Paul's Parish in Vicksburg, Mississippi. There he participates in the civil rights movement, helps to establish the state's first human rights council, and supports adult literacy programs. Church leaders consider him bright and capable, with a strong future ahead.

In January 1984, Law fulfills those expectations when he is selected Boston's new archbishop. Quickly thereafter, he announces that his priorities are to crusade against abortion, contraception, divorce, and homosexuality. His responsibilities also include delegating to others the day-to-day operations of the diocese. He retains primary responsibility over all personnel transfers and maintains ultimate possession of the diocese's confidential personnel files.

On September 6, 1984, Margaret Gallant again writes to the archdiocese, this time to inform the newly installed Archbishop Law about Geoghan's history of molestation:

> There is a priest at St. Brendan's in Dorchester who has been known in the past to molest boys. Cardinal [Medeiros] had sent father for treatment, and after returning to parish duties he maintained a low profile for quite a while. Lately, however, he has been seen in the company of many boys, to the extent of dropping them off at their homes as late as 9:30 p.m.

Law marks the envelope of Gallant's letter "Urgent, please follow through," and sends it to Bishop Daily. On September 18, Law terminates Geoghan's assignment at St. Brendan's, in the process informing him that he is "in between assignments."

On September 21, Gallant receives a reply from Law, thanking her for her "letter of September 6, 1984 concerning the priest at St. Brendan's Dorchester. . . . The matter of your concern is being investigated and appropriate pastoral decisions will be made for both the priest and God's people."

On October 31, Law assigns Geoghan to St. Julia's parish in Weston, a wealthy Boston suburb. He informs its parish priest, Monsignor Rossiter, of

Figure 61 **John Geoghan, 2002**
(AP)

Geoghan's history. They inform no one else in the parish, however. Geoghan again supervises the altar boys, along with two other youth groups. Law later acknowledges that he knew of Geoghan's alleged abuse when he reassigned him.

In 1985, Reverend Thomas Doyle, a canon law-yer, and Michael Peterson, a psychiatrist at St. Luke's, which is a treatment facil-ity in Maryland for abusive priests, publish a controver-sial study on the propensity of sexual abuse by clergy members. They report that the rate of repeat offenders is high among pedophiles, and controlled studies reveal that "traditional outpatient psychiatric or psychologi-cal treatment DOES NOT WORK" with this cohort of offenders. In addition, they observe that pedo-philia is "a lifelong disease with NO HOPE AT THIS TIME FOR A CURE." Law initially supports the study's conclusions but withdraws support by the time the National Conference of Catholic Bishops convenes. The Conference, according to its general counsel, decides not to consider the study because it merely reiterates information that the bishops have already gathered.

Meanwhile, under Law's direction, the Boston Archdiocese begins paying out settlements on claims against more than 70 priests. Victims maintain their anonymity, but are usually required to sign a confidentiality agreement as a condi-tion of receiving their settlement. (When later asked in a deposition why he did not institute policies to deal with the abuse when he became aware of complaints against the priests, Cardinal Law says, "I'm not certain that the judgment at that time would have been that we were facing a major, overwhelming problem.")

In February 1986, while Geoghan is still working at St. Julia's, the boy-friend of a ten-year-old boy's mother contacts the Department of Social Services and Boston Police alleging Geoghan sexually abused the boy. While at the Boys and Girls Club swimming pool, Geoghan reached inside the boy's trunks and grabbed his buttocks. When the victim fails to testify, however, the authorities drop the matter entirely, lacking any additional evidence. Shortly thereafter, Geoghan abuses twelve-year-old Patrick McSorley. While driving McSorley home, Geoghan puts his hands on the boy's genitals and starts masturbating McSorley and then starts masturbating himself. (McSorley does not tell his mother about the abuse until 1999, when, along with 85 other plaintiffs, he brings a civil suit against Geoghan.)

Figure 62 **Law speaking to a crowd in Boston after his elevation to Cardinal**
(Bettmann/Corbis)

In 1989, Geoghan tells Bishop Banks, a deputy of Cardinal Law, that he had been accused of fondling a boy but denies the allegations and says the matter was dropped because of discrepancies in the victim's story. (Ten years later, the victim contacts the Suffolk County District Attorney, who investigates and brings criminal charges for two counts of rape against Geoghan on December 11, 1999. In March 2002, a Superior Court judge dismisses the charges, ruling that the statute of limitations has run.)

Later in 1989, Cardinal Law pulls Geoghan from service and sends him to St. Luke's, which has a program for priests who are sex offenders. After three weeks of observation, the psychiatrists classify him as a "high-risk homosexual pedophile." Dr. Brennan, Geoghan's psychiatrist, recommends to Bishop Banks that the archdiocese "clip his wings before there is an explosion." Banks informs Geoghan that he may not return to his parish and sends him to Hartford's Institute for Living, which treats priests who are sex offenders. After three months, doctors report that despite being "a high-risk-taker," he is an "atypical pedophile in *remission*."

On November 13, 1989, Cardinal Law allows Geoghan to resume his duties as vicar at St. Julia's. He writes, "It is most heartening to know that things have gone well for you and that you are ready to resume your efforts with a renewed zeal and enthusiasm. I am confident that you will again render fine priestly service

Figure 63 **Patrick McSorley, December 2002**
(Reuters NewsMedia Inc./Corbis)

Figure 64 **Cardinal Law, 2002**
(AP)

to the people of God in Saint Julia Parish." Banks obtains written confirmation from the Institute for Living recommending that Geoghan is fit to return to parish work. Within a few weeks of his return, however, Geoghan is again abusing boys. (The lawsuits against Geoghan later include claims that he abused at least 30 boys during his time at St. Julia's.)

In 1992, the archdiocese passes over Geoghan in selecting a new pastor for St. Julia's. An administrator informs Geoghan, however, that he should not take this "in any negative way with reference to [him]self," and recommends contacting the archdiocese about any positions that interest him.

In January 1993, after new allegations surface, Law removes Geoghan from parish service and assigns him to the Office of Senior Priests at Regina Cleri. He also proposes several new policies, including a comprehensive review of old records, an offer to pay for victim counseling, and the appointment of a review board to consider allegations of abuse. Law makes it clear, however, that he will allow some priests treated for sexual disorders to return to parish work and that the archdiocese's procedures will be the primary means of investigating allegations of abuse. He says that priests and other church officials will report allegations in accordance with state law, but at the time state law does not require them to do so, unlike other professionals, such as teachers and physicians.

In May, Law and his staff meet with experts in the field of child sexual abuse to better understand how to treat the problem they face. The experts state forcefully that the archdiocese is mishandling the problem twofold: by permitting homosexual pedophiles, who have a high rate of repeat behavior, easy access to young boys, and by not reporting the allegations to authorities. However, the archdiocese politely declines the group's offer to help develop a policy to deal with the problem, and there is no subsequent follow-up.

By 1994, civil authorities are again investigating Geoghan. Law puts him on administrative leave, effective December 30, 1994, writing, "I realize this is a difficult time for you and for those close to you. If I can be of help to you in some way, please contact me. Be assured you are remembered in my prayers."

In 1995, Geoghan caresses the genitals of a ten-year-old Weymouth boy while driving. Some months earlier, Geoghan had caressed the same boy's genitals while helping him into his altar boy's robe in preparation for the christening of the boy's younger sister. Later, Geoghan is charged with indecent assault and battery of a child. This is the third set of criminal charges he faces.

On August 4, 1996, Law places Geoghan on sick leave. Two months later, Geoghan asks to retire. Law grants him senior priest retirement status on December 12, 1996, writing him, "Yours has been an effective life of ministry, sadly impaired by illness. On behalf of those you have served well, and in my own name, I would like to thank you. . . . God bless you, Jack."

1. Relying only on your own intuitions of justice, what liability and punishment, if any, does Cardinal Law deserve?

N	0	1	2	3	4	5	6	7	8	9	10	11
☐	☐	☐	☐	☐	☐	☐	☐	☐	☐	☒	☐	☐
no liability	liability but no punishment	1 day	2 wks	2 mo	6 mo	1 yr	3 yrs	7 yrs	15 yrs	30 yrs	life imprison- ment	death

2. What "justice" arguments could defense counsel make on the defendant's behalf?

3. What "justice" arguments could the prosecution make against the defendant?

4. What liability, if any, for Cardinal Law under the then-existing statutes? Prepare a list of all criminal code subsections and cases in the order in which you rely on them in your analysis.

5. What liability, if any, under the Model Penal Code? Prepare a list of all criminal code subsections in the order in which you rely on them in your analysis.

■ THE LAW

Massachusetts General Laws Annotated
(1988)

Crimes and Punishments

Chapter 265. Crimes Against the Person

Section 13A. Assault or Assault and Battery; Punishment

Whoever commits an assault or an assault and battery upon another shall be punished by imprisonment for not more than two and one half years in a house of correction or by fine of not more than five hundred dollars. . . .

Section 13B. Indecent Assault and Battery on Child Under Fourteen; Penalties; Subsequent Offenses; Eligibility for Parole, etc.

Whoever commits an indecent assault and battery on a child under the age of fourteen shall be punished by imprisonment in the state prison for not more than ten years, or by imprisonment in a jail or house of correction for not more than two and one-half years; and whoever commits a second or subsequent such offense shall be punished by imprisonment in the state prison for life or any term of years.

No person serving a sentence for a second or subsequent such offense shall be eligible for furlough, temporary release, or education, training or employment programs established outside a correctional facility until such person shall have served two-thirds of such minimum sentence or if such person has two or more sentences to be served otherwise than concurrently, two-thirds of the aggregate of the minimum terms of such several sentences.

In a prosecution under this section, a child under the age of fourteen years shall be deemed incapable of consenting to any conduct of the defendant for which said defendant is being prosecuted.

Section 13H. Indecent Assault and Battery on Child of Fourteen; Penalties

Whoever commits an indecent assault and battery on a person who has attained age fourteen shall be punished by imprisonment in the state prison for not more than five years, or by imprisonment for not more than two and one-half years in a jail or house of correction.

Section 22. Rape, Generally; Penalties; Eligibility for Parole, etc.

(a) Whoever has sexual intercourse or unnatural sexual intercourse with a person, and compels such person to submit by force and against his will, or compels such person to submit by threat of bodily injury, and if either such sexual intercourse or unnatural sexual intercourse results in or is committed with acts resulting in serious bodily injury, or is committed by a joint enterprise, or is committed during the commission or attempted commission of an offense defined in section fifteen A, fifteen B, seventeen, nineteen or twenty-six of this chapter, section fourteen, fifteen, sixteen, seventeen or eighteen of chapter two hundred and sixty-six or section ten of chapter two hundred and sixty-nine shall be punished by imprisonment in the state prison for life or for any term of years.

No person serving a sentence for a second or subsequent such offense shall be eligible for furlough, temporary release, or education, training or employment programs established outside a correctional facility until such person shall have served two-thirds of such minimum sentence or if such person has two or more sentences to be served otherwise than concurrently, two-thirds of the aggregate of the minimum terms of such several sentences.

(b) Whoever has sexual intercourse or unnatural sexual intercourse with a person and compels such person to submit by force and against his will, or compels such person to submit by threat of bodily injury, shall be punished by imprisonment in the state prison for not more than twenty years; and whoever commits a second or subsequent such offense shall be punished by imprisonment in the state prison for life or for any term of years.

No person serving a sentence for a second or subsequent such offense shall be eligible for furlough, temporary release, or education, training or employment programs established outside a correctional facility until such person shall have served two-thirds of such minimum sentence or if such person has two or more sentences to be served otherwise than concurrently, two-thirds of the aggregate of the minimum terms of such several sentences.

For the purposes of prosecution, the offense described in subsection (b) shall be a lesser included offense to that described in subsection (a).

Section 22A. Rape of Child; Use of Force

Whoever had sexual intercourse or unnatural sexual intercourse with a child under sixteen, and compels said child to submit by force and against his will or compels said child to submit by threat of bodily injury, shall be punished by imprisonment in the state prison for life or for any term of years; and whoever over the age of eighteen commits a second or subsequent such offense shall be sentenced to the state prison for life or for any term of years, but not less than five years.

Section 23. Rape and Abuse of Child

Whoever unlawfully has sexual intercourse or unnatural sexual intercourse, and abuses a child under sixteen years of age shall, for the first offense, be punished by imprisonment in the state prison for life or for any term of years, or, except as otherwise provided, for any term in a jail or house of correction, and for the second or subsequent offense by imprisonment in the state prison for life or for any term of years, but not less than five years.

Section 24. Assault with Intent to Commit Rape; Penalties; Eligibility for Parole, etc.

victim = adult

Whoever assaults a person with intent to commit a rape shall be punished by imprisonment in the state prison for not more than twenty years or by imprisonment in a jail or house of correction for not more than two and one-half years; and whoever commits a second or subsequent such offense shall be punished by imprisonment in the state prison for life or for any term of years.

No person serving for a second or subsequent such offense shall be eligible for furlough, temporary release, or education, training or employment programs established outside a correctional facility until such person shall have served two-thirds of such minimum sentence or if such person has two or more sentences to be served otherwise than concurrently, two-thirds of the aggregate of the minimum terms of such several sentences.

Section 24B. Assault of Child; Intent to Commit Rape; Punishment

victim = child, or under 16

Whoever assaults a child under sixteen with intent to commit a rape, as defined in section thirty-nine of chapter two hundred and seventy-seven, shall be punished by imprisonment in the state prison for life or for any term of years; and whoever over the age of eighteen commits a subsequent such offense shall be punished by imprisonment in the state prison for life or for any term of years but not less than five years.

Chapter 274. Felonies, Accessories and Attempts to Commit Crimes

Section 2. Aiders; Accessories Before Fact; Punishment

Whoever aids in the commission of a felony, or is accessory thereto before the fact by counseling, hiring or otherwise procuring such felony to be committed, shall be punished in the manner provided for the punishment of the principal felon.

aider or accessories is punished as if principal

Section 3. Prosecution; Time; Joinder with Felon; Felon's Conviction or Amenability to Justice. . . .

Whoever counsels, hires or otherwise procures a felon to be committed may be indicted and convicted as an accessory before the fact, either with the principal felon or after his conviction; or may be indicted and convicted of the substantive felony, whether the principal felon has or has not been convicted, or is or is not amenable to justice; and in the last mentioned case may be punished in the same manner as if convicted of being an accessory before the fact. . . .

Section 4. Accessories After Fact; Punishment; Relationship as Defense; Cross Examination; Impeachment

Whoever, after the commission of a felony, harbors, conceals, maintains, or assists the principal felon or accessory before the fact, or gives such offender any other aid, knowing that he has committed a felony or has been accessory thereto before the fact, with intent that he shall avoid or escape detention, arrest, trial, or punishment, shall be an accessory after the fact, and, except as otherwise provided, be punished by imprisonment in the state prison for not more than seven years or in jail for not more than two and one half years or by fine of not more than one thousand dollars. The fact that the defendant is the husband or wife, or by consanguinity, affinity, or adoption, the parent or grandparent, child or grandchild, brother or sister of the offender, shall be a defense to a prosecution under this section. . . .

Chapter 277. Indictments and Proceedings Before Trial Indictments and Complaints

Section 39. Construction of Words Used in Indictment

The words used in an indictment may, except as otherwise provided in this section, be construed according to their usual acceptation in common language; but if certain words and phrases are defined by law, they shall be used according to their legal meaning.

The following words, when used in an indictment, shall be sufficient to convey the meaning herein attached to them:

Adultery.—Sexual intercourse by a married person with a person not his spouse or by an unmarried person with a married person.

Affray.—Fighting together of two or more persons in a public place to the terror of the persons lawfully there.

Aggravated Rape.—Sexual intercourse or unnatural sexual intercourse by a person with another person who is compelled to submit by force and against his will or by threat of bodily injury; and either such sexual intercourse or unnatural sexual intercourse results in or is committed with acts resulting in serious bodily injury, or is committed by a joint enterprise, or is committed during the commission or attempted commission of an offense defined in section fifteen A, fifteen B, seventeen, nineteen or twenty-six of chapter two hundred and sixty-five, section fourteen, fifteen, sixteen, seventeen or eighteen of chapter two hundred and sixty-six, or section ten of chapter two hundred and sixty-nine.

False Pretenses.—False representations made by word or act of such a character, or made under such circumstances and in such a way, with the intention of influencing the action of another, as to be punishable.

Forgery.—The false making, altering, forging or counterfeiting of any instrument described in section one of chapter two hundred and sixty-seven, or any instrument which, if genuine, would be a foundation for or release of liability of the apparent maker.

Fornication.—Sexual intercourse between an unmarried male and an unmarried female.

Murder.—The killing of a human being, with malice aforethought.

Rape.—Sexual intercourse or unnatural sexual intercourse by a person with another person who is compelled to submit by force and against his will or by threat of bodily injury, or sexual intercourse or unnatural sexual intercourse with a child under sixteen years of age.

Robbery.—The taking and carrying away of personal property of another from his person and against his will, by force and violence, or by assault and putting in fear, with intent to steal.

Stealing. Larceny.—The criminal taking, obtaining or converting of personal property, with intent to defraud or deprive the owner permanently of the use of it; including all forms of larceny, criminal embezzlement and obtaining by criminal false pretenses.

Commonwealth v. Morrow

363 Mass. 601, 296 N.E.2d 468 (1973)

Defendant was held liable for a rape of a woman committed by an accomplice during the armed robbery of two men at the house. The court held that being an accessory before the fact involves counseling, hiring, or otherwise procuring, which means something more than mere acquiescence, but does not require physical participation if the defendant has associated himself with the criminal venture and in any significant way participated in it.

Commonwealth v. Stout
356 Mass. 237, 249 N.E.2d 12 (1969)

Defendant was held liable as an accessory before the fact for supplying guns employed in an attempted bank robbery. The court held that, in order for a person to be an accessory before the fact, the defendant must "in some way associate himself with the venture, that he participate in it as in something that he wishes to bring about, that he seek by his actions to make it succeed." (quoting U.S. v. Peoni, 100 F.2d 401 (2d Cir.)) Conviction affirmed.

Glover v. Callahan
299 Mass. 55, 12 N.E.2d 194 (1937)

The court held that the statutory crime of carnally knowing and abusing a female child under the age of sixteen "does not require . . . that the acts of the defendant were done with force or without consent of the victim." The offense is committed even if committed with full consent. The court explained that "the legislature as a matter of public policy, for the protection of female children under the age of sixteen, has fixed an age below which a female child is to be held legally incapable of consenting to assaults of this character." Thus, the court acknowledges that statutory rape is committed if the assault on the body is committed.

Model Penal Code
(Official Draft 1962)

Section 2.06. Liability for Conduct of Another; Complicity

(1) A person is guilty of an offense if it is committed by his own conduct or by the conduct of another person for which he is legally accountable, or both.

(2) A person is legally accountable for the conduct of another person when:

(a) acting with the kind of culpability that is sufficient for the commission of the offense, he causes an innocent or irresponsible person to engage in such conduct; or

(b) he is made accountable for the conduct of such other person by the Code or by the law defining the offense; or

(c) he is an accomplice of such other person in the commission of the offense.

(3) A person is an accomplice of another person in the commission of an offense if:

(a) with the purpose of promoting or facilitating the commission of the offense, he

(i) solicits such other person to commit it; or

(ii) aids or agrees or attempts to aid such other person in planning or committing it; or

(iii) having a legal duty to prevent the commission of the offense, fails to make proper effort so to do; or

(b) his conduct is expressly declared by law to establish his complicity.

(4) When causing a particular result is an element of an offense, an accomplice in the conduct causing such result is an accomplice in the commission of that offense, if he acts with the kind of culpability, if any, with respect to that result that is sufficient for the commission of the offense.

(5) A person who is legally incapable of committing a particular offense himself may be guilty thereof if it is committed by the conduct of another person for which he is legally accountable, unless such liability is inconsistent with the purpose of the provision establishing his incapacity.

(6) Unless otherwise provided by the Code or by the law defining the offense, a person is not an accomplice in an offense committed by another person if:

(a) he is a victim of that offense; or

(b) the offense is so defined that his conduct is inevitably incident to its commission; or

(c) he terminates his complicity prior to the commission of the offense and

(i) wholly deprives it of effectiveness in the commission of the offense; or

(ii) gives timely warning to the law enforcement authorities or otherwise makes proper effort to prevent the commission of the offense.

(7) An accomplice may be convicted on proof of the commission of the offense and of his complicity therein, though the person claimed to have committed the offense has not been prosecuted or convicted or has been convicted of a different offense or degree of offense or has an immunity to prosecution or conviction or has been acquitted.

● OVERVIEW OF COMPLICITY

Hypothetical: Bib Tries to Help (#65)

Having failed to pass several grades in grammar school, Muscle and Bib are twenty-one-year-old seniors at K Street High School. Muscle is interested in dating a freshman, Susan Rigg, but Susan's older brother, John, with whom she has lived since her parents died, has made it clear that he does not want Muscle associating with Susan. Susan nonetheless has encouraged Muscle's interest, and this has resulted in several confrontations between Muscle and John. The latest has left Muscle steaming and more determined than ever to pursue Susan.

Muscle arranges with Susan for a rendezvous at her house while John is away at his night job, and asks Bib to come along as a lookout. "Goin' over there's not a good idea," Bib warns. "She's probably jail bait."

"Let me worry about her age. You just keep your eyes open."

"Yeah, and what if big brother shows up?"

"He won't give me any trouble. I'll bring my .45."

Bib smiles. "You're a wild man."

Muscle and Bib drive to Susan's house where they find Susan waiting on the stoop. Muscle disappears upstairs with Susan. Bib settles in the car for a long wait, but soon slips into a snooze. A rattle at the front door wakes him. John Rigg is back. Bib hits the horn to alert Muscle, but it won't sound with the ignition off. As he heads for the house, he hears shouts, then a shot from inside. He finds John in a pool of blood just inside the front doorway. Muscle and Bib flee but are arrested within hours. Muscle is charged and convicted of the murder of John Rigg, who dies before police arrive, and of the statutory rape of Susan Rigg, who is 14 years old. Bib is charged as an accomplice to both offenses. Is Bib liable?

Notes

Objective Elements
  Common Law Requirements
    Accessory After the Fact
  Objective Elements Under Modern Codes
  Derivative vs. Personal Liability
  Objectivist vs. Subjectivist Views of Criminality
  Objective Elements Satisfied by Principal
Culpability Requirements
  Complicity as "Intentional": Does This Require Purpose or Knowledge?
    Significance of Degree of Assistance and Offense Seriousness
  Culpability as to Assistance vs. Culpability as to Offense
    Example: Loaning Keys to Car Used in DUI Homicide
    "Purpose of FaciLitating Commission of Offense"
  Elevating Culpability Requirements for Complicity
    No Elevation as to Result Under MPC
    Culpability as to Circumstance Element Less Clear
  Liability for Unplanned Offenses: "Natural and Probable Consequence" Rule
  Summary of Complicity Requirements
    Elements Satisfied by Perpetrator for Liability of Accomplice
Causing Crime by an Innocent
  Liability for Causing Crime by an Innocent Person
  Common Law Complicity Rules Create Need for Alternative Basis of Liability

Though accomplice liability superficially resembles other offenses defined in relation to some distinct "target" crime—conspiracy and attempt, for example—complicity is not an offense in itself. Rather, it is a basis of liability under which one person (the accomplice) is held accountable for the conduct of another person (the principal). An offense definition typically requires the performance of certain conduct. Yet a person may be held liable for the offense, although the person has not performed the required conduct, if he is legally accountable for the principal's conduct. The complicity doctrine thus *imputes* the principal's conduct to the accomplice if the special requirements for complicity are satisfied. Thus, while murder is defined to require knowingly *causing the death* of another, and statutory rape requires *intercourse* with a person under the age of 16, in the hypothetical above, if Bib satisfies the complicity rules, Muscle's conduct in committing these offenses may be imputed to Bib. Accountability for another's conduct requires proof of both special objective and culpability requirements.

OBJECTIVE ELEMENTS

Common Law Requirements   At Common Law, complicity required that the accomplice *assist* the perpetrator in committing the offense. (Such assistance was, and still is, sometimes called "aiding and abetting" another's crime.) The assistance did not need to be necessary for successful commission of the offense, nor did it need to be substantial.

> It is quite enough if the aid merely rendered it easier for the principal actor to accomplish the end intended by him and the aider and abettor, though in all human probability the end would have been attained without it.[1]

Indeed, the accomplice was not required to assist in a physical sense; encouragement was recognized as a form of assistance.

> [I]t nerves [the principal actor] to the deed, and helps him execute it through a consciousness—a purely mental condition—that another is standing by in a position to help him.

Thus, in the hypothetical above, because Bib's standing lookout provides some measure of confidence or encouragement to Muscle, it is sufficient for complicity at common law, even though Bib's attempt to warn Muscle by honking the horn fails.

Accessory After the Fact   At Common Law, one could also be held liable for complicity for aiding the perpetrator *after* the commission of the substantive offense. Such liability was, however, reserved for those aiding the perpetrator of a felony. To be a so-called *accessory after the fact* generally required that the accessory knew that a felony had been committed and personally gave aid to the felon for the purpose of hindering the apprehension or punishment of the offender.[2]

Objective Elements Under Modern Codes   The Model Penal Code, in section 2.06(3)(a)(ii), goes beyond the Common Law assistance rule and extends complicity liability to include cases where the accomplice simply "agrees or attempts to aid" the principal. Actual assistance, even in the form of psychological assistance through encouragement, is not required. The drafters intend that what constitutes an adequate "attempt to aid" will be determined by reference to the definition of the general inchoate offense of attempt in Model Penal Code section 5.01. That is, the accomplice must take a "substantial step" toward providing assistance. Similarly, whether an actor "agrees to aid" another is determined by the general inchoate offense of conspiracy, defined in Code section 5.03 as a unilateral agreement requirement. In the hypothetical above, by agreeing to serve as a lookout for Muscle, Bib did enough to be an accomplice under the "agrees to aid" language of the Code's complicity provision.

Derivative vs. Personal Liability   The difference in objective requirements—actual assistance versus an attempt or agreement to assist—reflects different conceptualizations of complicity at common law and in modern codes. Common Law viewed complicity as liability derivative from that of the principal; the principal's liability is extended to those who assist. The requirement of actual assistance, no matter how slight, served to tie the accomplice to the perpetrator

---

1. State ex rel. Martin v. Tally, 15 So. 722, 738-739 (Ala. 1894).
2. See 4 Blackstone, *Commentaries on the Laws of England* *35.

and his deed. Under modern codes, on the other hand, complicity liability is viewed as personal to the accomplice. Liability is based on *the actor's* own conduct and culpable state of mind, rather than that of the perpetrator.[3] It follows from this view that a perpetrator's knowledge of, or actual assistance from, an accomplice is not determinative. The central questions—whether the accomplice intended to assist and whether she externalized a willingness to act upon that intention—apply to the accomplice herself, not to the principal or the objective relation between them. (The derivative theory of the common law also supports a defense for the actor when the principal is unconvictable. Indeed, at early Common Law the accomplice was subject to prosecution only *after* the principal's liability was established. Modern codes explicitly reject an unconvictable perpetrator defense.)

Objectivist vs. Subjectivist Views of Criminality   The difference between derivative and personal views of complicity is one manifestation of the larger difference in perspective between the common law and modern codes, a difference described as that between an *objectivist* and a *subjectivist* view of criminality. The Common Law's objectivist view required actual assistance because objective harm or evil was viewed as essential to substantive criminality, and actual assistance causally tied the offender to the harm or evil of the offense. In contrast, the Model Penal Code's shift to a subjectivist view of criminality derives from its view that an actor's culpable state of mind, manifested in conduct, is itself a sufficient basis for criminality, even absent a causal connection with the harm or evil of an offense.

Objective Elements Satisfied by Principal   In addition to proof of assistance or an attempt or agreement to assist, there is one final objective requirement of complicity: the principal's commission of the offense conduct. That is, in order for *the accomplice* to be held liable for an offense, *the principal* must engage in the conduct comprising the offense. The Model Penal Code follows the common law on this point. Section 2.06(7) explicitly provides that accomplice liability requires "proof of the commission of the offense." Consistent with this, the Code states that complicity in a failed attempt is to be punished only as an attempt.[4] Even today, though accomplice liability is seen as personal to the accomplice, it remains an imputation rule, and unless the principal has performed the conduct constituting the offense, there is nothing to impute to the accomplice.

CULPABILITY REQUIREMENTS

Complicity as "Intentional": Does This Require Purpose or Knowledge? It is common for courts to describe complicity as necessarily being intentional. One cannot, it is claimed, accidentally be an accomplice. This raises several issues. The first concerns whether the common law's "intention" requirement should be taken to mean, in modern code terms, "purposeful" or "knowing." In *United States v. Peoni*, Judge Learned Hand concludes that the accomplice must "in some sort associate himself with the venture, . . . participate in it as in something that he wishes to bring about, . . . seek by his action to make it succeed." He must have a "purposive attitude towards it."[5] In *Backun v. United States*, in

3. See Model Penal Code § 2.06(7).

4. See Model Penal Code § 5.01(3).

5. 100 F.2d 401, 402 (2d Cir. 1938) (knowledge purchaser of counterfeit bills would sell to another insufficient to charge original seller as accessory to third-party possession).

contrast, Judge Parker concludes that knowing assistance is adequate for complicity liability. "[G]uilt as an accessory depends, not on . . . 'having a stake' in the outcome of crime . . . but on aiding and assisting the perpetrators. . . . [The actor] may not ignore" the aims of the perpetrator.[6] The Model Penal Code drafters initially proposed a knowledge standard,[7] but in the final draft a purpose requirement was adopted.[8]

Significance of Degree of Assistance and Offense Seriousness   The preference for requiring only knowing assistance, as reflected in Judge Parker's opinion in *Backun* and in the Model Penal Code's Tentative Draft formulation, stems from a belief that an actor ought not be free to assist what he knows to be a criminal offense, even if the actor does not affirmatively desire the offense. This view is particularly strong where the offense is serious and the assistance is substantial or necessary to its commission. Volunteering the whereabouts of an intended victim for a fee, *knowing* that the questioner intends murder, would seem to many people to be adequate for complicity liability. But permitting accomplice liability based on knowing assistance seems problematic in other cases, as reflected in Judge Hand's opinion in *Peoni*. While a knowledge requirement would appropriately impose liability for identifying the person another is seeking in order to murder, such a requirement also would impose liability on persons who provide minor, nonessential assistance toward less serious offenses, such as selling cigarette papers to customers knowing they will use them to smoke marijuana. Many would balk at holding the tobacconist liable as an accomplice to each of the multitude of illegal uses of marijuana that follow the sale, even if the seller knows of the intended illegal use. Consistent with this concern for the degree of assistance, statutes that adopt a knowing standard frequently increase the degree of assistance required to that of "substantial facilitation" or something similar.[9] Other "knowing" complicity statutes impose reduced liability.[10]

Culpability as to Assistance vs. Culpability as to Offense   The purpose-versus-knowledge issue is complicated by the common belief, held at Common Law and, unfortunately, in many modern cases, that there exists a single culpability requirement for complicity. This notion is typical of the "offense analysis" view prevalent at Common Law. In this context, offense analysis confuses two distinct aspects of an accomplice's culpability: (1) culpability as to assisting the perpetrator's conduct, and (2) culpability as to the elements of the object offense. One might intentionally assist someone else, yet have no culpability as to assisting that person's criminal objective: for example, intentionally loaning someone your car without knowing the person plans to use it to rob a bank. Or, one might be only negligent or reckless as to assisting an actor's conduct (e.g., accidentally leaving the car keys out where the perpetrator might take them), yet actually hope that

---

6. 112 F.2d 635, 637 (4th Cir. 1940) (seller of goods known to be stolen held liable for buyer transporting stolen property across state lines).

7. Model Penal Code § 2.04(3)(b) (Tent. Draft No. 1, 1953) (subsequently revised and renumbered § 2.06(3)(b)).

8. Model Penal Code § 2.06(3)(a).

9. See, e.g., Model Penal Code § 2.04(3)(b) (Tent. Draft No. 1, 1953) (establishes accomplice liability when "acting with knowledge that such other person was committing or had the purpose of committing the crime, he knowingly, substantially facilitates its commission").

10. N.Y. Penal Law § 115.00 (creates offense of criminal facilitation that adopts knowing standard but imposes liability for lesser offense).

the offense will occur. Even modern codes do not distinguish the two issues as clearly as they might and, as a result, they often give no clear answer on whether the "purpose" required for complicity liability requires that it be the accomplice's purpose to (a) assist the perpetrator's conduct, (b) advance commission of the offense, or (c) both.

Example: Loaning Keys to Car Used in DUI Homicide In *State v. Etzweiler*, excerpted below, the defendant gave his car keys to Bailey, a fellow worker he knew to be intoxicated. Ten minutes later, Bailey collided with another car and killed two people.[11] As a factual matter, Etzweiler might be *purposeful as to assisting* Bailey in Bailey's *conduct* constituting the offense (driving); that is, it was his purpose to give Bailey his car keys and to have Bailey drive his car. Yet Etzweiler might only be *negligent* as to whether his conduct assists Bailey *in causing the deaths*. While it was his conscious object (that is, purpose) to let Bailey drive his car, he was unreasonably unaware of a substantial risk (that is, negligent) that letting Bailey drive his car while intoxicated would cause another's death.

"Purpose of Facilitating Commission of Offense" Neither the majority nor the dissent in *Etzweiler* disagrees with the claim that an actor's culpability as to assisting the principal's conduct may differ from his culpability as to the offense elements, such as causing death. Their disagreement concerns whether the statute requires (and should require) a different level of culpability as to these matters. The New Hampshire statute at issue tracks Model Penal Code section 2.06, which requires that the accomplice assist the principal "with the purpose of promoting or facilitating the commission of the offense."[12] The majority concludes that this means that, to be liable as an accomplice, an actor must be purposeful not only as to assisting the perpetrator's conduct, but also as to all elements of the object offense. Thus, while Bailey (the principal) might be liable for *recklessly* causing the deaths, Etzweiler (the accomplice) can have no liability unless he was *purposeful* as to causing the deaths. He will be liable only if, in giving his keys to Bailey, it was his "conscious object" that Bailey kill another person.

Elevating Culpability Requirements for Complicity Such a view—that complicity requires purpose as to all elements of the object offense—obviously reduces the potential scope of accomplice liability, because "purpose" is such a demanding culpability level. An accomplice frequently may *know* of the circumstances and results of a perpetrator's planned conduct, but not be purposeful as to them. In fact, purpose is such a demanding level of culpability that even the offense of murder often does not require purpose, but only knowledge that one's conduct will cause a death. The terrorist is liable for murder if he blows up the embassy knowing that the blast will kill a night watchman, even though he may hope that the night watchman will go on break before the explosion and not be killed; he is knowing, but not purposeful, as to the killing. Under the majority view in *Etzweiler*, if an accomplice of the terrorist similarly knows that the bombing will cause the watchman's death but does not necessarily desire it, the accomplice will escape complicity liability for the killing. Applying this view to the "Bib" hypothetical, if Bib purposefully stands watch for Muscle at John's house and at the time is aware of a substantial risk (reckless) that Muscle will kill John,

---

11. 480 A.2d 870 (N.H. 1984).
12. N.H. Rev. Stat. Ann. § 626:8.

he nonetheless has no complicity in the homicide. He can be an accomplice in the homicide only if his conscious object is to assist in causing John's death.

No Elevation as to Result Under MPC   Perhaps for fear of this confusion, the Model Penal Code expressly provides that the "purpose" requirement does not apply to a result element of the offense. Section 2.06(4) provides that an accomplice need only have "the kind of culpability, if any, with respect to [a] result that is sufficient for the commission of the offense." In other words, the state could charge Etzweiler with negligent homicide under a complicity theory, and would have to prove only that he was negligent as to causing a death when he gave his keys to Bailey. This was the view of the dissent in *Etzweiler*,[13] which cites language in the New Hampshire statute that parallels the Model Penal Code language just quoted. The nonelevation of culpability as to a result is not only a more accurate reading of the statute, it is also a sounder policy. Applying this view to the hypothetical, Bib's purposeful assistance, with recklessness as to John's death, would not bar complicity liability, though his culpability as to the death would guide the *degree* of his liability. Whereas Muscle is liable for murder for intentionally killing John, because Bib is only reckless as to the killing, he is liable only for manslaughter. (If, at the time of his assistance, he knew or desired that Bib would kill John, he would be liable for murder.)

Culpability as to Circumstance Element Less Clear   The complicity requirements for culpability as to a circumstance are less clear under the Code. That the Code specifically provides for no elevation of culpability as to a result element might be interpreted as an expression of legislative intent to have circumstance elements treated differently from result elements—that is, elevated to purposeful. On the other hand, the policy arguments against elevation of culpability as to a result are equally applicable to circumstance elements. For example, in the "Bib" hypothetical, assume that when Bib purposefully assists Muscle by standing guard, he is reckless (i.e., aware of a substantial risk) as to the circumstance element of Susan being underage. If complicity requires purpose as to circumstance elements, although the statutory rape offense itself requires only negligence as to age (or may be a strict liability offense, as in the Model Penal Code[14]), Bib would have no complicity liability even though he is aware of substantial risk (i.e., reckless) that she is underage. The Model Penal Code fails to express a clear position as to whether complicity requires purpose as to circumstance elements, thereby leaving it to judges to sort out case by case. Whatever one thinks is the proper view—purpose as to all circumstance elements (elevation) or requiring only the culpability required for the target offense (no elevation)—this failure to express a clear position seems insensitive to the demands of the legality principle.

Liability for Unplanned Offenses: "Natural and Probable Consequence" Rule   Some courts, following the Common Law rule, extend accomplice liability to include offenses beyond those for which the accomplice satisfies the required culpability, imposing liability for any offense that was the "natural and probable consequence" of the offense(s) for which the defendant did have culpability.[15] In

---

13. 480 A.2d at 881.

14. Model Penal Code § 213.3(1)(a)

15. The U.S. Supreme Court, citing a party's brief, has expressed the view that "relatively few jurisdictions"—perhaps as few as ten—"have expressly rejected the 'natural and probable consequences' doctrine." Gonzales v. Duenas-Alvarez, 549 U.S. 183, 190-191 (2007).

People v. Luparello, for example, Luparello had enlisted his friends to compel one Martin to tell them where to find Luparello's former lover, who had left him.[16] Luparello was convicted of murder when, in his absence, his friends shot and killed Martin in trying to get the requested information. The court held that an actor may be liable "not only for the offense he intended to facilitate or encourage, but also [for] any reasonably foreseeable offense committed by the person he aids and abets." Under this foreseeable-offense rule, where a killing occurs during a felony, any accomplice to the underlying felony would become an accomplice to murder, whether or not that accomplice had any involvement in (or culpability toward) the killing itself. While the felony-murder rule remains popular, few jurisdictions extend the scope of accomplice liability for murder in this way, with good reason. It imposes liability beyond that which the actor's blameworthiness can justify.

Summary of Complicity Requirements   The better view is that the "purpose" requirement in complicity requires only that the accomplice purposely *assist* the perpetrator's *conduct*, not that the accomplice have purpose as to all offense elements. The culpability requirements of the substantive offense, as to both result and circumstance elements, ought to determine the culpability required for complicity in that offense. These, then, are the elements of complicity that the *accomplice* must satisfy: assisting the perpetrator (or, under the Model Penal Code, attempting or agreeing to assist), with the purpose to assist the perpetrator in his conduct that in fact constitutes the offense, and with the culpability as to the circumstance and result elements of the offense as required by the offense definition (though some interpretations require purpose as to circumstance elements, or even as to all elements).

Elements Satisfied by Perpetrator for Liability of Accomplice   In addition, complicity liability also may require that the *principal* satisfy some offense elements. The Common Law and modern codes require that, for the accomplice to be held liable, the principal must actually commit the offense, at least to the extent of satisfying the objective requirements of the offense. The Model Penal Code presents this requirement in section 2.06(7) when it requires "proof of commission of the offense." The Common Law also required that the principal satisfy the offense's culpability requirements (and that the principal have no general defense), but modern codes—in keeping with their subjectivist view of criminality, which focuses on the accomplice's own culpability—reject such a requirement.

CAUSING CRIME BY AN INNOCENT

Liability for Causing Crime by an Innocent Person   Under complicity liability, an actor who helps another person commit an offense is held accountable for the other person's criminal conduct. Both parties typically are guilty of the offense, one as the perpetrator or *principal*, the other as an *accomplice*. Where the perpetrator is not a confederate of the "accomplice," but is instead an innocent person being used as a pawn or instrumentality to commit a crime, the person causing the innocent person's conduct may be held accountable for that conduct

---

16. 187 Cal. App. 3d 410, 231 Cal. Rptr. 832 (1986).

through a doctrine analogous to, but distinct from, complicity. As the Model Penal Code states it,

> A person is legally accountable for the conduct of another person when, acting with the kind of culpability that is sufficient for the commission of the offense, he causes an innocent or irresponsible person to engage in such conduct.[17]

Common Law Complicity Rules Create Need for Alternative Basis of Liability   The Common Law also imposed liability for such "causing crime by an innocent." Recognition of such a doctrine was made a practical necessity by the common law's recognition of an unconvictable-perpetrator defense, under which an accomplice can be held liable only when the principal is also held liable. Absent a special rule, recognition of an unconvictable-perpetrator defense made it impossible to convict an actor who caused an innocent or irresponsible person to commit an offense. Also influential in creating this alternative theory of liability was the difference in fact patterns between complicity and innocent-perpetrator cases. Rather than merely assisting the perpetrator, as an accomplice does, the other party in the latter situation generally is the moving force in the offense. The innocent or irresponsible actor typically is more an "instrument" than a "perpetrator."

State v. Etzweiler

Supreme Court of New Hampshire
125 N.H. 57, 480 A.2d 870 (1984)

BATCHELDER, Justice, with whom BROCK, Justice, concurs.

The issues raised in these consolidated cases involve the applicability of New Hampshire's motor vehicle laws and Criminal Code to a simple fact situation. The State and Mark A. Etzweiler, one of the defendants, have stipulated to the following facts. On July 30, 1982, the defendants, Mark Etzweiler and Ralph Bailey, arrived in Etzweiler's automobile at the plant where both were employed. Bailey had been drinking alcoholic beverages and was, allegedly, intoxicated. Etzweiler, allegedly knowing that Bailey was intoxicated, loaned his car to Bailey and proceeded into the plant to begin work. Bailey drove Etzweiler's car away. Approximately ten minutes later, Bailey, driving recklessly, collided with a car driven by Susan Beaulieu. As a result of the accident, two passengers in the Beaulieu car, Kathryn and Nathan Beaulieu, were killed.

On August 26, 1982, the grand jury handed down two indictments charging Etzweiler with negligent homicide, and two indictments charging Bailey with manslaughter. Subsequently, on April 6, 1983, the grand jury issued two additional indictments charging Etzweiler with negligent homicide as an accomplice.

Etzweiler filed motions to quash all indictments against him, and the Superior Court transferred to this court the questions of law raised by the motions. . . .

The cases were consolidated on appeal. We dismiss all indictments against Etzweiler. . . .

The superior court transferred five questions of law. We need address only the first question: whether the legislature intended to impose criminal liability upon a person who lends his automobile to an intoxicated driver but does not

---

17. Model Penal Code § 2.06(2)(a).

accompany the driver, when the driver's operation of the borrowed automobile causes death. . . .

The second indictments charge Etzweiler with the offense of negligent homicide as an accomplice.

RSA 626:8 delineates all situations in which an individual may be held criminally liable for the conduct of another. One situation is when an individual "is an accomplice of [another] in the commission of the offense." RSA 626:8, II(c). Accomplice liability under RSA 626:8, II(c) is defined in two parts, RSA 626:8, III and IV. Section III sets forth the elements which must be present above, beyond, and regardless of the substantive offense. Section IV sets forth the elements of the substantive offense that must be present in order to charge the accomplice.

RSA 626:8, III provides:

> A person is an accomplice of another person in the commission of an offense if: (a) with the purpose of promoting or facilitating the commission of the offense, he aids . . . such other person in planning or committing it. . . .

The section sets forth the conduct element of accomplice liability, and the necessary accompanying mental state.

Under section III, the State has the burden of establishing that the accomplice acted with the purpose of promoting or facilitating the commission of the substantive offense. This encompasses the requirement that the accomplice's acts were designed to aid the primary actor in committing the offense, and that the accomplice had the purpose to "make the crime succeed." In other words, the accomplice must have the "purpose to advance the criminal end." Model Penal Code §5.03, comment at 107 (Tent. Draft No. 10, 1960) (RSA 626:8 is based upon the Model Penal Code).

Section IV sets forth the elements of the substantive offense that the State has the burden of establishing against the accomplice. "When causing a particular result is an element of an offense," the accomplice must act "with the kind of culpability, if any, with respect to that result that is sufficient for the commission of the offense." RSA 626:8, IV. See generally *Element Analysis in Defining Criminal Liability: The Model Penal Code and Beyond*, 35 Stan. L. Rev. 681, 739-41 (1983).

Our interpretation of the accomplice liability statute effectuates the policy that an accomplice's liability ought not to extend beyond the criminal purposes that he or she shares. Because accomplice liability holds an individual criminally liable for actions done by another, it is important that the prosecution fall squarely within the statute.

Applying these statutory prerequisites, we turn to the indictments charging Etzweiler as an accomplice to negligent homicide.

> Mark Etzweiler acted as an accomplice in the conduct which caused the death[s] of Kathryn [and Nathan] Beaulieu when, with a purpose to promote and facilitate the offense of driving under the influence of alcohol, he aided Ralph Bailey in the commission of that offense by lending Ralph Bailey his 1980 AMC automobile, knowing Ralph Bailey was under the influence of alcohol, and encouraging him to drive it on a public way in such condition, and Mark Etzweiler thereby acted negligently with respect to the death[s] of Kathryn [and Nathan] Beaulieu. . . .

The State has alleged that, with the purpose of promoting or facilitating the offense of driving under the influence of alcohol, Etzweiler aided Bailey in the commission of that offense. However, under our statute, the accomplice must aid the primary actor in the substantive offense with the purpose of facilitating the substantive offense—in this case, negligent homicide. Therefore, the indictments against Etzweiler must be quashed.

Even if the indictments tracked the statutory language of RSA 626:8, III and IV, Etzweiler, as a matter of law, could not be an accomplice to negligent homicide. To satisfy the requirements of RSA 626:8, III, the State must establish that Etzweiler's acts were designed to aid Bailey in committing negligent homicide. Yet under the negligent homicide statute, Bailey must be unaware of the risk of death that his conduct created. RSA 630:3, I, RSA 626:2, II(d). We cannot see how Etzweiler could intentionally aid Bailey in a crime that Bailey was unaware that he was committing. Thus, we hold, as a matter of law, that, in the present context of the Criminal Code, an individual may not be an accomplice to negligent homicide. We need not reach the question of whether the statute provides for accomplices to manslaughter or murder.

Need intent/ purpose to be an aider/ accomplice

Therefore, we answer the first question posed by the superior court in the negative in regard to both RSA 630:3, I and RSA 626:8. . . .

[Remanded.]

SOUTER, Justice, concurring specially:

I concur with the [result] reached by Justice Batchelder, and I join in his opinion, save in [one respect]. Although there would be no value in an extended analysis at this point, I do not read RSA 626:8, IV as my brother does. That section provides that

> [w]hen causing a particular result is an element of an offense, an accomplice in the conduct causing such result is an accomplice in the commission of that offense, if he acts with the kind of culpability, if any, with respect to that result that is sufficient for the commission of the offense.

I read this language as an attempt to provide that a person may be criminally liable as an accomplice even if he does not act "with the purpose of promoting or facilitating the commission of an offense." RSA 626:8, III(a).

The attempt fails because the meaning of "accomplice" in section IV is unclear. Section III provides what is necessary to be an "accomplice . . . in the commission of an offense." Among other things, such an accomplice must have a "purpose" to promote or facilitate the commission of the offense. Section IV purports to determine when an accomplice in "conduct" causing a particular result is also an accomplice in the commission of the offense defined by reference to that result. Section IV does not, however, define this new sense of "accomplice" in conduct. One can guess that it means "accomplice" as used in section III minus the "purpose." This is no more than a guess, however. The confusion is probably explained historically by tracing the revisions in the Model Penal Code, on which New Hampshire's provisions are based. Compare Tent. Draft No. 1, §2.04(3)(a), (b) and (4) with final draft §2.06(3)(a) and (4); compare Tent Draft No. 1, §2.04(4) with RSA 626:8, IV. See *Element Analysis in Defining Criminal Liability: The Model Penal Code and Beyond*, 35 Stanford L. Rev. 681, 733 (1983). Whatever the explanation, section IV fails to give any comprehensible, let alone fair, notice of its intended effect and is thus unenforceable. It is of course

← Need purpose to facilitate

open to the legislature to provide for accomplice liability more broadly than it has done in section III alone. . . .

KING, Chief Justice, dissenting in *Etzweiler* (with whom DOUGLAS, Justice, joins . . .).

For the reasons that follow, I would affirm [the] indictments against Etzweiler, as . . . an accessory to negligent homicide. . . .

In construing RSA 626:8—which imputes criminal liability to a person for the conduct of another—to determine whether the indictments in question properly state an offense under that statute, one must define the pertinent statutory language by reference to the definitions provided in the statute itself.

RSA 626:8, I and II(c) assign criminal liability to someone who is "an accomplice of another person in the commission of an offense." This phrase is defined by other provisions in the statute which designate three sets of circumstances under which a person may become "an accomplice of another person in the commission of an offense." They are:

(1) if, "with the purpose of promoting or facilitating the commission of that offense, he solicits such other person in committing it, or aids or agrees or attempts to aid such other person in planning or committing it," RSA 626:8, III(a); or

(2) if "his conduct is expressly declared by law to establish his complicity," RSA 626:8, III(b); or

(3) if, "[w]hen causing a particular result is an element of an offense," the person is "an accomplice in the conduct causing such result" and "he acts with the kind of culpability, if any, with respect to that result that is sufficient for the commission of the offense."

RSA 626:8, IV.

While the statutory phrase "accomplice in the conduct causing [a particular] result" provided by RSA 626:8, IV is not explicitly defined in the statute, when viewed as part of a totality it is implicitly defined by RSA 626:8, III(a). Under section III(a), a person is an accomplice in the principal's criminal conduct causing a particular result if, with the purpose of promoting or facilitating the principal's criminal conduct, the person solicits that conduct, or aids or agrees or attempts to aid that conduct. Section III also assigns liability in those situations in which the accomplice actively seeks the criminal result by aiding and abetting the principal without caring precisely how the principal achieves that result.

Therefore, for a person to be criminally liable under RSA 626:8, IV for the crime of a principal, that person must act purposefully with respect to the principal's criminal conduct. However, with respect to the result of the principal's criminal conduct, section IV requires a showing that the person acted with the same state of mind required of the principal. See ALI, *Model Penal Code and Commentaries*, Tentative Draft No. 1, Comments §2.04 (4), at 34 (1953); *Element Analysis in Defining Criminal Liability: The Model Penal Code and Beyond*, 35 Stan. L. Rev. 681, 739-40 (1983). A showing that a person merely acquiesced in or consented to a principal's conduct is not enough to prove purposefulness under section III. Rather, it must be demonstrated that the person participated actively in the principal's conduct.

The second indictments properly allege that Etzweiler acted purposefully to "promote and facilitate" Bailey's criminal conduct—Bailey's alleged intoxicated driving—causing the deaths and "aided" Bailey by "encouraging" him in that conduct. The indictments also allege, as they must, that Etzweiler "thereby acted negligently with respect to" the resulting deaths. Of course, to obtain a conviction of Etzweiler, the State must prove each alleged act and mental state as well as the causal link between Bailey's driving and the resulting deaths. Finally, it should be noted that to find Etzweiler guilty, the jury must conclude that he was criminally negligent under RSA 626:2, II(d), a showing of culpability substantially higher than ordinary civil negligence.

While other proffered interpretations of RSA 626:8 may be plausible, they effectively give principal meaning to either section III or section IV of the statute at the expense of the other section. The majority opinion, for example, essentially reads section IV of RSA 626:8 out of the statute, notwithstanding the court's failed attempt to infuse that section with meaning. The statutory analysis herein satisfies the rule of statutory construction that all parts of a statute be read as meaningful and consistent parts of a whole. This analysis also fulfills the court's duty to interpret a statute so as to effectuate its legislative intent: here, to inculpate persons who purposely further the criminal conduct of others while [culpably] unaware of the substantial and unjustifiable risks attending that criminal conduct.

The court's holding that as a matter of law "a person may not have a purpose of having another commit negligent homicide" is problematic. First, this holding is not supported by the language of RSA 626:8. Second, the court's holding requiring purposeful conduct with respect to the result of the principal's offense, effectively precludes criminal liability for aiding any homicide other than intentional homicide. The justification, theoretical or otherwise, for such an approach to accomplice liability is imperceptible. . . .

▲ **PROBLEMS**

Wrong Place, Wrong Race (#66)

Keith Mondello grows up in a predominantly white, working-class neighborhood in Brooklyn, New York. The vast majority of his community is either Italian immigrants or second- or third-generation Italian Americans. While the neighborhood has a close-knit, family feeling, it also has a darker side. Some in the neighborhood, particularly young men, believe that non-Italians, particularly racial and ethnic minorities, should be kept out. Mondello is one such young man. His feelings against perceived outsiders are particularly inflamed when his ex-girlfriend, Gina Feliciano, is seen dating black and Latino men. One day, some black and Latino friends of Feliciano have a run-in with Mondello and his group of friends. Mondello and his crowd force the men to leave without a physical confrontation, but threaten to hurt them if they ever come back. Feliciano tells Mondello and his friends that about 30 of her black and Puerto Rican friends are coming the next day to beat them up.

Fearing that Feliciano will follow through on her threat, Mondello gathers a group, eliciting help from a nearby group of older, tougher men, including Joey Fama. Fama has a mental impairment stemming from a car accident when he was younger, after which he became notably prone to violence. Mondello and around 30 of his friends meet near Feliciano's apartment, prepared for the fight. Many of them are carrying bats. Unknown to Mondello, Fama has brought a loaded gun.

Meanwhile, Yusuf Hawkins, a black sixteen-year-old, is out with three of his friends that same night. After spending most of the day watching movies, the four boys head to Mondello's neighborhood because one of them wants to look at a car he saw in a classified ad. They take the train to the neighborhood and begin walking to the address, stopping and asking for directions along the way. One of Mondello's group spots the four black boys and, because blacks are rare in the neighborhood, yells out "They're here!" The mob instantly surrounds the four friends, shouting and waving their bats. Some members of the group realize that Hawkins and his friends are not the friends of Feliciano they are anticipating and they back off. Fama, however, pulls out his .32 caliber semi-automatic pistol and points it at Hawkins. Someone yells for Fama not to shoot and Hawkins pleads for his life, but Fama pays no attention. Instead, he fires four shots at Hawkins from a distance of seven feet. The crowd flees. Hawkins dies on the way to the hospital.

What liability for Mondello, if any, under the Model Penal Code for Hawkins' death? Prepare a list of all criminal code subsections in the order in which you rely on them in your analysis.

Helping Lincoln's Assassin (#67)

The Civil War has just ended. General Robert E. Lee has surrendered at Appomattox, and the rebellious states are brought back into the Union. It is a grand victory for President Abraham Lincoln, who has persevered through the long and difficult war, refusing to let the nation dissolve. The Confederacy, however, still has many sympathizers, and some are not willing to give up the fight. John Wilkes Booth, bitter over the South's loss, hatches a plot to assassinate Lincoln. While Lincoln watches a play at Ford's Theatre in Washington, D.C., Booth is able to slip into the President's box, where he shoots Lincoln in the back of the head. As he jumps from the box to the stage to make his escape, Booth breaks his ankle. However, he still manages to make his way out of the theater and flee with a co-conspirator, David Herold.

On their way to Virginia, Booth and Herold stop in Bryantown, Maryland, at the farm of Dr. Samuel Mudd, a sympathizer of the Southern cause. They arrive in the middle of the night and give Mudd reason to suspect that they are on the run from authorities. Mudd, who has met Booth twice before, treats Booth's injured ankle and lets them spend the night in his house. He charges Booth $25 for setting his ankle, which he later claims was presented to him as sustained in a fall from a horse. At the time, news of Lincoln's assassination has not yet reached Bryantown. The next day, however, the news has spread. Mudd goes into town to fetch supplies and learns that Booth is being sought and why. When he returns, Booth and Herold have left. Mudd waits until the following day to report his encounter with Booth to the authorities.

What liability for Mudd, if any, under the Model Penal Code? Prepare a list of all criminal code subsections in the order in which you rely on them in your analysis.

What liability for Mudd, if any, under common law?

Cheering on Rapists (#68)

Cheryl Araujo, a twenty-one-year-old mother of two, has just celebrated her oldest daughter's third birthday. After some light tidying up following the festivities, Araujo goes out to pick up some cigarettes. It is getting late, and the only place open is Big Dan's Tavern, a bar known for its tough crowd. In the small town, it is widely considered an inappropriate place for women to venture into alone. However, there are only about a dozen patrons in the bar, and Araujo decides to stay for a drink.

Araujo begins to watch a group of men playing pool and goes over to play a song on the jukebox. Before long, two men approach her and ask her to leave with them. Araujo refuses and decides to leave. However, Daniel Silvia grabs her and forces her onto the pool table. There, she is stripped from the waist down, as two men take turns raping her. Araujo cries and screams for help, but instead of coming to her aid, the other patrons either watch or cheer on the rapists. Some of them yell "Go for it, go for it," as the two men rape Araujo repeatedly. After being raped by the men, Araujo manages to escape from the bar and runs half-naked into the street, where three passersby take her to a hospital.

What liability under the Model Penal Code, if any, for the bar-goers who cheered on the rapists?

What liability under the Model Penal Code, if any, for the bar-goers who watched the rape and did nothing?

Prepare a list of all criminal code subsections in the order in which you rely on them in your analysis.

Murder by Cop? (#69)

Joseph Bailey and Gordon Murdock each own citizens' band radios, which they use primarily to have long arguments with each other. Living just two miles apart, they mostly communicate over the radio waves. Bailey knows that Murdock is easily agitated and often intoxicated. He enjoys provoking him. Their fighting escalates this night when Bailey insults Murdock and Murdock's hero, General George Patton. Bailey challenges Murdock to grab his gun and be ready for him when he comes over. Murdock responds by saying that he will be waiting on his front porch and tells Bailey to "kiss your mother and wife and children goodbye because you will never go back home."

Instead of going to Murdock's, however, Bailey calls the police to report a man waving a weapon on the porch at Murdock's home. When police arrive, the porch is empty. Informed of this, Bailey goes back on his radio and chides Murdock for not showing up for their proposed duel. He again tells Murdock that he is on his way over and to have his gun ready. Bailey knows that Murdock is legally blind but is able to distinguish shapes and colors. He tells Murdock that he will be over in a blue and white car, the colors of the local police cars. Murdock again agrees to be out on his porch. Bailey calls the police a second time, telling them that Murdock is out on his porch again, threatening the neighbors with a gun. This time, when the officers arrive at Murdock's house, they find him on the porch with his gun. One officer tells him to "leave the gun alone and walk down the stairs away from it." Murdock responds by cursing them out and firing at the officer. Though his shot misses, all three officers return fire, fatally wounding Murdock. Before he dies, Murdock says several times, "I didn't know you was the police."

What liability for Bailey, if any, under the Model Penal Code for Murdock's death? Prepare a list of all criminal code subsections in the order in which you rely on them in your analysis.

✳ DISCUSSION ISSUE

Should Criminal Liability Be Imposed for Facilitating Conduct that One Knows Is a Crime, Even if Facilitating the Crime Is Not One's Purpose?

Materials presenting each side of this Discussion Issue appear in the Advanced Materials for Section 14 in Appendix A.

The Act Requirement and Liability for an Omission or Possession

Most offenses define prohibited conduct, such as engaging in conduct that causes a death. But a person sometimes can be criminally liable for failing to act if such failure is the violation of a legal duty. Thus, the effect of legal duties may be to treat offenders *as if they had* engaged in prohibited offense conduct—that is, to *impute* required offense conduct. What legal duties does the law create, and when should their violation lead to criminal liability?

◆ **THE CASE OF DAVID CASH (#70)**

It is Memorial Day weekend, 1997. Best friends Jeremy Strohmeyer and David Cash are seniors at Woodrow Wilson High School in Long Beach,

Figure 65 **Strohmeyer school yearbook photo**
(Las Vegas Review Journal)

Figure 66 **David Cash, May 1997**
(Las Vegas Review Journal)

California. Classmates consider Cash smart, but socially awkward. He acts cool by spiking his hair and growing sideburns, but is still baby-faced, short, and interested in subjects like engineering. In contrast, Strohmeyer is outgoing, wild, and worldly, after living in Singapore for several years while his mother was working there. He drinks, has a fake ID, and is very flirtatious. The two have a firm friendship, though, after meeting in a computer class during their junior year, just after Strohmeyer returned to the states. Both have aspirations for after gradation. Strohmeyer wants to be an officer in the Air Force, like his adoptive father, and Cash hopes to become a nuclear engineer.

Strohmeyer is responsible for introducing Cash to the wilder side of high school by taking him to parties and getting him drunk for the first time, even bringing a camcorder to tape the evening. Cash's parents, who are reconciling after being separated for years, are not terribly concerned. They treat him leniently because he has always been independent and trustworthy, and his grades remain high. Even when Cash returns home drunk with Strohmeyer, they do not get angry. Strohmeyer also shows off to Cash his upper-class lifestyle, which includes a maid, a jet, and four cars.

Strohmeyer's behavior is increasingly wild and erratic, and his grades have dropped since he returned from Singapore. For example, a teacher who once described him as one of the best students he ever taught has recently changed his mind; he now sees two different sides to Strohmeyer. In school, he is thought of as a hard partier with a violent temper. His Internet sign-in name is "Killer." He also has a secret interest in child pornography. Recently, he had an Internet chat under the screename "flyboy1030," where he wrote that he fantasizes about sex with five- or six-year-old girls. *ew* He even asked a girlfriend to dress up in a young girl's school uniform and put her hair in pigtails. (She refused.)

Figure 67 **Strohmeyer and Cash in Wilson High School senior class photo**
(Las Vegas Review Journal)

Over the past year, Strohmeyer has slowly spiraled into a destructive pattern. He uses drugs more often, drinks frequently, and is taking amphetamines, the combination of which explains his recent behavior at parties. At one, he spit in a jock's face and screamed profanities at a girl after she asked him to leave. On another occasion, he sneaked a kitten out of a host's house and threw it out of a car's window as he drove away. He even incited others to help him throw marshmallows, then books, and finally bottles down a hallway at a party, which he followed up by personally kicking holes in the walls. His parents think he is just going through a typical teenage rebellion stage, while classmates attribute his behavior to extreme senioritis. *how ignorant are these people?*

Nonetheless, Cash still looks up to Strohmeyer. Strohmeyer is one of the "cool kids," and helps Cash overcome his struggles of trying to fit in by introducing him to people and giving him the chance to hang out with other "cool kids." Cash sometimes joins Strohmeyer in a big group to cruise the town, which occasionally also includes harassing prostitutes and the homeless. Strohmeyer often brags about smashing eggs in the faces of prostitutes.

Strohmeyer also benefits from his friendship with Cash. As the more impressionable of the two, Cash makes Strohmeyer feel good about himself by laughing at Strohmeyer's jokes and pranks and defending his actions. Cash is also allowed to drive his mother's red Chevrolet convertible, while Strohmeyer's parents never allow him to drive their cars. The two recently used Cash's mother's car for a road trip to UC Berkeley, during which they got their tongues pierced. The university is Cash's top choice. A serious car crash ended their trip, but Strohmeyer's father bailed them out by purchasing them airline tickets back to Long Beach.

For the long Memorial Day weekend, Cash's father invites Strohmeyer along for a trip to Las Vegas as a thank you to his parents for letting Cash stay with them for three weeks. Cash is looking forward to the trip.

On the evening of Saturday, May 24, 1997, they leave for Las Vegas. On the way, they stop in several towns for food and gas, reaching Primm, on the

Figure 68 **The Primadonna Resort in Primm, Nevada, which changed its name to the Primm Valley Resort in 1998**

(Frank Reynolds, www.vegasgallery.com)

Nevada border, at midnight. There, they visit the Primadonna Casino. Cash's father gives the two some money and tells them to meet up again at 3:00 a.m. He then goes to play poker. Cash and Strohmeyer want to ride Wild Bill's Roller Coaster but cannot find the entrance. Instead, they end up at another casino and then an arcade before returning to the Primadonna.

Sitting by the pool at the Primadonna, Strohmeyer uses his fake ID to order some drinks. He has a whiskey and Coke, while Cash goes for a strawberry daiquiri. As the night creeps on, they grow restless. At one point, Strohmeyer tries sneaking into the gambling section, but casino security promptly kicks him out. They order more drinks and play arcade games. Strohmeyer starts talking to a girl who he thinks has a nice body. He asks for her beeper number, but she refuses, recalling

later that she thought he was creepy. Strohmeyer leaves to get more drinks, but when he returns he keeps trying to talk to her. He tries to impress her by showing off his nipple and tongue piercings. When her mother arrives, they quickly leave.

Cash and Strohmeyer are tired of playing the video games and decide to urinate on them instead to entertain themselves. They quickly become distracted, however, by two young children having a spitball fight. One of their wet paper towels hits Strohmeyer and he throws it back. He then starts playing with the kids, and they run through the rows of video games.

One of the children is seven-year-old Sherrice Iverson, of South Central Los Angeles. Like Strohmeyer and Cash, she has grown tired of waiting for her father. Casino security has twice taken her back to her father, and she had already fallen asleep in the driver's seat of a video game. She is used to the long nights that the Nevada casino trips bring, because her father, a diabetic on disability, is a gambling addict. While thinking it too dangerous to

Figure 69 **Sherrice Iverson**

(Las Vegas Metropolitan Police Department)

allow Sherrice to play in front of their house in South Central, he thinks the Primadonna is safe and lets her have the run of the place. Sherrice is generally well cared for; she always sports freshly pressed clothes and neatly braided hair. At age seven, she likes "The Little Mermaid," the color purple, and jumping rope but is still afraid of the dark. When she grows up, she wants to be a "nurse, policewoman, model, or dancer." She is less than 4 feet tall and weighs about 46 pounds. Strohmeyer is almost 6 feet tall and weighs about 150 pounds.

Figure 70 Iverson on Primadonna Resort arcade surveillance camera
(Las Vegas Sun/Ethan Miller)

Strohmeyer and Sherrice continue playing in the arcade for another ten minutes or so, until Sherrice runs into the women's restroom. Strohmeyer gets a drink of water, takes a puff of his cigarette, and follows her in. A few seconds later, Cash follows in after him. In the bathroom, Sherrice swings a plastic "Wet Floor" sign at Strohmeyer and he gets angry. He picks her up, placing one of his arms under her armpit with his hand over her mouth, while using the other arm to lift her into the large handicap stall, locking the door behind him.

Thinking that the game has gone too far, Cash tries to get Strohmeyer's attention by standing on the toilet in the stall adjacent to the handicap one. Cash tells him to let Sherrice go and tries to convince him to leave the bathroom. He then starts tapping on Strohmeyer's head to get his attention. Strohmeyer ignores him until Cash knocks off his friend's "Bruins" cap. Strohmeyer stares at Cash weirdly, as if "he [doesn't] care what [Cash] is saying." After this unsuccessful attempt to get Strohmeyer to stop, Cash gives up. He leaves the arcade and waits for Strohmeyer and his father on a bench in the resort's courtyard.

After Cash's attempted intervention, Strohmeyer quickly refocuses on Sherrice. He takes off her boots, followed by her pants and underwear. She screams when he "fingers" her a few times. He notices blood on his index finger. To quiet her down, he puts her on the floor, with her hands pulled around her neck. He holds her in this position for about ten minutes, and then puts her on the toilet and begins to masturbate against her body. He thinks she is unconscious, but alive.

When women suddenly come into the restroom, Strohmeyer quickly props Sherrice up on the toilet and sits on her, so that only his feet show under the stall's door. With people still there, he tries masturbating again but cannot maintain an erection. Strohmeyer quickly covers her mouth when he hears Sherrice gasping for air.

After the restroom empties, Sherrice is limp. Strohmeyer thinks that it would be cruel to leave Sherrice as she is. He considers her future as a "vegetable" and decides to "put her out of her misery." He tries to break her neck. Despite hearing a loud pop, he sees her still moving and uses all of his strength to do it again. This time he is convinced that she is dead.

Figure 71 **Surveillance tape of Strohmeyer outside the women's bathroom of the Primadonna resort**

(Las Vegas Sun/Ethan Miller)

Figure 72 **Cash and Strohmeyer (in hat) on arcade surveillance camera**

(Las Vegas Metropolitan Police Department)

Strohmeyer cleans up by putting Sherrice's boots, pants, and underwear in the toilet. He then wipes his forearm clean of white foam and blood before finally putting Sherrice's legs in the toilet and propping her up so that none of her limbs are visible from under the stall door. Twenty-two minutes after following Sherrice in, Strohmeyer leaves.

As he walks out of the casino, he stays close to the walls of the arcade in an attempt to avoid the security cameras. He meets Cash. On their way to the car, they talk to a valet and show off their piercings. Cash asks Strohmeyer what went on in the bathroom after he left. Looking Cash straight in the eye, Strohmeyer answers, bluntly, "I killed her." Cash later recalls being shocked by the revelation and having no idea how to react. His only other question of Strohmeyer is whether she was "wet" when he digitally raped her.

Shortly afterwards, Cash's father arrives and they finish driving to Las Vegas, arriving there on the morning of Sunday, May 25. They check into the Holiday Inn at noon. Strohmeyer and Cash play slot machines, drink beer, ride a roller coaster, and check out all the casinos. During their explorations, they discuss what happened at the Primadonna. Cash is convinced they will be caught because of the video surveillance cameras that were all over the resort. He is also worried that they made themselves conspicuous by showing off their piercings and saying they were from Long Beach. They make a pact not to tell anyone. If caught, they make up various excuses for Strohmeyer to use, ranging from sheer innocence to intoxication to insanity. Early Monday morning, the three arrive back in Long Beach. At the Primadonna, meanwhile, a female employee has found Sherrice's body and has informed the police and the girl's father.

On Tuesday, school is back in session, but Cash sleeps in and skips his classes. He hangs around the house all day and during the five o'clock news sees that there is a videotape of him and Strohmeyer entering and exiting the restroom. Realizing that they will certainly be found, the color drains from his face. He calls Strohmeyer to tell him about the video. Cash watches it again with Strohmeyer. To gain perspective, they decide they need to tell someone about the incident. They tell the whole story to a friend, James Trujillo, in a Kinko's parking lot. When Trujillo does not believe them, Cash tells another friend, Jeremy Phillips, who tells Cash to turn Strohmeyer in to the police.

The next day, a classmate, Melissa Ellis, sees the video on television before school. She immediately recognizes the pair, identifying Strohmeyer from his posture and walk and Cash by his sideburns and hair. Strohmeyer and Cash drive to school that day in Cash's mother's red convertible with an *LA Times* newspaper in the backseat. On the front page of the paper are pictures of the two (stills from the videotape). They talk with Justin Ware, whose mother called him at 10:00 p.m. the night before, to see if he recognized the boys in the video. Ware asks them if they really did it; Strohmeyer says he did. Ware is speechless. The pair go to class, and Strohmeyer acts normal the entire day, goofing off and flashing his piercings.

Later, Ellis runs into her friend, Lisa Cota, and finds out that she too recognized Strohmeyer and Cash in the video. They talk to Carmela Rhmyer, who says that Strohmeyer just told her that he and Cash were in Las Vegas over the weekend but that he was drunk and is innocent. Later, a girl in Ware's class says that the *LA Times* photo looks like Strohmeyer. Ware tells Strohmeyer about it and asks him what he is going to do. Strohmeyer says, "Nothing," and that another student has already confronted him. Strohmeyer and Cash go to Taco Bell for lunch and make "last supper" jokes throughout the meal. Cash thinks they will be arrested when they return to school. Acting on information from Ellis and Cota, Assistant Principal Greg Mendoza contacts Officer Birdsall about the video. Birdsall interviews the two students and arranges for surveillance on Strohmeyer's house.

Strohmeyer goes home after school, growing increasingly anxious. He calls an ex-girlfriend, Agnes Lee, and asks her to come over. Although she feels ill, she does not want to let him down and goes. They go to Jamba Juice, where she notices that he is nervous and fidgety. She drops him off at his house, just as his older sister, Heather, is arriving. He runs back to Lee's car and asks her to stay because he has to tell her something—that he has done something horrible. He tells her that he strangled a young black girl and asks her to leave the country with him. He also says the girl was sexually molested, but (falsely) blames it on Cash. Lee refuses to flee with him and tells him he deserves to be punished. When she gets back to her house, she sees the video and recognizes Strohmeyer and Cash. Lee calls her father and recounts her conversation with Strohmeyer. Her father immediately calls the Long Beach police. They contact Lee, who warns them of Strohmeyer's temper and desire to leave the country.

By now, Cash has received a phone call from his father instructing him to stay home. Cash is certain that his father is now aware of their involvement in the crime at the Primadonna. Cash calls Strohmeyer to explain that his father knows and he will probably be forced to talk to the police. Strohmeyer agrees and says that he understands the situation. He is now aware that he is being watched. He takes his ADD medication off the shelf, empties the bottle into his mouth, and writes a suicide note. He then goes out on the porch to smoke a cigarette while the police sit in their cars, watching patiently. Strohmeyer's sister drops their mother off at home, but he does not want her to see him in this state and scrambles out the door and down the street. He does not make it very far, however, before the police overtake him.

They take him to a community hospital after his mother alerts them to his drug ingestion. Meanwhile, Cash's father asks Cash if he saw the video. They go to the police department. Cash is scared, thinking, "Even though I didn't do anything,

Figure 73 **Cash driving by prom that he was unable to attend, June 1997**

(Las Vegas Review Journal)

I could get into more trouble." The police take his picture and interview him but do not charge him with any crime. Cash goes home to finish homework that is due the next day.

At the hospital, Strohmeyer tells the police he wants to talk and get things out in the open. They inform him of his rights. He tells them that Cash had nothing to do with the murder. He says that he "wanted to experience death." He describes that it was like a dream and he can only remember bits and pieces. After giving a full account of the evening, Strohmeyer adds that he hopes some good will come of his crime in the form of parents keeping better watch over their children.

At school the next day, Cash is curious whether things will be different and what people's reactions will be. His day is cut short, however, when he is thrown out of class for his project—a collage of pictures of pierced female genitalia. When he finally returns to school, Cash is shocked to learn that he will not be allowed to participate in his class's graduation or its prom. He is told that his diploma will be sent to him and the cost of his prom tickets refunded.

The story is sensational and the media quickly descend on Cash. They interview him and even pay for the video of him getting drunk for the first time with Strohmeyer. Cash sells the video for $1,500, keeps $500 for himself, and gives the rest to Philips for orchestrating the deal. Cash and Philips later show up outside the school prom, standing through the sunroof of a limo screaming, "I'm not going." The media cover the stunt heavily, and Cash later recalls that he enjoyed being in the limelight. He later goes with friends to watch a belly-dancing performance at a restaurant.

Figure 74 **Leroy Iverson at Sherrice's funeral**

(Las Vegas Review Journal)

On Saturday, May 31, Sherrice's funeral is held at Paradise Baptist Church. Her parents are not speaking to each other, and both are suing Strohmeyer and the Primadonna. (Sherrice's father is also involved in another lawsuit for slander, after a casino official told reporters that the father asked for $100, a six-pack, a hotel room, and payment for Sherrice's funeral after learning of her death.) The

Primadonna files cross-claims and third-party claims against Cash and Strohmeyer. Sherrice's mother says she still dreams about her daughter. Strohmeyer's parents are receiving death threats.

In an interview with the *LA Times*, Cash says that "if anything, the case has made it easier for [me] to score with women." When asked whether he is angry with Strohmeyer, Cash says no, only that he misses his friend. When asked if he feels sorry for Sherrice Iverson, he says that the "situation sucks in general." He says he feels worse for Strohmeyer because he knows him.

> It is very tragic, okay? But the simple fact remains I do not know this little girl. I do not know starving children in Panama. I do not know people that die of disease in Egypt. The only person I knew in this event was Jeremy Strohmeyer, and I know as his best friend that he had potential. . . . I'm sad that I lost a best friend. . . . I'm not going to lose sleep over somebody else's problem.

1. Relying only on your own intuitions of justice, what liability and punishment, if any, does David Cash deserve?

N	0	1	2	3	4	5	6	7	8	9	10	11
☐	☐	☐	☐	☐	☐	☐	☐	☐	☒	☐	☐	☒
no liability	liability but no punishment	1 day	2 wks	2 mo	6 mo	1 yr	3 yrs	7 yrs	15 yrs	30 yrs	life imprisonment	death *to everyone*

2. What "justice" arguments could defense counsel make on the defendant's behalf?

3. What "justice" arguments could the prosecution make against the defendant?

4. What liability for Cash, if any, under the then-existing statutes? Prepare a list of all criminal code subsections and cases in the order in which you rely on them in your analysis.

5. What liability, if any, under the Model Penal Code? Prepare a list of all criminal code subsections in the order in which you rely on them in your analysis.

▪ THE LAW

Nevada Revised Statutes Annotated
(1998)

Title 15. Crimes and Punishments

Chapter 200. Crimes Against the Person Homicide

Section 200.010. "Murder" Defined

Murder is the unlawful killing of a human being, with malice aforethought, either express or implied, or caused by a controlled substance, which was sold, given, traded or otherwise made available to a person in violation of chapter 453 of NRS. The unlawful killing may be effected by any of the various means by which death may be occasioned.

Section 200.020. Malice: Express and Implied Defined

1. Express malice is that deliberate intention unlawfully to take away the life of a fellow creature, which is manifested by external circumstances capable of proof.

2. Malice shall be implied when no considerable provocation appears, or when all the circumstances of the killing show an abandoned and malignant heart.

Section 200.030. Degrees of Murder; Penalties

1. Murder of the first degree is murder which is:
    (a) Perpetrated by means of poison, lying in wait, torture or child abuse, or by any other kind of willful, deliberate and premeditated killing;
    (b) Committed in the perpetration or attempted perpetration of sexual assault, kidnapping, arson, robbery, burglary, invasion of the home, sexual abuse of a child or sexual molestation of a child under the age of 14 years; or
    (c) Committed to avoid or prevent the lawful arrest of any person by a peace officer or to effect the escape of any person from legal custody.

2. Murder of the second degree is all other kinds of murder.

3. The jury before whom any person indicted for murder is tried shall, if they find him guilty thereof, designate by their verdict whether he is guilty of murder of the first or second degree.

4. A person convicted of murder of the first degree is guilty of a category A felony and shall be punished:
    (a) By death, only if one or more aggravating circumstances are found and any mitigating circumstance or circumstances which are found do not outweigh the aggravating circumstance or circumstances; or
    (b) By imprisonment in the state prison:
        (1) For life without the possibility of parole;
        (2) For life with the possibility of parole, with eligibility for parole beginning when a minimum of 20 years has been served; or
        (3) For a definite term of 50 years, with eligibility for parole beginning when a minimum of 20 years has been served.

A determination of whether aggravating circumstances exist is not necessary to fix the penalty at imprisonment for life with or without the possibility of parole.

5. A person convicted of murder of the second degree is guilty of a category A felony and shall be punished by imprisonment in the state prison:
    (a) For life with the possibility of parole, with eligibility for parole beginning when a minimum of 10 years has been served; or
    (b) For a definite term of 25 years, with eligibility for parole beginning when a minimum of 10 years has been served.

6. As used in this section:

(a) "Child abuse" means physical injury of a nonaccidental nature to a child under the age of 18 years;

(b) "Sexual abuse of a child" means any of the acts described in NRS 432B.100; and

(c) "Sexual molestation" means any willful and lewd or lascivious act, other than acts constituting the crime of sexual assault, upon or with the body, or any part or member thereof, of a child under the age of 14 years, with the intent of arousing, appealing to, or gratifying the lust, passions, or sexual desires of the perpetrator or of the child.

Section 200.040. "Manslaughter" Defined

1. Manslaughter is the unlawful killing of a human being, without malice express or implied, and without any mixture of deliberation.

2. Manslaughter must be voluntary, upon a sudden heat of passion, caused by a provocation apparently sufficient to make the passion irresistible, or, involuntary, in the commission of an unlawful act, or a lawful act without due caution or circumspection.

Section 200.070. "Involuntary Manslaughter" Defined

Except under the circumstances provided in NRS 484.348 and 484.377, involuntary manslaughter is the killing of a human being, without any intent to do so, in the commission of an unlawful act, or a lawful act which probably might produce such a consequence in an unlawful manner, but where the involuntary killing occurs in the commission of an unlawful act, which, in its consequences, naturally tends to destroy the life of a human being, or is committed in the prosecution of a felonious intent, the offense is murder.

Chapter 193. General Provisions

Section 193.0175. "Malice" and "Maliciously" Defined

"Malice" and "maliciously" import an evil intent, wish or design to vex, annoy, or injure another person. Malice may be inferred from an act done in willful disregard of the rights of another, or an act wrongfully done without just cause or excuse, or an act or omission of duty betraying a willful disregard of social duty.

Chapter 200. Crimes Against the Person
Homicide

Section 200.033. Circumstances Aggravating First Degree Murder

The only circumstances by which murder of the first degree may be aggravated are:

1. The murder was committed by a person under sentence of imprisonment.

2. The murder was committed by a person who was previously convicted of another murder or of a felony involving the use or threat of violence to the person of another.

3. The murder was committed by a person who knowingly created a great risk of death to more than one person by means of a weapon, device or course of action which would normally be hazardous to the lives of more than one person.

4. The murder was committed while the person was engaged, alone or with others, in the commission of or an attempt to commit or flight after committing or attempting to commit, any robbery, sexual assault, arson in the first degree, burglary, invasion of the home or kidnapping in the first degree, and the person charged:

    (a) Killed or attempted to kill the person murdered; or

    (b) Knew or had reason to know that life would be taken or lethal force used.

5. The murder was committed to avoid or prevent a lawful arrest or to effect an escape from custody.

6. The murder was committed by a person, for himself or another, to receive money or any other thing of monetary value.

7. The murder was committed upon a peace officer or fireman who was killed while engaged in the performance of his official duty or because of an act performed in his official capacity, and the defendant knew or reasonably should have known that the victim was a peace officer or fireman. For the purposes of this subsection, "peace officer" means:

    (a) An employee of the department of prisons who does not exercise general control over offenders imprisoned within the institutions and facilities of the department but whose normal duties require him to come into contact with those offenders, when carrying out the duties prescribed by the director of the department.

    (b) Any person upon whom some or all of the powers of a peace officer are conferred pursuant to NRS 281.0311 to 281.0353, inclusive, when carrying out those powers.

8. The murder involved torture or the mutilation of the victim.

9. The murder was committed upon one or more persons at random and without apparent motive.

10. The murder was committed upon a person less than 14 years of age.

11. The murder was committed upon a person because of the actual or perceived race, color, religion, national origin, physical or mental disability or sexual orientation of that person.

12. The defendant has, in the immediate proceeding, been convicted of more than one offense of murder in the first or second degree. For the purposes of this subsection, a person shall be deemed to have been convicted of a murder at the time the jury verdict of guilt is rendered or upon pronouncement of guilt by a judge or judges sitting without a jury.

Section 200.035. Circumstances Mitigating First Degree Murder

Murder of the first degree may be mitigated by any of the following circumstances, even though the mitigating circumstance is not sufficient to constitute a defense or reduce the degree of the crime:

    1. The defendant has no significant history of prior criminal activity.

2. The murder was committed while the defendant was under the influence of extreme mental or emotional disturbance.

3. The victim was a participant in the defendant's criminal conduct or consented to the act.

4. The defendant was an accomplice in a murder committed by another person and his participation in the murder was relatively minor.

5. The defendant acted under duress or under the domination of another person.

6. The youth of the defendant at the time of the crime.

7. Any other mitigating circumstance.

Chapter 200. Crimes Against the Person
Kidnapping

Section 200.310. Degrees

1. A person who willfully seizes, confines, inveigles, entices, decoys, abducts, conceals, kidnaps or carries away a person by any means whatsoever with the intent to hold or detain, or who holds or detains, the person for ransom or reward, or for the purpose of committing sexual assault, extortion or robbery upon or from the person, or for the purpose of killing the person or inflicting substantial bodily harm upon him, or to exact from relatives, friends, or any other person any money or valuable thing for the return or disposition of the kidnapped person, and a person who leads, takes, entices, or carries away or detains any minor with the intent to keep, imprison, or confine him from his parents, guardians, or any other person having lawful custody of the minor, or with the intent to hold the minor to unlawful service, or perpetrate upon the person of the minor any unlawful act is guilty of kidnapping in the first degree which is a category A felony.

2. A person who willfully and without authority of law seizes, inveigles, takes, carries away or kidnaps another person with the intent to keep the person secretly imprisoned within the state, or for the purpose of conveying the person out of the state without authority of law, or in any manner held to service or detained against his will, is guilty of kidnapping in the second degree which is a category B felony.

Section 200.320. Kidnapping in First Degree: Punishment

A person convicted of kidnapping in the first degree is guilty of a category A felony and shall be punished:

1. Where the kidnapped person suffers substantial bodily harm during the act of kidnapping or the subsequent detention and confinement or in attempted escape or escape therefrom, by imprisonment in the state prison:

(a) For life without the possibility of parole;

(b) For life with the possibility of parole, with eligibility for parole beginning when a minimum of 15 years has been served; or

(c) For a definite term of 40 years, with eligibility for parole beginning when a minimum of 15 years has been served.

2. Where the kidnapped person suffers no substantial bodily harm as a result of the kidnapping, by imprisonment in the state prison:

(a) For life with the possibility of parole, with eligibility for parole beginning when a minimum of 5 years has been served; or

(b) For a definite term of 15 years, with eligibility for parole beginning when a minimum of 5 years has been served.

Chapter 200. Crimes Against the Person
Sexual Assault and Seduction

Section 200.366. Sexual Assault: Definition; Penalties

1. A person who subjects another person to sexual penetration, or who forces another person to make a sexual penetration on himself or another or on a beast, against the victim's will or under conditions in which the perpetrator knows or should know that the victim is mentally or physically incapable of resisting or understanding the nature of his conduct, is guilty of sexual assault.

2. Except as otherwise provided in subsection 3, a person who commits a sexual assault is guilty of a category A felony and shall be punished:

(a) If substantial bodily harm to the victim results from the actions of the defendant committed in connection with or as a part of the sexual assault, by imprisonment in the state prison:

(1) For life without the possibility of parole;

(2) For life with the possibility of parole, with eligibility for parole beginning when a minimum of 15 years has been served; or

(3) For a definite term of 40 years, with eligibility for parole beginning when a minimum of 15 years has been served.

(b) If no substantial bodily harm to the victim results:

(1) By imprisonment in the state prison for life, with the possibility of parole, with eligibility for parole beginning when a minimum of 10 years has been served; or

(2) By imprisonment in the state prison for a definite term of 25 years, with eligibility for parole beginning when a minimum of 10 years has been served.

3. A person who commits a sexual assault against a child under the age of 16 years is guilty of a category A felony and shall be punished:

(a) If the crime results in substantial bodily harm to the child, by imprisonment in the state prison for life without the possibility of parole.

(b) If the crime does not result in substantial bodily harm to the child, by imprisonment in the state prison for:

(1) Life with the possibility of parole, with eligibility for parole beginning when a minimum of 20 years has been served; or

(2) For a definite term of not less than 5 years nor more than 20 years, without the possibility of parole.

Section 200.364. Definitions

As used in this section and NRS 200.364 to 200.3774, inclusive, unless the context otherwise requires:

1. "Perpetrator" means a person who commits a sexual assault.

2. "Sexual penetration" means cunnilingus, fellatio, or any intrusion, however slight, of any part of a person's body or any object manipulated or inserted

by a person into the genital or anal openings of the body of another, including sexual intercourse in its ordinary meaning.

3. "Statutory sexual seduction" means:

(a) Ordinary sexual intercourse, anal intercourse, cunnilingus or, fellatio committed by a person 18 years of age or older with a person under the age of 16 years; or

(b) Any other sexual penetration committed by a person 18 years of age or older with a person under the age of 16 years with the intent of arousing, appealing to, or gratifying the lust or passions or sexual desires of either of the persons.

4. "Victim" means a person who is subjected to a sexual assault.

Chapter 195. Parties to Crimes

Section 195.020. Principals

Every person concerned in the commission of a felony, gross misdemeanor, or misdemeanor, whether he directly commits the act constituting the offense or aids or abets in its commission, and whether present or absent; and every person who, directly or indirectly, counsels, encourages, hires, commands, induces, or otherwise procures another to commit a felony, gross misdemeanor, or misdemeanor is a principal, and shall be proceeded against and punished as such. The fact that the person aided, abetted, counseled, encouraged, hired, commanded, induced, or procured, could not or did not entertain a criminal intent shall not be a defense to any person aiding, abetting, counseling, encouraging, hiring, commanding, inducing, or procuring him.

Lee v. GNLV Corporation

22 P.3d 209, 212 (Nev. 2001)

Survivors of an intoxicated invitee who choked to death in a restaurant sued the restaurant for negligence, alleging that it breached a duty of reasonable care owed to the invitee when its employees failed to administer the Heimlich maneuver to him. The trial court granted summary judgment for restaurant. The Supreme Court held that, "In Nevada, as under the common law, strangers are generally under no duty to aid those in peril. This court, however, has stated that, where a special relationship exists between the parties, such as with an innkeeper-guest, teacher-student or employer-employee, an affirmative duty to aid others in peril is imposed by law." The restaurant owed a duty to the invitee to act reasonably, but the restaurant had no duty to administer the Heimlich maneuver to invitee.

Strangers — no duty

Special relationship — there is duty

Labastida v. State

931 P.2d 1334, 112 Nev. 1502 (1996)

The defendant's conviction for second-degree murder and child neglect charges were affirmed, upon the court holding that her failure to prevent severe and repeated abuse of her infant child by the child's father was sufficient to support the conviction. The seven-weeks-old infant was severely beaten and bitten by its father over the course of many weeks. Its bruises and bite marks were conspicuous and covered fifty to seventy-five percent of the baby's body. The court held that the statutes permitted the jury to find the defendant guilty of child abuse and first-degree murder on the grounds that she was responsible for the child, was aware of the abuse, could have taken preventive measures, but did nothing to stop it. By finding second-degree murder, the jury was simply being lenient.

Model Penal Code
(Official Draft 1962)

Section 2.01. Requirement of Voluntary Act; Omission As Basis of Liability; Possession As an Act

(1) A person is not guilty of an offense unless his liability is based on conduct which includes a voluntary act or the omission to perform an act of which he is physically capable. . . .

(3) Liability for the commission of an offense may not be based on an omission unaccompanied by action unless:

(a) the omission is expressly made sufficient by the law defining the offense; or

(b) a duty to perform the omitted act is otherwise imposed by law.

(4) Possession is an act, within the meaning of this section, if the possessor knowingly procured or received the thing possessed or was aware of his control thereof for a sufficient period to have been able to terminate his possession.

● OVERVIEW OF THE ACT REQUIREMENT

Notes

Purposes of the Act Requirement
> Excluding Mere Thoughts or Fantasies
> Demanding Objective Evidence of Mental State
> Providing Time and Place of Occurrence
> Distinguishing Multiple Offenses

Operation of the Act Requirement
> What is an "Act"?
> Intangible Acts
> Omissions as "Negative Acts"
> Possession as an Act
> Voluntary Act or Omission
> Voluntariness Requirement
> Act-Omission Distinction as Trigger for Special Omission Requirements
> The Act Requirement by Itself

Effect of the Act Requirement

PURPOSES OF THE ACT REQUIREMENT

It is commonly said that criminal law imposes an *act requirement*—that there typically can be no criminal liability unless the offender has performed some act. Why should there be such a rule? Several reasons are traditionally offered in support of an act requirement.

Excluding Mere Thoughts or Fantasies The act requirement allows criminal law to limit liability to those who have externalized a willingness to commit a crime. It is said that one cannot be held liable for thoughts alone, and it is in expression of this that an act requirement is needed. This is not to say that thoughts *never* impact criminal liability. Conduct that is otherwise lawful *can* be made criminal by virtue of an actor's accompanying state of mind. In that sense, one can be punished because of one's thoughts. Lighting one's pipe is not itself an offense, but it becomes attempted arson if it is a step in a plan to ignite a neighbor's haystack. Giving a young girl a ride is not an offense, but it becomes attempted sexual assault if it is done with the intention of subsequently sexually assaulting her. However, merely thinking about committing an offense—arson or sexual assault—is not an offense. It is only after the actor externalizes his thoughts by performing an act toward the offense, even an otherwise innocent act, that the actor may be subject to criminal liability. The act requirement is the criminal law's mechanism for requiring such externalization.

Similarly, by requiring an act, the law excludes from liability those persons who only fantasize about committing an offense, as well as those persons who may indeed form an intention to commit an offense but whose intention is not sufficiently firm that it would ever be externalized. One might argue that such people are dangerous, at least more dangerous than persons without such fantasies or intentions, and perhaps the criminal law ought to take jurisdiction. But many people may fantasize or form irresolute intentions, and most never act, thus use of criminal sanctions in those cases may be seen as wasteful and unfair. More important, as long as the criminal law continues to concern itself with punishing bad acts, not bad character, there is little justification for punishing pure fantasizing or the forming of irresolute intentions. Further, because one cannot easily control one's thoughts, it is difficult to blame an actor for the same. Condemnation sufficient for criminal liability typically attaches only after the actor externalizes her criminal intention in action.

Demanding Objective Evidence of Mental State Beyond barring punishment for non-externalized thoughts, the act requirement is thought to provide some minimal objective confirmation that an actor's intention does exist. That is, evidence of an actor's intention to commit an offense can gain additional confirmation from an act in furtherance of that intention. But the act requirement by itself performs this function poorly. Admittedly, some conduct may well manifest a mind unambiguously bent on crime, such as agreeing with another that one or the other will commit an offense. More frequently, however, conduct (especially that short of a substantive offense) does little by itself to indicate a culpable state of mind. The farmer lighting his pipe and the actor giving a ride to a young girl, to recall earlier examples, may in fact have no intention of committing arson or sexual assault.

Providing Time and Place of Occurrence The act requirement also is said to be useful in providing a time and place of occurrence for the offense. While one's intention may range over a long period of time and cover many places, the conduct constituting the offense can be identified with a particular time and place. This assists enforcement of the concurrence requirement by ensuring that the required mens rea exists at the time of the conduct constituting the offense. An identifiable time and place also ease application of procedural rules governing jurisdiction, venue, and time limitations for prosecution. Even here, however, the act requirement cannot be relied on for too much. Many offenses require several acts and some punish so-called "continuing acts" (such as concealment, criminal agreement, possession, or obstruction). The greater the number of acts, or the longer "a continuing act," the messier the application of these procedural rules. In some cases, the rationale of the procedural rules may be undercut, such as where jurisdiction and venue are appropriate everywhere and the statute of limitations never begins to run.

Distinguishing Multiple Offenses Some states, such as California, have tried to use the act requirement as a basis for resolving the thorny issue of liability and punishment for multiple offenses. The California Penal Code purports to allow punishment for only one offense for a single act.[1] Even the California courts have rejected a strict application of this provision where one act causes two results, such as two deaths, or constitutes two violations of the same offense provision, such as two instances of attempted murder.[2] The California courts continue to give deference to the provision, however, where one act violates different provisions, such as arson and attempted murder. But even this narrow application seems problematic. If an actor sets a house on fire with two people in it, intending to burn the house and the people, why should the state have to elect to punish for arson or for attempted murder? Why is it not appropriate to punish for both? One also may wonder about the logic of allowing multiple liability for the two instances of attempted murder arising from a single act, yet denying liability for the arson and attempted murder from the same act. Under what theory must the state choose between different kinds of harms from a single act, yet not need to choose between distinct but related harms from a single act? As the California experience illustrates, the act requirement is of minimal value in solving the difficult problem of multiple offenses. At best, it serves as a starting point for a more complex analysis.

---

1. Cal. Penal Code § 654 ("An act or omission which is made punishable in different ways by different provisions of this code may be punishable under either of such provisions, but in no case can it be punished under more than one").

2. See, e.g., Neal v. State, 357 P.2d 839 (Cal. 1960) (defendant convicted on two counts attempted murder and one arson; because both resulted from one act, defendant's conviction for arson dismissed, but not two convictions for attempted murder).

OPERATION OF THE ACT REQUIREMENT

What is an "Act"?   Writers disagree as to the precise definition of an "act." Some writers define "act" as simply a muscular movement.[3] This is the most common modern usage.[4] Others define it as a willed movement.[5] The disagreement is not of practical importance, because the act requirement is nearly always drafted to require not only an act but a *voluntary* act, as in Model Penal Code section 2.01(1). Other writers define "act" to include the circumstances and consequences of the act.[6] But this usage is not the modern view, and if it was adopted, it would undermine the modern offense-definition system that divides the objective components of an offense into conduct, circumstance, and result elements, each with a corresponding culpability requirement.

Intangible Acts   In some instances, the law assumes that an act has occurred although the actor has performed no muscular movement. A legal or intangible act, for example, may occur where an actor shows his "agreement" or "command" in some way other than by movement. "Let me know if I shouldn't kill him like the rest, Boss," may allow the Mafia chief to direct a killing by doing nothing. Such can be the basis for criminal liability; a muscular movement typically is not required in such a case. Similarly, courts have found the "agreement" required for conspiracy to be satisfied by the acquiescence of one party. The argument in support of liability in such cases focuses on the special circumstances that express the actor's intention and willingness to carry out the act. The special circumstances are said to be adequate to serve the primary rationales of the act requirement as effectively as an affirmative act does.

Omissions as "Negative Acts"   Liability frequently is imposed for an omission to perform an act that one has a legal duty to perform. An omission is sometimes called a "negative act,"[7] but this seems a dangerous practice, for it too easily permits an omission to be substituted for an act without requiring the special requirements for omission liability, such as a legal duty and the physical capacity to perform the act.

Possession as an Act   An almost universally recognized exception to the act requirement is the criminalization of possession. Rather than treating it as a formal exception to the act requirement, most codes simply define possession to be an act, similar to the way intangible acts are treated. Under the Model Penal Code, for example,

> Possession is an act, within the meaning of this Section if the possessor knowingly procured or received the thing possessed or was aware of his control thereof for a sufficient period to have been able to terminate his possession.[8]

---

3. Proposed Federal Criminal Code (S. 1722, 86th Cong., 1st Sess.) § 111; Paul H. Robinson & Jane A. Grall, *Element Analysis in Defining Liability: The Model Penal Code and Beyond*, 35 STAN. L. REV. 681, 719 (1983).

4. See, e.g., Model Penal Code § 1.13(2) ("'act' or 'action' means bodily movement whether voluntary or involuntary").

5. See, e.g., Oliver W. Holmes, *The Common Law* 54 (1881); Rollin M. Perkins & R. Boyce, Criminal Law 607 (3d ed. 1982).

6. Glanville Williams, *Criminal Law: The General Part* § 11 (2d ed. 1961).

7. 1 John Austin, *Jurisprudence* § 502 (Campbell Ed. 1875).

8. Model Penal Code § 2.01(4).

With the addition of the special requirement—*knowing* receipt or control—the intent-based rationales of the act requirement are sought to be satisfied. That is, where the actor has knowledge of receipt or control but fails to terminate possession, he has made a conscious choice to keep possession. The intent rationales also are satisfied by the additional requirement that an actor have control "for a sufficient period to have been able to terminate his possession." This ensures that the actor could have terminated possession, thus his retention can be viewed again as the manifestation of a choice. In this respect, possession and other intangible acts are analogous. The Mafia chief's silence is judged an "act" because the chief *knows* that his silence will be taken as assent, has the *opportunity* to speak, yet *chooses* to have the killing performed.

Voluntary Act or Omission   Model Penal Code section 2.01(1) requires that criminal liability be "based on conduct which includes a voluntary act or the omission to perform an act of which he is physically capable." By itself, this foundational section does not really seem to do much. It seems to say that liability requires either an act or omission—but how could it be otherwise? *Any* conduct, criminal or not, consists of either action or inaction. In truth, the significant effects of the doctrine arise from two less obvious features: first, from the requirement of voluntariness; and second, from the special requirements for omission liability, contained in the later subsections of section 2.01, which are triggered if liability is based on an omission rather than on an act.

Voluntariness Requirement   Note that under the Code provision, liability must be based on an act that is "voluntary" or an "omission to perform an act *of which [the actor] is physically capable.*" These are essentially parallel requirements of voluntariness. Such a requirement is essential, of course, if criminal liability is to be imposed only on blameworthy offenders: Entirely involuntary conduct cannot support the attribution of blame. This *voluntariness requirement* produces an *involuntariness defense* that is similar in function to other excuse defenses—such as insanity, involuntary intoxication, immaturity, and duress—that perform this same function.

Act-Omission Distinction as Trigger for Special Omission Requirements   A second function of section 2.01(1), beyond imposing a voluntariness requirement, is its explicit recognition that the distinction between an act and an omission is relevant to assessing criminal liability. By itself, the provision does not do much, but the distinction it introduces serves to trigger the special requirements for omission liability. In this role, then, the term *act requirement* is misleading; an act is not truly required, but its absence will lead other, additional requirements to arise.

The Act Requirement by Itself   Aside from its important functions as a vehicle for the voluntariness requirements and as a trigger for omission rules, does the act requirement have much effect on its own? Despite its prominence in the traditional literature, its independent effect is minimal, if not trivial, at least in the operation of criminal law under a modern code. This conclusion is somewhat surprising given the lofty purposes traditionally ascribed to the act requirement.

EFFECT OF THE ACT REQUIREMENT

Many of the goals of the act requirement are important, especially its exclusion from liability of fantasizing and forming irresolute intentions, but the effect of the doctrine in achieving those goals is modest. The act requirement can be satisfied by nearly trivial acts offering little assurance that the actor is engaged in culpable wrongdoing. It does not require that the actor perform the conduct element of a completed offense or *any* particular conduct. On the other hand, the attempt offense does provide some action requirement, vague as it may be: For example, Model Penal Code section 5.01(1) requires that conduct constitute "a substantial step" in a course of conduct planned to culminate in the substantive offense. Similarly, the offense of conspiracy, under section 5.03(1) of the Code, requires an "agreement" with another person that one of the two will commit an offense. Speaking—as in "I agree"—is an act. But nothing in *the act requirement* or in Model Penal Code section 2.01(1) requires that the act performed be sufficiently close to the completed offense or sufficiently expressive of an actor's intention or willingness to act on the intention.

Is Act Requirement Needed? It appears, then, that it is not the act requirement, but rather the definition of offenses, including inchoate offenses, that ensures that conduct is sufficiently related to the offense to support liability. Why, then, have a requirement of an act in section 2.01(1)?

Distinguishing Voluntariness Requirement from Act Requirement First, as noted previously, section 2.01(1) requires a "*voluntary* act." This voluntariness requirement is important. In discussing the act requirement one tends to assume, often without noting, that it is a voluntary act to which one refers. An *in*voluntary act would not satisfy the primary purposes of the act requirement. Permitting liability to be based on an involuntary act would do little or nothing to protect from punishment fantasizing or forming irresolute intentions, and would provide little or no objective evidence of intention. For these reasons, the "act" requirement typically is meant to require a voluntary act, even if such is not expressly provided.

Act Requirement Identifies Cases Needing Special Rules Holding aside the requirement of voluntariness, is there value in the "*act* requirement" itself? Consider the doctrines of liability for omission and possession. Each has a set of special requirements. When do those special requirements apply? Model Penal Code section 2.01(1) answers this question: Those rules apply when liability is not based on an act. In other words, as noted previously, the primary practical function of the act requirement is to identify those cases where the special rules of possession and omission liability are triggered. Apart from that function, the act requirement itself is of little consequence.

Act Requirement for Code Drafters What has been discussed so far is what might be called the act requirement in assessing liability. Criminal liability must be based on conduct that includes a voluntary act. If it is not, then the special requirements of possession or omission liability must be satisfied. A second kind of act requirement directs itself to the definition of offenses. Nothing in the act requirement in Model Penal Code section 2.01(1) requires that an offense definition contain any act as an element of the offense. The provision is addressed to adjudicators, not code drafters. But several Supreme Court cases do set an "act requirement" of sorts for code drafters. These cases may be read as constitutionalizing a requirement that an offense definition must contain a requirement of an act on its face, or something analogous to it. The effect and the rationale of such a requirement is found in the need to limit governmental power to define criminal offenses.

Voluntary Act or Possession or Omission Liability

Constitutionalization of Act Requirement In *Scales v. United States*, for example, the Court bars the government from criminalizing pure membership in the Communist Party. It does, however, allow liability for "active" members.[9] Similarly, vagrancy offenses that punish "not having any visible means of support" have been invalidated.[10] Also invalidated are statutes such as those criminalizing "keeping a place . . . with intent" to sell liquor unlawfully.[11] In *Robinson v. California*, the Court invalidated a state statute that made it an offense to "be addicted to the use of narcotics."[12] Yet, these cases limit governmental criminalization authority only in a modest way. It would not be a violation of this constitutional act requirement to criminalize using drugs or selling liquor. This act requirement may make the government's case more difficult to prove, but it only modestly limits what the government may criminalize.

Martin v. State

17 So. 2d 427 (1944)

SIMPSON, Judge.

Appellant was convicted of being drunk on a public highway, and appeals. Officers of the law arrested him at his home and took him onto the highway, where he allegedly committed the proscribed acts, viz., manifested a drunken condition by using loud and profane language.

The pertinent provisions of our statute are: "Any person who, while intoxicated or drunk, appears in any public place where one or more persons are present, . . . and manifests a drunken condition by boisterous or indecent conduct, or loud and profane discourse, shall, on conviction, be fined," etc. Code 1940, Title 14, Section 120.

Under the plain terms of this statute, a voluntary appearance is presupposed. The rule has been declared, and we think it sound, that an accusation of drunkenness in a designated public place cannot be established by proof that the accused, while in an intoxicated condition, was involuntarily and forcibly carried to that place by the arresting officer.

Conviction of appellant was contrary to this announced principle and, in our view, erroneous. . . .

Reversed and rendered.

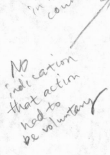

● OVERVIEW OF LIABILITY FOR AN OMISSION

Hypothetical: Dunning's Deal (#71)

Dunning's expenses for school are more than he can handle so he decides to earn extra money by working as an escort. He is relatively good looking and can

---

9. 367 U.S. 203, 222 (1961).

10. See, e.g., Goldman v. Knecht, 295 F. Supp. 897, 899 (D. Colo. 1969).

11. See Proctor v. State, 176 P. 771, 771 (Okla. Crim. App. 1918).

12. 370 U.S. 660, 667 (1962).

be very charming when necessary. Mrs. Harrington, an elderly widow, particularly enjoys Dunning's company and they agree that he will be an escort for her, exclusively, in exchange for a monthly salary. Both are pleased with the arrangement until Mrs. Harrington by chance sees Dunning with a young woman. When he arrives that evening at his usual time, she confronts him with her observation. "That's my girlfriend, not another customer," he insists. "We agreed that you would escort only me," she responds. They continue to argue. Concerned that Mrs. Harrington intends not to pay him what he has already earned, Dunning insists on getting paid for the past month. Mrs. Harrington snaps, "It's not due until tomorrow. Anyway, why should I pay you? You broke our agreement." She continues with a tirade on Dunning's breach of their agreement. As she gets more excited, Mrs. Harrington's face turns pale and she falls to the floor, gasping for air. She crawls toward her handbag, which contains her medicine, but is unable to get more than a few yards. Her breathing gets more labored and her color turns to chalk white. Dunning knows that she needs the medicine in her handbag, but he turns and leaves. Mrs. Harrington dies several minutes later.

Is Dunning liable under the following statute for his failure to aid Mrs. Harrington?

A person is guilty of involuntary manslaughter when as a direct result of the doing of an unlawful act in a reckless or grossly negligent manner, he causes the death of another person.[13]

Notes

Omission Liability as Exception to Act Requirement
    Relation to Act Requirement's Rationales
    Liability Requirements Beyond Those Special to Omissions
Requirement of Legal Duty; Sources of Duty
    Civil Sources
    Duty and Legality Principle
Knowledge of Legal Duty Not Required
    Constitutionalization of Knowledge-of-Duty Requirement
Should There Be a General Duty to Aid?

Omission Liability as Exception to Act Requirement   The earlier portion of this section discusses the virtues of the act requirement, yet criminal liability for an omission is also well accepted where the actor has a legal duty and the capacity to act.[14] It is said that this rather fundamental exception to the act requirement is permitted because an actor's failure to perform a legal duty of which he is capable satisfies the purposes of the act requirement, or at least satisfies them as well as an act does.

---

13. 18 Pa. Stat. Ann. ' 2504.

14. Most modern codes state that crimes may be committed either by an act or an omission. See, e.g., Ala. Code 1975, § 13A-2-3; Alaska Stat. 11.81.600; Ariz. Rev. Stat. Ann. 13–201; Ark. Stat. § 41–202; Del. Code tit. 11, § 242; Hawaii Rev. Stat. § 702–200; Ky. Rev. Stat. Ann. § 501.030; La. Rev. Stat. Ann. § 14:18; Me. Rev. Stat. Ann. tit. 17-A, § 31; Vernon's Ann. Mo. Stat. § 562.011; Mont. Code Ann. § 45–2-202; N.H. Rev. Stat. Ann. § 626:1; N.J. Stat. Ann. § 2C:2–1; New York Penal Law § 15.10 (McKinney); N.D. Cent. Code § 12.1–02-01; Ohio Rev. Code Ann. ' 2901.21; Or. Rev. Stat. § 161.095; 18 Pa. Cons. Stat. Ann. § 301; Vernon's Tex. Penal Code Ann. § 6.01.

Relation to Act Requirement's Rationales   Specifically, the special requirements for omission liability—the requirements of (1) a legal duty (2) of which
one is capable of performing—help to exclude from liability cases of fantasizing
and irresolute intentions, important purposes of the act requirement. However, a
failure to act, by itself, does nothing to screen out mere fantasies. It is the actor's
failure to act in light of her capacity to do so that suggests the actor's willingness to go beyond mere fantasizing and to have the harm or evil of the offense
occur. Even then, however, the screening effect seems weak; "letting something
happen" simply does not carry the same implication of resolute intention that is
shown in causing something to happen by affirmative action. While an actor's failure to perform a legal duty provides some evidentiary support for the existence of
an intention to have the harm or evil occur, the force of the implication is similarly
weak. Inaction often carries no implication of intention unless it is shown that the
actor knows of his or her duty to act and the opportunity to do so.

As to other rationales for the act requirement, an omission also does poorly
in limiting governmental criminalization authority. The government need only
create a legal duty in order to criminalize an omission. Nor is an omission helpful
in providing an identifiable time and place of occurrence. An omission necessarily
is a continuing state. On balance, then, while an omission itself serves none of the
rationales of the act requirement, the special requirements of duty and capacity
do something toward satisfying those rationales, but considerably less than even
the poor performance of the act requirement itself. It should be no surprise, then,
that omission liability traditionally is limited. Legal duties to act generally are few
in number and narrow in scope.

Liability Requirements Beyond Those Special to Omissions   Keep in mind that
where an actor fails to perform a legal duty, criminal liability does not necessarily
follow. Satisfaction of the special requirements for omission liability serves only to
substitute for the act requirement, as it were. As always, offense liability requires
proof of all elements of the offense (all objective elements [circumstance and
result elements], a causal connection between the omission and any result element, and all culpability elements) as well as the absence of all general defenses. In
Dunning's case, this means that even if Dunning had a legal duty and the capacity
to get Mrs. Harrington her medicine, he is criminally liable for her death only if
he also satisfies the requirements of the homicide offense: His omission caused
her death, an adequate causal connection between his omission and her death
(including proof that, if he had acted, she would not have died), and at the time
of his omission he must have had the required culpable state of mind as to his
omission causing her death.

Requirement of Legal Duty; Sources of Duty   Liability for an omission
requires a legal duty to act; a moral duty to act is not sufficient.[15] The duty may
arise either from the offense definition itself or from some other provision of
criminal or civil law. A duty arises from the former when an offense is defined
in terms of omission. This is the situation where the legislature has made it an
offense, for example, to fail to file a tax return, for a parent to neglect to furnish
medical care to a sick child, for a motorist to fail to stop after having an accident,

---

15. People v. Beardsley, 113 N.W. 1128, 1131 (Mich. 1907) (no legal duty to prevent death of mis-
tress, who overdosed on morphine).

or for a draftee to fail to report for induction.[16] In each instance, the offense makes the omission criminal and thereby creates the duty to act. A legal duty to act also may be created by a provision of either criminal or civil law separate from the offense charged. For example, a municipal regulation requiring homeowners to shovel the sidewalk in front of their homes creates a legal duty to act and, therefore, ultimately might provide the basis for criminal liability if an actor's failure to shovel is accompanied by the required elements of a criminal offense.

Civil Sources   A legal duty to act commonly is recognized in the following instances: (1) Landowners may have specific duties with regard to the condition of their property, as in the requirement that homeowners fence in their swimming pools; (2) a duty may arise from a relationship between the actor and the victim, as in the duty of a parent to protect a child; (3) a contract between parties may create a legal duty to act, such as a hotel lifeguard's duty to save a drowning guest (this might be viewed as a form of relationship created by contract, and thus a subset of (2) above); (4) tort law may create a continuing duty of care to an actor who voluntarily assumes responsibility for another; (5) also under tort law, an actor may have a duty to rescue if the actor has created the peril, even if such creation is neither tortious nor criminal (for example, an actor who sets a legal trap for vermin may be liable for failing to immediately release a trapped dog). These are the general categories of duties recognized by case law. Civil statutes have created any number of other miscellaneous duties. For example, a special provision may give dog owners a duty to keep their dogs on leashes.

Duty and Legality Principle   One may wonder whether this mechanism for defining the duties that may give rise to criminal liability—that is, by cross-reference to the entire body of civil law—is consistent with the spirit of the legality principle. The demands of the legality principle exist in part to ensure that citizens can know the law that they are obliged to follow on pain of criminal sanction. Yet no one would argue that it is realistic for a citizen to know the full breadth of civil (and criminal) law that might give rise to a duty to act. Indeed, this aspect of omission liability requires citizens not only to know all existing criminal and civil statutes and case law creating a duty, but also to be able to apply those statutes and case law at a moment's notice. Does Dunning have a duty to aid Mrs. Harrington? The answer depends on the nature of their contractual agreement. Does Dunning's escort duty extend to protecting Mrs. Harrington's health, getting her medicine? Does her refusal to confirm that Dunning will be paid give Dunning a right to declare an anticipatory breach? Has Dunning's "escorting" of his girlfriend breached his contract with Mrs. Harrington, thereby giving Mrs. Harrington a right to renegotiate that month's payment, making lawful her refusal to confirm full payment? Contract law no doubt has an answer to these questions, but it is unrealistic to think that Dunning would.

Knowledge of Legal Duty Not Required   The potential complexity in determining one's duty is all the more problematic because an actor's mistake as to the existence or extent of his duty typically is no defense. This is true of even a reasonable mistake as to one's legal duty. The absence of a knowledge-of-duty requirement follows from the rule that ignorance of the law is no excuse. But while that rule may have some justification in the context of affirmative acts, liability for omissions

---

16. See generally 1 Paul H. Robinson, *Criminal Law Defenses* § 86(b) (1984).

presents special problems and may justify a special rule. An actor's failure to know of her legal duty to act undercuts the moral implications that may be drawn from the actor's omission. To deal with the problem, one might urge adoption of a rule that a duty to act is an element of an offense and, therefore, is subject to the standard requirement of proof of a minimum culpability, usually recklessness.

Constitutionalization of Knowledge-of-Duty Requirement   In *Lambert v. California*,[17] the Supreme Court seems to recognize the unfairness of imposing omission liability where an actor is unaware of a duty to act. The Court suggests the possibility of a constitutional requirement, under the Due Process Clause, that an actor have some awareness of, or at least a reasonable opportunity to become aware of, their duty to act. Lambert failed to register with the police, as all convicted felons were required to do by a Los Angeles ordinance. She won a reversal by arguing that she was unaware of her obligation to register and could not reasonably have been expected to be aware of it. But *Lambert* has been given the narrowest of readings and its continuing significance is unclear. It can be argued that it applies only to cases of omission liability for minor offenses or regulatory offenses like the felon registration requirement, or only where the existence of a duty is not generally known and has not reasonably been made known, or only to cases where all of these special conditions are satisfied.[18]

Should There Be a General Duty to Aid?   Many writers have argued for a general duty to aid a stranger when the stranger is in danger of death or serious bodily injury. While such a duty is not uncommon in Europe,[19] few states have adopted such a general duty to aid.[20] The opponents of such a general duty argue that it would create undue governmental intrusion into the affairs of the individual and, further, that any general duty necessarily would be susceptible to overbroad interpretations. They prefer liability for an omission only where the law already has created a specific duty to act. Proponents of a general duty to rescue argue that a limited general duty to rescue is morally required and legally feasible. They would create a duty to save life if it could be done without personal danger or pecuniary loss. The most dramatic illustrations of the desirability of a general duty are provided by cases like the stabbing of Catherine Genovese outside of her New York apartment building, to which there were many witnesses, all of whom ignored her loud screams for some time.[21]

Jones v. United States
308 F.2d 307, 113 U.S. App. D.C. 352 (1962)

Wright, Circuit Judge.

Appellant, together with one Shirley Green, was tried on a three-count indictment charging them jointly with (1) abusing and maltreating Robert Lee Green, (2) abusing and maltreating Anthony Lee Green, and (3) involuntary manslaughter through failure to perform their legal duty of care for Anthony Lee

17. 355 U.S. 225 (1957).

18. 2 Paul H. Robinson, Criminal Law Defenses § 161(b)(4) (1984).

19. See Andrew Ashworth & Eva Steiner, *Criminal Omissions and Public Duties: The French Experience*, 10 Legal Studies 153 (1990).

20. See, e.g., R.I. Gen. Law §§ 11–56-1; Vt. Stat. Ann. Tit. 12 § 519; Wis. Stat. Ann. § 940.34(1), (2).

21. See "37 Who Saw Murder Didn't Call Police," N.Y. Times, Mar. 27, 1964, col. 4, at l.

Green, which failure resulted in his death. At the close of evidence, after trial to a jury, the first two counts were dismissed as to both defendants. On the third count, appellant was convicted of involuntary manslaughter. Shirley Green was found not guilty. . . .

. . . In late 1957, Shirley Green became pregnant, out of wedlock, with a child, Robert Lee, subsequently born August 17, 1958. Apparently to avoid the embarrassment of the presence of the child in the Green home, it was arranged that appellant, a family friend, would take the child to her home after birth. Appellant did so, and the child remained there continuously until removed by the police on August 5, 1960. Initially appellant made some motions toward the adoption of Robert Lee, but these came to naught, and shortly thereafter it was agreed that Shirley Green was to pay appellant $72 a month for his care. According to appellant, these payments were made for only five months. According to Shirley Green, they were made up to July, 1960.

Early in 1959 Shirley Green again became pregnant, this time with the child Anthony Lee, whose death is the basis of appellant's conviction. This child was born October 21, 1959. Soon after birth, Anthony Lee developed a mild jaundice condition, attributed to a blood incompatibility with his mother. The jaundice resulted in his retention in the hospital for three days beyond the usual time, or until October 26, 1959, when, on authorization signed by Shirley Green, Anthony Lee was released by the hospital to appellant's custody. Shirley Green, after a two or three day stay in the hospital, also lived with appellant for three weeks, after which she returned to her parents' home, leaving the children with appellant. She testified she did not see them again, except for one visit in March, until August 5, 1960. Consequently, though there does not seem to have been any specific monetary agreement with Shirley Green covering Anthony Lee's support, appellant had complete custody of both children until they were rescued by the police.

With regard to medical care, the evidence is undisputed. In March, 1960, appellant called a Dr. Turner to her home to treat Anthony Lee for a bronchial condition. Appellant also telephoned the doctor at various times to consult with him concerning Anthony Lee's diet and health. In early July, 1960, appellant took Anthony Lee to Dr. Turner's office where he was treated for "simple diarrhea." At this time the doctor noted the "wizened" appearance of the child and told appellant to tell the mother of the child that he should be taken to a hospital. This was not done.

On August 2, 1960, two collectors for the local gas company had occasion to go to the basement of appellant's home, and there saw the two children. Robert Lee and Anthony Lee at this time were age two years and ten months respectively. Robert Lee was in a "crib" consisting of a framework of wood, covered with a fine wire screening, including the top which was hinged. The "crib" was lined with newspaper, which was stained, apparently with feces, and crawling with roaches. Anthony Lee was lying in a bassinet and was described as having the appearance of a "small baby monkey." One collector testified to seeing roaches on Anthony Lee.

On August 5, 1960, the collectors returned to appellant's home in the company of several police officers and personnel of the Women's Bureau. At this time, Anthony Lee was upstairs in the dining room in the bassinet, but Robert Lee was still downstairs in his "crib." The officers removed the children to the D.C. General Hospital where Anthony Lee was diagnosed as suffering from severe malnutrition and lesions over large portions of his body, apparently caused by severe diaper rash. Following admission, he was fed repeatedly, apparently with no difficulty, and was described as being very hungry. His death, 34 hours after admission, was attributed without dispute to malnutrition. At birth, Anthony Lee weighed six pounds, fifteen ounces—at death at age ten months, he weighed seven pounds, thirteen ounces. Normal weight at this age would have been approximately 14 pounds.

[T]here is substantial evidence from which the jury could have found that appellant failed to obtain proper medical care for the child. Appellant relies upon the evidence showing that on one occasion she summoned a doctor for the child, on another took the child to the doctor's office, and that she telephoned the doctor on several occasions about the baby's formula. However, the last time a doctor saw the child was a month before his death, and appellant admitted that on that occasion the doctor recommended hospitalization. Appellant did not hospitalize the child, nor did she take any other steps to obtain medical care in the last crucial month. Thus there was sufficient evidence to go to the jury on the issue of medical care, as well as failure to feed.

Appellant also takes exception to the failure of the trial court to charge that the jury must find beyond a reasonable doubt, as an element of the crime, that appellant was under a legal duty to supply food and necessities to Anthony Lee. . . .

The problem of establishing the duty to take action which would preserve the life of another has not often arisen in the case law of this country. The most commonly cited statement of the rule is found in *People v. Beardsley*, 150 Mich. 206, 113 N.W. 1128, 1129, 13 L.R.A., N.S., 1020:

> The law recognizes that under some circumstances the omission of a duty owed by one individual to another, where such omission results in the death of the one to whom the duty is owing, will make the other chargeable with manslaughter. . . . This rule of law is always based upon the proposition that the duty neglected must be a legal duty, and not a mere moral obligation. It must be a duty imposed by law or by contract, and the omission to perform the duty must be the immediate and direct cause of death. . . .

There are at least four situations in which the failure to act may constitute breach of a legal duty. One can be held criminally liable: first, where a statute imposes a duty to care for another; second, where one stands in a certain status relationship to another; third, where one has assumed a contractual duty to care for another; and fourth, where one has voluntarily assumed the care of another and so secluded the helpless person as to prevent others from rendering aid.

It is the contention of the Government that either the third or the fourth ground is applicable here. However, it is obvious that in any of the four situations, there are critical issues of fact which must be passed on by the jury—specifically in this case, whether appellant had entered into a contract with the mother for the care of Anthony Lee or, alternatively, whether she assumed the care of the child and secluded him from the care of his mother, his natural protector. On both of these issues, the evidence is in direct conflict, appellant insisting that the mother was actually living with appellant and Anthony Lee, and hence should have been taking care of the child herself, while Shirley Green testified she was living with her parents and was paying appellant to care for both children.

In spite of this conflict, the instructions given in the case failed even to suggest the necessity for finding a legal duty of care. The only reference to duty in the instructions was the reading of the indictment which charged, inter alia, that the defendants "failed to perform their legal duty." A finding of legal duty is the critical element of the crime charged and failure to instruct the jury concerning it was plain error. . . .

Reversed and remanded.

● OVERVIEW OF LIABILITY FOR POSSESSION

Notes

Possession Liability Common, but Controversial
Act, Omission, and Possession
Possession as Act Versus Omission
    Degree and Duration of Necessary Control
Possession as Inchoate versus Consummate Crime
    Possession as Basis for Imputation
Imposing Liability Absent Both Action and Harm
Culpability as to Possession
    Culpability as to Future Unlawful Use
Specific Possession Offenses

Possession Liability Common, but Controversial   Possession of a prohibited item or substance is a common, but controversial, basis of criminal liability. The reason for the controversy is that possession, by itself, seems a rather thin degree of conduct to support punishment: it is not clear whether possession should be treated as an affirmative act, and even if so, it is not clear whether the act of possession per se is sufficiently harmful or wrongful, or sufficiently proximate to a harm or wrong, to merit criminal sanction.

Act, Omission, and Possession   As discussed above, concerning the act requirement, liability for possession is an exception to that formal requirement. Like omission liability, possession liability imposes special additional requirements, most notably the requirements that the actor (1) knowingly received the thing possessed and (2) was aware of his control of it for a period long enough to terminate his possession, as Model Penal Code section 2.01(4) provides.[22]

Possession as Act versus Omission   Some writers characterize possession as an affirmative act, others as an omission, still others as possibly either (or perhaps neither). If possession is seen not as an act, but as an omission—specifically, a failure to relinquish control over the property in question—then criminal offenses whose only objective requirement is possession would require no affirmative act. Moreover, such offenses might seem to extend the scope of omission liability

---

22. Model Penal Code § 2.01(4).

beyond its usual boundaries—that is, beyond situations where the law imposes an affirmative duty to act. These offenses prohibit possession across the board, so that the prohibition applies to all people at all times rather than only specified people in particular situations. Of course, the offenses could simply be seen as defining a new legal duty not to possess whatever the law defines as prohibited contraband, and the law is presumably free to define such new duties, so long as they do not run afoul of the Constitution. Still, even possession offenses that raise no obvious constitutional issues will seem troubling to the extent that they involve only minimal or even nonexistent demands in terms of the conduct required for liability.

Degree and Duration of Necessary Control   Whether possession is seen as act or omission, the Model Penal Code definition also underscores the importance of timing or duration in determining whether a person has possession of something. Mere momentary access or control is generally insufficient to constitute possession: One who takes contraband away from someone else for the sake of throwing it away has not "possessed" the contraband merely by having control for the time it took to dispose of it. Still, the required duration or extent of control is usually left unspecified, so a finding of possession is essentially up to the fact finder's discretionary judgment. Indeed, sometimes mere "constructive possession" rather than actual possession suffices for liability, but this term also is often left undefined, and amounts to a label for situations where clear physical control is lacking but a finding of possession seems appropriate.

Possession as Inchoate versus Consummate Crime   Like the ambivalence of possession's status as act or omission, there is some debate as to whether possession offenses are inchoate or consummate offenses. For example, criminal codes vary as to whether they locate possession offenses in the general part with inchoate offenses, in the special part with completed offenses, or both. Possession offenses impose inchoate liability insofar as possession itself is not typically seen as inherently harmful or wrongful but merely as creating a risk of some other harm or creating an opportunity for wrongful behavior. Indeed, many such offenses do not even explicitly require the offender to create a risk of any specified harm but simply ban a category of conduct that seems generally to correlate with a risk of harm, though specific instances of it may well be completely harmless. At the same time, possession offenses resemble consummate rather than inchoate offenses in that they are not always defined as preparatory efforts toward some other offense, but may stand as offenses all their own. Indeed, some jurisdictions allow liability for inchoate efforts toward possession itself, such that one can be held liable for attempt to possess or conspiracy to possess.

Possession as Basis for Imputation   At least some possession offenses might also be seen as a version of an imputation rule: The fact of possession is used as a substitute or proxy for the harm or wrong with which the law is truly concerned. (Depending on the requirements of the offense, possession might also amount to a basis for imputing *culpability* as to that harm or wrong; the offense might not explicitly demand proof of culpability, effectively presuming that possession itself amply demonstrates the offender's unlawful purpose. The appropriateness of this sort of imputation would depend in part on whether possession of the item in question was compatible with a lawful purpose.) Some materials may be seen as inherently dangerous, at least insofar as they have the potential to cause harm if

<!-- margin note: Not enough to have brief acces or control -->

they fall into the wrong hands, so possessing them might be viewed as a sort of per se risk creation, or at least a satisfactory basis for imputation on an equivalency theory. Possession might also serve an evidentiary imputation function, as possession is easy to discover and prove, whereas affirmative acts such as sale or use might be harder to establish (though likely to be occurring in many cases of possession). On such a theory, possession of large amounts of a prohibited drug might be good evidence of the likelihood of distribution, whereas a smaller amount would provide evidence of the likelihood of personal use.

Imposing Liability Absent Both Action and Harm Hence, offenses criminalizing mere possession seem to lack both of the normal touchstones of criminal liability, in terms of its objective requirements: action and harm. Accordingly, they combine the features of two distinct kinds of rules, each of which seems to expand the scope of criminal liability: omission liability, which dispenses with the usual requirement of an act, and inchoate liability, which dispenses with the usual requirement of a consummated harm or wrong. Possession offenses may be controversial precisely because they fit into this category: They differ from other offenses not only because they prohibit conduct whose status as action is dubious, or because they prohibit conduct that creates a mere likelihood of harm rather than actual harm, but because they combine both of these features.

Culpability as to Possession Possession offenses typically, though not always, require conscious (that is, knowing) possession, though the requirement of "knowing possession" may be satisfied where the possessor is aware only of the thing itself but not its nature or properties. Thus one might knowingly possess a bag of white powder without knowing that the powder is cocaine. Possession offenses vary with respect to the culpability they require, if any, as to the nature of the thing possessed. Markus Dirk Dubber describes the minimal culpability requirements of modern possession statutes as follows:

> In many cases, possession statutes also save prosecutors the trouble of proving that other major ingredient of criminal liability in American criminal law, mens rea, or a guilty mind. This means that many possession statutes, particularly in the drug area—where some of the harshest campaigns in the war on crime have been prosecuted—are so-called strict liability crimes. In other words, you can be convicted of them if you don't know that you are "possessing" a drug of any kind, what drug you are "possessing," how much of it you've got, or—in some states—even that you are possessing anything at all, drug or no drug.[23]

Culpability as to Future Unlawful Use Possession liability might also demand, explicitly or implicitly, some additional culpability as to using the possessed material toward some criminal end. Usually, as with other forms of inchoate liability, some degree of intent as to some future conduct, or as to causing some prohibited result, may be thought necessary (and sufficient) to justify imposition of punishment, and preventive intervention, where the offender has not yet consummated the criminal project. Indeed, some courts have rejected, as unconstitutional, possession statutes that do not explicitly require any form of intent as

---

23. Markus Dirk Dubber, *The Possession Paradigm: The Special Part and the Police Power Model of the Criminal Process, in Defining Crimes: Essays on the Criminal Law's Special* Part 91 (R. A. Duff & Stuart Green eds., 2005) at 859 (citing State v. Cleppe, 635 P.2d 435 (Wash. 1981)).

to future criminal conduct, at least where the nature of the materials possessed is not such as to manifest such an unlawful objective on its own. Even if prohibition of possession itself is constitutionally acceptable, the usual purposes of inchoate liability support a requirement of such culpability to demonstrate the offender's dangerousness or blameworthiness. Accordingly, many narcotics or obscenity offenses, for example, will prohibit *possession with intent to distribute* the good in question.

Specific Possession Offenses   In addition to specific possession offenses, many jurisdictions define several other possession offenses. Some jurisdictions, following the Model Penal Code, recognize a general offense of *possessing instruments of crime,* which does not specify the proscribed materials, but requires that they must be "specially made or specially adapted for criminal use" or at least "commonly used for criminal purposes."[24] Others adopt offenses that define the prohibited items more narrowly. It is relatively common, for example, to criminalize *possession of burglary tools,* such as lock-picking devices. Various other such possession offenses exist as well, banning possession of everything from "graffiti instruments" to fireworks to gambling equipment; indeed, New York alone recognizes over 150 possession offenses. Because the instruments or tools these offenses cover may be used for lawful as well as unlawful purposes, these offenses generally explicitly require not only possession, but the intent to use the possessed item for some criminal purpose. A number of jurisdictions also recognize an offense of *possession of stolen goods.* Typically these offenses require that the offender knows the goods to be stolen and has the intent to prevent the owner from recovering them.

▲ PROBLEMS

Can a Mother Rape a Daughter Through a Husband? (#72)

After a previous failed marriage, Mary Knox lives with her new husband, Charles Knox, and her daughter Debbie from her first marriage. Charles grows very attached to the young girl, who is under the age of 12. However, his affection for Debbie becomes sexual in nature, and he begins raping Debbie on a regular basis. Mary is aware of what is happening but chooses to ignore the situation, even after Debbie comes to her in tears, begging her mother to make Charles stop "messing" with her. Charles repeatedly rapes Debbie for nearly a year before Debbie confides in her school principal. The principal immediately reports the rapes to the authorities and both Charles and Mary Knox are arrested.

What liability for Mary Knox, if any, under the Model Penal Code? Prepare a list of all criminal code subsections in the order in which you rely on them in your analysis.

---

24. Model Penal Code § 5.06.

Possessing Cocaine? (#73)

In January 1992, Ruben de los Santos is a seaman serving on a boat docked in Cartagena, Colombia. He is given 16 packages of cocaine, amounting to 8 kilograms, by a drug dealer and instructed to transport the cocaine to the port of Ponce in Puerto Rico. Upon docking, he is to deliver the cocaine to a Mr. Palestino at the Hotel Melia. Unknown to the drug dealers involved, American law enforcement agents from the Customs Service had approached Santos regarding a cocaine sting. Thus, Santos had accepted the cocaine and the transport plan while under police surveillance and with their permission.

Upon arriving in Ponce, Santos goes to Hotel Melia to meet Mr. Palestino. He meets Rafael Angel Zavala Maldonado who says he is a friend of Palestino and gestures for Santos to follow him to room 302. Santos confides in Zavala that he has the cocaine for Palestino, and the pair try to get in contact with Palestino.

After waiting awhile, Santos and Zavala decide to leave room 302 to get a soda, and while in the corridor the customs agents detain them. Zavala is taken into custody for possession of cocaine even though Zavala never actually held the cocaine nor was he alone with it, nor had he taken control of it. Palestino and his driver are arrested in the hotel, but neither is ultimately charged. Zavala is charged with possession of cocaine under the theory that he had gained constructive possession when he and Santos had agreed to leave the bag of cocaine in room 302, since Zavala was the only one of the pair who had access to the room and thus to the drugs after that point.

Assume 21 U.S.C. §841(a)(1) applies:

> [I]t shall be unlawful for any person knowingly or intentionally
> To manufacture, distribute, or dispense, or possess with intent to manufacture, distribute, or dispense, a controlled substance.

What liability for Zavala, if any, under the Model Penal Code? Prepare a list of all criminal code subsections in the order in which you rely on them in your analysis.

Stepping Over the Corpse in Aisle 3 (#74)

LaShanda Callaway and Cherish McCullough are inside a convenience store when they begin arguing. The other customers ignore the women as the fight escalates. The store is located in a high-crime area of town, and physical violence is not uncommon. McCullough takes out a knife and stabs Callaway. The shoppers simply go about their business. After McCullough flees, Callaway attempts several times to get up and seek help, but she is unable to stand. She lies collapsed on the floor, bleeding profusely from her wounds. But even though McCullough has left the store, the shoppers are hesitant to become involved. Several shoppers step over Callaway as they take their purchases to the register to pay. One shopper uses her cell phone to photograph Callaway's bleeding body, but not to call 911. After some time has passed, someone finally calls for help. By the time medics arrive, Callaway is dead. An investigation later determines that if emergency aid had been promptly summoned, Callaway could have been saved.

What liability, if any, under the Model Penal Code for the shopper who used her phone to take Callaway's photograph but not to call 911? Prepare a list of all criminal code subsections in the order in which you rely on them in your analysis.

What liability, if any, under each of the Rhode Island, Vermont, and Wisconsin general-duty-to-rescue statutes in the Advanced Materials for this Section in Appendix A? The issue of whether there should be a general duty to aid a stranger is the Discussion Issue for this Section, and is examined in the Advanced Materials in the Appendix.

✳ DISCUSSION ISSUE

Should There Be a Criminal-Law-Enforced Duty to Protect, Rescue, or Assist a Stranger in Danger if One Can Do So Without Unreasonable Risk or Inconvenience?

Materials presenting each side of this Discussion Issue appear in the Advanced Materials for Section 15 in Appendix A.

PART VI

GENERAL DEFENSES

Absent Element "Defenses"
Offense Modifications
General Defenses: Three Types
    Justifications
    Excuses
    Nonexculpatory Defenses

In casual language, it is common to refer to anything that prevents conviction of a defendant as a "defense," but this blanket term includes concepts and doctrines that are very different from one another. An "alibi defense," for example, simply refers to a claim that the defendant was somewhere else when the offense was committed and therefore cannot be the perpetrator. It is not a legal doctrine at all, but a form of factual counterclaim. A defense of diplomatic immunity, on the other hand, may admit commission of the offense (although it need not), yet claim that the jurisdiction nonetheless cannot legally prosecute the offense. The legal doctrines that we refer to as defenses typically are one of five sorts:[1] Absent element "defenses," offense modifications, justifications, excuses, or nonexculpatory defenses.

Absent Element "Defenses" Many defenses are simply facts that prevent proof of the requirements of the offense definition: For example, mistake negating a culpability element and mental illness negating the culpability required for homicide ("diminished capacity"). Where they do not provide complete exculpation, but only a reduction in liability, these factors sometimes are called "mitigations." In truth, such mitigations are simply instances where a fact—such as mistake or mental illness—shows the absence of a required element for one offense, but not for a lesser included offense. It is true that an absent element "defense" has the effect of preventing or reducing liability, but this effect is not the result of some additional doctrine of defense or mitigation. It is, rather, the result of applying the normal rules for assessing the satisfaction of the offense elements.

---

1. For illustrations and authorities for each defense, and for a discussion of the relations among the five defense groups, see Paul H. Robinson, *Criminal Law Defenses: A Systematic Analysis*, 82 COLUM. L. REV. 199, 213-216 (1982).

Offense Modifications   Other defenses and mitigations are defined separately from offense definitions. They do more than simply describe the absence of a required offense element, but rather supplement those elements to create additional rules to determine liability. These *offense modifications* serve to refine the nature and scope of a particular offense or group of offenses. These include, for example, renunciation as a defense to inchoate liability and "inevitably incident" conduct as a defense to complicity liability. Though, as a formal matter, these rules are set out in a separate place from the offense definition, they are essentially additional parts of that definition. That is, the true legal definition of conspiracy is an agreement *that is not renounced*—yet the part of the definition relating to renunciation does not appear in the conspiracy provision itself, but in a separate provision. Locating different offense requirements in different provisions may seem confusing or undesirable, but can increase efficiency if the offense-modification rule applies to multiple offenses at once. For example, the distinct renunciation rule does not only modify the definition of conspiracy, but of all other inchoate offenses also. Placing it in a separate provision can avoid needless duplication of the same rule in multiple offense definitions, especially if the modification rule is itself fairly complex or elaborate.

General Defenses: Three Types   Other defenses, in contrast, do not just modify the requirements of specific offenses, but have general application to *all* offenses. Such *general defenses* represent independent principles that bar liability for reasons unrelated to the nature or scope of any particular offense. They relate not to matters of criminalization but rather to matters of exculpation, or at least reasons for exemption from liability despite the fact that a crime has been committed. General defenses are of three sorts: justifications, excuses, and nonexculpatory defenses.

Justification Defenses   These defenses, such as the lesser evils justification, self-defense, and law enforcement authority, exculpate on a theory that the actor's otherwise criminal conduct avoided a greater harm or evil than it created. That is, while an actor satisfies the elements of an offense, her offense is tolerated (or even encouraged) because its offsetting benefits in a particular situation are such that it does not cause a net societal harm. An actor who burns a firebreak on another's land to stop an oncoming fire may thereby commit arson, but also may have a justification defense (of lesser evils) because, by creating the firebreak, the actor saves innocent lives threatened by the initial fire.

Excuse Defenses   These defenses, such as insanity and duress, exculpate under a different theory. Excuses apply to actors who have caused a net societal harm or evil—and are thus not justified—but who cannot justly be held responsible for their conduct. Note the difference in focus between justifications and excuses: The first focus on the actor's conduct, the second on the actor's responsibility for that conduct. As a general matter we can say that an *act* (or series of acts) is justified, whereas an *actor* is excused.

Nonexculpatory Defenses   A final group of general defenses does not exculpate an actor, but does provide an exemption from liability. Even for actors whose criminal conduct is not justified and who are fully responsible for it (thus not excused), the law might prevent punishment through application of a *nonexculpatory defense*.

Such defenses are made available because each furthers important societal interests that are thought, in particular cases, to outweigh society's interest in just punishment of criminal offenders. Thus, diplomatic immunity may provide a defense, without regard to the guilt or innocence of the actor, because by doing so, a country's diplomats are protected from interference when abroad and diplomatic communications among nations can thereby be established and maintained.

JUSTIFICATION DEFENSES GENERALLY

● **OVERVIEW OF JUSTIFICATION DEFENSES GENERALLY**

Lesser Evils Defense
    Balancing Competing Interests as Underlying Principle
Public Authority Justifications
    Furthering Public Interests
Defensive Force Justification
    Defending Against Unlawful Force
Common Structure of Justifications
    Triggering Conditions
    Necessity Requirement
    Proportionality Requirement

Lesser Evils Defense   A forest fire rages toward a town of unsuspecting inhabitants. The actor burns a field of corn located between the fire and the town; the burned field serves as a firebreak, saving lives. The actor satisfies all elements of the offense of criminal mischief by setting fire to the field with the purpose of destroying it. The immediate harm he causes—the destruction of the field—is precisely the harm that the mischief statute seeks to prevent and punish. Yet the actor is likely to have a complete defense because his conduct and its harmful consequences are justified. His conduct is tolerated, even encouraged, by society.

Balancing Competing Interests as Underlying Principle   The forest fire case provides an example of the *lesser evils* justification (also called *choice of evils* or *necessity*). This justification defense most clearly reflects the general principle of justification. Where codified, the defense explicitly requires that "the harm or evil sought to be avoided by such conduct is greater than that sought to be prevented by the law defining the offense charged."[2] As we shall see, the public authority

---

2. Model Penal Code § 3.02(1)(a).

and defensive force justifications, the subject of the next two Sections, have no such general balancing language but nonetheless are rooted in the same balancing principle. In those defenses, the legislature has undertaken to establish the balance of competing interests and has promulgated specific rules that embody its conclusions. Neither the defendant nor a jury is permitted to strike the balance differently.

Public Authority Justifications   When a deputy sheriff uses force in the execution of a judicial arrest warrant, his conduct may satisfy all the elements of assault, and the arrest and subsequent detention may satisfy the elements of kidnapping. But these practices further effective criminal justice, as well as the effective exercise of judicial authority. These societal interests are thought to justify the corresponding harm, giving rise to the officer's *public authority* defense. Such defenses need not be triggered by a threat from another (as is required for defensive force justifications, discussed below). An actor may be justified if she affirmatively acts to further a legally recognized interest. For example, a bus driver might be authorized to forcibly eject passengers who refuse to pay or are disruptive. On the other hand, the use of public authority justifications often is limited to certain persons, whose position or training makes them particularly appropriate protectors of the interest at stake, whereas defensive force justifications are generally available to all citizens.

Furthering Public Interests   The interests furthered or protected by public authority justifications may be personal or societal. They include criminal law enforcement, child rearing and education, safety and order on public transportation vehicles or in public institutions, life or health (as in medical emergencies and suicide prevention), military operations, and effective exercise of judicial authority, to name the most prominent. In each instance, the interest gives rise to an authority for the appropriate persons to act in a way that otherwise would be criminal, if it furthers or protects the interest. Public authority justifications are distinguished from one another according to the interest protected. Legislatures may refine the basic principle to provide a suitably limited justification defense for each interest and authority. Thus, for example, the scope of law enforcement authority may be different from the scope of the authority of a bus driver to maintain safety and decorum.

Defensive Force Justification   A prowler attempts to steal chickens from a chicken coop. May the owner use physical force against the prowler to prevent the theft? Some limited degree of force commonly is permitted, if it is necessary to protect the property. It is not that society deems injury to a person as a less significant interest than the right to ownership of chickens. Rather, in weighing the interests at stake, the legislature considers not only the immediate physical harms—personal injury versus loss of a chicken—but also the intangible societal interest in maintaining a right to hold personal property. The threatened theft endangers not only the rightful possession by this owner, but also the stability and vitality of the rule of private possession generally. To state it negatively, society generally abhors unjustified aggressive takings because they undercut the security of private possession and social order generally. Society therefore tolerates the injury that must be inflicted to stop the aggressor. The same reasoning applies when the aggression is toward the actor himself or toward another person. Society's interest in maintaining a right to bodily integrity, when combined with the physical harm threatened, may outweigh the personal injury that must be inflicted to block the aggression.

Defending Against Unlawful Force Such *defensive force* justifications are each triggered by a threat of unlawful force. Like public authority justifications, they are distinguished from one another by the interest at issue: Defense of self, defense of others, defense of property. Legislatures often wish to make special rules to govern the use of defensive force, depending on the interest to be protected. For example, they may limit the defense-of-property justification to exclude the use of deadly force. They might permit the use of force to defend another person only if that other person would also be justified in using such force.

Common Internal Structure of Justifications The balancing of competing interests common to all justification defenses is part of the internal structure of each defense. Justifications share other characteristics as well. All justifications have the following internal structure, with three general elements: (1) Some enabling or *triggering condition* authorizes an otherwise illegal action (frequently the use of force), so long as that action (2) is *necessary* to protect or further the interest at stake, and (3) causes only such harm as is *proportional* or reasonable in relation to the harm threatened or the interest to be furthered. Each of these three requirements plays a role in ensuring that the conduct justified by the defense is indeed conduct that society would encourage or at least tolerate. The lesser evils defense describes these elements in the broadest terms; other justifications reflect more explicit and specific legislative determinations about the relevant conditions and the type and extent of conduct authorized.

Triggering Conditions *Triggering conditions* are the circumstances that must exist before an actor is eligible to act under the justification. Defensive force justifications are triggered when an aggressor threatens unjustified force against the protected interest, as, for instance, by attempting to steal the defendant's chickens. Public authority justifications are triggered when the circumstances evoke the use of the public authority given to the actor. A conductor's authority to act to maintain order and safety on a train may be triggered by a passenger who refuses to stop smoking or to pay for his ticket. The general justification defense, lesser evils, has the broadest triggering condition. In its purest form, the defense is available whenever any legally protected interest is threatened and some action is possible to avoid that threat. (The general defense is available, however, only in situations unrelated to the triggering conditions for one of the more specific justification defenses.)

Necessity Requirement The *necessity requirement* demands that the defendant act only when, and only to the extent, necessary to protect or further the interest at stake. Thus, where an aggressor announces his intention to assault the actor at noon of the next day, the threat triggers a right of self-defense. But if the actor is not in danger at the time of the announcement and can just as effectively defend the next morning, the actor is not justified in immediately using physical force against the would-be aggressor. Further, even when an actor must act immediately, the actor is privileged to use only the degree of force necessary for self-protection. Even if most persons would find it necessary to use greater force, the force used is not justified if this actor can protect himself or herself as effectively with less. Assume the actor is a karate expert who, with no risk of harm to himself, can dislodge an attacker's club with a high kick. While the average person might be justified in shooting the armed attacker, this actor may only use karate to disarm if greater force, such as shooting, is unnecessary to protect himself.

Proportionality Requirement The *proportionality requirement* places a maximum limit on the necessary force that may be used in protection or furtherance of an interest. Even necessary force will not be justified if it is too harmful in relation to the value of the interest at stake. To illustrate, assume an actor has no other option but to use deadly force to prevent the stealing of apples from his orchard. Most jurisdictions would deny a defense for use of deadly force, even if the actor had tried all less harmful means of preventing the thefts. It should be no surprise that there is some controversy surrounding these rules. They require the actor stoically to sacrifice a legally recognized interest, frequently for the protection of an aggressor (as in all defensive force justifications). But such commitment to proportionality—such as valuing human life, even that of a lawbreaker, over property interests—is the mark of a civilized society. It is under this same principle that deadly force against a nonaggressor is rarely, if ever, justified, suggesting that an innocent's life is a near-absolute interest that can almost never be outweighed.

Lesser Evils Defense

When should the law authorize conduct that would otherwise be an offense but that special circumstances would seem to justify? This Section begins the examination of this important group of general defenses: justifications.

◆ THE CASE OF THE ISRAELI GENERAL SECURITY SERVICE (#75)

For decades, Israelis and Palestinians have been locked in conflict. To force the Israeli government to compromise, Palestinian extremist groups regularly use car and suicide bombings against civilians. Over a recent two-and-a-half-year period, these types of bombings have killed 121 and injured 707. For example, two bus bombings in April 1994 killed 13 people in operations for which Hamas, a Palestinian extremist group, claimed responsibility. A few months later, another Hamas bus bombing killed 20 people and injured another 48. Yehuda Shloss, a witness to the explosion, describes how the explosion lofts the bus full of passengers a meter into the air and crushes the bus as it falls back to the ground. Passengers' dismembered body parts flew out, crashing through the widows of nearby stores and apartment buildings. Looking at the remains, a teenage girl expresses the Israelis' despair, "How much can we take?" Hamas is just one of several Palestinian groups whose stated purpose is the annihilation of the State of Israel.

To prevent these terrorist attacks, Israel established the General Security Service (GSS), which has had moderate success. In September 1995, state attorney Shai Nitzan reports that the GSS recently prevented ten attempted car bombings, seven attempts to kidnap soldiers, and several attempted murders. The GSS has also discovered a lab equipped to manufacture explosives and pipe bombs. In August 1995, Israel reports that the GSS has uncovered and arrested the commanders and planners of groups that attacked Jerusalem twice the previous year. Following those arrests, the GSS uncovers more Hamas organizations throughout

Figure 75 "Qas'at-a-Tawleh" Method: forcing the interrogee to kneel or sit down with his back to a table, while the interrogator places his arms, bound and stretched behind him, on the table. In that position, the interrogator sometimes pushes the interrogee's body forward or pulls his legs

(B'Tselem)

Figure 76 "Qambaz" Method: forcing the interrogee to crouch on his toes with his hands tied behind him

(B'Tselem)

Figure 77 "Standing Shabeh" Method: having the interrogee stand, with his hands tied and drawn upwards

(B'Tselem)

Figure 78 "Banana" Method: having the interrogee lie on his back on a high stool with his body arched backwards

(B'Tselem)

Figure 79 "Regular Shabeh" Method: tying the interrogee to a low chair, tilting forward

(B'Tselem)

Figure 80 "Violent shaking" method: interrogator grasps and violently shakes the detainee

(B'Tselem)

Judea and Samaria, including Eastern Jerusalem. The arrests of these members foil a number of planned recent attacks, including a suicide attack at the Jerusalem central bus station, a suicide attack on a civilian bus in Tel Aviv, the kidnapping of two Israeli soldiers, the killing of a settler in the Samaria region, the attempt to plant a bomb on a train in the Jerusalem area, and the killing of a settler in the Gaza Strip. In July 1995, Prime Minister Rabin reports that the GSS prevented a potentially devastating attack planned by Hamas for July 1, the date on which the Camp David Israel-Palestinian peace agreement was to be signed. In May 1998, it is revealed that the GSS foiled not only the usual suicide bombing attacks but also several attempts at kidnapping Israeli dignitaries.

The GSS commonly detains and questions alleged members of various radical or militant Palestinian groups. Ordinarily, the GSS does not formally charge the detainees; it holds them "administratively" to obtain information about planned or impending attacks. Their methods, which have successfully produced life-saving information, often involve the use of severe methods, including electrical shock, cold showers, and harsh beatings.

Formed during the 1987 intifada, Hamas vehemently opposes the existence of Israel and openly advocates the use of terrorist attacks against Israeli civilians. In April 1994, for example, Hamas claimed responsibility for separate suicide attacks that killed eight people on a bus in the center of Afula and five at the central bus station of Hadera. Later that year, Hamas undertook two more attacks in Jerusalem. The GSS is thus highly suspicious of any person having an affiliation with Hamas.

Abdel Zamed Hassan Harizat is an educated, thirty-year old computer operator who still lives at home with his parents and a brother in Hebron. He is a diminutive man at four feet six inches, but makes up for his lack of height with

Figure 81 **Fatma Harizat holds a photo of her son, Abdel-Samad Harizat, at her home in Hebron, Sept. 6, 1999**

(AP Photo/Nasser Shiyoukhi)

a pleasant personality. His employer is a Hebron publishing company that is known for supporting fundamentalists. His boss, Manager Jewad Said, is pleased with Harizat's performance.

Two years ago, Harizat spent three months in an Israeli prison and was fined $1,350 for distributing Hamas leaflets. The GSS now believes him to be a senior member of Izzadin Kassam, the military wing of Hamas. He is also suspected of being involved in three fatal attacks on Jewish settlers in Hebron.

The GSS has recently learned that Taher Kapisha, a Hamas terrorist, is planning an imminent attack. They believe Harizat can lead them to Kapisha and to other members of the Izzadin Kassam. (Kapisha is subsequently tracked down and killed by security forces in June.)

On the night of Saturday, April 22, 1995, GSS agents come to Harizat's home. They drag him outside blindfolded

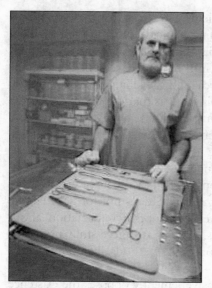

Figure 82 **Dr. Yehuda Hiss, who per-**
formed the autopsy of Harizat, 1999

(Jonathan Bloom, Jerusalem Post)

while several agents beat him. Other agents lock the rest of his family in one room before ransacking the house looking for intelligence and finding only Hamas leaflets. Meanwhile, other agents take Harizat to one of its facilities, the Russian Compound, in Jerusalem. A doctor who examines him concludes that he is in good health despite his protestations that he has a medical problem. Agents begin the interrogation, which for the first one-half hour involves beating him. They follow with banging his head against a wall and shaking him violently a dozen times by his shirt collar and shoulders. They stop when they notice he is having trouble breathing. Harizat is left in the interrogation room alone, bleeding, and eventually loses consciousness. Several hours later, agents take him to Jerusalem's Hadassah Hospital. He arrives still unconscious. The doctors treat him for severe head injuries. There are also visible signs of bruising on his chest and indications that he has multiple concussions.

Later that day, GSS agents return to Harizat's house and ask his brother and mother to accompany them to the hospital. There they see his beaten, unconscious, shackled body. Two days later, he dies of his wounds. He is the fourth detainee to die in custody since January. The following week, Dr. Yehuda Hiss, an Israeli pathologist, performs an autopsy despite Harizat's mother's initial opposition. At the family's request, an independent Scottish pathologist observes during the procedure. The autopsy confirms that Harizat died of traumatic causes.

In protest of Harizat's death, Hamas files a formal complaint with the International Committee of the Red Cross. It also issues a press release threatening that Israel "will pay a high price" for torturing Harizat to death. Palestinian Liberation Authority leader Yasser Arafat adds that, "what happened to Harizat is an execution. . . . Israel is not only killing Palestinian prisoners . . . but the whole peace process." A chief Israeli government spokesman says "that there is no systemized torture in Israel. But since we are threatened with a huge ring of terror, the main duty of the government is to protect its citizens, and therefore we have to resort to methods that are not so nice." Meanwhile, the Justice Minister initiates an official investigation, while a senior defense official believes that deviation from standard procedures caused the death.

1. Relying only on your own intuitions of justice, does the GSS official who authorized the interrogation techniques used on Harizat deserve liability and punishment and, if so, how much?

N	0	1	2	3	4	5	6	7	8	9	10	11
☐	☐	☐	☐	☐	☐	☐	☐	☐	☐	☐	☐	☐
no liability	liability but no punishment	1 day	2 wks	2 mo	6 mo	1 yr	3 yrs	7 yrs	15 yrs	30 yrs	life imprison-ment	death

2. What "justice" arguments could defense counsel make on the defendant's behalf?

3. What "justice" arguments could the prosecution make against the defendant?

4. What liability, if any, for the GSS official under the then-existing statutes? Prepare a list of all criminal code subsections or case in the order in which you rely on them in your analysis.

5. What liability, if any, under the Model Penal Code? Prepare a list of all criminal code subsections in the order in which you rely on them in your analysis.

■ THE LAW

Israeli Penal Law
(1995)
(5737-1977, as amended in 5754-1994)

Chapter Ten. Offenses Against the Person

Article One. Causing Death

Section 298. Manslaughter

If a person—by an unlawful act or omission—causes the death of another, he is guilty of manslaughter and is liable to twenty years imprisonment.

Section 300. Murder

(a) If a person does one of the following, he is guilty of murder and is liable to life imprisonment, and only to that penalty:

(1) he willfully causes the death of his father or mother or grandfather or grandmother by an unlawful act or omission;

(2) he premeditatively causes the death of any person;

(3) in the commission of an offense or while preparing for or facilitating the commission of an offense, he willfully causes the death of a person;

(4) having committed another offense, he causes the death of a person in order to secure the escape or to avoid punishment of himself or of a person who participated in the commission of that offense.

(b) A person convicted of murder under section 2(f) of the Nazis and Nazi Collaborators (Punishment) Law 5710-1950, is liable to the death penalty.

Section 300A. Reduced Penalty

Notwithstanding the provisions of section 300, a penalty lighter than that set in it may be imposed, if the offense was committed in one of the following situations:

(a) when, because of a severe mental disturbance or because of his limited intellectual capability, the defendant's ability to do one of the following was severely reduced, even though not to the point of the complete incapacity said in section 34H:

(1) to understand what he was doing or that his act is wrong; or

(2) to refrain from committing the act;

(b) when, under the circumstances of the case, the defendant's act exceeded by little what would have been reasonable, as required under section 34P, for the application of the exceptions of self defense, necessity or duress under sections 341, 34J and 34K can be applied;

(c) when the defendant was in a state of severe mental distress, because of severe or continued harassment of himself or of a member of his family by the person whose death the defendant caused.

Section 301. Premeditation

(a) For purposes of section 300, a person shall be deemed to have killed another person premeditatively, if he resolved to kill him and killed him in cold blood without immediate provocation, under circumstances in which he was able to think and understand the result of his actions, after having prepared to kill him or after having prepared the instrument with which he killed him.

(b) As regards the resolution and preparation to kill, it is immaterial whether the accused resolved to kill the other person or a particular member—or any member—of his family or race.

(c) To prove premeditation, it is not necessary to show that the accused was in any state of mind for any particular period before the offense was committed or that the instrument with which the offense was committed was prepared at any particular time before the act.

Section 304. Causing Death by Negligence

If a person causes another person's death by negligence, then he is liable to three years imprisonment.

Section 309. Definition of Causing Death

A person even though his act or omission is not the immediate or sole cause of death, shall be deemed to have caused the death of another person in any of the following cases:

(1) he inflicted bodily injury which necessitated medical or surgical treatment and the treatment caused the injured person's death; it is immaterial whether the treatment was mistaken, so long as it was given in good faith and with ordinary knowledge and skill; if it was not so given, the person who inflicted the injury shall not be deemed to have caused the injured person's death;

(2) he inflicted bodily injury which would not have caused the injured person's death, had he received proper medical or surgical treatment or had he observed proper precautions as to his way of life;

(3) he caused a person, by violence or threats of violence, to commit an act which caused his own death, if that act appeared to that person—under the circumstances—a natural way of avoiding the violence or threats;

(4) he hastened, by deed or by omission, the death of a person who suffers from a disease or injury, which—even without that deed or omission—would have caused death;

(5) the act or omission would not have caused death, unless accompanied by an act or omission of the person killed or of some other person.

Article Four. Endangering Life and Health

Section 329. Harm with Aggravating Intent

If a person does one of the following with intent to disable, disfigure or cause grievous harm to another, or with intent to resist or prevent the lawful arrest or detention of himself or of another, then he is liable to twenty years imprisonment:

(1) he unlawfully wounds or causes grievous harm to a person;

(2) he unlawfully attempts to strike a person with a projectile, knife or other dangerous or offensive weapon;

(3) he unlawfully causes an explosive substance to explode;

(4) he sends or delivers an explosive substance or other dangerous or noxious object to a person, or he causes a person to receive such a substance or object;

(5) he puts a destructive or explosive substance or a corrosive fluid in any place;

(6) he throws any substance or fluid said in paragraph (5) at a person or otherwise applies it to his body.

Section 333. Grievous Harm

If a person unlawfully does grievous harm to another person, he is liable to seven years imprisonment.

Section 334. Wounding

If a person unlawfully wounds another person, he is liable to three years imprisonment.

Section 341. Harm Through Negligence

If a person unlawfully commits any act, or omits anything which it is his duty to do, that act or omission not being one specified in sections 338 to 340, and if by that act or omission harm is caused to a person, then he is liable to one year imprisonment.

Article Eight. Assault

Section 378. Definition of Assault

If a person directly or indirectly strikes, touches, pushes or otherwise applies force to another without his consent or with his consent, which was obtained by fraud, he is said to commit assault; for this purpose, the application of force includes the application of heat, light, electricity, gas, smells or any other thing or substance, if it is applied to a degree that causes injury or discomfort.

Section 379. Common Assault

If a person unlawfully assaults another, he is liable to two years imprisonment, except to the extent that this Law provides a different punishment for the offense, in view of its circumstances.

Section 380. Assault that Causes Actual Bodily Harm

If a person commits assault that causes actual bodily harm, he is liable to three years imprisonment.

Section 381. Various Kinds of Assault

(a) If a person does one of the following, he is liable to three years imprisonment:
    (1) he assaults another in order to commit a felony;
    (2) he assaults another in order to steal anything;
    (3) he assaults another in order to resist or prevent the Lawful arrest or apprehension of himself or of another for any offense;

(b) If a person assaults a public servant, or a person who performs a duty or function assigned to him under law, or a person who renders a service to the public on behalf of a body that provides a service to the public—the assault being connected with the performance of the assaulted person's duty or function—he is liable to five years imprisonment.

Section 382. Assault Under Aggravating Circumstances

If any offense under sections 379, 380, or 381(a)(1) or (3) was committed in the presence of two or more persons, who combined for the commission of the act by one or some of them, each of them is liable to double the penalty prescribed for the offense.

Chapter Eleven. Offenses Relating to Property

Article One. Theft

Section 383. Definition of Theft

(a) A person commits theft—
    (1) if he takes and carries away—without the owner's consent, fraudulently, and without claiming a right in good faith—a thing capable of being

stolen, with the intention—when he takes it—of permanently depriving its owner;

(2) if he—while having lawful possession of a thing capable of being stolen, being its bailee or part owner—fraudulently converts it to his own use or to the use of another person who is not the owner.

(b) In respect of theft under subsection (a), it is immaterial that the person who takes or converts the object in question is a director or officer of a body corporate which is its owner, provided that the aggregate of other circumstances amounts to stealing—

(c) For the matter of stealing—

(1) "taking" includes obtaining possession—

(a) by a trick;

(b) by intimidation;

(c) by a mistake on the owner's part, the person who takes the object knowing that the possession has been so obtained;

(d) by finding, if the finder at that time believes that the owner can be discovered by reasonable means;

(2) "carrying away" includes the removal of a thing from the place which it occupies, but in the case of an attached object, only if it has been completely detached;

(3) "ownership" includes part ownership, possession, a right to possession and control;

(4) "thing capable of being stolen" —a thing which has value and is the property of a person, but if the thing is attached to an immovable object, only if it has been detached from it.

Section 384. Punishment for Theft

If a person commits theft, he is liable to three years imprisonment, unless some other punishment is provided in view of the circumstances of the theft or of the nature of the stolen object.

Chapter Five "A". Restrictions on Criminal Liability

Article Two. Restrictions on Criminal Nature of Act

Section 384J. Defensive Force

No person shall bear criminal responsibility for an act that was immediately necessary in order to repel an unlawful attack, which posed real danger to his own or another person's life, freedom, bodily welfare or property; however, a person is not acting in self defense when his own wrongful conduct caused the attack, the possibility of such a development having been foreseen by himself.

Section 384K. Necessity

No person shall bear criminal responsibility for an act that was immediately necessary in order to save his own or another person's life, freedom, bodily welfare or property from a real danger of severe injury, due to the conditions prevalent at the time the act was committed, there being no alternative but to commit the act.

Section 384M. Justification

No person shall bear criminal responsibility for an act that he committed under any of the following circumstances:

(1) he was lawfully obligated or authorized to commit it;

(2) he committed it under the order of a competent authority, which he lawfully was obligated to obey, unless the order is obviously unlawful;

(3) in respect of an act which lawfully requires consent, when the act was immediately necessary in order to save a person's life or his bodily welfare, or to prevent severe injury to his health, if, under the circumstances, he was not able to obtain the consent;

(4) he committed it on a person with lawful consent, in the course of a medical procedure or treatment, the objective of which was that person's or another person's benefit.

(5) he committed it in the course of a sports activity or of a sports game, such as are not prohibited by law and do not conflict with public order, in accordance with rules customary for them.

Section 384P. Unreasonableness

The provisions of sections 34J, 34K, and 34L shall not apply, if, under the circumstance, the act was not a reasonable one for the prevention of the injury.

Section 384R. Misinterpretation of Situation

(a) If a person commits an act, while imagining a situation that does not exist, he shall not bear criminal responsibility, except to the extent that he would have had to bear it, had the situation really been as he imagined it.

(b) Subsection (a) shall also apply to an offense of negligence, on condition that the mistake was reasonable, and to an offense of [strict liability] . . .

Chapter Five. Derivative Offences
Article One. Attempt

Section 25. What Constitutes an Attempt

A person attempts to commit an offense if he, with intent to commit the offense, does an act that constitutes more than mere preparation and the offense is not completed.

Section 26. Commission of the Offense Is Impossible

With regard to an attempt, it is immaterial whether the commission of the offense is impossible owing to a state of things of which the person attempting is not aware or about which he is mistaken.

The State of Israel v. Blesser
PD 59(2) 408 (2003), at p. 415, Criminal Appeal 9723/03, 9777/03

As the court explains, per Chief Justice BEINISH, "The objective element of the offense of homicide includes the broadly defined element 'a forbidden commission or omission' and the consequential element 'the death of a person.' A factual causal linkage is required between these two elements ('which have resulted in'). The requirement of causal linkage purports that the conduct of the accused has constituted, from a physical-objective perspective, a necessary significant cause of the result. Therefore, the prosecution has to demonstrate that the conduct of the accused has been a cause sine qua non of the death of the victim. It should be stressed, that the conduct of the accused does not have to be the only cause of the immediate cause of the death, but should have a necessary contribution to the deadly result in the way it has occurred."

Model Penal Code
(Official Draft 1962)

Section 3.02. Justification Generally Choice of Evils

(1) Conduct which the actor believes to be necessary to avoid a harm or evil to himself or to another is justifiable, provided that:

(a) the harm or evil sought to be avoided by such conduct is greater than that sought to be prevented by the law defining the offense charged; and

(b) neither the Code nor other law defining the offense provides exceptions or defenses dealing with the specific situation involved; and

(c) a legislative purpose to exclude the justification claimed does not otherwise plainly appear.

(2) When the actor was reckless or negligent in bringing about the situation requiring a choice of harms or evils or in appraising the necessity for his conduct, the justification afforded by this section is unavailable in a prosecution for any offense for which recklessness or negligence, as the case may be, suffices to establish culpability.

● OVERVIEW OF LESSER EVILS DEFENSE

Hypothetical: A Life-Saving Break-In (#76)

Burke and his two roommates, Tim and Henry, have AIDS. As yet, Burke has few debilitating symptoms. He remains physically and mentally strong. Tim is in very poor health and is getting worse rapidly. Henry was in the same condition several months ago until he began participating in a research study using a drug called IIR. His health, like that of many others in the study, dramatically improved after he started using the drug. While Burke is thrilled with Henry's recovery, he is angry that the study's sponsors will not let him and Tim participate. He has urged government authorities in the Food and Drug Administration to make IIR generally available, but his requests have been denied on grounds that insufficient research has been done to justify FDA approval. Burke is convinced that the only way he can save his own life and Tim's is to break into the research study's offices and steal sufficient doses of IIR for them both. He breaks into the building, but trips several silent alarms and is apprehended by police as he is leaving with the drug.

Burke is charged with burglary and offers a lesser evils justification defense. Should he get the defense?

Notes

Triggering Conditions
    Threat to Legally Protected Interest
    Opportunity to Promote Interest
Necessity Requirement
    Necessary in Time
        Requirement of "Imminent" Threat
        Alternative Requirement That Response Be "Immediately Necessary"
    Necessity of Degree of Harm
Proportionality Requirement
    Justifiability of Taking Life to Save More Lives
    Supremacy of Community's Balance of Interests
    Deference to Legislative Balance of Interests
        Rejection of Defense for Civil Disobedience
        Argument for Transcendent Legal Norms JustIfying Resistance to Positive Law
        Legislative Preemption Through Offense Exceptions
        More Specific Justification Governs Situations Where It Applies

The *lesser evils* defense—sometimes called *choice of evils* or *necessity*, or simply the *general justification* defense—is formally recognized in about half of the American jurisdictions.[3] It illustrates the structure and operation of justification defenses generally by relying explicitly on the rationale inherent in all justifications: While the actor may have caused the harm or evil of an offense, the justifying circumstances suggest that his conduct avoided a greater harm or evil than it caused. In the language of the Model Penal Code, an actor is justified if his conduct is:

> necessary to avoid a harm or evil to himself or to another . . . provided that: the harm or evil sought to be avoided by such conduct is greater than that sought to be prevented by the law defining the offense charged . . . . [4]

TRIGGERING CONDITIONS

The lesser evils defense was once limited to situations in which the threat was from natural forces, such as the threat of starvation to survivors in a drifting lifeboat. Modern codes, however, follow the lead of the Model Penal Code in doing away with that limitation. The rationale for the defense—that the conduct avoided a greater harm or evil than it caused—supports a defense no matter what the source of the threat may be. Modern codes typically require instead that the

---

3. See 2 Paul H. Robinson, *Criminal Law Defenses* § 124(a) (1984).
4. Model Penal Code § 3.02(1)(a).

threat must affect a legally protected interest and must be unjustified. In application, these requirements are quite broad and tend to exclude few cases.

Threat to Legally Protected Interest   Legally protected interests relevant to the defense include not only those interests the law expressly sanctions, such as one's right to freedom of political or religious expression, but may also include other interests, at least if the legal system does not specifically reject their legitimacy. The loss of an actor's opportunity to see his dying mother arguably might support a claim of the defense, although the law does not expressly recognize such visitation as a legal right. Thus, a defendant might receive a general justification defense if he violates a traffic law in his rush to the hospital, provided the jury concludes that the harm or evil avoided (inability to see his mother one last time) outweighs the harm or evil of the offense committed (speeding). In the "Break-In" hypothetical, Burke should have little difficulty arguing that his life and Tim's are interests worth protecting and that both are in danger.

Opportunity to Promote Interest   While the lesser evils defense is typically expressed to require a triggering threat—the offense conduct must be "necessary to avoid a harm or evil"—it is not difficult to argue that the defense may apply much more broadly, justifying opportunities to affirmatively advance an interest rather than to just react to a threat. The same conduct frequently can be described either in terms of furthering a good or avoiding a harm. Protestors who interfered with the selective service system to stop the Vietnam War might describe their acts either as advancing the interests of peace or as averting the evils of war. Private use of marijuana in the treatment of glaucoma can be seen as furthering the interest of the defendant's good health or as combating the threat of impending blindness.

NECESSITY REQUIREMENT

As with any other justification, the triggering of a lesser evils does not give an actor unlimited authority. Her response must be both necessary and proportionate. As to the first of these, statutes typically demand that, to be justified, conduct must be "necessary" to promote the relevant interest (or combat the relevant threat). Necessity has two distinct aspects: The conduct must be necessary in time and in the amount of harm it causes. That is, the necessity requirement is not satisfied if the conduct would have been as effective if delayed, or if a less harmful alternative is available and would suffice.

Necessary in Time   The famous case of *Regina v. Dudley and Stephens*[5] raises, among other things, the issue of the temporal aspect of the necessity requirement. One reason the court denied a necessity defense was that the defendants, who turned to murder and cannibalism after days at sea without food, might have survived until rescued if they had waited a few days more.[6] In the "Break-In" hypothetical above, Burke would have to clear a similar hurdle, showing that delay in taking the drugs would risk death or injury. His ability to show this will depend in part on the operation of the drug. Is a patient's prognosis improved when he begins the treatment earlier, or could Burke and Tim have started the drug later

---

5. 14 Q.B.D. 273 (1884).
6. Id. at 279.

with equal efficacy? Certainly Burke's best position is to argue that Tim's life was in immediate danger because of his quickly deteriorating condition, and, in any case, Tim's present suffering justified immediate action. He can argue that every moment of delay was an additional moment of suffering.

Requirement of "Imminent" Threat   The issue of temporal necessity arises not only from the general statutory requirement of "necessary" conduct, but also because many statutes require that the threat of harm must be "imminent" for the defense to apply. Underlying this requirement is a presumption that, unless the danger is imminent, action is not yet necessary. But such a presumption is not always valid. Suppose, for example, a ship's crew discovers a slow leak soon after leaving port. The captain unreasonably refuses to return to shore. In order to save themselves and the passengers, the crew must mutiny. If the leak would not pose an actual danger of capsizing the vessel for several days, should the crew be forced to wait until the danger is imminent, even though this would mean that the ship would be too far out to sea to reach shore before it sinks? Or should the crew be able to act before it is too late, even though it may be several days before the danger of capsizing is imminent? Requiring "imminent" harm, if it means the risk must be on the verge of materializing, sometimes may require the actor to wait until it is too late for any response to be effective. Since the lesser evils defense already justifies only "necessary" conduct, adding such an "imminence" require-ment is an unnecessary and potentially improper limitation.

Alternative Requirement That Response Be "Immediately Necessary"   Some necessity statutes require instead that the actor's conduct be "immediately necessary."[7] This formulation is less problematic. In the sinking-ship hypothetical, for example, the actors could argue that as soon as they discovered the serious leak, it became immediately necessary to act, even though the danger of capsizing was not yet imminent. There remain situations, however, where the "immediately nec-essary" language would force an actor to wait longer before acting than he would have to wait without the requirement. Commonly, the effect of such a require-ment is to force an actor to delay his actions in case subsequent events make the justified conduct unnecessary. Reasonable persons may disagree over whether it is appropriate to require such a delay, and one's views may vary with the situation. The "immediately necessary" requirement would seem always to force an actor to delay, rather than leaving it for a jury to decide whether it was reasonable under the circumstances to reduce the risk of the harm by acting earlier.

Necessity of Degree of Harm   The amount-of-harm aspect of the neces-sity requirement bars the lesser evils defense where a lawful, or less harmful, means exists to protect the threatened interest. Where prisoners escape or rebel in order to avoid or publicize life-threatening prison conditions, for example, courts frequently refuse the defense on grounds that less harmful alternatives are avail-able, including lawful alternatives such as registering complaints with the prison authorities.[8] The necessity requirement also implicitly requires a causal connection between the actor's conduct and avoiding the threatened harm: If the defendant's conduct could not actually prevent the threatened harm, then the conduct cannot

---

7. See, e.g., Ark. Stat. Ann. § 41-504(1)(a); Colo. Rev. Stat. § 18-1-702(1).

8. See, e.g., State v. Green, 470 S.W.2d 565 (Mo. 1971); see also 2 Paul H. Robinson, *Criminal Law Defenses* § 124(a) n.8 (1984).

be "necessary" to prevent the harm. In the "Break-In" hypothetical, Burke probably can show that no less harmful means of saving his life and Tim's is available. He has approached government officials to no avail. On the other hand, the implicit requirement that his conduct be effective in saving his life and Tim's requires a showing that IIR would have made a difference. If IIR would not have been an effective treatment for him or Tim, Burke can hardly argue that stealing it was necessary to save their lives.

PROPORTIONALITY REQUIREMENT

The lesser evils defense, like all other justifications, requires proportionality between the harm or evil the actor's conduct causes and the harm or evil it avoids. Indeed, the defense contains a more explicit proportionality requirement than other justifications, which tend either to provide specific rules that effectively codify a legislature's proportionality balance or to require proportionality through a requirement that conduct be "reasonable." The lesser evils requirement might be seen as more demanding. It is not enough for the defense that the actor's conduct is proportionate in that it caused *no more harm* or evil than it avoided. The actor's conduct must be *less* harmful than the threat it averts. For example, in the case where two lives are in conflict, neither actor could lawfully take the other's, unless some tangible interest (such as the law's abhorrence of unjustified aggression) favored one over the other. Thus one could kill an unjustified aggressor to save oneself, but could not kill an innocent nonaggressor to save oneself (in order to take the only available life preserver on the sinking ship, for example). In the "Break-In" hypothetical, Burke no doubt will feel that the harm threatened (two deaths) is greater than the harm he caused by breaking in and stealing IIR.[9] On the other hand, the prosecution may argue that important intangible interests are at stake, such as the dangerousness of effectively creating a rule allowing burglaries of researchers' offices. Any adverse effect on the operation of research generally ought to be included in the balancing.

Justifiability of Taking Life to Save More Lives   One of the more difficult issues that arises in lesser evils situations is whether to allow the taking of one innocent (nonaggressor's) life in order to save several innocent lives. The opinion of Lord Coleridge in *Queen v. Dudley and Stephens*[10] suggests a philosophy that the value of innocent human life is an absolute that can never be outweighed or justified by its possible consequences, not even by the potential to save a greater number of lives. This philosophy, consistent with the Kantian position that taking innocent life is a categorical wrong, is an alternative to the more utilitarian approach that might permit the taking of an innocent life to bring about a net saving of lives. But the situation in *Dudley and Stephens*, where one innocent life is taken to save only two or three others, does not present the strongest case for justifying the killing of an innocent. Where many lives are at stake, it becomes more difficult to hold to the absolutist position.[11] Yet even if one rejects that

---

9. The Model Penal Code asks the jury to focus not on the harm caused but on the harm "sought to be prevented by the law defining the offense charged." Model Penal Code § 3.02(1)(a).

10. L.R. 14 Q.B. 273 (1884).

11. This was the situation in the leading American case, United States v. Holmes, which approved the jettison of some passengers of a sinking lifeboat in order to prevent the death of all, but only if the selection for jettison is made by drawing lots. 26 F. Cas. 360 (1842) (No. 15,383).

position and takes the view that an innocent life can be outweighed by other interests (such as saving a greater number of innocent lives), one might nonetheless conclude that it would be dangerous, or wrongful, to establish a precedent condoning—or even seeming to approve—the choice to take the life of an innocent, and the concerns with setting such a precedent might weigh heavily against allowing a justification.

Supremacy of Community's Balance of Interests   In the balancing called for by the proportionality requirement, no jurisdiction delegates to individual actors the right to determine authoritatively the relative value of the harms they avoid and the harms they create. It is the community's view, not the individual's, that matters. Where the community view standard is not contained within the language of the defense provision, it is often judicially supplied. As a practical matter, in particular criminal cases involving the lesser evils defense, the community's view governs via the judgment of the jury, who ultimately determine the balance of interests in deciding whether to grant the defense.[12] Thus, in the "Break-In" hypothetical, it is of no consequence that the proper balance was clear to Burke; Burke's defense depends on whether the jury will agree, or be persuaded, that his calculations were correct.

Deference to Legislative Balance of Interests   It is a corollary of representative government that the ultimate power to judge the relative values of competing interests rests with the legislature. If an actor balances the competing interests differently from the legislature, the legislature's view must prevail. This limitation is expressed in part by language that withdraws the Model Penal Code lesser evils defense whenever "a legislative purpose to exclude the justification claimed" plainly appears.[13] Such superiority of legislative determinations explains the usual refusal of courts to grant a justification for a prison inmate's escape to avoid unhealthy or dangerous, but common, prison conditions. The legislature presumably was aware of the conditions, the argument goes, when it authorized prison sentences (and when it determined the prisons' annual funding). Apparently it was the legislature's view, the argument continues, that the harms those conditions impose are less grave than the public fear and institutional disorder that would result from allowing prisoners lawfully to escape. This limitation on the lesser evils defense, applied to the "Break-In" hypothetical, will give Burke some difficulty. That the FDA has expressly prohibited the use of IIR outside of the study reflects an authoritative governmental view. Presumably the agency's decision weighs the potential benefits and risks of allowing such use. While the agency is not the legislature, the authority to make such decisions probably has been delegated to it by the legislature. As long as the terms of that delegation have been met, the agency's view would seem to be beyond challenge.

Rejection of Defense for Civil Disobedience   This same limitation makes the lesser evils defense generally unavailable in cases of civil disobedience. A firm belief in the immorality of a particular national defense policy or abortion policy, for example, will not justify illegal interference with its execution if the policy is

---

12. As the Model Penal Code commentary explains: "The balancing of evils is not committed to the private judgment of the actor; it is an issue for determination at the trial." Model Penal Code § 3.02 comment 2 (1985).

13. Model Penal Code § 3.02(1)(c); see 2 Paul H. Robinson, *Criminal Law Defenses* 51 n.12 (1984).

lawfully arrived at and implemented.[14] Legitimately promulgated laws and administrative policies are conclusive evidence of the legislature's view and, through it, the community's view of the competing interests. The most controversial instances in which this issue arises are where a law is disobeyed in an exercise of civil disobedience to protest the immorality of the law. Examples include "sit-ins" to protest racial segregation policies and draft-card burnings to protest draft registration laws. But the supremacy of legislative judgment means that the enforcement of the law that the actor is charged with violating can never be a justifying harm or evil.

Argument for Transcendent Legal Norms Justifying Resistance to Positive Law Some writers argue that while the individual may not substitute her own personal judgment, the legislative view ought not be taken as conclusive. There exist, it is argued, some fundamental moral precepts outside the written law that an individual and a court may rely on to justify conduct without regard to contradictory legislative action. This is the point of conflict between a system of *positivist* jurisprudence and one that recognizes transcendent legal norms, such as natural law. Reliance on transcendent legal norms is said to create the danger that either defendants or courts might seek to use the law to further their own moral convictions (which, by hypothesis, differ from the convictions expressed in duly enacted legislation). On the other hand, to give absolute authority to a legislature is to assume that legislatures will always behave in a way consistent with fundamental human rights. The lawfully enacted, yet universally condemned, legislative acts of the Third Reich provide one obvious illustration of the dangerousness of such an assumption.[15]

Legislative Preemption Through Offense Exceptions The supremacy of legislative judgment also means that the lesser evils defense is not available where an offense definition addresses situations similar to those at issue. If the legislature exhaustively enumerates the situations where an offense shall not apply, a court may find that those exceptions are meant to be all-inclusive. The Model Penal Code lesser evils defense is expressly made unavailable when the "law defining the offense provides exceptions or defenses dealing with the specific situation involved."[16] This is simply the application of an accepted rule of statutory construction. In *Bice v. State*, the defendant sought to justify violation of a law against bringing liquor to church with a claim that his doctor deemed the liquor necessary for medicinal purposes.[17] The statute expressly provided that a practicing physician could bring liquor to church, thus, the court concluded, the legislature apparently intended to prohibit anyone other than a doctor from doing so. By specifying certain exceptions, the law makers impliedly rejected others and foreclosed the issue of additional exceptions—at least exceptions that arguably are

---

14. See, e.g., United States v. Schoon, 971 F.2d 193 (9th Cir. 1992) (rejecting necessity claim of demonstrators who splashed simulated blood in I.R.S. office and disrupted its operation in order to protest use of taxes for U.S. involvement in El Salvador).

15. Consider, for example, the "Law for the Protection of German Blood and German Honor," which forbade marriage between Jews and citizens of the so-called Aryan race. See Ingo Müller, *Hitler's Justice: The Courts of the Third Reich* 97 (1991). The growing body of international law, including United Nations "legislation," setting out a universal concept of basic human rights may make it more feasible in the future to give deference to existing law.

16. Model Penal Code § 3.02(1)(b).

17. 34 S.E. 202 (Ga. 1899).

of the sort that the legislature might have included on its list. This limitation on justification defenses does not pertain exclusively to proportionality concerns, but may reflect a legislative predetermination to exclude the defense for a variety of reasons.

More Specific Justification Governs Situations Where It Applies   One final means by which legislative judgment trumps other potential judgments as to the proper balancing of interests is found in the rule making the lesser evils defense unavailable when another justification defense specifically addresses the situation. That is, more specific justification defenses are given superiority over more general defenses, such as lesser evils. By defining more specific justifications, the legislature sets out the triggering conditions, necessity, and proportionality requirements that will apply for particular situations. Thus, an actor cannot rely on lesser evils to claim a defense for his use of force to protect himself; the self-defense justification specifically addresses that situation. Special rules frequently are provided for the most common justification situations, where an actor is given a special public authority to act or where defensive force is needed to defend against an aggressor. For example, the legislature may wish to limit the use of deadly force in self-defense to instances in which the actor cannot retreat in safety. Such more detailed rules help increase uniformity in the adjudication of justification cases and make the law's operation more predictable. A defendant ought not be able to circumvent such rules by claiming the general justification defense of lesser evils.

The Queen v. Dudley and Stephens
Queen's Bench Division
14 Q.B.D. 273 (1884)

Lord COLERIDGE, C.J.

The two prisoners, Thomas Dudley and Edwin Stephens, were indicted for the murder of Richard Parker on the high seas on the 25th of July in the present year. They were tried before my Brother Huddleston at Exeter on the 6th of November, and, under the direction of my learned Brother, the jury returned a special verdict, the legal effect of which has been argued before us, and on which we are now to pronounce judgment.

The special verdict . . . is as follows:

"That on July 5, 1884, the prisoners, Thomas Dudley and Edward Stephens, with one Brooks, all able-bodied English seamen, and the deceased, also an English boy, between seventeen and eighteen years of age, the crew of an English yacht, a registered English vessel, were cast away in a storm on the high seas 1,600 miles from the Cape of Good Hope, and were compelled to put into an open boat belonging to said yacht. That in this boat they had no supply of water and no supply of food, except two 1 lb. tins of turnips, and for three days they had nothing else to subsist upon. That on the fourth day they caught a small turtle, upon which they subsisted for a few days, and this was the only food they had up to the twentieth day when the act now in question was committed. That on the twelfth day the remains of the turtle were entirely consumed, and for the next eight days they had nothing to eat. That they had no fresh water, except such rain as they from time to time caught in their oilskin capes. That the boat was drifting on the ocean, and was probably more than 1,000 miles away from land. That on the eighteenth day, when they had been seven days without food and five without water, the prisoners spoke to Brooks as to what should be done if no succor came, and suggested that someone should be sacrificed to save the rest, but Brooks dissented, and the boy, to whom they were understood to refer, was not consulted. That on the 24th of July, the day before the act now in question, the prisoner Dudley proposed to Stephens and Brooks that lots should be cast who should be put to death to save the rest, but Brooks refused to consent, and it was not put to the boy, and in point of fact there was no drawing of lots. That on the day the prisoners spoke of their families, and suggested it would be better to kill the boy that their lives should be saved, and Dudley proposed that if there was no vessel in sight by the morrow morning the boy should be killed. That next day, the 25th of July, no vessel appearing, Dudley told Brooks that he had better go and have a sleep, and made signs to Stephens and Brooks that the boy had better be killed. The prisoner Stephens agreed to the act, but Brooks dissented from it. That the boy was then lying at the bottom of the boat quite helpless and extremely weakened by famine and by drinking sea water, and unable to make any resistance, nor did he ever assent to his being killed. The prisoner Dudley offered a prayer asking forgiveness for them all if either of them should be tempted to commit a rash act, and that their souls might be saved. That Dudley, with the assent of Stephens, went to the boy, and telling him that his time was come, put a knife into his throat and killed him then and there; that the three men fed upon the body and blood of the boy for four days; that on the fourth day after the act had been committed the boat was picked up by a passing vessel, and the prisoners were rescued, still alive, but in the lowest state of prostration. That they were carried to the port of Falmouth, and committed for trial at Exeter. That if the men had not fed upon the body of the boy they would probably not have survived to be so picked up and rescued, but would within the four days have died of famine. That the boy, being in a much weaker condition, was likely to have died before them. That at the time of the act in question there was no sail in sight, nor any reasonable prospect of relief. That under these circumstances there appeared to the prisoners every probability that unless they then fed or very soon fed upon the boy or one of themselves they would die of starvation. That there was no appreciable chance of saving life except by killing some one for the others to eat. That assuming any necessity to kill anybody, there was no greater necessity for killing the boy than any of the other three men. But whether upon the whole matter by the jurors found the killing of Richard Parker by Dudley and Stephens be felony and murder the jurors are ignorant, and pray the advice of the Court thereupon, and if upon the whole matter the Court shall be of opinion that the killing of Richard Parker be felony and murder, then the jurors say that Dudley and Stephens were each guilty of felony and murder as alleged in the indictment."

From these facts, stated with the cold precision of a special verdict, it appears sufficiently that the prisoners were subject to terrible temptation, to sufferings which might break down the bodily power of the strongest man, and try the conscience of the best. Other details yet more harrowing, facts still more loathsome and appalling, were presented to the jury, and are to be found recorded in my learned Brother's notes. But nevertheless this is clear, that the prisoners put to death a weak and unoffending boy upon the chance of preserving their own lives by feeding upon his flesh and blood after he was killed, and with the certainty of depriving him of any possible chance of survival. The verdict finds in terms that "if the men had not fed upon the body of the boy they would probably not have survived," and that "the boy being in a much weaker condition was likely to have died before them." They might possibly have been picked up next day by a passing ship; they might possibly not have been picked up at all; in either case it is obvious that the killing of the boy would have been an unnecessary and profitless act. It is found by the verdict that the boy was incapable of resistance, and, in fact, made none; and it is not even suggested that his death was due to any violence on his part attempted against, or even so much as feared by, those who killed him. Under these circumstances the jury say that they are ignorant whether those who killed him were guilty of murder, and have referred it to this Court to determine what is the legal consequence which follows from the facts which they have found.

[T]he real question in the case [is] whether killing under the circumstances set forth in the verdict be or not be murder. The contention that it could be anything else was, to the minds of us all, both new and strange, and we stopped the Attorney General in his negative argument in order that we might hear what could be said in support of a proposition which appeared to us to be at once dangerous, immoral, and opposed to all legal principle and analogy. . . .

Is there, then, any authority for the proposition [that this might not be murder]? Decided cases there are none. . . . The American case cited by my Brother Stephen in his Digest, from Wharton on Homicide, in which it was decided, correctly indeed, that sailors had no right to throw passengers overboard to save themselves, but on the somewhat strange ground that the proper mode of determining who was to be sacrificed was to vote upon the subject by ballot, can hardly, as my Brother Stephen says, be an authority satisfactory to a court in this country. . . .

The one real authority of former time is Lord Bacon, who, in his commentary on the maxim, "necessitas inducit privilegium quoad jura privata," lays down the law as follows:— "Necessity carrieth a privilege in itself. Necessity is of three sorts—necessity of conservation of life, necessity of obedience, and necessity of the act of God or of a stranger. First of conservation of life; if a man steal viands to satisfy his present hunger, this is no felony nor larceny. So if divers be in danger of drowning by the casting away of some boat or barge, and one of them get to some plank, or on the boat's side to keep himself above the water, and another to save his life thrust him from it, whereby he is drowned, this is neither se defendendo nor by misadventure, but justifiable." On this it is to be observed that Lord Bacon's proposition that stealing to satisfy hunger is no larceny is hardly supported by Staundforde, whom he cites for it, and is expressly contradicted by Lord Hale in the passage already cited. And for the proposition as to the plank or boat, it is said to be derived from the canonists. At any rate he cited no authority for it, and it must stand upon his own. . . . There are many conceivable states of things in which it might possibly be true, but if Lord Bacon meant to lay down the broad proposition that a man may save his life by killing, if necessary, an innocent and unoffending neighbour, it certainly is not law at the present day. . . .

It must not be supposed that in refusing to admit temptation to be an excuse for crime it is forgotten how terrible the temptation was; how awful the suffering;

how hard in such trials to keep the judgment straight and the conduct pure. We are often compelled to set up standards we cannot reach ourselves, and to lay down rules which we could not ourselves satisfy. But a man has no right to declare temptation to be an excuse, though he might himself have yielded to it, nor allow compassion for the criminal to change or weaken in any manner the legal definition of the crime. It is therefore our duty to declare that the prisoners' act in this case was wilful murder, that the facts as stated in the verdict are no legal justification of the homicide; and to say that in our unanimous opinion the prisoners are upon this special verdict guilty of murder.

The Court then proceeded to pass sentence of death upon the prisoners.*

▲ PROBLEMS

Torture to Save a Kidnap Victim (#77)

Wolgang Daschner is the officer in charge of the investigation of one of Frankfurt, Germany's most notorious crimes. Eleven-year-old Jakob von Metzler has been kidnapped. Police observe twenty-seven-year-old Magnus Gafgen, an acquaintance of Jakob's sister, picking up the ransom. Gafgen is arrested but during the interrogation proves evasive and uncooperative. He lies about facts police know to be true about his involvement. When confronted with evidence of the crime found at his apartment, he sends police on a fruitless search of a nearby lake-cabin. A police psychologist determines that Gafgen is being intentionally evasive in discussions of the child's safety. Because there does not appear to be an accomplice, with Gafgen in custody, police worry that the child is not receiving food or water.

As Gafgen continues to refuse to disclose Jakob's location, police become increasingly frantic. Officer Daschner decides that the only avenue to procure the child's location to possibly save his life is to use painful coercion in the interrogation to get the boy's location. Daschner orders a martial arts specialist to be helicoptered to Frankfurt who can impose the pain needed. His instructions are that the force used should inflict pain but not cause injury to the suspect and that a physician should supervise the proceedings. Some members of the police force have objections to the plan but Daschner decides to proceed anyway because, as the officer in charge of the investigation, he feels responsible for Jakob's life.

When told of the plan to use painful interrogation to obtain Jakob's location and of the imminent arrival of the martial arts specialist, Gafgen becomes cooperative and discloses Jakob's true location, where police do find him.

What liability for Daschner, if any, under the Model Penal Code for undertaking his plan to use pain in the interrogation of Gafgen? Prepare a list of all criminal code subsections in the order in which you rely on them in your analysis.

---

*Editor's Note.—Their sentence was afterward commuted by the Crown to six months' imprisonment.

Fight, Submit, or Escape (#78)

Only days after arriving in prison, John Charles Green is already in front of the disciplinary board for fighting. His explanation is that he had to resort to violence to fend off sexual advances by other prisoners. Within a month of the hearing, two inmates break into his prison cell, having easily picked the lock, and forcibly rape Green. Green tries yelling for the guard during the rape, but the guard on duty is separated from the wing by a heavy door and does not respond. Shortly after the two inmates leave his room, Green slices his arm in order to be removed to the prison hospital. Green reports the rape to Donald Hartness, the Assistant Superintendent of Treatment, but refuses to name his attackers for fear of being killed by the other inmates. Hartness denies Green's request to be moved in order to avoid future attacks, suggesting instead that Green go back and fight it out. Several days later three men pick the lock on Green's cell again, knock him unconscious before he can struggle, and rape him. Green again returns to the hospital after feigning swallowing glass. He appears once more before the disciplinary board, which is composed of Hartness, Mr. Baldwin (the Assistant Superintendent of Custody), and a guard. Green describes the attacks and asks for protective custody, which is denied. Baldwin offers Green a wing transfer and advises him to "fight it out, submit to the assaults, or go over the fence."

In his new wing, Green is repeatedly taunted by the other prisoners, who are aware of his struggles in the previous wing. Shortly after his transfer, at noon, five inmates come to Green's cell and tell him they will come for him that night to gang-rape him. They tell him that he will be their "punk" (by which they mean the person penetrated in male same-sex intercourse) for the remainder of his time in prison and threaten to seriously injure or kill him if he does not cooperate. Green decides not to tell authorities this time, as his previous attempts have all failed. Instead, around 6:00 p.m., he quietly escapes, climbing over the fence near the powerhouse on the west side of the prison. He walks down a railroad track, across several fields, and along the highway before he is picked up the next day by an officer. Green is taken into custody without incident.

What liability for Green, if any, under the Model Penal Code? Prepare a list of all criminal code subsections in the order in which you rely on them in your analysis.

What liability for Green, if any, under the common law rule?

No to Nuclear Power (#79)

John Warshow is strongly opposed to the operation of nuclear power plants. He believes them to pose a severe risk of harm because of the low-level radiation and nuclear waste they create, along with the possibility of a catastrophic nuclear accident. Warshow is particularly concerned about the Vermont Yankee nuclear power plant. When Vermont Yankee is shut down for repairs, Warshow and others attempt to go through political channels, raising public concern, and trying to get media attention in a bid to stop the plant from reopening. Warshow believes that there are defects in the plant's cooling system that will cause the plant to experience a meltdown within seven seconds of being restarted. He also believes that starting the plant up again poses an imminent danger to many people in the surrounding area from hazardous radiation, for which most would have little or no insurance coverage. However, all of his attempts to go through proper channels fail, and Vermont Yankee is scheduled to resume its operation.

On the day that Vermont Yankee is to be reopened, Warshow joins a group of protestors on the plant's private property. The demonstrators are rallying at the main gates of the nuclear power plant to protest its reopening. The protestors prevent workers from entering the plant and placing it online. Warshow and the others refuse to leave when representatives of Vermont Yankee asked them to leave the private property. The police are called in to break up the demonstration so that the workers can access the plant. While many of the protestors comply with police orders, Warshow and a small group of others refuse to leave. They are arrested.

What liability for Warshow, if any, under the Model Penal Code? Prepare a list of all criminal code subsections in the order in which you rely on them in your analysis.

Burning Out the Local Crack House (#80)

Sam Mohammed has always had a strong sense of protection. He is a large man in his mid-30s and has spent time serving as a bodyguard for several music groups, including Boyz II Men, TLC, and SWV. He now lives on a couch at a laundromat in West Palm Beach, in a bad part of town. In a three-block radius of his new home, there have been 35 robberies, 32 burglaries, 84 drug arrests, and 8 murders during the year, most of which have been attributed to drug trafficking and crack cocaine use. Police even hear of drug dealers who offer children ice cream to lure them into drug dens. The same year, Mohammed witnesses a shootout in the street, in which a young victim dies in his arms. Since then, Mohammed has been active in trying to clean up the community. He attends church regularly, stands guard for phone company employees as they collect change from the neighborhood pay phones, scolds boys for swearing in front of women, and looks out for elderly customers who do their laundry in the laundromat that he calls home.

Fed up with the drug-related violence in his community and the police force's inability to control the situation, Mohammed decides to attack the problem at its root. A boarded-up house across the street from his laundromat is a known crack house. It serves as a haven for crack users who Mohammed feels are ruining his community. Mohammed breaks down the door of the house and starts a small fire using lighter fluid. The fire is quickly put out by firefighters, but Mohammed remains undeterred. He returns several days later and pours gasoline throughout the house. He then flicks his lighter onto the gas and crosses the street to watch it burn. Mohammed turns himself in to police, stating that he burned the house down to "save the community" and made sure that it burned at a time when no one was inside and no children were nearby.

What liability for Mohammed, if any, under the Model Penal Code? Prepare a list of all criminal code subsections in the order in which you rely on them in your analysis.

The Bomb Thief (#81)

Motti Ashkenazi, a thin, thirty-year-old man from a poor, crime-ridden South Tel Aviv neighborhood, strolls along a crowded beach between Tel Aviv and Jaffa on a hot Friday afternoon in June 1997. A drug addict and petty thief who only a week ago was arrested after bungling a car burglary, Ashkenazi has been thinking about getting off drugs and putting his life together for a while. However, as he walks, he sees that someone has left a black backpack unattended by the sidewalk. He picks up the backpack and quickly sneaks off to an abandoned building to inspect his loot. Rather than valuables, he finds a clock with wires connected to a cookie tin, with loose nails surrounding the contraption. Ashkenazi quickly realizes he has just stolen a terrorist's bomb.

Leaving the bomb in the abandoned building, he runs to the nearby Savoy Hotel and tells the reception desk clerk what he found. The clerk calls the police. The bomb squad arrives in minutes and begins to deactivate the bomb. Meanwhile, Ashkenazi stands outside the building, keeping the street clear of passersby. The bomb squad finds that the bomb is packed with nearly three kilograms of explosives. After an hour's work, they use a robot to shoot the backpack in a way that neutralizes the bomb. Considering the amount of explosives and the number of people on the beach, police estimate that many would have been killed in a major terrorist attack.

During the police activity, Ashkenazi slips away. But because he is well known to the police, detectives easily track him down for questioning. At first, Ashkenazi lies to the police and tells them he found the backpack in the apartment building stairwell where he had gone to urinate, but he later confesses to having stolen the backpack from the beach.

What liability for Ashkenazi, if any, under the Model Penal Code? Prepare a list of all criminal code subsections in the order in which you rely on them in your analysis.

What liability, if any, under the Israeli statutes, reproduced in the Law section following the GSS case? Prepare a list of all criminal code subsections in the order in which you rely on them in your analysis.

Life-Saving Necrophilia—Revisited (#24)

Reconsider the facts of Problem Case "Life-Saving Necrophilia" (#24) in Section 5. When the case was first examined, imputation had not yet been addressed. Using your knowledge of imputation that you now have, as well as your new knowledge of the lesser evils justification, is your analysis of the case any different from what it was in Section 5? What liability, if any, for Giorgi under the Model Penal Code?

✳ DISCUSSION ISSUE

Are There Any Circumstances in Which It Would Be Justifiable to Use Torture in the Interrogation of a Suspected Terrorist to Save the Life of an Intended Victim?

Materials presenting each side of this Discussion Issue appear in the Advanced Materials for Section 16 in Appendix A.

SECTION 17

Public Authority Justifications

More typical than the open-ended lesser evils defense are the public authority justifications in which the legislature itself strikes the balance between competing interests. It is common for situations to arise in which societal interests would be furthered by aggressive use of force, such as when used to make an arrest or to maintain the order required for safety on public transportation. These defenses set out what officials can do under various circumstances.

◆ THE CASE OF OFFICER ELTON HYMON (#82)

Born in 1948, Elton Hymon grows up with two brothers and five sisters in a devout Christian family in Memphis. He goes to church and Sunday school each week. His father works at the Memphis Cemetery, and his mother is a cook at Tall Trees, a center for troubled youths. His neighborhood forms a tight community where people look out for one another; children go to neighbors for advice as if they were their parents. Hymon enjoys basketball and plays on Geeter High School's A team. He wants to be a doctor until he sees the burned back of a cousin who gets scalded by water and he decides he cannot deal with the gorier side of

Figure 83 **Officer Elton Hymon, circa 1984**
(NCJRS)

Figure 84 **Edward Garner, age unknown**
(NCJRS)

medicine. After graduating from high school, Hymon begins studying business at Tennessee State University in Nashville but switches to English in his sophomore year. He also plays on the Tennessee State basketball team until a back injury forces him to quit. He takes up judo and rises to become a brown belt. After graduating with a B.S. in 1970, Hymon takes a job as a treatment service counselor at Fort Pillow State Prison. The 65-mile commute to Fort Pillow from Memphis begins to wear on him, so Hymon begins to look for a job in his hometown. Though his parents are against it because they believe it too dangerous, Hymon joins the Memphis Police Department in July 1973, a month after getting married, and graduates as one of the top five in his class at the police academy.

Edward Garner is a fifteen-year-old who lives with his father and 5 other siblings in Memphis. At 5 feet 4 inches and less than 100 pounds, he is small for a teenager. His father, Cleamtee, works the second shift at the Memphis Defense Depot and has trouble keeping an eye on Garner. Like other boys in the neighborhood, Garner has already had minor troubles with the law. Three years ago, he and some friends were caught after illegally sneaking into a house. This past July, Garner stole a jar of pennies from a neighbor's house. Although the neighbor thought it unnecessary to call the police, the neighbor's family insisted on reporting the incident. Garner receives one year of probation, and his father imposes a curfew. Police subsequently arrest him for violating his probation but dismiss the matter when they learn he is working at a local store.

It is October 3, 1974, about 10:40 p.m., and Edward Garner is somewhat intoxicated as he walks toward 739 Vollintine Street, which is just a few blocks from his own house at 929 Tally Street. He pulls a garbage can beneath a window, climbs onto it, smashes the window, and climbs into the house. Inside the dark and empty house, he rummages around for valuables. Next door, at 737

Vollintine, Daisy Bell States thinks she hears a noise and calls the police to report what she thinks is a prowler. Her prudence is understandable because over the last 3 months her neighborhood has been plagued by a string of over 120 burglaries and larcenies.

Officers Elton Hymon and Leslie B. Wright are at a nearby fire station when they receive the call to investigate. It takes them about 15 minutes to arrive. States, a middle-aged African American woman, is standing on her porch in a housecoat. Hymon goes to the porch, and States explains to him quietly that she heard glass shatter next door. She also tells him that she thinks that a person is still inside the house. After conferring with Wright, both officers take flashlights and head to the back of the house from opposite sides. Wright calls in to report that they are investigating the scene, then circles around to the back of the house.

Hymon arrives first, with his .38 caliber revolver drawn. When he sees the broken window and a light on in the house, he thinks something is "wrong inside."

Figure 85 **Bedroom ransacked by Garner while looking for money and valuables**

(U.S. District Court, Western District Tennessee)

Figure 86 **Daytime view of the backyard. Officer Hymon stood at the short fence in the front left; Garner was along the fence in the far right-hand corner**

(U.S. District Court, Western District Tennessee)

Inside, Garner, hearing the officers outside, quickly glances around the room one last time and grabs a small purse with ten dollars. He heads to the back door and tries to make a run for it. Hymon hears the screen door slam and sees Garner sprint through a stream of light in the otherwise dark backyard. As Garner runs for the chain-link fence on the other side of the yard, he hears Hymon yell, "Police! Halt!" Garner freezes at the foot of the fence.

Scanning the backyard with his flashlight, Hymon sees a waist-high chicken-wire fence between him and Garner, as well as a clothesline and other clutter. Training his light on Garner, he sees the face of a young black man, who he thinks is about 17, crouching beside a 6-foot-high chain-link fence. Although Hymon is about 40 feet away, and despite seeing something unidentifiable in one of Garner's hands, Hymon believes that Garner is unarmed. When Wright arrives at

Figure 87 **The view Officer Hymon had of the backyard. Garner had accessed the house using the trash can in the front left**

(U.S. District Court, Western District Tennessee)

Figure 88 **Blood spot in corner where Garner was shot**

(U.S. District Court, Western District Tennessee)

the backyard, Hymon calls out to him to circle around the chain-link fence.

Hymon takes a step toward the fence, but Garner leaps up to climb over, almost making it to the top in a single jump. When he sees how fast Garner moves, Hymon is sure that Garner will escape because he cannot see beyond the fence and his boots and equipment will inevitably slow him down. Wright is too far away to catch up with Garner.

Hymon aims at Garner's torso, as he was trained to do, and fires one shot. Only when Hymon sees Garner slump over the fence does he realize that the shot hit him in the back of the head. This is the first time Hymon has fired at a suspect since joining the force.

Wright reaches Garner first and yells out that he is bleeding badly from the head. It is the most bleeding he has ever seen. They get Garner down from the fence and call an ambulance and their lieutenant. The ambulance arrives in minutes and rushes Garner to John Gaston Hospital, where he dies on the operating table. The news of Garner's death is devastating to Hymon, who had seen him alive and hoped he would survive. Hymon's supervisor later informs him that he faces a murder charge, despite apparently following departmental procedures.

1. Relying only on your own intuition of justice, what liability and punishment, if any, does Officer Hymon deserve?

N	0	1	2	3	4	5	6	7	8	9	10	11
☐	☐	☐	☐	☐	☐	☐	☐	☐	☐	☐	☐	☐
no liability	liability but no punishment	1 day	2 wks	2 mo	6 mo	1 yr	3 yrs	7 yrs	15 yrs	30 yrs	life imprisonment	death

2. What "justice" arguments could defense counsel make on the defendant's behalf?

3. What "justice" arguments could the prosecution make against the defendant?

4. What liability, if any, for Officer Hymon under the then-existing statutes? Prepare a list of all criminal code subsections and cases in the order in which you rely on them in your analysis.

5. What liability, if any, under the Model Penal Code? Prepare a list of all criminal code subsections in the order in which you rely on them in your analysis.

■ THE LAW

Tennessee Code Annotated
(1974)

Title 39. Criminal Offenses

Chapter 2. Offenses Against the Person
Part 2. Homicide

Section 39-2401. Murder Generally

If any person of sound memory and discretion, unlawfully kills any reasonable creature in being, and under the peace of the state, with malice aforethought, either express or implied, such person shall be guilty of murder.

Section 39-2402. Murder in the First Degree

An individual commits murder in the first degree if:

(1) he commits a willful, deliberate, malicious and premeditated killing or murder;

(2) he commits a willful, deliberate, malicious killing or murder, and:

(a) the victim is an employee of the department of correction having custody of the actor,

(b) the victim is a prison inmate in custody with the actor,

(c) the victim is known to the actor to be a peace officer or fireman acting in the course of his employment,

(d) the victim is a judge acting in the course of his judicial duties,

(e) the victim is a popularly elected public official,

(f) the offense is committed for hire; or,

(g) the offense is committed while attempting to evade law enforcement officials;

(3) he hires another to commit willful, deliberate, malicious and premeditated killing or murder, and such hiring causes the death of the victim; or,

(4) he commits a willful, deliberate, and malicious killing or murder during the perpetration of any arson, rape, robbery, burglary, larceny, kidnapping, aircraft piracy, or unlawful throwing, placing, or discharging of a destructive device or bomb.

Section 39-2403. Murder in the Second Degree

All other kinds of murder shall be deemed murder in the second degree.

Section 39-2404. Jury to Ascertain Degree

The jury before whom the offender is tried shall ascertain in their verdict whether it is murder in the first or second degree; and if the accused confess his guilt, the court shall proceed to determine the degree of crime by the verdict of a jury, upon the examination of testimony, and give sentence accordingly.

Section 39-2405. Punishment for Murder in the First Degree

Every person convicted of murder in the first degree, or as accessory before the fact to such crime, shall suffer death by electrocution.

Section 39-2406. Death Penalty Mandatory for Conviction of Murder in the First Degree

When a person is convicted of crime of murder in the first degree, or as an accessory before the fact of such crime, it shall be the duty of the jury convicting him in their verdict to fix his punishment at death as provided by law.

Section 39-2408. Punishment for Murder in the Second Degree

Every person convicted of murder in the second degree shall be imprisoned in the penitentiary for life or for a period of not less than ten (10) years.

Section 39-2409. Manslaughter

Manslaughter is the unlawful killing of another without malice, either express or implied, which may be either voluntary upon a sudden heat, or involuntary, but in the commission of some unlawful act.

Section 39-2410. Punishment for Voluntary Manslaughter

Whoever is convicted of the crime of voluntary manslaughter shall undergo confinement in the penitentiary not less than two (2) years nor more than ten (10) years.

Section 39-2411. Punishment for Involuntary Manslaughter

Whoever is convicted of involuntary manslaughter shall undergo confinement in the penitentiary for not less than one year nor more than five (5) years.

Chapter 6. Assaults, Attempts and Injuries to Persons

Section 39-601. Assault with Deadly Weapons—Penalty

If any person assaults and beats another with a cowhide, stick, or whip, having at the time in his possession a pistol or other deadly weapon, with intent to intimidate the persons assaulted, and prevent him from defending himself, he shall, on conviction, be imprisoned in the penitentiary not less than two (2) years nor more than ten (10) years.

Section 39-612. Shooting or Stabbing Without Malice—Assault and Battery

When any person is indicted for malicious stabbing or shooting, and the jury shall be of the opinion that the defendant is not guilty of the malice, they shall have the power to find the defendant guilty of an assault and battery.

Section 40-808. Resistance to Officer

If, after notice of the intention to arrest the defendant, he either flees or forcibly resists, the officer may use all the necessary means to effect the arrest.

Chapter 3. Offenses Against Property

Section 39-401. Burglary Generally

(a) Burglary is the breaking and entering into a dwelling house, or any other house, building, room or rooms therein used and occupied by any person or persons as a dwelling place or lodging either permanently or temporarily and whether as owner, renter, tenant, lessee or paying guest, by night, with intent to commit a felony.

(b) Every person convicted of this crime shall be imprisoned in the penitentiary not less than five (5) years nor more than fifteen (15) years.

(c) Provided, however, if the person convicted of this crime had in his possession a firearm at the time of the breaking and entering, he shall be imprisoned in the penitentiary not less than ten (10) nor more than fifteen (15) years.

Section 39-405. Treatment upon Conviction of Burglary or Safecracking

(a) . . .

(b)

    (1) Upon conviction for a violation of §39-3-401, if the district attorney general, or his designee, introduces a certified document to the court showing that such person has been previously convicted of such offense, such person shall not be considered for or granted parole or otherwise released until such time as he has served at least five (5) calendar years of the sentence received for the second such conviction. . . .

    (5) Notwithstanding any other provision of chapters 3 or 18 of title 41 to the contrary, no person serving a sentence for a third or subsequent conviction of one (1) of the offenses specified in subsection (c)(1) or (c)(2) of this section shall be eligible for any program whereby he may be granted supervised or unsupervised release into the community.

(c)

    (1) Upon conviction for a violation of §39-3-401, if the district attorney general, or his designee, introduces certified documents to the court

showing that such person has been previously convicted of such offense two (2) or more times, such person shall not be considered for or granted parole or otherwise released until such time as he has served at least five (5) calendar years of the sentence received for the third or subsequent such conviction. . . .

(5) Notwithstanding any other provision of chapters 3 or 18 of title 41 to the contrary, no person serving a sentence for a third or subsequent conviction of one (1) of the offenses specified in subsection (c)(1) or (c)(2) of this section shall be eligible for any program whereby he may be granted supervised or unsupervised release into the community.

(d) For purposes of this section, convictions for multiple offenses occurring as part of a single criminal episode shall constitute only one (1) offense.

Morelock v. State
460 S.W.2d 861 (Tenn. Crim. App. 1970)

The defendant was engaged in an illicit affair with the victim. While drinking and driving, the couple engaged in an argument over the future of their relationship. When the defendant tossed a beer can out of the car window, he attracted police attention and was pulled over. He suddenly panicked and shot the victim four times in the head, then shot himself. The court upheld his conviction for first-degree murder, despite his defense that he had not shown malice, because the "settled law in this State is that all homicides are presumed to be malicious, in the absence of evidence which would rebut the implied presumption." Further, the court reasoned that "[i]t is also no longer debatable or open to question that if a weapon is handled in a manner so as to make the killing a natural or probable result of such conduct, malice will be presumed from the use of the weapon."

Leake v. State
29 Tenn. 144, 149 (1849)

The defendant, a young man of small stature and missing his right hand, went to the house of deceased, a strong woman of ill repute to harass her. They quarreled, and she attacked him with a skillet, whereupon he shot her with his pistol. The defendant appealed his conviction of second-degree murder on the basis that his case was devoid of malice and his self-defense reduced the offense to manslaughter. The court set aside his verdict, finding that the evidence did not support malice. The court held that "the presumption of malice arising in law from this killing, and from the deadly character of the weapon used, is rebutted by the proof of the suddenness of the rencounter [sic], the violence of the assault on the part of the deceased, and the dangerous nature of the weapon used by her." Further, the court held that "in the absence of proof of express malice, this killing must be held to have been the result of sudden heat and excited passion, and, therefore, not murder in either the first or second degree."

Copeland v. State
154 Tenn. 7, 285 S.W. 565 (1926)

Plaintiff in error was convicted of involuntary manslaughter for causing the death of Robert Holland on the public highway at Saltillo, December 4, 1924, when he was struck and killed by an automobile driven by Copeland.

[I]nvoluntary manslaughter is not only an unintentional homicide occasioned by a person engaged at the time in an unlawful act. It may consist in doing a lawful act in an unlawful manner, as where one by his gross or culpable negligence causes the death of another. Or, if the homicide results from a criminal want of caution and circumspection, and not misadventure, it is involuntary and manslaughter.

In a charge otherwise accurate the trial judge failed to instruct the jury that, to convict for homicide caused from a lawful act committed in an unlawful manner, it must appear that the death was not the result of misadventure, but the natural and probable result of a reckless or culpably negligent act.

Allowance must always be made for misadventure and accident, as distinguished from culpable negligence.

> While the kind of negligence required to impose criminal liability has been described in different terms, it is uniformly held that it must be of a higher degree than is required to establish negligence upon a mere civil issue, and it must be shown that a homicide was not improbable under the facts as they existed which should reasonably have influenced the conduct of accused.

Reversed and remanded, for the failure of the trial court to charge that, if death did not result from Copeland's violation of the statute, there could be no conviction, unless the boy's death was the reasonable and probable result of Copeland's negligent or reckless act, and if he acted as a man of reasonable care in attempting to pass the wagons, and death was the result of an accident caused by the boy unexpectedly running from behind the wagon in front of the automobile, the homicide would not be unlawful.

Bouie v. City of Columbia
378 U.S. 347 (1964)

The defendants were two African American college students who took seats in a booth in the restaurant department at an Eckerd's, which had a policy of excluding non-whites. While they waited to be served, an employee of the store put up a "no trespassing" sign. After the defendants continued to sit quietly in the booth the store manager called the police. Once the police had arrived, the store manager twice asked the defendants to leave. When they did not, the police then asked them to leave. Upon final refusal, they were arrested and subsequently charged and convicted of criminal trespass under a provision that prohibited conduct as "entry upon the lands of another . . . after notice from the owner or tenant prohibiting such entry. . . . " The state supreme court affirmed their trespass convictions, interpreting the trespass statute to "cover not only the act of entry on the premises of another after receiving notice not to enter, but also the act of remaining on the premises of another after receiving notice to leave." The defendants appealed their trespass convictions to the U.S. Supreme Court, and in a 6-3 decision, the Court reversed their convictions stating that "by its terms, the statute prohibited only 'entry upon the lands of another . . . after notice from the owner . . . prohibiting such entry. . . .' There was nothing in the statute to indicate that it also prohibited the different act of remaining on the premises after being asked to leave." Furthermore, Justice Brennan, writing for the majority, decided that "by applying such a construction of the statute to affirm [the defendants'] convictions in this case, the State has punished them for conduct that was not criminal at the time they committed it, and hence has violated the requirement of the Due Process Clause that a criminal statute give fair warning of the conduct which it prohibits." The Court held that it is a violation of fair notice when a statute that is "precise on its face" is "unforeseeably and retroactively expanded by judicial construction." The Court limited its recognition of a defense to those extreme situations, like the case at bar, in which the state interprets a statute to hold other than its plain meaning, and in which prior judicial decisions would lead an individual to construe the statute in a different manner.

Model Penal Code
(Official Draft 1962)

Section 3.03. Execution of Public Duty

(1) Except as provided in Subsection (2) of this Section, conduct is justifiable when it is required or authorized by:

    (a) the law defining the duties or functions of a public officer or the assistance to be rendered to such officer in the performance of his duties; or

    (b) the law governing the execution of legal process; or

    (c) the judgment or order of a competent court or tribunal; or

    (d) the law governing the armed services or the lawful conduct of war; or

    (e) any other provision of law imposing a public duty.

(2) The other sections of this Article apply to:

    (a) the use of force upon or toward the person of another for any of the purposes dealt with in such sections; and

    (b) the use of deadly force for any purpose, unless the use of such force is otherwise expressly authorized by law or occurs in the lawful conduct of war.

(3) The justification afforded by Subsection (1) of this Section applies:

    (a) when the actor believes his conduct to be required or authorized by the judgment or direction of a competent court or tribunal or in the lawful execution of legal process, notwithstanding lack of jurisdiction of the court or defect in the legal process; and

    (b) when the actor believes his conduct to be required or authorized to assist a public officer in the performance of his duties, notwithstanding that the officer exceeded his legal authority.

Section 3.07. Use of Force in Law Enforcement

(1) Use of Force Justifiable to Effect an Arrest. Subject to the provisions of this Section and of Section 3.09, the use of force upon or toward the person of

another is justifiable when the actor is making or assisting in making an arrest and the actor believes that such force is immediately necessary to effect a lawful arrest.

(2) Limitations on the Use of Force.

(a) The use of force is not justifiable under this Section unless:

(i) the actor makes known the purpose of the arrest or believes that it is otherwise known by or cannot reasonably be made known to the person to be arrested; and

(ii) when the arrest is made under a warrant, the warrant is valid or believed by the actor to be valid.

(b) The use of deadly force is not justifiable under this Section unless:

(i) the arrest is for a felony; and

(ii) the person effecting the arrest is authorized to act as a peace officer or is assisting a person whom he believes to be authorized to act as a peace officer; and

(iii) the actor believes that the force employed creates no substantial risk of injury to innocent persons; and

(iv) the actor believes that:

(1) the crime for which the arrest is made involved conduct including the use or threatened use of deadly force; or

(2) there is a substantial risk that the person to be arrested will cause death or serious bodily harm if his apprehension is delayed.

(3) Use of Force to Prevent Escape from Custody. The use of force to prevent the escape of an arrested person from custody is justifiable when the force could justifiably have been employed to effect the arrest under which the person is in custody, except that a guard or other person authorized to act as a peace officer is justified in using any force, including deadly force, which he believes to be immediately necessary to prevent the escape of a person from a jail, prison, or other institution for the detention of persons charged with or convicted of a crime.

(4) Use of Force by Private Person Assisting an Unlawful Arrest.

(a) A private person who is summoned by a peace officer to assist in effecting an unlawful arrest is justified in using any force which he would be justified in using if the arrest were lawful, provided that he does not believe the arrest is unlawful.

(b) A private person who assists another private person in effecting an unlawful arrest, or who, not being summoned, assists a peace officer in effecting an unlawful arrest is justified in using any force which he would be justified in using if the arrest were lawful, provided that (i) he believes the arrest is lawful, and (ii) the arrest would be lawful if the facts were as he believes them to be.

(5) Use of Force to Prevent Suicide or the Commission of a Crime.

(a) The use of force upon or toward the person of another is justifiable when the actor believes that such force is immediately necessary to prevent such other person from committing suicide, inflicting serious bodily harm upon himself, committing or consummating the commission of a crime involving or threatening bodily harm, damage to or loss of property or a breach of the peace, except that:

(i) any limitations imposed by the other provisions of this Article on the justifiable use of force in self-protection, for the protection of others, the protection of property, the effectuation of an arrest or the prevention of an escape from custody shall apply notwithstanding the criminality of the conduct against which such force is used; and

(ii) the use of deadly force is not in any event justifiable under this Subsection unless:

(1) the actor believes that there is a substantial risk that the person whom he seeks to prevent from committing a crime will cause death or serious bodily harm to another unless the commission or the consummation of the crime is prevented and that the use of such force presents no substantial risk of injury to innocent persons; or

(2) the actor believes that the use of such force is necessary to suppress a riot or mutiny after the rioters or mutineers have been ordered to disperse and warned, in any particular manner that the law may require, that such force will be used if they do not obey.

(b) The justification afforded by this Subsection extends to the use of confinement as preventive force only if the actor takes all reasonable measures to terminate the confinement as soon as he knows that he safely can, unless the person confined has been arrested on a charge of crime.

Section 3.08. Use of Force by Persons with Special Responsibility for Care, Discipline or Safety of Others

The use of force upon or toward the person of another is justifiable if:

(1) the actor is the parent or guardian or other person similarly responsible for the general care and supervision of a minor or a person acting at the request of such parent, guardian or other responsible person and:

(a) the force is used for the purpose of safeguarding or promoting the welfare of the minor, including the prevention or punishment of his misconduct; and

(b) the force used is not designed to cause or known to create a substantial risk of causing death, serious bodily harm, disfigurement, extreme pain or mental distress or gross degradation; or

(2) the actor is a teacher or a person otherwise entrusted with the care or supervision for a special purpose of a minor and:

(a) the actor believes that the force used is necessary to further such special purpose, including the maintenance of reasonable discipline in a school, class or other group, and that the use of such force is consistent with the welfare of the minor; and

(b) the degree of force, if it had been used by the parent or guardian of the minor, would not be unjustifiable under Subsection (1)(b) of this Section; or

(3) the actor is the guardian or other person similarly responsible for the general care and supervision of an incompetent person; and:

(a) the force is used for the purpose of safeguarding or promoting the welfare of the incompetent person, including the prevention of his misconduct, or, when such incompetent person is in a hospital or other institution for his care and custody, for the maintenance of reasonable discipline in such institution; and

(b) the force used is not designed to cause or known to create a substantial risk of causing death, serious bodily harm, disfigurement, extreme or unnecessary pain, mental distress, or humiliation; or

(4) the actor is a doctor or other therapist or a person assisting him at his direction, and:

(a) the force is used for the purpose of administering a recognized form of treatment which the actor believes to be adapted to promoting the physical or mental health of the patient; and

(b) the treatment is administered with the consent of the patient or, if the patient is a minor or an incompetent person, with the consent of his parent or guardian or other person legally competent to consent in his behalf, or the treatment is administered in an emergency when the actor believes that no one competent to consent can be consulted and that a reasonable person, wishing to safeguard the welfare of the patient, would consent; or

(5) the actor is a warden or other authorized official of a correctional institution, and:

(a) he believes that the force used is necessary for the purpose of enforcing the lawful rules or procedures of the institution, unless his belief in the lawfulness of the rule or procedure sought to be enforced is erroneous and his error is due to ignorance or mistake as to the provisions of the Code, any other provision of the criminal law or the law governing the administration of the institution; and

(b) the nature or degree of force used is not forbidden by Article 303 or 304 of the Code; and

(c) if deadly force is used, its use is otherwise justifiable under this Article; or

(6) the actor is a person responsible for the safety of a vessel or an aircraft or a person acting at his direction, and

(a) he believes that the force used is necessary to prevent interference with the operation of the vessel or aircraft or obstruction of the execution of a lawful order, unless his belief in the lawfulness of the order is erroneous and his error is due to ignorance or mistake as to the law defining his authority; and

(b) if deadly force is used, its use is otherwise justifiable under this Article; or

(7) the actor is a person who is authorized or required by law to maintain order or decorum in a vehicle, train or other carrier or in a place where others are assembled, and:

(a) he believes that the force used is necessary for such purpose; and

(b) the force used is not designed to cause or known to create a substantial risk of causing death, bodily harm, or extreme mental distress.

Section 221.1. Burglary

(1) Burglary Defined. A person is guilty of burglary if he enters a building or occupied structure, or separately secured or occupied portion thereof, with purpose to commit a crime therein, unless the premises are at the time open to the public or the actor is licensed or privileged to enter.

It is an affirmative defense to prosecution for burglary that the building or structure was abandoned.

(2) Grading. Burglary is a felony of the second degree if it is perpetrated in the dwelling of another at night, or if, in the course of committing the offense, the actor:

> (a) purposely, knowingly or recklessly inflicts or attempts to inflict bodily injury on anyone; or

> (b) is armed with explosives or a deadly weapon. Otherwise, burglary is a felony of the third degree. An act shall be deemed "in the course of committing" an offense if it occurs in an attempt to commit the offense or in flight after the attempt or commission.

(3) Multiple Convictions. A person may not be convicted both for burglary and for the offense which it was his purpose to commit after the burglarious entry or for an attempt to commit that offense, unless the additional offense constitutes a felony of the first or second degree.

● OVERVIEW OF PUBLIC AUTHORITY JUSTIFICATIONS

Notes

Availability of Public Authority Justifications
    Justifications Promote a Broad Range of Interests
Common Internal Structure of Public Authority Justifications
Authorization Requirement Unique to Public Authority Justifications
    Rationale of Authorization Requirement
    Exceptions to Authorization Requirement
Evocation Requirement
Necessity Requirement
    "Purpose" as Substitute for Necessity
Proportionality Requirement
    Legislative Balancing of Interests
    Interest Protected vs. Force Used
General Public Authority

Availability of Public Authority Justification   Public authority justifications are available to actors specially authorized (and usually specially trained) to engage in conduct that would otherwise constitute an offense but is necessary to protect or further a societal interest. Unlike defensive force justifications, the actor's authority under these provisions is not limited to defensive action. She may act affirmatively to further a public interest, even one that is entirely intangible. These justification defenses are distinguished from one another according to the specific interests they foster. Different defenses authorize the use of force for: law enforcement purposes[1]; medical purposes; military purposes; judicial pur-

---

1. Model Penal Code § 3.07.

poses; maintaining order and safety on public carriers or in public places of assembly; or for use by parents or guardians.[2] A catchall public authority justification commonly provides a defense for performing public duties.[3]

Justifications Promote a Broad Range of Interests   These defenses may seek to further or protect the interests of individuals (such as parental, medical, or suicide prevention justification defenses, which are meant to allow the authorized parties to act in ways that promote the ultimate welfare of the child, patient, or potential suicide victim, respectively); or the interests of a class of citizens (such as authorizing transit officials to maintain order and safety, which protects the interests of all users of public transportation); or the interests of society as a whole (such as the defenses related to law enforcement, judicial, and military authority). The interests may be of immediate or more long-range concern; they may be physical, or intangible, or both. For example, not only are the personal interests of the child pertinent in parental authority, but also the more general societal interest in preserving the family structure (and protecting it from governmental intrusion). When a mother disciplines a child caught playing with matches, such disciplinary conduct has the immediate effect of preventing the child or others from being burned, and the long-range effect of advancing the child's proper discipline and upbringing. The wide variety of interests at stake—individual, group, or societal; immediate and long-range; physical and intangible—is reflected in the large number and diversity of public authority justifications.[4]

---

2. Model Penal Code § 3.08.

3. Model Penal Code § 3.03.

4. The following table illustrates some of the interests that one might describe as served by various common public authority justifications:

Public Authority Justification	Interests Furthered
Law enforcement authority	(1) Prevention of the threatened crime, apprehension and detention of the criminal (2) Establishment of credibility and respect for the criminal law generally
Authority to maintain order and safety	(1) Maintenance of order and safety on the present occasion (2) Effective operation of public facilities generally
Parental and benevolent custodial authority	(1) Maintenance of discipline, safety, and health on the present occasion (2) Promotion of general welfare and development of child or incompetent
Medical authority	(1) Provision of medical treatment (2) Promotion of individual's health and well-being generally
Authority to prevent suicide or self-inflection of serious injury	(1) Prevention of an immediate self-inflected harm (2) Promotion of the value of human life generally
Judicial authority	(1) Execution of a court order or judgment (2) Administration of justice; upholding respect for the authority of the judiciary
Military authority	(1) Achievement of a military objective (2) Establishment of effective armed forces
General public authority	(1) Execution of a particular legislative or executive enactment, decree, or defined duty (2) Administration of governmental authority not specifically provided for elsewhere

Common Internal Structure of Public Authority Justifications   The general form of public authority justifications may be summarized as follows: *Special authorization* and *evoking conditions* trigger an actor's right to use *necessary* and *proportional* force. The authorization and evocation elements act together, as triggering conditions, to describe the combination of persons and circumstances giving rise to an authority to act. The necessity and proportionality requirements, the response elements, describe the nature of the conduct that is justified once the authority to act is triggered. These general requirements resemble the elements of the lesser evils defense, except that they add the further requirement that the actor have special authorization.

Authorization Requirement Unique to Public Authority Justifications   The authorization requirement is unique to public authority justifications; the defensive force and lesser evils justifications have no such requirement and generally are available to all persons. The requirement of special authorization may appear to conflict with the general rule that justified conduct is equally justified for all actors in similar circumstances. This requirement is in keeping with that rule, however; the "circumstances" giving rise to the justifying societal interests here simply include the actor's authority to act. An unauthorized person engaging in the same conduct might not be able to further the societal or personal interests at stake, or at least not to the same extent and with the same efficiency and competence that an authorized person could. Indeed, the common interest of many of these defenses in maintaining law, order, and safety would be undermined if legal authority were completely diffuse, with no coordination or shared understanding of who should take control of (and responsibility for) a situation.

Rationale of Authorization Requirement   Assume a death warrant has been issued for a person found guilty of murder. After hearing the sentence, the victim's vengeful brother enters the prison on the day of execution, confines the executioner, takes his place, and executes the prisoner at the appointed time and in the prescribed manner. The brother's conduct conforms to that mandated by the judicial order, but he acts without the court's authority. The conduct furthers the immediate interest of enforcing the sanction, but not the similarly important societal interest in promoting the system's reputation for impartial punishment. For a more commonplace example, consider the authority given to train conductors or bus drivers to keep order on their vehicles. If a passenger becomes rowdy, another passenger might stop the disorder as effectively as the bus driver could. On the other hand, without special training and, more importantly, without special authority—which is typically signaled in some way, as with a uniform—another passenger's attempts to maintain order may only prompt resistance and the escalation of hostilities. In addition, even if successful, the passenger's actions would not further the societal interest in fostering compliance with the bus driver's efforts to maintain order. Respect for, and reaffirmation of, a bus driver's authority may help promote future cooperation when a driver seeks to exercise his authority.

Exceptions to Authorization Requirement   Two of the public authority justifications relax this requirement of special authorization: First, all persons are authorized to use force to prevent a suicide; second, under certain circumstances, persons without special authority are authorized to use force against a person who is preparing to commit, or who has just committed, a crime. Limiting authority to specially authorized persons is not feasible in these two instances because averting the threatened harm may require immediate action by whoever is present. Defensive force justifications do not require special authorization. Significantly, these two public authority justifications, suicide and crime prevention, resemble defensive force justifications in terms of the relevant triggering threat. In both situations there is an identifiable aggressor threatening physical harm to persons or property. If these two defenses were not included within a public authority defense—a location that makes sense, given their relation to the defense for law enforcement authority—they might alternatively be seen as defensive force justifications.

Evocation Requirement   In addition to requiring authorization to act, public authority justifications typically require circumstances that trigger or evoke the need for such action. Public authority justifications do not require a threat of harm to persons or property, as defensive force justifications do. They are evoked whenever a recognized interest is endangered or an opportunity to further an interest is presented. A violator may injure or endanger an interest without being an "aggressor" in the normal sense of that term. Neither the noisy bus passenger nor the escaping prisoner is an aggressor in the same way as a person who threatens physical injury for which defensive force is justified. (Of course, instances of physical aggression do arise in public authority situations, and when they do, an appropriate defensive force justification might also be triggered and might authorize even greater force than the public authority justification.) Yet even without physical aggression, both the passenger and the prisoner threaten important interests: the former, the decorum of the bus and the safety of its passengers; and the latter, the effective operation of the criminal justice and correctional systems. The specific conditions that will trigger a public authority defense frequently are set out in administrative regulations promulgated by the oversight body charged with regulating the conduct of the specially authorized group in question.

Necessity Requirement   Once the authorization and evocation requirements are satisfied, the actor has authority to act but must use the least harmful conduct necessary to protect or further the interests at stake, and the actor must act only when necessary. These necessity limitations are analogous to the necessity requirement of other justifications.

"Purpose" as Substitute for Necessity   The necessity requirement frequently is explicit but sometimes is replaced by a requirement that the actor act with a proper "purpose."[5] Conduct motivated by the purpose to protect the relevant interest often will be necessary for that purpose, thus satisfying a necessity requirement. But a "purpose" requirement does give an actor somewhat greater latitude than would a pure "necessity" requirement. The parent who acts with the proper purpose in spanking his child need not show that the conduct in fact was necessary, in the sense that no less harmful means could have been used as effectively. It is enough for the defense that the conduct is intended and designed to serve the disciplinary purpose. This substitution of a purpose requirement for a necessity requirement is another example of the Model Penal Code's subjectivization of justification defenses, in which it includes as "justified" the conduct of one who only mistakenly believes that she is justified. The parent gets the defense even if

---

5. See Model Penal Code §§ 3.08(1), 3.08(4).

her conduct is not in fact necessary, as long as she acted for the proper purpose and, therefore, presumably believed that the conduct was necessary.

Proportionality Requirement   The proportionality requirement ensures that, no matter how much force would be necessary to protect or further the interest at stake, no more force may be used than the relative importance of the interest warrants. The public authority justifications do not leave it to individual juries to determine the balance of conflicting interests. The legislature has predetermined the balance and promulgated a set of explicit limitations on the use of force. Public authority defenses rarely authorize the use of force that risks serious injury, even if it is necessary to stop the violation, and there are constitutional limits on the use of deadly force by law enforcement officers. The proportionality of the use of force is important in many situations. Under the Model Penal Code, for example, a bus driver may maintain order and decorum only with a degree of force that does not "create a substantial risk of causing death, bodily harm, or extreme mental distress."[6] (Greater force may be justified if the safety of the driver or a passenger is threatened, thereby triggering a defensive force justification.)

Legislative Balancing of Interests   As the bus driver limitation illustrates, the proportionality requirement, as expressed in statutes, typically does not permit ad hoc balancing, but rather is embodied in a series of specific limitations on the amount and kind of force that the justification will permit in a given situation. Each of these limitations is the result of a legislative assessment of the relative value of protecting the interest at stake and permitting injury to the person against whom the actor seeks to justify force. In setting these limits, the legislature ought to, and generally does, consider all aspects of the threatened interest, the long-range as well as the immediate, as discussed above. For example, in balancing disciplinary and protective interests against immediate threat of harm, the Model Penal Code's parental-discipline justification prohibits parents from using force that "create(s) a substantial risk of causing death, serious bodily harm, disfigurement, extreme pain or mental distress or gross degradation."[7]

Interest Protected vs. Force Used   Some public authority justifications further broad societal interests, while others rely primarily on personal interests to justify action. Not surprisingly, where the harm caused by the actor is balanced only against personal interests—especially the interests of the very person against whom the force is used—the force justified is strictly limited. A doctor clearly is not justified in undertaking a form of treatment that will cause more harm than it cures or prevents. In contrast, where broad societal interests are at stake, the harm the actor causes must be weighed against not only the physical harm threatened (if any), but also the harm to broader societal interests. Thus, law enforcement authority, judicial authority, and military authority all justify greater use of force and, under certain circumstances, even deadly force, as reflected in the legislative balances contained in the specific rules governing the each such defense.

General Public Authority   Model Penal Code section 3.03 describes the broadest public authority justification. It provides a defense for otherwise criminal conduct that is specifically "required or authorized" by the actor's public duty. The provision sets no specific limits on the use of force, and one might worry

---

6. Model Penal Code § 3.08(7)(b).
7. Model Penal Code § 3.08(1)(b).

that this general public authority defense could be used or applied too broadly, but the danger of abuse is reduced by section 3.03(2)(a), which states that more specific justification provisions are controlling for conduct that they address. In other words, the general public authority defense is, like the lesser evils defense, only a catchall for the instances where the situation is not covered by one of the more specific public authority defenses.

Scott v. Harris
Supreme Court of the United States
550 U.S. 372 (2007)

Justice SCALIA delivered the opinion of the Court.

We consider whether a law enforcement official can, consistent with the Fourth Amendment, attempt to stop a fleeing motorist from continuing his public-endangering flight by ramming the motorist's car from behind. Put another way: Can an officer take actions that place a fleeing motorist at risk of serious injury or death in order to stop the motorist's flight from endangering the lives of innocent bystanders?

In March 2001, a Georgia county deputy clocked respondent's vehicle traveling at 73 miles per hour on a road with a 55-mile-per-hour speed limit. The deputy activated his blue flashing lights indicating that respondent should pull over. Instead, respondent sped away, initiating a chase down what is in most portions a two-lane road, at speeds exceeding 85 miles per hour. The deputy radioed his dispatch to report that he was pursuing a fleeing vehicle and broadcast its license plate number. Petitioner, Deputy Timothy Scott, heard the radio communication and joined the pursuit along with other officers. In the midst of the chase, respondent pulled into the parking lot of a shopping center and was nearly boxed in by the various police vehicles. Respondent evaded the trap by making a sharp turn, colliding with Scott's police car, exiting the parking lot, and speeding off once again down a two-lane highway.

Following respondent's shopping center maneuvering, which resulted in slight damage to Scott's police car, Scott took over as the lead pursuit vehicle. . . . Scott applied his push bumper to the rear of respondent's vehicle. As a result, respondent lost control of his vehicle, which left the roadway, ran down an embankment, overturned, and crashed. Respondent was badly injured and was rendered a quadriplegic. . . .

Judging the matter on that basis, we think it is quite clear that Deputy Scott did not violate the Fourth Amendment. Scott does not contest that his decision to terminate the car chase by ramming his bumper into respondent's vehicle constituted a "seizure." . . . The question we need to answer is whether Scott's actions were objectively reasonable. . . .

In determining the reasonableness of the manner in which a seizure is effected, "[w]e must balance the nature and quality of the intrusion on the individual's Fourth Amendment interests against the importance of the governmental interests alleged to justify the intrusion." *United States v. Place*, 462 U.S. 696, 703 (1983). . . . So how does a court go about weighing the perhaps lesser probability of injuring or killing numerous bystanders against the perhaps larger probability of injuring or killing a single person? We think it appropriate in this process to take into account not only the number of lives at risk, but also their relative culpability. It was respondent, after all, who intentionally placed himself and the public in danger by unlawfully engaging in the reckless, high-speed flight that ultimately produced the choice between two evils that Scott confronted. Multiple police cars, with blue lights flashing and sirens blaring, had been chasing respondent for nearly 10 miles, but he ignored their warning to stop. By contrast, those who might have been harmed had Scott not taken the action he did were entirely innocent. We have little difficulty in concluding it was reasonable for Scott to take the action that he did. . . .

The car chase that respondent initiated in this case posed a substantial and immediate risk of serious physical injury to others; no reasonable jury could conclude otherwise. Scott's attempt to terminate the chase by forcing respondent off the road was reasonable, and Scott is entitled to summary judgment. The Court of Appeals' judgment to the contrary is reversed.

It is so ordered.

Justice STEVENS, dissenting,

Today, the Court asks whether an officer may "take actions that place a fleeing motorist at risk of serious injury or death in order to stop the motorist's flight from endangering the lives of innocent bystanders." . . . Depending on the circumstances, the answer may be an obvious "yes," an obvious "no," or sufficiently doubtful that the question of the reasonableness of the officer's actions should be decided by a jury, after a review of the degree of danger and the alternatives available to the officer. A high-speed chase in a desert in Nevada is, after all, quite different from one that travels through the heart of Las Vegas.

Relying on a *de novo* review of a videotape of a portion of a nighttime chase on a lightly traveled road in Georgia where no pedestrians or other "bystanders" were present, buttressed by uninformed speculation about the possible consequences of discontinuing the chase, eight of the jurors on this Court reach a verdict [in favor of Officer Scott.] . . . The Court's justification for this unprecedented departure from our well-settled standard of review of factual determinations . . . is based on its mistaken view . . . and that respondent's version of the events was "so utterly discredited by the record that no reasonable jury could have believed him."

Rather than supporting the conclusion that what we see on the video "resembles a Hollywood-style car chase of the most frightening sort," the tape actually confirms . . . the factual questions at issue. More importantly, it surely does not provide a principled basis for depriving the respondent of his right to have a jury evaluate the question whether the police officers' decision to use deadly force to bring the chase to an end was reasonable. . . .

My colleagues on the jury saw respondent "swerve around more than a dozen other cars," and "force cars traveling in both directions to their respective shoulders," but they apparently discounted the possibility that those cars were already out of the pursuit's path as a result of hearing the sirens. Even if that were not so, passing a slower vehicle on a two-lane road always involves some degree of swerving and is not especially dangerous if there are no cars coming from the opposite direction. At no point during the chase did respondent pull into the opposite lane other than to pass a car in front of him; he did the latter no more than five times and, on most of those occasions, used his turn signal. On none of these occasions was there a car traveling in the opposite direction. In fact, at one point, when respondent found himself behind a car in his own lane and there were cars traveling in the other direction, he slowed and waited for the cars traveling in the other direction to pass before overtaking the car in front of him while using his turn signal to do so. . . .

What would have happened if the police had decided to abandon the chase? We now know that they could have apprehended respondent later because they had his license plate number. Even if that were not true, and even if he would have escaped any punishment at all, the use of deadly force in this case was no more appropriate than the use of a deadly weapon against a fleeing felon in *Tennessee v. Garner*, 471 U.S. 1 (1985). [The facts of this case are recounted in the Elton Hymon narrative at the beginning of this section]. In any event, any uncertainty about the result of abandoning the pursuit has not prevented the Court from basing its conclusions on its own factual assumptions. The Court attempts to avoid the conclusion that deadly force was unnecessary by speculating that if the officers had let him go, respondent might have been "just as likely" to continue to drive recklessly as to slow down and wipe his brow. That speculation is unconvincing as a matter of common sense and improper as a matter of law. Our duty to view the evidence in the light most favorable to the nonmoving party would foreclose such speculation if the Court had not used its observation of the video as an excuse for replacing the rule of law with its ad hoc judgment. There is no evidentiary basis for an assumption that dangers caused by flight from a police pursuit will continue after the pursuit ends. . . .

In my view, the risks inherent in justifying unwarranted police conduct on the basis of unfounded assumptions are unacceptable, particularly when less drastic measures—in this case, the use of stop sticks[8] or a simple warning issued from a loudspeaker—could have avoided such a tragic result. In my judgment, jurors in Georgia should be allowed to evaluate the reasonableness of the decision to ram respondent's speeding vehicle in a manner that created an obvious risk of death and has in fact made him a quadriplegic at the age of 19.

I respectfully dissent.

▲ PROBLEMS

Aggressive Fishing (#83)

Charles Long and his friend, Hammond, are avid fishermen. They do not always respect the rules, however, including using gill nets to catch fish. Gill nets are large nets usually stretched across a river to catch fish by their gills as they swim through them and are an effective means of catching substantial quantities of fish with little effort. They are used by commercial fishermen, but are heavily regulated in order to prevent overfishing. Long's and Hammond's use of gill nets violates local fish and game law.

They are eventually spotted by a deputy game warden, James Durham. When the two row to shore, Durham attempts to arrest them. Long pushes Durham away, striking him in the process, then jumps back into the boat and both men

---

8. "Stop sticks" are a device that can be placed across the roadway and used to flatten a vehicle's tires slowly to safely terminate a pursuit.

begin rowing. Durham pursues them, wading out into the muddy water, yelling
for the men to stop. He grabs onto the bow of the boat to try to pull it back to
shore, while calling his partner for backup.

Long asks Hammond to hand him an oar. He then attacks Durham with the
oar, hitting him in the shoulder and knocking loose his grip on the boat. Durham
catches hold of a chain that is attached to the boat and struggles to pull the boat
back to shore. Durham orders Long to put the oar down, but Long continues to
hit him with it. Durham draws his gun and fires a warning shot into the water.
However, Long continues swinging the oar, hitting Durham in the neck and on
the side of the face. Durham is afraid that if he is hit hard enough, he may lose
consciousness and drown. After repeated warnings, Durham shoots Long in the
chest. Injured, Long then moves to the other side of the boat to help Hammond
row. Durham is unable to hold onto the boat any longer and lets go of the chain.
Following the incident, Durham is arrested for shooting Long.

What liability for Durham, if any, for his shooting of Long, under the Model
Penal Code? Prepare a list of all criminal code subsections in the order in which
you rely on them in your analysis.

Keeping Rodney King Down (#84)

Rodney King has just driven through a series of red lights. He had been
drinking earlier in the day with two of his friends and is driving with a blood-
alcohol level over twice the legal limit. When an officer attempts to pull him over,
King tries to lose him. He is on parole from prison following a robbery conviction and wishes to avoid his parole being revoked. Finally, after an eight-mile
chase, King pulls over. By this time there are more than ten officers involved in
the pursuit. King and his friends are ordered out of the car and are told to lie on
the ground. King's friends do as they are told and are arrested without incident.
King, however, refuses to follow the orders, dancing around and waving to police
helicopters that are circling the scene.

King is a large, muscular man, standing 6 feet, 3 inches and weighing 230
pounds. King is, in fact, larger than any of the police officers present. Sergeant
Stacey Koon arrives on the scene and takes command. Observing King's strange
behavior and refusal to lie down, Koon believes that King has been using PCP, a
drug that can make a person irrational, violent, strong, and impervious to pain.
After King once more fails to heed the officers' instructions, Koon orders four
officers to "swarm" King, bring him to the ground, and handcuff him. King is
thrown to the ground, but when officers attempt to restrain him he fights back
and begins to get up again. Koon decides to take a different approach. He pulls
out his Taser and shocks King. When King does not fall down, Koon shocks him
repeatedly. King drops to his knees but uses his hands to stop himself from falling
flat. Again ordered to lie down, King pulls himself back to a standing position and
runs toward an officer. Koon then orders the officers to use their batons to bring
King down. King is struck repeatedly with the metal batons, falling to the ground
after a severe blow to the head. By this time, King appears disoriented but is making some further movements on the ground.

At this point, King has been hit with the batons more than 25 times and
there are more than 11 officers present in his vicinity. Koon, more convinced that

King is on PCP and thus not acting rationally, orders hits to King's joints, knowing the risk of permanent injury and broken bones but hoping to bring King down without the use of deadly force. Finally, King looks up at an officer and says, "Please stop." Koon then orders his men back so that King can be cuffed. However, King begins struggling again as the handcuffs are placed on him, and the officers knock him face to the ground and stomp on his chest. They hog-tie King, binding his feet together after the handcuffs are in place. Koon then calls for an ambulance.

At the hospital, doctors determine that King has no drugs in his system apart from the alcohol. He has sustained multiple head injuries and facial fractures, nerve damage, a fractured fibia, as well as multiple superficial lacerations, bruises, and contusions.

A subsequent investigation finds that, while the officers involved did not violate then-existing regulations, they had not been adequately trained to deal with such situations in the most effective way.

What liability for Koon, if any, under the Model Penal Code? Prepare a list of all criminal code subsections in the order in which you rely on them in your analysis. (If Koon has lost his public authority justification, at what point in the incident did he lose it?)

Killing Your Co-Felon Through a Gun Battle with Police—Revisited (#30)

Reconsider the facts of Problem Case: Gun Battle with Police (#30) from Section 6.

Does the material in this Section give any additional arguments for the defendant in *Redline*? If so, what?

☀ DISCUSSION ISSUE

When Should Police Be Allowed to Shoot in Other than Defensive Situations?

Materials presenting each side of this Discussion Issue appear in the Advanced Materials for Section 17 in Appendix A.

Defensive Force Justifications

Perhaps the most common fact pattern that raises justification issues is that of a person using force in defense of person or property. Unlike the general justification defense of lesser evils, the law has developed explicit and detailed rules governing the case of defensive force, and typically these rules are embodied in modern criminal codes.

◆ THE CASE OF BERNHARD GOETZ (#85)

It is December 22, 1984. New York City faces problems of widespread drug use and rampant crime. Six hundred thousand crimes have already been committed this year. The steeply escalating rates of street and violent crime are linked to the introduction of crack cocaine. (In 1984 the New York City violent crime rate is almost four times what it is today: 2,566 in 1984 as compared to 551.8 in 2009 per 100,000.) On average 40 felonies are committed against subway riders every day.

The fear has caused people to change the way they live their lives. They have stopped wearing valuables. Some carry a wallet with enough cash to satisfy a

489

Figure 89 **Bernhard Goetz at his home, 1985**
(Bettmann/Corbis)

mugger. Many stay indoors at night and plan their daily commutes and errands to avoid certain streets and subway routes thought to be dangerous. Fewer tourists visit the Big Apple and people are moving to the suburbs in droves. Many feel that "the system" has let them down and no longer trust law enforcement to protect them.

One of three brothers, Bernhard ("Bernie") Goetz was raised in upstate New York, the son of a Jewish mother and a German father. When he was 13, his father was convicted of abusing two boys. The incident brought the family closer; Goetz always believed in his father's innocence. It was a profound experience for Goetz, and the first of many disappointments he feels toward the legal system.

Goetz left his hometown to study nuclear and electrical engineering at New York University. While there, he discovered he had a talent for fixing machines and after graduation took a job as nuclear engineer for submarines. Never a team player, Goetz had trouble interacting with people in college, and his difficulties continued when he worked for private contractors. He often reported defects to the military when they would have preferred his silence. Goetz finally came to realize that his aversion to both authority and people generally would make it difficult for him to work in a corporate environment. He decided to start his own business and today repairs electronics from his apartment, which is in New York City's rough Fourteenth Street neighborhood.

Goetz was recently victimized by crime, which makes his decision to stay in the city all the more surprising. In 1981, he was riding the subway home, carrying electronic equipment for his business, when he was mugged for the first time. Three young men jumped him by slamming him into a glass door, driving its handle into his chest, and then throwing him to the ground. With the help of a janitor, Goetz was able to grab hold of the ringleader, Fred Clark, until the police arrived.

The incident served only to solidify further Goetz's distrust of the criminal justice system. After the mugging, the police interrogated him for more than six hours while apparently releasing the criminals after just a few hours. His assailants were charged only with criminal mischief—for ripping Goetz's jacket—because authorities concluded that there was insufficient evidence for an attempted robbery charge. Goetz was frustrated; the justice system seemed so focused on details that it ignored the real harm of the crime.

The mugging and the system's inability to protect him so disturbed Goetz that he spent more than $2,000 trying to obtain a concealed weapon permit. The police turned him down. When pressed for a reason, an officer explained simply that the department cannot give every person a permit. The system's concern with "technicalities" again frustrated Goetz.

Even now, the physical and emotional scars of the mugging remain; his knees are permanently injured, and he is frightened of being "beaten to a pulp" by muggers. He likens himself to a caged rat that is continuously poked with red-hot needles. To feel safe, he now leaves his apartment only with a .38 caliber gun in a quick-draw holster. He also never wears gloves, even in the coldest weather, in order to be "fast on the draw." Despite Goetz's fears, he still engages in risky behavior. For example, one evening he stays on the wrong subway, going toward Harlem, rather than getting off and switching directions. He exits at a stop near the northern edge of Central Park, an area notorious for muggings and assaults, and goes for a walk. While walking, Goetz scares off a mugger with his gun.

Today, feeling depressed about his father's recent death, Goetz leaves his apartment in the early afternoon to head downtown. He catches the No. 2 train at the corner of Seventh Avenue and Fourteenth Street and sits in the first car, near four young African American men, Darrell Cabey, Barry Allen, Troy Canty, and James Ramseur. They are all high school dropouts with criminal records. Earlier in the year, Cabey had been arrested for armed robbery. Shortly before the subway shooting, Cabey is accused of robbing three other men at gunpoint. He and Allen also menaced a woman on a train, asking for money. Allen has twice pled guilty to disorderly conduct. Ramseur and Canty have been convicted of petit larceny. Ramseur has been accused of being involved in the gang rape of a pregnant woman.

Their aggressive and somewhat threatening behavior causes the 15 to 20 other passengers to move to the other end of the car. Canty, lying on the bench across the way, says to Goetz, "How are ya?" Along with Allen, he approaches Goetz and asks for five dollars. Canty and Allen stand to Goetz's left, between Goetz and the passengers who had distanced themselves from the situation. Goetz sees one of the other two men reach into his pocket, which appears to be bulging. (It is later determined that the men are carrying sharpened screwdrivers in their pockets, but at this point Goetz does not know what the bulge is.) Goetz asks them to repeat their request, later explaining that he wanted to be sure that they were "playing the game." They repeat themselves, saying, "Give us five dollars." Cabey later admits that they were intending to rob Goetz because "he looked like easy bait."

After their second request, Goetz pulls his gun and fires rapidly at them as they scatter. He hits each of them at least once. After some confusing moments, he sees Cabey sitting near the conductor's cab, grasping the seat. Goetz approaches

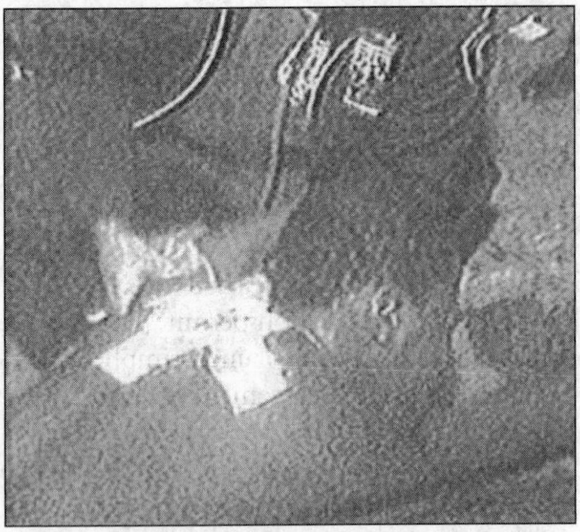

Figure 90 **Crime scene on the No. 2 train in New York City, 1984**

(CNN)

Figure 91 **Darrell Cabey entering Bronx State Supreme Court during civil suit against Goetz, April 12, 1996**

(CNN)

takes another shot when Cabey is down

him and says, "You seem to be doing all right. Here's another," and shoots him. Other passengers pull the emergency cord, jerking the train to a stop. Everyone exits except two terrified women whom Goetz tries to comfort. When the conductor enters the car and asks Goetz if he is a police officer, Goetz says no and explains that the young men were trying to rob him. Keeping his gun, Goetz walks off into the subway tunnel. He later describes his shooting the four men as wanting "to murder *MR* them, to hurt them, to make them suffer as much as possible." He was sick of being "played with . . . as a cat plays with a mouse."

The young men are left lying in pools of blood on the train car's floor. *serious physical injuries* Canty, Allen, and Ramseur are all injured in the upper body but eventually recover from their serious injuries. The shooting paralyzes Cabey and causes brain damage.

After Goetz surfaces from the tunnel, he rents a car and drives north to Vermont and New Hampshire. He thinks that the whole thing will blow over in a few days. Nine days later, he returns to New York and notices that things have quieted down for the most part. The police have left notes on his door and in his mailbox requesting that he come in for questioning. They have not singled out Goetz as their prime suspect but have information from a caller that he might be the shooter. Seeing the notes, he panics and returns to New Hampshire. Two days later, he walks into the Concord, New Hampshire, police station and gives a statement to police.

1. Relying only on your own intuitions of justice, what liability and punishment, if any, does Bernhard Goetz deserve?

N	0	1	2	3	4	5	6	7	8	9	10	11
☐	☐	☐	☐	☐	☐	☐	☐	☑	☐	☐	☐	☐
no liability	liability but no punishment	1 day	2 wks	2 mo	6 mo	1 yr	3 yrs	7 yrs	15 yrs	30 yrs	life imprisonment	death

2. What "justice" arguments could defense counsel make on the defendant's behalf?

3. What "justice" arguments could the prosecution make against the defendant?

4. What liability for Goetz, if any, under the then-existing statutes? Prepare a list of all criminal code subsections in the order in which you rely on them in your analysis.

5. What liability, if any, under the Model Penal Code? Prepare a list of all criminal code subsections in the order in which you rely on them in your analysis.

▪ THE LAW

New York Penal Law
(1984)

Section 120.00. Assault in the Third Degree

A person is guilty of assault in the third degree when:

1. With intent to cause physical injury to another person, he causes such injury to such person or to a third person; or

2. He recklessly causes physical injury to another person; or

3. With criminal negligence, he causes physical injury to another person by means of a deadly weapon or a dangerous instrument. Assault in the third degree is a class A misdemeanor.

Section 120.05. Assault in the Second Degree

A person is guilty of assault in the second degree when:

1. With intent to cause serious physical injury to another person, he causes such injury to such person or to a third person; or

2. With intent to cause physical injury to another person, he causes such injury to such person or to a third person by means of a deadly weapon or a dangerous instrument; or . . .

4. He recklessly causes serious physical injury to another person by means of a deadly weapon or a dangerous instrument;. . . .
Assault in the second degree is a class D felony.

Section 120.10. Assault in the First Degree

A person is guilty of assault in the first degree when:

1. With intent to cause serious physical injury to another person, he causes such injury to such person or to a third person by means of a deadly weapon or a dangerous instrument; or . . .

Hot show depraved indfference

3. Under circumstances evincing a depraved indifference to human life, he recklessly engages in conduct which creates a grave risk of death to another person, and thereby causes serious physical injury to another person; . . .

Assault in the first degree is a class C felony.

Section 125.00. Homicide Defined

Homicide means conduct which causes the death of a person or an unborn child with which a female has been pregnant for more than twenty-four weeks under circumstances constituting murder, manslaughter in the first degree, manslaughter in the second degree, criminally negligent homicide, abortion in the first degree or self-abortion in the first degree.

Section 125.10. Criminally Negligent Homicide

A person is guilty of criminally negligent homicide when, with criminal negligence, he causes the death of another person.

Criminally negligent homicide is a class E felony.

Section 125.15. Manslaughter in the Second Degree

A person is guilty of manslaughter in the second degree when:

1. He recklessly causes the death of another person; or . . .

3. He intentionally causes or aids another person to commit suicide.

Manslaughter in the second degree is a class C felony.

Section 125.20. Manslaughter in the First Degree

A person is guilty of manslaughter in the first degree when:

1. With intent to cause serious physical injury to another person, he causes the death of such person or of a third person; or

2. With intent to cause the death of another person, he causes the death of such person or of a third person under circumstances which do not constitute murder because he acts under the influence of extreme emotional disturbance, as defined in paragraph (a) of subdivision one of section 125.25. The fact that homicide was committed under the influence of extreme emotional disturbance constitutes a mitigating circumstance reducing murder to manslaughter in the first degree and need not be proved in any prosecution initiated under this subdivision; . . .

Manslaughter in the first degree is a class B felony.

Section 125.25. Murder in the Second Degree

A person is guilty of murder in the second degree when:

1. With intent to cause the death of another person, he causes the death of such person or of a third person; except that in any prosecution under this subdivision, it is an affirmative defense that:

(a) The defendant acted under the influence of extreme emotional disturbance for which there was a reasonable explanation or excuse, the reasonableness of which is to be determined from the viewpoint of a person in the defendant's situation under the circumstances as the defendant believed them to be. Nothing contained in this paragraph shall constitute a defense to a prosecution for, or preclude a conviction of, manslaughter in the first degree or any other crime; or . . .

2. Under circumstances evincing a depraved indifference to human life, he recklessly engages in conduct which creates a grave risk of death to another person, and thereby causes the death of another person;. . . .

Murder in the second degree is a class A-I felony.

Section 160.10. Robbery in the Second Degree

A person is guilty of robbery in the second degree when he forcibly steals property and when:

1. He is aided by another person actually present; or
2. In the course of the commission of the crime or of immediate flight therefrom, he or another participant in the crime:

(a) Causes physical injury to any person who is not a participant in the crime; or

(b) Displays what appears to be a pistol, revolver, rifle, shotgun, machine gun or other firearm.

Robbery in the second degree is a class C felony.

Section 160.15. Robbery in the First Degree

A person is guilty of robbery in the first degree when he forcibly steals property and when, in the course of the commission of the crime or of immediate flight therefrom, he or another participant in the crime:

1. Causes serious physical injury to any person who is not a participant in the crime; or
2. Is armed with a deadly weapon; or
3. Uses or threatens the immediate use of a dangerous instrument; or
4. Displays what appears to be a pistol, revolver, rifle, shotgun, machine gun or other firearm; except that in any prosecution under this subdivision, it is an affirmative defense that such pistol, revolver, rifle, shotgun, machine gun or other firearm was not a loaded weapon from which a shot, readily capable of producing death or other serious physical injury, could be discharged. Nothing contained in this subdivision shall constitute a defense to a prosecution for, or preclude a conviction of, robbery in the second degree, robbery in the third degree or any other crime.

Robbery in the first degree is a class B felony.

Section 10.00. Definitions of Terms of General Use in This Chapter

Except where different meanings are expressly specified in subsequent provisions of this chapter, the following terms have the following meanings:

1. "Offense" means conduct for which a sentence to a term of imprisonment or to a fine is provided by any law of this state or by any law, local law or ordinance of a political subdivision of this state, or by any order, rule or regulation of any governmental instrumentality authorized by law to adopt the same. . . .

4. "Misdemeanor" means an offense, other than a "traffic infraction," for which a sentence to a term of imprisonment in excess of fifteen days may be imposed, but for which a sentence to a term of imprisonment in excess of one year cannot be imposed.

5. "Felony" means an offense for which a sentence to a term of imprisonment in excess of one year may be imposed.

6. "Crime" means a misdemeanor or a felony. . . .

8. "Possess" means to have physical possession or otherwise to exercise dominion or control over tangible property.

9. "Physical injury" means impairment of physical condition or substantial pain.

10. "Serious physical injury" means physical injury which creates a substantial risk of death, or which causes death or serious and protracted disfigurement, protracted impairment of health or protracted loss or impairment of the function of any bodily organ.

11. "Deadly physical force" means physical force, which, under the circumstances in which it is used, is readily capable of causing death or other serious physical injury.

12. "Deadly weapon" means any loaded weapon from which a shot, readily capable of producing death or other serious physical injury, may be discharged, or a switchblade knife, gravity knife, dagger, billy, blackjack, or metal knuckles.

13. "Dangerous instrument" means any instrument, article or substance, including a "vehicle" as that term is defined in this section, which, under the circumstances in which it is used, attempted to be used or threatened to be used, is readily capable of causing death or other serious physical injury. . . .

Section 15.00. Culpability; Definitions of Terms

The following definitions are applicable to this chapter:

1. "Act" means a bodily movement.

2. "Voluntary act" means a bodily movement performed consciously as a result of effort or determination, and includes the possession of property if the actor was aware of his physical possession or control thereof for a sufficient period to have been able to terminate it.

3. "Omission" means a failure to perform an act as to which a duty of performance is imposed by law.

4. "Conduct" means an act or omission and its accompanying mental state.

5. "To act" means either to perform an act or to omit to perform an act.

6. "Culpable mental state" means "intentionally" or "knowingly" or "recklessly" or with "criminal negligence," as these terms are defined in section 15.05.

Section 15.05. Culpability; Definitions of Culpable Mental States

The following definitions are applicable to this chapter:

1. "Intentionally." A person acts intentionally with respect to a result or to conduct described by a statute defining an offense when his conscious objective is to cause such result or to engage in such conduct.

2. "Knowingly." A person acts knowingly with respect to conduct or to a circumstance described by a statute defining an offense when he is aware that his conduct is of such nature or that such circumstance exists.

3. "Recklessly." A person acts recklessly with respect to a result or to a circumstance described by a statute defining an offense when he is aware of and consciously disregards a substantial and unjustifiable risk that such result will occur or that such circumstance exists. The risk must be of such nature and degree that disregard thereof constitutes a gross deviation from the standard of conduct that a reasonable person would observe in the situation. A person who creates such a risk but is unaware thereof solely by reason of voluntary intoxication also acts recklessly with respect thereto.

4. "Criminal negligence." A person acts with criminal negligence with respect to a result or to a circumstance described by a statute defining an offense when he fails to perceive a substantial and unjustifiable risk that such result will occur or that such circumstance exists. The risk must be of such nature and degree that the failure to perceive it constitutes a gross deviation from the standard of care that a reasonable person would observe in the situation.

Section 15.10. Requirements for Criminal Liability in General and for Offenses of Strict Liability and Mental Culpability

The minimal requirement for criminal liability is the performance by a person of conduct which includes a voluntary act or the omission to perform an act which he is physically capable of performing. If such conduct is all that is required for commission of a particular offense, or if an offense or some material element thereof does not require a culpable mental state on the part of the actor, such offense is one of "strict liability." If a culpable mental state on the part of the actor is required with respect to every material element of an offense, such offense is one of "mental culpability."

Section 15.15. Construction of Statutes with Respect to Culpability Requirements

1. When the commission of an offense defined in this chapter, or some element of an offense, requires a particular culpable mental state, such mental state is ordinarily designated in the statute defining the offense by use of the terms "intentionally," "knowingly," "recklessly" or "criminal negligence," or by use of terms, such as "with intent to defraud" and "knowing it to be false," describing a specific kind of intent or knowledge. When one and only one of such terms appears in a statute defining an offense, it is presumed to apply to every element of the offense unless an intent to limit its application clearly appears.

2. Although no culpable mental state is expressly designated in a statute defining an offense, a culpable mental state may nevertheless be required for the commission of such offense, or with respect to some or all of the material elements thereof, if the proscribed conduct necessarily involves such culpable mental state. A statute defining a crime, unless clearly indicating a legislative intent to impose strict liability, should be construed as defining a crime of mental culpability. This subdivision applies to offenses defined both in and outside this chapter.

Section 110.00. Attempt to Commit a Crime

A person is guilty of an attempt to commit a crime when, with intent to commit a crime, he engages in conduct which tends to effect the commission of such crime.

Section 110.05. Attempt to Commit a Crime; Punishment

An attempt to commit a crime is a:
1. Class A-I felony when the crime attempted is the A-I felony of murder in the first degree, criminal possession of a controlled substance in the first degree or criminal sale of a controlled substance in the first degree;
2. Class A-II felony when the crime attempted is a class A-II felony;
3. Class B felony when the crime attempted is a class A-I felony except as provided in subdivision one hereof;
4. Class C felony when the crime attempted is a class B felony;
5. Class D felony when the crime attempted is a class C felony;
6. Class E felony when the crime attempted is a class D felony;
7. Class A misdemeanor when the crime attempted is a class E felony;
8. Class B misdemeanor when the crime attempted is a misdemeanor.

Section 25.00. Defenses; Burden of Proof

1. When a "defense," other than an "affirmative defense," defined by statute is raised at a trial, the people have the burden of disproving such defense beyond a reasonable doubt.
2. When a defense declared by statute to be an "affirmative defense" is raised at a trial, the defendant has the burden of establishing such defense by a preponderance of the evidence.

Section 35.00. Justification; a Defense

In any prosecution for an offense, justification, as defined in sections 35.05 through 35.30, is a defense.

Section 35.05. Justification; Generally

Unless otherwise limited by the ensuing provisions of this article defining justifiable use of physical force, conduct which would otherwise constitute an offense is justifiable and not criminal when:

1. Such conduct is required or authorized by law or by a judicial decree, or is performed by a public servant in the reasonable exercise of his official powers, duties or functions; or

2. Such conduct is necessary as an emergency measure to avoid an imminent public or private injury which is about to occur by reason of a situation occasioned or developed through no fault of the actor, and which is of such gravity that, according to ordinary standards of intelligence and morality, the desirability and urgency of avoiding such injury clearly outweigh the desirability of avoiding the injury sought to be prevented by the statute defining the offense in issue. The necessity and justifiability of such conduct may not rest upon considerations pertaining only to the morality and advisability of the statute, either in its general application or with respect to its application to a particular class of cases arising thereunder. Whenever evidence relating to the defense of justification under this subdivision is offered by the defendant, the court shall rule as a matter of law whether the claimed facts and circumstances would, if established, constitute a defense.

Section 35.10. Justification; Use of Physical Force Generally

The use of physical force upon another person which would otherwise constitute an offense is justifiable and not criminal under any of the following circumstances:

1. A parent, guardian or other person entrusted with the care and supervision of a person under the age of twenty-one or an incompetent person, and a teacher or other person entrusted with the care and supervision of a person under the age of twenty-one for a special purpose, may use physical force, but not deadly physical force, upon such person when and to the extent that he reasonably believes it necessary to maintain discipline or to promote the welfare of such person.

2. A warden or other authorized official of a jail, prison or correctional institution may, in order to maintain order and discipline, use such physical force as is authorized by the correction law.

3. A person responsible for the maintenance of order in a common carrier of passengers, or a person acting under his direction, may use physical force when and to the extent that he reasonably believes it necessary to maintain order, but he may use deadly physical force only when he reasonably believes it necessary to prevent death or serious physical injury.

4. A person acting under a reasonable belief that another person is about to commit suicide or to inflict serious physical injury upon himself may use physical force upon such person to the extent that he reasonably believes it necessary to thwart such result.

5. A duly licensed physician, or a person acting under his direction, may use physical force for the purpose of administering a recognized form of treatment which he reasonably believes to be adapted to promoting the physical or mental health of the patient if (a) the treatment is administered with the consent of the patient or, if the patient is under the age of eighteen years or an incompetent person, with the consent of his parent, guardian or other person entrusted with his care and supervision, or (b) the treatment

is administered in an emergency when the physician reasonably believes that no one competent to consent can be consulted and that a reasonable person, wishing to safeguard the welfare of the patient, would consent.

6. A person may, pursuant to the ensuing provisions of this article, use physical force upon another person in defense of himself or a third person, or in defense of premises, or in order to prevent larceny of or criminal mischief to property, or in order to effect an arrest or prevent an escape from custody. Whenever a person is authorized by any such provision to use deadly physical force in any given circumstance, nothing contained in any other such provision may be deemed to negate or qualify such authorization.

Section 35.15. Justification; Use of Physical Force in Defense of a Person

1. A person may, subject to the provisions of subdivision [2], use physical force upon another person when and to the extent he reasonably believes such to be necessary to defend himself or a third person from what he reasonably believes to be the use or imminent use of unlawful physical force by such other person, unless:

(a) The latter's conduct was provoked by the actor himself with intent to cause physical injury to another person; or

(b) The actor was the initial aggressor; except that in such case his use of physical force is nevertheless justifiable if he has withdrawn from the encounter and effectively communicated such withdrawal to such other person but the latter persists in continuing the incident by the use or threatened imminent use of unlawful physical force; or

(c) The physical force involved is the product of a combat by agreement not specifically authorized by law.

2. A person may not use deadly physical force upon another person under circumstances specified in subdivision one unless:

(a) He reasonably believes that such other person is using or about to use deadly physical force. Even in such case, however, the actor may not use deadly physical force if he knows that he can with complete safety as to himself and others avoid the necessity of so doing by retreating; except that he is under no duty to retreat if he is:

(i) in his dwelling and not the initial aggressor; or

(ii) a police officer or peace officer or a person assisting a police officer or a peace officer at the latter's direction, acting pursuant to section 35.30; or

(b) He reasonably believes that such other person is committing or attempting to commit a kidnapping, forcible rape, forcible sodomy, or robbery; or

(c) He reasonably believes that such other person is committing or attempting to commit a burglary, and the circumstances are such that the use of deadly physical force is authorized. . . .

Section 35.25. Justification; Use of Physical Force to Prevent or Terminate Larceny or Criminal Mischief

A person may use physical force, other than deadly physical force, upon another person when and to the extent that he reasonably believes such to be necessary to prevent or terminate what he reasonably believes to be the commission or attempted commission by such other person of larceny or of criminal mischief with respect to property other than premises.

Section 40.15. Mental Disease or Defect

In any prosecution for an offense, it is an affirmative defense that when the defendant engaged in the proscribed conduct, he lacked criminal responsibility by reason of mental disease or defect. Such lack of criminal responsibility means that at the time of such conduct, as a result of mental disease or defect, he lacked substantial capacity to know or appreciate either:

    1. The nature and consequences of such conduct; or

    2. That such conduct was wrong.

Section 70.00. Sentence of Imprisonment for Felony

1. Indeterminate sentence. Except as provided in subdivision four, a sentence of imprisonment for a felony shall be an indeterminate sentence. When such a sentence is imposed, the court shall impose a maximum term in accordance with the provisions of subdivision two of this section and the minimum period of imprisonment shall be as provided in subdivision three of this section.

2. Maximum term of sentence. The maximum term of an indeterminate sentence shall be at least three years and the term shall be fixed as follows:

    (a) For a class A felony, the term shall be life imprisonment;

    (b) For a class B felony, the term shall be fixed by the court, and shall not exceed twenty-five years;

    (c) For a class C felony, the term shall be fixed by the court, and shall not exceed fifteen years;

    (d) For a class D felony, the term shall be fixed by the court, and shall not exceed seven years; and

    (e) For a class E felony, the term shall be fixed by the court, and shall not exceed four years.

3. Minimum period of imprisonment. The minimum period of imprisonment under an indeterminate sentence shall be at least one year and shall be fixed as follows:

    (a) In the case of a class A felony, the minimum period shall be fixed by the court and specified in the sentence.

        (i) For a class A-I felony, such minimum period shall not be less than fifteen years nor more than twenty-five years.

        (ii) For a class A-II felony, such minimum period shall not be less than three years nor more than eight years four months.

    (b) Where the sentence is for a class B or class C violent felony offense as defined in subdivision one of section 70.02, the minimum period shall be fixed by the court pursuant to subdivision four of section 70.02. Where the sentence is for any other felony, the minimum period shall be fixed by the court and specified in the sentence and shall be not less than one year nor more than one-third of the maximum term imposed.

    (c) [Repealed]

4. Alternative definite sentence for class D, E, and certain class C felonies. When a person, other than a second or persistent felony offender, is sentenced for a class D or class E felony, or to a class C felony specified in article two hundred twenty or article two hundred twenty-one, and the court, having regard to the nature and circumstances of the crime and to the history and character of the defendant, is of the opinion that a sentence of imprisonment is necessary but that it would be unduly harsh to impose an indeterminate sentence, the court may impose a definite sentence of imprisonment and fix a term of one year or less.

Model Penal Code
(Official Draft 1962)

Section 3.04. Use of Force in Self-Protection

(1) Use of Force Justifiable for Protection of the Person. Subject to the provisions of this Section and of Section 3.09, the use of force upon or toward another person is justifiable when the actor believes that such force is immediately necessary for the purpose of protecting himself against the use of unlawful force by such other person on the present occasion.

(2) Limitations on Justifying Necessity for Use of Force.
   (a) The use of force is not justifiable under this Section:
       (i) to resist an arrest which the actor knows is being made by a peace officer, although the arrest is unlawful; or
       (ii) to resist force used by the occupier or possessor of property or by another person on his behalf, where the actor knows that the person using the force is doing so under a claim of right to protect the property, except that this limitation shall not apply if:
           (1) the actor is a public officer acting in the performance of his duties or a person lawfully assisting him therein or a person making or assisting in a lawful arrest; or
           (2) the actor has been unlawfully dispossessed of the property and is making a re-entry or recaption justified by Section 3.06; or
           (3) the actor believes that such force is necessary to protect himself against death or serious bodily harm.
   (b) The use of deadly force is not justifiable under this Section unless the actor believes that such force is necessary to protect himself against death, serious bodily harm, kidnapping or sexual intercourse compelled by force or threat; nor is it justifiable if:
           (i) the actor, with the purpose of causing death or serious bodily harm, provoked the use of force against himself in the same encounter; or
           (ii) the actor knows that he can avoid the necessity of using such force with complete safety by retreating or by surrendering possession of a thing to a person asserting a claim of right thereto or by complying with a demand that he abstain from any action which he has no duty to take, except that:

        (1) the actor is not obliged to retreat from his dwelling or place of work, unless he was the initial aggressor or is assailed in his place of work by another person whose place of work the actor knows it to be; and

        (2) a public officer justified in using force in the performance of his duties or a person justified in using force in his assistance or a person justified in using force in making an arrest or preventing an escape is not obliged to desist from efforts to perform such duty, effect such arrest or prevent such escape because of resistance or threatened resistance by or on behalf of the person against whom such action is directed.

    (c) Except as required by paragraphs (a) and (b) of this Subsection, a person employing protective force may estimate the necessity thereof under the circumstances as he believes them to be when the force is used, without retreating, surrendering possession, doing any other act which he has no legal duty to do or abstaining from any lawful action.

(3) Use of Confinement as Protective Force. The justification afforded by this section extends to the use of confinement as protective force only if the actor takes all reasonable measures to terminate the confinement as soon as he knows that he safely can, unless the person confined has been arrested on a charge of crime.

Section 3.05. Use of Force for the Protection of Other Persons

(1) Subject to the provisions of this Section and of Section 3.09, the use of force upon or toward the person of another is justifiable to protect a third person when:

    (a) the actor would be justified under Section 3.04 in using such force to protect himself against the injury he believes to be threatened to the person whom he seeks to protect; and

    (b) under the circumstances as the actor believes them to be, the person whom he seeks to protect would be justified in using such protective force; and

    (c) the actor believes that his intervention is necessary for the protection of such other person.

(2) Notwithstanding Subsection (1) of this Section:

    (a) when the actor would be obliged under Section 3.04 to retreat, to surrender the possession of a thing or to comply with a demand before using force in self-protection, he is not obliged to do so before using force for the protection of another person, unless he knows that he can thereby secure the complete safety of such other person; and

    (b) when the person whom the actor seeks to protect would be obliged under Section 3.04 to retreat, to surrender the possession of a thing or to comply with a demand if he knew that he could obtain complete safety by so doing, the actor is obliged to try to cause him to do so before using force in his protection if the actor knows that he can obtain complete safety in that way; and

(c) neither the actor nor the person whom he seeks to protect is obliged to retreat when in the other's dwelling or place of work to any greater extent than in his own.

Section 3.06. Use of Force for the Protection of Property

(1) Use of Force Justifiable for Protection of Property. Subject to the provisions of this Section and of Section 3.09, the use of force upon or toward the person of another is justifiable when the actor believes that such force is immediately necessary:

(a) to prevent or terminate an unlawful entry or other trespass upon land or a trespass against or the unlawful carrying away of tangible, movable property, provided that such land or movable property is, or is believed by the actor to be, in his possession or in the possession of another person for whose protection he acts; or

(b) to effect an entry or re-entry upon land or to retake tangible movable property, provided that the actor believes that he or the person by whose authority he acts or a person from whom he or such other person derives title was unlawfully dispossessed of such land or movable property and is entitled to possession, and provided, further, that:

(i) the force is used immediately or on fresh pursuit after such dispossession; or

(ii) the actor believes that the person against whom he uses force has no claim of right to the possession of the property and, in the case of land, the circumstances, as the actor believes them to be, are of such urgency that it would be an exceptional hardship to postpone the entry or re-entry until a court order is obtained.

(2) Meaning of Possession. For the purposes of subsection (1) of this Section:

(a) a person who has parted with the custody of property to another who refuses to restore it to him is no longer in possession, unless the property is movable and was and still is located on land in his possession;

(b) a person who has been dispossessed of land does not regain possession thereof merely by setting foot thereon;

(c) a person who has a license to use or occupy real property is deemed to be in possession thereof except against the licensor acting under claim of right.

(3) Limitations on Justifiable Use of Force.

(a) Request to Desist. The use of force is justifiable under this section only if the actor first requests the person against whom such force is used to desist from his interference with the property, unless the actor believes that:

(i) such request would be useless; or

(ii) it would be dangerous to himself or another person to make the request; or

(iii) substantial harm will be done to the physical condition of the property which is sought to be protected before the request can effectively be made.

(b) Exclusion of Trespasser. The use of force to prevent or terminate a trespass is not justifiable under this Section if the actor knows that the exclusion of the trespasser will expose him to substantial danger of serious bodily harm.

(c) Resistance of Lawful Re-Entry or Recaption. The use of force to prevent an entry or re-entry upon land or the recaption of movable property is not justifiable under this Section, although the actor believes that such re-entry or recaption is unlawful, if:

(i) the re-entry or recaption is made by or on behalf of a person who was actually dispossessed of the property; and

(ii) it is otherwise justifiable under paragraph (1)(b) of this Section.

(d) Use of Deadly Force. The use of deadly force is not justifiable under this Section unless the actor believes that:

(i) the person against whom the force is used is attempting to dispossess him of his dwelling otherwise than under a claim of right to its possession; or

(ii) the person against whom the force is used is attempting to commit or consummate arson, burglary, robbery or other felonious theft or property destruction and either:

(1) has employed or threatened deadly force against or in the presence of the actor; or

(2) the use of force other than deadly force to prevent the commission or the consummation of the crime would expose the actor or another in his presence to substantial danger of serious bodily harm.

(4) Use of Confinement as Protective Force. The justification afforded by this Section extends to the use of confinement as protective force only if the actor takes all reasonable measures to terminate the confinement as soon as he knows that he can do so with safety to the property, unless the person confined has been arrested on a charge of crime.

(5) Use of Device to Protect Property. The justification afforded by this Section extends to the use of a device for the purpose of protecting property only if:

(a) the device is not designed to cause or known to create a substantial risk of causing death or serious bodily harm; and

(b) the use of the particular device to protect the property from entry or trespass is reasonable under the circumstances, as the actor believes them to be; and

(c) the device is one customarily used for such a purpose or reasonable care is taken to make known to probable intruders the fact that it is used.

(6) Use of Force to Pass Wrongful Obstructor. The use of force to pass a person who the actor believes to be purposely or knowingly and unjustifiably obstructing the actor from going to a place to which he may lawfully go is justifiable, provided that:

(a) the actor believes that the person against whom he uses force has no claim of right to obstruct the actor; and

(b) the actor is not being obstructed from entry or movement on land which he knows to be in the possession or custody of the person obstructing him, or in the possession or custody of another person by whose authority the obstructor acts, unless the circumstances, as the actor believes them to be, are of such urgency that it would not be reasonable to postpone the entry or movement on such land until a court order is obtained; and

(c) the force used is not greater than would be justifiable if the person obstructing the actor were using force against him to prevent his passage.

● OVERVIEW OF DEFENSIVE FORCE JUSTIFICATIONS

Hypothetical: Rosie's Home Run (#86)

Rosie is playing ball with her friends in a vacant lot. In the bottom of the third, she hits a home run off Spano's fastball. "I'm dangerous low and inside," she yells to Spano as she rounds first at full tilt.

"I guess so," responds Spano with a smirk. "You just got Logan's window."

Sure enough, the ball has gone through Mr. Logan's bathroom window. Worse yet, Logan is screaming out of the window, shaking a fist with one hand and holding his eye with the other. "Game's over," Rosie yells as she rounds second and heads for her house.

As she slips through the front door, her mother and her mother's new boyfriend, Frankie, quickly sit up on the couch, clearing their throats and arranging their clothes. "How's it going, Rosie?" Frankie asks, a little too loudly. "Game over so soon?"

"Yeah, I hit the ball through Logan's window and I don't think he's in the mood to give it back."

"You leave it to me, Kitten. I'll talk to the bum. I'll have you guys playing ball again in no time."

"Not a good idea, Frankie, he's really pissed."

"Yeah? We'll see how tough he is." He turns to Rosie's mom, "I'll take care of this for you, Poopsy."

Frankie, who is 6 feet tall and weighs 210 pounds, walks up on Logan's porch and pounds on the front door. "Let's have that ball, Logan," he bellows. Logan pulls open the door and rushes out. He is 6 feet, 3 inches tall, and 230 pounds. "Get off my f——— porch. The only way you'll get this ball back is if I stick it up your a———."

Frankie, who takes two steps back in surprise when Logan rushes out, is momentarily speechless. He looks behind him to see who is watching and catches Rosie on the sidewalk looking up at him. He looks back to Logan, "Give me that ball, m——— f———, or you're dead meat." Frankie grabs the ball from Logan's hands. Logan tries to wrestle the ball away. Frankie punches Logan in the face, but Logan knees Frankie in the chest and smashes him on the back of the head with his two hands cupping the ball. Frankie goes down hard, hitting his head on the cinder block wall. He doesn't move. Someone calls an ambulance. Frankie dies at the hospital from head injuries suffered in the fall.[1]

Logan is charged with manslaughter. Is he liable?

Notes

Triggering Conditions
    Requirement of Physical Aggression
    Distinguishing Aggressive from Defensive Conduct
        Establishing Rules to Guide Finding of Defensiveness
        "Aggressors" Who Are Not Immediate Source of Threat
    Threatened Harm Must Be Unjustified
    Common Reference to "Unlawful," Rather Than "Unjustified," Force
    Resisting Conduct for Which Aggressor Has Defense
        Different Rule for Resisting Justified Conduct
    MPC Formulation Distinguishes "Privileged" and "Unprivileged" Justified Force
        Criticisms of Code's FormUlation
        Superiority of Distinguishing Objective Justification from Subjective Mistake
Necessity and Proportionality
    Necessity Requirement
    Comparison to Lesser Evils Necessity Requirement
    Necessity and Defense of Others
    Proportionality: Statutory Rules Codify Proper Balance of Interests
        Concern Not Only with Direct Harm, but Also Disapproval of Aggression
        Central Proportionality Issue for Defensive Force: When to Allow Deadly Force
        Deadly Force in Defense of Property Is Not Justified
        Deadly Force in Self-DefEnse: Weighing Defender's Life Over Aggressor's?
    Legislating Specific Limits on Defenses
        Retreat And Request to Desist Consistent with Necessity Principle
        Requiring Threat of Serious Harm Consistent with Proportionality
        Other Special Rules Depart From, or Alter, Normal Principles
    Desirability of Specific Versus General Justification Rules
        Seeking Consistency between Special Rules and General Requirements
    Summary of Hypothetical Analysis
    Shifting Right of Defense

Defensive force justifications provide a defense for the use of force necessary to protect persons or property from unjustified aggression. Three such defenses traditionally are recognized: self-defense, defense of another, and defense of property. (Some jurisdictions recognize a special defense of premises, and some combine self-defense and defense of another into a general defense-of-person formulation.[2]) These defenses reflect the same internal structure of other justifications: *triggering conditions* authorizing responsive force that must be *necessary* to protect against, and *proportional* in relation to, the harm threatened.

---

1. The facts are a variation on State v. Griffith, 589 P.2d 799 (Wash. 1979).

2. As to defense of premises, see, e.g., N.Y. Penal Law § 35.20; see also Model Penal Code § 3.06(3)(d)(I) (special force authorized for defense of dwelling). As to combined self-defense and defense of others, see, e.g., 720 Ill. Ann. Stat. 5/7-1; N.H. Rev. Stat. Ann. § 627:4.

aggressive physical use or threat of force

Defensive force justification

public authority justifications

TRIGGERING CONDITIONS

A defensive force justification is triggered when an aggressor unjustifiably threatens harm to persons or property. The name of each defense identifies the relevant threatened interest: self-defense, defense of others, and defense of property. These triggering conditions—requiring an unlawful, aggressive use (or threat) of force—are considerably more specific than those for the lesser evils or public authority justifications, which generally are triggered by any need to protect or further a public interest.

Requirement of Physical Aggression   That the person against whom the actor uses force is acting unlawfully is not sufficient to trigger a defensive force justification. Smoking on a bus or refusing to get out of the way of an emergency vehicle may be unlawful conduct and may even justify the use of force against the violator under some other defense (probably a public authority justification), but the defensive force defenses will not apply. For defensive force, active physical aggression is required. In the "Rosie's Home Run" hypothetical above, Logan will argue that Frankie was an unlawful aggressor, but a number of questions cloud this issue, as discussed below.

Distinguishing Aggressive from Defensive Conduct   The defensive character of an actor's conduct provides much of the rationale for these justifications. In practice, however, this critical distinction between defense and aggression can be unclear. Suppose *A* breaks into *B*'s house to steal his television. *B* discovers *A* in the act and wrestles with him, but *A* breaks loose and, still carrying the set, bolts for the door. Further action by *B* would, in a narrow sense, constitute aggressive rather than defensive action. *A* has physical possession of the television; *B*'s conduct would constitute an attempt to take it away from *A*. Even so, a strong argument can be made that, given the brief interval of *A*'s actual possession, *B*'s conduct is still essentially defensive. If, on the other hand, *B* tracks *A* for several days before attempting recapture, his conduct might now be characterized as aggressive, and thus outside the protection of the defensive force justifications. It is probably impossible to define a precise point where a struggle for repossession shifts from defensive to offensive.

Establishing Rules to Guide Finding of Defensiveness   Given the variety of possible factual situations, a careful study of each case as it arises seems preferable to drafting a universally applicable rule. At the very least, it would seem appropriate to require that the conduct of "recapture" offer some objective and intuitive indication of being defensive. (It is the appearance of a defense to another's aggression, after all, that weighs in favor of justifying the responsive force.) In establishing the justification for use of force to protect property, for example, the Model Penal Code creates a rule that property that another person has taken, but that is still located on the land of the person seeking to retain (or retake) it, remains in the landowner's "possession" so that the landowner may use force against the person who has taken it.[3] In the "Rosie's Home Run" hypothetical, Logan would still have access to a defense-of-property justification, even though Frankie had taken control of the ball at the moment and Logan was trying to get it back.

"Aggressors" Who Are Not Immediate Source of Threat   Defensive force justifications may extend to justify force against people other than the one most

---

3. Model Penal Code § 3.06(2)(a).

immediately applying the aggressive force or threat. Suppose that L, an underworld gang leader, orders one of his underlings, Υ, to kill D while both L and Υ are in D's presence. Suppose further that only L is vulnerable to D's defensive force (Υ is wearing a bulletproof vest) and that Υ will act only while L is alive. Although Υ presents the immediate threat, L is equally, or more, responsible for the presence of the threat. In one sense, Υ is simply L's instrument in making the attack. If D kills Υ, L may order someone else to do the job, and the threat to D will continue. Should D be able to claim self-defense, then, against L as well as against Υ, although L does not fit the traditional view of an aggressor? Many would think yes.

Threatened Harm Must Be Unjustified To trigger a defensive force justification, the aggressor must *unjustifiably* threaten harm to the actor. Thus, when a police officer uses justified force to effect an arrest, the arrestee has no right of self-defense, and others may not lawfully use defensive force on his behalf. Similarly, where one actor unjustifiably attacks another and his victim then uses (justified) defensive force to repel the attack, the initial aggressor has no right of self-defense against the justified response. On the other hand, where the intended victim uses unnecessary or disproportionate force in response—and hence is unjustified—the initial aggressor regains a right to use defensive force.

Common Reference to "Unlawful," Rather Than "Unjustified," Force A common formulation of defensive force triggering conditions permits an actor to defend only against "unlawful force." This is the language of the Model Penal Code.[4] There is the potential for confusion in this language, however, because some threats may be "lawful"—in the sense that the aggressor cannot be held criminally liable for the attack—yet still trigger a defensive force justification. Such is the case, for example, where the aggressor is not liable for the use of force because he lacks the required culpability for an offense (for example, if the aggressor is mistaken about the facts of the situation) or because he has an excuse for the aggressive conduct (for example, if the aggressor is insane or acting under duress). In these cases, the victim ought to be able lawfully to defend, even though the aggressor would face no liability for attack. Unfortunately, the phrase "unlawful force," by itself, can be misleading on this point. What is needed is a clear description of what kinds of defenses an aggressor might have that will allow a victim justifiably to defend, and what kind will not. What kind of aggressor defenses should bar a victim's defensive force?

Resisting Conduct for Which Aggressor Has Defense The soundest answer seems to be that a victim should be able to defend against an attack unless the aggressor is justified, in an objective sense. Thus, where an actor has an absent-element or offense-modification defense that hinges on the absence of a required culpability element, the objective elements of the offense are still satisfied, so the aggressor's attack properly may be resisted. Even though the attacker or apparent thief acts inadvertently due to mistake or intoxication, he properly is subject to defensive force. Of course, such an actor might be stopped with a simple, "excuse me, that is my umbrella," in which case using force would be unjustified (because unnecessary), as discussed below. Similarly, it should be lawful to resist

(handwritten margin notes:)
P1 unj attack
P2 just. defe force
P1 no right of self defense

P1 unj attack
P2 unj. def. force
P1 has right to self defense

---

an aggressor who has an excuse defense. The victim of a psychotic attacker should be able lawfully to defend herself and to have others assist in such defense. While the aggressor ultimately may be judged blameless, his conduct is clearly harmful and unjustified. When an attacker has only a nonexculpatory defense, such as diplomatic immunity, the case is clearest for permitting, indeed encouraging, resistance and interference. The conduct is harmful; the actor may be blameworthy. The immune diplomat may escape conviction for an unjustified and unexcused attack, but it hardly follows that the victim is bound to submit or the observer to acquiesce.

Different Rule for Resisting Justified Conduct   Where an aggressor has a justification defense, in contrast, the rule should be different: Justified aggression cannot be lawfully subject to resistance or interference. When conduct is objectively justified, it is by definition conduct that follows the rules of conduct (conduct that does not create a net harm or evil for society). The owner of a field should not be allowed to resist one who would burn the field to stop a spreading fire, and others should be encouraged to assist the burning and should not be permitted to interfere with it.

MPC Formulation Distinguishes "Privileged" and "Unprivileged" Justified Force   As noted above, the Model Penal Code authorizes defensive force only to defend against "unlawful" force. This provision, by itself, might seem too narrow, for it might be interpreted to bar a justification for resisting an attacker who has an excuse, a nonexculpatory defense, or an absent-element or offense-modification defense based on lack of culpability. But the Code drafters understand the distinctions that the law should make. Their "unlawful force" formulation does in fact give the results that it should, albeit through a rather awkward definition. Section 3.11(1) defines "unlawful force" to mean:

> force, . . . the employment of which constitutes an offense or actionable tort or would constitute such offense or tort except for a defense (such as the absence of intent, negligence, or mental capacity; duress; youth; or diplomatic status) not amounting to a privilege to use force.

The language of the definition seems consistent with the conclusions of the analysis above as to what kinds of attacks can justifiably be resisted. It includes within "unlawful force" aggression for which the actor has a "defense . . . such as the absence of . . . mental capacity; duress; [or] youth"—that is, an excuse; or "a defense . . . such as . . . diplomatic status" —that is, a nonexculpatory defense; or "a defense . . . such as the absence of intent [or] negligence" —that is, an absent-element or offense-modification defense based upon absence of culpability. By including such aggression within the definition of "unlawful force," the Model Penal Code formulation permits resistance to, and interference with, such aggression, as it should. Moreover, by including within the "unlawful force" definition "a defense . . . not amounting to a privilege," the provision suggests by implication that force "amounting to a privilege" is not "unlawful force" and, therefore, cannot lawfully be resisted—again the proper result, assuming that the drafters intend the phrase "privileged" force to mean objectively justified force.

Criticisms of Code's Formulation   The Code's provision is subject to several criticisms. First, such important distinctions as those defining the force that lawfully may be resisted ought not be hidden in a definitional section, for many lawyers and courts will miss it there. Second, as the previous discussion illustrates, even when discovered, the provision is a bit difficult to digest. Even several readings can lead to a misinterpretation. This is partly because the provision offers illustrations of the defenses that should be categorized as "unlawful force," but fails to provide a conceptual framework to classify or explain the illustrations. How is one to extrapolate from the illustrations provided to cases not addressed? Without a conceptual framework or principled categories, the Code drafters leave ambiguity as to which defenses are meant to be included and which excluded. Third, the Code never defines which defenses are those "amounting to a privilege." Independent reasoning is needed to infer that they apparently mean objective justifications.

Superiority of Distinguishing Objective Justification from Subjective Mistake In the end, the Code is forced to rely on a concept ("privilege") borrowed from tort law, because its own definition of "justification" makes it impossible to use that term in this context. The concept of "justification" the Code uses in its justification defense formulations includes both objective justification (what they call here "privilege") and subjective (that is, mistaken) justification: Throughout Article 3, the Code defines conduct as "justified" if the actor *believes* that it is justified. This approach—subjectivizing the formulation of justification defenses to find an actor "justified" even if he only mistakenly "believes" that he is justified— makes it impossible for the Code to easily distinguish the cases of objective (actual) justification and subjective (mistaken) justification. This is highly unfortunate, for the distinction is of great practical importance: Objectively justified conduct may not lawfully be resisted, but subjectively "justified" conduct may be. The better approach is that of the Draft Code of the National Commission: Define justification defenses objectively and provide a separate mistake provision that recognizes an *excuse* for reasonable mistakes as to a justification.[5] Under this approach, the

---

5. The National Commission's Draft Code formulated justifications objectively and provided a separate mistake excuse defense:

§ 603. Self-Defense

A person is justified in using force upon another person in order to defend himself against danger of imminent unlawful bodily injury, sexual assault or detention by such other person, except that:

(a) a person is not justified in using force for the purpose of resisting arrest, execution of process, or other performance of duty by a public servant under color of law, but excessive force may be resisted; and

(b) a person is not justified in using force if (i) he intentionally provokes unlawful action by another person in order to cause bodily injury or death to such other person, or (ii) he has entered into a mutual combat with another person or is the initial aggressor unless he is resisting force which is clearly excessive in the circumstances. A person's use of defensive force after he withdraws from an encounter and indicates to the other person that he has done so is justified if the latter nevertheless continues or menaces unlawful action.

§ 608. Excuse

(1) Mistake. A person's conduct is excused if he believes that the factual situation is such that his conduct is necessary and appropriate for any of the purposes which would establish a justification or excuse under this Chapter, even though his belief is mistaken, except that, if his belief is negligently or recklessly held, it is not an excuse in a prosecution for an offense for which negligence or recklessness, as the cause may be, suffices to establish culpability. Excuse under this subsection is a defense or affirmative defense according to which type of defense would be established had the facts been as the person believed them to be.

(2) Marginal Transgression of Limit of Justification. A person's conduct is excused if it would otherwise be justified or excused under this Chapter but is marginally hasty or excessive because he was confronted with an emergency precluding adequate appraisal or measured reaction.

Final Report of the National Commission on Reform of Federal Criminal Laws (1971).

triggering conditions of defensive force defenses may be defined clearly and simply: A right to use defensive force is triggered by an "unjustified" threat of force.

NECESSITY AND PROPORTIONALITY

As noted above, an unjustified threat to person or property triggers the right to use defensive force. The scope of this right is limited, however, by the requirements that only *necessary* and *proportional* force is allowed.

Necessity Requirement A common formulation of self-defense, for example, gives the actor the right to act when "such force is necessary to defend himself."[6] This necessity requirement includes two essential parts: Force may be used only (1) when necessary and (2) to the extent necessary. The actor may not use force when such force would be equally effective at a later time and the actor suffers no harm or risk by waiting. Nor may an actor use more force than is necessary for the defensive purpose. If the threat can be averted without force or with lesser force, the greater force is not justified.

Comparison to Lesser Evils Necessity Requirement The defensive force justifications typically contain an explicit necessity requirement and often include a specific temporal dimension to the requirement. The Model Penal Code, for example, requires that the force be "immediately necessary" to protect the person or property. (The common law and some codifications require that the threat be "imminent," which is a problematic formulation.) Thus, the necessity requirement in defensive force apparently is meant to be stricter in some sense than it is in lesser evils, where the conduct need only be "necessary."

Necessity and Defense of Others The Model Penal Code's defense-of-others provision allows the use of force when the actor (1) would be justified in using such force to defend himself, and (2) the person being defended would also be justified in using such force to defend himself.[7] However, the extent of force allowed in defending another may vary based on differences between the actor and the person being defended. If, for example, the person being defended is a world-class Judo competitor, the third-party defender is not justified in using deadly force if the Judo master could simply subdue the attacker without using deadly force. This is true even though, if the defender were in the Judo master's position (that is, facing a similar attack), he would be justified in using deadly force to defend himself. Similarly, if the defender of the victim is the Judo master, she may not use deadly force to protect another when she could subdue the attacker instead, even though the intended victim would be justified in using deadly force in self-defense.

Proportionality: Statutory Rules Codify Proper Balance of Interests The proportionality requirement also is apparent in defensive force justifications, but it differs from the proportionality rule for lesser evils. Rather than empowering juries to determine ad hoc the appropriate balance of conflicting interests in individual cases, as the open and explicit proportionality requirement of the lesser evils defense does, defensive force justifications impose specific rules reflecting a legislative predetermination of the proper balance. (This contrast may help explain why many legislatures are hesitant to formally codify the lesser evils defense; for

---

6. 2 Paul H. Robinson, *Criminal Law Defenses* § 131(c) n.18 (1984).
7. Model Penal Code §§ 3.05(1)(a) and 3.05(1)(b).

fear that it would too easily give juries a power to balance interests that the legislature wishes to reserve for itself.)

Concern Not Only with Direct Harm, but Also Disapproval of Aggression The competing interests in defensive force cases typically include more than tangible, physical harms. The legislative balancing weighs important intangible interests as well—in particular, society's abhorrence of unjustified aggression. In the balance of interests, such aggression may count against the aggressor, discounting the value of the aggressor's life relative to the nonaggressor or, in perhaps a better characterization of the analytic process, counting the unjustified aggressive force as a greater harm or evil than the reactive force, even if the objective magnitude of the forces are equivalent (such as a gunshot in response to a gunshot).

Central Proportionality Issue for Defensive Force: When to Allow Deadly Force The most significant issues in the legislative proportionality determination revolve around when to allow the use of *deadly force*. Frequently criminal codes will allow the use of "force"—a term that, interestingly, usually is left undefined—whenever necessary to defend a protected interest in person or property, but will impose limitations on the use of deadly force. Even when deadly force is necessary to defend a legitimate legal interest, these rules may prohibit its use on the ground that it is disproportionate in relation to the threat.

Deadly Force in Defense of Property Is Not Justified Legislative concern for proportionality is particularly obvious in the rules for governing defense of property. Recall the general structure of the defense: An aggressor who threatens property rights (by attempting to steal or destroy another's property) triggers a right to use physical force if necessary to resist the threat. But how much physical force against the oppressor is allowed to defend property—given that injury to a person is typically regarded as more serious than injury to property? That is the proportionality question. In this situation, the harm of physical injury to the aggressor (say, a thief) is balanced against both the owner's interest in retaining the threatened property, and society's general interests in preserving property rights and condemning unjustified aggression. The intangible societal interests may be more important in this balancing than the individual owner's interests. But even the combined weight of these important societal interests has a limit, and the taking of a human life is generally understood to exceed that limit. A human life, even that of a thief, is seen as having greater value than property rights and the deterrence of aggression against property. Accordingly, all American criminal codes bar the use of deadly force solely to defend property rather than personal safety. Looking at the "Rosie's Home Run" hypothetical, this rule might seem to be bad news for Logan, who has killed Frankie in defense of a baseball. However, he may argue that his use of force was not in protection of property, but rather a defense of his own safety against an unlawful threat from Frankie.

Deadly Force in Self-Defense: Weighing Defender's Life Over Aggressor's? The same balancing principles apply when the actor kills another to save his own life. Self-defense, however, is unique among defensive force justifications and can be conceptually troublesome. By definition only one human life is at stake on the side of the actor relying on self-defense; if there are more, a defense-of-others justification would apply. This presents a difficult situation: A balance of one life against one life, the aggressor against the defender, demands complete reliance on intangible societal interests to break the deadlock. There is no reason, however, that the method of analysis should vary. The community generally gives due weight to the intangible interests—protecting personal autonomy and condemning and deterring unjustified aggression—to tip the balance in favor if the defender's life over the aggressor's life, and thereby permit killing the aggressor. Most jurisdictions extend the analysis to allow use of deadly force to defend against unjustified threats not only of death, but also of serious bodily injury. Thus, in the "Home Run" hypothetical, if Logan can show that Frankie's aggression posed an unjustified threat of serious bodily injury, Logan would be justified in using deadly force to defend (that is, he may use force that creates a substantial risk of death or serious bodily injury).

Legislating Specific Limits on Defense Rules   The proportionality concern also is reflected in a variety of other rules that limit defensive force justifications. For example, defense provisions typically require that one must suffer an unlawful arrest rather than use force against a police officer and one must give up one's right to be in a particular public place before one can use deadly force (called the "retreat rule"). In some of the special rules, the legislature seeks only to make explicit what the requirements of necessity and proportionality normally would demand if properly applied. The special rule is useful in increasing uniformity and predictability in adjudication. In other instances, the legislature's special rule alters the result that the general principles would otherwise generate.

Retreat and Request to Desist Consistent with Necessity Principle   The common requirement that an actor must retreat rather than use deadly force, if the actor can do so in complete safety,[8] is consistent with what the necessity requirement generally would require. Where an actor fails to take an opportunity safely to retreat, the killing would not be the least harmful means of avoiding the threatened harm. Similarly, the requirement that an actor request the aggressor to desist[9] simply states more specifically what would already follow from the necessity requirement; the use of force is not *necessary* if a request to desist would stop the aggression.

Requiring Threat of Serious Harm Consistent with Proportionality   Typically, an actor may not use deadly force except to defend against the threat of death or serious bodily harm.[10] Such a limit is consistent with the usual proportionality principle; a human life, even that of an aggressor, is of greater value than the actor's right to stand his ground or avoid only minor injury. Similarly, the rule prohibiting the use of deadly force in defense of property, noted above, merely states explicitly what the general principle of proportionality would require. To be clear, the Code and other modern codes do permit deadly force to protect property, but only if the aggressor either is attempting to dispossess the actor of the actor's dwelling, or is committing one of certain enumerated offenses and has used or threatened deadly force. These exceptions also naturally follow from application of the general principle of proportionality, for such situations are likely to involve danger to persons as well as property.

Other Special Rules Depart From, or Alter, Normal Principles   Not all special rules are consistent with the standard defensive force requirements inherent in the basic triggering conditions, necessity, and proportionality requirements. For

---

8. See Model Penal Code § 3.04(2)(b); 2 Paul H. Robinson, *Criminal Law Defenses* § 131(d)(3).

9. See Model Penal Code § 3.06(3)(a).

10. See Model Penal Code § 3.04(2)(b); 2 Paul H. Robinson, *Criminal Law Defenses* § 131(d)(2) (1984).

example, special rules bar the use of defensive force to resist an unlawful arrest or to take possession from one unlawfully resisting under a mistaken claim of right.[11] These rules do alter the results that would follow from application of the general principle of self-defense: The general principle would allow an actor to resist "unlawful" force, including an unlawful arrest and an attempt to retain unlawful possession of property. The theory behind these modifications is that it is better to have the defendant sacrifice his or her lawful right to use defensive force than to allow the use of force and thereby invite retaliation, potentially resulting in injury to one or both parties. Determining the unlawfulness of the arrest or the possession, it is argued, is better left to a formal court proceeding, though this may necessitate a temporary deprivation of the victim's rights.

Desirability of Specific vs. General Justification Rules Given the frequency with which defensive force situations arise, at least relative to lesser evils situations, these special rules are no doubt valuable in improving consistency in the disposition of similar cases. In addition, it may be better to have the legislature codify the balancing of interests reflected in the proportionality judgment, rather than leaving that balancing to the judgment of individual judges or juries. On the other hand, the rules seem too complex reasonably to expect that an actor can refer to them for guidance at the moment he or she must decide whether to use defensive force. The conflict between these goals illustrates the tension that commonly arises because of the criminal law's dual functions of stating ex ante rules of conduct to guide the public's behavior and articulating principles of ex post adjudication in the criminal justice process.

Seeking Consistency between Special Rule and General Requirements While it seems unlikely that a citizen can know these special rules and follow them at the moment he is responding to an aggressor, a citizen might well be expected to appreciate and act according to the general requirements of necessity and proportionality, especially since these fundamental requirements appear to correspond to our intuitive notions of justice. One might argue, then, that special rules that do not alter the results of the general requirements of necessity and proportionality are desirable in all respects. They announce rules for future conduct that we can reasonably expect will be followed and they increase the consistency and ease of adjudication. In contrast, special rules that attempt to alter the results of the general principles can lead to unfairness to the many actors who cannot reasonably be expected to know or follow such rules. The more detailed the rules, the less likely they can be expected to affect people's conduct. The more they deviate from basic principles, the greater the likelihood of injustice.

Summary of Hypothetical Analysis To summarize the analysis of Logan's liability in the "Rosie's Home Run" hypothetical, Frankie's initial use of force against Logan in grabbing the ball appears to be unjustified; the initial owner may use force to recapture only if she was "unlawfully dispossessed," which Rosie was not. Thus, Logan's use of force to resist Frankie is justified, and Frankie's punching Logan in the face is unjustified. If the punch threatened serious bodily harm, Logan would be entitled to use deadly force in defending against it. (Note that although Frankie did die as a result of Logan's use of force, it is by no

---

11. See Model Penal Code § 3.04(2)(a).

means clear that Logan was using "deadly force"—the death may have been an unfortunate and unforeseeable accident.)

Shifting Right of Defense   The hypothetical's analysis reflects what might be called the potential "shifting right of self-defense": Whether use of defensive force is justified depends on whether the threat is justified, which in turn may depend on whether the threat to which that threat responds is justified. A justified actor will retain a right to use defensive force as long as he remains within the limits of justification. If he exceeds those limits, the right of self-defense may shift to the other party.

Judgment of the German Supreme Court of September 20, 1920
55 Decisions of the Supreme Court in Criminal Matters 82

The defendant held watch during the night in a shed amidst his fruit trees; he was accompanied by his dog and armed with a loaded rifle. In the early morning, he noticed two men taking fruit from his trees. Upon hearing the defendant both thieves took flight with the fruit that they had picked; the defendant shouted to both of them to halt and he threatened to shoot. When they did not stop, the defendant fired buckshots in their direction and injured one of them, not insignificantly. One may surmise from the judgment below that this result was intended by the defendant. The defendant was charged with intentional battery and was acquitted on the ground that he acted in self-defense. The trial court assumed that the defendant justifiably used force to regain the fruit and that there was "no other means" except the firing of the shot to force the thieves to stop thereby to regain the property. In appealing the decision, the prosecutor argued that this was not justly to be considered a case of self-defense (Notwehr); for at the moment that the shot was fired the thieves had completed their attack upon the defendant's property and had begun to flee from the scene of the crime. This meant that the risk to the defendant's property was no longer "imminent." The prosecutor also argued that the defendant used excessive defensive force because the fruit in question was an insignificant interest and the defendant endangered lives and health of the fleeing persons, and thereby thought to sacrifice the higher interest to save the lower.

This appeal does not prevail [i.e., acquittal affirmed]. . . .

If the defendant fired the shot in order to protect his property and the fruit, and if the defendant had no other equally effective means to this end, then this is a case of permissible defense against an imminent attack against property and possession. The legal conclusions of the trial court are therefore unexceptionable.

The attack of the thieves had not yet ended; and this would be true even if it is assumed that the act of theft had already been completed. So long as the thieves and the property they were stealing could be reached by the defendant, the defendant's act is to be construed as a defense against a continuing attack. . . . The use of defensive force against a continuing attack against property requires only that the force be fitted to the circumstances of the case, which means that no more force be used to achieve the permitted goal than is "necessary." Whether that requirement is satisfied, is a question for the trier-of-fact. . . . The opinion is occasionally expressed that the degree of permissible force should be determined not only by the severity of the attack and the available defensive means, but also by the principle that to preserve a minor interest one may not force the assailant to sacrifice a valuable interest. If this were the case, defensive force involving attacks upon life and bodily integrity would simply not be available against thieves. So weighing the relative merit of competing interests could not possibly be justified where someone in the Right is locked in struggle against someone in the Wrong; it is not to be expected of the party exercising the defensive force that in protecting his rights against a [wrongfully] acting assailant, he limit the harm he causes to the amount that is threatened to him by the [unjustified] attack. If that were the law governing the case in which one had to protect one's property or possession by threatening the life or bodily security of the assailant, the decision to fight on behalf of a relatively insignificant interest would frequently depend upon moral views, sensibilities of justice, and other views held by the party under attack. Accordingly, men might frequently choose not to endanger the lives of others and suffer the loss of their rights and thereby tolerate [unlawfulness]. . . . [The] statutory law does not provide any support for the view that the relative value of the conflicting interests imposes a limitation on the right of self-defense. The balancing of values may be justified where the conflict is between two rights, but not in a case in which balancing would serve to protect [unlawfulness] and would represent a limitation on the use of defensive force against attacks upon interests of a particular sort, and thus make the degree of defensive force dependent on the harm that might occur to the [wrongfully] acting assailant. . . .

▲ PROBLEMS

Archery and Arson in the Garage (#87)

For $150 a month, Michael Fairall rents the garage in Melody Downes's home, which houses a number of other tenants as well. He installs a loft bed and moves in his few possessions. Unable to meet his rent one month, he gives Melody his stereo in lieu of payment. Fairall believes that he is simply lending it to her as a goodwill gesture, seeing as there is no stereo in the house. Downes, however, thinks that she has been given the stereo and proceeds to sell it in order to recoup the missing rent. When Fairall discovers that his stereo has been sold, he goes ballistic. Fairall smashes in the windows of Downes's car, slashes the tires, and dents the body. He then returns to the house, trashes Downes's room, and frees her pet snake.

Downes goes to housemate Kelsey Gleghorn for help. She tells him everything that has happened, hoping that he will retaliate against Fairall. Gleghorn is enraged by Fairall's actions and goes to the garage to settle the matter. Fairall is sleeping in his loft. Gleghorn pounds on the garage door, screaming that he will kill him. Receiving no answer, Gleghorn breaks into the garage and begins hitting the support beams of the loft with a large stick. Fairall ignores him until Gleghorn lights a pile of Fairall's clothing on fire. Gleghorn tells Fairall that he can either come down or burn to death. Fairall, now taking Gleghorn's threats seriously, grabs his bow and arrow, which he keeps by his bed, and shoots an arrow through the smoke in the direction of Gleghorn's voice. He then descends from the loft. When he gets down, he realizes that the arrow has lodged in Gleghorn's back. Despite the arrow in his back Gleghorn nonetheless attacks Fairall as soon as he steps off the ladder. Hitting him repeatedly with the stick, Gleghorn breaks Fairall's jaw, tears his lips, knocks out nearly a dozen teeth and causes lacerations over much of Fairall's body. Fairall also suffers burns on his hands from trying to put out the fire that Gleghorn had started.

What liability for Gleghorn, if any, under the Model Penal Code? Prepare a list of all criminal code subsections in the order in which you rely on them in your analysis.

A Homemade Burglary System (#88)

George O's is a small tavern in Aurora, Illinois. The bar has many regulars, known by both the bartender and the owner, Jesse Ingram. The small wooden building is painted red with white trim, has four windows and two doors, and has such a quaint and familiar atmosphere that its patrons leave their money on top of the register and walk out. However, while the bar has no troubles during operating hours, it has recently been the target of several break-ins, which have cost Ingram thousands of dollars. Ingram purchases a silent alarm and video surveillance system, but George O's is burglarized three more times within weeks of installing the new security measures. Though the video system captures images of the thief, the police are unable to catch a suspect.

Ingram therefore decides to install his own security system. He places metal bars around the bar's two doorframes and under its four window sills. He then connects the metal bars to the tavern's 220-volt electrical system. His goal is to stun potential burglars long enough for the police to respond to the silent alarm. Ingram discusses the plan with a few electricians and is reassured that it will not cause serious harm to the burglar.

Less than a week later, the system is triggered by Lenny Harris as he attempts to burglarize the bar at night. When the police respond to the silent alarm, they find Harris's body lying on the floor of the tavern below a window that he had forced open. Harris died after the shock from the security system caused his heart to stop beating.

What liability for Ingram, if any, under the Model Penal Code for Harris' death? Prepare a list of all criminal code subsections in the order in which you rely on them in your analysis.

In Defense of an Unborn (#89)

Jaclyn Kurr and her boyfriend, Antonio Pena, have a rocky relationship. Pena is heavily into drugs, including cocaine, and is often violent. Kurr, afraid of how Pena might react, has rarely confronted him about the drugs or the violence. However, things change after Kurr becomes pregnant with multiple fetuses. She realizes that she can no longer put up with his behavior, for her children's sake if not for her own. She wants her children to grow up in a safe and drug-free environment.

She confronts Pena on the matter, telling him that she will leave unless he stops abusing drugs. He reacts violently, just as she feared. He punches Kurr twice in the stomach. She yells at him not to hit her because she is pregnant with his babies, but Pena does not listen and comes at Kurr again. Fearing for the safety of her fetuses, which are not yet viable, Kurr grabs a knife and stabs Pena in the chest, killing him.

What liability for Kurr, if any, under the Model Penal Code? Prepare a list of all criminal code subsections in the order in which you rely on them in your analysis.

---

* **DISCUSSION ISSUE**

Should the Criminal Law Give a Defense for the Use of Whatever Force Is Necessary to Defend Persons or Property Against an Unlawful Attack? Or, Should the Law Deny a Defense if the Force, Even Though Necessary for Defense, Would Injure Interests Greater Than Those Injured by the Unlawful Attack?

Materials presenting each side of this Discussion Issue appear in the Advanced Materials for Section 18 in Appendix A.

Mistake as to a Justification

The previous three Sections have addressed the conditions under which a person's conduct is actually, objectively justified—that is, the conditions under which the law would be happy to have (or at least tolerant of having) the person and other persons engage in the same conduct under the same circumstances in the future. But it is commonly the case that a person is mistaken in the belief that her conduct is justified, typically because she misperceives the actual situation. When should such mistaken justification be a defense, and what kind of defense should it be—a justification or an excuse?

◆ THE CASE OF RICHARD JOHN JAHNKE, JR. (#90)

Richard Jahnke, Jr., is a sixteen-year-old R.O.T.C. student in Laramie, Wyoming—a handsome, sensitive, all-American boy who has never been in trouble. Lately, however, Jahnke has been doing poorly in school. The problem is the cumulative effect of years of physical and mental abuse at the hands of his father. Himself a victim of child abuse, Richard Jahnke, Sr., is cruel and insensitive and a bully to his family, and has been for years. As a result, Jahnke, Jr., is frequently on edge and feels as though he lives in a state of near-constant danger.

The beatings are torturous. His father punches his back, slaps his head, and slams him into whatever surface is nearby. Jahnke has asthma, and his father commonly beats him to make him stop coughing. A beating also can be triggered for not finishing his food. (The children eat with plastic forks because the father thinks metal ones are too loud.) Jahnke's mother recalls that her husband was once a caring young soldier. He is now an I.R.S. investigator, and things are quite different.

One of Jahnke's early memories is of his father breaking a toy boat. With his father screaming and chasing his five-year-old son, Jahnke's mother stepped in to shield him from the blows. His father then beat his mother while calling her a slut and insulting her Mexican heritage. Jahnke, beaten almost daily, felt that his father enjoyed it. His father would whip him with a belt for walking with his mouth open and hit him even harder if he cried.

As Jahnke grew up, the beatings came slightly less frequently, though they were still violent. His father had become preoccupied with his older sister, Deborah. He began watching her in the shower and rubbing her breasts and groping her as discipline. He also sometimes would lie on top of her when she went

Figure 92 **Richard John Jahnke, Jr., circa 1984** (AP)

to bed. Jahnke is disgusted with the abuse and has discussed it with his mother. She responds by getting angry at Deborah, telling her it is her own fault for wearing shorts. At the same time, his mother is afraid of her husband and fears that he may kill Jahnke if he voices dissent about his father's treatment of Deborah.

Jahnke knows his father always carries a gun—when answering the door, in the bathroom, sitting on the couch, even in the middle of the night. (On one occasion, Jahnke got up to get food at 10 p.m. and found himself staring down the barrel of the gun.) He becomes increasingly scared for both his safety and that of his mother and sister. On a recent hunting trip, Jahnke's father tells him he is going to lose it one day and kill Jahnke. Jahnke is afraid to tell his teachers and friends about the rampant abuse, but his feelings of desperation are building.

On the afternoon of May 2, 1982, Jahnke's father gets irritated about something and begins to mercilessly beat Jahnke. When he is finished, he shoves him down the stairs and orders him to clean the basement, his usual chore. Jahnke obeys and begins to clean. He is startled, however, when he hears his father stomping down the stairs. Ever since he was little, Jahnke has associated his father's stomping with an imminent and severe beating. Jahnke's fears are realized; his father starts punching him again. Jahnke begins to cry, overcome by pain and helplessness. He runs from the house and reports his father to the sheriff. The sheriff sets up a meeting with a police officer and a social worker and the rest of the family. After a short discussion, everyone is sent home. As soon as they arrive at home, Jahnke's father says he will never forgive Jahnke for snitching on him.

Jahnke begins putting a chair in front of his bedroom door at night. His father does not beat him for a week, but then he starts again, increasing the frequency of the beatings to every day.

By Saturday, Jahnke has become desperate. That morning, his father beats Jahnke's sister for not combing her hair. After she is thoroughly battered, he puts his hands down her pants while Jahnke's mother is in the room. She ignores the scene and keeps cooking. Jahnke decides he needs to do something. As his father grabs his sister by the hair and starts to beat her again, Jahnke tells him to leave her alone. For a moment he feels a sense of pride for standing up for Deborah, but he soon pays the price. His father chases him and beats him instead. Later, badly hurt and upset, Jahnke begins to consider shooting his father as the only way to stop the brutality.

A few days later, Jahnke asks his mother for a ride to his school's open house. His mother gets angry with him. She tells Jahnke that she blames him for ruining her marriage. Jahnke, hurt and angered by the rebuke, tells her to shut up. His mother responds angrily by throwing a can of dog food at him, hitting him squarely on the head.

When Jahnke's father gets home, Jahnke's mother tells him that Jahnke sassed her. Cursing, the father starts to beat Jahnke, saying he is disgusted with the way Jahnke turned out and will find a way to get rid of him. His language is interspersed with cursing. His sister tries to intervene, but the father screams at her to get out. Jahnke's father gets his gun, turns back to his son, punches him again, and warns Jahnke that he had better not be there when he returns. Jahnke's parents leave for dinner to celebrate the anniversary of the day they met.

Jahnke is distraught. Deborah is hysterical. Jahnke feels he must do something to protect his sister and mother but feels trapped. He thinks that the sheriff will not take his allegations seriously and that his teachers would leak the embarrassing information to his peers. He can think of no one who will help him. Jahnke concludes that the only way to prevent a serious, perhaps life-threatening, beating upon his father's return is to kill his father first. Meanwhile, at their celebration dinner, Jahnke's father is telling his mother how much he hates his children and is disappointed in them. Jahnke's mother wonders whether her husband's earlier threat might have meant more than simply kicking Jahnke out of the house.

Having decided to kill his father, Jahnke changes his clothes to something less visible and places weapons throughout the house in case his initial attempt fails. In all, he has two shotguns, three rifles, a .38 caliber pistol, and a marine knife. He gives his sister a gun and quickly shows her how to use it. He feels it is important that she be protected even if his attempt fails. Jahnke puts the family pets into the basement so they will not be hurt. He goes to the garage, closes the door, and waits, selecting a spot where he cannot be seen but can see the driveway. His parents return from their romantic dinner at 6:30 p.m. As his father steps out of the car, Jahnke experiences a moment of hesitation. Part of him wants to run to his father and tell him that he loves him. But he remembers past attempts at reconciliation, all of which ended in the same way—with a violent beating.

The sound of his father's heavy steps jars him back, reminding him of the prelude to countless incidents of violence. With his twelve-gauge shotgun in one hand and his R.O.T.C. whistle in the other, Jahnke musters his courage. He blows the whistle for strength and opens fire as soon as he sees his father's head. He fires six shots, hitting his father four times. Jahnke later recalls that every shot at his father pained him. The most damaging shot hits his father in the chest and passes through his rib cage, lungs, liver, heart, and esophagus before ending up embedded in his back. Jahnke leaves his mother screaming in the driveway and runs into the house to get his sister. They go out a back window and run for a while, then go their separate ways. Jahnke ends up at his girlfriend's house, where he tells her father that he killed his father for revenge. His sister goes to a local mall. His father is pronounced dead one hour after the encounter.

1. Relying only on your own intuitions of justice, what liability and punishment, if any, does Richard Jahnke, Jr. deserve?

N	0	1	2	3	4	5	6	7	8	9	10	11
☐	☐	☐	☐	☐	☐	☐	☐	☐	☐	☐	☐	☐
no liability	liability but no punishment	1 day	2 wks	2 mo	6 mo	1 yr	3 yrs	7 yrs	15 yrs	30 yrs	life imprison- ment	death

2. What "justice" arguments could defense counsel make on the defendant's behalf?

3. What "justice" arguments could the prosecution make against the defendant?

4. What liability for Jahnke, if any, under the then-existing statutes? Prepare a list of all criminal code subsections and cases in the order in which you rely on them in your analysis.

5. What liability, if any, under the Model Penal Code? Prepare a list of all criminal code subsections in the order in which you rely on them in your analysis.

■ THE LAW

Wyoming Statutes
(1982)

Chapter 4. Offenses Against the Person

Article 1. Homicide

Section 6-4-101. Murder in the First Degree

(a) Whoever purposely and with premeditated malice, or in the perpetration of, or attempt to perpetrate any rape, sexual assault, arson, robbery or burglary, or by administering poison or causing the same to be done, kills any human being, or whoever purposely and with premeditated malice kills any peace officer, correction employee or fireman acting in the line of duty, is guilty of murder in the first degree.

(b) A person convicted of murder in the first degree shall be punished by death or life imprisonment according to the law.

Section 6-4-102. Presentence Hearing for Murder in the First Degree; Mitigating and Aggravating Circumstances

(a) Upon conviction of a person for murder in the first degree the judge shall conduct a separate sentencing hearing to determine whether the defendant should be sentenced to death or life imprisonment. The hearing shall be conducted before the judge alone if:

    (i) The defendant was convicted by a judge sitting without a jury;

    (ii) The defendant has pled guilty; or

    (iii) The defendant waives a jury with respect to the sentence.

(b) In all other cases the sentencing hearing shall be conducted before the jury which determined the defendant's guilt or, if the judge for good cause shown discharges the jury, with a new jury impaneled for that purpose.

(c) The judge or jury shall hear evidence as to any matter that the court deems relevant to a determination of the sentence, and shall include matters relating to any of the aggravating or mitigating circumstances enumerated in subsection (h) and (j) of this section. Any evidence which the court deems to have probative value may be received regardless of its admissibility under the exclusionary rules of evidence, provided the defendant is accorded a fair opportunity to rebut any hearsay statements and provided further that only such evidence in aggravation as the state has made known to the defendant or his counsel prior to his trial shall be admissible.

(d) Upon conclusion of the evidence and arguments the judge shall give the jury appropriate instructions, including instructions as to any aggravating or mitigating circumstances, as defined in subsections (h) and (j) of this section, or proceed as provided by paragraph (ii) of this subsection:

    (i) After hearing all the evidence, the jury shall deliberate and render a recommendation of sentence to the judge, based upon the following:

        (A) Whether one (1) or more sufficient aggravating circumstances exist as set forth in subsection (h) of this section;

        (B) Whether sufficient mitigating circumstances exist as set forth in subsection (j) of this section which outweigh the aggravation circumstances found to exist; and

        (C) Based upon these considerations, whether the defendant should be sentenced to death or life imprisonment.

    (ii) In nonjury cases, the judge shall determine if any aggravating or mitigating circumstances exist and impose sentence within the limits prescribed by law, based upon the considerations enumerated in (A), (B), and (C) of this subsection.

(e) The death penalty shall not be imposed unless at least one (1) of the aggravating circumstances set forth in subsection (h) of this section is found. The jury, if its verdict is a recommendation of death, shall designate in writing signed by the foreman of the jury the aggravating circumstance or circumstances which it found beyond a reasonable doubt. In nonjury cases the judge shall make such a designation. If the jury cannot, within a reasonable time, agree on the punishment to be imposed, the judge shall impose a life sentence.

(f) Unless the jury trying the case recommends the death sentence in its verdict, the judge shall not sentence the defendant to death but shall sentence the defendant to life imprisonment as provided by law. Where a recommendation of death is made, the court shall sentence the defendant to death.

(g) If the trial court is reversed on appeal because of error only in the presentence hearing, the new trial which may be ordered shall apply only to the issue of punishment.

(h) Aggravating circumstances are limited to the following:

(i) The murder was committed by a person under sentence of imprisonment;

(ii) The defendant was previously convicted of another murder in the first degree or a felony involving the use or threat of violence to the person;

(iii) The defendant knowingly created a great risk of death to two (2) or more persons;

(iv) The murder was committed while the defendant was engaged, or was an accomplice, in the commission of, or an attempt to commit, or flight after committing or attempting to commit, robbery, rape, sexual assault, arson, burglary, kidnapping, or aircraft piracy or the unlawful throwing, placing, or discharging of a destructive device or bomb;

(v) The murder was committed for the purpose of avoiding or preventing a lawful arrest or effecting an escape from custody;

(vi) The murder was committed for pecuniary gain;

(vii) The murder was especially heinous, atrocious, or cruel;

(viii) The murder of a judicial officer, former judicial officer, district attorney, former district attorney, or former county and prosecuting attorney, during or because of the exercise of his official duty.

(j) Mitigating circumstances shall be the following:

(i) The defendant has no significant history of prior criminal activity;

(ii) The murder was committed while the defendant was under the influence of extreme mental or emotional disturbance;

(iii) The victim was a participant in the defendant's conduct or consented to the act;

(iv) The defendant was an accomplice in a murder committed by another person and his participation in the homicidal act was relatively minor;

(v) The defendant acted under extreme duress or under the substantial domination of another person;

(vi) The capacity of the defendant to appreciate the criminality of his conduct or to conform his conduct to the requirements of law was substantially impaired;

(vii) The age of the defendant at the time of the crime.

Section 6-4-104. Murder in the Second Degree

Whoever purposely and maliciously, but without premeditation, kills any human being, is guilty of murder in the second degree, and shall be imprisoned in the penitentiary for any term not less then twenty (20) years, or during life.

Section 6-4-107. Manslaughter

Whoever unlawfully kills any human being without malice, expressed or implied, either voluntarily, upon the sudden heat of passion, or involuntarily, but in commission of some unlawful act, except as provided in W.S. 31-5-1117 [Homicide by vehicle; aggravated homicide by vehicle; penalties], or by any culpable neglect or criminal carelessness, is guilty of manslaughter, and shall be imprisoned in the penitentiary not more than twenty (20) years.

Chapter 1. General Provisions
Article 2. Conspiracy

Section 6-1-203. Conspiracy

(a) A person is guilty of conspiracy to commit a crime if he agrees with one (1) or more persons to commit a crime and he or another person does an overt act to effect the object of the agreement.

(b) A person is not liable under this section if after conspiring he withdraws from the conspiracy under circumstances manifesting voluntary and complete renunciation of his criminal intention.

(c) A conspiracy may be prosecuted in the county where the agreement was entered into, or in any county where any act evidencing the conspiracy or furthering the purpose took place.

Section 6-1-204. Penalty

The penalty for attempt, solicitation, and conspiracy is the same as the penalty for the most serious offense which is attempted, solicited or is an object of the conspiracy except that an attempt, solicitation or conspiracy to commit a capital crime is not punishable by the death penalty if the capital crime is not committed.

Loy v. State
26 Wyoming 381, 185 P. 796 (1919)

The defendant was convicted of murder in the first degree and sentenced to imprisonment in the penitentiary for life. The defendant was a white guest of a hotel in Laramie, who shot an African American porter during a brief altercation. The court approved the following jury instruction given to the jury regarding premeditation:

> The word "premeditated," as used in the information and in the statute, means to think beforehand. It implies an interval, however brief, between the formation of the intent or design and the commission of the act. To find the defendant guilty of murder in the first degree, you must find from the evidence beyond a reasonable doubt that he killed the deceased purposely and with premeditated malice as herein defined. But it is not necessary that such premeditation should have existed in the mind of the defendant for any particular length of time before the killing; it is sufficient if he has deliberately

formed in his mind a determination to kill and has thought over it before the shot was fired. . . . It is the fixed, deliberate, premeditated intention to kill which characterizes the crime of murder in the first degree, and the premeditated malice mentioned in the information need only be such deliberation and thought as enable a person to appreciate and understand at the time the act is committed the nature of the act and its probable results.

The defendant claimed that the porter approached him in a threatening way while touching his coat pocket. In response, the defendant pulled out a gun and shot the victim, as he claimed, in self-defense. The court affirmed his conviction and held that self-defense was permitted as a justification for murder when the "Defendant . . . not only believe[s] he is in danger, but the circumstances must be such as to afford reasonable grounds for the belief." In this case, the circumstances did not afford such reasonable grounds for his belief.

Ross v. State
57 P. 924 (Wyo. 1899)

The defendant was charged with first-degree murder, but convicted of second-degree murder and sentenced to life imprisonment for the shooting death of a competitor saloon owner. While the facts were in dispute, it was clear that the defendant had attempted to provoke the decedent with insults and disparaging remarks, and that his actions resulted in either a gun battle between the men or the defendant's unprovoked shooting of the decedent. The state's evidence showed that the decedent was unarmed. The defendant appealed his conviction and charged that the trial court erred by permitting a jury instruction as to implied malice. The supreme court affirmed the lower court's decision and held that the instruction that "[t]hough there was no premeditation, a charge that 'malice is implied from any deliberate and cool act done against another, however sudden, which shows an abandoned and malignant heart, and where one person assaults another with a deadly weapon in such a manner as is likely to cause death, although he had no previous malice or ill will against the party assaulted, yet he is presumed, in law, to have such malice at the moment of the assault, and, if death result therefrom, it is murder,' was not erroneous, as authorizing a conviction of murder in the first degree."

State v. Helton
73 Wyo. 92, 115, 276 P.2d 434, 442 (1954)

In reversing a conviction for murder and entering a judgment for voluntary manslaughter for the defendant's shooting of her husband, the court explained the offense of voluntary manslaughter in this way:

> Our laws recognize an intermediate crime lying someplace between the excusable, justifiable or privileged killing of a human being, and the unlawful taking of a life with malice [i.e., murder]. [W]e find in our law, that the intentional (i.e. voluntary) doing of the wrongful act, "upon a sudden heat of passion," although completely free of express, implied, constructive or legal malice, but committed without legal excuse, privilege or justification, is a punishable crime which we call voluntary manslaughter. This simply recognizes that there may be circumstances surrounding a killing which . . . while not producing that

degree of mental disturbance or aberration of the mind which is necessary in law to excuse the homicide, still leaves the mind devoid of that wicked, evil and unlawful purpose, or of that wilful disregard of the rights of others which is implied in the term "malice." Such circumstances mitigate or extenuate the act and make the homicide a crime of lesser degree. The "sudden heat of passion" contemplated by our voluntary manslaughter statute is descriptive of just such a state of mind, and it may occur from any emotional excitement of such intensity that it temporarily obscures reason, or leaves the mind bereft of reason.

Foley v. State

72 P. 627 (Wyo. 1903)

The defendant was convicted of second degree murder and appealed on an issue of error by the trial court for admitting hearsay testimony. Within its opinion, the court defined a defense for mistaken self-defense: "[h]omicide is justifiable on the ground of self-defense where the slayer, in the careful and proper use of his faculties, bona fide believes, and has reasonable ground to believe, that he is in imminent danger of death or great bodily harm, and that his only means of escape from such danger will be by taking the life of his assailant, although in fact he is mistaken as to the existence or imminence of the danger."

Harries v. State

650 P.2d 273 (Wyo. 1982)

The defendant was convicted of use of a weapon to commit assault and battery on another. He had been involved in a bar fight during which he was struck by an unknown assailant. He retaliated with a shot to the leg of a third party. He then went for a weapon in his friend's truck, pulled out a gun, and fired it when a third party tried to take the weapon from him. He claimed a reasonable belief that actions were justified as self-defense and defense of others based on the third party's movements toward him during the scuffle. The court dismissed his defense-of-others argument because it had not been raised at trial. It affirmed his conviction despite his self-defense claim because the defendant's belief was not one that an objectively reasonable person would hold. The court affirmed the trial court's jury instruction that the elements of self-defense required the defendant have "reasonable grounds for believing and does believe that bodily injury is about to be inflicted upon him. In doing so he may use all force and means which he believes to be necessary and which would appear to a reasonable person, in the same or similar circumstances, to be necessary to prevent the injury which appears to be imminent." (Quoting Instruction No. 10; Wyoming Pattern Jury Instructions 5.208). The court further held that "[t]o justify acting in self-defense, it is not necessary that the danger was real, or that the danger was impending and immediate, so long as the defendant had reasonable cause to believe and did believe these facts. If these two requirements are met, acting in self-defense was justified even though there was no intention on the part of the other person to do him harm, nor any impending and immediate danger, nor the actual necessity for acting in self-defense." (Quoting Instruction No. 11; Wyoming Pattern Jury Instructions Criminal, 5.210).

Delaney v. State
14 Wyo. 1, 81 P. 792 (1905)

Defendant was found guilty of assault with intent to murder one Stark. Because he was in his own home at the time of the assault, he objected to the following jury instruction, on the ground that it violated his right not to have to retreat from his own house before using deadly force:

> If you find from the evidence that the defendant could have retired to a place of safety before Stark reached his gun, then it was his duty to have done so, and he was not justified in shooting Stark because he may have believed that Stark was going after his gun. To justify the use of a deadly weapon by the defendant when an assault has been made upon him, the circumstances must appear to be such that there is no other reasonable means of escape from death or great bodily harm.

The court rejects the claim and affirms the conviction, saying:

> Having been the aggressor, the defendant placed himself in the attitude of one who assaults another on the highway, and upon whom the law imposes the duty of withdrawing in good faith from, and not for the purpose of renewing, the assault, before he can justify shooting his adversary on the ground of self-defense.

Model Penal Code
(Official Draft 1962)

Section 3.09. Mistake of Law as to Unlawfulness of Force or Legality of Arrest; Reckless or Negligent Use of Otherwise Justifiable Force; Reckless or Negligent Injury or Risk of Injury to Innocent Persons

(1) The justification afforded by Sections 3.04 to 3.07, inclusive, is unavailable when:

(a) the actor's belief in the unlawfulness of the force or conduct against which he employs protective force or his belief in the lawfulness of an arrest which he endeavors to effect by force is erroneous; and

(b) his error is due to ignorance or mistake as to the provisions of the Code, any other provision of the criminal law or the law governing the legality of an arrest or search.

(2) When the actor believes that the use of force upon or toward the person of another is necessary for any of the purposes for which such belief would establish a justification under Sections 3.03 to 3.08 but the actor is reckless or negligent in having such belief or in acquiring or failing to acquire any knowledge or belief which is material to the justiciability of his use of force, the justification afforded by those Sections is unavailable in a prosecution for an offense for which recklessness or negligence, as the case may be, suffices to establish culpability.

(3) When the actor is justified under Sections 3.03 to 3.08 in using force upon or toward the person of another but he recklessly or negligently injures or

creates a risk of injury to innocent persons, the justification afforded by those Sections is unavailable in a prosecution for such recklessness or negligence towards innocent persons.

Section 3.05. Use of Force for the Protection of Other Persons

(1) Subject to the provisions of this Section and of Section 3.09, the use of force upon or toward the person of another is justifiable to protect a third person when:

(a) the actor would be justified under Section 3.04 in using such force to protect himself against the injury he believes to be threatened to the person whom he seeks to protect; and

(b) under the circumstances as the actor believes them to be, the person whom he seeks to protect would be justified in using such protective force; and

(c) the actor believes that his intervention is necessary for the protection of such other person.

(2) Notwithstanding Subsection (1) of this Section:

(a) when the actor would be obliged under Section 3.04 to retreat, to surrender the possession of a thing or to comply with a demand before using force in self-protection, he is not obliged to do so before using force for the protection of another person, unless he knows that he can thereby secure the complete safety of such other person; and

(b) when the person whom the actor seeks to protect would be obliged under Section 3.04 to retreat, to surrender the possession of a thing or to comply with a demand if he knew that he could obtain complete safety by so doing, the actor is obliged to try to cause him to do so before using force in his protection if the actor knows that he can obtain complete safety in that way; and

(c) neither the actor nor the person whom he seeks to protect is obliged to retreat when in the other's dwelling or place of work to any greater extent than in his own.

Section 2.10. Military Orders

It is an affirmative defense that the actor, in engaging in the conduct charged to constitute an offense, does no more than execute an order of his superior in the armed services which he does not know to be unlawful.

● OVERVIEW OF MISTAKE AS TO A JUSTIFICATION

Hypothetical: Moro's Mistake (#91)

Moro loves to play the horses, and Snake, a local mobster, loves it when he does. Moro is almost always in the hole to Snake, paying Snake only the vig (interest) each week. Snake has been less than happy as of late, however, because Moro has not been covering even the vig. Things have gotten out of hand. Snake has his reputation to think about. If Moro doesn't keep up, others will think they don't have to either. To help make his point, Snake gave Moro a severe beating last week, with a warning that, if Moro missed another payment, he would be killed. Nothing personal; general deterrence and all that.

The payment is due today, but Moro doesn't have the money. He borrows a gun and hangs out at Joshua's Deli, the neighborhood grocery store, in the hopes that Snake will leave him alone in public. He is shocked when Snake comes in and walks straight at him. "I won't let you get me, Snake!" he says as he pulls his gun and aims. Just before he pulls the trigger, Joshua, the proprietor, who is directly across the counter from him, leans over and punches him. "That's not Snake. It's his brother, you moron." Joshua has made a point of learning to tell the identical twin brothers apart, because Snake never pays his bill. Joshua's punch deflects Moro's shot. Snake's brother is wounded but not killed.

At a preliminary hearing on an attempted murder charge, the court finds that, while Moro did intend to kill, he reasonably believed that he was in danger of being killed and acted in what he reasonably believed was self-defense. Moro is cleared of all charges.

Moro then files assault charges against Joshua. Is Joshua criminally liable for striking Moro?

Notes

An actor's mistake may exculpate the actor in any number of ways. Assume a hunter's companion violates basic safety rules by moving too far ahead of his partner and into the partner's line of fire. When the partner shoots the companion, reasonably mistaking him for a deer, the partner is properly exculpated, because his mistake negates the culpable state of mind required for murder; he lacks the requisite intent to kill another human being. (If reasonable, the mistake also negates the recklessness or negligence required for lesser degrees of homicide as well.) No justification or excuse defense is required, because the elements of the offense itself have not been satisfied. In contrast, in the "Moro's Mistake" hypothetical, when Moro shoots Snake's brother, he does intend to cause the brother's death. If he had successfully killed Snake's brother, Moro would satisfy the requirements of murder. Further, Moro's conduct is not justified, as Snake's brother does not actually present a threat to Moro. Nonetheless, Moro may have a defense if his shooting *would have been* justified in the circumstances he reasonably believed to exist—in other words, if he made a reasonable mistake as to being justified. Because of a mistaken belief, neither the hunter nor Moro is knowingly engaging in criminal conduct so their punishment would not serve the condemnatory function of the criminal law. In Moro's case, however, because the elements of murder would be satisfied had Snake's brother died—and the elements of attempted murder might be satisfied even without the death—Moro can avoid punishment only if he is able to rely on a general defense.

COMPETING THEORIES OF JUSTIFICATION

Every jurisdiction recognizes a defense for some class of mistake as to a justification. The often unpredictable and confrontational nature of justifying circumstances makes such mistakes particularly understandable. This is especially true for defensive force justifications, where the actor must make the decision to act under an impending threat of harm. An actor who reasonably believes he is justified is blameless; he could not reasonably have been expected to avoid the offense. Society encourages, or at least tolerates, justified conduct. If the law failed to recognize a defense for reasonable mistakes as to justification, fear of liability might discourage some people from engaging in justified, perhaps even desirable, conduct. Without a defense, people who could take action to avoid a greater harm might hold back if they have any doubt at all about the situation, as even a reasonable error could lead to criminal liability.

Justification for Actor Who "Believes" Conduct Is Justified Model Penal Code-based jurisdictions enable a defense for mistake as to justification by including the word "believes" or "reasonably believes" in the definition of justification defenses: An actor will get the justification defense if she (reasonably) believes her conduct is justified, even if in fact it is not. This common formulation has two potentially problematic effects. First, defining justifications in terms of "belief" treats equally, and mixes together, conduct that is objectively justified and conduct that is not. Giving the mistake defense is appropriate, even important, but doing so through this formulation confuses and blends justification and excuse. (For one example of the problems this confusion may create, recall that an attack by one who mistakenly believes he is justified triggers a right of the victim to use defensive force; the objectively justified attack does not.) The second effect of defining justifications subjectively—giving a justification defense to one who "believes" she is justified—is to deny a justification defense to an actor whose conduct actually is justified, but who does not "believe" that it is, a result inconsistent with most people's intuition of justice.[1] An alternative, and probably superior, formulation is to define justifications objectively (that is without the "believes"

---

1. See Paul H. Robinson & John M. Darley, *Testing Competing Theories of Justification*, 76 N.C. L. REV. 1095 (1998).

language) and to provide a separate general excuse defense for mistakes as to a justification. The National Commission recommended this approach.[2]

Two Theories of Justification: Reasons vs. Deeds   Defining justification defenses *subjectively*, to require that an actor "believes" his conduct is justified, reflects what has been called a *reasons* theory of justification, where the basis of the defense is the actor's proper motivation. Defining justification defenses *objectively*, to require that the actor's conduct actually satisfies the ex ante rules of conduct, reflects what may be called a *deeds* theory of justification, where the basis of the defense is the justified character of the actor's deed, rather than his motivation.

Analysis of "Moro's Mistake" Hypothetical   Turning to the "Moro's Mistake" hypothetical, should Joshua be liable for striking Moro? As earlier discussions have noted, (objectively) justified conduct is conduct that the law tolerates and may even encourage. It makes sense, then, to prohibit others from interfering with, or resisting, such justified conduct. In Moro's case, however, he only *thinks* his conduct is justified. Because the person he takes to be Snake is really Snake's brother, he is not actually in danger, and his use of force is not (objectively) justified. This being the case, it follows that Joshua should be justified in intervening to prevent Moro's unjustified conduct. There is general agreement with this result—allowing a justification defense for Joshua's interference with Moro's shooting—but it is not always clear how, or whether, current statutes reach this proper result.

Difficulty of Resolving Under Model Penal Code   Under the Model Penal Code, for example, Joshua is justified in using force to defend Snake's brother only if Snake's brother would be justified in using the same force to defend himself.[3] Snake's brother, in turn, is justified in using force against Moro only if Moro's force is "unlawful." In fact, Moro's shooting is "justified" under the Model Penal Code, because Moro "believes" the shooting is immediately necessary to protect himself. One might normally assume that because Moro's shooting of Snake's brother is "justified"—and therefore not subject to criminal punishment—it follows that it is not "unlawful," which would mean that Joshua has no right to resist or interfere with the shooting. But the Code's definition of "unlawful force" gives a different result. The Code abandons its own concept of "justified" force and shifts instead to rely on a new concept of "privileged" force (which may not lawfully be resisted) and "unprivileged" force (which may). Assuming Moro's force is not "privileged" (an undefined term in the Code), Moro's force may be "justified" yet still be "unlawful force," in which case Joshua can lawfully defend Snake's brother against it. Accordingly, the Model Penal Code seems to reach the proper resolution of the case, though the required analysis under the Code's framework is far from straightforward.

Subjective Definition of Justification Clouds Law's Commands   While the Model Penal Code's approach—giving a justification defense to an actor who mistakenly *believes* his conduct is justified—may cause some confusion in application, its greatest problem is the conceptual confusion it creates and the ensuing difficulty it presents for the law's ability to communicate its commands. Conduct that is actually, objectively justified—"privileged" conduct—creates no net harm

---

2. See Final Report of the National Commission on Reform of Federal Criminal Laws § 608 (1971).
3. See Model Penal Code § 3.05(1).

or evil, and may even create a net benefit, in terms of the interests the law protects. Accordingly, the law seeks to send the message that such conduct is to be publicly approved and will be encouraged (or at least tolerated) if performed under similar circumstances in the future. Conduct that is not objectively justified—as where the actor is mistaken about a justification—does create a net harm or evil. When an actor engages in such conduct, the law may grant him an *excuse* defense because of his mistake, but the law also wants to avoid any suggestion that others should engage in such conduct under similar circumstances in the future. Blurring the distinction between objectively justified and objectively unjustified conduct impedes the law's ability to state clearly what conduct it prohibits and what conduct it permits.

Ambiguity of Acquittals By treating mistaken conduct as "justified," current doctrine creates an ambiguity that risks distorting the true rules of conduct. An acquittal granted under a "justification" defense, but actually based on a mistake as to a justification, sends an ambiguous message as to the rules of conduct. Do the rules permit what the actor actually did, or just what he thought he was doing, or both? Giving the same "justification" defense to both the objectively justified actor and the mistaken actor leaves the ambiguity dangerously unresolved in every case. A case of mistaken justification might be misinterpreted as a case of true justification, thereby signaling approval of conduct that ought to be prohibited.[4] Meanwhile, cases involving objectively justified conduct might be misinterpreted as involving mistakes, thereby distorting the rules in a way that may discourage desirable or at least objectively justified conduct.

Increased Clarity of Objectively Defined Justifications The difficulty can be avoided by adopting an objective definition of "justification" and creating a separate excuse defense for mistaken justifications, as is done in some justification statutes.[5] Under this approach, an actor is justified only if her conduct is in fact objectively justified, not if the actor mistakenly believes that it is justified. This distinguishes the two cases and permits a clear communication of the rules of conduct. Only objective justifications can provide the unambiguous and invariant rules needed to announce the rules of proper conduct for the future.[6]

Example of Proposed Approach Objectively defined justifications might look something like the following, taken from the existing North Dakota statutes:

> *Section 12.1-05-03. Self-Defense.* A person is justified in using force upon another person to defend himself against danger of imminent unlawful bodily injury . . . by such other person. . . .

> *Section 12.1-05-04. Defense of Others.* A person is justified in using force upon another person in order to defend anyone else if:
> 1. The person defended would be justified in defending himself; and
> 2. The person coming to the defense has not, by provocation or otherwise, forfeited the right of self-defense.

---

4. See Paul H. Robinson, *Rules of Conduct and Principles of Adjudication*, 57 U. Chi. L. Rev. 729, 766 (1990) (arguing that acquittal based on absence of violation of rules of conduct announces approval of conduct, and that acquittal based on absence of blame announces disapproval of conduct).

5. See, e.g., North Dakota Cent. Code §§ 12.1-05-03 to -12.

6. See Paul H. Robinson, Competing Theories of Justification: Deeds vs. Reasons, in A.T.H. Smith & A. Simester, eds., Current Problems of Criminal Theory 45 (1995).

> *Section 12.1-05-07. Limitations on the Use of Force—Excessive Force.* A person is
> not justified in using more force than is necessary and appropriate under the
> circumstances.
>
> *Section 12.1-05-08. Excuse.* A person's conduct is excused if he believes that the
> facts are such that his conduct is necessary and appropriate for any of the pur-
> poses which would establish a justification . . . under this chapter, even though
> his belief is mistaken. However, if his belief is negligently or recklessly held, it
> is not an excuse in a prosecution for an offense for which negligence or reck-
> lessness, as the case may be, suffices to establish culpability. . . . [7]

The North Dakota self-defense statute uses the term *unlawful* rather than *unjustified*, although the latter would be preferable given how it defines the notion of
"justified" conduct. Instead of the complications that arise from combining actual
justification and a subjective belief in formulation, this scheme makes clear that
justifications are objective, whereas mistaken subjective beliefs about justification
warrant an excuse.

Case for Subjective Theory   Many codes and some writers insist on defining justifications subjectively. That is, they argue that one ought to be justified if
one (reasonably) believes that one's conduct is justified. According to this argument, such an actor has behaved properly; to convict the actor is to disapprove,
improperly, of the conduct as the actor saw it. One writer gives the example
of the *Young* case, in which the defendant bravely intervened to help defend a
youth being beaten by two men, only to be charged with criminal assault when
it turned out the two men were police officers trying to arrest the youth.[8] The
writer observes:

> Actions like Young's should not be the subject of criminal liability, but the
> question here is whether they should be labeled justified or excused. Young is
> to be praised, not blamed, for what he did, and *members of society would wish
> that others faced with similar situations requiring instant judgment would act as
> Young did*. A moral assessment of Young's act would treat it as justified.[9]

The argument is, in part, that a justification defense must be given to Young
because only in this way can the law (1) give the moral approval to his motivation
that it deserves, and (2) encourage others to intervene in similar situations in the
future. But the logic of this subjective theory is flawed.

Response to Arguments Favoring Subjective Theory   An excuse defense for
Young, rather a justification defense, also would judge him blameless. The argument above, however, goes further to claim that Young's act, not just Young's
motivation, should be judged proper—that we want "others faced with similar
situations [to] act as Young did." But this incorrectly assumes that we must label
as "justified" Young's mistaken act in order to encourage others in the future to
act as Young thought he was acting. In fact, the future actor who believes she
has come upon the mugging of an innocent youth will be encouraged to act by
a rule of conduct that allows, under an objective justification defense, the right
to defend another from an unjustified attack. Such an actor will not be deterred

---

7. N.D. Cent. Code, supra.
8. People v. Young, 183 N.E.2d 319 (N.Y. 1962).
9. Kent Greenawalt, *The Perplexing Borders of Justification and Excuse*, 84 COLUM. L. REV. 1897, 1919-
1920 (1984) (emphasis added).

by a rule that excuses rather than justifies reasonable mistakes as to a justification, because the actor believes that the circumstances are such that the intervention actually is justified. (If the actor is concerned about the possibility that she might be mistaken in her perception of the justifying circumstances—a concern that we might want to encourage—the actor can take comfort in the fact that an excuse defense is available for a reasonable mistake as to a justification.) A justification defense for objectively justified conduct should suffice to encourage future actors to act in situations where intervention appears to them to be justified.

CULPABLE MISTAKES AS TO JUSTIFICATION

For simplicity's sake, the discussion has so far assumed that the actor reasonably believed his conduct was justified, and would therefore be entitled to an excuse defense. Should the results differ if the actor were negligent or reckless in holding that belief? Both the objective-justification defense provisions quoted above and the Model Penal Code's subjective-justification provisions would allow an unreasonable mistake, such as a negligent or reckless mistake, to at least mitigate the degree of liability. A reckless mistake leading one to kill or injure another would make the person liable for reckless homicide or reckless wounding, if such an offense exists. A negligent mistake would render him liable for negligent homicide or wounding.[10] And of course, as with a reasonable mistake as to being justified, the conduct of an actor making a culpable mistake as to being justified is not justified, and thus can be lawfully resisted.

Denying Defense or Mitigation for Culpable Mistake Some jurisdictions, however, permit no defense—whether justification, excuse, or mitigation—if an actor's mistake is unreasonable.[11] Thus, a reckless or negligent mistake will leave the actor liable for an intentional assault or killing. Some writers, such as George Fletcher, support such a reasonableness requirement:

> If a mistaken claim of justification functions as an excuse, then one can expect it to meet the standard applied to other excusing conditions—namely, that it actually excuse the actor from blame. As the claim of duress must satisfy normative criteria, so must the claim of mistake as an excuse satisfy normative criteria—namely, the requirement of reasonableness—in order effectively to excuse the wrongful act.[12]

Case for Mitigation for Unreasonable Mistake While Fletcher is correct that excuses (such as an excuse for mistaken justification) normally require reasonableness—which is to say, blamelessness—it does not follow that any degree of blameworthiness should lead to full liability. Generally, an honest but unreasonable mistake ought to provide some degree of mitigation. The actor who kills under an unreasonable belief that such conduct is necessary in self-defense may not merit a complete excuse, but is less blameworthy than the actor who intentionally kills with no such mistaken belief, simply intending to kill the victim out of hate, greed, or whatever. The criminal law must not only avoid punishing the blameless, but must also ensure that each blameworthy actor's degree of

---

10. See Model Penal Code § 3.09(2); N.D. Cent. Code § 12.1-05-08.
11. See N.Y. Penal Law § 35.15; N.J. Stat. Ann. § 2C:3-4. See People v. Goetz, 497 N.E.2d 41 (N.Y. 1986); State v. Kelly, 478 A.2d 364 (N.J. 1984).
12. George Fletcher, Rethinking Criminal Law 696 (1978).

liability corresponds to the degree of the actor's blameworthiness. A negligent mistake as to whether force is necessary may justify some liability, but not as much liability as is suitable for an actor who knows the force is unnecessary. Just as an unreasonable mistake as to an objective offense element may provide a defense or mitigation (where the offense requires knowledge or intention), so too might an unreasonable mistake as to a justification form a legitimate basis for an excuse or mitigation. (Similar treatment of mistakes as to a justification and mistakes as to objective offense elements seems particularly appropriate given the similarity in function of many objective offense elements and justification defenses: Both serve to define the scope of proscribed conduct.)

Varying Liability Based on Culpability of Mistake For these reasons, many jurisdictions do not require a reasonable mistake to obtain a mitigation, but permit a defense for any mistake less culpable than the offense's required culpability. The Model Penal Code, for example, takes this approach of tying the culpability required for mistake as to justification to the culpability of the offense charged. The Code gives a defense to any actor who believes he is justified; but then, in a separate provision, the Code withdraws the defense for a reckless or negligent mistake, respectively, for any "offense for which recklessness or negligence, as the case may be, suffices to establish culpability."[13] Thus, mistakes as to justification provide an excuse for, but only for, offenses whose culpability requirement exceeds the culpability level of the mistake. For example, where a police officer negligently believes that a bank robber has a gun, and then (intentionally) kills the bank robber to protect herself and others, she would not be convicted of intentional homicide, as would occur if her culpable (i.e., unreasonable) mistake could play no excusing or mitigating role. Perhaps the ideal solution, and one that several modern codes adopt, is a specific homicide offense addressing deaths caused by actors making reckless or negligent mistakes as to a justification.[14] In lieu of creating such a special offense, the Model Penal Code drafters may have reasoned that the best available approximation is a lesser offense requiring reduced culpability. Thus, where the police officer is negligent in her mistake, the Code holds the mistaken officer liable for negligent homicide; if the mistake is reckless, for reckless homicide.

Culpability as to Justification vs. Causing Death While the Model Penal Code scheme is more refined than other codes, many of which deny a defense or mitigation in the presence of any culpability, the Code's approach nonetheless may be criticized as being too harsh. It treats culpability as to a justifying circumstance as equivalent to culpability as to causing another's death. But culpability as to, say, the existence of an attack may be less blameworthy than culpability as to causing another's death. The preferred resolution in such cases is to ask whether, in creating the circumstances that made him culpable as to the justification, the actor was culpable as to whether those circumstances would lead him to unjustifiably cause another's death.

Difficulties Where Offenses Have Multiple Culpability Levels One technical difficulty with the Model Penal Code's scheme is that, in setting the actor's liability to that of "an offense for which recklessness or negligence . . . suffices to establish culpability," the Code erroneously assumes that each offense has a single culpability level. The language is not a problem for homicide offenses, which require

---

13. Model Penal Code § 3.09(2).
14. For examples, see 2 Paul H. Robinson, *Criminal Law Defenses* § 184(e)(3) n.45 (1984).

the same culpability level as to all elements. Thus, a reckless mistake results in liability for reckless homicide (manslaughter); a negligent mistake means liability for negligent homicide; a faultless mistake gives a complete defense. It is less clear, though, how the section applies to offenses that have different culpability levels for different offense elements.

Standard of Reasonableness   A final issue relates to reasonable mistakes as to justification, which all agree should provide a complete excuse. "Reasonable" typically is defined as "non-negligent"[15]; thus the reasonableness of a mistake is to be judged, at least in the Model Code, by the partially individualized objective standard used for negligence.[16] But there can be confusion on this point. In *People v. Goetz*, for example, the trial court determined that the defendant's belief regarding his own justification need only be "reasonable as to him," which essentially amounted to a purely subjective standard.[17] The defendant shot several youths on a subway car after they had approached him in what he believed was an attempt to rob him. The court's interpretation of the "reasonable belief" requirement of the New York statute (an all-or-nothing scheme) was reversed on appeal, however, with the Court of Appeals making clear that the reasonableness of the defendant's belief was to be judged by an objective standard, albeit one individualized by certain characteristics of the defendant and his situation. This partial-individualization approach allows the court to admit, and the jury to consider, evidence of factors that may distort the defendant's perception of what is reasonable. In *State v. Kelly*, for example, the court allowed expert testimony concerning Battered Woman's Syndrome as relevant to establishing the reasonableness of the defendant's belief that she was in imminent danger of death.[18] The defendant in *Kelly* stabbed and killed her husband, believing that he was about to kill her but under circumstances where a reasonable person would not have come to such a conclusion. The testimony suggested that a pattern of past abuse tends to cause the abused to overestimate the extent and immediacy of the threat, and to underestimate her ability to avoid the threat by retreat. On appeal, the court directed that such evidence of battering and its effects could be relevant to a determination of the reasonableness of Kelly's belief. The issue of defense mitigation for an unreasonable but honest mistake, like that of a battered woman who kills her sleeping husband, is the subject of the Discussion Issue for this Section and is discussed in the Discussion Materials in the Appendix.

People v. Young

Court of Appeals of New York
11 N.Y.2d 274, 183 N.E.2d 319, 229 N.Y.S.2d 1 (1962)

PER CURIAM.

Whether one, who in good faith aggressively intervenes in a struggle between another person and a police officer in civilian dress attempting to effect the lawful

---

15. See, e.g., Model Penal Code § 1.13(16).

16. See, e.g., Model Penal Code § 2.02(2)(d).

17. 497 N.E.2d 41 (N.Y. 1986).

18. 478 A.2d 364 (N.J. 1984). But see State v. Norman, 378 S.E.2d 8 (N.C. 1989) (severely battered wife not entitled to jury instruction on perfect or imperfect self-defense).

arrest of the third person, may be properly convicted of assault in the third degree is a question of law of first impression here.

The opinions in the court below in the absence of precedents in this State carefully expound the opposing views found in other jurisdictions. The majority in the Appellate Division have adopted the minority rule in the other States that one who intervenes in a struggle between strangers under the mistaken but reasonable belief that he is protecting another who he assumes is being unlawfully beaten is thereby exonerated from criminal liability. The weight of authority holds with the dissenters below that one who goes to the aid of a third person does so at his own peril.

While the doctrine espoused by the majority of the court below may have support in some States, we feel that such a policy would not be conducive to an orderly society. We agree with the settled policy of law in most jurisdictions that the right of a person to defend another ordinarily should not be greater than such person's right to defend himself. Subdivision 3 of section 246 of the Penal Law, Consol. Laws, c. 40, [which authorizes the use of force in defense of another] does not apply as no offense was being committed on the person of the one resisting the lawful arrest. Whatever may be the public policy where the felony charged requires proof of a specific intent and the issue is justifiable homicide, it is not relevant in a prosecution for assault in the third degree where it is only necessary to show that the defendant knowingly struck a blow.

In this case there can be no doubt that the defendant intended to assault the police officer in civilian dress. The resulting assault was forceful. Hence motive or mistake of fact is of no significance as the defendant was not charged with a crime requiring such intent or knowledge. To be guilty of third degree assault, "It is sufficient that the defendant voluntarily intended to commit the unlawful act of touching." Since in these circumstances the aggression was inexcusable the defendant was properly convicted.

Accordingly, the order of the Appellate Division should be reversed and the information reinstated.

FROESSEL, Judge (dissenting).

The law is clear that one may kill in defense of another when there is reasonable, though mistaken, ground for believing that the person slain is about to commit a felony or to do some great personal injury to the apparent victim (Penal Law §1055); yet the majority now hold, for the first time, that in the event of a simple assault under similar circumstances, the mistaken belief, no matter how reasonable, is no defense.

Briefly, the relevant facts are these: On a Friday afternoon at about 3:40, Detectives Driscoll and Murphy, not in uniform, observed an argument taking place between a motorist and one McGriff in the street in front of premises 64 West 54th Street, in midtown Manhattan. Driscoll attempted to chase McGriff out of the roadway in order to allow traffic to pass, but McGriff refused to move back; his actions caused a crowd to collect. After identifying himself to McGriff, Driscoll placed him under arrest. As McGriff resisted, defendant "came out of the crowd" from Driscoll's rear and struck Murphy about the head with his fist. In the ensuing struggle Driscoll's right kneecap was injured when defendant fell on top of him. At the station house, defendant said he had not known or thought Driscoll and Murphy were police officers.

Defendant testified that while he was proceeding on 54th Street he observed two white men, who appeared to be 45 or 50 years old, pulling on a "colored boy" (McGriff), who appeared to be a lad about 18, whom he did not know. The men had nearly pulled McGriff's pants off, and he was crying. Defendant admitted he knew nothing of what had transpired between the officers and McGriff, and made no inquiry of anyone; he just came there and pulled the officer away from McGriff.

Defendant was convicted of assault third degree. In reversing upon the law and dismissing the information, the Appellate Division held that he is not "criminally liable for assault in the third degree if he goes to the aid of another who he mistakenly, but *reasonably*, believes is being unlawfully beaten, and thereby injures one of the apparent assaulters" (emphasis supplied). While in my opinion the majority below correctly stated the law, I would reverse here and remit so that the Appellate Division may pass on the question of whether or not defendant's conduct was reasonable in light of the circumstances presented at the trial.

As the majority below pointed out, assault is a crime derived from the common law. Basic to the imposition of criminal liability both at common law and under our statutory law is the existence in the one whom committed the prohibited act of what has been variously termed a guilty mind, a mens rea or a criminal intent.

Criminal intent requires an awareness of wrongdoing. When conduct is based upon mistake of fact reasonably entertained, there can be no such awareness and, therefore, no criminal culpability. . . .

It is undisputed that defendant did not know that Driscoll and Murphy were detectives in plain clothes engaged in lawfully apprehending an alleged disorderly person. If, therefore, defendant reasonably believed he was lawfully assisting another, he would not have been guilty of a crime. Subdivision 3 of section 246 of the Penal Law provides that it is not unlawful to use force "When committed either by the party about to be injured or *by another person in his aid or defense, in preventing or attempting to prevent an offense against his person,* . . . if the force or violence used is not more than sufficient to prevent such offense" (emphasis supplied). The law is thus clear that if defendant entertained an "honest and reasonable belief" that the facts were as he perceived them to be, he would be exonerated from criminal liability.

By ignoring one of the most basic principles of criminal law that crimes mala in se require proof of at least general criminal intent, the majority now hold that the defense of mistake of fact is "of no significance" . We are not here dealing with one of "a narrow class of exceptions" where the Legislature has created crimes which do not depend on criminal intent but which are complete on the mere intentional doing of an act malum prohibitum.

There is no need, in my opinion, to consider the law of other States, for New York policy clearly supports the view that one may act on appearances reasonably ascertained, as does New Jersey. Our Penal Law (§1055), to which I have already alluded, is a statement of that policy. The same policy was expressed by this court in *People v. Maine*, 166 N.Y. 50, 59 N.E. 696. There, the defendant observed his brother fighting in the street with two other men; he stepped in and stabbed to death one of the latter. The defense was justifiable homicide under the predecessor of section 1055. The court held it reversible error to admit into evidence the declarations of the defendant's brother, made before defendant happened upon the scene, which tended to show that the brother was the aggressor. We said: "Of course, the acts and conduct of the defendant must be judged solely with reference to the situation as it was when he first and afterwards saw it." Mistake of relevant fact, reasonably entertained, is thus a defense to homicide under section 1055, and one who kills in defense of another and proffers this defense of justification is to be judged according to the circumstances as they appeared to him.

The mistaken belief, however, must be one which is reasonably entertained, and the question of reasonableness is for the trier of the facts. "The question is not, merely, what did the accused believe? but also, what did he have the right to believe?" Without passing on the facts of the instant case, the Appellate Division had no right to assume that defendant's conduct was reasonable, and to dismiss the information as a matter of law. Nor do we have the right to reinstate the verdict without giving the Appellate Division the opportunity to pass upon the facts.

Although the majority . . . are now purporting to fashion a policy "conducive to an orderly society," by their decision they have defeated their avowed purpose. What public interest is promoted by a principle which would deter one from coming to the aid of a fellow citizen who he has reasonable ground to apprehend is in imminent danger of personal injury at the hands of assailants? Is it reasonable to denominate, as justifiable homicide, a slaying committed under a mistaken but reasonably held belief, and deny this same defense of justification to one using less force? Logic, as well as historical background and related precedent, dictates that the rule and policy expressed by our Legislature in the case of homicide, which is an assault resulting in death, should likewise be applicable to a much less serious assault not resulting in death.

I would reverse the order appealed from and remit the case to the Appellate Division . . . for determination upon the questions of fact raised in that court.*

▲ PROBLEMS

Killing a Batterer While He Sleeps (#92)

Judy and J. T. Norman have been married almost 25 years and have several children. Unfortunately, it is by no means a happy marriage. Since J. T. began drinking five years into their marriage, he has regularly abused Judy, cruelly. He puts cigarettes out on Judy's body, throws hot coffee on her, breaks glass against her face, and crushes food on her face. He has also on occasion forced Judy to

---

*Editor's Note.—New York courts have since determined that *Young* has been overruled by N.Y. Penal Law 35.15 and that "if the intervenor . . . reasonably should have known that the person being defended initiated the original conflict, then justification is not a defense" but that otherwise the mistake as to justification defense is available. People v. Melendez, 588 N.Y.S.2d 718, 722 (N.Y. Sup. Ct. 1992); see also People v. Wang, 625 N.Y.S.2d 413 (N.Y. Sup. Ct. 1995). (The New York Court of Appeals has not addressed the issue again since *Young*.)

engage in prostitution, beating her if she resists or if he is unhappy with the amount of money she earns. He routinely calls her "dog," "bitch," and "whore," and on a few occasions made her eat pet food out of the pets' bowls and bark like a dog. She is often made to sleep on the floor. At times, J. T. deprives Judy of food and refuses to let her get food for the children. During these years of abuse, J. T. threatens numerous times to kill her and to maim her in various ways.

Judy calls the police once to report J. T.'s abuse, but when advised to file a formal complaint, she says that she is afraid her husband would kill her if she had him arrested. The deputies tell her they cannot obtain a warrant for his arrest without a formal complaint and leave the house. Less than an hour later they return, after Judy has ingested an entire bottle of pills. J. T. curses at her and insults her while she is attended to by paramedics and tells them to let her die. The defendant's stomach is pumped out at the hospital, where she is visited by a therapist and discusses filing charges against her husband and having him committed for treatment. The therapist notes that the defendant seems depressed in the hospital and that she expresses considerable anger toward her husband, even threatening to kill him.

The next day when Judy returns home, she confronts her husband with the possibility of pressing charges or having him committed. J. T. tells her he will "see them coming" and will cut her throat before they get to him. That afternoon, one of the Normans' daughters comes to drop off her baby for Judy to look after. Later in the evening, when the Normans go to their bedroom to sleep, J. T. calls Judy a "dog" and makes her lie on the floor. After J. T. falls asleep, the baby begins to cry, and Judy takes him back to her daughter's house so as not to wake up J. T. While at her daughter's, she takes a pistol that she knows her daughter keeps in her purse. When she returns home, she goes into the bedroom where J. T. is sound asleep after drinking heavily. She attempts to shoot J. T. but the gun jams. While he is still asleep, she manages to fix the pistol and this time the gun works. She shoots J. T. once in the back of the head. She then feels his chest and determines that he is still breathing. Judy points the gun at him and shoots him twice more in the back of the head.

After the shooting, two experts in forensic psychology and psychiatry who examine Judy determine that she fits the profile of battered spouse syndrome. The condition, which can appear after a long period of battering, is characterized by the battered spouse coming to believe she is unable to help herself and cannot expect help from anyone else. She believes that she cannot escape the complete control of her husband and that he is invulnerable to law enforcement and other sources of help.

What liability for Judy Norman, if any, under the Model Penal Code? Prepare a list of all criminal code subsections in the order in which you rely on them in your analysis.

Warm-Up for Watergate (#93)

After World War II, Cuban Bernard Barker returns home and works for the Cuban police and for the C.I.A. When Castro comes to power, Barker flees to the United States and settles in Miami. His formal relationship with the C.I.A. ends in 1966. In 1970, his former C.I.A. supervisor, Howard Hunt, also leaves the

Agency but is soon thereafter hired as a consultant by the Executive Office of the President to work on covert special investigations. One such investigation involves Daniel Ellsberg. Ellsberg has been identified as the source of a leak that resulted in a series of articles in the *New York Times* concerning top-secret Pentagon reports about America's involvement in the Vietnam War. A special White House unit known as the Plumbers is convened to handle the situation and prevent future occurrences. John Ehrlichman, Assistant to the President for domestic affairs, heads the group, which includes persons from the National Security Council as well as G. Gordon Liddy, a former F.B.I. agent, and Hunt.

After determining Ellsberg to be the source of the leaks, the group decides to discredit him by gathering damaging personal information. In an effort to do so, the F.B.I. unsuccessfully tries to obtain records about Ellsberg from his psychiatrist, Dr. Lewis J. Fielding. The Plumbers then decide to use Hunt's former C.I.A. contacts to help. Hunt calls Barker in August 1971 but does not tell him that he has left the C.I.A. Rather, Hunt explains that he is part of a White House group that is "a sort of superstructure," with greater jurisdiction than the F.B.I. and C.I.A., "because the F.B.I. was tied by Supreme Court decisions and the Central Intelligence Agency didn't have jurisdiction in certain matters." He asks Barker to become "operational" again and to help them collect information about "a traitor to this country, who [is] passing classified information to the Soviet Embassy." Finally, he asks Barker to also recruit two experienced men with C.I.A. training.

Having worked for Hunt, Barker assumes that the government has authorized the mission and agrees to become operational. He recruits two other men, one of whom is on retainer with the C.I.A. and another who has worked as an intelligence officer in the United States Army. He provides them with the same minimal information that he was given about the operation. All three are accustomed to receiving operational information on a "need to know" basis. Shortly after he recruits the men, Hunt informs Barker that his recruits have received clearance and that the operation is a go. Hunt gives the team a briefing on the mission plan. Barker and the two other men are told to enter Fielding's office, without using force, to look for a file (unspecified at this point, but later revealed to be Ellsberg's treatment file), photograph it, and replace it. There is no discussion about obtaining a warrant or other judicial authorizations for the search. Barker is not concerned, however, because he sees the mission as a matter of national security, of high sensitivity, and typical by C.I.A. standards. He does not ask questions.

The operation, however, does not go smoothly. Finding it impossible to enter Fielding's office without using force, the men use a crowbar to open the door. Wearing gloves, they then pry open locked cabinets and flip through drawers of files. After almost 45 minutes of searching, they find nothing except Ellsberg's name in an address book. They photograph open file cabinets and the book to show they made a good faith attempt to complete their mission. Since force was used to enter the office, they follow Hunt's instructions to make it look as if a drug addict had broken in by scattering some of the doctor's pills on the floor. The next day, Barker and the two recruits are reimbursed for their expenses and given an additional $100 each. No other payment is forthcoming, nor do they expect any. On March 7, 1974, Barker is indicted for the break-in at Dr. Fielding's office.

What liability for Barker, if any, under the Model Penal Code? Prepare a list of all criminal code subsections in the order in which you rely on them in your analysis.

Executing Abortionists (#94)

Paul Hill is ordained as a Presbyterian minister. However, he has a difficult time keeping jobs as a minister owing to his extreme views about abortion. While opposition to the procedure is fairly common, Hill's views are widely considered extreme: He believes that killing abortion providers is justifiable homicide to save the lives of the "babies." After being fired from several churches for his inflammatory rhetoric, he takes his views to pro-life protests. He begins carrying signs saying, "Execute Abortionists." At one protest in front of an abortion clinic, Hill says, "We should have the right to shoot to kill anyone here. . . . "

A turning point for Hill comes when Dr. David Gunn, who frequently assists in abortions, is fatally shot by Michael Griffin outside of an abortion clinic. Upon hearing the news, Hill speaks out in favor of Griffin's actions, appearing on various syndicated television talk shows. Later, after thinking through his support of Griffin, Hill decides that he should act on his own beliefs. He goes one morning to the same abortion clinic at which Gunn had operated. Arriving before the clinic opens, he waits with his 12-gauge shotgun for the physicians to arrive. Dr. John Britton has just flown in to help keep appointments following Gunn's death. He is accompanied from the airport by James and June Barrett. The Barretts have been volunteering as clinic escorts following the murder of Gunn. James is a retired Air Force lieutenant colonel and is confident that he can protect Britton. However, as the Barretts' pickup truck pulls into the clinic's parking lot, Hill approaches the truck from the driver's side and opens fire. James and Britton are hit in the head and die instantly. June, who is riding in the back seat, is wounded in the arm. Hill walks away from the scene but is arrested moments later.

What liability for Hill for the killing of Dr. Britton, if any, under the Model Penal Code? Prepare a list of all criminal code subsections in the order in which you rely on them in your analysis.

✳ DISCUSSION ISSUE

Should the Criminal Law Recognize a Defense or Mitigation for an Honest but Unreasonable Mistake as to a Justification? For Example, Should a Battered Spouse Be Able to Get a Defense or Mitigation for Killing Her Sleeping Husband?

Materials presenting each side of this Discussion Issue appear in the Advanced Materials for Section 19 in Appendix A.

EXCUSE DEFENSES GENERALLY

● OVERVIEW OF THE NATURE OF EXCUSES

Justifications vs. Excuses
Rationale for Recognizing Excuses
    Distributive Principles That Would Not Recognize Excuses
Common Requirements of Excuses
    Disability vs. Mistake Excuses

Justifications vs. Excuses   Justifications and excuses are similar in that both are general defenses and both exculpate an actor because of his blamelessness. However, the two are also importantly different, for both practical and conceptual reasons. Justifications apply to *acts,* while excuses apply to *actors.* Justified conduct is behavior that is to be encouraged, or at least tolerated, if performed by others in similar circumstances in the future. In determining whether conduct is justified, the proper focus is on the act and its circumstances, not the actor. An excuse, in contrast, represents a conclusion that the conduct is wrong, undesirable, but that criminal liability is inappropriate because some characteristic of the actor or his situation undercuts his blameworthiness and, thereby, society's wish to punish him. Excuses do not suggest the absence of a net harm or evil, as do justifications, but rather suggest the absence of the actor's blameworthiness for the harm or evil, usually because the actor either could not control, or did not sufficiently understand or appreciate, what he was doing or its consequences.

    Rationale for Recognizing Excuses Not every distributive principle for criminal liability would necessarily recognize excuse defenses. A distributive principle based on just desert supports the recognition of excuses in order to exculpate blameless offenders. A distributive principle based exclusively on special deterrence might similarly support the recognition of excuses. That is, a sanction can hardly deter a specific offender from future misconduct if that offender cannot control his own behavior or apprehend its circumstances or wrongfulness. Accordingly, from a special-deterrence perspective, the costs of punishment would be wasted on such an offender.

Distributive Principles That Would Not Recognize Excuses   On the other hand, sanctioning such a blameless offender may well have a general deterrent value—that is, it may deter other, nonexcused potential offenders. Punishing even the blameless would signal to potential offenders just how serious the law is about punishing violations, thus discouraging anyone contemplating such violations, especially those who might hope to claim (or feign) an excuse. A distributive principle that looks only to incapacitation or rehabilitation of dangerous offenders similarly might deny an excuse to a blameless offender, at least where the source of the excuse continues or is likely to recur, making the offender likely to reoffend unless the law intervenes. The criminal law would want jurisdiction over such offenders in order to administer the needed incapacitation or rehabilitation. The widespread recognition of excuses under current doctrine suggests that in this respect, desert (and possibly special deterrence) are the guiding distributive principles, rather than general deterrence, incapacitation, or rehabilitation.

Common Requirements of Excuses   Many doctrines and defenses serve as excuses: The involuntary act requirement performs an excusing function, as do the defenses of insanity, subnormality, involuntary intoxication, immaturity, duress, mistake as to a justification, and certain mistake-of-law defenses. The common rationale of these excuses, to exculpate the blameless, gives rise to common requirements: A *disability* or *reasonable mistake* must cause an *excusing condition*. Under each doctrine, an actor is excused if, because of the special conditions of the defense, the actor could not reasonably have been expected to have avoided the violation. This conclusion may derive from either of two kinds of explanations. For the disability excuses, the actor can point to abnormal circumstances or abnormal characteristics that make it too difficult for her to appreciate the criminality or wrongfulness of her conduct or too difficult to conform her conduct to the requirements of law. For mistake excuses, no disabling abnormality exists, but the actor can claim that, because of a reasonable mistake, she did not realize that her conduct violated the law or was wrongful.

Disability vs. Mistake Excuses   The disability and mistake excuses generate the same conclusion of blamelessness, but in different ways. In the disability excuses, the disabling abnormality sets the actor apart from the general population. The mistake excuses seem to do the opposite: They claim that the actor should not be punished because he has acted just as anyone else would, and should, have acted in the same situation. That is, the actor's mistake is reasonable; any reasonable person would have made the same mistake. This path to blamelessness has complications, however, for no disabling abnormality exists that can be considered "responsible" for the actor's offense. Further, with no disability to distinguish the actor from the general population, there is greater danger that acquitting the apparently normal actor will undercut the law's prohibition of the actor's conduct. The absence of a disabling abnormality may help explain why the law is more hesitant to recognize mistake excuses and, when they are recognized, why it tends to severely restrict their reach. Objective appearances aside, however, the two mechanisms of excuse in fact are analogous. Both rely on a conclusion that the actor could not reasonably have been expected to have avoided the violation. Where a disabling abnormality exists, the claim of excuse is essentially a claim that the reasonable person suffering a similar disability would have been similarly unable to avoid a violation.

Mistake Excuses

◆ THE CASE OF JULIO MARRERO (#95)

Julio Marrero of the Bronx, New York, is a disabled Vietnam veteran who previously worked as an undercover agent in a Puerto Rican drug enforcement operation for the Departamento de Hacienda. He now works as a prison guard at the federal prison in Danbury, Connecticut, and is the father of 6: Sonya, 11; Hector Louis, 8; Ricardo, 6; Carina 4; and Joe and Vanessa, 3. His children Endira and Carlos will be born in a year and two years, respectively.

During his time as a guard at Danbury, Marrero has received death threats, as many guards have, including one from a recently released inmate. He regularly carries a pistol for protection, having received weapons training when he was in the Military Police. Marrero stores several weapons at the Military Police armory in Manhattan for use at the firing range.

Marrero purchases his pistol from a New York City gun dealer, Eugene DiMayo, who sells it to Marrero knowing

Figure 93

549

Figure 94. **Formerly a social club, now a Mexican restaurant, 207 Madison Street was where Julio Marrero was arrested on December 19, 1977**

(Photograph by the author)

that Marrero does not have a special New York gun permit, but believing and advising Marrero that, as a federal prison guard, Marrero does not need one. DiMayo knows several federal prison guards who similarly have bought weapons without a special New York gun permit. DiMayo explains to Marrero that "federal corrections officers" are considered "peace officers," under the New York firearms statute and "licenses are not required if proper identification is presented."

On December 19, 1977, while off duty, Marrero visits a social club at 207 Madison Street in New York City. As he enters the club, he is searched by police officer G. Dugan of the 7th precinct, who finds a loaded .38 caliber pistol on Marrero's person. Marrero explains that he does not have a permit but does not need one because he is a federal corrections officer. He shows his identification badge. The police call the Danbury prison and confirm that he is a guard there. Marrero is nonetheless arrested, and charges are filed. Ten days later Marrero is indicted for criminal possession of a weapon.

1. Relying only on your own intuitions of justice, what liability and punishment, if any, does Julio Marrero deserve?

N	0	1	2	3	4	5	6	7	8	9	10	11
☐	☐	☐	☐	☐	☐	☐	☐	☐	☐	☐	☐	☐
no liability	liability but no punishment	1 day	2 wks	2 mo	6 mo	1 yr	3 yrs	7 yrs	15 yrs	30 yrs	life imprison-ment	death

2. What "justice" arguments could defense counsel make on the defendant's behalf?[†]

3. What "justice" arguments could the prosecution make against the defendant?

4. What liability, if any, for Marrero under the then-existing statutes? Prepare a list of all criminal code subsections in the order in which you rely upon them in your analysis.

5. What liability, if any, under the Model Penal Code? Prepare a list of all criminal code subsections in the order in which you rely upon them in your analysis.

---

† In other words, articulate the intuitions of justice of this sort that guided the judgment you made on the liability scale in Question 1.

■ THE LAW

Consolidated Laws of New York Penal Law
(1977)

Section 265.01 Criminal possession of a weapon in the fourth degree

A person is guilty of criminal possession of a weapon in the fourth degree when:

(1) He possesses any firearm, electronic dart gun, gravity knife, switch-blade knife, cane sword, billy, blackjack, bludgeon, metal knuckles, chuka stick, sand bag, sandclub, or slingshot, or

(2) He possesses any dagger, dangerous knife, dirk, razor, stiletto, imitation pistol, or any other dangerous or deadly instrument or weapon with intent to use the same unlawfully against another; or

(3) He knowingly has in his possession a rifle, shotgun or firearm in or upon a building or grounds, used for educational purposes, of any school, college or university, except the forestry lands, wherever located, owned and maintained by the State University of New York college of environmental science and forestry, without the written authorization of such educational institution; or

(4) He possesses a rifle or shotgun and has been convicted of a felony or serious offense; or

(5) He possesses any dangerous or deadly weapon and is not a citizen of the United States; or

(6) He is a person who has certified not suitable to possess a rifle or shotgun, as defined in subsection sixteen of section 265.00, and refuses to yield possession of such rifle or shotgun upon the demand of a police officer. Whenever a person is certified not suitable to possess a rifle or shotgun, a member of the police department to which such certification is made, or of the state police, shall forthwith seize any rifle or shotgun possessed by such person. A rifle or shotgun seized as herein provided shall not be destroyed, but shall be delivered to the headquarters of such police department, or state police, and there retained until the aforesaid certificate has been rescinded by the director or physician in charge, or other disposition of such rifle or shotgun has been ordered or authorized by a court of competent jurisdiction.

Criminal possession of a weapon in the fourth degree is a class A misdemeanor.

Section 265.02 Criminal possession of a weapon in the third degree

A person is guilty of criminal possession of a weapon in the third degree when:

(1) He commits the crime of criminal possession of a weapon in the fourth degree as defined in subdivision one, two, three or five of section 265.01, and has been previously convicted of any crime; or

(2) He possesses any explosive or incendiary bomb, bombshell, fire-arm silencer, machine-gun or any other firearm or weapon simulating a machine-gun and which is adaptable for such use; or

(3) He knowingly has in his possession a machine-gun or firearm which has been defaced for the purpose of concealment or prevention of the detection of a crime or misrepresenting the identity of such machine-gun or firearm; or

(4) He possesses any loaded firearm. Such possession shall not, except as provided in subdivision one, constitute a violation of this section if such possession takes place in such person's home or place of business.

(5)(i) He possesses twenty or more firearms; or (ii) he possesses a fire-arm and has been previously convicted of a felony or a class A misdemeanor defined in this chapter within the five years immediately preceding the com-mission of the offense and such possession did not take place in the person's home or place of business.

Criminal possession of a weapon in the third degree is a class D felony.

Section 265.20 Exemptions

a. Sections 265.01, 265.02, 265.03, 265.04, 265.05, 265.10, 265.15 and 270.05 shall not apply to:

(1) Possession of any of the weapons, instruments, appliances or sub-stances specified in sections 265.01, 265.02, 265.03, 265.04, 265.05 and 270.05 by the following:

(a) Persons in the military service of the state of New York when duly authorized by regulations issued by the chief of staff to the governor to possess the same, members of the division of state police, and peace officers as defined in subdivision thirty-three of section 1.20 of the criminal procedure law and persons appointed as railroad policemen pursuant to section eighty-eight of the railroad law.

(b) Persons in the military or other service of the United States, in pursuit of official duty or when duly authorized by federal law, regu-lation or order to possess the same.

(c) Persons employed in fulfilling defense contracts with the gov-ernment of the United States or agencies thereof when possession of the same is necessary for manufacture, transport, installation and test-ing under the requirements of such contract.

(d) A person voluntarily surrendering such weapon, instrument, appliance or substance, provided that such surrender shall be made to the sheriff of the county in which such person resides and in the county of Nassau to the commissioner of police or a member of the police department thereof designated by him, or if such person resides in a city having a population of seventy-five thousand or more to the police commissioner or head of the police force or department, or to a member of the force or department designated by such commissioner or head; and provided, further, that the same shall be surrendered by such person only after he gives notice in writing to the appropriate authority, stating his name, address, the nature of the weapon to be surrendered, and the approximate time of day and the place where such surrender shall take place. Such notice shall be acknowledged immediately upon receipt thereof by such authority. Nothing in this paragraph shall be construed as granting immunity from prosecution for any crime or offense except that of unlawful possession of such weapons, instruments, appliances or substances surrendered as herein provided. A person who possesses any such weapon, instrument, appliance or substance as an executor or administrator or any other lawful possessor of such property of a decedent may continue to possess such property for a period not over fifteen days. If such property is not lawfully disposed of within such period the possessor shall deliver it to an appropriate official described in this paragraph or such property may be delivered to the superintendent of state police. Such officer shall hold it and shall thereafter deliver it on the written request of such executor, administrator or other lawful possessor of such property to a named person, provided such named person is licensed to or is otherwise lawfully permitted to possess the same. If no request to deliver the property is received within two years of the delivery of such property to such official he shall dispose of it in accordance with the provisions of section 400.05 of the penal law.

(2) Possession of a machine-gun, firearm, switchblade knife, gravity knife, billy or blackjack by a warden, superintendent, headkeeper or deputy of a state prison, penitentiary, workhouse, county jail or other institution for the detention of persons convicted or accused of crime or detained as witnesses in criminal cases, in pursuit of official duty or when duly authorized by regulation or order to possess the same.

(3) Possession of a pistol or revolver by a person to whom a license therefore has been issued as provided under section 400.00; provided, that such a license shall not preclude a conviction for the offense defined in subdivision three of section 265.01.

(4) Possession of a rifle, shotgun or longbow for use while hunting, trapping or fishing, by a person, not a citizen of the United States, carrying a valid license issued pursuant to section 11B0713 of the environmental conservation law.

(5) Possession of a rifle or shotgun by a person who has been convicted as specified in subdivision four of section 265.01 to whom a certificate of good conduct has been issued pursuant to section two hundred forty-two, subdivision three of the executive law.

(6) Possession of a switchblade or gravity knife for use while hunting, trapping or fishing by a person carrying a valid license issued to him pursuant to section 11B0713 of the environmental conservation law.

(7) Possession, at an indoor or outdoor rifle range for the purpose of loading and firing the same, of a rifle of not more than twenty-two caliber rim fire, the propelling force of which may be either gunpowder, air or springs, by a person under sixteen years of age but not under twelve, who

is a duly enrolled member of any club, team or society organized for educational purposes and maintaining as a part of its facilities, or having written permission to use, such rifle range under the supervision, guidance and instruction of (a) a duly commissioned officer of the United States army, navy, marine corps or coast guard, or of the national guard of the state of New York; or (b) a duly qualified adult citizen of the United States who has been granted a certificate as an instructor in small arms practice issued by the United States army, navy or marine corps, or by the adjutant general of this state, or by the National Rifle Association of America, a not-for-profit corporation duly organized under the laws of this state.

(8) The manufacturer of machine-guns, pilum ballistic knives, switchblade or gravity knives, billies or blackjacks as merchandise and the disposal and shipment thereof direct to a regularly constituted or appointed state or municipal police department, sheriff, policeman or other peace officer, or to a state prison, penitentiary, workhouse, county jail or other institution for the detention of persons convicted or accused of crime or held as witnesses in criminal cases, or to the military service of this state or of the United States.

(9) . . .

(a) The regular and ordinary transport of firearms as merchandise, provided that the person transporting such firearms, where he knows or has reasonable means of ascertaining what he is transporting, notifies in writing the police commissioner, police chief or other law enforcement officer performing such functions at the place of delivery, of the name and address of the consignee and the place of delivery, and withholds delivery to the consignee for such reasonable period of time designated in writing by such police commissioner, police chief or other law enforcement officer as such official may deem necessary for investigation as to whether the consignee may lawfully receive and possess such firearms.

(b) The transportation of such pistols or revolvers into, out of or within the city of New York may be done only with the consent of the police commissioner of the city of New York. To obtain such consent, the manufacturer must notify the police commissioner in writing of the name and address of the transporting manufacturer, or agent or employee of the manufacturer who is authorized in writing by such manufacturer to transport pistols or revolvers, the number, make and model number of the firearms to be transported and the place where the manufacturer regularly conducts business within the city of New York and such other information as the commissioner may deem necessary. The manufacturer must not transport such pistols and revolvers between the designated places of business for such reasonable period of time designated in writing by the police commissioner as such official may deem necessary for investigation and to give consent. The police commissioner may not unreasonably withhold his consent.

(10) Engaging in the business of gunsmith or dealer in firearms by a person to whom a valid license therefor has been issued pursuant to section 400.00.

(11) Possession of a pistol or revolver by a police officer or sworn peace officer of another state while conducting official business within the state of New York. . . .

b. At any time, any person who voluntarily delivers to a peace officer any weapon, instrument, appliance or substance specified in section 265.01, 265.02, 265.03, 265.04, or 265.05, under circumstances not suspicious, peculiar or involving the commission of any crime, shall not be arrested. Instead, the officer who might make the arrest shall issue or cause to be issued in a proper case a summons or other legal process to the person for investigation of the source of the weapon, instrument, appliance or substance.

c. Section 265.01 shall not apply to possession of that type of billy commonly known as a "police baton" which is twenty-four to twenty-six inches in length and no more than one and one-quarter inches in thickness by members of an auxiliary police force of a city with a population in excess of one million persons when duly authorized by regulation or order issued by the police commissioner of such city. Such regulations shall require training in the use of the baton and instruction in the legal use of deadly physical force pursuant to article thirty-five of this chapter. Notwithstanding the provisions of this section or any other provision of law, possession of such baton shall not be authorized when used intentionally to strike another person except in those situations when the use of deadly physical force is authorized by such article thirty-five.

Section 5.00 Penal law not strictly construed

The general rule that a penal statute is to be strictly construed does not apply to this chapter, but the provisions herein must be construed according to the fair import of their terms to promote justice and effect the objects of the law.

Section 15.00 Culpability; definitions of terms

The following definitions are applicable to this chapter:

(1) "Act" means a bodily movement.

(2) "Voluntary act" means a bodily movement performed consciously as a result of effort or determination and includes the possession of property if the actor was aware of his physical possession or control thereof for a sufficient period to have been able to terminate it.

(3) "Omission" means a failure to perform an act as to which a duty of performance is imposed by law.

(4) "Conduct" means an act or omission and its accompanying mental state.

(5) "To act" means either to perform an act or to omit to perform an act.

(6) "Culpable mental state" means "intentionally" or "knowingly" or "recklessly" or with "criminal negligence," as these terms are defined in section 15.05.

Section 15.05 Culpability; definitions of culpable mental states

The following definitions are applicable to this chapter:

(1) "Intentionally." A person acts intentionally with respect to a result or to conduct described by a statute defining an offense when his conscious objective is to cause such result or to engage in such conduct.

(2) "Knowingly." A person acts knowingly with respect to conduct or to a circumstance described by a statute defining an offense when he is aware that his conduct is of such nature or that such circumstance exists.

(3) "Recklessly." A person acts recklessly with respect to a result or to a circumstance described by a statute defining an offense when he is aware of and consciously disregards a substantial and unjustifiable risk that such result will occur or that such circumstance exists. The risk must be of such nature and degree that disregard thereof constitutes a gross deviation from the standard of conduct that a reasonable person would observe in the situation. A person who creates such a risk but is unaware thereof solely by reason of voluntary intoxication also acts recklessly with respect thereto.

(4) "Criminal negligence." A person acts with criminal negligence with respect to a result or to a circumstance described by a statute defining an offense when he fails to perceive a substantial and unjustifiable risk that such result will occur or that such circumstance exists. The risk must be of such nature and degree that the failure to perceive it constitutes a gross deviation from the standard of care that a reasonable person would observe in the situation.

Section 15.10 Requirements for criminal liability in general and for offenses of strict liability and mental culpability

The minimal requirement for criminal liability is the performance by a person of conduct which includes a voluntary act or the omission to perform an act which he is physically capable of performing. If such conduct is all that is required for commission of a particular offense, or if an offense or some material element thereof does not require a culpable mental state on the part of the actor, such offense is one of "strict liability." If a culpable mental state on the part of the actor is required with respect to every material element of an offense, such offense is one of "mental culpability."

Section 15.15 Construction of statutes with respect to culpability requirements

(1) When the commission of an offense defined in this chapter, or some element of an offense, requires a particular culpable mental state, such mental state is ordinarily designated in the statute defining the offense by use of the terms "intentionally," "knowingly," "recklessly" or "criminal negligence," or by use of terms, such as "with intent to defraud" and "knowing it to be false," describing a specific kind of intent or knowledge. When one and only one of such terms appears in a statute defining an offense, it is presumed to apply to every element of the offense unless an intent to limit its application clearly appears.

(2) Although no culpable mental state is expressly designated in a statute defining an offense, a culpable mental state may nevertheless be required for the commission of such offense, or with respect to some or all of the material elements thereof, if the proscribed conduct necessarily involves such culpable mental state. A statute defining a crime, unless clearly indicating a legislative intent to impose strict liability, should be construed as defining a crime of mental culpability. This subdivision applies to offenses defined both in and outside this chapter.

Section 15.20 Effect of ignorance or mistake upon liability

(1) A person is not relieved of criminal liability for conduct because he engages in such conduct under a mistaken belief of fact, unless:

(a) Such factual mistake negatives the culpable mental state required for the commission of an offense; or

(b) The statute defining the offense or a statute related thereto expressly provides that such factual mistake constitutes a defense or exemption; or

(c) Such factual mistake is of a kind that supports a defense of justification as defined in article thirty-five of this chapter.

(2) A person is not relieved of criminal liability for conduct because he engages in such conduct under a mistaken belief that it does not, as a matter of law, constitute an offense, unless such mistaken belief is founded upon an official statement of the law contained in:

(a) a statute or other enactment; or

(b) an administrative order or grant of permission; or

(c) a judicial decision of a state or federal court; or

(d) an interpretation of the statute or law relating to the offense, officially made or issued by a public servant, agency or body legally charged or empowered with the responsibility or privilege of administering, enforcing or interpreting such statute or law.

(3) Notwithstanding the use of the term "knowingly" in any provision of this chapter defining an offense in which the age of a child is an element thereof, knowledge by the defendant of the age of such child is not an element of any such offense and it is not, unless expressly so provided, a defense to a prosecution therefor that the defendant did not know the age of the child or believed such age to be the same as or greater than that specified in the statute.

Consolidated Laws of New York Annotated
Criminal Procedure Law
(1977)

Section 1.20C Definitions of terms of general use in this chapter

Except where different meanings are expressly specified in subsequent provisions of this chapter, the term definitions contained in section 10.00 of the penal law are applicable to this chapter, and, in addition, the following terms have the following meanings:

(1) "Accusatory instrument" means an indictment, an information, a simplified information, a prosecutor's information, a superior court information, a misdemeanor complaint or a felony complaint. Every accusatory instrument, regardless of the person designated therein as accuser, constitutes an accusation on behalf of the state as plaintiff and must be entitled "the people of the state of New York" against a designated person, known as the defendant.

(2) "Local criminal court accusatory instrument" means any accusatory instrument other than an indictment or a superior court information.

(3) "Indictment" means a written accusation by a grand jury, more fully defined and described in article two hundred, filed with a superior court, which charges one or more defendants with the commission of one or more offenses, at least one of which is a crime, and which serves as a basis for prosecution thereof.

(3)-a. "Superior court information" means a written accusation by a district attorney more fully defined and described in articles one hundred ninety-five and two hundred, filed with a superior court pursuant to article one hundred ninety-five, which charges one or more defendants with the commission of one or more offenses, at least one of which is a crime, and which serves as a basis for prosecution thereof.

(4) "Information" means a verified written accusation by a person, more fully defined and described in article one hundred, filed with a local criminal court, which charges one or more defendants with the commission of one or more offenses, none of which is a felony, and which may serve both to commence a criminal action and as a basis for prosecution thereof.

(5) [See, also, subd. 5 below.] "Simplified traffic information" means a written accusation, more fully defined and described in article one hundred, by a police officer or other public servant authorized by law to issue same, filed with a local criminal court, which, being in a brief or simplified form prescribed by the commissioner of motor vehicles, charges a person with one or more traffic infractions or misdemeanors relating to traffic, and which may serve both to commence a criminal action for such offense and as a basis for prosecution thereof.

(5) [See, also, subd. 5 above.]

(a) "Simplified information" means a simplified traffic information, a simplified parks information, or a simplified environmental conservation information.

(b) "Simplified traffic information" means a written accusation by a police officer, or other public servant authorized by law to issue same, more fully defined and described in article one hundred, filed with a local criminal court, which, being in a brief or simplified form prescribed by the commissioner of motor vehicles, charges a person with one or more traffic infractions or misdemeanors relating to traffic, and which may serve both to commence a criminal action for such offense and as a basis for prosecution thereof.

(c) "Simplified parks information" means a written accusation by a police officer, or other public servant authorized by law to issue same, filed with a local criminal court, which, being in a brief or simplified form prescribed by the commissioner of parks and recreation, charges a person with one or more offenses, other than a felony, for which a uniform simplified parks information may be issued pursuant to the parks and recreation law and the navigation law, and which may serve both to commence a criminal action for such offense and as a basis for prosecution thereof.

(d) "Simplified environmental conservation information" means a written accusation by a police officer, or other public servant authorized by law to issue same, filed with a local criminal court, which being in a brief or simplified form prescribed by the commissioner of environmental conservation, charges a person with one or more offenses, other than a felony, for which a uniform simplified environmental conservation simplified information may be issued pursuant to the environmental conservation law, and which may serve both to commence a criminal action for such offense and as a basis for prosecution thereof.

(6) "Prosecutor's information" means a written accusation by a district attorney, more fully defined and described in article one hundred, filed with a local criminal court, which charges one or more defendants with the commission of one or more offenses, none of which is a felony, and which serves as a basis for prosecution thereof.

(7) "Misdemeanor complaint" means a verified written accusation by a person, more fully defined and described in article one hundred, filed with a local criminal court, which charges one or more defendants with the commission of one or more offenses, at least one of which is a misdemeanor and none of which is a felony, and which serves to commence a criminal action but which may not, except upon the defendant's consent, serve as a basis for prosecution of the offenses charged therein.

(8) "Felony complaint" means a verified written accusation by a person, more fully defined and described in article one hundred, filed with a local criminal court, which charges one or more defendants with the commission of one or more felonies and which serves to commence a criminal action but not as a basis for prosecution thereof.

(9) "Arraignment" means the occasion upon which a defendant against whom an accusatory instrument has been filed appears before the court in which the criminal action is pending for the purpose of having such court acquire and exercise control over his person with respect to such accusatory instrument and of setting the course of further proceedings in the action.

(10) "Plea," in addition to its ordinary meaning as prescribed in sections 220.10 and 340.20, means, where appropriate, the occasion upon which a defendant enters such a plea to an accusatory instrument.

(11) "Trial." A jury trial commences with the selection of the jury and includes all further proceedings through the rendition of a verdict. A non-jury trial commences with the first opening address, if there be any, and, if not, when the first witness is sworn, and includes all further proceedings through the rendition of a verdict.

(12) "Verdict" means the announcement by a jury in the case of a jury trial, or by the court in the case of a non-jury trial, of its decision upon the

defendant's guilt or innocence of the charges submitted to or considered by it.

(13) "Conviction" means the entry of a plea of guilty to, or a verdict of guilty upon, an accusatory instrument other than a felony complaint, or to one or more counts of such instrument.

(14) "Sentence" means the imposition and entry of sentence upon a conviction.

(15) "Judgment." A judgment is comprised of a conviction and the sentence imposed thereon and is completed by imposition and entry of the sentence.

(16) "Criminal action." A criminal action (a) commences with the filing of an accusatory instrument against a defendant in a criminal court, as specified in subdivision seventeen; (b) includes the filing of all further accusatory instruments directly derived from the initial one, and all proceedings, orders and motions conducted or made by a criminal court in the course of disposing of any such accusatory instrument, or which, regardless of the court in which they occurred or were made, could properly be considered as a part of the record of the case by an appellate court upon an appeal from a judgment of conviction; and (c) terminates with the imposition of sentence or some other final disposition in a criminal court of the last accusatory instrument filed in the case.

(17) "Commencement of criminal action." A criminal action is commenced by the filing of an accusatory instrument against a defendant in a criminal court, and, if more than one accusatory instrument is filed in the course of the action, it commences when the first of such instruments is filed.

(18) "Criminal proceeding" means any proceeding which (a) constitutes a part of a criminal action or (b) occurs in a criminal court and is related to a prospective, pending or completed criminal action, either of this state or of any other jurisdiction, or involves a criminal investigation.

(19) "Criminal court" means any court defined as such by section 10.10.

(20) "Superior court" means any court defined as such by subdivision two of section 10.10.

(21) "Local criminal court" means any court defined as such by subdivision three of section 10.10.

(22) "Intermediate appellate court" means any court possessing appellate jurisdiction, other than the court of appeals.

(23) "Judge" means any judicial officer who is a member of or constitutes a court, whether referred to in another provision of law as a justice or by any other title.

(24) "Trial jurisdiction." A criminal court has "trial jurisdiction" of an offense when an indictment or an information charging such offense may properly be filed with such court, and when such court has authority to accept a plea to, try or otherwise finally dispose of such accusatory instrument.

(25) "Preliminary jurisdiction." A criminal court has "preliminary jurisdiction" of an offense when, regardless of whether it has trial jurisdiction

thereof, a criminal action for such offense may be commenced therein, and when such court may conduct proceedings with respect thereto which lead or may lead to prosecution and final disposition of the action in a court having trial jurisdiction thereof.

(26) "Appearance ticket" means a written notice issued by a public servant, more fully defined in section 150.10, requiring a person to appear before a local criminal court in connection with an accusatory instrument to be filed against him therein.

(27) "Summons" means a process of a local criminal court, more fully defined in section 130.10, requiring a defendant to appear before such court for the purpose of arraignment upon an accusatory instrument filed therewith by which a criminal action against him has been commenced.

(28) "Warrant of arrest" means a process of a local criminal court, more fully defined in section 120.10, directing a police officer to arrest a defendant and to bring him before such court for the purpose of arraignment upon an accusatory instrument filed therewith by which a criminal action against him has been commenced.

(29) "Superior court warrant of arrest" means a process of a superior court directing a police officer to arrest a defendant and to bring him before such court for the purpose of arraignment upon an indictment filed therewith by which a criminal action against him has been commenced.

(30) "Bench warrant" means a process of a criminal court in which a criminal action is pending, directing a police officer, or a uniformed court officer, pursuant to paragraph b of subdivision two of section 530.70 of this chapter, to take into custody a defendant in such action who has previously been arraigned upon the accusatory instrument by which the action was commenced, and to bring him before such court. The function of a bench warrant is to achieve the court appearance of a defendant in a pending criminal action for some purpose other than his initial arraignment in the action.

(31) "Prosecutor" means a district attorney or any other public servant who represents the people in a criminal action.

(32) "District attorney" means a district attorney, an assistant district attorney or a special district attorney, and, where appropriate, the attorney general, an assistant attorney general, a deputy attorney general or a special deputy attorney general.

(33) "Peace officer." The following persons are peace officers:

(a) A police officer;

(b) An attendant, uniformed court officer or an official of the supreme court in the first and second departments;

(c) An attendant, uniformed court officer or other official attached to the county courts of Nassau and Suffolk counties;

(d) A marshal, clerk or attendant of a district court;

(e) A clerk, uniformed court officer or other official of the criminal court of the city of New York;

(f) A uniformed court officer or an official of the civil court of the city of New York;

(g) An attendant, clerk or uniformed court officer of the family court;

(h) An attendant, or an official, or guard of any state prison or of any penal correctional institution.

(i) A parole officer in the department of correctional services;

(j) A harbor master appointed by a county, city, town or village;

(k) An investigator of the office of the state commission of investigation;

(l) Onondaga county park rangers;

(m) An officer or agent of a duly incorporated society for the prevention of cruelty to animals and children;

(n) An inspector or investigator of the department of agriculture and markets;

(o) An employee of the department of taxation and finance assigned to enforcement of the tax on cigarettes imposed by article twenty of the tax law by the commissioner of taxation and finance;

(p) An employee of the New York City finance administration assigned to enforcement of the tax on cigarettes imposed by section D46B2.0 of the administrative code of the city of New York by the finance administrator;

(q) A constable or police constable of a city, county, town or village; or a bay constable of the town of Hempstead;

(r) Suffolk county park rangers;

(s) A probation officer;

(t) The sheriff, under-sheriff and deputy sheriffs of New York City;

(u) Long Island railroad police.

(34) "Police officer." The following persons are police officers:

(a) A sworn officer of the division of state police;

(b) Sheriffs, under-sheriffs and deputy sheriffs of counties outside of New York City;

(c) A sworn officer of an authorized county or county parkway police department;

(d) A sworn officer of an authorized police department or force of a city, town, village or police district;

(e) A sworn officer of an authorized police department of an authority or a sworn officer of the state regional park police in the office of parks and recreation;

(f) A sworn officer of the capital police force of the office of general services;

(g) An investigator employed in the office of a district attorney;

(h) An investigator employed by a commission created by an interstate compact who is, to a substantial extent, engaged in the enforcement of the criminal laws of this state;

(i) The chief and deputy fire marshals, the supervising fire marshals and the fire marshals of the bureau of fire investigation of the New York City fire department;

(j) A sworn officer of the division of law enforcement in the department of environmental conservation;

(k) A sworn officer of a police force of a public authority created by an interstate compact; (l) [See, also, par. (l) below] Long Island railroad police.

(l) [See, also, par. (l) above] An employee of the department of taxation and finance assigned to enforcement of the tax on cigarettes imposed by article twenty of the tax law by the commissioner of taxation and finance for the purpose of applying for and executing search warrants under article six hundred ninety of this chapter in connection with the enforcement of such tax on cigarettes.

(34)-a. "Geographical area of employment." The "geographical area of employment" of certain police officers is as follows:

(a) New York state constitutes the "geographical area of employment" of any police officer employed as such by an agency of the state or by an authority which functions throughout the state;

(b) A county, city, town or village, as the case may be, constitutes the "geographical area of employment" of any police officer employed as such by an agency of such political subdivision or by an authority which functions only in such political subdivision; and

(c) Where an authority functions in more than one county, the "geographical area of employment" of a police officer employed thereby extends through all of such counties.

(35) "Commitment to the custody of the sheriff," when referring to an order of a court located in a county or city which has established a department of correction, means commitment to the commissioner of correction of such county or city.

(36) "County" ordinarily means (a) any county outside of New York City or (b) New York City in its entirety. Unless the context requires a different construction, New York City, despite its five counties, is deemed a single county within the meaning of the provisions of this chapter in which that term appears.

(37) "Lesser included offense." When it is impossible to commit a particular crime without concomitantly committing, by the same conduct, another offense of lesser grade or degree, the latter is, with respect to the former, a "lesser included offense." In any case in which it is legally possible to attempt to commit a crime, an attempt to commit such crime constitutes a lesser included offense with respect thereto.

(38) "Oath" includes an affirmation and every other made authorized by law of attesting to the truth of that which is stated.

(39) "Petty offense" means a violation or a traffic infraction.

(40) "Evidence in chief" means evidence, received at a trial or other criminal proceeding in which a defendant's guilt or innocence of an offense is in issue, which may be considered as a part of the quantum of substantive proof establishing or tending to establish the commission of such offense or an element thereof or the defendant's connection therewith.

Model Penal Code
(Official Draft 1962)

Section 2.04. Ignorance or Mistake

(1) Ignorance or mistake as to a matter of fact or law is a defense if:

(a) the ignorance or mistake negatives the purpose, knowledge, belief, recklessness or negligence required to establish a material element of the offense; or

(b) the law provides that the state of mind established by such ignorance or mistake constitutes a defense.

(2) Although ignorance or mistake would otherwise afford a defense to the offense charged, the defense is not available if the defendant would be guilty of another offense had the situation been as he supposed. In such case, however, the ignorance or mistake of the defendant shall reduce the grade and degree of the offense of which he may be convicted to those of the offense of which he would be guilty had the situation been as he supposed.

(3) A belief that conduct does not legally constitute an offense is a defense to a prosecution for that offense based upon such conduct when:

(a) the statute or other enactment defining the offense is not known to the actor and has not been published or otherwise reasonably made available prior to the conduct alleged; or

(b) he acts in reasonable reliance upon an official statement of the law, afterward determined to be invalid or erroneous, contained in (i) a statute or other enactment; (ii) a judicial decision, opinion or judgment; (iii) an administrative order or grant of permission; or (iv) an official interpretation of the public officer or body charged by law with responsibility for the interpretation, administration or enforcement of the law defining the offense.

(4) The defendant must prove a defense arising under Subsection (3) of this Section by a preponderance of evidence.

Section 2.02. General Requirements of Culpability

. . .

(9) Culpability as to Illegality of Conduct. Neither knowledge nor recklessness or negligence as to whether conduct constitutes an offense or as to the existence, meaning or application of the law determining the elements of an offense is an element of such offense, unless the definition of the offense or the Code so provides. . . .

● OVERVIEW OF MISTAKE OF LAW EXCUSE

Hypothetical: Sophie's Stand (#96)

Sophie is upset at the recent practice of "pro-life" groups, which have begun heckling women who enter the local Woman's Center, where abortions are performed. As an active member of a "pro-choice" group, she has joined in counter-demonstrations but is increasingly persuaded that they are ineffective at deterring or countering what she sees as unfair harassment. Because she is a law student, she is asked at a planning meeting of her group to investigate other methods for minimizing the effect of the pro-life picketing. All present agree that any course of action that they take as a group should remain lawful. While visiting the scene of the demonstrations, Sophie notices that the only way for a large group to access the Center is along the street from the park, where the pro-life people now assemble their group. If pro-choice forces congregated on both sidewalks at some point on the street, the pro-life demonstrators would have to switch to much longer and more narrow routes, which would both delay their arrival at the Center and force them to break into small groups that might not be quite as emotionally charged as the large excited groups that have done the harassing.

Sophie reviews applicable law and concludes that the planned action would not be unlawful, because the pro-life demonstrators would never be touched or detained in any way, they would have another means of access to where they wished to go, and the sidewalk blocking would last only a short time and therefore would not interfere with normal public use. Her group likes her idea, but asks that she check with officials to be sure that congesting the sidewalks in this way would not be unlawful. In response to Sophie's inquiry, the local police advise against the proposed plan or any other such confrontational activity. When Sophie presses for a formal legal opinion, the police point out that they are not lawyers and refer her to the State's Attorney's office, while also repeating their advice against this or any other confrontation. The State's Attorney's office responds to Sophie's inquiry by noting its longstanding policy against giving prior official interpretations of state law. Providing such legal advice, the response notes, would be impossible with the office's current legal staff, which is barely able to keep up with current court cases. Sophie reports back to her group about these communications, together with her own research and her legal opinion that the planned conduct would not be a violation of law. The group accepts her recommendation.

The next day the pro-choice supporters congregate on the sidewalk in the path of the pro-life demonstrators. No contact is made. The pro-life marchers split up and take other routes to the Center. Members of Sophie's group are arrested for "Obstructing a Public Passageway," a county ordinance that does expressly criminalize their conduct. It turns out that her law school's library collection, where she had done her research, does not include county ordinances.

Does Sophie have a defense? Do the other members of her group have a defense?

Notes

Venerable Maxim That "Ignorance of Law Is No Excuse"
    Desert Claim in Support of Maxim
    Utilitarian Claim in Support of Maxim
Two Common Exceptions to Maxim
    Unavailable Law
    Reliance on Official Misstatement
Exceptions to Maxim Rooted in Estoppel, Not Actor's Blamelessness

Mistake may serve as a defense in various ways. When an actor mistakes another's umbrella for his own, his mistake will negate the culpable state of mind required for theft (because he does not know the umbrella belongs to someone else). Such a mistake is an example of mistake as an absent-element defense. A mistake also may be the basis for a general defense, without regard to the elements of the offense charged. An actor who takes another's backpack, mistakenly believing it to contain a terrorist bomb that is endangering a restaurant full of people, satisfies all the elements of theft, yet if the actor's belief is reasonable, he may have a general excuse for mistake as to justification. If a new antiterrorism law makes it an offense to carry a sharply pointed object in a public place, an actor may have a defense to a violation if the law has not yet reasonably been made available to the public or if a public official has incorrectly advised the actor that the law does not apply to umbrellas. It is this latter kind of mistake, providing a general mistake excuse unrelated to offense elements and unrelated to a belief in justification, that is the subject of this Section.

Venerable Maxim That "Ignorance of Law Is No Excuse"   The common law followed, and modern courts still frequently note, the maxim that "ignorance or mistake of law is no excuse." At common law, the maxim frequently was applied even where the mistake of law negated an offense element. This extreme form of adherence to the maxim is no longer common. A mistake that negates an offense element, even a mistake of law, is now typically recognized as a defense. The maxim continues to be given effect otherwise, however, in denying a defense where an actor's mistake is not about the nature or circumstances of his conduct, but about the *lawfulness* of his conduct—that is, where the actor knows what he is doing, but does not know that what he is doing *is a crime*. Such mistakes rarely negate an offense element, because few offenses require culpability regarding the unlawfulness of one's conduct, as opposed to culpability regarding the circumstances and results that make the conduct a crime. Therefore, even under today's more limited application of the "ignorance is no excuse" maxim, an actor's belief, even a reasonable belief, that her conduct is not criminal typically will not provide a defense. In the "Sophie's Stand" hypothetical, if the maxim is applied, neither Sophie nor the members of her group would have a defense.

Desert Claim in Support of Maxim   The arguments in support of the maxim—the rationales for punishing even a reasonable mistake of law—are of two sorts: desert-based and utilitarian. The just-deserts argument may be stated as follows: All citizens have an absolute duty to learn the law, and ignorance or mistake is therefore a breach of that duty, deserving punishment.[1] But this argument misperceives what is required to show a reasonable mistake. A reasonable mistake

---

1. See Gerhard O. W. Mueller, *On Common Law Mens Rea*, 42 Minn. L. Rev. 1043, 1060 n.49 (1958).

is, by definition, a non-negligent,[2] faultless mistake, one a reasonable person similarly would have made in the actor's situation. An actor who is culpable in some way for the ignorance or mistake of law—perhaps because she did not take reasonable steps to find the law or took an unreasonable view of whether certain conduct falls within the prohibition of a criminal statute—would not satisfy an excuse for *reasonable* mistakes of law. By denying a defense for even a reasonable mistake, application of the maxim can lead to the conviction of morally blameless actors.

Utilitarian Claim in Support of Maxim A more coherent rationale for the maxim is the claim that a defense for a reasonable mistake of law would be easy to make and hard to disprove. Accordingly, a generalized excuse might enable or encourage defendants to make false claims of ignorance or mistake, thereby avoiding deserved liability, or at least making prosecution more difficult. The result, the argument continues, would not only frustrate justice but also reduce the criminal justice system's effectiveness or increase its costs. Moreover, to acquit an actor who has made a mistake of law, even a reasonable mistake, is to acquit one who has in fact violated the criminal law's prohibition. Such an acquittal, it is feared, can create dangerous ambiguity: It might be taken as approving the actor's conduct and thereby undercutting the prohibition. As one judge explained in arguing against giving a reasonable mistake of law defense: "We should refuse to cut away and weaken the core standards of behavior provided by the criminal law. Softening the standards of conduct . . . serves only to undermine the behavioral incentives the law was enacted to provide."[3]

Two Common Exceptions to Maxim Though still widely endorsed, the "ignorance is no excuse" maxim is not necessarily categorical. States following the Model Penal Code, as well as court opinions in some other states, recognize two general-defense exceptions to the maxim. A general defense commonly is available where an actor's ignorance or mistake of law occurs because (1) the law violated was not made reasonably available, or (2) the actor reasonably relied on an official misstatement of the law.[4] But these exceptions do not reflect a concern with the actor's blamelessness (the usual basis for an excuse defense) so much as an estoppel rationale independent of blameworthiness concerns.

Unavailable Law Even before the Model Penal Code, the impropriety of convicting an offender where the law was not made reasonably available occasionally was recognized as grounds for adopting an exception to the maxim. In *The Cotton Planter* case, for example, a ship set sail from St. Mary's in Georgia for Antigua in the West Indies. After the ship was beyond land communication, word was received at the port that sailing to Antigua had been made unlawful by a new statute that put an embargo on all ships and vessels in the ports and harbors of the United States.[5] The court reverses the lower court's judgment of forfeiture:

> A more abject state of slavery cannot easily be conceived than that the legislature should have the power of passing laws inflicting the highest penalties, without taking any measure to make them known to those whose property or

---

2. See Model Penal Code § 1.13(16).

3. United States v. Barker & Martinez, 546 F.2d 940, 972 (D.C. Cir. 1976) (Leventhal, J., dissenting).

4. See Model Penal Code § 2.04(3)&(4).

5. 6 F. Cas. 620, 620 (No. 3,270) (1810).

lives may be affected by them. It is not only necessary, therefore, in a country governed by laws, that they be passed by the supreme or legislative power, but that they be notified to the people who are expected to obey them.[6]

An unavailable-law defense is codified in the Model Penal Code as follows:

> A belief that conduct does not legally constitute an offense is a defense to a prosecution for that offense based upon such conduct when:
>
> the statute or other enactment defining the offense is not known to the actor and has not been published or otherwise reasonably made available prior to the conduct alleged; . . .
>
> The defendant must prove a defense arising under [this] Subsection by a preponderance of evidence.[7]

The requirements for making a law "available," however, tend to be minimal, demanding merely publication in a document that members of the public can access, even if only in limited locations.[8] In the "Sophie's Stand" hypothetical, Sophie and the members of her group could not claim a defense under this exception to the maxim. There is nothing to suggest that the county ordinance was not duly published as required by law, even if Sophie could only find it in a county office and a handful of other places.

Reliance on Official Misstatement   Similar arguments can be made in support of a defense for an actor who reasonably relies on an official misstatement of law. But in *United States v. Anthony*,[9] excerpted more extensively below, Susan B. Anthony relied on the (inaccurate) opinion of the election inspectors that she had a right to vote, and the court stuck to the maxim and denied a defense:

> One illegally voting was bound and was assumed to know the law, and that a belief that he had a right to vote gave no defense, if there was no mistake of fact. No system of criminal jurisprudence can be sustained upon any other principle.[10]

On the other hand, almost a century later, the Model Penal Code codifies a defense for reasonable reliance on an official misstatement:

> A belief that conduct does not legally constitute an offense is a defense to a prosecution for that offense based upon such conduct when:
>
> [the defendant] acts in reasonable reliance upon an official statement of the law, afterward determined to be invalid or erroneous, contained in (I) a statute or other enactment; (ii) a judicial decision, opinion or judgment; (iii) an administrative order or grant of permission; or (iv) an official interpretation of the public officer or body charged by law with responsibility for the interpretation, administration or enforcement of the law defining the offense.
>
> The defendant must prove a defense arising under [this] Subsection by a preponderance of evidence.[11]

---

6. Id. at 621.

7. Model Penal Code § 2.04(3)(a)&(4).

8. For a discussion of the problem of communicating criminal law to the public, see Paul H. Robinson, *Are Criminal Codes Irrelevant?*, 68 S. Cal. L. Rev. 159, 163-169 (1994).

9. 24 F. Cas. 829 (No. 14, 459) (1873).

10. Id. at 832.

11. Model Penal Code § 2.04(3)(b)&(4).

Sophie and the members of her group will not qualify for a defense under this section, either. They have not relied on an official misstatement of the law, but rather on Sophie's efforts to find out what the law is.

Exceptions to Maxim Rooted in Estoppel, Not Actor's Blamelessness One may be tempted to see these two exceptions to the maxim as the spearhead in a move toward outright rejection of the maxim. After all, the maxim does seem to conflict with the law's general requirement of blameworthiness as a precondition to criminal conviction: An actor who makes a reasonable mistake of law—a mistake that a reasonable person would have made—is blameless. Yet considerations of blamelessness, even if they support limitation or rejection of the maxim, do not provide the basis for these two narrow exceptions. They are explained instead by the governmental role in causing the mistake: The failure of the government, or its agent, to provide or describe the law to the public competently and accurately. There is a special unfairness, it may be argued, if the government misleads a person about the law's demands, or inadequately publicizes the law's existence, and then tries to prosecute for a resulting violation of that law. Further, if the government could prosecute notwithstanding its failure to satisfy its obligation to inform the public, it would have less incentive to satisfy that obligation. Accordingly, there is an intuition that the government should be barred, or estopped, from exploiting its own failure to disseminate or properly explain the law.

Continued Application of Maxim Outside Estoppel Context   Aside from such estoppel-based exceptions, the maxim apparently continues to enjoy vigorous support. Note, for example, that the Model Penal Code offers no defense for reasonable reliance on a statement of law from a person whom one reasonably, but mistakenly, believes is a government official; the person must in fact be such an official.[12] Where the statement does not come from an actual official, the government has not acted improperly and thus the estoppel rationale does not apply. Yet an actor who reasonably, but inaccurately, believed she was relying on an official would seem as blameless as one whose belief was accurate.

Great Defense for Reasonable Mistake of Law   The maxim is clearly rejected, however, by the New Jersey criminal code, which provides a true general excuse for a reasonable mistake of law, albeit in fairly restrictive form:

> A belief that conduct does not legally constitute an offense is a defense to a prosecution for that offense based upon such conduct when:
>
> The actor diligently pursues all means available to ascertain the meaning and application of the offense to his conduct and honestly and in good faith concludes his conduct is not an offense in circumstances in which a law-abiding and prudent person would also so conclude.
>
> The defendant must prove a defense arising under [this] subsection by clear and convincing evidence.[13]

In several ways, this statute minimizes the feared potential for abuse of a general mistake of law defense. It is not enough that the actor reasonably believes the conduct is not criminal; the New Jersey provision explicitly requires that the actor affirmatively seek to ascertain the proper meaning and application of the law to the contemplated conduct. The provision also appears to take into account the

---

12. See Model Penal Code § 2.04(3)(b).
13. N.J. Stat. Ann. § 2C:2-4(c)(3).

difficulties of proving the defendant's awareness of the law, or the unreasonableness of his ignorance of it by shifting the burden of proof to the defendant. The defendant must establish the defense by "clear and convincing" evidence, as compared to the Model Penal Code's less demanding "by a preponderance" of the evidence.

Analysis of Hypothetical Under N.J. Defense Despite the broader defense in New Jersey, the result of the "Sophie's Stand" hypothetical under the New Jersey provision is not at all certain, but the defense would at least afford Sophie, and the members of her group, the chance to persuade a jury that they had acted "diligently[,] . . . honestly, and in good faith" to determine whether their planned conduct was illegal, and that a "law-abiding and prudent person" would have come to the same conclusion they did. The prosecutor may argue that any possible defense would, at most, apply to Sophie alone, as she was the only defendant to actively investigate the law on the matter. The defense may counter that as Sophie was the only member of the group with legal training, a "prudent" person would defer to her superior knowledge and legal research skills. Here, one sees a potential conflict: On the one hand, it would seem odd to give Sophie an excuse, but hold the other members liable for relying on her; on the other hand, giving the members an excuse based on their reliance on Sophie, who is not an official or even a lawyer, would greatly expand the scope of the defense and open more avenues for potential abuse. Such a defense could encourage the hiring of persons to give desired legal opinions, thereby insulating from liability the person doing the hiring. The potential for abuse may be limited, however, if the burden is on each defendant to show both a reasonable belief in the lawfulness of the conduct and a reasonable effort to ascertain the law.

Arguments Opposing "No Excuse" Maxim and Favoring Defense Several reasons support recognizing a reasonable mistake-of-law excuse. First, and foremost, denying the excuse creates all the disadvantages inherent in convicting blameless persons: It is unjust to the individual defendant and it undermines the moral credibility of the criminal law, thereby weakening the condemnatory effects of criminal conviction. Further, it is unclear that recognizing a reasonable mistake of law defense will necessarily undermine the strength of the prohibition, as is claimed. The law could adopt a verdict system that makes clear that the defendant is being acquitted for a blameless violation, rather than because there was no violation. An "excused" verdict—based on a mistake of law or any other excuse defense—would operate just as the more specialized "not guilty by reason of insanity" verdict does today; it expressly condemns the conduct, while excusing the actor due to his blamelessness. Even without such a change in verdict system, it is not clear that recognizing a general reasonable mistake-of-law defense would be subject to the widespread and debilitating abuse that some predict. The New Jersey provision quoted above has been in effect since 1979. There is no evidence that the effectiveness of the criminal justice system in the State has suffered because of it, nor are there reports of abuse of the defense.

(Flawed) Alternative of De Facto *Defense via Jury Nullification* Even without a formal defense, some juries might simply return a verdict of "not guilty" based on their sense that, whatever the law says, a defendant does not deserve punishment. Such reliance on *jury nullification* might be seen as a useful practical solution to a difficult problem: It enables the system to announce that strict adherence

to the law is required, yet avoid actual punishment of many blameless defendants. But such a "solution" seems unwise, as it makes the defendant's (proper) acquittal hinge on the jury's willingness to disobey its legal instructions. Such pressures to nullify are also undesirable because every instance of nullification helps undermine the law's moral credibility. Finally, such a practice is likely to result in disparate treatment of similar cases. Because juries generally are not explicitly told about their nullification power, their exercise of the power is unpredictable and somewhat arbitrary, perhaps depending upon the personalities or knowledge of the particular group, rather than the facts of the case.

(Flawed) Alternative of Relying on Amelioration At Sentencing Another alternative to a formal mistake excuse is to rely on judges to use their sentencing discretion in favor of the reasonably mistaken defendant, to reduce such an offender's sentence. Yet this option seems even less attractive than jury nullification. First, because it comes after conviction, it does not avoid the unfairness of criminal conviction and its accompanying condemnation and collateral effects. Nor does it avoid the injury to the law's moral credibility that may come from convicting a blameless defendant. Further, modern sentencing guidelines have increasingly reduced judges' sentencing discretion, yet few guidelines take account of such factors as a defendant who has made a reasonable mistake of law. Further, without a formal mitigation, different judges are likely to have different views as to whether, and how much of, a mitigation is appropriate. A third and final mechanism for mitigating the injustice of the "no excuse" maxim is reliance on prosecutorial discretion. However, this suffers from many of the same shortcomings as jury nullification and sentencing discretion.

Superiority of Rules Over Reliance on Discretion Reliance on ad hoc discretionary judgments—whether made through jury nullification, sentencing discretion, or prosecutorial discretion—inevitably engenders all of the evils against which the legality principle stands, including the problems of unwarranted disparity among cases and the potential for abuse of discretion. Most objectionable, however, is that such outright dependence on discretion is a declaration of surrender in the search for a just criminal law. Reliance on discretion to ameliorate failings of the law reflects a resignation that liability rules cannot be crafted to reflect our notions of blameworthiness and justice. But taking this view—resorting to ad hoc discretion because rule refinement is too complex or too difficult—only assures that our future liability system will perpetuate the same injustices as our present system. The long-term stable trends toward more comprehensive criminal codes and toward guidelines for sentencing suggest that our society generally rejects this view and that current law is committed to seeking a more just system, although progress may be halting and slow.

United States v. Anthony
Circuit Court, N.D. New York
24 F. Cas. 829 (no. 14,459) (1873)

The defendant [Susan B. Anthony], a female, was indicted for a violation of the 19th section of the act of May 31st. 1870 (16 Stat. 144). . . . The trial took place before Hunt, Circuit Justice, and a jury. There was no dispute that the defendant had voted for a representative in the congress of the United States at an election therefor, in Rochester, Monroe county, New York, and that, under the constitution and laws of the state of New York, none but males were authorized to vote at an election for members of the most numerous branch of the state legislature, and that the defendant possessed all the qualifications entitling a person to vote at such election, except that she was not a male.

Hunt, Circuit Justice, after argument had been heard on the legal questions involved, ruled as follows:

The defendant is indicted under the act of congress of May 31st, 1870, for having voted for a representative in congress, in November, 1872. Among other things, that act makes it an offence for any person knowingly to vote for such representative without having a lawful right to vote. It is charged that the defendant thus voted, she not having a right to vote, because she is a woman. The defendant insists that she has a right to vote; and that the provision of the constitution of this state, limiting the right to vote to persons of the male sex, is in violation of the fourteenth amendment of the constitution of the United States, and is void. . . .

If she believed she had a right to vote, and voted in reliance upon that belief, does that relieve her from the penalty? It is argued, that the knowledge referred to in the act relates to her knowledge of the illegality of the act, and not to the act of voting; for, it is said, that she must know that she voted. Two principles apply here: First, ignorance of the law excuses no one, second, every person is presumed to understand and to intend the necessary effects of his own acts. Miss Anthony knew that she was a woman, and that the constitution of this state prohibits her from voting. She intended to violate that provision—intended to test it, perhaps, but, certainly, intended to violate it. The necessary effect of her act was to violate it, and this she is presumed to have intended. There was no ignorance of any fact, but, all the facts being known, she undertook to settle a principle in her own person. She takes the risk, and she cannot escape the consequences. . . .

[T]he counsel for the defendant requested the court to submit the case to the jury on the question of intent, and with the following instructions: (1) If the defendant, at the time of the voting, believed that she had a right to vote, and voted in good faith in that belief, she is not guilty of the offence charged. (2) In determining the question whether the defendant did or did not believe that she had a right to vote, the jury may take into consideration, as bearing upon that question, the advice which she received from the counsel to whom she applied, and, also, the fact, that the inspectors of the election considered the question and came to the conclusion that she had a right to vote. (3) The jury have a right to find a general verdict of guilty or not guilty, as they shall believe that the defendant has or has not committed the offence described in the statute.

The Court declined to submit the case to the jury, on any question, and directed the jury to find a verdict of guilty. A request, by the defendant's counsel, that the jury be polled, was denied by The Court, and a verdict of guilty was recorded. . . .

The defendant was thereupon sentenced to pay a fine of $100 and the costs of the prosecution.

▲ PROBLEMS

Parking Lot Lottery Ticket (#97)

Linda Ruschioni, a plaque maker, and her husband, Ricci, a firefighter, live with their son Ricci, Jr., 11, daughter Randi, 10, and daughter Traci, 8 in the middle-class town of Winchendon, Massachusetts. On Monday night, July 19, 1993, Linda and Traci go to the Family VideoLand store to rent a movie. Traci spots something on the ground in the parking lot once they leave the store. There are no cars around and no people. She bends down and picks up two instant "Twin Spins" lottery tickets that have yet to be scratched off. The tickets cost $2 each with the potential to pay from $1 to $20,000 as prizes and are sponsored by the Massachusetts Lottery Commission.

Traci gives the tickets to her mom who puts them in her pocketbook. Later that night, as Traci, her sister, and a friend watch the movie, Linda remembers the tickets and has Traci scratch them off. One of them is a $4 winner. The other scores $10,000, a 144,000-to-1 shot!

The next morning, Linda, Ricci, and Traci show up at the lottery commission's regional office in Worcester and present the $10,000 ticket. After taxes, the ticket pays $6,700. The commission determines that the winning ticket came from a book distributed to the Beverage Barn in Winchendon, next door to Family VideoLand.

Amazed by her daughter's good luck and thinking it is a wonderful story, Linda calls the local television station and tells them of Traci's find. Soon, stations and newspapers in Boston pick up the story, with national coverage close behind. Then "Good Morning America" even calls and Linda goes on television.

After paying a dentist bill and car insurance and splurging on a freezer, a new cage for Traci's birds, and a bicycle for Traci's sister, the Ruschionis plan to use the money to go back to Disney World, where they vacationed the year before.

Unknown to the Ruschionis at the time, a Massachusetts statute requires persons finding property worth over $3 to turn it in to the local police station. The true owner may reclaim the property within one year, otherwise it becomes the property of the finder. Another provision makes it a crime—a form of larceny—to "unlawfully convert" the property of another to one's own use.

What liability, if any, exists for Ruschioni under the Model Penal Code? What liability, if any, exists under the above stated Massachusetts law?

Cultural Marriage Differences (#98)

In some Islamic traditions, parents are allowed to contract their daughters (whether still as minors or as adults) into compulsory marriage. Dating and premarital sex are forbidden. Salem and Salima Al-Saidy were born in Iraq and come from families that follow these customs. However, they no longer live in Iraq. When Salem refused to join Saddam Hussein's army during the Persian Gulf War, he and his wife were forced to flee to America and settled in the Midwest. The Al-Saidys have 4 daughters, including two teenagers, 13 and 14 respectively. The older daughters have quickly become accustomed to American life; a teacher tells Salem that, having learned English in a matter of months, his eldest daughter could easily be mistaken for an American. Salem, however, does not see this as a compliment. He is distraught over the girl's apparent willingness to reject her family's cultural norms. At one point, he threatens his thirteen-year-old with a knife when she refuses to reveal whether or not her older sister has a boyfriend.

Salem decides finally that the only way to ensure that his daughters do not lose their way is to marry them off. It is not out of the ordinary in Iraq for marriages to be arranged between teenaged girls and older men, so Salem and Salima see no problem in their choice of Majed Al-Taminy, 28, and Latif Al-Hussani, 34, as grooms for their daughters. However, both girls vehemently object to the marriages. So too do friends of the Al-Saidys, who tell the parents that the marriages would be illegal in America due to the young ages of their daughters. The friends are unsuccessful at dissuading the Al-Saidys.

One month later, the two girls are married in traditional Islamic fashion. The grooms, who have recently come to the United States as laborers, have not integrated into American culture and are unaware that they may be violating the law by marrying such young girls. Following the wedding, a $3,000 bride price is paid by the men. To ensure that the girls are virgins, the men have intercourse with their new brides that night, despite the fact that both girls plead for them not to do so.

Assume that the state restricts marriage to those 16 and older. What liability, if any, for the grooms, Al-Hussani and Al-Taminy, under the Michigan sexual offense statutes excerpted in the Section 25 Law section? Assume that the jurisdiction otherwise has adopted the Model Penal Code. Prepare a list of all criminal code subsections in the order in which you rely on them in your analysis.

Would the grooms have a defense under the New Jersey reasonable mistake of law general excuse quoted in the Overview Notes?

What liability, if any, for the parents, the Al-Saidys?

✳ DISCUSSION ISSUE

Should the Criminal Law Recognize an Excuse Defense for a Reasonable Mistake of Law?

Materials presenting each side of this Discussion Issue appear in the Advanced Materials for Section 20 in Appendix A.

Insanity

Mistake excuses, the subject of the last two Sections, exculpate because the person acts reasonably given what he or she knows. A second group of general excuses—disability excuses—exculpate on a very different ground: because the person's offense conduct was heavily influenced by serious cognitive or control dysfunction such that we cannot reasonably have expected the person to remain law-abiding. This section takes up the highest profile disability excuse, insanity. The next section examines the other disability excuses.

◆ THE CASE OF ANDREW GOLDSTEIN (#99)

It is January 3, 1999. Yesterday, Andrew Goldstein, a shy, average-looking 29-year old, had been in the emergency room to have his ankle examined but the doctors told him that he was fine, and he returned to his apartment in Howard Beach, Queens. For Goldstein, yesterday's trip to the hospital is just another reason to be sad this holiday season. His family does not want to have much to

Figure 95　**Andrew Goldstein, circa 1990**
(Vern Lovic)

do with him. A few years ago, his parents divorced. His mother remains in New York, but his father moved to Delaware. Since he turned 16, Goldstein's relationship with his family (and the world) has been strained. Ten years ago, Goldstein was diagnosed with schizophrenia.

One of three brothers, Goldstein was raised in Queens and Little Neck, and attended Yeshiva Elementary School in central Queens. He graduated with honors and appeared to be on his way to a promising future. While his classmates report that he was a loner, his solitariness did not impede his academic performance, and he attended the elite Bronx High School of Science and then earned admission to SUNY Stony Brook. However, just before applying to SUNY, while riding a bus, he noticed something wrong—he could no longer understand anything in the book he was reading. His family was concerned and sought medical and psychiatric care. Goldstein was eventually diagnosed as a paranoid schizophrenic and prone to violence. He tried to overcome the disease by staying in school, but his symptoms only intensified.

After he pushed his mother and accused her of poisoning his food, Goldstein was hospitalized at Creedmoor Psychiatric Center. He tried returning to college several times after his release but found it too difficult to concentrate and to comprehend what he read. In December 1992, he was recommitted for assaulting a nurse and remained at Creedmoor until August 1993. He then lived in a community residence facility until he was discharged in November 1994. He later moved into the Leben Home for Adults in Elmhurst, New York, which provided him a place to live but did not offer any supervision or counseling.

Goldstein's disease has grown progressively worse. The frequency and duration of his hallucinations have increased, leading him to believe that aliens are sucking oxygen from the earth and that there is someone inside him controlling

29 yr old man estranged from family

diagnosed w/ schizo

in and out of psychiatric centers and adult homes

hallucinations got worse but he doesn't like taking them

his behavior and movements. His medication can help control the symptoms, but Goldstein does not like that it causes drowsiness, dissociation, and stiffness. He knows that there are newer medications without these side effects, but they are too expensive for him. He lives on $500 per month from welfare and an occasional $50 from his father.

He reports to psychiatrists that he is turning purple, that his penis is enlarged because his food is contaminated, and that a gay man is stealing his excrement from the toilet (by way of "interpolation") and eating it with a fork and knife. Goldstein has also hit at least a dozen people without provocation in restaurants, stores, hospitals, and subways. When police arrive, he always admits to what he did and asks to be taken to a hospital. Reflecting on these incidents, Goldstein describes that each time it happened, it felt as if a spirit or ghost had overtaken him.

Goldstein is uncomfortable and frustrated. He wants a normal life and on several occasions has requested to be placed in long-term care at a state hospital or given a bed at a group home. There are no vacancies, however, at either of these facilities, in part because of recent state budget cuts.

These days, Goldstein lives in a decrepit one-bedroom basement apartment for $300 a month. It has no lock; the bathroom does not work; and it smells of dead mice. Since he is prone to late-night walks, he does not often sleep there. He shares the apartment with two roommates who at times are kind to him. In November, one of them invited Goldstein to his family's Thanksgiving celebration, but the event turned out badly. After the visit, Goldstein was again hospitalized, at North General Hospital, from November 24 until December 15. When released, doctors advise him to seek counseling and provided him with a week's worth of medication. If unsupervised, Goldstein typically stops taking his medication, misses counseling appointments, and ignores letters requesting that he reschedule. With a lack of funding, the state mental health system is unable to do anything besides send a letter when a patient fails to show for an appointment.

Today, Goldstein forgoes his medication again before going into Manhattan for the day. It is his mother's birthday. He goes to a Virgin Records store and listens to Natalie Imbruglia's "Wishing I Was There" and Madonna's "Ray of Light." He enjoys listening to music because it allows him to draw pictures in his mind to go along with what he hears. He then watches scenes from *The Good, the Bad, and the Ugly*, in the video section and thinks that he would like to be a director someday. Getting hungry, he goes to Dunkin' Donuts for a donut with icing and a cup of water. He once worked at the donut chain but lasted only a day. Still hungry, he gets a McRib sandwich and Coke at a McDonald's. He then goes to visit his brother at his optical shop, but finds he is not there. It is now getting late, and feeling hungry again, he stops at Wendy's for a steak burger and another Coke.

After he finishes eating, he walks nine blocks uptown to Twenty-Third Street and enters the underground subway station. Dawn Lorenzino is walking behind him and sees that he is acting strangely and stumbling, "taking baby steps on his tiptoes." She also hears him mumbling to himself. When they reach the platform, Goldstein stares intensely at Lorenzino, until she finally asks what he is looking at. Troubled, Goldstein backs away and starts pacing so furiously that a man on the platform says to him, "Yo buddy, can you stop pacing, you're making us nervous." He stops and approaches another blond woman, Kendra Webdale.

Figure 96 **Andrew Goldstein being escorted by police the day after the attack, 1999**

(AP)

Webdale is originally from Fredonia, a small town near Buffalo in western New York. She majored in communications at SUNY Buffalo. After graduation, she worked for a couple of small weekly alternative papers in Buffalo before moving to New York City looking for more excitement. When she arrived, she worked for a Queens newspaper and now is a receptionist for a recording company. She is wearing her favorite black boots and is dressed up for an evening out.

Goldstein asks Webdale for the time. She replies and returns her attention to her magazine. He then steps back and leans on the wall just behind Webdale. Soon the train is rumbling toward the station. As it arrives, Goldstein darts from the wall and, as a witness later describes, "lurk[s] right behind Webdale with his fingers extend[ing] toward her shoulders." He then pushes her hard enough under her shoulder blades for people on the platform to hear it over the roar of the train. Webdale struggles to regain her balance but cannot, and falls directly into the train's path. The motorman, Jacque Lewis, pulls the emergency brake and closes his eyes, hoping to avoid her somehow. The train decapitates Webdale, killing her instantly. Its first three cars run over her body.

After the train stops, Lewis jumps out and asks Goldstein if he killed Webdale. He replies that he did but quickly asks for a doctor, explaining that he is a mental patient. Goldstein then begins to walk toward the north turnstile. Another commuter, Alston, screams "murderer" when she sees him walking off and orders him to stop where he is. She later recalls that he looked scared and "recoiled like a child, pulling his arms up to his chest with his fingers pointed downward and trembling." She wonders what is wrong with him. Some passengers stand guarding him as another fetches the police.

When the police arrive, one officer yells that he sees a leg. Goldstein looks at the other officers, glances toward the train, and says, "I don't know the woman. I pushed her." Detective William Hamilton, who first questions Goldstein, notes that he appears alert and answers all of the detective's questions promptly. Twelve hours later, in a videotaped session, police again question Goldstein. He admits to knowing that Webdale might be killed if he pushed her off the platform. When asked if pushing Webdale was wrong, Goldstein says yes but then adds, "Yeah, definitely. I would never do something like that." When they press the fact that he actually did push her, he says, "I know, but the thing is I would never do it on purpose." He explains that "I wasn't thinking about anything when I pushed her." Throughout the interview, Goldstein speaks with a "polite, chatty tone," and answers all of the questions posed. He becomes confused, however, whenever the conversation returns to him pushing Webdale. Trying to explain his actions and the spirits that overcame him, Goldstein says, "When it happens, I don't think; it just goes whoosh, whoosh, push, you know. It's like a random variable."

Psychiatric examinations show that at the time of the offense Goldstein continued to suffer from schizophrenia of the paranoid type, a disorder with these symptoms:

> The essential feature of the Paranoid Type of Schizophrenia is the presence of prominent delusions or auditory hallucinations in the context of a relative preservation of cognitive functioning and affect. . . . Delusions are typically persecutory or grandiose, or both, but delusions with other themes (e.g., jealousy, religiosity, or somatization) may also occur. The delusions may be multiple, but are usually organized around a coherent theme. Hallucinations are also typically related to the content of the delusional theme. Associated features include anxiety, anger, aloofness, and argumentativeness. The individual may have a superior and patronizing manner and either a stilted, formal quality or extreme intensity in interpersonal interactions. The persecutory themes may predispose the individual to suicidal behavior, and the combination of persecutory and grandiose delusions with anger may predispose the individual to violence. Onset tends to be later in life than the other types of Schizophrenia, and the distinguishing characteristics may be more stable over time. These individuals usually show little or no impairment on neuropsychological or other cognitive testing. Some evidence suggests that the prognosis for the Paranoid Type may be considerably better than for the other types of Schizophrenia, particularly with regard to occupational functioning and capacity for independent living.[1]

1. Relying only on your own intuition of justice, what liability and punishment, if any, does Andrew Goldstein deserve?

N	0	1	2	3	4	5	6	7	8	9	10	11
☐	☐	☐	☐	☐	☐	☐	☐	☐	☐	☐	☐	☐
no liability	liability but no punishment	1 day	2 wks	2 mo	6 mo	1 yr	3 yrs	7 yrs	15 yrs	30 yrs	life imprisonment	No punishment but civil preventive detention for as long as he is dangerous

2. What "justice" arguments could defense counsel make on the defendant's behalf?

3. What "justice" arguments could the prosecution make against the defendant?

4. What liability for Goldstein, if any, under the then-existing statutes? Prepare a list of all criminal code subsections or cases in the order in which you rely on them in your analysis.

5. What liability, if any, under the Model Penal Code? Prepare a list of all criminal code subsections in the order in which you rely on them in your analysis.

---

1. American Psychiatric Association, Diagnostic and Statistical Manual of Mental Disorders 313-314 (4th ed. text revision 2000).

▪ THE LAW

New York Penal Code
(1999)

Part 3. Specific Offenses

Title H. Offenses Against the Person Involving
Physical Injury, Sexual Conduct, Restraint and Intimidation
Article 125. Homicide, Abortion and Related Offenses

Section 125.00. Homicide Defined

Homicide means conduct which causes the death of a person or an unborn child with which a female has been pregnant for more than twenty-four weeks under circumstances constituting murder, manslaughter in the first degree, manslaughter in the second degree, criminally negligent homicide, abortion in the first degree or self-abortion in the first degree.

Section 125.10. Criminally Negligent Homicide

A person is guilty of criminally negligent homicide when, with criminal negligence, he causes the death of another person.

Criminally negligent homicide is a class E felony.

Section 125.15. Manslaughter in the Second Degree

A person is guilty of manslaughter in the second degree when:
    1. He recklessly causes the death of another person; . . .
Manslaughter in the second degree is a class C felony.

Section 125.20. Manslaughter in the First Degree

A person is guilty of manslaughter in the first degree when:
    1. With intent to cause serious physical injury to another person, he causes the death of such person or of a third person; or
    2. With intent to cause the death of another person, he causes the death of such person or of a third person under circumstances which do not constitute murder because he acts under the influence of extreme emotional disturbance, as defined in paragraph (a) of subdivision one of section 125.25. The fact that homicide was committed under the influence of extreme emotional disturbance constitutes a mitigating circumstance reducing murder to manslaughter in the first degree and need not be proved in any prosecution initiated under this subdivision; or . . .
Manslaughter in the first degree is a class B felony.

Section 125.25. Murder in the Second Degree

A person is guilty of murder in the second degree when:

1. With intent to cause the death of another person, he causes the death of such person or of a third person; except that in any prosecution under this subdivision, it is an affirmative defense that:

(a) The defendant acted under the influence of extreme emotional disturbance for which there was a reasonable explanation or excuse, the reasonableness of which is to be determined from the viewpoint of a person in the defendant's situation under the circumstances as the defendant believed them to be. Nothing contained in this paragraph shall constitute a defense to a prosecution for, or preclude a conviction of, manslaughter in the first degree or any other crime; or

(b) The defendant's conduct consisted of causing or aiding, without the use of duress or deception, another person to commit suicide. Nothing contained in this paragraph shall constitute a defense to a prosecution for, or preclude a conviction of, manslaughter in the second degree or any other crime; or

2. Under circumstances evincing a depraved indifference to human life, he recklessly engages in conduct which creates a grave risk of death to another person, and thereby causes the death of another person; or

3. Acting either alone or with one or more other persons, he commits or attempts to commit robbery, burglary, kidnapping, arson, rape in the first degree, sodomy in the first degree, sexual abuse in the first degree, aggravated sexual abuse, escape in the first degree, or escape in the second degree, and, in the course of and in furtherance of such crime or of immediate flight therefrom, he, or another participant, if there be any, causes the death of a person other than one of the participants; except that in any prosecution under this subdivision, in which the defendant was not the only participant in the underlying crime, it is an affirmative defense that the defendant:

(a) Did not commit the homicidal act or in any way solicit, request, command, importune, cause or aid the commission thereof; and

(b) Was not armed with a deadly weapon, or any instrument, article or substance readily capable of causing death or serious physical injury and of a sort not ordinarily carried in public places by law-abiding persons; and

(c) Had no reasonable ground to believe that any other participant was armed with such a weapon, instrument, article or substance; and

(d) Had no reasonable ground to believe that any other participant intended to engage in conduct likely to result in death or serious physical injury; or

4. Under circumstances evincing a depraved indifference to human life, and being eighteen years old or more the defendant recklessly engages in conduct which creates a grave risk of serious physical injury or death to another person less than eleven years old and thereby causes the death of such person. Murder in the second degree is a class A-I felony.

Part 1. General Provisions

Title B. Principles of Criminal Liability
Article 15. Culpability

Section 15.00. Culpability; Definitions of Terms

The following definitions are applicable to this chapter:
1. "Act" means a bodily movement.
2. "Voluntary act" means a bodily movement performed consciously as a result of effort or determination, and includes the possession of property if the actor was aware of his physical possession or control thereof for a sufficient period to have been able to terminate it.
3 "Omission" means a failure to perform an act as to which a duty of performance is imposed by law.
4. "Conduct" means an act or omission and its accompanying mental state.
5. "To act" means either to perform an act or to omit to perform an act.
6. "Culpable mental state" means "intentionally" or "knowingly" or "recklessly" or with "criminal negligence," as these terms are defined in section 15.05.

Section 15.05. Culpability; Definitions of Culpable Mental States

The following definitions are applicable to this chapter:
1. "Intentionally." A person acts intentionally with respect to a result or to conduct described by a statute defining an offense when his conscious objective is to cause such result or to engage in such conduct.
2. "Knowingly." A person acts knowingly with respect to conduct or to a circumstance described by a statute defining an offense when he is aware that his conduct is of such nature or that such circumstance exists.
3. "Recklessly." A person acts recklessly with respect to a result or to a circumstance described by a statute defining an offense when he is aware of and consciously disregards a substantial and unjustifiable risk that such result will occur or that such circumstance exists. The risk must be of such nature and degree that disregard thereof constitutes a gross deviation from the standard of conduct that a reasonable person would observe in the situation. A person who creates such a risk but is unaware thereof solely by reason of voluntary intoxication also acts recklessly with respect thereto.
4. "Criminal negligence." A person acts with criminal negligence with respect to a result or to a circumstance described by a statute defining an offense when he fails to perceive a substantial and unjustifiable risk that such result will occur or that such circumstance exists. The risk must be of such nature and degree that the failure to perceive it constitutes a gross deviation from the standard of care that a reasonable person would observe in the situation.

Section 15.10. Requirements for Criminal Liability in General and for Offenses of Strict Liability and Mental Culpability

The minimal requirement for criminal liability is the performance by a person of conduct which includes a voluntary act or the omission to perform an act which he is physically capable of performing. If such conduct is all that is required for commission of a particular offense, or if an offense or some material element thereof does not require a culpable mental state on the part of the actor, such offense is one of "strict liability." If a culpable mental state on the part of the actor is required with respect to every material element of an offense, such offense is one of "mental culpability."

Section 15.15. Construction of Statutes with Respect to Culpability Requirements

1. When the commission of an offense defined in this chapter, or some element of an offense, requires a particular culpable mental state, such mental state is ordinarily designated in the statute defining the offense by use of the terms "intentionally," "knowingly," "recklessly" or "criminal negligence," or by use of terms, such as "with intent to defraud" and "knowing it to be false," describing a specific kind of intent or knowledge. When one and only one of such terms appears in a statute defining an offense, it is presumed to apply to every element of the offense unless an intent to limit its application clearly appears.

2. Although no culpable mental state is expressly designated in a statute defining an offense, a culpable mental state may nevertheless be required for the commission of such offense, or with respect to some or all of the material elements thereof, if the proscribed conduct necessarily involves such culpable mental state. A statute defining a crime, unless clearly indicating a legislative intent to impose strict liability, should be construed as defining a crime of mental culpability. This subdivision applies to offenses defined both in and outside this chapter.

Part 1. General Provisions

Title C. Defenses
Article 25. Defenses in General

Section 25.00. Defenses; Burden of Proof

1. When a "defense," other than an "affirmative defense," defined by statute is raised at a trial, the people have the burden of disproving such defense beyond a reasonable doubt.

2. When a defense declared by statute to be an "affirmative defense" is raised at a trial, the defendant has the burden of establishing such defense by a preponderance of the evidence.

Article 40. Other Defenses Involving Lack of Culpability

Section 40.15. Mental Disease or Defect

In any prosecution for an offense, it is an affirmative defense that when the defendant engaged in the proscribed conduct, he lacked criminal responsibility by reason of mental disease or defect. Such lack of criminal responsibility means that at the time of such conduct, as a result of mental disease or defect, he lacked substantial capacity to know or appreciate either:

1. The nature and consequences of such conduct; or
2. That such conduct was wrong.

Part 2. Sentences

Title E. Sentences
Article 70. Sentences of Imprisonment

Section 70.00. Sentence of Imprisonment for Felony

1. Indeterminate sentence. Except as provided in subdivisions four, five and six, a sentence of imprisonment for a felony shall be an indeterminate sentence. When such a sentence is imposed, the court shall impose a maximum term in accordance with the provisions of subdivision two of this section and the minimum period of imprisonment shall be as provided in subdivision three of this section.

2. Maximum term of sentence. The maximum term of an indeterminate sentence shall be at least three years and the term shall be fixed as follows:

(a) For a class A felony, the term shall be life imprisonment;

(b) For a class B felony, the term shall be fixed by the court, and shall not exceed twenty-five years; provided, however, that where the sentence is for a class B felony offense specified in subdivision two of section 220.44, the maximum term must be at least six years and must not exceed twenty-five years;

(c) For a class C felony, the term shall be fixed by the court, and shall not exceed fifteen years;

(d) For a class D felony, the term shall be fixed by the court, and shall not exceed seven years; and

(e) For a class E felony, the term shall be fixed by the court, and shall not exceed four years.

3. Minimum period of imprisonment. The minimum period of imprisonment under an indeterminate sentence shall be at least one year and shall be fixed as follows:

(a) In the case of a class A felony, the minimum period shall be fixed by the court and specified in the sentence.

(i) For a class A-I felony, such minimum period shall not be less than fifteen years nor more than twenty-five years; provided that where a sentence, other than a sentence of death or life imprisonment without parole, is imposed upon a defendant convicted of murder in the first degree as defined in section 125.27 of this chapter such minimum period shall be not less than twenty years nor more than twenty-five years.

(ii) For a class A-II felony, such minimum period shall not be less than three years nor more than eight years four months.

(b) Where the sentence is for a class B felony offense specified in subdivision two of section 220.44, the minimum period must be fixed by the court at one-third of the maximum term imposed and must be specified in the sentence. Where the sentence is for any other felony, the minimum period shall be fixed by the court and specified in the sentence and shall be not less than one year nor more than one-third of the maximum term imposed.

4. Alternative definite sentence for class D, E, and certain class C felonies. When a person, other than a second or persistent felony offender, is sentenced for a class D or class E felony, or to a class C felony specified in article two hundred twenty or article two hundred twenty-one, and the court, having regard to the nature and circumstances of the crime and to the history and character of the defendant, is of the opinion that a sentence of imprisonment is necessary but that it would be unduly harsh to impose an indeterminate or determinate sentence, the court may impose a definite sentence of imprisonment and fix a term of one year or less.

5. Life imprisonment without parole. Notwithstanding any other provision of law, a defendant sentenced to life imprisonment without parole shall not be or become eligible for parole or conditional release. For purposes of commitment and custody, other than parole and conditional release, such sentence shall be deemed to be an indeterminate sentence. A defendant may be sentenced to life imprisonment without parole only upon conviction for the crime of murder in the first degree as defined in section 125.27 of this chapter and in accordance with the procedures provided by law for imposing a sentence for such crime.

6. Determinate sentence. Except as provided in subdivision four of this section and subdivisions two and four of section 70.02, when a person is sentenced as a violent felony offender pursuant to section 70.02 or as a second violent felony offender pursuant to section 70.04 or as a second felony offender on a conviction for a violent felony offense pursuant to section 70.06, the court must impose a determinate sentence of imprisonment in accordance with the provisions of such sections and such sentence shall include, as a part thereof, a period of post-release supervision in accordance with section 70.45.

People v. Segal
444 N.Y.S.2d 588, 591-592 (1981)

At a criminal trial the People bear the burden of proof, not only with respect to ordinary defenses which have been codified but more fundamentally they must prove every element of the crime, including intent whenever relevant. Although proof of a mental defect other than insanity may not have acquired the status of a statutory defense, and will not constitute a "complete" defense in the sense that it would relieve the defendant of responsibility for all his acts, it may in a particular case negate a specific intent necessary to establish guilt.

Model Penal Code
(Official Draft 1962)

Section 4.01. Mental Disease or Defect Excluding Responsibility

(1) A person is not responsible for criminal conduct if at the time of such conduct as a result of mental disease or defect he lacks substantial capacity either

to appreciate the criminality [wrongfulness] of his conduct or to conform his conduct to the requirements of law.

(2) As used in this Article, the terms "mental disease or defect" do not include an abnormality manifested only by repeated criminal or otherwise antisocial conduct.

Section 4.02. Evidence of Mental Disease or Defect Admissible When Relevant to Element of the Offense; [Mental Disease or Defect Impairing Capacity as Ground for Mitigation of Punishment in Capital Cases]

(1) Evidence that the defendant suffered from a mental disease or defect is admissible whenever it is relevant to prove that the defendant did or did not have a state of mind which is an element of the offense.

[(2) Whenever the jury or the Court is authorized to determine or to recommend whether or not the defendant shall be sentenced to death or imprisonment upon conviction, evidence that the capacity of the defendant to appreciate the criminality [wrongfulness] of his conduct or to conform his conduct to the requirements of law was impaired as a result of mental disease or defect is admissible in favor of sentence of imprisonment.]

● OVERVIEW OF THE INSANITY DEFENSE

Notes

Mental Illness Negating an Element vs. General Excuse
"Mental Disease or Defect" as Disability
    Intoxication Excluded
    Psychopathy Excluded
Excusing Conditions
    McNaughton Test: Unaware of Conduct's Nature or Wrongfulness
    Supplementing *McNaughton* Test with "Irresistible Impulse" Test
    Durham "Product" Test Expands Defense (and Proves Unpopular)
    Model Penal Code Test: "Lacks Substantial Capacity"
    Earlier ALI Formulation: Cannot Be "Justly Held Responsible"
    Federal Insanity Test Reverts Toward Original *McNaughton* Test
Practical Consequences of Insanity Verdict
Abolition of Insanity Defense
Insanity Defense in the United States—Survey
Adding Verdict of "Guilty but Mentally Ill" (Gbmi)
    Concerns with Gbmi Verdict
    Gbmi as (Improper) Replacement for Insanity Verdict
    Underlying Fear That Insanity Defense Will Be Abused
    Incapacitating Dangerous but Blameless Offenders as Civil Function

Mental Illness Negating an Element vs. General Excuse The effects of mental illness can sometimes make it impossible for the state to prove the culpability requirements for an offense. For example, an actor who hallucinates that a knife is a clothes brush may not have the required culpability for homicide if he kills someone thinking that he is brushing lint from the victim's chest. Similarly, mental illness can mitigate murder to manslaughter if the actor killed during an "extreme *mental* or emotional disturbance." Finally, mental illness can form the basis of a general excuse: the insanity defense. Unlike the other two doctrines, the insanity defense operates without regard to—that is, despite the defendant's satisfaction of—the elements of the offense definition. (Indeed, the excuse is only necessary if the defendant otherwise satisfies the offense requirements.) To get the insanity defense, the actor need only satisfy the conditions set out in the defense provision. The defense reflects the standard structure and requirements of disability excuses, namely, that a *disability* (in this instance, mental disease, or defect) cause an *excusing condition*.

"Mental Disease or Defect" as Disability   The disability required by the insanity defense is commonly described as a "mental disease or defect." For these purposes, "mental disease or defect" is a legal concept, not a medical one, and is thus for the jury rather than medical experts to resolve—though the jury will no doubt be influenced by the expert witnesses that they hear. Many experts testifying as to whether the defendant suffers from a mental disease or defect will rely on the classification system contained in the *Diagnostic and Statistical Manual* of the American Psychiatric Association, now in its fourth edition (DSM-IV-TR).[2] The APA gives the following definition of "mental disorder":

> In DSM-IV, each of the mental disorders is conceptualized as a clinically significant behavioral or psychological syndrome or pattern that occurs in an individual and that is associated with present distress (e.g., a painful symptom) or disability (i.e., impairment in one or more important areas of functioning) or with a significantly increased risk of suffering death, pain, disability, or an important loss of freedom. In addition, this syndrome or pattern must not be merely an expectable and culturally sanctioned response to a particular event, for example, the death of a loved one. Whatever its original cause, it must currently be considered a manifestation of a behavioral, psychological, or biological dysfunction in the individual. Neither deviant behavior (e.g., political, religious, or sexual) nor conflicts that are primarily between the individual and society are mental disorders unless the deviance or conflict is a symptom of a dysfunction in the individual, as described above.[3]

Intoxication Excluded   Intoxication may cause mental dysfunction, but it is excluded as a basis for the insanity defense, because it is not a form of mental disease or defect.[4] It is dealt with instead under the law's special intoxication defense. The habitual and excessive use of intoxicants, however, may cause a mental disease with resulting dysfunction apart from the intoxication, and this mental disease can be the basis for an insanity defense.[5] Addiction, for example, has been recognized as a mental disease.[6]

---

2. American Psychiatric Association, Diagnostic and Statistical Manual of Mental Disorders (4th ed. text revision 2000) (hereinafter DSM-IV-TR) at xxxi.

3. Id. at xxi.

4. Model Penal Code § 2.08(3).

5. See, e.g., United States v. Lyons, 731 F.2d 243 (5th Cir. 1984) (evidence on lack of substantial capacity to appreciate criminality of conduct due to physiological impairment due to drug addiction can be submitted to jury).

6. See DSM-IV-TR, at 199-200. Some cases, however, expressly reject the notion that addiction can qualify an actor for an insanity defense. See, e.g., United States v. Moore, 486 F.2d 1139 (D.C. Cir. 1973).

Handwritten margin note: Habitual/repeat Criminals also excluded

Psychopathy Excluded   The insanity defense also excludes any "abnormality manifested only by repeated criminal or otherwise anti-social conduct."[7] In other words, being a habitual criminal is not in itself a sufficient indication of a cognizable disability. Such an abnormality may be a mental disease for clinical purposes,[8] but to recognize it as a mental disease for the purposes of the insanity defense would generate results inconsistent with the theory of excuses as serving to exculpate blameless offenders. Such habitual criminality by itself may be fully volitional conduct, and thus fully blameworthy.

Excusing Conditions   It is not enough for an excuse that an actor suffers some abnormality, even one that causes dysfunction. To be held blameless, the actor's disability must cause effects so strong that it would not be reasonable to expect the actor to have avoided the violation. This *excusing condition*, or required effect of the disability, has been formulated in several different ways for the insanity defense. The most significant tests include: the *McNaughton* test, the *McNaughton* test plus the "irresistible impulse" test, the *Durham* "product" test, the Model Penal Code test, and the more recent federal insanity test.

McNaughton Test: Unaware of Conduct's Nature or Wrongfulness   In *McNaughton's Case*, the House of Lords held that an actor has a defense of insanity if, "at the time of committing the act, the party accused was laboring under such a defect of reason, from disease of the mind, as *not to know the nature and quality of the act he was doing, or, if he did know it, [he] did not know he was doing what was wrong*."[9] As the quote indicates, this test can be satisfied in two ways: The disabling mental defect may prevent the defendant from understanding (1) the nature, or (2) the wrongfulness, of his conduct. For both cases, the focus is on the defendant's impaired perception or cognition. The *McNaughton* test was an advance over prior case law, which set the standard for the defense as having no more understanding than "an infant, a brute, or a wild beast."[10] It gave the jury specific criteria to focus on rather than vague analogies. The test is in use in many American jurisdictions today, as detailed below, and remains the test for the insanity defense in England.

Supplementing McNaughton Test with "Irresistible Impulse" Test   As early as 1887, the *McNaughton* test was criticized as failing to reflect advances in the behavioral sciences. Mental illness, it was observed, can take away the *power to choose* as well as the *knowledge* of one's situation or of right and wrong.[11] To permit a defense in cases involving loss of the power to choose, some jurisdictions supplemented the *McNaughton* test with what is sometimes described as an "irresistible impulse" test. Under this supplemental test—which is said to add a "control prong" to *McNaughton*'s "cognition prong" of the insanity defense—an actor obtains the defense if he or she satisfies the *McNaughton* test or:

> (1) if, by reason of the duress of such mental disease, he had so far lost the *power to choose* between the right and wrong, and to avoid doing the act in question, as that his free agency was at the time destroyed; (2) and if, at the

---

7. Model Penal Code § 4.01(2).
8. DSM-IV-TR, supra, at 701-703.
9. M'Naghten's Case, 8 Eng. Rep. 718, 722 (1843) (emphasis added).
10. Arnold's Case, 16 How. State Tr. 695, 765 (1724).
11. Parsons v. State, 2 So. 854 (Ala. 1887).

same time, the alleged crime was so connected with such mental disease, in the relation of cause and effect, as to have been the product of it *solely*.[12]

Durham "Product" Test Expands Defense (and Proves Unpopular) The *McNaughton*-plus-irresistible-impulse test was criticized in turn as not fully reflecting more recent advances in the behavioral sciences. For example, the court in *Durham v. United States* observed that mental dysfunctions, of both the cognitive and control types, always are a matter of degree and are not, as was previously thought, absolute in their effect.[13] Further, the court found, the *McNaughton* and irresistible-impulse tests improperly focus on particular symptoms rather than on the key question of whether the mental illness, whatever its nature, *had the effect of causing the offense*. *Durham* then articulated a "product" test for insanity, under which an accused "is not criminally responsible if his unlawful act was the product of mental disease or mental defect."[14] *Durham*, however, was widely criticized as overstating the adequate grounds of exculpation. The critics argued that it should not suffice that the mental illness is a "but for" cause of the offense; the mental illness must cause a degree of impairment that renders the defendant blameless for the offense. The product test was adopted in only a few jurisdictions, and arguably remains in use in only one.[15]

Model Penal Code Test: "Lacks Substantial Capacity" In *United States v. Brawner*,[16] excerpted below, the Court of Appeals for the District of Columbia Circuit overruled its own earlier decision in *Durham* and adopted the test contained in Model Penal Code § 4.01(1) (also known as the "American Law Institute" or "ALI" test):

> A person is not responsible for criminal conduct if at the time of such conduct as a result of mental disease or defect he *lacks substantial capacity either to appreciate the criminality [wrongfulness] of his conduct or to conform his conduct to the requirements of law.*

This formulation concedes that there are *degrees* of impairment, as *Durham* had emphasized, but also requires a minimum degree of impairment: The actor must "lack substantial capacity" to behave properly. The Model Penal Code test reverts to the structure of the *McNaughton*-plus-irresistible-impulse test in specifically noting that the dysfunction may affect either cognitive or control capacities. It differs from *McNaughton*-plus-irresistible-impulse, however, in that the earlier formulation would appear to require absolute dysfunction: the total absence of knowledge of criminality or the total loss of power to choose. The Model Penal Code test, in contrast, requires only that the actor lack "substantial capacity" to control his conduct or "appreciate" criminality. As detailed further below, the test has gained wide acceptance, rivaling the popularity of *McNaughton* and *McNaughton*-plus-irresistible-impulse formulations.

---

12. *Parsons*, 2 So. at 866-867.

13. Durham v. United States, 214 F.2d 862 (D.C. Cir. 1954).

14. Id. at 874.

15. State v. Shackford, 506 A.2d 315 (N.H. 1986) (holding that insanity test is matter "to be weighed by the jury upon the question whether the act was the offspring of insanity," quoting State v. Jones, 50 N.H. 369, 398-399 (1871)).

16. 471 F.2d 969 (D.C. Cir. 1972).

Earlier ALI Formulation: Cannot Be "Justly Held Responsible" Another formulation of the insanity defense, which was considered but rejected by the ALI, calls for the jury's general assessment of an actor's responsibility and blameworthiness for the offense. It would provide the defense if the actor, because of mental disease or defect, lacked sufficient capacity to be "justly held responsible" for his conduct.[17] The approach is similar to the Model Penal Code's approach in other contexts, where the Code's rules explicitly call on the decision maker for a normative judgment. Its causation test, for example, asks the jury to decide whether a result's occurrence is too remote or accidental "to have a [just] bearing on the actor's liability or on the gravity of his offense."[18] Such an open formulation was rejected in the insanity context, however, because it was thought that the jury could and should be given greater guidance. The version ultimately included in the Code focused the jury's attention on the nature and effect of the dysfunction—with specific reference to cognitive or control dysfunction—and avoided having a jury incorporate considerations of general sympathy (or bias) that might come in under the broader "justice" standard.

Federal Insanity Test Reverts Toward Original McNaughton Test Some jurisdictions that previously adopted the Model Penal Code test have cut back on it. For example, the federal insanity statute[19] (enacted after *Brawner,* noted above and excerpted later in this Section, which had adopted the Model Code's test) uses the Code's "appreciates" language, rather than the *McNaughton* "know" language, thereby seeming to allow exculpation for degrees of cognitive dysfunction short of complete loss. On the other hand, the federal statute drops the "lacks substantial capacity" language, which makes it closer to the apparently absolute requirement of *McNaughton.* Most important, the federal formulation drops the control prong of the defense, reverting to the single cognitive prong. This reflects skepticism as to whether behavioral scientists can measure an actor's degree of control impairment and as to whether jurors can understand testimony about, or effectively judge, a defendant's degree of impairment.

Practical Consequences of Insanity Verdict A successful claim of the insanity defense leads to a special verdict of "not guilty by reason of insanity" (NGRI). Unlike the standard "not guilty" verdict, the NGRI verdict does not lead to the defendant's immediate release. Rather, the effect typically is to remand the defendant to state authorities for evaluation, supervision, and treatment.[20] Yet few laypeople realize that this result is the real consequence of a NGRI verdict; they assume that such a verdict is equivalent to a standard acquittal. Moreover, many jurisdictions have rules explicitly discouraging, or completely disallowing, jury instructions that would inform the jury of the consequences of issuing a NGRI verdict.[21] Accordingly, there is a significant likelihood that juries will erroneously conclude that a "guilty" verdict (or a GBMI verdict, discussed below) is either necessary to ensure that the defendant is not unconditionally released, or

---

17. This proposal appears as alternative (a) to paragraph (1) of Model Penal Code § 4.01 (Tent. Draft No. 4, 1955).

18. Model Penal Code § 2.03(2)(b) & (3)(b).

19. 18 U.S.C. § 17.

20. See, e.g., 730 Ill. Comp. Stat. 5/5-2-4.

21. See, e.g., People v. Stack, 613 N.E.2d 1175, 1183-1184 (Ill. App. 1993).

the only appropriate way to guarantee needed psychological treatment for the defendant, or both.

Abolition of Insanity Defense A few jurisdictions have abolished the insanity defense, but continue to allow mental disease or defect to provide a defense if it negates a required offense culpability element. Constitutional challenges to abolition have been successful in some cases, but not in others. Whether or not the federal or state constitutions bar it, abolition is a questionable policy. To the extent that the criminal law claims to express conclusions about an actor's blameworthiness—the characteristic that traditionally has distinguished criminal law from civil law—it cannot impose criminal liability and punishment on clearly insane offenders without destroying its moral credibility. If society has a need to protect itself against dangerous persons who are predicted to commit future crimes, it can and should do so. Typically, dangerous persons are blameworthy offenders. In the unusual case where an offender is dangerous yet blameless, as is true for some insane offenders, civil incarceration may be an alternative option and is preferable to criminal confinement for purposes of protecting the criminal law's moral credibility.[22]

Insanity Defense in the United States—Survey The alternative approaches to the insanity defense are reflected in the variety of approaches in American jurisdictions. Almost half of the jurisdictions apply the traditional *McNaughton* test,[23] with at least one jurisdiction adding the irresistible-impulse element.[24] Most of the jurisdictions that have adopted a control prong have done so by shifting to the somewhat broader Model Penal Code (ALI) formulation; close to 30% of the states have adopted that formulation in its entirety.[25] Another 20% have adopted only the cognitive prong of the Model Code's formulation.[26] Four jurisdictions have no insanity defense, though they continue to allow mental illness to negate

---

22. See Paul H. Robinson, *Punishing Dangerousness: Cloaking Preventive Detention as Criminal Justice*, 114 Harv. L. Rev. 1429 (2001).

23. Ariz. Rev. Stat. Ann. § 13-502; Cal. Penal Code § 25; Colo. Rev. Stat. Ann. § 16-8-101; Fla. Stat. Ann. § 775.027; Ga. Code Ann. § 16-3-2; Iowa Code Ann. § 701.4; La. Rev. Stat. Ann. § 14; Minn. Stat. Ann. § 611.026; Roundtree v. State, 568 So.2d 1173 (Miss. 1990); Mo. Ann. Stat. § 552.030 (modifying the standard language slightly to "incapable of knowing *and appreciating*"); State v. Harms, 650 N.W.2d 481 (Neb. 2002); N.J. Stat. Ann. § 2C:4-1; Finger v. State, 27 P.3d 66 (Nev. 2001) (finding unconstitutional the legislator's attempt to abolish the insanity defense and applying the McNaghten test instead); State v. Vickers, 291 S.E.2d 599 (N.C. 1982); Ohio Rev. Code Ann. § 2901.01; Okla. Stat. Ann. tit. 21 § 152; 18 Pa. Cons. Stat. Ann. § 314; S.C. Code Ann. § 17-24-10; S.D. Codified Laws § 22-1-2; Tex. Penal Code Ann. § 8.01; Price v. Commonwealth, 323 S.E.2d 106 (Va. 1984); Wash. Rev. Code Ann. § 9A.12.010.

24. State v. White, 270 P.2d 727 (N.M. 1954).

25. Ark Code Ann. § 5-2-312; Conn. Gen. Stat. Ann. § 53a-13; Patton v. US, 782 A.2d 305 (D.C. 2001); Haw. Rev. Stat. Ann. § 704-400; Ky. Rev. Stat. Ann. § 504.020; Md. Code Ann., Crim. Proc. § 3-109; Commonwealth v. Brown, 434 N.E.2d 973 (Mass. 1982); Mich. Comp. Laws Ann. § 768.21a; Or. Rev. Stat. § 161.295; State v. Johnson, 399 A.2d 469 (R.I. 1979); Vt. Stat. Ann. Tit. 13 § 4801; State v. Samples, 328 S.E.2d 191 (W.Va. 1985); Wis. Stat. Ann. § 971.15; Wyo. Stat. Ann. § 7-11-304.

26. Ala. Code § 13A-3-1; Alaska Stat. § 12.47.010; Del. Code Ann. Tit. 11, § 401; 720 Ill. Comp. Stat. Ann. 5/6-2; Ind. Code Ann. § 35-41-3-6; Me. Rev. Stat. Ann. tit. 14 § 14; N.Y. Penal Law § 40.15; N.D. Cent. Code § 12.1-04.1-01 (requiring also that "an essential element of the crime charged [is] that the individual act willfully"); Tenn. Code Ann. § 39-11-501.

an offense culpability element.[27] One state adopts what appears to be something close to the *Durham* product test.[28]

Adding Verdict of "Guilty but Mentally Ill" (GBMI) In the 1970s and 1980s, a number of jurisdictions adopted a verdict of "guilty but mentally ill" (GBMI). The verdict replaces the insanity defense in only a few states. More frequently, it provides the trier of fact with an additional verdict in cases where mental illness is an issue. The special verdict may be returned where a defendant is mentally ill, but where his mental illness is insufficient to provide either an insanity defense or a defense of mental illness negating an offense element. Following a GBMI verdict, the court typically has the same sentencing options that would follow from a typical "guilty" verdict. GBMI convicts must be examined by psychiatrists before beginning to serve the sentence and, if found to need treatment, will then be imprisoned in a criminal mental health facility. In most jurisdictions, however, such evaluation and treatment occurs for *all* convicted offenders, not just those receiving a GBMI verdict, in which case a GBMI verdict is indistinguishable from a guilty verdict in its practical effect. (As noted above, similar civil commitment required-examination procedures also often exist for defendants *acquitted* under a NGRI verdict.) In fact, although the GBMI verdict may seem designed to help mentally ill convicts, one of the few practical distinctions between GBMI convicts and typical sane convicts is that the GBMI convicts tend to receive *longer* sentences.[29]

Concerns with GBMI Verdict The GBMI verdict raises some significant concerns. First, one must question why the fact finder in a criminal trial is an appropriate body to determine whether an offender is in need of a psychiatric examination. The expertise of the jury is in finding the facts of past events and in applying that community's notion of blameworthiness. The need for psychiatric treatment is a clinical issue, appropriate for prison psychiatrists, for example. It is not within the lay judgment of the jury, and asking the jury to undertake such an inquiry can distract and confuse it in its task of assessing blameworthiness.

(margin note: should not be left up to jury to decide GBMI)

GBMI as (Improper) Replacement for Insanity Verdict A second concern arises from an analysis of the legislative history for the GBMI verdict. The history suggests that the verdict was not designed to perform a psychiatric screening function, which clinicians can do more reliably than juries, but rather arose as a device to reduce NGRI acquittals after constitutional mandates limited the use of civil commitment to preventively detain disturbed offenders.[30] The limitations on commitment were thought to create a risk of dangerously insane acquittees

---

27. Idaho Code § 18-207; Kan. Stat. Ann. § 22-3220; Mont. Code Ann. § 45-2-101; Utah Code Ann. § 76-2-305.

28. State v. Shackford, 506 A.2d 315 (N.H. 1986) (holding that insanity test is matter "to be weighed by the jury upon the question whether the act was the offspring of insanity") (quoting State v. Jones, 50 N.H. 369, 398-399 (1871)).

29. See Henry J. Steadman et al., Before and After Hinckley: Evaluating Insanity Defense Reform 8 (1993). This is likely due to a suspicion that mentally ill individuals are unusually dangerous and need to be incapacitated to prevent them from committing more crimes.

30. See, e.g., Donald H.J. Hermann & Yvonne S. Sor, *Convicting or Confining? Alternative Directions in Insanity Law Reform: Guilty But Mentally Ill Versus New Rules for Release of Insanity Acquittees,* 1983 B.Y.U. L. Rev. 499, 582 ("The rationale for the GBMI verdict stems from a legislative concern that the insanity defense is too easily proved, while the abolition of automatic commitment of insanity acquittees in some states has made civil commitment of persons found NGRI more difficult.").

being released back into the community. Adding the GBMI verdict combats this perceived danger indirectly, not by loosening civil commitment standards, but by diverting mentally ill offenders from civil commitment to the criminal justice system. A jury choosing between an NGRI verdict and a GBMI verdict may select the latter, not because the jury finds the defendant blameworthy, but because the latter verdict seems to guarantee what may be the obvious need for treatment and confinement. The difficulty with the GBMI verdict is that it invites jurors to consider matters unrelated to blameworthiness at a time when blameworthiness should be the sole issue before them. Moreover, the verdict plays on jurors' ignorance of the consequences of a NGRI verdict (or a standard "guilty" verdict), encouraging the misperception that a GBMI verdict is the only way to incapacitate dangerously mentally ill persons while also providing necessary psychological treatment. (Adding to the potential confusion is the likelihood that the jury will inadvertently confuse the statutory definition of "mental illness," relevant to the GBMI verdict, and the definition of "mental disease or defect," relevant to the insanity defense.) The use of such an improper compromise verdict may do as much to undermine the insanity defense as total abolition would. If effective abolition is the objective, abolishing the insanity test openly would better further the interests of informed debate and reform.

Underlying Fear That Insanity Defense Will Be Abused   The underlying purpose of adding the GBMI verdict, reducing insanity acquittals, is driven by fears that the insanity defense is granted too often and possibly subject to abuse. Yet the empirical evidence suggests that such fears are ill-founded. For example, people generally believe, inaccurately, that the insanity defense is a commonly offered defense in criminal trials: One study found that people estimate that 38% of all defendants charged with crime plead not guilty by reason of insanity (NGRI).[31] In reality, an insanity plea is exceedingly rare, raised in a fraction of a percent of even felony cases.[32] Also contrary to popular belief, more than half of the few cases where an insanity plea is introduced involve nonviolent offenses.[33] In addition, even in the rare cases in which the insanity defense is sought, it is usually not granted,[34] yet the public perception is that it is commonly granted.[35] Claims that the defense is abused and employed to manipulate juries are also belied by the fact that most NGRI pleas are not contested,[36] and the vast majority of NGRI verdicts—93%, in one study—are reached through negotiated pleas or rendered

---

31. See Valerie P. Hans, *An Analysis of Public Attitudes Toward the Insanity Defense*, 24 CRIMINOLOGY 393, 406 (1986); see also Eric Silver et al., *Demythologizing Inaccurate Perceptions of the Insanity Defense*, 18 LAW & HUM. BEHAV. 63, 67-68 (1994).

32. See Lisa A. Callahan et al., *The Volume and Characteristics of Insanity Defense Pleas: An Eight-State Study*, 19 BULL. AM. ACAD. PSYCHIATRY & L. 331, 334 (1991).

33. See Steadman et al., supra note 29, at 111.

34. One study reports that the average acquittal rate for an insanity plea is 26%. See Lisa Callahan et al., *The Volume and Characteristics of Insanity Defense Pleas: An Eight-State Study*, 19 BULL. AM. ACAD. PSYCHIATRY & L. 331, 334 (1991); Pasewark and McGinley report a success rate of 15% of pleas. See Richard A. Pasewark & Hugh McGinley, *Insanity Plea: National Survey of Frequency and Success*, 13 J. PSYCHIATRY & L. 101 at 106 (1985).

35. See, e.g., Hans, supra note 31, at 406 (reporting study indicating that public believes over 36% of all NGRI claims, constituting perceived 14% of all criminal cases, result in NGRI verdict).

36. See Michael J. Perlin, A Law of Healing, 68 U. CIN. L. REV. 407, 425 (2000) ("Nearly 90% of all insanity defense cases are 'walkthroughs'—stipulated on the papers.").

by judges in bench trials, rather than by juries.[37] The evidence directly refutes fears of rampant abuse and courtroom manipulation by attorneys representing sane defendants; in fact, most NGRI acquittees have significant prior histories of treatment for mental illness.[38]

Incapacitating Dangerous but Blameless Offenders as Civil Function   Protecting the public from potentially violent offenders, sane or insane, is an important, indeed irreproachable, goal. The GBMI verdict may protect the public from some dangerously insane offenders, but it does so not through rational reform of civil commitment, but rather by subverting the insanity defense and thereby perverting the criminal justice system to condemn, through criminal conviction, violators who may be blameless. Such condemnation of blameless offenders may have the long-term effect of weakening the criminal law's moral credibility, undermining its general condemnatory force and its ability to harness the powerful forces of social influence and internalized norms. The solution to the problem of dangerous but insane offenders lies not in the distortion of criminal justice, but in the adoption of civil commitment standards and procedures that will adequately protect the public. While there exist some serious constitutional limitations on civil commitment, the Supreme Court has held that the same limitations do not apply to commitment after an acquittal based on an insanity defense. Civil commitment after an NGRI verdict is made easier in part because the insanity acquittee's past offense provides evidence of dangerousness that may not exist in the normal civil commitment case.[39]

Lisa Callahan, et al., Insanity Defense Reform in the United States—Post-Hinckley

11 Mental and Physical Disability Law Reporter 54-60 (1987)

Study Design

To assess the types of insanity defense reform made following John Hinckley's shooting of President Ronald Reagan, we examined all insanity defense reforms in the 51 U.S. jurisdictions from 1978 through 1985. . . .

The reforms are categorized as follows: (1) changes in the test of insanity or in the entering of the plea; (2) addition of the GBMI ["guilty but mentally ill"] option; (3) changes in the burden and/or standard of proof; (4) changes in trial procedures; and (5) changes in commitment and release procedures. Clearly each state's reforms are idiosyncratic to its legal system. However, our classification system permits comparisons of the general types of reforms that have occurred after the Hinckley case.

Findings

First, it should be noted that 13 states made no changes in the insanity defense during our 6-year study period. It is acknowledged that some changes

---

37. See Callahan et al., supra note 34, at 334.
38. See, e.g., Michael R. Hawkins & Richard A. Pasewark, *Characteristics of Persons Utilizing the Insanity Plea*, 53 PSYCHOL. REP. 191, 194 (1983); Steadman et al., supra note 29, at 56.
39. See generally Robinson, Punishing Dangerousness, supra note 22.

may have occurred in other systems (e.g., civil commitment) that affect insanity acquitted, but these 13 states had no change in law that speaks directly to NGRI ["not guilty by reason of insanity"] procedures. We have identified 38 states that made significant reforms at some point between 1978 and 1985.

During the pre-Hinckley period, 11 states made changes in their insanity defense laws; two of the states made multiple changes. Five of these states made changes in the commitment/release procedures; in three of those states, this was the only change made. The two states that made multiple changes involved a change in commitment/release rules and a change in the test of insanity. Other single reforms were in three states that changed trial procedures—two that changed the burden and standard of proof, and one that changed the test of insanity (see Table 2).

Eight states made changes in their laws "during" Hinckley, the time between the shooting and the acquittal. One state made two reforms—adding the GBMI option and a change in commitment/release. The remaining seven states made single reforms: Three in commitment/release, two additions of GBMI, one in the test of insanity and one in the burden and standard of proof (see Table 2).

Twenty-five states that made no changes during or pre-Hinckley did make changes in the post-Hinckley period (see Table 2). Additionally, nine states made changes both pre- and post-Hinckley. Many states made multiple reforms during this period: 64 reforms occurred in 34 states. The most common reform made was in commitment/release (27 reforms in 26 states). Changes in the burden and standard of proof were made in 16 states. Eight states changed the test for insanity; eight states added the guilty but mentally ill option, and four states changed trial procedures.

Reforms that were made in the commitment process for persons acquitted by reason of insanity generally mandate some period of commitment for all such persons. This mandatory commitment is generally temporary "for evaluation," requiring court review at the end of a stated period of time. Distinctions are sometimes made among acquittees by the type of offense of which they were acquitted. Defendants acquitted of more serious crimes involving bodily injury may be automatically and indefinitely committed, while defendants convicted of less serious offenses may be entitled to a hearing to determine whether commitment is proper.

Reforms addressing release of persons acquitted by reason of insanity most often include mandatory court review prior to release of the person. Furthermore, some jurisdictions added provisions for conditional release, a program similar to parole. Only one of these changes could be interpreted outright as allowing more "due process" for insanity acquittees: in Florida the hearing for revocation of conditional release now must occur within seven days instead of "within a reasonable time" as the prior law provided.

In all reform jurisdictions but one (Utah) in which the burden of proof was changed, the burden was shifted from the state to the defendant. In conjunction with this reform, the standard of proof was changed from "beyond a reasonable doubt" to either the preponderance test or to "clear and convincing evidence."

In jurisdictions that altered the test of insanity, seven made changes that restricted the definition and use of insanity as a defense. Four jurisdictions changed from the American Law Institute (A.L.I.) or M'Naughten plus irresistible impulse tests to the simple M'Naughten test; two jurisdictions restricted the use of the insanity defense so that it could not be utilized to negate mens rea as a defense

Table 2: Instances of Insanity Defense Reforms

State	Test Used	Locus of Burden of Proof	Standard of Proof	GBMI	Trial Procedures	Release/ Commitment
Alabama						
Alaska				3		
Arizona		3	3			3
Arkansas						3
California	1, 2, 3					1
Colorado	3	3				3
Connecticut	3	3	3			3
Delaware				3	3	3
District of Columbia						
Florida						1, 3
Georgia		1	1	3		3
Hawaii		2, 3	2		1	3
Idaho	3					3
Illinois		3	3	2		3
Indiana	3			2		2, 3
Iowa		3	3			3
Kansas						
Kentucky				3		
Louisiana						
Maine						
Maryland		3	3		3	3
Massachusetts						
Michigan						
Minnesota		3				3
Mississippi						
Missouri						3
Montana	1					
Nebraska		3	3			1, 2
Nevada						
New Hampshire		1	1			2, 3
New Jersey						
New Mexico				2		
New York		3	3			3
North Carolina					1	2, 3
North Dakota	3	3	3		3	3
Ohio						1
Oklahoma					3	3
Oregon	3					1
Pennsylvania		3	3	3		
Rhode Island	1					
South Carolina				3		
South Dakota		3		3		3
Tennessee						3
Texas	3					3
Utah		3	3	3		3
Vermont		3	3			
Virginia						
Washington						3
Wisconsin					1	
Wyoming		3	3			

Key

1 = Pre-Hinckley (1/78-3/81)
2 = During Hinckley (4/81-6/82)
3 = Post-Hinckley (7/82-9/85)

to certain types of offenses; and one jurisdiction repealed the plea and the test of insanity altogether. Two jurisdictions, however, expanded the test for insanity by repealing the M'Naughten test and adopting the A.L.I. test.

Discussion

There have clearly been more reforms in the insanity defense during the post-Hinckley time than during a comparable period prior to the shooting and acquittal. While this may reinforce a conclusion that this increased activity resulted from the "notorious" case, there is at least one other plausible conclusion. Although our data cannot directly address the issue of causality, it seems plausible that a 1983 U.S. Supreme Court decision, *Jones v. U.S.*, accounts for much of the observed change being attributed to Hinckley.

The *Jones* decision requires that in states that have an automatic, indefinite commitment of persons acquitted by reason of insanity, the burden of proof must be on the defendant to demonstrate insanity by a preponderance of the evidence. Thus, states that wish to have an automatic, indefinite commitment retained or created must change the burden and standard of proof to comply with *Jones*. Such legal changes in reference to *Jones* could be attributed to states responding to public pressures to make sure "Hinckley couldn't happen in our state." In fact, the precipitant was case law, which at best was an indirect result of Hinckley.

It is just as likely that these reforms were enacted in compliance with *Jones*. Twelve of fourteen changes in the burden of proof at trial occurred in the period following *Jones*. Before attributing causality to the *Jones* decision, however, we must recognize that the legislative process is slow, and that changes occurring on the heels of the *Jones* decision nevertheless may have been initiated in response to Hinckley but not finalized until after *Jones*.

United States v. Brawner

United States Court of Appeals for the District of Columbia Circuit
471 F.2d 969 (1972) (en banc)

LEVENTHAL, Circuit Judge:

The principal issues raised on this appeal from a conviction for second degree murder and carrying a dangerous weapon relate to appellant's defense of insanity. After the case was argued to a division of the court, the court sua sponte ordered a rehearing en banc. We identified our intention to reconsider the appropriate standard for the insanity defense. . . .

We have stretched our canvas wide; and the focal point of the landscape before us is the formulation of the American Law Institute. The ALI's primary provision is stated thus in its Model Penal Code, see §4.01(1).

> Section 4.01 Mental Disease or Defect Excluding Responsibility. (1) A person is not responsible for criminal conduct if at the time of such conduct as a result of mental disease or defect *he lacks substantial capacity either to appreciate the criminality [wrongfulness] of his conduct or to conform his conduct to the requirements of the law.*

We have decided to adopt the ALI rule as the doctrine excluding responsibility for mental disease or defect, for application prospectively to trials begun after this date.

[The rule of Durham v. United States, 94 U.S. App. D.C. 228, 214 F.2d 862 (1954), which excused an unlawful act if it was the product of a mental disease or defect, will no longer be in effect.]*

---

* Chief Judge Bazelon, the author of the *Durham* decision, dissents in this case.

INSANITY RULE IN OTHER CIRCUITS

The American Law Institute's Model Penal Code expressed a rule which has become the dominant force in the law pertaining to the defense of insanity. The ALI rule is eclectic in spirit, partaking of the moral focus of McNaghten, the practical accommodation of the "control rules" (a term more exact and less susceptible of misunderstanding than "irresistible impulse" terminology), and responsive, at the same time, to a relatively modern, forward-looking view of what is encompassed in "knowledge." . . .

The core rule of the ALI has been adopted, with variations, by all save one of the Federal circuit courts of appeals, and by all that have come to reconsider the doctrine providing exculpation for mental illness. . . .

COMMENTS CONCERNING REASON FOR ADOPTION OF ALI RULE AND SCOPE OF RULE AS ADOPTED BY THIS COURT

Need to depart from "product" formulation and undue dominance by experts.

A principal reason for our decision to depart from the Durham rule is the undesirable characteristic . . . of undue dominance by the experts giving testimony. . . .

The doctrine of criminal responsibility is such that there can be no doubt "of the complicated nature of the decision to be made—intertwining moral, legal, and medical judgments," see King v. United States, 125 U.S. App. D.C. 318, 324, 372 F.2d 383, 389 (1967). Hence, as King and other opinions have noted, jury decisions have been accorded unusual deference even when they have found responsibility in the face of a powerful record, with medical evidence uncontradicted, pointing toward exculpation. The "moral" elements of the decision are not defined exclusively by religious considerations but by the totality of underlying conceptions of ethics and justice shared by the community, as expressed by its jury surrogate. The essential feature of a jury "lies in the interposition between the accused and his accuser of the commonsense judgment of a group of laymen, and in the community participation and shared responsibility that results from that group's determination of guilt or innocence."

The expert witnesses—psychiatrists and psychologists—are called to adduce relevant information concerning what may for convenience be referred to as the "medical" component of the responsibility issue. But the difficulty . . . is that the medical expert comes, by testimony given in terms of a non-medical construct ("product"), to express conclusions that in essence embody ethical and legal conclusions. There is, indeed, irony in a situation under which the Durham rule, which was adopted in large part to permit experts to testify in their own terms concerning matters within their domain which the jury should know, resulted in testimony by the experts in terms not their own to reflect unexpressed judgments in a domain that is properly not theirs but the jury's. The irony is heightened when the jurymen, instructed under the esoteric "product" standard, are influenced significantly by "product" testimony of expert witnesses really reflecting ethical and legal judgments rather than a conclusion within the witnesses' particular expertise. . . .

The experts have meaningful information to impart, not only on the existence of mental illness or not, but also on its relationship to the incident charged as an offense. In the interest of justice this valued information should be available, and should not be lost or blocked by requirements that unnaturally restrict communication between the experts and the jury. The more we have pondered the problem the more convinced we have become that the sound solution lies not in further shaping of the Durham "product" approach in more refined molds, but in adopting the ALI's formulation as the linchpin of our jurisprudence.

The ALI's formulation retains the core requirement of a meaningful relationship between the mental illness and the incident charged. The language in the ALI rule is sufficiently in the common ken that its use in the courtroom, or in preparation for trial, permits a reasonable three-way communication—between (a) the law-trained, judges and lawyers; (b) the experts and (c) the jurymen—without insisting on a vocabulary that is either stilted or stultified, or conducive to a testimonial mystique permitting expert dominance and encroachment on the jury's function. There is no indication in the available literature that any such untoward development has attended the reasonably widespread adoption of the ALI rule in the Federal courts and a substantial number of state courts.

Consideration and rejection of other suggestions

a. Proposal to abolish insanity defense

A number of proposals in the journals recommend that the insanity defense be abolished altogether. This is advocated in the amicus brief of the National District Attorneys Association as both desirable and lawful. . . .

This proposal has been put forward by responsible judges for consideration, with the objective of reserving psychiatric overview for the phase of the criminal process concerned with disposition of the person determined to have been the actor. However, we are convinced that the proposal cannot properly be imposed by judicial fiat.

The courts have emphasized over the centuries that "free will" is the postulate of responsibility under our jurisprudence. 4 Blackstone's Commentaries 27. The concept of "belief in freedom of the human will and a consequent ability and duty of the normal individual to choose between good and evil" is a core concept that is "universal and persistent in mature systems of law." Morissette v. United States, 342 U.S. 246, 250, 72 S. Ct. 240, 243, 96 L. Ed. 288 (1952). Criminal responsibility is assessed when through "free will" a man elects to do evil. And while, as noted in *Morissette*, the legislature has dispensed with mental element in some statutory offenses, in furtherance of a paramount need of the community, these instances mark the exception and not the rule, and only in the most limited instances has the mental element been omitted by the legislature as a requisite for an offense that was a crime at common law.

The concept of lack of "free will" is both the root of origin of the insanity defense and the line of its growth. This cherished principle is not undercut by difficulties, or differences of view, as to how best to express the free will concept in the light of the expansion of medical knowledge. We do not concur in the view of the National District Attorneys Association that the insanity defense should be abandoned judicially, either because it is at too great a variance with popular conceptions of guilt or fails "to show proper respect for the personality of the criminal [who] is liable to resent pathology more than punishment."

These concepts may be measured along with other ingredients in a legislative re-examination of settled doctrines of criminal responsibility, root, stock and branch. Such a reassessment, one that seeks to probe and appraise the society's processes and values, is for the legislative branch, assuming no constitutional bar. The judicial role is limited, in Justice Holmes's figure, to action that is molecular, with the restraint inherent in taking relatively small steps, leaving to the other branches of government whatever progress must be made with seven-league leaps. Such judicial restraint is particularly necessary when a proposal requires, as a mandatory ingredient, the kind of devotion of resources, personnel and techniques that can be accomplished only through whole-hearted legislative commitment. . . .

b. Proposal for defense if mental disease impairs capacity to such an extent that the defendant cannot "justly be held responsible."

We have also pondered the suggestion that the jury be instructed that the defendant lacks criminal responsibility if the jury finds that the defendant's mental disease impairs his capacity or controls to such an extent that he cannot "justly be held responsible."

This was the view of a British commission, adapted and proposed in 1955 by Professor Wechsler, the distinguished Reporter for the ALI's Model Penal Code, and sustained by some, albeit a minority, of the members of the ALI's Council. In the ALI, the contrary view prevailed because of a concern over presenting to the jury questions put primarily in the form of "justice."

The proposal is not to be condemned out of hand as a suggestion that the jury be informed of an absolute prerogative that it can only exercise by flatly disregarding the applicable rule of law. It is rather a suggestion that the jury be informed of the matters the law contemplates it will take into account in arriving at the community judgment concerning a composite of factors.

However, there is a substantial concern that an instruction overtly cast in terms of "justice" cannot feasibly be restricted to the ambit of what may properly be taken into account but will splash with unconfinable and malign consequences. The Government cautions that "explicit appeals to 'justice' will result in litigation of extraneous issues and will encourage improper arguments to the jury phrased solely in terms of 'sympathy' and 'prejudice.'"

Nor is this solely a prosecutor's concern. Mr. Flynn, counsel appointed to represent defendant, puts it that even though the jury is applying community concepts of blameworthiness "the jury should not be left at large, or asked to find out for itself what those concepts are."

The amicus submission of the Public Defender Service argues that it would be beneficial to focus the jury's attention on the moral and legal questions intertwined in the insanity defense. It expresses concern, however, over a blameworthiness instruction without more, saying "it may well be that the 'average' American condemns the mentally ill." It would apparently accept an approach not unlike that proposed by the ALI Reporter, under which the justice standard is coupled with a direction to consider the individual's capacity to control his behavior. Mr. Dempsey's recommendation is of like import, with some simplification. But the problem remains, whether, assuming justice calls for the exculpation and treatment of the mentally ill, that is more likely to be gained from a jury, with "average" notions of mental illness, which is explicitly set at large to convict or acquit persons with impaired mental capacity according to its concept of justice.

It is the sense of justice propounded by those charged with making and declaring the law—legislatures and courts—that lays down the rule that persons without substantial capacity to know or control the act shall be excused. The jury is concerned with applying the community understanding of this broad rule to particular lay and medical facts. Where the matter is unclear it naturally will call on its own sense of justice to help it determine the matter. There is wisdom in the view that a jury generally understands well enough that an instruction composed in flexible terms gives it sufficient latitude so that, without disregarding the instruction, it can provide that application of the instruction which harmonizes with its sense of justice. The ALI rule generally communicates that meaning. This is recognized even by those who might prefer a more explicit statement of the matter. It is one thing, however, to tolerate and even welcome the jury's sense of equity as a force that affects its application of instructions which state the legal rules that crystallize the requirements of justice as determined by the lawmakers of the community. It is quite another to set the jury at large, without such crystallization, to evolve its own legal rules and standards of justice. It would likely be counter-productive and contrary to the larger interest of justice to become so explicit—in an effort to hammer the point home to the very occasional jury that would otherwise be too rigid—that one puts serious strains on the normal operation of the system of criminal justice.

Taking all these considerations into account we conclude that the ALI rule as announced is not productive of injustice, and we decline to proclaim the broad "justly responsible" standard. . . .

Elements of the ALI rule adopted by this court

Though it provides a general uniformity, the ALI rule leaves room for variations. Thus, we have added an adjustment in the *McDonald* definition of mental disease, which we think fully compatible with both the spirit and text of the ALI rule. In the interest of good administration, we now undertake to set forth, with such precision as the subject will permit, other elements of the ALI rule as adopted by this court.

The two main components of the rule define (1) mental disease, (2) the consequences thereof that exculpate from responsibility.

a. Intermesh of components

The first component of our rule, derived from *McDonald*, defines mental disease or defect as an abnormal condition of the mind, and a condition which substantially (a) affects mental or emotional processes and (b) impairs behavioral controls. The second component, derived from the Model Penal Code, tells which defendant with a mental disease lacks criminal responsibility for particular conduct: it is the defendant who, as a result of this mental condition, at the time of such conduct, either (i) lacks substantial capacity to appreciate that his conduct is wrongful, or (ii) lacks substantial capacity to conform his conduct to the law.

The first component establishes eligibility for an instruction concerning the defense for a defendant who presents evidence that his abnormal condition of the mind has substantially impaired behavioral controls. The second component completes the instruction and defines the ultimate issue, of exculpation, in terms of whether his behavioral controls were not only substantially impaired but impaired to such an extent that he lacked substantial capacity to conform his conduct to the law.

b. The "result" of the mental disease

The rule contains a requirement of causality, as is clear from the term "result." Exculpation is established not by mental disease alone but only if "as a result" defendant lacks the substantial capacity required for responsibility. Presumably the mental disease of a kleptomaniac does not entail as a "result" a lack of capacity to conform to the law prohibiting rape.

c. At the time of the conduct

Under the ALI rule the issue is not whether defendant is so disoriented or void of controls that he is never able to conform to external demands, but whether he had that capacity at the time of the conduct. The question is not properly put in terms of whether he would have capacity to conform in some untypical restraining situation—as with an attendant or policeman at his elbow. The issue is whether he was able to conform in the unstructured condition of life in an open society, and whether the result of his abnormal mental condition was a lack of substantial internal controls. . . .

d. Capacity to appreciate wrongfulness of his conduct

As to the option of terminology noted in the ALI code, we adopt the formulation that exculpates a defendant whose mental condition is such that he lacks substantial capacity to appreciate the wrongfulness of his conduct. We prefer this on pragmatic grounds to "appreciate the criminality of his conduct" since the resulting jury instruction is more like that conventionally given to and applied by the jury. While such an instruction is of course subject to the objection that it lacks complete precision, it serves the objective of calling on the jury to provide a community judgment on a combination of factors. And since the possibility of analytical differences between the two formulations is insubstantial in fact in view of the control capacity test, we are usefully guided by the pragmatic considerations pertinent to jury instructions. . . .

e. Caveat paragraph

Section 4.01 of the Model Penal Code as promulgated by ALI contains in subsection (2) what has come to be known as the "caveat paragraph":

> (2) The terms "mental disease or defect" do not include an abnormality manifested only by repeated criminal or otherwise anti-social conduct.

The purpose of this provision was to exclude a defense for the so-called "psychopathic personality."

There has been a split in the Federal circuits concerning this provision. . . .

Our own approach is influenced by the fact that our rule already includes a definition of mental disease (from *McDonald*). Under that definition, as we have pointed out, the mere existence of "a long criminal record does not excuse crime." We do not require the caveat paragraph as an insurance against exculpation of the deliberate and persistent offender. Our *McDonald* rule guards against the danger of misunderstanding and injustice that might arise, say, from an expert's classification that reflects only a conception defining all criminality as reflective of mental illness. There must be testimony to show both that the defendant was suffering from an abnormal condition of the mind and that it substantially affected mental or emotional processes and substantially impaired behavioral controls.

In this context, our pragmatic approach is to adopt the caveat paragraph as a rule for application by the judge, to avoid miscarriage of justice, but not for inclusion in instructions to the jury.

The judge will be aware that the criminal and antisocial conduct of a person—on the street, in the home, in the ward—is necessarily material information for assessment by the psychiatrist. On the other hand, rarely if ever would a psychiatrist base a conclusion of mental disease solely on criminal and anti-social acts. Our pragmatic solution provides for reshaping the rule, for application by the court, as follows: The introduction or proffer of past criminal and anti-social actions is not admissible as evidence of mental disease unless accompanied by expert testimony, supported by a showing of the concordance of a responsible segment of professional opinion, that the particular characteristics of these actions constitute convincing evidence of an underlying mental disease that substantially impairs behavioral controls.

This formulation retains the paragraph as a "caveat" rather than an inexorable rule of law. It should serve to obviate distortions of the present state of knowledge that would constitute miscarriages of justice. Yet it leaves the door open—on shouldering the "convincing evidence" burden—to accommodate our general rule to developments that may lie ahead. It is the kind of imperfect, but not unfeasible, accommodation of the abstract and pragmatic that is often found to serve the administration of justice. . . .

The case is remanded for further consideration by the District Court in accordance with this opinion.

So Ordered.

▲ PROBLEMS

Cinema as Life: Assassinating the President (#100)

John Hinckley loves the movie *Taxi Driver*, particularly its leading actress, Jodie Foster. In fact, he is obsessed with both. After watching the film, over a period of four years he repeatedly attempts to meet Foster. As his attempts fail, Hinckley becomes increasingly depressed and isolated. He begins to mimic the character of Travis Bickle from *Taxi Driver*. In the film, Bickle attempts to assassinate a presidential candidate, which leads to a relationship with the beautiful woman played by Jodie Foster. Trying to replicate Bickle's success, Hinckley stalks President Jimmy Carter and later President Ronald Reagan. Finally, he decides he must act. Hinckley writes Foster a letter professing his love for her and stating that he intends to perform a historic act in order to gain her respect; specifically, he writes that he intends to kill Reagan. After completing the letter, Hinckley goes to the Washington Hilton Hotel, where Reagan is giving a speech. He joins a crowd of people outside the hotel who are waiting to catch a glimpse of the President as he leaves. When Reagan emerges with his entourage, Hinckley takes out his pistol and fires six shots at the President. No one is killed; however, Reagan, his Press Secretary, Bill Brady, a police officer, and a secret service agent are all injured. Reagan survives after extensive surgery, and Brady is paralyzed for life.

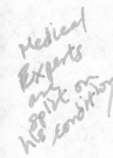

Psychiatric experts agree that Hinckley is suffering from severe depression and is often suicidal but are split on the exact nature of his condition. A majority find that Hinckley is schizophrenic and unable control his actions and only able to appreciate the wrongfulness of his conduct from a detached, intellectual standpoint.

What liability for Hinckley, if any, under the Model Penal Code? Prepare a list of all criminal code subsections in the order in which you rely on them in your analysis.

What liability, if any, under other insanity defense formulations?

Multiple Personalities, Same Body (#101)

Rodrigo Rodrigues lures young girls into secluded areas and performs sex acts on them, including sodomy and intercourse. He suffers from multiple personality syndrome (MPS). In this condition, there are distinct personalities that emerge within the same person, any one of which may be dominant at a certain time. Each personality is fully formed, with its own particular behavioral patterns, and whichever personality is dominant at the time has complete control over the individual's behavior. It is often the case that the nondominant personality experiences amnesia as to the times when it is not in control. Rodrigues's symptoms include two distinct personalities. One of the personalities is able to appreciate the wrongfulness of his acts and can control his behavior to conform to the law but is quite antisocial and does not care about the harm he causes to others. The other, however, lacks such capacity to conform his conduct to the requirements of law. After he is apprehended, several psychiatrists examine Rodrigues but disagree as to which personality was in control when he sexually assaulted the girls.

What liability for Rodrigues, if any, under the Model Penal Code? Prepare a list of all criminal code subsections in the order in which you rely on them in your analysis.

Saving Her Children from Eternal Damnation by Drowning Them (#102)

Rusty and Andrea Yates believe in having a large family. They want as many children as Andrea's health permits. Within their first year of marriage, they have their first child, Noah. Two more boys soon follow. Andrea and her husband are deeply religious and spend much time together in prayer. When Rusty wants to live a simpler life, the family moves from their trailer into a renovated bus. This becomes their permanent home as Andrea gives birth to a fourth baby boy. The bus is purchased from their minister, Michael Woroniecki, an evangelical who preaches that women derive their role from the sin of Eve and that bad mothers create bad children, who go to hell. The Yateses strictly follow Woroniecki's teachings. *sigh*

Andrea begins to experience symptoms of mental illness. She attempts to commit suicide by swallowing pills and is diagnosed with major depression. Though she is given prescriptions for multiple medications, including antipsychotics, Andrea does not take them. She often shakes, fails to feed her children, mutilates herself, and claims that there are cameras in the ceilings. Rusty manages to stop a second, nearly successful, suicide attempt but does not report the incident to her physicians. *sigh*

The Yateses are warned against having more children because of Andrea's precarious mental state, but in response to Rusty's pleading, they have a fifth child, a baby girl. The family moves from the bus into a house, and Andrea's condition initially improves. However, the improvement is short-lived. Soon, Andrea is again cutting herself and refusing to feed her children. She worries that her mental illness renders her a bad mother and that, as Woroniecki preaches, her children will be doomed to hell. One morning, after Rusty leaves for work, Andrea fills the bathtub with water. She drowns her three youngest boys and her daughter. Noah sees his mother kill his little sister. He tries to run, but Andrea grabs him and drowns him as he struggles. Andrea explains later that she believed that she was killing her children in order to save them from eternal torment in hell. *he's as insane as she #13*

What liability for Yates, if any, under the Model Penal Code? Prepare a list of all criminal code subsections in the order in which you rely on them in your analysis.

✳ DISCUSSION ISSUE

Should the Criminal Law Recognize an Excuse Defense for an Offender Who, Because of Mental Illness, Knows His Conduct Constituting the Offense Is Wrong But Lacks the Capacity to Control It?

Materials presenting each side of this Discussion Issue appear in the Advanced Materials for Section 21 in Appendix A.

Disability Excuses

The previous Section, concerning insanity, offers a case study of the principles of exculpation for disability excuses. Involuntary intoxication and duress, as well as the involuntary act excuse contained in the voluntary act requirement, also are classic disability excuses. Defendants have pressed for the recognition of other excuses, some of which would seem to satisfy the principles of excuse, while some would not.

◆ THE CASE OF PATTY HEARST (#103)

Patty Hearst is a nineteen-year old art history major at the University of California at Berkeley. She lives in an apartment close to campus with her fiancé,

Figure 97 **Patty Hearst, 1973**
(F.B.I.)

Figure 98 **Patricia Hearst's grandfather, William Randolph Hearst, 1935**
(AP)

Steven Weed, and finally feels happy. Hearst, always mature and independent, began dating Weed while she was attending the small, elite Crystal Springs School for Girls, close to her parents' California home. She graduated early and, much in love, had her parents hire Weed as her full-time math tutor. They moved in together during Hearst's first year of college at Menlo Park, where she finished in the top of her class. After Weed was accepted into Berkeley's Ph.D. program in Philosophy, Hearst decided to enroll there as well. She had become quite interested in art history while at Menlo Park, and Berkeley seemed like an ideal place to continue her studies.

Hearst is just now getting into the swing of college. She took the fall semester off and worked in the stationery section of a department store (her first job). She is enjoying her quiet domestic life. Weed does the cleaning; she does the cooking. Her chief aspiration in life is to have a collie, a station wagon, and two children. Such goals are quite tame for the granddaughter of William Randolph Hearst, a member of one of the most influential families in California and the world. But most people who meet Patty Hearst find her to be quite different from the affected elitist that her name might imply. Her faculty adviser at Crystal Springs describes her as "delightful" and "unpretentious. [She] never rode on the laurels of her family name." Hearst feels comfortable with her casual lifestyle but is still uncomfortable about her family and their wealth. Her recent engagement has improved her familial relationships. Her usually overbearing, politically far-right mother has often been disappointed with Hearst and her liberal, unrefined ways. But that has changed, now that they are shopping for china, silver, and crystal, and are planning a big society wedding.

On February 2, 1974, Hearst goes through her usual routine. She and Weed are quite domestic, often staying in for the evening, cooking, reading, and talking. Their quiet evening is interrupted by a knock on the door. Two people, acting strange and fidgety, say they were told the apartment is up for rent and ask whether they can see the inside. Weed replies that there has been a mistake and turns them away. Both Hearst and Weed are mildly shaken by the strange visitors. The next evening, Hearst is again disturbed

Figure 99 **Patricia Hearst and Steven Weed's apartment on Benvenue Avenue in Berkeley**

(San Francisco Examiner, Florence Fang)

Figure 100 **Steven Weed, Hearst's boyfriend, in the hospital after the kidnaping**

(San Francisco Examiner, Florence Fang)

when a stranger calls, persistently asking for Mary.

Two days later, Weed has an evening class, then walks home as usual. Hearst waits for him and then the pair has dinner. They settle down to watch the television program *Star Trek*, followed by *Mission: Impossible*. Their domestic scene is interrupted for the third evening in a row by a sharp knock on the door. Annoyed, Weed goes to answer. Two shabbily dressed people are outside, asking to use their phone. Moments later, the visitors push open the door and barge in, followed by two men. Weed is beaten, tied up, and dragged into the living room. Hearst tries to fight the intruders before being overwhelmed. When the intruders notice that Weed is still struggling, they hit him with a rifle butt several times. Hearst, dressed only in her bathrobe, screams, cries, and pleads with her captors to let her go. She is dragged outside and thrown into the trunk of a car.

When the police arrive, they question the neighbors. From the cyanide-tipped bullets that were left at the scene, they determine that the infamous Symbionese Liberation Army is behind the kidnapping. The SLA has become well known for its killing of Dr. Marcus Foster, the African American superintendent of schools for Oakland County. They are reputed to be dangerously driven by their far-left, slightly illogical politics, mixing Marxist theory with violent activism. Most of the members come from upper middle-class backgrounds.

Three days after the kidnapping, SLA leader Donald Defreeze releases a communiqué. They declare that Hearst is a prisoner of war and is being ransomed for the release of Joseph Remiro and Russell Little, two men held in connection with Foster's death. There is a tape of Hearst saying that she is being well treated in accordance with the Geneva Convention prisoner-of-war guidelines. The SLA calls for a good faith gesture requiring the Hearst family to distribute $70 worth of food to every needy Californian. Hearst's father distributes $2 million worth of

Figure 101 **General Field Marshall Cinque Mtume, aka Donald Defreeze**
(F.B.I.)

Figure 102 **Lines of people waiting to receive food from the giveaway sponsored by the Hearst family in response to SLA demands**
(UPI)

Figure 103 **Closet where Hearst was held**
(Bob McLeod, San Francisco Examiner)

food and makes arrangements for another $4 million distribution.

Hearst is kept captive and isolated in a stuffy bedroom closet all day long except for brief trips to the bathroom. There is a single bare bulb in the hot, windowless room. She is blindfolded at all times. Since her kidnapping, Hearst has been threatened with death, taunted, ruthlessly interrogated, and terrorized by the constant sounds of cleaning and loading of weapons. She is also raped by two of the SLA members. The leader, DeFreeze, comes into the closet to chide her for not cooperating with the "sisters." As he begins to talk to her, he grabs her pelvic region and breasts. He returns later and forces her to have sex with him. Then William Wolfe, another SLA member, visits her in her closet and rapes her. Hearst feels helpless and afraid and is unable to put up much of a fight. Her captors tell her that her parents are bourgeois pigs who have abandoned her and that she has no hope of survival. They say that when and if the F.B.I. raids the house, they will not be concerned about her getting killed in the exchange of gunfire. Hearst vacillates between defending her parents and feeling as if they do not care about her predicament. As a result of her treatment and fears, Hearst is having difficulty eating.

After a month in captivity, Hearst is a physical and emotional wreck. She cannot walk at all and can only stand briefly before collapsing. She finds that she is gradually becoming sympathetic to the SLA mission and position. Her captors latch onto this new sentiment and encourage her SLA education, inviting her to attend meetings and giving her reading materials (on poverty, injustice, inequality, and the evils of the Hearst family). After being isolated from all outside human contact, Hearst is buoyed by now being hugged and called "sister" by the SLA members.

On April 3, 1974, two months after being kidnapped, Hearst declares that she is joining the SLA. In a tape released to the public, Hearst says that she has taken the name "Tania" after one of Che Guevara's comrades. She derides her father, saying that his attempts to meet the SLA

Figure 104 **Hearst posing before a SLA banner, 1974** (Bettmann/Corbis)

demands were futile and weak. She now thinks that revolutionary action is the only way to make a difference. She says that she can never go back to her old life now that she is aware of the world's inequities. In addition to the tape, the SLA releases a poster depicting Hearst dressed in a jumpsuit and beret, crouching with a gun in front of a seven-headed cobra, the SLA symbol. Public and police sentiment turns against Hearst, but her parents maintain that she has been brainwashed by the group.

Figure 105 **The Hibernia Bank in the Sunset District of San Francisco, 1976** (AP)

On April 15th, "Tania" accompanies her new comrades to the Hibernia Bank in San Francisco. They park illegally in a bus zone and approach the bank with Tania in the rear, equipped with a cut-down carbine. There are 18 employees and 6 customers inside the bank on this sunny morning. The SLA women, wearing three-quarter-length pea coats, dark flared pants, and hiking boots, force the people to the ground and keep them under control. Witnesses note that the group acts like commandos, with each person assigned a discrete task. They are so well orchestrated that there is little need for communication among them during the robbery.

As she has been instructed, Tania announces that she is Patty Hearst. She threatens people if they do not stay horizontal on the floor. Upstairs, the bank manager is in the break room when he notices what is going on below. He activates the silent alarm, which in turn activates the security video cameras. Just before the robbery is completed, an SLA woman shoots two customers who walk into the midst of the robbery and try to leave again. (They recover from their injuries.) The group then escapes with more than $10,000 and dump their get-away cars at an elementary school.

The F.B.I. arrives on the scene and recognizes Hearst on the security tapes. News of Hearst's role in the robbery reaches her family, who has retreated to Desi Arnaz's home in Mexico. They are horrified and assert that she was coerced and brainwashed. The F.B.I. Director says that, for the time being, they will assume Hearst is a coercion victim. The Bureau wishes to arrest her only as a material witness. However, the Attorney General says Hearst is now nothing more than a common criminal. Media stories show no sympathy. The F.B.I. issues a wanted poster that becomes an immediate collectors' item and is offered for sale at alternative lifestyle stores in the Bay Area.

The next Wednesday, April 24th, Hearst issues a statement claiming that she willingly participated in the robbery and that she received one-ninth of the

Figure 106 **Patty Hearst holding gun inside the Hibernia Bank, 1974** (AP)

Figure 107 **William Harris**
(San Mateo County jail)

Figure 108 **Emily Harris**
(San Mateo County jail)

profits, just as did every other SLA participant. She also criticizes her parents and her former boyfriend, Steven Weed. After this statement, the SLA disappears from view, leaving their current hideout and moving to 1808 Oakdale Street. On May 10th, the SLA decides that San Francisco is no longer a safe place and move to the anonymity of Los Angeles.

On May 15th, Hearst is waiting for two SLA members, Emily and Bill Harris, in a car outside of Mel's Sporting Goods Store. The proprietor catches Bill attempting to steal a bandolier. He confronts Harris as Harris tries

Figure 109 F.B.I. Wanted Poster for Hearst (F.B.I.)

to leave the premises. A struggle ensues. Hearst fires cover shots from across the street to facilitate the Harrises' escape. Twenty-seven slugs slam into the storefront; three hit an adjoining building. The trio drives away and, a few blocks later, hijack a van belonging to Tom Matthews, a high school student from Lynwood. He stays in the van and spends the next day and a half with Hearst, Bill, and Emily. Hearst tells Matthews that she was not coerced into robbing the Hibernia Bank. (Hearst later says she told Matthews this information because the Harrises were there.) During their time together, Hearst pats Matthews's head, telling him that he will be okay. They drop him off at his house in time for his upcoming ball game and even offer him gas money for his troubles. They do not return to the SLA safe house.

The other SLA members evacuate their safehouse and find another refuge nearby. Police track them there and, during a shootout with police, all eight SLA members are killed. Patty and the Harrises watch the events unfold on television. They leave Los Angeles for the Bay Area and then travel, separately, across the country, meeting up in New York City. Together, they head to Pennsylvania for the summer. In September 1974, Patty makes her way to Las Vegas and then to Sacramento. The Harrises arrive a few days later, and the SLA (with some new recruits) becomes active again. On January 31st, Patty registers for classes at Sacramento City College under the assumed name of Sue Hendricks. In late May, Hearst moves to the Mission District. She shares an apartment at 625 Morse Street with other SLA members until September 18, 1975, when the F.B.I. finally catches up with her. By this point, the federal government has spent more than $3.5 million and twenty months tracking her.

When Agent Tom Padden crashes through the door shouting "F.B.I! Freeze!" Hearst is in the process of packing a loaded .38 caliber Smith and Wesson handgun and has twenty-three bullets in her purse.

1. Relying only on your own intuitions of justice, what liability and punishment, if any, does Patty Hearst deserve?

N	0	1	2	3	4	5	6	7	8	9	10	11
☐	☐	☐	☐	☐	☐	☐	☐	☐	☐	☐	☐	☐
no liability	liability but no punishment	1 day	2 wks	2 mo	6 mo	1 yr	3 yrs	7 yrs	15 yrs	30 yrs	life imprison- ment	No punish- ment but civil preventive detention for as long as she is dangerous

2. What "justice" arguments could defense counsel make on the defendant's behalf?

3. What "justice" arguments could the prosecution make against the defendant?

4. What liability for Hearst, if any, under the then-existing statutes? Prepare a list of all criminal code subsections and cases in the order in which you rely on them in your analysis.

5. What liability, if any, under the Model Penal Code? Prepare a list of all criminal code subsections in the order in which you rely on them in your analysis.

■ THE LAW

United States Code Title 18
(1974)

Section 2113. Bank Robbery and Incidental Crimes

(a) Whoever, by force and violence, or by intimidation, takes, or attempts to take, from the person or presence of another any property or money or any other thing of value belonging to, or in the care, custody, control, management, or possession of, any bank, credit union, or any savings and loan association; or

Whoever enters or attempts to enter any bank, credit union, or any savings and loan association, or any building used in whole or in part as a bank, credit union, or any savings and loan association, or building, or part thereof, so used, any felony affecting such bank, credit union, or any savings and loan association and in violation of any statute of the United States, or any larceny—

Shall be fined not more than $5,000 or imprisoned not more than twenty years, or both.

(b) Whoever takes and carries away, with intent to steal or purloin, any property or money or any other thing of value exceeding $100 belonging to, or in the care, custody, control, management, or possession of any bank, credit union, or any savings and loan association, shall be fined not more than $5,000 or imprisoned not more than ten years, or both.

Whoever takes and carries away, with intent to steal or purloin, any property or money or any other thing of value not exceeding $100 belonging to, or in the care, custody, control, management, or possession of any bank, credit union, or any savings and loan association, shall be fined not more than $1,000 or imprisoned not more than one year, or both.

(c) Whoever receives, possesses, conceals, stores, barters, sells or disposes of, any property of money or other thing of value knowing the same to have been taken from a bank, credit union, or any savings and loan association, in violation of subsection (b) of this section shall be subject to the punishment provided by said subsection (b) for the taker.

(d) Whoever, in commission, or in attempting to commit, any offense defined in subsections (a) and (b) of this section, assaults any person, or puts in jeopardy the life of any person by the use of a dangerous weapon or device, shall be fined not more than $10,000 or imprisoned not more than twenty-five years, or both.

(e) Whoever, in committing any offense defined in this section, or in avoiding or attempting to avoid apprehension for the commission of such offense, kills any person, or forces any person to accompany him without the consent of such person, shall be imprisoned not less than ten years, or punished by death if the verdict of the jury shall so direct.

(f) As used in this section the term "bank" means any member of the Federal Reserve System, and any bank, banking association, trust company, savings bank, or other banking institution organized or operating under the laws of the United States, and any bank the deposits of which are insured by the Federal Deposit Insurance Corporation.

(g) As used in this section the term "savings and loan association" means any federal savings and loan association and any "insured institution" as defined in section 401 of the National Housing Act, as amended, and any "Federal credit union" as defined in section 2 of the Federal Credit Union Act.

(h) As used in this section the term "credit union" means any federal credit union and any State-chartered credit union the accounts of which are insured by the Administrator of the National Credit Union Administration.

Section 924. [Use of a Firearm in Commission of a Felony;] Penalties

(a) . . .

(c) Whoever—

(1) uses a firearm to commit any felony for which he may be prosecuted in a court of the United States, or

(2) carries a firearm unlawfully during the commission of any felony for which he may be prosecuted in a court of the United States shall, in addition to the punishment provided for the commission of such felony, be sentenced to a term of imprisonment for not less that one year nor more than ten years. In the case of his second or subsequent conviction under this subsection, such person shall be sentenced to a term of imprisonment for not less than two nor more than twenty-five years and, notwithstanding any other

provision of law, the court shall not suspend the sentence in the case of a second or subsequent conviction of such person or give him a probationary sentence, nor shall the term of imprisonment imposed under this subsection run concurrently with any term of imprisonment imposed for the commission of such felony.

United States v. Gordon
526 F.2d 406 (9th Cir. 1975)

The defendant was convicted of possession and sale of amphetamine tablets, despite his claim of a duress defense arising from his belief that his life and the lives of his friends would be in danger if he did not complete the sale. The court of appeals applied the definition of duress, first appearing in *Shannon v. United States*, 76 F.2d 490, 493 (10th Cir. 1935), that "[c]oercion which will excuse the commission of a criminal act must be immediate and of such nature as to induce a well-grounded apprehension of death or serious bodily injury if the act is not done. One who has full opportunity to avoid the act without danger of that kind cannot invoke the doctrine of coercion. . . . For a defendant to successfully urge duress as a defense, he must show that the threat and the fear which the threat caused were immediate and involved death or serious bodily injury. He must also show that the fear was well-grounded and that there was no reasonable opportunity to escape." The court ultimately found that his situation lacked in immediacy because the threats were made during long-distance telephone calls by persons who were hundreds of miles away and that he held an opportunity to escape, as "[a]venues of escape were always available. . . . If they had not been selling drugs, they could have sought police protection."

D'Aquino v. United States
192 F.2d 338 (9th Cir. 1951)

The defendant was an American citizen of Japanese ancestry who was charged with treason for allegedly broadcasting over the radio from Japan during World War II. She claimed a defense of duress based on her fears that she would be harmed during her residency in Japan if she did not provide public support for their cause. However, the court held that the elements of duress would not be satisfied by her circumstances. She was not a military prisoner, for which there might have been an exception, and as such, was held to the standard that "in order to excuse a criminal act on the ground of coercion, compulsion or necessity, one must have acted under the apprehension of immediate and impending death or of serious and immediate bodily harm. Fear of injury to one's property or remote bodily harm do not excuse an offense." Further, the court noted:

> We know of no rule that would permit one who is under the protection of an enemy to claim immunity from prosecution for treason merely by setting up a claim of mental fear of possible future action on the part of the enemy. We think that the citizen owing allegiance to the United States must manifest a determination to resist commands and orders until such time as he is faced with the alternative of immediate injury or death. Were any other rule to be applied,

traitors in the enemy country would by that fact alone be shielded from any requirement of resistance. The person claiming the defense of coercion and duress must be a person whose resistance has brought him to the last ditch.

Model Penal Code
(Official Draft 1962)

Section 2.08. Intoxication

(1) Except as provided in Subsection (4) of this Section, intoxication of the actor is not a defense unless it negatives an element of the offense.

(2) When recklessness establishes an element of the offense, if the actor, due to self-induced intoxication, is unaware of a risk of which he would have been aware had he been sober, such unawareness is immaterial.

(3) Intoxication does not, in itself, constitute mental disease within the meaning of Section 4.01.

(4) Intoxication which (a) is not self-induced or (b) is pathological is an affirmative defense if by reason of such intoxication the actor at the time of his conduct lacks substantial capacity either to appreciate its criminality [wrongful-ness] or to conform his conduct to the requirements of law.

(5) Definitions. In this Section unless a different meaning plainly is required:

(a) "intoxication" means a disturbance of mental or physical capacities resulting from the introduction of substances into the body;

(b) "self-induced intoxication" means intoxication caused by substances which the actor knowingly introduces into his body, the tendency of which to cause intoxication he knows or ought to know, unless he introduces them pursuant to medical advice or under such circumstances as would afford a defense to a charge of crime;

(c) "pathological intoxication" means intoxication grossly excessive in degree, given the amount of the intoxicant, to which the actor does not know he is susceptible.

Section 2.09. Duress

(1) It is an affirmative defense that the actor engaged in the conduct charged to constitute an offense because he was coerced to do so by the use of, or a threat to use, unlawful force against his person or the person of another, which a person of reasonable firmness in his situation would have been unable to resist.

(2) The defense provided by this Section is unavailable if the actor recklessly placed himself in a situation in which it was probable that he would be subjected to duress. The defense is also unavailable if he was negligent in placing himself in such a situation, whenever negligence suffices to establish culpability for the offense charged.

(3) It is not a defense that a woman acted on the command of her husband, unless she acted under such coercion as would establish a defense under this Section. [The presumption that a woman, acting in the presence of her husband, is coerced is abolished.]

(4) When the conduct of the actor would otherwise be justifiable under Section 3.02, this Section does not preclude such defense.

● OVERVIEW OF DISABILITY EXCUSES

Hypothetical: The Brothers' Brawl (#104)

The Motan brothers, Acker and Ed, have a reputation for being a bit wild. Their wildness has given them near-celebrity status in some quarters, and they are happy to cultivate the image. They stop in at one of their favorite bars, The Wheel, and some "fans" buy them a round of beers. After the brothers guzzle them down, a woman in the group reveals that their drinks were spiked with a "gorilla" drug. "Watch out, everybody! You're going to get a show tonight!" she shouts to the crowd. Acker starts to feel strange, excited, and very aggressive. He starts dancing on the table. Ed joins in and before long both are kicking drinks and throwing pitchers of beer.

Jote, a man in the group who usually is a fan of their antics, takes offense and begins to scream at them. As a brawl begins, the bar's bouncer moves toward the group. At six-feet six-inches and 250 pounds, the sight of him is enough to make the Motan brothers quiet down. Jote, however, turns his anger toward the bouncer and is quickly ejected.

After a few more beers, the brothers leave for another favorite bar but find Jote waiting for them outside. He is highly belligerent and vocal. His shouting draws a crowd from inside the bar. The brothers decide to beat him senseless but then spot a patrol car across the street. They point it out to Jote, but he is undeterred. When Jote begins telling the assembled "fans" that the brothers are too "wimpy" and "yellow" to fight, the brothers conclude that they have no choice but to hurt him. Each takes turns punching him while the other holds him, but after a minute or two, the police intervene and arrest all three for their brawling.

Tired of the Motan brothers' relentless brawling, the prosecutor wants prison terms, but his case is complicated by the blood-test reports from the hospital. Acker and Jote (who mistakenly got the dose intended for Ed) had a level of Skopezine that would create uncontrollable feelings of aggression in the average person. In addition, the medical authorities explain that a belief that one has been subjected to an aggression-inducing drug, as Ed believed, could cause a loosening of psychological restraints to aggression that otherwise might prevent such conduct.

Jote is tried first and acquitted, on the ground that his behavior resulted from his involuntary intoxication. Should either, or both, of the brothers also be excused?

Notes

Common Structure of Disability Excuses
    Disability Requirement
    Disability Must Extend Beyond Criminal Conduct

COMMON STRUCTURE OF DISABILITY EXCUSES

One traditional disability excuse, insanity, is discussed in the previous section. Others include subnormality, involuntary intoxication, immaturity, and duress. With few (but important) variations, each defense reflects the same internal structure as insanity, requiring that a *disability* cause an *excusing condition*. Each defense, however, addresses a different disability requirement and recognizes a different combination of excusing conditions.

Disability Requirement   In this context, a *disability* means an abnormal condition of the actor at the time of the offense, such as insanity, intoxication, subnormality, or immaturity. Each such disability is a real-world condition with a variety of observable manifestations apart from the conduct constituting the offense. It may be a long-term or even permanent condition, such as subnormality, or a temporary state, such as intoxication, somnambulism, or hypnotism. Its source may be internal, as in insanity, or external, as in coercion from another person (duress). The disability requirement serves to distinguish the actor from the general population; it provides an object to which the blame may be shifted; and it allows the law to acquit the actor because he is different, while continuing to condemn and prohibit the offense conduct when performed by others. The existence of a disability also provides some evidence that a resulting excusing condition also exists. In the "Brothers' Brawl" hypothetical, Jote's and Acker's Skopezine-influenced state provides the disability required for the involuntary-intoxication defense. Ed, with only the mistaken belief that he was drugged, does not satisfy the disability requirement. While he might argue for an insanity defense, it may be difficult for him to show that the effects of his mistaken belief constitute even a temporary "mental disease or defect," as the defense requires.[1]

Disability Must Extend Beyond Criminal Conduct   The purposes of the disability requirement help explain why a disability typically must have confirmable manifestations beyond the criminal conduct at hand. The Model Penal Code intoxication defense, for example, requires "a disturbance of mental or physical capacities resulting from the introduction of substances into the body."[2] The insanity defense requires that the defendant be suffering from a "mental disease or defect,"[3] which is defined to exclude "an abnormality manifested only by repeated criminal or otherwise antisocial conduct."[4]

Nature of Disability Distinguishes Excuses from Each Other   Most excuses are defined and distinguished according to the disabilities to which they apply. Where a mental disease or defect is the cause of the excusing condition, the insanity defense is applicable. Even where the results of the defendant's disability are identical to those that may result from insanity—distortion in perception, ignorance of criminality, or impairment of ability to control one's conduct—if the underlying disability is not mental disease or defect, a defendant will not be eligible for an insanity excuse. Thus, it is the excusing condition's cause—be it involuntary intoxication, immaturity, subnormality, hypnotism, duress, or some other disability—rather than its results, that determines which excuse is applicable. This practice of defining excuses by their disability elements may have evolved because the disability is an independently observable phenomenon, while the resulting excusing condition is not.

Special Rules for Specific Disabilities   Such a disability-organized system of excuses probably developed also because it has practical value. As with justification defenses, it frequently is appropriate to attach special rules to govern in particular instances. For example, it may be more of a concern in practice that an actor voluntarily caused his own intoxication than that he caused his own insanity. Thus, special rules relating to an actor's culpability in becoming intoxicated are added to the intoxication excuse. On the other hand, as a theoretical matter, it would

---

1. "Mental disease or defect" has been defined as "any normal condition of the mind which substantially impairs behavior controls." McDonald v. United States, 312 F.2d 847, 851 (D.C. Cir. 1962).
2. Model Penal Code § 2.08(5).
3. Model Penal Code § 4.01(1).
4. Model Penal Code § 4.01(2).

seem that the same principles should apply, no matter what the disability. If it is appropriate to take account of an actor's causing his own disability, for example, there is no reason why the principle should not apply to all disabilities, whether the defendant causes his own intoxication, hypnotism, duress, or insanity.

EXCUSING CONDITIONS

A recognized disability, standing alone, does not qualify an actor for an excuse, for the disability itself does not provide the central reason for exculpating the actor. An actor is not excused because she is involuntarily intoxicated, but rather because the *effect* of the intoxication in the instant situation is to create a condition that renders her blameless for the conduct constituting the offense. The requirement of an *excusing condition*, then, is not independent of the actor's disability, but rather a requirement that the actor's disability cause a particular result—a particular exculpating mental or emotional condition in relation to the conduct constituting the offense. In the "Brothers' Brawl" hypothetical, while Acker may have had Skopezine in his body, an excuse defense requires that the Skopezine had a sufficiently strong effect in bringing about his assaultive behavior that he is blameless for that conduct.

Four Types of Excusing Conditions   Society generally is willing to excuse an actor under any of four types of conditions. In descending order of severity, they include situations where:

(1) The conduct constituting the offense is involuntary, that is, not the product of the actor's voluntary effort or determination (e.g., the actor is having a seizure);

(2) The offense conduct is voluntary, but the actor does not accurately perceive the physical nature or consequences of the conduct (e.g., the actor hallucinates that what in fact is a gun is a paint brush, or accurately perceives the physical characteristics of the gun but does not know that guns shoot bullets that can injure people), and therefore does not know that his conduct is wrong or criminal;

(3) The actor accurately perceives and understands the physical nature of the offense conduct and its consequences, but for some other reason does not know that his conduct is wrong or criminal (e.g., the actor thinks God has ordered him to sacrifice a neighbor for the good of mankind, or believes, because of paranoid delusions, that the man waiting for a bus is about to attack him); or

(4) The actor accurately perceives the nature and consequences of the offense conduct and knows its wrongfulness and criminality, but lacks the ability to control his conduct (e.g., because of an insane compulsion or duress) to such an extent that he cannot reasonably be expected to have avoided it.

The last of these is the kind of excusing condition that Acker claims in the "Brothers' Brawl" hypothetical.

Involuntary Act   The first excusing condition occurs where the conduct constituting an offense does not include a volitional act. Cases of this sort include "conduct" that is a reflex action or convulsion. This first excusing condition presents the clearest case of blamelessness. The absence of volition in the doing of a criminal act is only a step above the absence of an act at all; it seems clearly improper to punish someone merely for having, say, a muscular contraction, where the person did not will or choose the activity of her own body.

Nearly any disability causing this excusing condition is recognized as adequate for a defense; the resulting dysfunction is sufficiently gross that it tends to establish its own abnormality. Traditionally, such conditions bar conviction on the ground that they prevent satisfaction of the voluntary act requirement that is said to be an element of all offenses. There are advantages to recognizing that such cases are really providing a general excuse defense rather than negating a required offense element.

Ignorance of Act's Nature   In an excusing condition of the second sort, there is a voluntary act, but the actor is exculpated because she is unaware of the act's physical nature or normal consequences. Such is the case of an actor who, suffering from a delusion that she is squeezing an orange, strangles her spouse. The defect typically is one of perception, and commonly results from insanity or intoxication or from more exotic disabilities such as automatism or somnambulism. When this second excusing condition is relied on, the law limits the excuse to specific disabilities—such as involuntary intoxication or insanity—and requires independent proof of the relevant disability.

Ignorance of Act's Criminality or Wrongfulness   In the third category of excusing condition, the actor engages in conduct voluntarily and knows the nature of her act but does not know that the act is wrong or criminal. The defect is one of knowledge rather than perception. It can result from a simple lack of information or from a lack of the intelligence or cognitive function necessary to use available information to determine wrongfulness or criminality. The law is generally more suspicious of these claims for excuse. For example, the law typically rejects a "normal" person's plea for excuse based on ignorance or misunderstanding of the law that proscribes his conduct. Because anyone can make such mistakes, presence of this condition alone does little to distinguish the actor from the general population. Instances of this third excusing condition thus are more selectively excused, generally requiring either a disability with persuasive indications of abnormality or special circumstances suggesting a *reasonable* mistake and compelling a conclusion of blamelessness. This basis for exculpating an actor may support a disability excuse for insanity, subnormality, involuntary intoxication, or immaturity. The few mistake excuses that are recognized also use the excusing condition of this third sort.

Mistake Excuses as Example of Third Type of Excusing Condition   Three types of mistakes commonly are allowed as grounds for a general excuse defense (as distinguished from mistakes that provide an absent-element defense by negating a required culpability element). Reliance on an official misstatement of law, and mistake due to the unavailability of a law, are two such general mistake excuses. A mistake as to whether one's conduct is justified also is commonly recognized as a defense. In the latter instance, the actor does not know his conduct is wrong or criminal because, under the circumstances as he perceives and understands them, his actions are justified.

Impairment of Control   The fourth excusing condition exists where an actor engages in conduct voluntarily, correctly perceives the nature of her act, and is aware that it is wrong or criminal. The act is exculpated because she lacks the capacity to control her conduct and thus cannot justly be held accountable for it. For this fourth excusing condition, the law generally is unwilling to excuse unless there is a clear and confirmable disability that distinguishes the actor from others, a disability that explains the criminal conduct and can be deemed responsible for it. A loaded .357 Magnum pointed at the actor's head, for example, may provide the objective, confirmable criterion necessary to distinguish the actor's ability to control her conduct from that of the general population. Insanity and intoxication may cause this excusing condition, just as they may cause the previous two excusing conditions. The duress defense is based solely on this impairment of self-control. Hypnotism sometimes is recognized as an excuse because it may cause this fourth excusing condition, although it often is incorrectly listed as an example of the involuntary act defense, the first excusing condition.

Single Disability Causing Multiple Excusing Conditions   As the discussion above indicates, a single disability may cause more than one kind of excusing condition. Insanity and intoxication, for example, may cause excusing conditions of the second, third, and fourth types: They may create defects either in the perception of the nature of the act, in the evaluation of its wrongfulness or criminality, or in the actor's ability to resist performing it. Moreover, such a disability may cause two or more of these defects at one time. Where this occurs, the actor normally relies on a single excuse defense, according to the disability present. A single disability may, however, also give rise to two excuses: a disability excuse and a mistake excuse (where the disability adequately explains an otherwise unreasonable and unexcused mistake, for example). Thus, a mentally ill actor who has an insanity defense also may have a defense for a mistake as to a justification that would be denied to other actors, if his mistake is reasonable for a person in his situation—that is, suffering the mental illness that he suffers.

Multiple Disabilities Causing Single Excusing Condition   In some instances, multiple disabilities may contribute jointly to a single excusing condition. A mentally ill offender may become involuntarily intoxicated when his medication unexpectedly interacts with a common cold remedy he buys over the counter. The mental illness and the involuntary intoxication each may impair the actor. Even if the degree of impairment from either would be inadequate in itself to excuse the actor the cumulative impairment from the two may rise to a level suggesting blamelessness. If each of the disabilities are legally recognized, and if together they cause a legally adequate excusing condition, there seems little basis on which to deny an excuse.

Cumulative Excuses Under Current Law   Unfortunately, current excuse defense doctrine typically assumes that only a single disability is at work in a given case. Because excuses are divided into distinct defenses according to disability, to meet the requirements of any defense an adequate excusing condition must result from a single disability. To use the example above, both the insanity defense and the involuntary intoxication defense require that the necessary level of dysfunction result *from the mental illness* or *from the involuntary intoxication*, respectively.[5] No provision in modern codes allows an excusing condition to be satisfied by more than one disability, thus there is no formal mechanism that will recognize the cumulative effect of multiple disabilities.

---

5. An insanity defense is given if the excusing condition is satisfied "*as a result of* mental disease or defect[.]" Model Penal Code § 4.01(1). An involuntary-intoxication defense is given if the excusing condition is satisfied "*by reason of* such intoxication[.]" Model Penal Code § 2.08(4).

Combining Excuses by Assessing "Actor's Situation"   Although perhaps not intended for this use, the individualized reasonable-person tests might serve as means of recognizing a form of such "combined excuses." In duress, for example, an actor is excused if "a person of reasonable firmness in his situation would have been unable to resist."[6] One might argue that the effects of other disabilities ought to be taken into account as part of the actor's "situation." This technique is available whenever a defense formulation uses the term *reasonable* in its criteria. As noted previously, the Model Penal Code defines *reasonable* to mean non-negligent, which includes assessment of some individual characteristics of the actor.[7] In determining whether a mistaken reliance on an official misstatement was "reasonable," or whether there is a "reasonable" explanation for an actor's extreme emotional disturbance,[8] a court is to assess what is reasonable for a person "in the actor's situation." In each instance, this permits the decision maker to take account of duress, mental disease, involuntary intoxication, or other disabilities as part of "the actor's situation." This method of accounting for cumulative excuses does not provide a general solution, but only a patchwork remedy with less than comprehensive coverage. A comprehensive approach that would cover the cumulative effects of all disabilities would require a general provision.[9]

CONDITIONS INSUFFICIENT TO EXCUSE

The previous subsection provides a comprehensive list of conditions that will excuse an actor for his conduct. A successful claim of excuse demands that one (or more) of these conditions arose as a result of a legally recognized disability. It is not enough for the actor to have a disability, such as intoxication or subjection to duress; his intoxication or duress must cause an excusing condition. This may seem rudimentary, especially in the case of duress or intoxication, but the implications for other excuses can be dramatic.

Rejection of "Status Excuses"   Because a disability alone is inadequate to excuse, there ought to be no such thing as a "status excuse" where having the disability itself provides the defense. The Common Law recognized some such excuses, and some modern theorists appear to support them.[10] Yet the law does not recognize a class of, say, mentally ill persons who are *automatically* free of criminal responsibility for whatever they might do. Rather, the insanity defense requires that the actor's mental illness, at the time of the offense, must generate effects that excuse the offense at hand. A seriously mentally ill person may still be liable for an offense if the mental illness does not play a sufficient role in leading

---

6. Model Penal Code § 2.09(1).

7. See Model Penal Code § 2.02(2)(d).

8. See Model Penal Code §§ 3.03(3), 3.07(4), 210.3(1)(b).

9. A principle of cumulative excuses might be codified as follows:

Multiple Excuses. If an actor satisfies the requirements of more than one excuse, all such excuses shall be permitted as defenses. If an actor suffers from more than one disability that is recognized as the potential basis for an excuse, but does not satisfy the requirements of the required effects [i.e., the excusing condition element] of any one excuse defense, the actor nonetheless shall be excused if the cumulative effect of the multiple disabilities satisfies the requirements of the required effects of any one of the relevant excuse defenses.

10. Common Law recognition of "status excuses" is exemplified by Blackstone: "In criminal cases, therefore, idiots and lunatics are not chargeable for their own acts, if committed when under these incapacities." 4 William Blackstone, Commentaries *24.

him to commit the offense. In other words, the disability must cause an excusing condition *for the conduct constituting the offense charged.* If *A*, while knowingly preparing a false income tax return, hallucinates that a neighbor's barking dog has turned into an attacking tiger, he may be considered insane at the time of filing the false return, but he does not merit an insanity excuse if his hallucination plays no part in the preparation and filing of the return. If he kills the dog in perceived self-defense, of course, he may be excused for the killing, for in that case the disability has created an excusing condition (of the second type) that undercuts *A*'s responsibility for the offense.

Disability as "But For" Cause is Insufficient The importance of the excusing condition requirement is seen in the rule that an existing disability, without an adequate excusing condition, is insufficient to excuse *even if the disability is a "but for" cause of the offense.* The effect of this rule can be quite dramatic. Assume an elderly male, with no prior record of child abuse, is given a drug while in the hospital, and while under the influence of the drug, he goes to another room in the hospital and molests a young girl. Assume further that the evidence shows conclusively that the actor would not have committed the offense if he had not been given the drug. Should he be excused? One can appreciate the appeal of the defendant's claim that it was the drug, not his own free choice, that has caused the offense. Yet, under current excuse formulations, it is not enough that the drug created an impulse that would not otherwise have existed or that it eroded a restraint that otherwise would have existed. Standard excuse requirements insist that the compulsion be sufficiently overwhelming, or that the actor's capacity to resist be sufficiently impaired, that he could not reasonably have been expected to have avoided committing the offense. The excusing condition requirement does not only demand an objective causal connection, but also adds this normative standard in judging the legal significance of the compulsion or incapacity.

Uniform Obligation to Avoid Crime Harder for Some to Bear Than Others The result of this principle may be that the law's demands are harder for some people to bear than others. And the greater burden may be one for which the actor is not fully responsible, as with the hospitalized molester noted above. But then, many people may bear greater burdens than others in conforming their conduct to the law's requirements, perhaps because of where they live or grew up or the kinds of genes and physiology they have or for various other reasons. The law generally does not take account of such differing burdens unless the burden of obeying the law reaches a level of severity sufficiently gross and abnormal that compliance cannot reasonably be expected. Absent a clear abnormality causing an adequate excusing condition, each person is equally obliged, even if not equally predisposed, to resist the compulsions and overcome the incapacities tending toward crime.

Objective Limitation on Excuses To judge a person's capacity to avoid a violation, the law introduces objective standards into its excuses. While we may tend to think of excuses as being very subjective, in principle all modern excuses hold an actor to some form of objective standard in judging her efforts to remain law-abiding. Several excuses have explicit objective standards: For example, duress requires the actor to meet the standard of resistance of "the person of reasonable firmness."[11] (Recall that reasonableness, or non-negligence, is assessed through

---

11. Model Penal Code § 2.09(1).

a partially individualized objective standard that looks to the reasonable person in the actor's situation.[12]) Such objective limitations are what one would expect, given that excuses serve a normative function of assessing blameworthiness. Such an assessment is more complex than merely asking whether a person felt pressure or temptation, or had difficulty resisting some inclination toward crime. It looks to the objective *degree*, not just the subjective experience, of pressure or temptation. How strong was it? How difficult was it for the actor to resist? Inevitably, we may try to put ourselves in the actor's situation and try to imagine whether we would have been able to resist the violation.

Objective Standard Sometimes Unstated, but Still Implicit in Rules   Not all excuse defenses include an objective standard in their formal legal formulation. Defenses for involuntary acts, insanity, and involuntary intoxication have no explicit requirement of this sort. Yet these defenses have other limitations to ensure that they excuse only where the actor has met our collective normative expectations for efforts to avoid a violation. In the involuntary act defense, for example, relying on the first type of excusing condition, the required dysfunction is sufficiently great that it assures that compliance was unattainable. The act constituting the offense simply was not the product of the actor's effort or determination.

"Substantial Capacity" Language Inviting Normative Assessment   The formulations of the insanity and involuntary intoxication defenses take a somewhat different approach. A person is excused if, as a result of either disability, "he lacks *substantial* capacity either to appreciate the criminality [wrongfulness] of his conduct or to conform his conduct to the requirements of law."[13] The formulation leaves it to the jury to determine how much incapacity is enough to render the actor's violation blameless. Instead of explicitly providing a partially individualized objective standard, the formulation uses an openly vague term, *substantial*, knowing, indeed intending,[14] that it will call for a similar normative assessment based on the jury's collective judgment of blameworthiness. It seems likely that the analysis and the result will be the same under the "substantial capacity" standard as under the reasonableness standard used for the duress (and reasonable mistake) excuses. That is, an actor's lack of capacity to appreciate or control his conduct will be judged "substantial" only if "the reasonable person in the actor's situation" could not reasonably have been expected to have avoided the offense.

Analysis of "Brothers" Hypothetical   Considering the "Brothers' Brawl" hypothetical, the facts in Acker's case raise some serious questions about whether the effect of the Skopezine on him was sufficiently overwhelming that he could not have been expected to remain law-abiding. He was able to overcome his temptation to beat Jote in the bar when he saw the bouncer coming. (Recall that

---

12. Model Penal Code §§ 1.13(16) & 2.02(2)(d).

13. Model Penal Code §§ 2.08(4) & 4.01(1) (emphasis added).

14. The drafters of the Model Penal Code meant for the "substantial capacity" language to invite a normative evaluation by the jury:

> It was recognized, of course, that "substantial" is an open-ended concept, but its quantitative connotation was believed to be sufficiently precise for practical administration. The law is full of instances in which courts and juries are explicitly authorized to confront an issue of degree. Such an approach was deemed to be no less essential and appropriate in dealing with this issue. . . .

Model Penal Code § 4.01 comment 3 (1985).

Jote, in contrast, became abusive toward the bouncer, despite the obvious unde-sirable result.) Acker again initially restrained himself from beating Jote outside the bar when he noticed a police car nearby. (Jote, on the other hand, was unde-terred by the police car and the inevitable arrest that it signaled.) A jury might conclude on these facts that Acker, even if influenced by the Skopezine, nonethe-less retained sufficient control over his actions to be accountable for them. Ed's claim for excuse is subject to the same evidence suggesting a continuing capacity for some degree of control. Further, as noted previously, since Ed did not ingest Skopezine, he also lacks a clear disability.

No Defense for Mistake as to Excuse Even if he reasonably believed that he was drugged beyond control, Ed has little chance of gaining an excuse. Mistaken belief that one satisfies the conditions of an excuse is not itself an excuse. Thinking you are insane (even if it is reasonable to think so) will not get you an insanity defense. An actor who makes a reasonable mistake as to a justification can claim that, from his perspective, he reasonably believed that he was engaging in conduct that was justified and thus was not prohibited. The actor who is mistaken as to an excuse can make no similar claim. Even if the actor reasonably believed that an excusing condition existed, neither the actor's conduct nor the actor's motivation are desirable, even from the actor's own perspective. Absent a claim of justification or an *actual* excusing condition, the actor is aware that she is engaging in wrongful conduct and merits punishment on that basis; her mistaken belief that she qualifies for a legal excuse does not alter her blameworthiness.[15]

Aggressive Tendencies Do Not Modify Standard to Which Actor Is Held If the Motan brothers were being judged under a partially individualized objective standard, one might wonder whether their generally aggressive personalities, as reflected in their history of brawling, ought to be taken into account. They might argue that the standard of the "reasonable person *in the actor's situation*" means they must be judged with regard to their innate aggressive tendencies. That is, the brothers might argue that, while the average person might be able to resist violent action when made more aggressive by Skopezine, their higher baseline of aggres-siveness makes it much harder for them to resist violent action under the same conditions. It would not be surprising, however, if judges resisted the notion that an actor's historic aggressive tendency is a factor by which the reasonable person standard should be individualized. It is more likely that a judge would find an actor responsible for being aggression-prone, if such is the case, and would hold the actor to the standard of the reasonable person with a reasonably nonag-gressive character. While the involuntary intoxication defense on which Acker relies has no "reasonable person in the actor's situation" standard—it requires instead a determination of whether the person "lacked substantial capacity" to do otherwise—the analysis and the result are likely to be the same. Acker will be judged to have "lacked substantial capacity" by virtue of the Skopezine only if the reasonable person *without Acker's aggressive tendency* would also have lacked that capacity when similarly drugged.

---

15. For a further discussion of the issue of mistake as to an excuse, see Paul H. Robinson, *Causing the Conditions of One's Own Defense*, 71 Va. L. Rev. 1 (1985).

INVOLUNTARY INTOXICATION, ADDICTION, AND SUBNORMALITY

Involuntary Intoxication Excuse The *involuntary intoxication* excuse has a disability of intoxication and typically the same excusing conditions as the insanity defense: a sufficient cognitive or control dysfunction. That is, involuntary intoxication provides an excuse if it causes the level of dysfunction required by the jurisdiction's insanity defense (*McNaughton* test or Model Penal Code test, for example). *Voluntary* intoxication, even when severe enough to cause an excusing condition, will not provide an excuse defense.[16]

Addiction as a Claimed Excuse Addiction is also sometimes offered as a defense to crime. Addiction is a physiologically confirmable abnormal state, and thus may qualify as a disability, but it usually does not cause excusing conditions sufficient to render an actor blameless.[17] Compare this to instances in which long-term addiction causes mental illness. In such a case, an actor may have a defense under the standard insanity defense, not because of the actor's addiction per se, but because of the resulting mental illness.[18] Addiction also may serve another role for excuse purposes: It sometimes is offered as a ground for claiming that the actor's intoxication is involuntary, qualifying him for the involuntary intoxication excuse.

Subnormality Usually Addressed Under Insanity Defense Some writers and jurisdictions have contemplated a separate excuse of *subnormality*. Here low intelligence is the disability. It frequently is treated as a form of "mental defect" under the insanity defense and typically requires the same cognitive dysfunction excusing conditions as insanity does.[19] Low intelligence usually does not support a claim of excuse on control impairment grounds.

Insufficiency of Disability, without Excusing Condition, for Defense The involuntary intoxication defense illustrates the importance of the independent excusing condition and the normative assessment it embodies. As with insanity, the mere disability is not itself enough. To merit an excuse, the disability must cause sufficient dysfunction that the actor could not reasonably have been expected to have avoided the violation. In *State v. Mriglot*, for example, the defendant sought, as a defense to a forgery charge, an instruction on involuntary intoxication that would excuse him if the jury found he had been "involuntarily *under the influence* [of] or *affected* by the use of liquor or drugs."[20] The court rejected the defendant's instruction. Even if the defendant would not have committed the offense *but for* the involuntary intoxication, the court concluded, he would have no defense unless the involuntary intoxication caused sufficient dysfunction to render him blameless for the offense. The case underscores an important practical

---

16. See, e.g., Model Penal Code § 2.08(4) & (5), which requires both involuntary intoxication and resulting dysfunction similar to insanity.

17. See discussion in 2 Paul H. Robinson, *Criminal Law Defenses* § 194 (1984); see, e.g., United States v. Moore, 486 F.2d 1139 (D.C. Cir. 1973) (court rejects defendant's claim of defense to possession because of addiction's creation of overpowering need to use heroin).

18. See, e.g., People v. Kelly, 516 P.2d 875 (Cal. 1973) (when long-continued voluntary ingestion of drugs results in insanity, it is still complete defense); Anderson v. State, 380 N.E.2d 606 (Ind. App. 1978) (extended use of alcohol over extended periods of time can be basis for insanity defense).

19. See In re Ramon M., 584 P.2d 524 (Cal. 1978) (defendant, who, along with two other youths, attacked man with belts, did not deny charges, but presented defense of "idiocy;" court ruled that same test used to determine insanity was to be used to determine idiocy; defendant acquitted under A.L.I. test).

20. 550 P.2d 17, 17–18 (Wash. App. 1976) (emphasis in original).

and conceptual feature of excuses: As noted above, even though a disability may erode one's resistance to the extent that it becomes a but-for cause of one's crime, this does not suffice to excuse. Though an involuntarily intoxicated or mentally ill actor may, through no fault of her own, have more difficulty resisting temptations and compulsions toward a violation, the law nonetheless expects the actor to try to remain law-abiding, and exculpates only if the disability sufficiently overwhelmed her capacity to avoid the offense.

IMMATURITY

The elements of the *immaturity* excuse, sometimes called the *infancy* defense, are conceptually similar to the standard disability excuse requirements: a disability causing an excusing condition. It is common, for example, that in teenagers the dorsal lateral prefrontal cortex is not fully developed, and this part of the brain plays a role in decision making and in understanding future consequences. The extent of a young adult's life experience and social sophistication are also significant. A fair blameworthiness judgment must take account of what we can reasonably expect of each young person. What we can reasonably expect of many fifteen-year-olds may not be the same as what we expect of most adults.

Age as a Conclusive Presumption of Immaturity However, in most jurisdictions, the immaturity defense does not rely on an assessment of the individual, in the way that an insanity defense examines the mental capacity of a defendant. Maturity, or lack thereof, typically is conclusively presumed based on the actor's chronological age.[21] All actors below a specified cutoff age are conclusively presumed to be immature, and all those above that age are presumed mature. Further, current defense formulations irrebuttably presume not only the existence of the disability (immaturity), but also that the disability is of such a nature and degree as to cause an adequate excusing condition.

Errors in Presumption of Maturity Such an age cutoff formulation makes it quick and easy to apply the defense, but it also invites error. First, it results in a failure to excuse an older actor who is as immature as a typical underage actor and for whom we should have reduced expectations. In *State v. Jamison*, for example, the defendant was denied an immaturity defense despite his documented "mental age" of 11.7 years, because his chronological age of 17 put him over the statutory age cutoff for the immaturity defense.[22]

Errors in Presumption of Immaturity Conversely, a chronological age cutoff also creates the problem of understating our normative expectations for the fully mature but underage actor. As long as an actor's chronological age is less than the statutory cutoff age, the actor gets the excuse. This is the case even if the actor's level of maturity is such that the actor reasonably *could* have been expected to have avoided the violation. Application of the defense is reduced to firm, though inevitably arbitrary, timing rules: An actor who is one day younger than the cutoff is treated the same as a person ten years younger and categorically differently from a person a single day older.

Alternative of Making Age-Based Presumption Rebuttable Objective, easy-to-apply criteria are always a virtue. In the realm of excuses, however, where the goal

---

21. See authorities cited at 2 Paul H. Robinson, Criminal Law Defenses § 175 n.1 (1984).
22. 597 P.2d 424, 428 (Wash. App. 1980), aff'd, 613 P.2d 776 (Wash. 1979).

is a complex judgment of individual blameworthiness, subjective and judgmental criteria frequently are needed. In the case of the immaturity excuse, an approach more consistent with its goal would be to assess the individual actor's actual degree of immaturity. If a concession to easier application is needed, it can be achieved through rebuttable presumptions, rather than the irrebuttable presumptions most current formulations create. That is, an actor below a given age might be presumed immature unless the prosecution proves otherwise, while an actor above that age (or another age) might be presumed mature unless the defense proves otherwise. There is precedent for such a rebuttable-presumption approach both in some current state codes and at Common Law.[23] To rebut the presumption, the party should have to prove (or disprove) not only the disability of being abnormally immature, but also that the effect of such immaturity was to cause an excusing condition sufficient to render the actor blameless for the offense. (Many jurisdictions have a system of two cutoff ages, where there is discretion as to whether a defendant between the two ages will be treated as underage.[24] That discretionary determination is usually not made on an assessment of actual immaturity or blameworthiness, however, but on other criteria, such as susceptibility to rehabilitation or the availability of a suitable rehabilitation program.)

Immaturity as Determining Only Proper Court, Not Ultimate Liability Significantly, a successful immaturity "defense" typically does not lead to the defendant's release, but only transfers jurisdiction to the juvenile court. (This is similar to insanity acquittals, which often result in transfer to mental health authorities for evaluation and possible civil commitment, rather than the defendant's immediate release.) This procedural feature of the "defense" might seem to mitigate possible errors caused by the irrebuttable presumptions of most current immaturity defenses, as it suggests that offenders who are young, but blameworthy, will still be subject to adjudication and possible liability. But the criteria for juvenile detention may not be tied to matters of blameworthiness, so some blameworthy juveniles may be released (while some blameless juveniles may be confined).

Problem Arising from Defense's Jurisdictional Nature Further, the jurisdictional quality of the "defense" does nothing to avoid the second kind of error: denying an excuse to an overage, but immature, offender. Once an overage defendant's case is assigned to an adult court, no further claim of an immaturity excuse is available. Where the statutory cutoff age is 16 or higher, this may be a problem in the unusual case, but under the current trend of lowering the cutoff age to 12 or less in some jurisdictions,[25] there is real danger that a defendant's immaturity will undercut his blameworthiness but that no excuse defense will be available to recognize that blamelessness. If a cutoff age is to be used to select the court of jurisdiction, an immaturity defense should remain available in adult courts to allow a jury to excuse an actor whose immaturity satisfies the traditional conditions

---

23. In several states, the fact that the defendant is younger than a specified age creates only a rebuttable presumption of immaturity. See Ariz. Rev. Stat. Ann. § 13–501 (under 14); Cal. Penal Code § 26(1) (under 14); Nev. Rev. Stat. §§ 194.010(1)-(2), 193.210 (between age 8 and 14); Okla. Stat. Ann. tit. 21, § 152(1)-(2) (between age 7 and 14); S.D. Codified Laws Ann. § 22–3-1(1)-(2) (between age 10 and 14); Wash. Rev. Code Ann. § 9A.04.050 (between age 8 and 12).

24. See, e.g., Model Penal Code § 4.10.

25. See, e.g., Or. Rev. Stat. § 161.290; Ga. Code Ann. § 16–3-1.

of excuse. (Typically, insanity will not be available as an excuse in these cases. A 13-year-old may be entirely normal in his development and free from mental disease or defect, yet, due to his normal immaturity, have insufficient blameworthiness to merit criminal liability and punishment.)

DURESS

The duress excuse illustrates another variation in the formulation of disability excuses. Like the conclusive presumption of the immaturity defense, the structure of the duress defense is a variation that has its roots in the practical necessity of the situation. The defense has a disability requirement: The actor must have committed the offense while under *coercion* to do so.[26] The defense does not, however, require that the coercion cause in the actor a "substantial lack of capacity to conform his conduct to the requirements of law," or other similar description of the degree of control impairment contained in the excusing conditions for insanity or involuntary intoxication. Instead, the duress defense requires that the actor's disability, the coercion, come from a particular cause: a threat of force that "a person of reasonable firmness in the actor's situation would have been unable to resist."[27]

Relative Weakness of Coercion as Disability No other disability excuse requires that the disability come from a particular cause. Any drug of any amount can give rise to an involuntary intoxication defense, for example, as long as its intoxicating effect on the actor causes the degree of impairment called for by the excusing condition. The objective requirement for the cause of the coercion in the duress defense is not surprising, however, as it reflects the relative weakness of coercion in satisfying the functions of a disability requirement. A state of coercion is not as easy to verify or observe as the presence of alcohol or drugs in the blood, for example. Nor is coercion likely to manifest itself in continuing abnormalities or in abnormalities other than the offense conduct, as mental illness would. Coercion is a product of the actor's immediate external conditions and may disappear without trace when the threatening conditions disappear. For all of these reasons, the coercion by itself does a poor job at serving the functions of a disability. It does little to signal the actor as abnormal or different from the rest of the population, and also does little to provide an obvious and continuing cause to which to shift the blame for the violation.

Serious-Threat Requirement Bolsters Disability (and Replaces Excusing Condition) The effectiveness of coercion as a disability can be buttressed, however, by requiring that the coercion come from a sufficiently clear and powerful threat. Such a threat is objectively confirmable and sets the actor apart from others. Further, by requiring a sufficiently extreme threat, the law may presume that an adequate excusing condition is also present. If a reasonably strong-willed person would have been unable to resist the threat, then generally the actor in question cannot reasonably have been expected to have resisted either. In duress, the jury's normative judgment occurs through this cause-of-the-disability requirement rather than through an independent excusing condition.[28]

---

26. See, e.g., Model Penal Code § 2.09(1).

27. Model Penal Code § 2.09(1).

28. See, e.g., State v. Toscano, 378 A.2d 755 (N.J. 1977) (defendant's conviction for conspiring to obtain money by false pretenses overturned for lower court's failure to allow jury to consider whether threats of physical harm against defendant and family qualified as duress).

Potential Harshness of Objective Standard   A danger of such an objective cause-of-the-coercion requirement is that it may be too harsh. It may fail to excuse an actor who cannot meet the standard of the reasonably firm-willed person. The subnormal actor, for example, may be particularly susceptible to coercion, especially if the coercion plays on the actor's ignorance in order to exaggerate the degree of the threat.

Relaxing Standard Based on "Actor's Situation"   The Model Penal Code duress formulation addresses this potential problem by modifying the reasonable-person standard to allow consideration of an actor's individual circumstances and characteristics. The device used in duress is the same as that used to partially individualize the reasonable-person standard in negligence, recklessness, and extreme emotional disturbance. The seriousness of the threat is assessed in terms of whether it would coerce "a person of reasonable firmness *in [the actor's] situation*."[29] A judge may use this language as authority to take account of an actor's immaturity or subnormality, for example. Would the person whose will is reasonably strong, *given that he has such a condition*, have been unable to resist? The Code's Commentary gives little guidance as to the characteristics or circumstances that ought to be permitted as individualizations of the reasonable person standard.[30] Judges are left wide discretion to determine the issue ad hoc.

▲ PROBLEMS

Robbing for the I.R.A. (#105)

As a nineteen-year-old student in Northern Ireland in the mid-1970s, Charles Fitzpatrick is swept up in a revolutionary spirit. He joins the I.R.A. hoping to protect his hometown. The I.R.A. is an illegal organization in Northern Ireland. Fitzpatrick knows of the I.R.A.'s history and tactics and understands that he might become involved in criminal activities if he joins the group. He receives firearms training and begins carrying out armed vigilante duty on the streets. When his I.R.A. activities begin to interfere with his education, Fitzpatrick drops out of school.

After a time, however, he becomes depressed and decides that he would rather go back to school. He asks a superior officer about quitting. Fitzpatrick is sent to an I.R.A. club in Belfast and told that he cannot leave. He is further ordered to take part in a planned robbery and told that if he refuses, his parents will be killed. Fitzpatrick agrees to participate.

A few days later, Fitzpatrick and another I.R.A. member travel to the Whiterock Industrial Estate. Armed with a .38 caliber revolver, Fitzpatrick enters the estate's office intent on robbing the weekly wages. Fitzpatrick lines the six men in the office against the wall as his accomplice loads the money into bags. When

---

29. Model Penal Code § 2.09(1) (emphasis added).

30. Model Penal Code § 2.09 comment at 375 (noting that reference to actor's "situation" is meant to have same meaning for duress as for appraisal of recklessness or negligence); id. § 2.02 comment at 242 (noting, in negligence context, that "[t]here is an inevitable ambiguity in 'situation'").

Fitzpatrick asks one of the men if there is any more money, the man points to some loose change on a desk and then rushes at Fitzpatrick. Fitzpatrick shoots the man in the chest, fatally wounding him. In the commotion, the other men wrestle the gun from Fitzpatrick and detain him. The other I.R.A. member escapes.

What liability for Fitzpatrick, if any, under the Model Penal Code? Prepare a list of all criminal code subsections in the order in which you rely on them in your analysis.

Hypnotic Prison Break (#106)

Jack Cox, wanting to learn a new skill while he is serving time in prison, teaches himself hypnosis from reading books on the subject. He practices on many of the prisoners, perfecting his technique. Among others, Cox hypnotizes Thomas Marsh, a fellow inmate, who is serving a prison sentence for a first-degree robbery conviction. Wanting him to return to a childlike state, Jack directs Marsh to "go back where he . . . was having a good time" and other such directions. Rather than reverting to a childhood state of mind, Marsh follows the hypnotic suggestion literally and leaves prison, returning to his home in California.

Feeling responsible, Cox also leaves prison. After finding Marsh, he rehypnotizes him and revokes the earlier hypnotic direction. Cox explains to Marsh what has happened, and both decide to return to prison. Marsh claims to have no memory of anything that happened from the time he was hypnotized until Cox intervenes at Marsh's home. On their way back, they stop to get coffee at a restaurant and are apprehended.

What liability for Marsh, if any, under the Model Penal Code? Prepare a list of all criminal code subsections in the order in which you rely on them in your analysis.

Inducing Rape for Blackmail (#107)

Barry Kingston is hired by James and Diedre Forman to run a spa they own while the Formans are out of the country. Upon the Formans' return, Diedre becomes disenchanted with Kingston and fires him. However, after an acrimonious dismissal, the Formans are concerned that Kingston may report the couples' questionable tax practices to the authorities. Kevin Penn, a Brighton resident and acquaintance of Kingston, is aware of the situation. He offers to allay the Formans' fears by providing them with something they can use to blackmail Kingston.

Penn learns that Kingston has a sexual interest in teenage boys. Kingston has never been charged with any improper involvement with a minor, but Penn has a plan. He befriends Darren Child, a 15-year-old, and one evening invites him over to pick up a used stereo. Penn also calls Kingston and invites him to his apartment for the same evening. When Child arrives, Penn offers him a beer, which he accepts. The drink is laced with triazolam and temazepam, two sedatives that also induce memory loss. After the drinks' effects kick in, Penn removes Child's clothing and places him on the bed in the bedroom. When Kingston arrives, Penn offers him coffee laced with the same drugs, but in a dosage intended only to impair Kingston's judgment, not to render him unconscious like Child. As Kingston becomes increasingly groggy, Penn leads him to the bedroom, where he presents the boy lying naked on the bed and invites Kingston to have sex with him, which Kingston does. Penn audio-records the episode and takes photographs. The next day, neither Kingston nor Child remember what has happened.

Penn sells the negatives and the audiotape to the Formans. Mrs. Forman arranges a meeting with Kingston and informs him that she possesses the incriminating photos and audiotape. She explains to him that if he does anything to hurt the Formans' interests, they will give the material to his new employer, the Department of Social Services. Several months later, Mrs. Forman changes her mind and gives the photographs to the police, who arrest Kingston.

What liability for Kingston, if any, under the Model Penal Code? Prepare a list of all criminal code subsections in the order in which you rely on them in your analysis.

Bomb Collar Robbery Gone Bad (#108)

Pizza delivery man Robert Wells, 46, has fallen in with a questionable group of friends. Marjorie Diehl-Armstrong and William Rothstein have checkered backgrounds and less than noble aspirations for the future. Diehl-Armstrong is trying to raise enough money to have her father killed. She believes that he has blocked her from receiving the inheritance she was due when her mother died. To finance the hit, she and Rothstein devise a creative plot to rob a local bank. They tell Wells that they want him to commit the robbery while wearing a bomb secured around his neck. The plan is for him to claim that three men held him at gunpoint and forced him to wear the bomb-collar. If he is caught, he is to explain to police that he was told that he would get instructions on how to disarm the ticking bomb only after delivering the money to a designated location.

As the plan calls for, Diehl-Armstrong and Rothstein begin by ordering pizza, which Wells arrives to deliver. But when they begin to secure the bomb collar on Wells, he balks. Their response is to simply go ahead with their plan, forcing him to wear the bomb and telling him he must deliver the money to the specified location in order to get the deactivation instructions.

Wearing the live bomb, Wells goes to the bank. He asks a bank teller for money, explaining that he has a bomb strapped to him that is on a timer and will soon explode. He is apprehended by police as he leaves the bank with the money.

What liability for Wells, if any, under the Model Penal Code? Would it matter whether the bomb threatened just his life or also that of the teller? Prepare a list of all criminal code subsections in the order in which you rely on them in your analysis.

● OVERVIEW OF PROBLEMATIC EXCUSES

Notes

Chromosomal and Physiological Abnormalities
    Abnormality Presents Model Disability Element
      Resulting Dysfunction, or Its Excusing Effect, Less Clear

This section considers several excuses that the criminal law has occasionally recognized but typically rejected: chromosomal abnormality, brainwashing, cultural indoctrination, and "rotten social background." Studying these excuses sharpens our understanding of present theory and doctrine and, on occasion, illustrates its weaknesses. To explain why an excuse should not be given, especially in a situation where we feel some sympathy for the actor, sometimes requires us to examine more carefully, and to articulate with greater clarity, why the law does give an excuse and the conditions it imposes for doing so. Not infrequently, the study of problematic excuses reveals fundamental assumptions that we make about human nature and exculpation that are not otherwise apparent.

Chromosomal and Physiological Abnormalities Chromosomal abnormality is sometimes offered as an excuse because some studies suggest a causal connection between one's genetic composition and a predisposition toward criminality, particularly violence.[31] Other studies suggest that other physiological abnormalities, such as abnormalities in brain chemistry, predispose a person toward violence.[32] Some writers conclude that if an abnormality, such as the XYY chromosomal pattern occurring in some males, involuntarily causes an actor to be more aggressive, the actor ought to be excused when such aggression manifests as criminal conduct. However, more recent evidence casts some doubt as to the strength of the effect of such chromosomal or physiological abnormalities.[33]

Abnormality Presents Model Disability Element The appeal of recognizing chromosomal or physiological abnormality as the basis for excuse is understandable. The disability, the XYY pattern or the physiological misfunctioning, is easily shown to be abnormal. It is objectively observable, admitting of confirmation (or refutation) through scientific tests, rather than depending on therapists' judgments, as with most forms of mental illness. Further, especially in the case of chromosomal abnormality, it is beyond question that the abnormality is not the fault of the actor—unlike, say, intoxication, where it is always possible that the actor voluntarily caused it. As disabilities, then, such abnormalities combine the most attractive features of traditional disability excuses.

---

31. See Andrew Saulitis, *Chromosomes and Criminality: The Legal Implications of the XYY Syndrome*, 1 J. Legal Med. 269 (1979); Lee Ellis, *Genetics and Criminal Behavior*, 20 Criminology 43 (1982).

32. See Hill & Pond, *Reflections on One Hundred Capital Cases Submitted to Electroencephalography*, 98 J. Mental Sci. 23 (1952); D.W. Elliott, *Neurological Findings in Adult Minimal Brain Dysfunction and the Dyscontrol Syndrome*, 170 J. Nervous & Mental Disease 680 (1982).

33. See, e.g., James Q. Wilson and Richard J. Herrnstein, Crime and Human Nature 101 (1985); Deborah W. Denno, *Human Biology and Criminal Responsibility: Free Will or Free Ride?* 137 U. Pa. L. Rev. 615, 617 (1988).

Resulting Dysfunction, or Its Excusing Effect, Less Clear   While such abnormalities have qualities that make them attractive as disabilities, the effect of such abnormalities in causing excusing conditions is unclear. Most XYY males do not violate the law. Even if one assumes that the abnormality creates some predisposition toward violent conduct, a predisposition, even if involuntarily acquired, does not excuse. It is not enough that the disability was a but-for cause of committing the offense. The dysfunctional effect must be of such a degree that the actor could not reasonably have been expected to have avoided the violation. Even the strongest claims of researchers do not suggest that either the XYY chromosomal abnormality, or most physiological abnormalities, cause such a level of dysfunction. Accordingly, these conditions are rarely if ever grounds for a successful defense.

Brainwashing   *Brainwashing*, sometimes called *coercive persuasion, coercive indoctrination*, or *thought reform*, may be the most interesting of problematic excuses. It challenges many basic assumptions of excuse theory and, if recognized as a defense, arguably could pave the way for recognition of a cultural defense or a defense for a "rotten social background." In some ways, brainwashing presents the reverse case from chromosomal and physiological abnormalities: Brainwashing may cause excusing conditions, at least in one sense, but no apparent disability may exist.

Brainwashing Process as Source of Duress or Insanity Excuse   Isolation, close control, physiological debilitation, threats, and psychological manipulation are all part of the classic brainwashing process.[34] Under the right conditions, these qualify an actor for a duress defense. They also might produce effects that could qualify an actor for an insanity defense. If an actor commits an offense as a direct result of the pressures common in the brainwashing process or as a result of mental illness caused by the process, he may be able to rely on one of those traditional disability excuses.

No Lingering Disability After Brainwashing Is Complete   The difficulty in coping with brainwashing as a defense arises where a brainwashed actor commits an offense *after* the coercive brainwashing process is complete. A successful process may leave the person normal in every traditional sense, neither mentally ill nor subject to continuing duress or coercion. Yet the actor may hold a different set of beliefs and values than she did before the process. When such a person, who holds these different (perhaps radical) beliefs and values, commits an offense in furtherance of those beliefs and values, the person does not satisfy the disability or excusing condition of any traditional excuse. No coercion or mental illness exists—having radical beliefs or values is not a mental illness. (If it were, most radical terrorists would have an insanity defense simply because their conduct is a product of their radical beliefs, especially if, as is common, some outside source or group helped indoctrinate them into those beliefs.)

Accountability for One's Beliefs and Values   While the brainwashed actor presently suffers neither coercion nor mental illness, the actor's choices nonetheless have been highly influenced by others, and against his will, through the coercive indoctrination that the actor experienced. For that reason, it seems awkward to hold such an actor accountable for conduct in the same way as someone who has

---

34. See Delgado, *Ascription of Criminal States of Mind: Toward a Defense Theory for the Coercively Persuaded ("Brainwashed") Defendant*, 63 Minn. L. Rev. 1, 2 (1978).

(more) freely chosen or developed her own beliefs and values. Indeed, there was strong support for exculpating captured soldiers brainwashed by their captors during the Korean War, even those who refused repatriation and participated in propaganda activities for the enemy.[35] However, the law holds each person accountable for her own personality, beliefs, and values—and would face great difficulties if it did not.

Cultural Indoctrination Cases of "cultural indoctrination" highlight the line-drawing problems the law would confront if it enabled defendants to disclaim responsibility for their own beliefs and values. For example, in *People v. Kimura*, the defendant, a Japanese immigrant, walked into the ocean with her two young children.[36] She intended to die along with her children but was rescued after losing consciousness. The defendant, who was distraught over her husband leaving and intent on killing herself, killed her children as well so that they would not be raised with the shame of being orphans. The defendant's act is condemned in the United States, but such *Oyako-shinju*, or parent-child suicide, was estimated to occur about once a day in Japan at the time[37] and was considered honorable there, albeit illegal, as all suicide is. Should Kimura get a defense or mitigation because she was following one of the existing traditions of her culture? (In fact, after the court received petitions in Kimura's behalf with 25,000 signatures from the Japanese community, she was allowed to plead guilty to voluntary manslaughter and sentenced to time served plus five years' probation.)

Cultural Norms as Most Coercive Indoctrinators The power of Kimura's indoctrination derives in part from the fact that initially (when Kimura lived in Japan) her values represented the *norm*, not an abnormality. This aspect of Kimura's indoctrination highlights a point of conflict with an excuse defense. Excuses are made available only in the abnormal and unusual case; this is a central role of the disability requirement. Yet in the context of accountability for one's beliefs and values, the more pervasive the norm and the larger the group, the more "coercive" the indoctrination and arguably the stronger the excusing condition. The pressures on Kimura are all the more powerful because their development was long-term, subtle, and did not call for resistance, as indoctrination by a POW's captors might—quite the opposite, they were socially reinforced. For Kimura, the overwhelming influence and legitimacy of the culture powers the indoctrination. Is abnormality or is normality in the indoctrinating circumstances the more compelling ground for viewing the indoctrination as grounds for excuse?

"Rotten Social Background" Defense Relies on Claim of Corrupting Environment A variation on the cultural-indoctrination defense, which has come to be known as the "rotten social background" defense, relies on a claim that the defendant's social circumstances have caused his criminality. For example, in *United States v. Alexander*,[38] excerpted below, defense counsel argued that defendant Murdock "did not have control of his conduct," and that the reason for

35. Consider the facts of Problem #110 (The Brainwashed Defector).
36. People v. Kimura, No. A-091133 (Santa Monica Super. Ct. (Cal.), Nov. 21, 1985) (unpublished decision).
37. See Megan McCaslin, *Immigrant's Suicide Attempt Marks Death of a Dream, Birth of a Cause: Japanese American's Trial Widely Followed in Homeland*, Wash. Post., Sept. 5, 1985, at A12; Gordon Dillow, *When Legal Systems and Culture Collide*, L.A. Herald Examiner, Feb. 18, 1985, at A7.
38. 471 F.2d 923 (D.C. Cir. 1973).

that lack of control was rooted in his "rotten social background," which led to a deep-seated emotional disorder creating a tendency to overreact to perceived threats. As with *Kimura*, the indoctrination mechanism in *Alexander* seems quite powerful. Most of Murdock's daily existence was subject to his environment, which involved growing up nearly penniless in the violent, chaotic Watts section of Los Angeles. He was not responsible for being born into such a situation, and he had no obvious or easy means of escaping from it. On the other hand, not all people who grew up in Watts with him became criminals—just as not all Japanese parents who commit suicide kill their children also. That is, even admitting that Murdock's environment significantly influenced the development of his personality, the strength of its causal contribution to the offense at hand is unclear.

Problem of "Normal" Coercive Indoctrination   As with Kimura, Murdock's situation is not abnormal: He shares his social background, "rotten" or not, with a significant portion of the population. Indeed, having a rotten social background is not necessarily limited to being poor and deprived of material goods; a middle- or upper-class upbringing in a family devoid of emotional support and meaningful interpersonal relationships may be equally harmful to one's emotional and social development. The "rotten social background" defense would seem to support an excuse for many, if not most, offenders, and that result does not reflect the community's normative expectations.

Difficulty of Holding Offenders Blameless Where Their "Disability" Is Common This is not to deny that social background may well be the but-for cause of many crimes; there might be many fewer violations if all people had pleasant and supportive social backgrounds. However, despite the underlying assumption of the dissent in *Alexander*, which argued in support of a rotten-social-background defense, such a but-for causal connection is generally seen as inadequate to excuse. Recall that the *Durham* "product" test for insanity also demanded only that mental illness be a but-for cause of the offense (and drew widespread criticism for doing so). It is perhaps unsurprising that both the court's opinion in *Durham* and the dissenting opinion in *Alexander* have the same author, Judge Bazelon. Both opinions reflect a position out of step with the typical view that only offenders with severely reduced ability to satisfy the law should be "excused" from the requirements that bind the vast majority of citizens. The larger the number of people who share the actor's "disability" but are able to remain law-abiding, the more difficult it will be for the actor to argue persuasively that he could not reasonably have been expected to do the same, and accordingly, that he should be held blameless for his offense.

United States v. Alexander
United States Court of Appeals, District of Columbia Circuit
as amended, 471 F.2d 923 (1972)

BAZELON, Chief Judge (dissenting):

The Evidence Presented at Trial

Five United States Marine Lieutenants—Ellsworth Kramer, Thaddeus Lesnick, William King, Frank Marasco, and Daniel LeGear—attended a dinner at the Marine Corps Base in Quantico, Virginia, on the evening of June 4, 1968, in celebration of their near-completion of basic officers' training. After dinner, they drove to Washington, arriving about midnight, still wearing their formal dress white uniforms. They stopped for about an hour-and-a-half at a nightclub, where they each had a drink. They were well-behaved and "conducted themselves like gentlemen." At the nightclub they met Barbara Kelly, a good friend of Lieutenant Kramer. They accompanied her to her apartment, which she shared with another young woman, and visited there with the two women until about 2:40 a.m. When the five Marines departed, Miss Kelly accompanied them, intending to return to the nightclub to meet another friend. Along the way, they decided to stop at a hamburger shop to get some coffee and sandwiches before the trip back to Quantico. The six of them entered the shop, stood by the take-out counter, and ordered their food. They noticed three Negro males sitting at the other end of the counter. As described by Lieutenant Kramer, "[T]heir hair was in Afro-bush cut, wearing medallions, jersey knit shirts, sport jackets. [T]hey were what I consider in eccentric dress." The three men were Alexander, Murdock, and Cornelius Frazier. The critical events which subsequently took place in the restaurant were described by the four survivors of the Marine group and by Murdock and Frazier. Alexander chose not to take the stand.

According to the prosecution witnesses, Lieutenant Kramer realized that appellant Alexander was staring at him, and he returned the stare. "[I]t was on the order of a Mexican stand-off type thing where you just keep staring at one another for an indefinite period of time." No words were exchanged between the two men, and Lieutenant Kramer soon turned and faced the counter. Shortly thereafter Frazier, Murdock, and Alexander got up from where they were sitting and walked to the door behind the Marines. Murdock and Frazier left the shop, but Alexander stopped in the doorway. He tapped Lieutenant Kramer on the shoulder. When the Marine turned around, Alexander poked his uniform name tag and said, "You want to talk about it more? You want to come outside and talk about it more?" When Lieutenant Kramer replied, "Yes, I am ready to come out" or "Yes, I guess so," Alexander added, "I am going to make you a Little Red Ridinghood." At this point, Lieutenant King stepped up beside Lieutenant Kramer and made a remark variously reported by the prosecution witnesses as "What you God-damn niggers want?" "What do you want, you nigger?" ,"What do you want, dirty nigger bastard?" and "Get out of here nigger." Thereupon Alexander abruptly drew a long-barreled .38 caliber revolver, cocked it, and pointed it at the group or directly into Lieutenant King's chest, saying, "I will show you what I want," or "This is what I want."

The Marines possessed no weapons whatsoever and, according to their testimony, were not advancing toward Alexander. As they stood there, shocked at the sight of the gun, Murdock reentered the shop at Alexander's left and rear, and drew a short-barreled .38 caliber revolver. A series of shots suddenly rang out, and the Marines and Miss Kelly fell or dived to the floor. None attempted to retaliate because they all were taking cover and trying to get out of the line of fire. Alexander and Murdock withdrew from the shop, but one of them stuck his arm back into the shop and attempted—unsuccessfully—to fire his weapon several times more. Only Lieutenant Kramer attempted to identify this man, and he said it was Murdock.

Lieutenants King and Lesnick were mortally wounded in the fusillade; they died within minutes. Lieutenant Kramer was wounded in the head, but he remained conscious, as did Miss Kelly, who had been shot in the hip. Only Lieutenants LeGear and Marasco were not hit.

Alexander, Murdock, and Frazier fled to Alexander's automobile and drove off rapidly in the wrong direction on a one-way street. Alexander was driving, and as the car drove off, Murdock fired three more shots from the window of the car, at the door of the hamburger shop, and at people in the street. A nearby scout car raced after the fleeing car and stopped them within a few blocks. Two revolvers were recovered from the front floorboard of Alexander's automobile. . . .

The Hearing on Criminal Responsibility

. . . [I]n the charge to the jury [at a bifurcated insanity trial for Murdock], the court used language that seemed to tell the jury to disregard a portion of the evidence that was critical to Murdock's theory of the case.

The court has concluded, for the reasons set forth in Judge McGowan's separate opinion, that the record does not call for reversal [because of the jury charge]. Because the author of this opinion is persuaded that there is substantial merit [to defendant Murdock's claim], the author's views are set forth below.

Instructions to the Jury

I turn . . . to what I regard as a serious error in the jury charge on the issue of criminal responsibility. In order to put the problem in perspective, it will be necessary to review the testimony in some detail.

1. Murdock relied primarily on the testimony of Dr. Williams, a board-certified psychiatrist, and professor at Howard University Medical School. Dr. Williams had examined Murdock on two occasions during his confinement in St. Elizabeths Hospital [for psychiatric evaluation upon his plea of insanity]. According to the testimony of Dr. Williams, Murdock was strongly delusional, though not hallucinating or psychotic; he was greatly preoccupied with the unfair treatment of Negroes in this country, and the idea that racial war was inevitable. He showed compulsiveness in his behavior, emotional immaturity, and some psychopathic traits. Since his emotional difficulties were closely tied to his sense of racial oppression, it is probable that when the Marine in the Little Tavern called him a "black bastard" Murdock had an irresistible impulse to shoot. His emotional disorder had its roots in his childhood, in the Watts section of Los Angeles; particularly important was the fact that his father had deserted his mother, and he grew up in a large family with little money and little love or attention.

Dr. Williams stated firmly that in his view Murdock was suffering from an abnormal mental condition that substantially impaired his behavior controls. But he stated just as firmly that the condition did not amount to a mental illness. . . .

Counsel's strategy was to bypass the troublesome term "mental illness," and invite the jury to focus directly on the legal definition of that term. He conceded to the jury that Murdock "did not have a mental disease in the classic sense," i.e., he did not have a psychosis. But, counsel argued, the expert testimony showed that at the critical moment Murdock did not have control of his conduct, and the reason for that lack of control was a deep-seated emotional disorder that was rooted in his "rotten social background." Accordingly, he asked the trial court to omit the term "mental disease or defect" from the jury instructions. I think his proposal was ingenious; the trial court might well have framed a suitable instruction asking the jury to consider whether Murdock's act was the product, not of "mental illness," but of an "abnormal condition of the mind that substantially affects mental or emotional processes and substantially impairs behavior controls."

While the trial court denied the requested instruction, we cannot say that ruling was error. The judge carefully instructed the jury to resolve the question of mental illness in accordance with its legal definition; he told them they were not bound by medical conclusions as to what is or is not a mental disease, and he told them to ignore defense counsel's concession that Murdock was without mental disease. In this respect the instructions conform to the requirements set forth in our cases.

But the judge injected into the instructions a special note of caution, in response to the testimony and argument presented in this case. He told the jury:

> We are not concerned with a question of whether or not a man had a rotten social background. We are concerned with the question of his criminal responsibility. That is to say, whether he had an abnormal condition of the mind that affected his emotional and behavioral processes at the time of the offense.

Defense counsel had objected to that instruction before it was given, because his theory of the case was that Murdock had an abnormal mental condition caused in part by his "rotten social background." The trial court overruled his objection, deeming the instruction necessary to counteract what he saw as an attempt by defense counsel to appeal to the jurors on the basis of sympathy, or passion, or prejudice.

It may well be that the trial judge was motivated by a reasonable fear that the jury would reach its decision on the basis not of the law but of sympathy for the victims of a racist society. Nevertheless, I think that the quoted instruction was reversible error. It had the effect of telling the jury to disregard the testimony relating to Murdock's social and economic background and to consider only the testimony framed in terms of "illness." Such an instruction is contrary to law, and it clearly undermined Murdock's approach to the insanity defense in this case. For Murdock's strategy had two parts: first, he sought to convince the jury to disregard Dr. Williams' finding of no "mental illness," and then he sought to persuade them to find mental illness in the legal sense of the term. The jury could hardly consider the issue of mental illness without considering Murdock's background, in view of the fact that all the witnesses traced such disabilities as they found at least in part to his background.

No matter what the trial judge intended, his instruction may have deprived Murdock of a fair trial on the issue of responsibility. But even if that instruction had not been offered, Murdock could argue that he was denied a fair opportunity to present his particular responsibility defense—a defense not clearly grounded on any medically recognized "mental disease or defect." While the language of our responsibility test theoretically leaves room for such a defense, our experience reveals that in practice it imposes illogical constraints on the flow of information to the jury and also on the breadth of the jury's inquiry. Our test demands an "abnormal condition of the mind," and that term carries implications that may mislead counsel, the court, and the jury.

McDonald defined mental illness for purposes of the responsibility defense as an abnormal condition of the mind that "substantially affects mental or emotional processes and substantially impairs behavior controls." The thrust of Murdock's defense was that the environment in which he was raised—his "rotten social background"—conditioned him to respond to certain stimuli in a manner most of us would consider flagrantly inappropriate. Because of his early conditioning, he argued, he was denied any meaningful choice when the racial insult triggered the explosion in the restaurant. He asked the jury to conclude that his "rotten social background," and the resulting impairment of mental or emotional processes and behavior controls, ruled his violent reaction in the same manner that the behavior of a paranoid schizophrenic may be ruled by his "mental condition." Whether this impairment amounted to an "abnormal condition of the mind" is, in my opinion, at best an academic question. But the consequences we predicate on the answer may be very meaningful indeed.

We have never said that an exculpatory mental illness must be reflected in some organic or pathological condition. Nor have we enshrined psychosis as a prerequisite of the defense. But our experience has made it clear that the terms we use—"mental disease or defect" and "abnormal condition of the mind"—carry a distinct flavor of pathology. And they deflect attention from the crucial, functional question—did the defendant lack the ability to make any meaningful choice of action—to an artificial and misleading excursion into the thicket of psychiatric diagnosis and nomenclature. . . .

[W]e sacrifice a great deal by discouraging Murdock's responsibility defense. If we could remove the practical impediments to the free flow of information we might begin to learn something about the causes of crime. We might discover, for example, that there is a significant causal relationship between violent criminal behavior and a "rotten social background." That realization would require us to consider, for example, whether income redistribution and social reconstruction are indispensable first steps toward solving the problem of violent crime.

. . . It is a critical responsibility of courts, legislatures and commentators to undertake a purposive analysis of the responsibility defense, instead of merely paying it lip-service in deference to its historical significance and our "liberal" consciences. Under each of the prevailing tests of criminal responsibility, the operation of the defense has been haphazard, perfunctory, and virtually inexplicable. If we cannot overcome the irrational operation of the defense, we may have no honest choice but to abandon it and hold all persons criminally responsible for their action.

McGOWAN, Circuit Judge [writing for the majority]:
The tragic and senseless events giving rise to these appeals are a recurring byproduct of a society which, unable as yet to eliminate explosive racial tensions, appears equally paralyzed to deny easy access to guns. Cultural infantilism of this kind inevitably exacts a high price, which in this instance was paid by the two young officers who were killed. The ultimate responsibility for their deaths reaches far beyond these appellants.

As courts, however, we administer a system of justice which is limited in its reach. We deal only with those formally accused under laws which define criminal accountability narrowly. Our function on these appeals is to determine whether appellants had a fair opportunity to defend themselves, and were tried and sentenced according to law. . . .

Judge Bazelon . . . finds reversal to be compelled by reason of a statement made to the jury by the court in the course of its instructions. The bare words used are not a faulty statement of the law. They remind the jury that the issue before them for decision is not one of the shortcomings of society generally, but rather that of appellant Murdock's criminal responsibility for the illegal acts of which he had earlier been found guilty; and, the court added in the next breath, that issue turns on "whether [appellant] had an abnormal condition of the mind that affected his emotional and behavioral processes at the time of the offense." This last is, of course, an unexceptionable statement of what we have declared to be the law in this jurisdiction. . . .

[Affirmed.]

▲ PROBLEMS

Chromosome Criminality (#109)

Chromosomes help determine who we are as people, carrying important genetic material that impacts physical and mental development. Variations in people's chromosomes can contribute to significant differences in behavior.

One particular chromosomal pattern appears to be a strong predictor of criminal and, in particular, violent behavior. People born with the condition produce greater quantities of a hormone that scientists have linked to increased physical aggressiveness. A person with this chromosomal pattern is nearly four times more likely to commit a criminal offense and more than six times more likely to commit an offense of physical aggression and violence. Not surprisingly, such persons are dramatically over-represented in the prison population. They are nearly six times more likely to be imprisoned than a person without the pattern, and twelve times more likely to be convicted of a violent felony. The data is clear: The chromosomal pattern contributes to greater violence and criminality.

Given that people cannot choose the chromosomal pattern they have, should people with this pattern receive an excuse for their criminal behavior?

The Brainwashed Defector (#110)

Richard Tenneson is a 17-year-old who grew up on a farm in rural Minnesota. Though he has never left his home state, he is deeply patriotic, and at the outbreak of the Korean War he does not hesitate to quit high school and enlist to fight overseas. During his visit home after basic training he tells his mother, "If I should win the Congressional Medal of Honor, I still wouldn't have done enough for my country." Within months he is on the front line in Korea with the 2nd Army Division, south of the 38th parallel. The Communist Chinese are in the midst of a spring offensive that pushes the 2nd Division back toward Seoul, and cuts it off from the main body of American forces. Communist forces overrun Tenneson's position and take him prisoner, along with hundreds of others. During the next five months, Tenneson and the other prisoners are marched north. More than half die of starvation before the march ends 300 miles north, at a prison camp on the Yalu River near Chungsong.

A few weeks after reaching the camp, Tenneson is removed from the general population; his captors say he is being hospitalized for pneumonia. When Tenneson emerges from his "hospital" stay, his world view has changed. He is now a devoted believer in the Communist Chinese cause. Tenneson makes propaganda broadcasts for his captors and works to promote their cause among the prisoners as a means of undermining the morale of POWs and the United Nations forces generally. He does this as his "hosts" are killing Tenneson's former brothers-in-arms. A few months later Tenneson, now 18, formally renounces his United States citizenship and defects to Communist China. In December 1953, when the Korean hostilities cease, Tenneson joins 20 other POWs who refuse repatriation to the United States and elect to stay with their former captors.

In the aftermath of the revolution in China, the Communists developed considerable expertise in what is now called "coercive indoctrination." Their methods have been studied by Westerners and their effectiveness proven. Rather than mere physical torture, the indoctrination techniques follow a series of stages in which the subject is first isolated, then disoriented, through malnutrition and constant provocation of anxiety, and finally made to participate in symbolic acts of self-betrayal. This renders the subject's previous personality subject to degradation. The captors then build up a new personality, one that agrees with the belief structure of the indoctrinators, by offering positive reinforcement when the subject expresses the desired views. Eventually, the subject does not feel manipulated and comes to truly hold the beliefs of his captors.

Two years after hostilities with Korea end, the Communists have little use for Tenneson, his value as an instrument of propaganda having run its course. He is given a farming job and is left to his own devices. To fully maintain the effectiveness of coercive indoctrination, the belief structure must be regularly reaffirmed in the subject. Without continued reinforcement, Tenneson becomes homesick and eventually arranges to be repatriated to the United States. On his return he is arrested for treason. While he initially expresses some sympathy for his former captors, he renounces their Communist ideology. Eventually he becomes quite bitter toward his former captors.

A soldier aiding the enemy during a time of war might normally be punished by death or by life imprisonment. What liability for Tenneson, if any, under the Model Penal Code? Should Tenneson receive a defense?

The Abused Becomes the Abuser (#111)

When Alex Cabarga is five, his parents give up their traditional life and move to an "experimental community" named Project Two, which is located in a vacant warehouse. Several weeks after the family's arrival, a thirty-three-year-old man named Luis "Tree Frog" Johnson joins the group. He is a transient who shares the group's goals of throwing off old taboos. He especially favors complete freedom for children. Tree Frog befriends five-year-old Alex and his two older brothers, and the boys begin spending their days with him. The parents do not like Tree Frog but allow him unfettered access to their children in order to have the open-mindedness that their new lifestyle calls for.

[handwritten margin note: that's the problem w/ no-judgment zones]

Two years later, Alex's parents separate. His mother takes legal custody of the boys and moves to a trailer near the warehouse. Tree Frog lives in an old school bus on the same property and continues his relationship with the boys. Tree Frog courts seven-year-old Alex as he would a sexual partner. As Alex's older brothers grow older, they move out of the trailer and break contact with Tree Frog. Alex's mother suspects that Tree Frog has been having sex with Alex for some time but does nothing about it. When Alex is nine, his mother hands over parental custody to Tree Frog, and Alex moves in with him. His mother explains later that she was simply tired of being a parent.

After he gains custody, Tree Frog's physical and sexual abuse of Alex becomes regular. He hits Alex and denies him food if Alex resists having sex or otherwise disobeys. Tree Frog and Alex move away from the warehouse community. They live a nomadic life in a dilapidated bread van with cardboard on the windows, moving the van from one seedy San Francisco neighborhood to another. For money, Tree Frog sells pornographic movies of Alex. Tree Frog believes in a radical dogma that advocates open sexual relations between adults and children and argues that even a very young girl can conceive a child. Tree Frog decides that they will kidnap a little girl and raise her according to his radical tenets, including having her conceive Tree Frog's child, who then also will be so raised.

Alex, now 17, helps Tree Frog kidnap a two-year-old girl named Tara Burke from her parents' van in an auto supply store parking lot. Tree Frog treats Tara as he treated Alex after gaining custody. She is denied food unless she obeys directions, which include having sex with Tree Frog and Alex. Tree Frog takes pictures and sometimes movies of Alex and Tara having sex. Tara is not allowed to wash and is kept naked from the waist down. Her once blond hair becomes dirty brown. Tree Frog soon crops it close to her head. Two months later, an eleven-year-old Vietnamese runaway, Mac Lin Nguyen, is befriended by Tree Frog and offered $200 to babysit Tara. He moves into the van to live with the group. He is treated like Alex was, originally courted, then, once isolated and dependent, increasingly made Tree Frog's subject of abuse. Tree Frog continues his practice of taking pic-) *can be please be executed?* tures and movies as he directs sex between the children. After eight months, Mac escapes and reports the activities in the van to the police. Police find Alex and Tara under blankets, both naked from the waist down. When Tara is reunited with her parents, they do not recognize her. She has an extensive vocabulary, including all the most vulgar words imaginable. A therapist later concludes that her ten-month ordeal has scarred her for life.

What liability for Cabarga, if any, under the Model Penal Code? Should Cabarga receive a defense? *⊖ insanity*

Child Gang Murderer (#112)

Robert Sandifer is the third of eight children. His mother is a drug addict and prostitute who had her first child at 15. By the time she is 29, she has been arrested 41 times. Robert's father deals drugs and weapons when he is not in prison. The children frequently are left home alone. When the mother is home, she generally beats the children. Before age three, Robert has injuries showing regular whippings with an electrical cord and burns from cigarettes butts. He and his siblings are placed by Family Services with his grandmother, who is little better. A psychiatric report finds the grandmother to be suffering a "severe borderline personality disorder." At various times, 40 children are in her 3-bedroom house—10 of her own and 30 grandchildren. Neighbors launch a petition drive to force her to move out of the neighborhood. Robert's direction of development shows itself early. During a hospital stay when he is not yet three, he is angered by something a social worker says to him. He grabs a toy knife and charges the woman, screaming "Fuck you, you bitch." He tries to stab the woman with the rubber knife, saying "I'm going to cut you." The source of his behavior is no mystery. The County Public Guardian describes Robert, saying that he was "in trouble from the moment he was conceived. His family made him a sociopath." Robert misses more first grade than he attends and, increasingly, lives on the street, where his reputation is bad. As he grows older, his reputation gets worse; the local grocer bars Robert from his store for stealing. Robert often challenges older, bigger kids to fights, sometimes beating them, and earns a reputation as a street fighter and a bully. He also develops a habit of stealing cars, preferring large ones—Lincolns and Cadillacs. Because he is still too young to be locked up, when Robert is arrested, he is usually taken back to his grandmother's house, then heads back out on the street.

At the ripe age of eight years old, with his father in prison, his mother absent, and his grandmother disconnected, Robert joins the "Black Disciples," one of Chicago's largest street gangs. Young members are prized because they are immune from detention for more than 30 days. In the gang Robert finds a family. He picks up the nickname "Yummy" because of his love of cookies and Snickers bars. Although small—4 feet tall, 86 pounds—Robert is an active and devoted gang member. He has the gang insignia tattooed on his forearm. His first officially recorded offense, at age 9, is an armed robbery. By age 11, he has compiled a rap sheet of 28 crimes, all but 5 of which are felonies. His short detentions become less frequent when, because of his violence toward other detained children, Family Services refuses to accept even temporary custody.

Robert is assigned by gang higher-ups to shoot a member of a rival gang, the "Gangster Disciples." The attack is part of a larger ongoing conflict between the two groups. Robert, still only 11 years old, walks up to rival gang member Kianta Britten, 16, who is standing on a street corner with other gang members. Kianta turns to run when Robert draws a gun. Robert shoots him twice in the back. Though Kianta survives, he is permanently disabled. Two hours later, still acting under orders, Robert runs out of a viaduct toward a group of boys playing football and opens fire with his 9-mm semiautomatic. He wounds Sammy Saey, 17, and hits Shavon Dean, a 14-year old girl, in the head, killing her.

What liability for Robert Sandifer, if any, under the Model Penal Code? Should Robert receive a defense?

✳ DISCUSSION ISSUE

*Should the Criminal Law Recognize an Excuse Defense
for a Person Who Commits an Offense Because Coercively
Indoctrinated with Values and Beliefs that Make the Person
Want to Do So?*

Materials presenting each side of this Discussion Issue appear in the Advanced
Materials for Section 22 in Appendix A.

NONEXCULPATORY DEFENSES GENERALLY

Nonexculpatory Defenses

Justifications and excuses exculpate. A third group of general defenses—nonexculpatory defenses—give a defense not because the person is blameless but because by forgoing prosecution or punishment some other important societal interest is thought to be advanced.

◆ THE CASE OF MELVIN IGNATOW (#113)

Since divorcing his wife of 13 years (and gaining custody of their 3 children) in 1973, Melvin Ignatow has become more cocky and flashy. He wears expensive jewelry, drives a Corvette, has his hair dyed and permed, belongs to singles clubs, and dates younger women. A college dropout, he works for Rosalco Company, an import-export firm in Louisville, Kentucky, which is where he met Mary Ann Shore. The two have dated for ten years, during which time Mary Ann has cared for Ignatow's children when he traveled on business. But in September 1986, a friend of the forty-eight-year-old Ignatow has set him up on a blind date with thirty-four-year-old Brenda Schaefer, an X-ray technician in the office of Dr. William

Spalding. Ignatow's friend is dating Schaefer's best friend, Joyce Smallwood. The couples double-date for a river cruise on Ignatow's 32-foot boat.

Schaefer is also divorced. She met her ex-husband, Charles Van Pelt, in 1968 and married him in December 1971, but the marriage began to crumble after a few years, in part because of problems with physical intimacy. Although Brenda liked to kiss and hug her husband, she was very inhibited with respect to more physical acts. Money was also a problem; Charles complained that Brenda was too materialistic, and Brenda complained that Charles was financially irresponsible. They divorced after four years, after which, like Ignatow, Schaefer changed her appearance and lifestyle. She got a nose job, had her breasts augmented, and straightened her teeth; and she began to frequent singles bars and date men with money who would buy her jewelry and take her on trips. When she meets Ignatow, she is living with her parents, even though she owns a condominium, in order to care for her mother, Essie Schaefer, who is ill with lupus, high blood pressure, and heart problems.

Ignatow and Schaefer's relationship becomes serious, and on Valentine's Day, 1987, Ignatow proposes. Ignatow gives Schaefer a custom-designed 2.3-carat engagement ring, but they do not set a wedding date. Ignatow is in awe of his relationship with this younger, beautiful woman, describing their relationship as an "ego trip," yet he continues to have sexual encounters with Mary Ann Shore, who is bitter about being "dumped" for Schaefer. Schaefer's work schedule usually permits her to see Ignatow only on weekends, and several of Schaefer's coworkers and friends believe her relationship with Ignatow has more to do with her material needs than any emotional attachment to him.

Schaefer becomes increasingly depressed. Coworkers at Dr. Spalding's office notice that her work is suffering and that she seems very nervous. Schaefer tells many friends and family that she has come to dislike and to fear Ignatow and that she intends to break off her engagement. She tells Linda Love that one time she woke up with Ignatow leaning over her with a rag doused in chloroform. When asked what he was doing, he said that he was trying to help her sleep. Schaefer confides to some that Ignatow has occasionally forced her to take "sex drugs" and that after taking the pills, she wakes without clothing or any idea of what has happened.

Meanwhile, Ignatow complains to Shore that Schaefer is "frigid" and that he wants to hold a "sex therapy" session at Shore's home "to bring [Schaefer] out of that." The session is scheduled for September 24, 1988. Ignatow also asks Shore to help him dig a hole behind her house. She objects, telling him that she does not want to be part of whatever it is he plans to do. Ignatow assures

Figure 110 **Mel Ignatow and Brenda Schaefer as a couple**
(Courtesy Schaefer family)

Shore that he only intends to scare Schaefer, and Shore acquiesces. The pair test Shore's house to see if screams inside the house can be heard outside.

On September 21, Schaefer tells the women at the office that she has left Ignatow. He calls her at work that Friday, but LaVerne Burnside, Schaefer's coworker, tells him that Schaefer is busy. Ignatow becomes belligerent, so Schaefer reluctantly accepts the call and says to him, "I told you never to call me again." Schaefer later tells Joyce Basham, another coworker, that she intends to meet Ignatow the next day to give him back his jewelry and fur coat. She also tells Basham that she is frightened of Ignatow.

That same day, Ignatow brings a shovel, a wooden paddle, a camera, film, plastic garbage bags, a vibrator, lubricating jelly,

Figure 111 **Mary Ann Shore testifying in court**
(Photo by Michael Hayman, ©Courier-Journal)

tape, a pair of gloves, rope, and a bottle of chloroform to Shore's house. Later that night, Schaefer speaks with her sister-in-law and tells her that she suspects that Ignatow has followed her home from work. She also says she has plans to see Dr. Jim Rush, her former serious romantic interest, that Sunday. The two are trying to rekindle their romance. By 4:00 p.m. on Saturday, September 24, Schaefer is at Ignatow's door to pick him up for their last meeting. They go to the Gold Star Chili restaurant at Hike's Point, where Ignatow suggests that they visit a friend of his who has expressed interest in buying Schaefer's jewelry.

Around 5:30 or 6:00 p.m., Ignatow and Schaefer arrive at Shore's home. Ignatow sits Schaefer down on the couch and tells her about his "sex therapy" idea. She gets up to leave, but he forces her back down on the couch. Ignatow tells her that "she [needs] to have this because she [is] just very cold-natured, and he [needs] that sex." He has a checklist on a yellow piece of paper listing all of the steps of his "sex therapy." First, he forces Schaefer to stand against a wall and disrobe while he takes pictures. Next, Ignatow strips off his clothing, leaving on only his dark socks, ties Schaefer to a coffee table, and forces her to have anal sex for two hours. Ignatow orders Shore to photograph him and Schaefer but tells Shore to leave his head out of the pictures. Ignatow then moves Schaefer to the bedroom, where he performs more sex acts on her. He ties Schaefer to the bed and orders her to perform fellatio on him. Schaefer's terror continues as Ignatow positions her legs over her head and ties them to the bed rails. Ignatow rapes her and takes more pictures. He tells Shore to stick her finger into Schaefer's anus and then tells her to hit Schaefer. Schaefer cries during the assault and at one point starts screaming as Ignatow strikes her with the wooden paddle. Shore, scared and disgusted by further indecencies by Ignatow, flees to the kitchen, leaving Schaefer in the bedroom with Ignatow.

Ignatow pours chloroform onto a handkerchief and covers Schaefer's mouth and nose with the soaked rag. Unsure of whether Schaefer is dead, Ignatow ties a rope tightly around her neck to choke her. Ignatow later emerges from the bedroom and announces that Schaefer is dead. Shore enters the bedroom and sees Schaefer on the bed with her hands tied and a rope tight around her neck. Ignatow folds Schaefer's body into the fetal position and ties it tightly with ropes. Ignatow and Shore then wrap Schaefer's body in garbage bags and bury her in the backyard.

Ignatow changes his clothes and throws away the dirty ones. He puts the vibrator, bottle of chloroform, camera, tape, and rope in the trunk of Shore's car. He then punctures the rear tire of Schaefer's car and pushes a nail into the hole. Wearing gloves, he gets into Schaefer's car and drives to Interstate 64. Shore follows him in her car. Ignatow leaves the car on the side of the highway and tells Shore to drive him home. Alone at his house, Ignatow puts Schaefer's jewelry and the photographic film of the torture in a plastic bag and tapes it to the inside of a floor heating duct.

Figure 112 "Missing Person" poster
(Courtesy Schaefer family)

The next morning, at 6:08 a.m., Officer Tom Gilsdorf of the St. Matthews Police Department spots Schaefer's white, two-door 1984 Buick Regal on the shoulder near the Breckinridge Lane overpass. The car has a flat right rear tire, a broken rear window, a missing radio, and an unlocked passenger side door. There is damage to the left rear corner of the trunk lid, and the trunk lock has been pried. The backseat and the outside of the car are splattered with what looks like blood.

At noon, having discussed Brenda's apparent disappearance with her mother, Essie, earlier that morning, Ignatow visits the Schaefers and spends the afternoon with them. He seems nervous and jittery, and occasionally he whimpers like a child, but he does not shed tears. Schaefer's brother Tom and his girlfriend, Linda Love, go to the police station and meet with detective Jim Wesley. After Love tells Wesley everything Schaefer has said about Ignatow and describes Ignatow's creepy behavior, Wesley decides to interview Ignatow. Wesley and two other officers question him at his home, where he carefully recounts the events of the previous day—speaking, oddly enough, from prepared notes. He tells the officers that Schaefer picked him up at 3:00 Saturday afternoon and they went for a drive. He fills them in on the details of the drive, mentioning every stop. The officers leave, feeling very unsatis-fied and agreeing that Ignatow seems cold and methodical.

The investigation continues with little progress. Ignatow is asked to take a lie detector test, but he refuses, claiming that such a test would put too much stress on his weak heart. Other people come forth with stories of Schaefer's whereabouts on the day of her disappearance that conflict with Ignatow's claims. Members of the Kentucky Rescue Association spend 80 hours searching for Schaefer's body in the Ohio River but come up empty-handed. Dr. Spalding starts a reward fund for information about Schaefer's disappearance that grows to $16,000 in just two weeks. Ignatow does not contribute to the fund.

Joyce, Schaefer's coworker, eventually provides information that helps investigators. She knows a hair stylist, Lauren Lechleiter, who has known Mary Ann Shore for ten years and who has cut Ignatow's hair. Shore had confided to Lechleiter about Ignatow's control over her and her inability to get over her relationship with him. Suspicion of Shore's involvement in Schaefer's disappear-ance is heightened by information from Robert Spoelker, who pays Shore $125 a week to babysit his children. Spoelker's records show that Shore did not work on Saturday, September 24. A background check also reveals five arrest warrants for bad checks. Wesley and the F.B.I. decide that the bad check charges may be used as leverage if Shore refuses to cooperate.

Shore comes to the police station for questioning and takes a polygraph test, which she fails. When Wesley confronts Shore about her test results, she becomes agitated and refuses to say anything else. Wesley allows her to leave but has a police officer follow her. That night, Shore is seen walking in the rain with Ignatow. Wesley is notified at home of the situation. Unmarked police cars pull up next to the couple. Ignatow remains calm and tells Shore to cooperate. At the station, Wesley grills Shore, demanding to know what she knows. He tells her that he knows Ignatow killed Schaefer and that Ignatow does not care about Shore. Shore does not budge. Wesley can sense that she has something she wants to say so he pulls out all the stops, threatening her with the bad check charges. Still, she does not cooperate. At 12:45 a.m. on February 14, 1989, Shore is fingerprinted and put in jail on five warrants for bad checks under $100.

Some months later, Shore is called to testify before a federal grand jury. U.S. Attorney Scott Cox asks Shore how many times she had seen Schaefer before the disappearance. Shore replies that she had seen Schaefer only once. When Cox later asks what Schaefer looked like when she saw her, Shore responds, "You mean the last time?" Cox then points out the discrepancy in Shore's statements as Shore turns pale and leaves the jury room. On January 9, 1990, Shore confesses to the F.B.I. and the police that she was present when Ignatow killed Schaefer at Shore's rented house. She leads the police to the woods behind her house, where she and Ignatow buried Schaefer, and also agrees to wear a concealed microphone for a conversation with Ignatow. In return, the authorities agree to charge Shore only with tampering with physical evidence.

Shore tapes a conversation with Ignatow in which he orders her to resist inves-tigators' requests for a lie-detector test and refers to Schaefer's burial site by way of

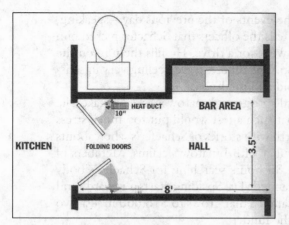

Figure 113 **Diagram of the hallway of Mel Ignatow's home where photos of Brenda Schaefer's sexual torture are discovered in a heating duct hidden beneath a carpet**

(Court discovery document.)

assuring Shore that the body will not be found. The next day, Ignatow is arrested and charged with multiple offenses in connection to Brenda Schaefer.

On January 10, after hours of digging in Shore's backyard, the police bring in Bingo, a German shepherd. Within fifteen minutes, Bingo picks up a scent, and after the officers dig for a few minutes, their shovels hit a black plastic bag. A smaller plastic bag is found a couple of hours later. The bags are brought to the autopsy room of Humana Hospital University. Dr. George Nichols II, Kentucky's chief medical examiner, removes Schaefer's clothes from the smaller bag. Then he turns to the larger bag. The body is wrapped in four overlapping plastic bags sealed by tan plastic tape. Her skin is badly decomposed and her facial features have disappeared. A forensic odontologist helps identify Schaefer by her teeth.

On December 2, 1991, the day before jury selection for the murder trial is scheduled to begin, Mary Ann Shore pleads guilty to tampering with physical evidence. On December 3, a jury is selected. On December 9, trial begins.

On December 21, the jurors begin deliberating. Most believe that Ignatow is involved somehow, but there are problems they can't get over. First, Shore does not seem to be a reliable witness. Ignatow's attorney has done a good job portraying her as a jealous, vindictive ex-girlfriend. Second, the 13-minute taped conversation between Shore and Ignatow has turned out to be a disappointment for prosecutors. The defense argues that Ignatow is simply talking about a safe that he had loaned to Shore. Ultimately, the jury acquits Ignatow of kidnapping and murdering Schaefer.

On February 3, 1992, Mary Ann Shore is sentenced to the maximum five years in prison for tampering with physical evidence.

On October 1, 1992, Ronald and Judith Watkins, the current owners of Ignatow's former home, are changing the carpet. In a plastic bag taped to the inside of a floor duct, they discover undeveloped film and jewelry and notify the F.B.I. The film is developed, revealing about 100 pictures of "sexual acts, sadomasochistic bondage, disrobing, and torture of Brenda Sue Schaefer" that indisputably show Ignatow's guilt.

1. Relying only on your own intuitions of justice, what liability and punishment, if any, does Melvin Ignatow deserve?

N	0	1	2	3	4	5	6	7	8	9	10	11
☐	☐	☐	☐	☐	☐	☐	☐	☐	☐	☐	☐	☐
no liability	liability but no punishment	1 day	2 wks	2 mo	6 mo	1 yr	3 yrs	7 yrs	15 yrs	30 yrs	life imprisonment	death

2. What "justice" arguments could defense counsel make on the defendant's behalf?

3. What "justice" arguments could the prosecution make against the defendant?

4. What liability for Ignatow, if any, under the then-existing statutes? Prepare a list of all criminal code subsections in the order in which you rely on them in your analysis.

5. What liability, if any, under the Model Penal Code? Prepare a list of all criminal code subsections in the order in which you rely on them in your analysis.

▲ THE LAW

Kentucky Revised Statutes Annotated
(1988)

Title L. Kentucky Penal Code

Chapter 507. Criminal Homicide

Section 507.020. Murder

(1) A person is guilty of murder when:

(a) With intent to cause the death of another person, he causes the death of such person or of a third person; except that in any prosecution a person shall not be guilty under this subsection if he acted under the influence of extreme emotional disturbance for which there was a reasonable explanation or excuse, the reasonableness of which is to be determined from the viewpoint of a person in the defendant's situation under the circumstances as the defendant believed them to be. However, nothing contained in this section shall constitute a defense to a prosecution for or preclude a conviction of manslaughter in the first degree or any other crime;

(b) Including, but not limited to, the operation of a motor vehicle under circumstances manifesting extreme indifference to human life, he wantonly engages in conduct which creates a grave risk of death to another person and thereby causes the death of another person.

(2) Murder is a capital offense.

Section 507.030. Manslaughter in the First Degree

(1) A person is guilty of manslaughter in the first degree when:

(a) With intent to cause serious physical injury to another person, he causes the death of such person or of a third person; or

(b) With intent to cause the death of another person, he causes the death of such person or of a third person under circumstances which do not constitute murder because he acts under the influence of extreme emotional disturbance, as defined in subsection (1)(a) of KRS 507.020.

(2) Manslaughter in the first degree is a Class B felony.

Section 507.050. Reckless Homicide

(1) A person is guilty of reckless homicide when, with recklessness he causes the death of another person.

(2) Reckless homicide is a Class D felony.

Section 507.010. Definitions

A person is guilty of criminal homicide when he causes the death of another human being under circumstances which constitute murder, manslaughter in the first degree, manslaughter in the second degree, or reckless homicide.

Chapter 508. Assault and Related Offenses

Section 508.010. Assault in the First Degree

(1) A person is guilty of assault in the first degree when:

(a) He intentionally causes serious physical injury to another person by means of a deadly weapon or a dangerous instrument; or

(b) Under circumstances manifesting extreme indifference to the value of human life he wantonly engages in conduct which creates a grave risk of death to another and thereby causes serious physical injury to another person.

(2) Assault in the first degree is a Class B felony.

Section 508.020. Assault in the Second Degree

(1) A person is guilty of assault in the second degree when:

(a) He intentionally causes serious physical injury to another person; or

(b) He intentionally causes physical injury to another person by means of a deadly weapon or a dangerous instrument; or

(c) He wantonly causes serious physical injury to another person by means of a deadly weapon or a dangerous instrument.

(2) Assault in the second degree is a Class C felony.

Chapter 509. Kidnapping and Related Offenses

Section 509.040. Kidnapping

(1) A person is guilty of kidnapping when he unlawfully restrains another person and when his intent is:

(a) To hold him for ransom or reward; or

(b) To accomplish or to advance the commission of a felony; or

(c) To inflict bodily injury or to terrorize the victim or another; or

(d) To interfere with the performance of a governmental or political function; or

(e) To use him as a shield or hostage.

(2) Kidnapping is a Class B felony when the victim is released alive and in a safe place prior to trial, except as provided in this section. Kidnapping is a Class A felony when the victim is released alive but the victim has suffered serious physical injury during the kidnapping or as a result of not being released in a safe place or as a result of being released in any circumstances [that] are intended, known or should have been known to cause or lead to serious physical injury. Kidnapping is a capital offense when the victim is not released alive or when the victim is released alive but subsequently dies as a result of:

(a) Serious physical injuries suffered during the kidnapping; or

(b) Not being released in a safe place; or

(c) Being released in any circumstances which are intended, known or should have been known to cause or lead to the victim's death.

Section 509.010. Definitions

The following definitions apply in this chapter unless the context otherwise requires:

(1) "Relative" means a parent, ancestor, brother, sister, uncle, or aunt.

(2) "Restrain" means to restrict another person's movements in such a manner as to cause a substantial interference with his liberty by moving him from one place to another or by confining him either in the place where the restriction commences or in a place to which he has been moved without consent. A person is moved or confined "without consent" when the movement or confinement is accomplished by physical force, intimidation, or deception, or by any means, including acquiescence of a victim, if he is under the age of sixteen (16) years, or is substantially incapable of appraising or controlling his own behavior.

Chapter 510. Sexual Offenses

Section 510.040. Rape in the First Degree

(1) A person is guilty of rape in the first degree when:

(a) He engages in sexual intercourse with another person by forcible compulsion; or

(b) He engages in sexual intercourse with another person who is incapable of consent because he:

1. Is physically helpless; or

2. Is less than twelve (12) years old.

(2) Rape in the first degree is a Class B felony unless the victim is under twelve (12) years old or receives a serious physical injury in which case it is a Class A felony.

Section 510.060. Rape in the Third Degree

(1) A person is guilty of rape in the third degree when:

(a) He engages in sexual intercourse with another person who is incapable of consent because he is mentally retarded or mentally incapacitated; or

(b) Being twenty-one (21) years old or more, he engages in sexual intercourse with another person less than sixteen (16) years old.

(2) Rape in the third degree is a Class D felony.

Section 510.070. Sodomy in the First Degree

(1) A person is guilty of sodomy in the first degree when:

(a) He engages in deviate sexual intercourse with another person by forcible compulsion; or

(b) He engages in deviate sexual intercourse with another person who is incapable of consent because he:

(1) Is physically helpless; or

(2) Is less than twelve (12) years old.

(2) Sodomy in the first degree is a Class B felony unless the victim is under twelve (12) years old or receives a serious physical injury in which case it is a Class A felony.

Section 510.110. Sexual Abuse in the First Degree

(1) A person is guilty of sexual abuse in the first degree when:

(a) He subjects another person to sexual contact by forcible compulsion; or

(b) He subjects another person to sexual contact who is incapable of consent because he:

(1) Is physically helpless; or

(2) Is less than twelve (12) years old.

(2) Sexual abuse in the first degree is a Class D felony.

Section 510.140. Sexual Misconduct

(1) A person is guilty of sexual misconduct when he engages in sexual intercourse or deviate sexual intercourse with another person without the latter's consent.

(2) Sexual misconduct is a Class A misdemeanor.

Section 510.010. Definitions

The following definitions apply in this chapter unless the context otherwise requires:

(1) "Deviate sexual intercourse" means any act of sexual gratification between persons not married to each other involving the sex organs of one (1) person and the mouth or anus of another;

(2) "Forcible compulsion" means physical force or threat of physical force, express or implied, which places a person in fear of immediate death or physical injury to himself or another person or in fear that he or another person will be immediately kidnapped; . . .

(8) "Sexual contact" means any touching of the sexual or other intimate parts of a person not married to the actor done for the purpose of gratifying the sexual desire of either party; and

(9) "Sexual intercourse" means sexual intercourse in its ordinary sense but is limited to sexual intercourse between persons not married to each other. Sexual intercourse occurs upon any penetration, however slight; emission is not required.

Section 510.020. Lack of Consent

(1) Whether or not specifically stated, it is an element of every offense defined in this chapter that the sexual act was committed without consent of the victim.

(2) Lack of consent results from:

    (a) Forcible compulsion;

    (b) Incapacity to consent; or

    (c) If the offense charged is sexual abuse, any circumstances in addition to forcible compulsion or incapacity to consent in which the victim does not expressly or impliedly acquiesce in the actor's conduct.

(3) A person is deemed incapable of consent when he is:

    (a) Less than sixteen (16) years old;

    (b) Mentally retarded or suffers from a mental illness;

    (c) Mentally incapacitated; or

    (d) Physically helpless.

Chapter 515. Robbery

Section 515.020. Robbery in the First Degree

(1) A person is guilty of robbery in the first degree when, in the course of committing theft, he uses or threatens the immediate use of physical force upon another person with intent to accomplish the theft and when he:

    (a) Causes physical injury to any person who is not a participant in the crime; or

    (b) Is armed with a deadly weapon; or

    (c) Uses or threatens the immediate use of a dangerous instrument upon any person who is not a participant in the crime.

(2) Robbery in the first degree is a Class B felony.

Section 515.010. Definition

The following definition applies in this chapter, unless the context otherwise requires: "Physical force" means force used upon or directed toward the body of another person.

Chapter 524. Interference with Judicial Administration

Section 524.100. Tampering with Physical Evidence

(1) A person is guilty of tampering with physical evidence when, believing that an official proceeding is pending or may be instituted, he:

    (a) Destroys, mutilates, conceals, removes, or alters physical evidence which he believes is about to be produced or used in the official proceeding with intent to impair its verity or availability in the official proceeding; or

(b) Fabricates any physical evidence with intent that it be introduced in the official proceeding or offers any physical evidence, knowing it to be fabricated or altered.

(2) Tampering with physical evidence is a Class D felony.

Chapter 505. Protection Against Unfair or Oppressive Prosecution

Section 505.030. Effect of Former Prosecution for Same Offense

When a prosecution is for a violation of the same statutory provision and is based upon the same facts as a former prosecution, it is barred by the former prosecution under the following circumstances:

(1) The former prosecution resulted in:

(a) An acquittal, or

(b) A conviction which had not subsequently been set aside; or

(2) The former prosecution resulted in a determination by the court that there was insufficient evidence to warrant a conviction; or

(3) The former prosecution was terminated by a final order or judgment, which has not subsequently been set aside, and which required a determination inconsistent with any fact or legal proposition necessary to a conviction in the subsequent prosecution; or

(4) The former prosecution was improperly terminated after the first witness was sworn but before findings were rendered by a trier of fact. Termination under either of the following circumstances is not improper:

(a) The defendant expressly consents to the termination or by motion for mistrial or in some other manner waives his right to object to the termination; or

(b) The trial court, in exercise of its discretion, finds that the termination is manifestly necessary.

United States Constitution

Fifth Amendment

No person shall be held to answer for a capital, or otherwise infamous crime, unless on a presentment or indictment of a Grand Jury, except in cases arising in the land or naval forces, or in the Militia, when in actual service in time of War or public danger; *nor shall any person be subject for the same offence to be twice put in jeopardy of life or limb*; nor shall be compelled in any criminal case to be a witness against himself, nor be deprived of life, liberty, or property, without due process of law; nor shall private property be taken for public use, without just compensation.

Model Penal Code
(Official Draft 1962)

Section 1.08. When Prosecution Barred by Former Prosecution for the Same Offense

When a prosecution is for a violation of the same provision of the statutes and is based upon the same facts as a former prosecution, it is barred by such former prosecution under the following circumstances:

(1) The former prosecution resulted in an acquittal. There is an acquittal if the prosecution resulted in a finding of not guilty by the trier of fact or in a determination that there was insufficient evidence to warrant a conviction. A finding of guilty of a lesser included offense is an acquittal of the greater inclusive offense, although the conviction is subsequently set aside.

(2) The former prosecution was terminated, after the information had been filed or the indictment found, by a final order or judgment for the defendant, which has not been set aside, reversed, or vacated and which necessarily required a determination inconsistent with a fact or a legal proposition that must be established for conviction of the offense.

(3) The former prosecution resulted in a conviction. There is a conviction if the prosecution resulted in a judgment of conviction which has not been reversed or vacated, a verdict of guilty which has not been set aside and which is capable of supporting a judgment, or a plea of guilty accepted by the Court. In the latter two cases failure to enter judgment must be for a reason other than a motion of the defendant.

(4) The former prosecution was improperly terminated. Except as provided in this Subsection, there is an improper termination of a prosecution if the termination is for reasons not amounting to an acquittal, and it takes place after the first witness is sworn but before verdict. Termination under any of the following circumstances is not improper:

(a) The defendant consents to the termination or waives, by motion to dismiss or otherwise, his right to object to the termination.

(b) The trial court finds that the termination is necessary because:

(1) it is physically impossible to proceed with the trial in conformity with law; or

(2) there is a legal defect in the proceedings which would make any judgment entered upon a verdict reversible as a matter of law; or

(3) prejudicial conduct, in or outside the courtroom, makes it impossible to proceed with the trial without injustice to either the defendant or the State; or

(4) the jury is unable to agree upon a verdict; or

(5) false statements of a juror on voir dire prevent a fair trial.

● OVERVIEW OF NONEXCULPATORY DEFENSES

Notes

THE NATURE OF NONEXCULPATORY DEFENSES

In 1991, an old woman is robbed, raped, and beaten. The crime goes unsolved until 1998, when the offender is identified and arrested. Although he cannot legitimately claim that his conduct is justified or excused, the actor nonetheless may have a defense to liability for his offenses. The statute of limitations may bar his conviction for some or all of his crimes, despite his clear blameworthiness, because forgoing the conviction is thought to further other public interests.

Examples of Nonexculpatory Defenses   Other *nonexculpatory defenses*, as they may be called, include diplomatic immunity; judicial, legislative, and executive immunities; immunity after compelled testimony or pursuant to a plea agreement; and incompetency to stand trial. Each of the forms of immunity furthers an important societal interest, respectively: reciprocal protection of our diplomats abroad, protection of governmental officials from interference with their official duties, the need to compel incriminating testimony from some offenders in order to successfully prosecute others, and the avoidance of the costs and risks of trials through inducement of plea agreements. The incompetency defense is based primarily on concerns of fairness to the defendant. It prohibits trial unless the defendant has "the capacity to participate in his defense and understand the proceedings against him."[1]

Nonexculpatory Defenses Provided by Constitution   Nonexculpatory policy interests also serve as the basis for many constitutional defenses. The Double Jeopardy Clause of the Fifth Amendment, for example, may foreclose the trial of even a blameworthy and (otherwise) convictable offender, by barring the state from making repeated attempts to convict him. Notions of procedural fairness are said to prohibit the state from subjecting a defendant to the embarrassment, expense, and ordeal of trial more than once, or compelling him to live in a continuing state of anxiety and insecurity about the possibility of a second prosecution. Dismissals based on the operation of the Fourth Amendment exclusionary rule, or on prosecutorial misconduct, also may be nonexculpatory in nature, especially because the dismissals may be entirely unrelated to the reliability of the evidence against the defendant. The public policies served by such nonexculpatory defenses may seek broadly to protect all members of society (from unlawful searches, for example), or they may focus narrowly on assuring fair treatment of individual defendants.

Nonexculpatory Defenses Distinguished from Justifications   The balancing of competing interests that underlies nonexculpatory defenses should be distinguished from the balancing that occurs in justification defenses. With justifications, the harm created by the defendant's conduct is weighed against the harm or evil avoided or the benefit gained from that same conduct. The actor whose conduct causes no *net* societal harm or evil is given a justification defense. With nonexculpatory defenses, the defendant's conduct neither creates a societal benefit nor avoids a societal harm or evil; the defendant has caused a harm or evil for which he or she is fully blameworthy. The societal benefit from the nonexculpatory defense does not arise from (or even relate to) the actor's conduct, but from some interest that is thought to weigh against *punishing* the actor for that

---

1. Medina v. California, 505 U.S. 437, 448 (1992).

conduct. Thus, the defendant escapes liability not because of his level of blameworthiness, but rather despite it.

Detrimental Effects of Nonexculpatory Defenses It should be clear that the criminal justice system incurs a cost each time a nonexculpatory defense is permitted. Most obviously, nonexculpatory defenses run contrary to retributive principles by permitting blameworthy offenders to escape the punishment they deserve. Further, such defenses subvert the utilitarian purposes for which criminal liability is imposed. Acquitting culpable offenders who admittedly have caused the harm or evil prohibited by the criminal law undercuts the aims of special and general deterrence. The offender's acquittal shows others (and the offender) that it is possible culpably to violate the criminal law without suffering the threatened sanction. In addition, nonexculpatory defenses deprive the criminal justice system of the authority to incapacitate or rehabilitate such offenders, thereby increasing the likelihood of future offenses.

COMMON NONEXCULPATORY DEFENSES

The most common nonexculpatory defenses include the statute of limitation (setting a maximum time period from the end of an offense to the commencement of its prosecution), diplomatic immunity, governmental immunities (judicial, legislative, and executive), testimonial or plea-bargained immunity, and incompetency. The scope, requirements, and rationale of each are examined below. The entrapment defense presents special issues and is discussed in the following section.

Statutes of Limitation Nearly every American jurisdiction imposes some form of time constraint for instituting a criminal prosecution, under rules set out in what is commonly called a *statute of limitation*.[2] The length of the period of limitation generally increases with the seriousness of the offense.[3] For murder, and sometimes other serious offenses (such as other capital offenses, where recognized), there is commonly no time limitation.[4] Some courts have imposed additional due-process constraints on the timing of prosecution, such that even a prosecution within the limitation period will be dismissed where a long period has elapsed since the offense, and the delay creates prejudice to the defendant.

Diplomatic Immunity Another commonly recognized nonexculpatory defense is diplomatic immunity. The diplomatic agents of foreign states and many of the members of their missions[5] are granted immunity from criminal prosecution by the federal Diplomatic Relations Act of 1978[6]: "[A] diplomatic agent shall enjoy immunity from the criminal jurisdiction of the receiving state."[7] The

---

2. See the authorities collected at 2 Paul H. Robinson, Criminal Law Defenses § 202 n.1 (1984).

3. See, e.g., Model Penal Code § 1.06(1), (2) (murder—no limit; felony of first degree—6 years from commission; any other felony—3 years from commission; misdemeanor—2 years from commission; petty misdemeanor or violation—6 months from commission).

4. See, e.g., Model Penal Code § 1.06(1); 18 U.S.C.A. § 3281.

5. Members of the mission include "the head of a mission and those members of a mission who are members of the diplomatic staff or who, pursuant to law, are granted equivalent privileges and immunities . . . , members of the administrative and technical staff of a mission and . . . members of the service staff of the mission . . . " 22 U.S.C.A. § 254a(1)(A)-(C).

6. 22 U.S.C.A. §§ 254a-254d.

7. Vienna Convention of Diplomatic Relations, Apr. 18, 1961, art. 31, 23 U.S.T. 3227, T.I.A.S. No. 7502, 500 U.N.T.S. 95 (ratified by U.S. Senate, Sept. 14, 1965; ratification deposited, Nov. 13, 1972; entered into force for the United States, Dec. 13, 1972, adopted by the Diplomatic Relations Act of 1978, 22 U.S.C.A. § 254).

Act grants full immunity to the "diplomatic agent" (that is, the ambassador) and her family and administrative and technical staff, but grants only limited immunity to other members of the mission. The diplomatic agent's service staff, for example, is granted immunity only for acts committed in the performance of official duties. The agent's personal staff receives no immunity, nor do members of the mission who happen to be citizens of the United States. The 1978 Act requires the diplomat, or someone acting on the diplomat's behalf, to assert a claim of immunity by appropriate motion.[8] In practice, however, the State Department intervenes regularly on behalf of foreign diplomats, although it has the option not to do so.

Governmental Immunities   Judicial, legislative, and executive immunities, or what as a group might be called *governmental* or *official immunities*, generally protect government agents and officials from criminal prosecution and conviction for conduct that they engage in as part of their official duties. A distinct governmental immunity exempts officials not only from prosecution, but from arrest; such immunity generally is only temporary and is designed to permit the performance of official business without interference. Officials also commonly enjoy broad immunity from civil liability.[9]

Paul H. Robinson & Michael Cahill, Law Without Justice, "Controlling Police and Prosecutors" and "Promoting Interests Unrelated to Criminal Justice"
137–155, 186, 195–201 (2006)

Controlling Police and Prosecutors

[A] justification offered in support of deviations from desert is the need to curb misconduct by criminal-justice officials, whose zealous pursuit of criminals has the potential to overwhelm the desire for fair play and respect for individual rights. In turn, our desire to limit governmental intrusion and to promote procedural integrity sometimes appears to require a sacrifice for justice. What is at stake here is a tradeoff between the societal interest in effective law enforcement and the countervailing interest in preventing abusive or overly intrusive law enforcement . . . .

Some people may see little complexity here. One might adopt a categorical stance that the desert/control-of-government tradeoff should always be resolved in favor of effective law enforcement or, on the other hand, that it should always be resolved in favor of recognizing individual rights. Members of both of these groups, the diehard desert fundamentalists and the diehard anti-government-overreaching fundamentalists, would view the proper resolution of the conflict as obvious: Each group would argue that its favored concerns should simply trump the other all the time.

---

8. See 22 U.S.C.A. § 254d.

9. See, e.g., Imbler v. Pachtman, 424 U.S. 409 (1976) (prosecutors immune from civil liability for conduct in initiating and pursuing prosecutions); see generally 63 Am. Jur. 2d, Public Officers and Employees §§ 362–368.

But others, probably most people, fall outside these groups and have strong principled commitments to *both* substantive desert and procedural restraints. Even for this camp, however, it may seem at first blush that the two principles are simply at loggerheads, and one must simply adopt a normative preference for one or the other. We seek to argue that, in at least some cases, there may be a method of accommodating both interests, and in other cases of balancing the two goals in a reasoned manner. That balancing turns on the relative value of the principles, not *as* principles, but as *practical* influences on the criminal justice system's moral authority and therefore on its effectiveness.

Released to Kill

[Larry Eyler, 30, is a man of contradictions. He has a round baby face and a shy, quiet manner, but his 6'1" body is all muscle. His behavior is childlike and naive, yet he can be cunning when necessary. Eyler's greatest inner conflict, however, revolves around his sexuality. Though attracted to men ever since he can remember, he can barely even talk about the subject. Possibly a consequence of his strict religious upbringing, he is terribly ashamed of his sexual orientation, and with Eyler, this shame translates into violence. When he engages in sex, he is brimming with rage. He has a sadomasochist bondage fetish and enjoys tying up his partners and inflicting pain.

Late at night, he likes to cruise the roads to gay bars in uptown Chicago, carrying in his pickup truck a "torture kit," which includes knives, a metal-tipped whip, a sword, handcuffs, and tear gas. Steven Agan is hitchhiking when Eyler passes by and picks him up. Eyler drives north on Route 63 to an abandoned farm near the tiny town of Newport. At knifepoint, he orders Agan to take off his shirt, then handcuffs him, gags his mouth, and drags him into a shed. With a rope, he ties the terrified Agan to a beam. He unbuckles Agan's belt and pulls his pants down. Eyler meticulously sets up a stage of ritual torture: He sets flashlights for dramatic lighting and puts his torture kit in order. Then he slowly stabs Agan in the chest. Agan, unable to scream through his gagged mouth, tries to avoid the knife. His actions, however, only excite Eyler. In a frenzy of rage, Eyler makes deeper and deeper horizontal gashes on his victim's abdomen and throat. Agan bleeds to death, but Eyler does not stop; he continues to mutilate the dead body. After he calms down, he drags the body into a wooded area and drives away.

Bodies of young men slowly pile up along nearby stretches of highway. Many of the men found are homosexual prostitutes. All are found mutilated in a similar fashion, and the police suspect a serial killer. A special multiagency task force is established. The task force receives a break when an informant calls in and identifies Eyler as the murderer. At times they put surveillance on Eyler. The task force also issues a bulletin telling police departments that Eyler is a suspect and that officers should contact them with reports if they have reason to come in contact with Eyler.

Unaware of the ongoing investigation, Eyler continues to prey upon young men, next murdering Ralph Calise in a fashion similar to Agan's. This time, though, Eyler does not make a clean getaway. The earth is damp, and his boots and his pickup truck's tires leave marks.

Eyler spots his next victim, Daryl Hayward, a young drifter from Arkansas, a few days later. After some conversation, Eyler offers Hayward $100 to let Eyler tie him up for a sex act to satisfy a fetish. He promises he will not hurt Hayward in any way. They pull over to the shoulder and go into the woods, with Eyler bringing a bag containing his torture kit. As they begin, Hayward becomes uneasy about being so close to the highway and suggests they go somewhere more private. Eyler readily agrees. As they are heading back up to the truck, state trooper Kenneth Buehrle pulls up to tell the men that parking on the interstate shoulder is not permitted. He asks the reason for their stop. Eyler tells him they were going to the bathroom. Buehrle knows the men just passed one rest stop and that another lies a few miles ahead. He becomes suspicious and asks to look inside the bag he saw Eyler carry from the woods, which Eyler has been attempting to hide. Eyler appears to consent, but actually shows Buehrle a second bag. This bag contains some personal effects, but no toilet paper. Eyler tells Buehrle that they used all the toilet paper and buried it in the woods.

Buehrle returns to his car to radio for a warrant check and to write a ticket for illegal parking on the interstate. While he learns that there is no warrant out for Eyler, the dispatcher realizes Eyler's description matches that of the suspect on a task force flyer. The dispatcher asks for Buehrle's location in code, signaling to Buehrle that something abnormal regarding the person he has stopped. Buehrle does not know he has stumbled upon a potential serial killer.

Two other officers are sent to join Buehrle. The dispatcher tells one of them, Sergeant Peter Popplewell, that he believes Eyler is the suspect listed on an information sheet regarding the serial murders. The officers are instructed to bring Eyler and Hayward to the station for questioning regarding the current events and impound the truck. Eyler is patted down, handcuffed, and placed in the back of a squad car. Hayward is then handcuffed and placed in a different car. A search of Eyler's truck turns up the other bag, containing various lengths of rope and tape. Eyler is read his Miranda warnings and is driven to the station, where his belt and boots are taken.

While this occurs, Sergeant Popplewell questions Hayward, who is still in the back of his squad car. Hayward breaks down when Popplewell begins reading his Miranda warnings and tells the officer that Eyler offered him $100 for bondage sex. The tow truck arrives and transports Eyler's truck to the police station. Hayward is also driven to the station, where he gives a written statement. Neither man is told whether they are under arrest or on what charges.

At the station, Eyler is put in a cell and the task force is contacted to urgently come and deal with the situation. When the task force arrives, a task force officer says that, while they lack probable cause to arrest Eyler for the murders, there is probable cause to arrest him on the prostitution charge. Eyler still is not charged, which is problematic because it could be viewed as an illegal arrest. The task force quickly determines that the boots and truck tires match those taken by Lake County detectives at Calise's murder scene. They ask Eyler if they may keep the boots, and Eyler agrees. In the meantime, police technicians process the truck for fingerprints and tire impressions. They find Eyler's knife with blood on it and are able to arrest and charge him with Ralph Calise's murder.

Eyler's lawyer files pretrial suppression motions based on the contention that Eyler was illegally arrested after the initial traffic stop. The judge agrees that although the original stop was valid, there was no legal justification for taking Eyler into custody after the stop. The judge grants the motions to suppress the evidence gathered and following the decision, Eyler is released.]

Exclusionary Rules

The so-called Fourth Amendment exclusionary rule provides that when police obtain evidence from an improper search or seizure, that evidence is inadmissible in a subsequent prosecution of the person whose rights were violated.[10] Other, similar exclusionary rules prevent admission of criminal confessions obtained in violation of the Fifth Amendment or of the warning rules established in *Miranda v. Arizona*.[11]

These rules, and the rule requiring dismissal in cases involving violations of the Sixth Amendment speedy-trial right, enforce vital constitutional protections. Yet at the same time, the remedy they employ to do so has great potential to undermine the significant competing goal of punishing the guilty. . . .

How often exclusionary rules operate, as in *Eyler*, to prevent conviction of defendants is hotly debated. As to the *Miranda* warnings, for example, estimates of their impact vary widely. One analysis looked at numerous prior studies and concluded that *Miranda* led to lost convictions in 3.8 percent of all criminal cases, meaning that "[r]oughly 28,000 arrests for serious crimes of violence and 79,000 arrests for property crimes slip through the criminal justice system due to *Miranda,* and almost the same number of cases are disposed of on terms more favorable for defendants," in any given *year.* Another analysis, though, countered that proper examination of the same studies leads to a finding that "the properly adjusted attrition rate is not 3.8 percent but *at most* only 0.78 percent . . . for the immediate post-*Miranda* period, and most likely even less today."[12] As for the Fourth Amendment exclusionary rule, the Supreme Court has cited statistics claiming that the rule causes the release of between 0.6 and 2.35 percent of felony arrestees—a seemingly small percentage but one that translates into a large absolute number of cases. . . . In one recent study of 400 judges, prosecutors, and defense counsel, the respondents estimated, based on their own practical experience, that Fourth Amendment claims were offered in about 7% of all criminal cases and Fifth Amendment claims in about 4% of all cases—but estimated success rates for those claims were quite low, ranging between about 10 and 12%. . . .

[T]he Supreme Court repeatedly has noted that the [exclusionary] rules are not directly mandated by the Constitution, but are a remedy designed to achieve the goal of preventing misconduct by police and prosecutors. The deterrence objective is not the only possible justification for an exclusionary rule, . . . but because the Court has relied on that particular objective when making its decisions about the rule's scope, the rule has evolved such that its current formulation is incompatible with any other basis.

The same rationale underlies other related rules, such as the "fruit of the poisonous tree" doctrine, which prevents introduction not only of the evidence obtained directly as a result of the illegal activity, but of any other evidence it leads to. In fact, the curbing-misconduct rationale underlies the fruit of the poisonous tree rule even where the justification for denying the initially obtained evidence is not misconduct curbing but rather a concern about reliability. For example, if the

---

10. See Weeks v. United States, 232 U.S. 383 (1914) (establishing exclusionary rule for federal courts); Mapp v. Ohio, 367 U.S. 643 (1961) (extending *Weeks's* exclusionary rule to state proceedings).

11. 384 U.S. 436 (1966).

12. Stephen J. Schulhofer, *Miranda's Practical Effect: Substantial Benefits and Vanishingly Small Social Costs, in The Miranda Debate,* 175, 191, 192 (Richard A. Leo & George C. Thomas III eds., Northeastern U. 1998.)

police beat a confession out of a murderer, the confession might be unreliable, and it makes sense to exclude it on that ground alone. But if the murderer then tells them where the bodies are hidden, the later-found bodies are quite reliable evidence, and the reliability concern alone would not warrant their exclusion. (Note that the later-found bodies do *not*, however, make the confession itself any more reliable. The confession, considered *in vacuo* as a piece of evidence, is unreliable; to the extent extrinsic evidence makes it appear more trustworthy, it is that extrinsic evidence that truly indicates the defendant's guilt and on which the prosecutor should have to rely to demonstrate that guilt.)

The curbing-misconduct rationale, then, is critical to a number of key exclusionary rules and other related rules. Yet that rationale is based on an empirical assumption—that the rules actually deter misconduct—which should require some support. . . . A deterrence strategy is only effective if it creates a significant likelihood of a meaningful penalty for engaging in the conduct it aims to deter, yet it remains highly uncertain whether the existing rules manage to do this. . . .

Consider, for example, the potential penalty for a police officer's failure to follow constitutional requirements. The exclusion of evidence against an offender is, to be sure, a significant sanction, but its costs are borne largely by society as a whole, and experienced only indirectly by the officer. The officer may suffer some reputation costs when his misconduct leads an offender to go free, but the extent of such costs is unclear, as is the issue of whether the benefits of obtaining convictions using similar improper practices that go undetected in other cases offset those costs in part or in full.

Moreover, the likelihood of experiencing the cost may not be significant enough to make up for its small magnitude. Even if an exclusionary rule operates to exclude evidence, the offender may be convicted anyway, in which case the officer will think, "No harm done." Additionally, the officer may figure that there is little risk involved in conducting a search and seizure, for without the evidence obtained thereby there may be *no* chance of obtaining a conviction. And in the situations where obtaining a conviction is not the sole, or even the central, motivation for conducting the search, the officer simply will not care about the prospect of exclusion leading to acquittal. There are a variety of such situations, including:

> arrest or confiscation as a punitive sanction (common in gambling and liquor law violations), arrest for the purpose of controlling prostitutes and transvestites, arrest of an intoxicated person for his own safety, search for the purpose of recovering stolen property, arrest and search and seizure for the purpose of "keeping the lid on" in a high crime area or of satisfying public outcry for visible enforcement, search for the purpose of removing weapons or contraband such as narcotics from circulation, and search for weapons that might be used against the searching officer.[13]

The Supreme Court itself has recognized that an exclusionary rule will be "powerless to deter invasions of constitutionally guaranteed rights where the police either have no interest in prosecuting or are willing to forgo successful

---

13. Dallin H. Oaks, *Studying the Exclusionary Rule in Search and Seizure*, 37 U. Chi. L. Rev. 665, 721–722 (1970).

prosecution in the interest of serving some other goal."[14] Thus, even if resulting evidence is likely to be excluded—in some situations, even if it is *certain* to be excluded—a police officer will often have little incentive to avoid conducting an improper search. . . .

But as mentioned, deterrence is not the only possible justification for the exclusionary rules, and perhaps not even the best one. It may also be argued that exclusionary rules are important mechanisms for promoting the legitimacy of the criminal justice system, insofar as they are seen as necessary means of maintaining the integrity of the judicial branch as an institution charged with upholding the Constitution. This view was emphasized in some of the Supreme Court's early exclusionary-rule cases. In more recent years, however, the court has subordinated judicial integrity concerns to, or merged them with, the goal of deterring law-enforcement abuses. Accordingly, the Supreme Court has created exceptions for the rule for various situations where its deterrence value seems minimal. . . .

Accordingly, the impact of the exclusionary rules (as they are currently formulated) on the perceived integrity of the judicial branch is likely quite attenuated—the very inconsistency of the rules themselves suggests that they do only a poor job of maintaining judicial integrity. For example, if the courts' integrity demands that they refuse to countenance, or to become complicit in, any violation of the Constitution, one would expect that the courts would exclude all such evidence, whether obtained by an official within or outside their jurisdiction, and regardless of the type of proceeding in which it was to be introduced. Yet such is not the case. Additionally, we would expect the existing "good-faith" exception to the exclusionary rule to undermine judicial integrity; if the courts are supposed to forswear complicity with any violation of the Fourth Amendment, they should not care about the mental state of the officials who committed the violation.

At least as currently conceived, then, the exclusionary rules hardly seem to promote recognition of the judicial branch's integrity, and so any legitimacy cost from abandoning them altogether would likely be limited. On the other hand, great potential benefits might support expansion of the rules to properly promote the goal of integrity, if doing so would enhance the system's legitimacy. But at present, the rules seem constructed to maximize their own cost and minimize their own benefit: they clearly sacrifice desert and are so defined as to render any possible enhancement of the system's integrity negligible, in the name of serving a deterrence goal whose basis is empirical, yet unproved, both in terms of absolute effect and *relative* advantage over other methods.

The exclusionary remedy, then, is troublesome in terms of desert and questionable in its deterrent effect. Moreover, it may be counterproductive in terms of protection of the underlying right, to the extent that the unappealing prospect of imposing the remedy discourages courts from finding any violation of the right. Indeed, one key question regarding the exclusionary rules, and the speedy-trial rules we discuss below, is whom these powerful remedies deter more effectively: the police and prosecutors, from engaging in wrongful conduct; or the courts, from finding that such conduct amounts to a constitutional violation mandating the remedy. The first effect is the rules' aim; yet the second effect, which is the last

---

14. Terry v. Ohio, 392 U.S. 1, 14 (1968).

thing the rules' advocates (or anyone else) would want, may also be as powerful, or more so . . . .

As to the specific question of illegally obtained confessions (such as those resulting from *Miranda* violations), an additional potential solution also may exist: mandatory videotaping of police interrogations of suspects. Videotaped or recorded interrogation has long been advocated and has been implemented for some time. Britain imposed a recording requirement in 1988, and by 1990, about one in six police departments in the United States—one in three, for departments serving populations over 50,000—had instituted videotaping for at least some interrogations. Minnesota and Alaska mandate recording of interrogations, and Texas effectively imposes a similar rule by barring admission of an oral confession unless it has been recorded. Illinois recently created a statewide pilot program to videotape interrogations in all first-degree murder cases. The ABA's House of Delegates recently approved a report urging law enforcement officials to adopt videotaping.

Promoting Interests Unrelated to Criminal Justice

[Another] justification offered for departures from desert is that such departures are sometimes necessary to promote an interest external to the criminal law. Sometimes these departures involve rules that impose punishment where none is deserved. [In the case of diplomatic immunity, there is] a policy interest outside the criminal law . . . used to prevent the imposition of deserved punishment. Permitting diplomatic immunity from criminal prosecution in this country prevents acts of retaliation against our diplomats abroad . . . .

THE DIPLOMATIC RAPIST

["Jane" (not her real name) stops in the entryway of her apartment building in the Upper East Side of Manhattan, as always, to check her mailbox before unlocking the inside door. After she enters but before the door locks behind her, a young black man, Manuel Ayree, catches the closing door and follows her inside. Short but powerfully built, he is dressed nicely in a tie and well-pressed slacks and is carrying keys in his hand. Jane assumes he lives in the building. He leisurely climbs the stairs behind her, lighting a cigarette on his way up. As Jane goes to her apartment, Ayree approaches the door across the hallway from hers.

As soon as she unlocks her door, she feels him press against her back. In a thick accent, he says, "Do everything I say or I'll kill you. I have a gun." Jane tells him that she will do anything he wants and pleads with him not to kill her. As they enter the kitchen, he grabs a steak knife. Once again, he threatens her, prodding her stomach with it. She offers him money to leave her alone. He ignores the offer and orders her into the studio. The convertible sofa is still open from the previous night. He tells her to take off her pants and lie face down on the mattress. He pulls down his own pants and enters her anus. She screams from the pain and starts crying. After intercourse, he orders her under her bed and tells her to go to sleep and never wake up. At this point, she is sure that he means to kill her, but then she hears him walk out the door and down the stairs. She picks herself up and eventually telephones the police.

Later that winter, Ayree victimizes Carol Holmes, a freelance proofreader in New York, using a similar modus operandi. Within a month, at least ten similar rapes, in addition to Jane's and Carol's, are reported. Nearly all the rapes occur on the Upper East Side. Told by the police that the attacker probably lives in the area and feeling continually upset and fearful about the attack, Carol and her boyfriend Bruce frequently walk the neighborhoods of the attacks looking for the attacker. On one afternoon, their search pays off. They spot Ayree walking toward them. Bruce grabs him as Carol runs to call police.

At the station, however, Ayree announces that he has diplomatic immunity and demands to be released immediately. Shortly thereafter, officials from the Ghanaian mission to the United Nations arrive and identify the rapist as the 19-year-old son of the third attaché to the mission. Forty-five minutes after arriving at the station, Ayree is released. He snickers at Carol and laughs tauntingly as he walks by Carol and Bruce on his way out.]

DIPLOMATIC IMMUNITY

The diplomatic agents of foreign states and many of the members of their missions are granted immunity from criminal prosecution by the Diplomatic Relations Act of 1978,[1] which adopted the Vienna Convention of Diplomatic Relations: "[A] diplomatic agent shall enjoy immunity from the criminal jurisdiction of the receiving state."[2] The Act grants full immunity to the "diplomatic agent" (that is, the ambassador) and the agent's family and administrative and technical staff, but grants only limited immunity to other members of the mission. The diplomatic agent's service staff, for example, is granted immunity only for acts committed in the performance of official duties. The personal staff of the ambassador receives no immunity, nor do members of the mission who happen to be citizens of the United States. Some 200,000 residents of the United States—mostly in Washington, D.C., and New York—are entitled to diplomatic immunity, and roughly 40 to 50 of those people commit a crime in the United States each year.

Underlying the immunity rule is the fear that subjection of foreign diplomats to criminal prosecution in this country might lead to reprisals abroad. . . . At some level, such immunity is a necessary evil, for there is no other practical way to accomplish the goal of reciprocal protection and prevention of reprisals. But two useful limitations can minimize the deviations and their effects . . . .

[I]mmunity can be extended only to the degree that it is necessary to achieve its purpose—and in fact, this is often done. The modern scope of diplomatic immunity has been narrowed in many instances to limit its breadth to that which is functionally necessary for the performance of the diplomat's duties. Further, a diplomatic agent's grant of immunity is not a grant of total impunity. The host state may declare a diplomat to be *persona non grata* and request the sending state to recall the diplomat or terminate the diplomat's service. If its request is denied, the receiving state may refuse to recognize the person as a member of the mission. While the diplomat who has lost protected status in this fashion may not be punished for previous offenses, most legal authorities suggest that the injured state may restrain the offending diplomat until expulsion is possible. Further, the agent enjoys the immunity as a representative of, and by the grace of, the sending country. A diplomat may be liable for trial and punishment under the laws of the sending country. Or that country may waive its diplomat's immunity and thereby subject the diplomat to criminal prosecution in the host state. These alternatives offer at least some prospect of bringing an immune criminal to justice. But . . . even these mechanisms often do not prevent serious failures of justice.

Josh Bowers & Paul H. Robinson, Perceptions of Fairness and Justice: The Shared Aims & Occasional Conflicts of Legitimacy and Moral Credibility
2–6, 56–58, 60–61, 63 (2011)

A growing literature suggests that a criminal justice system derives practical value by generating societal perceptions of fair enforcement and adjudication.[15] Specifically, perceptions of procedural fairness—resulting in perceptions of the system's "legitimacy," as the term is used—may promote systemic compliance with substantive law, cooperation with legal institutions and actors, and deference to even unfavorable outcomes. A separate literature suggests that a criminal justice system derives practical value by distributing criminal liability and punishment according to principles that track societal intuitions of justice.[16] Specifically, perceptions of substantive justice—resulting in perceptions of the system's "moral credibility"—would seem to promote compliance, cooperation, and deference. By contrast, a criminal justice system perceived to be procedurally unfair or substantively unjust may provoke resistance and subversion, and may lose its capacity to harness powerful social and normative influence.

This Article examines the shared aims and overlaps in operation and effect of these two criminal justice dynamics—the "legitimacy" that derives from fair adjudication and professional enforcement and the "moral credibility" that derives from just results—as well as the occasional potential for conflict. Specifically, in this article, we aim to isolate and define the parameters of each dynamic, to compare and examine their similarities and differences, and to explore the settings in which the two run together or (more rarely) cross-wise . . .

. . . we endorse the prevailing view that moral credibility and legitimacy are promising—indeed, critical—systemic enterprises, and we make a number of tentative claims about when and to what degree a system ought to pursue or prioritize each enterprise. Particularly, we anticipate significant crime-control advantages for a system that enjoys perceptions of both moral credibility and legitimacy, but we conclude that—for empirical and theoretic reasons—moral credibility ought to be the principal objective in uncommon circumstances in which a system may effectively pursue only one. . . .

---

15. Tom R. Tyler & Yuen J. Huo, Trust in the Law xiv (2002); Tom R. Tyler, *Procedural Justice, Legitimacy, and the Effective Rule of Law*, 30 Crime & Just. 283, 286 (2003) [hereinafter, *Effective Rule of Law*].

16. Paul H. Robinson, *Distributive Principles of Criminal Law: Who Should be Punished How Much?* chs. 7–8, 11–12 (2008); Paul H. Robinson & John M. Darley, *The Utility of Desert*, 91 Nw. U.L. Rev. 453 (1997); Paul H. Robinson, *Why Does the Criminal Law Care What the Lay Person Thinks is Just? Coercive vs. Normative Crime Control*, 86 Va. L. Rev. 1839–1869 (2000); Paul H. Robinson & John M. Darley, *Intuitions of Justice: Implications for Criminal Law and Justice Policy*, 81 S. Cal. L. Rev. 1 (2007).

THE SHARED AIMS OF LEGITIMACY AND MORAL CREDIBILITY

Legitimacy

In law, as in life, legitimacy is a term invoked so casually that it sometimes seems to signify little more than a vague aspiration. However, in the criminal justice context, the term has come to represent something more precise. Criminologists, social psychologists, and political scientists have refined the concept to mean a "belief that legal authorities are entitled to be obeyed and that the individual ought to defer to their judgments."[17] . . .

Procedure is legitimacy's starting point. People come to obey law and cooperate with legal authorities because they perceive their institutions to operate fairly. In this way, perceptions of procedural fairness facilitate a kind of normative, as opposed to purely instrumental, crime control. Put differently, citizens of a procedurally just state comport their behavior to the substantive dictates of law not because the state exercises coercive power (or, at least, not exclusively because of it), but because they feel a normative commitment to the state. Unlike conventional deterrence theory, which presumes the necessity of carrots and sticks, legitimacy harnesses the power of internal commitment and volitional participation. . . .

Critically, perceptions of procedural fairness are outcome independent. In other words, a defendant or victim need not realize her objective in order to conclude that enforcement or adjudicatory practices are legitimate. Likewise, an ordinary citizen need not determine that the law expresses her personal notion of morality in order to accept its validity. In this way, procedural fairness differs from outcome-driven normative and psychological approaches to criminal justice (like distributive justice generally and moral credibility specifically), which examine whether law produces results that accord with communal intuitions of just deserts. Because the concept of procedural fairness is not dependent upon piecemeal review of substantive outcomes, positive or negative perceptions possess significant potential to motivate or undermine deference to power and thereby to transfer to the state broad discretionary authority. In this way, legitimacy may produce compliance and cooperation with not just an immediate enforcement effort, but across codes, cases, and even actors and institutions. Thus, for legal authorities, cultivating perceptions of legitimacy is a particularly useful and flexible value.

But what does the public perceive to be legitimate procedures and practices? What minimum standards are shared across demographics and cultures? We can provide no definitive answers to these questions in this space. Nevertheless, a fair consensus has developed over the principal criteria that typify procedural fairness. Legitimacy may be measured by the quality of decision making or the quality of treatment of defendants. More specifically, procedures are legitimate when they are neutral, accurate, consistent, trustworthy, and fair—when they provide opportunities for error correction and for interested parties to be heard. Legal authorities are legitimate when they act impartially, honestly, transparently, respectfully, ethically, and equitably. The criminal justice system that optimally expresses these values is not only morally defensible, but also quite probably stable and effective. . . .

---

17. Tom R. Tyler and Yuen J. Huo, *Trust in the Law*, supra note 1, at xiv.

The Occasional Conflicts Between Legitimacy and Moral Credibility

. . . perceptions of fairness in enforcement and adjudication are distinct from and independent of perceptions of justice in the distribution of liability and punishment. This is not to say that the two dynamics—legitimacy and moral credibility—are unrelated. To the contrary, they are often mutually reinforcing. Significantly, however, they are not always symbiotic. A procedurally fair system may generate seriously unjust results, and a procedurally unfair system may nonetheless produce just results. In short, the police practices, criminal adjudication procedures, and the criminal liability rules within a jurisdiction may be in very different states. More importantly for our purposes, not only is it possible for fair practices and procedures and just punishment to be on different tracks, but sometimes they are on a collision course. Specifically, practices and procedures that advance fairness sometimes can undermine justice. And enforcement practices and adjudication procedures that would most effectively advance justice may be seen as unfair.

Points of Tension

Consider, for example, such stalwarts of the American criminal justice system as the prohibition against allowing prosecutors to rely on illegally seized evidence, or to retry acquitted defendants, or to delay trials as best suits effective prosecution. The rights against double jeopardy and to a speedy trial, as well as the exclusionary rule, all have been constitutionally enshrined to some extent. Yet it may well be that the virtues that drive these procedural rules are not accuracy in truth finding or reliability in doing justice. On the contrary, each of these rules, and many others, can easily frustrate justice.

The exclusionary rule can exclude reliable evidence that allows the perpetrator of even a serious offense to go free, a result that cannot help but draw the criminal justice system into disrepute, at least with regard to its commitment for doing justice. In the case of Larry Eyler, for example, police suspected Eyler of a string of gruesome killings of young gay men. When a state trooper just happened upon Eyler parked on the side of the highway preparing for another kill of a young hitch-hiker, he became suspicious, called headquarters and heard of prior suspicions, and took Eyler to the station, probably saving the hitch-hiker's life. A search of Eyler's vehicle turned up conclusive proof of his previous crimes, but the court excluded the evidence because the search was unlawful. Eyler was released to kill again, and, indeed, did so before subsequently being captured and convicted for the later crime. Many may wonder whether this frustration of justice, together with its high cost in human life, is worth the benefits that the exclusionary rule offers.

The double jeopardy bar may present a similar situation. In the case of Melvin Ignatow, for example, Brenda Schaefer was brutally raped, tortured, and killed by Ignatow and his former girlfriend. At trial, the girlfriend testified for the prosecution but came off as an unreliable witness and Ignatow simply lied his way to reasonable doubt. He was acquitted. Ten months later, as the new owners of Ignatow's former house were putting down new carpeting, they found film taped inside a floor duct. When the film was developed, it provided a grisly record of

Ignatow's horrendous offense, yet Ignatow could not be retried for the murder. Again, this gross failure of justice is likely to undermine in many peoples' minds the system's commitment to doing justice.

Or imagine that an Eyler or an Ignatow is released because of a speedy trial violation, or because a statute of limitations has run, or because the text of an offense statute was ambiguous (even though the defendant knew his conduct was wrong). The fairness interests may be clear—speedy trial rights, statutes of limitation, and the legality principle are common and well established—but the justice costs can be significant.

Nonetheless, there are good reasons to insist on adhering to the conventional standards and rules that are premised on fairness concerns. First, and obviously, fairness is an important value in itself. . . . there are practical crime-control reasons beyond this. . . . But one can say more. For example, the system's adherence to these fairness rules, even in such costly cases, advertises the extent of its commitment to them. Indeed, it is the costs of undermining justice in discrete cases that may do the most to advertise just how devoted the system is to these fairness interests. If the system is willing to follow such rules even when they undermine justice in such egregious cases, the message says, then citizens can have confidence that the rules certainly will be followed in the more common less egregious cases. That demonstration of high commitment enhances the system's legitimacy, with it's the consequent benefits of greater deference and compliance.

However, one can imagine ways in which a society might strike a different balance between fairness and justice on these, and other, issues. A system might limit application of the rules, perhaps by applying them less rigorously in case of serious offenses, as some have suggested. Or a system might shift to alternative procedures that could effectively advance fairness interests without jeopardizing justice—for example, by replacing the exclusionary rule with a robust civil compensation or administrative disciplinary regime that could punish police for unlawful searches of any individual (and not just for unlawful searches of accused offenders). Or a system might narrow application of rules and standards in circumstances where the threat of injustice is high, but the threat of unfairness is low. For example, the system might bar application of double jeopardy when a defendant's deceptive conduct helped generate the original acquittal.

Resolving the Conflict

As the last section demonstrates, although a system should strive to realize both values, this may not always be possible. Specifically . . . we explored tensions between legitimacy and moral credibility and identified a number of discrete rules and standards—the exclusionary rule, speedy trial guarantees, and protections against double jeopardy—that may be defensible on fairness grounds even where they promote injustice. More generally, the question arises: Which objective is superior where a system might achieve only one? . . .

For a number of reasons, we believe that moral credibility should be expected to more effectively motivate optimal deference. First, moral credibility entails a concrete assessment of the substantive law or enforcement effort at hand.

Legitimacy, by contrast, entails institutional analyses that operate at higher levels of abstraction. To produce deference, then, legitimacy is mediated by a cognitive move: The prospective offender must contemplate illegal conduct, then consider what he thinks of the set of procedures used to enforce it, and then decide whether to engage in the forbidden conduct based on his feelings—not toward the law itself—but toward the system that prescribes it. For moral credibility to produce deference, the prospective offender need only contemplate the illegal conduct and then consider what he thinks of that conduct. . . .

Second, moral judgments are innately comprehensible. We are all social beings with moral compasses that we instinctively consult. We require no auxiliary understanding to access perceptions of just deserts. But we must achieve a certain level of socialization for legitimacy to do its work. We must grasp the objectives, structure, and methods of a justice system and the implications of its procedural practices and strategic choices. For this reason, perceptions of moral credibility are not just easier to tap, they are likelier to be right. Fewer external variables cloud our moral valuations. By contrast, perceptions of legitimacy may fail to reflect reality in fact, because these perceptions may be based on incomplete or inaccurate information about supplementary matters of enforcement and adjudication. Indeed, the fact that perceptions of procedural fairness rely on more than intuition may explain the somewhat greater dissensus that we think we see on questions of procedural as opposed to distributive justice.

Third, legitimacy is an umbrella concept that covers everything from discourteous to discriminatory behavior. And even if we lack a comprehensive rank ordering of legitimacy criteria, it simply stands to reason that mere rudeness is less likely to undermine deference than perceived immorality.

Fourth, perceptions of procedural fairness are more likely to be socially-constructed than perceptions of substantive justice. Therefore, the corrupt state may more easily manipulate the legitimacy project to serve its bad ends, as we detail below. . . .

Summary and Conclusion

A growing literature on procedural fairness suggests that there is practical value in enhancing a criminal justice system's "legitimacy" with the community. A separate literature suggests that there is practical value in enhancing the system's "moral credibility" with the community it governs by distributing criminal liability and punishment according to principles that track the community's shared intuitions of justice. . . .

. . . the normative influences of the two dynamics are indeed similar, and that they may be mutually reinforcing. On the other hand, the extent of our knowledge about the two dynamics are different. While the "legitimacy" dynamic is the better known and is more frequently used as a justification by scholars, we know less about what practices and procedures will produce legitimacy than we do about what liability and punishment rules will produce moral credibility. Similarly, at present there is less empirical support for the claimed beneficial practical effects of legitimacy in producing deference and compliance than there is for moral credibility doing the same.

▲ PROBLEM

Too Late for Justice? (#114)

On the evening of March 16, 1978, sixteen-year-old Lauren Kustudick makes plans to meet friends at an early St. Patrick's Day party at a local dance club known as Some Other Place Lounge. Lauren, known to friends and family as Lori, lives with her family in Glenview, Illinois, a suburb of Chicago. Her friends are not at the club when Lori gets there so she passes the time by having a few drinks and talking to a few familiar faces she has seen at the club before.

Around 2:30 a.m., a young man (later identified as Herbert Howard) approaches Lori and offers her a ride home. Lori accepts the ride with Howard and the pair leaves the club with another young man. The other young man drives Howard and Lori in a blue, two-door car with white vinyl bucket seats. Instead of driving Lori home, the young man drives on while Howard then proceeds to jump into the backseat where he cracks Lori in the face with his fist, then begins to severely beat her. Lori begs the driver to stop the car but he ignores her pleas. Howard is screaming obscenities at Lori and spitting on her. He then rips off Lori's clothes and forcibly rapes her. Howard chokes and bites Lori and burns her with a cigarette. The beating is so severe that it fractures her skull in multiple places.

After the ordeal, the driver pulls the car into a gas station and Lori is able to flee from the car. At 4:04 a.m. on March 17, Officer Jack Hartmann of the Cook County Sheriff's Department spots Lori running diagonally across an intersection, completely naked. Officer Hartmann picks Lori up, wraps her in a blanket, and rushes her to Lutheran General Hospital.

Following the incident, the police, led by Investigator William Behrens, attempt to locate Lori's attacker. Robert Fenton, a doorman at Some Other Place Lounge, helps identify Howard as one of the men who left with Lori. Unfortunately, Lori is unable to select Howard's picture from a book of photos, and she is unable to bring herself to enter the local courthouse in the weeks following the rape in order to identify Howard in person. With no witness to testify against Howard, he is released.

In 1991, Lori begins seeing Lynn James, a rape therapist. Through therapy, Lori is able to remember the details of the attack and come to terms with the incident. Lori contacts the Cook County police for the case record as well as Lutheran General Hospital to obtain her file from the night of the incident. Lori consults with Officer Kathy Lee who had comforted Lori in the aftermath of the rape, and Lori goes on to identify Howard in a book of potential assailants. After years of searching, Lori is prepared to bring a case against Howard around October of 1993. However, legal research determines that Howard cannot be tried. In the state of Illinois at the time of Lori's attack, all rape prosecutions carried a five-year statute of limitation. Because the time limit has passed, the state is powerless to pursue Howard for the rape.

What liability for Howard, if any, under the Model Penal Code? Prepare a list of all criminal code subsections in the order in which you rely on them in your analysis.

✳ DISCUSSION ISSUES

Should the Double Jeopardy Rule be Modified to Provide Fewer Acquittals of Blameworthy Offenders?

Should the Statute of Limitations be Lengthened or Eliminated to Provide Fewer Acquittals of Blameworthy Offenders?

Should the Exclusionary Rule be Modified to Provide Fewer Acquittals of Blameworthy Offenders?

Materials presenting each side of the Discussion Issues appear in the Advanced Materials for Section 23 in Appendix A.

Entrapment

Some defenses, such as diplomatic immunity or statutes of limitations are clearly nonexculpatory. An actor may be entirely blameworthy but not prosecutable because of her role as an ambassador or the passing of time. However, for other defenses, the relationship between the actor's offense and the rationale for not holding the actor liable may be less straightforward. While "undercover" operations are commonplace, when the government plays too direct a role in helping (or causing) an actor to commit an offense, the law may recognize an entrapment defense. Does entrapment satisfy the traditional requirements for an excuse? If not, are there non-exculpatory policy rationales that explain why the defense is recognized?

◆ THE CASE OF JOHN DELOREAN (#115)

John Zachary DeLorean is born on January 6, 1925, on Detroit's Near Eastside. He is the oldest of Zachary and Kathryn DeLorean's four boys. His

Figure 114 **John DeLorean in his high-rise Manhattan office**

(Anthony Howarth)

father is a hard-drinking French Alsatian who works off and on for Ford. His mother is a factory worker with Eastern European heritage. DeLorean's commitment to hard work yields early success; for example, he attends a better high school after winning a clarinet scholarship. After following his father into the car industry, DeLorean is quickly recognized as a brilliant engineer. Although some people consider him brusque and erratic, he seems to know what people want and swiftly moves up the ranks of Detroit's elite.

He becomes one of GM's youngest division managers and is subsequently put in charge of Pontiac. In the 1970s, however, DeLorean and GM's administration increasingly clash over his attitude, the company's structure, and even his style of dress—sideburns and bell-bottoms, rather than blue suits. People say that he has "gone Hollywood" because of his frequent business travels to California, which have brought him in contact with new social circles and pleasant sunny weather. By 1973, he has divorced two wives, the second a 20-year-old, and marries his third, fashion model Christina Ferrare, in Los Angeles. A few months before his third marriage, he loses his $650,000 annual salary when GM asks him to resign. He announces that he will start his own company and build a luxury car that will be more fuel-efficient and have more safety features than any other on the market. The car also will have "gull-wing" doors that open from the top.

DeLorean knows that the endeavor will not be easy. He belatedly tries to block the publication of his exposé on the problems at GM, fearing that the book could have a detrimental effect on his new car project. However, when he is unsuccessful at persuading the publisher to hold the book's release and it quickly sells out its first 600,000 copies, DeLorean immediately shifts gears and supports the book, claiming that he might "give [any money he receives from it] to some charity."

Although DeLorean is an advocate for several charities and a vocal proponent of civil rights, he gives people reason to question his motives when it comes to money. For example, an inventor, Peter Avrea, claims that DeLorean cheated him out of hundreds of thousands of dollars when DeLorean did not maintain the patents he was hired to protect. A couple claims that they lost a ranch that he sold to them because he failed to inform them of a large existing mortgage on the property. A Wichita car dealer claims that DeLorean ruined his dealership and stole his gull-winged Mercedes 300SL to use as a "model." The accusations do not seem to bother DeLorean.

Figure 115 **DeLorean seated inside the DMC-12 model of his car at Earl's Court Motor Fair in London in 1981**

(Hulton-Deutsch Collection/Corbis)

In 1977, he establishes the DeLorean Motor Company. He locates its production plant in Dunmurry, Northern Ireland, an area desperately in need of jobs, in exchange for

$134.1 million in financing from the British government. DeLorean is able to start the company without much of his own money by obtaining investments from other Americans, such as Sammy Davis, Jr., who see DeLorean's company as a good tax shelter.

The company's first model, the DMC-12, is plagued with design problems from the start. Time and fiscal constraints created by technical conflicts between engineers that DeLorean had wooed away from GM and his new partners from Lotus make it impossible to incorporate into its design many of the innovations that DeLorean had hoped for. Critics suggest that the DMC-12 is quite different from the small, safety-motivated car DeLorean has been hyping for five years. Beyond failing to satisfy critics, the DMC-12's design problems contribute to the company's chronic cash flow difficulties. DeLorean personally adds to the company's cash-flow problems by using its assets to make private purchases, such as a small Nevada-based snowmobile company and art for his New York office.

When first released, the stainless-steel DMC-12 sells well, but a slowdown in the luxury-car market concerns some at the company. They see the market for an expensive monochrome, non-convertible two-seater as limited, especially when priced higher than a comparable Porsche or Mercedes. Moreover, the cars have mechanical problems.

Johnny Carson, the company's official spokesman, has his car break down within just a few miles. The company rushes over a new part, but that too breaks. On another occasion, a man climbs into a display model at the Cleveland Museum and is trapped when the doors will not open.

In 1980, after providing an additional $33 million in loans, the British government announces that DeLorean's company will receive no further government support. The following year, in October 1981, Prime Minister Margaret Thatcher orders a police investigation of the company's finances after a disgruntled former employee provides company memorandums and files suggesting both mismanagement of the company's finances and that DeLorean's personal investment in the company is much less than his deal with the government requires.

Meanwhile, the company's cars continue to suffer from mechanical problems, and by late November the company has recalled most of the 2,000 DMC-12s on the road. After the British government refuses to provide additional loans, DeLorean authorizes the firing of almost half of his company's 2,600-person workforce in January 1982. The government begins a review to determine the company's likelihood of survival.

DeLorean initially reacts to the review meetings by asking Sir Cork, a respected financier, for advice on how to sue the British government for "war damages and criminal damages and breach of contract and other things." He drops the effort after being advised against it. By February, the company is in receivership—tantamount to declaring bankruptcy—and placed under the total control of an appointed financier, Sir Cork. During an interview, DeLorean responds that he is "delighted at the outcome," explaining that the government now has to deal with the company's debt problem.

In May 1982, the British government announces that it is closing the plant by the end of the month. Within hours of the announcement, DeLorean releases a statement that he has new backers who will provide the $37 million necessary to keep the plant open. He keeps the sources secret, describing them only as "an individual

Figure 116 **DeLorean at bankruptcy conference, February 19, 1982**
(Bettmann/Corbis)

and a bank." Having heard vague promises of funding from unknown sources before, those closest to him are skeptical.

DeLorean is now seemingly out of ideas but recalls conversations he has had with a former neighbor, James Timothy Hoffman. They know each other through their sons and have discussed in general terms their respective business troubles. Several days earlier, Hoffman had tried to reach DeLorean.

Hoffman did not find his success in the business world. Rather, he is involved in drug trafficking, which by the early 1980s is a very lucrative venture. The Drug Enforcement Agency (DEA) estimates that during that period more than $30 billion are spent yearly on cocaine alone. In 1981, the F.B.I. arrests the 40-year old Hoffman, who agrees to act as a government informant in exchange for a reduced sentence, and since January 1982 has been an F.B.I. informant. When DeLorean calls, Hoffman mentions that he has made money smuggling drugs from Colombia and Thailand. On July 11, the two meet at the Marriott in Newport Beach, California. DeLorean raises the idea of arranging a drug deal. The following day, after Hoffman informs his contacts about DeLorean's suggestion to sell drugs, the F.B.I. opens an official file on DeLorean.

On July 13, in the first of many videotaped conversations, DeLorean explains to Hoffman that his company has $40 million in cars but no cash, and he would like to proceed with the proposition they discussed. During the meeting, an F.B.I. camera hidden underneath the table records DeLorean's shoes, trouser legs, and muffled voice explaining that his tax man can reconstruct records to make anything look legitimate. Hoffman explains to DeLorean that they can channel the profits from the cocaine sales through Eureka Federal Savings, in San Carlos, California, to make the transaction appear legal. DeLorean comments that he does not really care what the money's source is—drugs, organized crime, anything—so long as it eventually filters through a recognized financial institution.

On September 4, DeLorean meets with Hoffman in Washington, D.C. At this meeting, which the F.B.I. is again secretly videotaping, they specifically discuss the importation of heroin and cocaine as a way for DeLorean to generate capital; the drug deal could raise the estimated $40 million he needs to save his company. DeLorean agrees to provide $1.8 million in funding for the deal. Hoffman reassures him that he will not be easily connected to the transaction but warns DeLorean that, once they start, he had better have a good reason not to follow through with the plan. Hoffman also reminds DeLorean not to take part in anything with which he is uncomfortable. "I won't be mad, I won't be hurt, I won't be anything. If you can get the money somewhere else and it's better circumstances, I'd say do it," Hoffman says. Although he appreciates the option to withdraw, DeLorean tells him, "I want to proceed."

During his meetings with Hoffman and his associates, DeLorean makes a vague claim that he has a tight relationship with the Irish Republican Army (I.R.A.), and warns that drug dealers should be warned not to mess with him. (When this claim becomes known, the United States government takes it quite seriously and conducts an investigation, but is unable to confirm or deny the claim. Upon hearing the claim later, the I.R.A. strongly denies any connection to DeLorean. In Belfast, the I.R.A. issues a statement: "In Ireland, we treat as an offense anyone who falsely uses the name of the Irish Republican Army to impress people, abuse people, or extricate themselves from situations of their own making. . . . We do not take lightly Mr. DeLorean's lies, nor will we forget them should he ever bump into us.")

On September 8, DeLorean travels to San Carlos, California, and meets with a person he believes to be the drug dealers' banker, James Benedict (F.B.I. agent Benedict Tisa). Benedict outlines a plan to hire William Hetrick, a 50-year old pilot, who is "very successful for bringing in cocaine." The F.B.I. suspects that Hetrick, who maintains a lifestyle beyond the means of a flight operator with no clients, is one of southern California's major cocaine traffickers but have been unsuccessful in catching him.

Unwilling to risk his own money, DeLorean calls Benedict a week later to tell him that the $1.8 million he promised is unavailable because his I.R.A. contact has made it impossible for him to get access to the money. Benedict does not hide his disappointment. He tells DeLorean that he is letting them down.

On September 17, DeLorean calls Benedict again to inform him that he has found another way to get the money needed for the deal and is ready to make the arrangements with pilot Hetrick. The three meet

Figure 117 **The DA's evidence against John DeLorean**

(AP)

together on September 20 at the Bel Air Sands Hotel to discuss DeLorean's new plan. Eleven days later, at the Bonaventure Hotel in Washington, D.C., Hoffman introduces DeLorean to the bearded Mafia kingpin, Mr. Vicenza (DEA agent Valenstra). While eating lunch, Vicenza discusses rates of return on investment with DeLorean, estimating that DeLorean could have $10 million within 48 hours "from that particular cocaine purchase."

Trying to finalize the deal, DeLorean offers Vicenza a 50 percent ownership stake in his company as collateral if Vicenza will purchase the cocaine with his money. (In a September 29 letter, DeLorean signs over 500 shares of DeLorean Motor Company stock to Vicenza, and 5,000 to Benedict, which according to later estimates is his entire voting block in the company.) From the table, DeLorean calls pilot Hetrick and says awkwardly, "They'd like to go ahead with those monkeys [code for a kilo of cocaine] you had up in San Francisco." They agree to meet in Los Angeles after the drugs have been flown in.

On Monday, October 18, the F.B.I. arrests Hetrick and his assistant, Steven Arrington, at the Los Angeles airport with more than 60 pounds of cocaine, worth about $24 million. Meanwhile, Hoffman calls DeLorean, who arranges a flight to Los Angeles the next morning, October 19.

While DeLorean is en route to Los Angeles, the British government announces that it is permanently closing his company's plant. Both are unaware that a legitimate banker has been desperately trying to contact DeLorean's office with loan papers for his signature that could provide the funds necessary to salvage his company. She is told that he is unreachable because he is on a flight to Los Angeles.

Upon arrival, DeLorean goes to Room 501 of the airport's Bel Air Sands Hotel. The room is being audio- and videotaped. DeLorean enters the room to see an open suitcase with 60 pounds of cocaine worth $24 million. Picking up one of the bags, DeLorean says it is better than gold. "Just in the nick of time," he beams. They pass glasses of champagne around and DeLorean toasts, "A lot of success for everyone."

A knock at the door interrupts the celebration. Agent Jerry West enters, announcing, "I'm with the F.B.I. You are under arrest for narcotics law violations."

1. Relying only on your own intuitions of justice, what liability and punishment, if any, does John DeLorean deserve?

N	0	1	2	3	4	5	6	7	8	9	10	11
☐	☐	☐	☐	☐	☐	☐	☐	☐	☐	☐	☐	☐
no liability	liability but no punishment	1 day	2 wks	2 mo	6 mo	1 yr	3 yrs	7 yrs	15 yrs	30 yrs	life imprison- ment	death

2. What "justice" arguments could defense counsel make on the defendant's behalf?

3. What "justice" arguments could the prosecution make against the defendant?

4. What liability for DeLorean, if any, under the then-existing statutes? Prepare a list of all criminal code subsections and cases in the order in which you rely on them in your analysis.

5. What liability, if any, under the Model Penal Code? Prepare a list of all criminal code subsections in the order in which you rely on them in your analysis.

■ THE LAW

United States Code
(1982)

Title 21. Food and Drugs

Chapter 13. Drug Abuse Prevention and Control
Subchapter I. Control and Enforcement

Section 802. Definitions

As used in this subchapter: . . .

(4) The term "Drug Enforcement Administration" means the Drug Enforcement Administration in the Department of Justice.

(5) The term "control" means to add a drug or other substance, or immediate precursor, included in schedule I, II, III, IV or V of part B of this subchapter, whether by transfer from another schedule or otherwise.

(6) The term "controlled substance" means a drug or other substance, or immediate precursor, included in schedule I, II, III, IV or V of part B of this subchapter. The term does not include distilled spirits, wine, malt beverages, or tobacco, as those terms are defined or used in subtitle E of the Internal Revenue Code of 1954.

(7) The term "counterfeit substance" means a controlled substance which, or the container or labeling of which, without authorization, bears the trademark, trade name, or other identifying mark, imprint, number, or device, or any likeness thereof, or a manufacturer, distributor, or dispenser other than the person or persons who in fact manufactured, distributed, or dispensed such substance and which thereby falsely purports or is represented to be the product of, or to have been distributed by, such other manufacturer, distributor, or dispenser.

(8) The terms "deliver" or "delivery" mean the actual, constructive, or attempted transfer of a controlled substance, whether there exists an agency relationship.

(9) The term "depressant or stimulant substance" means—

(A) a drug which contains any quantity of (i) barbituric acid or any of the slats of barbituric acid; or (ii) any derivative of barbituric acid which has been designated by the Secretary as habit forming under section 352(d) of this title; or

(B) a drug which contains any quantity of (i) amphetamine or any of its optimal isomers; (ii) any slat of amphetamine or any slat of an optical isomer of amphetamine; or (iii) any substance which the Attorney General, after investigation, has been found to be, and by regulation designated as, habit forming because of its stimulant effect on the central nervous system; or

(C) lysergic acid diethylamide; or

(D) any drug which contains any quantity of a substance which the Attorney General, after investigation, has found to have, and by regulation designated as having, a potential for abuse because of its depressant or stimulant effect on the central nervous system or its hallucinogenic effect.

(10) The term "dispense" means to deliver a controlled substance to an ultimate user or research subject by, or pursuant to the lawful order of, a practitioner, including the prescribing and administering of a controlled substance and the packaging, labeling or compounding necessary to prepare the substance for such delivery. The term "dispenser" means a practitioner who so delivers a controlled substance to an ultimate user or research subject.

(11) The term "distribute" means to deliver (other than by administrating or dispensing) a controlled substance. The term "distributor" means a person who so delivers a controlled substance.

(12) The term "drug" has the meaning given that term by section 321(g) (1) of this title.

(13) The term "felony" means any Federal or State offense classified by applicable Federal or State law as a felony. . . .

(16) The term "narcotic drug" means any of the following, whether produced directly or indirectly by extraction from substances of vegetable origin, or independently by means of chemical synthesis, or by a combination of extraction and chemical synthesis:

(A) Opium, coca leaves, and opiates.

(B) A compound, manufacture, salt, derivative, or preparation of opium, coca leaves, or opiates.

(C) A substance (and any compound manufacture, salt, derivative, or preparation thereof) which is chemically identical with any of the substances referred to in clause (A) or (B).

Such term does not include decocainized coca leaves or extracts of coca leaves which extracts do not contain cocaine or ecgonine.

(17) The term "opiate" means any drug or other substance having an addiction-forming or addiction-sustaining liability similar to morphine or being capable of having such addiction-forming or addiction-sustaining liability. . . .

Section 841. Prohibited Acts

(a) Unlawful acts: Except as authorized by this subchapter, it shall be unlawful for any person knowingly or intentionally—

(1) to manufacture, distribute, or dispense, or possess with intent to manufacture, distribute, or dispense, a controlled substance; or

(2) to create, distribute, or dispense, or possess with intent to distribute or dispense, a counterfeit substance.

(b) Penalties: Except as otherwise provided in section 845 of this title, any person who violates subsection (a) of this section shall be sentenced as follows:

(1) (A) In the case of a controlled substance in schedule I or II which is a narcotic drug, such person shall be sentenced to a term of imprisonment of not more than 15 years, a fine of not more than $25,000, or both. If any person commits such violation after one or more prior convictions of him for an offense punishable under this paragraph, or for a felony under any other provision of this subchapter of subchapter II of this chapter or other law of the United States relating to narcotic drugs, marihuana, or depressant or stimulant substances, have become final, such person shall be sentenced to a term of imprisonment of not more than 30 years, a fine of not more

than $50,000, or both. Any sentence imposing a term of imprisonment under this paragraph shall, in the absence of such prior conviction, impose a special parole term of at least 3 years in addition to such term of imprisonment and shall, if there was such a prior conviction, impose a special parole term of as least 6 years in addition to such term of imprisonment.

(B) In the case of a controlled substance in schedule I or II which is not a narcotic drug or in the case of any controlled substance in schedule III, such person shall, except as provided in paragraphs (4), (5) and (6) of this subsection, be sentenced to a term of imprisonment of not more than 5 years, a fine of not more than $15,000, or both. If any person commits such a violation after one or more prior convictions of him for an offense punishable under this paragraph, or for a felony under any other provision of this subchapter or subchapter II of this chapter of other law of the United States relating to narcotic drugs, marihuana, or depressant or stimulant substances, have become final, such person shall be sentenced to a term of imprisonment of not more than 10 years, a fine of not more than $30,000, or both. Any sentence imposing a term of imprisonment under this paragraph shall, in the absence of such a prior conviction, impose a special parole term of at least 2 years in addition to such term of imprisonment and shall, if there was such a prior conviction, impose a special parole term of at least 4 years in addition to such term of imprisonment. . . .

Section 843. Prohibited Acts C

(a) . . .

(b) Communication facility. It shall be unlawful for any person knowingly or intentionally to use any communication facility in committing or in causing or facilitating the commission of any act or acts constituting a felony under any provision of this subchapter. . . . Each separate use of a communication facility shall be a separate offense under this subsection. For purposes of this subsection, the term "communication facility" means any and all public and private instrumentalities used or useful in the transmission of writing, signs, signals, pictures, or sounds of all kinds and includes mail, telephone, wire, radio, and all other means of communication.

Section 846. Attempt and Conspiracy

Any person who attempts or conspires to commit any offenses defined in this subchapter is punishable by imprisonment or fine or both which may not exceed the maximum punishment prescribed by the offense, the commission of which was the object of the attempt or conspiracy.

Section 847. Additional Penalties

Any penalty imposed for violation of this subchapter shall be in addition to, and not in lieu of, any civil or administrative penalty or sanction authorized by law.

Title 18. Crimes and Criminal Procedure

Part I. Crimes
Chapter 95. Racketeering

Section 1952. Interstate and Foreign Travel or Transportation in Aid of Racketeering Enterprises

(a) Whoever travels in interstate or foreign commerce or uses any facility in interstate of foreign travel, including the mail, with intent to—

(1) distribute the proceeds of any unlawful activity; or

(2) commit any crime of violence to further any unlawful activity; or

(3) otherwise promote, manage, establish, carry on, or facilitate the promotion, management, establishment, or carrying on, of any unlawful activity, and thereafter performs or attempts to perform any of the acts specified in subparagraph (1), (2), and (3), shall be fined not more than $10,000 or imprisoned for not more than five years, or both.

(b) As used in this section "unlawful activity" means (1) any business enterprise involving gambling, liquor on which the Federal excise tax has not been paid, narcotics or controlled substances, . . . or prosecution offenses in violation of the laws of the State in which they are committed or of the United States or (2) extortion, bribery, or arson in violation of the laws of the State in which committed or of the United States.

(c) Investigations of violations under this section involving liquor shall be conducted under the supervision of the Secretary of the Treasury.

Chapter 96. Racketeer Influenced and Corrupt Organizations

Section 1961. Definitions

As used in this chapter—

(1) "racketeering activity" means (A) any act or threat involving murder, kidnapping, gambling, arson, robbery, bribery, extortion, or dealing in narcotic or other dangerous drugs, which is punishable under State law and punishable by imprisonment for more than one year; (B) any act which is indictable under any of the following provisions of title 18, United States Code: Section 201 (relating to bribery), section 224 (relating to sports bribery), section 471, 472, and 473 (relating to counterfeiting), section 569 (relating to theft from interstate shipment) if the act indictable under section 659 is felonious, section 664 (relating to embezzlement from pension and welfare funds, sections 891–894 (relating to extortionate credit transactions), section 1084 (relating to the transmission of gambling information), section 1341 (relating to wire fraud), section 1503 (relating to obstruction of justice), section 1510 (relating to obstruction of criminal investigations), section 1511 (relating to the obstruction of State or local enforcement), section 1951 (relating to interference with commerce, robbery, or extortion), section 1952 (relating to racketeering), section 1953 (relating to interstate transportation of wagering paraphernalia), section 1954 (relating to unlawful welfare fund payments), section 1955 (relating to the prohibition of

illegal gambling businesses), sections 2314 and 2315 (relating to interstate transportation of stolen property), section 2341–2346 (relating to trafficking in contraband cigarettes), sections 2421–24 (relating to white slave traffic), (C) any act which is indictable under title 29, United States Code, section 186 (dealing with restrictions on payments and loans to labor organizations) or section 501(c) (relating to embezzlement from union funds), or (D) any offense involving fraud connected with a case under title 11, fraud in the sale of securities, or the felonious manufacture, importation, receiving, concealment, buying, selling, or otherwise dealing with narcotic or other dangerous drugs, punishable under any law of the United States;

(2) "State" means any State of the United States, District of Columbia, the Commonwealth of Puerto Rico, any territory or possession of the United States, any political subdivision, or any department, agency, or instrumentality thereof;

(3) "person" includes any individual or entity capable of holding a legal or beneficial interest in property;

(4) "enterprise" includes any individual, partnership, corporation, association, or other legal entity, and any union or group of individuals associated in fact although not a legal entity;

(5) "pattern of racketeering activity" requires at least two acts of racketeering activity, one of which occurred after the effective date of this chapter and the last of which occurred within ten years (excluding any period of imprisonment) after the commission of a prior act of racketeering activity; . . .

Section 1962. Prohibited Activities

(a) It shall be unlawful for any person who has received any income derived, directly or indirectly, from a pattern of racketeering activity or through collection of an unlawful debt in which such person has participated as a principal within the meaning of section 2, title 18, United States Code, to use or invest, directly or indirectly, any part of such income, or the proceeds of such income, in acquisition of any interest in, or the establishment or operation of, any enterprise which is engaged in, or the activity of which affect, interstate or foreign commerce. A purchase of securities on the open market for purposes of investment, and without the intention of controlling or participating in the control of the issuer, or of assisting another to do so, shall not be unlawful under this subsection if the securities of the issuer held by the purchaser, the members of his immediate family, and his or their accomplices in any pattern of racketeering activity or the collection of an unlawful debt after such purchase do not amount in the aggregate to one percent of the outstanding securities of any one class, and do not confer, either in law or in fact, the power to elect one or more directors of the issuer.

(b) It shall be unlawful for any person through a pattern of racketeering activity or through collection of an unlawful debt to acquire or maintain, directly or indirectly, any interest in or control of any enterprise which is engaged in, or the activities of which affect, interstate or foreign commerce.

(c) It shall be unlawful for any person employed by or associated with any enterprise engaged in, or the activities of which affect, interstate or foreign commerce, to conduct or participate, directly or indirectly, in the conduct of such enterprise's affairs through a pattern of racketeering activity or collection of unlawful debt.

(d) It shall be unlawful for any person to conspire to violate any of the provisions of subsections (a), (b), or (c) of this section.

Section 1963. Criminal Penalties

(a) Whoever violates any provision of section 1962 of this chapter shall be fined not more than $25,000 or imprisoned not more than twenty years, or both, and shall forfeit to the United States (1) any interest he has acquired or maintained in violation of section 1962, and (2) any interest in, security in, claim against, or property or contractual right of any kind affording a source of influence over, any enterprise which he has established operated, controlled, conducted, or participated in the conduct of, in violation of section 1962.

(b) In any action brought by the United States under this section, the district courts of the United States shall have jurisdiction to enter such restraining orders or prohibitions, or to take such other actions, including, but not limited to, the acceptance of satisfactory performance bonds, in connection with any property or other subject to forfeiture under this section, as it shall deem proper.

(c) Upon conviction of a person under this section, the court shall authorize the Attorney General to seize all property or other interest declared forfeited under this section upon such terms and conditions as the court shall deem proper. If property right or other interest is not exercisable or transferable for value by the United States, it shall expire, and shall not revert to the convicted person. All provisions of law relating to the disposition of property, or the proceeds from the sale thereof, or the remission or mitigation of forfeitures for violation of the customs laws, and the compromise of claims and the award of compensation to informers in respect of such forfeitures incurred, or alleged to have been incurred, under the provisions of this section, insofar as applicable and not inconsistent with the provisions hereof. Such duties as are imposed upon the collector of customs or any other person with respect to the disposition or property under the customs laws shall be performed under this chapter by the Attorney General. The United States shall dispose of all such property as soon as commercially feasible, making due provision for the rights of innocent persons.

Grimm v. United States

156 U.S. 604 (1895)

Defendant was indicted for mailing letters in violation of Rev. St. §3893, which provided that lewd pictures, books or pamphlets, and information on how to receive them, could not be sent through the mail. He had responded to a letter requesting the quantity and price of lewd pictures, which came from a government agent using a fictitious name. The Court affirmed his indictment and denied his defense of entrapment. The Court held that "[t]he law was actually violated by the defendant; he placed letters in the post office which conveyed information as to where obscene matter could be obtained . . . with a view of giving such information. . . . The fact that the person who wrote under these assumed names and received his letters was a government detective in no manner detracts from his guilt."

Sorrells v. United States
287 U.S. 435 (1932)

Nearly forty years after *Grimm*, the Court had moved away from it and found a rationale to provide a defense of entrapment. In *Sorrells*, the defendant was convicted of possessing and selling one-half gallon of whiskey in violation of the National Prohibition Act, and argued that he was entrapped by a prohibition agent. The agent testified that on July 13, 1930, he visited the defendant's home with three of the defendant's acquaintances for a couple of hours, and at least three times, asked the defendant to procure him some whiskey. The government admitted that "[t]here was no evidence that the defendant had ever possessed or sold any intoxicating liquor prior to the transaction in question." The Court held that the defense of entrapment was available to the defendant in such circumstances. It stated that "[i]t is clear that the evidence was sufficient to warrant a finding that the act for which defendant was prosecuted was instigated by the prohibition agent, that it was the creature of his purpose . . . and that the agent lured defendant, otherwise innocent, to its commission by repeated and persistent solicitation. . . . Such a gross abuse of authority given for the purpose of detecting and punishing crime, and not for the making of criminals, deserves the severest condemnation." In support for its new rule, the Court found that "the weight of authority in the lower federal courts is decidedly in favor of . . . the defense of entrapment [being] available." To set limitations on its use, the Court held that "[t]he defense is available, not in the view that the accused though guilty may go free, but that the government cannot be permitted to contend that he is guilty of a crime where the government officials are the instigators of his conduct." At the same time, the defendant's intent must be investigated to determine the applicability of the defense, for "if the defendant seeks acquittal by reason of entrapment he cannot complain of an appropriate and searching inquiry into his own conduct and predisposition as bearing upon that issue."

(Roberts, concurrence.) "There is common agreement that where a law officer envisages a crime, plans it, and activates its commission by one not theretofore intending its perpetration, for the sole purpose of obtaining a victim through indictment, conviction and sentence, the consummation of so revolting a plan ought not to be permitted by any self-respecting tribunal. . . . The enforcement of this policy calls upon the court [as opposed to the jury], in every instance where alleged entrapment of a defendant is brought to its notice, to ascertain the facts, to appraise their effect upon the administration of justice, and to make such order with respect to the further prosecution of the cause as the circumstances require." The Court's opinion weighs the intent of the accused against that of the government agents. Instead, "[t]he applicable principle is that courts must be closed to the trial of a crime instigated by the government's own agents. No other issue, no comparison of equities as between the guilty official and the guilty defendant, has any place in the enforcement of this overruling principle of public policy."

United States v. Russell
411 U.S. 423 (1973)

The *Russell* opinion is excerpted following the Notes section below.

Hampton v. United States
425 U.S. 484 (1976)

The defendant was convicted of distributing heroin. He invited a DEA informant to produce buyers, who turned out to be undercover officers. The defendant argued that, while his disposition might normally exclude him from an entrapment defense, his case fit the potential exception noted in *Russell*, in which the officers' conduct was "so outrageous . . . [as to] bar the government from . . . obtain[ing] a conviction." However, the Court rejected his argument and found that the defendant's case differed from *Russell* only in degree, and that "in each case the Government agents were acting in concert with the defendant, and in each case either the jury found or the defendant conceded that he was predisposed to commit the crime for which he was convicted. The Court reaffirmed that the defendant's predisposition to commit the crime "rendered this defense unavailable to him."

(Brennan, dissent.) The court should "refuse to convict an entrapped defendant, not because his conduct falls outside the proscription of the statute, but because, even if his guilt be admitted, the methods employed on behalf of the Government to bring about conviction cannot be countenanced." Instead, the court has adopted a "subjective" approach to the defense of entrapment that focuses on the "conduct and propensities of the particular defendant in each case and, in the absence of a conclusive showing, permits the jury to determine as a question of fact the defendant's 'predisposition' to the crime. This jury determination produces an improper weighing of the defendant's intent against that of the government agent, when the propensities and predisposition of a specific defendant should not be at issue. Therefore, if the police conduct "falls below standards, to which common feelings respond, for the proper use of governmental power," the determination of the "lawfulness of the Government's conduct must be made—as it is on all questions involving the legality of law enforcement methods—by the trial judge, not the jury."

Model Penal Code
(Official Draft 1962)

Section 2.13. Entrapment

(1) A public law enforcement official or a person acting in cooperation with such an official perpetrates an entrapment if for the purpose of obtaining evidence of the commission of an offense, he induces or encourages another person to engage in conduct constituting such offense by either:

(a) making knowingly false representations designed to induce the belief that such conduct is not prohibited; or

(b) employing methods of persuasion or inducement which create a substantial risk that such an offense will be committed by persons other than those who are ready to commit it.

(2) Except as provided in Subsection (3) of this Section, a person prosecuted for an offense shall be acquitted if he proves by a preponderance of evidence that

his conduct occurred in response to an entrapment. The issue of entrapment shall be tried by the Court in the absence of the jury.

(3) The defense afforded by this Section is unavailable when causing or threatening bodily injury is an element of the offense charged and the prosecution is based on conduct causing or threatening such injury to a person other than the person perpetrating the entrapment.

● OVERVIEW OF ENTRAPMENT

Hypothetical: JJ's Out (#116)

Waldoro Williams, known as "JJ," has a string of arrests and convictions for various drug offenses. Recently out of prison, he is anxious to get back into the drug business because the money is so good. He decides to work for another dealer while he reestablishes his connections.

Garrett, an undercover narcotics agent, hears about JJ and works out a plan to catch him dealing. He approaches JJ and, after some preliminary conversation, asks him if he wants a job. JJ replies, "Sounds good, but I don't even know you. How do I know you're not a cop?" Garrett assures JJ that he is not a cop and invites him to a party the following evening. For the party, Garrett hires JJ's ex-girlfriend, a prostitute, who left JJ after his last arrest. Garrett hopes that the party and the ex-girlfriend will remind JJ of the "good life" and that he will then be willing to take the risk of working with Garrett. On instructions from Garrett, JJ's ex-girlfriend has intercourse with JJ and tells him that if he starts working for Garrett, they can get back together again. At the end of the night, JJ agrees to work for Garrett.

Garrett arranges for JJ to deliver eight ounces of cocaine the following day. At the delivery point, JJ is arrested by narcotics officers and charged with possession of cocaine with intent to distribute. He offers an entrapment defense.[1] Will he get it?

Notes

Objective Formulations Focus on Police (Mis)conduct
Subjective Formulations Ask If Actor Was "Predisposed" to Commit Offense
    Evidence Supporting Finding of Predisposition
    Where Evidence of Predisposition Is Held Insufficient
Supreme Court Adopts Subjective Federal Defense, Despite Criticism
Separate "Due Process" Defense for Police Misconduct
Entrapment as Nonexculpatory Defense, Rather Than Excuse
    Subjective Entrapment Falls Short of Excusing Condition
    Lack of Defense for Private Inducements Confirms NonexCulpatory Nature
Defense May Be Unavailable for Some Offenses
Summary of Rationales For Entrapment Defense

---

1. This hypothetical is a variation on the facts of *State v. Taylor*, 599 P.2d 496 (Utah 1979).

Where a police officer or agent has some hand in leading an actor to commit an offense, the actor may claim an entrapment defense.[2] The United States is one of the few countries in the world that recognizes such a defense, and within the United States, jurisdictions disagree over how the defense should be formulated. The disagreement largely concerns how much the defense should focus on the *police conduct*, as opposed to focusing on the entrapping conduct's *effect on the defendant*. The first view supports what are known as *objective* formulations of the defense, while the second supports *subjective* formulations. Which focus is preferable may depend on what we seek to achieve in recognizing an entrapment defense.

Objective Formulations Focus on Police (Mis)conduct Objective formulations of the entrapment defense focus on the impropriety of the police conduct. The Model Penal Code, for example, defines entrapping conduct as police conduct that "creates a substantial risk that such an offense will be committed by persons other than those who are ready to commit it."[3] The defense does not require that the *defendant* actually be a person "other than those ready to commit it." Regardless of the defendant's pre-existing willingness to commit the offense, the defense is available if the police conduct is such that it might cause an offense by someone who is not "ready to commit it." Indeed, the Code does not even require (as some codes do) that the defendant actually be "induced" by the police conduct, but only that the defendant's offense be "in response to" the police conduct.[4] Thus, even if the entrapping police conduct did not cause or induce the defendant to commit the offense, he would have a defense under the Model Penal Code if the police conduct is judged to be improper. Under this formulation, in the "JJ's Out" hypothetical, JJ may be able to claim that the defense should be given because the police conduct in holding the party with the ex-girlfriend was improper inducement, even though JJ was already eager to get back into the drug business.

Subjective Formulations Ask If Actor Was "Predisposed" to Commit Offense Subjective formulations of the entrapment defense focus on the degree to which the entrapping conduct, rather than the actor's own choice, is responsible for the actor committing the offense. The Delaware statute, for example, permits an entrapment defense only if the defendant is "induced" to commit an offense that *he*—this defendant in particular—"is not otherwise disposed" to commit.[5] Under this formulation, the defense is given "because the wrongdoing of the officer originates the idea of the crime and then induces the other person to [commit the offense] when the other person is not otherwise disposed to do so."[6] In other words, the subjective formulation is centrally concerned with the defendant's own (lack of) predisposition to commit the crime: Unless the police conduct, rather than the defendant's own predisposition toward crime, caused the offense, no defense is available. In the "JJ's Out" hypothetical, JJ is not likely to have a defense under this formulation, as he was willing, indeed seeking, to commit the offense even before the police efforts to encourage him.

---

2. See authorities collected at 2 Paul H. Robinson, Criminal Law Defenses § 209 n.1 (1984).
3. Model Penal Code § 2.13(1)(b).
4. Model Penal Code § 2.13(2).
5. Del. Code Ann. tit. 11, § 432.
6. Id.

Evidence Supporting Finding of Predisposition　Evidence of predisposition, for purposes of a subjective entrapment defense, is not necessarily limited to the defendant's conduct *prior* to the entrapping conduct. In *Harrison v. State*, for example, the defendant, a prison guard, agrees to smuggle marijuana to a prisoner (who, it turns out, is acting as an agent for the police).[7] The defendant had never smuggled drugs into prison before, and would not have done so on this occasion but for the inducement of the police, yet she is denied an entrapment defense. The court explains that even without any prior acts showing predisposition, the defendant's response to the police inducement may itself offer highly relevant evidence of the defendant's predisposition to commit the offense. In *Harrison*, the defendant took an active role in planning the smuggling once she was approached, then failed to seize any of several opportunities to withdraw, and committed two offenses one month apart.

Where Evidence of Predisposition Is Held Insufficient　In contrast, in *Jacobson v. United States*, the evidence of predisposition was found legally insufficient, and the defense was granted. The defendant in *Jacobson* mail-ordered from a bookstore two magazines depicting naked children, at a time when it was lawful to do so.[8] Subsequent federal legislation made it illegal to obtain by mail sexually explicit depictions of children. Federal agents found Jacobson's name on the bookstore mailing list and then, acting through several fictitious organizations, tried to induce him to order more of the (now illegal) magazines. For two and a half years, the government sent Jacobson various catalogs offering child pornography, as well as correspondence decrying censorship and calling for lobbying to prevent it. Finally Jacobson ordered a magazine from one of the catalogs—and was arrested upon its delivery. A search of his home revealed no relevant materials other than the original, legally purchased magazines and the material sent to him by the government. The Supreme Court reversed Jacobson's conviction, holding that no reasonable jury could find beyond a reasonable doubt that Jacobson was predisposed to commit the offense.

Supreme Court Adopts Subjective Federal Defense, Despite Criticism　The United States Supreme Court cases formulating the federal entrapment defense—there is no federal entrapment statute—reveal debate about the merits of the objective and the subjective formulations. In *Sorrells v. United States*, the Supreme Court adopted the subjective view that the entrapment defense is intended to prevent conviction of "otherwise innocent" individuals who have been lured into crimes they had no predisposition to commit.[9] The opinion "left no doubt that the gravamen of the defense of entrapment was not the propriety of the conduct of the government agents but rather the subjective guilt of the defendant, that is, his predisposition to commit the offense."[10] A long line of cases have upheld this characterization of the defense. On the other hand, an equally long line of concurrences and dissents, beginning with the concurrence of Justice Roberts in *Sorrells*, have opposed this view. Justice Roberts argued that the basis of the entrapment defense is a concern about the system's integrity being sullied by allowing improper police conduct to procure convictions. Under this rationale, the defen-

---

7. 442 A.2d 1377, 1379–80 (Del. 1982).
8. 503 U.S. 540 (1992).
9. 287 U.S. 435, 442 (1932).
10. S. Rep. No. 95–605, Part I, 95th Cong., 1st Sess. 111 (1977) (federal).

dant's predisposition is immaterial; the only relevant question is the degree to which the police have overstepped the bounds of appropriate behavior.[11]

Separate "Due Process" Defense for Police Misconduct Authority also exists for a "due process" defense, independent of the entrapment defense, for cases involving improper police behavior.[12] Based as it is on constitutional grounds, it supplements whatever statutory entrapment defense a state's legislature may have adopted. The due process defense arises from a belief that, as the *Sorrells* dissent claims, allowing police misconduct to support a conviction offends both the dignity of the courts and the rights of the defendant. The test for a due process violation differs from the entrapment standard, as it does not ask whether the police conduct induced this defendant, or even whether it would have induced an innocent person, as all but the most objective formulations of entrapment require. Rather, a due process claim arises if the police conduct offends "the canons of fundamental fairness, shocking to the universal sense of justice."[13] The availability of a due process claim is most relevant in jurisdictions adopting a subjective formulation of entrapment, because such a formulation gives no defense for improper police conduct if the defendant is predisposed, no matter how shocking the police conduct may be. On the other hand, the vast majority of police conduct satisfying the due process test would likely support an objectively defined entrapment defense also, so the due process claim would be less significant, or even superfluous, in jurisdictions with an objective formulation.

Entrapment as Nonexculpatory Defense, Rather Than Excuse Objective formulations of the entrapment defense, as well as the possible due process claim for police misconduct, clearly provide nonexculpatory defenses; they exist not as a reflection of the defendant's lack of blameworthiness, but as a means of deterring improper police conduct. A subjective ("predisposition") formulation might appear, in contrast, to be an excuse, similar to duress that exculpates the defendant because he or she is coerced to commit an offense. More careful analysis, however, suggests that such a characterization is unfounded. The subjective formulation of the entrapment defense does not satisfy the traditional requirements for an excuse. The "inducement" in entrapment may be analogous to the coercion that supports a duress defense. But a duress defense requires more than the existence of coercion, just as an insanity defense requires more than the existence of mental illness. The actor merits an excuse only if the relevant disability is sufficiently strong in its effect that one could not reasonably have expected the actor to have

11. See Sorrells v. United States, 287 U.S. 435, 458 (1932) (Roberts, J., concurring) ("Whatever may be the demerits of the defendant or his previous infractions of law these will not justify the instigation and creation of a new crime, as a means to reach him and punish him for his past misdemeanors"); Sherman v. United States, 356 U.S. 369, 380 (1958) (Frankfurter, J., concurring) ("The courts refuse to convict an entrapped defendant, not because his conduct falls outside the proscription of the statute, but because . . . the methods employed on behalf of the government to bring about conviction cannot be countenanced.").

12. See, e.g., Hampton v. United States, 425 U.S. 484, 491 (1976) (Powell, J., concurring) (holding open possibility of such a defense); United States v. Twigg, 588 F.2d 373 (3d Cir. 1978) (due process rights of defendant violated when government involvement in manufacture of methamphetamine was indispensable element in commission of crime). But cf. United States v. Russell, 411 U.S. 423 (1976) (undercover agents' participation in manufacturing of methamphetamine did not violate due process rights of defendant).

13. Russell, 411 U.S. at 432, quoting Kinsella v. United States ex rel. Singleton, 361 U.S. 234, 246 (1960).

avoided the violation. In the context of duress, an excuse is permitted only if the coercion was such that "a person of reasonable firmness would have been unable to resist." In the context of insanity and involuntary intoxication, those disabilities could be the "but for" cause of an offense and yet still not provide a defense. The disability—the actor's mental illness or involuntary intoxication, or the coercion—must not only contribute to the offense, it must be sufficiently strong in its effect to render the actor blameless for the offense conduct.

Subjective Entrapment Falls Short of Excusing Condition For insanity, recall, courts have rejected the *Durham* "product" test, under which the offense must only be the "product" of the actor's mental disease or defect. The subjective formulation of entrapment essentially imposes a similar "product" test: At most, it requires a showing that the actor would not have committed the offense *but for* the officer's inducement. A but-for causal connection between a disability and the offense is insufficient to render the actor blameless for the offense in other excuse contexts, and there is no reason judgments of blameworthiness should differ in this context.

Lack of Defense for Private Inducements Confirms Nonexculpatory Nature If the subjective formulation represented a true excuse, based on the pressure brought to bear on the defendant, there would be no reason to limit the defense to cases of inducement by government agents. Equal inducement from a private citizen should render the defendant equally blameless, so private entrapment logically should be recognized as an excuse also. Yet private entrapment is not a recognized defense. In *United States v. Perl*,[14] for example, defendant Dr. Perl was induced by a private citizen to commit minor acts of terrorism to help the plight of Soviet Jews. After the inducement, the private citizen turned Dr. Perl in to the police. The court denied an entrapment defense, reasoning that Dr. Perl may well have been induced to commit the offense, but forgoing his conviction would do nothing toward deterring improper police conduct. One must conclude that the subjective formulation of entrapment, like the objective formulation, is centrally oriented toward regulating law enforcement, not adjudicating an offender's blameworthiness for the offense. The subjective formulation merely makes a different tradeoff between the competing goals of punishing the guilty and deterring police misconduct, promoting relatively more offender punishment and less police deterrence than the objective formulation.

Defense May Be Unavailable for Some Offenses In keeping with the defense's nonexculpatory basis, its scope is often limited, as by prohibiting the defense for certain serious offenses. The Model Penal Code, for example, makes its entrapment defense "unavailable" for offenses in which "causing or threatening bodily injury is an element."[15] In attempting to deter improper police conduct, it is reasonable for a jurisdiction to conclude that acquitting violent offenders is too high a price to pay for deterrence of improper police entrapment. Of course,

---

14. 584 F.2d 1316 (4th Cir. 1978).
15. Model Penal Code § 2.13(3).
   It will not seem generally unfair to punish someone who has caused or threatened bodily injury to another, even though he was induced to his action by law enforcement officials. It is unlikely that a law-abiding person could be persuaded by any tactics to engage in such behavior, and a person who can be persuaded to cause such injury presents a danger that the public cannot safely disregard.
   Model Penal Code § 2.13 comment at 420 (1985).

a jurisdiction might also reasonably decide to allow the defense in such cases, concluding that the official misconduct is also especially gross when the police are inducing others to commit violent crimes.

Summary of Rationales for Entrapment Defense To summarize, some reduced blameworthiness may be present where an actor is induced to commit an offense, at least where the actor is not otherwise predisposed to do so. But such inducement alone, without a showing that the actor could not reasonably have been expected to have avoided the violation, is insufficient to support an excuse. Nor does the reduced blameworthiness rationale for the entrapment defense explain why only police officers or agents can trigger the defense. In reality, the primary reasons for the defense are nonexculpatory interests of deterrence and estoppel: Deterring improper police inducement, and avoiding the apparent unfairness of allowing the government to induce an offense and then prosecute it. Given the nonexculpatory status of an entrapment defense, it seems most appropriate that the judge determine the defense before trial, rather than a jury at trial, as some statutes provide.[16] Certainly a "not guilty" verdict for entrapment is misleading to the extent that it suggests that the defendant has either engaged in no wrongdoing or is blameless for his wrongdoing.

United States v. Russell
Supreme Court of the United States
411 U.S. 423 (1973)

Mr. Justice REHNQUIST delivered the opinion of the Court.

[The respondent Richard Russell was convicted, along with co-defendants John and Patrick Connolly, of unlawfully manufacturing and processing methamphetamine. Russell's sole defense was one of entrapment. The undisputed facts indicated that Russell and the Connolly brothers were already involved in the manufacturing of methamphetamine when they were approached by an undercover federal narcotics agent, Joe Shapiro, posing as a representative of a West Coast crime syndicate. Shapiro offered to provide an essential and difficult to obtain chemical necessary for the production of methamphetamine in exchange for one half of the profits from the Connollys' operation. The offer was conditioned on viewing the existing laboratory and receiving a sample of their methamphetamine. After the defendants complied with both requests, Shapiro provided the defendants with the necessary chemical. He later observed the preparation of two batches of methamphetamine made with the chemical he had provided and received a sample of the finished product. The defendants were arrested a month later after Shapiro had confirmed their desire to continue the "arrangement."

Russell was convicted after a jury trial, but the conviction was overturned by the United States Court of Appeals for the Ninth Circuit.]

At the close of the evidence, and after receiving the District Judge's standard entrapment instruction, the jury found the respondent guilty on all counts charged. On appeal, the respondent conceded that the jury could have found

---

16. See Model Penal Code § 2.13(2); cf. U.S. v. Russell, 411 U.S. 423 (1976) (reversing Ninth Circuit's decision to overturn jury finding of no entrapment).

him predisposed to commit the offenses, but argued that on the facts presented there was entrapment as a matter of law. The Court of Appeals agreed, although it did not find the District Court had misconstrued or misapplied the traditional standards governing the entrapment defense. Rather, the court in effect expanded the traditional notion of entrapment, which focuses on the predisposition of the defendant, to mandate dismissal of a criminal prosecution whenever the court determines that there has been "an intolerable degree of governmental participation in the criminal enterprise." In this case the court decided that the conduct of the agent in supplying a scarce ingredient essential for the manufacture of a controlled substance established that defense.

This new defense was held to rest on either of two alternative theories. One theory is based on two lower court decisions which have found entrapment, regardless of predisposition, whenever the government supplies contraband to the defendants. The second theory, a nonentrapment rationale, is based on a recent Ninth Circuit decision that reversed a conviction because a government investigator was so enmeshed in the criminal activity that the prosecution of the defendants was held to be repugnant to the American criminal justice system. The court below held that these two rationales constitute the same defense, and that only the label distinguishes them. In any event, it held that "(b)oth theories are premised on fundamental concepts of due process and evince the reluctance of the judiciary to countenance 'overzealous law enforcement.'"

This Court first recognized and applied the entrapment defense in Sorrells v. United States, 287 U.S. 435 (1932). In *Sorrells*, a federal prohibition agent visited the defendant while posing as a tourist and engaged him in conversation about their common war experiences. After gaining the defendant's confidence, the agent asked for some liquor, was twice refused, but upon asking a third time the defendant finally capitulated, and was subsequently prosecuted for violating the National Prohibition Act.

Mr. Chief Justice Hughes, speaking for the Court, held that as a matter of statutory construction the defense of entrapment should have been available to the defendant. Under the theory propounded by the Chief Justice, the entrapment defense prohibits law enforcement officers from instigating a criminal act by persons "otherwise innocent in order to lure them to its commission and to punish them." Thus, the thrust of the entrapment defense was held to focus on the intent or predisposition of the defendant to commit the crime. "(I)f the defendant seeks acquittal by reason of entrapment he cannot complain of an appropriate and searching inquiry into his own conduct and predisposition as bearing upon that issue."

Mr. Justice Roberts concurred but was of the view "that courts must be closed to the trial of a crime instigated by the government's own agents." The difference in the view of the majority and the concurring opinions is that in the former the inquiry focuses on the predisposition of the defendant, whereas in the latter the inquiry focuses on whether the government "instigated the crime." . . .

In the instant case, respondent asks us to reconsider the theory of the entrapment defense as it is set forth in the majority opinions in *Sorrells* and *Sherman*. His principal contention is that the defense should rest on constitutional grounds. He argues that the level of Shapiro's involvement in the manufacture of the methamphetamine was so high that a criminal prosecution for the drug's manufacture violates the fundamental principles of due process. The respondent contends that the same factors that led this Court to apply the exclusionary rule to illegal searches and seizures, and confessions, should be considered here. But he would have the Court go further in deterring undesirable official conduct by requiring that any prosecution be barred absolutely because of the police involvement in criminal activity. The analogy is imperfect in any event, for the principal reason behind the adoption of the exclusionary rule was the Government's "failure to observe its own laws." Mapp v. Ohio, supra, 367 U.S., at 659. Unlike the situations giving rise to the holdings in *Mapp* and *Miranda*, the Government's conduct here violated no independent constitutional right of the respondent. Nor did Shapiro violate any federal statute or rule or commit any crime in infiltrating the respondent's drug enterprise.

Respondent would overcome this basic weakness in his analogy to the exclusionary rule cases by having the Court adopt a rigid constitutional rule that would preclude any prosecution when it is shown that the criminal conduct would not have been possible had not an undercover agent "supplied an indispensable means to the commission of the crime that could not have been obtained otherwise, through legal or illegal channels." Even if we were to surmount the difficulties attending the notion that due process of law can be embodied in fixed rules, and those attending respondent's particular formulation, the rule he proposes would not appear to be of significant benefit to him. For, on the record presented, it appears that he cannot fit within the terms of the very rule he proposes.

The record discloses that although the propanone was difficult to obtain, it was by no means impossible. The defendants admitted making the drug both before and after those batches made with the propanone supplied by Shapiro. Shapiro testified that he saw an empty bottle labeled phenyl-2-propanone on his first visit to the laboratory on December 7, 1969. And when the laboratory was searched pursuant to a search warrant on January 10, 1970, two additional bottles labeled phenyl-2-propanone were seized. Thus, the facts in the record amply demonstrate that the propanone used in the illicit manufacture of methamphetamine not only could have been obtained without the intervention of Shapiro but was in fact obtained by these defendants.

While we may some day be presented with a situation in which the conduct of law enforcement agents is so outrageous that due process principles would absolutely bar the government from invoking judicial processes to obtain a conviction, the instant case is distinctly not of that breed. Shapiro's contribution of propanone to the criminal enterprise already in process was scarcely objectionable. The chemical is by itself a harmless substance and its possession is legal. While the Government may have been seeking to make it more difficult for drug rings, such as that of which respondent was a member, to obtain the chemical, the evidence described above shows that it nonetheless was obtainable. The law enforcement conduct here stops far short of violating that "fundamental fairness, shocking to the universal sense of justice," mandated by the Due Process Clause of the Fifth Amendment.

The illicit manufacture of drugs is not a sporadic, isolated criminal incident, but a continuing, though illegal, business enterprise. In order to obtain convictions for illegally manufacturing drugs, the gathering of evidence of past unlawful conduct frequently proves to be an all but impossible task. Thus in drug-related offenses law enforcement personnel have turned to one of the only practicable means of detection: the infiltration of drug rings and a limited participation in their unlawful present practices. Such infiltration is a recognized and permissible means of investigation; if that be so, then the supply of some item of value that the drug ring requires must, as a general rule, also be permissible. For an agent will not be taken into the confidence of the illegal entrepreneurs unless he has something of value to offer them. Law enforcement tactics such as this can hardly be said to violate "fundamental fairness" or "shocking to the universal sense of justice."

Respondent also urges, as an alternative to his constitutional argument, that we broaden the nonconstitutional defense of entrapment in order to sustain the judgment of the Court of Appeals. This Court's opinions in Sorrells v. United States, supra, and Sherman v. United States, supra, held that the principal element in the defense of entrapment was the defendant's predisposition to commit the crime. Respondent conceded in the Court of Appeals, as well he might, "that he may have harbored a predisposition to commit the charged offenses." Yet he argues that the jury's refusal to find entrapment under the charge submitted to it by the trial court should be overturned and the views of Justices Roberts and Frankfurter, in *Sorrells* and *Sherman*, respectively, which make the essential element of the defense turn on the type and degree of governmental conduct, be adopted as the law.

We decline to overrule these cases. *Sorrells* is a precedent of long standing that has already been once reexamined in *Sherman* and implicitly there reaffirmed. Since the defense is not of a constitutional dimension, Congress may address itself to the question and adopt any substantive definition of the defense that it may find desirable. . . .

Several decisions of the United States district courts and courts of appeals have undoubtedly gone beyond this Court's opinions in *Sorrells* and *Sherman* in order to bar prosecutions because of what they thought to be, for want of a better term, "overzealous law enforcement." But the defense of entrapment enunciated in those opinions was not intended to give the federal judiciary a "chancellor's foot" veto over law enforcement practices of which it did not approve. The execution of the federal laws under our Constitution is confided primarily to the Executive Branch of the Government, subject to applicable constitutional and statutory limitations and to judicially fashioned rules to enforce those limitations. We think that the decision of the Court of Appeals in this case quite unnecessarily introduces an unmanageably subjective standard which is contrary to the holdings of this Court in *Sorrells* and *Sherman*.

Those cases establish that entrapment is a relatively limited defense. It is rooted, not in any authority of the Judicial Branch to dismiss prosecutions for what it feels to have been "overzealous law enforcement," but instead in the notion that Congress could not have intended criminal punishment for a defendant who has committed all the elements of a proscribed offense but was induced to commit them by the Government.

Sorrells and *Sherman* both recognize "that the fact that officers or employees of the Government merely afford opportunities or facilities for the commission of the offense does not defeat the prosecution." Nor will the mere fact of deceit defeat a prosecution, for there are circumstances when the use of deceit is the only practicable law enforcement technique available. It is only when the Government's deception actually implants the criminal design in the mind of the defendant that the defense of entrapment comes into play.

Respondent's concession in the Court of Appeals that the jury finding as to predisposition was supported by the evidence is, therefore, fatal to his claim of entrapment. He was an active participant in an illegal drug manufacturing enterprise which began before the Government agent appeared on the scene, and continued after the Government agent had left the scene. He was, in the words of *Sherman*, supra, not an "unwary innocent" but an "unwary criminal." The Court of Appeals was wrong, we believe, when it sought to broaden the principle laid down in *Sorrells* and *Sherman*. Its judgment is therefore

Reversed.

[Justices DOUGLAS, BRENNAN, STEWART, and MARSHALL dissented.]

▲ PROBLEMS

A Pickpocket Sting (#117)

Crime has become a major problem in the downtown area of Reno, which many people now avoid for fear of being robbed. Statistics for the last two months indicate that the bulk of the cases are "crimes of convenience," where the perpetrators do not plan the crimes in advance but seize an opportunity for an easy score when it presents itself. The perpetrators are typically young men in their late teens or twenties. The victims are generally tourists, most of them female, elderly, or disabled. Responding to complaints from local businesses, who are feeling the economic sting of fewer tourists and residents venturing to their stores, the police increase uniformed squad car and foot patrols, as well as plainclothes officers downtown. However, despite these responses, crime continues to increase. Frustrated by the failures, the police and district attorney's office decide to put in place a decoy operation that will focus on the high-risk areas and the profiled offenders.

Officer Roger Linscott serves as the decoy. He plays the part of a defenseless elderly man lying intoxicated in a building alcove near First and Center Streets. His dress and demeanor are intended to give the appearance of a tourist who has passed out after drinking too much. Linscott faces away from pedestrian traffic and is unresponsive to passing pedestrians. Sticking out of his right-rear pants pocket are the edges of some U.S. currency, a total of $126, but Linscott is positioned so that he can move slightly to make the money obvious or keep it out of sight. During the hour and a half that Linscott lies on the sidewalk, a number of people pass by. Linscott does not expose the bait money to everyone. It is Officer Linda Peters' job to keep constant visual contact from the third floor of the parking garage across the street and to alert Linscott when passersby fit the profile offender.

David Kenney Hawkins, 28, and a friend fit the profile, so Linscott leaves the bait exposed as the pair approach. They appear to notice the intoxicated "tourist" but do not stop. They enter the saloon, stay for about 45 minutes, then leave.

As they approach Linscott the second time, they stop and inspect him. Hawkins' friend jumps up and down on the ground and yells to see if the prone man is passed out. Linscott does not move. Hawkins takes a few more moments to look the man over and then bends down and slowly removes the money from the decoy's right-rear pocket. Without searching any other pockets, Hawkins and his friend continue walking and cross the street. Hawkins is immediately arrested.

What liability for Hawkins, if any, under the Model Penal Code? Prepare a list of all criminal code subsections in the order in which you rely on them in your analysis.

Would the liability be different under the federal rules described in the Law Section after the DeLorean narrative?

Government as Pornographer (#118)

Keith Jacobson is a 56-year old farmer who lives with his elderly father on an 80-acre farm in a town of 800 people. He drives a school bus and grows corn and soybeans to support himself and his father. A Korean War veteran, Jacobson attends church and is well liked in his community. Jacobson also has a hidden secret: He enjoys child pornography. Jacobson comes to the attention of the Postal Inspection Service for ordering two child porn magazines, titled Bare Boys I and Bare Boys II. The magazines consist almost entirely of photographs of nude pre-teen and teenage boys in various poses, some of which focused on the boys' genitalia. These magazines were legal at the time Jacobson ordered them; however, later that month, Congress changed the law and passed an act criminalizing the receipt through the mails of sexually explicit depictions of children.

The next year, based on Jacobson's previous purchases, a postal inspector sends him a letter from a fictitious organization called the American Hedonist Society (AHS), as well as a membership application that includes a survey of sexual attitudes. Jacobson returns the survey one month later, ranking "pre-teen sex" as something he enjoys. He also applies for membership in AHS and remits the $4 membership fee. The following year a new "prohibited mail specialist" finds Jacobson's name in a file and sends him a letter from a second fictitious company, Midlands Data Research (MDR). It offers Jacobson an opportunity to share with others of similar interest his pleasures with viewing underage sex. Jacobson replies, asking for more information, and states his interest in teenage sexuality. Two months later, the postal inspector sends Jacobson a letter and a survey from the Heartland Institute for a New Tomorrow (HINT), a third fictitious organization, describing itself as an organization "founded to protect and promote sexual freedom and freedom of choice." HINT seeks to "eliminate any legal definition of the 'age of consent'" and "to repeal all statutes which regulate sexual activities, except . . . rape." Jacobson returns the letter and the survey, indicating an interest in "pre-teen sex—homosexual." The postal inspector, posing as HINT, then sends Jacobson a list of names and addresses of potential "pen pals" with similar backgrounds and interests. When Jacobson does not initiate any correspondence, the postal inspector poses as one of the people from the list and begins discussing child porn with Jacobson.

A few months later, Jacobson is sent yet another fictitious letter, this time prepared by the Customs Service. The brochure, from a fictitious Canadian company called Produit Outaouais, advertises photograph sets of "young boys in sex action fun." Jacobson orders a photo set, which is never delivered. That same month, the Far Eastern Trading Company Limited, another front for the Postal Inspection Service's undercover operation, sends Jacobson a letter and a catalog of child porn videos and magazines. Jacobson orders a magazine called Boys Who Love Boys. A month later, Jacobson is arrested when the magazine is delivered. When authorities search his home after the arrest, the only items found in Jacobson's home are Bare Boys I and II, the brochure from which he ordered the Bare Boys magazines, the Far Eastern catalog, and the Produit Outaouais brochure.

Assume the Model Penal Code criminalizes the purchase of pornography, including magazines like those at issue here. What liability for Jacobson, if any, under the Code?

Would the liability be different under the federal rules described in the Law Section after the DeLorean narrative?

Undercover Trolling at an AA Meeting (#119)

At age 15, Amy Lively finds out that she is pregnant and decides to give up her cocaine habit. She had begun drinking alcohol and using cocaine the previous year but never sold any drugs, and she now wants to start a new life with her new family. By age 18, Amy has two children and a husband who is stationed in Korea. She does not take up cocaine again after her pregnancy but has difficulty escaping her heavy drinking. She checks into a detoxification program and begins attending Alcoholics Anonymous/Narcotics Anonymous (AA/NA) meetings. She suffers one relapse but then checks back into a detoxification program and continues her AA/NA meetings.

At one of her AA/NA meetings, Lively meets Kamlesh "Koby" Desai. Desai is an undercover police informant who attends the meetings with the approval and supervision of drug enforcement detectives in the hopes of identifying repeat addicts who might continue to sell drugs. Two weeks after their first meeting, Desai asks Lively out on a date. He is very responsive to her emotions and supportive of Lively as she struggles with fighting her addiction. Their relationship becomes intimate, and Desai asks her to divorce her husband stationed in Korea and to marry him. They move in together over the summer, and Lively becomes emotionally reliant on Desai during that time.

When Lively mentions in conversation that she knows a person who sells marijuana and cocaine, Desai asks if a good friend of his could purchase some cocaine through her. She initially refuses, but after two weeks of repeated requests from Desai, she finally agrees. Desai sets up the deal with one of the detectives, who arrests Lively when she sells him 1.3 grams of cocaine.

Assume the Model Penal Code criminalizes Lively's sale of cocaine. What liability for Lively, if any, under the Code?

Would the liability be different under the federal rules described in the Law Section after the DeLorean narrative?

✳ DISCUSSION ISSUE

Should the Criminal Law Recognize an Entrapment Defense?

Materials presenting each side of this Discussion Issue appear in the Advanced Materials for Section 24 in Appendix A.

DISCUSSION ISSUE

PART VII

CHANGING PATTERNS OF CRIMINALITY

Changing social norms and political and economic shifts have brought waves of criminal law reform to many areas. The materials in this Part focus on four of the most active areas. Sexual offense reforms, the subject of Section 25, reflect changing norms but also considering evolving norms further. The new formulations are calculated to make people think differently about what is and is not acceptable conduct. Hate crimes, the subject of Section 26, reflect both an increased sensitivity to the dangers of bigotry and an attempt to create a still greater public awareness of those dangers. Section 27 examines whether and how criminal liability should be imposed on nonhuman entities, like corporations. If criminal law's unique brand involves moral condemnation, how can that apply to a legal fiction? Finally, Section 28 focuses on the growing area of criminality on the Internet and through computers. Technological advances have not only created new ways for people to commit old wrongs, such as taking another's property, but they also create new wrongs, and even new issues, such as what counts as "property."

Rape

◆ THE CASE OF ERIC STEVEN CARLSON (#120)

It is January 2000 in Grand Haven, Michigan, a small community on the edge of Lake Michigan. Eric Carlson is an eleventh-grader who is about to turn 17 years old. He has asked one of the girls in his class, "Jane," who is 17, if she wants to go for a ride with him. Although they have attended the same school for two years, Carlson only knows her through their mutual friend, "Amy," whom he dated a few times several months ago.

Jane considers Carlson an acquaintance and is familiar with him only through Amy. Jane also knows that Amy was upset after she last went out with Carlson. Amy says he would not take "no" for an answer and raped her. Jane nonetheless agrees to go out with him.

Carlson picks her up in the afternoon and they drive to the parking lot of Meijer—a large grocery store. They sit for awhile in the front bucket seats talking and writing notes to each other. Things eventually escalate sexually and they begin kissing and groping one another. Consensually, he digitally penetrates her,

Figure 118 **Lot where Carlson and Jane parked and groped**

and she manually masturbates him. She describes it later as having "made out and stuff."

On January 23, about two weeks later, Carlson calls her "to hang out" again. She agrees and he picks her up. She is wearing jeans and a long-sleeve shirt. They drive around a little before ending up in the YMCA parking lot. They quickly resume the activities as before, kissing "and stuff." Jane allows Carlson to unbutton her jeans and to digitally penetrate her. Carlson then tells her that he wants to have intercourse. She says no. He asks her why not, and she says that she does not want to. (She has had sex before, in her last relationship, in August.)

Now completely undressed, they continue groping one another. Carlson continues asking if she wants to have sex; he even asks to just stick his penis in once. She eventually tires of his asking and just stops answering. He leans over her, but she does not react. He then climbs on top of her and penetrates her. He asks whether she is enjoying it; she again tells him that she does not want to "do it," but he continues anyway. She is unsure how to react, but she does not resist physically or push him away. After about five minutes, he stops and they put their clothes on. They stop at a gas station when she asks for a drink. Although she is not interested in talking, there is some forced conversation. He asks if she wants to go home and she replies, "I don't care." He then asks whether she still wants to go out with him. She does not respond.

The next day, she writes Carlson a note, sometimes addressing him in the note by his nickname, "Beeker," and sometimes as "sweetie," as she does with most people. Handing it to him personally, the note explains that she does not want a relationship and asks whether this will make him mad. She also writes that he owes her a note in response.

The same day she tells Amy what happened. Amy says that it was rape and again alleges that Carlson raped her. When Jane remembers that Carlson was

Figure 119 **Grand Haven High School**

not wearing a condom, she becomes worried about being pregnant or having contracted a sexually transmitted disease.

She subsequently talks to the school counselor about the incident, who has her report it to the Ottawa County Sheriff's Department. Deputy Sarah Flick interviews Jane and three other students who claim that Carlson also sexually assaulted them. On February 9, Flick interviews Carlson. With his attorney, Philip Sielski present, Carlson voluntarily surrenders himself to the authorities on March 10.

1. Relying only on your own intuitions of justice, what liability and punishment, if any, does Eric Carlson deserve, based on the incident with Jane?

N	0	1	2	3	4	5	6	7	8	9	10	11
☐	☐	☐	☐	☐	☐	☐	☐	☐	☐	☐	☐	☐
no liability	liability but no punishment	1 day	2 wks	2 mo	6 mo	1 yr	3 yrs	7 yrs	15 yrs	30 yrs	life imprison-ment	death

2. What "justice" arguments could defense counsel make on the defendant's behalf?

3. What "justice" arguments could the prosecution make against the defendant?

4. What liability for Carlson, if any, under the then-existing statutes? Prepare a list of all criminal code subsections and cases in the order in which you rely on them in your analysis.

5. What liability, if any, under the Model Penal Code? Prepare a list of all criminal code subsections in the order in which you rely on them in your analysis.

▪ THE LAW

Michigan Statutes Annotated
(2000)

Title 28. Crimes

Part Two. Substantive Criminal Law
Chapter 286a. Penal Code

Chapter LXXVI. Criminal Sexual Conduct

Section 520a. Definitions

As used in sections 520a to 520-l:

(a) "Actor" means a person accused of criminal sexual conduct. . . .

(c) "Intimate parts" includes the primary genital area, groin, inner thigh, buttock, or breast of a human being. . . .

(i) "Physically helpless" means that a person is unconscious, asleep, or for any other reason is physically unable to communicate unwillingness to an act.

(j) "Personal injury" means bodily injury, disfigurement, mental anguish, chronic pain, pregnancy, disease, or loss or impairment of a sexual or reproductive organ.

(k) "Sexual contact" includes the intentional touching of the victim's or actor's intimate parts or the intentional touching of the clothing covering the immediate area of the victim's or actor's intimate parts, if that intentional touching can reasonably be construed as being for the purpose of sexual arousal or gratification.

(l) "Sexual penetration" means sexual intercourse, cunnilingus, fellatio, anal intercourse, or any other intrusion, however slight, of any part of a person's body or of any object into the genital or anal openings of another person's body, but emission of semen is not required.

(m) "Victim" means the person alleging to have been subjected to criminal sexual conduct.

Section 520b. Criminal Sexual Conduct in First Degree

(1) A person is guilty of criminal sexual conduct in the first degree if he or she engages in sexual penetration with another person and if any of the following circumstances exists:

(a) That other person is under 13 years of age.

(b) That other person is at least 13 but less than 16 years of age and any of the following:

(i) The actor is a member of the same household as the victim.

(ii) The actor is related to the victim by blood or affinity to the fourth degree.

(iii) The actor is in a position of authority over the victim and used this authority to coerce the victim to submit.

(c) Sexual penetration occurs under circumstances involving the commission of any other felony.

(d) The actor is aided or abetted by 1 or more other persons and either of the following circumstances exists:

(i) The actor knows or has reason to know that the victim is mentally incapable, mentally incapacitated, or physically helpless.

(ii) The actor uses force or coercion to accomplish the sexual penetration. Force or coercion includes but is not limited to any of the circumstances listed in subdivision (f)(i) to (v).

(e) The actor is armed with a weapon or any article used or fashioned in a manner to lead the victim to reasonably believe it to be a weapon.

(f) The actor causes personal injury to the victim and force or coercion is used to accomplish sexual penetration. Force or coercion includes but is not limited to any of the following circumstances:

(i) When the actor overcomes the victim through the actual application of physical force or physical violence.

(ii) When the actor coerces the victim to submit by threatening to use force or violence on the victim, and the victim believes that the actor has the present ability to execute these threats.

(iii) When the actor coerces the victim to submit by threatening to retaliate in the future against the victim, or any other person, and the victim believes that the actor has the ability to execute this threat. As used in this subdivision, "to retaliate" includes threats of physical punishment, kidnapping, or extortion.

(iv) When the actor engages in the medical treatment or examination of the victim in a manner or for purposes which are medically recognized as unethical or unacceptable.

(v) When the actor, through concealment or by the element of surprise, is able to overcome the victim.

(g) The actor causes personal injury to the victim, and the actor knows or has reason to know that the victim is mentally incapable, mentally incapacitated, or physically helpless.

(h) That other person is mentally incapable, mentally disabled, mentally incapacitated, or physically helpless, and any of the following:

(i) The actor is related to the victim by blood or affinity to the fourth degree.

(ii) The actor is in a position of authority over the victim and used this authority to coerce the victim to submit.

(2) Criminal sexual conduct in the first degree is a felony punishable by imprisonment in the state prison for life or for any term of years.

Section 520c. Criminal Sexual Conduct in Second Degree

(1) A person is guilty of criminal sexual conduct in the second degree if the person engages in sexual contact with another person and if any of the following circumstances exists:

(a) That other person is under 13 years of age.

(b) That other person is at least 13 but less than 16 years of age and any of the following:

(i) The actor is a member of the same household as the victim.

(ii) The actor is related by blood or affinity to the fourth degree to the victim.

(iii) The actor is in a position of authority over the victim and the actor used this authority to coerce the victim to submit.

(c) Sexual contact occurs under circumstances involving the commission of any other felony.

(d) The actor is aided or abetted by 1 or more other persons and either of the following circumstances exists:

(i) The actor knows or has reason to know that the victim is mentally incapable, mentally incapacitated, or physically helpless.

(ii) The actor uses force or coercion to accomplish the sexual contact. Force or coercion includes but is not limited to any of the circumstances listed in sections 520b(1)(f)(i) to (v).

(e) The actor is armed with a weapon, or any article used or fashioned in a manner to lead a person to reasonably believe it to be a weapon.

(f) The actor causes personal injury to the victim and force or coercion is used to accomplish the sexual contact. Force or coercion includes but is not limited to any of the circumstances listed in section 520b(1)(f)(i) to (v).

(g) The actor causes personal injury to the victim and the actor knows or has reason to know that the victim is mentally incapable, mentally incapacitated, or physically helpless.

(h) That other person is mentally incapable, mentally disabled, mentally incapacitated, or physically helpless, and any of the following:

(i) The actor is related to the victim by blood or affinity to the fourth degree.

(ii) The actor is in a position of authority over the victim and used this authority to coerce the victim to submit.

(2) Criminal sexual conduct in the second degree is a felony punishable by imprisonment for not more than 15 years.

Section 520d. Criminal Sexual Conduct in the Third Degree; Felony

(1) A person is guilty of criminal sexual conduct in the third degree if the person engages in sexual penetration with another person and if any of the following circumstances exist:

(a) That other person is at least 13 years of age and under 16 years of age.

(b) Force or coercion is used to accomplish the sexual penetration. Force or coercion includes but is not limited to any of the circumstances listed in section 520b(1)(f)(i) to (v).

(c) The actor knows or has reason to know that the victim is mentally incapable, mentally incapacitated, or physically helpless.

(d) That other person is related to the actor by blood or affinity to the third degree and the sexual penetration occurs under circumstances not otherwise prohibited by this chapter. It is an affirmative defense to a prosecution under this subdivision that the other person was in a position of authority over the defendant and used this authority to coerce the defendant to violate this subdivision. The defendant has the burden of proving this defense by a preponderance of the evidence. This subdivision does not apply if both persons are lawfully married to each other at the time of the alleged violation.

(2) Criminal sexual conduct in the third degree is a felony punishable by imprisonment for not more than 15 years.

Section 520e. Criminal Sexual Conduct in the Fourth Degree; Misdemeanor

(1) A person is guilty of criminal sexual conduct in the fourth degree if he or she engages in sexual contact with another person and if any of the following circumstances exist:

(a) That other person is at least 13 years of age and under 16 years of age, and the actor is 5 or more years older than that other person.

(b) Force or coercion is used to accomplish the sexual contact. Force or coercion includes but is not limited to any of the following circumstances:

(i) When the actor overcomes the victim through the actual application of physical force or physical violence.

(ii) When the actor coerces the victim to submit by threatening to use force or violence on the victim, and the victim believes that the actor has the present ability to execute these threats.

(iii) When the actor coerces the victim to submit by threatening to retaliate in the future against the victim, or any other person, and the victim believes that the actor has the ability to execute this threat. As used in this subdivision, "to retaliate" includes threats of physical punishment, kidnapping, or extortion.

(iv) When the actor engages in the medical treatment or examination of the victim in a manner or for purposes which are medically recognized as unethical or unacceptable.

(v) When the actor achieves the sexual contact through concealment or by the element of surprise.

(c) The actor knows or has reason to know that the victim is mentally incapable, mentally incapacitated, or physically helpless.

(d) That other person is under the jurisdiction of the department of corrections and the actor is an employee or a contractual employee of, or a volunteer with, the department of corrections who knows that the other person is under the jurisdiction of the department of corrections.

(e) That other person is a prisoner or probationer under the jurisdiction of a county for purposes of imprisonment or a work program or other probationary program and the actor is an employee or a contractual employee of or a volunteer with the county who knows that the other person is under the county's jurisdiction.

(f) The actor knows or has reason to know that the juvenile division of the probate court, the circuit court, or the recorder's court of the city of Detroit has detained the victim in a facility while the victim is awaiting a trial or hearing, or committed the victim to a facility as a result of the victim having been found responsible for committing an act that would be a crime if committed by an adult, and the actor is an employee or contractual employee of, or a volunteer with, the facility in which the victim is detained or to which the victim was committed.

(g) That other person is related to the actor by blood or affinity to the third degree and the sexual contact occurs under circumstances not otherwise prohibited by this chapter. It is an affirmative defense to a prosecution under this subdivision that the other person was in a position of authority over the defendant and used this authority to coerce the defendant to violate this subdivision. The defendant has the burden of proving this defense by a preponderance of the evidence. This subdivision does not apply if both persons are lawfully married to each other at the time of the alleged violation.

(2) Criminal sexual conduct in the fourth degree is a misdemeanor punishable by imprisonment for not more than 2 years or a fine of not more than $500.00, or both.

Section 520i. Resistance by Victim

A victim need not resist the actor in prosecution under sections 520b to 520g.

Section 520j. Admissibility of Evidence

(1) Evidence of specific instances of the victim's sexual conduct, opinion evidence of the victim's sexual conduct, and reputation evidence of the victim's sexual conduct shall not be admitted under sections 520b to 520g unless and only

to the extent that the judge finds that the following proposed evidence is material to a fact at issue in the case and that its inflammatory or prejudicial nature does not outweigh its probative value:

(a) Evidence of the victim's past sexual conduct with the actor.

(b) Evidence of specific instances of sexual activity showing the source or origin of semen, pregnancy, or disease.

Section 750.81. Assault and Assault and Battery; Domestic Assault

(1) Except as otherwise provided in this section, a person who assaults or assaults and batters an individual, if no other punishment is prescribed by law, is guilty of a misdemeanor punishable by imprisonment for not more than 93 days or a fine of not more than $500.00, or both.

(2) Except as provided in subsection (3) or (4), an individual who assaults or assaults and batters his or her spouse or former spouse, an individual with whom he or she has or has had a dating relationship, an individual with whom he or she has had a child in common, or a resident or former resident of his or her household, is guilty of a misdemeanor punishable by imprisonment for not more than 93 days or a fine of not more than $500.00, or both.

(3) An individual who commits an assault or an assault and battery in violation of subsection (2), and who has previously been convicted of assaulting or assaulting and battering his or her spouse or former spouse, an individual with whom he or she has or has had a dating relationship, an individual with whom he or she has had a child in common, or a resident or former resident of his or her household, under any of the following, may be punished by imprisonment for not more than 1 year or a fine of not more than $1,000.00, or both:

(a) This section or an ordinance of a political subdivision of this state substantially corresponding to this section.

(b) Section 81a, 82, 83, 84, or 86.

(c) A law of another state or an ordinance of a political subdivision of another state substantially corresponding to this section or section 81a, 82, 83, 84, or 86.

(4) An individual who commits an assault or an assault and battery in violation of subsection (2), and who has 2 or more previous convictions for assaulting or assaulting and battering his or her spouse or former spouse, an individual with whom he or she has or has had a dating relationship, an individual with whom he or she has had a child in common, or a resident or former resident of his or her household, under any of the following, is guilty of a felony punishable by imprisonment for not more than 2 years or a fine of not more than $2,500.00, or both:

(a) This section or an ordinance of a political subdivision of this state substantially corresponding to this section.

(b) Section 81a, 82, 83, 84, or 86.

(c) A law of another state or an ordinance of a political subdivision of another state substantially corresponding to this section or section 81a, 82, 83, 84, or 86.

(5) This section does not apply to an individual using necessary reasonable physical force in compliance with section 1312 of the revised school code, 1976 PA 451, MCL 380.1312.

(6) As used in this section, "dating relationship" means frequent, intimate associations primarily characterized by the expectation of affectional involvement. This term does not include a casual relationship or an ordinary fraternization between 2 individuals in a business or social context.

Section 750.87. Assault with Intent to Commit Felony Not Otherwise Punished

Any person who shall assault another, with intent to commit any burglary, or any other felony, the punishment of which assault is not otherwise in this act prescribed, shall be guilty of a felony, punishable by imprisonment in the state prison not more than 10 years, or by fine of not more than 5,000 dollars.

Section 750.520g. Assault with Intent to Commit Criminal Sexual Conduct

(1) Assault with intent to commit criminal sexual conduct involving sexual penetration shall be a felony punishable by imprisonment for not more than 10 years.

(2) Assault with intent to commit criminal sexual conduct in the second degree is a felony punishable by imprisonment for not more than 5 years.

People v. Premo
540 N.W.2d 715 (Mich. Ct. App. 1995)

The defendant was charged with three counts of fourth degree criminal sexual conduct and moved to quash the information. The district court denied the motion, and the appeals court affirmed. Defendant contended that pinching the victims' buttocks, the alleged unlawful sexual conduct, is insufficient to satisfy the requirement that force or coercion be used to accomplish the sexual contact. The court held that "Defendant's pinching of the victims' buttocks satisfies the force element of the statute because the act of pinching requires the actual application of physical force. The definition of the term 'force' includes, among other things, 'strength or power exerted upon an object.' We believe that the act of pinching is an act of physical force because it requires a person to exert strength or power on another person." (Quoting *The Random House College Dictionary: Revised Edition*). Alternatively, the court found the acts to be by coercion because the defendant was the teacher and the victims were his students.

People v. Berlin
507 N.W.2d 816 (Mich. Ct. App. 1993)

Defendant gynecologist was charged with fourth-degree criminal sexual conduct when, after examining a patient, he took her hand and placed it on his crotch over his clothes. She quickly removed her hand. The patient testified that the defendant "took her hand and placed it on his crotch. She stated that he did not grab it or pull it and that he did not hurt her. She also testified that he did not resist at all when she pulled her hand away and that he did not threaten her." Given the ordinary meaning of the words "force or coercion," and the legislature's exclusion of the concealment or surprise provision from the fourth-degree criminal sexual conduct statute, the Court of Appeals held that the force or coercion required for such an offense was absent.

People v. Jansson
323 N.W.2d 508 (Mich. Ct. App. 1982)

The defendant was convicted of third degree criminal sexual conduct. On appeal, he asserted that, "because there was no indication in the record that the complainant advised or communicated to the defendant that she did not wish to engage in sexual intercourse, the defendant did not know that the sexual relations were nonconsensual and, therefore, could not have intended to engage in those relations by force or coercion. Without some manifestation of the complainant's unwillingness to engage in sexual relations [the] defendant could not have known of her nonconsent and, therefore, may have assumed that signs of physical resistance by the complainant were 'the final token manifestations of modesty.'" The court held that "[a]lthough consent precludes conviction of criminal sexual conduct in the third degree by force or coercion, the prosecution is not required to prove nonconsent as an independent element of the offense. If the prosecution offers evidence to establish that an act of sexual penetration was accomplished by force or coercion, that evidence necessarily tends to establish that the act was nonconsensual."

People v. Hale
370 N.W.2d 382 (Mich. Ct. App. 1985)

The defendant was convicted of third-degree criminal sexual conduct. He appealed his conviction based on the instruction regarding consent that was given to the jury. The jury was instructed: "If the evidence does not convince you beyond a reasonable doubt that the sexual acts complained of were not consented to, then the defendant is not guilty of the crime." The defendant claimed that "the instruction was inadequate because it predicated criminal responsibility on the victim's subjective consent rather than on defendant's reasonable belief that the victim consented." He argued that the court should have instructed the jury that "if a defendant entertains a reasonable and bona fide belief that a prosecutrix voluntarily consented to engage in sexual intercourse," the jury should find the defendant not guilty. The appeals court rejected this standard for consent, noting that "no Michigan case law requires the trial court to define consent in terms of a defendant's reasonable and honest belief."

People v. Lardie & Hudick
452 Mich. 231, 239, 551 N.W.2d 656, 660 (1996)

"In order to determine whether a statute imposes strict liability or requires proof of a mens rea, that is, a guilty mind, this Court first examines the statute itself and seeks to determine the Legislature's intent. In interpreting a statute in which the Legislature has not expressly included language indicating that fault is a necessary element of a crime, this Court must focus on whether the Legislature nevertheless intended to require some fault as a predicate to finding guilt.

"Criminal intent is ordinarily an element of a crime even where the crime is created by statute. Statutes that create strict liability for all of their elements are not favored. Nevertheless, a state may decide under its police power that certain acts or omissions are to be punished irrespective of the actor's intent. Many of the crimes that impose strict liability have been termed 'public welfare regulation.' Chief Justice Thomas Cooley succinctly described the general rule that a criminal statute requires a mens rea:

> I agree that as a rule there can be no crime without a criminal intent; but this is not by any means a universal rule. One may be guilty of the high crime of manslaughter when his only fault is gross negligence; and there are many other cases where mere neglect may be highly criminal. Many statutes which are in the nature of police regulations impose criminal penalties irrespective of any intent to violate them; the purpose being to require a degree of diligence for the protection of the public which shall render violation impossible."

Model Penal Code
(Official Draft 1962)

Section 213.1. Rape and Related Offenses

(1) Rape. A male who has sexual intercourse with a female not his wife is guilty of rape if:

(a) he compels her to submit by force or by threat of imminent death, serious bodily injury, extreme pain or kidnapping, to be inflicted on anyone; or

(b) he has substantially impaired her power to appraise or control her conduct by administering or employing without her knowledge drugs, intoxicants or other means for the purpose of preventing resistance; or

(c) the female is unconscious; or

(d) the female is less than 10 years old. Rape is a felony of the second degree unless (i) in the course thereof the actor inflicts serious bodily injury upon anyone, or (ii) the victim was not a voluntary social companion of the actor upon the occasion of the crime and had not previously permitted him sexual liberties, in which cases the offense is a felony of the first degree.

(2) Gross Sexual Imposition. A male who has sexual intercourse with a female not his wife commits a felony of the third degree if:

(a) he compels her to submit by any threat that would prevent resistance by a woman of ordinary resolution; or

(b) he knows that she suffers from a mental disease or defect which renders her incapable of appraising the nature of her conduct; or

(c) he knows that she is unaware that a sexual act is being committed upon her or that she submits because she mistakenly supposes that he is her husband.

Section 213.2. Deviate Sexual Intercourse by Force or Imposition

(1) By Force or Its Equivalent. A person who engages in deviate sexual intercourse with another person, or who causes another to engage in deviate sexual intercourse, commits a felony of the second degree if:

(a) he compels the other person to participate by force or by threat of imminent death, serious bodily injury, extreme pain or kidnapping, to be inflicted on anyone; or

(b) he has substantially impaired the other person's power to appraise or control his conduct, by administering or employing without the knowledge of the other person drugs, intoxicants or other means for the purpose of preventing resistance; or

(c) the other person is unconscious; or

(d) the other person is less than 10 years old.

(2) By Other Imposition. A person who engages in deviate sexual intercourse with another person, or who causes another to engage in deviate sexual intercourse, commits a felony of the third degree if:

(a) he compels the other person to participate by any threat that would prevent resistance by a person of ordinary resolution; or

(b) he knows that the other person suffers from a mental disease or defect which renders him incapable of appraising the nature of his conduct; or

(c) he knows that the other person submits because he is unaware that a sexual act is being committed upon him.

Section 213.4. Sexual Assault

A person who has sexual contact with another not his spouse, or causes such other to have sexual contact with him, is guilty of sexual assault, a misdemeanor, if:

(1) he knows that the contact is offensive to the other person; or

(2) he knows that the other person suffers from a mental disease or defect which renders him or her incapable of appraising the nature of his or her conduct; or

(3) he knows that the other person is unaware that a sexual act is being committed; or

(4) the other person is less than 10 years old; or

(5) he has substantially impaired the other person's power to appraise or control his or her conduct, by administering or employing without the other's knowledge drugs, intoxicants or other means for the purpose of preventing resistance; or

(6) the other person is less than [16] years old and the actor is at least [4] years older than the other person; or

(7) the other person is less than 21 years old and the actor is his guardian or otherwise responsible for general supervision of his welfare; or

(8) the other person is in custody of law or detained in a hospital or other institution and the actor has supervisory or disciplinary authority over him. Sexual contact is any touching of the sexual or other intimate

parts of the person for the purpose of arousing or gratifying sexual desire.

Section 213.6. Provisions Generally Applicable to Article 213

(1) Mistake as to Age. Whenever in this Article the criminality of conduct depends on a child's being below the age of 10, it is no defense that the actor did not know the child's age, or reasonably believed the child to be older than 10. When criminality depends on the child's being below a critical age other than 10, it is a defense for the actor to prove by a preponderance of the evidence that he reasonably believed the child to be above the critical age.

(2) Spouse Relationships. Whenever in this Article the definition of an offense excludes conduct with a spouse, the exclusion shall be deemed to extend to persons living as man and wife, regardless of the legal status of their relationship. The exclusion shall be inoperative as respects spouses living apart under a decree of judicial separation. Where the definition of an offense excludes conduct with a spouse or conduct by a woman, this shall not preclude conviction of a spouse or woman as accomplice in a sexual act which he or she causes another person, not within the exclusion, to perform.

(3) Sexually Promiscuous Complainants. It is a defense to prosecution under Section 213.3 and paragraphs (6), (7) and (8) of Section 213.4 for the actor to prove by a preponderance of the evidence that the alleged victim had, prior to the time of the offense charged, engaged promiscuously in sexual relations with others.

(4) Prompt Complaint. No prosecution may be instituted or maintained under this Article unless the alleged offense was brought to the notice of public authority within [3] months of its occurrence or, where the alleged victim was less than [16] years old or otherwise incompetent to make complaint, within [3] months after a parent, guardian or other competent person specially interested in the victim learns of the offense.

(5) Testimony of Complainants. No person shall be convicted of any felony under this Article upon the uncorroborated testimony of the alleged victim. Corroboration may be circumstantial. In any prosecution before a jury for an offense under this Article, the jury shall be instructed to evaluate the testimony of a victim or complaining witness with special care in view of the emotional involvement of the witness and the difficulty of determining the truth with respect to alleged sexual activities carried out in private.

Section 213.0 Definitions

In this Article, unless a different meaning plainly is required:

(1) the definitions given in Section 210.0 apply;

(2) "Sexual intercourse" includes intercourse per os or per anum, with some penetration however slight; emission is not required;

(3) "Deviate sexual intercourse" means sexual intercourse per os or per anum between human beings who are not husband and wife, and any form of sexual intercourse with an animal.

Section 211.1. Assault

(1) Simple Assault. A person is guilty of assault if he:

(a) attempts to cause or purposely, knowingly or recklessly causes bodily injury to another; or

(b) negligently causes bodily injury to another with a deadly weapon; or

(c) attempts by physical menace to put another in fear of imminent serious bodily injury. Simple assault is a misdemeanor unless committed in a fight or scuffle entered into by mutual consent, in which case it is a petty misdemeanor.

(2) Aggravated Assault. A person is guilty of aggravated assault if he:

(a) attempts to cause serious bodily injury to another, or causes such injury purposely, knowingly or recklessly under circumstances manifesting extreme indifference to the value of human life; or

(b) attempts to cause or purposely or knowingly causes bodily injury to another with a deadly weapon. Aggravated assault under paragraph (a) is a felony of the second degree; aggravated assault under paragraph (b) is a felony of the third degree.

Section 2.11. Consent

(1) In General. The consent of the victim to conduct charged to constitute an offense or to the result thereof is a defense if such consent negatives an element of the offense or precludes the infliction of the harm or evil sought to be prevented by the law defining the offense.

(2) Consent to Bodily Injury. When conduct is charged to constitute an offense because it causes or threatens bodily injury, consent to such conduct or to the infliction of such injury is a defense if:

(a) the bodily injury consented to or threatened by the conduct consented to is not serious; or

(b) the conduct and the injury are reasonably foreseeable hazards of joint participation in a lawful athletic contest or competitive sport or other concerted activity not forbidden by law; or

(c) the consent establishes a justification for the conduct under Article 3 of the Code.

(3) Ineffective Consent. Unless otherwise provided by the Code or by the law defining the offense, assent does not constitute consent if:

(a) it is given by a person who is legally incompetent to authorize the conduct charged to constitute the offense; or

(b) it is given by a person who by reason of youth, mental disease or defect or intoxication is manifestly unable or known by the actor to be unable to make a reasonable judgment as to the nature or harmfulness of the conduct charged to constitute the offense; or

(c) it is given by a person whose improvident consent is sought to be prevented by the law defining the offense; or

(d) it is induced by force, duress or deception of a kind sought to be prevented by the law defining the offense.

● OVERVIEW OF RAPE

Notes

FORCE OR THREAT

Definition of Rape Covers Situations Where Consent Is Manifestly Absent   The Model Penal Code defines the offense of *rape* to cover instances where a male has sexual intercourse with a female[1] and:

(a) he compels her to submit by force or by threat of imminent death, serious bodily injury, extreme pain or kidnapping, to be inflicted on anyone; or
(b) he has substantially impaired her power to appraise or control her conduct by administering or employing without her knowledge drugs, intoxicants or other means for the purpose of preventing resistance; or
(c) the female is unconscious; or
(d) the female is less than 10 years old.[2]

Each of these conditions presents relatively incontrovertible objective evidence that effective consent does not exist, so that the wrongfulness of the conduct

---

1. Under this definition, females cannot commit rape, nor can males be rape victims. Both of these aspects of the definition have been widely abandoned at this point.
2. Model Penal Code § 213.1(1)(a)-(d).

and the actor's culpability generally are clear. (For the last case, where the sexual partner is underage, consent may exist but is deemed ineffective and irrelevant.)

Requiring Force (or Threat) versus Requiring Resistance   Note that the definition of rape as forcible intercourse does not require that the victim have physically resisted the attack, but asks whether the attacker "compels . . . by force or by threat." Requiring resistance, as some jurisdictions once did, would require victims to put themselves in danger of additional injuries if their resistance is met with greater force, as is often likely. (Of course, resistance is also impossible where the actor sedates or knocks out the victim in advance, rather than using contemporaneous force.) The victim may lawfully use force to resist, even deadly force,[3] but if the victim chooses to submit to the offender's force rather than risk additional injury, the offender's liability is not reduced. (At least one court has ruled that the "force" requirement may be satisfied by the force inherent in the sexual penetration itself; no additional force need be shown.[4] This interpretation of the "force" requirement essentially does away with the requirement and redefines the offense as one of unconsented-to intercourse.)

Demanding Serious Threat for Rape Liability   Where no force is used, but only a threat, some jurisdictions—in keeping with the Model Penal Code formulation, noted above—require that the threat be such as to make the victim reasonably believe she is in danger of serious injury if she resists.[5] At the same time, the victim's belief that the actor has made a threat is not conclusive; as in most criminal offenses, the focus is on the *defendant's* state of mind and whether the defendant intended the words as a threat.[6]

Lesser Offense for Coerced Intercourse Using Lesser Threat   A less serious Code offense addresses intercourse coerced by a threat less serious than the "threat of imminent death, serious bodily injury, extreme pain or kidnapping" required for rape. An actor commits the offense of *gross sexual imposition* "if he compels her to submit by any threat that would prevent resistance by a woman of ordinary resolution[.]"[7] The drafters explain:

> Examples might include threat to cause her to lose her job or to deprive her of a valued possession. This provision extends liability for coercion by threat far beyond anything contemplated by prior law. It rests on the judgment that using one's ability to cause harm in order to override the will of a reluctant female is wrongful and should be punished. Although threat of economic injury may be deemed less serious than threat of physical attack, threat of either description may be sufficient to deny the freedom of choice that the law of rape and related offenses seeks to protect and to subject a woman to unwanted and degrading sexual intimacy. Realistic assessment of the many modes of sexual aggression requires that the penal law reach beyond the narrow confines of threat of violence to include more figurative kinds of assault.[8]

While the threat sufficient to constitute a sexual offense has been broadened, it is nonetheless required that some threat be made; procuring intercourse by making

---

3. See Model Penal Code § 3.03(2)(b).
4. See, e.g., State in Interest of M.T.S., 609 A.2d 1266 (N.J. 1992).
5. See, e.g., State v. Rusk, 424 A.2d 720 (Md. 1981).
6. See, e.g., People v. Evans, 85 Misc. 2d 1088, 379 N.Y.S.2d 912 (S. Ct., N.Y. County, T.T. 1975).
7. Model Penal Code § 213.1(2)(a).
8. Model Penal Code § 213.1 comment at 312 (1980).

some false promise or claim generally is not a crime, except for limited situations such as pretending to be the victim's husband.

Limitations to Contain Reach of Threat-Based Liability　Yet the Code drafters are concerned that the broad definition of gross sexual imposition creates a danger of "extending the prospect of criminal sanctions into the shadow area between coercion and bargain. To take an extreme example, the man who 'threatens' to withhold an expensive present unless his girlfriend permits his advances is plainly not a fit subject for punishment under the law of rape."[9] To limit this potential overcriminalization, the Code limits the offense in three respects. First, the threat must meet an objective standard. Specifically, it must be such as would prevent resistance "by a woman of ordinary resolution,"[10] and the actor must disregard the risk that his threat is of this nature. Second, the statutory language "compels to submit" is intended to require that the victim's submission result from coercion rather bargaining.[11] Finally, the Code reduces the grade of liability for this offense relative to rape: While rape is a first- or second-degree felony, gross sexual imposition is a third-degree felony.

Why a Threat Requirement?　The Model Penal Code's definition of rape covers a subset of cases where consent is lacking. Yet the Code creates no general criminal offense of intercourse without consent. One may wonder why not. Taking property without consent is theft; entering on property without consent is trespass. Why no offense for intercourse without consent? It might make sense to aggravate liability where the offender uses force or a threat—just as the offense of robbery aggravates liability for thefts involving force or threat—but there is no obvious reason to require force or threat for *any* liability to arise. At the same time, a general offense of nonconsensual sex introduces its own issues and complications.

LACK OF CONSENT (AND INEFFECTIVE CONSENT)

Criminalizing Nonconsensual Intercourse　It has become increasingly common for states to criminalize nonconsensual sexual relations, without requiring any overt force or threat (or other means of physically overcoming the victim, such as drugging).[12] For example, Wisconsin has the following offense:

---

9. Model Penal Code § 213.1 comment at 312 (1980).

10. This standard is sufficiently general that it is likely to change with time and culture.

11. The commentary states:

> This inquiry into the essential character of the threat is distinct from, though complementary to, the requirement that it achieve a gravity sufficient to "prevent resistance by a woman of ordinary resolution." Thus, if a wealthy man were to threaten to withdraw financial support from his unemployed girlfriend, it is at least arguable under the circumstances that he is making a threat "that would prevent resistance by a woman of ordinary resolution." The reason why this case is excluded from liability . . . is not the gravity of the harm threatened—it may be quite substantial—but its essential character as part of a process of bargain. He is not guilty of compulsion overwhelming the will of his victim but only of offering her an unattractive choice to avoid some unwanted alternative.

Model Penal Code § 213.1 comment at 314.

12. See Michelle J. Anderson, *All-American Rape*, 79 St. John's L. Rev. 625, 629-633 (2005) (stating that "[s]ixteen states and the District of Columbia do criminalize sexual penetration that is nonconsensual and without force"; providing citations and noting offense grades, finding that more than half of jurisdictions impose misdemeanor liability).

Third Degree Sexual Assault. Whoever has sexual intercourse with a person without the consent of that person is guilty of a Class D felony.

Consent. "Consent," as used in this section, means words or overt actions by a person who is competent to give informed consent indicating a freely given agreement to have sexual intercourse . . . . [13]

MPC Does Not Contain Offense for Nonconsensual Sex   The Model Penal Code drafters considered and expressly rejected the possibility of criminalizing intercourse without consent:

> [O]veremphasis on nonconsent can be troublesome . . . . Evidentiary considerations aside, consent appears to be a conceptually simple issue. Either the female assented to intercourse, or she did not. Searching for consent in a particular case, however, may reveal depths of ambiguity and contradiction that are scarcely suspected when the question is put in the abstract. Often the woman's attitude may be deeply ambivalent. She may not want intercourse, may fear it, or may desire it but feel compelled to say "no." Her confusion at the time of the act may later resolve into nonconsent. Some have expressed the fear that a woman who subconsciously wanted to have sexual intercourse will later feel guilty and "cry rape." It seems plain, on the other hand, that a barrage of conflicting emotions at the time of the assault does not necessarily imply the victim's consent, although it may lead to misperception by the actor. Further ambiguity may be introduced by the fact that the woman may appear to consent because she is frozen by fear and panic, or because she quite rationally decides to "consent" rather than risk being killed or injured.

The point, in any event, is that inquiry into the victim's subjective state of mind and the attacker's perceptions of her state of mind often will not yield a clear answer. The deceptively simple notion of consent may obscure a tangled mesh of psychological complexity, ambiguous communication, and unconscious restructuring of the event by the participants. Courts have not been oblivious to this difficulty, but in attempting to resolve it they have often placed disproportionate emphasis upon objective manifestations of nonconsent by the woman. It seems plain that some courts have gone too far in this direction, although it is equally plain that one can go too far in the opposite direction.[14]

Concern That Ambiguity Creates Risks of Improper Liability   The drafters seem concerned that the "depths of ambiguity and contradiction" in the situation mean that the defendant might not know whether the sexual partner (for the Code, the "woman") has consented; indeed, the partner might not know herself. But one might respond that if an actor does not know whether a potential sex partner is consenting, the actor ought not to have intercourse with that person. On the other hand, perhaps the situation and history of the relationship may give rise to implied or presumed consent, and in such a situation, perhaps the partner ought to be obliged to withdraw or rebut that presumed consent through word or action. Yet even with such contextual presumptions of consent or nonconsent, some potential for error remains. For the Code drafters, a requirement of force or threat is preferable because it gives clear objective proof of lack of consent.

---

13. Wis. Stat. Ann. § 940.225(3)&(4).
14. Model Penal Code § 213.1 comment at 302-03 (1980).

Yet Culpability Requirements May Minimize Risk The drafters' concern seems to assume that the ambiguity of the situation works against the defendant in an unfair way, making inappropriate convictions likely. But it may be the prosecution, not the defendant, whose legal burden becomes more difficult because of that ambiguity. If an offense prohibits intercourse without consent, the state would have to prove not only the actual absence of consent, but also that the defendant had the required culpability (presumably at least recklessness) as to the victim's lack of consent.[15] That is, the drafters' fear that an offense of nonconsensual intercourse would invite improper convictions may give inadequate weight to the protection of the culpability requirement. Further, in cases where the prosecutor *can* prove beyond a reasonable doubt that, at the time of intercourse, the sex partner was not consenting and the actor was aware of a substantial risk of that nonconsent, why should the actor escape all liability? Today, the criminal codes of roughly one-third of American jurisdictions have rejected the Model Penal Code's position and adopted a general offense for sexual intercourse without consent.

Ineffective Consent, Based on Victim's Incompetency, Mistake or Status In addition to intercourse compelled by force or threat, and (increasingly) intercourse without consent, modern codes also punish intercourse with an adult victim whose apparent consent is *ineffective* or *invalid* because of the victim's mental incapacity or mistake. (Where the incapacity is sufficiently obvious, as where the victim is unconscious, the code may provide for aggravated liability.) Frequently, liability is imposed only if the actor knows of the victim's incompetency or mistake. Under the Model Penal Code, for example, an actor commits the offense of *gross sexual imposition* if:

> he knows that [the sexual partner] suffers from a mental disease or defect which renders her incapable of appraising the nature of her conduct; or
>
> he knows that she is unaware that a sexual act is being committed upon her or that she submits because she mistakenly supposes that he is her husband.[16]

> The Code also recognizes four other instances of invalid consent in its offense of *corruption of minors and seduction*, which punishes intercourse where:

> (a) the other person is less than [16] years old and the actor is at least [4] years older than the other person; or
>
> (b) the other person is less than 21 years old and the actor is his [or her] guardian or otherwise responsible for general supervision of his [or her] welfare; or
>
> (c) the other person is in custody of law or detained in a hospital or other institution and the actor has supervisory or disciplinary authority over him [or her]; or
>
> (d) the other person is a female who is induced to participate by a promise of marriage which the actor does not mean to perform.[17]

The first of these is graded as seriously as gross sexual imposition; the remainder are treated as less serious offenses.[18] The Code provides a defense to this offense

---

15. See Model Penal Code § 2.02(3).
16. Model Penal Code § 213.1(2)(b)&(c).
17. Model Penal Code § 213.3(1)(a)-(d) (first two sets of brackets in original).
18. Model Penal Code § 213.3(2).

where the victim has been previously promiscuous,[19] on the theory that "proof of prior sexual promiscuity rebuts the presumption of naiveté and inexperience that supports the imposition of criminal liability,"[20] but the defense has not been widely adopted by the states.[21]

"Statutory Rape" Offenses Criminalize Sexual Conduct with Minor Minors comprise one significant category of people whose consent to sexual activity is legally ineffective. The first form of the corruption-of-minors offense noted above—intercourse with a minor under age 16 where the actor is at least 4 years older—provides one example of the category of sexual offenses commonly known as *statutory rape*, which ban sexual relations with minors. It is common for states to define different categories of statutory rape for victims of different ages: The base offense might apply where the sexual partner is under 16 or 18 years of age,[22] with aggravated offenses covering cases where the victim is below some lower cutoff, such as 9 or 10 or 11 years of age.[23] It is also common to specify that the offender must be a certain number of years older than the victim.[24] Some states have no such limitation, however; in those states, two minors who have intercourse with each other have both committed statutory rape.[25]

Reduced, or No, Culpability Required as to Victim's Age An actor's mistake as to an offense element typically will give the actor a mistake defense if it negates the offense's required culpability. In the context of sexual offenses, it is common to limit such a mistake defense—or lower the culpability requirement itself—when the element in question is the victim's age. The Model Penal Code, for example, imposes strict liability as to whether a victim is under ten, an element of its most aggravated form of statutory rape.[26] Thus, no mistake as to the victim's age will provide a defense. One argument in favor of strict liability here is the position that any mistake as to the age of a child under ten is per se unreasonable, hence negligent. At best, even if the actor believed the sexual partner was older than 10, he could not reasonably believe the partner to be older than 16, so that even based on his mistaken view, the actor would still be committing a statutory rape offense, albeit a lesser one.[27] Normally, mistake rules would allow a mitigation in grade to the less serious offense the actor believed he was committing,[28] but such a mitigation is rejected here. For the less serious offense of intercourse with a female less than 16, a reasonable mistake as to age will provide a defense,[29] which essentially

---

19. Model Penal Code § 213.6(3).

20. Model Penal Code § 213.6 comment at 420 (1980).

21. See Maryanne Lyons, Comment, *Adolescents in Jeopardy: An Analysis of Texas' Promiscuity Defense for Sexual Assault*, 29 HOUS. L. REV. 583, 616 (1992) (noting that "[o]f the fifty states, only Mississippi, Tennessee, and Texas have statutory provisions dealing with the 'prior chastity' of the complainant").

22. See, e.g., Model Penal Code § 213.3(1)(a).

23. See, e.g., Model Penal Code § 213.1(1)(d).

24. See Charles A. Phipps, *Misdirected Reform: On Regulating Consensual Sexual Activity Between Teenagers*, 12 CORNELL J.L. & PUB. POL'Y 373, 390 nn.115-116 (2003) (listing state provisions that impose liability only where defendant is above a certain age, or more than a specified number of years older than victim).

25. See id. at n.118 (listing provisions for 12 states that require no minimum age for offender and require no age differential).

26. See Model Penal Code § 213.6(1).

27. See Model Penal Code § 213.6 comment at 414 (1980).

28. See Model Penal Code § 2.04(2).

29. Model Penal Code § 213.6(1).

creates a negligence requirement for that element. These special rules for mistake as to age effectively modify the culpability elements of the relevant offenses, for which the Code would otherwise "read in" a higher requirement of recklessness.

Grading Sexual Offenses   The variety of sexual offenses creates a challenge for code drafters in making grading distinctions. Some of the grading differences among offenses have already been mentioned. Under the Model Penal Code, rape is a first- or second-degree felony; gross sexual imposition is a third-degree felony; corruption of minors, seduction, sexual assault, and indecent exposure generally are misdemeanors. The grading distinctions reflected in these categorizations, and other special grading rules contained in the offenses, focus on several factors to aggravate or mitigate the seriousness of an offense. The level of violence accompanying the offense affects its grade. Serious bodily harm results in a first-degree felony;[30] force or a threat of serious bodily harm results in a second-degree felony[31]; compulsion by a threat of less serious harm results in a third-degree felony.[32] The youthfulness of the victim also affects the offense grade, reflecting society's view that the younger the victim, the more harmful or egregious the conduct (and the greater the inability to give meaningful consent). Intercourse with a victim less than 10 years old results in a first- or second-degree felony,[33] intercourse with a victim between 10 and 16 results in a third-degree felony.[34] Other grading distinctions focus on the means by which an ineffective "consent" was obtained. Having intercourse with a victim who is unconscious or drugged[35] is classed as more serious than intercourse with a victim who is mentally defective or tricked into thinking the actor is her husband,[36] which in turn is classed as more serious than intercourse with a victim who is under the supervision or disciplinary authority of the actor, or who is induced by a promise of marriage that the actor does not mean to perform.[37] Just as the definitions of sexual offenses are likely to change with changing social norms, so too are the grading factors and their relative effect on the offense grade.

Special Evidentiary Rules for Sexual Offenses   Much of the controversy related to sexual offenses surrounds the special evidentiary rules commonly imposed.[38] One such rule requires the victim to register a complaint within a specified period of time.[39] A special corroboration requirement is also sometimes imposed, requiring corroboration of a complainant's testimony before allowing

---

30. Model Penal Code § 213.1(1)(i).

31. Model Penal Code § 213.1(1)(a).

32. Model Penal Code § 213.1(2).

33. Model Penal Code § 213.1(1)(d). Because a ten-year old child is not likely to have been a voluntary social companion nor previously permitted sexual liberties, the offense is likely to be a first-degree felony, under Model Penal Code § 213.1(1)(ii).

34. Model Penal Code § 213.3(1)(a). For liability, the actor must be at least four years older than the victim.

35. Model Penal Code § 213.1(1)(b)&(c).

36. Model Penal Code § 213.1(2)(b)&(c).

37. Model Penal Code § 213.3(1)(c)&(d)&(2).

38. For a discussion of the special evidentiary problems in the law of rape, see, e.g., Kim Lane Scheppele & Susan Estrich, *Real Rape: How the Legal System Victimizes Women Who Say No*, 54 U. Chi. L. Rev. 1095 (1987).

39. See, e.g., Model Penal Code § 213.6(4).

felony conviction for a sexual offense.[40] Some courts have sought to make the requirement flexible, however, allowing corroboration by anything that "would permit the jury to conclude beyond a reasonable doubt that the victim's account of the crime was not a fabrication."[41] Such provisions have received mixed reviews in the states. Many of these provisions have not been widely adopted, and some that were adopted have subsequently been repealed. Where adopted, most continue to be controversial. Also controversial are rules that allow the admission into evidence of past unchaste acts by the victim of a sexual offense. Some jurisdictions have adopted *rape shield* laws to bar such evidence or limit its use to narrowly defined situations,[42] although the exclusion of evidence is sometimes successfully challenged as a violation of the right to effective cross-examination.[43] The evolution of these evidentiary rules reflects broader changes in the understanding of sexual offenses over time.

Evolving Standards of Sexual Conduct

MPC Retains Common Law's "Marital Exemption" The Common Law recognized a *marital* (or *spousal*) *exception* to rape: It was legally impossible for a husband to rape his wife. This exception was rooted in the view that wives were chattels, or possessions, of their husbands. Obviously, this view is now seen as backward and oppressive. The Model Penal Code, drafted in the second half of the twentieth century, retains the Common Law's marital exemption for each of its sexual offenses, albeit for different reasons. The Code's justification derives from its concern that the relationship between husband and wife creates a different context for sexual conduct between them than exists for unmarried partners. The Code drafters contend that coercion or assault between husband and wife, even in a sexual context, is more appropriately dealt with through nonsexual assault offenses against the person.[44] The Code's exclusion applies not only to persons legally married, but also to "persons living as man and wife," though not to "spouses living apart under a decree of judicial separation."[45]

Abolishing marital exemption Commentators have challenged the Code's assumption that marital rape is less harmful than other forms of rape:

> [W]ife rape can be as terrifying and life-threatening to the victim as stranger rape. In addition, it often evokes a powerful sense of betrayal, deep disillusionment, and total isolation. Women often receive very poor treatment by friends, relatives, and professional services when they are raped by strangers. This isolation can be even more extreme for victims of wife rape. And just as they are more likely to be blamed, they are more likely to blame themselves.[46]

For these reasons and others, nearly all states have dropped the spousal exception to rape, and some courts have found it to be unconstitutional, as a violation of

---

40. See, e.g., S.D. Codified Laws Ann. § 23-44-4 through § 23-44-16; Model Penal Code § 213.6(5).
41. United States v. Wiley, 160 U.S. App. D.C. 781, 492 F.2d 547 (1974).
42. See, e.g., Ala. Code § 12-21-203; Fed. R. Evid. 412.
43. See, e.g., State v. DeLawder, 344 A.2d 446 (Md. App. 1975).
44. See Model Penal Code § 213.1 comment at 341-346 (1980).
45. Model Penal Code § 213.6(2).
46. Diana E.H. Russell, Rape in Marriage 198 (1982).

equal protection.[47] For related reasons, states now uniformly reject the Code's so-called date rape grading reduction, which authorizes a lower offense grade for the rape of a "voluntary social companion" who has had prior intercourse with the defendant.

Gender-Based Definition of Sexual Offenses   Again following the Common Law, the Model Penal Code defines both rape and statutory rape as offenses that can only be committed by males against females. The drafters point out that distinct Code offenses criminalize analogous conduct involving female offenders or male victims, making the gender-based limitation on rape essentially a grading device.[48] They defend the grading difference for rape in part as a reflection of the practical reality that most offenses involve male offenders and female victims, and that is where the greatest deterrent threat is needed. The desert-based rationale for such a limitation, if there is one, would relate to a claim of differential harm to women along the lines elaborated in the statutory-rape context, discussed immediately below.

Gender-Based Statutory Rape   The arguments for and against a gender-based statutory rape offense are slightly different than those for rape. In *Michael M. v. Sonoma County Superior Court*,[49] the constitutionality of a gender-based statutory rape law was challenged on Equal Protection grounds. A plurality of the United States Supreme Court upheld the statute:

> The justification for the statute offered by the State, and by the Supreme Court of California, is that the legislature sought to prevent illegitimate teenage pregnancies. . . .

> We need not be medical doctors to discern that young men and women are not similarly situated with respect to the problems and the risks of sexual intercourse. Only women become pregnant, and they suffer disproportionately the profound physical, emotional, and psychological consequences of sexual activity. The statute at issue here protects women from sexual intercourse at an age when those consequences are particularly severe.[50]

The dissent argued, among other things:

> Until very recently, no California court or commentator had suggested that the purpose of California's statutory rape law was to protect young women from the risk of pregnancy. Indeed, the historical development of § 261.5 demonstrates that the law was initially enacted on the premise that young women, in contrast to young men, were to be deemed legally incapable of consenting to an act of sexual intercourse. Because their chastity was considered particularly precious, those young women were felt to be uniquely in need of the State's protection. In contrast, young men were assumed to be capable of making such decisions for themselves; the law therefore did not offer them special protection.

---

47. See, e.g., People v. Liberta, 474 N.E.2d 567 (N.Y. 1984).

48. Model Penal Code § 213.1 comment 8(a) at 335-37 (1980) (pointing to offenses of deviate sexual intercourse, § 213.2; corruption of minors and seduction, § 213.3; and sexual assault, § 213.4).

49. 450 U.S. 464 (1981).

50. Id. at 471-472.

It is perhaps because the gender classification in California's statutory rape law was initially designed to further these outmoded sexual stereotypes, rather than to reduce the incidence of teenage pregnancies, that the State has been unable to demonstrate a substantial relationship between the classification and its newly asserted goal. But whatever the reason, the State has not shown that Cal. Penal Code § 261.5 is any more effective than a gender-neutral law would be in deterring minor females from engaging in sexual intercourse.[51]

MPC Permits Consensual (but Aggravates for Nonconsensual) "Deviate Intercourse"   At first glance, the Model Penal Code might also appear to retain the Common Law offenses that prohibited certain types of intercourse judged to be immoral. The Code provides a special offense punishing so-called *deviate sexual intercourse*, defined as: "sexual intercourse per os or per anum between human beings who are not husband and wife, and any form of sexual intercourse with an animal."[52] In actuality, the Code departs from prior law and *decriminalizes* oral and anal intercourse—for unmarried as well as married partners, and for same-sex as well as opposite-sex partners—except where it occurs in the absence of meaningful consent, in parallel fashion to the prohibitions involving "standard" intercourse (under the offenses of rape, gross sexual imposition, corruption of minors, and seduction). Thus, the effect of the formal distinction between types of intercourse is simply to aggravate the penalty for nonconsensual intercourse when it constitutes "deviate" sexual intercourse. For example, while intercourse with one who is mentally defective ordinarily is gross sexual imposition, a third-degree felony, it is elevated to a second-degree felony if the conduct amounts to "deviate sexual intercourse."

Decriminalization of Consensual Conduct, Within or Outside Marriage Decriminalization of consensual "deviate" sexual intercourse between husband and wife is supported by a growing sense that such conduct may not be deviate after all. As the Model Penal Code drafters explain:

> So-called deviate sexual intercourse between spouses may contravene an ethical or religious notion that there is only one "right" way to achieve sexual gratification, but there is nothing approaching societal consensus on this point. Both the popular literature and available empirical data reveal that such practices are anything but uncommon. Moreover, current scientific thinking confirms that so-called deviate sexual intercourse may be part of a healthy and normal marital relationship. While it is difficult to see that nonstandard sexual intimacy between spouses occasions any harm of which the state properly might take cognizance, it is easy to identify criminal sanctions for such conduct as inconsistent with the societal goal of protecting the marital relationship against outside interference.[53]

Once it is determined that consensual sexual conduct is no longer to be criminalized for its "deviancy," the only basis for criminalization is disapproval of sexual conduct outside of marriage.[54] But the Model Code, and other modern criminal codes, generally decriminalize consensual sex outside of marriage, as manifested

---

51. Id. at 494-496 (Brennan, J., dissenting).
52. Model Penal Code § 213.2(1).
53. Model Penal Code § 213.2 comment at 363-64 (1980).
54. Model Penal Code § 213.1 comment at 365 (1980).

by the widespread rejection of the Common Law offenses of *adultery* (extra-marital sex by or with a married person) and *fornication* (sex between unmarried persons). The Code drafters cite nonenforcement, difficulties in enforcement, and abuse through selective prosecution as the primary reasons for discontinuing these offenses.[55] The same reasons, together with the changed norms regarding deviancy, support discontinuation of the prohibition against deviate sexual intercourse outside of marriage.

Decriminalization of Homosexual Relations Because sexual intercourse between persons of the same sex generally involves conduct the Code defines as "deviate" sexual intercourse, the decriminalization of deviate intercourse also decriminalizes homosexual relations. The Code intends this result. After discussing three views of homosexuality—as a sin, as a disease, and as merely a difference—the drafters conclude:

> Only one of the three conceptions—i.e., the view that homosexual conduct is a sin—provides an appropriate starting point for imposition of penal sanctions. No principle is more broadly accepted than that the criminal law, involving as it does both punishment and condemnation, should be concerned with conduct that is morally reprehensible or culpable. To the extent that it seems inappropriate to regard homosexual relations as blameworthy—that is, as representative of moral failing by the actor—the essential premise for assigning criminal punishment is vitiated. Of course, many in the community view homosexual conduct as morally reprehensible, but it is equally clear that many do not. Given the absence of harm to the secular interests of the community occasioned by atypical sexuality between consenting adults, the problematical nature of the underlying ethical issue should suggest the need for caution in continuing criminal proscription of this kind of behavior.[56]

Constitution Prohibits Ban on Consensual Sexual Relations In addition to the policy justifications, criminalization of consensual sexual relations, whether "deviate" or not, between consenting adults—married or unmarried, opposite-sex or same-sex—is now considered to run afoul of constitutionally protected privacy interests. The United States Supreme Court has held that criminalization of consensual homosexual conduct violates the Constitution, based on protected liberty and autonomy interests in making personal decisions about intimate relations.[57]

Margaret T. Gordon & Stephanie Riger, The Female Fear: The Social Cost of Rape
2, 26-28, 32-36 (1991)

Most women experience fear of rape as a nagging, gnawing sense that something awful could happen, an angst that keeps them from doing things they want or need to do, or from doing them at the time or in the way they might otherwise do. Women's fear of rape is a sense that one must always be on guard, vigilant and alert, a feeling that causes a woman to tighten with anxiety if someone is walking too closely behind her, especially at night. . . . It is worse than fear of other crimes

---

55. Model Penal Code art. 213 comment at 434-36 (1980).
56. Model Penal Code § 213.2 comment at 369 (1980).
57. See Lawrence v. Texas, 539 U.S. 558 (2003).

because women know they are held responsible for avoiding rape, and should they be victimized, they know they are likely to be blamed. . . .

[I]n 1986 there were 90,434 forcible rapes reported by police across the country to the F.B.I., representing an increase of 3.2 percent over 1985 and a rate of 73 per 100,000 women. . . .

Analyses of how UCR (Uniform Crime Reports) data are gathered and compiled (by the F.B.I.) have indicated errors of omission and commission, most of which lead to the under-representation of the actual rate of rape. . . . [The authors discuss the shortcomings of UCR data.]

These findings and others gave rise to the National Crime Surveys (also often referred to as the victimization surveys) now regularly conducted in conjunction with the U.S. Census. [R]apes reported to surveyors in 1986 yield a rate of about 140 per 100,000 . . . women a rate [double] that indicated by the UCR data. . . .

Perhaps the greatest source of error in the reported rate of rape is the non-reported incidents. This "doubly dark" figure of crime, which is reported *neither* to the police *nor* to a victimization survey interviewer, remains elusive. Research indicates that rapes by known assailants are particularly likely to go unreported, resulting in a serious underestimation of the extent of violence against women.

When women living in [three] selected cities were asked in telephone interviews if they had ever been raped *or* sexually assaulted *at some time during their lives*, 2 percent said yes. That is a rate of 2,000 per 100,000, much higher than either yearly UCR or survey rates for these cities. But when women were asked the same question in person, the figures were even more startling. Eleven percent (or 11,000 in 100,000) said they had been raped or sexually assaulted. These rates are surprisingly high and help to underscore the problems with any of the figures now available. . . .

While stranger rapes may constitute people's image of what is typical, acquaintance rapes or nonstranger rapes are an increasingly large proportion of actual rapes and now account for 55 to 60 percent of rapes reported to police. . . .

But the words "nonstranger" or "acquaintance" cover a wide range of types of relationships. [One] type of acquaintance rape is referred to as date rape; this occurs when the victim initially is willing to be in the company of a man who then becomes violent toward her. For several reasons, many of these rapes are not reported. . . . Although the victim may have resisted and been forced, she herself may not recognize it as rape *because* she was on a date. . . . Most important, date-rape victims often feel they won't be believed or will be perceived as having "asked for it"—by the police, the courts, and everyone else and, therefore, there is no point in reporting it.

A special form of date rape is being increasingly reported on college campuses. In what may have become a typical campus rape, a young woman is assaulted by a young man she has met (often the same evening) at a party on campus. She may have danced with him, gone for a walk with him, gone to his room, or allowed him to walk her to her room. Many campus rapes seem to involve the use of excessive amounts of alcohol by one or both persons involved. One victim of campus rape blamed herself because she was drunk. When a faculty member reminded her that it is a crime to rape, but not a crime to get drunk, the coed decided to file charges. Experts in this field say, "Clearly, among college students sexual aggression is rare among strangers and common among acquaintances." . . .

[R]esearchers argue that campus rape may be so prevalent because of norms in our society that condone sexual violence. People are conditioned to accept sexual roles in which male aggression is an acceptable part of our modern courtship culture. According to this line of reasoning, campus rapists are ordinary males operating in an ordinary social context, not even knowing they are doing something wrong, let alone against the law.

Commonwealth v. Fischer

Superior Court of Pennsylvania
721 A.2d 1111 (1998)

BECK, J.:

. . . Appellant, an eighteen year-old college freshman, was charged with involuntary deviate sexual intercourse (IDSI), aggravated indecent assault and related offenses in connection with an incident that occurred in a Lafayette College campus dormitory. The victim was another freshman student appellant met at school.

At trial, both the victim and appellant testified that a couple of hours prior to the incident at issue, the two went to appellant's dorm room and engaged in intimate contact. The victim testified that the couple's conduct was limited to kissing and fondling. Appellant, on the other hand, testified that during this initial encounter, he and the victim engaged in "rough sex" which culminated in the victim performing fellatio on him. According to appellant, the victim acted aggressively at this first rendezvous by holding appellant's arms above his head, biting his chest, stating "You know you want me," and initiating oral sex.

After the encounter, the students separated and went to the dining hall with their respective friends. They met up again later and once more found themselves in appellant's dorm room. While their accounts of what occurred at the first meeting contained significant differences, their versions of events at the second meeting were grossly divergent. The victim testified that appellant locked the door, pushed her onto the bed, straddled her, held her wrists above her head and forced his penis into her mouth. She struggled with appellant throughout the entire encounter. . . . She also . . . repeatedly stated that she did not want to engage in sex, but her pleas went unheeded.

According to the victim, appellant [stated] "I know you want it," . . . and "Nobody will know where you are." When the victim attempted to leave, appellant blocked her path. Only after striking him in the groin with her knee was the victim able to escape.

Appellant characterized the second meeting in a far different light. He stated that as he led the victim into his room, she told him it would have to be "a quick one." . . . Thereafter, according to appellant, he began to engage in the same type of behavior the victim had exhibited in their previous encounter. Appellant admitted that he held the young woman's arms above her head, straddled her and placed his penis at her mouth. . . . When she [said] "no," appellant answered "No means yes." After another verbal exchange that included the victim's statement that she had to leave, appellant again insisted that "she wanted it." This time she answered "No, I honestly don't." Upon hearing this, appellant no longer sought to engage in oral sex and removed himself from her body. However, as the two lay side by side on the bed, they continued to kiss and fondle one another.

. . . According to appellant, the victim enjoyed the contact and responded positively to his actions. At some point, however, she stood up and informed appellant that she had to leave. When appellant again attempted to touch her, this time on the thigh, she told him she was "getting pissed." Before appellant could "rearrange himself," so that he could walk the victim to her class, she abruptly left the room.

At trial, . . . [m]edical personnel testified to treating the victim on the night in question. Many of the victim's friends and classmates described her as nervous, shaken and upset after the incident.

Defense counsel argued throughout the trial and in closing that appellant, relying on his previous encounter with the victim, did not believe his actions were taken without her consent. . . . In light of his limited experience and the victim's initially aggressive behavior, argued counsel, appellant's beliefs were reasonable. Further, . . . as soon as appellant realized that the victim truly did not wish to engage in oral sex a second time, appellant stopped seeking same. As a result, appellant's actions could not be deemed forcible compulsion.

The jury returned a verdict of guilty on virtually all counts. Appellant was sentenced to two to five years in prison. On direct appeal, he retained new counsel who has raised a single issue . . . that trial counsel provided ineffective assistance in failing to request a jury charge on the defense of mistake of fact. Specifically, appellant claims that counsel should have asked the court to instruct the jurors that if they found appellant reasonably, though mistakenly, believed that the victim was consenting to his sexual advances, they could find him not guilty.

The standard of review for ineffectiveness challenges is clear. Appellant must establish: 1) an underlying issue of arguable merit; 2) the absence of a reasonable strategy on the part of counsel in acting or failing to act; and 3) prejudice as a result of counsel's action or inaction. . . .

Our initial inquiry is whether counsel would have been successful had he requested a mistake of fact instruction. Counsel cannot be deemed ineffective for failing to pursue a baseless claim. Further, the quality of counsel's stewardship is based on the state of the law as it existed at time of trial; counsel is not ineffective if he fails to predict future developments or changes in the law.

The Commonwealth relies . . . on an opinion by a panel of this court. Commonwealth v. Williams, 294 Pa. Super. 93, 439 A.2d 765 (Pa.Super.1982), concerned the rape and assault of a Temple University student. The facts established that the victim accepted a ride from the appellant on a snowy evening in Philadelphia. Instead of taking the young woman to the bus station, appellant drove her to a dark area, threatened to kill her and informed her that he wanted sex. The victim told Williams to "go ahead" because she did not wish to be hurt.

[The appellant in that case] argued, among other things, that the trial court erred in refusing to instruct the jury "that if the defendant reasonably believed that the prosecutrix had consented to his sexual advances that this would constitute a defense to the rape and involuntary deviate sexual intercourse charge." This court rejected Williams's claim and held:

> . . . When one individual uses force or the threat of force to have sexual relations with a person not his spouse and without the person's consent he has committed the crime of rape. *If the element of the defendant's belief as to the victim's state of mind is to be established as a defense to the crime of rape then it should be done by our legislature which has the power to define crimes and offenses. We refuse to create such a defense.*

Id. (emphasis supplied.) The Commonwealth insists that under *Williams*, appellant was not entitled to the instruction he now claims trial counsel should have requested.

In response, appellant makes two arguments. First, he argues that the "stranger rape" facts of *Williams* were far different from those of this case, making the case inapplicable. Second, he maintains that the law with respect to rape and sexual assault has changed significantly over the last decade, along with our understanding of the crime and its permutations, making a mistake of fact instruction in a date rape case a necessity for a fair trial. . . .

Although the rape and IDSI laws have always required the element of "forcible compulsion," that term was not initially defined. . . . [58] Not long after *Williams* was decided, our supreme court published Commonwealth v. Rhodes, 510 Pa. 537, 510 A.2d 1217 (1986). In that case, a twenty-year-old man was accused of raping an eight-year-old girl. The evidence established that the appellant took the victim, whom he knew, to an abandoned building and sexually assaulted her. The child complied with all of the appellant's instructions. . . . A panel of this court reversed Rhodes's rape conviction based on insufficient evidence. The panel held that while the crime of statutory rape clearly was established given the victim's age, there was no evidence of the forcible compulsion necessary for the rape conviction. Our supreme court disagreed. . . . Defining forcible compulsion as including "not only physical force or violence but also moral, psychological or intellectual force," the court held that forcible compulsion was established. . . . The *Rhodes* court's inclusion of types of forcible compulsion other than physical was a significant change in the law. Of course, defining those new types was not an easy task. [In 1995,] the legislature amended the sexual assault law by adding a definition for forcible compulsion. The language of the amendment closely followed that used by the *Rhodes* court:

> "Forcible Compulsion." Compulsion by use of physical, intellectual, moral, emotional or psychological force, either express or implied. . . .

It is this broader definition, argues appellant in this case, that prompts the necessity for a mistake of fact jury instruction. . . . According to appellant:

> The language of the present statute inextricably links the issues of consent with *mens rea*. To ask a jury to consider whether the defendant used "intellectual or moral" force, while denying the instruction as to how to consider

---

58. It is clear from a reading of the relevant statutes and accompanying case law that the rape and IDSI statutes rely on the same definitions. Therefore, despite the fact that this is an IDSI case, our discussion of rape laws and cases involving rape convictions is relevant to and probative of the issue before us.

the defendant's mental state at the time of alleged encounter is patently unfair to the accused.

Appellant's argument is bolstered by the fact that the concept of "mistake of fact" has long been a fixture in the criminal law. The concept is codified in Pennsylvania and provides [18 Pa. C.S.A. §304]:

> Ignorance or mistake as to a matter of fact, for which there is reasonable explanation or excuse, is a defense if:
> (1) the ignorance or mistake negatives the intent, knowledge, belief, recklessness, or negligence required to establish a material element of the offense; or
> (2) the law provides that the state of mind established by such ignorance or mistake constitutes a defense

. . . Courts in other jurisdictions have likewise held that jury instructions regarding the defendant's reasonable belief as to consent are proper.

Although the logic of these other cases is persuasive, we are unable to adopt the principles enunciated in them because of the binding precedent with which we are faced, namely, *Williams*. In an effort to avoid application of *Williams*, appellant directs our attention to the Subcommittee Notes of the Pennsylvania Criminal Suggested Standard Jury Instructions. The possible conflict between *Williams* and §304 (Mistake of Fact) was not lost on the Subcommittee. . . .

> In the opinion of the Subcommittee there may be cases, especially now that *Rhodes* has extended the definition of force to psychological, moral and intellectual force, where a defendant might non-recklessly or even reasonably, but wrongly, believe that his words and conduct do not constitute force or the threat of force and that a non-resisting female is consenting. An example might be "date rape" resulting from mutual misunderstanding. The boy does not intend or suspect the intimidating potential of his vigorous wooing. The girl, misjudging the boys' character, believes he will become violent if thwarted; she feigns willingness, even some pleasure. In our opinion the defendant in such a case ought not to be convicted of rape.

. . . We agree with the Subcommittee that the rule in *Williams* is inappropriate in the type of date rape case described above. Changing codes of sexual conduct, particularly those exhibited on college campuses, may require that we give greater weight to what is occurring beneath the overt actions of young men and women. Recognition of those changes, in the form of specified jury instructions, strikes us an appropriate course of action.

Despite appellant's excellent presentation of the issues, there remain two distinct problems precluding relief in this case. First . . . [t]his case . . . is not one of the "new" varieties of sexual assault contemplated by the amended statute. This is a case of a young woman alleging physical force in a sexual assault and a young man claiming that he reasonably believed he had consent. In such circumstances, *Williams* controls.

We are keenly aware of the differences between *Williams* and this case. Most notable is the fact that Williams and his victim never met before the incident in question. Here, appellant and the victim not only knew one another, but had engaged in intimate contact just hours before the incident in question. It is clear however, that the *Williams* court's basis for denying the jury instruction was its conclusion that the law did not require it and, further, that the judiciary had no authority to grant it. Even if we were to disagree with those conclusions, we are powerless to alter them.

In any event, distinguishing *Williams* on the basis of the parties' previous contacts . . . is not enough to allow appellant the relief he seeks. Even if we . . . are persuaded by appellant's arguments chronicling the history of sexual assault law . . . , we face a second barrier. Because this appeal raises ineffective assistance of counsel, we are required to find that appellant's trial lawyer made a mistake. That mistake is the failure to ask the trial court for an instruction that the *Williams* case held is unwarranted. In other words, we would have to find that counsel's failure to argue for a change in the law constituted ineffectiveness. This, of course, is not possible. We simply cannot announce a new rule of law and then find counsel ineffective for failing to predict same.

. . . The relief appellant seeks represents a significant departure from the current state of the law. Despite its compelling nature, it cannot be the basis for an ineffective assistance of counsel claim.

Judgment of sentence affirmed.

▲ PROBLEM

Acquiescence on a Mountain Top (#121)

Sarah Lawler and Stephen Austin[59] work together and have developed a mutual respect for one another. As the two become closer in their friendship, Austin begins to find Lawler more and more attractive. He invites her on a weekend getaway up into the mountains. Austin owns a few acres and knows the perfect spot to take Lawler for a night alone. Lawler, admiring Austin's "back-to-the-land" approach, accepts his offer. She considers warning Austin not to get any romantic or sexual ideas about their trip together, but does not want to insult him and stays quiet, hoping that Austin will understand that they are just friends.

Alone, high in the mountains, beneath the stars, Austin and Lawler unroll their sleeping bags and prepare to go to sleep after a long drive. Austin brings up having sex to Lawler, stroking her as he talks. He starts with a soft whisper. "Oh, come on. You'll love it." She declines. "Why'd you come up here with me then? Just once. It's such a beautiful night. You'll enjoy it, really. Come on. Please?" Eventually the whining turns into an argument. As he starts touching her, Lawler blindly slaps him away.

Austin does not give up. His cajoling and pressuring goes on for several hours. There is no one around, nowhere for Lawler to run, and Austin has the keys to the only car. Lawler finally relents. As Austin is having sex with her, Lawler cries, but does not scream and does not tell him to stop. Afterwards, Lawler curls into a ball and falls asleep.

---

59. While the story is based on a real event, the names have been changed.

What liability for Austin, if any, under the Model Penal Code? Prepare a list of all criminal code subsections in the order in which you rely on them in your analysis.

What liability, if any, under the Michigan statutes excerpted in the Law Section after the principal case above?

✳ DISCUSSION ISSUE

Should Rape Liability Be Allowed in the Absence of Force or Threat of Force? Should It Be Allowed on Use of Nonphysical Coercion to Gain Acquiescence?

Materials presenting each side of this Discussion Issue appear in the Advanced Materials for Section 25 in Appendix A.

Hate Crimes

◆ THE CASE OF TODD MITCHELL (#122)

It is October 7, 1989, in Kenosha, Wisconsin, an industrial community of 80,000, just north of the Illinois border. The city's population is 90 percent white and counts among its numbers many German, Irish, and Polish immigrants. Over the past decade, however, its minority population has increased, with African Americans now accounting for 3 percent. For the most part, the different ethnic groups seem to live together comfortably, without the kind of racial problems that exist in larger communities. Like other Midwest factory towns, Kenosha has suffered economically with the decline of the American auto industry. Two years ago, the American Motor Company went out of business, and more recently a Chrysler plant closed, which have served to exacerbate the city's economic problems of high unemployment and empty industrial parks.

Figure 120 **Todd Mitchell at his trial in December 1989**

(Kenosha News)

Figure 121 **Viewpoint Mitchell and the others would have had while standing in front of the apartment complex and looking across the street to where Reddick was walking**

(Kenosha Joint Services)

On Forty-fifth Street, near the defunct American Motor Company plant, several African American teenagers are sitting in the hallway of an apartment complex, drinking wine and beer, and talking. Many have criminal histories for offenses like battery, disorderly conduct, and shoplifting. Some are also members of either the Vice Lords or Disciples, which are both street gangs that first appeared in the early 1980s. Officials consider these "spin-off gangs" to be a growing and potentially dangerous import from Chicago, but estimate that presently there are only about twenty to thirty hard-core gang members in the city.

After a while, the group's conversation turns to the recently released movie, "Mississippi Burning," which a number of them have seen. It is a fictionalized account of an F.B.I. investigation into the disappearance of three civil rights workers, two white, one black, in Jessup County, Mississippi. Several in the group are upset by one scene in particular. In the movie, evening services are just concluding with a hymn when trucks of hooded Ku Klux Klan men pull up and surround the exit of the church. The men and women of the congregation pause momentarily, but begin to run when the Klansmen firebomb the church. The Klansmen start chasing down people and beating those they catch. While the violence is swirling about, one boy stops to stare at the church and drops to his knees to pray. One of the hooded men approaches the boy and kicks him hard in the face and stomach, warning him that things will not change. As the boy curls up in pain, the man kicks him one last time before striding away.

Figure 122 **Intersection of 40th Avenue and 45th Street. Mitchell and the others were gathered in front of the apartment complex on the left**

(Kenosha Joint Services)

Discussing the scene makes the teenagers increasingly angry. Some of them have now moved outside and continue to talk and drink. After they have been talking for about forty-five minutes, nineteen-year old Todd Mitchell and his younger brother, Jermaine, who are also African American and live nearby on Forty-third Avenue, join them.

The older Mitchell brother remains generally quiet during the discussion of the movie, but grows enraged listening to the description of the firebombing scene. Seeing that the discussion angers everyone, Mitchell asks, "Do you all feel hyped up to move on some white people?" Looking across the street, he spots Gregory Reddick, a white fourteen-year old, walking home to Fifty-second Avenue from a nearby pizza parlor. Several in the group attend Bullen Junior High with Reddick, but nobody recognizes him. Mitchell turns to the group and says, "There goes a white boy. Go get him!"

Pointing left and right to signal that they should encircle him, Mitchell counts to three, and ten of them take off after Reddick. Knocking him to the ground, they kick, punch, and stomp on him for about five minutes. The beating leaves Reddick unconscious on the ground. One attacker thinks he is dead. Another takes Reddick's British Knight sneakers, a status symbol to some in the neighborhood, and later shows them off around the apartment complex. Throughout the attack, Mitchell watches from across the street.

Mitchell then flags down a police officer and shows him where Reddick lies. Emergency officials rush Reddick to St. Catherine's Hospital, where he remains comatose for four days. Doctors fear that his brain damage may be permanent.

1. Relying only on your own intuitions of justice, consider what liability and punishment, if any, Todd Mitchell would deserve, if he had done what he did with no racially related motivation. (Assume the victim was African American and assume his motivation was simply a dislike for the victim).

Now consider, and indicate below, what *additional liability and punishment above and beyond this amount,* if any, Todd Mitchell deserves on the actual facts of this case.

N	0	1	2	3	4	5	6	7	8	9	10	11
☐	☐	☐	☐	☐	☐	☐	☒	☐	☐	☐	☐	☐
no liability	liability but no punishment	1 day	2 wks	2 mo	6 mo	1 yr	3 yrs	7 yrs	15 yrs	30 yrs	life imprison-ment	death

2. What "justice" arguments could defense counsel make on the defendant's behalf?

3. What "justice" arguments could the prosecution make against the defendant?

4. What additional liability for Mitchell, if any, under the then-existing statutes? Prepare a list of all criminal code subsections in the order in which you rely on them in your analysis.

5. What additional liability, if any, under the Model Penal Code? Prepare a list of all criminal code subsections in the order in which you rely on them in your analysis.

■ THE LAW

Wisconsin Statutes
(1989)

Criminal Code

Section 940.19. Battery; Aggravated Battery   *All P mr*

(1) Whoever causes bodily harm to another by an act done with intent to cause bodily harm to that person or another without the consent of the person so harmed is guilty of a Class A misdemeanor.

(1m) Whoever causes great bodily harm to another by an act done with intent to cause bodily harm to that person or another without the consent of the person so harmed is guilty of a Class E felony.

(2) Whoever causes great bodily harm to another by an act done with intent to cause great bodily harm to that person or another with or without the consent of the person so harmed is guilty of a Class C felony.

(3) Whoever intentionally causes bodily harm to another by conduct which creates a high probability of great bodily harm is guilty of a Class E felony. A rebuttable presumption of conduct creating a substantial risk of great bodily harm arises:

(a) If the person harmed is 62 years of age or older; or

(b) If the person harmed has a physical disability, whether congenital or acquired by accident, injury or disease, which is discernible by an ordinary person viewing the physically disabled person.

Section 939.22. Words and Phrases Defined

In chs. 939 to 948 and 951, the following words and phrases have the designated meanings unless the context of a specific section manifestly requires a different construction of the word or phrase as defined in §948.01 for purposes of ch. 948: . . .

(4) "Bodily harm" means physical pain or injury, illness, or any impairment of physical condition. . . .

(14) "Great bodily harm" means bodily injury which creates a substantial risk of death, or which causes serious permanent disfigurement, or which causes a permanent or protracted loss or impairment of the function of any bodily member or organ or other serious bodily injury. . . .

Section 943.32. Robbery

(1) Whoever, with intent to steal, takes property from the person or presence of the owner by either of the following means is guilty of a Class C felony:

(a) By using force against the person of the owner with intent thereby to overcome his physical resistance or physical power of resistance to the taking or carrying away of the property; or

(b) By threatening the imminent use of force against the person of the owner or of another who is present with intent thereby to compel the owner to acquiesce in the taking or carrying away of the property.

(2) Whoever violates sub. (1) by use or threat of use of a dangerous weapon or any article used or fashioned in a manner to lead the victim reasonably to believe that it is a dangerous weapon is guilty of a Class B felony.

(3) In this section "owner" means a person in possession of property whether his possession is lawful or unlawful.

Section 939.05. Parties to Crime

(1) Whoever is concerned in the commission of a crime is a principal and may be charged with and convicted of the commission of the crime although he did not directly commit it and although the person who directly committed it has not been convicted or has been convicted of some other degree of the crime or of some other crime based on the same act.

(2) A person is concerned in the commission of the crime if he:

(a) Directly commits the crime; or

(b) Intentionally aids and abets the commission of it; or

(c) Is a party to a conspiracy with another to commit it or advises, hires, counsels or otherwise procures another to commit it.

Such a party is also concerned in the commission of any other crime which is committed in pursuance of the intended crime and which under the circumstances is a natural and probable consequence of the intended crime. This paragraph does not apply to a person who voluntarily changes his mind and no longer desires that the crime be committed and notifies the other parties concerned of his withdrawal within a reasonable time before the commission of the crime so as to allow the others also to withdraw.

Section 939.645. Penalty; Crimes Committed Against Certain People or Property

(1) If a person does all of the following, the penalties for the underlying crime are increased as provided in sub. (2):

(a) Commits a crime under chs. 939 to 948.

(b) Intentionally selects the person against whom the crime under par. (a) is committed or selects the property which is damaged or otherwise affected by the crime under par. (a) because of the race, religion, color, disability, sexual orientation, national origin or ancestry of that person or the owner or occupant of that property.

(2)(a) If the crime committed under sub. (1) is ordinarily a misdemeanor other than a Class A misdemeanor, the revised maximum fine is $10,000 and the revised maximum period of imprisonment is one year in the county jail.

(b) If the crime committed under sub. (1) is ordinarily a Class A misdemeanor, the penalty increase under this section changes the status of the crime to a felony and the revised maximum fine is $10,000 and the revised maximum period of imprisonment is 2 years.

(c) If the crime committed under sub. (1) is a felony, the maximum fine prescribed by law for the crime may be increased by not more than

$5,000 and the maximum period of imprisonment prescribed by law for the crime may be increased by not more than 5 years.

(3) This section provides for the enhancement of the penalties applicable for the underlying crime. The court shall direct that the trier of fact find a special verdict as to all of the issues specified in sub. (1).

(4) This section does not apply to any crime if proof of race, religion, color, disability, sexual orientation, national origin or ancestry is required for a conviction for that crime.

Section 939.23. Criminal Intent

(1) When criminal intent is an element of a crime in chs. 939 to 951, such intent is indicated by the term "intentionally," the phrase "with intent to," the phrase "with intent that," or some form of the verbs "know" or "believe."

(2) "Know" requires only that the actor believes that the specified fact exists.

(3) "Intentionally" means that the actor either has a purpose to do the thing or cause the result specified, or is aware that his or her conduct is practically certain to cause that result. In addition, except as provided in sub. (6), the actor must have knowledge of those facts which are necessary to make his or her conduct criminal and which are set forth after the word "intentionally."

(4) "With intent to" or "with intent that" means that the actor either has a purpose to do the thing or cause the result specified, or is aware that his or her conduct is practically certain to cause that result.

(5) Criminal intent does not require proof of knowledge of the existence or constitutionality of the section under which he is prosecuted or the scope or meaning of the terms used in that section.

(6) Criminal intent does not require proof of knowledge of the age of a minor even though age is a material element in the crime in question.

Section 939.24. Criminal Recklessness

(1) In this section, "criminal recklessness" means that the actor creates an unreasonable and substantial risk of death or great bodily harm to another human being and the actor is aware of that risk.

(2) If criminal recklessness is an element of a crime in chs. 939 to 951, the recklessness is indicated by the term "reckless" or "recklessly."

(3) A voluntarily produced intoxicated or drugged condition is not a defense to liability for criminal recklessness if, had the actor not been in that condition, he or she would have been aware of creating an unreasonable and substantial risk of death or great bodily harm to another human being.

Section 939.25. Criminal Negligence

(1) In this section, "criminal negligence" means ordinary negligence to a high degree, consisting of conduct which the actor should realize creates a substantial and unreasonable risk of death or great bodily harm to another.

(2) If criminal negligence is an element of a crime in chs. 939 to 951 or § 346.62, the negligence is indicated by the term "negligent."

● OVERVIEW OF HATE CRIMES

Notes

Hate Crimes
  Concern with Punishing Based on Offender's Motivation
  Acceptable to Punish Based on Motive, but Not Character
  Alternative Formulation Based on Culpability as to Sending Hateful Message

Hate Crimes   The most significant category of crimes punishing offenses against shared public values—in this case, values upholding human equality and dignity—is the category of *hate crimes*. A hate crime occurs when the offender targets the victims based on a bias against some characteristic or trait the victim possesses, or some group to which the victim belongs. (Hate crime laws frequently address crimes motivated by the victim's race, color, religion, national origin, or gender, but coverage of other traits, such as sexual orientation, varies across jurisdictions.) The underlying conduct—often an offense against the person such as assault or homicide, but potentially also a property crime such as theft or arson—is already criminalized and thus subject to punishment, but here the offender's bigotry is considered to make that crime especially heinous or outrageous, meriting an aggravation relative to the punishment such an offense would typically receive. Accordingly, hate crime provisions frequently are not enacted as separate offenses, but as grading or sentencing enhancements for existing crimes.[1]

  Concern with Punishing Based on Offender's Motivation   The antibigotry moral values that support hate crime provisions are widely shared and important, yet these provisions, which were widely adopted in the 1980s and 1990s, have always been highly controversial. The primary objection to hate crimes is the claim that the offender's *motive*, or underlying reason for acting, should not be relevant to criminal liability. By contrast, it is generally accepted that criminal law often does, and should, focus on an offender's *purpose* or *intention*—*what* the person is trying to achieve, as opposed to *why*.

  Acceptable to Punish Based on Motive, but Not Character   The purported distinction between motive and intention can be slippery and elusive, however. Here and elsewhere, the criminal law does sometimes consider an offender's reasons for acting in deciding whether the offender's conduct is criminal, or determining the proper degree of liability. For example, burning one's own house down is often lawful, but becomes criminal if one's underlying motivation is to obtain insurance money. In the grading or sentencing context, the degree of liability for criminal homicide may depend on the actor's motivation, which might either mitigate punishment (as in the provocation context) or aggravate it (as with a murder performed for hire or otherwise for the sake of financial gain[2]). Such a concern with motivation is important, as an actor's goals and reasons for having those goals seem highly relevant to the actor's blameworthiness. Indeed, taking

---

  1. See, e.g., Ala. Code § 13A-5-13; Fla. Stat. § 775.085; Ky. Rev. Stat. § 532.031; Minn. Stat. § 244.10.5a(11); Mo. Stat. § 557.035; N.Y. Penal Law § 485.10; Tenn. Code Ann. § 40-35-114(17); Utah Code § 76-3-203.3; Wis. Stat. § 939.645.
  2. See, e.g., Model Penal Code § 210.6(3)(g).

account of motive has the virtue of facilitating a moral evaluation while making sure to focus the inquiry on a person's actual conduct, rather than engaging in some broader investigation of the person's character. It is generally understood that criminal law should focus on bad acts and intentions, not overall character assessments—the law's concern is triggered only when character is manifested in conduct.

Alternative Formulation Based on Culpability as to Sending Hateful Message While considering an offender's motive may be consistent with traditional criminal law, it does not follow that focusing on the offender's subjective hate-based motivation is the best means of defining crimes of this sort. Rather than considering the individual person's reasons for acting, which may be multiple and complex, a hate crime provision might focus instead on the actor's culpability with respect to the factor justifying the prohibition: the propensity of this particular conduct to express improper bigotry, with all its ensuing tangible and intangible harms (traumatizing the victim, intimidating and demeaning the group to which the victim belongs, and outraging the community at large). In other words, such a formulation would focus not on the offender's own purposes for acting, but on the impact of the action on other people, including the outrage it will generate.[3] Such an offense (or grading or sentencing provision) could impose liability not only where the offender is affirmatively motivated by hatred, but also where the offender is knowing or reckless (or even negligent) as to the hateful message his conduct sends.

When an actor commits an offense against a person that is motivated by bias rooted in the person's membership in a certain kind of groups, hate crime laws may dictate more liability than would have been imposed without the prejudicial motivation. The limits of these laws are, however, still being defined. The following article by James Jacobs and Kimberly Potter explores the rationales behind hate crime laws and the debate over their scope. The authors survey the various state positions and address what offenses and biases are covered, the extent to which the biases must be manifest in order to incur liability, and the relationship between hate crime laws and the Civil Rights Act.

James B. Jacobs & Kimberly Potter, Hate Crime Laws
Hate Crimes: Criminal Law & Identity Politics 29–44 (1998)

> [O]ur single most effective weapon is the law. I implore you to support the Bias Related Violence and Intimidation Act I have proposed, and make it clear to the people of this state that behavior based on bias will not be ignored or tolerated.
>
> —*Letter from New York State Governor Mario M. Cuomo to the New York State Legislature, August 16, 1991*

By 1995, the federal government, thirty-seven states, and the District of Columbia had passed hate crime laws that fall into four categories: (1) sentence enhancements; (2) substantive crimes; (3) civil rights statutes; and (4) reporting statutes. The diversity of these laws demonstrates the plasticity of the hate crime concept.

---

3. See, e.g., Paul H. Robinson, *Hate Crimes: Crimes of Motive, Character, or Group Terror?*, 1993 Ann. Survey Am. L. 605.

Sentence Enhancements

The majority of hate crime statutes are of the sentence enhancement type. Typically, these laws bump up the penalty for a particular crime when the offender's motivation is an officially designated prejudice. The Montana and Alabama sentence enhancement statutes are typical. Montana provides that

> a person who has been found guilty of any offense that was committed because of the victim's race, creed, religion, color, national origin, or involvement in civil rights or human rights activities, *in addition to* the punishment provided for commission of the offense, *may be* sentenced to a term of imprisonment of not less than two years or more than 10 years.

Alabama provides a mandatory minimum sentence for violent crimes motivated by an officially designated bias.

> On a conviction of a Class A felony that was found to have been motivated by the victim's actual or perceived race, color, religion, national origin, ethnicity, or physical or mental disability, the sentence shall not be less than 15 years.

The size of the penalty enhancement varies from state to state. In Vermont, a hate crime is subject to *double* the maximum prison term. Under Florida's enhancement provision, the maximum possible sentence is tripled. The hate crime statute challenged before the Supreme Court in *Wisconsin v. Mitchell* provided for a two-year maximum prison term for aggravated battery, but if the perpetrator was motivated by bias, the maximum punishment jumped to seven years.

On the federal level, the Violent Crime Control and Law Enforcement Act of 1994 mandated that the U.S. Sentencing Guidelines provide a sentence enhancement of three "offense levels" above the base level for the underlying federal offense, if the sentencing court finds

> beyond a reasonable doubt that the defendant intentionally selected any victim or any property as the object of the offense because of the actual or perceived race, color, religion, national origin, ethnicity, gender [but not in the case of a sexual offense], disability, or sexual orientation of any person.

Applying the Sentencing Guidelines in the case of an aggravated assault, for example, the ordinary base level offense score of 15 is increased to 18, elevating the sentencing range from 18–24 months to 27–33 months.

The Enumerated Prejudices

The various state substantive and sentence enhancement hate crime laws differ from one another with respect to which prejudices transform ordinary crime into hate crime. All hate crime laws are designed to punish criminals motivated by prejudice based on race, color, religion, and national origin, but all uniformity ends there. Only eighteen states and the District of Columbia include gender and/or sexual orientation bias as hate crime triggers. Prejudice against Native Americans, immigrants, the physically and mentally handicapped, union members, nonunion members, right-to-life and pro-choice groups are included in some hate crime laws. Vermont's law applies to offenders motivated by prejudice against service in the armed forces. Montana condemns prejudice against "involvement in civil rights or human rights activities." The District of Columbia statute is the most inclusive; in addition to race, color, religion, national origin, gender, and sexual orientation, it prohibits targeting an individual or group by reason of physical disability, age, personal appearance, family responsibility, marital status, political affiliation, and matriculation.

Predicate Offenses

State hate crime laws also differ with respect to which predicate offenses, when motivated by prejudice, qualify as hate crimes. The Anti-Defamation League (ADL) model statute, which many states used as a prototype for their statutes, covers only harassment or intimidation. By contrast, in Pennsylvania, Vermont, and Alabama, *any offense* is a hate crime if the offender was motivated by race, religion, national origin, or other selected prejudices. The Alabama statute, which covers all misdemeanors and felonies:

> The purpose of this section is to impose additional penalties where it is shown that a perpetrator committing the underlying offense was motivated by the victim's actual or perceived race, color, religion, national origin, ethnicity, or physical or mental disability.

Other states limit hate crimes to certain predicate offenses. Some states reserve hate crime designation for low-level offenses, such as harassment, menacing, or criminal mischief. The Ohio hate crime statute covers only menacing, aggravated menacing, criminal damage or endangering, criminal mischief, and phone harassment. Similarly, in New Jersey, only simple assault, aggravated assault, harassment, and vandalism can be classified as hate crimes. New York has a single hate crime offense—aggravated harassment. Illinois designates nine predicate offenses: assault, battery, aggravated assault, misdemeanor theft, criminal trespass to residence, misdemeanor criminal damage to property, criminal trespass to vehicle, criminal trespass to real property, and mob action. Washington, D.C., includes arson, assault, burglary, injury to property, kidnaping, manslaughter, murder, rape, robbery, theft, or unlawful entry as possible hate crimes.

Defining and Proving Prejudiced Motivation

Most state hate crime laws do not use the word "motivation," rather, they prohibit *choosing* the victim "by reason of" or "because of" certain characteristics. Other states prohibit choosing the victim "maliciously and with specific intent."

The hate crime statutes differ on whether the offender's prejudice has to be "manifest" in the commission of the crime itself, or whether prejudice can be based on character evidence and evidence of the defendant's actions or words prior to the crime. In Washington, D.C., an ordinary crime becomes a hate crime when the conduct "*demonstrates* an accused's prejudice." Florida requires that the crime "evidences prejudice." One would think that what has to be demonstrated is (1) that the defendant harbors prejudiced beliefs, and (2) that this particular crime, in the way it was committed, demonstrates or reaffirms the existence of such prejudice.

But some juries and/or courts, perhaps hostile to the idea of hate crimes or wary of applying the statutes in an unconstitutional manner, seem to require that the crime demonstrate hard core prejudice.

In interpreting Florida's hate crime statute, which requires that the crime "evidences prejudice," the Florida Supreme Court held that

> [t]he statute requires that it is the commission of the crime that must evidence the prejudice; the fact that racial prejudice may be exhibited during the commission of the crime is itself insufficient.

The court explained that the statute was not meant to cover disputes, such as arguments over a parking space, which escalate into fist fights accompanied by racial or other slurs. If that restricted interpretation of hate crime law prevailed, hate crime laws would be reserved for hard core ideologues like neo-Nazis and thus rarely used.

Other states, such as Wisconsin and California, deal with the motivation element by requiring that the offender have "intentionally selected" the victim "because of" or "by reason of" race, color, religion, and so forth. Read literally, this type of statute would not require proof of *prejudice*, but merely color consciousness in the selection of a victim. For example, it would be a hate crime for a white defendant to attack and rob only Asian women because he perceived them as more vulnerable and less likely to resist. The defendant, although not prejudiced against Asians, would be a hate criminal for selecting the victim by reason of race. However, it is doubtful that prosecutors and judges would interpret the hate crime statute this way, because they recognize the legislative intent to penalize prejudice. Despite differences in the language used to set forth motivation requirements (manifest, evidences, motivated in whole, or in part, because of, etc.), the majority of courts hold that prejudice must be a *substantial* motivating factor.

In Pittsburgh, Pennsylvania, Emmitt Harris, a black male, and Matthew Chapman, a white male, were throwing trash in a dumpster behind the deli where Harris worked. The defendant, Theresa Ferino, a white woman whom Harris and Chapman knew as a deli customer, walked up the alley to the rear of the deli, pointed a gun at Harris and Chapman, and stated, "I'm going to kill, you fucking nigger." Ferino fired the gun in the direction of both Harris and Chapman, but injured no one. The state supreme court, in less than straightforward language, reversed the conviction for ethnic intimidation on the grounds that

> the singularity of the act committed by the [defendant], directed as it was against both Harris [a black man] and his companion (a Caucasian), the antecedent of which was neither a harsh word, gesture nor conduct exhibited between the victim and the [defendant], we do not believe rises to the proof-level sufficient to constitute a contravention of the ethnic intimidation statute.

In other words, use of the word "nigger," plus the firing of the gun, was not sufficient to sustain a hate crime conviction, when a second possible victim was someone of the same race as the defendant.

Substantive Offenses

ADL Model Hate Crime Law

Some hate crime statutes define new substantive offenses. They redefine conduct that is already criminal as a new crime or as an aggravated form of an existing crime. The ADL model statutes, which many states have adopted, provide for new substantive offenses of "intimidation" and "institutional vandalism."

> A person commits the crime of intimidation if, by reason of the actual or per-ceived race, color, religion, national origin or sexual orientation of another indi-vidual or group of individuals, he violates Section _____ of the Penal Code (insert provision for criminal trespass, criminal mischief, harassment, menac-ing, assault and/or appropriate statutorily proscribed criminal conduct).
>
> Intimidation is a _____ misdemeanor/felony (the degree of liability should be at least one degree more serious than that imposed for commission of the offense).

Intimidation, a new substantive offense, recriminalizes several existing low-level offenses, in effect *enhancing the maximum possible sentence* when the offender is motivated by one of the enumerated biases. Whether a hate crime law takes the form of a new substantive offense, or a sentence enhancement, the end result is the same—a more severe punishment. Hate crime laws in general, and this statute in particular, do not seem aimed at the archetypal racists, anti-Semites, misogynists, and homophobes. Instead, they seem aimed at the ad hoc disputes, arguments, and fights that frequently erupt in a multiracial, multiethnic, multire-ligious society. The following [cases are] typical:

- In 1989, David Wyant and his wife, both white, were playing loud music at their campsite in Ohio's Alum Creek State Park. Two black campers at the adjoining campsite, Jerry White and Patricia McGowan, complained to park officials. When asked by park officials to turn off the music, Wyant complied, but fifteen minutes later turned on the radio again. White and McGowan then overheard Wyant shouting that "[w]e didn't have this problem until those nig-gers moved in next to us. I ought to shoot that black motherfucker. I ought to kick his black ass." Wyant was convicted of ethnic intimidation, a fourth degree felony, and sentenced to one and one-half years imprisonment, *triple* the maximum sentence for the underlying offense of aggravated menacing, a first degree misdemeanor, with a sentence range of 0–6 months imprisonment or a fine.
- In 1991, a white police officer, Stephen Keyes, responded to a domestic dis-turbance call at the Florida home of Michael Hamm, an African American. When Officer Keyes attempted to arrest him, Hamm shouted, "I'll shoot you white cracker motherfucker." Believing that Hamm was armed, Keyes radioed for back-up. In the meantime, Hamm escaped, but was later apprehended. No gun was found. Hamm was charged with aggravated assault for "evidencing prejudice based on race, color, [etc.]." All charges were later dropped because there was not enough evidence (primarily, the lack of a weapon) that Hamm intended to assault Officer Keyes.
- In 1994, Herbert Cohen accompanied Denise Avard to Richard Stalder's Florida home to retrieve Avard's earrings; allegedly, Avard had some sort of dispute with Stalder. Stalder pushed Cohen and called him a "Jew boy," "Jewish lawyer," "you fat Jewish lawyer, get off my property," "Jewish kike, come on Jewish lawyer, I'm going to kick your ass." Stalder was charged with battery subject to a hate crime sentence enhancement.

ADL Model Institutional Vandalism Statute

The ADL recommends a second substantive hate crime statute for the destruction of property that belongs to religious groups. Its "Institutional Vandalism" law provides:

> A person commits the crime of institutional vandalism by knowingly vandalizing, defacing or otherwise damaging:
>
> i. Any church, synagogue, or other building, structure or place used for religious worship or other religious purposes;
>
> ii. Any cemetery, mortuary or other facility used for the purpose of burial or memorializing the dead;
>
> iii. Any school, educational facility or community center;
>
> iv. The grounds adjacent to, and owned or rented by any institution, facility, building, structure or place described in subsections (i), (ii), or (iii) above.

This statute increases penalties for vandalism of sacred buildings. "It is critical . . . that the enhanced penalties be sufficiently severe for the new statute to have its desired deterrent impact."

Some states combine the ADL intimidation and institutional vandalism model statutes. For example, Connecticut's hate crime statute provides:

> A person is guilty of intimidation based on bigotry or bias if such person maliciously, and with specific intent to intimidate or harass another person because of such other person's race, religion, ethnicity or sexual orientation does any of the following: (1) causes physical contact with such other person; (2) damages, destroys or defaces any real or personal property of such other person; or (3) threatens, by word or act, to do an act described in subdivision (1) or (2).

Under this statute, a hate crime prosecution could be brought if an offender spray paints anti-gay graffiti on the facade of a gay bar, but not if the offender spray paints misogynistic graffiti on *Ms. Magazine's* headquarters. While both hypothetical acts of vandalism express prejudice, gender-based prejudice is not covered by Connecticut's statute. In contrast, the Alaska and Michigan hate crime laws would produce the opposite result; the definition of hate crime includes gender bias, but not sexual orientation bias.

In New York, the substantive hate crime statute is called "aggravated harassment." It provides:

> A person is guilty of aggravated harassment . . . when with intent to harass, annoy, threaten, or alarm another person, he: Strikes, shoves, kicks, or otherwise subjects another person to physical contact, or attempts to threaten to do the same, because of the race, color, religion or national origin of such person.

Essentially, when a crime is motivated by bias, the defendant is charged with the underlying crime, assault for example, plus an added count of aggravated harassment. If convicted of aggravated harassment, the defendant faces a significantly more severe sentence. For example, in *People v. Grupe*, the defendant was convicted of aggravated harassment for striking a Jewish man while shouting anti-Semitic epithets, such as "Is that the best you can do? I'll show you Jew bastard." The maximum sentence under the aggravated harassment statute is one year imprisonment, whereas the maximum sentence for the same conduct, absent the anti-Semitic epithets, is 15 days imprisonment. Such significant differences in sentencing based on the words uttered during the crime have led some critics to call hate crime statutes "thought crime laws."

The Federal Civil Rights Acts

Some commentators refer to the federal criminal civil rights laws as hate crime statutes. However, they are actually quite different in intent, formulation, and operation—especially the post-Civil War statutes. They do not deconstruct criminal law into various offender/victim configurations based upon race, religion, sexual orientation, and the like; neither do they politicize "the crime problem" in the manner of the contemporary state hate crime laws.

Post-Civil War Rights Acts

After the Civil War, in many places within the former Confederacy, local law enforcement agencies would not prosecute crimes committed by whites against blacks, nor would local governments permit blacks to exercise rights guaranteed by the Fourteenth Amendment. So, Congress passed laws to authorize federal prosecution of the Ku Klux Klan and others, including law enforcement and government officials, who denied the newly freed slaves their civil rights. The authority for these statutes was Congress's power to enforce the Thirteenth and Fourteenth Amendments.

The federal statutes did not aim to enhance punishment or to *recriminalize* conduct already covered by criminal law. At the time, these statutes provided the only de facto law enforcement option. If local law enforcement officers had investigated and prosecuted those who victimized the former slaves, there would have been no need for the federal laws. The federal criminal civil rights statutes are not directed exclusively at hate crimes (although they can be used for that purpose), but at what law professor Frederick Lawrence calls "rights interference crimes." The civil rights statutes and hate crime laws both respond to issues of race and discrimination, but any similarity ends there. The civil rights statutes are not framed in terms of identity politics and group rights, but in terms of everyone's *individual* civil rights.

The first of the two post–Civil War statutes, 18 United States Code § 241, provides punishment for conspiracies to violate federally guaranteed rights. It provides that

> [i]f two or more persons conspire to injure, oppress, threaten, or intimidate any person in the free exercise or enjoyment of any right or privilege secured to him by the Constitution or laws of the United States or;
>
> If two or more persons go in disguise on the highway [i.e., the Ku Klux Klan], or on the premises of another, with intent to prevent or hinder [the] free exercise or enjoyment of any right or privilege so secured, [t]hey shall be fined not more than $10,000, or imprisoned not more than 10 years or both.

The second post–Civil War statute, 18 U.S.C. § 242, is explicitly concerned with federal, state, or local government officials who deprive private citizens of their federally guaranteed rights on the basis of certain characteristics. Its purpose is to guarantee even-handed, color-blind law enforcement:

> Whoever, under color of any law, . . . willfully subjects any person . . . to the deprivation of any rights, privileges, or immunities secured or protected by the Constitution or laws of the United States, or to different punishments, pains, or penalties, on account of such person being an alien, or by reason of his color, or race, than are prescribed for the punishment of citizens, shall be fined . . . or imprisoned. . . .

Neither of these statutes was meant to single out the prejudices of common criminals for special condemnation and more severe punishment; rather, their purpose was to ensure that laws were enforced equally on behalf of all victims, no matter what race, and against all offenders, whatever their race, prejudice, or criminal motivation. Unlike modern-day state hate crime statutes, which cover only those victims who fall within the groups listed in the hate crime statute, the post-Civil War statutes apply to everyone.

Sections 241 and 242 have been used to prosecute a wide variety of conduct, including ballot tampering, extortion by a public defender, unlawful searches, obstruction of federal witness's testimony, and the abuse of a state hospital patient by hospital staff. When the federal civil rights statutes have been used to prosecute cases of racially motivated violence, the crimes have almost always been committed "under color of law" as, for example, the 1964 murders by Mississippi police of civil rights workers Michael Henry Schwerner, James Early Chaney, and Andrew Goodman, or the 1992 attack of black motorist Rodney King by a group of Los Angeles police officers.

The 1968 Civil Rights Act

Passed as part of the Civil Rights Act of 1968, 18 United States Code §245, might be considered a precursor to the modern state hate crime laws. Indeed, §245 was one component of the legislation that marks the beginning of the modern civil rights movement. Titled "Federally Protected Activities," §245 was designed to provide a remedy for the violence resulting from opposition to civil rights marches, voter registration drives and other voting issues, enrollment of black students in formerly all-white schools and universities, and efforts to abolish Jim Crow laws.

The first subsection of Section 245 mirrors §§241 and 242 by specifically enumerating federal activities, the enjoyment of which the Act seeks to protect against infringement by anybody for any reason. The second subsection specifically protects a broad category of "state and local activities" from interference motivated by certain prejudices. It protects participants in state and local activities from victimization based on race, color, religion, and national origin. The prosecution must prove that the defendant, motivated by bias, attacked a victim who was participating in a state or local activity. The offender's prejudice need not have been the sole motivating factor. Subsection (b)(2) provides that

Whoever, whether or not acting under color of law, by force or threat of force willfully injures, intimidates or interferes with, or attempts to interfere with . . . any person because of his race, color, religion, or national origin and because he is or has been . . . enrolling in or attending a public school or university; participating in any benefit, program, service or facility provided by a state or local government; applying or working for any state or local government or private employer; serving as a juror; traveling in or using any facility of interstate commerce, or using any vehicle, terminal, or facility of any common carrier; or using any public facility, such as a bar, restaurant, store, hotel, movie theater, or stadium shall be punished. . . . [The statute provides a range of different punishments depending on the conduct, whether firearms or explosives are used, and the degree of injury to victims.]

Perhaps because of its complexity and abstruseness, this statute has rarely been used. The Department of Justice estimates that it "seeks indictments [for violations of §§241, 242, and 245] in 50–60 cases per year." These statutes were never intended, and have never served, as all-purpose federal hate crime statutes. Rather, they function as insurance which can be called upon if, for discriminatory or other improper reasons, state and local law enforcement officers fail to prosecute violations of civil rights.

At least ten states have civil rights-type statutes, patterned on the federal laws. These statutes are quite justifiably referred to as hate crime laws, since they aim at criminals who are prejudiced. West Virginia's statute, titled "Prohibiting Violations of an Individual's Civil Rights," provides:

All persons within the boundaries of the state of West Virginia have the right to be free from any violence, or intimidation by threat of violence, committed against their persons or property because of their race, sex, color, religion, ancestry, national origin, political affiliation, or sex.

If any person does by force or threat of force, willfully injure, intimidate or interfere with, or attempt to injure, intimidate or interfere with, or oppress or threaten any other person in the free exercise or enjoyment of any right or privilege secured to him or her by the Constitution or laws of the state of West Virginia or of the United States, because of such other person's race, color, religion, ancestry, national origin, political affiliation, or sex, he or she shall be guilty of a felony, and upon conviction, shall be fined not more than five thousand dollars or imprisoned not more than ten years or both.

Conclusion

In the mid-1980s, Congress and a majority of state legislatures passed hate crime laws that do not criminalize previously *noncriminal* behavior, but enhance punishment for conduct that was already a crime. The well-known federal criminal civil rights statutes are often assumed to be the model for these new laws, but they are quite different. They do not recriminalize prohibited behavior, enhance sentences, or designate a finite list of prejudices. They protect the federal, constitutional, and statutory rights of all citizens by making it a criminal offense to interfere with those rights. They provide federal insurance that crime will be prosecuted if state and local law enforcement authorities default in carrying out their responsibilities.

There are significant differences in the ways that federal and state legislatures define hate crimes. A number of states, following the ADL's lead, treat hate crime as a low-level offense, such as intimidation or harassment. Other states have more general hate crime laws and sentence enhancements that mandate higher sentences for most or all crimes when motivated by prejudice. The statutes also differ as to which prejudices transform ordinary crime into hate crime and as to whether those prejudices must be manifest in the criminal conduct itself or can be proved by evidence concerning the defendant's beliefs, opinion, and character. The diversity of hate crime laws means that we cannot assume that people are talking about the same thing when they discuss "hate crime" or that hate crime reports and statistics from one jurisdiction can be compared with reports and statistics from other jurisdictions.

Wisconsin v. Mitchell

Supreme Court of the United States
508 U.S. 476 (1993)

Chief Justice REHNQUIST delivered the opinion of the Court.

Respondent Todd Mitchell's sentence for aggravated battery was enhanced because he intentionally selected his victim on account of the victim's race. The question presented in this case is whether this penalty enhancement is prohibited by the First [Amendment]. We hold that it is not.

[The facts of the case can be found in the *Mitchell* case narrative at the beginning of this Section.]

After a jury trial in the Circuit Court for Kenosha County, Mitchell was convicted of aggravated battery. That offense ordinarily carries a maximum sentence of two years' imprisonment. But because the jury found that Mitchell had intentionally selected his victim because of the boy's race, the maximum sentence for Mitchell's offense was increased to seven years. . . . That provision enhances the maximum penalty for an offense whenever the defendant "[i]ntentionally selects the person against whom the crime . . . is committed . . . because of the race, religion, color, disability, sexual orientation, national origin or ancestry of that person. . . . " The Circuit Court sentenced Mitchell to four years' imprisonment for the aggravated battery.

Mitchell unsuccessfully sought postconviction relief in the Circuit Court. Then he appealed his conviction and sentence, challenging the constitutionality of Wisconsin's penalty-enhancement provision on First Amendment grounds. The Wisconsin Court of Appeals rejected Mitchell's challenge, . . . but the Wisconsin Supreme Court reversed. The Supreme Court held that the statute "violates the First Amendment directly by punishing what the legislature has deemed to be offensive thought." It rejected the State's contention "that the statute punishes only the 'conduct' of intentional selection of a victim." According to the court, "[t]he statute punishes the 'because of' aspect of the defendant's selection, the *reason* the defendant selected the victim, the *motive* behind the selection." (emphasis in original). And under R.A.V. v. St. Paul, 505 U.S. 377 (1992), "the Wisconsin legislature cannot criminalize bigoted thought with which it disagrees."

The Supreme Court also held that the penalty-enhancement statute was unconstitutionally overbroad. It reasoned that, in order to prove that a defendant intentionally selected his victim because of the victim's protected status, the State would often have to introduce evidence of the defendant's prior speech, such as racial epithets he may have uttered before the commission of the offense. This evidentiary use of protected speech, the court thought, would have a "chilling effect" on those who feared the possibility of prosecution for offenses subject to penalty enhancement. Finally, the court distinguished antidiscrimination laws, which have long been held constitutional, on the ground that the Wisconsin statute punishes the "subjective mental process" of selecting a victim because of his protected status, whereas antidiscrimination laws prohibit "objective acts of discrimination."

We granted certiorari because of the importance of the question presented and the existence of a conflict of authority among state high courts on the constitutionality of statutes similar to Wisconsin's penalty-enhancement provision. We reverse. . . .

The State argues that the statute does not punish bigoted thought, as the Supreme Court of Wisconsin said, but instead punishes only conduct. While this argument is literally correct, it does not dispose of Mitchell's First Amendment challenge. To be sure, our cases reject the "view that an apparently limitless variety of conduct can be labeled 'speech' whenever the person engaging in the conduct intends thereby to express an idea." Thus, a physical assault is not by any stretch of the imagination expressive conduct protected by the First Amendment.

But the fact remains that under the Wisconsin statute the same criminal conduct may be more heavily punished if the victim is selected because of his race or other protected status than if no such motive obtained. Thus, although the statute punishes criminal conduct, it enhances the maximum penalty for conduct motivated by a discriminatory point of view more severely than the same conduct engaged in for some other reason or for no reason at all. Because the only reason for the enhancement is the defendant's discriminatory motive for selecting his victim, Mitchell argues (and the Wisconsin Supreme Court held) that the statute violates the First Amendment by punishing offenders' bigoted beliefs.

Traditionally, sentencing judges have considered a wide variety of factors in addition to evidence bearing on guilt in determining what sentence to impose on a convicted defendant. The defendant's motive for committing the offense is one important factor. Thus, in many States the commission of a murder, or other capital offense, for pecuniary gain is a separate aggravating circumstance under the capital sentencing statute.

But it is equally true that a defendant's abstract beliefs, however obnoxious to most people, may not be taken into consideration by a sentencing judge. In [Dawson v. Delaware, 503 U.S. 159 (1992)], the State introduced evidence at a capital sentencing hearing that the defendant was a member of a white supremacist prison gang. Because "the evidence proved nothing more than [the defendant's] abstract beliefs," we held that its admission violated the defendant's First Amendment rights. In so holding, however, we emphasized that "the Constitution does not erect a *per se* barrier to the admission of evidence concerning one's beliefs and associations at sentencing simply because those beliefs and associations are protected by the First Amendment." Thus, in Barclay v. Florida, 463 U.S. 939 (1983) (plurality opinion), we allowed the sentencing judge to take into account the defendant's racial animus towards his victim. The evidence in that case showed that the defendant's membership in the Black Liberation Army and desire to provoke a "race war" were related to the murder of a white man for which he was convicted. Because "the elements of racial hatred in [the] murder" were relevant to several aggravating factors, we held that the trial judge permissibly took this evidence into account in sentencing the defendant to death.

[margin note: 1st amend not violated]

Mitchell suggests that *Dawson* and *Barclay* are inapposite because they did not involve application of a penalty-enhancement provision. But in *Barclay* we held that it was permissible for the sentencing court to consider the defendant's racial animus in determining whether he should be sentenced to death, surely the most severe "enhancement" of all. And the fact that the Wisconsin Legislature has decided, as a general matter, that bias-motivated offenses warrant greater maximum penalties across the board does not alter the result here. For the primary responsibility for fixing criminal penalties lies with the legislature.

[margin note: case comparison]

Mitchell argues that the Wisconsin penalty-enhancement statute is invalid because it punishes the defendant's discriminatory motive, or reason, for acting. But motive plays the same role under the Wisconsin statute as it does under federal and state antidiscrimination laws, which we have previously upheld against constitutional challenge. . . .

Nothing in our decision last Term in *R.A.V.* [v. St. Paul, 505 U.S. 377 (1992)] compels a different result here. That case involved a First Amendment challenge to a municipal ordinance prohibiting the use of "'fighting words' that insult, or provoke violence, 'on the basis of race, color, creed, religion or gender.'" Because the ordinance only proscribed a class of "fighting words" deemed particularly offensive by the city—i.e., those "that contain . . . messages of 'bias-motivated' hatred," we held that it violated the rule against content-based discrimination. But whereas the ordinance struck down in *R.A.V.* was explicitly directed at expression (*i.e.*, "speech" or "messages"), the statute in this case is aimed at conduct unprotected by the First Amendment.

[margin note: conduct vs. expression]

Moreover, the Wisconsin statute singles out for enhancement bias-inspired conduct because this conduct is thought to inflict greater individual and societal harm. For example, according to the State and its amici, bias-motivated crimes are more likely to provoke retaliatory crimes, inflict distinct emotional harms on their victims, and incite community unrest. The State's desire to redress these perceived harms provides an adequate explanation for its penalty-enhancement provision over and above mere disagreement with offenders' beliefs or biases. . . .

For the foregoing reasons, we hold that Mitchell's First Amendment rights were not violated by the application of the Wisconsin penalty-enhancement provision in sentencing him. The judgment of the Supreme Court of Wisconsin is therefore reversed, and the case is remanded for further proceedings not inconsistent with this opinion.

It is so ordered.

✳ DISCUSSION ISSUE

Should the Criminal Law Impose Additional Liability and Punishment for an Offense that Is Motivated by Hatred Toward an Identifiable Group?

Materials presenting each side of this Discussion Issue appear in the Advanced Materials for Section 26 in Appendix A.

Corporate Criminality

Corporate criminality has become an increasingly popular area of law over the past few decades. Criminal law is seen as providing a means of gaining greater compliance by corporations than would civil law alone. However, corporate criminal liability is necessarily based on a legal fiction, since only individuals can be moral beings. The advantages of treating corporations as fit criminal defendants, as well as the limitations, are explored throughout the Section.

◆ THE CASE OF FORD MOTOR COMPANY (#123)

It is about 5:30, the evening of August 10, 1978, in Elkhart County, Indiana. Lyn Ulrich, 16, hops into the back of her sister Judy's 1973 Ford Pinto. The Ulrichs' cousin Donna, 18, who is visiting from Illinois, climbs in after her. With Judy behind the wheel, they set off out of Osceolo down Highway 33 toward Elkhart. Elkhart County is a small conservative community in northern Indiana, east of South Bend. About 45,000 of the 125,000 residents live in the city of Elkhart itself. Many in the community share a common Amish or Mennonite heritage or, like the Ulrichs, a strong fundamentalist Christian faith. The girls are on their way to play volleyball at a Baptist church near Goshen, about 20 miles away.

Figure 123 **1973 Ford Pinto**
(FordPinto.com)

The Pinto is Judy's first car. Her parents, Earl and Mattie, are helping with payments as a graduation present. Judy knows that Pintos have been popular for years and has seen many on the road. Ford has sold almost 2 million, but recently they have become a major problem for the company.

The development of the car in the early 1970s was rushed from the start. Lee Iacocca, then president of Ford, insisted that the car be under 2,000 pounds and cost less than $2,000, which did not leave the engineers a great deal of flexibility in design features. Although the first Pinto passed all federal regulations, it did not hold up well in rear-end collisions. Horrible accidents involving Pintos eventually led to more than 50 civil suits against Ford. In one case in Southern California, a new Pinto stalls and is hit from behind by a car going about 30 mph. The Pinto immediately catches fire. Richard Grimshaw, a 13-year-old riding in the car, survives but is left with burns on 90 percent of his body. He loses his nose, left ear, and most of his left hand, and endures 65 surgeries and four months in the hospital. A jury awards him almost $128 million in punitive damages, in addition to $2.8 million in compensatory funds. At the time, it is the largest award ever made by a jury for a personal injury case, though the judge later reduces it to $6.6 million. There are several more accidents, and Ford soon learns to avoid jury trials.

Media attention increases dramatically when, in September 1977, Mark Dowie publishes an article in Mother Jones titled "Pinto Madness." In the award-winning article, Dowie reports that Ford knew the Pinto gas tank was unsafe. The car had failed every collision test when the gas tank was not altered using one of three relatively simple methods. A Ford engineer is quoted as saying that even though they knew it was not safe, no one necessarily would tell Lee Iacocca, who had personally pushed the development of the car to be completed in almost half the normal time. "That person would have been fired. Safety was not a popular subject around Ford in those days. With Lee it was taboo. Whenever a problem was raised that meant a delay in the Pinto, Lee would chomp on his cigar, look out the window, and say, 'Read the product objectives again and get back to work.'" At that time, safety was not one of the product objectives. Dowie went on to detail the internal Ford documents that used cost-benefit analysis to evaluate the costs of the Pinto casualties. The document showed that Ford rounded down the National Highway Traffic Safety

Figure 124 **Henry Ford II (right) announces restructuring of President Lee Iacocca's job, 1977**
(Bettmann/Corbis)

Administration's (NHTSA) calculation that a human life is worth $200,275, and by estimating 180 fiery deaths, 180 serious burn injuries and 2,100 burned vehicles, determined that damages would be about $49.5 million. According to company calculations, it was therefore less expensive to leave the flawed gas tank alone than to spend the $137 million estimated for an $11 adjustment to each of the 11 million cars and 1.5 million light trucks. Dowie questions the calculations as well as the underlying process, arguing that crashes would result in many more injuries than the company allowed, and that the cost to make the car safer could have been as low as $5.08. Ford contests most aspects of Dowie's evaluation, arguing as well that their decisions were not based on such cost-benefit calculations.

Public announcement of the Dowie report at a D.C. press conference began a public outcry against the Pinto. The next day, the NHTSA begins a formal investigation. On May 8, 1978, the NHTSA issues a report stating that the 1.9 million Ford Pintos and 30,000 Mercury Bobcats (a similar model) built between 1971 and 1976 have a system defect that could lead to fires in a rear-end collision. The Department of Transportation is then authorized to order a formal recall. Ford has thirty days to review the results before a public hearing set for June 14.

As a result of the bad publicity, on June 9 Ford recalls all Pintos made between 1971 and 1976, including Judy's car. The company reports that it will take a few months to get all the letters out; owners probably will not receive them until September. On this cool August evening, the girls are not thinking about any of these car troubles. Their family has not yet received word of the recall or the particular susceptibility of the gas tank to leaks during collisions. Enjoying the sun and the cool evening breeze on their way, the Ulrichs chat with their cousin, Donna. Born just a few days after Judy, Donna is president of her Mennonite church's youth group and is thinking about doing a full-time volunteer program now that she has graduated. She tells her cousins about the volunteer trip in rural Kentucky that her group just completed.

Judy has also just graduated from high school and plans to study interior design in college in the fall. She is working at an ice cream shop in South Bend to make money for college. Her younger sister, Lyn, is about to start her junior year at Penn High School and is a straight-A student. She thinks that she might study mathematics in college and works as a cashier at the local supermarket.

After they have driven for about half an hour, Judy notices that the gas is running low. She pulls into a Checker

Figure 125 **Judy Ulrich** (And Books)

Figure 126 **Lyn Ulrich** (And Books)

Figure 127 **Donna Ulrich** (And Books)

Figure 128 **Close-up view of the van and Pinto**
(And Books)

gas station and rests the gas cap on the roof of the car. After paying, she forgets to put the gas cap back on and starts driving with it still resting on the roof of the car. They do not notice until they have driven about a mile and a half and the cap suddenly flies off the roof and lands on the other side of the five-lane highway.

Traffic is not too bad. Judy waits until it seems safe, then carefully makes a U-turn and puts on her hazard flashers. She slowly drives westward toward the lost cap. There is an eight-inch curb along the side of the road that keeps her from pulling off the road.

At the same time, Robert Duggan is driving westward along Highway 33 in a gold van with Peace Train written across the hood. He is on his way to a friend's to get the van tuned up and ready for a vacation. He also needs to clean it up a bit; there are two Budweiser cans, the ends of two marijuana cigarettes, some rolling papers, and a baggie of what he thinks are amphetamines (actually caffeine pills). He had just gotten his license back a few weeks before, after speeding, running a stop sign, and failing to yield enough times that the authorities suspended his driving privileges. He is trying to be more careful now, so when he sees a police car coming the other way, he checks his speedometer to make sure he is still driving under the 55 mph limit. Relieved that he is, he reaches down to grab his pack of cigarettes, which has fallen to the floor of the van. When he looks up, he sees the Ulrich's Pinto about ten feet ahead. There is no time to stop.

Witnesses see Duggan's van slowing to what looks like about 30 mph before he hits the girls' car. The pine board bumper of the gold van slams into the back of the Pinto. The rear of the car is jammed into the highway and leaves three gouges in the road. Duggan is thrown forward but is not shaken too badly.

Rear steel sub-frames that might have protected the gas tank were rejected from the early Pinto design as too heavy and expensive to fit the self-imposed design requirements. The back bumper in these models can withstand a collision of only about 5 or 10 mph. Ford, with other car manufacturers, successfully lobbied to hold off federal requirements for resisting even 20 mph rear collisions until 1977. In a 30 mph collision, the car's back half entirely crumples.

The gas tank of Judy's Pinto is about six inches away from the bumper. From the force of the crash, the tank slams into the differential housing, the block in the middle of the rear axle, and ruptures on one of the four sharp bolts that stick out from the housing. Gas spills from these holes all over the road. The impact also pulls out the tube leading from the gas tank, leaving a two and one-half inch hole. More gas spills out through this hole. Then the tank bursts along the seams, and the seam rips, leaving a six-inch gap. More gas pours out.

All of this happens in a moment. The passenger compartment of Judy's car is splashed with a sheet of gasoline. Duggan can smell it from the road. The impact sets steel scraping against steel as the car grinds along the road. As a spark ignites the gasoline, a long flame shoots out, then a huge explosion, as the car bursts into flames.

Witnesses are shocked by the explosion and by the fire. For a 30-mph collision, they expected a mild fender bender, instead; the car looked "like a large napalm bomb." Bystanders can no longer see the girls in the backseat. It is "a solid mass of orange flame." Black smoke and flames billow out 20 feet into the air. The temperature in the back of the car reaches almost 1,000 degrees. The plastic dashboard and steering wheel melt almost completely, and the vinyl seats are burnt down to the springs. Lyn's sunglasses melt around her eyes. Donna and Lyn die in less than a minute.

Judy is thrown from the car, still alive, but is burned over more than 95 percent of her body. Her right ankle is caught in the door, and as her sneaker melts on her foot she begins to call for help. Bystanders, stunned that she is still alive, run to try to help, and use a board to pry the door open. They pull her to the side of the road.

Duggan is on his knees, watching in horror and sobbing. When someone checks to see if he is all right, he beats the ground with his fists, and cries for people to help the girls.

Bradley McCalim, one of the first EMTs to arrive, has not seen a similarly severe burn victim since Vietnam. He cannot believe Judy is still alive; in fact, until she speaks, he is sure she is dead. Judy asks him if the other girls are all right. A bystander, without looking into the burnt shell of the car, reassures her that they are.

The medics, thankful that Judy cannot feel the extent of her injuries because the nerve endings are burned, reassure her about her chances, telling her that she will make it, even though they know that there is no hope. She dies eight hours later.

Neil Graves, a six-and-a-half year veteran state trooper, is soon radioed to report to the scene. He has seen 987 accidents and does not expect this to be anything new. But the scene is not what he expects. He has seen only three car fires, and they were usually only after high speed collisions. Here the cars do not look like they are from the same accident. One of the van's headlights is cracked, the

Figure 129 **The accident scene**
(And Books)

grill is pushed in, and there are a few dents. The back of the Pinto is completely buckled, and only the burnt shell of the car remains.

Looking inside, he sees two charred bodies in the back seat, a gruesome sight he will never forget. Then he notices the smell of gasoline in the interior of the car. At some point, he remembers the article he read in Mother Jones the year before about the Pinto and starts wondering about the role the car might have played in the accident.

News of the accident gets out. After a local television station calls Terry Shewmaker, the county's assistant prosecutor, to ask him about the case, Shewmaker calls the sheriff to find out what happened. Then he calls his boss, Mike Consentino. Hearing of the severity of the deaths, injuries, and damage, Consentino tells Shewmaker to treat it as a potential homicide.

Mike Consentino is a hard-working Republican who ran for and won the elected position of county prosecutor on a "law and order" platform. He was raised by his mother, and as a teenager earned an athletic scholarship to Beloit College, where he majored in philosophy. He briefly served in the military, then put himself through evening classes at the University of Wisconsin. His job as prosecutor is only part-time; he spends the rest of his time in private practice, often defending corporations and others in the community. But he is proud of his record as a prosecutor: He has won convictions in every one of the 25 murder cases he has tried.

On Friday, Duggan is arrested for possession of an illegal drug after the pills are found in his van. They are later determined to be caffeine. Meanwhile, national media track down the state trooper, Graves, where he works at his part-time job. They ask about the car, not the drivers. Consentino calls "Pinto Madness" author Dowie and gets more details about Ford's development of the car and suggestions on whom to contact at the company.

Evidence from the accident site is collected and processed during the weekend. Consentino and Shewmaker meet with Graves and the rest of the staff to discuss the charges for the case. Pictures of the dead girls are passed around, leaving the men horrified and upset. No one should die that way, they think. Something must have gone wrong, and they feel that they need to find out who was responsible.

Lawyers with civil cases pending against Ford start calling Consentino offering corporate documents that would be damaging to Ford. The criminal case could have great influence over other Pinto civil suits. A verdict against Ford in a criminal case, which has a stricter burden of proof than in civil cases, would hurt Ford's position in civil trials and give civil lawyers an edge.

Seeing the volume of evidence against Ford that points to the company's knowledge of the Pinto's dangerousness and the company's delay in acting on a recall, Consentino concludes that the company had a role in the girls' deaths. Looking at the case as a prosecutor, he concludes that Ford's development of the Pinto makes the company criminally culpable, not just tangentially responsible. The company has done something morally wrong that resulted in three individuals' deaths, he reasons. It should be prosecuted. Mattie and Earl Ulrich strongly support the idea of going after Ford in a criminal prosecution.

Consentino files an indictment that charges Ford Motor Company, a corporation, with causing the Ulrichs' deaths "through the acts and omission of its agents acting within the scope of their authority with said corporation

Figure 130 **Prosecutor Mike Consentino** (And Books)

[when they] did recklessly design and manufacture a certain 1973 Pinto . . . in such a manner as would likely cause said automobile to flame and burn upon rear-end impact, . . . [and such] reckless disregard for the safety of other persons [caused the girls] to languish and die by incineration."

It is the first time that a major corporation has been indicted on homicide charges for making an allegedly defective product that led to a consumer's death. The maximum penalty is a fine of $10,000 for each death. The van driver, Duggan, is not charged with an offense.

1. Relying only on your own intuitions of justice, what liability and punishment, if any, does the Ford Motor Company deserve? (As a corporate defendant cannot physically be imprisoned, use the scale below simply as a device by which to communicate the quantum of punishment you think is deserved. That punishment, if any, would be imposed through a mechanism other than imprisonment.)

N	0	1	2	3	4	5	6	7	8	9	10	11
☐	☐	☐	☐	☐	☐	☐	☒	☐	☐	☐	☐	☐
no liability	liability but no punishment	1 day	2 wks	2 mo	6 mo	1 yr	3 yrs	7 yrs	15 yrs	30 yrs	life imprison-ment	death

2. What "justice" arguments could defense counsel make on the defendant's behalf?

3. What "justice" arguments could the prosecution make against the defendant?

4. What liability, if any, for Ford under the then-existing statutes? Prepare a list of all criminal code subsections or cases in the order in which you rely on them in your analysis.

5. What liability, if any, under the Model Penal Code? Prepare a list of all criminal code subsections in the order in which you rely on them in your analysis.

■ THE LAW

Burns Indiana Statutes Annotated
(1978)

Division 5. Courts and Judicial Proceedings

Title 35, Book 2. Criminal Law and Procedure
Article 42. Offenses Against the Person

Section 35-42-1-1. Murder

A person who:
    (1) Knowingly or intentionally kills another human being; or
    (2) Kills another human being while committing or attempting to commit arson, burglary, child molesting, criminal deviate conduct, kidnapping, rape, or robbery;
commits murder, a felony.

Section 35-42-1-4. Involuntary Manslaughter

A person who kills another human being while committing or attempting to commit:
    (1) A class C or class D felony that inherently poses a risk of serious bodily injury;
    (2) A class A misdemeanor that inherently poses a risk of serious bodily injury; or
    (3) Battery;
commits involuntary manslaughter, a class C felony. However, if the killing results from the operation of a vehicle, the offense is a class D felony.

Section 35-42-1-5. Reckless Homicide

A person who recklessly kills another human being commits reckless homicide, a Class C felony. However, if the killing results from the operation of a vehicle, the offense is a Class D felony.

Section 35-42-2-2. Recklessness

(a) A person who recklessly, knowingly, or intentionally performs an act that creates a substantial risk of bodily injury to another person commits criminal recklessness, a Class B misdemeanor. However, the offense is a Class A misdemeanor if the conduct includes the use of a vehicle or deadly weapon.

(b) A person who recklessly, knowingly, or intentionally inflicts serious bodily injury on another person commits criminal recklessness, a Class D felony.

Article 41. Crimes—General Substantive Provisions

Chapter 2. Basis of Liability

Section 35-41-2-1. Voluntary Conduct

(a) A person commits an offense only if he voluntarily engages in conduct in violation of the statute defining the offense. However, a person who omits to perform an act commits an offense only if he has a statutory, common law, or contractual duty to perform the act.

(b) If possession of property constitutes any part of the prohibited conduct, it is a defense that the person who possessed the property was not aware of his possession for a time sufficient for him to have terminated his possession.

Section 35-41-2-2. Culpability

(a) A person engages in conduct "intentionally" if, when he engages in the conduct, it is his conscious objective to do so.

(b) A person engages in conduct "knowingly" if, when he engages in the conduct, he is aware of a high probability that he is doing so.

(c) A person engages in conduct "recklessly" if he engages in the conduct in plain, conscious, and unjustifiable disregard of harm that might result and the disregard involves a substantial deviation from acceptable standards of conduct.

(d) Unless the statute defining the offense provides otherwise, if a kind of culpability is required for commission of an offense, it is required with respect to every material element of the prohibited conduct.

Section 35-41-2-3. Liability of a Corporation, Partnership or Unincorporated Association

(a) A corporation, partnership, or unincorporated association may be prosecuted for any offense; it may be convicted of an offense only if it is proved that the offense was committed by its agent acting within the scope of his authority.

(b) Recovery of a fine, costs, or forfeiture from a corporation, partnership, or unincorporated association is limited to the property of the corporation, partnership, or unincorporated association.

Howell v. State
200 Ind. 345; 163 N.E. 492; 1928 Ind. LEXIS 78 (1928)

Defendant drove an automobile along a paved road at an unlawful speed of thirty-five miles per hour and collided with a nine-year-old girl, who, with two companions, was proceeding along the road facing the oncoming automobile, but on the opposite side of the road. When the car was within ten feet of her, the deceased suddenly darted in front of the automobile. The court held that the unlawful act of the defendant was not the proximate cause of her death.

Model Penal Code
(Official Draft 1962)

Section 2.07. Liability of Corporations, Unincorporated Associations and Persons Acting, or Under a Duty to Act, in Their Behalf

(1) A corporation may be convicted of the commission of an offense if:

(a) the offense is a violation or the offense is defined by a statute/other than the Code in which a legislative purpose to impose liability on corporations plainly appears (and) the conduct is performed by an agent of the corporation acting in behalf of the corporation within the scope of his office or employment./except that if the law defining the offense designates the agents for whose conduct the corporation is accountable (or) the circumstances under which it is accountable, such provisions shall apply; (or)

(b) the offense consists of an omission to discharge a specific duty of affirmative performance imposed on corporations by law; or

Iacocca (c) the commission of the offense was authorized, requested, commanded, performed or <u>recklessly tolerated</u> by the board of directors or by a high managerial agent acting in behalf of the corporation within the scope of his office or employment.

(2) When absolute liability is imposed for the commission of an offense, a legislative purpose to impose liability on a corporation shall be assumed, unless the contrary plainly appears.

(3) An unincorporated association may be convicted of the commission of an offense if:

(a) the offense is defined by a statute other than the Code which expressly provides for the liability of such an association and the conduct is performed by an agent of the association acting in behalf of the association within the scope of his office or employment, except that if the law defining the offense designates the agents for whose conduct the association is accountable or the circumstances under which it is accountable, such provisions shall apply; or

(b) the offense consists of an omission to discharge a specific duty of affirmative performance imposed on associations by law.

(4) As used in this Section:

(a) "corporation" does not include an entity organized as or by a governmental agency for the execution of a governmental program;

(b) "agent" means any director, officer, servant, employee or other person authorized to act in behalf of the corporation or association and, in the case of an unincorporated association, a member of such association;

(c) "high managerial agent" means an officer of a corporation or an unincorporated association, or, in the case of a partnership, a partner, or any other agent of a corporation or association having duties of such responsibility that his conduct may fairly be assumed to represent the policy of the corporation or association.

(5) In any prosecution of a corporation or an unincorporated association for the commission of an offense included within the terms of Subsection (1)(a) or Subsection (3)(a) of this Section, other than an offense for which absolute liability has been imposed, it shall be a defense if the defendant proves by a preponderance of evidence that the high managerial agent having supervisory responsibility over the subject matter of the offense employed due diligence to prevent its commission. This paragraph shall not apply if it is plainly inconsistent with the legislative purpose in defining the particular offense.

(6)(a) A person is legally accountable for any conduct he performs or causes to be performed in the name of the corporation or an unincorporated association or in its behalf to the same extent as if it were performed in his own name or behalf.

(b) Whenever a duty to act is imposed by law upon a corporation or an unincorporated association, any agent of the corporation or association having primary responsibility for the discharge of the duty is legally accountable for a reckless omission to perform the required act to the same extent as if the duty were imposed by law directly upon himself.

(c) When a person is convicted of an offense by reason of his legal accountability for the conduct of a corporation or an unincorporated association, he is subject to the sentence authorized by law when a natural person is convicted of an offense of the grade and the degree involved.

● OVERVIEW OF CORPORATE CRIMINALITY

Hypothetical: Evergreen Greenbacks (#124)

Garden Centers Supply, Inc. (GCS) supplies independent retailers with flowers, bushes, trees, and other plants. During the two months before Christmas, GCS hires additional help to handle the large increase in business generated by Christmas tree sales. Bob and Chester Turner have recently been hired to tour the many small local tree farms. They are authorized to buy trees for up to $2.25 per foot. If they negotiate a lower price, they receive a bonus equal to 20% of any amount saved.

Because demand is high this year, trees are harder to find and those available are bringing higher prices. As the first three weeks of hauling close, Bob and Chester find that they are far from the bonuses they were counting on. Indeed, they have failed to meet their quota and are concerned that they may not be hired again next year.

They hit on a plan that they think will improve their situation. A state forest within their territory has suitable trees. By adding state trees to their farm purchases and doctoring their transport slips, they can both fill their quota and reduce the per-foot cost of each load. The company handbook for drivers specifically prohibits such unauthorized cuttings, but Bob and Chester see little chance of being caught either by the state foresters or by the company.

By week five, their record has improved dramatically and they are in line for big bonuses. Company officials are surprised by the dramatic improvement, especially given the poor condition of the market supply. When asked to explain their sudden success, Bob and Chester have no explanation other than, "We're just lucky." Officials are puzzled and suspicious, but see no way to effectively pursue the matter further. They remind Bob and Chester of the company's policy against unauthorized cuttings.

A state forester in Flemington is shocked to find a Z-type spruce on sale when she takes her children to buy their Christmas tree. Z-types are an experimental tree bred for their capacity to quickly absorb large amounts of water, an important characteristic for successful plantings in sandy soil. She relates her discovery to state investigators, who paper-trace the tree to a purchase by Bob and Chester from the Elliott farm, which has no Z-types. Interviews with the Elliotts reveal alterations in the transport slips. The illegal cuttings from the state forest are discovered.

State officials institute a prosecution not only against Bob and Chester, but also against GCS for the actions of its employees. The officials, noting the difficulty of effectively policing the large stands of state evergreens found in unpopulated areas throughout the state, cite the special need for this case to send a message that will deter others. By prosecuting GCS, they hope to motivate all wholesalers to more actively discourage illegal state cuttings. They also believe that the publicity surrounding the prosecution will discourage the traditional increase in state tree thefts immediately preceding Christmas.

Is GCS liable for the thefts of state trees by Bob and Chester?

Notes

Organizational Liability as Imputation
Shift from Common Law Reluctance to Find Organizations Criminally Liable
Offenses Authorized by Upper Management
Liability for Conduct "Recklessly Tolerated" by Management
Liability for Agent's Unauthorized Regulatory Violation
Liability for Agent's Unauthorized Criminal Offense
    Example: Liability for Agent's Unauthorized Antitrust Violation
Deterrence Rationale of Expansive Corporate Liability
Other Relaxations of Liability Requirements

Organizational Liability as Imputation Because an organization can neither act nor think except through its agents and officers, it cannot satisfy the elements of an offense except through imputation. Thus, if criminal liability is to be imposed on an organization, as opposed to its individual members, the criminal law must specify the rules enabling imputation of conduct and culpability to the organization.

Shift from Common Law Reluctance to Find Organizations Criminally Liable Courts in the Common Law period were reluctant to impose criminal liability on corporations. Such liability seemed impossible: How could a legal entity have the *mens rea* required by criminal law? Many procedural requirements, such as the presence of the defendant at trial, also seemed to suggest that organizations were inappropriate subjects for criminal prosecutions. Further, the most common forms of criminal punishment—imprisonment or execution—were unavailable for corporations. However, growing industrialization and public pressure for more effective control of corporate behavior brought about a change of view.[1] Prosecution of corporations was first allowed for strict liability offenses. Because such offenses required no *mens rea* and rarely involved a sentence of imprisonment, their use against an incorporeal, purely legal entity seemed less objectionable. The potential for corporate criminality then spread to general-intent offenses. Common Law rules often presumed a required "general intent" from the offense conduct. This made it possible to prosecute organizations without any special rules for imputing *mens rea*. Corporations could not be held liable for specific-intent offenses, however, because of the impossibility of proving that the corporation itself possessed such intent. Only more recently has corporate liability expanded to include intentional crimes.

Offenses Authorized by Upper Management While it is sometimes criticized as double vicarious liability—the shareholders being punished without regard to their ability to control the management, and the management being punished without regard to their ability to control the offending employee— many jurisdictions tend to avoid the most egregious instances of vicarious liability by imposing important limitations. In *State v. Christy Pontiac-GMC, Inc.*, a salesman for the Christy Pontiac car dealership swindled two customers out of cash rebates and kept the money for the corporation. Under the rules of organizational liability used in *Christy*, the criminal acts of a corporation's agent are imputed to the corporation if they are (1) performed within the scope of employment, (2) in furtherance of the interests of the corporation, and (3) authorized, tolerated, or ratified by corporate management.[2] Because the corporation received the swindled funds and the conduct was ratified, if not authorized, by the corporation's president, the corporation was held liable for the employee's criminal act. Applying this approach to the "Evergreen Greenbacks" hypothetical, GCS is not likely to be held liable because there is no indication that management knew anything about the illegal cutting of state trees.

Liability for Conduct "Recklessly Tolerated" by Management Some jurisdictions follow the Model Penal Code in extending liability not only to conduct authorized or ratified by corporate management, but also to conduct "recklessly tolerated."[3] This seeks to prevent management from simply turning a blind eye

---

1. See, for example, the discussion in New York Central & Hudson River R.R. Co. v. United States, 212 U.S. 481 (1909).

2. 354 N.W.2d 17, 18-20 (Minn. 1984).

3. Model Penal Code § 2.07(1)(c). This form of liability is not available under the Code for the prosecution of unincorporated associations.

to violations because the violations further the corporate interest. This approach, focusing on the acts or omissions of upper management, stems from a belief that punishing management misconduct is the most effective and fair means of deterring future corporate misconduct. Applying this approach to the hypothetical, prosecutors may claim that GCS management consciously disregarded the substantial risk that the trees were procured illegally, as management was indeed suspicious that the trees could have been procured through legal means given the existing shortage.

Liability for Agent's Unauthorized Regulatory Violation   Some jurisdictions, again following the Model Penal Code, also allow organizational liability for quasi-criminal offenses (often called "violations") and regulatory offenses (typically defined outside of the criminal code) even where there is no showing of authorization (or reckless toleration) by upper management. As MPC section 2.07(1)(a) provides:

> A corporation may be convicted of the commission of an offense if . . . the offense is a violation or the offense is defined by a statute other than the Code in which a legislative purpose to impose liability on corporations plainly appears and the conduct is performed *by an agent of the corporation acting in behalf of the corporation within the scope of his office or employment*, except that if the law defining the offense designates the agents for whose conduct the corporation is accountable or the circumstances under which it is accountable, such provisions shall apply. . . .

As the italicized language makes clear, liability can arise from any conduct an agent performs on behalf of the corporation, even if the corporation did not directly authorize that particular conduct. But where such is the basis for liability, many jurisdictions follow the Model Penal Code in allowing a "due diligence defense," such as under MPC section 2.07(5):

> [I]t shall be a defense if the defendant proves by a preponderance of evidence that the high managerial agent having supervisory responsibility over the subject matter of the offense employed due diligence to prevent its commission. This paragraph shall not apply if it is plainly inconsistent with the legislative purpose in defining the particular offense.[4]

Liability for Agent's Unauthorized Criminal Offense   Other jurisdictions, including federal law, provide a still broader form of corporate liability. These jurisdictions simply impute to the corporation the conduct of any agents acting within the scope of their employment to the corporation. Under this rule, corporate liability even for serious offenses is not limited to violations authorized by, or recklessly tolerated by, upper management. Nor do most of these jurisdictions provide a due-diligence defense for upper-management attempts to prevent the offense. Under this approach, corporate criminal liability is not significantly different from corporate tort liability under the doctrine of *respondent superior*. In fact, some courts have put it in just those terms.[5] Thus, a corporation may be

---

4. Model Penal Code § 2.07(5).
5. Judge Learned Hand concludes that "there is no distinction in essence between the civil and the criminal liability of corporations based upon the element of intent or wrongful purpose. Each is merely an imputation to the corporation of the mental condition of its agents." U.S. v. Nearing, 252 F. 223, 231 (D.N.Y. 1918).

liable for a serious offense committed by its agent, even where the management expressly forbade and diligently sought to prevent the agent's acts.

Example: Liability for Agent's Unauthorized Antitrust Violation   In United States v. Hilton Hotels Corp.,[6] for example, a group of hotels, restaurants, and hotel and restaurant supply companies organized an association with other businesses in Portland, Oregon to attract conventions to their city. Members were to contribute money to help fund the association. To aid collections, hotel members, including appellant, agreed to give preferential treatment to suppliers who paid their assessments, and to curtail purchases from those who did not. The agreement was later held to violate the Sherman Antitrust Act. Although the hotel's president and manager disapproved of the scheme, the purchasing agent abided by the agreement. The *Hilton* court concluded that imputation does not require official authorization or toleration of the agent's criminal conduct; the corporate entity can be held liable even if management specifically prohibited the agent's conduct. *Hilton* requires only that the conduct be within the scope of employment and that outsiders might reasonably assume that the agent's conduct was authorized.[7] Applying the *Hilton* approach to the hypothetical, GCS may well be liable for the thefts by Bob and Chester. Neither management's lack of actual knowledge of their conduct, nor the specific prohibition of their actions in the company handbook, would protect the company from liability.

Deterrence Rationale of Expansive Corporate Liability   The *Hilton* approach reasons that a corporation's express prohibition of the criminal conduct ought not protect the corporation from liability because, after issuing formal orders against a violation, the upper management nonetheless may facilitate or endorse the violation in less visible ways. Further, high management is likely to know about violations—or if not, should be encouraged to learn about them— and thus ought to have the burden of doing whatever is necessary to prevent them. But these concerns may be satisfied by using a "reckless toleration" standard of liability, as do the jurisdictions following the Model Penal Code. Perhaps the broader liability of the *Hilton* approach provides greater deterrence than if liability were limited to only the offending agent: In a large corporation, the offending agent may be difficult to identify and, even if caught and punished, the agent may not be in a position to change the practices of other corporate agents. Under this view, only high management has the opportunity and authority effectively to avoid violations, so the law must target high management to create incentives for it to prevent criminal activity.[8] This line of argument indicates a strictly utilitarian deterrence basis for corporate criminal liability, as it openly abandons any pretense that criminal liability for corporations rests upon the traditional blameworthiness criterion that governs criminal liability in nonorganizational contexts. In doing so, such a broad imputation rule threatens to blur the distinction between criminal and civil liability.

Other Relaxations of Liability Requirements   For reasons similar to those offered by the *Hilton* court, many jurisdictions have done much to relax the normal rules of imputation and proof. Some hold that it need not be shown that

---

6. 467 F.2d 1000, 1002 (9th Cir. 1972).
7. *Hilton*, 467 F.2d at 1007.
8. *Hilton*, 467 F.2d at 1006.

any agent of the company satisfies both the objective and culpability elements of the offense, although concurrence between the two normally would be required. Indeed, many courts do not require the identification of the agent who performed the criminal conduct. The requirement that the agent be acting within the scope of his employment has been similarly broadened to include nearly any job-related activity. Also, it need not be shown that the corporation actually received any benefit from the agent's offense, although conduct that is against the corporation's interest will not support liability for the corporation.

Commonwealth v. Beneficial Finance Co.

Supreme Judicial Court of Massachusetts
360 Mass. 188, 275 N.E.2d 33 (1971)

SPIEGEL, Justice.

[Beneficial Finance Co. was convicted, along with other defendants, both individual and corporate, of bribing and conspiring to bribe state banking officials in order to receive preferential treatment from the state Small Loans Regulatory Board. The acts of bribery were committed by corporate employees. John M. Farrell worked as an officer and director of Beneficial Management Co., a subsidiary of Beneficial Finance, and Francis T. Glynn reported to Farrell but was paid through Industrial Bankers, another subsidiary of Beneficial Finance. Both men were implicated in the bribery scheme, as Glynn personally met with the state banking officials, and Farrell oversaw Glynn's contact with the officials and adopting the bribery plan. Neither, however, were officers or directors of Beneficial Finance itself.]

The defendants and the Commonwealth have proposed differing standards upon which the criminal responsibility of a corporation should be predicated. The defendants argue that a corporation should not be held criminally liable for the conduct of its servants or agents unless such conduct was performed, authorized, ratified, adopted or tolerated by the corporations' directors, officers or other "high managerial agents" who are sufficiently high in the corporate hierarchy to warrant the assumption that their acts in some substantial sense reflect corporate policy. This standard is that adopted by the American Law Institute Model Penal Code. . . . Section 2.07 of the Code provides that, except in the case of regulatory offences and offences consisting of the omission of a duty imposed on corporations by law, a corporation may be convicted of a crime if "the commission of the offence was authorized, requested, commanded, performed or recklessly tolerated by the board of directors or by a high managerial agent acting in behalf of the corporation within the scope of his office or employment." The section proceeds to define "high managerial agent" as "an officer of a corporation . . . or any other agent . . . having duties of such responsibility that his conduct may fairly be assumed to represent the policy of the corporation."

The Commonwealth, on the other hand, argues that the standard applied by the judge in his instructions to the jury was correct. These instructions, which prescribe a somewhat more flexible standard than that delineated in the Model Penal Code, state in part, as follows:

[T]he Commonwealth does not have to prove that the individual who acted criminally was expressly requested or authorized in advance by the corporation to do so, nor must the Commonwealth prove that the corporation expressly ratified or adopted that criminal conduct on the part of that individual or those individuals. It does not mean that the Commonwealth must prove that the individual who acted criminally was a member of the corporation's board of directors, or that he was a high officer in the corporation, or that he held any office at all. If the Commonwealth did prove that an individual for whose act it seeks to hold a corporation criminally liable was an officer of the corporation, the jury should consider that. But more important than that, it should consider what the authority of that person was as such officer in relation to the corporation. The mere fact that he has a title is not enough to make the corporation liable for his criminal conduct. The Commonwealth must prove that the individual for whose conduct it seeks to charge the corporation criminally was placed in a position by the corporation where he had enough power, duty, responsibility and authority to act for and in behalf of the corporation to handle the particular business or operation or project of the corporation in which he was engaged at the time that he committed the criminal act with power of decision as to what he would or would not do while acting for the corporation, and that he was acting for and in behalf of the corporation in the accomplishment of that particular business or operation or project, and that he committed a criminal act while so acting. . . .

The difference between the judge's instructions to the jury and the Model Penal Code lies largely in the latter's reference to a "high managerial agent" and in the Code requirement that to impose corporate criminal liability, it at least must appear that its directors or high managerial agent "authorized . . . or recklessly tolerated" the allegedly criminal acts. The judge's instructions focus on the authority of the corporate agent in relation to the particular corporate business in which the agent was engaged. The Code seems to require that there be authorization or reckless inaction by a corporate representative having some relation to framing corporate policy, or one "having duties of such responsibility that his conduct may fairly be assumed to represent the policy of the corporation." Close examination of the judge's instructions reveals that they preserve the underlying "corporate policy" rationale of the Code by allowing the jury to infer "corporate policy" from the position in which the corporation placed the agent in commissioning him to handle the particular corporate affairs in which he was engaged at the time of the criminal act.

[Reviewing Massachusetts criminal cases on vicarious liability, the court finds] a long line of decisions in this Commonwealth holding that before criminal responsibility can be imposed on the master, based on a master-servant relationship under the doctrine of *respondeat superior*, actual participation in, or approval of, the servant's criminal act must be shown. [The rule concerns both mala in se and mala prohibitum offenses.] . . .

The thrust of each of the cases cited above involving a human principal is that it is fundamental to our criminal jurisprudence that for more serious offences guilt is personal and not vicarious. . . . [But] the very nature of a corporation as a "person" before the law renders it impossible to equate the imposition of vicarious liability on a human principal with the imposition of vicarious liability on a corporate principal. "A corporation can act only through its agents. . . .

[C]orporate criminal liability is necessarily vicarious." Note, Criminal Liability of Corporations for Acts of Their Agents, 60 Harv. L. Rev. 283. . . . Thus, the issue is not whether vicarious liability should be imposed on a corporation under the "direct participation and assent rule" of the master-servant cases cited above, but rather, whether the acts and intent of natural persons, be they officers, directors or employees, can be treated as the acts and intent of the corporation itself. For the foregoing reasons, despite the strenuous urging of the defendants, we are unconvinced that the standard for imposing criminal responsibility on a human principal adequately deals with the evidentiary problems which are inherent in ascribing the acts of individuals to a corporate entity. . . .

Examining several federal cases, the Court discussed New York Central & Hudson River Railroad Co. v. United States, 212 U.S. 481 (1909), in which corporations were subject to criminally liability for their employees' actions. The Court then dismissed the defendants' argument that they were not subject to any of the federal precedent, as all of the cases involved crimes that did not require intent as an element, or, where there was an intent element, someone of authority in the corporation agreed with or approved of the criminal action taken by the employee, concluding that, even when the actor is a minor employee, the federal cases supported liability for corporations for intentional crimes.

[Responding to defendant's objection to the use of a civil law standard to impose criminal liability, the Court granted that] the theoretical principles underlying this standard are, in general, the same as embodied in the rule of respondeat superior. Nevertheless, as we observed at the outset, the judge's instructions, as a whole and in context, required a greater quantum of proof in the practical application of this standard than is required in a civil case. In focusing on the "kinship" between the authority of an individual and the act he committed, the judge emphasized that the jury must be satisfied "beyond a reasonable doubt" that the act of the individual "*constituted*" the act of the corporation. Juxtaposition of the traditional criminal law requirement of ascertaining guilt beyond a reasonable doubt (as opposed to the civil law standard of the preponderance of the evidence), with the rule of respondeat superior, fully justifies application of the standard enunciated by the judge to a criminal prosecution against a corporation for a crime requiring specific intent.

The foregoing is especially true in view of the particular circumstances of this case. In order to commit the crimes charged in these indictments, the defendant corporations either had to offer to pay money to a public official or conspire to do so. The disbursal of funds is an act peculiarly within the ambit of corporate activity. These corporations by the very nature of their business are constantly dealing with the expenditure and collection of moneys. It could hardly be expected that any of the individual defendants would conspire to pay, or would pay, the substantial amount of money here involved, namely $ 25,000, out of his own pocket. The jury would be warranted in finding that the disbursal of such an amount of money would come from the corporate treasury. A reasonable inference could therefore be drawn that the payment of such money by the corporations was done as a matter of corporate policy and as a reflection of corporate intent, thus comporting with the underlying rationale of the Model Penal Code, and probably with its specific requirements.

Moreover, we do not think that the Model Penal Code standard really purports to deal with the evidentiary problems which are inherent in establishing the quantum of proof necessary to show that the directors or officers of a corporation authorize, ratify, tolerate, or participate in the criminal acts of an agent when such acts are apparently performed on behalf of the corporation. Evidence of such authorization or ratification is too easily susceptible of concealment. As is so trenchantly stated by the judge: "Criminal acts are not usually made the subject of votes of authorization or ratification by corporate Boards of Directors; and the lack of such votes does not prevent the act from being the act of the corporation." . . .

Additional factors of importance are the size and complexity of many large modern corporations which necessitate the delegation of more authority to lesser corporate agents and employees. As the judge pointed out: "There are not enough seats on the Board of Directors, nor enough offices in a corporation, to permit the corporation engaged in widespread operations to give such a title or office to every person in whom it places the power, authority, and responsibility for decision and action." This latter consideration lends credence to the view that the title or position of an individual in a corporation should not be conclusively determinative in ascribing criminal responsibility. In a large corporation, with many numerous and distinct departments, a high ranking corporate officer or agent may have no authority or involvement in a particular sphere of corporate activity, whereas a lower ranking corporate executive might have much broader power in dealing with a matter peculiarly within the scope of his authority. Employees who are in the lower echelon of the corporate hierarchy often exercise more responsibility in the *everyday operations* of the corporation than the directors or officers. Assuredly, the title of office that the person holds may be considered, but it should not be the decisive criterion upon which to predicate corporate responsibility. . . .

Considering everything we have said above, we are of opinion that the quantum of proof necessary to sustain the conviction of a corporation for the acts of its agents is sufficiently met if it is shown that the corporation has placed the agent in a position where he has enough authority and responsibility to act for and in behalf of the corporation in handling the *particular* corporate business, operation or project in which he was engaged at the time he committed the criminal act. The judge properly instructed the jury to this effect and correctly stated that this standard does not depend upon the responsibility or authority which the agent has with respect to the entire corporate business, but only to his position with relation to the particular business in which he was serving the corporation.

[The court then considered the question of whether Beneficial could be convicted for Farrell and Glynn's actions. After reviewing the extent of their relationship with Beneficial, the court concluded that, because of the manner in which Beneficial was structured, there was] sufficient evidence to support a finding that there existed between defendants Farrell and Glynn and the corporation Beneficial Management a relationship of agency with the corporation Beneficial which empowered Farrell and Glynn to act on behalf of Beneficial in dealing with [the state officials.]

▲ PROBLEMS

The Shield that Hurts (#125)

It is the late 1960s, and a new birth control method has become available. Along with "the pill," the intrauterine device (IUD) is now widely used by women as a reliable form of birth control. However, only one IUD is being marketed. Seeing opportunity, A.H. Robins Co. decides to enter the IUD market. Robins is best known for nonprescription products such as cough medicine and lip balm and does not have an obstetrician or gynecologist on staff. However, Robins is able to acquire the rights to a new IUD, the Dalkon Shield, from its inventor, Irwin Lerner, and despite a lack of in-house medical expertise, immediately begins production.

While Robins is urged to seek outside research from an unbiased party, the company instead relies on the research of Dr. Hugh Davis, a co-owner of Lerner's Dalkon Corp. Lerner himself warns Robins that pregnancy rates with the Dalkon Shield were actually higher than the Davis research reports. Undaunted, Robins begins marketing and selling its new IUD device six months after acquiring the rights. The Shield is very popular and quickly becomes a major source of income for the company. However, soon after the product hits the market it becomes apparent that its failure to be effective in preventing pregnancies in certain cases is not the only concern. Of the unwanted pregnancies, one internal memo cites 248 cases of miscarriages, as compared to 55 cases for users of all other IUDs who become pregnant. Worse, some users of Robins' product develop pelvic inflammatory disease, which can lead to sterility, removal of the woman's reproductive organs, or even death. In the United States alone, 20 women die from complications arising from their use of the Dalkon Shield. Company memos suggest that executives are aware of the problems with the device and its potential of doing harm but do nothing so as not to jeopardize sales of what has become one of the most popular IUDs on the market.

What criminal homicide liability for A.H. Robins Co., if any, under the Model Penal Code? Prepare a list of all criminal code subsections in the order in which you rely on them in your analysis.

What liability, if any, under Commonwealth v. Beneficial Finance Co.?

C.E.O. of the Baltimore Rodents (#126)

Acme Markets is a national retail food chain with approximately 36,000 employees, 874 retail outlets, 12 general warehouses, and four special warehouses. Its headquarters, including the office of the president, are located in Philadelphia, Pennsylvania. In 1971, president and C.E.O. Park is advised by letter from the F.D.A. of unsanitary conditions in Acme's Baltimore warehouse. In March 1972, a second inspection of the Baltimore warehouse finds that, while improvements have been made, there nonetheless remains evidence of rodent activity and rodent-contaminated food items. Upon receiving a letter from the F.D.A. reporting the results of the inspection, C.E.O. Park confers with the vice president for legal affairs, who informs him that the Baltimore division vice president "was investigating the situation immediately and will be taking corrective action and would be preparing a summary of the corrective action to reply to the [F.D.A.] letter."

The government charges Acme Markets, Inc., and Park personally, as its C.E.O., with violations of the F.D.A. arising from the rodent contamination at Acme's Baltimore warehouse. The company pleads guilty to each of the five counts but C.E.O. Park pleads not guilty.

C.E.O. Park testifies that all of Acme's employees are in a sense under his general direction but that the company had an "organizational structure for responsibilities for certain functions" according to which different phases of its operations were "assigned to individuals who, in turn, have staff and departments under them." On cross-examination he admits receiving the F.D.A. letter regarding insanitary conditions at Acme's Baltimore warehouse and admits that the existence of these problems indicated that the system for handling sanitation "wasn't working perfectly" and that as Acme's C.E.O. he is responsible for "any result which occurs in our company."

What criminal liability, if any, for Park personally under the Model Penal Code? Prepare a list of all criminal code subsections in the order in which you rely on them in your analysis. A deeper analysis of this case can be found in the Advanced Materials in this Section's Appendix.

❊ DISCUSSION ISSUE

Should Criminal Liability Be Imposed Upon a Legal Fiction, Such as a Corporation?

Materials presenting each side of this Discussion Issue appear in the Advanced Materials for Section 27 in Appendix A.

28

Criminal Law in the Technological Age

The advent of computers and the Internet has changed the way that people work, play, interact with one another, and communicate around the world. Technology has made many things easier and more convenient, including committing some kinds of crime. Further, a wide array of cybercrimes have cropped up, many of which are particularly difficult to monitor, prevent, and punish. Computer fraud, identity theft, and the easy availability of child pornography are difficult for local, state, and even federal law enforcement to curb. And the criminal law itself has had difficulty keeping up. The Model Penal Code, for example, promulgated in 1962, would fail to prohibit some conduct that nearly everyone would agree should be criminal. This section gives an overview of this growing area of criminal law and examines how law enforcement and criminal law might adapt to the changing patterns of criminality.

● OVERVIEW OF COMPUTER RELATED CRIMES

Jessica L. McCurdy, Computer Crimes
47 American Criminal Law Review 287 (Spring 2010)

Defining Computer Crime

The U.S. Department of Justice ("DOJ") broadly defines computer crime as "any violations of criminal law that involve a knowledge of computer technology for their perpetration, investigation, or prosecution."[1] Because of the diversity of computer-related offenses, a narrower definition would be inadequate. While the term "computer crime" includes traditional crimes committed with the use of a computer, the rapid emergence of computer technologies and the exponential expansion of the Internet spawned a variety of new, technology-specific criminal behaviors that must also be included in the category of "computer crimes." To combat these new criminal behaviors, Congress passed specialized legislation.

Experts have had difficulty calculating the damage caused by computer crimes due to: the difficulty in adequately defining "computer crime;" victims' reluctance to report incidents for fear of losing customer confidence; the dual system of prosecution; and the lack of detection. . . .

Types of Computer-Related Offenses

1. Object of Crime

DOJ divides computer-related crimes into three categories according to the computer's role in the particular crime. First, a computer may be the "object" of a crime. This category primarily refers to theft of computer hardware or software. Under state law, computer hardware theft is generally prosecuted under theft or burglary statutes. Under federal law, computer hardware theft may be prosecuted under 18 U.S.C. § 2314, which regulates the interstate transportation of stolen or fraudulently obtained goods. Computer software theft is only included in this category if it is located on a tangible piece of hardware because the theft of intangible software is not prosecutable under 18 U.S.C. § 2314.

2. Subject of Crime

Second, a computer may be the "subject" of a crime. In this category, the computer is akin to the pedestrian who is mugged or the house that is robbed, it is the subject of the attack and the site of any damage caused. These are computer crimes for which there is generally no analogous traditional crime and for which special legislation is needed. This category encompasses spam, viruses, worms, Trojan horses, logic bombs, sniffers, distributed denial of service attacks, and unauthorized web bots or spiders. In the past, malice or mischief rather than

---

1. National Institute of Justice, Department of Justice, Computer Crime: Criminal Justice Resource Manual 2 (1989) [hereinafter DOJ Computer Crime Manual].

financial gain motivated most offenders in this category. Now, many crimes are driven by personal profit or malice. These types of crimes were frequently committed by juveniles, disgruntled employees, and professional hackers as a means of showing off their skills. Disgruntled employees are widely thought to pose the biggest threat to company computer systems. In sentencing juvenile offenders, courts have had a particularly difficult time in finding appropriate penalties. However, in recent years, more of these crimes have been committed for financial gain.[2] . . .

3. Instrument of Crime

Third, a computer may be an "instrument" used to commit traditional crimes. These traditional crimes include identity theft, child pornography, copyright infringement, and mail or wire fraud.

GENERAL ISSUES
Constitutional Issues

. . . First Amendment

The First Amendment protects the same forms of speech in cyberspace that it does in the real world. Hate speech and other forms of racist speech receive the same protection on the Internet as they have always received under traditional First Amendment analysis. The guarantee of the First Amendment extends well beyond personally held beliefs to include speech that advocates conduct, even when that conduct is illegal. Racist speech is also probably protected on the Internet, as it is not likely to fit within the "fighting words" exception to the First Amendment.

There is an exception to this general free speech principle for "true threats," such as sending threatening e-mail messages to a victim or even a public announcement on the Internet of an intention to commit an act that is racially motivated. A similar exception exists for harassment on e-mail or the Internet, as long as it is sufficiently persistent and malicious as to inflict, or is motivated by desire to cause, substantial emotional or physical harm and is directed at a specific person. Child pornography is not protected either, but finding a sufficiently narrow description to prevent its spread on the Internet has proven difficult. . . .

Fourth Amendment

A number of difficult Fourth Amendment issues inhere in computer crimes. The Fourth Amendment prohibits unreasonable searches and seizures by the government. However, what constitutes a search or seizure with respect to computers

---

2. See, e.g., Cassell Bryan-Low, *Virus for Hire: Growing Number Of Hackers Attack Web Sites for Cash—Entrepreneur Asked a Team To Mastermind Strikes Against Rivals, U.S. Says—WeaKnees on Its Knees,* WALL ST. J., Nov. 30, 2004, at A1 (describing the indictment of a businessman who paid someone to launch a virus attack against WeaKnees over a proposed business deal); see also Bob Sullivan, *Consumers Still Falling for Phish: FTC, DOJ Announce Prosecution of Teen-ager,* MSNBC, Mar. 22, 2004, http://www.msnbc.msn.com/id/4580909 (last visited Mar. 9, 2010) (discussing case of 19-year-old college student who pleaded guilty to stealing identities by using a "phishing" scam).

is not always clear. There is disagreement as to whether there should be a special approach created for computer-related searches and seizures, or whether it is adequate to draw comparisons from traditional Fourth Amendment analysis. . . .

The Supreme Court has held that a search occurs within the meaning of the Fourth Amendment when government actions violate an individual's legitimate or "reasonable" expectations of privacy. Generally, a person has a reasonable expectation of privacy in a computer they own in their home, but this is less clear-cut in the workplace. Fourth Amendment issues may also arise when law enforcement intercepts address information on the Internet, such as e-mail addresses and website addresses. Before 2001, the FBI routinely searched similar information on Internet communications without much mention of constitutional issues. The Ninth Circuit has held that obtaining Internet address information by installing a surveillance program at the Internet Service Provider's ("ISP") facility is "constitutionally indistinguishable" from the use of a pen register and, therefore, Internet users have no expectation of privacy in such information.[3] The Fourth Circuit has similarly held that a criminal defendant has no reasonable expectation of privacy in the information he provides to his ISP.[4]

The use of investigative tools devised for eavesdropping on Internet communications may present additional Fourth Amendment questions. The use of a keystroke logger system appears to be constitutional. The constitutionality of other techniques, however, will likely be tested as the government discloses more information about both the nature of its capabilities and the frequency of their application.

Although the Fourth Amendment generally requires specificity in search warrants, broad search warrants have been upheld when addressed to computer crimes. Broad searches have been justified as "about the narrowest definable search and seizure reasonably likely to obtain the [evidence]."[5] . . .

Jurisdiction

1. Federal Jurisdiction

The majority of federal computer crimes statutes have been enacted under Congress' power "to regulate Commerce . . . among the several States." As the Internet is considered to be both a channel and instrumentality of interstate commerce, it falls under the Commerce Clause's broad power. Most courts have held that the courts should treat jurisdictional components of federal statutes as meaningful restrictions. Therefore, they must judge whether the activity in question implicates interstate commerce on a case-by-case basis. This analysis has centered on there being a sufficient nexus between the offending activity and interstate commerce. Where there has been movement of people or materials in interstate commerce in furtherance of the offending activity, or where the Internet has been employed, the application of the statute has been held constitutional. However, a serious question remains as to whether the

---

3. United States v. Forrester, 495 F.3d 1041, 1049 (9th Cir. 2007).

4. See id. at 539-540 (claiming that skeptics believe the FBI is acquiring more information when it uses its Internet surveillance software, "Carnivore," than it should be entitled to under the Constitution).

5. United States v. Upham, 168 F.3d 532, 535 (1st Cir. 1999).

statute can reach purely intrastate activity. Under the Supreme Court's holding and reasoning in *Gonzales v. Raich*, courts considering the question have answered "yes."

2. State Jurisdiction

A significant challenge to state officials in prosecuting computer crimes is one of jurisdiction. Jurisdictional problems arise for state prosecutors when the acts are committed out of state because the jurisdictional rules of criminal law require the prosecutor to prove that the defendant intended to cause harm within his state. As a result, many states have broadened their jurisdictional rules to address the new concerns that arise from the global nature of the Internet. For example, Wisconsin's criminal statute permits jurisdiction even when no result occurs in the state. Alabama, California, and South Dakota have statutes providing for jurisdiction where an offense begins outside the state and "consummates" within the state. . . .

FEDERAL APPROACHES

. . . The government can charge computer-related crimes under at least forty different federal statutes.[6] There are also a number of traditional criminal statutes whose application to computer crime is unclear. In addition, the federal government has sometimes used the United States Sentencing Guidelines ("Guidelines") to enhance sentences for traditional crimes committed with the aid of computers. . . .

Federal Statutes

Since 1984, Congress has pursued a dual approach to combating computer crime. The Counterfeit Access Device and Computer Fraud and Abuse Act of 1984 and subsequent amending acts address crimes in which the computer is the "subject." This line of statutes culminated in the Computer Fraud and Abuse Act ("CFAA"). . . . The federal government's other approach to regulating computer crime has been to update traditional criminal statutes to reach similar crimes involving computers.

1. Child Pornography Statutes

Federal child pornography statutes have not fared well under the First Amendment. In *Reno v. American Civil Liberties Union*,[7] the Supreme Court gave an unqualified level of First Amendment protection to Internet communications. Under *Reno*, legislation will not withstand scrutiny if it requires web surfers or Internet content providers to estimate the age of those with whom they communicate or to tag their communications as potentially indecent or offensive, prior to engaging in "cyberspeech." The Court found that less regulation

---

6. See U.S. Sentencing Commission, Computer Fraud Working Group, Report Summary of Findings 3 (1993).

7. 521 U.S. 844 (1997).

is necessary to protect children on the Internet compared to television or radio because users rarely come across content on the Internet accidentally and warnings often precede sexually explicit images. The global nature of the Internet also renders it difficult, if not impossible, for users to predict when their potentially offensive communications will reach a minor. Consequently, *Reno* requires courts to apply unqualified First Amendment scrutiny to speech restrictions affecting the Internet. Note that "unqualified" protection does not cover obscenity or child pornography, which the government may ban. . . .

2. Computer Fraud and Abuse Act

18 U.S.C. § 1030, which many courts refer to as the Computer Fraud and Abuse Act ("CFAA"), protects against various crimes involving "protected computers." Because "protected computers" include those used in interstate commerce or communications, the statute covers any computer attached to the Internet, even if all the computers involved are located in the same state. . . .

The CFAA prohibits seven specific acts of computer-related crime. First, it is a crime to access computer files without authorization and to subsequently transmit classified government information if the information "could be used" to the injury of the United States. Second, the CFAA prohibits obtaining, without authorization, information from financial institutions, the United States, or private computers that are used in interstate commerce. Third, it proscribes intentionally accessing a United States department or agency nonpublic computer without authorization. If the government or a government agency does not use the computer exclusively, the illegal access must affect the government's use. Fourth, it prohibits accessing a protected computer, without authorization, with the intent to defraud and obtain something of value.

The fifth prohibition, which addresses computer hacking, has two categories of offenses depending on whether there is intent to cause damage. The first category criminalizes knowingly causing the transmission of a program, code, or command, that intentionally causes damage to a protected computer. . . .

The second category of offenses prohibits intentional access without authorization that results in damage but does not require intent to damage. . . . Sixth, the CFAA prohibits someone from trafficking in passwords knowingly and with intent to defraud. . . .

3. Controlling the Assault of Non-Solicited Pornography and Marketing Act of 2003

Unsolicited commercial e-mail or "spam" has been a growing problem in the United States for many years. Congress has considered many proposed federal anti-spam bills since 1995, but did not enact a comprehensive statute until December of 2003. The Controlling the Assault of Non-Solicited Pornography and Marketing Act of 2003 ("CAN-SPAM") was enacted to establish a national standard for e-mail solicitations. The CAN-SPAM Act has several key provisions that affect persons or companies sending commercial solicitations via email. Section 1037 of Title 18 prohibits a number of well-known deceptive and/or fraudulent practices commonly used in commercial emails. These techniques include using deceptive subject lines, providing false or misleading header information, and using another computer to relay e-mail messages without authorization to prevent anyone from tracing the e-mail back to its sender. Section 7704 of Title 15 further prohibits similar deceptive practices, as well as requiring that a commercial e-mail include a method for the recipient to "opt-out" of future solicitations and that the subject line warn if the e-mail contains sexually oriented material.

4. Copyright Statutes

Copyright violations are particularly harmful to computer software developers. Software piracy presents unique challenges to law enforcement because of the various ways the crime can be committed, the ease and minimal cost of reproduction, and the slight degradation in the quality of pirated software. The difficulty of detection also exacerbates the problem of electronic infringement. Many of these issues also apply to other media in digital form.

a. Criminal Copyright Infringement in the Copyright Act

Persons who unlawfully copy and distribute copyrighted material by computer may be subject to punishment for criminal copyright infringement. The criminal copyright infringement statute has four elements: (i) existence of a valid copyright; (ii) that the defendant willfully; (iii) infringed; and (iv) "either (1) for commercial advantage or private financial gain, (2) by reproducing or distributing infringing copies of works with a total retail value of over $1,000 over a 180-day period, or (3) by distributing a 'work being prepared for commercial distribution' by making it available on a public lyaccessible computer network." . . .

Digital Millennium Copyright Act

The Digital Millennium Copyright Act of 1998 ("DMCA") generally prohibits tampering with any access control or copy control measures applied to digital copies of copyrighted works. . . .

5. Electronic Communications Privacy Act

The Electronic Communications Privacy Act of 1986 ("ECPA") regulates crimes with no close "traditional crime" analog, such as hacking. Unlike CFAA, ECPA approaches such crimes by updating existing federal prohibitions against intercepting wire and electronic communications. ECPA updated Title III and created the Stored Communications Act ("SCA"). ECPA attempts to curb hacking activities by fortifying the privacy rights of computer users and enabling law enforcement officers to employ electronic surveillance in the course of investigating computer crimes. The government has used ECPA to prosecute hackers, although they generally rely on CFAA for such prosecutions. Prosecutors have invoked ECPA, however, against piracy of electronically encrypted, satellite-transmitted television broadcasts. Devices used to intercept cable television signals likewise fall within ECPA's purview.

a. Stored Communications Act

Congress intended for the SCA to protect stored e-mail and voicemail. The SCA prohibits any person from gaining (1) intentional access (2) without or exceeding authorization (3) to a facility that provided an electronic communication service and (4) using that access to obtain, alter, or prevent authorized access to a communication in electronic storage. . . . [T]he SCA does not apply to ISPs reading stored communications on their own systems. Nor does it apply if one of the parties to the stored communication gives permission to access.

For violations of the SCA a first-time offender shall be fined under Title 18, imprisoned for not more than one year, or both. If the SCA is violated for purposes of private financial gain or malicious destruction or damage, a first-time offender shall be fined under Title 18, imprisoned for not more than five years, or both. A repeat offender shall be fined under Title 18, imprisoned for not more than ten years, or both. A repeat offender shall be fined under Title 18, imprisoned for not more than five years, or both. Additionally, the SCA's provisions for money damages can address governmental as well as private transgressions.

b. Title III (Wiretap Act)

ECPA extended the prohibitions in Title III of the Omnibus Crime Control and Safe Streets Act of 1968 ("Title III") on intercepting oral and wire communication to include electronic communications intercepted during transmission. . . .

Under Title III, the government needs a court order for a wiretap. The court may require a showing that normal investigative techniques for obtaining the information have failed or are likely to fail. . . .

6. Identity Theft

Section 1028 of Title 18 prohibits the knowing transfer, possession, or use of a means of identification, such as names, social security numbers, and dates of birth, to commit a crime. It prohibits the production, transfer, or possession, in certain circumstances, of false or illegally issued identification documents. It further prohibits production, transfer, or possession of a "document-making implement," specifically including computers, with the intent to use it in the production of a false identification document. The term "transfer" includes making either false identification documents or the software or data used to make them available online. . . .

7. Wire Fraud Statute

The federal wire fraud statute[8] prohibits the use of interstate wire communications to further a fraudulent scheme to obtain money or property. Several

---

8. 521 U.S. 844 (1997).

cases have held that the wire fraud statute applies to computer crimes. District courts have taken divergent positions as to whether the wire fraud statute reaches copyright infringement. Congress later amended the Copyright Act to address this issue. . . .

STATE APPROACHES

. . . Like the federal statutes, many of the state statutes divide computer crimes into the same three categories: "crimes where a computer is the target, crimes where a computer is a tool of the crime, and crimes where a computer is incidental."[9]

Reforms in state computer crime statutes have included provisions expanding forfeiture of computer equipment used in crimes, allowing state authorities to seize property involved in computer crimes.[10] Some states have begun to respond to the growing concerns of online harassment by criminalizing online threats by including electronic communications under "unconsented contact" in anti-stalking statutes,[11] and incorporating computers and electronic communications devices into general telephone harassment statutes.[12] Other state statutes specifically address the problem of offenders whose target victims are minors.[13] These statutes, however, may face significant constitutional challenges on First Amendment grounds.[14]

CHILD PORNOGRAPHY AND OBSCENITY ON THE INTERNET

Lori J. Parker, Validity, Construction, and Application of Federal Enactments Proscribing Obscenity and Child Pornography or Access Thereto on the Internet
7 American Law Reports F.2d 1 (2005)

As noted by the U.S. Court of Appeals for the Armed Forces, "[n]ew technologies create interesting challenges to long established legal concepts,"[15] and the Internet represents new technology over which a body of existing law regulating obscenity and child pornography has been superimposed. The Internet has also spawned new legislation that specifically addresses obscenity and child pornography transmitted over, received from, produced for, and possessed as a result

---

9. See Marc D. Goodman, *Why the Police Don't Care About Computer Crime*, 10 HARV. J. L. & TECH. 465, 468-69 (1997).

10. See Cal. Penal Code § 502.01 (West 1998 & Supp. 2004); N.J. Stat. Ann. § 2C:64-1 (West 1995 & Supp. 2000); N.M. Stat. Ann. § 30-45-7 (1997).

11. See Alaska Stat. § 11.41.270 (2000); Mich. Comp. Laws Ann. § 750.411(h)(e)(vi) (West Supp. 2000); Okla. Stat. Ann. tit. 21, § 1173 (West Supp. 2001); Wis. Stat. § 947.0125 (2001); Wyo. Stat. Ann. § 6-2-506 (1999).

12. Ala. Code § 13A-11-8(b)(1)(a) (1994 & Supp. 2000); Conn. Gen. Stat. § 53a-183 (2001); Idaho Code Ann. § 18-6710(3) (1997); N.Y. Penal Law § 240.30 (McKinney 1989 & Supp. 2001).

13. E.g., Mich. Comp. Laws Ann. § 750.145(d) (West Supp. 2004).

14. See Vives v. City of New York, 405 F.3d 115 (2d Cir. 2005); State v. Brobst, 857 A.2d 1253 (N.H. 2004); ACLU v. Johnson, 194 F.3d 1149 (10th Cir. 1999); ACLU of Georgia v. Miller, 977 F. Supp. 1228, 1231 (N.D. Ga. 1997).

15. U.S. v. Maxwell, 45 M.J. 406 (C.A.A.F. 1996).

of perusal of the Internet. This blend of old and new legislation is woven together by a strand of significant cases.

For regulations on adult pornography to square with the First Amendment, the regulated material must be obscene under Miller v. California, 413 U.S. 15, 93 S. Ct. 2607, 37 L. Ed. 2d 419, 1 Media L. Rep. (BNA) 1441 (1973). *Miller* sets forth a three-part test that guides the trier of fact in determining whether a given work is obscene: first, whether the average person, applying contemporary community standards would find that the work, taken as a whole, appeals to the prurient interest; second, whether the work depicts or describes, in a patently offensive way, sexual conduct specifically defined by the applicable state law; and third, whether the work, taken as a whole, lacks serious literary, artistic, political, or scientific value. More than 30 years later, the Miller test remains the standard by which obscenity is assessed, and has provided the foundation for some statutes that address obscenity and other sexually oriented content on the Internet. . . .

With the growing use and influence of the Internet, Congress sought, in its 1996 passage of the Child Pornography Prevention Act (CPPA), 18 U.S.C.A. §§ 2252A, 2256(8)(B), (D), to go beyond the scope of 18 U.S.C.A. § 2252, and address not only child pornography involving real children, but also "virtual child pornography"—depictions that look like real children, but are not. Such depictions might include those that do not depict any real person, but rather, are generated by computer software, as well as depictions of real people who are actually adults, but are portrayed as children. Unlike § 2252, § 2252A utilizes the term "child pornography", and two of the definitions of child pornography for § 2252A, which are set forth in 18 U.S.C.A. § 2256(8)(B), (D), encompass virtual child pornography. Under § 2256(8)(B), "child pornography" included a visual depiction that "appears to be a minor engaging in sexually explicit conduct." "Child pornography" under § 2256(8)(D) included sexually explicit images that are "advertised, promoted, presented, described, or distributed in such a manner that conveys the impression" that they depict minors engaging in sexually explicit conduct. . . .

In Ashcroft v. Free Speech Coalition, 535 U.S. 234, . . . (2002), the United States Supreme Court, characterizing its opinion as addressed to that universe of speech that was neither obscenity as defined by *Miller* nor child pornography depicting real children, . . . struck down as overbroad the definitions of "child pornography" from §§ 2256(8)(B) and (D). . . .

[C]ourts have upheld 18 U.S.C.A. § 1470 and provisions of the Communications Decency Act (CDA), 47 U.S.C.A. §§ 223 et seq., both of which prohibit transmission, including via the Internet, of "obscene" messages to minors (§§ 4, 13, 14, respectively) in the face of First Amendment overbreadth challenges. In one instance, a court, finding that the overbreadth determination is fact-based, refused to dismiss a claim to enjoin enforcement of provisions of the CDA utilizing "community standards" to assess whether Internet communications are "obscene" or "patently offensive" until the plaintiffs had an opportunity to establish the facts necessary to demonstrate the CDA's purported substantial overbreadth in violation of the First Amendment (§ 9). On the other hand, the United States Supreme Court has held that use of the term "indecent" in provisions of the CDA prohibiting Internet transmission of "obscene . . . or indecent" messages to minors rendered those provisions unconstitutionally overbroad in violation of the First Amendment (§ 6), and has likewise, along with at least one other court, held that the First Amendment cannot tolerate the CDA's prohibition of "patently offensive" Internet communications to minors (§ 8). . . .

United States v. Romm
455 F.3d 990 (9th Cir. 2006)

Justice BEA delivered the opinion of the Court.

We are called upon to decide whether, absent a search warrant or probable cause, the contents of a laptop computer may be searched at an international border and, if so, what evidence is sufficient to convict its owner of receiving and possessing child pornography. We also address an error in the jury instructions on the mental state required for knowingly possessing child pornography. . . .

BACKGROUND

From January 23, 2004, to February 1, 2004, Romm attended a training seminar held by his new employer in Las Vegas, Nevada. When the training seminar ended on February 1, 2004, Romm flew from Las Vegas, Nevada to Kelowna, British Columbia, on business.

At the British Columbia airport, Canada's Border Services Agency discovered that Romm had a criminal history and stopped him for questioning. Romm admitted he had a criminal record and was currently on probation. Agent Keith Brown then asked Romm to turn on his laptop and briefly examined it. When Brown saw several child pornography websites in Romm's "internet history," Brown asked Romm if he had violated the terms of his probation by visiting these websites. Romm answered "Yes," and also said, "That's it. My life's over."

Meanwhile, Canada's immigration service had decided not to admit Romm into the country. Romm withdrew his application for entry and was placed under detention until the next flight to Seattle. Agent Brown then informed U.S. Customs in Seattle that Romm had been denied entry and possibly had illegal images on his computer. On February 2, 2004, Romm returned to Seattle. At the Seattle-Tacoma airport, Romm was interviewed by Agents Macho and Swenson of Immigration and Customs Enforcement ("ICE"). The agents told Romm they needed to search his laptop for illegal images, and could arrange for the examination to be completed that night. Romm agreed. He told the agents he had been in sole possession of the laptop for the previous six to eight weeks. He also told the agents he had "drifted" away from his "therapy," and experienced "occasional lapses" during which he would view child pornography. But Romm repeatedly denied having any child pornography on his laptop.

ICE conducted a preliminary forensic analysis of the hard drive in Romm's laptop. When the preliminary analysis revealed ten images of child pornography, Agent Macho confronted Romm with this information and asked Romm why he had lied about having images on his computer. Romm looked down, adopted a "confessional mode," made little eye contact with his interrogators, and said that "he knew [the agents] were gonna find something on the computer." He also stated the agents had every right to arrest him and would probably do so.

Romm then described to the agents how he used Google to search for child pornography websites. When he found pictures he liked, Romm would keep them on his screen for five minutes and then delete them. Romm used the terms "save" and "download" to describe this operation. While staying in his hotel room in Las Vegas, Romm viewed child pornography and masturbated twice, while or shortly after viewing the child pornography; he claimed to have then deleted such images. In all, Romm used the internet for approximately six-and-a-half hours during his week-long stay in Las Vegas. . . .

ANALYSIS

. . .

II. SUFFICIENCY OF THE EVIDENCE

Romm challenges the sufficiency of the evidence that he committed the acts of "possessing" and "receiving" child pornography. .. Romm concedes there was sufficient evidence for the jury to find he acted with the requisite mental state of "knowingly," but rather contends that the act he committed was merely the viewing of child pornography, not the possession or receipt of it. We disagree. In the electronic context, a person can receive and possess child pornography without downloading it, if he or she seeks it out and exercises dominion and control over it. *See United States v. Tucker,* 305 F.3d 1193, 1204 (10th Cir. 2002), *cert. denied,* 537 U.S. 1223, 123 S.Ct. 1335, 154 L.Ed.2d 1082 (2003) (*"Tucker II"*). Here, we hold Romm exercised dominion and control over the images in his cache by enlarging them on his screen, and saving them there for five minutes before deleting them. While the images were displayed on Romm's screen and simultaneously stored to his laptop's hard drive, he had the ability to copy, print, or email the images to others. Thus, this evidence of control was sufficient for the jury to find that Romm possessed and received the images in his cache.

Possession of Child Pornography

. . . [W]hether Romm "received" the images in his cache depends on whether he knowingly took possession of them. Thus, we begin by analyzing his conviction for knowingly possessing child pornography. It is a federal crime to "knowingly possess[ ] any book, magazine, periodical, film, videotape, computer disk, or any other material that contains an image of child pornography. . . ." 18 U.S.C. § 2252A(a)(5)(B). . . .

Romm's first argument is that files in the Internet cache are not "visual depictions" and, therefore, lie beyond the reach of 18 U.S.C. § 2252A. Specifically, Romm argues the files in the cache are not "data . . . which is capable of conversion into a visual image," because they must be copied to another location on the disk before they are fully accessible. . . .

In essence, Romm's argument is that the cached files do not become "visual depictions" until the user takes the additional step of converting them into ordinary files. The statute, however, speaks of data files that are *capable* of conversion into a viewable form, not data files that are immediately viewable without any further affirmative steps. *See* 18 U.S.C. § 2256(5). Here, Romm could convert the image files in his Internet cache into a viewable form by right-clicking his mouse.

Also, when Romm had the images displayed on his screen that were contemporaneously stored to the cache, he could copy, print, or e-mail them to another person, just as with ordinary files. Therefore, we hold there was sufficient evidence from which the jury could find that the images stored in Romm's internet cache were "visual depictions."

Second, Romm challenges the sufficiency of evidence of his control over the images in the internet cache. We begin with the text of 18 U.S.C. § 2252A. We interpret the term "knowing possession" according to its plain meaning, and presume Congress intended to apply traditional concepts of possession. . . . to establish possession, " '[t]he government must prove a sufficient connection between the defendant and the contraband to support the inference that the defendant exercised dominion and control over [it].' " *United States v. Carrasco*, 257 F.3d 1045, 1049 (9th Cir. 2001) (quoting *United States v. Gutierrez*, 995 F.2d 169, 171 (9th Cir. 1993) (internal quotation marks and alterations omitted)). . . .

By his own admission to ICE, Romm repeatedly sought out child pornography over the Internet. When he found images he "liked," he would "view them, save them to his computer, look at them for about five minutes [ ] and then delete them." Either while viewing the images or shortly thereafter, Romm twice masturbated. He described his activities as the "saving" and "downloading" of the images. While the images were displayed on screen and simultaneously stored to his cache, Romm could print them, e-mail them, or save them as copies elsewhere. Romm could destroy the copy of the images that his browser stored to his cache. And according to detective Luckie, Romm did just that, either manually, or by instructing his browser to do so. Forensic evidence showed that Romm had enlarged several thumbnail images for better viewing. In short, given the indicia that Romm exercised control over the images in his cache, there was sufficient evidence for the jury to find that Romm committed the act of knowing possession. . . .

. . . [W]e hold there was sufficient evidence for the jury to conclude that the images in the cache were "visual depictions" because they could be accessed and viewed by Romm. Further, given Romm's ability to control the images while they were displayed on screen, and the forensic and other evidence that he actually exercised this control over them, there was sufficient evidence to support the jury's finding that Romm possessed three or more images of child pornography. Coupled with Romm's conceded knowledge that the images were saved to his disk, the prosecution produced sufficient evidence to establish every element of knowingly possessing child pornography under 18 U.S.C. § 2252A.

Receiving Child Pornography

Since Romm knowingly possessed the files in the internet cache, it follows that he also knowingly received them. Federal law makes it a crime to "knowingly receiv[e] or distribut[e] . . . any child pornography that has been mailed, or shipped or transported in interstate or foreign commerce. . . ." 18 U.S.C. § 2252A(a)(2). . . . Here, we have held that the files stored to the cache were possessed by Romm, and thus, that the caching of files, on the facts of this case, is analogous to downloading for the purpose of possession. . . . Therefore, we hold that the evidence was sufficient to sustain Romm's conviction for receiving child pornography.

. . . Romm's convictions are **AFFIRMED.** His sentences are **VACATED,** and the case is **REMANDED.**

COMPUTER FRAUD, SPAM, AND IDENTITY THEFT

Jennifer Lynch, Identity Theft in Cyberspace: Crime Control Methods and Their Effectiveness in Combating Phishing Attacks
20 Berkeley Tech. L.J. 259 (2005)

. . .

OVERVIEW OF THE IDENTITY THEFT PROBLEM IN THE DIGITAL AGE

Identity theft is one of the fastest growing crimes in the United States. A broad survey commissioned by the Federal Trade Commission (FTC) in September 2003, estimated that 9.9 million Americans had had their personal information stolen in the prior year, collectively costing businesses $47.6 billion and consumers $5.0 billion. The FTC Identity Theft Survey revealed an exponential increase in identity theft, with the number of victims nearly doubling each year for the previous 2-3 years.

Identity theft is not a new crime. Long before the Internet, thieves used low-tech methods to obtain and misuse people's credit and identification documents. But the Internet and the increased use of databases for storing consumer information has allowed thieves easier access to greater quantities of individual information at one time. In close to the same amount of time it would take for a thief to monitor a physical mailbox and steal one individual's new credit card, the thief can now set up a phishing scam and potentially steal hundreds or thousands of individuals' personal identifying information. . . .

Many laws criminalize identity theft and offer protection for consumers. At the federal level, laws against credit card fraud, wire fraud, bank fraud, and identity theft can be used against identity thieves. Consumers are also protected by the Truth in Lending Act, which among other things limits their losses to $50 for unauthorized credit card use, and the Gramm-Leach-Bliley Act (GLB Act), which prohibits a person from using false pretenses to obtain financial information from a customer. In addition, almost every state has its own criminal and consumer protection laws that deal with identity theft. . . .

PHISHING

Phishing is a particularly pernicious form of identity theft because it exacts a price on both the individual consumer and on Internet use in general. . . .

Phishing scams involve a spoofed e-mail and a spoofed website, both of which use company trademarks and logos to appear to represent a legitimate financial institution or Internet Service Provider (ISP) with which the consumer has an account. Phishing scams focus almost exclusively on banks and online shopping sites: 30% are linked to eBay or PayPal, while almost 60% target US Bank or CitiBank.[16]

Phishers use scare tactics to catch a recipient off guard. . . . In the most basic phishing scams, the e-mail states that the recipient needs to update her account by clicking on a link and entering her personal and financial information in the website to which she is directed. The e-mail contains a "link alteration" that directs the recipient to a URL that looks like it should belong to the financial institution but in fact links to the phisher's website. After the recipient has entered her personal and financial information on the fraudulent website, she will then be redirected to the actual financial institution's website, to make the experience seem authentic. . . .

Current attacks have become more prevalent and more sophisticated. They use spyware, take advantage of software security flaws, and are able to avoid fraud and spam filters. . . .

Like other forms of computer crime, phishing is difficult to deter because normal barriers to offline crime do not apply. Computer crime's effective anonymity means that social norms that might deter offline criminals are inapplicable to cybercriminals. This anonymity also means that the chance of getting caught is significantly lower. In addition, cybercrimes such as phishing attacks are much less expensive to commit, in part because the thief's computer substitutes for the accomplices who would be needed to commit a similar crime offline. . . .

RECENT DEVELOPMENTS IN COMBATING IDENTITY THEFT AND HOW THEY STAND UP TO PHISHING ATTACKS

. . . Many federal agencies, including the FTC, Justice Department, FBI, and Secret Service, are involved in efforts to protect consumers against identity theft and in prosecuting criminals who have committed theft. But the federal government cannot operate alone. Most commentators recognize that government must work with other constituents, including private business entities and potential victims, for crime control to be effective. . . .

Crime control, both in the physical world and in cyberspace, can be seen as occurring on three levels: primary, which includes "self-help" steps the potential victim can take to educate herself about and insulate herself from the initial crime and resulting harms; secondary, which includes architecture and fraud prevention mechanisms that private parties can institute to prevent crime and lessen the harms associated with it; and tertiary, which includes public law enforcement efforts to deter crime and track down and prosecute criminals. . . .

The main federal criminal laws used against identity thieves include the Credit Card (or "Access Device") Fraud Act and the Identity Theft and Assumption Deterrence Act of 1998 (ID Theft Act). The Credit Card Fraud Act makes it a felony to "knowingly and with intent to defraud," use, purchase goods aggregating $1,000 or more with, or possess fifteen or more unauthorized "access devices." Access devices include account numbers and personal identifiers that can be used to "to obtain money, goods, services, or any other thing of value, or that can be

---

16. Brian Krebs, *Phishing Feeds Internet Black Markets*, WASH. POST., Nov. 18, 2004, available at http://www.washingtonpost.com/wp-dyn/articles/A59347-2004Nov18.html.

used to initiate a transfer of funds." The Credit Card Fraud Act includes penalties of up to 15 years and a fine. It also allows for restitution to the "victim," although the Act considers the bank, credit issuer, or merchant to be the victim rather than the person whose identity was stolen, because the credit issuer is financially liable for the fraudulent purchases. . . .

Various problems with law enforcement specific to phishing and other sophisticated forms of identity theft make the use of federal and state laws difficult. For example, jurisdictional issues can prevent proper investigation at the state or local level. Victims' first line of defense is their local police department, but while victims may be able to file a police report in their own state, they may not be able to do so in the location where their information was actually used fraudulently. . . . [P]hishing attacks and other online scams present a challenge to law enforcement because they are designed to appear to be disconnected and small-scale, when in fact they are coordinated and large-scale. The FTC is trying to combat all of these problems through a program called the "Consumer Sentinel Network," which is accessible to law enforcement agencies across the country and links to an "Identity Theft Data Clearinghouse" containing over 666,000 consumer complaints. However, out of an estimated 18,000 state and local law enforcement agencies in the United States, only about 1,040 agencies have signed up for access to the network so far. Thus, both the FTC and local law enforcement have a long way to go to provide more of a benefit to the phishing victim. . . .

. . . [T]here is no one solution at any one level that will solve the phishing problem. Stakeholders at each level can and must make greater efforts and institute new practices to prevent identity theft. Stakeholders among the levels also must collaborate with each other to find cross-level solutions.

ILLEGAL PRESCRIPTION DRUGS

Statement of Joseph T. Rannazzisi, Current Awareness: From the Drug Enforcement Agency
Congressional Testimony before the Senate Judiciary Committee (May 16, 2007)

The Internet as a Method of Diversion

The Internet has become one of the fastest methods used today to divert huge quantities of controlled pharmaceuticals. Certainly there are benefits to allowing individuals with a valid prescription to get their prescriptions over the Internet, ranging from simple convenience to providing individuals in remote areas or with limited mobility with access to needed medications they may not otherwise obtain. As with many other products, the Internet affords businesses access to a customer base not possible for a traditional "brick and mortar" location. The convenience appeals to consumers as well. Legitimate pharmacies operate everyday providing services over the Internet and operate well within the bounds of both the law and sound medical practice. In support of these legitimate efforts, the National Association of Boards of Pharmacy (NABP) has established a registry of pharmacies that operate online and meet certain criteria, including compliance with licensing and inspection requirements of their state and each state to which they dispense pharmaceuticals.

Unfortunately, other so-called pharmacy sites on the Internet today illegally sell controlled substance pharmaceuticals. These rogue Internet sites are not there to benefit the public, but to generate millions in illegal sales. To the uninformed individual these sites may seem convenient, cost-effective and safe, but to the investigator and the drug-seeking individual there are indicators on the rogue sites which should serve as a warning that the site is operating beyond the bounds of what's safe and legal.

A consumer will notice a level of authorization and accountability with legitimate sites that is very rare to find with a "rogue" site. Before you even access its main page, an illicit site will draw you in by advertising powerful prescription medicines. The drugs and their cost (often designed to convey the sense that the consumer is saving money, when in actuality, they're frequently spending far more via "rogue" sites) are the first pieces of information these sites typically publish in order to get the customer's attention. More often than not, a "rogue" site will also validate and process prescriptions based on the completion of a cursory questionnaire. This process is designed to elicit what drug the customer wants and what the method of payment will be, rather than diagnosing a health problem and establishing a sound course of medical treatment.

. . .

Rogue sites . . . may provide bogus pictures of individuals wearing white lab coats designed to imply a level of trustworthiness, but these sites have structured themselves to avoid accountability for the products they sell. DEA believes a majority of the rogue sites operating today are based in the United States and work in concert with unscrupulous doctors and pharmacies. The fact that all of these individuals are complicit in this operation defeats the important checks and balances that have been established in the legitimate process of supplying controlled substance prescriptions to patients in need. While DEA has had some law enforcement successes against these organizations, the criminals promoting this activity are becoming more sophisticated. Their business model takes advantage of the anonymity of the Internet, the ease with which new websites can be created, and the trust of the American people in the safety and efficacy of pharmaceutical products.

While this business model has evolved significantly over time (and we expect it to keep doing so), there are three primary players that facilitate these websites: the doctor, the pharmacy, and the Internet facilitator. These three players collaborate in an almost seamless fashion.

Illegal pharmaceutical sales are promoted by Internet facilitators who have no medical training and are not DEA registrants. These facilitators start by targeting doctors who may be carrying a significant debt, such as a young doctor fresh out of medical school, or those who have retired and are looking for some extra income. The facilitator convinces these doctors that it's OK to approve the prescriptions because they will be provided with some "medical history" (submitted by the "patient" through a website). Increasingly common is for the facilitator to provide an opportunity for the doctor to have a telephone conversation with the "patient" or for the "patient" to fax or email "medical" information to the doctor. . . . This poorly constructed veil of medical evaluation is designed to provide added justification for the requested medicine. And for every prescription the doctor authorizes, the Internet facilitator will pay the doctor ten to twenty-five dollars. Law enforcement has discovered website-affiliated doctors who authorize hundreds of prescriptions a day.

The Internet facilitators will also recruit pharmacies into their scheme. They often target small, independent pharmacies struggling to make ends meet. The Internet facilitator will tell the pharmacist that all they have to do is fill and ship these prescriptions to customers. The prescriptions have all been approved by a doctor, and they are only for schedule III or schedule IV substances. In addition to paying the pharmacy for the cost of the medicine, the Internet facilitator will also pay the pharmacy an agreed upon amount that may reach into the millions of dollars. DEA has seen pharmacies close their doors completely to walk-in customers and convert their entire business to filling these orders.

The Internet facilitator generates the websites that draw customers into this scheme. Websites used by Internet facilitators often mislead the public by advertising themselves as pharmacies, but they do not operate in the same manner as brick-and-mortar pharmacies. These rogue sites offer only a few pharmaceutical products for sale, and are typically limited to only controlled substance and life-style drugs. Advertising typically emphasizes the ability to acquire controlled substances without a prescription or an appropriate examination, and none include a face-to-face medical examination from a licensed physician. They provide the customer with a widevariety of quick and easy payment methods, ranging from cash-on-delivery to credit "gift" cards. Various steps of the ordering process will link and shift the buyer to different websites, making it difficult to connect payments, products, and web providers together. Rarely is there any identifying information on the website about where the Internet pharmacy is located or who owns or operates the website. . . .

The Effects of Rogue Internet Pharmacies

In calendar year 2006, thirty-four known or suspected rogue Internet pharmacies dispensed 98,566,711 dosage units of hydrocodone combination-products.[17] To put this in perspective, controlled substances account for 11 percent of dosages at legitimate "brick and mortar" pharmacies in the United States versus 95 percent at these rogue Internet pharmacies. . . .

Controlled pharmaceuticals in the United States are legitimately prescribed and dispensed within a closed system of distribution. Importers and manufacturers of controlled substances as well as physicians who dispense or prescribe them and pharmacies that fill controlled substance prescriptions are all DEA registrants subject to the Controlled Substance Act and the Code of Federal Regulations. As a closed system there are built-in checks and balances. Each registrant has a corresponding liability to keep the integrity of the closed system intact. However, with rogue Internet pharmacies there is complicity amongst all of the participants, effectively eliminating all of the normal checks and balances. Even some major corporations may turn a blind eye to obvious warning signs when supplying these rogue pharmacies. . . .

The sheer volume of controlled substances being dispensed anonymously over the Internet contributes significantly to other downstream methods of diversion, (e.g. children and young adults getting controlled substances from the medicine cabinet or family and friends). While studies such as *National Survey on Drug*

---

17. Information gathered from information reported to DEA and recorded in the ARCOS database.

Use and Health indicate that only a small percentage of youth get controlled pharmaceuticals via the Internet (the majority obtaining them from family and friends), it's important to remember that when these individuals obtain these substances they generally acquire only a few pills at a time. In contrast, individuals ordering via the Internet frequently receive 100-120 pills at a time, making it a potentially much higher-volume source than friends or the family medicine cabinet. . . .

Enforcement Challenges

As this threat has grown, DEA has also increased its effort to go after these cyber drug dealers. There no longer needs to be a direct interaction between these modern criminals and the drug seeker, they have the ability to reach directly into every computer on the Internet. Whether temptation in the form of a cleverly worded "spam" e-mail or someone actively seeking to acquire narcotics without seeing a doctor, the Internet has created a whole new delivery and sales system for drug traffickers. . . .

In short, the Internet has provided drug-trafficking organizations with the perfect medium. It connects individuals from anywhere in the globe at any time; it provides anonymity, and it can be deployed from almost anywhere with very little formal training. All of these features allow for a more rapid means of diverting larger and larger quantities of controlled substances. The proliferation of rogue Internet pharmacies has also brought new legal challenges. . . .

Conclusion

Drug traffickers continue to exploit the Internet and threaten the health and safety of Americans. Nevertheless, the DEA has refined its methods by which we identify, pursue, and ultimately dismantle these groups and we remain committed to bringing to bear all of the resources at our disposal to fight this growing problem while simultaneously ensuring an uninterrupted supply of controlled pharmaceuticals for legitimate demands. DEA's core mission of disrupting and dismantling drug-trafficking organizations, including those who seek to illegally distribute licit drugs, is an integral component to the 2006 Synthetic Drug Control Strategy and we will continue to implement this aspect of the Strategy with our inter-agency partners to combat controlled substance pharmaceutical diversion.

MALICIOUS COMMUNICATIONS, HATE CRIMES, AND CYBERBULLYING

Todd D. Erb, A Case for Strengthening School District Jurisdiction to Punish Off-Campus Incidents of Cyberbullying

40 Arizona State Law Journal (Spring 2008)

. . . Cyberbullying occurs when students use electronic means, including the use of Internet websites, chat rooms, instant messaging, text and picture messaging on phones, and blogs, to bully peers. "The only real difference between cyberbullying and traditional bullying is that cyberbullying takes place on the Internet," and thus "cyberbullying results in greater impact because Internet content is widely distributed and more public than traditional bullying." Furthermore, most of the content produced by cyberbullying originates away from the school campus on personal computers; however, the effects of such content can be felt every day within the schoolhouse gates.

. . . [A]dolescent threats, teasing, and harassment over the Internet are occurring at an alarming rate throughout the nation, and many of these incidents follow a natural progression into the hallways of the local schools. According to a 2007 study by the Federal Probation Juvenile Department, "90 percent of middle-school students have had their feelings hurt online," while seventy-five percent had visited a website that bashed another student. . . .

Despite the efforts of state legislatures, state antibullying statutes fail to address off-campus Internet communications between students. The court system has also struggled with how to handle cyberbullying incidents. . . .

Where to Turn for Redress: A No Man's Land

. . .

Conflicting Messages in State Laws and School Board Policies: Some Bullying Will Be Punished, Some Bullying Will Not

In response to the deadly consequences of allowing bullying to go unchecked, states have scrambled to strengthen school districts' jurisdiction over incidents of bullying taking place on their campuses, at school activities, or on the way to and from school. Schools have now developed procedures to track incidents of bullying, inform parents of such incidents, and enact disciplinary measures to punish breaches of the antibullying policies.[18]

When it comes to cyberbullying, school administrators are now hearing the familiar justification that comments on websites are sophomoric, childish, and made in a joking nature. But bullying is still bullying, no matter what the medium. Many commentators argue that cyberbullying is even worse than traditional bullying because the Internet content is widely distributed, causing constant harassment and compounding the emotional wreckage that arrives at the schoolhouse gate. . . .

. . . [T]he legal system has supplied mixed messages about bullying. A bully that harasses another student will be subject to discipline as long as it occurs on campus, at a school activity, or on the way to and from school. But the instant the bully enters his home, sits down at his computer, and spends hours creating a website to intimidate, scare, and ruin the reputation of another student, he will face no consequences for his actions. It is a good time to be a cyberbully.

The Inadequacy of Criminal Law as a Remedy

Scholars that have criticized school district jurisdiction over Internet speech are quick to point out that other methods of recourse, such as criminal or civil

---

18. See, e.g., Peoria Unified School District No. 11 Policy Manual, Governing Board Policy, Bullying § 5.1.7.6.2 (2006), available at http://portal.peoriaud.k12.az.us/Governing%20Board/Governing%20 Board%C20Policy%20Manual/PUSD%20Governing%C20Board%20Policy/Governing%20 Board%C20Policy%C20Section%05.htm#_Toc18089089.

proceedings, are better able to punish incidents of cyberbullying. However, cyberbullying victims have had little success using civil and criminal laws to prosecute cyberbullies. For example, the Horace Greeley High School seniors that posted the sexual history, names, and addresses of their fellow female students on a website were initially charged with second-degree harassment, which carries a sentence of up to one year in jail and a $1,000 fine.[19] Nonetheless, a few days later the Westchester District Attorney announced that, although the material on the website was "offensive and abhorrent," it did not meet the legal definition of harassment, resulting in the criminal charges against the boys being dropped. In the rare cases where a student is criminally convicted of Internet harassment, appellate courts have been reluctant to enforce such penalties.

States have enacted laws to govern behavior by individuals over the Internet, but many of these laws require a high threshold of threatening speech to trigger indictment. . . .

Although these laws may be effective for victims of stalking in the community at large, such laws do not help school children combat the cyberbullying problem. The primary deficiency is that if the speech on the Internet puts another student in apprehension that he or she may be subject to bodily harm, the schools will most likely be able to reach such speech through a true threat analysis. Furthermore, it is more difficult to prosecute bullies under anti-harassment or anti-stalking statutes due to the mens rea requirement in criminal proceedings that is not required in a "true threat" analysis. Thus, criminal statutes do not offer victims of cyberbullying a viable option to seek redress against their harassers. . . .

Finding Solutions to the Cyberbullying Problem

. . . As mediating institutions, public schools are better equipped to handle student speech that is not actionable in the criminal or civil courts, but still disrupts the lives of teachers and students in the educational community. . . . [T]he educational system provides a "low-risk" medium to perhaps allow children to experience a limited set of consequences for writing or speaking their minds in a way that is offensive or hurtful to other members of society. . . .

. . . [I]t is more practical to allow schools to reassume the role of mediating institutions that they traditionally held by deferring to administrators' discretion when punishing incidents of cyberbullying. . . .

Policymakers and judges have two distinct options if they want to truly address the problem of cyberbullying in our schools: either strengthen civil and criminal remedies with which victims could deter harassers, or defer to school discretion in punishing abusive Internet speech. Strengthening civil and criminal judicial remedies is not appealing for two primary reasons. First, the stakes are much higher for children in such proceedings. Convictions would show up on criminal records and could affect a student's chances to get admitted into college or the military after high school. Second, there is not a structure already in place to track bullying speech on websites throughout the community. Asking police officers and judges to make time in their daily schedules to address these

---

19. Amy Benfer, *Cyber Slammed*, Salon.com, July 3, 2001, http://archive.salon.com/mwt/feature/2001/07/03/cyber_bullies/index.html? source=search&aim=/mwt/feature.

comparatively petty issues (although not petty in the eyes of the students) would not make for good public policy or efficient government. . . .

Conclusion

The problem of cyberbullying on school campuses closely parallels the traditional problems associated with off-campus speech that has made its way onto school campuses. However, the current trend to treat all off-campus speech equally, whether it be political or harassing in nature, has failed many of the students in our nation's schools and has deprived them of the right to receive an undisturbed education. Therefore, policymakers and judges should revert to the former practice of treating schools as mediating institutions and expand school jurisdiction to punish cyberbullying incidents.

Courts can implement the expansion of school district jurisdiction by replacing the current "sufficient nexus" and "substantial disruption" tests with an "impact analysis." By doing such, the school will be able to reach an off-campus cyberbullying incident that directly affects the school environment, even if it affects only a handful of students. Alternatively, courts could adopt the practice of reviewing school district disciplinary measures with a more deferential standard of review such as "abuse of discretion." By expanding school district jurisdiction to punish off-campus cyberbullying incidents that impact the in-school learning environment, courts will protect innocent students and teachers from undue harassment and simultaneously allow schools to reassume their role as the mediating social institutions.

United States v. Drew
259 F.R.D. 449 (C.D. Ca. 2009)

Justice Wu delivered the opinion of the Court.

This case raises the issue of whether (and/or when will) violations of an Internet website's[20] terms of service constitute a crime under the Computer Fraud and Abuse Act ("CFAA"), 18 U.S.C. § 1030 . . . Drew was . . . acquitted by a jury of the felony CFAA counts but convicted of misdemeanor CFAA violations.

. . . Drew, a resident of O'Fallon, Missouri, entered into a conspiracy in which its members agreed to intentionally access a computer used in interstate commerce without (and/or in excess of) authorization in order to obtain information for the purpose of committing the tortious act of intentional infliction of emotional distress upon . . . Megan Meier ("Megan"). Megan was a 13-year-old girl living in O'Fallon who had been a classmate of Drew's daughter Sarah. . . . Pursuant to the conspiracy, on or about September 20, 2006, the conspirators registered and set up a profile for a fictitious 16-year-old male juvenile named "Josh Evans" on the www.MySpace.com website ("MySpace"), and posted a

---

20. There is some disagreement as to whether the words *Internet* and *website* should be capitalized and whether the latter should be two words (*i.e. web site*) or one. "Internet" is capitalized, as that is how the word appears most often in Supreme Court opinions. See, e.g., *Pac. Bell Tel. Co. v. Linkline Comms., Inc.,* 555 U.S. __, 129 S.Ct. 1109, 1115, 172 L.Ed.2d 836 (2009).

photograph of a boy without that boy's knowledge or consent. . . . Such conduct violated MySpace's terms of service. The conspirators contacted Megan through the MySpace network (on which she had her own profile) using the Josh Evans pseudonym and began to flirt with her over a number of days. On or about October 7, 2006, the conspirators had "Josh" inform Megan that he was moving away. On or about October 16, 2006, the conspirators had "Josh" tell Megan that he no longer liked her and that "the world would be a better place without her in it." Later on that same day, after learning that Megan had killed herself, Drew caused the Josh Evans MySpace account to be deleted. . . .

At the trial, after consultation between counsel and the Court, the jury was instructed that, if they unanimously decided that they were not convinced beyond a reasonable doubt as to the Defendant's guilt as to the felony CFAA violations of 18 U.S.C. §§ 1030(a)(2)(C) and 1030(c)(2)(B)(ii), they could then consider whether the Defendant was guilty of the "lesser included" misdemeanor CFAA violation of 18 U.S.C. §§ 1030(a)(2)(C) and 1030(c)(2)(A). . . .

The jury did find Defendant "guilty" "of [on the dates specified in the Indictment] accessing a computer involved in interstate or foreign communication without authorization or in excess of authorization to obtain information in violation of Title 18, United States Code, Section 1030(a)(2)(C) and (c)(2)(A), a misdemeanor." . . .

During the relevant time period herein, the misdemeanor 18 U.S.C. § 1030(a)(2)(C) crime consisted of the following three elements:

First, the defendant intentionally [accessed without authorization] [exceeded authorized access of] a computer;

Second, the defendant's access of the computer involved an interstate or foreign communication; and

Third, by [accessing without authorization] [exceeding authorized access to] a computer, the defendant obtained information from a computer . . . [used in interstate or foreign commerce or communication]. . . .

Ninth Circuit Model Criminal Jury Instruction 8.79 (2003 Ed.)
(brackets in original).

In this case, a central question is whether a computer user's intentional violation of one or more provisions in an Internet website's terms of services (where those terms condition access to and/or use of the website's services upon agreement to and compliance with the terms) satisfies the first element of section 1030(a)(2)(C). If the answer to that question is "yes," then seemingly, any and every conscious violation of that website's terms of service will constitute a CFAA misdemeanor.

Initially, it is noted that the latter two elements of the section 1030(a)(2)(C) crime will always be met when an individual using a computer contacts or communicates with an Internet website. Addressing them in reverse order, the third element requires "obtain[ing] information" from a "protected computer," which is defined in 18 U.S.C. § 1030(e)(2)(B) as a computer "which is used in interstate or foreign commerce or communication. . . ." "Obtain[ing] information from a computer" has been described as " 'includ[ing] mere observation of the data. Actual aspiration . . . need not be proved in order to establish a violation. . . .' S.Rep. No. 99-432. at 6-7 (1986). *reprinted at* 1986 U.S.C.C.A.N. 2479, 2484." Comment, Ninth Circuit Model Criminal Instructions 8.77. As for the "interstate or foreign commerce or communication" component, the Supreme Court in *Reno v. American Civil Liberties Union*, 521 U.S. 844, 849, 117 S.Ct. 2329, 138 L.Ed.2d 874 (1997), observed that: "The Internet is an international network of interconnected computers." . . .

As to the first element (*i.e.* intentionally accessing a computer without authorization or exceeding authorized access), the primary question here is whether any conscious violation of an Internet website's terms of service will cause an individual's contact with the website via computer to become "intentionally access[ing] . . . without authorization" or "exceeding authorization." . . .

Treating a violation of a website's terms of service, without more, to be sufficient to constitute "intentionally access[ing] a computer without authorization or exceed[ing] authorized access" would result in transforming section 1030(a)(2)(C) into an overwhelmingly overbroad enactment that would convert a multitude of otherwise innocent Internet users into misdemeanant criminals. . . . utilizing a computer to contact an Internet website by itself will automatically satisfy all remaining elements of the misdemeanor crime in 18 U.S.C. §§ 1030(a)(2)(C) and 1030(c)(2)(A). . . .

Given the incredibly broad sweep of 18 U.S.C. §§ 1030(a)(2)(C) and 1030(c)(2)(A), should conscious violations of a website's terms of service be deemed sufficient by themselves to constitute accessing without authorization or exceeding authorized access, the question arises as to whether Congress has "establish[ed] minimal guidelines to govern law enforcement." *Kolender,* 461 U.S. at 358, 103 S.Ct. 1855. . . . For instance, section 1030(a)(2)(C) is not limited to instances where the website owner contacts law enforcement to complain about an individual's unauthorized access or exceeding permitted access on the site. Nor is there any requirement that there be any actual loss or damage suffered by the website or that there be a violation of privacy interests. . . .

In sum, if any conscious breach of a website's terms of service is held to be sufficient by itself to constitute intentionally accessing a computer without authorization or in excess of authorization, the result will be that section 1030(a)(2)(C) becomes a law "that affords too much discretion to the police and too little notice to citizens who wish to use the [Internet]." *City of Chicago v. Morales,* 527 U.S. 41, 64 (1999).

Defendant's motion to dismiss was GRANTED

DISCUSSION MATERIALS & ADVANCED ISSUES

APPENDIX A: SECTION 2

The Legality Principle

DISCUSSION MATERIALS
Issue: Should the Criminal Law Recognize an Exception to the Legality Principle When the Crime Is Serious?
    Report to the President from Justice Robert H. Jackson, Chief of
        Counsel for the United States in the Prosecution of Axis
        War Criminals
    Gerry J. Simpson, Didactic and Dissident Histories in War Crimes Trials

✳ DISCUSSION MATERIALS

Issue: Should the Criminal Law Recognize an Exception to the Legality Principle When the Crime Is Serious?

In his capacity as Chief of Counsel for the United States in the prosecution of Axis war criminals, Justice Robert Jackson argues in the excerpt below in favor of flexibility in the legality principle in the context of the Nuremberg trials. The excerpt from Gerry Simpson offers a contrasting view.

Report to the President from Justice Robert H. Jackson, Chief of Counsel for the United States in the Prosecution of Axis War Criminals

Reprinted in 39 American Journal of International Law 178-190 (Supp. 1945)

My dear Mr. President:

I have the honor to report accomplishments during the month since you named me as Chief of Counsel for the United States in prosecuting the principal Axis War Criminals. . . .

. . . What specifically are the crimes with which these individuals and organizations should be charged, and what marks their conduct as criminal?

There is, of course, real danger that trials of this character will become enmeshed in voluminous particulars of wrongs committed by individual Germans throughout the course of the war, and in the multitude of doctrinal disputes which are part of a lawyer's paraphernalia. We can save ourselves from those pitfalls if our test of what legally is crime gives recognition to those things which fundamentally outraged the conscience of the American people and brought them finally to the conviction that their own liberty and civilization could not persist in the same world with the Nazi power.

Those acts which offended the conscience of our people were criminal by standards generally accepted in all civilized countries, and I believe that we may proceed to punish those responsible in full accord with both our own traditions of fairness and with standards of just conduct which have been internationally accepted. I think also that through these trials we should be able to establish that a process of retribution by law awaits those who in the future similarly attack civilization. . . .

I believe that those instincts of our people, [that the Nazis were a "band of brigands,"] were right and that they should guide us as the fundamental tests of criminality. We propose to punish acts which have been regarded as criminal since the time of Cain. . . .

In arranging these trials we must also bear in mind the aspirations with which our people have faced the sacrifices of war. After we entered the war, and as we expended our men and our wealth to stamp out these wrongs, it was the universal feeling of our people that out of this war should come unmistakable rules and workable machinery from which any who might contemplate another era of brigandage would know that they would be held personally responsible and would be personally punished. Our people have been waiting for these trials in the spirit of Woodrow Wilson, who hoped to "give to international law the kind of vitality which it can only have if it is a real expression of our moral judgment."

Against this background it may be useful to restate in more technical lawyer's terms the legal charges against the top Nazi leaders and those voluntary associations such as the S.S. and Gestapo which clustered about them and were ever the prime instrumentalities, first, in capturing the German state, and then, in directing the German state to its spoliations against the rest of the world:

(a) Atrocities and offenses against persons or property constituting violations of International Law, including the laws, rules, and customs of land and naval warfare. The rules of warfare are well established and generally accepted by the nations. They make offenses of such conduct as killing of the wounded, refusal of quarter, ill treatment of prisoners of war, firing on undefended localities, poisoning of wells and streams, pillage and wanton destruction, and ill treatment of inhabitants in occupied territory.

(b) Atrocities and offenses, including atrocities and persecutions on racial or religious grounds, committed since 1933. This is only to recognize the principles of criminal law as they are generally observed in civilized states. These principles have been assimilated as a part of International Law at least since 1907. The Fourth Hague Convention provided that inhabitants and belligerents shall remain under the protection and the rule of "the principles of the law of nations, as they result from the usage established among civilized peoples, from the laws of humanity and the dictates of the public conscience."

(c) Invasions of other countries and initiation of wars of aggression in violation of International Law or treaties.

The persons to be reached by these charges will be determined by the rule of liability, common to all legal systems, that all who participate in the formulation or execution of a criminal plan involving multiple crimes are liable for each of the offenses committed and responsible for the acts of each other. All are liable who have incited, ordered, procured, or counselled the commission of such acts, or who have taken what the Moscow Declaration describes as "a consenting part" therein.

The legal position which the United States will maintain, being thus based on the common sense of justice, is relatively simple and non-technical. We must not permit it to be complicated or obscured by sterile legalisms developed in the age of imperialism to make war respectable.

Doubtless what appeals to men of good will and common sense as the crime which comprehends all lesser crimes, is the crime of making unjustifiable war. War necessarily is a calculated series of killings, of destructions of property, or oppressions. Such acts unquestionably would be criminal except that International Law throws a mantle of protection around acts which otherwise would be crimes, when committed in pursuit of legitimate warfare. In this they are distinguished from the same acts in the pursuit of piracy or brigandage which have been considered punishable wherever and by whomever the guilty are caught. But International Law as taught in the Nineteenth and the early part of the Twentieth Century generally declared that war-making was not illegal and is no crime at law. Summarized by a standard authority, its attitude was that "both parties to every war are regarded as being in an identical legal position, and consequently as being possessed of equal rights." This, however, was a departure from the doctrine taught by Grotius, the father of International Law, that there is a distinction between the just and the unjust war—the war of defense and the war of aggression.

International law is more than a scholarly collection of abstract and immutable principles. It is an outgrowth of treaties or agreements between nations and of accepted customs. But every custom has its origin in some single act, and every agreement has to be initiated by the action of some state. Unless we are prepared to abandon every principle of growth for International Law, we cannot deny that our own day has its right to institute customs and to conclude agreements that will themselves become sources of a newer and strengthened International Law. International Law is not capable of development by legislation, for there is no continuously sitting international legislature. Innovations and revisions in International Law are brought about by the action of governments designed to meet a change in circumstances. It grows, as did the Common-law, through decisions reached from time to time in adapting settled principles to new situations. Hence I am not disturbed by the lack of precedent for the inquiry we propose to conduct. After the shock to civilization of the last World War, however, a marked reversion to the earlier and sounder doctrines of International Law took place. By the time the Nazis came to power it was thoroughly established that launching an aggressive war or the institution of war by treachery was illegal and that the defense of legitimate warfare was no longer available to those who engaged in such an enterprise. It is high time that we act on the juridical principle that aggressive war-making is illegal and criminal. . . .

Respectfully yours,
(s) Robert H. Jackson*

Gerry J. Simpson, Didactic and Dissident Histories in War Crimes Trials
60 Albany Law Review 801, 801-803, 804, 814-819 (1997)

I. INTRODUCTION

During the trial of Adolf Eichmann in Jerusalem in 1960, Hannah Arendt's moral certainty about both the defendant's unsurpassable evil and the rectitude of the trial itself gave way to a debilitating array of jurisprudential doubts, ethical quandaries and emotional ambivalence. For Arendt, what began with some excitement as "an obligation I owe my past" was transformed into a feeling that "the whole thing is stink normal [sic], indescribably inferior, worthless." Fourteen years earlier, in 1946, when a team of six army lawyers was appointed defense counsel for the Japanese General Yamashita prior to his trial for war crimes in the Philippines, these lawyers were indignant. For them, Yamashita was the ultimate war criminal, a man responsible for the dreadful and literally indefensible atrocities that had taken place in Manila at the end of the war. Slowly, however, Yamashita was transformed in their eyes from the "Beast of Bataan" to an innocent victim of American injustice. This perception of injustice took them, at some risk to their careers, to the Supreme Court. There, Supreme Court Justice Murphy, in a moving dissent, described Yamashita's trial as the "uncurbed spirit of revenge and retribution, masked in formal legal procedure for purposes of dealing with a fallen enemy commander." Yamashita was hanged, but thirty years later defense counsel and legal experts continue to assert his innocence.

Similar ambiguities have attended more recent war crimes prosecutions. The trial and subsequent acquittal of John Demjanjuk in Israel forced a review of U.S. Department of Justice extradition procedures. In Australia, the acquittal of Ivan Polyukhovich led to the disbanding of the Special Investigations Unit and its successor, the War Crimes Prosecutions Support Unit. Even successful prosecutions cause cultural upheaval and unease. For example, Klaus Barbie was put on trial and eventually convicted of having committed crimes against humanity in 1944 in occupied France. His trial, however, became an ordeal for the French nation. At times, France itself appeared to stand beside Barbie as a co-defendant accused of having collaborated with the Nazis during the occupation, or of having carried

---

* Editor's Note.—In his closing argument for the Nazi war crime trials, Justice Jackson argued that the principle of analogy was one of the mechanisms that the Nazis used to seize power.

> The doctrine of punishment by analogy was introduced to enable conviction for acts which no statute forbade. [They] considered every violation of the goals of life which the community set up for itself to be a wrong per se, and that the act could be punished even though it was not contrary to existing "formal law."

Jackson, Closing Arguments for Conviction of Nazi War Criminals, 20 Temp. L.Q. 85-87 (1946).

out crimes against humanity in Algeria during the colonial struggle there. Finally, even Nuremberg, the war crimes trial par excellence, is shadowed by its morally and legally defective twin at Tokyo by the continuing sense that here, again, was victor's justice, and by the spectral presence of those crimes against humanity left unpunished since.

This journey from certainty to doubt may be the price paid by all those who examine individual war crimes trials critically and closely. The accused is often monstrous, sometimes banal, but always human. The trials are most often well-intentioned, occasionally transformative, but always fraught with the gravest moral implications for the accusers. Meanwhile, the law usually is an accomplice to ideology, sometimes an enemy of justice, and always the narrator of a series of complex and deeply ambiguous stories. . . .

II. WAR CRIMES TRIALS: SOME PROBLEMS . . .

B. The Problem of Legality

War crimes trials have been impugned on many grounds over the last half-century. Perhaps the most serious group of objections deals with the legality or procedural fairness of these trials from Nuremberg to Barbie and beyond. Judith Shklar, for example, has argued that war crimes trials bear an uneasy resemblance to the political or show trials regarded as the antithesis of the Western tradition of legalism. There is no question that war crimes trials raise delicate matters of procedure and jurisdiction. . . .

1. Nullem Crimen Sine Lege

War crimes suffer from vagueness deficiencies. The lack of any systematic definition of international criminal law (only now being remedied by the International Law Commission, but the process is still in the reform stage) means that categories such as crimes against humanity or crimes against peace remain underdeveloped. Meanwhile, the notion of war crime itself has given rise to a proliferation of meanings. These include: (1) the generic everyday usage of the term to signify abhorrent acts carried out in war or peace, including genocide and crimes against humanity; (2) the legalistic definition of war crime as a technical breach of the laws of war; (3) the grave breaches enumerated in the Geneva Conventions and Protocols; (4) the category "exceptionally serious violations of the laws of war" contained in the Statute for War Crimes Tribunal for the Former Yugoslavia; and (5) the term "exceptionally serious war crimes" used by the International Law Commission in its Draft Code on Crimes Against the Peace and Security of Mankind (Draft Code). Each of these definitions may or may not be distinct, but the variable terminology leads to real difficulties. Similarly, confusion continues to exist over the definition of crimes against humanity and their relationship to war crimes and aggression. Does the category possess an independent existence? At Nuremberg, Julius Streicher was tried exclusively on this ground, and even then it was made clear that crimes against humanity could be carried out only in the context of an aggressive war. Yet, in the Eichmann trial, it was suggested that this link was not necessary to sustain a conviction on the count of crimes against humanity. Meanwhile, in the Barbie trial, the defendant himself, in a rare outburst, accused the Tribunal of blurring the distinction between war crimes and crimes against humanity.

The absence of clear standards or precedents is another ground for suggesting that war crimes prosecutions have the potential to offend the principles *nullem crimen sine lege* and *nullem poena sine lege*. This is particularly the case in international criminal law where the laws are rarely self-applying. The definition of "international crime," in a generic sense, remains in dispute. The International Law Commission's definition in Article 19(2) of the Draft Code is too imprecise to offer much guidance in this area. On the other hand, as Ruth Wedgwood recognized, this lack of precision can work to the advantage of the accused. Indeed, nearly all applicable war crimes law is hedged with problems of definition that need to be resolved. The major categories of war crimes remain somewhat blurred. Crimes against humanity is defined in the International Military Tribunal Charter as war-time acts and genocide requires an intent that may be difficult to show. International humanitarian law is hedged by military necessity defenses and has not been fully extended to cover civil wars, which are the major sources of war crimes in the contemporary world. Each of these factors makes enforcement more difficult.

War crimes trials are also quite often criticized as an ex post facto application of alien law to acts the criminality of which was not at all obvious at the time the acts were carried out. Indeed, this problem was fully exploited by the defense in the Nuremberg trial, arguing that the absence of an international criminal law regime prior to 1945 meant that the Nazi defendants could not possibly know that they had offended any universal principles of criminality. These defenses were rejected, but only after a rather unconvincing trawl through pre-war international law for evidence of an incipient criminal law system. The retroactivity problem is likely to be less acute in future war crimes trials given the various developments in the law since 1945. However, even recent trials of suspected Nazi war criminals have prompted defenses on the basis of the rule of law prohibition on retroactive application of law. . . .

It is clear that in an area of law so thoroughly politicized, culturally freighted and passionately punitive as war crimes, there is a need for even greater protections for the accused. As the dissenting Justice Rutledge said in In re Yamashita, quoting Thomas Paine: "He that would make his own liberty secure must guard even his enemy from oppression; for if he violates this duty he establishes a precedent that will reach to himself."

APPENDIX A: SECTION 3

Theories of Punishment

DISCUSSION MATERIALS

Issue: What Are the Strengths and Weaknesses of Deterrence as a Principle for Distributing Criminal Liability and Punishment?

Jeremy Bentham, The Theory of Legislation

Johannes Andenaes, The General Preventive Effects of Punishment

Paul H. Robinson & John M. Darley, The Role of Deterrence in the Formulation of Criminal Law Rules: At Its Worst When Doing Its Best

DISCUSSION MATERIALS

Issue: What Are the Strengths and Weaknesses of a Principle for Distributing Criminal Liability and Punishment that Would Optimize Rehabilitation and, Failing that, Incapacitate Dangerous Persons?

James Q. Wilson, Thinking About Crime

Andrew von Hirsch, Incapacitation

Paul H. Robinson, Punishing Dangerousness: Cloaking Preventive Detention as Criminal Justice

DISCUSSION MATERIALS

Issue: What Are the Strengths and Weaknesses of Desert as a Principle for Distributing Criminal Liability and Punishment?

Paul H. Robinson, Competing Conceptions of Modern Desert: Vengeful, Deontological, and Empirical

DISCUSSION MATERIALS

Issue: What are the Strengths and Weaknesses of Using "Restorative" Processes, Rather than Traditional Criminal Justice Adjudication?

Erik Luna, In Support of Restorative Justice

Paul H. Robinson, Restorative Processes & Doing Justice

✳ DISCUSSION MATERIALS

Issue: What Are the Strengths and Weaknesses of Deterrence as a Principle for Distributing Criminal Liability and Punishment?

The following excerpts explore the issues arising in the use of deterrence doctrine as a distributive principle. The criteria for an incapacitative distributive principle—dangerousness—and for a just deserts principle—moral blameworthiness—may be self-evident, at least in a general sense. However, the criteria for a deterrence distributive principle may not be evident. As background, then, the Bentham excerpt gives some guidance. Johannes Andenaes speaks primarily to the inherent ethical obstacles of using the deterrence rationale, specifically as to "exemplary" punishments. Robinson and Darley use empirical evidence to critically explore the implementation and overall effectiveness of the doctrine in its current application.

Jeremy Bentham, The Theory of Legislation
322-324, 325-326, 336 (1931 ed.)

The Utility Principle as a Limit on Punishment

The cases in which punishment ought not be inflicted may be reduced to four heads; when punishment would be—1st, Misapplied; 2nd, Inefficacious; 3rd, Superfluous; 4th, too expensive.

I. Punishments Misapplied.—Punishments are misapplied wherever there is no real offence, no evil of the first order or of the second order; or where the evil is more than compensated by an attendant good, as in the exercise of political or domestic authority, in the repulsion of a weightier evil, in self-defence, &c. . . .

II. Inefficacious Punishments.—I call those punishments inefficacious which have no power to produce an effect upon the will, and which, in consequence, have no tendency towards the prevention of like acts.

Punishments are inefficacious when directed against individuals who could not know the law, who have acted without intention, who have done the evil innocently, under an erroneous supposition, or by irresistible constraint. Children, imbeciles, idiots, though they may be influenced, to a certain extent, by rewards and threats, have not a sufficient idea of futurity to be restrained by punishments. In their case laws have no efficacy. . . .

III. Superfluous Punishments.—Punishments are superfluous in cases where the same end may be obtained by means more mild—instruction, example, invitations, delays, rewards. A man spreads abroad pernicious opinions: shall the magistrate therefore seize the sword and punish him? No; if it is the interest of one individual to give currency to bad maxims, it is the interest of a thousand others to refute him.

IV. Punishments Too Expensive.—If the evil of the punishment exceeds the evil of the offence, the legislator will produce more suffering than he prevents. He will purchase exemption from a lesser evil at the expense of a greater evil. . . .

1. Punishments

First Rule.—The evil of the punishment must be made to exceed the advantage of the offence. . . .

[E]rror is committed whenever a punishment is decreed which can only reach a certain point, while the advantage of the offence may go much beyond.

Some celebrated authors have attempted to establish a contrary maxim. They say that punishment ought to be diminished in proportion to the strength of temptation; that temptation diminishes the fault; and that the more potent seduction is, the less evidence we have of the offender's depravity.

This may be true; but it does not contravene the rule above laid down: for to prevent an offence, it is necessary that the repressive motive should be stronger than the seductive motive. The punishment must be more an object of dread than the offence is an object of desire. An insufficient punishment is a greater evil than an excess of rigour; for an insufficient punishment is an evil wholly thrown away. No good results from it, either to the public, who are left exposed to like offences, nor to the offender, whom it makes no better. What would be said of a surgeon, who, to spare a sick man a degree of pain, should leave the cure unfinished? Would it be a piece of enlightened humanity to add to the pains of the disorder the torment of a useless operation?

Second Rule.—The more deficient in certainty a punishment is, the severer it should be.

No man engages in a career of crime, except in the hope of impunity. If punishment consisted merely in taking from the guilty the fruits of his offence, and if that punishment were inevitable, no offence would be committed; for what man is so foolish as to run the risk of committing an offence with certainty of nothing but the shame of an unsuccessful attempt? In all cases of offence there is a calculation of the chances for and against; and it is necessary to give a much greater weight to the punishment, in order to counterbalance the chances of impunity.

It is true, then, that the more certain punishment is, the less severe it need be. . . . For the same reason it is desirable that punishment should follow offence as closely as possible; for its impression upon the minds of men is weakened by distance, and, besides, distance adds to the uncertainty of punishment, by affording new chances of escape.

Third Rule.—Where two offences are in conjunction, the greater offence ought to be subjected to severer punishment, in order that the delinquent may have a motive to stop at the lesser.

Two offences may be said to be in conjunction when a man has the power and the will to commit both of them. A highwayman may content himself with robbing, or he may begin with murder, and finish with robbery. The murder should be punished more severely than the robbery, in order to deter him from the greater offence. . . .

Fourth Rule.—The greater an offence is, the greater reason there is to hazard a severe punishment for the chance of preventing it.

We must not forget that the infliction of punishment is a certain expense for the purchase of an uncertain advantage. To apply great punishments to small offences is to pay very dearly for the chance of escaping a slight evil. . . .

In order that a punishment may adapt itself to the rules of proposition above laid down, it should . . . be susceptible of more or less, or divisible, in order to conform itself to variations in the gravity of offences. Chronic punishments, such as imprisonment and banishment, possess this quality in an eminent degree.

Johannes Andenaes, The General Preventive Effects of Punishment

114 University of Pennsylvania Law Review 949, 981-983 (1966)

Ethical Problems Connected with General Prevention

The use of any coercive measure raises ethical problems. This is so even when the motive rests upon the need to treat the person in question. To what extent are we justified in imposing upon someone a cure which he does not desire, and how are we to balance considerations in favor of his liberty against the need to eliminate the hazards he inflicts on society? Such problems are encountered in the public health services as well as in the exercise of criminal justice.

The conflict, however, assumes special proportions in connection with general prevention. It has often been said that punishment, in this context, is used not to prevent future violations on the part of the criminal, but in order to instill lawful behavior in others. The individual criminal is merely an instrument; he is sacrificed in a manner which is contrary to our ethical principles. This objection carries least weight in relation to general preventive notions connected with legislation. The law provides, for example, that whoever is found guilty of murder is liable to life imprisonment or that whoever drives a car when he is intoxicated is to be given a prison sentence of thirty days. Such penal provisions have been laid down with an aim to preventing *anyone* from performing the prohibited acts. If we accept the provisions as ethically defensible, we also have to accept the punishment prescribed in each individual case. As H. L. A. Hart has stated:

> The primary operation of criminal punishment consists simply in announcing certain standards of behavior and attaching penalties for deviation, making it less eligible, and then leaving individuals to choose. This is a method of social control which maximizes individual freedom within the coercive framework of law in a number of different ways.

The question, however, comes to a head when the individual penalty is decided by general preventions considerations, in other words, exemplary penalties. I have previously mentioned the sentences given in connection with the race riots in London in 1958. According to the newspaper bulletins, the penalties assessed in the earlier cases were lenient, ranging from six weeks to three months. As the riots continued, the courts introduced heavy penalties of four years imprisonment. "A groan of surprise came from the audience when the judgments were read," a correspondent reported. "On the galleries were seated the mothers of several of the boys, and they were led outside, weeping. Two of the boys were themselves totally paralyzed by the sentences and had to be helped out of the dock to their cells below the courtroom." The reporter continues: "After the encounters in West London, however, the race riots have waned away just as quickly as they started. The reason why they came to an end is undoubtedly the strong public reaction against racial persecution together with the resolute intervention of the police and the courts."

If the correspondent is right, the unusually heavy penalties in this case had a desirable effect, but the judgment is nevertheless felt to be ethically problematic. There is an element of ex post facto law involved in such sentences. Although the judge operates within the framework of the law, such sentences are not, in fact, applications of previously established norms. The judge establishes a norm to suit the situation. Nor does the result square with the ideal of equality before the law. The procedure calls to mind a practice which—at least according to historical novels—was commonly used in former times when a number of soldiers committed mutiny or similar grave violations: the commanding officer would have a suitable number of soldiers shot in order to instill fear and give warning, and the remaining soldiers were readmitted to service without penalty.

Such ethical doubts become even stronger if the individual sentence depends the kind of publicity—and hence the kind of preventive effect—which is ted. Suppose a judge is faced with two similar cases within a short interval. first case, the courtroom is filled with journalists, and the outcome of the likely to become known to millions of readers. In the second case, the r's benches are empty and, in all probability, the verdict will not spread far d the circles of those who are present in the courtroom. Is it defensible for ge to pass heavy judgment in the first instance because the sentence is likely much publicity and consequently bring about strong general preventive while the defendant in the second case is merely given a warning because ment in his case would only mean personal suffering, and would not yield from a social point of view? Such speculation upon the general preventive f the individual sentence easily become tinged with cynicism and for ethi- ons this approach is only acceptable within very narrow limits.

Paul H. Robinson & John M. Darley, The Role of Deterrence in the Formulation of Criminal Law Rules: At Its Worst When Doing Its Best

91 Georgetown Law Journal 949, 950-956 (2003)

For the past several decades, the deterrence of crime has been a centerpiece of criminal law reform. Law-givers have sought to optimize the control of crime by devising a penalty-setting system that assigns criminal punishments of a magnitude sufficient to deter a thinking individual from committing a crime. Although this seems initially an intuitively compelling strategy, we are going to suggest that it is a poor one; poor for two reasons. First, its effectiveness rests on a set of assumptions that on examination cannot be sustained. Second, the attempt to employ the strategy generates a good many crimogenic costs that are hidden if one is functioning within a deterrence paradigm.

Experience has taught us to be precise about exactly what we are saying about the effectiveness of a deterrence strategy. There seems little doubt that having a criminal justice system that punishes violators, as every organized society has, does have an general effect in influencing the conduct of potential offenders. This we concede: having a punishment system does deter. But there is growing evidence to suggest skepticism about the criminal law's deterrent effect—that is, skepticism about the ability to deter crime through the manipulation of criminal law rules and penalties. The general existence of the system may well deter prohibited conduct but the formulation of criminal law rules within the system according to a deterrence-optimizing analysis may have a limited effect or even no effect beyond the system's broad deterrent warning that has already been achieved.

We will suggest that it may be true that criminal law manipulation can influence behavior, but the conditions under which this can happen are unusual, rather than typical, in criminal justice systems of modern societies. By contrast, criminal law makers and adjudicators formulate and apply criminal law rules on the assumption that they always influence conduct. And it is this taken-for-granted assumption that we find so disturbing and so dangerous.

Let us briefly sketch our line of argument and conclusions: [T]he social science literature . . . suggests a skeptical view of criminal law deterrence. There is reason to think that potential offenders do not know the law, do not make rational choices, and/or do not perceive an expected cost for a violation that outweighs the expected gain.

In sharp contrast, criminal law has been formulated on the assumption that those legal formulation decisions will have a direct deterrent effect on conduct, and that assumption has been used in formulating nearly every aspect of criminal law, from defining the rules of conduct, to formulating principles of liability, to determining offense grades, to setting sentencing rules and practice.

Even if one concludes that deterrence skepticism overstates its case, there remain reasons for serious concern. We argue that even on the most cautious reading of the available studies enough is known to urge an end to the past practice of formulating criminal law based on a deterrence-optimizing analysis. [W]e offer four primary arguments.

First, a disabling problem for deterrence as a distributive principle is its need for information that is not available and not likely to be available any time in the foreseeable future. Formulating criminal law rules according to a deterrence analysis can produce erroneous results if based upon missing or unreliable data. In fact, inadequately informed analyses could produce criminal law rules that reduce rather than increase the possibility of deterrence. In such an informational void, we argue, it makes sense to follow a distributive principle that at the very least can achieve its objectives.

Further, even if full and perfect information were available, we argue that the dynamics of deterrence are dramatically more complex than has been supposed. The deterrent process involves complex interactions, like substitution effects, that make deterrent predictions enormously difficult. And the deterrent process is a dynamic rather than a static one. A criminal law rule manipulation may well increase deterrent effect as hoped, but that effect can itself change the existing conditions and require a new and different deterrence calculation. . . .

Second, once it is recognized that any distributive principle for criminal liability and punishment will produce some deterrent effect (if any is to be had). A deterrence-based distribution makes sense only if it can provide meaningfully greater deterrent effect than that already inherent in competing distributions that advance other valuable goals, such as doing justice.

So, and third, there is an important implication here. Deterrence can only do better than another distribution—such as a justice distribution (by "justice distribution" we mean a distribution according to the shared intuitions of justice of the community bound by the law)—only if and where it deviates from it. Thus, a deterrence-based distribution can deter better than a justice-based distribution only if and where it deviates from a just result. But it is just these instances of deviation from justice in which it is most difficult to get a deterrent effect.

People assume the law is as they think it should be, which is according to their own collective notions of justice. Thus, the simple prerequisite of making the deterrence-based rule now becomes a serious task. Further, it is these deviation-from-justice cases in which the system's deterrence-based rules are least likely to be followed. Because people commonly think of criminal liability and punishment in terms of justice, rather than deterrence, the exercise of police, prosecutorial, and judicial discretion, as well as jury nullification, commonly subvert application of deterrence-based deviation rules, thus subverting the deterrence program and confusing the deterrence message.

Fourth, even if one assumes for the sake of argument that a deterrence-based distribution produces a greater deterrent effect than a justice-based distribution despite its special deviation problems, there is reason to be concerned that the deterrence-based distribution simultaneously produces crime, because its deviation from the community's shared intuitions of justice can undercut the criminal law's moral credibility, lessening its crime-control power as a moral authority, a dynamic that we suspect can have significant crimogenic effect. Thus, even if a deterrence-based distribution did successfully produce a greater deterrent effect than a justice-based distribution, that greater deterrent effect might be offset by its greater crimogenic effect in undercutting the moral authority of the criminal law. These are the potential costs that we referred to above, that are incurred by a deterrence-based system.

We believe that optimizing deterrence through doctrinal manipulation is possible, but only under narrow conditions not typical in American criminal justice. There are possibilities for reform that might broaden these conditions, but also serious limitations, due in large part to the sacrifices such reforms would demand: in greater financial cost, in infringing interests of privacy and freedom from governmental intrusion, in compromising basic notions of procedural fairness, and in doing injustice and failing to do justice. Our conclusion is that if one takes a realistic view of deterrence, even after plausible reforms are made, little increase in the deterrent effect of doctrinal manipulation would be produced, and not enough to justify its continued use as the standard mechanism of criminal law-making. . . .

I. GROWING REASONS TO BE SKEPTICAL OF CRIMINAL LAW DETERRENCE

If a criminal law rule is to deter violators, three prerequisites must be satisfied: the potential offender must know of the rule, he must perceive the cost of violation as greater than the perceived benefit, and he must be able and willing to bring such knowledge to bear on his conduct decision at the time of the offense. But typically, one or more of these three hurdles block any material deterrent effect of doctrinal manipulation. The social science literature suggests that potential offenders commonly do not know the law, do not perceive an expected cost for a violation that outweighs the expected gain, and do not make rational self-interest choices. Let us summarize the central conclusions of the literature that are relevant to our current inquiry.

The available studies suggest that most people do not know the law, that even career criminals who have a special incentive to know it do not, and that even when people think they know the law they frequently are wrong. Potential offenders typically do not read law books and their ability to learn the law even indirectly through hearing or reading of particular cases is limited by the fact that the legal rule is just one of hundreds of variables that have play in a case disposition. To devine the operative liability rule, hidden under the effects of all the other variables, would require both a higher number of reported cases than potential offenders are exposed to and a mind for complex calculation beyond that which is reasonable to expect.

As to the perceived net-cost hurdle, the possibilities of deterrent effect are weakened by the difficulties in establishing a punishment rate that would be meaningful to potential offenders, the difficulties in avoiding the delay in imposition of punishment that seriously erodes its deterrent effect, and the difficulties in establishing and modulating the amount of punishment imposed, as an effective deterrence distribution of punishment must do.

Establishing some base expectation of a meaningful chance of punishment is also a necessary condition to any deterrent effect. Yet, the perceived probability of punishment is low, to the point where the threatened punishment commonly is not thought to be relevant to the potential offender.

A delay between violation and punishment can dramatically reduce the perceived cost of the violation. Even if the punishment is certain, the more distant it is, the more its weight as a threat will be discounted. Further, the strength of the punishment memory—that is, its recalled punitive "bite" as a perceived threat for a future violation—is dramatically reduced as the length of delay increases. Unfortunately, in modern criminal justice such delay is substantial.

As to amount of punishment, there is no question that any system that can impose punishment can produce a credible deterrent "bite". The challenge for a deterrence-based system is to modulate the threatened punishment bite as the program for optimum deterrence requires. Lawmakers assume they have the greatest control over this aspect of the cost-benefit calculus in that they can modulate bite by simply altering the length of prison term. But in reality, the studies suggest that this aspect of the cost-benefit balance is neither simple nor predictable. The forces at work in determining the perceived amount of punishment are complex. For example, the "hedonic adaptation" and "subjective well-being" studies suggest that one's standard for judging perceived punitive effect changes over time and conditions. (Both paraplegics and lottery winners return to their original state of well-being despite their dramatically changed circumstances.) Thus, as a prison term continues, it can become increasingly less painful in effect, although its cost per unit time remains constant, making it increasingly less cost effective.

Further, it appears that it is the intensity of the punishment experience, rather than its duration, that is of significant effect. Indeed, because the remembered intensity is highly influenced by the end-point intensity, which we note above decreases over time, it is possible that the overall remembered "bite" of a prison term decreases as it gets longer! The point here is that, while legislatures (and judges) believe they can reliably manipulate the amount of punishment threatened by simply manipulating the length of the prison term, such manipulation does not provide the punishment bite they assume.

As to the rational decision-making hurdle, there are a host of conditions that interfere with the rational calculation of self-interest by potential offenders: drug or alcohol use, personality types inclined toward impulsiveness and toward discounting consequences, and social influences such as the arousal effect of group action and the tendency of group members to calculate in terms of group rather than individual interests. Further, these conditions are disproportionately high among deterrence's primary target group: those persons for whom criminal conduct is not already ruled out by their own internalized norms or by those of their family or peers. This bodes ill for effective deterrence because it precludes, or at least diminishes, a rule's deterrent effect even if the rule is known and is backed by what is perceived as a meaningful threat of punishment. We can expect greater deterrent possibilities when dealing with more rational target audiences, such as white collar offenders. Unfortunately, the more serious and the more common offenses tend to be committed by persons less likely to exercise rationality.

The most serious problems for deterrent effect stem from the combined effect of all three of these hurdles. A well known rule carrying a credible threat of punishment that exceeds the benefit of the offense will be ineffective nonetheless in deterring a person caught up in rage, group arousal, and drug effects, as in many gang-related offenses. A rational calculator who fears any form of punishment even if the likelihood of it is slight, nonetheless will not be deterred by a rule that he does not know, as where a homeowner shoots to protect his home, unaware that the law does not allow deadly force in protection of property alone. And a rule well known by a rational calculator as carrying a meaningful penalty nonetheless will not deter if the chance of getting caught is seen as trivial, as with rampant tax cheating.

❋ DISCUSSION MATERIALS

Issue: What Are the Strengths and Weaknesses of a Principle for Distributing Criminal Liability and Punishment that Would Optimize Rehabilitation and, Failing that, Incapacitate Dangerous Persons?

In these materials Andrew von Hirsch traces the development of the incapacitation and rehabilitation rationales while James Wilson evaluates some of the scientific research done to implement an effective incapacitation system. Finally, Robinson offers a conceptual look at the relationship between prevention and punishment, and the conflict that inheres, and at its broad effects on the criminal justice system.

James Q. Wilson, Thinking About Crime
145-158 (rev. ed. 1983)

When criminals are deprived of their liberty, as by imprisonment . . . , their ability to commit offenses against citizens is ended. We say these persons have been "incapacitated," and we try to estimate the amount by which crime is reduced by this incapacitation.

. . . [T]here is one great advantage to incapacitation as a crime control strategy—namely, it does not require us to make any assumptions about human nature. By contrast, deterrence works only if people take into account the costs and benefits of alternative courses of action and choose that which confers the largest net benefit (or the smallest net cost). . . . Rehabilitation works only if the values, preferences, or time-horizon of criminals can be altered by plan. . . .

Incapacitation, on the other hand, works by definition: Its effects result from the physical restraint of the offender and not from his subjective state. More accurately, it works provided at least three conditions are met: Some offenders must be repeaters; offenders taken off the streets must not be immediately and completely replaced by new recruits; and prison must not sufficiently increase the post-release criminal activity of those who have been incarcerated sufficiently to offset the crimes prevented by their stay in prison.

The first condition is surely true. Every study of prison inmates shows that a large fraction (recently, about two-thirds) of them had prior criminal records before their current incarceration; every study of ex-convicts shows that a significant fraction (estimates vary from a quarter to a half) are rearrested for new offenses within a relatively brief period. In short, the great majority of persons in prison are repeat offenders, and thus prison, whatever else it may do, protects society from the offenses these persons would commit if they were free.

The second condition—that incarcerating one robber does not lead automatically to the recruitment of a new robber to replace him—seems plausible. Although some persons, such as Ernest van den Haag, have argued that new offenders will step forward to take the place vacated by the imprisoned offenders, they have presented no evidence that this is the case, except, perhaps, for certain crimes (such as narcotics trafficking or prostitution), which are organized along business lines. For . . . predatory street crimes . . . —robbery, burglary, auto theft, larceny—there are no barriers to entry and no scarcity of criminal opportunities. . . . In general, the earnings of street criminals are not affected by how many "competitors" they have.

The third condition that must be met if incapacitation is to work is that prisons must not be such successful "schools for crime" that the crimes prevented by incarceration are outnumbered by the increased crimes committed after release attributable to what was learned in prison. It is doubtless the case that for some offenders prison is a school; it is also doubtless that for other offenders prison is a deterrent. The former group will commit more, or more skillful, crimes after release; the latter will commit fewer crimes after release. The question, therefore, is whether the net effect of these two offsetting tendencies is positive or negative. . . . In general, there is no evidence that the prison experience makes offenders as a whole more criminal, and there is some evidence that certain kinds of offenders (especially certain younger ones) may be deterred by a prison experience. . . .

To determine the amount of crime that is prevented by incarcerating a given number of offenders for a given length of time, the key estimate we must make is the number of offenses a criminal commits per year free on the street. If a community experiences one thousand robberies a year, it obviously makes a great deal of difference whether these robberies are the work of ten robbers, each of whom commits one hundred robberies per year, or the work of one thousand robbers, each of whom commits only one robbery per year. In the first case, locking up only five robbers will cut the number of robberies in half; in the second case, locking up one hundred robbers will only reduce the number of robberies by 10 percent.

. . . Working with individual adult criminal records of all those persons arrested in Washington, D.C., during 1973 for any one of six major crimes (over five thousand persons in all), Alfred Blumstein and Jacqueline Cohen suggested that the individual offense rate varied significantly for different kinds of offenders. For example, it was highest for larceny and lowest for aggravated assault. But they also found, as had other scholars before them, that there was not a great deal of specialization among criminals—a person arrested today for robbery might be arrested next time for burglary. The major contribution of their study was the ingenious method they developed for converting the number of times persons were arrested into an estimate of the number of crimes they actually committed, a method that took into account the fact that many crimes are not reported to the police, that most crimes known to the police do not result in arrest, and that some crimes are likely to be committed by groups of persons rather than by single offenders. Combining all the individual crimes rates, the offenders in this study (a group of adults who had been arrested at least twice in Washington, D.C.) committed between nine and seventeen serious offenses per year free.

. . . [C]onfidence in the Blumstein-Cohen estimates was increased when the results of a major study at the Rand Corporation became known. Researchers there had been interviewing prisoners . . . to find out directly from known offenders how much crime they were committing while free. . . . [T]he Rand researchers cross-checked the information against arrest records and looked for evidence of internal consistency in the self-reports. Moreover, the inmates volunteered information about crimes they had committed but for which they had not been arrested. . . .

The Rand group found that the average California prisoner had committed about fourteen serious crimes per year during each of the three years he was free. . . . To state the California findings in slightly different terms, if no one was confined in state prison, the number of armed robberies in California would be about 22 percent higher than it is now. . . .

But the Rand group learned something else which would turn out to be even more important. The "average" individual offense rate was virtually a meaningless term because the inmates they interviewed differed so sharply in how many crimes they committed. A large number of offenders committed a small number of offenses while free and a small number of offenders committed a very large number of offenses. In statistical language, the distribution of offenses was highly skewed. For example, the median number of burglaries committed by the inmates in the three states was about 5 a year, but the 10 percent of the inmates who were the highest-rate offenders committed an average of 232 burglaries a year. The median number of robberies was also about 5 a year, but the top 10 percent of offenders committed an average of 87 a year. As Peter W. Greenwood, one of the members of the Rand group, put it, incarcerating one robber who was among the top 10 percent in offense rates would prevent more robberies than incarcerating eighteen offenders who were at or below the median. . . .

[A]ll the evidence we have implies that, for crime-reduction purposes, the most rational way to use the incapacitative powers of our prisons would be to do so selectively. Instead of longer sentences for everyone, or for persons who have prior records, or for persons whose present crime is especially grave, longer sentences would be given primarily to those who, when free, commit the most crimes. . . .

But how do we know who these high-rate, repeat criminals are? Knowing the nature of the present offense is not a good clue. The reason for this is quite simple—most street criminals do not specialize. Today's robber can be tomorrow's burglar and the next day's car thief. When the police happen to arrest him, the crime for which he is arrested is determined by a kind of lottery—he happened to be caught red-handed, or as the result of a tip, committing a particular crime that may or may not be the same as either his previous crime or his next one. If judges give sentences based entirely on the gravity of the present offense, then a high-rate offender may get off lightly because on this occasion he happened to be caught snatching a purse. The low-rate offender may get a long sentence because he was unlucky enough to be caught robbing a liquor store with a gun. . . . [W]hile society's legitimate desire for retribution must set the outer bounds of any sentencing policy, there is still room for flexibility within those bounds. We can, for example, act so that all robbers are punished with prison terms, but give, within certain relatively narrow ranges, longer sentences to those robbers who commit the most crimes.

If knowing the nature of the present offense and even knowing the prior record of the offender are not accurate guides to identifying high-rate offenders, what is? . . . In the Rand study, Greenwood and his colleagues discovered . . . that the following seven factors, taken together, were highly predictive of a convicted person being a high-rate offender: he (1) was convicted of a crime while a juvenile (that is, before age sixteen), (2) used illegal drugs as a juvenile, (3) used illegal drugs during the previous two years, (4) was employed less than 50 percent of the time during the previous two years, (5) served time in a juvenile facility, (6) was incarcerated in prison more than 50 percent of the previous two years, and (7) was previously convicted for the present offense.

Using this scale, Greenwood found that 82 percent of those predicted to be low-rate offenders in fact were, and 82 percent of those predicted to be medium- or high-rate offenders also were. To understand how big these differences are, the median California prison inmate who is predicted to be a low-rate offender will in fact commit slightly more than one burglary and slightly less than one robbery per year free. By contrast, the median California inmate who is predicted to be a high-rate offender will commit ninety-three burglaries and thirteen robberies per year free. . . .

Andrew von Hirsch, Incapacitation

In Principled Sentencing 101-108 (von Hirsch & Ashworth eds., 1992)

Incapacitation is the idea of simple restraint: rendering the convicted offender incapable, for a period of time, of offending again. Whereas rehabilitation involves changing the person's habits or attitudes so he or she becomes less criminally inclined, incapacitation presupposes no such change. Instead, obstacles are interposed to impede the person's carrying out whatever criminal inclinations he or she may have. Usually, the obstacle is the walls of a prison, but other incapacitative techniques are possible—such as exile or house arrest.

Incapacitation has, usually, been sought through predicting the offender's likelihood of reoffending. Those deemed more likely to reoffend are to be restrained, for example, by imposition of a term of imprisonment—or of a prison term of longer duration than they otherwise would receive. . . .

Who, then, is likely to reoffend? Prediction research in criminology has had a more than sixty-year history. . . . The basic research technique has been straightforward enough. Various facts about convicted criminals are recorded: previous arrests and convictions, social and employment history, prior drug use, and so forth; and those factors that are, statistically, more strongly associated with recidivism are identified. The prediction instrument, based on these factors, is then constructed and tested. The studies suggest that a limited capacity to predict does exist. Certain facts about offenders—principally, their previous criminal records, drug habits, and histories of unemployment—are (albeit only to a modest extent) indicative of increased likelihood of recidivism.

Incapacitation was an important (although often less visible) element in the traditional rehabilitative penal ethic. Sentencing judges and correctional officials were supposed to gauge not only offenders' treatment needs but their likelihood of recidivism. "Curable" offenders were to be treated (in the community, if possible), but those judged bad risks were to be restrained. The traditional view had its appeal precisely because it thus offered both therapy and restraint. One did not have to assume that all criminals really were treatable, but merely that some might be. Therapy could be tried on the potentially responsive, but always with a fail-safe: the offender who seemed unsuitable for treatment could be separated from the community. . . .

In the early 1970s, some penologists began raising doubts about predictive restraint in sentencing. . . . [Critics noted] that prediction in sentencing does not have to be left to judge's personal judgment. Before a defendant is incarcerated on incapacitative grounds, the degree of harmfulness of the predicted conduct, and its required degree of likelihood, could be specified in advance. The predictions could also rely, not on someone's intuitive sense of who is a bad risk, but on statistically tested forecasting methods. The question asked is whether—once these threshold requirements are met—it is fair to rely on forecasts of dangerousness in deciding the sentence.

In this connection, [commentators pointed] to the tendency of forecasts of criminality to overpredict. Although statistical forecasting methods can identify groups of offenders having higher than average probabilities of recidivism, these methods show a disturbing incidence of "false positives." Many of those classified as potential recidivists will, in fact, not be found to offend again. The rate of false positive is particularly high when forecasting serious criminality—for example, violence. The majority of those designated as dangerous turn out—when the predictions are followed up—to be persons who are not found to commit the predicted acts of violence when allowed to remain at large. . . .

False positives put the justice of predictive sentencing into question. Ostensibly, the offender classified as dangerous is confined to prevent him or her from infringing the rights of others. But to the extent the classification is mistaken, the offender would not have committed the infringement. The person's liberty is lost merely because people *like* him or her will offend again, and we cannot specify which of them will actually do so. . . .

[Some defenders of predictive sentencing concede the false positive problem and admit that in predicting dangerousness] at least half of those classified as risks will mistakenly be so classified. With such a high incidence of error, how then can sentencing on the basis of dangerousness be justified? It can only be [justified, these defenders suggest,] by the idea of shifting the burden of risk. An unconvicted dangerous person is entitled to remain at large, and any risk to potential victims must be borne by them. Once the person acts on the dangerous inclinations and is convicted for seriously harming others, however, we become entitled to shift the risk of victimization (in this case, of mistaken confinement) to the offender. Error is unavoidable, and the question is, who should bear its costs? . . .

[Such views raise a number of questions.] [E]ven if restraining the danger-ous were justifiable on . . . such . . . "shifting of risk" [grounds,] one still has not explained why an offender's *punishment* should be extended on that ground. Punishment, [for many commentators,] involves not only deprivation but blame—so that increasing punishment implies the offender to be more blame-worthy. . . . There is nothing about a convicted offender's dangerousness—that is, the mere likelihood of offending again as contrasted with the degree of culpability for crimes already committed—which renders him or her more to blame. Thus if confining offenders beyond their deserved term of punishment were justifiable at all, that confinement would be civil, not criminal. . . .

In the early 1980s. a number of studies, based mainly on interviews with incarcerated offenders, suggested that offense patterns are highly skewed, even among those individuals who recidivate after being convicted. While some recidi-vists reoffended only occasionally, others appeared to revert to serious criminality frequently. If incapacitative techniques could be targeted to the latter group—to the frequent, serious violators—might these techniques not offer hope, after all, for reducing crime?

It was during this period that Peter Greenwood, a Rand Corporation researcher, published a report on a prediction technique which he termed "selec-tive incapacitation." The technique, derived from interviews with confined offend-ers, made use of a few simple indicia of dangerousness, concerned mainly with the offender's criminal, unemployment, and drug-use histories. It was designed to identify "high-rate" predators—those who would commit violent offenses (such as robbery) frequently. Because so many robberies were being committed by a small group of active predators, he argued, identifying and isolating these per-sons could considerably reduce the incidence of such crimes. Greenwood devised a method of projecting the resulting crime reduction effect. He estimated that imposing longer prison terms for the high-rate offenders could reduce the rob-bery rate by as much as 15 to 20 percent, without even any significant increase in prison populations.

Greenwood's suggestions generated considerable interest among criminolo-gists and policymakers [who argued, among other things, that selective incapacita-tion is] not unfair or undeserved . . . because desert sets merely the broadest outer limits on permissible punishments. Reliance on status factors such as employment is no serious problem, because such factors are used by the criminal justice system in other contexts. The possible inaccuracies of the prediction technique should be no bar to use, because the technique is superior to the informal predictive judg-ments that judges and prosecutors make today. . . .

The optimism . . . about selective incapacitation was soon challenged, however. Objections were raised both about the empirical soundness of the technique and about its ethics. . . .

The empirical objections [questioned] whether Greenwood's factors can identify high-rate offenders, once official data that courts must rely upon are utilized, instead of offenders' self-reports of their own criminal activities. The projections of large crime-reduction effects are also suspect. Those projections rely on questionable extrapolations, from the criminal activity of *incarcerated* offenders to the activity of offenders generally. The projections also appear to make unrealistic estimates of such important factors as the anticipated length of offenders' criminal careers. In 1986, a research panel of the National Academy of Science examined these issues, and concluded that selective incapacitation at least today, has a much more modest crime-reduction potential than Greenwood . . . claim[s].

The ethical objection to selective incapacitation . . . consists chiefly in the strategy's conflict with the requirements of proportionality. Selective incapacitation relies upon factors (e.g. early criminal history, drug use, and so forth) that have little bearing on the blameworthiness of the criminal conduct for which the offender stands convicted. The strategy can have significant crime prevention effects by its own proponents' reckoning, moreover, only if disparities among those convicted of comparable offenses are very large: the prison sentences visited on "high-risk" felons must be *much* longer than those visited on lower-risk felons convicted of the same offense. To sustain such large disparities, proportionality must either be disregarded or be treated as only marginal constraint.

Paul H. Robinson, Punishing Dangerousness: Cloaking Preventive Detention as Criminal Justice

114 Harvard Law Review 1429-1432, 1434-1439, 1444-1446, 1450-1454 (2001)

Laypersons have traditionally thought of the criminal justice system as being in the business of doing justice: punishing offenders for the crimes they commit. Yet during the past several decades, the justice system's focus has shifted from punishing past crimes to preventing future violations through the incarceration and control of dangerous offenders. Habitual offender statutes, such as "three strikes" laws, authorize life sentences for repeat offenders. Jurisdictional reforms have decreased the age at which juveniles may be tried as adults. Gang membership and recruitment are now punished. "Megan's Law" statutes require community notification of convicted sex offenders. "Sexual predator" statutes provide for the civil detention of sexual offenders who remain dangerous at the conclusion of their criminal commitment. New sentencing guidelines increase the sentence of offenders with criminal histories because these offenders are seen as the most likely to commit future crimes. These reforms boast as their common denominator greater official control over dangerous persons, a rationale readily apparent from each reform's legislative history.

Although the individual legislative histories make clear that a preventive rationale has motivated each of these reforms, the system's general shift from punishment toward prevention has not been accompanied by a corresponding shift in how the system presents itself. While increasingly designed to prevent dangerous persons from committing future crimes, the system still alleges that it is doing criminal "justice" and imposing "punishment." Yet it is impossible to "punish dangerousness." To "punish" is "to cause (a person) to undergo pain, loss, or suffering for a crime or wrongdoing" —therefore, punishment can only exist in relation to a past wrong. "Dangerous" means "likely to cause injury, pain, etc." —that is, dangerousness describes a threat of future harm. One can "restrain," "detain," or "incapacitate" a dangerous person, but one cannot logically "punish" dangerousness.

Why the shift to preventive detention? Why the wish to keep the old criminal "punishment" facade? These are the starting points of inquiry in this Commentary. It concludes that the trend of the last decade—the shifting of the criminal justice system toward the detention of dangerous offenders—is a move in the wrong direction. The difficulty lies not in the laudable attempt to prevent future crime but rather in the use of the criminal justice system as the vehicle to achieve that goal. The approach perverts the justice process and undercuts the criminal justice system's long-term effectiveness in controlling crime. At the same time, the basic features of the criminal justice system make it a costly yet ineffective preventive detention system.

Segregation of the punishment and prevention functions offers a superior alternative. Punishment and prevention are fundamentally different; they rely on different criteria and call for different procedures. Punishment, especially through imprisonment, happily produces a beneficial collateral effect of incapacitation. If preventive detention is needed beyond the prison term of deserved punishment, it ought to be provided by a system that is open about its preventive purpose and is specifically designed to perform that function.

The Justice Problems

From this perspective, it is understandable that today's citizens are demanding greater protection and that legislators are seeking new ways to provide it. But the use of the criminal justice system as the primary mechanism for preventing future crimes seriously perverts the goals of our institutions of justice.

Lowering the age for adult prosecution, with its longer terms of imprisonment, is likely to increase societal protection. Juveniles are committing an increasing number of serious crimes. But decreasing the age at which a juvenile can be prosecuted as an adult increases the number of cases in which a young offender lacking the capacity for moral choice is nonetheless held criminally liable.

There is little dispute that many young offenders, especially those below the age of fifteen, lack the cognitive and control capacities of normal adults. Some may not appreciate the enormity of the consequences of their acts and others may lack normal behavior control mechanisms. If an adult offender is similarly dysfunctional, due to insanity or involuntary intoxication for example, an excuse defense is generally available. Yet a young offender impaired in a similar way by immaturity has no defense or mitigation, because adult courts traditionally have not recognized an immaturity excuse. Courts have had no need to make such an excuse available in the past for the obvious reason that juvenile courts dealt with the cases involving youthful offenders. The recent trend toward trying youths in adult courts has created the need for such an excuse defense, but none has been developed, perhaps because the defense would interfere with the goal of gaining control over dangerous offenders without regard to their blamelessness.

A more common and more damaging distortion of justice derives from the use of "three strikes" and other habitual offender statutes, and the use of prevention-oriented sentencing guidelines that dramatically increase sentences for offenders with prior criminal records. These reforms affect nearly every case in which an offender has a prior criminal record.

Shocking cases of long-term imprisonment for minor offenses are well known. In Rummel v. Estelle, for example, the defendant took $129.75 from a bar owner to fix the bar's air conditioner with no intention of actually doing so. His conviction for fraud was his third, qualifying him for a term of life imprisonment without the possibility of parole under an early "three strikes" statute.

But problems are inherent not only in the shocking cases but in every case in which a habitual offender statute or prior-record-based sentencing guideline applies. In these cases, the sentence imposed exceeds the deserved punishment, albeit to a less dramatic extent than life imprisonment for minor check fraud. The imposition of that excess punishment is, of course, the motivating goal of such statutes: they significantly increase the sentence beyond the level deserved for the crime because a prior record may predict future offenses. But the effect of such a policy is that the criminal justice system regularly imposes sentences that exceed the punishment deserved. Sentencing guidelines that give great weight to prior criminal records and "three strikes" and related habitual offender provisions commonly double, triple, or quadruple the punishment imposed on repeat offenders. An initial portion of the sentence may well be deserved, but what follows is a purely preventive detention portion that cannot be justified as deserved punishment.

One can construct a theory that makes a prior criminal record relevant to deserved punishment, as Andrew von Hirsch has done. By committing an offense after a previous conviction, an offender might be seen as "thumbing his nose" at the justice system. Such disregard may justify some incremental increase in punishment over that deserved by a first-time offender, but it seems difficult to justify the doubling, tripling, or quadrupling of punishment because of nose-thumbing. The recidivist nature of a second robbery is only one of many characteristics that determine blameworthiness. Lay intuitions may see the nose-thumbing as making the second robbery more condemnable than the first but not more condemnable than the second robbery itself, and certainly not twice as condemnable as the second robbery. But note that, although nose-thumbing may justify a minor portion of the dramatic increases imposed for a prior record, the theory allows proponents of preventive detention to implement their program unobtrusively within a system of criminal punishment.

Further, if such disrespect for law provided the impetus for these statutes, the aggravation of blameworthiness and increased punishment would apply to all offenses. That is, if nose-thumbing is itself condemnable, then it ought to be condemnable in every context, not just in selected contexts. Nose-thumbing through a second violent offense might be more condemnable than nose-thumbing through a second theft offense, but nose-thumbing through a second theft would hardly be irrelevant. Yet the three strikes provisions typically apply only to a limited class of offenses—commonly violent offenses—and typically account for only certain kinds of criminal history—again, commonly a history of violent offenses. It seems difficult to construct a desert theory of nose-thumbing disrespect that allows for such selective increases in punishment. But note that applying habitual-offender schemes only to violent offenses does make sense under a prevention rationale, however, because these offenses most demand prevention.

The criminal justice system's focus on dangerousness also causes, albeit less frequently, distortions of the reverse sort: failures of justice in which a person fails to receive the punishment he or she deserves. This kind of error can occur both in the assignment of liability and in the assessment of the proper amount of punishment. For example, the Model Penal Code provides a defense to inchoate liability if a person "presents [no] public danger" and the person's attempt was "inherently unlikely" to succeed. Such a defense may make sense for a system designed to incapacitate the dangerous person because incarcerating the nondangerous attempter is a waste of preventive resources. But if the person believes his conduct will cause a criminal harm, the person deserves punishment whether or not the chosen method is likely to succeed. For example, the HIV-positive son who attempts to kill his long-hated father by spitting on him can escape liability if the killing method is impossible and he is not otherwise dangerous. But if the son's intention to kill his father unjustifiably is real and he has shown a willingness to carry out the intention fully, his blameworthiness is clear.

Such failures of justice are more common in sentencing, at least in the discretionary systems that abounded two decades ago and that still exist in many jurisdictions. The judge who focuses on prevention instead of desert will give a minor sentence for a serious offense if the offender is no longer dangerous. Thus, the recently discovered, elderly former Nazi concentration camp official can escape the punishment he deserves.

These conflicts between pursuing justice and incapacitating dangerous persons should come as no surprise. Dangerousness and desert are distinct criteria that commonly diverge. Desert arises from a past wrong, whereas dangerousness arises from the prediction of a future wrong. A person may be dangerous but not blameworthy, or vice versa. Consider, for example, a mentally ill offender. A desert distributive principle acquits the dysfunctional person of all criminal liability because the person is not to blame for the offense; he deserves no punishment. But an incapacitation principle would impose liability and require incapacitation because the offender is dangerous.

In a reverse set of cases, an incapacitation principle does not call for punishment of an offender even though the desert principle calls for conviction, as with the elderly Nazi official and the HIV-positive spitter. Because the person's conduct is harmless and the person is not otherwise dangerous, an incapacitation principle suggests that imposing criminal sanctions is a waste of resources. The desert principle, in contrast, takes the person's attempt to kill as evidence of blameworthiness deserving punishment.

Cloaking Preventive Detention as Criminal Justice

It is ironic that the perversions of justice suffered in the name of prevention actually produce a seriously flawed prevention system. These prevention difficulties arise primarily because of the perceived need to cloak preventive measures as doctrines of criminal punishment to make them appear consistent with a criminal justice system that imposes punishment.

Why should this be so? If reformers want to detain dangerous offenders, why not adopt a system that is open about its preventive detention nature and its intention to fill any preventive need remaining after criminal justice incarceration? Most jurisdictions allow civil commitment of persons who are dangerous because of mental illness, drug dependency, or contagious disease. Why is there reluctance to detain preventively offenders who remain dangerous at the conclusion of their deserved criminal terms of imprisonment?

The intense controversy surrounding the preventive detention legislation of the 1960s may help to explain this reluctance. Critics denounced the legislation as "Clockwork Orange" and "'Alice in Wonderland' justice" in which the punishment precedes the offense and as introducing a "police state" and "fostering tyranny." Opponents described it as "intellectually dishonest," characterized it as "one of the most tragic mistakes we as a society could make," and feared that it "would change the complexion of American justice." Preventive detention was "simply not the American way."

A large part of the perceived problem with the 1960s preventive detention legislation was that it provided pretrial preventive detention. In contrast, most current reforms provide preventive detention only after trial and conviction, an important difference.

Yet the primary criticism of pretrial preventive detention—that the sentence precedes the trial—can also be applied to the postconviction preventive detention reforms. Detention for longer than the deserved term of imprisonment is justified as preventing predicted future crimes. Such detention not only punishes an offense for which the detainee has not yet been convicted, but also punishes an offense that he has not yet committed.

But the ability to punish the uncommitted crime, and thereby prevent it, is the genius of the current system's cloaking of preventive detention as criminal justice. By obscuring the preventive nature of the liability and sentence, by making it appear not so entirely different from a criminal justice system of deserved punishment, the preventive detention controversy can be avoided entirely.

The Preventive Detention Problems

It is evident, then, that there are various ways in which the current criminal justice system surreptitiously provides preventive detention at the expense of just punishment. Ironically, such cloaked preventive detention also seriously impedes the system's preventive effectiveness. For example, instead of examining each offender to determine the person's actual present dangerousness, the current system uses prior criminal record as a proxy for dangerousness. Prior record has some correlation with dangerousness and, with the assertion of the "nose-thumbing" theory, has plausible deniability as to its perverting justice. But prior record is only a rough approximation of actual dangerousness, and its use in preventive detention guarantees errors of both inclusion and exclusion.

A scientist's ability to predict future criminality using all available data is poor; using just the proxy of prior criminal history, a scientist's prediction is even less accurate. It is often true that a person who has committed an offense will do so again. But it is also frequently false—many offenders do not commit another offense. An explicit assessment of dangerousness would reveal that many second-time offenders are no longer dangerous, yet these offenders receive long preventive terms under three strikes statutes and criminal-history-based guidelines. At the same time, an explicit assessment of dangerousness would reveal that many first-time offenders are dangerous; yet these offenders are not preventively detained under three strikes statutes and criminal-history-based guidelines.

Indeed, this particular cloaking device stands good prevention on its head. Evidence suggests that criminality is highly age-related. Whether due to changes in testosterone levels or something else, the offending rate drops off steadily for individuals beyond their twenties. The prior-record cloak leads us to ignore younger offenders' future crimes when they are running wild, and to begin long-term imprisonment, often life imprisonment under "three strikes," just when the natural forces of aging would often rein in the offenders. Offenders with their criminal careers before them are not detained because they have not yet compiled their criminal resumes, whereas offenders with their criminal careers behind them are detained because they have the requisite criminal records. Such a scheme produces a costly prevention system of prisons full of geriatric life-termers. Simultaneously, the scheme leads to ineffective prevention, because the system does little during the period in a criminal's life when the need for preventive detention is greatest. A rational and cost-effective preventive detention system would more readily detain young offenders during their crime-prone years and release them for their crime-free older years. Yet the need to cloak preventive detention with deserved punishment prompts the use of prior record as a substitute for actual dangerousness.

An equally counterproductive aspect of the cloaked system is its mandating of fixed ("determinate") sentences immediately following a guilty verdict. In determining the length of a deserved sentence, all of the relevant information is known at the time of sentencing—the nature of the offense and the personal culpability and capacities of the offender. Thus, sentencing judges determining deserved punishment have little reason to impose any sentence other than a fully determinate one (that is, one that sets the actual release date) immediately after trial. A system that instead allows a subsequent reduction of sentence, as by a parole board, undercuts deserved punishment. Citizens become cynical that a just sentence will be undermined by early release. It is this cynicism that gives rise to demands for "truth in sentencing" and to the legislative response of establishing determinate terms and abolishing early release on parole.

Therefore, to maintain its justice cloak, the preventive system must follow this practice of imposing determinate sentences soon after trial. But this practice is highly inappropriate for effective prevention. It is difficult enough to determine a person's present dangerousness—whether he would commit an offense if released today. It is much more difficult to predict an offender's future dangerousness—whether he would commit an offense if released at the end of the deserved punishment term in the future. It is still more difficult, if not impossible, to predict today precisely how long the future preventive detention will need to last. Yet that is what determinate sentencing demands: the imposition now of a fixed term that predicts preventive needs far in the future.

A sentencing judge or guideline drafter is left to the grossest sort of speculation, inevitably doomed to setting either a term too long—thus unfairly detaining a nondangerous offender and wasting preventive resources—or a term too short—thus failing to provide adequate prevention. In deciding between these two bad choices, decision makers commonly opt for errors of the first sort rather than the second, resulting in the recent increases in the terms of imprisonment.

A rational preventive detention system would do what current civil commitment systems do: make a determination of present dangerousness in setting detention for a limited period, commonly six months, and then periodically revisit the decision to determine whether the need for detention continues.

Other inefficiencies resulting from the use of the cloak are found in the method of restraint. A rational preventive detention system would follow a principle of minimum intrusion: a detainee would be held at the minimum level of restraint necessary for community safety. If house arrest or regular medication would provide the same level of community safety as imprisonment, then the former choices would be preferred as less intrusive to the offender and less costly to society. Implementing deserved punishment, in contrast, may often require a prison term to reaffirm the community's strong condemnation of the offense. House arrest or regular medication may be unacceptable substitutes if they are perceived as trivializing the offense. If preventive detention must operate under the cloak of criminal justice, it too often must follow the punishment preference for imprisonment even in situations in which prevention would be satisfied with less intrusive restraint.

The preventive detention system hidden behind the cloak of criminal justice not only fails to protect the community efficiently but also fails to deal fairly with those being preventively detained. As noted above, the inaccuracies created by the use of prior record as a substitute for actual dangerousness result in the unnecessary detention of a greater number of nondangerous offenders. The inaccuracies created by the use of determinate sentences can have the same effect. In cases in which a nonincarcerative sentence would provide adequate protection, the use of a prison term provides one more example of needless restraint.

But the unfairness generated by the cloak of criminal justice extends to other aspects of the preventive detention system, such as the conditions of detention. Punitive conditions are entirely consistent with a punishment rationale for the incarceration. But if an offender has served the portion of his sentence justified by deserved punishment and continues to be detained for entirely preventive reasons, punitive conditions become inappropriate.

Similarly, an offender being preventively detained should logically have a right to treatment, especially if such treatment can reduce the length or intrusiveness of the preventive detention—this constitutes a specialized application of the principle of minimum restraint. If treatment can reduce the necessary individual sacrifice, the offender ought to receive it.

❋ DISCUSSION MATERIALS

Issue: What Are the Strengths and Weaknesses of Desert as a Principle for Distributing Criminal Liability and Punishment?

Paul H. Robinson, Competing Conceptions of Modern Desert: Vengeful, Deontological, and Empirical
67 Cambridge Law Journal (2008)

The dispute over the role desert should play, if any, in assessing criminal liability and punishment has a long and turbulent history. There is some indication that "deserved punishment" —referred to variously as desert, just punishment, retributive punishment, or simply "doing justice" —may be in ascendance, both in academic debate and in real world institutions. A number of modern sentencing guidelines have adopted it as their distributive principle. And desert is increasingly given deference in the "purposes" section of state criminal codes, where it can be the guiding principle in the interpretation and application of the code's provisions. Indeed, the American Law Institute will soon take up a proposed change to the Model Penal Code (the first since the Code's promulgation in 1962) that would set desert as the official dominant principle for sentencing. And courts have identified desert as the guiding principle in a variety of contexts, as with the Supreme Court's enthroning retributivism as the "primary justification for the death penalty."

But there remains a good deal of controversy over the reliance upon desert. It is strenuously argued by some that desert is inappropriate as a distributive principle because it is mean-spirited and harsh, because it has an unhealthy preference for prison, because it is based upon only vague notions that at most mark punishment extremes to be avoided, because people are in hopeless disagreement about what it requires, because it fails to avoid avoidable crime, because it is immoral, and because it is impractical to implement.

This Article argues that many of these objections are valid, at least when applied to some conceptions of desert, but that there are at least three distinct conceptions of desert to be found in the current debates, typically without distinction being made between them. The three include what might be called vengeful desert, deontological desert, and empirical desert. Each of the offered criticisms of desert is a fair objection to one of these conceptions of desert but an unfair objection to another. Thus, an accurate assessment of desert as a distributive principle requires that these three conceptions of desert be distinguished from one another, and that the strengths and weaknesses of each conception be judged on its own.

I. COMPETING CONCEPTIONS OF DESERT: VENGEFUL, DEONTOLOGICAL, AND EMPIRICAL

Three conceptions of desert are evident in the present debates over the propriety of desert as a distributive principle for criminal liability and punishment.

A. Vengeful Desert

A conception of desert used by many writers, what might be called "vengeful desert," is captured in the often-quoted biblical phrase: "eye for eye, tooth for tooth, hand for hand, foot for foot, burning for burning, wound for wound, stripe for stripe." It urges punishing an offender in a way that mirrors the harm or suffering he has caused, typically identified as lex talionis: "the principle or law of retaliation that a punishment inflicted should correspond in degree and in kind to the offense of the wrongdoer." In Kant's words:

> For the only time a criminal cannot complain that a wrong is done to him [by punishment] is when he brings his evil deed back upon himself, and what is done to him in accordance with penal law is what he has perpetrated on others.

Some writers argue that lex talionis does not require inflicting the exact same harm on the offender that the offender inflicted on his victim, but only requires the imposition of a relevantly similar deprivation. This variation thus takes a less demanding form, requiring only that the punishment be proportionate to the harm caused, sometimes captured by the suggestion that "the punishment should fit the crime." But even in this diluted form, the primary focus of vengeful desert remains the extent of the harm of the offense.

Because of this focus on the harm done, the vengeful conception of desert commonly is associated with the victim's perspective. Retributive justice "consists in seeking equality between offender and victim by subjecting the offender to punishment and communicating to the victim a concern for his or her antecedent suffering." "[I]n willing the crime, he willed that he himself should suffer in the same degree as his victim." And the association with the victim's suffering, in turn, associates vengeful desert with the feelings of revenge and hatred that we commonly see in victims. Thus, punishment under this conception of desert is sometimes seen as essentially an institutionalization of victim revenge; it is "injury inflicted on a wrongdoer that satisfies the retributive hatred felt by that wrongdoer's victim and that is justified because of that satisfaction."

B. Deontological Desert

The deontological conception of desert focuses not on the harm of the offense but on the blameworthiness of the offender, and is drawn primarily from the arguments and analyses of moral philosophy. "It is morally fitting that a person who does wrong should suffer in proportion to his wrongdoing. That a criminal should be punished follows from his guilt, and the severity of the appropriate punishment depends on the depravity of his act."

Thus, the criterion for assessing punishment is broader and richer than that for vengeful desert: Anything that affects an offender's moral blameworthiness is taken into account in judging the punishment he deserves. The extent of the harm caused or the seriousness of the evil done will be part of that calculation but so too will be a wide variety of other factors, such as the offender's culpable state of mind or lack thereof and the existing conditions at the time of the offense, including those that might give rise to claims of justification, excuse, or mitigation. A typical expression of this conception might be: "The offender deserves a particular punishment not simply for an act which causes harm but according to his personal responsibility for committing the act. This evaluation necessarily includes a review of the broad array of forces operating upon the individual to ascertain the extent of the individual's responsibility."

A key aspect of the deontological conception of desert, which distinguishes it from empirical desert, discussed immediately below, is that it transcends the particular people and situation at hand and embodies a set of principles derived from fundamental values, principles of right and good, and thus will produce justice without regard to the political, social, or other peculiarities of the situation at hand. As Henry Sidgwick famously put it, moral judgments are made "from the point of view of the universe."

C. Empirical Desert

Empirical desert, like deontological desert, focuses on the blameworthiness of the offender. But in determining the principles by which punishment is to be assessed, it looks not to philosophical analyses but rather to the community's intuitions of justice. The primary source of the principles, then, is empirical research into those factors that drive people's intuitions of blameworthiness. The existing studies suggest that the variety of factors at work are as rich and varied as those at work in determining deontological desert. The extent of the harm or evil plays an important role, but is only one of a wide variety of factors, including many related to the offender's situation and personal capacities.

It is not the community's view of deserved punishment in a given case that is relevant here. This conception of justice envisions a set of liability and punishment rules to be applied identically to all defendants, not ad hoc case dispositions. Further, in collecting data to construct the rules, real cases, especially publicly known cases, typically are not a useful source. People's views on such cases are commonly biased by political or social context or by other factors, such as race, that all would agree have no proper role in setting principles of justice. Instead, the community's intuitions of justice are derived from controlled social science studies that determine the factors that influence people's assessment of a violator's blameworthiness, not by asking people about abstract factors but rather by having them "sentence" a variety of carefully constructed cases to see what factors in fact influence their punishment judgments. The principles drawn from such studies are then applied in a like manner to all defendants.

It is obvious why one might support a deontological desert distribution: to do justice. But why would one support an empirical desert distribution? Why should we care about the community's intuitions of justice? Just because the community's intuitions think something is justice, it does not make it so, even if there is a strong agreement on those intuitions.

The reasons offered in support of an empirical desert distribution lie not in its moral implications but in its practical consequences. If the criminal law tracks the community's intuitions of justice in assigning liability and punishment, it is argued, the law gains access to the power and efficiency of stigmatization, it avoids the resistance and subversion inspired by an unjust system, it gains compliance by prompting people to defer to it as a moral authority in new or grey areas (such as insider trading), and it earns the ability to help shape of powerful societal norms. . . .

D. Vengeful Versus Other Conceptions of Desert

Vengeful desert differs from deontological and empirical desert in several ways that ultimately have important implications.

1. The Role of Punishment Amount: Ordinal Ranking of Cases Versus Punishment Continuum Endpoint

The most important difference between vengeful desert and the other two conceptions of desert is the importance the former gives to the absolute amount of punishment to be imposed. For vengeful desert, this absolute amount is its central focus: It must be equal in amount, if not also in means, to the suffering caused by the offense conduct. But for deontological and empirical desert, the absolute amount of punishment is of limited interest. Their central concern is the relative amount of punishment among cases of differing degrees of moral blameworthiness. These latter conceptions of justice focus primarily on ensuring that the offender is given not a particular amount of punishment, but rather is given that amount of punishment that puts him in his proper ordinal rank among all cases of differing degrees of blameworthiness.

Once a society has committed itself to a particular endpoint for its punishment continuum, which all societies must do—be it the death penalty, life imprisonment, fifteen years imprisonment, or something less—the ordinal rank of any given case necessarily converts to a specific amount of punishment: that amount of punishment that sets the offender at his appropriate ordinal rank. But for deontological and empirical desert, the amount of punishment has no other significance. If the endpoint of the punishment continuum changes, the amount of punishment that an offender deserves under these two conceptions of justice also changes, to that amount of punishment necessary to keep its proper ordinal rank.

Thus, while the absolute severity of punishment is central to vengeful desert—it ought to approximate the suffering of the offense—it is of limited relevance to deontological and empirical desert. Those latter conceptions of desert may play some role in a society's setting its punishment continuum endpoint, but, even in performing this role, these conceptions of desert operate differently than they do when performing their core function of establishing the proper ordinal rank of each case. In setting the punishment continuum endpoint, these conceptions of desert typically can offer only general guidance as to extremes that should be avoided, rather than to give guidance as the specific endpoint to pick.

2. The Role of Punishment Method: Punishment Method Versus Amount

Another characteristic that deontological and empirical desert share, which is not shared by vengeful desert, is the role given punishment method. The latter cares about the method of punishment: Ideally, it matches the means by which the victim was made to suffer. Failing this, it should be imposed in a way that is at least relevant to the nature of the offense, if that is possible. Thus, for example, the vengeful conception of desert is thought to support the use of the death penalty in cases of murder.

In contrast, deontological and empirical conceptions of desert have no such interest in the method of punishment. Their focus is on the amount of punishment—an amount that will put the offender in his proper ordinal rank according to his blameworthiness. As long as the total punitive "bite" of the punishment achieves this ranking, these conceptions of desert have little reason to care about the method by which that amount of punitive "bite" is imposed.

Of the course, where a variety of different sanctioning methods are used, the offender should get punishment "credit" for each only in proportion to the punitive "bite" of that method. This requires, then, establishment of ratios between the different punishment methods that reflect the differences in their punitive "bite." If the "bite" of one week in jail is equivalent to that of a month of weekends in jail or is equivalent to that of 80 hours of community service, these conceptions of desert would be satisfied with any of these sentences, so long as that amount of punishment was the amount deserved given the offender's blameworthiness. The ideal equivalency table would be one that generates alternative sanctions about which an offender and a community are indifferent as to which is imposed. . . .

II. RESULTING CONFUSIONS ABOUT THE NATURE OF DESERVED PUNISHMENT

It is argued here that the failure to appreciate the existence of these three quite different conceptions of desert commonly leads to confusion in the critique of desert as a principle for the distribution of criminal liability and punishment. That is, criticisms of "desert" are sometimes offered without appreciating that the criticism may be valid with regard to one conception of desert but not another, thus leading writers to reject "desert" generally while in fact their criticisms only suggest rejecting one or another specific conception of desert. Further, even when the issue is not the propriety of desert as a distributive principle generally but rather its implications on a specific issue—such as whether it calls for use of prison or the death penalty—the failure to appreciate the existence of these different conceptions of desert leads writers to use arguments based upon an analysis of one conception of desert to draw conclusions that they apply to a different conception of desert.

Consider the range of criticisms offered against desert.

A. Harsh?

. . . Because vengeful desert focuses primarily on the harm done, with little reference to the offender's situation and capabilities, it is easy to see how the resulting punishment can be perceived as being overly harsh (at least from the perspective of deontological or empirical desert), for it ignores many factors that both moral philosophers and the community would think are relevant in assessing blameworthiness. Thus, while the harshness criticism may seem valid to some people, it is valid only when applied to vengeful desert; it is misguided when applied to deontological and empirical desert. Indeed, the primary criterion of deontological desert is that the punishment be precisely that which is deserved, no more and no less. Similarly, empirical desert seeks to give offender exactly what he deserves according to principles of justice derived from the community's intuitions of justice. It would be odd indeed, then, to find substantial complaint that a distribution of liability and punishment based upon empirical desert was judged to be systematically harsh. . . .

Contrast this with application of the same complaint against vengeful desert. There the complaint goes not simply to a disagreement with one or another liability rule but to the foundational criterion by which punishment is to be distributed: to match the suffering caused the victim. In that context, the complaint may have traction, for the distributive criterion of vengeful desert fails to take account of factors, such as culpable state of mind and excusing conditions, thus will regularly and systematically produce punishment that is unduly harsh, at least from the point of view of deontological and empirical desert.

B. Based on Anger and Hatred?

. . . Complaints that deserved punishment is necessarily the product of anger and hatred are similar to complaints that deserved punishment is harsh, but also different. One might respond to the two complaints in a similar way: by suggesting that each reveals a confusion between vengeful desert on the one hand and deontological and empirical desert on the other. That is, to the extent that vengeful desert is associated with the special view of victims, it is easy to see how that association might suggest anger and hatred toward the victimizer, a reaction often felt by victims. Thus, one might observe that deontological and empirical desert, in contrast to vengeful desert, take no such victim's perspective and therefore this complaint has no application to them. They focus on the offender, in particular on his blameworthiness, not the victim and his injury, and certainly not the victim's anger or hatred. Indeed, because their goal is to assess as accurately as possible an offender's blameworthiness, it follows that the presence of anger or hatred would be anathema to these conceptions of desert because it risks distorting the accuracy of the blameworthiness judgment. In other words, the complaint that deserved punishment necessarily is the product of anger and hatred reflects a failure to distinguish vengeful desert on the one hand from deontological and empirical desert on the other—a response analogous to the response above to the complaint that deserved punishment is necessarily harsh.

But the complaint that desert is based upon anger and hatred also is problematic for another reason: It is a complaint about *motivation in punishing* rather than about the *distribution of punishment*. While the complaint is mixed with substantive complaints about lack of justness, it has nothing to do with justness. A distribution consistent with deontological or empirical desert could be motivated by anger in any particular case or by any particular punisher, but the motivation itself does not make the punishment any more or less just. The same is true of punishment based upon a vengeful desert distribution. If a vengeful desert distribution just happens as a matter of dumb luck in a given case to produce a sentence that exactly matches an offender's blameworthiness, the fact that it is motivated by anger or hatred does not make the sentence unjust. And conversely, if a vengeful desert distribution produces an unjust sentence (from the perspective of deontological or empirical desert), the absence of anger in its imposition does not make it just. A society has every reason to want its determinations of punishment to be free of anger and hatred for a wide variety of reasons, but the presence of that emotion itself can be only the basis upon which to criticize the punisher, not the punishment.

C. A Preference for Prison, or Worse?

Desert is sometimes associated with a preference for imprisonment, or worse. . . .

If, under the vengeful conception of desert, "the punishment should fit the crime," it might be argued that prison ought to have a preferred place among punishment methods because it best reproduces the victim's suffering, given the limitations placed on punishment methods by liberal democracies. Any less severe form of punishment would fail to match the victim suffering caused by the offender. By the same token, the vengeful conception of desert might logically suggest the death penalty for murder.

But, because neither deontological nor empirical desert have an interest in reproducing the suffering of the victim upon the offender, they have no reason to give special preference to prison or to any other punishment method. Their interest is only in insuring that a certain amount of punishment is imposed—the amount that will put the offender in his proper ordinal rank among other cases according to his relative blameworthiness. Any method or methods of punishment that achieve that result would be fully consistent with the demands of deontological and empirical desert.

Indeed, because their focus is on the amount rather than the method of punishment, deontological and empirical desert can provide greater flexibility in the method by which punishment is imposed than is commonly available today. A sentencing system or sentencing judge could be allowed complete discretion in fashioning any particular sentencing method or combination of methods for a given case, as long as the total amount of punishment imposed was that deserved given the offender's blameworthiness. All that would be needed would be a table that gave punishment "credit" for each punishment method according to the relative punitive "bite" of that method. Once such a table of punishment equivalencies is established (such tables already exist)—setting equivalencies between fine, weekend jail, supervised probation, community service, and any other sanctioning method—a sentencing judge can be left to translate a prison sentence into any other method or combination of methods, so long as the total punitive "bite" totaled the amount deserved. The ideal punishment equivalency table would be one that sets punishment ratios such that an offender is indifferent as to which of the punishment methods is used. . . .

D. Only Vague Demands? Only Marks Punishment Extremes to Be Avoided?: "Limiting Retributivism" in Setting the Punishment Continuum Endpoint

. . . If one has in mind the vengeful conception of desert, the claim of vagueness may make sense under the theory that the demand that the punishment be "proportional" to the harm caused leaves a good deal of flexibility in application. That proportionality requirement might be taken to suggest only the need for an approximation. On the other hand, the strict form of lex talionis—that punishment "should correspond in degree and in kind to the offense of the wrongdoer" is not so vague. Admittedly, there may remain some application questions: Exactly how is victim suffering to be measured, and how is it to be reproduced? Doesn't every victim experience a crime differently?

But the same vagueness complaint is even more misguided when applied to deontological and empirical desert, with their focus on offender blameworthiness rather than on victim suffering, although the vagueness complaint is made about blameworthiness too. . . .

But such complaints are based in part on a failure to appreciate the specific demands of these two conceptions of desert: the demands of ordinal ranking, as opposed to the issue of punishment continuum endpoint. . . . Those who complain about desert's vagueness seem to assume, incorrectly, that deontological and empirical desert seek to provide a universal, absolute amount of punishment as deserved for a given offense. Their criticism is an appropriate criticism only if one assumes that desert requires a specific amount of punishment in all societies but deontological and empirical desert make no such claim. The goal of empirical and deontological desert is to ensure that offenders of different blameworthiness are given different amounts of punishment, each to receive an amount that reflects their differences in blameworthiness. And that ordinal ranking does not require a specific amount of punishment in a universal sense. It requires imposition of only that specific amount of punishment that will put the offender at his appropriate ordinal rank *given punishment continuum endpoint in that society*. That is, the uncertainty about deserved punishment amount that Morris and others observe arises not because of any vagueness in the ordinal ranking of offenses according to offender blameworthiness but rather because of differences in the punishment continuum endpoint that a society might adopt. It is the proper ordinal rank that is the focus of deontological and empirical desert, not the punishment continuum endpoint. Once that endpoint is set, vagueness in deserved punishment amount disappears.

Deontological and empirical conceptions of desert may have something useful to say about placing the punishment continuum endpoint, but the nature of their contribution on this point is quite different than when they serve as a distributive principle for punishment: Here they identify only extremes beyond which placement of the endpoint would be problematic. . . .

But this does not settle the issue of the vagueness complaint against deontological and empirical desert. Some writers argue that even ordinal ranking is something that can be done only in the vaguest terms, that establishing specific rankings is impossible. . . .

Many moral philosophers may have an answer to this challenge and may be able to give a reasoned account of how to make the kinds of judgments called for here. But it is admittedly a problem that different moral philosophers will have different answers. But this is not a problem of vagueness but rather a problem of disagreement, . . . discussed immediately below. . . .

As to empirical desert, it may still be argued that the blameworthiness ranking of offenses is beyond the ability of people's intuitions of justice, that those intuitions are simply too vague to do more than to roughly distinguish between "serious" cases and "not serious" cases and cannot provide the nuance needed to do more.

But the empirical studies paint a quite different picture. The evidence comes from a wide variety of empirical studies. In some studies subjects were asked to put offenses or offense scenarios into one of a set of predetermined categories; in another kind of study, subjects were asked to rank order offenses or offense scenarios; in a third kind of study, subjects were asked to assign numerical values to each of a number of offenses or offense scenarios. The results in all of these studies are consistent: Subjects displayed a good deal of nuance in the judgments they make. Small changes in facts produce large and predictable changes in punishment. Durham summarizes the surveys this way: "Virtually without exception, citizens seem able to assign highly specific sentences for highly specific events." The conclusion suggested by the empirical evidence is that people take account of a wide variety of factors and often give them quite different effect in different situations. That is, people's intuitions of justice are not vague or simplistic, as claimed, but rather quite sophisticated and complex.

What this suggests is that, while the vagueness complaint may be valid with regard to vengeful desert, it is misguided when applied to deontological desert at least in principle, and simply wrong in both principle and practice when applied to empirical desert.

E. Subject to Profound Disagreement?

Another common objection to using desert as a distributive principle for criminal liability and punishment is the concern that, even if individual people may have a clear notion of what desert demands, there is simply no agreement among people. Against this complaint, both vengeful and deontological desert have weak responses. The problem for vengeful desert arises from the vagueness of its criterion: the vagueness of "proportionality" to victim suffering and the subjectivity inherent in the victim perspective. The problem for deontological desert is slightly different. The focus of its distributive principle is fixed and specific—an offender's moral blameworthiness—but moral philosophers simply disagree about just how this principle translates into specific punishment in a given case. . . .

But the common wisdom simply does not match the empirical reality. In fact, empirical studies show broadly shared intuitions that serious wrongdoing should be punished, and broadly shared intuitions about the relative blameworthiness of different cases. The striking extent of the agreement on intuitions of justice is illustrated in a recent study that asks subjects to rank order 24 crime scenario descriptions according to the amount of punishment deserved. The researchers found that the subjects displayed an astounding level of agreement in the ordinal ranking of the scenarios. . . .

A more sophisticated statistical measure of concordance is found in Kendall's W coefficient of concordance, in which 1.0 indicates perfect agreement and 0.0 indicates no agreement. In this study, the Kendall's W is .95 (with $p < .001$), an astounding level of agreement. One might expect to get this high a Kendall's W if subjects were asked to judge the relative brightness of different groupings of spots, for example. When asked to perform more subjective or complex comparisons, such as asking travel magazine readers to rank the attractiveness of eight different travel destinations, one gets a Kendall's W of .52. When asking economists to rank the top 20 economics journals according to quality, one gets a Kendall's W. of .095.

Indeed, the ordinal ranking of different cases generally is consistent across demographics, including cultural differences examined in cross-cultural studies that replicated domestic studies. Typical of the conclusions in these studies,

Newman reports that, "it is apparent that there was considerable agreement as to the amount of punishment appropriate to each act" and that looking at relative rankings indicates "general agreement in ranks across all countries."

The level of agreement is strongest for those core wrongs with which criminal law primarily concerns itself—physical aggression, taking property, and deception in exchanges—and becomes less pronounced as the nature of the offense moves farther from the core of wrongdoing. But even where there is disagreement, empirical desert offers a ready means by which the disagreements can be resolved: by adopting the majority view. No such means exists to resolve conflicting views for deontological desert. From the perspective of empirical desert, it is best to avoid deviation from community views, but where disagreement exists among the community and therefore some deviation from some people's views is inevitable, the law should adopt whatever rule will undermine its moral credibility the least. That commonly will mean adopting the majority rule over the minority rule. . . .

F. Fails to Avoid Avoidable Crime?

The most fundamental complaint by utilitarians against a desert distributive principle is its disutility. . . .

Traditionally, the utilitarian preference has been for distributing liability to optimize deterrence, rehabilitation, incapacitation, or some combination of them. And those consequentialists who seek to minimize future crime would be right to point out that deontological desert as a distributive principle would allow future crimes that could have been avoided by a utilitarian distributive principle, such as one that relied upon these traditional utilitarian distributive principles.

But of course this classic challenge of utilitarianism to a deontological desert does not work against empirical desert because its distribution of liability and punishment is specifically designed to minimize future crime—by harnessing the crime-control power of social influence that comes with building the criminal law's moral credibility. In other words, empirical desert is a utilitarian, consequentialist theory of punishment. A deontological desert distribution would indeed be ineffective at gaining the crime-control benefits. The beneficial consequences flow not from following a deontological desert distribution but only from following an empirical desert distribution. It is the community's perception that justice is being done that pays crime-control dividends, not the system's actual success as measured by deontological desert.

G. Immoral?

Just as the utilitarian objection of poor crime control has been leveled at a desert distributive principle—with some force when applied to deontological desert but missing the mark when applied to empirical desert—the reverse sort of objection also can be made: that a desert distribution is immoral. Some writers complain about "the injustice of 'just' punishment."

As one might expect, the response to the immorality complaint is essentially the reverse of the response to the disutility complaint discussed in the previous section: The objection may have weight against empirical desert but makes little sense with regard to deontological desert. That is, while moral philosophers may well disagree among themselves about how to translate desert into specific principles of justice, all would agree that the primary goal of a deontological desert distribution would be to produce criminal liability and punishment that was, above all else, moral.

On the other hand, the criticism is fair when applied to empirical desert: What empirical desert produces is not justice, but only liability and punishment consistent with the community's views about what constitutes justice. The community's intuitions of justice could be wrong, even if there is a high degree of agreement about them. At any particular time and place, there may be widespread support for the morality of conduct that only later is revealed to be immoral and unjust, as with slave owning. To protect against this error, to be able to identify when people's shared intuitions of justice are unjust, a system must turn to deontological desert to provide that transcendent check on the justness of its liability rules. It is only deontological desert that can give us the truth of what is deserved, insulated from the vicissitudes of human irrationality and emotions. . . .

✳ DISCUSSION MATERIALS

Issue: What are the Strengths and Weaknesses of Using "Restorative" Processes, Rather than Traditional Criminal Justice Adjudication?

Erik Luna, In Support of Restorative Justice

Criminal Law Conversations (Paul H. Robinson, Stephen P. Garvey, & Kimberly Kessler Ferzan ed. 2009)

The Theory of Restorative Justice

. . . Restorative justice can be described as an approach to punishment that includes all relevant parties to a crime in a group decision-making process to reach a mutually agreeable outcome. As a general rule, the participants are those who have been directly affected by the crime and/or have a cognizable stake in its resolution: victims, offenders, family members, law enforcement representatives, and others within a "community of interest."[1] Although it has been subject to various interpretations by scholars and practitioners, restorative justice can be separated into (at least) two distinct conceptions: one that takes the form of a substantive theory challenging retributivism, utilitarianism, and other philosophies of punishment; and another that sees restorative justice as merely a procedure that allows all legitimate sentencing theories, as represented by the participants, to have a say in the decision-making process and ultimate outcome.

---

1. Allison Morris and Warren Young, *Reforming Criminal Justice: The Potential of Restorative Justice* , *in* Restorative Justice: Philosophy to Practice 11, 14 (Heather Strang and John Braithwaite eds., 2000).

A. *The Substantive Conception of Restorative Justice*

In seeking to justify restorative justice as a substantive theory of punishment, some advocates rely upon religious tenets or non-Western traditions. But many proponents view restorative justice as a set of secular practices oriented toward restitution, for instance, or having numerous psychological benefits for participants and a greater impact on consequential goals like deterrence.

Of special note is the work of John Braithwaite, who has developed both a positive account and normative justification for substantive restorative justice[2] . . .

. . . [S]ubstantive restorative justice is usually presented as an alternative to pure utilitarianism or retributivism. Unlike the traditional theories, restorative justice claims that a punishment should be both backward-looking—condemning the offense and uncovering its causes—and forward-looking—making amends to the victim and the general community while facilitating moral development and constructive behavior in the offender. Metaphorically, restorative justice views crime as a point in the middle of a motion picture, with action both before and after the criminal event. In contrast to the temporal bracketing of retributivism and utilitarianism—with the former interested only in past acts and mental states and the latter focusing solely on future consequences—restorative justice is concerned with the causes of crime and issues of personal responsibility *and* the effects of sentencing on individuals, families, and communities.

Advocates often speak of "healing rather than hurting," rejecting punishment as just deserts, for instance, or as a means of incapacitation. With this in mind, substantive restorative justice incorporates a few core principles, beginning with the notion that crime is not just an action against the state but against specific victims and the relevant community. Offending is reframed as a violation of social relationships that also violates the law, with the source of beneficial norms and crime control located in families, support networks, and communities, rather than penal codes and courts. Accordingly, restorative justice promotes the involvement of victims, families, community representatives, and other stakeholders to deal with the causes and consequences of wrongdoing. Moreover, the substantive conception views crime as creating affirmative duties that offenders must meet with active responses instead of passive submission to a penalty.

In particular, a central ambition is making amends for the offense—especially for the physical, emotional, and economic harm to the victim—not just imposing pain upon the offender. Accountability tends to be characterized as an offender acknowledging the wrongfulness of his behavior, communicating remorse for the damage he has caused, and taking actions to mend the breach in social relationships. Toward this end, substantive restorative justice envisions a collaborative sanctioning process that involves all stakeholders concerned with the offense and offender. The primary feature is largely uninhibited dialogue among the parties, allowing all present to express their emotions and ideas in an open forum. Through discussion and deliberation, this approach contemplates mutual agreement on the steps that must be taken to heal the victim and the community,

---

2. See, e.g., John Braithwaite, Crime, Shame, and Reintegration (1989); John Braithwaite and Philip Pettit, Not Just Deserts: A Republican Theory of Criminal Justice (1990).

resulting in the formation of a plan to confront the factors contributing to the offender's conduct and to facilitate his development as a law-abiding citizen.

Substantive restorative justice also offers a fairly straightforward challenge to the actual practice of punishment, questioning the very foundation of modern criminal justice systems. An offense is not merely a "breach of the King's peace," to use the historical phrase, but a direct violation of the victim's rights and interests, a grave concern to loved ones (both of the victim and of the offender), and a threat to the community. Although state intervention stems the brutality of a private settling of scores, contemporary criminal justice systems are premised not on public intercession but government domination, often drastically limiting the input of affected parties or wholly excluding them from the process. Restorative justice recognizes that the victim, families, and community members have, in Nils Christie's words, a type of "property" interest in the case as a matter of process and outcome.[3]

In addition, substantive restorative justice argues that crime cannot be isolated or reduced to a problem with the criminal. Offending has a context, a history surrounding the event, and thoughtful solutions to crime will not focus on the offender alone. Although the wrongdoing must be firmly denounced and the nature of the harm made clear to the perpetrator, the substantive conception insists that the needs of the victim must be addressed as well, including repairing any harm caused by the offense. In addition, the occasion should be an opportunity for the community to reflect: *Did the social environment contribute to the offending and, if so, how are the relevant criminogenic influences remedied? What must be done to regain a sense of security and reaffirm pro-social values? How can the community and its members facilitate the moral education and social integration of the offender?* These questions are not asked as a means to exonerate a defendant for his harmful wrongdoing, but instead to restore the community's sense of wellbeing and to take affirmative, prophylactic steps against future offending. . . .

B. The Procedural Conception of Restorative Justice

. . . [R]estorative justice need not be seen as just another substantive theory of punishment. Rather, it can be viewed as a procedural approach that includes all stakeholders in a specific offense in a process of group decision making on how to handle the crime and its implications for the future. This conception would not embody a particular justification of punishment but instead would view restorative justice as providing a process that does not take a stand on the merits of utilitarianism, retributivism, communicative and compensatory models, and so forth. Each punishment rationale will have virtues for its sponsors and vices for its detractors, and as noted above, perfectly sensible people can and will adopt their own visions of justice in sentencing.

Procedural restorative justice tries to steer clear of the ongoing debate among philosophers of punishment. After all, real-world cases do need to be resolved regardless of enduring uncertainties about punishment theories, and what does seem feasible is that a dialogic process might lead affected individuals to agree on a sanction without necessarily agreeing on its justification. By bringing together victims, offenders, their supporters, and various other stakeholders,

---

3. See Nils Christie, *Conflicts as Property*, 17 BRIT. J. CRIMINOLOGY 1 (1977).

and then providing them an opportunity to express their opinions in an undominated forum, procedural restorative justice offers a broad framework for parties to find common ground on outcomes—an "overlapping consensus"[4] of sorts—while maintaining their personal interpretations of justice.

This does not mean that the victim may demand any sanction or none whatsoever, applying his chosen justification of punishment. The offender has rights, too, and he will have his own perspective on justice, something that would inform a punishment rationale. And although not as direct or compelling as those of the victim and offender, the rights of others may be at stake in the resolution of a criminal episode. The commission of a crime can place third parties in fear for their lives and property, impeding full enjoyment of their rights and fulfillment of their visions of the good life. Of course, government has an important job as well, protecting against an atavistic state of nature where crimes result in undue punishment or, conversely, no sanction at all.

Officials must establish a fair process by which conflicting rights and punishment rationales—those of victims, offenders, and affected third parties—can be mediated toward a reasonable outcome. If an agreement among all the stakeholders proves impossible—because the victim or offender refuses to participate, for instance, or their dialogue fails to reach a resolution—the traditional criminal justice system would need to be invoked to achieve an appropriate punishment in light of the views of the interested parties. But what the procedural conception does not foresee is a particular theory of punishment being foisted upon these parties in the first instance. . . .

Conclusion

Restorative justice cannot substitute for many of the core functions of modern legal systems. It is not an investigative tool for determining whether a crime has been committed and who is responsible, and it certainly lacks the fact-finding apparatus of the traditional court process. In other words, restorative justice can address neither the "whodunit" questions nor various aspects of culpability—whether an individual committed the crime at issue, whether an affirmative defense like mental illness or self-defense has any validity, whether the defendant is guilty of the highest charged crime or a lesser included offense, and so on. Likewise, restorative justice has no capacity to interpret penal codes or constitutional provisions, for example, a claim that the statute of limitations bars prosecution or that a government search violated the defendant's Fourth Amendment rights.

Nor is restorative justice a panacea for the problems mentioned at the outset, such as America's high rates of crime, victimization, and imprisonment. But studies have shown numerous cognitive, affective, and behavioral benefits from restorative justice, including a reduction in recidivism and the fear of revictimization. In addition, the substantive conception of restorative justice largely eschews incarceration, while the procedural conception empowers affected individuals to craft appropriate resolutions, with the process engendering feelings of fairness and satisfaction among the participants.

If nothing else, restorative justice cannot do any worse than the current approaches to punishment, and it may well check the opportunistic tendency of

---

4. See generally, John Rawls, Political Liberalism (1993).

political demagogues to put forward ruthless sentencing policies. The theory and principles of restorative justice can be tremendously stimulating, forcing punishment philosophers and state actors alike to reevaluate their own intellectual commitments and the merits of their chosen sentencing methodologies.

Paul H. Robinson, Restorative Processes & Doing Justice
3.3 Univ of St. Thomas Law Review 421 (2006)

I. Introduction

. . . I want to quarrel with some of the "restorative justice" advocates: victims and offenders are not the only people who have a stake in how we deal with offenders. The adjudication of criminal wrongs is not a private affair, which is why we treat these cases as state prosecutions and not civil trials. There are important societal interests at stake. Let me give just one case example to help bring the issues into focus: the *Clotworthy* case,[5] a case from New Zealand about which John Braithwaite, one of the major proponents of "restorative justice," speaks in admiring terms.[6] During a vicious robbery, Clotworthy stabbed the victim six times, puncturing the victim's lung and diaphragm and seriously disfiguring his face. It was the disfigurement that had the most devastating effect on the victim, for the result was sufficiently repulsive to people that it interfered with his normal social interactions. In the mediation session, it was agreed that Clotworthy would not go to prison but, instead, would work to earn money to pay the fifteen thousand dollars needed for the surgical operation to diminish the victim's disfigurement. Braithwaite thought this a wonderful disposition, an example of a restorative justice success. I think it an example of what is wrong with his vision of "restorative justice." I understand why the victim would agree to such a disposition: he was desperate to reestablish his social relationships. And I can understand why Clotworthy thought this was a great disposition: it was as if he was just paying civil compensation, and not even fair compensation at that since there was no compensation for the horrors that the victim had been put through.

But the victim should never have been put to a choice of getting justice or getting his life back. To take advantage of his desperate situation in order to get him to agree to such a disposition is simply to victimize him again—this time with official institutions approving the dirty deed. The result is appalling; to see it as a desirable disposition is even more so. But it nicely illustrates how unfortunately indifferent the restorative justice proponents can be to the importance of doing justice not just to victims but to the rest of society. Society has an important interest at stake here—doing justice, in the sense that the offender receive deserved punishment for his wrongdoing—and dispositions like *Clotworthy* undermine that interest. Justice would have been having Clotworthy stay out of prison long enough to make the money needed for the operation, then go to prison, or suffer some other form of punishment. . . .

---

5. The Queen v. Clotworthy, T.971545 (D.C. April 24, 1998) (N.Z.).

6. John Braithwaite, *Restorative Justice: Assessing Optimistic and Pessimistic Accounts*, 25 CRIME & JUST. 1, 87-88 (1999).

The crime-control benefits of doing justice may help explain the recent ascendance of desert as a principle for distributing criminal liability and punishment. A number of sentencing guidelines have adopted desert as the dominant criterion for sentencing.[7] Indeed, the American Law Institute, which drafted the Model Penal Code—the foundation for criminal codes in probably three quarters of the States[8]—has for the first time in forty-five years proposed a change to the Model Code: to set the guiding purpose in sentencing as that of doing justice, giving offenders the punishment they deserve.[9] Standing in a quite obvious contrast to this desert trend is the "restorative justice" movement, at least that portion of it advanced by academics like John Braithwaite, who use it in their anti-desert campaign. . . .

III. Justice and Restorative Measures Can Coexist

For these academics, it may be the potential of restorative processes to undermine deserved punishment that makes them attractive. I see their anti-desert attitude as being both odd and unfortunate. It is odd because there is nothing in the use of restorative processes themselves that is necessarily in conflict with desert. On the contrary, we have every reason to believe that it is the shared intuitions of justice of the persons participating in the restorative process that is shaping punishment determination. As social science research has confirmed, the criterion that drives people in assessing appropriate punishment is desert—an offender's blameworthiness. Thus, when members of a sentencing circle are sorting out an appropriate disposition for a case, what is driving their thinking is in large measure their intuitions of justice, in other words, desert. Studies suggest that these intuitions are quite strongly held and widely shared. It seems quite odd, then, that the "restorative justice" proponents approve of restorative processes that commonly run on the participants' shared intuitions of justice, yet at the same time claim that desert is to be opposed as a basis for assessing punishment.

Nor is desert as a distributive principle inconsistent with the common use of non-incarcerative sanctions that are encouraged in restorative processes. Distributing punishment consistent with the degree of an offenders' blameworthiness can be done through punishment in any form. Prison is one possibility but there are many other possibilities, including the full range of things that restorative processes might agree upon for an offender. All that desert demands is that the sum total of all punishment add up to a total that matches the amount

---

7. See, e.g., David Boerner and Roxanne Lieb, *Sentencing Reform in the Other Washington*, 28 CRIME & JUST. 71, 71-72 (2001) ("[Washington's] Sentencing Reform Act of 1981 rejected many core tenets of indeterminate sentencing, putting into place a sentencing system based on principles of just desert and accountability."); Michele Cotton, *Back with a Vengeance: The Resilience of Retribution as an Articulated Purpose of Criminal Punishment*, 37 AM. CRIM. L. REV. 1313, 1358 (2000) ("California endorsed retribution as "the" purpose for its punishment in 1977 and Pennsylvania identified it as the "primary" purpose in 1982 . . . ").

8. See ALI, Annual Report 21 (1984) (listing the states that have replaced their criminal codes since the promulgation of the Model Penal Code). The Code also is an influential source of authority even in those states without modern criminal codes, where courts regularly cite and follow its provisions.

9. See ALI, Model Penal Code Sentencing Report 41 (April 11, 2003), *available at* www.ali.org (follow "ALI Projects Online" hyperlink, then follow "Model Penal Code: Sentencing, Report (April 11, 2003)" hyperlink) ("[B]road support has been voiced for the theory of limiting retributivism as the philosophical cornerstone of sentencing decision under the revised Model Penal Code.").

of punishment that the offender deserves according to the degree of his blame-worthiness. In a penal code I just helped draft under UNDP sponsorship, the sentencing guidelines have a punishment method equivalency table that encourages sentencing judges to use non-incarcerative sanctions by letting them "translate" a prison term under the guidelines into a non-incarcerative sentence using the conversion table.[10] So, for example, a prison term of X amount might be "converted" into a fine of Y amount or Z hours of community service, etc. The goal is to provide as much flexibility as possible in the selection of sentencing method, while at the same time ensuring that offenders get the amount of punishment they deserve, no more, no less.

So, if there is nothing in restorative processes that is inconsistent with desert, why is it that Braithwaite and other "restorative justice" proponents are so opposed to desert? I think it is in part a misunderstanding of what modern notions of desert mean. These desert opponents may assume that desert means harsh punishment. Certainly the biblical phrase, "An eye for an eye," which they regularly repeat,[11] has the connotation of harsh, if not barbaric, punishment. And it is true that politicians sometimes talk about "desert" as if it means being more harsh. But no modern desert theorist would intend this meaning of desert when they propose using it as a principle for the distribution of criminal liability and punishment. On the contrary, to be "harsh" is to suggest that a person get more punishment than they deserve, which clearly would violate the principle of desert.

Indeed, desert typically has little interest in assuring punishment of any particular severity; more important to it is the proper ordinal ranking of cases along the continuum of punishment according to the relative degree of blameworthiness of the offenders. Different societies take different views about what should be the endpoint of the punishment continuum: some set it at the death penalty, some at life imprisonment, some at twenty years, some lower still. What desert says is that, once that endpoint on the continuum of punishment is marked, offenders should be set on that continuum according to the relative degree of their blameworthiness. Thus, the amount of punishment that an offender deserves is not a product of some magical connection between that offense and that amount of punishment. Rather, it is simply the amount of punishment that is needed to put that offender in his appropriate rank-order with other offenders. Modern desert is about giving each offender his or her appropriate amount of punishment in relation to other offenders. So you can see how odd it is when the restorative justice anti-desert supporters base their anti-desert campaign on a complaint that deserved punishment would be harsh.

---

10. Paul H. Robinson with the Univ. of Pa. Law School's Criminal Law Research Group, Final Report of the Maldives Penal Law & Sentencing Codification Project 129-30, 138-40 (2006), *available at* http://www.law.upenn.edu/fac/phrobins/draftislamicpenalcode/(follow "Volume 1" hyperlink).

11. See, e.g., Andrew J. Hosmanek, *Cutting the Cord: Ho'oponopono and Hawaiian Restorative Justice in the Criminal Law Context*, 5 Pepp. Disp. Resol. L. J. 359, 370 (insisting that retribution focuses on the "eye for an eye" model where society has the "right or obligation" to injure the offender to the same degree the offender has injured society); Christopher Slobogin, *The Civilization of the Criminal Law*, 58, Vand. L. Rev. 121, 147 (2005) (characterizing retributive punishment as punishment that adopts the Biblical "eye for an eye" philosophy).

APPENDIX A: SECTION 4

Culpability Requirements

✳ DISCUSSION MATERIALS

Issue: What Is the Minimum Culpability, if Any, That Should Be Required for Criminal Liability?

Notes on Minimum Culpability Requirements: Negligence and Strict Liability

Negligence
    Individualized objective standard
    Deterrence argument
    Utilitarian counterargument
    Deterrability of inattentiveness

NEGLIGENCE

Negligence differs from recklessness in that the actor is not, but should be, aware of a substantial risk that the prohibited result will occur or that the required circumstance exists. Recklessness and negligence are similar, however, in that both set a minimum standard for the kind of risk taking that will give rise to a finding of culpability. Not every risk is one for which an actor is negligent if he is unaware of it. In language parallel to that used in the definition of recklessness, the Model Penal Code provides that an actor is negligent if he or she is unaware of a substantial risk and the risk is of the sort of which the actor should have been aware:

> The risk must be of such a nature and degree that the actor's failure to perceive it, considering the nature and purpose of his conduct and the circumstances known to him, involves a gross deviation from the standard of care that a reasonable person would observe in the actor's situation.[1]

The "gross deviation" requirement makes clear that the civil standard of negligence in tort law is insufficient to sustain criminal liability for negligence.[2]

Individualized objective standard The objective standard represented by the "reasonable person" is modified—individualized—to include the facts known to the actor and the "actors situation." The commentary makes clear that this last requirement may be interpreted broadly. It may include not only the objective circumstances of the actor's "situation," but also characteristics of the actor. Thus, criminal negligence requires a finding that the circumstances are such that the actor rightfully could have been expected to have been aware of the risk. This makes his unawareness condemnable. The common law was much less likely to individualize the objective standard of negligence, tending instead to ignore differences in education, intelligence, age, background, and the like, that might alter expectations of the risks of which one could expect the actor to be aware.

Deterrence argument One argument against liability for negligence focuses on what is said to be the law's inability to deter negligent conduct. Where there is awareness of risk, as with recklessness, the threat of punishment may cause

---

1. Model Penal Code § 2.02(2)(d).

2. See Santillanes v. State, 849 P.2d 358 (N.M. 1993) (conviction for child abuse, which requires negligently endangering child, reversed because trial court instructed jury using civil negligence standard).

an actor to avoid the risk. The threat of criminal sanction can make the actor pause and perhaps reconsider, before choosing to disregard the risk. In the case of negligence, in contrast, an actor cannot be deterred, it is said, because she has no awareness of the facts that make her conduct criminal. It is argued that imposing liability in such a case is a futile and wasteful use of sanctioning resources.

Utilitarian counterargument   One might respond to this argument by noting that it is too narrow in focusing only on special deterrence as the crime prevention mechanism. Punishing the negligent actor may serve general deterrence goals: Others may pay closer attention to possible risks if they see offenders punished for such inadvertent risk taking. Or, one might even argue that incapacitative or rehabilitative goals can be served by imposing such liability. That is, it might bring within the jurisdiction of the correctional system people who are needlessly inattentive, as a means of protecting society from them or reforming them.

Deterrability of inattentiveness   A better response, however, may challenge the underlying assumption of the special deterrence argument that inattentiveness to risk taking is not deterrable. There is every indication that people can chose to pay more (or less) attention to their surroundings and the consequences of their conduct. In fact, the deterrability of inattentiveness is an underlying assumption of the general deterrence and rehabilitation counterarguments. They each assume that seeing inattentive risk taking punished in others can make an actor more careful.

Desert counterargument   But once it is admitted that inattentiveness can be deterred, that it is not hopelessly inevitable, then it becomes clear that there can be moral blame in the failure to be attentive. If an actor can choose how attentive he or she is to a particular kind of risk taking, the actor can be blamed for not being as attentive as the situation demands. Obviously there are limits to attentiveness. A person cannot be attentive to every possibility, nor should a person. Such a standard would paralyze all action and punish actors for inattentiveness when attentiveness could not reasonably be expected of them. If negligence is determined by a standard of absolute perfection, it becomes strict liability and punishes in the absence of blame. Under the requirements of modern codes, however, as illustrated by the Model Penal Code's definition of negligence described above, negligence is blameworthy. An actor is held negligent only if he fails to be reasonably attentive to risks, with the reasonableness of his attentiveness judged in light of "the circumstances known to him" and his "situation." He will be found negligent only if it is determined that, in the situation as it existed, he could have and should have been aware of the risk.

STRICT LIABILITY

Actors may be held liable for an offense of strict liability regardless of their culpability at the time of the offense. (An offense of strict liability only omits the culpability requirement; the full range of general defenses remains available.) Traffic offenses, such as speeding, commonly are strict liability offenses. More serious offenses also can be strict liability offenses.[3] For example, statutory rape is

---

3. See, e.g., United States v. Freed, 401 U.S. 601 (1971) (offense of unlawful possession of hand grenades requires no *mens rea*)

commonly defined as requiring no culpability as to the partner being underage.[4] An offense may be made one of strict liability either by a determination that no culpability is required or a determination that a reasonable mistake is no defense.

Case against strict liability   The arguments against the use of strict liability have been made above in discussing the appropriate restrictions upon negligent liability: An individualized standard of negligence is used by modern codes to ensure that negligent liability is imposed only on actors who could have done otherwise. To punish any infraction, without regard to the circumstances or the actor's situation, mental and physical, is to permit punishment in cases where the actor could not reasonably be expected to have avoided the violation. The fact is, strict liability punishes even in instances where the perfectly reasonable person could not have avoided the violation. That is, even the purely objective standard used at common law—the unindividualized "reasonable person" standard—ensures that liability is imposed only where the actor's conduct falls below a set standard. It is for these reasons that even jurisdictions without modern criminal codes generally assume that some culpability is required, even where an offense definition carries no culpability requirement on its face.

Case for strict liability   How might one seek to justify liability for a violation of the rules without regard to the reasonableness of the actor's conduct? Three sorts of arguments typically are given in support of strict liability: (1) that strict liability is limited in application to situations where the actor probably is at least negligent, (2) that the use of strict liability will lead people to be more careful, and (3) that only civil-like penalties are imposed for strict liability, so no serious injustice is done.

Limited application argument   It is true that strict liability is used sparingly in most modern codes. The Model Penal Code permits strict liability in three classes of offenses. The first two classes are described as follows:

> The requirements of culpability prescribed by Sections 2.01 and 2.02 do not apply to:
> (a) offenses which constitute violations, unless the requirement involved is included in the definition of the offense or the Court determines that its application is consistent with effective enforcement of the law defining the offense; or
> (b) offenses defined by statutes other than the Code, insofar as a legislative purpose to impose absolute liability for such offenses or with respect to any material element thereof plainly appears.[5]

Thus, where no culpability is provided in a criminal code offense definition, recklessness is read in by Model Penal Code section 2.02(3), except in the case of violations, which are typically only quasi-criminal offenses, having only a fine, forfeiture, or other civil penalty as a sentence.[6] Strict liability can also be imposed for offenses outside of the criminal code, but only if a legislative purpose to do so plainly appears. Again, offenses outside the code tend to be of minimal seriousness, with only minor penalties attached; at least, this was the situation when the Model Code was drafted.

---

4. See, e.g., Model Penal Code § 213.6(1).
5. Model Penal Code § 2.05(1).
6. See Model Penal Code § 1.04(5).

Strict Liability for Serious Offenses   However, the quoted provision only prevents the operation of sections 2.01 and 2.02, which would read in a culpability requirement where an offense definition is silent. The provision does not limit the legislature's ability expressly to provide for strict liability, even for a serious offense defined by the Code. This is a third class of strict liability offenses. For example, the Model Penal Code provides strict liability as to the age of the victim when an offense punishes sexual conduct with a partner under ten years old.[7] The point of the provision quoted above is simply to ensure that, absent such express legislative provision of strict liability, strict liability is not presumed from a silent statute. It is this third class of offenses in which the use of strict liability is most problematic and controversial.

Negligence Per Se Claim   Even when strict liability is used in more serious offenses, it is argued, it typically is limited to instances where an actor necessarily is at least negligent. For example, it seems unlikely that an actor would not be at least negligent as to whether a sexual partner is under the age of ten. On the other hand, it might happen that, "under the circumstances known to [the actor]," a reasonable person "in the actor's situation" might well make a mistake as to a sexual partner being under ten years old. And, in such a case, the Model Penal Code will impose significant liability in the absence of blameworthiness. Similarly, many states impose strict liability in holding an actor liable for murder when an accomplice kills a person in the course of a felony. Admittedly, many accomplices will be negligent as to contributing to such a death; they should have been aware that, by engaging in a felony where one of them planned to have a gun, a death might result. Yet, under the felony-murder rule, as it is called, murder liability will be imposed even if under the facts of the case no one could have guessed that there was any chance that someone could be killed. The fact is, unless negligence is explicitly required, liability can be imposed even if an actor is clearly non-negligent as to the offense. One might argue that we can rely upon the discretion of prosecutors to forego prosecution in such cases of non-negligence, but others would claim that such an expectation is unrealistic. What is more important, such an argument concedes that the law itself fails to make the distinctions necessary for a just result, adopting a position inconsistent with the legality principle or with modern notions of justice.

Constitutional Bar to an Attractive Solution   The advocates of strict liability that rely upon the negligence *per se* argument may respond by pointing to the significant burden placed on prosecutors when they must prove negligence, and may also cite the dangers to society that may arise if such prosecutions are less successful. Moreover, they may cite the additional cost of prosecutions if strict liability were not permitted. One response to this argument, adopted in many countries other than the United States, is to require negligence rather than permitting strict liability, but shift the burden of persuasion to the defendant, provided that a case can be made for the special difficulties of prosecution together with the special need for effective prosecution.[8] In other words, these countries exchange the *irrebuttable* presumption of negligence embodied in strict liability for a *rebuttable*

---

7. Model Penal Code § 213.6(1).

8. In Canada, for example, "strict liability" allows the defendant to rebut the presumption of culpability, while "absolute liability" does not. See Regina v. City of Sault Ste. Marie, 85 D.L.R.3d 161 (S. Ct. 1978); Eric Colvin, Principles of Criminal Law 22 (1986).

presumption. Unfortunately, by constitutionalizing the requirement that the state must carry the burden of persuasion on all offense elements, the Supreme Court has foreclosed this reform option.

Deter inattentiveness argument　Another argument in support of strict liability, that its use will cause people to be more careful, may well be accurate. Strict liability may make people more careful. What is left unclear is whether strict liability is more effective in this regard than a negligence standard would be. The negligence standard requires an actor to do all that he or she reasonably can be expected to do to be attentive and careful. What can the use of strict liability add to that? Strict liability might be able to encourage people to be even more careful than the circumstances reasonably would require. But this seems a questionable goal. As noted above, some risks ought to be taken and it may be harmful to society to have an actor unreasonably preoccupied with all potential risks. One might argue that, in a few instances, the potential harm is sufficiently serious that the law ought to do everything within its power to avoid a violation, and strict liability provides that special "superpunch." But this argument does not explain the current use of strict liability, which is most common in minor offenses and less common in more serious offenses. What is even more important is that the argument misunderstands the nature of negligence. In judging an actor's negligence, the seriousness of the harm is taken into account. As the potential harm becomes greater, an actor's ability to avoid negligence liability for his or her inattentiveness disappears.

Minor penalties argument　Another argument in support of strict liability focuses on its use in primarily minor offenses with minor penalties. When liability is imposed in the absence of culpability, it is argued, the penalties at stake—typically fines—make the prosecution essentially civil in nature. The argument finds support in modern codes, which typically limit the available penalties when strict liability is imposed.

> Notwithstanding any other provision of existing law and unless a subsequent statute otherwise provides, when absolute liability is imposed with respect to any material element of an offense defined by a statute other than the Code and a conviction is based upon such liability, the offense constitutes a violation.[9]

Indeed, the Code does not even class a "violation" as a crime:

> A violation does not constitute a crime and conviction of a violation shall not give rise to any disability or legal disadvantage based on conviction of a criminal offense.[10]

No term of imprisonment is authorized for a violation.

Limited Application of Minor Penalty Limitations　There are two difficulties with the minor penalties argument. First, the quoted Code provisions do not bar serious penalties for strict liability. They apply only to offenses "defined by a statute other than the Code." In other words, they serve only to ensure that significant penalties based upon strict liability are provided only if the legislature makes a deliberate choice to do so, manifested by their inclusion of the provision in the

---

9. Model Penal Code § 2.05(2)(a).
10. Model Penal Code § 1.04(5).

criminal code. Sexual offenses with persons under ten and felony murder, noted above, are examples of instances where legislatures have made this choice.

Limitation to Civil Penalties Suggests Civil Liability   Even if strict liability were limited to minor offenses, the minor penalties argument is problematic. If strict liability is to be justified on the grounds that only minor, civil-like penalties like fines are imposed, one may reasonably ask: Why not use civil liability? One might counter that criminal procedures are faster and have other enforcement advantages. But if special procedures are needed, the legislature has the authority to alter the procedures for civil actions or create special procedures for this special group of civil violations. The real reason that the criminal process is preferred is its potential to impose the stigma associated with criminal liability, a stigma that civil liability cannot impose.

Strict Liability as Undercutting Criminal Law's Moral Credibility   The stigma of criminal conviction does admittedly provide a deterrent threat that civil liability does not. But to impose *criminal* liability where the violation is morally blameless is to dilute the moral condemnation of criminal conviction. Where the criminal law is routinely used to punish blameless offenders, its ability to stigmatize, and thereby to deter, is weakened. Each time the system seeks to stigmatize where condemnation is not deserved, it reduces incrementally the system's ability to stigmatize even in cases where it is deserved. More importantly, such punishment of blameless offenders undermines the criminal law's moral credibility, thereby undermining the crime-control power that derives from harnessing the powerful forces of social influence.[11] Thus, any crime-control advantage gained from using criminal law to punish blameless violations is purchased at a serious cost.

Glanville Williams, Reasons for Punishing Negligence
Criminal Law: The General Part 122-124 (2d ed. 1961)

The use of the criminal law to punish negligence has been challenged. An American writer expressed the objection as follows:

If the defendant, being mistaken as to material facts, is to be punished because his mistake is one which an average man would not make, punishment will sometimes be inflicted when the criminal mind does not exist. Such a result is contrary to fundamental principles, and is plainly unjust, for a man should not be held criminal because of lack of intelligence.

The retributive theory of punishment is open to many objections, which are of even greater force when applied to inadvertent negligence than in crimes requiring *mens rea*. Some people are born reckless, clumsy, thoughtless, inattentive, irresponsible, with a bad memory and a slow "reaction time." With the best will in the world, we all of us at some times in our lives make negligent mistakes. It is hard to see how justice (as distinct from some utilitarian reason) requires mistakes to be punished.

[T]he deterrent theory, which is normally accepted as a justification for criminal punishment, finds itself in some difficulty when applied to negligence.

---

11. See Paul H. Robinson & John M. Darley, *The Utility of Desert*, 91 Nw. U. L. Rev. 453 (1997); Paul H. Robinson et al., *The Disutility of Injustice*, 85 N.Y.U. L. Rev. 1940 (2010).

At best the deterrent effect of the legal sanction is a matter of faith rather than of proved scientific fact; but there is no department in which this faith is less firmly grounded than that of negligence. . . . Even if a person admits that he occasionally makes a negligent mistake, how, in the nature of things, can punishment for inadvertence serve to deter? . . .

The argument in favour of punishment is that, just as it is possible for punishment to cause a person to exercise greater control over his acts in view of the known dangers, so it is possible for punishment to bring about greater foresight, by causing the subject to stop and think before committing himself to a course of conduct. . . .

A supporting consideration is that punishment may deter in respect of some subsidiary rule of prudence the breach of which is intentional. Although the harmful result of careless driving is not intended, there is often an element in the careless driving that is intended (e.g., pulling out on a blind corner), and the punishment, coupled with a recollection of the circumstances of the accident, may "condition" the driver not to repeat his mistake, and may even cause him to be more careful in other respects. Conceivably it may also improve the conduct of others who come to know of the mistake that was made. In the same way, although the threat of punishment may not be able to make me remember something that I have already forgotten, it may cause me so to impress a fact on my mind that I do not forget.

This justification for the punishment of inadvertence does not go very far, and the law acts wisely in making such punishment exceptional. Even where punishment is imposed, it best takes the form of a fine, operating as a warning for the future rather than as a substantial punishment for the past. Loss of liberty is not a necessary measure for those who cause harm inadvertently. If the offender is so incompetent as to be a social danger in his present occupation, the remedy is not to incarcerate him but (if milder methods of correction fail) to exclude him from the activity in which he is a danger.

The chief problem concerns negligent driving, and this has been partly solved by turning some jury rules of prudence into rules of law, as by the imposition of speed limits and by the requirement of halting at major roads. The intentional breach of such rules can be punished without enquiry into negligence. In 1930 Parliament took the new step of allowing the negligent driver to be disqualified from driving; and this, regarded not as a punishment but as society's method of removing a source of danger, is certainly the most fitting way of dealing with accident-prone motorists.

Model Penal Code Section 2.02 Commentary
Official Draft and Revised Comments 243-244 (1985)

No one has doubted that purpose, knowledge, and recklessness are properly the basis for criminal liability, but some critics have opposed any penal consequences for negligent behavior. Since the actor is inadvertent by hypothesis, it has been argued that the "threat of punishment for negligence must pass him by, because he does not realize that it is addressed to him." So too, it has been urged that education or corrective treatment, not punishment, is the proper social method for dealing with persons with inadequate awareness, since what is implied is not a moral defect. This analysis, however, oversimplifies the issue. When people have knowledge that conviction and sentence, not to speak of punishment, may follow conduct that inadvertently creates improper risk, they are supplied with an additional motive to take care before acting, to use their faculties and draw on their experience in gauging the potentialities of contemplated conduct. To some extent, at least, this motive may promote awareness and thus be effective as a measure of control. Moreover, moral defect can properly be imputed to instances where the defendant acts out of insensitivity to the interests of other people, and not merely out of an intellectual failure to grasp them. In any event legislators act on these assumptions in a host of situations, and it would be dogmatic to assert that they are wholly wrong. Accordingly, negligence, as here defined, should not be wholly rejected as a ground of culpability that they may suffice for purposes of penal law, though it should properly not generally be deemed sufficient in the definition of specific crimes and it should often be differentiated from conduct involving higher culpability for the purposes of sentence. . . .

Most recent legislative revisions and proposals have adopted definitions of negligence similar to that of the Model Code. . . .

Samuel H. Pillsbury, Crimes of Indifference
49 Rutgers Law Review 105, 106, 150-151 (1996)

[T]he modern trend to require that the defendant have actual awareness of fatal risks for either or both of these offenses is a mistake, based on a misconception of responsible choice. . . .

We may blame persons for failing to perceive risks to others when we can trace their lack of awareness to bad perception priorities. In such a case, we judge the person guilty of a bad choice. In setting his or her perception priorities, the individual assigned too low a priority to the value of other human beings. The key to culpability for failure to perceive is why the person failed to perceive. Assume two cases in which a driver runs a red light and fatally injures a pedestrian in the cross-walk. One case involves a father rushing his severely injured child to the hospital. Another involves a teenager showing off for his friends. Assume that in both cases the driver saw neither the light nor the pedestrian. Culpability should depend on the drivers' reasons for perceptive failure, not on the failure itself. The father's lack of perception may be attributed to his overriding and morally worthy desire to help his child. The teenager's failure to perceive may be attributed to morally blameworthy perception priorities. The teenager placed a higher value on winning the admiration of friends than on attending to the risks of fast driving. The teenager's conduct demonstrates an attitude of indifference toward others, a morally culpable state to which society should forcefully respond by conviction and punishment. Meanwhile, the father's conduct demonstrates a tragic conflict between valuing his child and valuing others.

Individuals deserve punishment for all acts displaying serious disregard for the moral worth of other human beings. Such acts involve many different levels of awareness. . . . In all cases we should judge the actor's choices: what she has chosen to care about and perceive, and what she has chosen not to care about and perceive. These choices give the individual's conduct a distinct moral meaning.

Laurie L. Levenson, Good Faith Defenses: Reshaping Strict Liability Crimes

78 Cornell Law Review 401, 419-427 (1993)

Justifications for Strict Liability Crimes

1. Public Welfare Offenses

The strict liability doctrine often applies to so-called "public welfare" offenses or regulatory crimes promulgated to address the dangers brought about by the advent of the industrial revolution. Public welfare offenses include the sale of impure or adulterated foods or drugs, driving faster than the speed limit, the sale of intoxicating liquor to minors, and improper handling of dangerous chemicals or nuclear wastes. Defendants violate these laws regardless of their intent or absence of negligent conduct.

There are several reasons the strict liability doctrine is used to redress invasions of the public welfare. First, the doctrine is employed for these offenses because it shifts the risks of dangerous activity to those best able to prevent a mishap. For example, a pharmaceutical manufacturer is liable if that product becomes contaminated for any reason. The risk of mishap is shifted to the manufacturer, who can be assured of avoiding liability only by not engaging in the particular high risk activity.

Yet, this reason alone cannot justify the doctrine. The strict liability doctrine is not the only possible method for shifting risk onto the manufacturer. A criminal negligence standard also shifts the risk to the party engaging in the activity and punishes those who act carelessly. Under a negligence standard, a defendant is liable for failure to act as a reasonable person would have under the circumstances, even if he did not intend or appreciate the risks of his activities. Under a negligence standard, if the defendant acts reasonably and harm results, no punishment follows. Nonetheless, the burden to learn and operate within society's standards rests with the defendant.

The strict liability doctrine operates in a fundamentally different way. While both negligence and strict liability shift the burden of risk avoidance to the defendant, only under strict liability are individuals imprisoned even if they take all possible precaution to act reasonably. The sole question for the trier of fact is whether the defendant committed the proscribed act. The jury may not decide whether the defendant could have done anything else to prevent the unlawful act.

Thus, there must be additional reasons for selecting the strict liability doctrine over the negligence standard. Among these reasons is the need by the legislature to assure that juries will treat like cases alike when judging conduct involving public welfare. Juries may be ill-suited to decide what is reasonable in complex high risk activities. For example, in order for juries to decide what is reasonable conduct when dealing with nuclear waste, they would have to be educated on the nuclear industry, the risks posed by it, and the safeguards that might be taken. Legislatures prefer to make this assessment themselves, rather than relying on the competence of juries. Moreover, jurors may be swayed by sympathies or prejudices of a particular case. By dictating what is *per se* unreasonable, an individual jury cannot reassess the standard of reasonableness. Accordingly, a second reason for using the strict liability doctrine is that it assures uniform treatment of particular, high risk conduct.

A third justification often offered for the strict liability doctrine is that it eases the burden on the prosecution to prove intent in difficult cases. Strict liability is based largely on the assumption that an accident occurs because the defendant did not take care to prevent it. No showing of intent or negligence is required, because the fact that a prohibited act occurred demonstrates the defendant's negligence. As with most irrefutable presumptions, the legislature believes individual inquiries are unnecessary because the overwhelming majority of cases will show that the defendant acted at least negligently. Seen in this light, strict liability is a procedural shortcut to punish those who would be culpable under traditional theories of criminal law.

Fourth, even if the presumption is incorrect in a particular case, legislatures determine that this risk is outweighed by the need for additional protection of society and expeditious prosecution of certain cases. For example, driving in excess of a posted speed limit is typically a strict liability crime. With nearly 398,000 annual traffic cases in one state alone, processing these cases as quickly as possible is important. The most efficient way to process such cases is to presume defendants drive carelessly when exceeding speed limits. The presumption is generally accurate and, even when it is not, the need for public safety and the relatively minor punishment minimizes any concern about injustice.

Finally, the strict liability doctrine is attractive as a powerful public statement of legislative intolerance for certain behavior. By labeling an offense as strict liability, the legislature can claim to provide the utmost protection from certain public harms. By affording no leniency for defendants causing harm, the legislature affirms society's interest in being protected from certain conduct. In this sense, strict liability expresses emphatically that such conduct will not be tolerated regardless of the actor's intent.

2. Morality Offenses

Similar justifications have been offered for the application of the strict liability doctrine to "morality crimes," offenses involving transgressions of society's sexual and social norms. Examples of these crimes are statutory rape, adultery, and bigamy.

Consider the classic case of *Regina v. Prince*. In *Prince*, the defendant was convicted for eloping with a minor without her father's permission. Although the jury accepted the defendant's claim that he did not know the girl was underage, the court denied a defense, finding "[t]he act forbidden is wrong in itself, . . . not . . . illegal, but wrong."

The court in *Prince* did not require that defendant know the age of the girl with whom he eloped. Eloping with any young woman without her father's permission was considered morally wrong. Because of this, the court felt it appropriate to impose punishment regardless of defendant's knowledge of the girl's age. The defendant bore the risk that his borderline conduct would violate a provision of the law.

As with the public welfare offenses, the less comfortable society is with certain types of behavior, the more likely the legislature will turn to the strict liability doctrine to transfer the risks of the behavior to the defendant. These risks include the possibility of physical or moral harm, and the possibility that a culpable defendant would escape punishment by feigning ignorance or mistake.

To assure that all juries assess the risks of a particular activity uniformly, the legislature designates an offense as a strict liability crime. By not allowing evidence as to why the defendant transgressed, the legislature can avoid the whims of any particular jury. Rather than having an individual jury decide what conduct is reasonable, the legislature decides for all strict liability cases. In this manner, firm social and moral lines are clearly drawn.

Application of the strict liability doctrine to morality offenses offers an additional justification for the doctrine. As already discussed, in strict liability offenses it is presumed that the defendant took an unjustifiable risk in his conduct and was therefore at least negligent. When the defendant's conduct is already morally questionable—"borderline" conduct—concern for punishing an innocent person decreases. Society does not approve of the defendant's conduct, although the limits of the law may seem to permit it. If the defendant crosses those limits, intentionally or unintentionally, society will seek to punish the defendant's behavior. The strict liability doctrine thereby serves an important function of setting firm limits on conduct that society is loath to tolerate. The interests in efficient punishment and maximum deterrence of certain conduct is seen as outweighing the risk that a nonculpable person will be punished.

Thus, for both public welfare and morality offenses, relieving the prosecution of the burden of proving a culpable mens rea is justified by the presumption that the defendant engaging in marginal and/or highly risky conduct deserves some punishment. Moreover, even if that presumption is incorrect in a given case, society receives valuable protection from such conduct.

3. Opposition to the Strict Liability Doctrine

Opponents of the strict liability doctrine argue that its justifications are inconsistent with both utilitarian and retributivist theories of punishment. Under utilitarian theory, punishment is justified if it deters unlawful behavior. If punishing those who commit prohibited acts will deter others from acting similarly, punishment is justified. Under the retributivist approach, an individual should be punished for choosing to violate the law. Punishment reflects respect for an individual's autonomy to choose to do "wrong." If an individual chooses to transgress the boundaries established to protect society, he "deserves" punishment.

The strict liability doctrine, especially when applied to defendants misled into committing an unlawful act, is not supported by either theory of punishment. Under retributivist theory, criminal law should hold individuals responsible for only those acts for which they are blameworthy. An individual is blameworthy, not because of accidental conduct, but because of a conscious and knowing breach of the law. At a minimum, the defendant must have acted below the standard of care that a reasonable person would have exercised under the same conditions. A strict liability defendant punished for an act that he has been misled into committing has not consciously decided to violate society's norms. Accordingly, under classic retributivist theory, this defendant does not "deserve" to be punished.

Additionally, the strict liability doctrine conflicts with utilitarian theories of punishment. Strict liability laws are inefficient because they tend to over deter individuals' behavior. If the strict liability defendant can be punished for *any* conduct crossing a certain proscribed line, the defendant will be inclined to abstain from *all* activities that could conceivably result in illegal behavior. In some situations, certain individuals might abstain from entering a high risk industry. [I]ndividuals may be deterred from engaging in constitutionally protected activity. Thus, strict liability may deter individuals from engaging in activities that are socially necessary or desirable, constitutionally protected, or both. In this manner, strict liability over deters conduct.

More fundamentally, the strict liability doctrine violates utilitarian theories of criminal punishment because an individual who has no basis for believing he is engaging in unlawful conduct will not be deterred from engaging in that behavior. If an individual has no indication that he is doing anything wrong until the harmful act is completed, then he has no reason to alter his conduct.

Given the conflicts with both the retributivist and utilitarian theories of punishment, it is understandable why opponents of strict liability do not want to use the doctrine against defendants who have made an affirmative effort to comply with the law but have been misled into committing a violation. Classic Anglo-American legal philosophy is that "[I]t is better that ten guilty persons escape than one innocent suffer." Strict liability theory operates from the opposite perspective. Under the strict liability doctrine, an occasional innocent may be punished to assure the safety of the majority. Thus, the prosecution of good faith defendants under strict liability laws appears to conflict with the most fundamental principles of just punishment.

✳ DISCUSSION MATERIALS

Issue: Should a Person's Negligence (and Recklessness) Be Judged Against an Objective or an Individualized Standard?

In the readings below, H.L.A. Hart examines the role of a partially individualized standard in negligence and of absolute liability. The Model Penal Code Commentary excerpt recognizes the existence of both standards in assessing liability, approving of the partially individualized standard but only in a somewhat confined manner that remains largely at the court's discretion. George Fletcher argues for the use of the partially individualized standard in a broader way.

H. L. A. Hart, Punishment and Responsibility
154-155 (1984)

When negligence is made criminally punishable, this . . . leaves open the question: whether, before we punish, both or only the first of the following two questions must be answered affirmatively:

(i) Did the accused fail to take those precautions which any reasonable man with normal capacities would in the circumstances have taken?

(ii) Could the accused, given his mental and physical capacities, have taken those precautions?

One use of the dangerous expressions "objective" and "subjective" is to make the distinction between these two questions: given the ambiguities of those expressions, this distinction would have been more aptly expressed by the expressions "invariant" standard of care, and "individualized conditions of liability." It may well be that, even if the "standard of care" is pitched very low so that individuals are liable only if they fail to take very elementary precautions against harm, there will still be some unfortunate individuals who, through lack of intelligence, powers of concentration or memory, or through clumsiness, could not attain even this low standard. If our conditions of liability are invariant and not flexible, i.e., if they are not adjusted to the capacities of the accused, then some individuals will be held liable for negligence though they could not have helped their failure to comply with the standard. In such cases, indeed, criminal responsibility will be made independent of any "subjective element," since the accused could not have conformed to the required standard. But this result is nothing to do with negligence being taken as a basis for criminal liability. . . . "Absolute liability" results, not from the admission of the principle that one who has been grossly negligent is criminally responsible for the consequent harm even if "he had no idea in his mind of harm to anyone," but from the refusal in the application of this principle to consider the capacities of an individual who has fallen below the standard of care.

Model Penal Code Section 2.02 Commentary
Official Draft and Revised Comments 240-242 (1985)

Negligence. The fourth kind of culpability is negligence. It is distinguished from purposeful, knowing or reckless action in that it does not involve a state of awareness. A person acts negligently under this subsection when he inadvertently creates a substantial and unjustifiable risk of which he ought to be aware. He is liable if given the nature and degree of the risk, his failure to perceive it is, considering the nature and purpose of the actor's conduct and the circumstances known to him, a gross deviation from the care that would be exercised by a reasonable person in his situation. As in the case of recklessness, both the substantiality of the risk and the elements of justification in the situation form the relevant standards of judgment. And again it is quite impossible to avoid tautological articulation of the final question. The tribunal must evaluate the actor's failure of perception and determine whether, under all the circumstances, it was serious enough to be condemned. The jury must find fault, and must find that it was substantial and unjustified; that is the heart of what can be said in legislative terms.

As with recklessness, the jury is asked to perform two distinct functions. First, it is to examine the risk and the factors that are relevant to its substantiality and justifiability. In the case of negligence, these questions are asked not in terms of what the actor's perceptions actually were, but in terms of an objective view of the situation as it actually existed. Second, the jury is to make the culpability judgment, this time in terms of whether the failure of the defendant to perceive the risk justifies condemnation. Considering the nature and purpose of his conduct and the circumstances known to him, the question is whether the defendant's failure to perceive a risk involves a gross deviation from the standard of care that a reasonable person would observe in the actor's situation.

Formulation of the standard in these terms is believed to be a substantial improvement over the traditional approach to defining negligence for purposes of criminal liability. . . .

A further point in the Code's concept of negligence merits attention. The standard for ultimate judgment invites consideration of the "care that a reasonable person would observe in the actor's situation." There is an inevitable ambiguity in "situation." If the actor were blind or if he had just suffered a blow or experienced a heart attack, these would certainly be facts to be considered in a judgment involving criminal liability, as they would be under traditional law. But the heredity, intelligence or temperament of the actor would not be held material in judging negligence, and could not be without depriving the criterion of all its objectivity. The Code is not intended to displace discriminations of this kind, but rather to leave the issue to the courts. . . .

George P. Fletcher, The Theory of Criminal Negligence: A Comparative Analysis

119 University of Pennsylvania Law Review 401, 426-427, 429-430, 433-434 (1971)

Is Negligence Invariably Measured Against an Objective Standard?

In the preceding section, we explored one sense in which negligence is conceptually objective or external and argued that this kind of externality—the absence of a subjective mental state—does not denigrate negligence as a basis for criminal liability. Despite this kind of externality or objectivity, there are good reasons to regard negligence as culpable, to regard it therefore as a form of *mens rea*, and to subject negligent conduct to criminal sanctions. A totally different argument, however, asserts that negligence is suspect because it is objective, not subjective. This argument holds that a subjective standard of negligence is conceptually untenable because it would take each individual as the measure of the propriety of his own conduct, thus rendering evaluation impossible by merging the standard of evaluation with the conduct to be evaluated.

This point is nicely captured in Tindal's famous admonition to avoid a standard of negligence that would be "as variable as the length of the foot of each individual." And again by Holmes: The standards of the law are standards of general application. The law takes no account of the infinite varieties of temperament, intellect, and education which make the internal character of a given act so different in different men.

The argument is undoubtedly sound—as far as it goes. It is true that legal rules, like all other rules, must apply to a range of cases. It follows that if liability for negligence is to be based on legal rules, the standard of liability must transcend individual differences; in this sense, the standard of liability is general, abstract, and objective. With this much we can agree.

It is the next step that provokes disagreement. On the basis of the invariable objectivity of the standard of negligence, common law analysts are inclined to view negligence as significantly different from intentional conduct. Their reasoning would run like this: A man's intentions are gauged by an individualized, subjective standard; it is his intention we try to establish, not that of an average man. But this is not the case with negligence where the issue is the behavior of an average member of the community. Therefore, the standard of negligence is less sensitive to individual culpability than the standard of intentional conduct; and accordingly, it should be used sparingly, if at all, as a ground for liability.

Although this line of reasoning may seem plausible, it derives from the false premise that standards of liability must be either subjective or objective, but not both. . . .

[T]he standard for negligence [is,] at once, objective and subjective. The objective issue is whether the risk is justified under the circumstances; the subjective issue is whether the actor's taking an unjustified risk is excusable on the ground of duress, insanity, or some other condition rendering his conduct involuntary and thus blameless. German theorists have recently come to conceptualize negligence as consisting of dimensions both of legality and culpability. There is also considerable evidence that common law analysts have long flirted with the same basic insight about the nature of negligence. For example, Holmes stresses that negligence is an objective standard; yet he concedes that conditions like blindness, infancy, and insanity should constitute excuses from liability. It seems contradictory for Holmes to admit the relevance of individualized excuses in the same passage in which he postulates that the "standards of the law are standards of general application . . . [taking] no account of the infinite varieties of temperament, intellect, and education. . . . " . . . In emphasizing the generality of standards, he acknowledged the dimension of legality in the structure of negligence. This interpretation establishes the consistency of Holmes' views by providing an account of how the standards of negligence can, at once, be of general application and yet accommodate excuses based on individual incapacities.

The Model Penal Code also displays an appreciation for the distinction between the dimensions of legality and culpability in the structure of negligence. Its definition of negligence specifies first that the risk in question be "substantial and unjustifiable." Secondly, it provides that "the actor's failure to perceive [the risk] . . . involves a gross deviation from the standard of care that a reasonable person would observe in the actor's situation." The first prong of the definition focuses on the justification and the legality of the risk; the second, on the culpability of the actor's ignorance of the risk. This definition invites criticism for its obvious circularity: it seeks to define negligence as a "kind of culpability," yet the key factor in the definition is whether the actor was culpable in failing to perceive particular risk. This duplicative reliance on the concept of culpability derives from the Code's confused use of the concept to refer sometimes to mental states, as in the definition of "purposely," —and sometimes to the blameworthiness of inadvertence, as in the definition of negligence. Thus negligence emerges as a "kind of culpability" that requires a special finding of culpability. . . .

Culpability and Difference Among Individuals

Although we have stressed the symmetry of liability for negligent and intentional criminality, we have yet to explain the frequent irrelevance of individual differences of "temperament, intellect, and education" in assessing liability for negligence. This characteristic of negligence inspired much of Holmes' analysis in *The Common Law*. It is another line of defense for those who insist that negligent criminality is significantly different from intentional criminality.

Individual differences are ignored in determining the legality of risks; the point of distinguishing between permissible and impermissible risks is to formulate a rule applicable to all men in the same situation. But many individual differences are also ignored in specifying the excuses bearing on culpability. Insanity is an excuse, but not awkwardness. If it is impossible for an actor to appreciate the illegality of the risk that he is running, he ought to be excused; if it is merely difficult for him to appreciate what others readily understand, his ignorance is not excusable. That differences among men are not always manifested in the criteria of excuses requires explanation.

It is important to note first that the practice of disregarding individual differences also prevails in assessing liability for intentional offenses. Duress is a defense to theft, but greediness is not. An irascible man, one easily provoked into fights, has a more difficult time avoiding liability for battery and homicide than does a man of even temperament. Legal systems inevitably impose greater burdens of compliance on some than on others. Norms of legal conduct cut across a wide range of human inclinations and capacities. Some men have an easier time than others in complying with prohibitions against negligent and intentional conduct; those for whom compliance is relatively easy are, to that degree, more culpable than others transgressing the law. Although this excess of culpability may be relevant in sentencing, it has no bearing on the issue of liability.

The point of excusing conditions is not to gauge degrees of culpability, but to determine when the actor's culpability falls below the threshold required for a fair conviction. Some men may be more culpable than is necessary for conviction; others may barely pass the required threshold. So long as the minimum threshold of culpability requires a finding that the defendant has a fair chance to avoid liability, it is immaterial whether some violators are more culpable than he. The goal of justly distributing sanctions is not one of finding the most culpable offenders, but one of assessing whether each alleged violator is sufficiently culpable to forfeit his freedom from sanctions.

❉ ADVANCED MATERIALS

Notes on Conduct, Circumstance, and Result Elements

Three categories of offense elements
Failure to define categories
Terms that combine categories
Need for category definitions
Proposed definitions
Illustration: "Obstructing a highway"

Three categories of offense elements The Model Penal Code devised a useful system to enable precise definition of offenses. Section 1.13(9), defining "elements of an offense," distinguishes between (1) conduct, (2) attendant circumstances, and (3) a result of conduct. These three categories form the objective building blocks for offense definitions under the MPC (and nearly all of the state codes based on it). Each offense definition typically has at least one *conduct* element, which satisfies the requirement of an act (which we discuss in § 3.3). Most offense definitions include one or more *circumstance* elements as well, defining the precise nature of the prohibited conduct (for example, having intercourse with a person *under 14 years old*) or the precise nature of a prohibited result (for example, causing the death of *another human being*). A minority of offenses contain a *result* element. For example, homicide offenses, personal injury offenses, and property destruction offenses require a resulting physical harm. Also, other offenses—such as endangerment, indecent exposure, and falsification—may require a resulting *risk* of harm or an intangible harm, such as danger, alarm, or a false impression.

Failure to define categories   Some of the potential benefit of this categorization of objective elements is lost by the common failure of codes, including the Model Penal Code, to define those categories. When does an element constitute a conduct element, as opposed to a circumstance element or a result element? In the illustrations above, for example, one might argue that "under 14 years old" is not a distinct circumstance element but rather is part of the single conduct element of "having intercourse with a person under 14 years old." Similarly, "another human being" might be interpreted to be part of the result element of "causing the death of another human being," rather than as an independent circumstance element. Without definitions of the categories, such interpretive questions cannot be resolved.

Terms that combine categories   Adding to the confusion, offense definitions commonly use terms that combine what might be different categories of elements. Some active verbs (like *kill, obstruct, destroy, falsify, mutilate,* and *desecrate*) simultaneously capture both conduct and a result of that conduct. For example, "to kill" means to engage in conduct that causes the result of another's death. Other complex verbs (like *compel* and *agree*) define both conduct and some of the attendant circumstances of that conduct. For example, the concept of "compelling" another does not describe some mere physical action, but is comprehensible only in terms of context: One can "compel" another only in a situation in which the other is not consenting, a circumstance that exists independently of one's own conduct.

Need for category definitions   The inability authoritatively to distinguish conduct, circumstance, and result elements has practical significance because the categorizations in turn form the basis of several important General Part code provisions. The Model Penal Code's widely followed culpability provisions, for example, define the central culpability terms differently for each kind of objective element. The definitions are asymmetrical. For example, "purpose" as to a *result* or *conduct* exists only if an actor has the element in question as his "conscious object" or goal. This contrasts with the lesser culpability level of knowledge, which involves awareness of the element but not the affirmative desire for it to exist. Yet for a *circumstance,* purpose requires only that one is "aware" of the circumstance—the same requirement set out for the lesser culpability of being "knowing" as to a circumstance. In other words, if an element is classed as a circumstance, a requirement of purpose as to the element requires no more proof than a requirement of knowledge. Similarly, special causation rules apply to elements classified as results, but not to conduct or circumstance elements. Thus, if "obstructs" is interpreted to be a pure conduct element, for example, the state need only prove the conduct. It need not also satisfy the special requirements of causation, such as proof that the obstruction would not have occurred but for the actor's conduct. But if "obstructs" is viewed as embodying both a conduct element and a result element, then the state must prove that the actor's conduct was responsible for bringing about a resulting obstruction.

Proposed definitions The following proposed definitions seem consistent with the spirit and intention of the Model Penal Code scheme: Define "conduct" elements narrowly to refer to the actual physical acts of the actor. Define all characteristics of the conduct to be separate "circumstance" elements; similarly, all results caused by the conduct should be defined as separate "result" elements. Define "result" elements to be any *change* in the surrounding circumstances, brought about by the offender's conduct, that the offense requires to occur. As with conduct, define the characteristics of a result to be separate "circumstance" elements.

Illustration: "Obstructing a highway" Thus, an offense of "obstructing a public highway" would essentially require proof that the actor "engaged in conduct that caused the obstruction of a public highway." "Obstruction" would be a result element; the state would have to prove that the actor's conduct caused the obstruction, which is a change in circumstance required under the offense (prior to the offense conduct the highway was not obstructed, afterward it was). On the other hand, the requirement of a "public highway" would be a circumstance element, as it would involve the context in which the offense occurred rather than a change the actor brought about—the public highway exists both before and after the offense. The "conduct" element here, as in many offenses, requires simply some act by the actor. No particular act is required, other than one that causes the required result (obstruction) in the required context (a public highway). Under this definitional scheme, the conduct element commonly will have little significance beyond satisfying the act requirement. Generally, courts have not addressed the problem of distinguishing conduct, circumstance, and result elements.

Hypothetical: Raimer Sets a Record

Raimer works in the office of the university registrar to help pay his tuition. Anna, a student, asks for a copy of her official file. The photocopying machine in the office is not working at the moment, so Anna asks if she can take the file to copy it on another machine. Because Raimer is new, he is unsure of the office policy. He thinks it is probably all right and that he probably has the authority to let her do it. When Bob, another student who works in the office, returns from his coffee break and learns that Raimer has allowed Anna to take her file, he berates Raimer for what he says is Raimer's irresponsibility and his insensitivity to the importance of proper handling of the files. This is a serious matter, Bob explains, and shows Raimer a copy of the following criminal statute:

> Tampering with Records. A person commits a misdemeanor if, knowing that he has no privilege to do so, he falsifies, destroys, removes or conceals any writing or record, with purpose to deceive or injure anyone or to conceal any wrongdoing.[12]

---

12. Model Penal Code § 224.4.

Bob is usually pleasant, so Raimer is taken aback by Bob's sternness and haughty tone. To lighten the mood, Raimer looks up Bob's official grade file and changes the As in criminal law and advanced criminal law classes to Fs. He shows Bob the new criminal law grade, and Bob launches into another lecture, including a description of how hard he worked to get Bs in his two criminal law courses. He insists that Raimer change his grade in criminal law back, which Raimer does. Raimer decides not to show Bob the second change he made—the one to the grade in advanced criminal law. After Bob leaves the room, Raimer changes that grade back as well. Raimer assumes that Bob knows what grades he got, especially given what an issue it apparently is with him. He concludes that the original As probably were an error and changes the joke F grades back to Bs.

A few moments later, Anna returns, very upset. She was on her way to photocopy her official file when a sudden gust of wind blew it out of her hand. She chased down as many sheets as she could but was only able to catch two and a half letters of recommendation. Raimer is concerned about losing his job. He asks Anna what her grades are but she is able to remember only some of them. He nonetheless prepares a new file that will look like the old one, making up the grades that Anna cannot remember. Later that afternoon, Bob, who has taken to reviewing all of Raimer's work, notices the half letter of recommendation in Anna's file. Further investigation by the registrar, including questioning of Anna, reveals the full story of Anna's file and Bob's criminal law grades. (In fact, Bob had gotten an A in criminal law and advanced criminal law; Raimer simply misunderstood Bob.) Raimer is dismissed from his job and charged with four counts of violating the Tampering with Records statute: for causing Anna's file to be removed without authority; for altering Bob's criminal law grades as a joke; for changing Bob's criminal law grades "back" to Bs; and for fabricating a file for Anna. Is he liable?

Notes on Determining Offense Culpability Requirements

Culpability Defined in Terms of Differing Objective Elements
    Failure to define recklessness and negligence with respect to conduct
    Interpretations of culpability as to "conduct"
        Narrow interpretation of "conduct"
        Advantages of narrow definition of "conduct"
    Asymmetry in definition of "purpose"
Determining Offense Culpability Requirements
    Assuming strict liability from absence of culpability requirement
    Culpability requirements supplied by general provision
    "Reading in" recklessness
    Providing a culpability other than recklessness
    Illustration: Tampering with records
Conflict and Inconsistency in the Modern Culpability Scheme
    Distinguishing conduct, circumstance, and result elements
    Objective element categories and culpability requirements
    Ambiguities from failure to define categories
        Implication of ambiguities
    Combining conduct and result or conduct and circumstance
        Implication of combined elements
Proposed Revisions to the Scheme
    Define conduct narrowly

CULPABILITY DEFINED IN TERMS OF DIFFERING OBJECTIVE ELEMENTS

The description of culpability levels in Section 4 uses culpability as to causing a result to illustrate the differences between levels. In fact, Model Penal Code section 2.02(2) defines each of the four kinds of culpability in relation to each of the three kinds of objective elements: conduct, circumstance, and result. The following chart gives the section 2.02(2) definition for each variation provided by section 2.02(2). A person acts [culpability level] with respect to [kind of objective element] when:

	Result	Circumstance	Conduct
Purposely	"it is his conscious object . . . to cause such a result"	"he is a aware of such circumstances or hopes that they exist"	"it is his conscious object to engage in conduct of that nature"
Knowingly	"he is aware that it is practically certain that his conduct will cause such a result"	"he is aware [of a high probability[13]] that such circumstances exist"	"he is aware his conduct is of that nature"
Recklessly	"he consciously disregards a substantial and unjustifiable risk that the material element . . . will result from his conduct"	"he consciously disregards a substantial and unjustifiable risk that the material element exists"	—
Negligently	"he should be aware of a substantial and unjustifiable risk that the material element . . . will result from his conduct"	"he should be aware of a substantial and unjustifiable risk that the material element exists"	—

Failure to define recklessness and negligence with respect to conduct The Code's precision does much to bring clarity to what previously had been a troubled area, but some details in the definitional scheme leave several ambiguities. For example, note that the Code does not expressly define "recklessness"

---

13. See Model Penal Code § 2.02(7).

and "negligence" with respect to a conduct element. One explanation for this failure is that the drafters determined that, as a practical matter, neither reckless-ness nor negligence as to conduct is likely to arise. That is, it is unlikely that a person would not at least *know* the nature of conduct she is performing. The Model Penal Code Commentary notes that "[w]ith respect to each of [the] three types of elements, the draft attempts to define each of the kinds of culpability *that may arise.*"[14] Other sections of the Commentary, however, might be inter-preted to suggest that the drafters did contemplate the possibility of recklessness or negligence as to conduct. Indeed, certain Code offenses appear specifically to proscribe reckless conduct. For example, one who "recklessly tampers with tan-gible property of another so as to endanger person or property" commits criminal mischief.[15] Similarly, one who "purposely or recklessly kills or injures any animal" is guilty of cruelty to animals.[16]

Interpretations of culpability as to "conduct" One might resolve this ambiguity in the Code's definitional scheme by reasoning that, because some culpability is required as to each element of an offense, and "recklessness" and "negligence" as to conduct are not defined, then "knowledge"—which is the minimum culpability that is defined with respect to conduct—should be required. This argument can be buttressed by referring to section 2.02(5), which states that "[w]hen recklessness suffices to establish an element, such element also is established if a person acts purposely or *knowingly.*" Some jurisdictions specifi-cally provide that while "reckless" is to be read in when an offense is silent as to the culpability required for a circumstance or result element (that is, "reckless" is implied by the absence of a specific culpability), "knowing" is read in for a conduct element.[17] Another approach may be for a court to define "recklessness" and "negligence" with respect to conduct by extrapolating from the definition of those terms that exist with regard to circumstance and result elements.

Narrow interpretation of "conduct" This ambiguity as to the definitions of "reckless" and "negligent" as to conduct may be insignificant if "conduct" ele-ments are defined narrowly to include only literally the *conduct* (muscular move-ment) of the actor. Under this approach, culpability as to an actor's "conduct" is relevant in the rare case that he does not know that he is engaging in a muscular movement, and these instances are likely to be exempt from liability under the involuntary-act defense. Culpability as to the *nature* of one's conduct, in the sense of culpability as to its circumstances and its results, would be represented by the culpability required as to the circumstance and result elements of the offense. Thus, the conduct of "obstructing a public roadway" would be understood to be conduct, whatever the particular actions might be, that caused the obstruction of (a result) a public roadway (a circumstance). The important culpability that might be in dispute at trial, then, is the actor's culpability as to causing the *result* of obstructing and his culpability as to the *circumstance* of it being a public road-way. Thus an actor's culpability as to his conduct itself, the actions he performed

14. Model Penal Code § 2.02 comment 2 at 124 (Tent. Draft No. 4, 1955) (emphasis added).
15. Model Penal Code § 220.3(1)(b) (1980).
16. Model Penal Code § 250.11.
17. See e.g., S.1437, 95th Cong., 2d Sess. §§ 302(c), 303(b)(1) (1978) (recklessness as to conduct undefined; minimum state of mind that must be proved with respect to conduct is knowledge).

to cause the obstruction, are rarely an issue (and where they are—where, for example, he blocks the roadway because he faints in his tractor trailer—a general excuse defense arising from his involuntariness will govern the matter, not the offense culpability requirements).

Advantages of narrow definition of "conduct" This narrow interpretation of what constitutes a "conduct" element not only gives a clear definition, without need for judicial extrapolation, but also has the important advantage of maximizing the legislature's ability to provide a different culpability level for different elements of a single offense. To treat "conduct" as including the circumstances and results of one's conduct would be to treat the conduct (narrow sense) and the circumstances and results of the conduct as a single element. This would require that a single culpability level must apply to all. To strip the circumstances and results of conduct from the "conduct" element, on the other hand, and treat them as independent circumstance and result elements, is to create several elements and thereby allow different culpability as to different elements.

Asymmetry in definition of "purpose" Another asymmetry revealed by the chart above is found in the definition of "purposely" with respect to a circumstance element. Recall that the hallmark of purposeful culpability in the context of result elements is the actor's *conscious object* to cause that result; "knowing" as to a result requires only that the actor be aware that his conduct will cause the result, not that he desires or hopes that it will. "Purposely" as to a conduct element has an analogous meaning: It must be the actor's conscious object to engage in conduct of that nature. It is not enough that he is aware that his conduct is of that nature ("knowing" as to conduct). In the context of circumstance elements, however, "purposely" requires only that the actor "[be] *aware* of such circumstances or hope(s) that they exist." In other words, "purpose" as to a circumstance can be shown by proving no more than is required to show "knowing" as to a circumstance. The distinction between "purposely" and "knowingly" is thereby eliminated for circumstance elements. The Model Penal Code Commentary gives no explanation and, indeed, does not acknowledge the variation. One can only speculate that the drafters thought the purposeful-knowing distinction to be irrelevant in the context of culpability as to circumstances, as opposed to the context of result and conduct elements in which it is relevant.[18]

DETERMINING OFFENSE CULPABILITY REQUIREMENTS

As described above, the Model Penal Code features significant innovations with regard to culpability requirements. This subsection describes how these innovations are applied in practice. The ultimate goal of the Code is to provide for each offense a precise list of the culpability elements that must be proven to establish liability. Typically, some of the culpability requirements for an offense are stated on the face of the offense definition. Other requirements must be determined by referring to other provisions in the Code.

---

18. The Code Commentary states as follows:

Knowledge that the requisite external circumstances exist is a common element of [purpose and knowledge]. But action is not purposive with respect to the nature or result of the actor's conduct unless it was his conscious object to perform an action of that nature or to cause such a result.

Model Penal Code § 2.02 comment 2 at 233 (1985).

Assuming strict liability from absence of culpability requirement The absence of a specified culpability requirement in an offense definition does *not* mean that culpability is not required. Modern codes permit strict liability in very limited instances—generally only for the least serious offenses, such as traffic violations. Model Penal Code sections 2.02(1) and 2.05, and similar provisions in state codes, are meant to require culpability for all elements of all offenses other than offenses classified as mere "violations." In some jurisdictions, when the drafters intend that culpability is not to be required, a phrase such as "in fact" is inserted at the appropriate place in the offense definition to signal the absence of a culpability requirement.

Culpability requirements supplied by general provision Where the offense definition does not explicitly provide a culpability requirement, Model Penal Code section 2.02(3) supplies one. Section 2.02(3) reads in a requirement of "recklessness" with respect to all circumstance and result elements and, because the Code fails to define "recklessness" as to conduct, is frequently interpreted to read in "knowing" with respect to all conduct elements. Consider, for example, the Model Penal Code's indecent exposure offense:

> A person commits a misdemeanor if, for the purpose of arousing or gratifying sexual desire, he exposes his genitals under circumstances in which he knows his conduct is likely to cause affront or alarm.[19]

An application of section 2.02(3), reading in culpability requirements, results in the following complete offense definition:

> A person commits a misdemeanor if, for the *purpose* of arousing or gratifying sexual desire, he [*knowingly* engages in conduct by which he *recklessly* causes the exposure of what he is aware of is a substantial risk (i.e., he is *reckless* as to the exposed parts being)] his genitals under circumstances in which he *knows* his conduct is likely to cause affront or alarm.

"Reading in" recklessness Obviously, such an explicit statement generates a grammatically awkward definition. A general provision that reads in a fixed culpability can provide the necessary guidance while leaving offense definitions readable. Such a general read-in-reckless provision also is useful because recklessness generally is the minimum culpability required for criminal liability. Reading in "recklessness" when no culpability is stated articulates this norm. Special circumstances may lead Code drafters to use a higher or a lower level in particular instances, but, absent special reasons, recklessness will be the minimum culpability required. Thus, a general provision such as Model Penal Code section 2.02(3) at once provides a comprehensive statement of all culpability requirements, a readable offense definition, and a standard minimum culpability of recklessness.

Providing a culpability other than recklessness Legislatures are free to deviate from the norm of recklessness in either of two ways. First, the legislature can explicitly provide a culpability requirement other than recklessness for a specific element of an offense definition. This is what the legislature has done in requiring "a purpose to arouse" and "know[ledge] [that the conduct] is likely to

---

19. Model Penal Code § 213.5.

affront" in the indecent exposure offense. In addition, a legislature can provide that a stated culpability requirement applies to more than a single element of the offense. This second alternative is provided in the Model Penal Code by section 2.02(4), which codifies a general rule of statutory construction requiring that a stated culpability term that does not distinguish among the elements, be applied to all elements of the offense. Thus, where the offense of causing a suicide is defined to punish one who "purposely causes such suicide by force,"[20] the actor must be purposeful as to using force and as to the result of causing the suicide. Normal rules of statutory construction would undoubtedly generate the same result.

Illustration: Tampering with records Application of these Model Penal Code provisions to the tampering-with-records statute suggests the following. On the face of the offense definition, the elements of "tampering with records" are:

Objective elements	Culpability requirements
(1) no privilege to do so	"Knowing" is expressly required.
(2) falsifies, destroys, removes, or conceals	(What culpability level applies?)
(3) a writing or record	(What culpability level applies?)
(4) — (There is no requirement that anyone actually be deceived.)	"Purpose to deceive" is expressly required.

"Knowing" is expressly provided as to "no privilege." It is unclear from the face of the offense definition what culpability level applies to the objective elements of "falsifies, etc." and "a writing or record." We can assume that some culpability level is required; strict liability is not to be presumed from the absence of a culpability requirement. Also explicitly required is the "purpose to deceive." Note that the corresponding objective element—that someone actually be deceived—is not required. Such a culpability element without a corresponding objective element is one of the things the common law called a "specific intent." To be liable for the offense of "assault with intent to rape," for example, the actor did not actually have to rape; he only had to intend to do so.

With this starting point from the language of the offense definition, and the foregoing explanation of how to determine culpability requirements, consider the following analysis of the hypothetical above:

Under Model Penal Code sections 224.4 and 2.02(3), Raimer's liability for the four counts might be analyzed as follows:

(Count 1) Raimer causes or permits Anna's record to be removed believing that he probably has the authority (privilege) to do so. That he believes he probably has the authority suggests that Raimer is aware of a risk that he does not have the authority. But "knowing" is required as to lack of privilege. Thus Raimer is not liable for this count because he is only reckless as to lacking the privilege.

(Count 2) As a joke on Bob, Raimer changes Bob's grade card to show an F in criminal law and advanced criminal law and shows Bob the criminal law change. As to the change that he shows Bob, the "purpose to deceive" requirement

---

20. Model Penal Code § 210.5(1).

probably is not satisfied, thus no liability. As to the advanced criminal law change that he does not show Bob, he may well have the purpose to deceive; he decides it best that Bob not know that he changed this other grade. But Raimer's intention to hide this change apparently emerged only after he showed the first grade to Bob; it did not exist at the time of his conduct in changing the grade. Thus there is no concurrence between his conduct and the required purpose to deceive.

(Count 3) Raimer changes Bob's grades back to Bs because he erroneously believes that they were originally recorded incorrectly as As. Because of Bob's lecture, Raimer now knows that he has no authority to alter a grade, thus he satisfies the requirement of "knowing he has no privilege." Liability under the statute also requires a "purpose to deceive," which Raimer may not have. (But the prosecutor might argue that in changing the advanced criminal law grade "back" to a B, Raimer was trying to hide the fact that he had changed the grade in the first place, and thus has a purpose to deceive.) In any case, the offense requires culpability as to whether the change "falsifies" the record. One might conclude that Raimer is negligent as to whether his entry of Bs is a falsification of the record. Would such negligence be sufficient for liability? While no culpability requirement is apparently provided on the face of the statute as to "falsifies," a requirement of recklessness is read in by section 2.02(3). Thus Raimer's negligence would not satisfy this recklessness requirement. (If a jury concludes that Raimer was aware of a risk that his changing the grades "back" to Bs was a falsification, then Raimer would be liable, provided that the other culpability requirements also are satisfied.)

(Count 4) To hide his earlier decision to let Anna take her file and its disastrous consequences, Raimer fabricates a new file for Anna that he knows is inaccurate. He knows he has no authority to do so—his purpose is to deceive the people in the office—and he knows the record is false (only recklessness as to falsification is required). Under the above reading of the statute, Raimer will be liable for the fourth count, fabricating Anna's file.

CONFLICT AND INCONSISTENCY IN THE MODERN CULPABILITY SCHEME

The Model Penal Code culpability scheme is a great improvement over "the variety, disparity, and confusion" of judicial definitions of "the requisite but elusive mental element" that existed prior to the Code's advent.[21] As is frequently the case with reform, however, the Code makes great advances but inevitably has shortcomings. All jurisdictions that follow the Model Penal Code's culpability scheme face a variety of common difficulties. Some states have changed the Code's provisions to avoid some of the problems. Others have created additional difficulties by tinkering with the scheme's provisions without fully understanding the implications of their changes.

Distinguishing conduct, circumstance, and result elements   One defect of the Code, already noted, is its failure to define the three categories of objective elements: conduct, circumstance, and result elements. For example, is "obstructs" a conduct or a result element? Does "insults another in a manner likely to provoke violent response" consist of a single conduct element or of one conduct element and one or more circumstance elements? Does "the death of another human being" consist of a single result element or of a result element and a circumstance

---

21. Morissette v. United States, 342 U.S. 246, 252 (1952).

element? The definitions of the three categories of objective elements are important because the categories are used as terms of art in many places in the Code. For example, by the terms of section 2.03, the special requirements of causation must be satisfied where an offense contains a "result" element.[22]

Objective element categories and culpability requirements Perhaps even more important, a precise definition of the "objective-element" categories is essential for proper application of the defined culpability terms. Recall the asymmetries in the Code's culpability definitions, discussed previously. To act "purposely" with respect to "conduct," or in causing "a result," an actor must have such conduct or result as his conscious object. But to act "purposely" with respect to "an attendant circumstance," an actor need only be aware of such circumstance, which is nothing more than what is required to prove "knowing" as to a circumstance. Recall also that "recklessness" and "negligence" are defined as to circumstance and result elements but are not defined as to conduct elements. Thus, if an element is categorized as a conduct element, there is some ambiguity as to what is to be required. Some jurisdictions would require that "knowing" be proven, for that is the lowest culpability with respect to conduct that is defined. Because of these asymmetries, the categorization of an objective element becomes essential in determining the precise culpability requirements that will apply.

Ambiguities from failure to define categories Consider the offense of theft by deception, which entails purposely obtaining another's property through deceit. A person "deceives" if he purposely "[c]reates or reinforces a false impression [as to value]."[23] One might argue that this requirement is a single elaborate conduct requirement: "creates or reinforces a false impression as to value." Or the prohibited conduct element might be "creates" or "reinforces" and the proscribed result might be interpreted as either (a) a false impression as to value (with no "attendant circumstance"), (b) a false impression (with value as a "circumstance"), or (c) an impression (with both falsity and value as "circumstances"). Selecting the proper interpretation requires a definition of what constitutes a "conduct," "circumstance," or "result," and the interpretation selected will determine the culpability required.

Implication of ambiguities Assume that a court applies section 2.02(4) to require that the stated culpability requirement, "purposely," apply to all elements of the offense of theft by deception. The actor's *conscious object* must then encompass all required conduct and results; but, because of the way "purposeful" as to a circumstance is defined, the actor need only be *aware* of the existence of a circumstance element. If the court applies interpretation (a) described above, the actor's *conscious object* must encompass every element of the offense because all elements are either conduct or results. If interpretation (b) is applied, however, the actor's *conscious object* must encompass only "creating" and a "false impression"; it need not be the actor's conscious object or hope—he need only be aware—that the false impression concerns "value." Finally, if the court applies interpretation (c), the actor's *conscious object* need only encompass "creating an impression"; he need only be *aware* of the fact that the impression is "false" and concerns "value." These differences create the potential to improperly manipulate a defendant's

---

22. See Model Penal Code § 2.03.
23. Model Penal Code § 223.3(a).

liability by altering the content of the categories "conduct," "result," and "circumstance," thereby altering the applicable culpability requirement.

Combining conduct and result or conduct and circumstance   Difficulties in distinguishing conduct, circumstance, and result elements also arise because most modern codes, including the Model Penal Code, use terms that combine conduct and a result as a single element or combine conduct and an attendant circumstance as a single element. Verbs like "damages," "obstructs," "destroys," "falsifies," "kills," and "desecrates" each combine both an act and a result of that act. Verbs like "compels"[24] combine conduct and circumstance elements. Such combinations create ambiguities and undermine consistency in the operation of the Code.

Implication of combined elements   Consider a statute that forbids "recklessly obstructing any highway."[25] What culpability should be required as to "obstructing"? A court might take any of three approaches. Because "obstructing" appears to be a conduct element and "recklessly" is not defined with respect to conduct, the court might determine that "knowing" is the appropriate culpability as to "obstructing" because it is the minimum culpability defined with respect to conduct. Or a court might attempt to invent a definition of recklessness as to conduct and require that newly defined culpability. Given the enactment of a comprehensive culpability scheme, such a definition of "culpability" seems properly a legislative task. A third, and perhaps the best, approach might be for a court to observe that "obstructing" is a combination of separate conduct and result elements: To obstruct is to "*render impassable* without unreasonable inconvenience or hazard."[26] In essence, the offense imposes liability when an actor engages in conduct by which he causes—that is, "renders"—any highway to be impassable. The stated culpability term *recklessly* under this approach can be meaningfully read to apply to the result element of causing the highway to be impassable. The same term could be interpreted to require "knowing" conduct, because "knowing" is the minimum culpability defined as to conduct.

PROPOSED REVISIONS TO THE SCHEME

The difficulties of the Model Penal Code scheme—arising from the failure to define the categories of objective elements and the use of terms that combine elements of different categories—can be avoided by use of a few thoughtful revisions, most of which may be done through judicial interpretation of existing provisions.[27] With revision, the Code's scheme can be made workable and can realize the full benefits of the insights and advances of the drafters. Here are some of the reforms that might be helpful.

Define conduct narrowly   Define "conduct" elements literally, that is, narrowly, to mean pure conduct: bodily movement of the actor (which is the way Model Penal Code section 1.13 defines "act"). Thus, objective elements of an offense definition that might otherwise be classified as conduct elements but that actually describe *characteristics* of the conduct, would be treated as separate circumstance

---

24. Model Penal Code § 213.1(1)(a) (defining offense of rape). The term "compels" implies an unstated yet required circumstance element: lack of consent.

25. See, e.g., Model Penal Code § 250.7.

26. Model Penal Code § 250.7(1).

27. See Paul H. Robinson & Jane A. Grall, *Element Analysis in Defining Criminal Liability: The Model Penal Code and Beyond*, 35 STAN. L. REV. 681 (1983).

or result elements. For example, the definition of "harassment" makes it an offense if an actor "insults another in a manner likely to provoke violent response." Under a narrow view of the conduct element, the required conduct is the simple act of speaking. The conduct's characteristics—its insulting character, its likelihood of provoking a violent response—would be treated as circumstance or result elements. Under this narrow view of conduct, the conduct element emerges as a relatively unspecific and unimportant aspect of an offense definition. In homicide, for example, the particular conduct that the actor engages in to cause the death of another human being does not matter. What matters is that the actor's conduct, of whatever nature, did cause the prohibited result. The most significant elements of an offense definition, then, typically are the circumstance and result elements.

Narrow conduct element as act requirement Such a narrowly defined conduct element continues adequately to serve the important purposes of the act requirement (at least as well as any act requirement can serve those purposes): to distinguish fantasy from intention and to exclude from liability intentions too irresolute ever to be carried out, to provide some minimal objective evidence confirming *mens rea*, and to set a minimal objective limit on the government's criminalization power. A narrow conduct element can improve on the act requirement function of providing a temporal point of reference for doctrines that need one, such as the concurrence requirement, statutes of limitation, and jurisdiction and venue. A broader definition of conduct makes application of these doctrines more difficult.

Distinguish combined elements As a corollary to this first revision, the legislature should redraft the language or, absent such redrafting, courts should distinguish the two aspects of the element in determining the culpability requirements whenever a single verb compounds a conduct element with a result element or with a circumstance element. By identifying the existence of a result element more clearly, this approach also identifies where the special requirements of causation apply.

Proposed distinction between circumstance and result Recall the problem of the Code's failure to define categories of objective elements: Is causing the "obstruction of a public highway" a single result element? Or is it a result element of causing an "obstruction" and a circumstance element of "a public highway"? A third proposal would resolve the problem by defining a "result" as a *circumstance changed by the actor*. All elements that did not fit this definition would be independent circumstance elements. In the short hypothetical above, the actor creates only the obstruction; he cannot create or alter the road's legal status as a "public highway." Thus, causing the "obstruction" would be a result element and "public highway" would be a circumstance element. To summarize, the conduct element in each offense is segregated, although it may be linguistically merged with other elements. It simply performs the function of the act requirement. Result elements are easy to identify as circumstances changed by the actor. All other elements are circumstance elements.

Culpability as to conduct similarly narrow Another corollary to the narrow scope of the conduct element is that the culpability requirement accompanying the conduct element is given a similarly narrow meaning. If the conduct element encompasses only an actor's act and not the characteristics of the accompanying circumstances or the results of the act, the required culpability as to the conduct encompasses only the actor's mental state as to engaging in the bare act itself, not his mental state as to the circumstances or results of the conduct. Any broader interpretation of conduct would make the culpability as to the conduct element all-encompassing. A requirement of "knowing" as to conduct, which would most frequently be required, would set "knowing" as the required culpability as to the pertinent attendant circumstances and the pertinent results of an actor's conduct. But to assume that the culpability required as to "conduct" controls the culpability as to the circumstances and results of the conduct as well, as the broader interpretation of conduct would do, is to undermine element analysis generally. Such an approach would short-circuit the Code's attempt to allow separate, and sometimes different, culpability requirements with respect to the circumstances and results of one's conduct.

Conduct culpability rarely an issue   Under the narrow definition of "conduct," an actor's culpability as to his conduct—for example, being aware of the nature of one's conduct—rarely will be a matter of dispute; instead, his culpability as to the circumstances and result of his conduct will be of primary practical importance. Culpability as to conduct simply requires, for example, that an actor be aware that he is moving his trigger finger or swinging his arm. The only cases that would present an issue under the narrowly defined conduct element would involve an actor who suffers from a considerable and abnormal disability. Such abnormalities typically are given more detailed consideration under provisions governing the voluntariness requirement and excuse defenses. The culpability requirements of an offense definition, in contrast, operate primarily to assess the culpability of normal persons. The normal person typically desires to move his body in the way that he actually moves it and therefore satisfies the narrow culpability-as-to-conduct requirement. The narrow interpretation of conduct avoids the problems inherent in the drafters' failure to define "recklessness" and "negligence" as to conduct. An actor who is only "aware of a substantial risk" or is "unaware of a substantial risk" that he is moving his trigger finger or arm is an actor who will have an excuse defense. Thus, no definitions of "recklessness" or "negligence" as to conduct are necessary.

MPC Section 2.02(4): Apply Stated Culpability to All Elements

One final but important difficulty with the Model Penal Code scheme results from too broad a reading of section 2.02(4):

> *Prescribed Culpability Requirement Applies to All Material Elements.* When the law defining an offense prescribes the kind of culpability that is sufficient for the commission of an offense, without distinguishing among the material elements thereof, such provision shall apply to all the material elements of the offense, unless a contrary purpose plainly appears.

The Commentary describes this provision as one that will embody the most probable legislative intent.[28] The provision may be interpreted too broadly, however, to allow what may be an exceptional culpability requirement, such as purposeful, which is meant by the legislature to apply only to one element of the offense, to govern the culpability requirements of all other offense elements. In other instances, the provision may have the equally undesirable effect of having an

---

28. Model Penal Code § 2.02 comment 6 at 245 (1985).

unusually low culpability requirement, such as negligence, apply to all elements, when it was meant only to apply to one.

Concerns with literal reading of rule Consider, for example, the offense of burglary. An actor commits burglary when he "enters a building or occupied structure with purpose to commit a crime therein, unless the premises are at the time open to the public or the actor is licensed or privileged to enter."[29] As "purpose" is the only culpability element prescribed, and as no contrary legislative purpose plainly appears, a provision like Model Penal Code section 2.02(4) might be interpreted to require that an actor must not only have the purpose to commit a crime within, but also must be purposeful with respect to every other element in order to be held liable for burglary. In other words, the actor must be aware of or believe or hope that *all the required circumstance* elements for burglary exist. He would escape liability if he thinks it likely, but is not certain and does not necessarily hope, that he is not "licensed or privileged to enter" or that he is entering a "building or occupied structure."[30] But burglary typically is understood to require purpose only as to the "intent to commit a crime therein." "Purpose" is an unusually stringent culpability requirement.[31] There are few areas where legislatures want so demanding a requirement. Too broad a reading of section 2.02(4) allows the exceptional case where purpose is required to become the standard for all elements of the offense. An analogous difficulty arises with the use of negligence. Where only negligence is required as to an offense element, strict application of section 2.02(4) applies this stated culpability term to all elements, although recklessness normally is the minimum culpability required.

Workable interpretation of rule A better reading of section 2.02(4) would apply its rule only to that part of the offense definition within the grammatical clause in which the stated term appears. This is consistent with the provision's direction that the rule applies only where the offense definition prescribes culpability, "without distinguishing among the material elements thereof." That is, grammatical structure should be taken as providing such distinction among elements. In the context of burglary, this interpretation would apply "purpose" only to "to commit a crime therein." The other elements of the offense would be governed by the other rules of construction; the culpability requirements would be derived either from other stated culpability terms or from section 2.02(3)'s reading in the standard "recklessness."

Interaction with section 2.02(3) This discussion gives some guidance in suggesting rules for how Model Penal Code sections 2.02(3) and 2.02(4) ought to interact. Consider the definition of "harassment":

> A person commits a petty misdemeanor if, with purpose to harass another, he . . . insults . . . another in a manner likely to provoke violent or disorderly response.[32]

29. Model Penal Code § 221.1.

30. "Purpose" as to a circumstance requires either a hope *or awareness*; the latter requirement is no more than is required for "knowledge." See supra. Thus, "knowledge" as to a circumstance element— "aware of high probability of its existence," § 2.02(7)—satisfies the requirement, but "recklessness"— "aware of a substantial risk," § 2.02(2)(c)—does not.

31. "[A]cting knowingly is ordinarily sufficient." Model Penal Code § 2.02 comment 2 at 234 (1985).

32. Model Penal Code § 250.4(2).

Model Penal Code section 2.02(3) requires recklessness whenever an offense definition fails to specify the culpability with respect to a particular element. On the other hand, when the offense definition specifies a culpability element, without distinguishing among elements, section 2.02(4) requires that the stated culpability apply to all elements, unless a contrary purpose appears. If section 2.02(4) were applied to require the stated culpability of "purpose" to all elements, even those elements outside of its grammatical clause, the actor would have to be purposeful with respect to all elements—for example, it must be his conscious object to "insult another" and his conscious object that the insult be "likely to provoke violent or disorderly response." Yet, as noted above, purpose is a special and very demanding culpability requirement, while recklessness is well-established as the "norm" for criminal liability. If section 2.02(3) is applied to all elements outside the grammatical clause in which "purpose" appears, the defendant must be purposeful only as to harassing another and need only be reckless with respect to all other elements. The section 2.02(3) recklessness requirement should be preferred. Section 2.02(4) admittedly should apply to the entire grammatical clause in which it appears, but it should apply outside that clause only when the placement and effect of the stated culpability term suggest that it is intended to govern culpability requirements outside of the clause.

Offenses containing two stated culpability terms? Another piece of evidence suggesting a restrictive interpretation of section 2.02(4) is illustrated by the "Raimer" hypothetical above, involving the offense of tampering with records. The definition contains two stated culpability requirements on its face. A broad interpretation of section 2.02(4)—which would have a stated term apply beyond its grammatical clause—presents the issue of which of the two terms should be applied to the elements outside of the two clauses, such as "falsifies" or "renames." The broad interpretation seems to assume that an offense definition will have only one stated culpability requirement. That this offense has two stated terms itself suggests a need for care in the interpretation of section 2.02(4). It seems safe to assume that each of the two requirements are intended to apply at least within the grammatical clause in which each appears. Thus, "knowing" is still required as to "no privilege," and a "purpose to deceive" is still required. But which of these stated terms, if either, will apply to the element outside of these two phrases? The best approach is to leave these other elements to the operation of section 2.02(3)'s reading of a requirement of recklessness.

These issues are explored in the further analysis of the Raimer hypothetical below.

More on Raimer's records   The proper interpretation of Model Penal Code section 2.02(4) can be examined in the context of Raimer's liability. What result if a broad reading of section 2.02(4) were used to determine the culpability requirements of Tampering with Records? Under a broad reading of section 2.02(4), what is the culpability required as to "falsifies," which is outside of both of the clauses in which the stated culpability terms of "knowing" and "purposeful" appear? Reconsider Raimer's liability for Counts 3 and 4, this time taking into account possible interpretations of section 2.02(4):

(Count 3) Recall that Raimer changes Bob's grades back to Bs because he erroneously believes that they were originally recorded incorrectly as As. Earlier we assumed that Raimer was negligent as to whether his entry of Bs "falsifies" the record. This time, assume Raimer is reckless as to whether his conduct "falsifies" the record. That is, assume that he is aware of a substantial risk that the Bs he is entering might be incorrect. If section 2.02(4) controls, which would require either knowing or purposeful as to falsifying, the culpability requirement is not satisfied and Raimer still has no liability; his recklessness is insufficient. If section 2.02(4) is limited in application to the grammatical clauses in which the stated culpability terms appear, and section 2.02(3) is relied upon to read in recklessness for elements outside of those clauses, Raimer's recklessness is sufficient. (However, recall that even if Raimer satisfies the culpability requirement, as to falsification, he nonetheless may claim that he had no "purpose to deceive" with regard to the first grade.)

(Count 4) Recall that to hide his earlier decision to let Anna take her file and the disastrous consequences that came out of this, Raimer fabricates a new file for Anna that he knows is inaccurate. He knows he has no authority to do so; his purpose is to deceive the people in the office, and he knows the record is false. Under a narrow interpretation of section 2.02(4), Raimer is liable for the fourth count, fabricating Anna's file, because he satisfies section 2.02(3)'s requirement that he be at least reckless as to falsifying. Under a broad reading of 2.02(4), however, the result is unclear. It depends upon whether the stated purposeful requirement or the stated knowing requirement is applied to the falsification element. Raimer knows that his conduct will falsify the record. Is he "purposeful" as to such falsification? No; he would prefer to reproduce Anna's record accurately. Thus, Raimer's liability will depend on which of the two stated terms applies to the element of falsification: If purpose is required, he is not liable; if only knowing is required, he is liable.

Aside from the obvious difficulty in the unresolved conflict between the two stated terms, the case illustrates the dangers of a broad reading of 2.02(4) in spreading a purpose requirement too broadly. It would seem odd that an actor who knew he had no authority to change a record, knew he was falsifying the record, and had the purpose to deceive others by his conduct, would nonetheless have no liability for the offense (because he did not have the falsification itself as his purpose). Application of section 2.02(3) to the falsification element would require only recklessness (or possibly knowing).

Proposed interpretation of sections 2.02(3) & 2.02(4) The better interpretation of section 2.02(4), as noted above, is to view it as requiring that a stated culpability term apply to the grammatical clause in which it appears unless the context demonstrates that it is intended to apply to other, subsequent clauses as well. Section 2.02(3) is best interpreted as supplying the culpability requirements to any elements to which section 2.02(4) does not apply. For example, in the absence of legislative direction to the contrary, recklessness would be required as to the circumstance element of "an unlicensed or unprivileged entry" in burglary. This interpretation of section 2.02(4) is not inconsistent with its language, which requires application of stated culpability only when such culpability is provided "without distinguishing among the material elements thereof." The interpretation rests on an assumption that, when a stated culpability is placed within a grammatical clause, such placement distinguishes the elements within the clause from those without. This use of section 2.02(3) to fill in any gaps after application of section 2.02(4) is consistent with the Model Penal Code's view that the culpability level of recklessness should be applied when the required culpability is unstated, a view that is supported by the fact that recklessness generally is accepted as the appropriate norm for imposing criminal liability.

Application to homicide   In many offenses, section 2.02(3) will have no application. Consider homicide, for example.

> A person is guilty of criminal homicide if he purposely, knowingly, recklessly
> or negligently causes the death of another human being.

The different degrees of homicide are then identified as dependent on the actor's level of culpability: Purposefully or knowingly causing the death is murder, recklessly is manslaughter, and negligently is negligent homicide.[33] Even under the more limited application of section 2.02(4), the culpability stated in homicide is likely to apply to both offense elements, causing death and the victim being a "human being." Because the offense is defined in a single clause, the stated culpability requirement would apply to all elements, including the circumstance element of "human being." Thus, if "human being" were defined for homicide purposes to include a "viable fetus," the doctor who purposely kills a fetus and is reckless as to its being a viable fetus would be liable for manslaughter, but not for murder.

Proposals affecting drafting technique, not content   Note that the interpretations of sections 2.02(3) and 2.02(4) proposed here are not designed either to raise or to lower the culpability requirements of offense definitions. They are, rather, designed to create a system in which the legislature can effectively, easily, and clearly define the culpability requirements it desires. If a culpability requirement other than recklessness is to apply to a particular element, the legislature need only state such culpability requirement in the offense definition. If the legislature desires the stated requirement to apply to more than one element, it can achieve this by its choice of placement of the stated culpability term within the offense definition. The legislature can provide an explicit culpability requirement to apply to particular elements (those within the clause) without fear that the requirement will be interpreted to apply more broadly than intended.

---

33. See Model Penal Code §§ 210.2, 210.3, and 210.4.

APPENDIX A: SECTION 5

Culpability and Mistake

✳ DISCUSSION MATERIALS

Issue: What Kind of Mistake as to Consent, if Any, Should Be Permitted to Provide a Defense to Rape?

Susan Estrich, in an article calling for criminal liability for the negligent rapist, examines the American system's limited mistake defense for rape and argues
that the current formulation has an adverse effect on victims. Lynne Henderson's
review of the article purports to uncover various flaws in Estrich's argument and
rejects her conclusions. Joshua Dressler explores the various dangers of rejecting
the *mens rea* requirement, advocated by many rape law reformers, while Lani Anne
Remick advocates an overhaul of the consent requirement, supporting instead an
affirmative verbal consent standard.

Susan Estrich, Rape

95 Yale Law Journal 1087, 1096-1097, 1098-1101, 1102-1105 (1986)

It is difficult to imagine any man engaging in intercourse accidentally or
mistakenly. It is just as difficult to imagine an accidental or mistaken use of force,

at least as force is conventionally defined. But it is not at all difficult to imagine cases in which a man might claim that he did not realize that the woman was not consenting to sex. He may have been mistaken in assuming that no meant yes. He may not have bothered to inquire. He may have ignored signs that would have told him that the woman did not welcome his forceful penetration.

In doctrinal terms, such a man could argue that his mistake of fact should exculpate him because he lacked the requisite intent or *mens rea* as to the woman's required nonconsent. American courts have altogether eschewed the *mens rea* or mistake inquiry as to consent, opting instead for a definition of the crime of rape that is so limited that it leaves little room for men to be mistaken, reasonably or unreasonably, as to consent. The House of Lords, by contrast, has confronted the question explicitly and, in its leading case, has formally restricted the crime of rape to men who act recklessly, a state of mind defined to allow even the unreasonably mistaken man to avoid conviction.

This Section argues that the American courts' refusal to confront the *mens rea* problem works to the detriment of the victim. In order to protect men from unfair convictions, American courts end up defining rape with undue restrictiveness. The English approach, while doctrinally clearer, also tends toward an unduly restricted definition of the crime of rape.

While the defendant's attitude toward consent may be considered either an issue of *mens rea* or a mistake of fact, the key question remains the same. In *mens rea* terms, the question is whether negligence suffices, that is, whether the defendant should be convicted who claims that he thought the woman was consenting, or didn't think about it, in situations where a "reasonable man" would have known that there was not consent. In mistake of fact terms, the question is whether a mistake as to consent must be reasonable in order to exculpate the defendant. . . .

To treat what the defendant intended or knew or even should have known about the victim's consent as irrelevant to his liability sounds like a result favorable to both prosecution and women as victims. But experience makes all too clear that it is not. To refuse to inquire into *mens rea* leaves two possibilities: turning rape into a strict liability offense where, in the absence of consent, the man is guilty of rape regardless of whether he (or anyone) would have recognized nonconsent in the circumstances; or defining the crime of rape in a fashion that is so limited that it would be virtually impossible for any man to be convicted where he was truly unaware or mistaken as to nonconsent. In fact, it is the latter approach which has characterized all of the older, and many of the newer, American cases. In practice, abandoning *mens rea* produces the worst of all possible worlds: The trial emerges not as an inquiry into the guilt of the defendant (is he a rapist?) but of the victim (was she really raped? did she consent?). The perspective that governs is therefore not that of the woman, nor even of the particular man, but of a judicial system intent upon protecting against unjust conviction, regardless of the dangers of injustice to the woman in the particular case.

The requirement that sexual intercourse be accompanied by force or threat of force to constitute rape provides a man with some protection against mistakes as to consent. A man who uses a gun or knife against his victim is not likely to be in serious doubt as to her lack of consent, and the more narrowly force is defined, the more implausible the claim that he was unaware of nonconsent.

But the law's protection of men is not limited to a requirement of force. Rather than inquire whether the man believed (reasonably or unreasonably) that his victim was consenting, the courts have demanded that the victim demonstrate her nonconsent by engaging in resistance that will leave no doubt as to nonconsent. The definition of nonconsent as resistance—in the older cases, as utmost resistance, while in some more recent ones, as "reasonable" physical resistance—functions as a substitute for *mens rea* to ensure that the man has notice of the woman's nonconsent.

The choice between focusing on the man's intent or focusing on the woman's is not simply a doctrinal flip of the coin.

First, the inquiry into the victim's nonconsent puts the woman, not the man, on trial. Her intent, not his, is disputed; and because her state of mind is key, her sexual history may be considered relevant (even though utterly unknown to the man). Considering consent from *his* perspective, by contrast, substantially undermines the relevance of the woman's sexual history where it was unknown to the man.

Second, the issue for determination shifts from whether the man is a rapist to whether the woman was raped. A verdict of acquittal thus does more than signal that the prosecution has failed to prove the defendant guilty beyond a reasonable doubt; it signals that the prosecution has failed to prove the woman's sexual violation—her innocence—beyond a reasonable doubt. Thus, as one dissenter put it in disagreeing with the affirmance of a conviction of rape: "The majority today . . . declares the innocence of an at best distraught young woman." Presumably, the dissenter thought the young woman guilty.

Third, the resistance requirement is not only ill-conceived as a definition of nonconsent, but is an overbroad substitute for *mens rea* in any event. Both the resistance requirement and the *mens rea* requirement can be used to enforce a male perspective on the crime, but while *mens rea* might be justified as protecting the individual defendant who has not made a blameworthy choice, the resistance standard requires women to risk injury to themselves in cases where there may be no doubt as to the man's intent or blameworthiness. The application of the resistance requirement has not been limited to cases in which there was uncertainty as to what the man thought, knew or intended; it has been fully applied in cases where there can be no question that the man knew that intercourse was without consent. Indeed, most of the cases that have dismissed claims that *mens rea* ought to be required have been cases where both force and resistance were present, and where there was no danger of any unfairness.

Finally, by ignoring *mens rea*, American courts and legislators have imposed limits on the fair expansion of our understanding of rape. As long as the law holds that *mens rea* is not required, and that no instructions on intent need be given, pressure will exist to retain some form of resistance requirement and to insist on force as conventionally defined in order to protect men against conviction for "sex." Using resistance as a substitute for *mens rea* unnecessarily and unfairly immunizes those men whose victims are afraid enough, or intimidated enough, or, frankly, smart enough, not to take the risk of resisting physically. In doing so, the resistance test may declare the blameworthy man innocent and the raped woman guilty. . . .

My view is that . . . a "negligent rapist" should be punished, albeit—as in murder—less severely than the man who acts with purpose or knowledge, or even knowledge of the risk. First, he is sufficiently blameworthy for it to be just to punish him. Second, the injury he inflicts is sufficiently grave to deserve the law's prohibition.

The traditional argument against negligence liability is that punishment should be limited to cases of choice, because to punish a man for his stupidity is unjust and, in deterrence terms, ineffective. Under this view, a man should only be held responsible for what he does knowingly or purposely, or at least while aware of the risks involved. As one of *Morgan*'s most respected defenders put it:

> To convict the stupid man would be to convict him for what lawyers call inadvertent negligence—honest conduct which may be the best that this man can do but that does not come up to the standard of the so-called reasonable man. People ought not to be punished for negligence except in some minor offences established by statute. Rape carries a possible sentence of imprisonment for life, and it would be wrong to have a law of negligent rape.

If inaccuracy or indifference to consent is "the best that this man can do" because he lacks the capacity to act reasonably, then it might well be unjust and ineffective to punish him for it. But such men will be rare, and there was no evidence that the men in *Morgan* were among them, at least as long as voluntary drunkenness is not equated with inherent lack of capacity. More common is the case of the man who could have done better but didn't; could have paid attention, but didn't; heard her say no, or saw her tears, but decided to ignore them. Neither justice nor deterrence argues against punishing this man.

Certainly, if the "reasonable" attitude to which a male defendant is held is defined according to a "no means yes" philosophy that celebrates male aggressiveness and female passivity, there is little potential for unfairness in holding men who fall below *that* standard criminally liable. Under such a low standard of reasonableness, only a very drunk man could honestly be mistaken as to a woman's consent, and a man who voluntarily sheds his capacity to act and perceive reasonably should not be heard to complain here—any more than with respect to other crimes—that he is being punished in the absence of choice.

But even if reasonableness is defined—as I argue it should be—according to a rule that "no means no," it is not unfair to hold those men who violate the rule criminally responsible, provided that there is fair warning of the rule. I understand that some men in our society have honestly believed in a different reality of sexual relations, and that many may honestly view such situations differently than women. But, it is precisely because men and women may perceive these situations differently, and because the injury to women stemming from the different male perception may be grave, that it is necessary and appropriate for the law to impose a duty upon men to act with reason, and to punish them when they violate that duty.

In holding a man to such a standard of reasonableness, the law signifies that it considers a woman's consent to sex to be significant enough to merit a man's reasoned attention. In effect, the law imposes a duty on men to open their eyes and use their heads before engaging in sex—not to read a woman's mind, but to give her credit for knowing her own mind when she speaks it. The man who has the inherent capacity to act reasonably, but fails to do so, has made the blameworthy choice to violate this duty. While the injury caused by purposeful conduct may be greater than that caused by negligent acts, being negligently sexually penetrated without one's consent remains a grave harm, and being treated like an object whose words or actions are not even worthy of consideration adds insult to injury. This dehumanization exacerbates the denial of dignity and autonomy which is so much a part of the injury of rape, and it is equally present in both the purposeful and negligent rape.

By holding out the prospect of punishment for negligence, the law provides an additional motive for men to "take care before acting, to use their faculties and draw on their experience in gauging the potentialities of contemplated conduct." We may not yet have reached the point where men are required to ask verbally. But if silence does not negate consent, at least the word "no" should, and those who ignore such an explicit sign of nonconsent should be subject to criminal liability.

Lynne N. Henderson, Review Essay: What Makes Rape a Crime?

Review of *Estrich, Real Rape*
3 Berkeley Woman's Law Journal 193, 211-219 (1987-1988)

Mens Rea as to Consent

Estrich thinks the focus of reform legislation should be on the offender, but that it should be done via a mens rea requirement as to consent rather than via an emphasis on force. She begins with a discussion of the English gang rape case *Director of Public Prosecutions v. Morgan*, a horrible case often taught in first year criminal law classes to illustrate mistake of fact. *Morgan* held that an honest but unreasonable belief, or negligence, as to a woman's consent was *not* a culpable mental state for the crime of rape. Although Estrich disagrees with the holding of *Morgan*, she agrees with its focus on consent and the defendant's intent. She then criticizes American courts for failing to discuss intent or mistake, because the resulting definition of rape effectively excludes the acquaintance or date rape situation: American courts, she claims, "have provided protection for men who find themselves in . . . potentially ambiguous situations through the doctrines of consent, defined as nonresistance, and force, measured by resistance." Estrich argues that this leads to an almost exclusive focus on the victim by making "her intent, not his" the issue in dispute.

Estrich's analysis has two flaws. First, her assertion that American courts ignore the issue of mens rea as to consent is wrong. Second, she is mistaken in thinking that shifting attention to the man's mental state about consent and reducing the mens rea requirement to negligence will relieve the victim of the burden of physical resistance and of having to "prove" she was raped. Estrich contends that absent a mens rea requirement for consent, the question becomes "was this woman raped?" rather than "is this man a rapist?" In fact, focusing on whether or not the man believed he had consent is no solution at all. First, it returns us to the dangers of the focus on consent of the nineteenth century. Second, the methods of proving mens rea will continue to focus attention on the woman and her credibility. . . .

. . . Absent a confession or an admission by the defendant, the prosecutor must introduce evidence of the circumstances surrounding the event to prove mens rea. Consequently, although the woman's subjective state may not be an issue, her behavior is certainly relevant to establishing whether the defendant "honestly and reasonably" believed that she consented. Thus, resistance . . .

becomes an issue. As the court in *Barnes* noted, "Absence of resistance may . . . be probative of whether the accused honestly and reasonably believed he was engaging in consensual sexuality." It is likely that the victim would be scrutinized every bit as closely under Estrich's proposed standard as under prior standards. Thus, resistance once more becomes an issue. . . .

Concentrating on the defendant's mens rea as to consent may bring back another nightmare: the survivor's sexual history. As of this writing, forty-nine states have rape shield laws limiting the introduction and use of a rape survivor's sexual history in rape trials. These statutes do far more than prevent "humiliating questions" in rape trials—they block the introduction of highly prejudicial evidence having little or no relevance to a victim's credibility. Traditionally, the premise underlying the use of this type of evidence has been that unchaste women are liars and should not be believed. A more recent premise is that if a woman previously consented to sex, she likely consented this time. Because the defendant in a criminal prosecution has the sixth amendment right to confront his accuser, inquiries focusing on a defendant's mens rea as to consent are likely to reopen the door to more extensive explorations of a victim's sexual past. For example, Vivian Berger's article on rape shield laws specifically mentions an exception for a man's claim of reasonable mistake as to consent. According to Berger, if a man has heard a woman is "easy," or if she behaves in a "seductive" way, the man may reasonably believe she *is* consenting regardless of whether she says no. "Therefore, a wisely drafted statute will not prohibit proof of the woman's sexual history offered to show the defendant's honest (reasonable) belief that she yielded (sic) to him voluntarily." Indeed, Berger's "model" rape shield statute permits exceptions to general prohibitions on evidence of sexual history. . . .

Estrich's solution lies in her definition of consent and her opposition to the resistance requirement. Throughout the book, she argues that "no means no," not yes. Under Estrich's proposal, the "reasonable man" is presumed to know that no means no. Although verbal manifestations of non-consent certainly should be sufficient, concentrating on the rapist's mens rea is not necessary to accomplish this objective. If verbal non-consent is sufficient, Estrich's proposal for making negligence the culpable mens rea as to consent is unnecessary: a woman's "no" would put a man on notice and alert him to the risk of committing rape. For the man to continue his sexual advances would seem, at the very least, to constitute recklessness. Rather than get tied into mens rea knots that lead back to the consent-force-resistance conundrum, it might be better to define consent in unequivocal terms—"no means no"—and presume recklessness by imposing strict liability on men who continue. Of course, this approach raises problems under our culture's existing models of sexual interaction—it raises the questions did the victim really *mean* "no," and did she really *say* "no." This inevitably leads back to an examination of the victim's credibility.

Estrich dismisses strict liability as an answer to the consent issue. Her reluctance to impose strict liability on the element of consent, even after it is established that the woman did not consent, reflects the very male nightmare that she seeks to combat. Estrich states that strict liability regarding consent would result in punishment of men who engaged in intercourse when "no one would realize the woman was not consenting." Yet as Kelman has observed:

> If . . . we view the decision to have intercourse where consent is ambiguous
> as a separate decision [from the negligent perception as to consent], we are

prone to be less sympathetic to the defendant. It is not as if the defendant is "trapped" into criminality either unavoidably or in the course of doing perfectly ordinary or protected acts. By avoiding sexual intercourse with women who are not clearly consenting, the defendant can avoid criminality.

The question becomes whether, as a society, we wish to continue to allow aggressive unwanted male sexual advances.

Moreover, if the standard is "no means no," how can any man possibly claim not to have known of the woman's lack of consent? Such a belief can only be justified if one assumes that men need not accept a woman's "no," that male persistence pays off, and that such persistence is in fact what women desire. The survival of Byron's phrase "[a]nd saying she would n'er consent, consented" certainly captures a vision of how male-female relationships are perceived in this culture, and it does not carry entirely negative connotations.

If Estrich's rejection of strict liability reflects a concern about women engaging in sexual relations who fail to outwardly manifest their non-consent, that is a different problem. Sexual intercourse with an adult woman who has not indicated her subjective opposition may be beyond the scope of what modern society can or should punish. That is, we must accept the notion that men should not be punished for engaging in sexual activity when the woman does not convey her subjective state in any tangible way. But, once the woman has managed *some* manifestation of that subjective state, whether by verbal, physical, or emotional behavior, imposing strict liability if the man proceeds seems justified.

What about the woman who does not want intercourse but fails to say anything because she is frightened of the man? Estrich's solution, because it focuses solely on the *verbal* "no"—although one assumes crying would count—fails to address the problem of what constitutes sufficient fear and/or force to make it seem pointless for the woman to speak the word "no." By focusing solely on the defendant's mens rea as to consent, Estrich leaves unprotected the woman who, frozen with fear, neither cries nor says "no." Estrich also offers little protection to the woman who says "no" long before the actual event, but who finally, giving up, "consents," as did the victims in both *Mayberry* and *Barnes*. Further, when must the "no" be said? At "the crucial genital moment," as Susan Griffin put it, or at any time during the interaction? Traditionally, women were supposed to fight and resist until actual penetration occurred: this extremely narrow time frame remains a potential problem. In a situation where the victim says "no" early on and then becomes paralyzed, speechless with fear—does the focus on consent or the "reasonable man" standard help or hurt? What if she says no, he persists, and she decides to go along—under the male persistence paradigm the reasonable man would think he has consent.

The definition of fear should include consideration of differences in size, verbal threats including harassment ("you bitch," etc.) and, as the court in *Barnes* observed, the generally threatening circumstances created by a particular man. In this type of situation, focus on force may be superior to Estrich's focus on consent. When the victim has been frightened into passive silence, justice is better served by focusing on the victim's fear and the nature of the threatening situation created by the defendant than on his mens rea as to her consent, or on whether she consented. Weapons negate consent; fear should too.

If it seems I do not trust Estrich's "reasonable man" standard, it is for a reason: Indications are that the reasonable man would infer consent where the reasonable woman would not. A woman might think it is reasonable to engage in necking, or invite a date into her home for coffee, as the end of an evening, without inevitably having it signal consent to intercourse. The reasonable man may consider the same conduct as foreplay rather than a pleasant exercise in itself. The reasonable woman might believe a verbal "no," said breathlessly or placatingly, sufficiently conveys her non-consent. The reasonable man may believe he is justified in disregarding anything short of a firm "no" followed by an implicit threat to do him physical harm. Reasonable men have determined the law of rape all along, and it has not helped us much; so calling it "mens rea" and concentrating on consent seems only to promote stereotypical attitudes, not combat them. Estrich's "answer" to this problem is in reality an abandonment of the "reasonable man" standard in any event. She writes that the law should hold "a man to a higher standard of reasonableness" than it has in the past, presumably by redefining non-consent to mean "no means no."

The focus on mens rea as to consent has theoretical as well as practical flaws. Arguably, women do not voluntarily consent to heterosexual sex in a society in which they are subordinate to male power. Some feminists go so far as to argue that heterosexual intercourse itself is the evil. While I disagree with this claim, I do think that women do not experience the same freedom and autonomy in heterosexual relations as men experience. Consensual sex is not an "arm's length bargain." No one reads women their rights before seeking "consent." Women may *hope* men will ask, but they do not take the initiative in sex unless they are "bad" girls, or incredibly lucky in their relationships. Women frequently consent because they are frightened, because they want to please men, or because they think it is their duty. (And, there is also the ironic consequence of the "sexual revolution": women are no longer virgins so how can they say no?). The word "consent," therefore, does not adequately encompass women's experience of unwanted sex.

The absence of an objective manifestation of non-consent does not necessarily mean consent; a woman may experience sex in such a situation as tantamount to rape. Yet, if women are regarded as absolutely choiceless in the face of male sexuality, women will always and forever be victims. Women must not only take responsibility for their sexuality, but use the law to empower themselves when their sexuality is expropriated. Estrich's proposal is one of two possible approaches to this problem. The other approach involves a statutory redefinition of consent as "words or overt actions by a person who is competent . . . indicating a freely given agreement to have sexual intercourse or sexual contact," or as "positive cooperation in act or attitude pursuant to an exercise of free will. . . . The person must act freely and voluntarily. . . . "

Estrich's definition of consent ("no means no") empowers women formally by offering them a method of expressing non-consent men must heed. Statutes requiring *positive* manifestations of consent minimize the relevance of resistance and protect women who are completely passive because of fear, even if those statutes embody *male* understandings of what constitutes consent. (An unsympathetic court could conceivably find that woman who, out of fear, submits to sexual acts at the defendant's demand, has manifested "positive cooperation," I suppose.) Perhaps a combination of approaches, "no means no" and "positive cooperation," would adequately encompass the possible variations in women's experiences of and reactions to rape.

Joshua Dressler, Where We Have Been, and Where We Might Be Going: Some Cautionary Reflections on Rape Law Reform

46 Cleveland State Law Review 409, 430-439 (1998)

Mens Rea

It is a fundamental principle of the criminal law—"no provincial or transient notion"—that we do not send people to prison and stigmatize them as serious wrongdoers in the absence of culpability for their actions. No matter how serious the harm caused, the general rule is that a person is not guilty of a criminal offense in the absence of *mens rea*. Imagine for a moment that you are driving safely on the highway, under an overpass, when a piece of the bridge crumbles, strikes your windshield, and causes you to lose control of your car. As a consequence, your car strikes and kills another. You are likely to feel awful about what happened, and in criminal law terms, you have committed the *actus reus* of criminal homicide. That is, you have caused precisely the type of harm that the criminal law wishes to prevent, the death of another human being. But, of course, you are guilty of no crime. You did not kill the pedestrian intentionally, or even recklessly or negligently.

Increasingly, we are forgetting—or, at least, at risk of forgetting—this basic culpability principle in the context of rape. In one sense, this is understandable. The female who is the victim of undesired sexual contact is initially apt to feel just as violated, whether the male knew he was acting against her will or, at the other extreme, was understandably clueless. The harm to her, after all, is the same. But, of course, the harm to the dead person on the highway in the imagined overpass accident is the same whether you killed *him* purposely or innocently—nonetheless, the law will exculpate you for the death assuming non-culpability in causing the harm. Unfortunately, as obvious as this seems, some people find the notion of a *mens rea* requirement in the rape context silly. The principle that a male should not be convicted of rape if he reasonably (but incorrectly) believed that the female consented has been trivialized (or distorted) to mean that "a woman [was] raped but not by a rapist"?

Before rape law reform, the issue of *mens rea* rarely arose in rape trials. As a practical matter, the *actus reus* proved the *mens rea*. If a male used or threatened force to obtain intercourse, then it was evident that he purposely or knowingly had nonconsensual sexual relations. If his conduct was not forcible, the female had to resist, and this gave the male reasonable warning of her lack of consent: if he proceeded against her resistance, a jury could reasonably assume that he knew she did not want sexual relations. At a minimum, the resistance meant that the male acted recklessly or negligently in regard to her wishes. Thus, there was always some form of culpability proven.

With the abandonment or softening of the resistance requirement and the increased willingness of lawmakers to permit prosecutions for nonforcible forms of nonconsensual intercourse—an appropriate change, as I have suggested—the risk of conviction in the absence of *mens rea* is enhanced. A person who sincerely believes that his partner has consented to sexual intimacy should not be convicted of rape if his belief was one that a reasonable person in the same circumstances might hold. And, indeed, this has been the traditional rule for "general intent" offenses, such as rape.

It is too early to know where rape law is going in regard to *mens rea*, but there are some distressing signs. One concern I have is that courts may abandon altogether the requirement of *mens rea* in the rape context. Recently, the Supreme Judicial Council of Massachusetts, an historically liberal court, and thus one that might be expected to honor the requirement of culpability, held that even a reasonable (but incorrect) belief as to a female's consent, is not a defense in a rape prosecution. Thus, even if a reasonable person in the actor's situation would have believed that the female was consenting, the male is guilty of rape, although the victim did not physically or verbally resist his overtures, and although he did not use or threaten to use any force. It would be as if you were convicted as a murderer for killing accidentally when the bridgework crumbled.

An appellate court in Massachusetts explained that the no-defense rule was "in harmony with the analogous rule that a defendant in a statutory rape case is not entitled to an instruction that a reasonable mistake as to the victim's age is a defense." But, it is only in harmony if one ignores the basic point that statutory rape is *a grave exception to the general rule that mens rea matters*. Wisely or not, most (although not all) jurisdictions treat statutory rape as an exceptional strict liability offense, in order to protect young females from the effects of their own decisions. Ordinary rape, however, has not been viewed as strict liability in character. There is simply no more principled basis for dispensing with the *mens rea* requirement in rape cases than there is in regard to any other serious crime.

Massachusetts, of course, is just one state. I do not mean to cry wolf here, but certain other judicial decisions suggest that courts might be prepared to erode, if not abolish, the *mens rea* requirement. Even if a person is entitled to be acquitted on the ground of a reasonable mistake of fact, courts might impose special rules regarding mistake claims in rape prosecutions that would effectively strip the defendant of the claim. For example, consider Justice Frederick Brown's remarks in *Commonwealth v. Lefkowitz*:

> The essence of the offense of rape is lack of consent on the part of the victim. I am prepared to say that when a woman says "no" to someone any implication other than a manifestation of non-consent that might arise in that person's psyche is legally irrelevant, and thus no defense. Any further action is unwarranted and the person proceeds at his peril. In effect, he assumes the risk. In 1985, I find no social utility in establishing a rule defining non-consensual intercourse on the basis of the subjective (and quite likely wishful) view of the more aggressive player in the sexual encounter.

In short, if a female says no (I assume he means in words or actions) to intercourse, not only does this prove the *actus reus* of the offense, but it automatically proves the *mens rea*. If the defendant asserts a mistake claim, Justice Brown would consider the mistake unreasonable *as a matter of law*. Thus, the issue would not go to the jury.

"No means no" is an excellent rule to teach men (and women) in our culture. And, it is an excellent starting point—initial premise—in rape trials. But, bright-line rules such as this can only result, at best, in the correct outcome *most* of the time. Such rules do not insure justice to the individual whose case might not fit the bright-line assumptions. As troubling as it is to acknowledge, no does *not* always—in one hundred percent of the cases—mean no in sexual relations, even today. If no does not always mean no, there can surely be cases in which a reasonable person could *believe* that no does not mean no in the specific incident, *even when it does.* Such cases will be relatively few in number, but it is improper to convict a person on the basis of the law of averages. It is wrong to use the bludgeon of the criminal law to impose rules intended to change cultural attitudes when this means punishing an individual for rape who made a mistake that the community, represented by the jurors, would characterize as reasonable. If the mistake was, indeed, unreasonable—or if the jurors don't believe the defendant's claim that he was mistaken—they can convict on the facts. The jury should not be deprived of the issue of *mens rea* through bright-line rules. Each case should be considered on its own merits.

Lani Anne Remick, Read Her Lips: An Argument for a Verbal Consent Standard in Rape
141 University of Pennsylvania Law Review 1103-1105 (1993)

Always take "no" for an answer. Always stop when asked to stop. Never assume "no" means "yes." If her lips tell you "no" but there's "yes" in her eyes, keep in mind that her words, not her eyes, will appear in the court transcript.

Violence against women has reached an all-time high. An estimated fifteen to forty percent of all women are victims of attempted or completed rapes at some point in their lifetimes. Most of their rapists are never criminally punished.

The criminal justice system's failure to bring most rapists to justice means that women's right to decide "who may touch their bodies, when, and under what circumstances" is often unenforceable. One of the causes of this problem is that the law of rape does not recognize women's right to sexual autonomy as absolute. Instead, rape law reflects the sexually coercive society in which it operates. Although frowning upon aggressive sexual behavior at the extremes, our male-dominated society accepts a certain amount of coercion, aggression or violence against women as a normal, even desirable, part of sexual encounters. Similarly, the law of rape is founded on a paradigm of violent stranger rape which fails to clearly proscribe less violent rapes or rapes in which some elements of a consensual sexual encounter are present. An estimated sixty to eighty percent of all rapes fit this description. The inability of victims of these "nontraditional" rapes to vindicate their rights through use of the criminal system is thus one of the biggest impediments to the comprehensive protection of female sexual autonomy under the law of rape. If such protection is to be afforded, therefore, "[m]uch, much more needs to be done. . . . The message that should go out today is that rape is a crime, whether it be date rape, intrafamilial rape, acquaintance rape, stranger rape or spousal rape. Rape is rape."

This Comment suggests a change in the law of rape that would bring all instances of nontraditional rape clearly within the boundaries of the criminal law. Its chosen vehicle for change is a redefinition of the consent standard. In searching for a solution to the current legal system's inadequate protection of women, several commentators have concluded that "the road to that solution presents itself clearly enough as a need for a reformulation of the criterion of consent." Other reformers call for simplicity and clarity in a new criterion, noting that "[c]ontinuous juggling of the elements of the crime by courts and commentators reflects an urge toward administrative simplicity, a search for an external standard by which to measure the subjective element of nonconsent. [Yet] . . . this interplay reveals a conviction that the central substantive issue in rape is consent."

In answer to the call for a new, clearer consent standard, this Comment proposes a rape law based on a norm of *affirmative verbal consent*. Under this standard, "no" would mean "no," "yes" would mean "yes," and the lack of any verbal communication as to consent would be presumed to mean "no." In more specific terms, a "no" or its verbal equivalent would be dispositive of the issue of consent, as would a freely-given "yes" or its verbal equivalent. The lack of a "yes" or its verbal equivalent would raise a presumption of non-consent. Such a standard would criminalize even "nonaggravated sexual assault, [that is,] nonconsensual sex that does not involve physical injury, or the explicit threat of physical injury." By establishing the threshold for rape at this level, the suggested standard clearly incorporates all instances of nontraditional rape. It also underscores the gravity of the harm of more traditional violent stranger rape. Finally, rather than simply mirroring our sexually coercive society, such a law declares that a woman's right to sexual autonomy is absolute.

It is because rape law currently operates in the context of a sexually coercive society and because rape victims are overwhelmingly female that this Comment argues for a change in the law on the ground of assuring sexual autonomy for women. . . .

✳ ADVANCED MATERIALS ON FUNCTIONAL ANALYSIS

Functional Analysis by Doctrine Type

	Rules of Conduct (ex ante)	Principles of Adjudication (ex post)	
	Doctrines needed to tell people ex ante what the law requires of them	**Liability Rules** Doctrines needed to determine ex post who should be punished	**Grading Rules** Doctrines needed to set the general range of punishment for a person held liable
Offense objective elements	conduct and circumstance offense elements		result elements
Offense culpability elements	(inchoate culpability requirements)	baseline (i.e., minimum) culpability requirements	aggravation culpability requirements
General defenses	(objective) justification defenses	excuse defenses (including mistake as to a justification)	

Flow Chart of Functions of Criminal Law

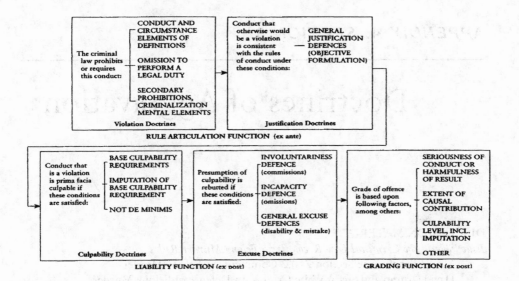

APPENDIX A: SECTION 6

Doctrines of Aggravation

DISCUSSION MATERIALS
Issue: Should the Criminal Law Recognize a Felony-Murder Rule?
     Model Penal Code Section 210.2 Commentary, Felony Murder
     David Crump and Susan Waite Crump, In Defense of Felony Murder
ADVANCED MATERIALS
     California Penal Code Sections 187, 188, 189, 192 (2006), Homicide
     Offenses

✳ DISCUSSION MATERIALS

Issue: Should the Criminal Law Recognize a Felony-Murder Rule?

The materials begin with a Model Penal Code Commentary discussion of the conceptual problems facing the felony-murder rule and its relationship to the mens rea requirement. David Crump and Susan Waite Crump offer an opposing view, positing arguments in favor of the rule.

Model Penal Code Section 210.2 Commentary
Felony Murder
Official Draft and Revised Comments 30 (1980)

The classic formulation of the felony-murder doctrine declares that one is guilty of murder if a death results from conduct during the commission or attempted commission of any felony. Some courts have made no effort to qualify the application of this doctrine, and a number of earlier English writers also articulated an unqualified rule. At the time the Model Code was drafted, a number of American legislatures, moreover, perpetuated the original statement of the rule by statute. As thus conceived, the rule operated to impose liability for murder based on the culpability required for the underlying felony without separate proof of any culpability with regard to the death. The homicide, as distinct from the underlying felony, was thus an offense of strict liability. This rule may have made sense under the conception of *mens rea* as something approaching a general criminal disposition rather than as a specific attitude of the defendant towards each element of a specific offense. Furthermore, it was hard to claim that the doctrine worked injustice in an age that recognized only a few felonies and that punished each as a capital offense.

In modern times, however, legislatures have created a wide range of statutory felonies. Many of these crimes concern relatively minor misconduct not inherently dangerous to life and carry maximum penalties far less severe than those authorized for murder. Application of the ancient rigor of the felony-murder rule to such crimes will yield startling results. For example, a seller of liquor in violation of a statutory felony becomes a murderer if his purchaser falls asleep on the way home and dies of exposure. And a person who communicates disease during felonious sexual intercourse is guilty of murder if his partner subsequently dies of the infection.

The prospect of such consequences has led to a demand for limitations on the felony-murder rule. American legislatures had responded to these demands at the time the Model Code was drafted primarily by dividing felony-homicides into two or more grades or by lowering the degree of murder for felony homicide. Only Ohio had abandoned the rule completely.

In addition, the courts had imposed restrictions, both overt and covert, on the reach of the felony-murder doctrine. . . .

These limitations confine the scope of the felony-murder rule, but they do not resolve its essential illogic. This doctrine aside, the criminal law does not predicate liability simply on conduct causing the death of another. Punishment for homicide obtains only when the deed is done with a state of mind that makes it reprehensible as well as unfortunate. Murder is invariably punished as a heinous offense and is the principal crime for which the death penalty is authorized. Sanctions of such gravity demand justification, and their imposition must be premised on the confluence of conduct and culpability. Thus, under the Model Code, as at common law, murder occurs if a person kills purposely, knowingly, or with extreme recklessness. Lesser culpability yields lesser liability, and a person who inadvertently kills another under circumstances not amounting to negligence is guilty of no crime at all. The felony-murder rule contradicts this scheme. It bases conviction of murder not on any proven culpability with respect to homicide but on liability for another crime. The underlying felony carries its own penalty and the additional punishment for murder is therefore gratuitous—gratuitous, at least, in terms of what must have been proved at trial in a court of law.

It is true, of course, that the felony-murder rule is often invoked where liability for murder exists on another ground. One who kills in the course of armed robbery is almost certainly guilty of murder in the form of intentional or extremely reckless homicide without any need of special doctrine. Similarly, a man who burns another's house will scarcely be heard to complain that he lacks the culpability for murder if the blaze kills a sleeping occupant. For the vast majority of cases it is probably true that homicide occurring during the commission or attempted commission of a felony is murder independent of the felony-murder rule. At bottom, continued adherence to the doctrine may rest on assessments of this sort.

The problem is that criminal liability attaches to individuals, not generalities. It is a weak rejoinder to a complaint of unjust conviction to say that for most persons in the defendant's situation the result would have been appropriate. To be sure, limiting the rule to specified felonies increases the probability that conviction in a particular case will be warranted. Criminal punishment should be premised, however, on something more than a probability of guilt. Requiring that the defendant's conduct in committing the underlying felony create a foreseeable risk to human life is a roundabout way of limiting felony murder to cases of negligent homicide. This is a worthwhile reform, for it effectively excludes extreme applications of the rule to instances in which the actor would not otherwise be guilty of any homicide offense. Yet murder and negligent homicide are not interchangeable; they carry vastly different sanctions. Punishment for the greater offense, on proof that should suffice only for conviction of the lesser, works within reduced compass the same essential violence to the general principles of criminal liability as does the unqualified rule.

Principled argument in favor of the felony-murder doctrine is hard to find. The defense reduces to the explanation that Holmes gave for finding the law "intelligible as it stands":

> [I]f experience shows, or is deemed by the law-maker to show, that somehow or other deaths which the evidence makes accidental happen disproportionately often in connection with other felonies, or with resistance to officers, or if any other ground of policy it is deemed desirable to make special efforts for the prevention of such deaths, the law-maker may consistently treat acts which, under the known circumstances, are felonious, or constitute resistance to officers, as having a sufficiently dangerous tendency to be put under a special ban. The law may, therefore, throw on the actor the peril, not only of the consequences foreseen by him, but also of consequences which, although not predicted by common experience, the legislator apprehends.

The answer to such argument is twofold. First, there is no basis in experience for thinking that homicides *which the evidence makes accidental* occur with disproportionate frequency in connection with specified felonies. Second, it remains indefensible in principle to use the sanctions that the law employs to deal with murder unless there is at least a finding that the actor's conduct manifested an extreme indifference to the value of human life. The fact that the actor was engaged in a crime of the kind that is included in the usual first-degree felony-murder enumeration or was an accomplice in such crime, as has been observed, will frequently justify such a finding. Indeed, the probability that such a finding will be justified seems high enough to warrant the presumption of extreme indifference that Subsection (1)(b) creates. But liability depends, as plainly it should, upon the crucial finding. The result may not differ often under such a formulation from that which would be reached under some form of the felony-murder rule. But what is more important is that a conviction on this basis rests solidly upon principle.

David Crump and Susan Waite Crump, In Defense of Felony Murder

8 Harvard Journal of Law and Public Policy 359, 362-364, 367-371 (1985)

Such diverse philosophers and judges as Jeremy Bentham, H.L.A. Hart, Sir James Fitzjames Stephen, Joel Feinberg, and Chief Justice Warren Burger have noted the disrespect that the law engenders when its response is disproportionate to public evaluations of the severity of an alleged violation. Many penal codes declare proportionality to be among their major objectives. The classification and grading of offenses so that the entire scheme of defined crimes squares with societal perceptions of proportionality—of "just deserts" —is a fundamental goal of the law of crimes.

The felony murder doctrine serves this goal. . . . Felony murder reflects a societal judgement that an intentionally committed robbery that causes the death of a human being is qualitatively more serious than an identical robbery that does not. Perhaps this judgement could have been embodied in a newly defined offense called "robbery-resulting-in-death;" but while a similar approach has been adopted in some areas of the criminal law, such a proliferation of offense definitions is undesirable. Thus the felony murder doctrine reflects the conclusion that a robbery that causes death is more closely akin to murder than to robbery. If this conclusion accurately reflects societal attitudes, and if classification of crimes is to be influenced by such attitudes in order to avoid depreciation of the seriousness of the offense and to encourage respect for the law, then the felony murder doctrine is an appropriate classificatory device.

There is impressive empirical evidence that this classification does indeed reflect widely shared societal attitudes. . . . [C]haracterizing a robbery-homicide solely as robbery would have the undesirable effect of communicating to the citizenry that the law does not consider a crime that takes a human life to be different from one that does not—a message that would be indistinguishable, in the minds of many, from a devaluation of human life.

Another aspect of condemnation is the expression of solidarity with the victims of crime. If we as a society label a violent offense in a manner that depreciates its significance, we communicate to the victim by implication that we do not understand his suffering. He may be left with the impression that he is unprotected—or even that he is disoriented, having himself failed to understand the rules of the game. Felony murder is a useful doctrine because it reaffirms to the surviving family of a felony-homicide victim the kinship the society as a whole feels with him by denouncing in the strongest language of the law the intentional crime that produced his death.

Deterrence is often cited as one justification for the felony murder doctrine. . . . Deterrence is the policy most often recognized in the cases. Scholars, however, tend to dismiss this rationale, using such arguments as the improbability that felons will know the law, the unlikelihood that a criminal who has formed the intent to commit a felony will refrain from acts likely to cause death, or the assertedly small number of felony-homicides.

The trouble with these criticisms is that they underestimate the complexity of deterrence. There may be more than a grain of truth in the proposition that felons, if considered as a class, evaluate risks and benefits differently than members of different classes in society. The conclusion does not follow, however, that felons cannot be deterred, or that criminals are so different from other citizens that they are impervious to inducements or deterrents that would affect people in general. There is mounting evidence that serious crime is subject to deterrence if consequences are adequately communicated. The felony murder rule is just the sort of simple, common sense, readily enforceable, and widely known principle that is likely to result in deterrence.

The argument against deterrence often proceeds on the additional assumption that felony murder is addressed only to accidental killings and cannot result in their deterrence. By facilitating proof and simplifying the concept of liability, however, felony murder may deter intentional killings as well. The robber who kills intentionally, but who might claim under oath to have acted accidentally, is thus told that he will be deprived of the benefit of this claim. By institutionalizing this effect and consistently condemning robbery homicides as qualitatively more blameworthy than robberies, the law leads the robber who kills intentionally to expect treatment for himself. Furthermore, the contrary argument proves too much even as to robbery-killings that are factually accidental. The proposition that accidental killings cannot be deterred is inconsistent with the widespread belief that the penalizing of negligence, and even the imposition of strict liability, may have deterrent consequences.

＊ ADVANCED MATERIALS

California Penal Code Sections 187, 188, 189, 192
(2006)

Homicide Offenses

Section 187. Murder Defined; Death of Fetus

(a) Murder is the unlawful killing of a human being, or a fetus, with malice aforethought. . . .

Section 188. Malice Defined

Such malice may be express or implied. It is express when there is manifested a deliberate intention unlawfully to take away the life of a fellow creature. It is implied, when no considerable provocation appears, or when the circumstances attending the killing show an abandoned and malignant heart.

When it is shown that the killing resulted from the intentional doing of an act with express or implied malice as defined above, no other mental state need be shown to establish the mental state of malice aforethought. Neither an awareness of the obligation to act within the general body of laws regulating society nor acting despite such awareness is included within the definition of malice.

Section 189. Degrees of Murder

All murder which is perpetrated by means of a destructive device or explosive, a weapon of mass destruction, knowing use of ammunition designed primarily to penetrate metal or armor, poison, lying in wait, torture, or by any other kind of willful, deliberate, and premeditated killing, or which is committed in the perpetration of, or attempt to perpetrate, arson, rape, carjacking, robbery, burglary, mayhem, kidnapping, train wrecking . . . or any murder which is perpetrated by means of discharging a firearm from a motor vehicle intentionally at another person outside of the vehicle with the intent to inflict death, is murder of the first degree. All other kinds of murders are of the second degree.

As used in this section, "destructive device" means any destructive device as defined in Section 12301, and "explosive" means any explosive as defined in Section 12000 of the Health and Safety Code.

As used in this section, "weapon of mass destruction" means any item defined in Section 11417.

To prove the killing was "deliberate and premeditated," it shall not be necessary to prove the defendant maturely and meaningfully reflected upon the gravity of his or her act.

Section 192. Manslaughter

Manslaughter is the unlawful killing of a human being without malice. It is of three kinds:

(a) Voluntary—upon a sudden quarrel or heat of passion.

(b) Involuntary—in the commission of an unlawful act, not amounting to felony; or in the commission of a lawful act which might produce death, in an unlawful manner, or without due caution and circumspection. That this subdivision shall not apply to acts committed in the driving of a vehicle.

APPENDIX A: SECTION 7

Death Penalty

DISCUSSION MATERIALS
Issue: Should Capital Punishment Be Allowed?
    Hugo A. Bedau, Arguments For and Against Capital Punishment
    Hugo A. Bedau, Innocence and the Death Penalty
    Ernest van den Haag, Punishing Criminals
    Robert Weisberg, Deregulating Death

✳ DISCUSSION MATERIALS

Issue: Should Capital Punishment Be Allowed?

The following discussion materials begin with two articles by Hugo Bedau. The first summarizes the development of the capital punishment debate and identifies the key arguments among the distributive principles. Bedau then argues against capital punishment, pointing specifically to the racially skewed execution rate in the first excerpt and describing the problem of false positives in capital punishment in the second. In response, Ernest van den Haag offers a retributive justification for capital punishment even in the face of error. Finally, Robert Weisberg examines optimal execution rates to satisfy the criminal justice principles and comments on the current trend of sentencing many but executing few.

Hugo A. Bedau, Arguments For and Against Capital Punishment
Encyclopedia of Crime and Justice 138-141 (S. Kadish ed., 1983)

With the rise of rationalist thought in European culture during the Renaissance and Enlightenment (1550-1750), and the concurrent decline in an exclusively religious foundation for moral principles, philosophers and jurists increasingly lent their support to the doctrine of "the rights of man" as the foundation for constitutional law and public morality. The most influential continental, British, and American Enlightenment thinkers—John Locke, Jean-Jacques Rousseau, Cesare Beccaria, William Blackstone, Immanuel Kant, and Thomas Jefferson—all agreed that the first and foremost of these rights is "the right to life." Few of these thinkers, however, opposed the death penalty (Beccaria was the notable exception); most endorsed it explicitly. They argued, typically, that since each person is born with a "natural" right to life, murder must be viewed as a violation of that right; accordingly, executing the murderer is not wrong since the murderer has forfeited his own right to life by virtue of his crime.

Modern thinkers, under the influence of the human rights provisions advocated by the United Nations in various resolutions, declarations, and covenants, have sought to appeal to a more complex line of considerations embedded in other human rights, as well as in the idea of the right to life. This view was advocated most prominently in the 1970s by Amnesty International, the human rights organization awarded the Nobel Peace Prize in 1978 for its worldwide campaign against torture. On this view, the death penalty violates human rights because (1) its administration is inevitably surrounded by arbitrary practices and unreliable procedures that violate offenders' rights; (2) erroneous executions are an irrevocable and irremediable violation of the right to life; and (3) there are less severe and equally effective alternatives—notably, long-term imprisonment.

In the United States since the 1960s, these themes have been argued most vigorously by the American Civil Liberties Union and by attorneys for the NAACP Legal Defense and Educational Fund and the Southern Poverty Law Center on behalf of nonwhite and indigent clients accused of murder. Their basic argument has been that the death penalty as it is actually used in contemporary American criminal justice systems is inherently and irredeemably class- and race-biased, so that a self-respecting civilized society cannot afford to employ it.

Racism

The central evidence for the main criticism—racist administration of the death penalty—comes from research conducted in several states, particularly in the South, in which it has been shown that a person is more likely to be sentenced to death if the victim is white than if nonwhite. These results are consistent with the generally acknowledged results of earlier research on the death penalty for rape, in which it was shown that the overwhelming preponderance of death penalties for black offenders could be explained only by the race of the offender taken in conjunction with that of the victim: the death penalty was highly probable only if the victim was white.

Defenders of the death penalty have, or could have, replied as follows: (1) all current capital laws are color-blind and impose equal liability on all persons regardless of race, color, class, or sex of offender or of victim; (2) racism in the current administration of the death penalty cannot be inferred from evidence relating to the admittedly racist practices of the distant past; (3) the evidence tending to show that the race of the victim is the chief explanation for whether an offender is sentenced to death (white victim) or to prison (non-white victim) is incomplete and inconclusive; (4) since justice requires that all murderers be sentenced to death and executed, some racial bias (if there is any) in the day-to-day administration of capital punishment is merely another case of the regrettable but tolerable imperfect enforcement of a just law; and (5) the deterrent and incapacitating effects of executions provided by even a somewhat racially biased death penalty are better for society than are the results of a less potent (even if less biased racially) alternative mode of punishment.

Retribution

Many defenders of the death penalty rest their position on principles of retributive justice and the appropriateness of moral indignation at murder, which they believe can be expressed adequately only by punishing that crime (and others, if any, no less heinous) by death. Whether such retributive reasoning has its origins in a passion for vengeance is less important than whether the principles to which it appeals are sound. Most opponents of the death penalty do not dispute (1) the principle that convicted offenders deserve to be punished; (2) the principle that a suitable punishment is, like a crime itself, some form of harsh treatment; and (3) the principle that the severity of the punishment should be proportional to the gravity of the offense. What is disputed is whether the third principle *requires* the death penalty for murder (and other crimes) or whether this principle is merely *consistent* with such a punishment, so that the further step in favor of death as the ideally fitting penalty must be taken by reference to other (perhaps nonretributive) considerations. Making the punishment fit the crime in any literal sense is either impossible or morally unacceptable, given the horrible nature of many murders. Interpreting the third principle so that it entails, "a life for a life" thus verges on begging the question. As a result, the focus of controversy between proponents and opponents of the death penalty who agree in arguing the issue primarily on grounds of retributive justice is on how closely it is necessary and desirable to model a punishment on the crime for which it is meted out. . . .

Utility and the Prevention of Crime

Quite apart from considerations rooted in principles of retributive justice or of constitutional law, arguments for and against the death penalty often proceed by reference to essentially utilitarian considerations, in which the consequences for overall social welfare—especially as this involves the reduction of crime—are the criteria to which both sides appeal. For example, defenders of the death penalty have argued that executions are a far less costly mode of punishment than any alternative. Abolitionists have replied that this is untrue if one takes into account the enormous cost to society of the extremely complex and lengthy litigation that surrounds a capital case, beginning with the search for an acceptable jury and culminating in postsentencing appeals and hearings in both state and federal courts. The chief issue of utilitarian concern, however, has always been whether the death penalty is an effective means of preventing crime and whether it is more effective than the alternative of imprisonment.

Incapacitation

Both sides concede that execution is a perfectly incapacitative punishment and that in this respect it is preferable to imprisonment. How much difference this makes to the crime rate is a matter of sharp dispute: the issue turns on

(1) whether persons who have been executed would have committed further capital (or other) offenses if they had not been executed, and (2) whether persons convicted and imprisoned for capital crimes but not executed will commit further capital offenses when and if released. There is no direct evidence available regarding the first question. Evidence relevant to the second question from parole and recidivism records indicates that a very small number of capital offenders commit subsequent crimes. Roughly 1 convicted homicide offender out of every 340 such persons released from prison commits another homicide within the first year after release. Defenders of the death penalty often argue that it is inexcusable for society not to take measures guaranteeing that a convicted murderer is incapable of repeating his crime. Abolitionists argue that the alternatives open to society, if it abandons the present system of parole and release practices, are even worse: either society must execute *all* convicted murderers, at intolerable moral cost (these thousands of executions are unnecessary, since so few murderers recidivate), or society must imprison *all* convicted murderers until their natural death, also intolerable because of the prison management problems that such a policy would create.

General Deterrence

Still more important and controversial is the adequacy of the death penalty as a general deterrent. During the 1950s, evidence based on several different comparisons convinced most criminologists that there was no superior deterrent effect associated with the death penalty. The comparisons were between homicide rates in given states before, during, and after abolition; homicide rates in given jurisdictions before and after executions; homicide rates in adjacent states, some with and others without the use of capital punishment; and rates of police killings in abolitionist and death-penalty jurisdictions. In the 1970s, this conclusion was challenged by research which used new methods borrowed from econometrics and which asserted that each execution in the United States between 1930 and 1969 prevented between eight and twenty murders. Subsequent investigators, however, soon showed that the alleged deterrent effect was an artifact of arbitrary if not dubious statistical methods. A panel of the National Academy of Science (NAS) went even further and expressed extreme skepticism about the results of all available research studies; none, the panel said, provided any useful evidence on the deterrent effect of capital punishment. No reliable scientific investigations support the common sense inference that since the death penalty is more severe than long-term imprisonment, the death penalty must be a better deterrent.

It is difficult to say whether skepticism (as recommended by the NAS panel) or a more positive conclusion against the deterrent efficacy of the death penalty is justified by the totality of all research. Some research, based on the study of executions and homicides in New York, has even suggested the initially implausible hypothesis that executions may actually exert a "brutalizing" effect upon society and that instead of deterring murders it incites them. What does seem true is that any argument for the death penalty based primarily on the claim of its superior deterrent efficacy is untenable. It is worth noting that the Supreme Court, in its series of death-penalty decisions during the 1970s, skirted this controversy and never spoke with a clear and unanimous voice one way or the other. (The sole exception is its decision in *Gregg*, where the majority of the Court conjectured that in such cases as "calculated murders," for example, terrorist attacks, sanctions less severe than death may not be adequate.) How much evidence proponents of the death penalty should be expected to produce in favor of the superior deterrent power of executions is also unclear, and perhaps imponderable.

Hugo A. Bedau, Innocence and the Death Penalty

The Death Penalty in America: Current Controversies 344, 345, 350-359
(H. Bedau, ed., 1997)

The most conclusive evidence that innocent people are condemned to death under modern death sentencing procedures comes from the surprisingly large number of people whose convictions have been overturned and who have been freed from death row. [In the period 1973-1992], at least 48 people have been released from prison after serving time on death row . . . with significant evidence of their innocence. In 43 of these cases, the defendant was subsequently acquitted, pardoned, or charges were dropped. [O]ne defendant was released when the parole board became convinced of his innocence.

[Professor Bedau describes the circumstances for each of the 48 cases. Many involved complete factual innocence—definitive proof that the defendant was in no way involved in the offense. Some involved what might be termed "legal innocence" —the defendant was not definitively exonerated but there was prosecutorial misconduct and/or incompetent defense, together with insufficient evidence of actual guilt. In the latter cases, he notes, there may have been "a lingering doubt" about complete innocence, but the evidence fell far short of proving guilt beyond a reasonable doubt. Bedau then summarizes the factors that led to conviction and a death sentence in these cases.]

. . . The cases outlined above might convey a reassuring impression that although mistakes are made, the system of appeals and reviews will ferret out such cases prior to execution. In one sense that is occasionally true: the system of appeals sometimes allows for correction of factual errors. But there is another sense in which these cases illustrate the inadequacies of the system. [Many of t]hese men were found innocent *despite the system* and only as a result of [unusual media attention or other] extraordinary efforts not generally available to death row defendants.

Indeed, in some cases, these men were found innocent as a result of sheer luck. In the case of Walter McMillian, his volunteer outside counsel had obtained from the prosecutors an audio tape of one of the key witnesses' statements incriminating Mr. McMillian. After listening to the statement, the attorney flipped the tape over to see if anything was on the other side. It was only then that he heard the same witness complaining that he was being pressured to frame Mr. McMillian. With that fortuitous break, the whole case against McMillian began to fall apart. . . .

Most of the releases from death row over the past twenty years came only after many years and many failed appeals. . . . Too often, the reviews afforded death row inmates on appeal and habeas corpus do not offer a meaningful opportunity to present claims of innocence. . . . After trial, the legal system becomes locked in a battle over procedural issues rather than a re-examination of guilt. . . . Accounts which report that a particular case has been appealed numerous times before many judges may be misleading. [W]hen Roger Keith Coleman was executed in Virginia [in 1992,] it was reported that his last appeal to the Supreme Court "was Coleman's 16th round in court." However, the Supreme Court had earlier declared that Coleman's constitutional claims were barred because his prior attorneys had filed an appeal too late in 1986. His evidence was similarly excluded from review in state court as well. Instead, Coleman's innocence was debated only in the news media and considerable doubt concerning his guilt went with him to his execution. . . .

Investigation of innocence ends after execution. . . . Judging by past experience, a substantial number of death row inmates are innocent and there is a high risk that some of them will be executed. The danger is enhanced by the failure to provide adequate counsel and the narrowing of opportunities to raise the issue of innocence on appeal. Once an execution occurs, the error is final.

Ernest van den Haag, Punishing Criminals
219-220 (1975)

Errors would not justify the abolition of the death penalty for retributionists. Many social policies have unintended effects that are statistically certain, irrevocable, unjust and deadly. Automobile traffic unintentionally kills innocent victims; so does surgery (and most medicines); so does the death penalty. These activities are justified, nevertheless, because benefits (including justice) are felt to outweigh the statistical certainty of unintentionally killing innocents. The certain death of innocents argues for abolishing the death penalty no more than for abolishing surgery or automobiles. Injustice justifies abolition only if the losses to justice outweigh the gains—if more innocents are lost than saved by imposing the death penalty compared to whatever net result alternatives (such as no punishment or life imprisonment) would produce. If innocent victims of future murderers are saved by virtue of the death penalty imposed on convicted murderers, it must be retained, just as surgery is, even though some innocents will be lost through miscarriage of justice—as long as more innocent lives are saved than lost. More justice is done with than without the death penalty. . . .

Robert Weisberg, Deregulating Death
Supreme Court Review 303, 386-387 (1983)

There may never be a social consensus on the role of capital punishment, but a social engineer might try to identify a sort of culturally optimal number of executions that would best compromise among the competing demands made by the different constituencies of the criminal justice system.

The most obvious approach is to have some executions, but not very many. A small number of executions offers a logical, if crude, compromise between the extreme groups who want either no executions or as many as possible. It would also satisfy those who believe that execution is appropriate only for a small number of especially blameworthy killers, at least if the right ones are selected. It might further satisfy those who do not believe there is a discernible and small category of most blameworthy killers, but who believe that a small number of executions might adequately serve general deterrence and make a necessary political statement about society's attitude toward crime. But our hypothetical social engineer would want to consider other points of view or factors as well in designing his culturally optimal number. Too many executions might have the opposite effect of morally offending people with the spectacle of a blood-bath. On the other hand, if the number were too low in comparison with the number of murders, capital punishment might not serve general deterrence. Or if we execute too few people, we may not produce a big enough statistical sample to prove that the death penalty meets any tests of rationality and nondiscrimination.

We might therefore imagine a socially stabilizing design for the death penalty which leads to just the right number of executions to keep the art form alive, but not so many as to cause excessive social cost. It is, of course, fanciful to imagine any political institution having the will or authority to take a systematic approach to executions. Under the current capital punishment laws, judges have some opportunity to manipulate the rate of execution. Legislators theoretically can affect the execution rate by changing the substantive laws of murder and punishment. But between the constitutional restrictions on death sentencing and the voters' general demand for capital punishment, legislators in most states probably do not have a great deal of room to maneuver. A prosecutor can ensure that any given murder defendant will not face execution, but because he cannot control the jury or judges he can never guarantee that a defendant is executed. A juror can at best control the rate of execution in one case. But judges, especially appellate judges, have a good deal of freedom to control the number of executions within the pool of capital claimants who come before them.

Viewing the statistics of the last decade, one might imagine that in a rough, systematic way, judges have indeed manipulated death penalty doctrine to achieve a culturally optimal number of executions. That number is very close to zero, but it must be viewed in light of a very different number—the number of death sentences.

If we somewhat fancifully treat the judiciary as a single and calculating mind, we could say that it has conceived a fiendishly clever way of satisfying the competing demands on the death penalty: We will sentence vast numbers of murderers to death, but execute virtually none of them. Simply having many death sentences can satisfy many proponents of the death penalty who demand capital punishment, because in a vague way they want the law to make a statement of social authority and control. It will also satisfy jurors who want to make that statement in a specific case with the reassurance that the death sentence will never really be carried out. And we can at the same time avoid arousing great numbers of people who would vent their moral and political opposition to capital punishment only on the occasion of actual executions. Once a murderer enters the apparently endless appellate process, much of the public ceases to pay attention.

APPENDIX A: SECTION 8

Homicide: Doctrines of Mitigation

DISCUSSION MATERIALS
Issue: Should One Have the Right to End One's Own Life? If So, Should Others Be Able to Help if Necessary?
Model Penal Code Section 210.5 Commentary
Neil M. Gorsuch, The Right to Assisted Suicide and Euthanasia
Robert M. Hardaway et al., The Right to Die and the Ninth Amendment: Compassion and Dying After Glucksberg and Vacco

✳ DISCUSSION MATERIALS

Issue: Should One Have the Right to End One's Own Life? If So, Should Others Be Able to Help if Necessary?

The first of the discussion materials comes from the Model Penal Code's Commentary on the offense of causing or aiding suicide and explains why the code does not criminalize suicide or attempted suicide but does criminalize causing, aiding, or soliciting the suicide of another. Neil M. Gorsuch's piece argues that assisted suicide should remain a criminal act on the grounds that human life has an inherent value to it. Finally, Robert M. Hardaway presents an opposing view on the issue, discussing a right to die as being linked to having compassion for the chronically ill.

Model Penal Code Section 210.5 Commentary
Official Draft and Revised Comments 91, 93-94, 98-104 (1985)

Suicide and Attempted Suicide as Crimes

The Model Code does not recognize either suicide or attempted suicide as a crime. This is accomplished with respect to suicide itself by the restriction of the homicide provisions to cases where the actor causes the death "of another human being" and by the provisions in Section 1.05(1) that "no conduct constitutes an offense unless it is a crime or violation under this Code or under another statute of this State." . . . It follows that attempted suicide is also not criminal under the Model Code, for Section 5.01 is limited to situations where the actor engages in inchoate behavior that has as its object the completion of conduct that the law declares to be criminal.

This result accords with current law in most jurisdictions. . . .

The judgment underlying the Model Code position is that there is no form of criminal punishment that is acceptable for a completed suicide and that criminal punishment is singularly inefficacious to deter attempts to commit suicide. There is scant reason to believe that the threat of punishment will have deterrent impact upon one who sets out to take his own life. By definition, the person who commits what could be denominated a criminal attempt to commit suicide intends to succeed. It seems preposterous to argue that the visitation of criminal sanctions upon one who fails in the effort is likely to inhibit persons from undertaking a serious attempt to take their own lives. Moreover, it is clear that the intrusion of the criminal law into such tragedies is an abuse. There is a certain moral extravagance in imposing criminal punishment on a person who has sought his own self-destruction, who has not attempted direct injury to anyone else, and who more properly requires medical or psychiatric attention.

Causing Suicide of Another

. . . It is the purpose of Section 210.5(1) to preclude [problematic causation outcomes] by limiting the occasions when one can be guilty for "causing another to commit suicide" to those cases where the actor "purposely causes such suicide by force, duress, or deception." Criminal liability is limited to purposeful conduct on the ground that merely creating the risk that another will commit suicide would cast the net of liability too wide. . . . [T]here are many human-relations situations where the risk of another's suicide may arise and yet where the actor should be free to act independently of that risk. . . . The effect of Subsection (1), therefore, would be to forbid prosecution under the ordinary criminal homicide provision of the Model Code except where this limiting language is satisfied.

Aiding or Soliciting Suicide of Another

Section 2.06 deals with the general problem of complicity in criminal conduct. Since suicide itself is not a crime, and since Section 2.06 applies only where one aids another to commit criminal conduct, the general complicity provisions of the Model Code have no application to the situation where one aids another to commit suicide. . . .

Subsection (2) creates a separate offense of aiding or soliciting suicide. Criminal punishment in this area raises an issue of some complexity. Self-destruction is surely not conduct to be encouraged or taken lightly. The fact that penal sanctions will prove ineffective to deter the suicide itself does not mean that the criminal law is equally powerless to influence the behavior of those who would aid or induce another to take his own life. Moreover, in principle it would seem that the interests in the sanctity of life that are represented by the criminal homicide laws are threatened by one who expresses a willingness to participate in taking the life of another, even though the act may be accomplished with the consent, or at the request, of the suicide victim. On the other hand, cases such as *People v. Roberts*,[1] where a husband yielded to the urging of his incurably sick wife to provide her with the means of self-destruction, sorely test the resiliency of a principle that completely fails to take account of the claim for mitigation that such a circumstance presents.

The law has wavered in its treatment of this issue in the past. At the time the Model Code was under consideration, some decisions reached aiding suicide on the theory that it established complicity in another's self-murder. Other jurisdictions held that, because suicide itself was not criminal, aiding the suicide of another was also not criminal. Many states dealt with the matter by statute, treating such conduct as manslaughter or as a separate crime of comparable grade. In Switzerland, the criminality of such conduct turned upon the presence of a selfish motive, a position one commentator in the Anglo-American tradition has embraced.[2] . . .

Several modern statutes omit any reference to causation and instead use a variety of phrases to describe the kinds of conduct that constitute the offense. It seems that these statutes fail to deal at all with the difficulty of potential overinclusiveness. The majority of the statutes that do mention the concept of causation in this context follow the provision in New York, which declares a person guilty of a felony if he "intentionally causes or aids another person to commit suicide."[3] This language must be read in connection with the specific provision of an affirmative defense to murder in cases where "[t]he defendant's conduct consisted of causing or aiding, without the use of duress or deception, another person to commit suicide."[4] It thus appears that if the defendant causes suicide by duress or deception he is guilty of murder, much as he could be under the provisions of Subsection (1) of Section 210.5.

Neil M. Gorsuch, The Right to Assisted Suicide and Euthanasia
23 Harvard Journal of Law & Public Policy 599, 696-701

An Argument for Respecting Life As A Sacrosanct Good

[Here I argue] that a persuasive argument against any form of assisted suicide or euthanasia has been largely overlooked in contemporary debate. This moral (and legal) argument does not claim to resolve end-of-life questions objectively, but it concedes that reference to a necessarily subjective conception of right and wrong is required. It is an argument concerning the sanctity of human life.

Under this view, the intentional taking of human life by private persons is always wrong. Publicly authorized forms of killing—in war or in the criminal justice system—fall in a separate category. . . . But, inherent in any version of the sanctity-of-life position is an exceptionless norm against the intentional taking of human life by private persons. This view seeks to establish both an absolute rule

---

1. 211 Mich. 187, 178 N.W. 690 (1920).
2. G. Williams, The Sanctity of Life and the Criminal Law 308-309 (1957).
3. N.Y. § 125.15(3).
4. N.Y. § 125.25(1)(b).

against intentionally taking innocent human life and reasons "why one should not kill an innocent person, even if that killing should violate no norm of fairness or, for that matter, any other relevant moral norm," like autonomy or utility.[5]

Life as a Basic Good

The sanctity-of-life position starts with the supposition that there are certain irreducible and categorical moral goods and evils. . . . A categorical moral good is one understood as intrinsically worthwhile. It is an end that is a reason, in and of itself, for action and choice and decision. Reference to some prior premises need not—and cannot—deduce its value; instead, its truth is self-evident. . . . Society's understanding of basic moral goods comes not from logical constructs, but from practical reasoning and experience. Neither are basic human goods Platonic forms that are unrealizable in daily life. They are reasoned practically from human experience. Such goods and evils are fundamental aspects of human nature and fulfillment. No logical truth about what "is" can be used to derive these collection of moral "oughts."

Likewise, as basic reasons for action, basic goods are not instrumental or merely useful for the purpose of achieving some other end. By definition, these ends in and of themselves are fulfilling in their own right. In claiming something as a basic good, one claims that an indefinite number of persons can participate in this inherent good in an indefinite number of valuable ways, many of which may be beyond what is presently imaginable.

Human life qualifies as such a basic value. Its status as such is suggested by the fact that people everyday and in countless ways do something to protect human life (one's own or another's) without thinking about any good beyond life itself. . . .

The fundamental and irreducible value of human life is further evidenced by the fact that it is essential to well-being. To have a good and fulfilled life, one must have life. Human beings are not merely rational beings, but corporeal bodies. Their fulfillment depends on their having physical lives. Life is intrinsic to human fulfillment.

Naturally, these considerations only indicate that life qualifies as a basic human good; fundamental premises and principles are not capable of syllogistic demonstration. Still, some objections to life's status as a basic good can be convincingly addressed. One might object that human life is not an intrinsically valuable or categorical good, but merely an instrumental one valuable only to the extent that it permits us to enjoy other goods, such as friendship and family. Most of us, for instance, would see little inherent good in a life spent in a coma. What is valuable to people about living is not the chance to exist, but the opportunity existence brings for pursuing other objectives and ends—family, friends, play, and work.

This objection, however, founders on the fact that family, friends, and medical workers often choose to provide years of loving care to persons who exist only physically, comatose or semicomatose, even linked to a respirator and feeding tubes.

---

5. See, e.g., Joseph M. Boyle, Jr., Sanctity of Life and Suicide: Tensions and Developments Within Common Morality, in Suicide and Euthanasia 221, 221 (Baruch A. Brody ed., 1989).

Members of religious orders and hospice organizations choose to devote their entire adult lives caring for such persons precisely because they are human persons, not because doing so instrumentally advances some other hidden objective. Even though all persons would not make a similar choice, "the fact that some people have made [such a choice] gives evidence that life is a basic human good—one which offers for choice an intelligible ground which need have no ulterior" motive.[6] . . .

Respecting Human Life as a Basic Good

. . . To intend freely and deliberately to do wrong, moreover, necessarily reveals something about character and commitments that no unintended side effect ever could. At an irreducible minimum, therefore, to respect human life means avoiding intentionally doing harm to it, even if we cannot always avoid actions that have the unintended side effect of harming human life. Applying that rule here eliminates assisted suicide and euthanasia—acts which, by definition, involve an intentional assault against the basic good of life.

The alternative to an absolute rule against private intentional killing, moreover, is troubling territory. Once some intentional killings become acceptable, society becomes enmeshed in making moral decisions about which ones it deems permissible. In the assisted suicide and euthanasia context, unless we unleash the full-throttle neutralist and harm principle right open to all adults, society is forced into a debate over the relative value of different kinds of human life. Judging whose lives may and may not be taken in turn depends upon assessments of quality of life—whether one is young and fit or old and sick. Different human lives are thus left with different moral and legal statuses based on their perceived "quality of life."

Robert M. Hardaway et al., The Right to Die and the Ninth Amendment: Compassion and Dying After *Glucksberg* and *Vacco*
7 George Mason Law Review 313 (Winter 1999)

A majority of Americans support legalizing physician-assisted suicide.[7] Clearly, many doctors are willing to help patients who wish to end their lives. A 1994 study of physicians in Washington State published in the Journal of the American Medical Association found that physicians had assisted 25 percent of all patient requests for assisted suicide. A 1997 study of physicians in the San Francisco Bay area reported that 53 percent of physicians admitted to assisting in the suicide of their patient. Yet physician-assisted suicide is legal in only one state in the country—Oregon. . . .

The Oregon Death with Dignity statute passed just in time. The Death with Dignity statute permits, but does not require, doctors to prescribe life-ending medication. . . .

---

6. Id. at 238-239.

7. See Marilyn Webb, The Good Death 393 (1997) (citing 1996 *Washington Post* survey); see also David A. Levine, *Legalizing Physician-Assisted Suicide: Michigan and Oregon*, 8 Brown U. Long-Term Care Quality Letter, Apr. 29, 1996, available in 1996 WL 9006372 (citing Michigan survey on physician-assisted suicide).

Right to Die statutes may not only reduce the pain and suffering of the terminally ill, but may also prove to be an effective antidote to an epidemic of suicides. . . . In her landmark compendium, *The Good Death*, Marilyn Webb tells the story of Glenn Leung. Paralyzed from the neck down, constantly gasping for breath, unable even to adjust his eyeglasses, wallowing in his own filth and degradation, his greatest fear had been that "he'd be trapped inside himself and now he is."[8] Many suicide victims are desperate to avoid such a fate, and therefore commit suicide prematurely, even though they must do so violently, away from friends and family. They have no assurance that they will be in control when their agony becomes unbearable. The tragedy is that thousands of people will die prematurely in the remaining 49 states where citizens are deprived of the right to physician-assisted suicide.

An optimistic view is that once fundamental rights are recognized in one state, it will be difficult for other states, or even for the federal government, to deny those same rights to others. The *Seattle Times* recently predicted that the Oregon statute could soon begin drawing out-of-state residents who want a physician's help in ending their lives. A pessimistic view is that the Supreme Court's refusal to recognize physician-assisted suicide as a fundamental right will needlessly prevent many terminally ill Americans from dying with dignity.

In *Washington v. Glucksberg*[9] and *Vacco v. Quill*,[10] the Supreme Court held that the right to physician-assisted suicide is neither a fundamental liberty interest protected by the Due Process Clause, nor a freedom protected by the Equal Protection Clause of the Fourteenth Amendment. According to the Court, a properly drafted ban on physician-assisted suicide is rationally related to legitimate government interests, and therefore passes constitutional muster. . . .

This Article argues that the right to determine the manner and method of one's own death should be protected as a fundamental right under the Ninth Amendment. . . . [This article] also provides recommendations for a model Dignity in Dying statute that would comply with the Ninth Amendment. . . .

Current Medical Practices

Physician-assisted suicide is a common practice in the United States. Physicians face increasing pressure to assist suffering patients end their lives. One of the most recent studies of current practices surveyed physicians treating AIDS victims in the San Francisco Bay area. Fifty-three percent of the physicians surveyed admitted to assisting patients with suicide.[11] A survey conducted by the New England Journal of Medicine revealed that one in five physicians prescribed medication with the intent to aid their patients' desire to terminate their suffering.

A 1996 Michigan survey questioned 1,119 physicians in those specialties most likely to encompass patients with terminal illnesses, and 998 adults within the general public. When asked whether physician-assisted suicide should be legalized, 56 percent of the physicians and 66 percent of the general public said yes. If physician assisted suicide were legalized, 35 percent of the physicians polled indicated that they might aid in a patient's suicide upon request. . . .

---

8. See Marilyn Webb, The Good Death 353 (1997).
9. 117 S. Ct. 2258 (1997).
10. 117 S. Ct. 2293 (1997).
11. See Marilyn Webb, The Good Death 386 (1997).

A Right to Die Under the Ninth Amendment

The right to die cries out for Ninth Amendment analysis. No right is as personal as the right to control one's own body. . . . Personal rights, whether the right to use contraception or control the time and nature of one's own death, are precisely the kind of rights which can and must be considered under the Ninth Amendment.

The key to identifying what rights are protected under the Ninth Amendment, is Justice Harlan's proposed "clear and direct harm to others" standard. The Ninth Amendment should protect the right to physician-assisted suicide because there is no clear and direct harm inflicted upon others when a terminal patient decides to end his suffering sooner with the assistance of a physician. . . .

. . . Ninth Amendment analysis . . . would vindicate the right of free persons in a democratic, compassionate, and humane society, to control their own bodies and avoid the agonies of a hard and painful death. Despite attempts to deny the right to die with a physician's humane assistance, terminal patients will continue to try to control how and when they die. . . .

Recommendations for a Model Right to Die Statute

The Oregon Death with Dignity Act provides the right to die only to Oregon residents who are diagnosed by a physician to be suffering from a terminal disease (defined as a disease which will cause death within six months) and who "voluntarily" express their wish to die.[12] Although this statute represents an admirable first step toward recognition of a right to die, there are several problems with the statute. . . .

Oregon's Death with Dignity Act should be viewed as a tentative first step on the road to full recognition of the right to die. If the right exists, then it can and should not depend upon a physician's unreviewed and arbitrary "guess" as to how long a patient has to live. Physician predictions of this sort are clearly unreliable since the amount of time a patient has to live is dependent on so many variable factors beyond the knowledge of the physician.

Thus the Oregon statute has two serious defects. First, it provides no judicial review of the doctor's opinion. Under such a statute, patients seeking the right will flock to a small group of doctors who gain a reputation for liberally predicting death within six months. Second, it removes the right to die from the person who seeks to exercise the right, and places it in the hands of another person. A true and fundamental right to die can and should not depend upon the actions of third parties. The person wishing to exercise the right should be the sole determiner of when to exercise the right. . . .

Leaving an individual clinician to determine a person's competence makes the right to die depend on unreviewed judgments or guesses of a third person. There is ample precedent for judicial review and oversight of a determination of competency. Competency is judicially determined in insanity commitments, will probates, and criminal cases. The competency of a criminal defendant is never left to the unreviewed discretion of a doctor or "clinician." The doctor may testify

---

12. Oregon Death with Dignity Act § 3.01, Or. Rev. Stat. § 127.815 (1997).

at the competency hearing, of course, as may another doctor who disagrees. The judge or jury, however, makes the final determination.

The same should be true for determining the competency of a person seeking to assert his right to die. The following procedure is submitted as a means of insuring that the right to die is fully recognized:

First, a person seeking to assert the right should have to file a petition with a court having jurisdiction in the place where the right is to be asserted. The person seeking the right to die should not have to provide a reason for asserting the right.

Second, an appropriate officer of the state should be entitled to file an answer to the petition, opposing the exercise of the petitioner's right to die on grounds that the petitioner is not competent to exercise the right. . . .

Third, a hearing before a judicial officer should be held to adjudicate the issue of competency. Whether the final decision should be by judge or jury should be decided by local law. . . .

Finally, upon a finding of competence, the court shall issue a document permitting petitioner to exercise the right to die, which document may be submitted to any licensed physician willing to assist the patient to assert his right.

APPENDIX A: SECTION 9

Causation

DISCUSSION MATERIALS

✳ DISCUSSION MATERIALS

Issue: Should Resulting Harm Be Relevant to Criminal Liability? Should a Completed Offense Be Punished More than an Unsuccessful Attempt?

Michael Moore responds to the problem of "moral luck" by arguing that it is not a problem at all, but only a symptom of a mistaken notion that there can only be responsibility if there is complete control. George Fletcher places the resulting-harm dispute in the context of what he calls the competing "traditionalist" and "modernist" approaches to criminal law. After refining Fletcher's distinction (and shifting to an "objectivist" and "subjectivist" terminology), Robinson explores why most jurisdictions adopt an objectivist view in assessing the significance of resulting harm and examines the Model Penal Code's inconsistencies in attempting to implement its stated preference for a subjectivist view.

Michael S. Moore, The Independent Moral Significance of Wrongdoing

5 Journal of Contemporary Legal Issues 237, 253-258 (1994)
Recasting the Problem of "Moral Luck"

Before we try to solve the problem of moral luck, perhaps we should first investigate whether we might dissolve it by showing that it is not a real problem at all. That there is a real problem here has been most influentially stated in contemporary philosophy by Tom Nagel:

> The problem develops out of the ordinary conditions of moral judgment. . . . It is intuitively plausible that people cannot be morally assessed . . . for what is due to factors beyond their control. . . . Without being able to explain exactly why, we feel that the appropriateness of moral assessment is easily undermined by the discovery that the act or attribute . . . is not under the person's control. . . . [A] clear absence of control, produced by involuntary movement, physical force, or ignorance of the circumstances, excuses what is done from moral judgment. But what we do depends in many more ways than these on what is not under our control. . . . And external influences in this broader range are not usually thought to excuse what is done from moral judgment. . . .

We do not control the normal wind pattern that carries our bullet without deviation into the brain of our intended victim, we do not control that a child did not stop at the last moment and so ran out in front of our speeding car, so it seems that our lack of control should vitiate any increased responsibility in such situations for the deaths that result from our intention or our recklessness/negligence. This is the problem of moral luck:

> Where a significant aspect of what someone does depends on factors beyond his control, yet we continue to treat him in that respect as an object of moral judgment, it can be called moral luck. . . . And the problem posed by this phenomenon . . . is that the broad range of external influences here identified seems on close examination to undermine moral assessment as surely as does the narrower range of familiar excusing conditions.

The problem of moral luck, as Nagel frames it, is how we can justify holding people more responsible for causing harm than for merely intending or risking harm when they lack that control (over whether the harm occurs or not) we generally require for responsibility.

Moral luck is good when an actor fails to cause the harm he has intended or risked, for the actor gets moral credit for something over which he lacked control; moral luck is bad when the actor does cause the harm he intended or risked, because he gets moral demerits for something over which he lacked control. Nagel's question is how such luck could be justified in the face of our control requirement for responsibility. . . .

We do have a criminal law doctrine that explicitly deals with the question of luck with regard to consequences. This is the doctrine of proximate causation. The proximate cause tests in criminal law have as their function the separation of harms in fact caused by a defendant's voluntary act into two camps: those freakishly so caused, in which event the actor is liable only for lesser crimes of attempt, specific intent, or risk-imposition; and those more normally so caused, in which event the actor is liable for the more serious punishments reserved for completed crimes. Sometimes these tests are explicit about their being tests of luck. The Model Penal Code, for example, provides that an act is the cause of a harm when the harm would not have happened but for the act, and [with complications here ignored] the "actual result is not too remote or accidental in its occurrence to have a just bearing on the actor's liability or on the gravity of his offense." Even when the proximate cause tests are not explicitly directed to this freakishness or luck question, they implicitly aim at just this factor. The foreseeability test of proximate causation, for example, seems to be aimed at an actor's culpability: could he have foreseen that such a harm would result from his action? In reality, given the well-known conundrum about specifying the details of the harm about which to ask foreseeability questions, what the test really asks is whether the "freakishness of the facts refuses to be drowned" or not. . . .

The notion of luck always involves some baseline of comparison. As the proximate cause tests of the criminal law use the notion, the baseline is the normal way things come about. When a defendant negligently operates a train too fast, so that he cannot stop it before it hits another's railroad car, there is no luck involved in his injuring the second car because that is how such things normally happen. When, however, the same negligently speeding defendant causes the same damage to the same car, but does so because the first collision (which does no damage) throws the defendant against the reverse throttle of his engine, thereby knocking him unconscious, whereupon his engine goes in reverse around a circular track, colliding with the other's car and then causing it damage, there is luck involved because of the abnormal conjunction of events taking place between defendant's act and the harm.

Moral luck on this concept of luck, would exist whenever the consequence of moral blame or credit is brought on one in an abnormal, freakish, or chance way. If one were truly to blame for someone else's actions over whom one had no control, for example, that would be a case of (bad) moral luck. But if one's blameworthiness only comes about in the normal, non-freakish, not-by-chance way, there is no moral luck involved in such blameworthiness, wherever it exists, even if there is luck involved.

The crucial question, of course, is to spell out when blameworthiness attaches in a normal, as opposed to an abnormal, way. Nagel thinks that this notion of normalcy is to be fleshed out with his idea of control: blameworthiness for a harm would attach in a normal way only if the agent was in control of all factors causally contributing to that harm. Yet this is surely not the notion of normalcy presupposed by the criminal law's notion of luck. And this last observation is not the observation that Nagel requires complete control (of all factors) while the criminal law and the morality that underlies it only requires control of some factors; rather, the observation is that the notion of control is alien to the criminal law's idea of luck. The baseline is freakishness of causal route, not degree of control by the agent of the intervening factors. . . . It is the normalcy of causal route that decides the normalcy of moral blameworthiness in such cases, ideas of normalcy to which control is simply irrelevant.

Of course, one might respond: "but the different notion of luck involved in the criminal law and in the morality that underlies it is just what Nagel is questioning." Yet where is Nagel's beachhead within that system of criminal law and the morality that underlies it from which to launch this question? . . . Nagel is simply proposing a different notion of luck than the one we employ in our everyday moral and legal assessments, and we are entitled to ask for justification of this conception revision. By our ordinary moral and legal notions, the freakishness or chance of the causal route does make a moral difference, but there is no moral luck involved in being more to blame for the non-freakish result of one's acts. Luck, in Nagel's sense that is dependent upon partial lack of control, is simply alien to this analysis.

Another way to see the same thing is to focus on Nagel's notion of control. Here Nagel sees clearly that he needs a beachhead (within our ordinary moral notions) from which to extend his idea of control:

> The condition of control does not suggest itself merely as a generalization from certain clear cases. It seems correct in the further cases to which it is extended beyond the original set. When we undermine moral assessment by considering new ways in which control is absent, we are not just discovering what would follow given the general hypothesis, but are actually being persuaded that in itself the absence of control is relevant in these cases too. The erosion of moral judgment emerges not as the obscure consequence of an over-simple theory, but as a natural consequence of the ordinary idea of moral assessment, when it is applied in view of a more complete and precise account of the facts.

Yet Nagel is surely wrong about his idea of control being built into our ordinary idea of moral assessment. When we proximately cause just the harm we intended to cause by our action, we have not lacked control as we use that phrase in ordinary moral assessments. The actor who lights the bushes in order to burn the forest, and whose act causes the burning of the forest without the intervention of any abnormal or freakish factors, is in control of that result, as we ordinarily use the word "control." Only would-be forest burners whose acts bring about the destruction of the forest in a chance or freakish way lack control in this sense, because their choices do not cause the harm. Nagel's stringent idea of control—where to control a result is to control all factors necessary to that result, even the normally occurring factors—finds no resonance in the ordinary notion of control, nor in the ordinary notion of moral assessment.

That, again, leaves Nagel having to argue for his notion of control as being morally correct, despite its not being an extension of our ordinary notion of responsibility. It is not obvious what such an argument would look like, since Nagel does not make it. My suspicion is that the only arguments available here are the same arguments as have been trotted out by incompatibilists on the free will issue for centuries. Incompatibilists have long sought to show that we must be in control over all factors that cause our choices in order for us to be responsible for both those choices and the wrongdoings such choices initiate. The question for incompatibilists has always been how they can support this demand for control, since it is not built into our ordinary notions of control. By our ordinary notions, we control our choices whenever such choices are not subject to threats or other coercion and when we have enough information to make them. There are no beachheads within our ordinary moral criteria for the incompatibilists' alien idea of control.

Nagel is in the same position as the more traditional incompatibilist about responsibility, except that in Nagel's case he wishes to import his alien notion of control into the causal chain that succeeds, rather than precedes, choice. Despite this last difference, Nagel needs exactly what the traditional incompatibilist needs, which is some reason supporting the importation of this requirement of control into the causal aetiology of wrongdoing. Neither Nagel nor the more traditional incompatibilist give us any such reason, because both of them think that this idea of control is already presupposed by our ordinary notions of moral assessment. Reject that claim, as I have in this section, and the "problem of moral luck" disappears—at least, as a problem of luck (in its ordinary sense) determining our moral deserts.

George P. Fletcher, A Crime of Self-Defense: Bernhard Goetz and the Law on Trial
64-67 (1988)

. . . Two conflicting schools of thought have emerged about the essential nature of criminal wrongdoing. A traditional approach emphasizes the victim's suffering and the actor's responsibility for bringing about irreversible damage. A modern approach to crime takes the act—the range of the actor's control over what happens—as the core of the crime. It is a matter of chance, the modernists say, whether a shot intended to kill actually hits its target. . . .

The traditionalists root their case in the way we feel about crime and suffering. Modernists hold to arguments of rational and meaningful punishment. Despite what we might feel, the modernist insists, reason demands that we limit the criminal law to those factors that are within the control of the actor. The occurrence of harm is beyond his control and therefore ought not to have weight in the definition of crime and fitting punishment. The tension between these conflicting schools infects virtually all of our decisions in designing a system of crime and punishment.

Historically, it is hard to deny the relevance of actual harm and suffering in our thinking about crime. The criminal law would never have come into being unless people actually harmed each other. Our thinking about sin and crime begins with a change in the natural order, a human act that leaves a stain on the world. The sin of Eden was not looking at the apple, not possessing it, but eating it. Oedipus's offense against the gods was not lusting, but actually fornicating with his mother. Cain's crime was not endangering Abel, but spilling his blood. The notions of sin and crime are rooted in the harms that humans inflict on each other.

The classical conception of retributive punishment, the *lex talionis*, reenacts the crime on the person of the offender. This is expressed metaphorically in the biblical injunction to take any eye for an eye, a tooth for a tooth, and life for a life. In *Discipline and Punish*, the philosopher Michel Foucault argues that classically, punishment symbolically *expiated* the crime by replicating on the body of the criminal the harm he inflicted on another. It is hard even to think about punishment without perceiving the relationship between the harm wrought by the criminal and the harm he suffers in return. . . .

This is not the way many or perhaps most policy makers think about crime in the modern world. Sometime in the last two or three centuries, our scientific thinking about crime began to shift from the harm done to the act that brings about the harm. The fortuitous connection between acts and their consequences did not trouble the great jurists of the past, but today, in the thinking of the moderns, a great divide separates the actor and his deed from the impact of his act on others. "There is many a slip 'twixt the cup and the lip." And all those slips, all those matters of chance, have undermined the unity we once felt between a homicidal act and the death of the victim.

The notions of risk, probability, and chance circumscribe the modern way of thinking about action and harm. Instead of seeing harm first and the action as the means for bringing about the harm, we are now inclined to see the action first and the harm as a contingent consequence of the action. And if we see the action first and the harm second, we invite the question, Why should we consider the harm at all . . . ? Many radical reformers hold that indeed the harm is totally irrelevant. If you shoot and miss, you should be punished as though you had killed someone. All that matter are the acts that you can control. And you cannot control the bullet after it leaves the barrel. Power may come from the barrel of a gun, as Chairman Mao said, but according to the modernists, you exhaust your power as soon as you fire the gun.

Modernists pride themselves on the rationality of their theory. If the purpose of punishment is *either* to punish wickedness *or* to influence and guide human behavior, the criminal law should limit its sights to conduct and circumstances within human control. There is nothing wicked about the way things fortuitously turn out. The actor's personal culpability is expressed in his actions—not in the accidents of nature that determine the consequences of his actions. And so far as the purpose of punishment is to set an example and deter future offenders, the only conduct that can be deterred is that within our control. The arguments of reason seem almost unbeatable.

The shift toward arresting and prosecuting those who merely attempt crimes reflects a practical concern as well. The legal system should arguably not only react to crimes already committed, but should intervene before the harm is done. The police should arrest the would-be offender before he has a chance to realize the harm his conduct bespeaks. Crimes should be defined and jail sentences inflicted not only to expiate previous wrongs and deter future offenders, but to prevent harm from occurring. This makes a good deal of sense in a world in which we try to manage the resources of government in order to maximize the welfare of all. This approach to punishment is typically called "preventive" as opposed to the traditional "retributive" practice of punishing past crimes, measure for measure.

The rationalists have held sway over English and American criminal law for most of the period since World War II. The prevailing view is that criminal law should serve social goals, rationally determined and efficiently pursued. Punishment should serve the goal of control either by rehabilitating offenders or, when we despair of changing criminals with doses of therapy, by deterring people in the future from choosing crime as a profitable career. The modern approach to crime dismisses as subrational the argument that people simply *feel* that actually killing someone is far worse than trying to kill. The Model Penal Code, a rationalist document that reflects the attitudes of reform-minded lawyers in the 1950s, goes so far as to recommend punishing attempted murder the same way we punish murder. Yet the concern for the suffering victims is too deep-seated to be rejected simply because the reformers have so limited a conception of fair and decent punishment.

We punish convicted criminals not only because as social planners we see a need to deter crime in the future, but because we recognize the irrepressible need of victims to restore their faith in themselves and in the society in which they live. The imperative to do justice requires that we heed the suffering of the victims, that we inquire at trial whether the defendant is responsible for that suffering, and we adjudge him guilty, if the facts warrant it, not for antiseptically violating the rules of the system, but for inflicting a wrong on the body and to the dignity of the victim. . . .

Whether the defendant actually causes the harm to the victim becomes, therefore, a pivotal question in every trial responding to the fact of suffering. . . .

Paul H. Robinson, The Role of Harm and Evil in Criminal Law: A Study in Legislative Deception?
5 Journal of Contemporary Legal Issues 304-322 (1994)

[The author argues that Fletcher oversimplifies when he portrays the disagreement as one between "traditionalists" and "modernists." The most common view of present codes and laypersons is to discount the significance of resulting harm in defining the minimum requirements of liability but to see it as highly relevant in issues of grading. To avoid confusion, the author suggests that use of the "objectivist" and "subjectivist" labels is preferable.]

Objectivist Versus Subjectivist View of Grading: The Arguments

Why do modern codes take what Fletcher calls the "traditionalist" (objectivist) view of harm and evil in grading? Why do they reject the modernist (subjectivist) view of grading? To set the stage for this discussion, let me review briefly the primary provisions that implement a subjectivist or objectivist view of grading. I will use the Model Penal Code as representative of the subjectivist view.

The most important provision is § 5.05(1), which grades all inchoate offenses the same as the grade of substantive offense, with the exception that the inchoate form of a first degree felony (e.g., murder) is graded as a second degree felony. Thus, an unsuccessful conspiracy to commit arson is the same grade offense as if the arson occurs. An uncompleted plan to rape is graded the same as if the rape occurs. A solicitation to illegally dump toxic chemicals is graded the same as if the chemicals were dumped.

Subjectivist grading also is employed in the Code's complicity provision, which stipulates that an actor is as an accomplice if he "aids or agrees or attempts to aid" in the commission of an offense.[1] Thus, an unfulfilled agreement or unsuccessful attempt to assist or encourage is graded the same as the substantive offense that does not materialize. The actor who agrees to stand watch for a perpetrator bent on arson is liable for arson even if he gets the date confused and does not show. In other words, inchoate complicity is punished not as inchoate liability but as full substantive liability.

---

1. Editor's Note—Complicity is the subject of Section 14.

Adhering to an objectivist view of grading, a majority of jurisdictions reduce the grade of inchoate conduct below that of the corresponding substantive offense. Similarly, many jurisdictions require actual assistance or encouragement for full complicity; an unsuccessful attempt at complicity can only be punished as an attempt. Where the actor takes steps to burn a building but another arsonist gets to it first, the actor is liable only for attempted arson, graded less than the substantive offense. Where the actor tries but fails to aid an arsonist, unbeknownst to the arsonist, and therefore has no causal connection with the offense harm or evil, his liability similarly is attempt liability, not substantive offense liability, and accordingly graded less. These objectivist views are adopted even by jurisdictions that otherwise are heavily influenced by the Model Penal Code and generally accept its subjectivist view of the minimum requirements of liability.

Why these differences in perspective on the significance of harm and evil in grading? The objectivist's preference for increasing liability where the actor causes or contributes to the actual occurrence of the offense harm or evil may be explained in part by a strong intuitive sense. . . . The community's shared intuitive sense that resulting harm and evil increases blameworthiness is confirmed by recent empirical studies. [The author reviews the studies.] Assume, then, that a strong community intuition exists for increasing punishment where harm or evil actually occurs and is attributable to the actor. Why precisely should the community intuition be of interest to drafters of the community's criminal code? Code drafters typically are guided by either retributivist or utilitarian considerations (or a combination of the two) in determining the rules for the distribution of liability and punishment. . . .

[The author reviews the arguments.]

To summarize, one can find both consequentialist and non-consequentialist arguments in support of giving significance to the occurrence of harm or evil in grading, but one also can find counterarguments of both sorts. If desert is the guiding principle, moral philosophers disagree over the significance of resulting harm or evil. If efficient crime prevention is the goal, the traditional arguments support the subjectivist view but more recent empirical data suggests there may be greater utility in following the community's sense of justice, which would take account of resulting harm and evil, the objectivist view.

Inconsistency in Application of the Subjective View of Grading

Given the arguments available to the subjectivist, one would expect to find a fairly consistent and complete execution of that view in the jurisdictions that adopt it. But no jurisdiction, even those that claim adherence to the principles of the subjectivist view of grading, is consistent or complete in its execution. The reasons for this failure are worth examining, but let me first demonstrate the inconsistencies and incompleteness, using the Model Penal Code again as an instructive subjectivist vehicle.

If the occurrence of the offense harm or evil should play no role in grading, one may wonder, for example, why the Code creates an exception for first degree felonies in grading inchoate offenses. If the arguments for grading inchoate conduct the same as the completed offense are sound, why should they not apply to first degree felonies as well? The Code's commentary offers a deterrent efficacy explanation:

> It is doubtful . . . that the threat of punishment for the inchoate crime
> can add significantly to the net deterrent efficacy of the sanction threatened

for the substantive offense that is the actor's object, which he, by hypothesis, ignores. Hence, there is a basis for economizing in use of the heaviest and most afflictive sanctions by removing them from the inchoate crimes. The sentencing provisions for second degree felonies, including the provision for extended terms, should certainly suffice to meet whatever danger is presented by the actor.

Thus, the drafters seem to concede that deterrence arguments in support of their policy are unpersuasive; dangerousness is the key. Whether the harm or evil actually occurs does not affect the actor's dangerousness.

But then one may wonder why the Code, like all other modern codes, distinguishes between offenses that differ only in that one punishes an actor when harm or evil occurs and the other punishes an actor, at a lower grade, when the harm or evil does not occur. Note, for example, the dramatic difference in grading between manslaughter and endangerment. The Model Penal Code grading is typical: the former is a second degree felony, the latter, a misdemeanor. Yet, the actor's conduct and culpability may be the same under the two offenses; the sole distinguishing variable is existence of a resulting harm or evil. Similarly, recklessly causing a catastrophe is a third degree felony, while the same recklessness where the catastrophe does not occur is punished as a misdemeanor. The deterrent-efficiency arguments that the drafters give to explain the exception for grading inchoate first degree felonies does not apply to any of these offenses; in each instance, the no-harm offense is punished only as a misdemeanor, a grade that may not "suffice to meet whatever danger is presented by the actor." Perhaps because the drafters do not see the apparent contradiction in their position, the commentary gives no explanation for why the occurrence of harm or evil should not be relevant in the general grading of inchoate conduct but should be relevant when two substantive offenses are defined and graded disparately to take account of the occurrence of harm or evil.

Other incongruities in the standard implementation of the subjective view are equally mystifying. Recall that, under the subjectivist view, an attempt or agreement to aid in an offense results in full substantive liability for the attempted complicity, not merely inchoate liability. This is consistent with the subjectivist view that an actor's liability ought to be based on the actor's own conduct and attendant state of mind, rather than on subsequent events over which the actor has no control, such as whether the attempt to aid is successful. Yet, the standard subjectivist complicity formulation also provides that an accomplice may not be liable for full substantive liability unless the perpetrator actually commits the offense. For example, Model Penal Code §2.06 provides that, while a perpetrator's defense does not redound to the benefit of the accomplice, as it would have at common law, an accomplice cannot be liable for the substantive offense except upon "proof of the commission of the offense." It is unclear what exactly this requires; presumably, at the least, the objective harm or evil of the offense must have occurred. Consistent with this, the Code explicitly provides that complicity in a perpetrator's failed attempt can only be punished as an attempt.

But one might ask, 'If causing the occurrence of the offense harm or evil is immaterial to the grading inquiry, why should it matter to an accomplice's liability whether the perpetrator does or does not actually commit the offense?' To echo the subjectivist argument in support of full substantive liability for inchoate assistance, the accomplice is no less dangerous (or blameworthy) simply because the perpetrator subsequently fails to commit the offense. The accomplice has shown a willingness to aid such an offense. Similarly, if the unsuccessful accomplice is to be held for full substantive liability, based solely upon his or her subjective culpability, why should not the successful accomplice (to the unsuccessful perpetrator) be held to the same result? Indeed, one could argue that the successful accomplice (to the unsuccessful perpetrator) has more clearly demonstrated his dangerousness, by carrying through with all of his complicit conduct, than the unsuccessful accomplice. If subjective culpability is to be the sole criterion, is it not wrong to distinguish the two cases? And, if a distinction is to be made, does not the standard formulation have it backwards based on a subjectivist perspective?

The obvious difference between unsuccessful complicity in a complete offense and successful complicity in an unsuccessful offense is that the harm or evil of the offense has occurred only in the former, which is the only one for which the supposedly subjectivist Code imposes full substantive liability. But the subjectivist can hardly rely on this difference, at least not without renouncing the subjectivist view in grading that the occurrence of harm and evil ought to be irrelevant.

The care taken to distinguish unsuccessful complicity in a complete offense from successful complicity in an unsuccessful offense is all the more peculiar when one remembers that attempt liability, in the latter case, will be punished at the same grade as the substantive offense, the liability in the former case. If the grading ultimately is the same, what is the point of having such a carefully structured distinction within criminal law doctrine?

To make the same point more broadly, one may ask, 'Why would the subjectivist in grading have result elements in any offense definition?' Result elements are found in a variety of offenses, including such offenses as felonious restraint, sexual assault, and arson. In each instance, where all elements of an offense are proven except the result element, an actor is liable for an attempt to commit the offense. Yet, after the doctrine carefully distinguishes the presence and absence of the prohibited result, by including the result as a requirement of the substantive offense's definition, it then imposes the same grade of liability for both the inchoate and the completed conduct! What is the point of the exercise? If the result element is to be ignored in answering the grading inquiry, why not define the offense without it? Why define offenses to include elements that are supposedly irrelevant to the liability inquiry?

Similar observations can be made with regard to the standard subjectivist treatment of offenses other than those with result elements. If the actual occurrence of the evil conduct is irrelevant, why define offenses to distinguish the substantive offense and the attempt? Why not define each offense as "an actor is liable for [the offense] if he does or attempts to do . . . ?" (What constitutes an "attempt" could be defined just as it is now.) The Code's careful segregation of inchoate offenses from complete offenses is, again, peculiar in light of its general policy to punish the attempt at the same grade as the substantive offense.

Illogical Inconsistencies or Useful Deception? . . .

The most plausible explanation is that subjectivist drafters sought to create the appearance of doctrine that takes account of the occurrence of harm and evil because only that would give the doctrine the moral credibility with the community that it needs, while in reality making the occurrence of harm or evil insignificant because that is what the subjectivist drafters believed better serves the goal of crime prevention.

This grand illusion theory suggests another explanation for the inchoate grading exception for first degree felonies: these offenses, such as murder and kidnapping with serious bodily injury, are the most serious offenses and a failure to grade inchoate conduct lower in these cases would create the greatest and most obvious disparity between the community's intuitive judgment and the legal rules. A similar explanation exists for the subjectivists' giving only inchoate liability for complicity in an unsuccessful offense: full liability for such complicity would be too obvious a deviation from the community's expectations.

The concern for preserving the appearance of a code that mirrors community intuitions is illuminated in several other provisions of modern codes. . . .

The drafters' desire for a code that seems to take account of the occurrence of harm and evil, while generally seeking to ignore the same, may well have been a clever strategy, given the arguments presented above concerning the importance of criminal law mirroring community notions of justice. To deviate too conspicuously or too greatly is to risk the law's moral credibility and the cooperation, acquiescence, and coercion to compliance that moral credibility perpetuates. The drafters have every reason, then, to want the code to seem to mirror the community's moral intuitions, especially on matters such as the occurrence of harm and evil for which the intuitions are nearly universal and strongly held.

. . . If the community comes to understand the deception, the system may well lose more credibility than if the code simply overtly deviated from community views. Further, the deception may make it difficult for subsequent reform measures to regenerate credibility for the system. Once deceived, the community understandably may be suspicious and cynical about even genuine reforms meant to make grading more credible. They may understandably ask, another calculated deception? . . .

To put a more admirable gloss on the subjectivist structuring of the Model Penal Code, one might speculate that such was an attempt to make the Code a useful model even if its position on the insignificance of resulting harm and evil were rejected. Perhaps the drafters knew that their view on harm and evil was not shared by most members of the community and that in the political process surrounding adoption of a criminal code it was likely that many jurisdictions would seek to deviate from the Model Code to make harm and evil matter. To maximize the chance that other valuable contributions of the Code would be adopted, the drafters may have thought it best to make it easy to alter the Code into a document that takes account of harm and evil. Thus, by defining distinct substantive and inchoate offenses, and equating their grade in a single provision, a jurisdiction could simply alter that inchoate grading provision if it rejected the Code's view of the insignificance of resulting harm and evil.

If this was the drafters' strategy, they should be congratulated for their political acumen. In the United States, three-quarters of the jurisdictions reject the notion of grading inchoate offenses the same as the completed offense. Nearly two-thirds of American jurisdictions have adopted codes that have been heavily influenced by the Model Penal Code, but less than 30% of these have adopted the Code's inchoate grading provision or something akin to. To the many jurisdictions that disagree with the Code on the significance of harm and evil, the drafters' use of the inchoate grading provision, rather than defining all offenses in their inchoate form, no doubt seems a blessing. They can reverse the Code's position simply by altering the relevant grading provisions. The remainder of the Code, with result elements intact, provides many useful advances over prior law in many important respects.

But even this strategy of the Model Penal Code drafters, if that is what it was, can be deceptive, if perhaps inadvertently so. While it may seem that dropping the inchoate grading provision will purge the Code of its disregard for harm and evil, the truth is that the Code's indifference to harm and evil is more pervasive. Recall, the example, that the Code's complicity provision requires only that the actor "aids *or agrees or attempts to aid*." If a jurisdiction rejects the subjectivist view of grading, it would want to delete the italicized language. Yet, of the States heavily influenced by the Model Penal Code that have dropped the Code's inchoate grading provision, more than a third have failed to drop the "agrees or attempts to aid" language from the complicity provision.

✳ ADVANCED MATERIALS RELATING TO CAUSATION

Notes on the Model Penal Code Causation Provision

The Model Penal Code drafters unfortunately confuse the drafting of the Code's causation provision. They clearly see the importance of the proximate cause requirement. Section 2.03(2)(b)&(3)(b) contains the language implementing it: the result must not be "too remote or accidental in its manner of occurrence to have a [just] bearing on the actor's liability or in the gravity of his offense." But under the structure of the section as drafted, the language has application only where culpability as to a result is being imputed to a defendant; it is not available as a "remoteness" defense!

One can speculate that the confusion comes from the apparent belief of the drafters that, in result element offenses, the prosecution must prove not only that the defendant had the required culpability as to causing the prohibited result but that the prosecution also must prove that the defendant had the required culpability as to the manner in which the result came about. But there is nothing in any of the Code's language to suggest such a demanding requirement.

But having assumed (incorrectly) that culpability as to manner of occurrence was required, one can see that the drafters were much concerned that this was a difficult and unwise burden to place on the prosecution and therefore created Section 2.03(2)(b)&(3)(b) to take away the burden. It imputes to the defendant culpability as to manner of occurrence of the result in most instances, as long as the defendant was culpable as to the result itself. Of course, having done that, they also needed to except from that imputation those cases of inadequate proximate cause—such as the falling piano hypothetical—and therefore added the proximate cause language that we see in Section 2.03(2)(b)&(3)(b).

They were attempting to solve a problem that did not in fact exist. Section 2.02(2) requires only proof of culpability as to the result element contained in the offense definition. The drafters could have and should have simply added a positive proximate cause requirement to Section 2.03(1), as in the following redraft:

Section 2.03. Causal Relationship Between Conduct and Result

(1) Conduct is the cause of a result if:

(a) the conduct is an antecedent but for which the result in question would not have occurred; and

(b) the result is not too remote or accidental in its occurrence to have a just bearing on the actor's liability or on the gravity of his offense; and

(c) the relationship between the conduct and result satisfies any additional causal requirements imposed by the Code or by the law defining the offense.

(2) Concurrent Causes. Where the conduct of two or more persons each causally contributes to a result and each alone would have been sufficient to cause the result, the requirement of Subsection (1) of this section is satisfied as to both persons.

Section 2.03A. Divergence Between Consequences Intended or Risked and Actual Consequences

(1) When culpability as to a particular consequence of a person's conduct is required by an offense definition and the consequence that actually occurs is not that designed, contemplated, or risked by the person, as the case may be, the required culpability nonetheless is established if the actual consequence differs from the consequence designed, contemplated, or risked only in the respect that:

(a) a different person or different property is injured or affected, or

(b) the consequence intended, contemplated, or risked was as or more serious or extensive an injury or harm than the actual consequence.

(2) "Consequence," as used in this Section, means a result element of an offense definition and the attendant circumstance elements that characterize the result.

Notes on Causation When Multiple Causes Are Present

Imputing co-criminal's causal conduct
"Combined effect" analysis
    Dangers of "combined effect"
Serial vs. intersecting causes
    Assessing serial dimension with proximate cause test
    Assessing accountability among intersecting causes
Necessary-cause test and simultaneous sufficient causes
    Necessary-cause test and intervening sufficient cause
    Accountability dependent on sufficiency of other cause

[The persons referred to are the characters in the "Manny the Master" (#40) Hypothetical Case in the main text.]

We may tend to think that the number of possible causes depends on the facts of the case. Where the actor shoots the victim in the head, we say the gunshot is the cause of death. In the more complicated case of Baylor's death in the "Manny the Master" hypothetical, we may say that the cause is either Manny's push or Baylor's curiosity or possibly both. Thus, more complicated cases like Baylor's seem to raise the issue of multiple causes. In fact, every result is necessarily the product of many causes, some acting immediately on and some acting long before the present result. The train was as necessary as Baylor's curiosity to bring about the death. If the local bar had not closed early, there would not have been as many people on the platform at the time, so Baylor would not have had to lean out as he did to see, so he would not have been hit. By closing early, then, the bar owner caused the death, in the but-for sense. Technically, every causation case is a multiple-cause case. It is accordingly crucial for the law to design rules to determine the causal accountability of one particular cause among multiple causes of a result. The proximate cause requirement is highly useful in this effort. The bar owner's conduct in closing early is clearly so remote from Baylor's death that it ought not be seen as a proximate cause. Importantly, the causation issue is distinct from the question of the bar owner's culpability: Even if the bar owner were a proximate cause, he does not have the required culpability. If he did have the required culpability—if he hoped that closing early somehow might cause Baylor's death—then he still cannot be liable for murder if his conduct is held not to be a proximate cause.

Imputing co-criminal's causal conduct   Legal doctrine sometimes avoids the problem of determining which of multiple causes is accountable for a result by treating the multiple causes as a single cause. This occurs most often where the two causes spring from accomplices or co-conspirators who are legally accountable for each other's conduct, as noted previously. In *Henderson v. State*, for example, the defendant father stabbed the deceased during a struggle. The son then shot and killed the victim.[2] The father might argue that, even if the stab wound was lethal, his conduct was not a but-for cause of the resulting death, because the victim would have died when he did from the gunshot even without the father's stab wound. However, if the father and son were accomplices, the court observes, the father is legally accountable for the conduct of the son, and it does not matter whether the father's conduct alone was a necessary cause.

"Combined effect" analysis   Some jurisdictions recognize a second kind of situation in which the conduct of two actors may be combined and treated as one. In *Henderson*, for example, the court concluded that, even if the father and son were not accomplices, their independent conduct ought to be treated as one causal force if the two forces combined in their effect. Thus, the father was to be held liable for the death if the stab wound that he inflicted had combined in effect with the gunshot by his son. If this doctrine were simply an application of the but-for test, it would be unobjectionable. That is, if the two causes were said to combine and were to be treated as one whenever neither alone would have been lethal, then each in fact is necessary for the result and therefore is a but-for cause.

Dangers of "combined effect"   Unfortunately, by thinking in terms of "combined effect," courts sometimes apply the doctrine too broadly. In *Henderson*, for example, if the father's stabbing of the victim were *not* necessary for the resulting

---

2. 65 So. 721, 722-723 (Ala. App. 1914).

death, then the father's conduct should not be taken to be a factual cause of the death even if its effect combined in some way with that of the son's shooting of the victim. Taking the "Manny the Master" hypothetical as an example, assume that Squeeze's poison had caused Baylor to become dizzy and thus made it even more likely that Manny would be successful in pushing Baylor in front of the train. If Baylor would have been killed at the same time even without the dizziness from Squeeze's poison, then Squeeze's conduct is not a but-for cause, even though a court might say that its effect combined with Manny's push. "Combined effect" analysis tends to be used by courts when it is unclear whether the defendant's cause was necessary for the result or was just a contributing but non-necessary factor. Would the son have successfully shot the victim even without the father's stabbing? Would Manny's push have made Baylor fall even without the dizziness from Squeeze's poison? These may be difficult factual questions for a jury to resolve. But if a necessary cause really is a requirement for establishing causation, then the state should have to prove this element beyond a reasonable doubt, as the state must prove every other offense element. To resort to "combined effect" analysis is to release the state from this burden and to substitute a lesser requirement of showing merely that the defendant's conduct contributed in some way to the result. On the other hand, in many cases, application of a combined-effect analysis seems entirely appropriate, as when two fires combine before causing the prohibited harm.

Serial vs. intersecting causes Multiple causes may interact with one another in any number of ways. The train, Manny's push, Baylor's curiosity, the early closing of the local bar, and many other circumstances came together at the moment before Baylor's death. Each represents an independent chain of events that intersects at that moment. And each of these intersecting chains of events has many links, a serial dimension in which each link has a causal connection with the links before and after. Kenny "The Hat" is a cause of Baylor's death, it might be said, by motivating Manny to do his pushing. Kenny's contract is not a cause independent of Manny's push in the same way that the train and Manny's push are independent. The contract stands in serial relation to Manny's push; the train intersects with the push. (There is nothing in the legal doctrine that requires this conceptualization of causation problems, but many people find it useful to think about the problem in this way.) In sorting out which causes will come within the realm of legal causal accountability, the doctrine must address two distinguishable questions. Which of the intersecting causal chains are eligible for causal accountability? And how far back along a causal chain, the serial dimension, should accountability extend?

Assessing serial dimension with proximate cause test The proximate cause test is the law's device for assessing the reach of accountability along the serial dimension. If Manny had successfully pushed Baylor in front of the train, his push clearly would be judged a proximate cause of the death. Kenny's contract, which motivated Manny, probably would be considered a sufficiently proximate cause as well. But the informant's report of the investigation, which motivated Kenny's contract, might be judged too remote to be a proximate cause, even if it were given with the intention that it would cause Kenny to have Baylor killed. The problem of serial causes is particularly troublesome when one of the links in the causal chain is another person.

Assessing accountability among intersecting causes   In addition to the issue of how far causal accountability travels down the chain of serial causes, the law must identify which among the many intersecting causal chains are eligible for being held accountable for the result. The law does this through the factual cause requirement, most commonly by using the necessary-cause test. Only those conditions that are necessary for the result are judged to be a factual cause of the result. The necessary-cause test is as clear and precise in application as the proximate cause test is judgmental and vague. Yet it generates a different sort of difficulty, as it tends to exclude from causal accountability at least two kinds of cases that some people think ought to be included: simultaneous sufficient causes (such as in *Jones*, below) and intervening sufficient causes (such as in *Wood*, below).

Necessary-cause test and simultaneous sufficient causes   In *Jones v. Commonwealth*, two actors simultaneously shot the deceased and inflicted similar chest wounds.[3] Either shot was itself sufficient to cause death; thus each actor can (correctly) claim that his conduct was not a necessary cause of the death. That is, each can claim that his shot did not satisfy the "but for" requirement, as the deceased would have died when he did (from the other actor's shot) even if that actor had not shot. Under a necessary-cause test, then, *both* actors would escape liability (for murder; as in most failure-of-causation situations, each may be liable for attempted murder). Most people find this result to be unacceptable. The court in *Jones* imposed liability despite the failure of the necessary-cause test. Most courts and legislatures appear to agree with this view. The escape from accountability permitted by the simultaneous-sufficient-cause flaw in the necessary-cause test sometimes is avoided through enactment of a special statutory provision.[4]

Necessary-cause test and intervening sufficient cause   There is less agreement, however, as to the impropriety of a second peculiarity in application of the necessary-cause test. In intervening-sufficient-cause cases, an actor's conduct may be sufficient to cause the prohibited result, yet the actor may nonetheless escape liability if a subsequent sufficient cause intervenes to cause the result earlier than it would otherwise have occurred. Recall from the "Manny the Master" hypothetical that this is the situation with Squeeze's poisoning of Baylor. While Baylor would have died from the poison within 45 minutes, he was killed by earlier events. Because Squeeze's poisoning was not necessary for the death by train, she will escape liability for the death. (Thus, if the death is judged too remote or accidental in relation to Manny's push, no one will be liable for Baylor's death.) Similarly, in *State v. Wood*, the defendant shot the deceased, inflicting a lethal wound. Before the deceased could die from the defendant's shot, however, he was killed by a subsequent lethal shot by another actor.[5] Because the defendant's earlier conduct was not necessary to cause the death, it did not satisfy the "but for" test, and the *Wood* court reversed the defendant's conviction on this ground.

Accountability dependent on sufficiency of other cause   The result in *Wood* is criticized by some, but is for the most part a popular view and one that most criminal codes would reflect. The criticism comes from the result's illustration of an effect of the necessary-cause test that in broad outline may seem unsettling:

---

3. 281 S.W.2d 920 (Ky. 1955).
4. See, e.g., Illinois Proposed Criminal Code § 203(2).
5. 53 Vt. 558 (1881).

An actor's liability depends not on the sufficiency of his own conduct to cause the result, but rather on *the sufficiency of the other cause(s)*. Indeed, it is this same effect that leads to the troubling result in *Jones*, the simultaneous-sufficient-cause case. The two tables below illustrate the application of the necessary-cause test for homicide in these two kinds of cases. Note that in each instance an actor's conduct will be accountable for the death if *the other cause* is non-lethal, and the actor will not be accountable if *the other cause* is lethal. This is true without regard to whether the actor's conduct is itself lethal or non-lethal. This effect—having an actor's accountability depend on the nature of another's conduct, not on his own conduct—may seem contrary to basic notions of accountability. On the other hand, to the extent that it reflects people's shared intuitions of justice, at least in the intervening-cause situation, there is good reason to adhere to it (as most jurisdictions do) if one seeks to promote the criminal law's moral credibility with the community it governs.

Table: Causal Accountability Of Actors A And B Under Necessary-Cause Test Where Simultaneous Causes Result In Homicide

		Cause B	
		Lethal	Non-Lethal
Cause A	Lethal	A: no causation B: no causation (the situation in Jones)	A: causation B: no causation
	Non-Lethal	A: no causation B: causation	A: causation* B: causation*

*For a death to occur in this situation, there must have been a combined effect of the two non-lethal causes.

Table: Causal Accountability Of Actor Under Necessary-Cause Test Where an Intervening Sufficient Cause Results in Homicide

		Intervening Cause	
		Lethal	*Non-Lethal*
Actor's (Prior) Cause	*Lethal*	no causation (the situation in *Wood*)	Causation
	Non-Lethal	no causation	Causation

Attempt Liability

✳ DISCUSSION MATERIALS

Issue: What Conduct Toward an Offense Should Be Sufficient to Constitute a Criminal Attempt?

The articles that follow urge different theories for determining the point at which one's conduct toward the commission of a crime becomes subject to criminal liability. The Model Penal Code Commentary compares the Code's proposed "substantial step" test to the other traditional tests, noting the benefits from its broadening of the scope of attempt liability. Andrew Ashworth compares the American and English approaches to attempt, posing the objectivist objections to England's subjectivist approach and concluding that although no test is precise, the "substantial step" test is the best available formulation.

Model Penal Code Section 5.01
Commentary General Distinction Between
Preparation and Attempt
Official Draft and Revised Comments 321, 329-330, 331 (1985)

It is clear . . . that . . . liability should extend beyond the cases where the defendant has engaged in the "last proximate act." If, as is generally assumed, every act done with intent to commit a crime is not to be made criminal, it becomes necessary to establish a means of inclusion and exclusion. The formulation of a general standard for that purpose in Subsection (1)(c) [the substantial-step provision] presents the most difficult problem in defining criminal attempt. . . .

(a) Requirements of "Substantial Step" and Corroboration of Purpose. Whether a particular act is a substantial step is obviously a matter of degree. To this extent, the Code retains the element of imprecision found in most of the other approaches to the preparation-attempt problem. There are, however, several differences to be noted:

First, this formulation shifts the emphasis from what remains to be done, the chief concern of the proximity tests, to what the actor has already done. That further major steps must be taken before the crime can be completed does not preclude a finding that the steps already undertaken are substantial. It is expected, in the normal case, that this approach will broaden the scope of attempt liability.

Second, although it is intended that the requirement of a substantial step will result in the imposition of attempt liability only in those instances in which some firmness of criminal purpose is shown, no finding is required as to whether the actor would probably have desisted prior to completing the crime. Potentially the probable desistance test could reach very early steps toward crime, depending on how one assesses the probabilities of desistance; but since in practice this test follows closely the proximity approaches, rejection of a test of probable desistance will not narrow the scope of attempt liability.

Finally, the requirement of proving a substantial step generally will prove less of a hurdle for the prosecution than the res ipsa loquitur approach, which requires that the actor's conduct itself have manifested the criminal purpose. The basic rationale of the requirement that the actor's conduct shall strongly corroborate his purpose to commit a crime is, of course, the same as that underlying the res ipsa loquitur view. But framed in terms of corroboration, the present formulation does not so narrowly circumscribe the scope of attempt liability. Rigorously applied, the res ipsa loquitur doctrine would provide immunity in many instances in which the actor had gone far toward the commission of an offense and had strongly indicated a criminal purpose.. . .

Under the Model Code formulation, the two purposes to be served by the res ipsa loquitur test are, to a large extent, treated separately. Firmness of criminal purpose is intended to be shown by requiring a substantial step, while problems of proof are dealt with by the requirement of corroboration—although under the reasoning previously expressed the latter will also tend to establish firmness of purpose.

In addition to assuring firmness of purpose, the requirement of a substantial step will remove very remote preparatory acts from the ambit of attempt liability and the relatively stringent sanctions imposed for attempts. On the other hand, by broadening liability to the extent suggested, apprehension of dangerous persons will be facilitated and law enforcement officials and others will be able to stop the criminal effort at an earlier stage, thereby minimizing the risk of substantive harm, but without providing immunity for the offender.

A number of recent [criminal code] revisions have adopted the substantial step formula, some including the requirement that the actor's conduct strongly corroborate his criminal purpose.. . .

Andrew Ashworth, Criminal Attempts and the Role of Resulting Harm under the Code, and in the Common Law
19 Rutgers Law Journal 725, 750-753 (1988)

The Conduct Element in Attempts

The English Court of Criminal Appeal has said that, if a person is charged with an attempt, "the intent becomes the principal ingredient of the crime." On the fully subjective principle . . . the paramountcy of the mens rea is assured. Does this dispense entirely with the need for proof of some conduct which might be described as an actus reus? Even in its most virulent form the fully subjective principle would not lead to this result: the theory turns on a "trying," which goes beyond a mere intention and requires some effort to put it into effect. Yet this is only a minimal actus reus, which might be satisfied by the doing of any overt act with the necessary intention. Those who might be described as "objectivists" in relation to the law of attempts would criticize this approach on two grounds: first, it would give too much power to law enforcement agents and would thus leave individuals vulnerable; second, it would leave insufficient room for an individual voluntarily to renounce a criminal endeavor.

The first objection is a qualifying principle which derives from a concern for individual rights and freedom from interference. One of the justifications for having a law of inchoate crimes. . .is to enable the police to intervene so as to prevent criminal activity before any harm is caused. But this police power should not be allowed to encroach upon individual rights and liberties. The English Law Commission referred to a need "to strike a balance in this context between individual freedom and the countervailing interests of the community" in other words, the justifications for penalising attempts must be tempered by considerations of individual liberty. If any overt act were to suffice as the actus reus, wrongful arrests might be more numerous; the police might be tempted to exert pressure in order to obtain a confession, since the mental element would be the overriding concern; miscarriages of justice might increase. The law should protect an individual's right not to be subjected to such treatment. Since an "overt act" test might in practice increase the risk of violation of that right, there is a strong argument for moving the actus reus somewhat further towards the substantive offence. The second objection is that, the earlier in the chain of events the actus reus of an attempt is placed, the less opportunity there is for the individual to change his mind before incurring criminal liability. This is particularly relevant to English law, which refuses to recognize any defense of abandonment and leaves its significance entirely to the courts' discretion when sentencing. It is perhaps less relevant when, as in the Model Penal Code, a defence of voluntary abandonment is available—partly on the reasoning that the voluntary renunciation negatives the inference of dangerousness and partly as an incentive to an attempter to desist even at the last moment.

Both these objections turn, to some extent, on judgements of degree which are also relevant in assessing other conceptions of the actus reus of an attempt. The "last act" or "final state" test might be thought to go too far in the direction of protecting the interests of would-be offenders. The English Law Commission rejected this approach, and rightly so. It would certainly maximize the defendant's opportunity to change his mind and abandon the attempt. However, if a defendant might exculpate himself from a charge of attempt by showing that he had not done the last act necessary to commit the crime, this would substantially reduce the preventive efficacy of the offence and would make it difficult for the police to intervene so as to forestall any harm.

A Working Party of the law Commission has earlier favored the concept of a "substantial step," following the Model Penal Code. In its final report, the Law Commission itself rejected the "substantial step" test for three reasons: first, they thought that it would be too imprecise; second, they disagreed with the Working Party's proposal that it should be for the judge to rule on whether certain conduct might amount to a substantial step; third, they believed that the test might extend the law of attempts so as to comprehend some acts of preparation. The Law Commission concluded that "the first element in a statutory test of proximity should be the drawing of the distinction between acts of preparation and acts which are sufficiently proximate to the offence." Their proposed test kept close to this rationale, and it is the test now embodied in Section 1 of the Criminal Attempts Act, 1981: ". . .an act which is more than merely preparatory to the commission of the offence." Yet, the first criticism which the Law Commission made against the "substantial step" test seems to have some application to the new test. Is it not an imprecise test, particularly if it is left for juries to determine in individual cases? Moreover, if the protection of individual rights and the confining of police discretion are regarded as important goals, does not its imprecision count against the test?

The fully subjective principle would be satisfied by the "overt act" test, but the objectivists are right to draw attention to the probable practical consequences of moving the threshold of criminal liability so far away from the last act in an attempt. It would be unworkable to require that the act should be unequivocally referable to the defendant's intent before liability for an attempt is established. Therefore, in order to strike an acceptable balance, there must be concrete discussion of specific examples based on experience of administering the law. The "substantial step" test classifies as an attempt certain forms of conduct which the new English test, "more than merely preparatory," is designed to exclude from the law of attempts. The American Law Institute, in proposing the "substantial step" test for the Model Penal Code, adopts the view that conduct such as reconnoitering and possession of incriminating equipment should amount to a criminal attempt (so long as they are strongly corroborative of the actor's criminal purpose); the English Law Commission disagreed, and believed that their new test would exclude these cases. Neither test is precise. And Sheriff Gordon's strictures on the Scots' distinction between preparation and perpetration might be applied to the English test:

It has one inestimable advantage as a working authority, and that is its vagueness. It offers an impressive-sounding and apparently precise rationalization for doing justice in any particular case: if the jury think the accused should be punished for what he did they will characterize what he did as [more than merely preparatory]; if they do not, they will characterize it as [mere] preparation. What was a question of law related to how restricted the scope of the criminal law should be, becomes a value-judgment related to the jury's assessment of blameworthiness.

Tests of this kind are unduly vague, and purchase flexibility at much too high a cost in terms of insufficient guidance to the police and to courts and, therefore, inconsistences in the administration of justice.

In order to achieve a solution which maximizes both certainty and flexibility, it is necessary to seek a formulation which combines several specific examples with a generalized test. The illustrative and authoritative examples of the Model Penal Code follow this approach, and, since maximum certainty is one aim, it would be preferable to use legislation of this purpose rather than awaiting the gradual development of judicial authority. The courts would retain the important role of interpreting and applying the generalized test. The legislative scheme should be such as to make it proper to argue by analogy from the illustrative examples when interpreting the test. In choosing between the Model Penal Code's "substantial step" test and the "more than merely preparatory" test, the English Law Commission argues that the former was wider and unduly so, whereas the natural meaning of the two tests does not suggest any such simple division. My own preference remains with the "substantial step" test, with the insistence that neither test meets the requirements of a modern system of criminal law if it is not supported by authoritative examples.

✳ ADVANCED MATERIALS

Notes on the Culpability Requirements and Defenses for Attempt Liability

Elevation as to Result Elements; Code Commentary Says Purpose Is Needed
    Exception for completed conduct: Elevate only to "knowing"
    Critique of exception's limitation to completed attempts
    Case for expanding exception to include incomplete attempts
    Case for removing any elevation as to result element
    Cannot accidentally attempt, but can attempt to cause an "accident"
Summary of Attempt Requirements Table
Attempt Defenses
Renunciation
    No renunciation defense for completed offense
    Common Law also provided no such defense for inchoate crimes
    Absent defense, modern attempt rules would offer little incentive to stop
    Desert-based rationale for defense
    Renunciation must be "complete and voluntary"
    Where attempt is complete, less reason to provide defense
        Model Penal Code allows defense for some completed attempts
        Code's position reflects deterrence, rather than desert, orientation

Requirement that renunciation must prevent offense's occurrence
Rule (again) suggests harm-prevention, rather than desert, rationale
Termination of Complicity
Prior to principal's completion of crime, complicity is essentially inchoate
Termination need not prevent crime or be "complete and voluntary"
Termination, unlike renunciation, is not a full defense

ELEVATION AS TO RESULT ELEMENTS; CODE COMMENTARY SAYS PURPOSE IS NEEDED

The modern treatment of culpability as to a result is less clear. The Model Penal Code's commentary explains that it generally seeks to follow the common law rule for attempt, elevating the culpability required as to a result element. "The general principle is . . . that the actor must affirmatively desire . . . to cause the result that will constitute the principal offense."[1] This is said to follow from the common law's rule that attempt is a specific-intent offense. In this respect, the Code's drafters appear to adopt the broad interpretation of section 5.01(1)'s "purpose" language, discussed above. The drafters fear that punishing cases where an actor recklessly or negligently disregards a possible result, but where the result does not occur, would unduly extend criminal liability. (This type of risk-creating conduct, such as recklessly creating a risk of death, is covered by the distinct substantive offense of reckless endangerment.[2] But then an issue arises as to the availability of—and the culpability required for—liability for attempted endangerment, where the actor attempts but fails to create the risk.) Thus, the drafters apparently wish the purpose and knowing requirements in the subsections to 5.01(1) to be interpreted as applying not only to the offense conduct, but also to any result element of the offense (though not to any circumstance elements). The statute's explicit language offers little to suggest such an intermediate reading between the narrow and broad interpretations; it gives no indication that the "purposely" requirement applies to result elements, while only the "acting with the culpability otherwise required" language governs circumstance elements.

Exception for completed conduct: Elevate only to "knowing" The Code creates an exception to its usual requirement of purpose as to a result. For completed attempts—where the actor performs all conduct needed to cause the result, yet the result does not occur—section 5.01(1)(b) requires only a "belief" (knowing) as to the result:

> [W]hen causing a particular result is an element of the crime, [the actor is liable if he] does or omits to do anything with the purpose of causing or with the belief that it will cause such result without further conduct on his part.[3]

Such a rule is justified, in the drafters' view, because:

> the manifestation of the actor's dangerousness is just as great—or very nearly as great—as in the case of purposive conduct. In both instances a deliberate

---

1. Model Penal Code § 5.01 comment at 301 (1985).
2. Model Penal Code § 5.01 comment at 303-04 (1985).
3. Model Penal Code § 5.01(1)(b) (emphasis added). The Code's commentary notes:

Thus when the charge is attempted murder or assault with intent to kill, it is error to permit conviction on a finding of reckless disregard for human life or intent to inflict grievous bodily harm.

Model Penal Code § 5.01 comment at 306-307 (1985).

is made to bring about the consequence forbidden by the criminal laws,
e actor has done all within his power to cause this result to occur.[4]

have reached the same conclusion, including a number of cases hold-
nmon law's specific-intent requirement to be satisfied by a belief that
vill occur.[5] English law no longer requires a desire to cause the result
but only a belief that the conduct will cause the result.[6] Under this
however, recklessness as to a result remains inadequate for attempt
liability, even if it would be adequate for the substantive offense.

Critique of exception's limitation to completed attempts This exception to the purpose requirement—allowing liability for knowledge as to a result—
applies only where the actor has completed all of the offense conduct. The actor
who sets the bomb knowing it will kill persons in the building, but not wanting
to kill such persons, will be liable for attempted murder if the bomb malfunctions
and does not explode. But if the bomb is fully functional and the actor is caught a
moment before flipping the switch, he cannot be held liable for attempted murder
under the Code. Because his attempt is incomplete, he will fall under the purpose
requirement of subsection $5.01(1)(c)$ rather than the belief requirement of subsection $5.01(1)(b)$. One may wonder whether the Code is wise to allow knowledge of a result to suffice for liability only for completed attempts. It is unclear
why the bomber should have no liability for attempted murder because the police
are lucky enough to stop him a moment before he is finished setting the bomb.

Case for expanding exception to include incomplete attempts One
might also argue that the larger difficulty with the Code's formulation is that it
elevates culpability as to a result at all. A handful of American statutory attempt
formulations drop the Model Penal Code's purpose or belief language altogether,
leaving only the requirement that the actor be "acting with the kind of culpability
otherwise required for commission of the offense."[7] Colorado has such a statute,
and has interpreted it to require intent only as to the actor's planned future conduct, but not as to circumstance or result elements:

> [I]n order to be guilty of criminal attempt, the actor must act with the kind
> of culpability otherwise required for commission of the underlying offense
> and must engage in the conduct which constitutes the substantial step with
> the further intent to perform acts which, if completed, would constitute the
> underlying offense.[8]

This approach allows liability not only based on knowledge as to a result, but also
recklessness or potentially even negligence, if that is all the completed offense
requires. Indeed, Colorado explicitly recognizes the offense of "attempted reckless manslaughter":

> Attempted reckless manslaughter requires that the accused have the intent to
> commit the underlying offense of reckless manslaughter. The "intent to com-
> mit the underlying offense" of which People v. Frysig [quoted above] speaks
> is the intent to engage in and complete the risk-producing act or conduct. It

---

4. Model Penal Code § 5.01 comment at 305 (1985).

5. See, e.g., State v. Krovarz, 697 P.2d 378, 380, 382 (Colo. 1985) (noting that relevant attempt
standard required intent, but concluding that "a knowing attempt to attain a proscribed result is a sufficient
culpable mental state to justify imposition by the legislature of attempt liability").

6. See Andrew Ashworth, Principles of Criminal Law 445 n.7 (2d ed. 1995).

7. Ind. Code Ann. § 35-41-5-1(a).

8. People v. Frysig, 628 P.2d 1004, 1010 (Colo. 1981).

does not include an intent that death occur even though the underlying crime, reckless manslaughter, has death as an essential element.[9]

Similarly, under this approach, an actor could presumably also be charged with attempted reckless endangerment where he did not create the risk of injury or death required for the offense. (The Model Penal Code's formulation of the endangerment offense actually reaches the same result; it requires only conduct that "places or may place" another person in danger, and thus does not require actual risk creation.[10] One may wonder, then, why the drafters think the absence of risk creation should trigger elevated culpability under the attempt offense.) Thus, an actor caught as he is about to dump toxic chemicals next to a school yard, aware that they might cause the death of one or more of the school children, could be held liable for attempted reckless endangerment because he purposely engages in conduct while knowing, or reckless that, it creates a risk of death.

Cannot accidentally attempt, but can attempt to cause an "accident" The drafters defend the Code's position by arguing that a general rule punishing reckless or negligent conduct that does not create or risk harm would be unduly broad.[11] However, while it is true that there should not be such a thing as an "accidental attempt," in the sense that attempt liability should not apply where the actor's conduct was unintentional, there nonetheless may be sound reasons to punish the attempt to cause an "accident," that is, an intentional act (or planned act) that would culpably risk an "accident" (in the sense of an unintended harm). The law has good reason to require the intent to engage in the conduct constituting the offense, but there seems little reason that attempts to create risks of harm ought not be punished.

Summary of Attempt Requirements Table

The requirements of attempt liability may be summarized as follows:

Summary of Requirements for Attempt Liability

Objective Requirements	Culpability Requirements
CONDUCT conduct constituting substantive offense not required; instead offense requires: CL: proximity / *res ipsa* tests MPC: substantial-step test	CONDUCT culpability as to conduct constituting substantive offense: CL and MPC: purpose
CIRCUMSTANCES CL: circumstance elements of substantive offense required (legal impossibility is a defense) MPC: circumstance elements of substantive offense not required (legal impossibility is not a defense)	CIRCUMSTANCES CL: elevate to require purpose as to circumstances MPC: as required by substantive offense; do not elevate (per commentary)
RESULT CL and MPC: result elements of substantive offense, if any, not required (nor is factual impossibility of it occurring a defense)	RESULT CL: elevate to require purpose as to result MPC: elevate to require purpose, but only to knowledge for completed conduct attempt

MPC = Model Penal Code
CL = Common Law

---

9. People v. Thomas, 729 P.2d 972, 974 (Colo. 1986).
10. Model Penal Code § 211.2.
11. See Model Penal Code § 5.01 comment at 303-305 (1985).

ATTEMPT DEFENSES

Where an actor engages in some efforts toward a criminal offense, but stops short and seeks to desist before the offense is completed, three sorts of claims may be available for her to avoid or mitigate criminal liability. The first is a claim of renunciation. After a conspiracy has formed, or preparation has progressed to the point of constituting a criminal attempt, one or all of the actors may renounce the criminal project so that the completed crime never occurs. A successful renunciation claim generates a complete defense, even for the inchoate crime already committed. The second type of claim, discussed earlier, is specific to conspiracy and is known as withdrawal or abandonment. Where one member of a conspiracy abandons prior to its completion of the target crime, she may avoid liability for the completed offense if the remaining group members proceed to carry it out, and she may also avoid the collateral consequences that flow from being a member of a conspiracy, but she will not obtain a full defense—her inchoate conspiracy liability will remain. The third type of claim, termination, arises for potential accomplices seeking to back out before the offense's commission. As with withdrawal and abandonment, successful termination will provide a defense to accomplice liability for the substantive offense, but not (necessarily) to inchoate liability. (Unfortunately, courts and legislatures are not always careful to distinguish these concepts, and sometimes use the terms "abandonment" and "withdrawal," as well as or instead of "renunciation" and "termination," to refer to the rules discussed in this section.)

RENUNCIATION

No renunciation defense for completed offense   If you steal a classmate's notes, suffer an attack of conscience, and return them before your classmate is injured by (or even knows of) their absence, you nonetheless are liable for theft. Generally, once the elements of a substantive offense are satisfied, the offense cannot be "undone."

Common Law also provided no such defense for inchoate crimes   The common law, and some current codes, take the same view toward inchoate offenses: The offense is complete, and irrevocable, the moment the actor satisfies its elements.[12] The common law's proximity test for attempt, under which attempt liability did not attach until the offense was nearly complete, greatly reduced the need for a renunciation defense to encourage potential offenders to stop short of the offense. Most actors who stopped before completing their efforts would not yet be subject to attempt liability, and would therefore need no defense. Even after the point where conduct becomes a criminal attempt, the actor would still have an incentive to stop before completion, because the completed offense typically would be subject to much greater liability than an

---

12. See, e.g., Blaylock v. State, 598 P.2d 251 (Okla. Crim. App. 1979) (because defendant met with undercover agents posing as hitmen to plan death of colleague, defendant guilty of conspiracy, even though plan not carried out).

inchoate offense. By stopping, the actor might not be able to avoid all liability, but could limit it.

Absent defense, modern attempt rules would offer little incentive to stop Modern formulations of, and grading schemes for, attempt (and other inchoate offenses) provide much less incentive to stop one's efforts after inchoate liability attaches. For example, the Model Penal Code generally grades inchoate offenses the same as the completed offense,[13] so that once an actor's conduct has become a criminal attempt, following through to complete the crime will not increase the liability he faces. In addition, the Code moves the point at which conduct becomes criminal to an earlier point in the process, requiring only a "substantial step" toward the crime instead of conduct very close to completion.[14] The combination of these rules means that minor conduct toward a crime will generate liability equal to that for the completed offense—thereby creating a situation in which most attempters and conspirators have little incentive to discontinue their efforts. Because of this, it becomes imperative for the Code to offer a renunciation defense to provide such an incentive to desist.

Desert-based rationale for defense If providing an incentive to stop were the only rationale for the defense, perhaps a mitigation, rather than a complete defense, would be adequate. Retaining some liability might be useful because one who tries to commit a crime, but then renounces, might nonetheless be dangerous. Yet a complete defense for renunciation may also find support on desert grounds. Recall that the desert-based rationale for punishing inchoate offenses relies on the actor's demonstrated willingness to commit the substantive offense, which shows the actor to be blameworthy. Where an actor voluntarily and completely renounces before committing the offense, any initial presumption about the actor's willingness to commit the offense has been undercut and the grounds for blameworthiness have been undermined. (The common law's stricter conduct test for attempt reflected, in part, a concern that the actor must have a locus penitentiae, or opportunity to repent of his criminal intention, before liability would be appropriate.[15])

Renunciation must be "complete and voluntary" This desert-based rationale justifies a renunciation defense, however, only in cases where the actor's sole reason for renouncing is that his intention is not (and quite possibly never was) sufficiently resolute. The rationale would not support a defense where the actor stops because of, say, changed conditions or new information making the offense look more difficult or less profitable than initially supposed. Accordingly, under this view, it makes sense to limit the defense to situations involving what the Model Penal Code calls "complete and voluntary" renunciation:

> Within the meaning of this Article, renunciation of criminal purpose is not voluntary if it is motivated, in whole or in part, by circumstances, not present or apparent at the inception of the actor's course of conduct, which increase

---

13. Model Penal Code § 5.05(1).

14. Model Penal Code § 5.01(1)(c).

15. See, e.g., Commonwealth v. Peaslee, 59 N.E. 55, 56, (Mass. 1901); see generally R.A. Duff, Criminal Attempts 35-38 (1996).

the probability of detection or apprehension or which make more difficult the accomplishment of the criminal purpose. Renunciation is not complete if it is motivated by a decision to postpone the criminal conduct until a more advantageous time or to transfer the criminal effort to another but similar objective or victim.[16]

Where attempt is complete, less reason to provide defense   The desert-based rationale for the defense does not apply in cases of completed attempts— where all the conduct has been performed, but the offense does not occur because a circumstance or result is absent—for in such cases, the actor has fully demonstrated her willingness to commit the offense. Nor does the concern with providing an incentive to stop before completing the offense apply in such cases. Thus, the Model Penal Code excludes a renunciation defense for some completed attempts by making the defense unavailable for attempts under section 5.01(1)(a), which covers impossible attempts: cases where the actor has engaged in conduct "which would constitute the crime if the attendant circumstances were as he believes them to be."

Model Penal Code allows defense for some completed attempts   Yet the Code allows a renunciation defense for attempt prosecutions under section 5.01(1)(b), which also covers a group of completed attempts: cases where the actor believes that his or her conduct will cause a required result (will cause death, in a homicide offense, for example) "without further conduct on his part." As with impossible attempts under subsection (1)(a), attempts under subsection (1)(b) involve actors who have shown their willingness to commit the offense and, indeed, think they have already done enough to commit the offense. The Code permits a defense in the latter cases, despite the actor's demonstrated willingness to commit the offense, in an effort to provide an incentive for the actor to prevent the harmful result that has not yet occurred.[17] Where the harm remains a threat and can yet be avoided, the incentive may be useful. (In the impossibility cases that subsection (1)(a) addresses, of course, the offense never can occur, so the incentive has no practical value.)

Code's position reflects deterrence, rather than desert, orientation   This may offer another illustration of the Code's underlying orientation toward utilitarian ends. Allowing a renunciation defense for completed attempts suggests that the central motivation behind the defense is deterrence, rather than punishing moral blameworthiness. A code focusing on desert would deny the defense where the actor has fully demonstrated his willingness to commit the offense. As with a completed offense, efforts to "undo" a completed attempt after the fact might

---

16. Model Penal Code § 5.01(4).

17. Indeed, the Code's commentary asserts that the incentive-to-prevent rationale is strongest here:

[One] reason for allowing renunciation of criminal purpose as a defense to an attempt charge is to provide actors with a motive for desisting from their criminal designs, thereby diminishing the risk that the substantive crime will be committed. While under the proposed subsection such encouragement is held out at all stages of the criminal effort, its significance becomes greatest as the actor nears his criminal objective and the risk that the crime will be completed is correspondingly high. At the very point where abandonment least influences a judgment as to the dangerousness of the actor—where the last proximate act has been committed but the resulting crime can still be avoided—the inducement to desist stemming from the abandonment defense achieves its greatest value.

Model Penal Code § 5.01 comment at 359 (1985).

merit consideration at sentencing, but would not obviate the actor's liability for her past violation.

Requirement that renunciation must prevent offense's occurrence   The Code demands not only that the actor must "completely and voluntarily" renounce his criminal efforts, but also that he must prevent the offense from happening.[18] The attempter must abandon his attempt "or otherwise prevent its commission."[19] The renouncing conspirator must "thwart the success of the conspiracy."[20] The renouncing solicitor must "persuade [the perpetrator] not to [commit the offense] or otherwise prevent commission of the crime."[21]

Rule (again) suggests harm-prevention, rather than desert, rationale   The prevention requirement again illustrates the Code's use of the renunciation defense primarily as a device to prevent criminal harms, rather than to exculpate actors who lack an adequately resolute intent. If the defense's rationale rested on the desert-based claim that renunciation rebuts an earlier appearance of blameworthiness, a complete and voluntary renunciation alone would be adequate for the defense. One might require proper effort to prevent the offense, which would confirm that the actor has truly repudiated the offense plan. But requiring actual prevention of the offense, no matter how heroic the effort to prevent, allows liability for an actor who truly has renounced but who, because of the particular circumstances, does not or cannot stop the crime from happening. For completed attempts, as noted above, the Code's renunciation rule denies liability for some cases where a desert rationale would allow it; here, it allows liability for some cases where a desert rationale would deny it. These variations from a desert-based distribution again indicate that the Code's subjectivist orientation is based primarily on a utilitarian rationale, rather than a blameworthiness rationale.

Termination of Complicity

As discussed in the previous section, the Model Penal Code's renunciation defense to inchoate liability requires actual prevention of the offense. Yet the Code's termination defense to complicity does not require actual prevention. Where a potential accomplice seeks to back out of his or her participation in the crime, the Code provides a defense if:

> he terminates his complicity prior to the commission of the offense and
> > (i) wholly deprives [his complicity] of effectiveness in the commission of the offense; or
> > (ii) gives timely warning to the law enforcement authorities or otherwise makes proper effort to prevent the commission of the offense.[22]

Even if the offense does occur after the accomplice's termination, the accomplice obtains a defense so long as he takes out what he put into the offense, or makes "proper effort" to prevent commission.

Prior to principal's completion of crime, complicity is essentially inchoate   Complicity can generate full substantive liability for the offense. As noted

---

18. See Model Penal Code §§ 5.02(3), 5.03(6).
19. Model Penal Code § 5.01(4) (tense changed).
20. Model Penal Code § 5.03(6) (tense changed).
21. Model Penal Code § 5.02(3) (tense changed).
22. Model Penal Code § 2.06(6)(c) (emphasis added).

earlier in this chapter, the usual rule holds that a substantive offense cannot be undone once completed; a renunciation defense exists, if at all, for inchoate crimes only. Why, then, should there be a termination defense to complicity? The defense recognizes that complicity, during the time before the perpetrator completes the offense, amounts to a form of inchoate liability for the accomplice. Once the perpetrator has committed an attempt, the accomplice is liable as an accomplice to that attempt. Like that of a coconspirator, the accomplice's conduct before the offense is in the nature of preparation. Even if the accomplice finishes providing his assisting conduct before the offense occurs, substantive liability will not arise until the principal completes the offense itself—after all, until then, there is no offense (except, perhaps, an inchoate attempt) to impute to the accomplice. Indeed, modern codes specifically provide for complicity to be treated as an attempt where the perpetrator does not ultimately commit the offense.[23] From that perspective, it seems appropriate to give a renunciation-like defense for would-be accomplices before the crime is complete.

Termination need not prevent crime or be "complete and voluntary"   If the termination defense for complicity parallels the renunciation defense, why does it not, like renunciation, require the accomplice actually to prevent the offense? Presumably this would maximize the accomplice's incentive to prevent the crime. Indeed, the difference between these rules at first may seem to have things backwards. Complicity, as a source of full substantive liability, might merit a more demanding requirement for a renunciation-like defense, if any at all. Inchoate offenses might warrant a less demanding defense, based as they are upon the actor's subjective culpability, which is undercut by his renunciation. A similar critique may be raised against the termination defense's failure to require that the termination be "complete and voluntary," as is required for the comparable renunciation defense to inchoate liability.

Termination, unlike renunciation, is not a full defense   These differences are sensible, however, because they are rooted in another, more fundamental difference between termination and renunciation. The termination "defense" is truly only a mitigation, as it only impacts the grading of the accomplice's liability, reducing it from full substantive liability to inchoate liability. (Of course, this mitigation is meaningful only if inchoate and substantive offenses are graded differently. Under the Model Penal Code scheme, which generally makes no such grading distinction, the explanation for the termination-renunciation difference is less clear.) Even if an actor escapes full complicity liability because he "terminates his complicity" and "makes proper effort to prevent the offense," he nonetheless may face attempt liability, either under the general attempt rules or under the specific rule treating "conduct designed to aid another" as an attempt. To escape inchoate liability, as well, and to get a complete defense, the actor would have to satisfy the more demanding requirements of the renunciation defense.

Hypothetical: Gambling Life

Bertie Graham works at a convalescent hospital for cardiac patients. She has recently learned that her friend Iva, who also works at the hospital, made some

---

23. Model Penal Code § 5.01(3).

Table: Summary of the Requirements of Attempt Liability

The doctrinal requirements for attempt liability may be summarized as follows:

Objective Requirements	Culpability Requirements
Conduct constituting substantive offense: Not required, instead: CL — proximity & res ipsa loquitur tests MPC — substantial step test	Culpability as to conduct constituting substantive offense: CL & MPC — purposeful
Result elements of substantive offense: CL & MPC — not required (nor is factual impossibility of it occurring a defense)	Culpability as to result elements of substantive offense: CL — elevate to purposeful MPC — elevate to purposeful, but only to knowing if conduct complete Other (e.g., Utah) — as required by substantive offense; do not elevate
Circumstance elements of substantive offense: CL — required (legal impossibility is a defense) MPC — not required (legal impossibility is not a defense)	Culpability as to circumstance elements of substantive offense: CL — elevate to purposeful MPC — as required by substantive offense; do not elevate (per commentary)

MPC = Model Penal Code

CL = Common Law

extra money by selling the heart medication of the patient she cares for, substituting aspirin. Bertie would like to do the same but is concerned that she might get caught and held criminally liable if her patient dies from an attack because the medication is not immediately available. Iva explains that on many occasions when patients take the medication, they are not really having an attack. Bertie decides to make the substitution.

After Bertie acquires the aspirin that she plans to substitute and changes the label to make it look like heart medicine but before she can make the switch, a patient dies from an attack and the authorities discover that the patient's medication had been switched. The offending employee, Jenkins, is found and charged with manslaughter (reckless homicide). Later that day, Iva's patient dies from a heart attack. All medication bottles are seized, and a review uncovers several more medication switches. To Iva's surprise and confusion, her patient's medication is found to be heart medication, not the aspirin she thought she had substituted. Those employees who made medication switches are charged with endangerment (recklessly creating a risk of death to another). In the hopes of getting better treatment from prosecutors, Iva turns in Bertie, who admits to investigators that she planned to make the switch later that day.

What, if anything, are Iva and Bertie liable for?

APPENDIX A: SECTION 11

Impossibility

DISCUSSION MATERIALS

Issue: If It Is Impossible for a Person to Commit the Offense Attempted, Should the Attempt Nonetheless Constitute a Crime? In Other Words, Should a Potential for Actual Commission Be Required, or Is a Subjective Belief in the Potential for Commission Enough?

George P. Fletcher, A Crime of Self-Defense: Bernhard Goetz and the Law on Trial

Model Penal Code Section 5.01 Commentary, Impossibility—Policy Considerations

Lawrence Crocker, Justice in Criminal Liability: Decriminalizing Harmless Attempts

ADVANCED MATERIALS

Notes on Impossibility

✳ DISCUSSION MATERIALS

Issue: If It Is Impossible for a Person to Commit the Offense Attempted, Should the Attempt Nonetheless Constitute a Crime? In Other Words, Should a Potential for Actual Commission Be Required, or Is a Subjective Belief in the Potential for Commission Enough?

George Fletcher's article on the significance of resulting harm, which was excerpted in Section 9, is worth reexamining here to refresh your recollection of his distinction between the "objectivist view of criminality" and the "subjectivist view of criminality." The Model Penal Code Commentary excerpt discusses the strengths and weaknesses of the impossibility doctrine as it relates to punishing dangerousness, purpose that guides the Code's formulation of the doctrine. Lawrence Crocker, taking an opposing objectivist view of criminality, challenges the Model Penal Code's subjectivist perspective and argues that such a subjectivist view of criminality risks punishing without blameworthiness and that objectivist principles are and ought to be the core of many current criminal codes.

George P. Fletcher, A Crime of Self-Defense: Bernhard Goetz and the Law on Trial
64-67 (1988)

[Reread the Fletcher excerpt in the Section 9 (Causation) Discussion Materials.]

Model Penal Code Section 5.01 Commentary
Impossibility—Policy Considerations
Official Draft and Revised Comments 315-316 (1985)

Insofar as it has not rested on conceptual tangles that have been largely independent of policy considerations, the defense of impossibility seems to have been employed to serve a number of functions. First, it has been used to verify criminal purpose; if the means selected were absurd, there is good ground for doubting that the actor really planned to commit a crime. Similarly, if the defendant's conduct, objectively viewed, is ambiguous, there may be ground for doubting the firmness of his purpose to commit a criminal offense. A general defense of impossibility is, however, an inappropriate way of assuring that the actor has a true criminal purpose.

A second function that the defense of impossibility seems to have served in some cases is to supplement the defense of entrapment. In situations in which the technical entrapment rules do not exonerate the defendant, there is a temptation to find that the presence of traps and decoys makes the actor's endeavor impossible. The Model Code has a separate formulation on entrapment which is believed to state the appropriate considerations for a defense on this ground.

A third consideration that has been advanced in support of an impossibility defense is the view that the criminal law need not take notice of conduct that is innocuous, the element of impossibility preventing any dangerous proximity to the completed crime. The law of attempts, however, should be concerned with manifestations of dangerous character as well as with preventive arrests; the fact that particular conduct may not create an actual risk of harmful consequences, though it would if the circumstances were as the defendant believed them to be, should not therefore be conclusive. The innocuous character of the particular conduct becomes relevant only if the futile endeavor itself indicates a harmless personality, so that immunizing the conduct from liability would not result in exposing society to a dangerous person.

Using impossibility as a guide to dangerousness of personality presents serious difficulties. What is needed is a guideline that can inform judgment in particular cases, so that those that involve a danger to society can be successfully prosecuted while those that do not can be dismissed. Such a vehicle is provided in Section 5.05(2), which authorizes the court to reduce the grade of the offense, or dismiss the prosecution, in situations where the conduct charged to constitute an attempt is "so inherently unlikely to result or culminate in the commission of

a crime that neither such conduct nor the actor presents a public danger warranting" the normal grading of the offense as an attempt. Section 5.05(2) thus takes
account of those cases where neither the offender nor his conduct presents a serious threat to the public. There is also, of course, prosecutorial discretion, which
seems to have eliminated most such cases from litigation in the past.

Lawrence Crocker, Justice in Criminal Liability: Decriminalizing Harmless Attempts
53 Ohio State Law Journal 1057, 1069-1072 (1992)

Among theories of criminal liability, two are polar opposites. On one theory, or more accurately family of theories, society's license to punish the offender
derives from her dangerousness or wickedness. On pure versions of these theories
wicked thoughts and plans unaccompanied by concrete acts fail to be punishable
only because the trier of fact would have insufficient evidence to infer the appropriate level of personal dangerousness or depravity. Such theories are "subjective."

On the opposite theory, society's license to punish the offender derives from
her commission of criminal acts that actually impose upon society. In the absence
of these acts, we cannot justly punish the offender even if we know with certainty
that she is desperately wicked and dreadfully dangerous. This is sometimes called
an "objective" theory, but because that label can cover a great deal of ground, I
will refer to this theory, which I endorse, by the more descriptive if less elegant
phrase "imposition theory."

A theory is not "subjective" in the sense I have in mind merely because the
mental state of the offender is an element of liability. In that weak sense we are
all subjectivists—so long as we recognize the propriety of distinguishing among
different degrees of homicide in terms of mental states. For the purposes of this
Article a theory is "purely subjective" if an act is not a necessary condition of
liability, and it is "subjective" if, for at least some offenses, an imposition upon
discrete victims or society is not a necessary condition of liability.

I doubt that there is anyone who holds a pure version of a subjective theory.
A purist would insist that the criminal act is only of evidentiary significance. In
principle a machine that perfectly assessed subjective depravity or predicted future
criminality could substitute for the criminal act as the predicate for criminal liability. Some may eschew this extreme view only because they believe such a machine
to be impossible. Most would, I hope, concede that such a machine, even if it
were possible, ought not be used for reasons of justice. In the end, this concession will take the modern subjectivist further than he may have anticipated. My
present purpose, however, is only to avoid seeming to overstate my opponents'
initial commitments.

Still, if there may be no "pure" subjectivists, the criminal justice community
has taken on board a very heavy load of subjectivism. The Model Penal Code,
for example, although it purports to forbid "conduct that unjustifiably and inexcusably inflicts or threatens substantial harm," apparently sees as the purpose of
punishment "to subject to public control persons whose conduct indicates that
they are disposed to commit crimes." Correspondingly, the official commentators
concluded that "the primary purpose of punishing attempts is to neutralize dangerous individuals and not to deter dangerous acts." . . .

Commentators are so nearly unanimous that the key to criminal liability ought to be the dangerousness or depravity of the offender, rather than the extent of his actual imposition upon his victim or society, that this subjective theory is sometimes simply called the "modern" theory. . . .

I want to emphasize, however, that what is at stake here is not simply a matter of theories of attempts, though harmless attempts—attempts that impose no risk—focus the dispute in a particularly sharp way. What is at stake is the general theory of criminal liability. Subjective theories and the imposition theory are fundamentally different ways of understanding what it is for conduct to be criminal. The imposition theory has its roots in retributive justice. Those of the subjective theories are primarily in utilitarianism.

The objective theory has differing consequences from subjective theories throughout the substantive criminal law including for such matters as punishment theory, victimless crimes, felony-murder, misdemeanor-manslaughter, conspiracy, possession offenses, and even criminal causation. Except for a brief excursion into punishment theory, this Article ignores these other matters to concentrate on the pivotal test case of attempts. My hope is thereby to show that there is some plausibility, after all, to an approach that has been all but universally rejected by academic commentators. . . .

. . . I submit that there is nothing mysterious or terribly difficult about an imposition theory. It resonates with considerations that have long been staples of the jurisprudence of crime and punishment—legality, responsibility, autonomy, and "proportionality." There is surely some initial plausibility to the proposition that free people should not become criminally liable unless they trespass upon someone else's moral space, that is unless they impose in some way. Similarly, there is at least some intuitive support for the further proposition that free people ought not to acquire liability for serious crimes unless they have imposed in some serious way. The common sense appeal of the imposition theory is reflected in the old common law, for which there was no criminal liability for any unsuccessful attempt.

It will be the burden of. . .this Article to argue that the imposition theory's initial plausibility is, in fact, well founded. In large part I do this through arguing against subjective theories. Of course every argument against the class of subjective theories is simultaneously an argument for the imposition theory and vice versa inasmuch as I have defined the two to be mutually exclusive and jointly exhaustive. Everyone who rejects the requirement of an imposition for liability, and a sufficiently objective imposition at that, I stuff together into the subjectivist pigeonhole.

In fact, despite the obviousness of the imposition theory, I have identified no contemporary commentator who escapes consignment to the subjectivist pigeonhole. That is not to say that no one in the recent past has argued for any form of an imposition theory. But the few who have argued for a requirement of an imposition for criminal liability have slid back into subjectivism by watering down what would count as an imposition. . . .

Let me anticipate with a few examples. Lying in wait for a victim who is still some distance away is, I will argue, not yet an "attempt" at all, but even if it were, it would be a harmless attempt because there is no immediate risk imposed upon the victim until he comes within range. When he does come within range, and is fired upon with live ammunition, there is an attempt, and not a harmless one. Even if the shooter missed, the attempt was possible and properly gives rise to liability because it did impose immediate risk upon the intended victim. Firing a stage prop pistol and firing at a tree stump in the mistaken belief it is a person are harmless attempts. There is no immediate imposition. Similarly there is no risk, and hence ought not be attempt liability, for spooning what is in fact sugar out of an arsenic box into one's aunt's tea, for buying goods in the mistaken belief they are stolen, for the smuggling of lace in the mistaken belief it is dutiable, for picking an empty pocket, for shooting into a bed believed on good grounds to be occupied, or for trying to rape a deceased or secretly consenting victim. . . .

II. Arguments Against Subjectivism and for the Imposition Theory

I will here set out seven arguments in favor of the imposition theory of attempts and against the modern subjective theory.

The first argument is partially descriptive in character. It looks to the fact that existing criminal codes are built upon the concept of imposition. Most obvious is the fact that offenses are largely graded in terms of the seriousness of their effects. In particular, the seriousness of the offense increases with the size of the theft, the seriousness of the physical injury, and the degree of the sexual imposition. Moreover, successful attempts, despite the complaints of subjectivists, are almost always of higher grade than unsuccessful attempts. The incompatibility of the subjective theory with these basic features of criminal law is not just an apparent incompatibility.

My second argument is that the subjective theory is radically incomplete. There are fact situations in which subjectivism is committed to there being criminal liability, but for which it lacks the resources to specify the offense for which the offender is liable.

For my third argument I draw upon the fact that the concept of criminal liability is closely bound to that of criminal responsibility. There is no liability unless the offender is responsible for the creation of some condition. In the end, only impositions have enough substance to count as such conditions. [This argument is excerpted below, under the "C." heading.]

The fourth argument is linguistic. It turns on the fact that ordinary usage does not recognize as attempts two broad and important groups of cases that count as attempts on subjectivist theories.

Political philosophy is the heart of my rather more extended fifth argument, which deals with the first category of harmless attempts—those that have not gone far enough to impose immediate risk. The argument focuses on the value of individual autonomy and liberty. The imposition theory leaves more scope for individual liberty, and less for state coercion, than do its rivals. In the course of establishing this, I will argue that the imposition theory is to be preferred because the pure subjective theory is flatly and unquestionably unacceptable in its treatment of liberty and autonomy and because there is no tenable middle ground between the pure subjective theory and the pure imposition theory. In short, no satisfactory alternative to the imposition theory is available.

Moreover, even if there were such an alternative, it would encounter grave difficulties drawing the line between liability and nonliability. Just what step is it on the path from plan to executed crime that crosses the line? My sixth argument is that the criterial verbal formulae of subjective theories are inevitably far too vague to provide adequate notice. These theories, then, fall short of minimal conditions of legality and due process.

My final, and weightiest, argument is one of retributive justice or fairness. It would be fundamentally unfair for society to impose upon the individual in the dramatic, serious, and stigmatizing fashion of the criminal law unless the individual has done something that imposes upon society.. . .

C. The Conflict Between Subjective Theories and Criminal Responsibility

A defendant has committed a murder only if the victim died and only if the defendant's actions causally contributed to that death. If the latter condition fails, the defendant is not responsible for the death. If the former, then there is nothing for which the offender could be responsible. It is no accident or mere linguistic convention that there should be this connection between criminal liability and responsibility. The sanctions of the criminal law are among the most serious interferences that a state makes in the lives of individuals. Unchecked, these sanctions would be the stuff of social terrorism of the most threatening sort. Criminal law's chief internal protection against such excesses is the requirement that there be no criminal liability without criminal responsibility. The requirement of responsibility is what separates criminal justice from other forms of social protection.. . .

Consider three cases in turn. In the first, the defendant, with intent to kill, fires a bullet that strikes the victim in the head killing her. In the second, with the same intent, the defendant fires a bullet that just misses the victim's head. In the third the defendant, again with the same intent, fires a pistol that is, unknown to him, a harmless stage prop.

In the first case, the defendant is unequivocally responsible for the death. In the second, it is not difficult to find something for which the defendant is responsible. Even in the absence of causing fright or the like, the defendant is responsible for the substantial risk to the victim's life that existed as the bullet sped through the air.

In the case of the stage pistol, one's first reaction ought, I think, to be that there is nothing here for which the defendant could be responsible.. . .

Does it properly describe the situation to say that we hold the defendant liable because he is responsible for this state of affairs? Such a description would be proper only if there is in this situation something that society takes to be an evil sufficiently great to sanction and if the offender is responsible for that evil. I will contend that, although there is something in this situation that society takes seriously and although there is something for which the defendant is responsible, the two are not the same.

In what does the seriousness of the situation consist? There would seem to be three possibilities: the defendant's evil character as evidenced by the act, the risk induced by the act, and the alarm actually caused by the act.

The last of these elements, of course, is perfectly at home in the imposition theory. If the victim was put in fear by the episode, then there was an imposition. Such lesser offenses as harassment or menacing are chargeable based on this imposition. This component of what the defendant did, however, clearly could not support a charge of attempted murder, as the subjective view would have it.

By contrast, the evil character evidenced is very different from an imposition. If we find in it the predicate for liability, then the imposition theory must be in error. Imposition would not be a necessary condition of liability.

It would be hard to deny that there is something that society regards as serious about so evil a state of mind. An evil state of mind is not, however, something that one can be said to be responsible for, in the sense of criminal responsibility. Under normal circumstances, we are not even causally responsible for our own desires or intents. We simply have this or that desire or intent.

More generally, when we are focusing upon the defendant's state of mind we are not really making use of the concept of moral responsibility at all. Moral assessment of character is a different and quite independent enterprise. Thus, insofar as the seriousness of the shooting with a stage prop is a matter of evidence of bad character, it falls outside the category of criminal responsibility.. . .

What follows from all this is that there is no account of such impossible attempts—as shooting with a stage pistol—on which what society finds worthy of condemning in them is comprehended under the concept of criminal responsibility. Indeed, a close look reveals that what tempts us to impose liability for such attempts comes down in the end to the wicked character of the defendant or to his future dangerousness. Now perhaps there is a corner of the criminal law in which criminal responsibility is unnecessary for criminal liability and in which bad character or dangerousness is sufficient to send to jail those who have done no harm. The concept of criminal responsibility, however, plays a crucial role in protecting us from overreaching in the name of public safety. For this reason, we should be cautious in accepting the proposition that there may be criminal liability without criminal responsibility. We should avoid this conclusion unless the moral force of arguments supporting it is overwhelming. In fact, the opposite turns out to be true.

▲ ADVANCED MATERIALS

Notes on Impossibility

Objectivist and subjectivist views of criminality; desert and dangerousness
Objectivist rationale for common law impossibility rules
Modern rules consistent with subjectivist view focusing on dangerousness
Alternative form of subjectivism focusing on moral desert
Defense for inherently unlikely attempt reveals dangerousness rationale for subjectivist view
    Desert-based view might permit mitigation, but not defense

Objectivist and subjectivist views of criminality; desert and dangerousness The common law's rules for impossibility—which distinguish legal from factual impossibility and give a defense only for the former—are in keeping with its objectivist view of criminality. Under this view, the central focus is not on culpability (as a subjectivist view would hold), but on coming close to the objective harm or evil. (Certainly, however, an actor's culpable state of mind remains an important prerequisite to liability even under an objectivist view of criminality, for this is the means by which innocent people are protected from mistaken conviction.) Under an objectivist view of criminality, attempts are punishable because they create a danger of completion that disrupts the social order in a real way or, at the very least, appears to come close to causing such a harm.

Objectivist rationale for common law impossibility rules From such an objectivist view of criminality, the factual-legal impossibility distinction may make somewhat more sense. If the missing element is a required circumstance that exists only in the actor's mind (in other words, if the case involves a legally impossible attempt), there may be less likelihood of any real danger of completion; moreover, because only the attempter may know of his mistake as to the circumstance, such conduct is less likely to be known by others and, therefore, less likely to be socially disruptive. Purchasing sugar (or nonstolen goods), or offering money to a nonofficial or nonjuror, does not manifest one's disregard for law in an obvious and easily observable way. By contrast, the types of attempts treated as factually impossible, which involve missing conduct or result elements—picking an empty pocket, shooting with an unloaded gun—may be more visibly and self-evidently attempts at unlawful conduct, thus warranting liability under an objectivist view. This analysis may not be entirely persuasive in arguing for a defense in legal impossibility cases, but it may at least give some sense of why the common law took this view.

Modern rules consistent with subjectivist view focusing on dangerousness The Model Penal Code rejects a defense for legal impossibility, but retains a possible defense or mitigation for an inherently unlikely attempt. These rules, as well as the Code's rejection of the common law proximity tests in favor of a substantial-step test for attempt, logically follow from the Code's general adoption of a subjectivist orientation concerned specifically with dangerousness. The actor who reaches the point of a "substantial step" toward an offense generally has sufficiently demonstrated his dangerousness, even if he has not yet reached close proximity to the crime or actual commission of the offense is (factually or legally) impossible. The Code's grading of an attempt equal to the substantive offense reflects a similar view: Whether the attempter is successful or unsuccessful, she has demonstrated similar dangerousness. In those rare cases where neither the method of attempt nor the actor is dangerous, however, the Code's rationale for liability evaporates, and a defense becomes appropriate; hence the Code's "inherently unlikely" defense, discussed in the previous subsection. In conspiracy, the shift from the common law's bilateral agreement requirement to a unilateral agreement requirement is similarly consistent with a dangerousness focus. An actor demonstrates dangerousness by agreeing with an apparent co-conspirator to commit an offense, whether or not the co-conspirator is really agreeing back.

Alternative form of subjectivism focusing on moral desert Yet a subjectivist view of criminality need not be rooted in adoption of dangerousness as the central criterion for criminal liability. A subjectivist view is useful not only to identify dangerous offenders, but also to identify blameworthy offenders. The attempt and conspiracy rules noted above improve on their common law counterparts in their ability to impose liability in accord with moral desert, as well as dangerousness. Actors who have performed a substantial step toward a crime (even if not yet proximate to it), or who seek to commit an offense but are mistaken about the immediate circumstances, or who mistakenly believe they are conspiring with another to commit an offense, have shown a willingness to act on an intention to break the law, and thus satisfy a desert-based rationale for punishment.

Defense for inherently unlikely attempt reveals dangerousness rationale for subjectivist view   The dangerousness and blameworthiness rationales frequently generate similar results, and this is not surprising, since dangerous people commonly do blameworthy things, and people who have done blameworthy things in the past are often likely to do something unlawful in the future. This is not always the case, however. One who commits an inherently unlikely attempt may not be dangerous now or in the future, but nonetheless may be blameworthy for his past attempt. For example, the actor who tries to kill using voodoo, in light of her belief that the voodoo pins will work, has demonstrated her intention and willingness to kill. The Model Penal Code's recognition of a defense for an inherently unlikely attempt gives evidence that the Code's subjectivist view of criminality is based on dangerousness rather than blameworthiness. A jurisdiction following a desert-based subjectivist view of criminality might adopt most of the Code's subjectivist changes to common law, but reject the Code's "inherently unlikely" defense, as many, if not most, modern codes do.

Desert-based view might permit mitigation, but not defense   One could argue that a mitigation, if not a defense, for an inherently unlikely attempt is appropriate even under a desert-based rationale. Many things, in addition to an actor's subjective culpability, may affect an actor's blameworthiness, including the extent of the harm caused or the degree of the danger created. Thus, an inherently unlikely attempt, where there is no danger of a resulting harm or evil, might be judged less blameworthy than a feasible attempt (all other things being equal), just as an unsuccessful attempt to kill may be judged less blameworthy than a successful attempt. The first pair of cases are distinguished from one another by the creation of a risk of death; the second pair are distinguished by an actual resulting death. Hence under a desert-based view, some mitigation in liability (beyond the usual mitigation for attempt relative to the completed crime) may be appropriate for an inherently unlikely attempt, but a complete defense would be inconsistent with the actor's demonstrated blameworthiness.

APPENDIX A: SECTION 12

Conspiracy

✳ DISCUSSION MATERIALS

Issue: In Addition to Using Conspiracy as an Inchoate Offense of Conspiracy, Should the Law Also Recognize It as a Substantive Offense in Order to Aggravate Punishment for Group Criminality?

The Harvard Law Review "Developments" excerpt traces the doctrinal development of the conspiracy offense, noting its procedural and theoretical short-comings but ultimately supporting its use. The Model Penal Code Commentary describes the Code's attempt to mitigate some of the major objections to the offense and the reasons for its present formulation in the Code as only an inchoate offense. In his "Why They Hate Us" article, Cass Sunstein reviews social science research that suggests the special potential for dangerousness in group action.

Developments in the Law: Criminal Conspiracy
72 Harvard Law Review 920, 922-925 (1959)

With the growth of organized criminal activity the conspiracy indictment has become an increasingly important weapon in the prosecution's armory. In some cases this weapon serves to nullify the opportunities for escaping punishment that the defendant might otherwise obtain from the anonymity of his position within a group or from the difficulty of tracing his precise contribution to any given substantive offense. In other cases it facilitates the intervention of the law at a stage when antisocial consequences can still be prevented. However, the flexibility and formlessness—both procedural and substantive—which account for the effectiveness of conspiracy as a tool of enforcement also create a serious danger of unfairness to the defendant, and have consequently evoked widespread criticism from judicial and law-review commentators. By means of evidence inadmissible under usual rules the prosecutor can implicate the defendant not only in the conspiracy itself but also in the substantive crimes of his alleged coconspirators. In a large conspiracy trial the effect produced upon the jury by the introduction of evidence against some defendants may result in conviction for all of them, so that the fate of each may depend not on the merits of his own case but rather on his success in dissociating himself from his codefendants in the minds of the jury.

These and other procedural problems, however, are perhaps less basic than the conceptual difficulties involved in any attempt to explain the underlying theory of conspiracy and to relate this theory to generally applicable principles of criminal law. Conspiracy is usually defined as an agreement between two or more persons to achieve an unlawful object or to achieve a lawful object by unlawful means. The gist of the crime is the agreement itself rather than the action pursuant to it.. . .At this point it is enough to suggest a rationale for what might appear to be a somewhat inharmonious element in a system of criminal law which purports to punish intent only when objectively manifested by action resulting, or likely to result, in socially harmful consequences.

The history of conspiracy, as Mr. Justice Jackson has pointed out, exemplifies the "tendency of a principle to expand itself to the limit of its logic." Originating in a statute of 1305 which prohibited confederacies for the false and malicious procurement of indictments, conspiracy became a common-law crime only at the beginning of the seventeenth century. Whereas prior to that time the writ of conspiracy would not lie unless the victim had actually been indicted and acquitted, the Star Chamber decided in the landmark Poulterers Case of 1611 that the agreement itself was punishable even if its purpose remained unexecuted. Once the focal point of the offense had shifted from the object of the agreement to the agreement itself, it was a short step to the proposition that an agreement to commit any crime was a criminal conspiracy. The eagerness of the courts, particularly the Star Chamber, to extend the scope of conspiracy was an aspect of the exceptionally vigorous growth of the criminal law generally during the seventeenth century and a reflection of the contemporary tendency to identify law with morality. The same factors probably account also for the widespread and permanent acceptance accorded a statement of Hawkins [a well-known treatise writer of the Common Law], doubtfully supported by previous case law, that the acts contemplated by a conspiracy need not themselves be criminal but need only be "wrongful" in order to make the conspiracy punishable.

Possibly the concept of conspiracy in such a highly generalized form could have been developed only within a system of judge-made law. In any event, a comparably broad doctrine of conspiracy has not emerged in civil-law countries. European penal codes frequently make concerted action a basis for aggravating the penalties for completed substantive crimes, but when no substantive offense has been completed, only certain types of conspiracies are proscribed—notably those directed against the security of the state, those involving many participants organized for the purpose of committing numerous crimes, and those contemplating particularly serious offenses. By applying the conspiracy doctrine only in situations involving a very great danger to society, continental legislators seem to have wisely limited the crime to the scope required by its underlying rationale

The heart of this rationale lies in the fact—or a least the assumption—that collective action toward an antisocial end involves a greater risk to society than individual action toward the same end. Primarily, the state is concerned with punishing conduct that has actually resulted in antisocial consequences. It is reluctant to intervene as long as the actor can still withdraw and as long as his conduct is still consistent with the absence of any criminal intent. However, as action toward a criminal end nears execution, a point is reached at which the increasing risk to society is thought to outweigh the diminishing likelihood of a change of heart or of a misreading of intent, and at this point mere "preparation" become punishable as "attempt." When the defendant has chosen to act in concert with others, rather than to act alone, the point of justifiable intervention is reached at an earlier state. In this situation the reasons for which the law is reluctant to intervene are considerably weaker. The agreement itself, in theory at least, provides a substantially unambiguous manifestation of intent; it also reduces the probability that the defendant can stop the wheels he has set in motion, since to restore the status quo would now require the acquiescence and cooperation of other wills than his own. More important, the collaboration magnifies the risk to society both by increasing the likelihood that a given quantum of harm will be successfully produced and by increasing the amount of harm that can be inflicted. A conspirator who has committed himself to support his associates may be less likely to violate this commitment than he would be to revise a purely private decision. Moreover, encouragement and moral support of the group strengthen the perseverance of each member. Furthermore, the existence of numbers both facilitates a division of labor which promotes the efficiency with which a given object can be pursued, and makes possible the attainment of objects more elaborate and ambitious than would otherwise be attainable. The notion of increased social risk also provides a possible rationale for the punishment of agreements to engage in certain types of conduct that would not otherwise be criminal, since the absence of any specific prohibition against such conduct may be due to the fact that the likelihood that a single person will engage in it is small, or that its harmful impact when engaged in by a single person is slight. A further rationale may be that reliance on social pressure alone to deter certain forms of antisocial conduct becomes unwarranted when this pressure is countered by that of the conspiratorial group itself.

The antisocial potentialities of a conspiracy, unlike those of an attempt, are not confined to the objects specifically contemplated at any given time. The existence of a grouping for criminal purposes provides a continuing focal point for further crimes either related or unrelated to those immediately envisaged. Moreover, the uneasiness produced by the consciousness that such groupings exist is in itself an important antisocial effect. Consequently, the state has an interest in stamping out conspiracy above and beyond its interest in preventing the commission of any specific substantive offense. This additional interest may explain, for example, why some courts have imposed cumulative sentences for a conspiracy and for the crime which was its object.. . . .

A further distinction between the law of conspiracy and that of attempt emerges when each is regarded not as a means of enabling official intervention to prevent the fruition of the crime in a particular case, but rather as a means of deterring potential criminal conduct. In its deterrent function the law operates on the mechanism of choice, seeking to make the disadvantages of criminal activity appear to outweigh its advantages. Since one who has decided to commit a crime does not confront the further choice whether to attempt that crime, the deterrent function of the proscription against attempt is not additional to that of the proscription against the completed offense. By contrast, conspiracy is simply a route by which a given criminal object can be approached. Because the antisocial potentialities of this route are peculiarly great, it is arguable that even those who have not been deterred by the penalty for the completed offense should nevertheless be discouraged from embarking upon their criminal venture in concert with others. The role of conspiracy as a subordinate deterrent may provide further support for the imposition of cumulative sentences for conspiracy and the completed substantive offense.

Model Penal Code Section 5.03 Commentary
Criminal Conspiracy—Introduction
Official Draft and Revised Comments 386-393 (1985)

Though conspiracy has been an offense at common law as well as under statutes existing before the Model Code, there was only fragmentary legislative treatment of the scope and the components of the crime, and this was usually limited to statements of the conspiratorial objectives that suffice for criminality and the requirement, in some but not all cases, of an overt act. The law defining the offense and dealing with the many special problems in its prosecution has been, on the whole, the product of the courts.

This product has been a controversial one on many grounds. Putting aside such special grievances as those based on the early condemnation of the labor union as a criminal conspiracy and the use of the charge against political offenders, the general critique has pointed to the danger of a dragnet in the broad, uncertain ground of liability, the wholesale joinder of defendants, the imposition of vicarious responsibility, the relaxation of the rules of evidence, and some or all of these in combination.

The Model Penal Code attempts to meet or mitigate objections of this kind to the extent that it is feasible to do so in a legislative treatment of the crime.

It is worthwhile to note preliminarily that conspiracy as an offense has two different aspects, reflecting the different functions it serves in the legal system. In the first place, conspiracy is an inchoate crime, complementing the provisions dealing with attempt and solicitation in reaching preparatory conduct before it has matured into commission of a substantive offense. Second, it is a means of striking against the special danger incident to group activity, facilitating prosecution of the group, and yielding a basis for imposing added penalties when combination is involved.

As an inchoate crime, conspiracy fixes the point of legal intervention at agreement to commit a crime, or at agreement coupled with an overt act which may, however, be of very small significance. Conspiracy thus reaches further back into preparatory conduct than attempt, raising the question of whether this extension is desirable. The Institute believed it was, for the following reasons:

First: The act of agreeing with another to commit a crime, like the act of soliciting, is concrete and unambiguous; it does not present the infinite degrees and variations possible in the general category of attempts. The danger that truly equivocal behavior may be misinterpreted as preparation to commit a crime is minimized; purpose must be relatively firm before the commitment involved in agreement is assumed.

Second: If the agreement was to aid another to commit a crime or if it otherwise encouraged the crime's commission, complicity would be established in the commission of the substantive offense. It would be anomalous to hold that conduct that would suffice to establish criminality, if something else is done by someone else, is insufficient if the crime is never consummated. Although this reason covers less than all the cases of conspiracy, it is significant that it covers many others.

Third: In the course of preparation to commit a crime, the act of combining with another is significant both psychologically and practically, the former because it crosses a clear threshold in arousing expectations, the latter because it increases the likelihood that the offense will be committed. Sharing lends fortitude to purpose. The actor knows, moreover, that the future is no longer governed by this will alone; others may complete what he has had a hand in starting, even if he has a change of heart.

There is little doubt, therefore, that as a basis for preventive intervention by the agencies of law enforcement and for the corrective treatment of persons who reveal that they are disposed to criminality, a penal code properly provides that conspiracy to commit crime is itself a criminal offense.

In its aspect as a sanction against group activity, conspiracy presents quite different problems.

First: One function to be noted in this area is the use of conspiracy to proscribe agreements having objectives that would not be criminal if pursued or achieved by single individuals, on the ground that combination towards such ends presents a danger a lone actor could not create on his own. There are, of course, important areas of conduct in which such a delineation of the scope of criminality may be appropriate; it is commonplace, for instance, in the field of antitrust. But judgments of this kind must be made sparingly and in the context of the specific conduct that is involved, taking into consideration other weapons in the legal arsenal that may be brought to bear upon these acts. It is not a matter to be dealt with in a general provision on conspiracy and it is not so dealt with in the Model Code.

To the extent that earlier decisional and statutory law performed this function by defining conspiracy to embody condemnation of all combinations with objectives that are "unlawful," "malicious," "oppressive," or "injurious," as distinct from criminal, the approach was regarded as too vague for penal prohibitions and was rejected in the Code.

Second: Group prosecution is undoubtedly made easier by the procedural advantages enjoyed by the prosecution when conspiracy is charged. Acts and declarations of participants may be admissible against each other under an exception to the hearsay rule, and ordinarily will be received, subject to later ruling, even before the required basis has been laid. Vicarious responsibility may relax venue rules and the conception of conspiracy as a continuous offense extends the period of limitations. The presentation in the case of a full picture of the workings of a large and complex network of related criminal activities will often help the jury to grasp the part played by individuals who otherwise might be forgotten, but a strong case against some defendants may unduly blacken all; the need to work a root and branch extermination of the organized activity may overcome doubts that would otherwise prevail.

Not all the difficulties posed by these procedures are intrinsic to conspiracy as an offense, notwithstanding belief by prosecutors that it is by virtue of indictment for conspiracy that procedural advantages are gained. The same rules as to joinder and venue, and the same rules of evidence, will normally apply when the prosecution is for substantive offenses in which joint complicity is charged. Nevertheless, the Code makes some attempt to treat the problems that are raised, focusing separately upon the substantive conceptions that have bearing on procedure, as, for example, the scope of a conspiracy, and upon the strictly procedural issues that are involved.

Third: The older common law rule that conspiracy, like attempt, merges in the completed crime that is its object, with the result that conviction and sentence on both grounds are barred, has been superseded on the whole in modern law. The act of combination is regarded as "an independent crime condemned by the statute for the primary purpose of discouraging organized and concerted efforts by two or more people to violate the law." Indeed, the conspiracy is often said to be more dangerous than "the mere commission of the contemplated crime."

The Code embraces this conception in part and rejects it in part. When a conspiracy is declared criminal because its object is a crime, it is entirely meaningless to say that the preliminary combination is more dangerous than the forbidden consummation; the measure of its danger is the risk of such culmination. On the other hand, the combination may and often does have criminal objectives that transcend any particular offenses that have been committed in pursuance of its goals. In the latter case, cumulative sentences for conspiracy and substantive offenses ought to be permissible, subject to the general limits on cumulation that the Code prescribes. In the former case, when the preliminary agreement does not go beyond the consummation, double conviction and sentence are barred.

The barrier to double sentence thus erected does not, however, prevent taking due account of a combination when it has real bearing on the sentence that should be imposed. Such cases are, in the Institute's view, limited to situations in which organized, professional criminality is involved, and the sentencing provisions of the Code thus permit the use of an extended term. This seems a far better way to effect needed aggravation in the sentence than a cumulation based on an antecedent combination to commit a consummated crime.

It should be added that the Code rejects what was the usual sentencing provision for conspiracy, one that fixed sentence at a level unrelated to the sanction for the crime that is its object when the purpose is commission of a major crime. Under Section 5.05(1), conspiracy, like attempt and solicitation, is a crime of the same grade and degree as the most serious of its criminal objectives, except that it is never graded higher than a second degree felony. This is a further indication that the sentencing provisions do not suffer from weakness in dealing with the combinations incident to organized group crime.

Fourth: It was argued in the Advisory Committee that the Code should build on European models in shaping conspiracy explicitly as a crime of criminal organization, rather than as an inchoate crime. Under this approach, apart from exceptional provisions dealing with crimes against the state, whether and to what extent conspiratorial activity is criminal, or the gravity of the offense, has depended on such special factors as the size and continuity of the group involved, the number of its criminal objectives, and the character of the individual's participation. In the treatment of completed crimes by groups, the same factors have sometimes aggravated the sentence.

The Italian Code of 1930 afforded the best example of this treatment of the subject. As to inchoate activity, it declared that "whenever two or more persons agree for the purpose of committing an offence, and it is not committed, none of them is punishable for the sole fact of making the agreement," although in such cases the judge may apply a "police measure." It provided for penal servitude of from 3 to 7 years, however, for the leaders and promoters of an association of "3 or more persons. . .for the purpose of committing more than one crime. . ." and penal servitude of from 1 to 5 years for those who only participated in the association; the punishment is increased "if the number of persons associating is 10 or more." As to crimes that have been committed, the Italian Code provided for aggravation of the penalty "(1) [i]f the number of persons co-operating in the offence is 5 or more. . ." and "(2) [i]n the case of individuals who. . .have promoted or organised co-operation in the offence, or have directed the action of the persons who co-operated in that offence."

To the extent that legislation of this kind serves to immunize from liability conspiracies with only two participants or with a single criminal objective, the Institute perceived no solid case for limitation. The inchoate crime function sustains the broader scope of the offense that is traditional in our system. To the extent that these provisions permit sterner sanctions to suppress the more potent combinations, there is certainly no weakness in the sentencing provisions of the Code. For these reasons, the distinctive pattern of the continental codes was rejected.

Cass R. Sunstein, Why They Hate Us: The Role of Social Dynamics

25 Harvard Journal of Law & Public Policy 429, 429-433, 439-440 (2002)

I. THE THESIS

My goal in this brief Essay is to cast some new light on a question that has been much discussed in the aftermath of the attacks of September 11. The question is simple: Why do they hate us? I suggest that a large part of the answer lies, not in anything particular to Islam, to religion, or even to the ravings of Osama bin Laden, but in social dynamics and especially in the process of group polarization. When group polarization is at work, like-minded people, engaged in discussion with one another, move toward extreme positions. The effect is especially strong with people who are already quite extreme; such people can move in literally dangerous directions. It is unfortunate but true that leaders of terrorist organizations show a working knowledge of group polarization. They sharply discipline what is said. They attempt to inculcate a shared sense of humiliation, which breeds rage, and group solidarity, which prepares the way for movement toward further extremes and hence for violent acts. They attempt to ensure that recruits speak mostly to people who are already predisposed in the preferred direction. They produce a cult-like atmosphere.

With an understanding of group polarization, we can see that when "they hate us," it is often because of social processes that have been self-consciously created and manipulated by terrorist leaders. These social processes could easily be otherwise. If they were, terrorism would not exist, or at least it would be greatly weakened and its prospects would be diminished. There is no natural predisposition toward terrorism, even among the most disaffected people in the poorest nations. When terrorism occurs, it is typically a result of emphatically social pressures and indeed easily identifiable mechanisms of interaction. More broadly, ethnic identification and ethnic conflict are a product of similar pressures; an understanding of "why they hate us" is thus likely to promote an increased understanding of social hatred in general.

We can draw some conclusions here for the law of conspiracy, for freedom of association, for the idea of "political correctness," for the system of checks and balances, and for possible responses to terrorist threats. Thus I shall identify the distinctive logic behind the special punishment of conspiracy: those who conspire are likely to move one another in more extreme and hence more dangerous directions. I shall also urge that freedom of association helps to fuel group polarization—a healthy phenomenon much of the time, but a potentially dangerous one in some contexts. I shall urge, finally, that an especially effective way to prevent terrorism is to prevent "terrorist entrepreneurs" from creating special enclaves of like-minded or potentially like-minded people. It might seem tempting to object to such efforts on the ground that they interfere with associational liberty, which is of course prized in all democratic nations. But we are speaking here of terrorism and conspiracy to kill American citizens; in such cases, the claims for associational liberty are very weak. Conspiracy is the dark side of freedom of association, and it is a form of conspiracy that I am discussing here. One of my largest goals is thus to provide a window on the nature and consequences of conspiracy in the particular context of terrorism.

II. THE BASIC PHENOMENON

A. What Groups Do

Let us begin with some social science research that seems very far afield from the area of terrorism. In 1962, J. A. F. Stoner, an enterprising graduate student, attempted to examine the relationship between individual judgments and group judgments. He did so against a background belief that groups tended to move toward the middle of their members' predeliberation views. Stoner proceeded by asking people a range of questions involving risk-taking behavior. People were asked, for example, whether someone should choose a safe or risky play in the last seconds of a football game; whether someone should invest money in a low-return, high-security stock or instead a high-return, lower-security stock; whether someone should choose a high prestige graduate program in which a number of people fail to graduate or a lower prestige school from which everyone graduates.

In Stoner's studies, the subjects first studied the various problems and recorded an initial judgment; they were then asked to reach a unanimous decision as a group. People were finally asked to state their private judgments after the group judgment had been made; they were informed that it was acceptable for the private judgment to differ from the group judgment. What happened? For twelve of the thirteen groups, the group decisions showed a repeated pattern toward greater risk-taking. In addition, there was a clear shift toward greater risk-taking in private opinions as well. Stoner therefore found a "risky shift," in which the effect of group dynamics was to move groups, and the individuals that composed them, in favor of increased risk-taking.

What accounts for this remarkable result? The answer is emphatically not that groups always move toward greater risk-taking. Some groups—asking, for example, about whether and when someone should get married, or travel despite a possibly serious medical condition—tend to move toward greater caution. Subsequent studies have shown a consistent pattern, one that readily explains Stoner's own findings: deliberating groups tend to move toward a more extreme point in line with their pre-deliberation tendencies. If like-minded people are talking with one another, they are likely to end up thinking a more extreme version of what they thought before they started to talk. It follows that, for example, a group of people who tend to approve of an ongoing war effort will, as a result of discussion, become still more enthusiastic about that effort; that people who think that environmentalists are basically right, and that the planet is in serious trouble, will become quite alarmed if they talk mostly with one another; that people who tend to dislike the Rehnquist Court will dislike it quite intensely after talking about it with one another; that people who disapprove of the United States, and are suspicious of its intentions, will increase their disapproval and suspicion if they exchange points of view. Indeed, there is specific evidence of the latter phenomenon among citizens of France. It should be readily apparent that enclaves of people, inclined to terrorist violence, might move sharply in that direction as a consequence of internal deliberations.

Three aggravating factors are of special relevance to the issue of terrorism. First, if members of the group think that they have a shared identity, and a high degree of solidarity, there will be heightened polarization. One reason is that if people feel united by some factor (for example, politics or necessity), internal dissent will be dampened. Second, if members of the deliberating group are connected by affective ties, polarization will increase. If they tend to perceive one another as friendly, likable, and similar to them, the size and likelihood of the shift will increase. These points obviously bear on the cult-like features of terrorist organizations, in which shared identity helps fuel movement toward extremes.

Third, extremists are especially prone to polarization. When they start out an extreme point, they are likely to go much further in the direction with which they started. Note in this regard that burglars in a group act more recklessly than they do as individuals.. . . .

IV. IMPLICATIONS AND LESSONS

What are the lessons for policy and for law? The simplest and most important is that if a nation aims to prevent terrorist activities, a good strategy is to prevent the rise of enclaves of like-minded people. Many of those who become involved in terrorist activities could end up doing something else with their lives. Their interest in terrorism comes, in many cases, from an identifiable set of social mechanisms (generally from particular associations). If the relevant associations can be disrupted, terrorism is far less likely to arise.

The second lesson has to do with the idea of "political correctness." That idea is far more interesting than it seems. It is true that some groups of left-leaning intellectuals push one another to extremes, and tow a kind of party line, in part through a limited argument pool, and in part through imposing reputational sanctions on those who disagree, or even ostracizing them. But political correctness is hardly limited to left-leaning intellectuals. It plays a role in groups of all kinds. In its most dangerous forms, it is a critical part of groups that are prone to violence and terrorism, simply because such groups stifle dissent.

The third lesson has to do with the system of checks and balances and even constitutional design. Citizens in democratic nations are hardly immune from the forces discussed here. Within legislatures, civic organizations, and even courts, group polarization might well occur. Nor is this necessarily bad. A movement in a more extreme direction might well be a movement in a better direction. But serious problems can arise when extremism is a product of the mechanisms discussed here, and not of learning through the exchange of diverse opinions. The institutions of checks and balances can be understood as a safeguard against group polarization, simply because those institutions ensure that like-minded people, operating within a single part of government, will not be able to move governmental power in their preferred direction. Consider, for example, the idea of bicameralism and the power of the president to veto legislation; through these routes, it is possible to reduce the risk that government policy will be a product of the forces I have discussed.

The fourth lesson has to do with the treatment of conspiracy, including but not limited to terrorist conspiracies. Why does the law punish conspiracy as a separate offense, independent of the underlying "substantive" crime? It is tempting to think that this kind of "doubling up" is indefensible, a form of overkill. But if the act of conspiring leads people moderately disposed toward criminal behavior to be more than moderately disposed, precisely because they are conspiring together, it makes sense, on grounds of deterrence, to impose independent penalties. Some courts have come close to recognizing this point. The key point is that the act of conspiracy has an independent effect, that of moving people in more extreme directions. The point holds for terrorists as well as for everyone else.

The discussion also offers some lessons about freedom of association in general, showing some of its many complexities. Associational freedom is of course an indispensable part of democracy. No one should deny that point. But when associational freedom is ensured, group polarization will inevitably ensue, as people sort themselves into groups that seem congenial. From the standpoint of liberty, this is extremely important. It is also valuable from the standpoint of democracy, not least because any society's "argument pool" will be expanded by a wide variety of deliberating groups. If groups move to extremes, then social fragmentation may be desirable insofar as it ensures that society as a whole will hear a wide range of positions and points of view. On the other hand, freedom of association can increase the risk of social fragmentation, and social antagonisms, potentially even violence, can result.

Almost all of the time, the risk is worth tolerating. But when we are dealing with conspiracies to kill American citizens, freedom of association is literally dangerous. Hatred itself is hardly against the law. By itself it is no reason for war. But when hatred is a product of the social forces outlined here, and when it makes terrorism possible, there is every reason to disrupt associations that drive people to violent acts. The line between associational freedom and conspiracy is not always crisp and certain. But in the cases I am emphasizing, there is no real puzzle. When they hate us, it is not a product of deprivation, individual rage, or religiously grounded predisposition; it is a result of social forces and, much of the time, self-conscious conspiracies to fuel hatred. A nation that seeks to win a war against terrorism must try to disrupt those conspiracies.

▲ ADVANCED MATERIALS

Further Notes on Conspiracy Culpability Requirements

Case against elevation to purpose for circumstance elements
    Questioning rationale for elevation as to result elements
    Case for limiting purpose requirement to conduct elements
        Elevation prevents liability for conspiracies to create risks
    Common Law rationale for elevation inapplicable

CASE AGAINST ELEVATION TO PURPOSE FOR CIRCUMSTANCE ELEMENTS

There is reason to think conspiracy liability, like attempt liability, should require the same culpability as to circumstances that the target offense requires, rather than elevating the culpability requirement. If there were no elevation, two persons could be liable for conspiring to have intercourse with a child they know is nine years old, although it is not their "purpose" that the child be underage. There is some case-law support for this view. In United States v. Feola, for example, the Supreme Court concluded that defendants need not know that their intended victims were federal officers in order to be convicted of conspiracy to assault a federal officer.[1] Such culpability was not required by the target offense, and therefore, the court reasoned, would not be required for conspiracy to commit that offense.

---

1. 420 U.S. 671 (1975).

Questioning rationale for elevation as to result elements   For that matter, the Code's elevation of the culpability requirement for result elements is also questionable. While there is a surface appeal to the Code's rationale of increasing the required culpability to offset the minimal conduct required, perhaps that reasoning is not ultimately sound. If a sliding scale is appropriate for result elements, why is it not equally appropriate for circumstance elements? More fundamentally, why a sliding scale at all: Why exactly should the preparatory nature of conspiracy require higher culpability? The concern is presumably twofold, worrying that the more preliminary the conduct, the more ambiguity exists as to (1) whether it is truly directed toward a criminal end, and (2) even if so, whether the actor truly intends to carry through to the completed offense. As to the first concern, conspiracy arguably presents a stronger case than many attempts for showing criminal intent, as the agreement element of conspiracy requires the actor to externalize his intent clearly enough for someone else to understand it, leaving little room for ambiguity about whether the intended objective is criminal. A substantial-step attempt carries no such evidence of criminal intent on its face. As to the second concern, requiring proof of the actor's purpose to promote the conduct constituting the offense would seem to provide adequate confirmation of the firmness of the actor's resolve. (Note as well that the renunciation defense is available for conspiracy and will give a defense to those with an intention too equivocal to carry through with the offense.)

Case for limiting purpose requirement to conduct elements   Accordingly, perhaps a better interpretation of the Code's "purpose" requirement—consistent with the drafters' own proposed interpretation of similar language in other contexts—is to require purpose only as to the conduct constituting the object offense. That is, it must be the actor's conscious object and desire that one of the conspirators engage in the conduct that would constitute the object offense. To this extent, the Common Law's view of conspiracy as a specific-intent crime is sensible: Conspiracy liability should not arise unless the actor truly intends to conspire and intends that the conduct constituting the offense will be committed. This interpretation of the purpose requirement does not demand purpose as to the result or circumstance elements of the target offense. Rather, the culpability required by that offense should suffice for such elements. This more narrow interpretation of the "purpose" requirement generates different results. On the facts in Beccia, for example, this view would hold that the defendant need only intend that he or the other conspirator set the fire, but he need not intend that the fire destroy or damage the building. As to that result, he need only be reckless, as required by the offense of third-degree arson.

Elevation prevents liability for conspiracies to create risks   The peculiarity of the elevation rule is apparent from the results it generates. Assume two actors agree that one will dump toxic waste down a bore hole leading to an abandoned mine shaft. They are aware of a substantial risk that such conduct will cause serious injury, death, or widespread damage to property. Police, learning of their plan, arrest them before they are able to carry it out, and charge them with conspiracy to risk a catastrophe.[2] These are essentially the facts in Commonwealth v. Scatera.[3] The defendants have the required culpable state of mind for the offense

---

2. See, e.g., Model Penal Code § 220.2(2).
3. 481 A.2d 855 (Pa. Super. 1984), rev'd, 498 A.2d 1314 (Pa. 1985).

(reckless disregard of a risk of catastrophe), but their conduct has not progressed beyond their agreement and an overt act. The elevation rule would bar conviction, requiring that the actors have the purpose to risk (or cause) a catastrophe. But why is it not enough that these actors had the purpose to engage in the conduct constituting the offense—dumping toxic waste into the bore hole—and had the culpability the offense requires?

Common Law rationale for elevation inapplicable The retention of an elevation rule may be shaped in part by the Common Law's position that conspiracy, like attempt, is a "specific intent" offense. But the rule made more sense at Common Law than it does under modern codes. Common Law allowed any number of evidentiary presumptions to prove culpable state of mind (for example, the presumption that a person intends the natural and probable consequences of his acts). In this environment, a true danger existed that any culpability requirement short of the maximum, coupled with the minimal conduct requirement, might lead to improper convictions. Modern codes, of course, do away with such evidentiary presumptions and require proof beyond a reasonable doubt of all required culpable states of mind.

Hypothetical: Selling Death

New national regulations requiring smoke detectors have just gone into effect. Because of anticipated enforcement difficulties, the authorities undertake a major advertising campaign announcing serious fines for any house or apartment dweller caught without the required number of detectors. Hans and Fri have seized on this as an opportunity to make some easy money. They plan to purchase several thousand unfinished smoke detectors from a scrap dealer. The detectors appear complete, and the warning buzzer sounds when tested, but the detection circuitry has not been installed. Hans and Fri estimate that they can make several thousand dollars each week selling their defective units door to door. When Hans calls the scrap dealer and confirms that the dealer has the units, the dealer becomes suspicious. He notifies the police, who trace the call back to Hans and Fri. Only Fri is at home when the police arrive; Hans is out purchasing a supply of the defective detectors. Under questioning Fri reveals their plan. On his return, Hans notices the police presence and keeps driving.

The next day Hans begins selling the faulty detectors. Business is even better than expected. Two weeks later, as a result of two nonfunctional detectors that Hans sold, a fire in a local rowhouse kills a mother and her child. The fire investigation reveals the defective detectors and ties them to the scheme by Fri and Hans. On a tip, police learn that Hans is a frequent customer at a local bar. An undercover officer approaches him and, presenting himself as a longtime con man, he suggests that Hans let him join the sales operation for half of the profit from his sales. Hans is happy to have a new partner. The next morning, Hans and the officer work together selling detectors so that Hans can show his new partner the ropes. As they work, they talk about many things, including the fire deaths from earlier sales. The officer then arrests Hans. The defective detectors sold that morning are retrieved for evidence. What can Hans be held liable for? What can Fri be convicted of?

Table: Summary of Conspiracy Requirements

The requirements for conspiracy liability for the defendant may be summarized as follows:

The defendant must satisfy these requirements:

Objective Requirements:	Culpability Requirements
Conduct constituting substantive offense: Not required, instead: CL & MPC—actor must agree with another that one of them will engage in the conduct that would constitute the substantive offense	*Culpability as to conduct constituting substantive offense:* CL & MPC §5.03(1)—"purpose of promoting or facilitating" the offense
Result elements of substantive offense: CL & MPC—not required (nor is factual impossibility of it occurring a defense)	*Culpability as to result elements of substantive offense:* CL—elevate to purposeful MPC—elevate to purposeful Other (e.g., *Feola* reasoning)—as required by substantive offense; do not elevate
Circumstance elements of substantive offense: CL—required (legal impossibility is a defense) MPC—not required (legal impossibility is not a defense)	*Culpability as to circumstance elements of substantive offense:* CL—elevate to purposeful MPC—perhaps do not elevate, left to "interpretation" (per commentary) Other (e.g., *Feola*)—as required by substantive offense; do not elevate

A co-conspirator must satisfy these requirements:

Objective Requirements:	Culpability Requirements
Agreement requirement: CL—at least one other conspirator must actually agree (bilateral agreement: "two or more persons agree to. . ."); MPC—no conspirator need agree (unilateral agreement; defendant "agrees. . .that one of them. . .")	*Intent to agree:* CL—Bilateral requires that coconspirator intend to agree back MPC—Unilateral does not
Overt act requirement: CL & MPC §5.03(5)—act in pursuance of conspiracy by any conspirator	*Unconvictable coconspirator defense:* CL—requires that coconspirator satisfy all elements of conspiracy and has not defense MPC §5.04: rejects defense(1)

MPC = Model Penal Code
CL = Common Law

APPENDIX A: SECTION 13

Voluntary Intoxication

DISCUSSION MATERIALS

Issue: What Level of Culpable Mental State, if Any, Should Be Imputed When It Is Absent Because the Offender Voluntarily Intoxicated Himself?

Commonwealth v. Daniel Lee Graves
Stephen J. Morse, Fear of Danger, Flight from Culpability
Paul H. Robinson & John M. Darley, Study 10: Voluntary Intoxication
Paul H. Robinson, Causing the Conditions of One's Own Defense: A Study in the Limits of Theory in Criminal Law Doctrine

LAW (Subsequent)

Current Indiana Law Statutes

✳ DISCUSSION MATERIALS

Issue: What Level of Culpable Mental State, if Any, Should Be Imputed When It Is Absent Because the Offender Voluntarily Intoxicated Himself?

The *Graves* dissent argues for a more severe position than the traditional voluntary: It would allow voluntary intoxication to justify the imputation of all culpable mental states. Stephen Morse then offers objections to the full range of rules that impute offense culpability because of voluntary intoxication, including that of the Model Penal Code, arguing that all are based on an unreliable assumption that the culpability in becoming intoxicated is comparable to, and a justified basis for imputing, culpability as to committing an offense. Based on a study of community perspectives, Robinson and Darley conclude that lay intuitions differ from most code voluntary intoxication rules; laypersons tend to assign liability based on the pre-intoxication culpability toward committing the offense. Finally, Robinson proposes, on jurisprudential grounds, an alternative approach that better tracks the community's shared intuitions of justice.

Commonwealth v. Daniel Lee Graves

Supreme Court of Pennsylvania
461 Pa. 118, 334 A.2d 661, 1975 Pa. LEXIS 729 (1975)

EAGEN, Justice (dissenting).

In the past, this Court has never deviated from the position that voluntary intoxication, no matter how gross or long continued, neither exonerates nor excuses a person from his criminal acts. "If it were [so], all crimes would, in a great measure, depend for their criminality on the pleasure of their perpetrators, since they may pass into that state when they will." *Keenan v. Commonwealth, 44 Pa. 55, 58 (1862)*. Today, however, the majority has adopted a new position which, in effect, will allow voluntary intoxication to serve as an excuse for criminal responsibility.

The rationale behind our long-standing rule as to voluntary ingestion of intoxicants and drugs is apparent. An individual who places himself in a position to have no control over his actions must be held to intend the consequences. Such a principle is absolutely essential to the protection of life and property. There is, in truth, no injustice in holding a person responsible for his acts committed in a state of voluntary intoxication. It is a duty which everyone owes to his fellowmen and to society, to preserve, so far as it lies in his own power, the inestimable gift of reason. If such reason is perverted or destroyed by fixed disease, though brought on by his own vices, the law holds him not accountable. But if by a voluntary act he temporarily casts off the restraints of reason and conscience, no wrong is done him if he is considered answerable for any injury which he, in that state, may do to others or to society.

While adhering to the above-mentioned rule, this Court has recognized there may be instances where an individual has voluntarily placed himself in a state of intoxication so as to be incapable of conceiving any intent. In those instances, we have permitted evidence of such intoxication to lower the *degree of guilt* within a crime, but only where the Legislature has specifically provided for varying degrees of guilt within a crime. Thus "[i]f the charge is *felonious* homicide, intoxication, which is so great as to render the accused incapable of forming a wilful, deliberate and premeditated design to kill or incapable of judging his acts and their consequences, may properly influence a finding by the trial court that no specific intent to kill existed, and hence to conclude the killing was murder in the second degree." [Emphasis in original.] *Commonwealth v. Tarver, 446 Pa. at 239, 284 A.2d at 762*. As the *Tarver* Court recognized, this exception to the general rule does not change the nature of the crime. Murder still remains murder. Only the degree of the crime has been affected. Because there exist no analogous degrees of robbery (and instantly burglary), the *Tarver* Court refused to extend this exception beyond the homicide area. To hold otherwise, and allow evidence of voluntary intoxication to negate the necessary specific intent required of both robbery and burglary, would permit an individual's voluntary intoxication to serve as a complete exoneration for all criminal acts committed while in that state. This cannot be tolerated.

The majority, while paying lip-service to the fundamental rule that voluntary intoxication is no defense to an individual's criminal acts, nevertheless sanctions such a defense. In ruling that evidence of voluntary intoxication can be offered for the purpose of negating the presence of the required specific intent in both robbery and burglary, the majority has, without good reason, discarded the traditional rule. It matters little that the majority regards such evidence as only bearing upon an element of the crime, the specific intent of the perpetrator, rather than serving as a defense to such crime. The end result is the same and no amount of legal jargon will make it otherwise. If a criminal defendant, charged with either robbery or burglary, is found by the jury, because of voluntary intoxication, not to have had the requisite specific intent, he must be found not guilty. Only a person blind to reality could fail to perceive that there is no practical difference between the admission of evidence to negate an element of the crime and the admission of evidence to constitute a defense. The end result is that human life and property would hardly be considered any longer as being under legal protection. An individual will, henceforth, be permitted to avail himself of his voluntary intoxication to exempt him from any legal responsibility which would attach to him, if sober. As one noted annotator said in speaking of voluntary intoxication as a defense to criminal responsibility, " . . . all that the crafty criminal would require for a well planned [robbery or burglary] would be a revolver in one hand to commit the deed, and a quart of intoxicating liquor in the other. . . . "

Today, all too many murderers, robbers, burglars, rapists and other felons escape the imposition of justice for unsound and unrealistic reasons. The present ruling of this Court widens that avenue of escape.

I emphatically dissent.

Stephen J. Morse, Fear of Danger, Flight from Culpability
4 Psychology, Public Policy, and the Law 250, 253-256 (1998)

Montana's statute, which prohibits defendants from using evidence of voluntary intoxication to rebut an allegation that a crime was committed with a required, subjective mens rea, expresses moral condemnation of behaving badly when drunk. Aristotle, for example, thought that a person who did harm when drunk was undoubtedly culpable. But getting drunk is one wrong, and whatever else an agent does while drunk is another. With the notable exceptions of felony-murder and certain forms of accomplice liability, the common law does not allow the mens rea for one crime to substitute for the mens rea required for a second crime. . . . The exceptions to this rule already noted are highly controversial precisely because they permit strict liability. . . .

The influential Model Penal Code tries to have it both ways about intoxication. While rejecting strict liability generally, the Code provides that a voluntarily intoxicated defendant may use evidence of such intoxication to negate purpose and knowledge but not to negate recklessness. The Code thus equates the culpability for becoming drunk with the conscious awareness of anything criminal that the agent might do while drunk. This "equation" permits the state to meet its burden of persuasion concerning recklessness without actually proving that the defendant was ever actually aware that getting drunk created a grave risk that the defendant would then commit the specific harm the statute prohibited. As an empirical matter, however, this equation is often preposterous. An agent will not be consciously aware while becoming drunk that there is a substantial and unjustifiable risk that he or she will commit a particular crime when drunk, unless the person has a previous history of becoming unconsciously involved when drunk in the creation of great risk of committing this specific crime. If such a prior history or other circumstances indicating previous conscious awareness exists, then the prosecution is capable of proving and should be required to prove the existence of previous awareness. The prosecution should not be able to rely on what is, in effect, the conclusive presumption that becoming drunk demonstrates the same culpability as the actual conscious awareness of a substantial and unjustifiable risk that the defendant would commit the specific harm.

The Montana statute goes even further toward strict liability than the Model Penal Code, of course, by providing that a defendant cannot use evidence of voluntary intoxication to negate purpose or knowledge. One interpretation of the statute—rejected by Montana's own Supreme Court, but adopted by Justice Ginsburg—is that the intoxication provision simply works to redefine the mental state element for murder to include an objective mens rea: negligence. Ever since the Court's opinion in Patterson v. New York, it has been clear that the states have the federal constitutional authority to effect such a redefinition, but this was not Montana's interpretation of its own law. More important for my analysis, this redefinition undermines the standard view that culpability is hierarchically arrayed depending on the blameworthiness of the various mental states. Our society's dominant morality simply does not accept, and with good reason, that negligent harmdoing is as blameworthy as committing the same harm purposely or with conscious awareness. The latter mental states indicate that the agent is consciously lacking in concern for the interests and well-being of an identifiable victim or class of victims, an attitude toward moral obligations that is more blameworthy than lack of awareness. Few except Oliver Wendell Holmes think that objective and subjective blameworthiness ought to be equated. Characterizing a negligent killer as a murderer does violence to our ordinary notions of culpability and desert.

With these observations in mind, consider Egelhoff's culpability again. First, assume that as the result of voluntary intoxication, James Allen Egelhoff was actually in a mental state that would meet the law's requirement of unconsciousness when he killed Pavola and Christenson. It is not unthinkable morally to condemn drinking oneself purposely or recklessly into a state of unconsciousness, but this behavior is not a crime per se. Criminal law theorists dispute the basis for the exculpatory effect of unconsciousness, but all agree that it does exculpate. Thus, if one believes Egelhoff's claim that he was legally unconscious, or to put it more accurately, if the prosecution were unable to prove beyond a reasonable doubt that he was legally conscious, then Egelhoff is not guilty of purposely or knowingly killing. Moreover, there is no evidence that Egelhoff was consciously aware when he was drinking that he would become homicidal when drunk. Thus, he did not kill recklessly, even if one looks back to his earlier mental states to find culpability. Once again, Egelhoff might be fully responsible for becoming unconscious, but without proof of the mental states usually required, it is a form of strict liability to hold him fully accountable for anything that he did while unconscious. He culpably caused the condition that would negate the prima facie case, but not with purpose, knowledge, or recklessness that he would be exculpated.

Egelhoff is a dangerous agent, and it is undeniable that the State might have great difficulty proving beyond a reasonable doubt on these facts that he was legally conscious and thus guilty of purposely or knowingly killing. If he was legally conscious at the time of the killings, of course, the precision of the executions suggests that the most sensible inference is that he killed purposely or knowingly, even if one believes his claim that he did not remember the homicides. Without the crutch of strict liability, however, the State might be able to convict only for negligent homicide, typically graded as involuntary manslaughter, which carries a substantially shorter term of years than murder. But our fear of Egelhoff and revulsion at his deeds should not be allowed to prove too much. The Constitution's requirement that in criminal cases the state must prove each element of the crime charged beyond a reasonable doubt almost always makes it more difficult for the prosecution to prove its most serious charge. Our society bears this risk because, except in a small number of inevitable cases, we believe that it is unacceptable to convict a legally innocent person. Concern with culpability thus almost always conflicts with concern for public safety.

Egelhoff signals weakened commitment to the importance of culpability. Negligent homicide is not the same as intentional killing, and the culpability of becoming drunk and unconscious is not the same as the culpability for murder. The Supreme Court's acceptance of the equation of these morally distinguishable cases is disquieting. . . .

Paul H. Robinson & John M. Darley, Study 10: Voluntary Intoxication

Justice, Liability and Blame 114-115 (1995)

[The authors summarize as follows the findings of their empirical study of lay intuitions of justice with regard to offenses during which the offender is voluntarily intoxicated:]

In the subjects' view, the factor that is highly determinative of liability is the person's pre-intoxication culpability as to committing the offense. A person who becomes intoxicated—purposefully, recklessly, or negligently—and at the time of becoming intoxicated is purposeful as to causing death, is treated by the subjects as a murderer and . . . is seen as having a highly culpable state of mind as to the killing at the time he causes the death. A person who is reckless as to whether he will cause a death, as shown by his plans to severely beat another individual, becomes intoxicated either purposefully, recklessly, or negligently, and while intoxicated beats and kills the other, is assigned liability similar to one committing reckless homicide (manslaughter). In the faultless [pre-intoxication culpability] cases, [the killer] receives quite high sentences, although ones that are diminished from the reckless and purposeful cases.

These results suggest that the differences between our respondent's moral intuitions and most codes are occasionally different, but not as different as some other cases that we have considered. Certainly the codes' position is consistent with the subjects' view in the cases where a person culpably intoxicates himself and, before his intoxication, has no purpose as to causing another's death. He is treated as liable for manslaughter by most codes and nearly so by the subjects.

The major code-community difference arises in the consideration of the person's pre-intoxication degree of culpability as to causing death. It makes a great deal of difference to our respondents and none in the codes. For instance, when a person is purposeful as to causing death before he becomes intoxicated, the subjects would impose liability for murder while the codes' voluntary intoxication provision imposes liability only for manslaughter. That is, the codes, counterintuitively, do not discriminate the case of the individual who is purposeful about killing another beforehand, and then gets drunk and kills, from the individual who has no such pre-intoxication purpose. But . . . the codes do not prevent a prosecutor from using as the basis for homicide liability the person's conduct in becoming intoxicated and his culpable state of mind as to causing death at that time. Such a theory of prosecution would produce the murder liability that the subjects impose.

Higher culpability than negligence as to becoming intoxicated generally has some but not a major effect in increasing the liability assigned by our subjects, and is given no such effect in the legal codes. Apparently culpability as to getting intoxicated is only slightly a determinant of degree of liability but serves mainly to provide a fixed minimum requirement for liability. [To match lay intuitions,] codes could be altered to give a slightly higher degree of liability for greater culpability in becoming intoxicated, or such could be taken into account as a factor in sentencing.

Paul H. Robinson, Causing the Conditions of One's Own Defense: A Study in the Limits of Theory in Criminal Law Doctrine

71 Virginia Law Review 1, 14-17, 27, 30-31, 35-36, 51 (1985) (abridged)

Most jurisdictions allow a defense of voluntary intoxication negating an offense element for offenses requiring purpose or knowledge but deny it for other, lesser-included offenses. . . . The most common rationale given for this rule is that the actor's culpability in becoming intoxicated is an adequate basis on which to impute recklessness as to committing the offense.

Denying a failure of proof defense for voluntary intoxication that negates the recklessness required for manslaughter is troubling, however, for a number of reasons. . . . First, the imputation of culpability—recklessness under codes following the Model Penal Code, and greater culpability under many other codes—is generally triggered by a definition of "voluntariness" in becoming intoxicated that requires only negligence. . . .

Second, the imputation of recklessness is objectionable because even if the actor is reckless, or even purposeful, as to *getting intoxicated*, it does not follow that he is reckless as to *causing the death of the pedestrian*. The notion that a person risks all manner of resulting harm when he voluntarily becomes intoxicated is common, but is obviously incorrect.[1]

Finally, the imputation of a culpable state of mind when none truly exists seems particularly strange for the Model Penal Code drafters, who opposed placing the burden of persuasion on the defendant for most defenses. Yet as to

---

1. Hawaii rejects the Model Penal Code provision for just this reason: "[The Model Penal Code] equates the defendant's becoming drunk with the reckless disregard by him of risks created by his subsequent conduct and thereby forecloses the issue." Hawaii Rev. Stat. § 702-230 commentary (1976).

intoxication, the drafters permit what is in essence an irrebuttable presumption as to the existence of an element of the offense.

Proposal: Maintaining the Defense for the Offense Conduct But Imposing Liability for Conduct in Causing the Defense Conditions

As has been illustrated above, the current treatment of an actor who is culpable in causing the conditions of his defense is problematic in several respects. An alternative approach suggested here would continue to allow the actor a defense for the immediate conduct constituting the offense, but would separately impose liability on the basis of the actor's earlier conduct in culpably causing the conditions of his or her defense.

This alternative "conduct-in-causing" analysis avoids the problems arising from current law treatment and has several advantages. It avoids the improper assumption that an actor who intends to cause (or risks causing) the conditions under which an offense is committed necessarily intends to commit (or risks committing) the offense. It also properly distinguishes among levels of culpability at the time of causing one's defense in determining the level of liability to be imposed. . . .

This analysis has several advantages. For example, it properly accounts for different levels of culpability as to causing the subsequent offense. Assume an actor knows that he always beats his wife uncontrollably after he returns from drinking with his buddies and that he knows that the severity of the beating is directly proportional to the extent of his drinking. He decides to kill his wife, goes to the bar intending to drink heavily to cause the desired beating, and returns homes and uncontrollably beats his wife to death. The evidence suggests that at the time of the beating, because of his gross intoxication, he was unaware of a risk that his conduct would kill his wife. He may not even have been aware of his conduct. The Model Penal Code would permit his intoxication to negate purpose or knowledge as to the death of his wife; it would impute recklessness and thereby convict him of reckless homicide (manslaughter). It seems clear, however, that a conviction for an intentional killing (murder) would be appropriate here. The proposed conduct-in-causing analysis would hold the actor liable for murder, based on his conduct in causing his intoxication and his then-existing intention to kill his wife.

Not only does the proposed analysis avoid treating such a grand schemer too leniently, but it also protects a less-culpable actor from being treated too harshly. The Model Penal Code would impute recklessness to the drinker who at the time of his imbibing is unaware of any risk that he may kill or even beat his wife, and thus would convict him of reckless homicide. The proposed analysis would avoid such an unwarranted result. The jury would examine his state of mind as to killing his wife at the time he began to drink and would probably conclude that at that time he was at most negligent as to causing his wife's death. He would thus be liable for, at most, negligent homicide. Indeed, a jury might conclude that a *reasonable person* under the same circumstances would have been unaware of a risk of causing his wife's death; thus, the actor might escape liability even for negligent homicide, [although he might be liable for some lesser offense about which he might have been reckless, such as reckless assault].

The theory . . . suggests reformulation of the doctrine [of] intoxication negating an offense element . . . :

Intoxication Negating An Offense Element

(1) Evidence of intoxication, voluntary or involuntary, may be admitted into evidence to negate a culpability element of an offense.

(2) If an actor's intoxication negates a required culpability element at the time of the offense, such element is nonetheless established if:

(a) the actor satisfied such element immediately preceding or during the time that he was becoming intoxicated or at any time thereafter until commission of the offense, and

(b) the harm or evil intended, contemplated, or risked is brought about by the actor's subsequent conduct during intoxication. . . .

Thus, the translation from theory to doctrine is relatively easy. Difficulties arise, however, in guaranteeing the feasibility or workability of the resulting doctrine. . . .

■ LAW (SUBSEQUENT)

Current Indiana Statutes
(2006)

Section 35-41-2-5. Intoxication Not a Defense

Intoxication is not a defense in a prosecution for an offense and may not be taken into consideration in determining the existence of a mental state that is an element of the offense unless the defendant meets the requirements of IC 35-41-3-5.

Section 35-41-3-5. Intoxication

It is a defense that the person who engaged in the prohibited conduct did so while he was intoxicated, only if the intoxication resulted from the introduction of a substance into his body:

(1) without his consent; or

(2) when he did not know that the substance might cause intoxication.

Sanchez v. State
749 N.E.2d 509 (Ind. 2001)

The court notes that in 1996, the United States Supreme Court held, in *Montana v. Egelhoff*, 518 U.S. 37 (1996), that the Fourteenth Amendment Due

Process Clause is not offended by a statute that bars the use of evidence of voluntary intoxication to negate a culpable state of mind required by an offense definition. In response, the Indiana legislature enacted Section 35-41-2-5. Relying on *Egelhoff* as to the federal constitution and reaching a similar conclusion with regard to their state constitution, the court held *Terry v. State* to no longer be good law and the new statute constitutional. [In *Egelhoff*, a plurality of the Court concluded that due process is offended only if an exclusion of evidence "offends some principle of justice so rooted in the traditions and conscience of our people as to be ranked as fundamental."]

APPENDIX A: SECTION 14

Complicity

DISCUSSION MATERIALS
*Issue: Should Criminal Liability Be Imposed for Facilitating Conduct that One
Knows Is a Crime, Even if Facilitating the Crime Is Not One's Purpose?*
Model Penal Code Section 2.04, Tentative Draft No. 1 Commentary, Liability of
Accomplices
New York Criminal Facilitation Statutes
Model Penal Code Section 2.06 Commentary, Liability of
Accomplices—Culpability
ADVANCED MATERIALS
Table: Summary of Requirements for Complicity Liability
Hypothetical: The Egg Hunt
Notes on the Requirements for Liability for Causing Crime by an Innocent
Table: Summary of Requirements for Causing Crime by an Innocent

---

✳ DISCUSSION MATERIALS

Issue: Should Criminal Liability Be Imposed for Facilitating Conduct that One Knows Is a Crime, Even if Facilitating the Crime Is Not One's Purpose?

The first Model Penal Code Commentary excerpt comes from a proposed draft, subsequently rejected by the A.L.I., that attempts to justify imposing complicity liability on merely "knowingly" assisting an offense (but also requires substantial facilitation of the crime). The New York Criminal Facilitation Statute demonstrates a different approach to complicity than that taken by the Model Penal Code: It extends liability to those who are aware of providing aid but treats it as a lesser offense than the crime itself. The second Commentary excerpt is taken from the final official Commentary and offers the Institute's reasons for adopting instead the more demanding "purposeful" assistance requirement.

Model Penal Code Section 2.04, Tentative Draft
No. 1 Commentary Liability of Accomplices
11-12, 27-32 (1953)

Section 2.04 Liability based on behavior; Liability for behavior of another; Complicity . . .

(3) A person is an accomplice of promoting or facilitating the commission of the crime if:

(a) with the purpose of promoting or facilitating the commission of the crime, he

(1) commanded, requested, encouraged or provoked such other person to commit it; or

(2) aided, agreed to aid or attempted to aid such other person in planning or committing it; or

(3) having a legal duty to prevent the crime, failed to make proper effort so to do; or

(b) acting with knowledge that such other person was committing or had the purpose of committing the crime, he knowingly, substantially facilitated its commission; or

[Alternate: (b) acting with knowledge that such other person was committing or had the purpose of committing the crime, he knowingly provided means or opportunity for the commission of the crime, substantially facilitating its commission; or]

(c) his behavior is expressly declared by law to establish his complicity. . . .

The draft does not confine [accomplice liability] to the case where there is a true purpose to promote or to facilitate commission of the crime. It also reaches those who, with knowledge that another is committing or has the purpose of committing an offense, knowingly facilitate its commission. In this event, however, it requires that the actor knowingly facilitate substantially. This is a median position on a much debated issue that requires explanation.

This issue is whether knowingly facilitating the commission of a crime ought to be sufficient for complicity, absent a true purpose to advance the criminal end. The problem, to be sure, is narrow in its focus: often, if not usually, aid rendered with guilty knowledge implies purpose since it has no other motivation. But there are many and important cases where this is the central question in determining liability. A lessor rents with knowledge that the premises will be used to establish a bordello. A vendor sells with knowledge that the subject of the sale will be used in commission of a crime. A doctor counsels against an abortion but, at the patient's insistence, refers her to a competent abortionist. A utility provides telephone or telegraph service, knowing it is used for book-making. An employee puts through a shipment in the course of his employment though he knows the shipment is illegal. A farm boy clears the ground for setting up a still, knowing that the venture is illicit. Such cases can be multiplied indefinitely; they have given the courts much difficulty when they have been brought, whether as prosecutions for conspiracy or for the substantive offense involved.

The problem has had most attention in the federal courts where there is division of opinion as to the criterion . . . [author reviews Learned Hand's opinion in

Peoni, discussed in the Overview materials, which argues for a purposeful require-ment in complicity].

The Supreme Court has quoted the *Peoni* formulation with approval and it has had some influence on other Circuits. Strong disagreement has, however, been expressed. Judge Parker, for example, has declared that guilt "as an acces-sory depends, not on 'having a stake' in the outcome of the crime . . . but on aiding and assisting the perpetrators. . . . The seller may not ignore the purpose for which the purchase is made if he is advised of that purpose, or wash his hands of the aid that he has given the perpetrator of a felony by the plea that he has merely made a sale of merchandise. One who sells a gun to another, knowing that he is buying it to commit a murder, would hardly escape conviction as an accessory to the murder by showing that he received full price for the gun. . . . " Even the Second Circuit has been less than rigorous in application of the doc-trine of *Peoni*, finding such factors as the contraband quality of the article sup-plied and failure to report the sale, as legally required, sufficient to meet its demands. Such factors seem, however, to have smaller bearing on the actor's pur-pose, which *Peoni* treats as crucial, than they have on the effects of his behavior, the extent to which it actually does facilitate commission of the crime.

The draft, it is submitted, should not embrace the *Peoni* limitation. Conduct which knowingly facilitates the commission of crimes is by hypothesis a proper object of preventive effort by the penal law, unless, of course, it is affirmatively justifiable. It is important in that effort to safeguard the innocent but the require-ment of guilty knowledge adequately serves this end—knowledge both that there is a purpose to commit a crime and that one's own behavior renders aid. There are, however, infinite degrees of aid to be considered. This is the point, we think, at which distinctions should be drawn. Accordingly, when a true purpose to further the crime is lacking, the draft requires that the accessorial behavior substantially facilitate commission of the crime and that it does so to the knowledge of the actor. This qualification provides a basis for discrimination that should satisfy the common sense of justice. A vendor who supplies materials readily available upon the market arguably does not make substantial contribution to commission of the crime since the materials could have easily been gotten elsewhere. The minor employee may win exemption on this ground, though he minded his own business to preserve his job. What is required is to give the courts and juries a criterion for drawing lines that must be drawn. The formula proposed accomplishes this purpose by a standard that is relevant, it is submitted, to all the legal ends involved. There will, of course, be arguable cases; they should, we think, be argued in these terms.

It has been urged in criticism of section 3(b) that "substantially facilitates" lays down too vague a test of liability to guide a jury verdict and that the legis-lature should determine whether or not in specific types of situations aid with knowledge but without purpose to further the commission of a crime ought to suffice for criminality. Whether a vendor, for example, must forego a sale because he knows of the illegal purpose of his would-be customer requires, it is argued, resolution of competing interests: that of vendors in freedom to refrain from the policing of vendees and that of the community in reducing the incidence of behavior that facilitates the commission of crimes.

We readily concede the vagueness of "substantially facilitates" but defend the formula by the submission that no less vague alternative has been proposed that both affirms a liability without a purpose to facilitate the crime and gives the court and jury a discretion to avoid it when its imposition would be deemed extreme. This practical consideration, coupled with the requirement of *scienter*, serves to allay a constitutional problem upon this score.

We also agree that a problem of conflicting interests is presented but submit that, absent special grounds that constitute legal justification, it ought to be resolved in favor of a principle that regards crime prevention as the prior value to be served. The justification provisions (Article 3) must, of course, be adequate for this case as for others and, when they are submitted, should be studied with this case in mind. But when the only interest of the actor is his wish for freedom to forego concern about the criminal purposes of others, though he knowingly facilitates in a substantial measure the achievement of such purposes, it is an interest that, we think, is properly subordinated generally to the larger interest of preventing crime. . . .

New York Criminal Facilitation Statutes
New York Penal Law §115.00 (2007)[1]

Section 115.00. Criminal Facilitation in the Fourth Degree

A person is guilty of criminal facilitation in the fourth degree when, believing it probable that he is rendering aid:

(1) to a person who intends to commit a crime, he engages in conduct which provides such person with means or opportunity for the commission thereof and which in fact aids such person to commit a felony; or

(2) to a person under sixteen years of age who intends to engage in conduct which would constitute a crime, he, being over eighteen years of age, engages in conduct which provides such person with means or opportunity for the commission thereof and which in fact aids such person to commit a crime.

Criminal facilitation in the fourth degree is a class A misdemeanor.

Section 115.01. Criminal Facilitation in the Third Degree

A person guilty of criminal facilitation in the third degree, when believing it probable that he is rendering aid to a person under sixteen years of age who intends to engage in conduct that would constitute a felony, he, being over eighteen years of age, engages in conduct which provides such person with means or opportunity for the commission thereof and which in fact aids such person to commit a felony.

Criminal facilitation in the third degree is a class E felony.

Section 115.05. Criminal Facilitation in the Second Degree

A person is guilty of criminal facilitation in the second degree when, believing it probable that he is rendering aid to a person who intends to commit a class A felony, he engages in conduct which provides such person with means or opportunity for the commission thereof and which in fact aids such person to commit such class A felony.

---

1. For similar provisions, see Ariz. § 13-604; Ky. §§ 506.080 to .100; N.D. § 12.1-06-02. See also Brown Commn. Final Report § 1002; Mass. ch. 263, § 46; W. Va. §§ 61-4-8 to -4-10.

Criminal facilitation in the second degree is a class C felony.

Section 115.08. Criminal Facilitation in the First Degree

A person is guilty of criminal facilitation in the first degree when, believing it probable that he is rendering aid to a person under sixteen years of age who intends to engage in conduct that would constitute a class A felony, he, being over eighteen years of age, engages in conduct which provides such person with means or opportunity for the commission thereof and which in fact aids such person to commit such a class A felony.

Criminal facilitation in the first degree is a class B felony.

Section 115.10. Criminal Facilitation; No Defense

It is no defense to a prosecution for criminal facilitation that:

(1) The person facilitated was not guilty of the underlying felony owing to criminal irresponsibility or other legal incapacity or exemption, or to unawareness of the criminal nature of the conduct in question or to other factors precluding the mental state required for the commission of such felony; or

(2) The person facilitated has not been prosecuted for or convicted of the underlying felony, or has previously been acquitted thereof; or

(3) The defendant himself is not guilty of the felony which he facilitated because he did not act with the intent or other culpable mental state required for the commission thereof.

Section 115.15. Criminal Facilitation; Corroboration

A person shall not be convicted of criminal facilitation upon the testimony of a person who has committed the felony charged to have been facilitated unless such testimony be corroborated by such other evidence as tends to connect the defendant with such facilitation.

Model Penal Code Section 2.06 Commentary
Liability of Accomplices—Culpability
Official Draft and Revised Comments 318-319, 321-322 (1985)

Though the Chief Reporter favored a formulation that would broaden liability beyond merely purposive conduct, the Institute rejected that position, principally on the argument that the need for stating a general principle in this section pointed toward a narrow formulation in order not to include situations where liability was inappropriate. Many recent revisions and proposals reflect a similar judgment about accomplice liability.[2] The possibility that a broadened

---

2. See Ala. § 13A-2-23; Ariz. § 13-301; Ark. § 41-303(1); Colo. § 18-1-603; Del. tit. 11, § 271(2); Haw. § 702-222(1); Ill. ch. 38, § 5-2(c); Ky. § 502.020(1); Mo. § 562.041(1)(2); Mont. § 94-2-107(3) (but see § 94-2-107(1)); N.H. § 626.8(III)(a); N.J. § 2C:2-6(c)(1); N.D. § 12.1-03-01(1)(b); Ore. § 161.155(2); Pa. tit. 18, § 306(c)(1); Tex. § 7.02(a)(2); Alas. § 11.16.110(2) (H.B. 661, Jan. 1978); S.C. § 11.1; Tenn. § 502(a)(2); W. Va. § 61-2-13(a).

liability should obtain in particular contexts is one that can be, and has been dealt with in the drafting of the substantive offenses themselves,[3] a situation explicitly left open by Subsection (3)(b), as well as by Subsection (2)(b). There is thus still room for the judgment that when the only interest of the actor is his wish to forego concern about the criminal purposes of others, though he knowingly facilitates in a substantial measure the achievement of such purposes, his interest is properly subordinated generally to the larger interest of preventing crime.

Some states have gone further, following the lead of New York, and have adopted general facilitation provisions.[4] These extend accessorial liability to persons who engage in conduct with the awareness that it will aid others to commit serious crimes, but treat such facilitation as a less grave offense than the crimes that are aided. This approach may well constitute a sensible accommodation of the competing considerations advanced at the Institute meeting. . . .

7. Result Elements. Subsection (4) makes it clear that complicity in conduct causing a particular criminal result entails accountability for that result so long as the accomplice is personally culpable with respect to the result to the extent demanded by the definition of the crime. Thus, if the accomplice recklessly endangers life by rendering assistance to another, he can be convicted of manslaughter if a death results,[5] even though the principal actor's liability is at a different level. In effect, therefore, the homicidal act is attributed to both participants, with the liability of each measured by his own degree of culpability toward the result.

The most common situation in which Subsection (4) will become relevant is where unanticipated results occur from conduct for which the actor is responsible under Subsection (3). His liability for unanticipated occurrences rests upon two factors: his complicity in the conduct that causes the result, and his culpability towards the result to the degree required by the law, that makes the result criminal. Accomplice liability in this event is thus assimilated to the liability of the principal actor; the principal actor's liability for unanticipated results, of course, would turn on the extent to which he was reckless or negligent, as required by the law defining the offense, toward the result in question. There is also room for application of Subsection (4) to the common felony-murder situation. An accomplice in a felony where one of the felons causes a death could be convicted for manslaughter or murder upon proof that, under Subsection (3), he was an accomplice in the conduct that caused the death and, under Subsection (4), he had the requisite culpability as to the death imposed by the relevant provision.[6]

---

3. See Section 242.6(2): "Any person who knowingly causes or facilitates an escape commits an offense."

4. [The MPC Commentary footnote cites the New York Substantial Facilitation Statutes reproduced above.]

5. See Section 210.3.

6. A manslaughter prosecution could be brought on the theory that the defendant consciously disregarded a substantial and unjustifiable risk that death would result from the assisted conduct, the risk being of such a nature and degree that, considering the nature and purpose of the defendant's conduct and the circumstances known to him, its disregard involved a gross deviation from the standard of conduct that a law-abiding person would have observed in the defendant's situation. See Sections 2.02(2)(c); 210.3(1)(a). A murder prosecution could be brought on the theory that the defendant was reckless as described, and moreover that he was reckless under circumstances manifesting extreme indifference to the value of human life. See Section 210.2(1)(b). In addition, of course, and by the explicit terms of Section 210.2(1)(b), the presumption that the requisite recklessness and indifference to make out a case of murder exist is afforded by the fact that "the actor is . . . an accomplice in the commission of . . . robbery. . . . "

This formulation combines the policy that accomplices are equally account-able within the range of their complicity with the policies underlying those crimes defined according to results. It is thus a desirable extension of accomplice liability beyond the principles stated in Subsection (3). A number of recent revisions have similar coverage.[7]

❋ ADVANCED MATERIALS

Table: Summary of Requirements for Complicity Liability

	Defendant (Accomplice)	Perpetrator (Principal)
Objective requirements	CL: assist (or encourage) MPC: aid or agree or attempt to aid	CL: objective elements of object offense MPC: same ("on proof of commission of the offense," § 2.06(7)
Culpability requirements	As to Conduct — CL and MPC: "purpose of promoting or facilitating the commission of the offense" (§ 2.06(3)(a))	CL: culpability requirements of object offense MPC: none (§ 2.06(7) rejects unconvictable perpetrator defense)
	As to Circumstances — CL: elevate to purposeful MPC: unclear; probably left to "interpretation," as in conspiracy	
	As to Result — CL: elevate to purposeful MPC: do not elevate (§ 2.06(4))	

MPC = Model Penal Code
CL = Common Law

Hypothetical: The Egg Hunt

Zander lives in an apartment at Cottage 12 of Southbury Training School. His charges are retarded men. "Pop," as they call Zander, shaves the men, helps them dress and shower, and generally supervises their activities. They are gentle

---

7. Editor's Note—The Model Penal Code drafters say this about the required culpability as to a circum-stance element of the substantive offense:

There is deliberate ambiguity as to whether the purpose requirement extends to circumstance ele-ments of the contemplated offense or whether, as in the case of attempts, the policy of the substantive offense on this point should control. The reasoning is the same as in the case of conspiracy, which is set forth in some detail in Section 5.03 Comment 2(c)(ii). The result, therefore, is that the actor must have a purpose with respect to the proscribed conduct or the proscribed result, with his attitude towards the circumstances to be left to resolution by the courts. His attitude towards the criminality of the conduct, see Section 2.02(9), is irrelevant here as it is in the other cases, subject of course to the limitations in Section 2.04(3).

Model Penal Code §2.06 Commentary at n.37 (1985).

people, but their mental impairment sometimes creates difficult situations. The "boys," as the staff call them, have recently taken to collecting anything small and shiny, calling such items "eggs." A recent visitor became frightened when her car was surrounded by a group of men three-deep, pressing their faces against the glass, pointing at the chrome dials on her console, and shouting "Egg! Egg!" The boys' interest in shiny objects is not accidental. Zander has cultivated it as a means of motivating them to steal silverware from the large restaurant where many of them work during the day as dishwashers.

Attie Winter, the house mother at Cottage 20, disapproves of the way Zander runs his cottage. In her view, the strip-baseball and tackle-badminton games, which Zander allows and the "boys" love, breed bad habits. Attie suspects Zander has the boys doing even more objectionable things but cannot prove it.

Zander knows of Attie's attempts to have him fired. He decides that a little intimidation may be useful. During lunch and again at dinner, he describes to the boys, in detail, "Mom" Winter's beautiful necklace of small silver "eggs." After the boys have gone to bed, Zander leaves to meet a friend for drinks at a nearby bar, as he often does. The night janitor is under instructions to call the central office if any problem arises. Zander leaves the front door to the dormitory unlocked, expecting that the boys will take the opportunity to sneak past the sleeping night janitor and head for Cottage 20 to find Mom Winter's necklace, undoubtedly scaring her plenty in the process.

Halfway to the bar, Zander remembers that he has forgotten to lock his room, where his loaded gun is stored. He has let the boys play cops and robbers with his gun when it was unloaded. They might think to take it with them when they go to Cottage 20 on their "egg hunt." After debating with himself, he concludes that it is more likely that they will not think of it.

As it happens, the boys have been calculating their attack on Cottage 20 ever since lunch. They notice immediately when Zander does not lock the dormitory door and his room. After waiting until they are sure he will not be returning soon, they take his gun and head en masse in search of the now-legendary necklace. They confront Mom Winter. When she resists turning over her necklaces, they point the gun at her and "shoot." But this time the gun is loaded, and to the boys' horror, Mom Winter falls to the floor bleeding. Zander is fired from his position when an investigation reveals his part in the affair.

Zander is also charged with the silverware thefts and with the murder of Attie Winter. Is he liable?

Notes on the Requirements for Liability for Causing Crime by an Innocent

Bases for finding perpetrator to be "innocent or irresponsible"
Objective requirement: "Causing" the offense
    Innocents as mere instruments
Culpability requirements track underlying offense
    Rule's ambiguity as to "offense analysis" versus "element analysis"
Culpability as to causing innocent to act vs. culpability as to object offense
    Analysis of "Egg Hunt" hypothetical: Culpability as to offense
    Culpability as to causing the conduct: Variable or fixed?
    Case for recklessness as to causing conduct
Requirements of innocent person for liability of instigator

Bases for finding perpetrator to be "innocent or irresponsible" The person engaging in the conduct constituting the offense may be "innocent or irresponsible" for any number of reasons. Perhaps he or she does not satisfy the culpability requirements of the offense, such as, for instance, when the actor asks another to retrieve her yellow umbrella from the coatroom, knowing that she does not own a yellow umbrella. The person taking the umbrella may satisfy the objective elements of theft, but does not have the culpability required, believing instead that the umbrella's owner has requested the taking. The person engaging in the criminal conduct also may be "innocent" because of a justification or excuse defense. In *State v. Dowell*, for example, the defendant compelled another man at gunpoint to attempt to rape the defendant's wife.[8] The coerced man would have an excuse of duress in most jurisdictions, yet the defendant nonetheless may be liable for causing the rape. In *Bailey v. Commonwealth*, the defendant tricked the deceased and the police into a confrontation during which the police justifiably shot the deceased.[9] While the police conduct is justified and thus exempt from liability, Bailey nonetheless is liable for the homicide, because he caused the conditions giving rise to the need for their justified conduct. In the "Egg Hunt" hypothetical, Zander's "boys" should be excused for the silverware thefts; because of the degree of their retardation they are unaware of the circumstances that make their conduct criminal. Yet Zander remains accountable: Because he intentionally caused their conduct and has the culpability required for theft, he is liable for the theft even though they are not.

Objective requirement: "Causing" the offense The objective requirement for liability for causing crime by an innocent is more demanding than that for complicity. An accomplice need only assist in some way—even a mere attempt to assist will typically suffice. Here, however, the actor must "cause" the innocent person to commit the offense, meaning that the usual demands of the causation rules apply: The actor must be both a necessary ("but for") and a proximate cause of the innocent person's conduct. In the "Egg Hunt" hypothetical, it seems clear that the boys would not have gone to Cottage 20 and shot Mom Winter if Zander had not manipulated them to seek shiny objects, told them of Mom Winter's shiny egg necklace, and left his loaded gun where they could get it.

Innocents as mere instruments The causation requirement does not explicitly require that the actor be the moving force in the offense; but where the "perpetrator" is innocent, it is common that another person will not be considered the cause of the conduct unless he instigated it. Indeed, in some cases, the role of the actor causing the perpetrator's conduct is so prominent that the case is prosecuted without reference to the causing-crime-by-an-innocent doctrine. Instead, the actor is treated as the principal and the innocent party is treated as simply an "instrument" of the actor, equivalent to an inanimate object such as a weapon or device.[10] While this may seem natural enough in many cases, it is undesirable as a general practice because it short-circuits the special requirements contained in both the doctrine of causing crime by an innocent and the doctrine of causation.

---

8. 11 S.E. 525 (N.C. 1890).

9. 329 S.E.2d 37 (Va. 1985).

10. See, e.g., State v. Dowell, 11 S.E. 525 (N.C. 1890) (defendant referred to as "instigator" and other actor as "instrumentality").

Culpability requirements track underlying offense The culpability requirements for causing crime by an innocent are more explicit than those for complicity. The Model Penal Code requires that the actor have "the kind of culpability that is sufficient for the commission of the offense."[11] Thus, one may be liable, under this theory of liability, for negligent homicide or statutory rape, either of which would require less than "purpose" as to some element of the offense: a result and a circumstance element, respectively. (Recall the ambiguity under complicity theory as to whether such liability is permissible: There is confusion as to whether the culpability elements of the object offense are all elevated to "purposeful" for the accomplice although they may be lower for the perpetrator. The absence of an elevation requirement for causing crime by an innocent might provide additional evidence to support the "no-elevation" interpretation of the complicity statute. If heightened culpability is not necessary for imputation of an innocent's conduct, one might argue, why should it be necessary for imputation of a fellow criminal's conduct?)

Rule's ambiguity as to "offense analysis" versus "element analysis" While the culpability requirements for causing crime by an innocent seem clear in comparison to the murky picture for complicity, the language of the Code provision is not without ambiguity. That the drafters spoke in the singular— *"the kind* of culpability that *is* sufficient for the commission of the offense" —might suggest that they envision a single culpability level for each offense. The same phrase is used in other parts of the Code where the implication is even stronger.[12] Such a reference is a throwback to "offense analysis," yet the Code generally (and rightly) repudiates offense analysis in favor of "element analysis." Under the Code's element analysis system, an offense may require different culpability levels as to different elements of the same offense. There seems little difficulty in this instance in concluding that the Code's drafters intended section 2.06(2)(a) to mean that the actor who causes an innocent's crime must satisfy each of the culpability requirements— each culpability requirement as to each objective element—of the object offense. Despite its misleading language, then, the causing-crime-by-an-innocent doctrine is consistent with the Code's overarching scheme of element analysis.

Culpability as to causing innocent to act vs. culpability as to object offense Recall that in complicity there exist two distinct kinds of culpability requirements: culpability as to assisting the perpetrator in the conduct that constitutes the offense, and culpability as to the elements of the object offense. An actor might have different degrees of culpability as to each of these two things. For example, an actor who gives his drunken friend car keys might be purposeful as to assisting the friend's driving, but he might simultaneously be only negligent as to whether the driving will cause the death of another motorist. Similarly, in cases of causing crime by an innocent, an actor may have one level of culpability as to causing the innocent person to act and a different level of culpability as to the elements of the object offense. An actor might be "purposeful" in causing his immature or impaired brother to shoot a hunting rifle, but may be only reckless as to whether the shot will accidentally cause the death of another person.

---

11. Model Penal Code § 2.06(2)(a).
12. See, e.g., Model Penal Code §§ 3.02(2), 3.09(2).

Analysis of "Egg Hunt" hypothetical: Culpability as to offense   In the "Egg Hunt" hypothetical above, it is Zander's purpose to cause the boys to go to Cottage 20 and scare Attie Winter, but he is probably only reckless as to causing the boys to kill her. When he decides not to return to lock his room, he does not desire that the boys will take his gun and shoot Attie, though he is aware of a risk that they might. Because he is only reckless as to causing Attie's death, he ought to be liable only for manslaughter (reckless homicide). As to the silverware thefts, Zander has the culpability required for theft: He knows the silverware is another's property, and it is his purpose to deprive the owner of it. He therefore ought to be liable for the thefts.

Culpability as to causing the conduct: Variable or fixed?   As to Zander's culpability toward causing the boys' conduct, he is purposeful as to causing the conduct constituting the thefts (taking the silverware), but it is less clear that he has the purpose to cause the conduct constituting the killing (pointing the gun at Attie Winter and "shooting"). The Model Penal Code provision that addresses causing an innocent's crime is silent regarding what culpability is required as to "causing" the innocent to engage in the conduct constituting the offense. One interpretation of the provision is that the drafters intend the culpability as to "causing" the offense conduct to be "the kind of culpability that is sufficient for the commission of the offense." But such an interpretation seems to repeat the false "offense analysis" assumption that each offense has only a single culpability level: If the offense were to have different culpability requirements as to different objective elements, it would not be clear which of these should apply to the requirement of causing the offense conduct by the innocent. Another approach may be to set a fixed, minimum level of culpability as to causing the innocent person to act. One might argue, using Model Penal Code section 2.02(3), that although the provision is silent on the culpability required as to causing the innocent person to act, strict liability should not be assumed, and instead a minimum requirement of recklessness should be "read in." If the offense contains a single stated culpability level, another approach, using Model Penal Code section 2.02(4), may be to apply this stated culpability level to all of the offense elements, including the causing-the-offense-conduct requirement.

Case for recklessness as to causing conduct   Though recklessness is a considerably lower requirement than the purpose required in the analogous context for complicity, it might be an appropriate level here, where the actor is the chief instigator and has caused the innocent's criminal conduct. By contrast, an accomplice need only assist, or attempt or agree to assist, the perpetrator in some way. In other words, complicity's high culpability requirement as to aiding the offense might be appropriate given its minimal, or non-existent, demands as to the accomplice making a causal contribution to the offense's occurrence—the high culpability requirement may counterbalance the low causal contribution requirement. Where the causal contribution requirement is high, however, as in causing crime by an innocent, a lower culpability requirement as to causing the offense conduct may be appropriate. And of course, in both instances, the actor must also satisfy all of the culpability requirements of the object offense.

Requirements of innocent person for liability of instigator   As with complicity, the actor's liability for causing crime by an innocent depends on the innocent person actually engaging in the conduct constituting the offense. In the "Egg Hunt" case, the boys must actually steal silverware and shoot Mom Winter if Zander is to be convicted of theft and homicide. It is not enough that they only attempt (unsuccessfully) to steal or kill, or that Zander only attempts (unsuccessfully) to cause them to so act. These requirements reflect the traditional view that full substantive liability is not appropriate unless the harm or evil of the offense actually occurs—though attempt liability might be appropriate if one causes an innocent to engage in an attempt. In this respect, complicity and causing crime by an innocent are similar. Note, however, that an actor who unsuccessfully attempts to cause an innocent to commit a crime is *not* liable for the full offense if the innocent nonetheless commits the offense (upon the urging of another instigator, for example).

Summary Requirements Table   The requirements for complicity liability might be summarized this way:

Table: Liability Requirements for Causing an Innocent's Crime

	Defendant (Accomplice)	Perpetrator (Principal)
Objective requirements	**CL and MPC**: cause an innocent or irresponsible person to engage in the conduct constituting the offense (MPC § 2.06(2)(a)); "cause" is defined by the normal requirements of causation	**CL and MPC**: objective elements of offense
Culpability requirements	*Culpability as to causing person to perform* **conduct** *constituting object offense:* **CL and MPC**: unspecified; recklessness read in by MPC § 2.02(3)? *Culpability as to elements of object offense:* **CL and MPC**: as required by the substantive offense ("acting with the kind of culpability that is sufficient for the commission of the offense," MPC § 2.06(2)(a))	**CL and MPC**: none (person performing offense conduct may be "innocent or irresponsible," MPC § 2.06(2)(a))

MPC = Model Penal Code
CL = Common Law

APPENDIX A: SECTION 15

The Act Requirement and Liability for an Omission

DISCUSSION MATERIALS
Issue: Should There Be a Criminal-Law-Enforced Duty to Protect, Rescue, or Assist a Stranger in Danger if One Can Do So Without Unreasonable Risk or Inconvenience?
    37 Who Saw Murder Didn't Call Police
    Rhode Island General Laws Section 11-56-1 (2006)
    Vermont Statutes Annotated, Title 12, Chapter 23, Section 519 (2006)
Wisconsin Statutes Annotated Section 940.34(1), (2), (3) (2006)
Joshua Dressler, Some Brief Thoughts (Mostly Negative) About "Bad Samaritan" Laws
Daniel B. Yeager, A Radical Community of Aid: A Rejoinder to Opponents of
    Affirmative Duties to Help Strangers
LAW (Subsequent)
    Nevada Revised Statutes (1999)

✳ DISCUSSION MATERIALS

Issue: Should There Be a Criminal-Law-Enforced Duty to Protect, Rescue, or Assist a Stranger in Danger if One Can Do So Without Unreasonable Risk or Inconvenience?

In its portrayal of Catherine Genovese's murder in front of more than thirty witnesses, the *New York Times* article below offers a look at the disturbing outcome of not imposing a duty to rescue or to assist. The obvious moral concerns have inspired three state provisions creating a duty to assist—those adopted by Rhode Island, Vermont, and Wisconsin. Even in the face of cases like the Genovese murder, Joshua Dressler opposes enacting "Bad Samaritan" laws by appealing to retributive, utilitarian, practical, and liberty-oriented arguments. In support of rescue statutes, Daniel Yeager examines what personal and societal motivations lead people not to rescue and evaluates the duty-to-rescue laws in place in some states.

37 Who Saw Murder Didn't Call Police
N.Y. Times, March 27, 1964

For more than half an hour thirty-eight respectable, law-abiding citizens in Queens watched a killer stalk and stab a woman in three separate attacks in Kew Gardens. Twice the sound of their voices and the sudden glow of their bedroom lights interrupted him and frightened him off. Each time he returned, sought her out and stabbed her again. Not one person telephoned the police during the assault; one witness called after the woman was dead. That was two weeks ago today. But Assistant Chief Inspector Frederick M. Lussen, in charge of the borough's detectives and a veteran of twenty-five years of homicide investigations, is still shocked.

He can give a matter-of-fact recitation of many murders. But the Kew Gardens slaying baffles him—not because it is a murder, but because the "good people" failed to call the police. "As we have reconstructed the crime," he said, "the assailant had three chances to kill this woman during a thirty-five minute period. He returned twice to complete the job. If we had been called when he first attacked, the woman might not be dead now."

This is what the police say happened beginning at 3:20 a.m. in the staid, middle-class, tree-lined Austin Street area:

Twenty-eight-year-old Catherine Genovese, who was called Kitty by almost everyone in the neighborhood, was returning home from her job as manager of a bar in Hollis. She parked her red Fiat in a lot adjacent to the Kew Gardens Long Island Rail Road Station, facing Mowbray Place. Like many residents of the neighborhood, she had parked there day after day since her arrival from Connecticut a year ago, although the railroad frowns on the practice. She turned off the lights of her car, locked the door and started to walk the 100 feet to the entrance of her apartment at 82-70 Austin Street, which is in a Tudor building, with stores on the first floor and apartments on the second.

The entrance to the apartment is in the rear of the building because the front is rented to retail stores. At night the quiet neighborhood is shrouded in the slumbering darkness that marks most residential areas.

Miss Genovese noticed a man at the far end of the lot, near a seven-story apartment house at 82-40 Austin Street. She halted. Then, nervously, she headed up Austin Street toward Lefferts Boulevard, where there is a call box to the 102d Police Precinct in nearby Richmond Hill. She got as far as a street light in front of a bookstore before the man grabbed her. She screamed. Lights went on in the ten-story apartment house at 82-67 Austin Street, which faces the bookstore. Windows slip open and voices punctured the early-morning stillness. Miss Genovese screamed: "Oh, my God, he stabbed me! Please help me! Please help me!" From one of the upper windows in the apartment house, a man called down: "Let that girl alone!"

The assailant looked up at him, shrugged and walked down Austin Street toward a white sedan parked a short distance away. Miss Genovese struggled to her feet. Lights went out. The killer returned to Miss Genovese, now trying to make her way around the side of the building by the parking lot to get to her apartment. The assailant stabbed her again.

"I'm dying!" she shrieked. "I'm dying!"

Windows were opened again, and lights went on in many apartments. The assailant got into his car and drove away. Miss Genovese staggered to her feet. A city bus, Q-10, the Lefferts Boulevard line to Kennedy International Airport, passed. It was 3:35 a.m.

The assailant returned. By then, Miss Genovese had crawled to the back of the building, where the freshly painted brown doors to the apartment house held out hope of safety. The killer tried the first door; she wasn't there. At the second door, 82-62 Austin Street, he saw her slumped on the floor at the foot of the stairs. He stabbed her a third time—fatally.

It was 3:50 by the time the police received their first call from a man who was a neighbor of Miss Genovese. In two minutes they were at the scene. The neighbor, a seventy-year-old woman and another woman were the only persons on the street. Nobody else came forward. The man explained that he had called the police after much deliberation. He had phoned a friend in Nassau County for advice and then he had crossed the roof of the building to the apartment of the elderly woman to get her to make the call.

"I didn't want to get involved" he sheepishly told the police.

Six days later, the police arrested Winston Moseley, a twenty-nine-year-old business-machine operator, and charged him with the homicide. Moseley had no previous record. He is married, has two children and owns a home at 133-19 Sutter Avenue, South Ozone Park, Queens. On Wednesday, a court committed him to Kings County Hospital for psychiatric observation.

The police stressed how simple it would have been to have gotten in touch with them. "A phone call," said one of the detectives, "would have done it." The police may be reached by dialing "0" for operator or SPring 7-3100.

The question of whether the witness can be held legally responsible in any way for failure to report the crime was put to the Police Department's legal bureau. There, a spokesman said: "There is no legal responsibility, with few exceptions, for any citizen to report a crime."

Under the statutes of the city, he said, a witness to a suspicious or violent death must report it to the medical examiner. Under state law, a witness cannot withhold information in a kidnaping.

Today witnesses from the neighborhood, which is made up of one-family homes in the $35,000 to $60,000 range with the exception of the two apartment houses near the railroad station, find it difficult to explain why they didn't call the police.

Lieut. Bernard Jacobs, who handled the investigation by the detectives, said: "It is one of the better neighborhoods. There are few reports of crimes. You only get the usual complaints about boys playing or garbage cans being turned over."

The police said most persons had told them they had been afraid to call, but had given meaningless answers when asked what they had feared.

"We can understand the reticence of people to become involved in an area of violence," Lieutenant Jacobs said, "but where they are in their homes, near phones, why should they be afraid to call the police?"

He said his men were able to piece together what happened—and capture the suspect—because the residents furnished all the information when detectives rang doorbells during the days following the slaying.

"But why didn't someone call us that night?" he asked unbelievingly.

Witnesses—some of them unable to believe what they had allowed to happen—told a reporter why.

A housewife, knowingly if quite casually, said, "We thought it was a lover's quarrel." A husband and wife both said, "Frankly, we were afraid." They seemed aware of the fact that events might have been different. A distraught woman, wiping her hands in her apron, said, "I didn't want my husband to get involved."

One couple, now willing to talk about that night, said they heard the first screams. The husband looked thoughtfully at the bookstore where the killer first grabbed Miss Genovese. "We went to the window to see what was happening," he said, "but the light from our bedroom made it difficult to see the street." The wife, still apprehensive, added: "I put out the light and we were able to see better."

Asked why they hadn't called the police, she shrugged and replied: "I don't know."

A man peeked out from a slight opening in the doorway to his apartment and rattled off an account of the killer's second attack. Why hadn't he called the police at the time? "I was tired," he said without emotion. "I went back to bed."

It was 4:25 a.m. when the ambulance arrived for the body of Miss Genovese. It drove off. "Then," a solemn police detective said, "the people came out."

Rhode Island General Laws Section 11-56-1
(2006)

Duty to Assist

Any person at the scene of an emergency who knows that another person is exposed to or has suffered grave physical harm shall, to the extent that he or she can do so without danger or peril to himself or herself or to others, give reasonable assistance to the exposed person. Any person violating the provisions of this section shall be guilty of a petty misdemeanor and shall be subject to imprisonment for a term not exceeding six (6) months or by a fine of not more than five hundred dollars ($500.00), or both.

Vermont Statutes Annotated, Title 12, Chapter 23, Section 519
(2006)

Emergency Medical Care

(a) A person who knows that another is exposed to grave physical harm shall, to the extent that the same can be rendered without danger or peril to himself or without interference with important duties owed to others, give reasonable assistance to the exposed person unless that assistance or care is being provided by others.

(b) A person who provides reasonable assistance in compliance with subsection (a) of this section shall not be liable in civil damages unless his acts constitute gross negligence or unless he will receive or expects to receive remuneration. Nothing contained in this subsection shall alter existing law with respect to tort liability of a practitioner of the healing arts for acts committed in the ordinary course of his practice.

(c) A person who willfully violates subsection (a) of this section shall be fined not more than $ 100.00.

Wisconsin Statutes Annotated Section 940.34(1), (2), (3)
(2006)

Duty to Aid Endangered Crime Victim

(1) . . .

    (a) Whoever violates sub. (2) (a) is guilty of a Class C misdemeanor.
. . .

(2) . . .

    (a) Any person who knows that a crime is being committed and that a victim is exposed to bodily harm shall summon law enforcement officers or other assistance or shall provide assistance to the victim. . . .

    (d) A person need not comply with this subsection if any of the following apply:

        1. Compliance would place him or her in danger.

        2. Compliance would interfere with duties the person owes to others.

        3. In the circumstances described under par. (a), assistance is being summoned or provided by others. . . .

(3) If a person renders emergency care for a victim, §895.48 (1) applies. Any person who provides other reasonable assistance under this section is immune from civil liability for his or her acts or omissions in providing the assistance. This immunity does not apply if the person receives or expects to receive compensation for providing the assistance.

Joshua Dressler, Some Brief Thoughts (Mostly Negative) About "Bad Samaritan" Laws
40 Santa Clara Law Review 971-975, 980-988 (2000)

"Soulless Individuals" in Our Midst?   [The author recounts the events of the Cash-Strohmeyer-Iverson case and the events of the Kitty Genovese case.]

What is to be done with persons like David Cash? He violated no Nevada criminal law when he purportedly left Sherrice Iverson in the clutches of Strohmeyer. But if some legislators get their way, future David Cashes will not get away so easily. Legislators of all political stripes may find it hard to resist the opportunity to enact Bad Samaritan ("BS") criminal laws. After all, who would possibly want to defend the "soulless" David Cashes or "rabies-infected animals . . . disguised as . . . human beings" of this world?

I, too, have no intention of defending the indefensible. . . . But it is precisely because the case for punishing people like Cash seems so obvious and so comforting to our psyche—it allows us to express our moral revulsion and, perhaps less charitably, feel morally superior—that we should hesitate long and hard before enacting BS legislation. Although such laws are morally defensible, there are also powerful reasons for rejecting them. . . .

Refuting the Justifications for Bad Samaritan Laws Although [some] retributive arguments support punishment of a Bad Samaritan, there are significant reasons—some retributive-based, some utilitarian, and some founded in political theory—that should give responsible lawmakers considerable pause before endorsing general duty-to-aid legislation.

Criticisms of BS laws begin with legalist concerns with retributive overtones. First, why is the offense called a "Bad Samaritan" law? The name suggests, I think, that we punish the bystander for being a bad person, i.e., for his "selfishness, callousness, or whatever it was" that caused him not to come to the aid of a person in need. However, the criminal law should not be (and, ordinarily, is not) used that way: criminal law punishes individuals for their culpable acts (or, perhaps here, culpable non-acts), but not generally for bad character. As mortals, we lack the capacity to evaluate another's soul. It is wrongful conduct, and not an individual's status as a bad person or even an individual's bad thoughts, that justify criminal intervention. BS laws may violate this principle. At a minimum, there is a serious risk that juries will inadvertently punish people for being (or seeming to be) evil or "soulless," rather than for what occurred on a specific occasion. One need only consider David Cash and the public's intense feelings of disgust and anger toward him to appreciate why jurors might convict Bad Samaritans less on the basis of the "technicalities" of a statute, and more on the basis of character evaluation.

Second, for retributivists, punishment of an innocent person is always morally wrong, and the risk of false positives—punishing an innocent person—is especially high with BS laws. . . .

Notice the inherent problem of punishing people for not-doings rather than wrongdoings. When a person points a loaded gun at another and intentionally pulls the trigger, it is reasonable to infer that the actor intended to cause harm. His mens rea is obvious. It is far harder to determine why a person does not act. . . .

[W]hy did the Genovese bystanders hear the woman scream but fail to act, if in fact that was the case? Is it at least possible that some of the bystanders did not know she was in dire jeopardy? A person who wakes up from a sleep often fails to appreciate her surroundings. Also, perhaps some of them—even all of them— believed that someone else had already called the police. It may be that, despite the condemnation directed at the Genovese bystanders, few, if any, of them were guilty of Bad Samaritanism. In view of the inherent ambiguities in such circumstances, if juries take their duties seriously—including the presumption of innocence—few, if any, BS convictions will result. If emotions and bad character attributions rule the day, however, innocent persons will be improperly convicted.

Third, the threat of convicting innocent persons points to a related danger. BS statutes are so rubbery in their drafting that they grant police and prosecutors too much discretion to determine whether and whom to prosecute. The due process clause prohibits the enforcement of penal laws that "fail to establish guidelines to prevent arbitrary and discriminatory enforcement of the law." However, even if the issue is seen as a non-constitutional matter, it is difficult to see how a prosecutor can fairly determine when charges are proper.

Again, the distinction between actions and non-actions demonstrates the vagueness problem. BS laws compel people to make the world (or, at least, a small part of it) better, rather than punish actors for actively making it worse. In the latter case, the identifiable conduct of the accused, and the demonstrable harm caused by those actions, serve to single out the actor as a plausible candidate for prosecution. With laws that punish for nothing, rather than something, there is a need for alternative objective criteria. At least with commission-by-omission liability, there are identifiable criteria, such as the status relationship of the parties, contractual understandings, or the suspect's personal connection to the emergency by having created the initial risk. In contrast, with BS laws, which impose a duty to aid strangers (potentially, anyone), criminal responsibility is based on imprecise factors (e.g., the duty to provide "reasonable assistance") and nearly unknowable circumstances (e.g., that the stranger is exposed to "grave" physical harm, and that assistance can be rendered without any "danger or peril" to the actor or others).

As the Genovese case demonstrates, these omission criteria are far less helpful in determining whether and against whom a prosecution should be initiated than are identifiable acts of commission. There is a significant risk with BS laws that the decision to prosecute will be based on a prosecutor's perceived need to respond to public outrage, which in turn, may be based less on the merits of the case and more on media coverage (which, in turn, may be founded on inappropriate factors, such as race, background, or even the physical attractiveness of the victim and/or the supposed poor character of the bystander). Not only may persons guilty of Bad Samaritanism avoid conviction because of selective enforcement, but the process may result in prosecution of persons who, upon cooler reflection, we might realize are innocent of wrongful not-doing.

There are also utilitarian reasons to question the wisdom of BS legislation. First, if such laws are taken seriously, the costs of investigating and potentially prosecuting bystanders might be prohibitive. Imagine the investigation necessary to decide whether to prosecute any of the Genovese bystanders and, if the decision were to proceed, to determine which of them to prosecute. Second, to the extent that BS statutes are narrowly drafted to reduce the risk of unfairness, prosecutions are likely to be rare (and convictions even rarer). Therefore, it is unlikely that the threat of punishment will have the desired effect of inducing bystanders to help persons in peril. The muted threat of a misdemeanor conviction is less likely to promote good behavior than the threat of public scorn that follows the publicity of such cases, or a Samaritan's own conscience.

Third, to the extent that such laws do, in fact, compel "Good Samaritanism," there is a risk that the Samaritan will hurt the person she is trying to assist, hurt others in the process, or unforeseeably harm herself. Fourth, since BS statutes are not linked to any prevention-of-harm causal requirement (i.e., it is not necessary to successfully prevent the threatened harm from occurring; it is enough to give it "the old college try"), the costs of such laws may easily outweigh their limited practical benefits. Even supporters of BS legislation concede that the law only helps at the boundaries.

There is one final reason to question the wisdom of BS statutes. Not only are positive duties morally less powerful than negative ones, but they also restrict human liberty to a greater degree. A penal law that prohibits a person from doing X (e.g., unjustifiably killing another person) permits that individual to do anything other than X (assuming no other negative duty). In contrast, a law that requires a person to do Y (e.g., help a bystander) bars that person from doing anything other than Y. . . .

What is the significance of this point? It is that the United States is a country that highly values individual liberty:

> Each person is regarded as an autonomous being, responsible for his or her own conduct. One aim of the law is to maximize individual liberty, so as to allow each individual to pursue a conception of the good life with as few constraints as possible. Constraints there must be, of course, in modern society: but freedom of action should be curtailed only so far as is necessary to restrain individuals from causing injury or loss to others.

Few people, except the most ardent libertarians, accept the latter statement in full. The point, however, is that in a society that generally values personal autonomy, we need to be exceptionally cautious about enacting laws that compel us to benefit others, rather than passing laws that simply require us not to harm others. The issue here, after all, is whether criminal law (as distinguished from tort law and religious, educational, and family institutions) should try to compel Good Samaritanism. Traditionally, Anglo-American criminal law sets only minimalist goals. The penal law does not seek to punish every morally bad act that we commit (aren't we glad of that?), and it leaves to other institutions the effort "to purify thoughts and perfect character."

Daniel B. Yeager, A Radical Community of Aid: A Rejoinder to Opponents of Affirmative Duties to Help Strangers
71 Washington University Law Quarterly 1-8, 13-38 (1993)

Introduction The use of law to coerce strangers to help one another always has been suspect in American legal thought. Laws that attempt to balance autonomy and a minimally acceptable level of neighborliness by imposing affirmative duties to help others are unpopular because they interfere with personal autonomy and the American "obsession with privacy." Even the most well-intentioned balance seems to prefer soulless individualism to creeping involuntary servitude and "unforeseen partnership." Our freedom to ignore those in need of immediate aid, however, may be a sign that we are "too free to consult the general good," or at least too free to acquiesce in our neighbors' misery.

This "crescendo of self-centeredness" downplays the cramped view of communal obligations that the rejection of a duty to aid others implies. By elevating rights over responsibilities, critics have argued, the law discourages the positive acts of communal solidarity that are part and parcel of citizenship. Adherents of the view that good citizenship entails communal obligations include Cicero, Plato, Mill, Bentham, Darwin, and Kant. Together they intimate that Jesus' admonition in the Good Samaritan parable, to go and do as the Samaritan did, should be perceived as duty, not charity. Because community membership inevitably involves dependency and vulnerability, these exceptional voices suggest that "the claim of each of us on the resources of the others is equal," even if we are not equally dependent in matters of strength, wealth or usefulness.

Contemporary sociologist Robert Wuthnow adds to this dialogue his studies, which challenge the assumption that individualism and altruism are antagonistic. . . . Wuthnow's studies support his conclusion that those who claim to be most intensely committed to self-realization and material pleasure are also most likely to value helping others.

Despite the arguments of many influential critics, the American reluctance to impose a legal duty to help others "shows remarkable staying power." Apparently fed up with a view so pessimistic and unsatisfying from an imperiled's standpoint (if not from that of a disinterested by-stander), Vermont, Rhode Island, and Wisconsin have adopted criminal statutes that impose an affirmative duty to help those in grave danger. Minnesota has imposed civil liability for failure to rescue under identical circumstances. Modeling their legislation on European precursors, this minority of states imposes liability for knowingly failing to undertake "easy rescue." Florida, Massachusetts, Ohio, Rhode Island, Washington, and Wisconsin have established slightly more stringent criminal penalties for the failure to report the commission of a serious crime. Although the laws are rarely invoked, they not only encourage a climate of increased personal security, but they also betray a view of community, solidarity, and humanity that is worth aspiring toward and expressing by law.

A Critique of the Majority Approach   The majority view of duties among strangers is bleak. A passerby need not "warn a blind man of an open manhole, . . . lift the head of a sleeping drunk out of a puddle of water, . . . throw a rope from a bridge to a drowning swimmer, [or] rescue or even report the discovery of a small child wandering lost in a wood." The harshness of the law reflects that even if in a moral sense all men are brothers, they are not their brothers' keepers. Thus moral philosophy and theology, not law, govern beneficence among strangers. The problem is purely one of individual empathy, not one of social or legislative importance.

Several writers have suggested ways to bring brotherhood to law. Most suggestions resemble the Vermont statute, substantially duplicated by Minnesota and Rhode Island, which penalizes omitters who knowingly fail to undertake easy rescues. An easy rescue is one which involves no danger to the rescuer and does not interfere with important duties that the rescuer owes to others. Through these laws, "common humanity . . . forges between us a link, but a weak one," given that the rescuer may opt out at the first sign of danger. Realistically, the law cannot require much more, since each of us should be permitted to remain a live coward rather than a dead public servant. . . .

Why Bystanders Fail to Intervene   Why those who see others in danger so often do nothing is unclear. In the case of witnesses to crimes, danger—real or imagined—and fear of retaliation account for some failures to intervene or notify authorities. In addition, because emergencies are, for most of us, exotic, a bystander's lack of opportunity for planning and rehearsal and the difficulty of quickly selecting the appropriate type of intervention might make her assistance less likely.

Some commentators, however, do not place the blame on individuals, but on urban conditions. Our "Cold Society" is a "fragmented," dispassionate "megalopolis" of crumbling morality, of "apathy" and "indifference," where "homo urbanis," charged by "T.V. sadism," "fear of police" and "unconscious sadistic impulses," ignores the suffering of others. Despite the deterioration of urban life, American cities remain densely populated because "few of us are attracted to the stifling small-town images of community we find championed in social-science textbooks."

The presence of other bystanders may reduce each potential rescuer's individual sense of responsibility to the imperiled, and increase the probability of free-riding. Each is lulled into a state of "pluralistic ignorance," which induces multiple bystanders to interpret others' nonaction as a sign of no danger. Despite the apparent incentive that risk-sharing would provide to potential co-intervenors, because of social inhibitions that arise in groups, people are more prone to respond to another's distress when alone than when accompanied by other witnesses.

Bystanders thus face a "choice of nightmares": fail to intervene and experience the empathic distress of watching another human being suffer, the guilt of failing to live up to a minimal threshold of decency, and the shame of having that failure witnessed by others; or, intervene and risk retaliation by an assailant, the ridicule and derision of nonintervening bystanders, and the threat of being mistaken for the cause of the harm. Moreover, the victim may spurn, attack, or become completely dependent on the rescuer, while the legal system may enlist the rescuer as a witness subject to innumerable encounters with police, lawyers, and judges. The nightmare then may be most easily resolved by convincing oneself that the victim is not imperiled.

Contradictory norms further complicate the bystander-imperiled episode and tend to produce inaction. Specifically, the controlling norm to "mind one's own business" clashes with the equally dominant norm to "do unto others." Even "do unto others" carries social baggage. Citizens may actively censor themselves to avoid the pejorative labels "bleeding heart," "dogooder," and "goody two-shoes," perhaps because compassion and altruism are often explained as no more than masks for self-interest.

A duty to report clashes with settled concepts such as loyalty and privacy when, based on relational affinity among family, friends, or ethnic or other groups, one has agreed not to disclose an incriminating fact. For example, in *Roberts v. United States*, a drug defendant appealed his sentence, which the lower court had increased when he failed to name his suppliers. Affirming his sentence, the Supreme Court condemned his contumacy as "antisocial conduct." In dissent, Justice Marshall strongly disagreed with the majority's conclusion that the defendant had a duty to become an informer, explaining:

> . . . The countervailing social values of loyalty and personal privacy have prevented us from imposing on the citizenry at large a duty to join in the business of crime detection. If the Court's view of social mores were accurate, it would be hard to understand how terms such as "stool pigeon," "snitch," "squealer," and "tattletale" have come to be the common description of those who engage in such behavior.

In its use of terms such as "stool pigeon" and "snitch," Justice Marshall's comment seems most apt when applied to an "informer," defined as "someone who betrays a comrade, i.e., a fellow member of a movement, a colleague, or a friend, to the authorities." His statement has less force, however, for a victim or stranger who witnesses a crime. Even the relationships among doctors, lawyers, or police officers, which are guided by institutionally imposed affirmative reporting requirements, also carry informal pressures to refuse to testify against a fellow member. The duty among strangers, however, involves no affinity-based obstacles, not even those endemic to the criminal milieu, such as the honor that is said to exist among thieves. . . .

A Contemporary Illustration: "The Accused" In 1983, six patrons of "Big Dan's," a New Bedford, Massachusetts bar, raped and sodomized a twenty-two-year-old mother of two while other patrons cheered. The setting was a working-class tavern in a largely Portuguese, economically depressed waterfront town of 98,000. The victim initially entered the bar to buy cigarettes, ordered a "high-ball," and talked briefly both with a woman she recognized and with her future assailants. She was then "'dragged literally kicking and screaming' across the floor," and "'thrown' onto the pool table, where one assailant tried to pull her jeans off." After two of the attackers tried unsuccessfully to force the victim to perform fellatio, two others raped her. "I could hear yelling, laughing, down near the end of the bar," she said. "My head was hanging off the edge of the pool table. . . . I was screaming, pleading, begging. . . . One man held my head and pulled my hair. The more I screamed, the harder he pulled. . . . " Finally, "clothed only in a shirt and one shoe, the victim escaped and ran into the street where she flagged down a passing truck."

In forty-three states, the nonfeasant witnesses committed no crime, although those who cheered on the assailants may have committed acts subjecting them to accomplice liability. No special relationship existed between the victim and the witnesses, with the possible exception of the bartender, who testified at trial but was not indicted. In these states, inaction in such a situation remains a matter of the passive witnesses' private morality, not law. In the substantial majority of states where the law is content to punish only active assailants, "rape is . . . a lawful spectator sport."

▪ LAW (SUBSEQUENT)

Nevada Revised Statutes
(1999, Current through the 2010 26th Special Session of the Nevada Legislature)

Section 202.882. Duty to report violent or sexual offense against child 12 years of age or younger; penalty for failure to report; contents of report.

1. Except as otherwise provided in [§§] 202.885 [limiting prosecution or conviction for failure to report to cases where the culpable actor has been convicted; providing a statute of limitations]; and 202.888 [listing persons exempt from duty to report, including persons less than 16 years of age, certain blood-relatives of the victimized child or the perpetrator, persons mentally impaired or disabled, persons in a situation where a report would enhance the danger to the

child, or persons whose knowledge of the offense was acquired in confidentiality], a person who knows or has reasonable cause to believe that another person has committed a violent or sexual offense against a child who is 12 years of age or younger shall:

   (a) Report the commission of the violent or sexual offense against the child to a law enforcement agency; and

   (b) Make such a report as soon as reasonably practicable but not later than 24 hours after the person knows or has reasonable cause to believe that the other person has committed the violent or sexual offense against the child.

2. A person who knowingly and willfully violates the provisions of subsection 1 is guilty of a misdemeanor.

3. A report made pursuant to this section must include, without limitation:

   (a) If known, the name of the child and the name of the person who committed the violent or sexual offense against the child;

   (b) The location where the violent or sexual offense was committed; and

   (c) The facts and circumstances which support the person's belief that the violent or sexual offense was committed.

APPENDIX A: SECTION 16

Lesser Evils Defense

✳ DISCUSSION MATERIALS

Issue: Are There Any Circumstances in Which It Would Be Justifiable to Use Torture in the Interrogation of a Suspected Terrorist to Save the Life of an Intended Victim?

These materials regarding torture and the lesser evils defense illustrate the challenges to properly defining its limitations. The Michael Levin essay argues that torture does not create a slippery slope issue and should be a viable interrogation tactic. Jeannine Bell argues for seriously restricting torture or abandoning torture altogether as an interrogation technique. Alan Dershowitz proposes permitting torture after authorization of a warrant to instill clarity into the system while still retaining democratic principles. David Luban rejects the ticking bomb scenario and criticizes torture as being inherently opposed to a liberal outlook.

Michael Levin, The Case for Torture

Newsweek, 1982 (Reprinted in The Phenomenon of Torture:
Readings and Commentary, Edited by William F. Schulz, 2007)

It is generally assumed that torture is impermissible, a throwback to a more brutal age. Enlightened societies reject it outright, and regimes suspected of using it risk the wrath of the United States.

I believe this attitude is unwise. There are situations in which torture is not merely permissible but morally mandatory. Moreover, these situations are moving from the realm of imagination to fact.

Suppose a terrorist has hidden an atomic bomb on Manhattan Island which will detonate at noon on July 4 unless . . . (here follow the usual demands for money and release of his friends from jail). Suppose, further, that he is caught at 10 a.m. of the fateful day but—preferring death to failure—won't disclose where the bomb is. What do we do? If we follow due process—wait for his lawyer, arraign him—millions of people will die. If the only way to save those lives is to subject the terrorist to the most excruciating possible pain, what grounds can there be for not doing so? I suggest there are none. In any case, I ask you to face the question with an open mind.

Torturing the terrorist is unconstitutional? Probably. But millions of lives surely outweigh constitutionality. Torture is barbaric? Mass murder is far more barbaric. Indeed, letting millions of innocents die in deference to one who flaunts his guilt is moral cowardice, an unwillingness to dirty one's hands. If you caught the terrorist, could you sleep nights knowing that millions died because you couldn't bring your-self to apply the electrodes?

Once you concede that torture is justified in extreme cases, you have admitted that the decision to use torture is a matter of balancing innocent lives against the means needed to save them. You must now face more realistic cases involving more modest numbers. Someone plants a bomb on a jumbo jet. He alone can disarm it, and his demands cannot be met (or if they can, we refuse to set a precedent by yielding to his threats). Surely we can, we must, do anything to the extortionist to save the passengers. How can we tell 300, or 100, or 10 people who never asked to be put in danger, "I'm sorry, you'll have to die in agony, we just couldn't bring ourselves to . . . "

Here are the results of an informal poll about a third, hypothetical, case. Suppose a terrorist group kidnapped a newborn baby from a hospital. I asked four mothers if they would approve of torturing kidnappers if that were necessary to get their own newborns back. All said yes, the most "liberal" adding that she would like to administer it herself.

I am not advocating torture as punishment. Punishment is addressed to deeds irrevocably past. Rather, I am advocating torture as an acceptable measure for preventing future evils. So understood, it is far less objectionable than many extant punishments. Opponents of the death penalty, for example, are forever insisting that executing a murderer will not bring back his victim (as if the purpose of capital punishment were supposed to be resurrection, not deterrence or retribution). But torture, in the cases described, is intended not to bring anyone back but to keep innocents from being dispatched. The most powerful argument against using torture as a punishment or to secure confessions is that such practices disregard the rights of the individual. Well, if the individual is all that important—and he is—it is correspondingly important to protect the rights of individuals threatened by terrorists. If life is so valuable that it must never be taken, the lives of the innocents must be saved even at the price of hurting the one who endangers them.

Better precedents for torture are assassination and pre-emptive attack. No Allied leader would have flinched at assassinating Hitler, had that been possible. (The Allies did assassinate Heydrich.) Americans would be angered to learn that Roosevelt could have had Hitler killed in 1943—thereby shortening the war and saving millions of lives—but refused on moral grounds. Similarly, if nation A learns that nation B is about to launch an unprovoked attack, A has a right to save itself by destroying B's military capability first. In the same way, if the police can by torture save those who would otherwise die at the hands of kidnappers or terrorists, they must.

There is an important difference between terrorists and their victims that should mute talk of the terrorists' "rights." The terrorist's victims are at risk unintentionally, not having asked to be endangered. But the terrorist knowingly initiated his actions. Unlike his victims, he volunteered for the risks of his deed. By threatening to kill for profit or idealism, he renounces civilized standards, and he can have no complaint if civilization tries to thwart him by whatever means necessary.

Just as torture is justified only to save lives (not extort confessions or recantations), it is justifiably administered only to those known to hold innocent lives in their hands. Ah, but how can the authorities ever be sure they have the right malefactor? Isn't there a danger of error and abuse? Won't We turn into Them?

Questions like these are disingenuous in a world in which terrorists proclaim themselves and perform for television. The name of their game is public recognition. After all, you can't very well intimidate a government into releasing your freedom fighters unless you announce that it is your group that has seized its embassy. "Clear guilt" is difficult to define, but when 40 million people see a group of masked gunmen seize an airplane on the evening news, there is not much question about who the perpetrators are. There will be hard cases where the situation is murkier. Nonetheless, a line demarcating the legitimate use of torture can be drawn. Torture only the obviously guilty, and only for the sake of saving innocents, and the line between Us and Them will remain clear.

There is little danger that the Western democracies will lose their way if they choose to inflict pain as one way of preserving order. Paralysis in the face of evil is the greater danger. Someday soon a terrorist will threaten tens of thousands of lives, and torture will be the only way to save them. We had better start thinking about this.

Jeannine Bell, "Behind This Mortal Bone": The (In)Effectiveness of Torture
Indiana Law Journal (2008)

Conclusion: Where Do We Go from Here? Maximizing Information Gain and Minimizing Harm

So what is the interrogator who wants accurate information to do? Realistically, interrogators who employ physically coercive interrogation practices—whether using torture or torture lite—to obtain information only gain when the useful information they garnered exceeds their costs. False positives—situations in which innocent people that possess no useful intelligence agree to having done something to stop the pain—are very costly. First, and most important, there is the cost to the innocent victim. In addition to the obvious physical consequences—broken bones, and other maladies caused by physical coercion—there is the neurological and psychological damage. Forceful shaking can cause brain damage, and even death. Studies of torture victims show that other physically coercive methods, even those that fall into the torture lite category, may cause lasting neurological damage. Moreover, methods that leave no physical scars may mark an individual psychologically for the rest of her life. Water boarding, considered by some a form of torture lite, subjects the suspect to near-asphyxiation and can cause severe psychological effects for years to come. In the words of one German P.O.W. tortured by the Nazis, "Whoever was tortured stays tortured. Torture is ineradicably burned into him, even when no clinically objective traces can be detected."

In addition to the human costs, torture is also costly politically. Once the news media acquire knowledge of such behavior, the reputation of the torturer—and his country—is damaged. While the reason for which the information is being acquired can help blunt the damage (i.e., torturing the suspect leads to lives being saved), this cannot occur if torture doesn't lead to more intelligence. In addition, regardless of whether it is useful or not, the use of coercive practices during interrogation may jeopardize the safety of prisoners of war from the torturer's own country as other countries decide that they should "take the gloves off, too."

Finally, and for those who tout torture's effectiveness, most importantly, there is the cost empirically. Recently, particularly in connection with the coercive interrogations at Abu Ghraib, we have seen that the widescale use of torture and torture lite yield false positives. Interrogators will not immediately know that a person who confesses falsely actually does not have sound information. Thus, I argue because of incentives placed on the suspect to confess, confessions procured as a result of torture and other physically coercive means must be investigated to determine their truthfulness. This is a time-consuming, and in the case of large numbers of false positives, ultimately a wasteful use of scarce investigative resources.

There is a potential solution. To decrease the number of false positives and increase the amount of overall information garnered, interrogators could torture only those most likely to give up valuable intelligence. This would mean limiting torture to: 1) suspects who the investigator has a strong feeling (or better yet, clear evidence), possess valuable intelligence; and 2) those who are weak-willed enough to succumb to pressure when faced with a high level of pain. I have added the second caveat because suspects who possess information but are strong-willed enough not to surrender it, like the prisoner in the above cited Emily Dickinson poem, may create just as many problems from an intelligence perspective—no useable information may be garnered from them.

This Essay does not advocate that approach for three reasons, all of which are practical. The first reason has to do with the difficulty, perhaps impossibility, of determining who possesses information and is weak-willed enough to surrender it under torture. Those alleged terrorists identified for interrogation have a range of experience, dedication, training and abilities. For instance, studies have shown variations in individuals who have different triggers and different abilities to withstand pain. Especially in ticking time bomb scenarios, there is neither time nor the facility during an interrogation to mine individuals' ability to withstand pain.

The second reason that this Essay eschews torture even when employed in a narrow set of circumstances has to do with the nature of both interrogation and torture. Studies of interrogation suggest that, by its very nature, the presumption of guilt underlies interrogation. This presumption sets into motion a process of behavioral confirmation which shapes the interrogator's, as well as the suspect's, behavior. Studies have shown that frequently, interrogators approach the task of interrogation with the belief that suspects are guilty. Even when dealing with suspects who are later proven to be innocent, interrogators have a tendency not to reevaluate their presumption of the suspect's guilt. Rather, seeing protestations of innocence as proof of the guilty person's resistance, this causes them to redouble their efforts to elicit a confession. Imagine the effects of this phenomenon if interrogators are allowed to torture the strong-willed: interrogation might be plunged into a death spiral as the suspect refuses to confess and the interrogator becomes more convinced of the suspect's guilt. This could be a recipe for torturing suspects to death, or, at the very least, causing irreparable bodily injury.

Finally, even it was possible to identify those likely to "give up the goods," such an approach might still be unworkable. It simply may be impossible to restrict interrogators' ability to torture to a limited number of suspects. This again stems from the very nature of torture. Torture is its own master. It controls the torturer just as surely as it controls its victims. Ordinary individuals' susceptibility to becoming torturers and willingly torturing others even to death has been demonstrated both by laboratory experience and in excesses in the field. In the Milgrim experiments, conducted in the early 1960s at Yale, ordinary individuals were willing to follow instructions to administer powerful electric shocks (in some cases as high as 450 V) to screaming victims, and even to continue administering the shocks when the screams stopped, presumably because the victim had lost consciousness or died. All of this suggests that it doesn't take a sadist to become a torturer. It is easy for this practice to become second nature, at which point it will be quite difficult to maintain any type of restrictions on its use.

Given the high costs of torture, and the absence of data on its effectiveness, are interrogators left with nothing? Clearly not. Police in the United States do not have torture available to them, and they have been quite successful in securing confessions. Those interrogating suspected terrorists are engaged in a similar task—trying to deduce information. It may be that not using torture will be more effective than having it at one's disposal. Studies, interviews with experienced interrogators, and interrogation manuals all suggest that one of the best ways of getting a suspect to talk is to use a highly skilled, well-trained interrogator who has a variety of tools at his or her disposal and, more importantly, recognizes which ones are most applicable, given the situation. As one veteran interrogator interviewed by Bowden said:

You want a good interrogator? . . . Give me somebody who people like and who likes people. Give me somebody who knows how to put people at ease. Because the more comfortable they are, the more they talk, and the more trouble they're in—the harder it is to sustain a lie.

How successful can interrogators who don't use torture be? Richard Leo, one of the foremost scholars of police interrogation found that police have developed techniques which are remarkably successful at producing confessions. Leo spent several months observing police interrogators in a major urban police department and also based his observations on tapes of interrogations at another department. Police in the United States are of course forbidden to torture suspects during interrogation. Leo observed no behavior that could be classified as torture. Moreover, in all of the interrogations he observed, the use of coercive interrogation methods was exceedingly rare, occurring in only 2% of cases. Despite the absence of physical and most psychological coercion, detectives were remarkably successful at getting suspects to confess. Leo found that when detectives actually attempted to gain incriminating information, their techniques yielded a partial admission or full confession more than three-fourths of the time. It is not clear from Leo's work how widespread such success is. He did believe that this success could be exported, hypothesizing that the level of success he found would be similar in departments where similar techniques are in use. While their precise effectiveness in the terrorism context has not been evaluated systematically, the methods used in American police departments are very similar to what those experienced with interrogation—both in the U.S. and abroad assert to be the most effective. Similar methods are also described in CIA interrogation manuals and used to train interrogators.

Paradoxically, the moral and legal prohibition of physically coercive mechanisms may have had unintended consequences. Instead of steering interrogators to other mechanisms, it has increased inexperienced interrogators' bloodlust. For poorly-trained investigators, physical coercion had become the longed-for instrument of last resort. They believe that torture will get the recalcitrant detainee to talk. Unfortunately, the infliction of pain becomes its own master. When interrogators resort to applying force, any knowledge they have regarding other methods that might be employed goes right out of the window. From an intelligence perspective, this might be more acceptable if there were clear evidence of torture's effectiveness.

In the war on terrorism, the risks of not catching terrorists are even higher than in the domestic context. Thinking about the quest to capture the most useful intelligence from an interrogator's perspective suggests that we should take a harder look at what methods work and reevaluate whether tangible benefits actually stem from brutal methods like torture.

Alan Dershowitz, Should the Ticking Bomb Terrorist Be Tortured?
Why Terrorism Works: Understanding the Threat Responding to the Challenge (2002)

This argument is reminiscent of the ones my students make in desperately seeking to avoid the choice of evils by driving the hypothetical railroad train off the track. The tragic reality is that torture sometimes works, much though many people wish it did not. There are numerous instances in which torture has produced self-proving, truthful information that was necessary to prevent harm to civilians. The *Washington Post* has recounted a case from 1995 in which Philippine authorities tortured a terrorist into disclosing information that may have foiled plots to assassinate the pope and to crash eleven commercial airliners carrying approximately four thousand passengers into the Pacific Ocean, as well as a plan to fly a private Cessna filled with explosives into CIA headquarters. For sixty-seven days, intelligence agents beat the suspect "with a chair and a long piece or wood [breaking most of his ribs], forced water into his mouth, and crushed lighted cigarettes into his private parts"—a procedure that the Philippine intelligence service calls "tactical interrogation." After successfully employing this procedure they turned him over to American authorities, along with the lifesaving information they had beaten out of him.[1] . . .

It is precisely because torture sometimes does work and can sometimes prevent major disasters that it still exists in many parts of the world and has been totally eliminated from none. It also explains why the U.S. government sometimes "renders" terrorist suspects to nations like Egypt and Jordan, "whose intelligence services have close ties to the CIA and where they can be subjected to interrogation tactics—including torture and threats to families—that are illegal in the United States," as the *Washington Post* has reported. "In some cases, U.S. intelligence agents remain closely involved in the interrogation. . . . 'After September 11, these sorts of movements have been occurring all of the time,' a U.S. diplomat said. 'It allows us to get information from terrorists in a way we can't do on U.S. soil.'" As former CIA counterintelligence chief Vincent Cannistraro observed: "Egyptian jails are full of guys who are missing toenails and fingernails." Our government has a "don't ask, don't tell" policy when it comes to obtaining information from other governments that practice torture.[2] All such American complicity in foreign torture violates the plain language of the Geneva Convention Against Torture, which explicitly prohibits torture from being inflicted not only by signatory nations but also "at the instigation of or with the consent or acquiescence of" any person "acting in an official capacity." As we began to come to grips with the horrible evils of mass murder by terrorists, it became inevitable that torture would return to the agenda, and it has. The recent capture of a high-ranking al-Qaeda operative, possibly with information about terrorist "sleeper cells" and future targets, has raised the question of how to compel him to disclose this important information. We must be prepared to think about the alternatives in a rational manner. We cannot evade our responsibility by pretending that torture is not being used or by having others use it for our benefit.

The modern resort to terrorism has renewed the debate over how a rights-based society should respond to the prospect of using nonlethal torture in the ticking bomb situation. In the late 1980s the Israeli government appointed a commission headed by a retired Supreme Court justice to look into precisely that situation. The commission concluded that there are "three ways for solving this grave dilemma" between the vital need to preserve the very existence of the state

---

1. Matthew Brzezinski, *Bust and Boom: Six Years Before the September 11 Attacks, Philippine Police Took Down an al Qaeda Cell That Had Been Plotting, Among Other Things, to Fly Explosives-Laden Planes into the Pentagon—and Possibly Some Skyscrapers,* WASH. POST, December 30, 2001, at W09.

2. Rajiv Chandrasekaran and Peter Finn, *U.S. Behind Secret Transfer of Terror Suspects,* WASH. POST, March 11, 2002, at A01; Kevin Johnson and Richard Willing, *Ex-CIA Chief Revitalizes "Truth Serum" Debate,* USA TODAY, April 26, 2002, *available at* http://www.usatoday.com/news/nation/2002/04/26/torture.htm.

and its citizens, and maintain its character as a law-abiding state. The first is to allow the security services to continue to fight terrorism in "a twilight zone which is outside the realm of law." The second is "the way of the hypocrites: they declare that they abide by the rule of law, but turn a blind eye to what goes on beneath the surface." And the third, "the truthful road of the rule of law," is that the "law itself must insure a proper framework for the activity" of the security services in seeking to prevent terrorist acts.[3]

There is of course a fourth road: namely to forgo any use of torture and simply allow the preventable terrorist act to occur. After the Supreme Court of Israel outlawed the use of physical pressure, the Israeli security services claimed that, as a result of the Supreme Court's decision, at least one preventable act of terrorism had been allowed to take place, one that killed several people when a bus was bombed. Whether this claim is true, false, or somewhere in between is difficult to assess.[4] . . .

Several important values are pitted against each other in this conflict. The first is the safety and security of a nation's citizens. Under the ticking bomb scenario this value may require the use of torture, if that is the only way to prevent the bomb from exploding and killing large numbers of civilians. The second value is the preservation of civil liberties and human rights. This value requires that we not accept torture as a legitimate part of our legal system. In my debates with two prominent civil libertarians, Floyd Abrams and Harvey Silverglate, both have acknowledged that they would want nonlethal torture to be used if it could prevent thousands of deaths, but they did not want torture to be officially recognized by our legal system. As Abrams put it: "In a democracy sometimes it is necessary to do things off the books and below the radar screen." Former presidential candidate Alan Keyes took the position that although torture might be necessary in a given situation it could never be right. He suggested that a president should authorize the torturing of a ticking bomb terrorist, but that this act should not be legitimated by the courts or incorporated into our legal system. He argued that wrongful and indeed unlawful acts might sometimes be necessary to preserve the nation, but that no aura of legitimacy should be placed on these actions by judicial imprimatur.

This understandable approach is in conflict with the third important value: namely, open accountability and visibility in a democracy. "Off-the-book actions below the radar screen" are antithetical to the theory and practice of democracy. Citizens cannot approve or disapprove of governmental actions of which they are unaware. We have learned the lesson of history that off-the-book actions can produce terrible consequences. Richard Nixon's creation of a group of "plumbers" led to Watergate, and Ronald Reagan's authorization of an off-the-books foreign policy in Central America led to the Iran-Contra scandal. And these are only the ones we know about! . . .

In a democracy governed by the rule of law, we should never want our soldiers or our president to take any action that we deem wrong or illegal. A

---

3. A special edition of the *Israel Law Review* in 1989 presented a written symposium on the report on the Landau Commission, which investigated interrogation practices of Israel's General Security Services from 1987 to 1989.

4. Charles M. Sennott, *Israeli High Court Bans Torture in Questioning 10,000 Palestinians Subjected to Tactics*, Boston Globe, September 17, 1999.

good test of whether an action should or should not be done is whether we are prepared to have it disclosed—perhaps not immediately, but certainly after some time has passed. No legal system operating under the rule of law should ever tolerate an "off-the-books" approach to necessity. Even the defense of necessity must be justified lawfully. The road to tyranny has always been paved with claims of necessity made by those responsible for the security of a nation. Our system of checks and balances requires that all presidential actions, like all legislative or military actions, be consistent with governing law. If it is necessary to torture in the ticking bomb case, then our governing laws must accommodate this practice. If we refuse to change our law to accommodate any particular action, then our government should not take that action.

Only in a democracy committed to civil liberties would a triangular conflict of this kind exist. Totalitarian and authoritarian regimes experience no such conflict, because they subscribe to neither the civil libertarian nor the democratic values that come in conflict with the value of security. The hard question is: which value is to be preferred when an inevitable clash occurs? One or more of these values must inevitably be compromised in making the tragic choice presented by the ticking bomb case. If we do not torture, we compromise the security and safety of our citizens. If we tolerate torture, but keep it off the books and below the radar screen, we compromise principles of democratic accountability. If we create a legal structure for limiting and controlling torture, we compromise our principled opposition to torture in all circumstances and create a potentially dangerous and expandable situation.

In 1678, the French writer François de La Rochefoucauld said that "hypocrisy is the homage that vice renders to virtue." In this case we have two vices: terrorism and torture. We also have two virtues: civil liberties and democratic accountability. Most civil libertarians I know prefer hypocrisy, precisely because it appears to avoid the conflict between security and civil liberties, but by choosing the way of the hypocrite these civil libertarians compromise the value of democratic accountability. Such is the nature of tragic choices in a complex world. As Bentham put it more than two centuries ago: "Government throughout is but a choice of evils." In a democracy, such choices must be made, whenever possible, with openness and democratic accountability, and subject to the rule of law.[5]

Consider another terrible choice of evils that could easily have been presented on September 11, 2001—and may well be presented in the future: a hijacked passenger jet is on a collision course with a densely occupied office building; the only way to prevent the destruction of the building and the killing of its occupants is to shoot down the jet, thereby killing its innocent passengers. This choice now seems easy, because the passengers are certain to die anyway and their somewhat earlier deaths will save numerous lives. The passenger jet must be shot down. But what if it were only probable, not certain, that the jet would crash into the building? Say, for example, we know from cell phone transmissions that passengers are struggling to regain control of the hijacked jet, but it is unlikely they will succeed in time. Or say we have no communication with the jet and all we know is that it is off course and heading toward Washington, D.C., or some other densely popu-

---

5. Quoted in W. L. Twining and P. E. Twining, *Bentham on Torture*, 24 N. IRELAND LEG. Q. 305, p. 345 (1973).

lated city. Under these more questionable circumstances, the question becomes who should make this life and death choice between evils—a decision that may turn out tragically wrong?

No reasonable person would allocate this decision to a fighter jet pilot who happened to be in the area or to a local airbase commander—unless of course there was no time for the matter to be passed up the chain of command to the president or the secretary of defense. A decision of this kind should be made at the highest level possible, with visibility and accountability.

Why is this not also true of the decision to torture a ticking bomb terrorist? Why should that choice of evils be relegated to a local policeman, FBI agent, or CIA operative, rather than to a judge, the attorney general, or the president?

There are, of course, important differences between the decision to shoot down the plane and the decision to torture the ticking bomb terrorist. Having to shoot down an airplane, though tragic, is not likely to be a recurring issue. There is no slope down which to slip. Moreover, the jet to be shot down is filled with our fellow citizens—people with whom we can identify. The suspected terrorist we may choose to torture is a "they"—an enemy with whom we do not identify but with whose potential victims we do identify. The risk of making the wrong decision, or of overdoing the torture, is far greater, since we do not care as much what happens to "them" as to "us." Finally, there is something different about torture—even nonlethal torture—that sets it apart from a quick death. In addition to the horrible history associated with torture, there is also the aesthetic of torture. The very idea of deliberately subjecting a captive human being to excruciating pain violates our sense of what is acceptable. On a purely rational basis, it is far worse to shoot a fleeing felon in the back and kill him, yet every civilized society authorizes shooting such a suspect who poses dangers of committing violent crimes against the police or others. In the United States we execute convicted murderers, despite compelling evidence of the unfairness and ineffectiveness of capital punishment. Yet many of us recoil at the prospect of shoving a sterilized needle under the finger of a suspect who is refusing to divulge information that might prevent multiple deaths. Despite the irrationality of these distinctions, they are understandable, especially in light of the sordid history of torture.

We associate torture with the Inquisition, the Gestapo, the Stalinist purges, and the Argentine colonels responsible for the "dirty war." We recall it as a prelude to death, an integral part of a regime of gratuitous pain leading to a painful demise. We find it difficult to imagine a benign use of nonlethal torture to save lives.

Yet there was a time in the history of Anglo-Saxon law when torture was used to save life, rather than to take it, and when the limited administration of nonlethal torture was supervised by judges, including some who are well remembered in history.[6] This fascinating story has been recounted by Professor John Langbein of Yale Law School, and it is worth summarizing here because it helps inform the debate over whether, if torture would in fact be used in a ticking bomb case, it would be worse to make it part of the legal system, or worse to have it done off the books and below the radar screen.

---

6. Sir Edward Coke was "designated in commissions to examine particular suspects under torture." Langbein, *Torture and the Law of Proof*, p. 73 (1977).

In his book on legalized torture during the sixteenth and seventeenth centuries, *Torture and the Law of Proof*, Langbein demonstrates the trade-off between torture and other important values. Torture was employed for several purposes. First, it was used to secure the evidence necessary to obtain a guilty verdict under the rigorous criteria for conviction required at the time—either the testimony of two eyewitnesses or the confession of the accused himself. Circumstantial evidence, no matter how compelling, would not do. As Langbein concludes, "no society will long tolerate a legal system in which there is no prospect in convicting unrepentant persons who commit clandestine crimes. Something had to be done to extend the system to those cases. The two-eyewitness rule was hard to compromise or evade, but the confession invited 'subterfuge.'" The subterfuge that was adopted permitted the use of torture to obtain confessions from suspects against whom there was compelling circumstantial evidence of guilt. The circumstantial evidence, alone, could not be used to convict, but it was used to obtain a torture warrant. That torture warrant was in turn used to obtain a confession, which then had to be independently corroborated—at least in most cases (witchcraft and other such cases were exempted from the requirement of corroboration).[7]

Torture was also used against persons already convicted of capital crimes, such as high treason, who were thought to have information necessary to prevent attacks on the state.

Langbein studied eighty-one torture warrants, issued between 1540 and 1640, and found that in many of them, especially in the "higher cases of treasons, torture is used for discovery, and not for evidence." Torture was "used to protect the state" and "mostly that meant preventive torture to identify and forestall plots and plotters." It was only when the legal system loosened its requirement of proof (or introduced the "black box" of the jury system) and when perceived threats against the state diminished that torture was no longer deemed necessary to convict guilty defendants against whom there had previously been insufficient evidence, or to secure preventive information.[8] . . .

It is always difficult to extrapolate from history, but it seems logical that a formal, visible, accountable, and centralized system is somewhat easier to control than an ad hoc, off-the-books, and under-the-radar-screen nonsystem. I believe, though I certainly cannot prove, that a formal requirement of a judicial warrant as a prerequisite to nonlethal torture would decrease the amount of physical violence directed against suspects. At the most obvious level, a double check is always more protective than a single check. In every instance in which a warrant is requested, a field officer has already decided that torture is justified and, in the absence of a warrant requirement, would simply proceed with the torture. Requiring that decision to be approved by a judicial officer will result in fewer instances of torture even if the judge rarely turns down a request. Moreover, I believe that most judges would require compelling evidence before they would authorize so extraordinary a departure from our constitutional norms, and law enforcement officials would be reluctant to seek a warrant unless they had compelling evidence that the suspect had information needed to prevent an imminent terrorist attack. A record would be kept of every warrant granted, and although it

---

7. Ibid., p. 7.
8. Ibid., p. 90, quoting Bacon.

is certainly possible that some individual agents might torture without a warrant, they would have no excuse, since a warrant procedure would be available. They could not claim "necessity," because the decision as to whether the torture is indeed necessary has been taken out of their hands and placed in the hands of a judge. In addition, even if torture were deemed totally illegal without any exception, it would still occur, though the public would be less aware of its existence.

I also believe that the rights of the suspect would be better protected with a warrant requirement. He would be granted immunity, told that he was now compelled to testify, threatened with imprisonment if he refused to do so, and given the option of providing the requested information. Only if he refused to do what he was legally compelled to do—provide necessary information, which could not incriminate him because of the immunity—would he be threatened with torture. Knowing that such a threat was authorized by the law, he might well provide the information. If he still refused to, he would be subjected to judicially monitored physical measures designed to cause excruciating pain without leaving any lasting damage. . . .

David Luban, Liberalism, Torture, and the Ticking Bomb
91 Virginia Law Review 1425 (October 2005)

[Torture] used to be incompatible with American values. Our Bill of Rights forbids cruel and unusual punishment, and that has come to include all forms of corporal punishment except prison and death by methods purported to be painless. Americans and our government have historically condemned states that torture; we have granted asylum or refuge to those who fear it. . . .

Then came September 11. . . . Six weeks after September 11, the press reported that frustrated FBI interrogators were considering harsh interrogation tactics; a few weeks after that, the *New York Times* reported that torture had become a topic of conversation "in bars, on commuter trains, and at dinner tables." . . . American abhorrence to torture now appears to have extraordinarily shallow roots.

. . . Henceforth, when I speak of "liberalism," I mean it in the broad sense used by political philosophers from John Stuart Mill on, a sense that includes conservatives as well as progressives, so long as they believe in limited government and the importance of human dignity and individual rights.

. . . I will examine the place of torture within liberalism. I hope to demonstrate that there are reasons that liberals find torture peculiarly abhorrent to their political outlook—but also reasons why liberal revulsion toward torture may be only skin deep. . . . I will criticize the liberal ideology of torture and suggest that ticking-bomb stories are built on a set of assumptions that amount to intellectual fraud. . . .

The Ticking Bomb

Suppose the bomb is planted somewhere in the crowded heart of an American city, and you have custody of the man who planted it. He won't talk. Surely, the hypothetical suggests, we shouldn't be too squeamish to torture the information out of him and save hundreds of lives. Consequences count, and abstract moral prohibitions must yield to the calculus of consequences.

Everyone argues the pros and cons of torture through the ticking time bomb. Senator Schumer and Professor Dershowitz, the Israeli Supreme Court and indeed every journalist devoting a think-piece to the unpleasant question of torture, begins with the ticking time bomb and ends there as well. The Schlesinger Report on Abu Ghraib notes that "[f]or the U.S., most cases for permitting harsh treatment of detainees on moral grounds begin with variants of the 'ticking time-bomb' scenario." At this point in my argument, I mean to disarm the ticking time bomb and argue that it is the wrong thing to think about. If so, then the liberal ideology of torture begins to unravel. . . .

The ticking-bomb scenario cheats its way around these difficulties by stipulating that the bomb is there, ticking away, and that officials know it and know they have the man who planted it. Those conditions will seldom be met. Let us try some more realistic hypotheticals and the questions they raise:

The authorities know there may be a bomb plot in the offing, and they have captured a man who may know something about it, but may not. Torture him? How much? For weeks? For months? The chances are considerable that you are torturing a man with nothing to tell you. If he doesn't talk, does that mean it's time to stop, or time to ramp up the level of torture? How likely does it have to be that he knows something important? Fifty-fifty? Thirty-seventy? Will one out of a hundred suffice to land him on the waterboard? . . .

The point of the examples is that in a world of uncertainty and imperfect knowledge, the ticking-bomb scenario should not form the point of reference. The ticking bomb is the picture that bewitches us. The real debate is not between one guilty man's pain and hundreds of innocent lives. It is the debate between the certainty of anguish and the mere possibility of learning something vital and saving lives. And, above all, it is the question about whether a responsible citizen must unblinkingly think the unthinkable and accept that the morality of torture should be decided purely by totaling up costs and benefits. Once you accept that only the numbers count, then anything, no matter how gruesome, becomes possible. . . .

Torture as a Practice

There is a second, insidious, error built into the ticking-bomb hypothetical. It assumes a single, ad hoc decision about whether to torture, by officials who ordinarily would do no such thing except in a desperate emergency. But in the real world of interrogations, decisions are not made one-off. The real world is a world of policies, guidelines, and directives. It is a world of practices, not of ad hoc emergency measures. Therefore, any responsible discussion of torture must address the practice of torture, not the ticking-bomb hypothetical. . . .

Treating torture as a practice rather than as a desperate improvisation in an emergency means changing the subject from the ticking bomb to other issues like these: Should we create a professional cadre of trained torturers? That means a group of interrogators who know the techniques, who learn to overcome their instinctive revulsion against causing physical pain, and who acquire the legendary surgeon's arrogance about their own infallibility. . . . Do we really want to create a torture culture and the kind of people who inhabit it? The ticking time bomb distracts us from the real issue, which is not about emergencies, but about the normalization of torture.

This is why Alan Dershowitz has argued that judges, not torturers, should oversee the permission to torture, which in his view must be regulated by warrants. . . . Politicians pick judges, and if the politicians accept torture, the judges will as well. Once we create a torture culture, only the naive would suppose that judges will provide a safeguard. Judges do not fight their culture—they reflect it.

For all these reasons, the ticking-bomb scenario is an intellectual fraud. In its place, we must address the real questions about torture—questions about uncertainty, questions about the morality of consequences, and questions about what it does to a culture and the torturers themselves to introduce the practice. Once we do so, I suspect that few Americans will be willing to accept that everything is possible. . . .

Conclusion

The only reasonable inference to draw from these recent efforts by the government to defend its actions is that the torture culture is still firmly in place, notwithstanding official condemnation of torture. . . . The persistence of interrogational brutality should surprise no one, because the liberal ideology of torture fully legitimizes it. The memos illustrate the ease with which arguments that pretend that torture can exist in liberal society, but only as an exception, quickly lead to erecting a torture culture, a network of institutions and practices that regularize the exception and make it standard operating procedure.

For this reason, the liberal ideology of torture, which assumes that torture can be neatly confined to exceptional ticking-bomb cases and surgically severed from cruelty and tyranny, represents a dangerous delusion.

✳ ADVANCED MATERIALS

Hypothetical: Bikers' Break

Ranger Yardley, 70, retired from service several years ago but still hangs around the station. He helped lay out the fire roads that crisscross the Pine Barrens. At the moment, both crews at the station are out on small fire calls. Yardley is alone. The Southwest Tower signals: "Class 4 fire . . . burn all of A-11 . . . Atsion endangered." Yardley calls the crews, but they are too far from road A-11 to get there before the blaze. He jumps in the flame truck, which is used to burn firebreaks to stop advancing forest fires, and heads out on his own. With no firefighting crews within reach, there will be no stopping the fire if it gets across A-11. He starts at the north end of A-11 and prepares to lay a strip of burning kerosene beside the road as he drives. But then he starts to feel faint, his chest starts to hurt, and he can't breathe. He jumps from the truck to the ground, gasping for air, and starts heading back on foot in the direction he came, staggering and incoherent.

Meanwhile, Lorenzo and Katherine are out for a ride, keeping an eye out for rangers. They aren't allowed to have their motorcycles on the Pine Barrens' fire roads, but it's a great ride. They spot a flame truck up ahead and pull over into the bush, afraid of being spotted. But after a few minutes they realize that no rangers are around, and the truck even has its flame going! "Maybe the rangers are in the woods answering nature's call," Lorenzo suggests.

"Talk about great rides!" blurts Katherine, as she jumps off the bike and heads for the truck cab. With Lorenzo alongside on the bike watching for rangers, Katherine roars off, spreading fire as she goes. When the road ends at the state highway, Katherine dumps the truck, jumps onto Lorenzo's motorcycle, and they're off down the highway. To Katherine, it was her best ride ever, and both are screaming and laughing, until a highway patrolman pulls them over and arrests them both for a third-degree felony (causing a catastrophe) for spreading fires with the flame truck.

Lorenzo argues the point. "Don't you know about the forest fire, man? We just saved Atsion. You should be giving us a medal."

Katherine is shocked. "Are you kidding?" she asks Lorenzo, before Lorenzo can signal her not to talk in front of the trooper. Investigation shows that many people would have died but for Katherine and Lorenzo's burning of A-11, and that Lorenzo realized the situation at the time they took the truck, but Katherine did not.

Can Lorenzo or Katherine, or both of them, get a justification defense?

Notes on the Unknowingly Justified Actor

Disagreement under current law
"Deeds" theory vs. "reasons" theory of justification
    "Deeds" theory rejects full liability for unknowingly justified actor
    "Deeds" theory would allow attempt liability
    "Reasons" theory denies defense and imposes full liability
Does "reasons" theory require purpose or knowledge?
Resisting unknowingly justified actor
Assisting unknowingly justified actor
"Deeds" theory enhances law's ability to communicate clear conduct rules
"Deeds" theory better matches community views

Disagreement under current law The Model Penal Code gives a justification defense to an actor who "believes" that her conduct is justified. In the "Bikers' Break" hypothetical, Katherine's conduct saved many lives, but at the time she drove the truck she did not "believe" that justifying circumstances existed. The language of the Model Code's formulation has the effect of denying the defense to an *unknowingly* justified actor, because she does not "believe" her conduct is justified.[9] The few authorities to have explicitly addressed the issue are divided: Some permit a defense for the unknowingly justified actor; others do not.[10] There also is disagreement in the academic literature as to which result should be preferred, although lay institutions support the defense (with a qualification, attempt liability, to be discussed in a moment).[11]

---

9. The commentary specifically addresses the issue, and rejects a defense for the unknowingly justified actor. See Model Penal Code § 3.02 comment 2 (1985) ("[T]he actor must actually believe his conduct is necessary to avoid an evil. If a druggist who sells a drug without a prescription is unaware that the recipient requires it immediately to save his life, the actual necessity of the transaction will not exculpate the druggist.").

10. George Fletcher claims that the "consensus of Western legal systems is that actors may avail themselves of justifications only if they act with a justificatory intent." George P. Fletcher, Rethinking Criminal Law 557 (1978).

11. See Paul H. Robinson & John M. Darley, *Testing Competing Theories of Justification*, 76 N.C. L. Rev. 1095 (1998).

"Deeds" theory vs. "reasons" theory of justification The issue of the unknowingly justified actor is of special significance because it forces an inquiry into the basic nature of justification defenses, specifically, whether it is the *act* or the *actor* that is justified. If the theory of justification defenses is that *conduct* is justified when, and because, it avoids a net harm or evil, then the defense should focus on purely objective criteria—the balance of conflicting interests. Under this "deeds" theory of justification, an unknowingly justified actor, such as Katherine in the "Bikers' Break" hypothetical, should have a justification defense to liability for the full substantive offense, despite her ignorance (although she may be liable for the lesser attempt liability). If, instead, the theory of justifications is that an *actor* is justified when, and because, she has tried to act properly—irrespective of the ultimate effect of that effort—then the defense should focus on the actor's state of mind and purposes. Under this "reasons" theory, Lorenzo might be justified—he knew of the justifying circumstances—but Katherine is not.

"Deeds" theory rejects full liability for unknowingly justified actor Under a "deeds" theory of justification, the primary role of justification defenses is as supplemental rules of conduct, designed to guide behavior by specifying what is prohibited and what is allowed. A defense is given when the otherwise criminal conduct is not, on balance, inappropriate here: The harm or evil it avoids outweighs the harm or evil it creates. Whatever the actor's attitude, the conduct itself is not conduct the law seeks to prohibit. By analogy, we do not impose liability on an actor who mistakenly believes she has committed an offense, but has not. Liability for the substantive offense requires that the harm or evil of the offense in fact occur. Where the harm or evil is absent, the actor's culpability may warrant attempt liability, but full liability is inappropriate. So, too, with the unknowingly justified actor. In the "Bikers' Break" hypothetical, a "deeds" theory would allow both Lorenzo and Katherine to claim a lesser evils defense.

"Deeds" theory would allow attempt liability While the "deeds" theory rejects full liability for the unknowingly justified actor, it does not reject all liability: Such an actor has committed an (impossible) attempt. A majority of jurisdictions allow attempt liability for an actor who, in the Model Penal Code's language, "purposely engages in conduct which would constitute the crime if the attendant circumstances were as [s]he believes them to be."[12] Attempt liability acknowledges that the harm or evil of the offense has not occurred. It bases liability instead on the actor's culpability—her demonstrated willingness to act in a way that she believes constitutes an offense. Such attempt liability seems well-suited for the unknowingly justified actor, who has not caused a net harm or evil but mistakenly believes that she has. In the "Bikers' Break" hypothetical, because Katherine mistakenly believed she was causing an unjustified harm, she would be liable for an attempt to cause such harm.

"Reasons" theory denies defense and imposes full liability Under a "reasons" theory of justification, in contrast, an unknowingly justified actor gets no justification defense and therefore is liable for the full offense, even though her conduct in fact avoids a greater harm or evil than it creates. Under this view, the existence of the justifying circumstances and the harm avoided is irrelevant in assessing the actor's liability, because the actor is unaware of these factors. In the "Bikers'

---

12. Model Penal Code § 5.01(1)(a).

Break" hypothetical, this theory would give Katherine no defense, because her conduct is not properly motivated. Without such a defense, because the harm of the offense did occur (even if it was offset or outweighed by a corresponding benefit), she is subject to full liability for the substantive offense, not just to attempt liability.

Does "reasons" theory require purpose or knowledge?   The "reasons" theory's reliance on an actor's motivation as a foundation for the defense creates a complication: Must the actor have the *purpose* of engaging in justified conduct, or merely the *knowledge* that a justification exists? Fletcher, for example, claims the rule to be that "actors may avail themselves of justifications only if they act with a *justificatory intent*."[13] As Greenawalt expresses the theory: "[J]ustified action is morally proper action. [T]o be justified is to have sound, good reasons for what one does."[14] This account of the defense, rooted in the actor's underlying reasons or motivations, would seem to require that the person act for the justificatory *purpose*, not just with knowledge of the justifying circumstances. In the "Bikers' Break" hypothetical, this account would mean that not only Katherine, but also Lorenzo, should be denied a defense, if it is shown that Lorenzo *knew* of the justifying circumstances but his *purpose* was to joyride rather than to save the town. However, the Model Penal Code would give Lorenzo the defense, because he does "believe" that he is justified—such a belief satisfies the Code's requirements, even if the belief does not provide the reason for Lorenzo's action. This result suggests that the Code's formulation is inconsistent with the underlying rationale for the "reasons" theory, which looks to (and demands) the actor's proper purpose.

Resisting unknowingly justified actor   Under a "reasons" theory, because the unknowingly justified actor is not justified, that actor's conduct may be lawfully resisted. Taking the "Bikers' Break" hypothetical as an example, if a land owner wished to resist the firebreak burning of his property out of pure selfishness, the Code would allow him lawfully to resist Katherine's burning *even though he knows of the forest fire and the circumstances that justify the burning*. Because Katherine's lack of "belief" in the justifying circumstances denies her a justification defense, her conduct is "unlawful" and therefore triggers a defense-of-property justification for the land owner.[15] Under a "deeds" theory, in contrast, the unknowingly justified actor's conduct remains justified, thus no one lawfully may interfere with that conduct. The selfish property owner who knows of the justifying circumstances could not lawfully resist Katherine's burning of the firebreak.

Assisting unknowingly justified actor   The "reasons" theory can lead to different liability results for two people who engage in, or assist, the same conduct at the same time. For example, in the "Bikers' Break" hypothetical, Ranger Yardley and Lorenzo will both obtain justifications for assisting Katherine (at least if "belief" rather than purpose is required for Lorenzo, as noted above), while Katherine, whose conduct is the same, will be held unjustified. Under an objective "deeds" theory, in contrast, the unknowingly justified actor remains justified, and

---

13. Fletcher, supra note 10, at 557.

14. Kent Greenawalt, *The Perplexing Borders of Justification and Excuse*, 84 Colum. L. Rev. 1897, 1903 (1984).

15. See, e.g., Model Penal Code § 3.06(1)(a).

anyone may assist that person. If one person is justified in performing the conduct, then all persons performing the same conduct, or assisting it, will similarly be justified.

"Deeds" theory enhances law's ability to communicate clear conduct rules   As noted previously, an advantage of the "deeds" theory is that its distinction between objective and mistaken justification facilitates the law's ability to communicate its rules of conduct to the public that is bound by those rules. By including both mistaken and actual justification within the single term *justified*, a "reasons" conceptualization invites the public to misconstrue acquittals of "justified" defendants, causing confusion as to whether the acquittal effectively declares the defendant's conduct acceptable or merely holds that the defendant is not to be punished for his improper conduct. This impedes a correct understanding of what the law condones and what it condemns.[16]

"Deeds" theory better matches community views   However, the unknowingly justified actor analysis reveals a different sort of advantage of the "deeds" theory: It accurately reflects community views, while the "reasons" theory conflicts with them. There is practical crime-control value in criminal law that earns moral credibility with the community it governs, thereby harnessing the powerful forces of social and normative influence.

---

16. For a full discussion of these points, see Paul H. Robinson, Objective Versus Subjective Justification: A Case Study in Function and Form in Constructing a System of Criminal Law Theory, in Criminal Law Conversations 343 (Paul H. Robinson et al. eds., 2009)

APPENDIX A: SECTION 17

Public Authority Justifications

DISCUSSION MATERIALS
Issue: When Should Police Be Allowed to Shoot in Other than Defensive Situations?
  Abraham N. Tennenbaum, The Influence of the *Garner* Decision on Police Use of
     Deadly Force
  Gregory Howard Williams, Controlling the Use of Non-Deadly Force: Policy and
     Practice

✳ DISCUSSION MATERIALS

Issue: When Should Police Be Allowed to Shoot in Other than Defensive Situations?

In an interesting follow-up to the *Tennessee v. Garner* Supreme Court decision, Abraham Tennenbaum looks at the effects of the *Garner* case on police
homicide rates and the benefits and costs of the changes in police procedure
prompted by the decision. The Gregory Williams excerpt takes up the issue of
controlling police use of non-deadly force.

Abraham N. Tennenbaum, The Influence of the *Garner* Decision on Police Use of Deadly Force

85 Journal of Criminal Law & Criminology 241-242, 257-260 (1994)

I. INTRODUCTION

People have criticized use of deadly force ever since police officers began
carrying guns. . . .

In March of 1985, the United States Supreme Court, in *Tennessee v.
Garner,* held that laws authorizing police use of deadly force to apprehend fleeing, unarmed, non-violent felony suspects violate the Fourth Amendment, and

therefore states should eliminate them. This paper investigates the impact of the *Garner* decision on homicides committed by police nationwide. . . .

IV. DISCUSSION

a. The Facts

Three conclusions seem to be self-evident from the data presented here. The first, and most important one is that *Garner* had a clear effect on justifiable police homicides. It reduced the total number of police homicides by approximately sixty homicides a year (more than sixteen percent). Second, *Garner* had an influence in both unconstitutional states and constitutional states. The magnitude of the reduction, however, was greater in unconstitutional states. Finally, *Garner* influenced not only a reduction in the number of police shootings of fleeing felons, but of all shootings, even those that are not correlated to defending life. This conclusion, however, needs more empirical support before it can be unequivocally accepted.

b. Why Did the *Garner* Decision Have Such an Impact?

The impact of *Garner* is surprising. Even before *Garner,* many police departments had already restricted their guidelines, and repealed the Any-Felony Rule. Accordingly, observers did not expect *Garner* to have such a dramatic impact.

A recent study on the influence of the *Garner* decision on the Memphis Police Department (MPD) may explain this phenomenon. Sparger & Giacopassi investigated MPD shootings in three different periods: 1969-1974; 1980-1984; 1985-1989. They concluded that *Garner* definitely reduced police shootings. Even though Memphis' policy before *Garner* was consistent with the Supreme Court's decision, the police restricted the policy even further after the decision. In fact, the policy after *Garner* emphasized "that deadly force should be used only as a last resort to protect life, not merely to apprehend fleeing dangerous felons."

This tendency by police departments to restrict their shooting guidelines beyond legal requirements is not a new one. Kenneth Matulia, who conducted a survey among fifty-seven big city police departments, wrote that "the individual police department rules generally place a more restrictive standard of conduct than permitted by law." Professors Geller and Scott also described a tendency in law enforcement agencies to move towards guidelines which were more restrictive than *Garner* required.

Thus, the adoption of more restricted policies by police departments nationwide after the Court's decision in *Garner* seems to have caused the reduction in police homicides. This is consistent with the evidence that restricted policies can reduce police shootings, and therefore police homicides. The magnitude of the change can explain the differences in reduction between the unconstitutional states (23.8% reduction in police homicides), and the constitutional states (12.96% reduction). The modifications which should have been made in department policies were higher in states that had the Any-Felony Rule than in states which did not. As a result, *Garner*'s influence was more accentuated in the unconstitutional states.

The self-restrictions on police behavior concerning deadly force were not only the result of good will but were also a political necessity. Police shootings of civilians have huge social costs, including riots. This has happened not only in the United States but in other nations too, and it is almost anticipated in some neighborhoods. Aside from public disturbances, police use of deadly force often spawns civil lawsuits. The fear of riots and law suits may explain why mayors and police chiefs prefer to severely limit the instances in which their officers may use deadly force.

In sum, the *Garner* decision seems to have reduced police homicides directly (by reducing police shooting at fleeing felons), and indirectly (by influencing police departments to reduce and modify their guidelines beyond *Garner* to appear just and sensitive to the public). As a result, all police shooting unrelated to protecting life seems to be declining.

c. Some Undesirable Outcomes

Until the 1960s, the number of homicides in the United States was relatively stable. There were fewer homicides then [than] there are today, and the percentage of homicides which qualified as justifiable (by police or civilians) was much higher than today. As Professor Brearley wrote in 1932, "it may be safely concluded that justifiable homicides comprise from one-fourth to one-third of the total number of slayings."

These statistics suggest that the more society views police and civilian homicides as justifiable, the more criminals these homicides deter. Professor Cloninger investigated the connection between police homicides and the crime rate in fifty cities. He found that non-homicide violent crime rates are inversely related to the police's lethal response rate, and concluded that police use of deadly force has a deterrent effect on the crime rate.

Further, police officers believe that the threat of deadly force deters felony criminals, and that harsh statutory limitations on police discretion is dangerous. In fact, some officers have already complained that the *Garner* decision, and resulting restrictive practices, have made their work frustrating and more dangerous.

Arguably, Justice O'Connor recognized this concern in her dissenting opinion: "I cannot accept the majority's creation of a constitutional right to flight for burglary suspects seeking to avoid capture at the scene of the crime." The majority of the Court considered this concern, but decided that the deterrent effect does not justify the risk of unnecessary police homicides. While the data is not sufficient to answer the empirical questions, the possibility that the Court's decision in *Garner* eroded the deterrent effect of police homicide should be considered in any evaluation of Garner's influence.

Gregory Howard Williams, Controlling the Use of Non-Deadly Force: Policy and Practice

10 Harvard BlackLetter Law Journal 79, 79-80, 82-93, 95-96, 102-104 (1993)

I. INTRODUCTION

The Los Angeles police beating of Rodney King, the Detroit killing of Malice Green, and the Nashville police beating of a Black citizen who turned out to be an undercover police officer illustrate the dilemma posed by the broad discretion given police to use non-deadly force. In recent years, courts and policy-makers have more clearly defined the circumstances that justify the use of deadly force. However, this is not the case with the use of non-deadly force. Because non-deadly force encompasses a broad range of activities, from a finger-hold to the use of a baton or chemical weapons such as mace, the potential misuse of non-deadly force is an urgent problem. Police officers are more likely to encounter the myriad situations that lead to the use of non-deadly force than those that result in the use of deadly force. . . .

This Article attempts to analyze the multi-dimensional problem with police use of non-deadly force.

[W]hile fully appreciating the practical problems surrounding the issue, this Article attempts to lay the groundwork for policy approaches to limit the use of non-deadly force. Although charting a course that limits but does not immobilize police in their attempts to maintain peace and order is difficult, it can be done. As I reflect on my own experience as a deputy sheriff, I recall how much power and authority I desired in order to deal effectively with the challenges I faced daily. Yet, I also remember watching my father being beaten by the police when I was eleven years old. These experiences motivate me to seek a middle ground—a policy that authorizes police to exercise the power necessary to confront situations demanding the use of force, but one that simultaneously circumscribes and controls the use of such force.

II. DEFINING THE PROBLEM

A. Police Use of Discretionary, Non-deadly Force

2. Social and Monetary Costs

"Reckless, careless or unjustified use of force causes public indignation and erodes citizen trust and support, thereby making the police task much more difficult." The failure of officers to provide reasonable explanations for their actions "creates great resentment, fear, and distrust in civilians, and may ultimately create actual resistance."

While evidence shows that police brutality actually has declined in recent years in New York, Chicago, New Orleans and even Los Angeles, the costs of unbridled discretion are huge. In the 1980s, riots resulting from police-citizen conflicts in Miami caused more than $100 million in damage. The riots set off by the acquittal of the officers accused of beating Rodney King in the spring of 1992 resulted in more than fifty deaths and approximately $800 million in damage. These events have created a "crisis of confidence in law enforcement." Since the ability of the police to carry out their duties largely depends on the degree to which the public is willing to assist and support them, a public not only skeptical of the police but antagonistic to them has tremendous repercussions on how well the police can accomplish the myriad of tasks they are assigned. While the public expects the police to exercise discretion in the performance of their duties, that discretion is expected to be reasonable and kept within appropriate boundaries. As evidenced by the public reaction following the Rodney King beating, there is little that can have a more negative impact on the public view of the police than examples of polices officers' flagrant abuse of physical power and authority. This has special significance in minority communities across America, as the skepticism about even-handed treatment by the police has always been higher in those communities than in predominantly white communities. Vivid public events like the Rodney King beating intensify and reinforce pervasive feelings of mistreatment by the police in minority communities. This mistrust of the police spills over into all areas of interaction between the police and the public.

B. Attempts to Control Non-deadly Force

Many police departments either have no formal rules on the use of non-deadly force, or have policies that are too vague to provide effective guidance. Unfortunately, there are few good examples of formal rules that can be used to formulate a forward-looking policy regarding the use of non-deadly force. The Model Rules for Law Enforcement Officers simply state that police officers may use non-deadly force only to achieve a lawful objective and that they must employ the least amount of force necessary to achieve that objective before escalating to the next, more forceful method. "However, nothing in the rules should be interpreted to mean that an officer is required to engage in prolonged hand-to-hand combat or struggle." Another model policy manual urges the use of only "the minimum force reasonable and necessary." It adds that force should not be used when unnecessary to effect an arrest, but it gives few specific examples of situations in which the use of such force is either appropriate or not. When officers are left to formulate policy on their own, the misuse of force is a likely result.

Although there are many police departments that can be singled out for criticism, the LAPD has been in the news most recently. It serves as a striking example of a police department that fails to specify and carefully monitor the use of force. In the early 1980s, a series of federal cases, emanating from Los Angeles citizens, challenged the police department's excessive use of "chokeholds." Compared to the use of force in other departments nationwide, the Los Angeles police appeared to use the chokeholds indiscriminately, even on offenders arrested for minor traffic violations. Despite the fact that the litigation revealed that between 1975 and 1982 sixteen persons were killed by the use of the "chokehold," primarily African Americans, Los Angeles police officials virtually ignored the need to address the problem of controlling the use of non-deadly force. (Not) surprisingly, former Los Angeles Police chief Daryl Gates blamed the disproportionate deaths of African American males from the use of chokeholds on his presumption of physiological differences between whites and Blacks. This type of leadership undoubtedly had a substantial impact on how use-of-force issues were viewed by officers on the street. In fact, in a remarkably counter-intuitive justification, Sergeant Stacey Koon, the supervising sergeant in the Rodney King beating, blamed the ban of the use of the chokehold for the beating. In what may have been a case of pigeons coming home to roost, Koon expressed shock and surprise when he and his fellow officers were reprimanded by Chief Gates for the Rodney King beating.

Contrary to the sentiments articulated by Sergeant Koon and others, civil rights committees in several states have noted the lack of guidance for officers on the escalating use of non-deadly force. These committees have called for more explicit instructions and limitations on the use of force and for increased training in the areas of persuasion and other non-physical coercive tactics. An Ohio committee, for example, warned that police officers "must learn to control their fears and anxiety, they must learn to examine people for signs of resistance, flight and threat. . . . They must learn how to establish and express authority by cajoling, requesting and negotiating to avoid using force." A Kansas committee urged for additional training on the use of force at police academies and during in-service programs, "so as to thoroughly indoctrinate the officers." A Minnesota committee has also sought formal education of officers in non-physical techniques such as negotiation and arbitration, noting that the lack of training impedes professional maturity, so that "civilians continue to bear the brunt of unnecessarily heavy-handed police conduct."

The mandate expressed in these and other reports is for more intensive efforts to teach police to remain calm, even though they may be taunted and provoked. "[P]olice training programs must do a more effective job in anticipating the situations that create the greatest stress and challenge for a police officer, and they must devise ways in which an officer can meet them." Oral and verbal tactics and body stance also are cited as effective methods for achieving police objectives without resorting to force. In general, police officers should be instructed that they cannot arbitrarily determine the level of force to be used; rather they can only use the minimum degree of force necessary to take a person into custody.

C. Theoretical Considerations: The Paradox of Police Work

Commentators have suggested that there is an inverse relationship between the use of force by police officers and their effectiveness as law enforcement agents. Paradoxically "the ultimate police resource is the legitimate use of force, [but] policing is more successful the less it has to be resorted to." If violence is to be used—and it should be resorted to only when absolutely necessary—it must be used efficiently. The incidence of violence should not be aggravated by the incompetence of the officer.

In his book, *Policing Liberal Society*, Steve Uglow assessed the paradox of police work: police are delegated the authority (at least implicitly) to use physical force, and they are expected to use it. At the same time, their duty is to serve and protect the public. Uglow states that "It is difficult for police officers to dwell in both camps, ready to help old ladies across the street but prepared to inflict fatal violence on other citizens." Uglow's study of the British approach to policing suggests that a more limited resort to force may reap dividends in terms of keeping the peace. Unarmed constables, for example, must rely on their ability to defuse situations, rather than on firepower. Apparently this approach has been effective.

Perhaps a more effective means than controlling the use of non-deadly force through punitive sanctions is that of fostering an internal "respect for justice" that prevents a police officer from using excessive force in the first place. Police officers often see themselves as isolated and separated from the communities in which they serve. The Christopher Commission, established to review the LAPD following the Rodney King beating, detailed vivid examples of feelings of separateness and an attitude of disdain on the part of Los Angeles officers serving Los Angeles' ethnic minority communities. Racial epithets and disparaging comments about minority citizens in the recorded radio transmission are clear evidence that minority citizens are considered less than human by many police officers. Similar remarks repeatedly documented in the records of the LAPD further demonstrate the violent and antagonistic mentality that has developed toward minority communities. If police officials continue to refuse to bring officers under control, citizens will have to demand political accountability through their government officials.

In some respects, one could argue that the problems we are facing as a result of police abusing their power speaks to the failure of previous and ongoing efforts to develop "politically independent" police agencies. Around the turn of the century, efforts were made to insulate the police from "politics." For example, in Los Angeles the position of Police Chief was established as a life tenure appointment. However, rather than establishing a position through which an appointee could rise above the vicissitudes of local politics, the police chief became a major political figure, with no constituency other than the officers whom he commanded. Consequently, departmental positions on such issues as the use of force have been largely shaped and formed internally and not subjected to external review and criticism.

APPENDIX A: SECTION 18

Defensive Force Justifications

DISCUSSION MATERIALS

Issue: Should the Criminal Law Give a Defense for the Use of Whatever Force Is Necessary to Defend Persons or Property Against an Unlawful Attack? Or Should the Law Deny a Defense if the Force, Even Though Necessary for Defense, Would Injure Interests Greater than Those Injured by the Unlawful Attack?

John Q. LaFond, The Case for Liberalizing the Use of Deadly Force in Self-Defense

Model Penal Code Section 3.04 Commentary, Limitations on Use of Deadly Force

Model Penal Code Section 3.06 Commentary, Deadly Force

Garrett Epps, Any Which Way But Loose: Interpretive Strategies and Attitudes Toward Violence in the Evolution of the Anglo-American "Retreat Rule"

Paul H. Robinson & John M. Darley, Study 6: Use of Force in Defense of Property

---

✳ DISCUSSION MATERIALS

Issue: Should the Criminal Law Give a Defense for the Use of Whatever Force Is Necessary to Defend Persons or Property Against an Unlawful Attack? Or Should the Law Deny a Defense if the Force, Even Though Necessary for Defense, Would Injure Interests Greater than Those Injured by the Unlawful Attack?

John LaFond's piece argues for dispensing with the proportionality requirement, for both practical and theoretical reasons. In two Model Penal Code Commentary excerpts, justification is offered for the necessity and proportional requirements as codified, elaborating on the debates that preceded the Code's current formulation and examining the scope of the rule. In a rather provocative article, Garrett Epp advocates limitations on the use of defensive force, including, most dramatically, doing away with the right altogether. Robinson and Darley offer empirical evidence that society supports a defensive force doctrine and examine community views on proportionality and the limits of defense of property.

John Q. LaFond, The Case for Liberalizing the Use of Deadly Force in Self-Defense

6 University of Puget Sound Law Review 237, 237-238, 274-284 (1983)

Introduction

For at least a century the common law of Washington and of virtually every state in the United States has permitted a citizen to use deadly force in self-defense, but only if he was unlawfully threatened, or appeared to be threatened, with death or serious bodily harm. Despite growing public fear of violent crime and recent statistics which provide a strong empirical basis for that fear, almost no state has expanded the common law right to permit a citizen to use deadly force to resist unlawful violence to his person if he was not threatened with death or serious bodily harm. It is no longer clear that the common law's stringent rules limiting the use of deadly force to instances in which the victim's life may be at stake are in accord with a shifting public value system or are sufficiently protective of the individual in these increasingly violent times. . . .

A Critique of the Law Governing the Use of Deadly Force in Self-Defense

. . . The law can thus be perceived as granting, in many violent confrontations not involving threatened deadly force, death or great bodily harm, an illusory right of self-defense; that is, as a practical matter, no right at all. The public may well react adversely to this hypocrisy in the law, considering it of minimal help at best and at worse debilitating.

Insisting that a citizen threatened "only" with physical force or a "mere" battery forego the immediate private right of effective self-defense in exchange for a deferred public remedy of criminal prosecution may have made more sense in an era in which subsequent arrest and successful prosecution of the aggressor were more likely. Given the increased violence of our times and the statistical likelihood that a majority of violent aggressors will in fact not be successfully apprehended and punished, many victims will be without any remedy, private or public. The better social policy is to recognize the extremely contingent nature of the public remedy and to increase the availability and efficacy of private remedies authorized by the law, lest unlawful violence continue without any effective restraint, private or public.

The present formulation of the law of self-defense, in its attempt to minimize social loss, has adopted a utilitarian scheme of justice without explicitly acknowledging its underlying philosophic premise. Adopting this premise condemns many individual victims to bear the primary cost of minimizing social loss. Maximizing the preservation of human life by inexorably distributing a significant personal burden of physical harm and psychic scarring to many innocent citizens chosen at random by violent aggressors may no longer accord with society's sense of social good. The abstract goal of preserving human life must be tempered with the recognition that the people whose lives are being protected by the law are frequently violent criminals who are thus free to prey again on society.

Even if one accepts this utilitarian premise, it is not clear that society currently agrees with the answer generated many years ago by the common law's reckoning on the utilitarian calculus. It is submitted that society today would not choose to preserve the lives of violent aggressors at the expense of physical and psychic harm to innocent victims. Interest balancing always contains a large degree of subjective value preference and courts may not be the institution best suited to gauge society's preferences. In any event, it seems quite clear that the legislature can reach a different conclusion in measuring the utilitarian preferences of society.

There are other cogent criticisms that can be made of the limitation on the use of deadly force in self-defense. As observed previously, limiting the right to use deadly force to instances in which deadly force is threatened may insure an ineffective response to violence. The victim may, once subjugated, only suffer physical harm together with the psychic scarring which usually accompanies such violence. It is also possible, however, that the aggressor will proceed to inflict even more serious damage on a victim once subjugation is complete and the possibility of resistance has been terminated. Indeed, the very helplessness of the victim may invite further aggression since there is virtually no present risk of resistance and harm to the aggressor. This fear is not unfounded. For it is precisely the random and unpredictable nature of violence, the possibility of unforeseen shifting aggressor objectives, and the escalation in the level of aggressor violence after the initial confrontation that are so bewildering today. It is not unusual to read about purse snatchings, muggings, and other crimes initially involving nondeadly force that result in appalling harm to the victim, including death. If initial aggressor threats of mere physical harm in fact frequently explode unpredictably into instances in which aggressors cause death or serious bodily harm, then even utilitarian objectives may not be furthered by the present law.

In its current formulation, the law of self-defense effectively creates a strong evidentiary presumption about the nature of the harm threatened to the victim based on the nature of the force threatened by the aggressor. As a practical matter most juries are unlikely to conclude that a victim reasonably feared death or serious bodily injury at the hands of the aggressor unless the aggressor was armed with a deadly weapon or other deadly force. This inference of fact seems both unnecessarily rigid and incongruent with experience.

Predicting violence is at best a difficult task. Predicting the level of violence or the outcome of a violent confrontation is no easier. Nor is there any necessary logical correlation between what harm an aggressor intends to inflict and the force he has at his disposal. Certainly, the actual threat or use of deadly force ought to permit the victim reasonably to fear that the aggressor intends to inflict death or serious bodily harm on him. It is not clear, however, that the presence of deadly force is a necessary factual predicate for such fear. Rather the presence, use, or threat of deadly force ought simply to be one fact among others for the jury to consider in determining what the victim reasonably feared.

Violent confrontations normally occur under conditions of uncertainty. Frequently they are of short duration and without warning. They may also occur in situations in which the victim may be at an extreme disadvantage in gauging the level of violence or harm threatened or the intention of the aggressor. . . .

Requiring further factual inquiry on the part of the victim may well disadvantage him even more and shift the odds enormously in favor of the aggressor.

With the possible exception of the problem of mistakes, no compelling argument can be offered that would justify requiring the victim to bear the risk of uncertainty generated by the aggressor's unlawful conduct. The aggressor has initiated the violent confrontation and the concomitant uncertainty. It is difficult to accept the logic and value of rules which, most citizens probably believe, generate an intolerable allocation of risk to innocent citizens in such paradigmatic cases. It seems far more preferable that all disadvantages which flow from such uncertainty should be allocated to the person who has caused the situation to occur.

Finally, an organized police force and the other apparatus of public security are simply not adequate by themselves to the tasks of controlling violent crime and of protecting ordinary people. Enhancing the ability of the private citizen to engage in effective self-defense will help provide the means of assuring personal security that the state can no longer insure.

The Proper Formulation of the Right of Self-Defense

The private right of self-defense should be grounded primarily in the theory of personal autonomy. The utilitarian theory of self-defense as a form of necessity should continue to be relevant to the scope of the right but only as a subordinated principle of limitation.

Accordingly, the private right of self-defense should be carefully expanded in order to permit innocent victims to respond effectively to unlawful violence against their persons. At the very core of the proposed change is the premise that effectiveness of response should be the paramount principle of authorization rather than proportionality. This change will acknowledge that an innocent victim need not endure unlawful violence to his person (with all its attendant risk of unknown outcome, including his possible death) in exchange for the forlorn hope of subsequent arrest and successful prosecution of the aggressor at some unknown time in the future.

Model Penal Code Section 3.04 Commentary
Limitations on Use of Deadly Force
Official Draft and Revised Comments 47-48, 52-55 (1985)

Subsection (2)(b) adds . . . limitations on the use of force, dealing with force that the actor uses with the purpose of causing or that he knows will create a substantial risk of causing death or serious bodily injury. As defined by Section 3.11(2), "deadly force" explicitly includes purposely firing a firearm in the direction of another person or at a vehicle in which another person is believed to be. Clearly, deadly force, as so conceived, should be privileged only in extreme situations. Subsection (2)(b) represents an effort to describe what those situations are.

Apprehension of Serious Injury. Subsection (2)(b) denies justification to the use of deadly force unless the actor believes that such force is necessary to protect himself against death, serious bodily injury, kidnaping or sexual intercourse compelled by force or threat. The formulation rests on the common law principle that the amount of force used by the actor must bear a reasonable relation to the magnitude of the harm that he seeks to avert. It is not reasonable "that for every assault . . . a man should be banged with a cudgel."

To give the law a measure of precision, force is divided into two categories, deadly and moderate. Force threatening only moderate harm may be inflicted by way of defense against any harm apparently threatened, while deadly force may be employed only by way of defense against the type of serious harm noted above. The premise is, of course, that the discouragement of the infliction of death or serious bodily injury is so high on the scale of preferred societal values that such infliction cannot be justified by reference to the protection of an interest of any lesser pretensions, with the possible exception of dispossession from one's own dwelling. Since the actor's own concept of morality will normally indicate that he sacrifice a lesser interest rather than engage in such behavior, the limitation of the privilege can be expected to have substantial deterrent effect.

There is no complete agreement on the nature of the extreme harm against which it is permissible to defend oneself by the use of deadly force. All authorities agree that it includes death or serious bodily injury. The Restatement of Torts adds "ravishment," which is defined in its Comment to mean not only rape but "any form of carnal intercourse which is criminal in character as, for example, sodomy." As well as including these forms of harms, Subsection (2)(b) of the Code adds kidnaping to the enumeration. Whether that inclusion will be appropriate in a particular jurisdiction will depend largely on how kidnaping is defined. Deadly force is not an appropriate response when one parent attempts to abduct a beloved child from the custody of another parent; under the Model Code that act is not kidnaping but it is under the law of some states.

The harms to one's person for which deadly force may appropriately be used are similar to those specified in the Model Code in many states that have undertaken recent legislative revisions.

Model Penal Code Section 3.06 Commentary, Deadly Force
Official Draft and Revised Comments 91-92, 94-97 (1985)

Subsection (3)(d) deals with the occasions when more than moderate force can be used in contexts where the main objective is the protection of property. It follows the common law in limiting the force that may generally be used in the protection of property to moderate nondeadly force, reflecting a value judgment that in most situations surely is sound. The principle controls, moreover, even though the person against whom force is used is making such resistance to the protective force that the defender must either proceed to extreme measures or give up the use of protective force. For example, suppose a trespasser in being ejected so defends himself that the occupier cannot eject him except by shooting him. The occupier is not entitled to shoot, and should not be.

The difficulty, and the controversy, comes in deciding to what extent exceptions to this general principle should be admitted. As originally drafted, this section included only the exception that is now found in Subsection (3)(d)(i). The matter was hotly debated on the floor of the Institute, however, terminating in directions to the Reporter to draft a more expansive exception to encompass the most serious and potentially violent situations that are likely to arise. The result is Subsection (3)(d)(ii). . . .

Paragraph (A) of Subsection (3)(d)(ii) permits the use of deadly force in a number of . . . situations where any danger to the life or well-being of the actor, though once existing, has passed. [It] permits the use of deadly force to prevent the commission or the consummation of the offense if the aggressor "has employed or threatened deadly force against or in the presence of the actor." It thus affords a privilege to kill even though drastic action may no longer be necessary in order to preserve the safety of the actor. For if the thief has once manifested or threatened deadly force in the attempt to commit or to consummate one of the enumerated property crimes, deadly force may be used in order to prevent him from capitalizing upon his offense. To give an illustration, one who commits robbery on the streets at gunpoint and who is in the course of fleeing from the offense may be shot by the victim if in the victim's judgment such force is immediately necessary in order to prevent the consummation of the offense.

The policy issues that such an extension exposes proved deeply divisive within the Institute. On the one hand is the basic value judgment, breached in this instance, that the protection of property interests should not justify the taking of life. On the other is the judgment that resort to deadly force in this context is a predictable response of reasonable people, and should not be met with condemnation by the criminal law. Moreover, since the use of deadly force is limited to situations where the aggressor has himself used or threatened deadly force, and his willingness to resort to such force on one occasion may be thought to indicate a willingness to do so again, the privilege afforded here may be thought to protect the bodily safety of potential future victims. In response to this point, however, one should note the deliberate judgment underlying Section 3.07(2)(b)(ii) that resort to deadly force in effecting an arrest should be limited to law enforcement officials or persons assisting them. Private citizens are not authorized to use deadly force to make an arrest of someone who has previously used deadly force and who may be thought likely to use it against future victims. Thus, to rely on the theory that prevention of harm to future victims justifies the use of deadly force by citizens to prevent successful commission of a crime against property would not be consonant with the judgment underlying Section 3.07.

It is clear, however, that the Institute determined to go beyond the use of deadly force for the prevention of the violent crime. It chose to permit actors to use deadly force to prevent escape with the fruits of such crimes by those who have used or threatened violence, as well as to permit the use of such force where the actor apprehends that the use of lesser force would expose him to danger. Hence, the Institute resolved the policy debate in favor of the broadened privilege, and the formulation could not well have been narrower than that presented in Subsection (3)(d)(ii) without nullifying those decisions.

Most recently enacted and proposed revised codes formulate justifications for the use of deadly force in defense of property, but they follow a variety of approaches.

Garrett Epps, Any Which Way But Loose: Interpretive Strategies and Attitudes Toward Violence in the Evolution of the Anglo-American "Retreat Rule"

55 Law and Contemporary Problems 303-305, 327-331 (1992)

If any one be in danger of receiving a buffet,[1] or the like evil, some hold that he has a right to protect himself by killing his enemy. If merely corrective

---

1. Editor's Note: A blow, stroke; now usually one given with the hand.

justice be regarded, I do not dissent. For though a buffet and death are very unequal, yet he who is about to do me an injury, thereby gives me a Right, that is a moral claim against him, in infinitum, so far as I cannot otherwise repel the evil. And even benevolence per se does not appear to bind us to advantage of him who does us wrong. But the Gospel law has made every such act unlawful: for Christ commands us to take a buffet, rather than hurt our adversary; how much less may we kill him? . . . Hence it appears also that that is wrong which is delivered by most writers, that defense with slaying is lawful, that is by Divine law (for I do not dispute that it is by Natural Law,) when flight without danger is possible: namely, because flight is ignominious, especially in a man of noble family. In truth, there is, then, no ignominy, but a false opinion of ignominy, to be despised by those who follow virtue and wisdom. . . .

On the Right of War and Peace
Hugo Grotius

A traveler on a dark road is set upon by an armed stranger. The stranger's assault threatens death or atrocious physical harm. The traveler pulls out a knife or a gun and kills the assailant. Has the traveler done something wrong—or, more precisely, something for which the legal system should punish him or her? Most contemporary Americans, faced with the facts above, would likely say that the traveler has killed in self-defense and thus has committed no crime. Further, most would likely perceive the scene described above as an easy case. H. L. A. Hart writes, "Killing in self-defense is an exception to a general rule making killing punishable; it is admitted because the policy or aims which in general justify the punishment of killing (for example, protection of human life) *do not include cases such as this.*"

But easy cases may make bad law. Two problems arise in the analysis of the uncomplicated narrative above. First, the very ease of the case conceals a contradiction: If "protection of human life" is a paramount goal of the criminal law, the incident on the highway, so far from falling outside the policy, must fall squarely within its purview. An act of violence has been committed, human life has been taken by another human being, and a legal system sincerely concerned with protecting human life should explain the exception in more rigorous terms than Hart admits. The case above seems easy to contemporary thinkers only because considerable historical grappling has been done by the legal system over half a millennium.

Second, the case cited above, in its very archetypicality, has the potential to distort legal analysis of actual cases. Available evidence suggests that most killings, even those in which the killer successfully pleads self-defense, are not of the "pure" variety cited above, in which an unknown assailant begins an unprovoked assault on a surprised victim. Instead, the majority of homicides take place after ambiguous confrontations between persons who know each other and have a history of involvement and conflict. The criminal justice system must assess the culpability of the survivor and decide what, if any, atonement is to be exacted for the act of killing. This complex investigation is powerfully shaped, and often distorted, by the belief of those in the system that are comparing the actual case before them with the archetype cited above. Our "intuition" about the "easy case," which is in fact a historically shaped perception about a troubling moral dilemma, leads us to view actual events as instances of that case. If there were different "easy cases" available . . . the outcome might often be different.

One aspect of the doctrine of self-defense has proved unusually problematic for theoreticians and courts. What if the traveler, menaced by the stranger's assault, could escape by dashing into a nearby house and closing a sturdy oaken door? To what extent should the law, if satisfied that the opportunity existed and that the traveler knew of it, penalize the traveler for using deadly force instead of running away?

The law's answer to this is most authoritatively stated by the Model Penal Code:

> The use of deadly force is not justifiable under this Section unless the actor believes that such force is necessary to protect himself against death, serious bodily injury, kidnaping or sexual intercourse compelled by force or threat; nor is it justifiable if . . . the actor knows that he can avoid the necessity of using such force with complete safety by retreating . . . except that . . . the actor is not obliged to retreat from his dwelling or place of work, unless he was the initial aggressor or is assailed in his place of work by another person whose place of work the actor knows it to be. . . .

But at the time they adopted the "retreat rule," the drafters of the Code recognized that "American jurisdictions [are] divided on the question . . . with the preponderant position favoring the right to stand one's ground." In fact, the "retreat rule" has spawned a strong argument—one that has attained the status of law in many jurisdictions—for the contrary rule, a rule of "no retreat." . . .

It would certainly be defensible to use the retreat cases as evidence for the proposition, advanced by legal realists, that courts do not use rules to decide cases, but simply to rationalize their own intuitive decisions; and by critical legal scholars, that "the law" as a construct is inherently incoherent, self-contradictory, and unprincipled, and that criminal-law rules cannot be drawn in a way that would successfully prevent courts from using their interpretive discretion to achieve results actually determined by class, race, or sexual bias. . . .

Much criminal doctrine remains grounded in largely obsolete nineteenth-century notions of free will and individualism. Legal analysis uses rights theory to analyze interactions between persons who are members of a social context and for whom largely unconscious reciprocal relationships are often more important determinants of behavior than are rational calculations about rights. Ideas and attitudes formulated during the sparsely populated, heavily rural, expanding frontier culture of nineteenth century America serve badly a crowded, multiracial, technological, urbanized society trembling on the lip of the twenty-first century. One of the chief needs of the evolving society of the United States is a reduction in the use of violence, whether expressed as crime, unprincipled law enforcement and corrections, or war and militarism. The law need not necessarily play a passive role in the attempt to wean our society from its uniquely violent mores; it could be used to restrict the tolerance and use of violence by all levels of society.

The law of self-defense is a logical place to begin this inquiry because contemporary thinkers tend to see the area of self-defense as one in which the general rules against violence simply do not apply. But if, as this note suggests, cases of "self-defense" represent a fragile, socially mediated interpretive construct, a determined effort to bring them more closely within a general proscription of violence might serve the purpose of awakening legal thinkers to the ways we use such "exceptions" to negate the rules we claim to live by.

Accordingly, I close with a few suggestions for change in the self-defense area. These are intended, at least at present, more as "thought experiments" than as formal proposals for statutory reform. . . .

[M]ost radically, the very idea of self-defense could be changed or negated altogether. Few things are more strange and threatening to the contemporary mind than a suggestion that the law should withdraw recognition of the "right" to use violence in any circumstances, even those historically recognized as self-defense. Self-defense is seen as a natural right, one that arises independently of the social context in which it is exercised and that can be recognized easily without reference to that context. I believe that what we call self-defense is in fact socially constructed and created by those who, after the fact, interpret events. And it is arguable that for every occasion on which the right of self-defense is invoked by a wronged party who has successfully resisted an aggressor, it is invoked at least once by an aggressive party seeking to justify unprovoked violence. Few aggressive wars are ever begun without a solemn declaration that the aggressor is defending itself against the weaker party;[2] in daily life, few violent acts are undertaken in which the aggressor does not claim, and usually believe, that he or she was in some sense acting in self-defense. A world without a concept of permissible violent self-defense—in which all acts of violence are seen as culpable to some degree—is difficult to imagine. I have not successfully imagined it; I cannot confidently argue that it would be better or less violent than the world we currently live in. But contemporary ethical theories, and the traditions bequeathed to us by all the major world religions, uniformly reveal a deep ambivalence about the use of force in self-defense. The Judeo-Christian tradition is often unable to choose between "an eye for an eye" and "turn the other cheek." It might be useful to imagine what the law would be like if it began turning more cheeks and plucking fewer eyes.

---

2. In the Persian Gulf War, Iraqi President Saddam Hussein justified his invasion of Kuwait on the grounds that Kuwait, by allegedly pumping oil from a disputed oil field on the Iraqi-Kuwaiti border and selling oil at a price lower than that at which he wanted to sell, had commenced "economic warfare" against Iraq, which Iraq was justified in resisting by military force. "Some of the Gulf states, [Hussein] said, were keeping the price of oil too low by pumping too much of it. Since every dollar off the price of a barrel cost Iraq $1 billion a year in lost revenues, this was an 'economic war' on Iraq. . . . [In a note to the Arab League,] Iraq accused Kuwait of planting military posts inside Iraq and stealing from an Iraqi oilfield. Both Kuwait and the U[nited] A[rab] E[mirates] were indeed, said the note, part of an 'imperialist-Zionist plot against the Arab nation.'" *Kuwait: How the West Blundered*, THE ECONOMIST (Sept 29, 1990), reprinted in Micah L. Sifry & Christopher Cerf, eds., The Gulf War Reader 99, 103, 104 (Times Books 1991). Saddam told the American ambassador to Iraq that "some brothers are fighting an economic war against us. And . . . not all wars use weapons and regard this war as a military against us." *The Glaspie Transcript: Saddam Meets the U.S. Ambassador*, reprinted in The Gulf War Reader at 122, 131. After the invasion, the United States then justified its organization and leadership of a multinational force that devastated Iraq on the grounds, inter alia, that Iraq represented an economic and military threat to the West. "Our country now imports nearly half the oil it consumes and could face a major threat to its economic independence." George Bush, *In Defense of Saudi Arabia* (Speech of Aug. 8, 1990), reprinted in The Gulf War Reader at 197, 198. "While the world waited, Saddam sought to add to the chemical weapons he now possesses, an infinitely more dangerous weapon of mass destruction—a nuclear weapon." George Bush, The Liberation of Kuwait Has Begun (Speech of Jan. 16, 1991), reprinted in *The Gulf War Reader* at 311, 312.

Paul H. Robinson & John M. Darley, Study 6: Use of Force in Defense of Property

Justice, Liability & Blame 65, 66, 71-72 (1995)

In this defense of property study, we tested the current defense of property rules against our subjects' assignment of liability in analogous defense of property situations. Subjects were given seven scenarios in which the person uses force to defend against an attempt to steal his motorcycle. One scenario presented a baseline case in which necessary, nondeadly force is used, which would receive complete exculpation under current doctrine. The other six scenarios presented variations in which the person deviates from the baseline case in one or more ways, typically in violation of one of the limitations on the use of force to defend property. The liability results are shown in Table 3.5. Notice that column *e* contains the various liabilities assigned to the person who attempts the theft. As one would expect, the thief is assigned some liability, and it is roughly constant across the cases.

With respect to perceptions of the use of necessary nondeadly force (the baseline case results in row 1), our subjects agree that complete exculpation is appropriate. Of the respondents, 89 percent judge that no liability should be assigned to the property defender; the remaining 11 percent assign liability but no punishment. . . .

Study 6 Summary

Even where the force used in defense of property is unnecessary or disproportionate, according to legal codes, the vast majority of subjects impose no punishment. The subjects also show a tendency to interpret a person's conduct as necessary to defend his property even in instances where such a conclusion is difficult to support on the objective facts. As with self-defense, the defensive nature of the person's situation appears to have a significant effect on the subjects' judgement. Even where the person's defensive response is knowingly improper— i.e., he knows that the law does not justify his conduct—the subjects significantly reduce the person's liability. Again, the subjects appear to distinguish a person who improperly defends his property from a person who uses the same force in other than a defensive context. This argues in favor of providing reduced grades of liability for those who err in defending against an attack. It remains a question for further research as to whether the value of the property being defended enters into the respondents' calculus.

If the legal code were modeled after the subjects' responses, it would give a complete defense for non-deadly force, necessary or not, used in the defense of property. The use of deadly force would be disapproved of but would result in low liability and punishment if the force appeared to be necessary (and the thief is not actually killed). In further research it would be important to address the question of what "philosophies" lie behind the judgements of individuals. Are there some individuals who believe that even deadly force is allowable in the defense of property? Does this belief reflect the view that the criminal justice system has become ineffective in defending property? The results may well be consistent with a public that is angry with what they see as the criminal justice system's failure to protect. "At the very least," the argument might go, "if the system will not protect my property, I should be permitted to do what is necessary (and perhaps more) to protect it myself."

Table 3.5 Liability for the Use of Force in Protection of Property

Scenarios	(a) Liability	(b) % No Liability (N)	(c) % No Liability or No Punishment (N+0)	(d) Model Penal Code Result for Defender	(e) Liability for Thief	(f) Maximum Force That Should be Permitted
1. Necessary force	0.00	89	100	Complete defense[a]	4.58	3.80
2. Questionably necessary force	0.00	77	98	Unclear[a]	4.70	3.91
3. Necessary force applied by device	0.19	77	93	Complete defense[b]	5.11	3.91
4. No imminent threat (perceived as not immediately necessary)	0.48	48	82	Unclear[c]	4.14	3.36
5. More than necessary force by choice	0.14	55	93	No defense: liable for simple assault, a misdemeanor	4.05	3.41
6. Deadly force, knowing not lawful	2.58	21	46	No defense; liable for aggravated assault, a second-degree felony	5.39	4.32
7. Deadly force, mistakenly believing it lawful	2.53	18	48		5.45	4.25

Liability Scale: N = No criminal liability, 0 = Liability but no punishment, 1 = 1 day, 2 = 2 weeks 3 = 2 months, 4 = 6 months, 5 = 1 year, 6 = 3 years, 7 = 7 years, 8 = 15 years, 9 = 30 years, 10 = life, and 11 = death.

Key to scenarios:

1. Necessary force: "Joe arrives home from work to find a man attempting to steal his motorcycle. Joe yells at him to get away and the thief ignores him. Joe then approaches him and grabs his arm, and the thief shrugs him off and continues hot wiring. *Finally Joe punches the thief, hitting him in the face. The thief runs off.*" In this, as well as in all the following scenarios, the thief is later apprehended by the police.

2. Questionable necessary force: "Joe punches the man, believing at the time that it is necessary. Joe's wife begins to yell at Joe that the man was small and not very muscular and Joe probably could have scared him off with a yell. Joe later realizes that his wife was right."

3. Necessary force applied by device: The owner of the motorcycle has "rigged a protective device to the garage door so that if anyone tried to break into the garage and steal the motorcycle, the device is triggered, firing a beanbag at the intruder." The thief breaks in and triggers the device, which breaks his nose.

4. No imminent threat (perceived as not immediately necessary): "The thief agrees to leave when Joe yells at him, but the thief makes it clear that he has an imprint of the keyhole and will return for the motorcycle. Joe resorts to force in order to retrieve the imprint."

5. More than necessary by force of choice: "Joe realizes that he can simply scare the man away by yelling at him. He nonetheless approaches the man and punches him in the face."

6. Deadly force: "A thief is detected attempting to steal a motorcycle and the owner attempts to get him to stop. The thief persists, and the owner gets a gun and shoots him." Respondents are told that the thief is wounded but not killed. The facts are manipulated slightly in scenarios 6 and 7 to create the knowing and mistaken belief scenarios.

Key to Column Heads:

(f) What is the maximum amount of force that someone should be permitted to use to protect his property in this situation? 0 = "no force," 2 = "risk of bodily injury," 4 = "bodily injury," 6 = "serious bodily injury," 8 = "serious bodily injury with risk of death," and 10 = "death."

[a] This scenario was intended to present the case of a mistaken actor. Such an actor might get a defense under current law, especially if his mistake was reasonable; he might only get a mitigation if his mistake was not reasonable. In fact, the scenario was perceived as a case of necessary force, for which the actor would have a defense under current doctrine.

[b] If the scenario had been perceived as the device creating a substantial risk of serious bodily injury, as was intended, there would be no defense. But no such risk was perceived by the subjects. See column d of Table 3.6. in a case of no risk of serious bodily injury, a complete defense is available.

[c] An "imminent threat" was required by common law; modern codes such as the Model Penal Code require only that the "force used be immediately necessary."

APPENDIX A: SECTION 19

Mistake as to a Justification

DISCUSSION MATERIALS

Issue: Should the Criminal Law Recognize a Defense or Mitigation for an Honest but Unreasonable Mistake as to a Justification? For Example, Should a Battered Spouse Be Able to Get a Defense or Mitigation for Killing Her Sleeping Husband?

Herbert Wechsler & Jerome Michael, The Rationale of the Law of Homicide
Model Penal Code Section 3.09(2) Commentary, Reckless or Negligent Belief

✳ DISCUSSION MATERIALS

Issue: Should the Criminal Law Recognize a Defense or Mitigation for an Honest but Unreasonable Mistake as to a Justification? For Example, Should a Battered Spouse Be Able to Get a Defense or Mitigation for Killing Her Sleeping Husband?

Under the harshest view, when one believes one is acting justifiably, one acts at one's own peril; even a reasonable mistake gives no defense. The first article, by Herbert Wechsler and Jerome Michael, captures the earlier debate on this point and generally rejects the harsh view in favor of granting a defense for a reasonable mistake.

The Model Penal Code Commentary accepts as fundamental the need for a defense for a reasonable mistake as to a justification and goes a step farther, to provide a mitigation (but not a defense) for even an unreasonable mistake. While some modern state codes adopt the all-or-nothing approach—that is, giving a complete defense for a reasonable mistake but full liability for an unreasonable mistake—the Model Code rejects that approach and instead varies the degree of liability with the defendant's level of culpability in making the mistake.

Herbert Wechsler & Jerome Michael, The Rationale of the Law of Homicide
37 Columbia Law Review 701, 736 (1937)

The most obvious case of homicidal behavior that serves the end of preserving life is that of the victim of a wrongful attack who finds it necessary to kill his assailant to save his own life. We need not pause to reconsider the universal judgment that there is no social interest in preserving the lives of aggressors at the cost of those of their victims. Given the choice that must be made, the only defensible policy is one that will operate as a sanction against unlawful aggression. But here the simplicity of the matter ends. The initial problem arises from the fact that men sometimes believe that they are being attacked, that their lives are in immediate peril and that it is necessary to kill to save themselves when such is not the case. So long as the belief is reasonable, it seems quite clear, however, that the original policy still obtains. Men must act on the basis of what was known or could have been known to them at the moment of action, not at some later time. To concede a privilege to kill only in cases of actual necessity is to lay down a rule that must either be disregarded or else must operate to deny freedom of action even in cases where the necessity exists and not merely in those where it does not. On the other hand, no such onerous limitation on freedom of action is imposed by requiring that men exercise the degree of care to appraise the facts correctly which is appropriate to the situation. It is desirable to deter men from acting without exercising such care; unless such care is taken, death is not a justifiable means even to the preservation of their own lives.

Model Penal Code Section 3.09(2) Commentary Reckless or Negligent Belief
Official Draft and Revised Comments 150-153 (1985)

Against the requirement of reasonable belief in justification defenses, there has been little more than a thin line of academic criticism. Keedy argued against the rule that a mistake must be reasonable on the ground that "[i]f the mistake, whether reasonable or unreasonable, as judged by an external standard, does negative the criminal mind, there should be no conviction." He thought that negligence should establish mens rea only where the actor failed to use the care that appeared proper to him under the circumstances and that the proper test must be: "Did the defendant act up to his own standard?" This attempted "subjective" definition of negligence has not been followed.

It is, however, commonly agreed that negligence at common law means for criminal purposes something more gross than civil negligence in that it implies a wide departure from the reasonable standard. On this view, it might be said that for a mistake to preclude justification it must be not merely unreasonable but grossly unreasonable. Even with this qualification, however, a person should not be convicted of a crime of intention where he has labored under a mistake that, had the facts been as he supposed, would have left him free from guilt. The unreasonableness of an alleged belief quite properly is considered as evidence that it was not in fact held, but if the tribunal is satisfied that the belief was held, the defendant, in a prosecution for crime founded on wrongful purpose, should be entitled to be judged as if his belief was true. To convict for a belief arrived at on an unreasonable ground is to convict for negligence. Where the crime otherwise requires greater culpability for a conviction, it is neither fair nor logical to convict when there is only negligence as to the circumstances that would establish a justification.

The solution in this section, as indicated earlier, is that such situations should be taken out of the category of purposeful crime and dealt with as cases of recklessness or negligence. If the belief is recklessly arrived at, i.e., with awareness of the risk that it may be unfounded, then it is appropriate to assess the defendant as one would be assessed who had acted recklessly with respect to the material elements of the offense. In homicide, for example, the distinction between purposeful and reckless homicide has enormous import when it comes to the degree of the offense and to the sentence. And it makes more sense to assimilate the defendant who is reckless as to the existence of justifying circumstances to one who recklessly takes life than to assimilate him to one who purposefully does so.

Sections 3.03 to 3.08 accordingly provide that the actor's belief alone will qualify him for the justification. Subsection (2) imposes as a general qualification the principle that when the actor's belief in the necessity for using the force that he used was recklessly or negligently formed, or when he was reckless or negligent in acquiring or failing to acquire any knowledge that is otherwise material to the justification for his use of force, the justification is lost in a prosecution for an offense for which recklessness or negligence, as the case may be, suffices for conviction. By the same token, the justification is retained in a prosecution for an offense that can only be committed purposely or knowingly, irrespective of recklessness or negligence in assessing the grounds for the justification. Recklessness and negligence as to the factors that establish justification, in short, are treated on a parity with recklessness or negligence as to the other material elements of the offense involved.

This subsection rejects the views of those who would have gone even further and accepted any honest belief as to justification as exculpating an actor from conviction for crimes of negligence and recklessness as well as crimes of purpose. Glanville Williams, who urged this position, contended that the concept of negligence was not a useful legal one in this context. The judgment of the Institute was that although caution should be exercised in finding recklessness or negligence in forming the beliefs that are material to justification, nevertheless cases do arise where such judgments can fairly be made.

No jurisdiction has gone as far as Professor Williams suggested. A number of recently revised codes and proposals follow the approach of this subsection toward reckless and negligent beliefs about justifying circumstances; but many of them adopt the older principle that no justification exists if a belief in justifying circumstances is unreasonable, thus permitting conviction for a crime of purpose when an actor has negligently concluded that a circumstance that would sustain a justification exists.

APPENDIX A: SECTION 20

Mistake Excuses

DISCUSSION MATERIALS
Issue: Should the Criminal Law Recognize an Excuse Defense for a Reasonable Mistake of Law?
   Thomas W. White, Reliance on Apparent Authority as a Defense to Criminal Prosecutions
   George P. Fletcher, Arguments for Strict Liability: Mistakes of Law
   Dan M. Kahan, Ignorance of the Law Is an Excuse—But Only for the Virtuous
LAW (Subsequent)
   United States v. Ehrlichman

❋ **DISCUSSION MATERIALS**

Issue: Should the Criminal Law Recognize an Excuse Defense for a Reasonable Mistake of Law?

In commenting on the denial of a mistake of law defense in the *Barker* case (Problem Case #93, Warm-up for Watergate, in Section 19), Thomas White discusses the rationale of the defense and argues against its use. George Fletcher's piece similarly argues in favor of the defense based on what he perceives as the complexity of today's criminal law system. He rejects the utilitarian and conceptual counter-arguments and adopts a Kantian perspective. Finally, Dan Kahan attempts to defend the result in *People v. Marrero*, the principal case for this Section, rejecting a reasonable mistake of law defense, by arguing that rejecting the defense makes sense as a device to prevent people from taking advantage of legal certainty in order to skate close to the line of legality and perhaps over the line of morality.

Thomas W. White, Reliance on Apparent Authority as a Defense to Criminal Prosecutions

77 Columbia Law Review 775, 779, 801 (1977)

[T]he values promoted by the general mistake of law rule do not obtain when the actor honestly and reasonably relies on what seems to be an authoritative statement of law. By seeking to inform himself of the law and then relying on it, the individual demonstrates his law-abiding nature; this exception to the rule advances, rather than hinders, the social value of making individuals know and obey the law.

Allowing the defense in the circumstances of the *Barker* cases does not serve to advance these policy interests. Reliance on a government official's apparent status as carrying with it all the legal authorization necessary for the operation is inconsistent with an affirmative effort to know the law. The burglars did not seek from Hunt an interpretation as to the legality of the break-in. Their reliance demonstrated not a law-abiding nature, but rather a failure to inquire into the law.

[T]he defense should be rejected on policy grounds: because of the societal interest in deterring conduct by government officials that infringes the civil rights of citizens, a person who purports to act on behalf of the government should be held to a high standard of knowledge of the important restrictions imposed by the law on governmental action. Only where such a person has made a reasonable effort to know the basis of legality of his actions, should he be granted a defense. An uninformed subjective belief in the legality of one's actions, unsupported by a reasonable basis for that belief, should not provide a defense.

George P. Fletcher, Arguments for Strict Liability: Mistakes of Law

Rethinking Criminal Law 731-736 (1978)

Various efforts have been made to defend the principle that even a reasonable mistake of law should not constitute an excuse for wrongdoing. In the early stages of the criminal law, when the range of offenses was limited to aggression against particular victims and other obvious moral wrongs, it was more plausible to assume that everyone knew the law. If someone did not realize that rape or homicide was wrong, one might properly expect a proof of mental illness in order to make out a believable claim. It is not surprising that the M'Naghten test of insanity is linked to the question whether, because of a mental disease or defect, the actor did not realize that the particular act was wrong.

The tight moral consensus that once supported the criminal law has obviously disappeared. This has happened as a result both of the vast expansion of the criminal law into regulatory offenses and the disintegration of the Judeo-Christian moral consensus. In a pluralistic society, saddled with criminal sanctions affecting every area of life, one cannot expect that everyone know what is criminal and what is not. The problem is compounded in some fields, such as abortion and obscenity, by constantly changing standards of permissible conduct. The "obscenity" that could send Ralph Ginzburg to jail for five years is now readily exhibited at adult theaters around the United States. Assuming that everyone who violates the law does so in disregard and disrespect of the law is obviously outdated. Maintaining that policy today verges on blindness to the problem of individual justice.

Oliver Wendell Holmes confronted the problem directly and found a harmonic consistency between disregarding mistakes of law and his favorite chord: "to admit the excuse at all would be to encourage ignorance . . . and justice to the individual is rightly outweighed by the larger interests on the other side of the scales." This utilitarian rationale for the traditional rule is hardly convincing to those who try to assess whether, in a particular case, the interests of society outweigh the interests of the individual. Surely, Holmes would not favor sacrificing the individual, however innocent, for the sake of the general good, however minimal. Therefore in a particular case, we have to assess whether or not the scales weigh more heavily on one side or on the other. If we wish to embark on this task of adjudication, how do we decide, and how should lawyers demonstrate, that one side of the scale outweighs the other? The problem with pursuing the general good is that the results of one instance of applying the criminal sanction are so speculative as to be chimerical. The problem with punishing a morally innocent person is that if one is willing to do that at all, the harm entailed is likely to appear either minimal or infinite: either because one does not perceive the evil of punishing the innocent, or because one does perceive the evil and regards it as so great as not to be worth any transient benefits. In either event, Holmes' proposal bears witness to his own famous aphorism about legal method: "General propositions do not decide concrete cases." The utilitarian calculus is too commodious a crucible for resolving concrete problems of mistakes of law.

Another rationale for disregarding mistakes of law is Jerome Hall's theory that there is a fundamental logical contradiction between deferring to the suspect's view of the law and the theory of legality. This argument merits consideration, for it illustrates the confusion engendered by a failure to recognize the distinction between wrongdoing and culpability. Hall's argument on mistake of law is best stated in his own words:

> If that plea [mistake of law] were valid, the consequence would be: whenever a defendant in a criminal case thought the law was thus and so, he is to be treated as though the law were thus and so, *i.e., the law actually is thus and so.* But such a doctrine would contradict the essential requisites of a legal system.

The fallacy in this line of reasoning consists in shifting the meaning of the word "law" as we move from the premise to the conclusion. In the phrase, "whenever a defendant thought the law was thus and so," the word "law" refers to the norms about which the defendant might be mistaken. In the conclusion, "the law actually is thus and so," the word "law" no longer refers to a norm or a rule about which the defendant is mistaken, but to an empirical concept of the law equivalent to whether the court actually acquits in the particular case. These two concepts of law have little to do with each other. The norms of the law provide reasons for acting and reasons for convicting those who transgress the law. The empirical set of decisions— "what the courts do in fact" —does not provide a reason for convicting or acquitting anyone. The practice of the courts does not justify itself.

The norms of the law do not change when a jury finds that a particular suspect could not have been expected to know, say, that posting a particular sign violated the law against soliciting marriages. If the suspect violates the rule in reasonable reliance on advice of the attorney general, the conduct may be subject to an excuse, but it does not follow that the court has engrafted an exception onto the norm. The proof of that proposition is that if the suspect, acquitted on grounds of mistake, left the courthouse and posted exactly the same sign, he would obviously be guilty. Recognizing a mistake of law as an excuse does not alter the norm any more than recognizing insanity as an excuse alters the prohibition against the conduct in question.

The more general flaw in Jerome Hall's system of criminal law is the failure to recognize the profound significance of distinguishing between wrongdoing and accountability or culpability. Recognizing a claim of justification does in fact acknowledge an exception to the norm; but recognizing an excuse means merely that in the particular case, the actor cannot be fairly held accountable for his wrongdoing. Mistake of law is an excuse that leaves the norm intact. Its effect is merely to deny the attribution of the wrongdoing to the particular suspect.

If there were any doubts about this, we need only ask how the norms of the criminal law would read if a mistake of law precluded a finding that the norm was violated. Norms are designed to guide and influence conduct. The norm itself cannot include a condition about what should happen in the event that the norm was violated involuntarily or by mistake. If it is unlawful to possess brass knuckles, the norm could not be read to say: Thou shalt not possess brass knuckles unless thou art reasonably mistaken about whether it is legal to do so. Nor does it say: Thou shalt not do X unless thou art insane or under duress or involuntarily intoxicated. The norm only includes those elements about which the actor should make a decision in seeking to conform his conduct to the law. It is not up to the actor to decide whether he is insane, whether the duress of another is sufficient to excuse a violation, or whether he is reasonably mistaken about the legality of his conduct. It is impossible to give an account of excuses by referring to the content of the norm and the question whether the norm is violated. The question of excusing arises after it is established that the norm is violated. The grounds for excusing are extrinsic to the norm and reserved for assessment by the trier of fact.

These two arguments rejecting mistake of laws—one associated with Holmes and the other with Hall—correspond to the two themes that run through this section on disregarding mistakes. One general strategy for suppressing mistakes is utilitarian: It is socially beneficial to eliminate the possibility of acquittal on some claims of mistake. The other strategy is moral or conceptual: There is some reason in the nature of the things why the mistake ought to be irrelevant. . . .

Utilitarian arguments raise broader questions of moral philosophy and, therefore, they resist refutation by laying bare their premises. There is nothing hidden in Holmes' argument. "Public policy," he tells us, "sacrifices the individual to the common good." An assault on this explicit and coherent premise requires far more than the feeble claim that it is unjust to sacrifice the individual to the common good. Unjust it may be, but one needs to ground the imperative to do justice in a set of values at least as compelling as the value of furthering the social good. The most compelling argument offered to date is the Kantian thesis that the categorical imperative requires us to respect persons as ends in themselves, and we violate this imperative when we punish a person solely to further interests of other persons. The skeptic might wonder how the practice of punishing criminals can escape the charge of using persons as means to the end of deterrence and social order. The answer to this objection takes us back to the classical theory of punishment. If punishment is based on accountability for wrongdoing, then the punishing agency does not act in disregard for the wrong-doer's autonomy. On the contrary, the imposition of punishment—as contrasted with civil commitment—expresses respect for the wrongdoer's autonomy and his capacity to avoid liability under the law.

Dan M. Kahan, Ignorance of the Law Is an Excuse—But Only for the Virtuous

96 Michigan Law Review 127, 131, 133, 141-142 (1997)

> If you want to know the law and nothing else, you must look at it as a bad man, who cares only for the material consequences which such knowledge enables him to predict, not as a good one, who finds his reasons for conduct, whether inside the law or outside of it, in the vaguer sanctions of conscience.
>
> *Oliver Wendell Holmes, Jr.*

> It is no doubt true that there are many cases in which the criminal could not have known that he was breaking the law, but to admit [mistake of law as an] excuse at all would be to encourage ignorance where the law-maker has determined to make men know and obey, and justice to the individual is rightly outweighed by the larger interests on the other side of the scales.
>
> *Oliver Wendell Holmes, Jr.*

It's axiomatic that "ignorance of the law is no excuse." My aim in this essay is to examine what the "mistake of law doctrine" reveals about the relationship between criminal law and morality in general and about the law's understanding of moral responsibility in particular.

The conventional understanding of the mistake of law doctrine rests on two premises, which are encapsulated in the Holmesian epigrams with which I've started this essay. The first is liberal positivism. As a descriptive claim, liberal positivism holds that the content of the law can be identified without reference to morality: one needn't be a good man to perceive what's lawful, Holmes tells us; one need only understand the consequences in store if one should choose to act badly. The normative side of liberal positivism urges us to see the independence of law from morality as a good thing. In a pluralistic society, the law should aspire to be comprehensible to persons of diverse moral views. What's more, it should avoid embodying within itself a standard of culpability or blame that depends on an individual's acceptance of any such view as orthodox; in a liberal society, even the bad man can be a good citizen so long as he lives up to society's rules.

Liberal positivism supports denying a mistake of law defense when combined with a second premise: the utility of legal knowledge. Under the liberal positivist view, the law disclaims any reliance on the moral knowledge of citizens, as well as any ambition to make them value morality for its own sake. Accordingly, to promote good (that is, law-abiding) conduct, it becomes imperative that citizens be made aware of the content of the law and the consequences of breaking it. Hence, the law shows no mercy for those who claim to be ignorant of what the criminal law proscribes, a position that maximizes citizens' incentive to learn the rules that "the law-maker has determined to make men know and obey."

I want to challenge the accuracy of this account of why ignorance of law does not excuse. In its place, I'll suggest an alternative understanding, which rests on premises diametrically opposed to the Holmesian aphorisms that undergird the classic account.

The first premise of this anti-Holmesian conception is legal moralism. This principle asserts that law is suffused with morality and, as a result, can't ultimately be identified or applied to law without the making of moral judgments. It asserts, too, that individuals are appropriately judged by the law not only for the law-abiding quality of their actions but also for the moral quality of their values, motivations, and emotions—in a word, for the quality of their characters.

The second premise of the anti-Holmesian view can be called the prudence of obfuscation. Moral judgments are too rich and particular to be subdued by any set of abstract rules; as a result, law will always embody morality only imperfectly. That means that from the standpoint of legal moralism, private knowledge of the law isn't unambiguously good. The more readily individuals can discover the law's content, the more readily they'll be able to discern, and exploit, the gaps between what's immoral and what's illegal. The law must therefore employ strategies to discourage citizens from gaining knowledge for this purpose. One is to deny an excuse for ignorance of law. Punishing those who mistakenly believe their conduct to be legal promotes good (that is, moral) behavior less through encouraging citizens to learn the law—an objective that could in fact be more completely realized by excusing at least some mistakes—than by creating hazards for those who choose to rely on what they think they know about the law. By denying a mistake of law defense, the law is saying, contra Holmes, that if a citizen suspects the law fails to prohibit some species of immoral conduct, the only certain way to avoid criminal punishment is to be a good person rather than a bad one.

This anti-Holmesian account, I'll argue, not only offers a superior explanation of why ignorance of the law is not ordinarily regarded as an excuse; it also does a better job in explaining why it sometimes is. Sometimes it's a crime to engage in an act—for example, omitting to file a tax return or failing to report certain financial transactions—that wouldn't be viewed as immoral were it not for the existence of a legal duty. Crimes of this sort are often referred to as *malum prohibitum*—wrong because prohibited and are distinguished from crimes that are *malum in se*—wrong in themselves independent of law. *Malum prohibitum* crimes are the ones most likely to be interpreted as permitting mistake of law defenses. This aspect of the doctrine defies both premises of the classic position: to distinguish *malum prohibitum* crimes from *malum in se* ones, courts must employ moral judgments of the sort that liberal positivism forbids; and by allowing a mistake of law defense for *malum prohibitum* crimes, courts relax citizens' incentives to learn the law. Excusing someone for ignorance of a *malum prohibitum* crime makes perfect sense, however, under the anti-Holmesian view since morality abstracted from law has nothing to say about the underlying conduct, a person can't be expected to rely on her perception of morality rather than her understanding of what such laws prohibit; because even a good person could make that kind of mistake in such circumstances, the defendant is excused.

A final advantage associated with the anti-Holmesian understanding of mistake of law is that it more completely defends the doctrine from the standard criticism made of it. Denying a mistake of law defense, it is said, sanctions punishment of the morally blameless. The classic conception demurs: "[J]ustice to the individual is rightly outweighed by the larger interests on the other side of the scales." But the anti-Holmesian conception goes further, showing that the standard criticism rests on a truncated understanding of when punishment is just a person is rightly condemned as a criminal wrongdoer not only for knowingly choosing to violate the law, but also for exhibiting the kind of character failing associated with insufficient commitment to the moral norms embodied in the community's criminal law. . . .

This account makes it easier to see why *Marrero* came out the way it did. Marrero ignored the law's injunction to do what's right rather than what one thinks is legal. New York's restrictive gun possession law embodies its citizens' strong antipathy toward, and fear of, handguns. But rather than defer to those norms, Marrero decided to be strategic, availing himself of what must have appeared even to him to be a largely fortuitous gap in the law. That's the attitude that made the court see in Marrero's efforts to decode the law not an earnest and laudable attempt to obey but rather a "false and diversionary stratagem," a form of "game playing and evasion."

Other facts, not even mentioned by the court, also likely played a role: that the policy of the federal prison at which Marrero worked forbade guards to carry guns either on or off duty; that Marrero had supplied his girlfriend and another companion with guns, even though they clearly had no grounds for believing their possession to be lawful; and that Marrero menacingly reached for his weapon when the police approached him in the Manhattan club. These facts might not have been formally relevant to the court's disposition, but they no doubt helped the court to see Marrero as a Holmesian bad man. And in the eyes of the court, a Holmesian bad man is plenty bad enough to be designated a criminal.

▪ LAW (SUBSEQUENT)

United States v. Ehrlichman
376 F. Supp. 29 (D.D,C. 1974)

The defendants were indicted for conspiring to contravene a psychiatrist's Fourth Amendment rights by entering his offices without a warrant to obtain a patient's medical records. They sought pre-trial discovery with respect to alleged national security of their case. The defendants contended that "even if the break-in was illegal, they lacked the specific intent necessary to violate section 241 because they reasonably believed that they had been authorized to enter and search Dr. Fielding's office." The district court granted their discovery request, but held that "it is well established that a mistake of law is no defense in a conspiracy case to the knowing performance of acts which, like the unauthorized entry and search at issue here, are malum in se." Unlike an exception that "resulted from good faith reliance on a court order or upon the legal advice of an executive officer charged with interpreting or enforcing the law in question [t]his principle cannot be stretched to encompass a mistake based upon the assurances of an alleged co-conspirator with regard to the criminality of acts that are malum in se."

APPENDIX A: SECTION 21

Insanity

DISCUSSION MATERIALS

Issue: Should the Criminal Law Recognize an Excuse Defense for an Offender Who, Because of Mental Illness, Knows His Conduct Constituting the Offense Is Wrong but Lacks the Capacity to Control It?

    United States v. Robert Lyons

    Legislative History to Public Law 98-473, Title IV, Insanity Defense Reform Act of 1983

    Jodie English, The Light Between Twilight and Dusk: Federal Criminal Law and the Volitional Insanity Defense

---

✳ DISCUSSION MATERIALS

Issue: Should the Criminal Law Recognize an Excuse Defense for an Offender Who, Because of Mental Illness, Knows His Conduct Constituting the Offense Is Wrong but Lacks the Capacity to Control It?

In limiting the insanity defense, to exclude a control prong, the majority in *United States v. Lyons* and the excerpted legislative history to the Insanity Defense Reform Act of 1983 justify their rejection of the earlier Model Penal Code's formulation. The dissenting *Lyons* opinion and Jodie English, in arguing against this rejection, question the motivations and sources used by the court and Congress and offer alternative approaches that would restrict the control prong without abolishing it.

United States v. Robert Lyons
United States Court of Appeals, Fifth Circuit
731 F.2d 243, 739 F.2d 994 (1984)

GEE, Circuit Judge:

    Defendant Robert Lyons was indicted on twelve counts of knowingly and intentionally securing controlled narcotics by misrepresentation, fraud, deception and subterfuge in violation of *21 U.S.C. §843(a)(3) (1976)* and *18 U.S.C. §2 (1976)*. Before trial Lyons informed the Assistant United States Attorney that he intended to rely on a defense of insanity: that he had lacked substantial capacity to conform his conduct to the requirements of the law because of drug addiction. Lyons proffered evidence that in 1978 he began to suffer from several painful ailments, that various narcotics were prescribed to be taken as needed for his pain, and that he became addicted to these drugs. He also offered to present expert witnesses who would testify that his drug addiction affected his brain both physiologically and psychologically and that as a result he lacked substantial capacity to conform his conduct to the requirements of the law.

In response to the government's motion *in limine,* the district court excluded any evidence of Lyon's drug addiction, apparently on the ground that such an addiction could not constitute a mental disease or defect sufficient to support an insanity defense. A panel of this Court reversed, holding that it was the jury's responsibility to decide whether involuntary drug addiction could constitute a mental disease or defect depriving Lyons of substantial capacity to conform his conduct to the requirements of the law. *United States v. Lyons, 704 F.2d 743 (5th Cir. 1983).* We agreed to rehear the case en banc.

I.

For the greater part of two decades our Circuit has followed the rule that a defendant is not to be held criminally responsible for conduct if, at the time of that conduct and as a result of mental disease or defect, he lacked substantial capacity either to appreciate the wrongfulness of his conduct *or to conform his conduct to the requirements of the law.*

II.

Because the concept of criminal responsibility in the federal courts is a congeries of judicially-made rules of decision based on common law concepts, it is usually appropriate for us to reexamine and reappraise these rules in the light of new policy considerations. We last examined the insanity defense in *Blake v. United States, 407 F.2d 908 (5th Cir. 1969)* (en banc), where we adopted the A.L.I. Model Penal Code definition of insanity: that a person is not responsible for criminal conduct if, at the time of such conduct and as a result of mental disease or defect, he lacks substantial capacity either to appreciate the wrongfulness of his conduct or to conform his conduct to the requirements of the law. Following the example of sister circuits, we embraced this standard in lieu of our former one, defined in *Howard v. United States, 232 F.2d 274, 275 (5th Cir. 1956)* (en banc), because we concluded that then current knowledge in the field of behavioral science supported such a result. Unfortunately, it now appears our conclusion was premature—that the brave new world that we foresaw has not arrived.

Reexamining the *Blake* standard today, we conclude that the volitional prong of the insanity defense—a lack of capacity to conform one's conduct to the requirements of the law—does not comport with current medical and scientific knowledge, which has retreated from its earlier, sanguine expectations.

Consequently, we now hold that a person is not responsible for criminal conduct on the grounds of insanity only if at the time of that conduct, as a result of a mental disease or defect, he is unable to appreciate the wrongfulness of that conduct.

We do so for several reasons. First, as we have mentioned, a majority of psychiatrists now believe that they do not possess sufficient accurate scientific bases for measuring a person's capacity for self-control or for calibrating the impairment of that capacity. "The line between an irresistible impulse and an impulse not resisted is probably no sharper than between twilight and dusk." *American Psychiatric Association Statement on the Insanity Defense*, 11 (1982) [APA Statement]. . . .

In addition, the risks of fabrication and "moral mistakes" in administering the insanity defense are greatest "when the experts and the jury are asked to speculate whether the defendant had the capacity to 'control' himself or whether he could have 'resisted' the criminal impulse." Moreover, psychiatric testimony about volition is more likely to produce confusion for jurors than is psychiatric testimony concerning a defendant's appreciation of the wrongfulness of his act. It appears, moreover, that there is considerable overlap between a psychotic person's inability to understand and his ability to control his behavior. Most psychotic persons who fail a volitional test would also fail a cognitive test, thus rendering the volitional test superfluous for them. Finally, Supreme Court authority requires that such proof be made by the federal prosecutor beyond a reasonable doubt, an all but impossible task in view of the present murky state of medical knowledge. Davis v. United States, 160 U.S. 469, 16 S. Ct. 353, 40 L. Ed. 499 (1895).[1]

One need not disbelieve in the existence of Angels in order to conclude that the present state of our knowledge regarding them is not such as to support confident conclusions about how many can dance on the head of a pin. In like vein, it may be that some day tools will be discovered with which reliable conclusions about human volition can be fashioned. It appears to be all but a certainty, however, that despite earlier hopes they do not lie in our hands today. When and if they do, it will be time to consider again to what degree the law should adopt the sort of conclusions that they produce. But until then, we see no prudent course for the law to follow but to treat all criminal impulses—including those not resisted—as resistible. . . .

III.

Thus, Lyons' claim that he lacked substantial capacity to conform his conduct to the requirements of the law will not raise the insanity defense. It would be unfair, however, to remit him retroactively to our newly restricted insanity defense without allowing him the opportunity to plan a defense bearing its contours in mind. Consequently, we vacate his conviction and remand for a new trial in accordance with our new insanity standard. . . .

Vacated and Remanded.

ALVIN B. RUBIN, Circuit Judge, with whom TATE, Circuit Judge, joins dissenting. . . .

---

1. Editor's Note. In *Rivera v. Delaware*, 429 U.S. 877 (1976), the Supreme Court dismissed, and consequently sustained, the constitutionality of a Delaware statute that required a criminal defendant raising an insanity defense to prove his or her mental illness or defect by a preponderance of the evidence.

The majority offers several reasons for its decision both to reexamine and to change the method by which we determine who is criminally responsible. . . .

The first is the potential threat to society created by the volitional prong of the insanity defense. Public opposition to any insanity-grounded defense is often based, either explicitly or implicitly, on the view that the plea is frequently invoked by violent criminals who fraudulently use it to evade just punishment. . . .

Despite the prodigious volume of writing devoted to the plea, the empirical data that are available provide little or no support for these fearsome perceptions and in many respects directly refute them. . . .

Another set of objections to the plea is based on the thesis that factfinders—especially juries—are confused and manipulated by the vagueness of the legal standards of insanity and the notorious "battle of the experts" who present conclusory, superficial, and misleading testimony. These conditions, the argument runs, conspire to produce inconsistent and "inaccurate" verdicts. . . .

The manipulated-jury argument is supported largely by declamation, not data. . . . [O]ne major study . . . found that jurors responsibly and carefully consider the evidence presented, do recognize that the final responsibility for the defendant's fate rests with them, do appreciate the limits and proper use of expert testimony, and do grasp the instructions given them. Although the evidence does not warrant the conclusion that juries function better in insanity trials than in other criminal cases, it certainly does not appear that they function *less* effectively. And no source has been cited to the court to support the conclusion that, as an empirical matter, pleas based upon the volitional prong present an especially problematic task for the jury.

Indeed, the majority opinion does not assert that the insanity defense, particularly the control test, *doesn't* work; it contends that the defense *can't* work. The principal basis for this contention is the belief, held by "a majority of psychiatrists," that they lack "sufficient accurate scientific bases for measuring a person's capacity for self-control or for calibrating the impairment of that capacity." This argument raises practical and important questions regarding the usefulness of expert testimony in determining whether a person has the ability to conform his conduct to law; but the absence of useful expert evidence, if indeed there is none, does not obviate the need for resolving the question whether the defendant ought to be held accountable for his criminal behavior. . . .

The relevant inquiry under either branch of the insanity test is a subjective one that focuses on the defendant's actual state of mind. Our duty to undertake that inquiry is not based on confidence in the testimony of expert witnesses, but on the ethical precept that the defendant's mental state is a crucial aspect of his blameworthiness. . . . The availability of expert testimony and the probative value of such testimony are basically evidentiary problems that can be accommodated within the existing test.

A recent Second Circuit case demonstrates that the volitional test can be reasonably cabined to prevent abuse. In *United States v. Torniero*, the court . . . . established two guidelines: (1) a defendant seeking to rely on a newly recognized disorder to meet the volitional test must show "that respected authorities in the field share the view that the disorder is a disease or defect that could have impaired the defendant's ability to desist from the offense charged . . . " ; and (2) the alleged disease or defect must be relevant to the crime charged. . . .

Even the few cases in which the trial develops into a battle of experts provide no basis for the majority's conclusion that the prosecution faces an "all but impossible task." The prosecution appears to be able to locate experts as readily as the defense. Indeed, a defendant pleading insanity typically faces both a judge and a jury who are skeptical about psychiatry in general and the insanity plea in particular. Sharply adversarial presentation of conflicting psychiatric testimony may increase this skepticism, and thus make acquittal more unlikely. Usually the defendant will have been adjudicated sane enough to understand the proceedings against him and to assist in his defense; otherwise he would be incompetent to stand trial. The formal allocation of the persuasion burden notwithstanding, the defendant to prevail must convince the doubting factfinder that, despite present outward appearances, he was insane at the time he committed the crime.

The majority's fear that the present test invites "moral mistakes" is difficult to understand. The majority opinion concedes that some individuals cannot conform their conduct to the law's requirements. . . . Without citing any data that verdicts in insanity cases decided under a control test are frequently inaccurate, the majority embraces a rule certain to result in the conviction of at least some who are not morally responsible and the punishment of those for whom retributive, deterrent, and rehabilitative penal goals are inappropriate. A decision that virtually ensures undeserved, and therefore unjust, punishment in the name of avoiding moral mistakes rests on a peculiar notion of morality. . . .

The majority opinion is a radical departure from the established jurisprudence of every federal circuit that has spoken on the issue. It is based only on intuitive reactions and the published recommendations, to which no one has testified, of a few professional groups. We would permit no jury to decide even an unimportant issue on such hearsay. The purposes to be served by this innovation are unclear. . . . Its effect will be felt by only two small groups: a few who otherwise might have made a case for the jury but who will be deprived of a plea that in any event would likely have been bootless, and those few unfortunate persons so afflicted by mental disease that they knew what the law forbade but couldn't control their actions sufficiently to avoid violating it. . . .

In sum, I cannot join in a decision that, without supporting data, overturns a widely used rule that has not been shown to be working badly in order to adopt a change that will likely produce little or no practical benefit to society as a whole, conflicts with the fundamental moral predicates of our criminal justice system, and may inflict undeserved punishment on a few hapless individuals.

Legislative History to Public Law 98-473, Title IV, Insanity Defense Reform Act of 1983

225-228, reprinted in U.S. Code Congressional and Administrative News 3407-3410 (1984)

Provisions of the bill, as reported . . .

Section 402 adds a new section 20 to title 18 of the United States Code to define the scope of the insanity defense for Federal offenses and to shift the burden of proof to the defendant. In its entirety the new section would provide:

§20. Insanity defense

(a) Affirmative Defense—It is an affirmative defense to a prosecution under any Federal statute that, at the time of the commission of the acts constituting the offense, the defendant, as a result of a severe mental disease or defect, was unable to appreciate the nature and quality or the wrongfulness of his acts. Mental disease or defect does not otherwise constitute a defense.

(b) Burden of Proof—The defendant has the burden of proving the defense of insanity by clear and convincing evidence.

The principal difference between the statement of the defense in S. 1762 and that presently employed in the Federal courts is that the volitional portion of the cognitive-volitional test of the A.L.I. Model Penal Code is eliminated. The Committee, after extensive hearings, concluded that it was appropriate to eliminate the volitional portion of the test.

While there has been criticism of the "right-wrong" *M'Naghten* test, the "irresistible impulse" part of the current Federal insanity defense has received particularly strong criticism in recent years. Conceptually, there is some appeal to a defense predicated on lack of power to avoid criminal conduct. If one conceives the major purpose of the insanity defense to be the exclusion of the nondeterrables from criminal responsibility, a control test seems designed to meet that objective. Furthermore, notions of retributive punishment seem particularly inappropriate with respect to one powerless to do otherwise than he did.

A strong criticism of the control test, however, is associated with a determinism which seems dominant in the thinking of many expert witnesses. As noted by [Professor] David Robinson of George Washington University, "[m]odern psychiatry has tended to view man as controlled by antecedent hereditary and environmental factors." [The Report goes on to support this position with quotes from Freud and a psychiatric text.]

Such a view is consistent with a conclusion that *all* criminal conduct is evidence of lack of power to conform behavior to the requirements of law. The control tests and volitional standards thus acutely raise the problem of what is *meant* by lack of power to avoid conduct or to conform to the requirements of law which leads to the most fundamental objection to the control tests—their lack of determinate meaning.

Richard J. Bonnie, Professor of Law and Director of the Institute of Law, Psychiatry and Public Policy at the University of Virginia, while accepting the moral predicate for a control test, explained the fundamental difficulty involved:

Unfortunately, however, there is no scientific basis for measuring a person's capacity for self-control or for calibrating the impairment of such capacity. There is, in short, no objective basis for distinguishing between offenders who were undeterrable and those who were merely undeterred, between the impulse that was irresistible and the impulse not resisted, or between substantial impairment of capacity and some lesser impairment. Whatever the precise terms of the volitional test, the question is unanswerable—or can be answered only by "moral guesses." To ask it at all, in my opinion, invites fabricated claims, undermines equal administration of the penal law, and compromises its deterrent effect.

Professor [David] Robinson states the same idea as follows:

> No test is available to distinguish between those who cannot and those who will not conform to legal requirements. The result is an invitation to semantic justice, metaphysical speculation and intuitive moral judgments masked as factual determinations.

Similarly, The Royal Commission on Capital Punishment stated:

> Most lawyers have consistently maintained that the concept of an "irresistible" or "uncontrollable" impulse is a dangerous one, since it is impracticable to distinguish between those impulses which are the product of mental disease and those which are the product of ordinary passion, or, where mental disease exists, between impulses that may be genuinely irresistible and those which are merely not resisted.

A brief but perceptive discussion of the problem is contained in the concurring opinion of Mr. Justice Black, joined by Mr. Justice Harlan, in *Powell v. Texas*, upholding the constitutionality of criminal penalties applied to alcoholics whose public drunkenness is alleged to be beyond volitional control:

> When we say that appellant's appearance in public is caused not by "his own" volition but rather by some other force, we are clearly thinking of a force which is nevertheless his except in some special sense. The accused undoubtedly commits the proscribed act and the only question is wither the act can be attributed to a part of "his" personality that should not be regarded as criminally responsible. . . .
>
> [T]he question whether an act is "involuntary" is, as I have already indicated, an inherently elusive question, and one which the State may, for good reasons wish to regard as irrelevant.

The American Psychiatric Association also has commented on the ability of expert witnesses to provide adequate information to resolve issues inherent in the current insanity test:

> The above commentary [concerning the legal standards for an insanity defense] does not mean that given the present state of psychiatric knowledge psychiatrists cannot present meaningful testimony relevant to determining a defendant's understanding or appreciation of his act. Many psychiatrists, however, believe that psychiatric information relevant to determining whether a defendant understood the nature of his act, and whether he appreciated its wrongfulness, is more reliable and has a stronger scientific basis than, for example, does psychiatric information relevant to whether a defendant was able to control his behavior. The line between an irresistible impulse and an impulse not resisted is probably no sharper than that between twilight and dusk.

Jodie English, The Light Between Twilight and Dusk: Federal Criminal Law and the Volitional Insanity Defense

40 Hastings Law Journal 1, 45-52 (1988)

The Policy Perspective

If not unconstitutional, Congress' complete omission of a volitional insanity defense is bad policy. The abolition of this defense constitutes a radical departure from widely held federal and state understandings of the scope of a proper insanity defense. Prior to *Hinckley*, all of the federal courts that had considered the matter favored inclusion of a volitional test. . . .

The NMHA convened a National Commission on the Insanity Defense that explicitly considered the ABA's proposal to eliminate the control test. The Commission rejected the proposal in favor of a formulation including both cognitive and volitional elements, comporting with "the modern view of the mind as a unified entity whose functioning may be impaired in numerous ways." In the aftermath of the *Hinckley* acquittal, however, what was once viewed as proper policy-making has drastically changed.

By abolishing the volitional prong and recasting the cognitive prong in language requiring absolute rather than substantial incapacitation, and by mandating that the potential class of exculpating mental diseases be restricted to those denominated as "severe," the Act has turned back the jurisprudential clocks to the unenlightened days of *M'Naghten*. . . .

M'Naghten terminology is based on an antiquated perception of human psychology that defines reason as the sole determinant of human behavior. This view ignores contemporary psychiatric understandings of man as an integrated personality and is, consequently, an inadequate yardstick by which to assess responsibility. . . . In short, the *M'Naghten* test is both bad psychiatry and bad law.

The arguments in favor of a return to *M'Naghten* and, concomitantly, an abolition of a federal control test are few. In *United States v. Lyons*, the arguments are distilled to their critical essence. The criticisms are directed at a professed inability of psychiatry to scientifically calibrate human incapacity for control and a concern that jurors, cast "adrift upon a sea of unfounded scientific speculation," will end up making the "moral mistake" of wrongfully acquitting. The allegations regarding inadequacies in current psychiatric discernment are only skeletally supported. The same conclusory record undergirded the congressional debate, which relied upon APA and ABA position papers to support an abolitionist posture toward volitional insanity. None of these sources presented any empirical analysis to justify their conclusions. Moreover, no contrary positions were either referred to or summarized. . . .

[Richard] Rogers' work on the development of empirical scales to objectively measure both cognitive and volitional impairment has been widely respected. Contemporaneously with the congressional debate, Rogers perfected clinical tests to calibrate both defects of reason and defects of control. These tests exhibited near perfect interexaminer reliability (ninety-seven percent), a high concordance rate with subsequent legal disposition (eighty-eight percent), and theoretically consistent and statistically significant differences between sane and insane subjects. Neither this research, nor any like it, ever informed the congressional debate.

Concededly, even if statistical reality rather than rhetoric characterized the legislative colloquy, there was not a perfect clinical measure for assessment of either cognitive or volitional impairment, nor will there ever be one. Yet, as was acknowledged in response to like concern over problems of proving volitional defects in *Parsons v. State*, "[i]t is no satisfactory objection to say that the rule above announced by us is of difficult application. The rule in *McNaghten's Case* is equally obnoxious to a like criticism. The difficulty does not lie in the rule, but is inherent in the subject of insanity itself."

These matters are simply not amenable to absolute psychiatric certitude. Even if they were, the resolution of the dividing line between responsibility and non-responsibility is the purview of the jury, not the medical expert. . . .

The second concern which dominated the congressional debate, and the *Lyons* majority opinion, centered on a fear that moral mistakes would result from juror speculation regarding the defendant's capacity for self-control. Such a concern is sorely misplaced. The existence of persons who cannot conform their conduct to the requirements of the law is fully conceded. Neither Congress nor the *Lyons* court, however, provide for the exculpation of such mentally infirm individuals. By eliminating the volitional prong altogether, Congress implied that the law "would achieve morally correct results more often. The objective of the law, however, should not be to achieve morally correct results more often, but rather to avoid morally incorrect results at all times." . . .

. . . Congress should have considered less restrictive measures rather than completely abdicate its obligation to fairly administer the criminal justice system on behalf of this population. . . .

In *United States v. Torniero*, for example, the Second Circuit declined invitations to abolish the insanity defense generally and the volitional prong specifically, but did adopt a narrowing of the A.L.I. volitional standard. Under *Torniero*, a defendant had to establish that his mental infirmity was widely understood by respected authorities in the field as being a mental disease or defect that impairs behavioral controls, and that there was a relevant connection between this condition and the defendant's incapacity to control his conduct. . . . Professor Bonnie also acknowledges a middle ground: "The volitional inquiry probably would be manageable if the insanity defense were permitted only in cases involving psychotic disorders." Since Congress adopted such a compromise position by limiting the availability of the insanity defense to those suffering from "severe" mental diseases or defects, abolition of the volitional prong was unnecessary from a policy perspective.

Similarly, Professor Morse has suggested that retention of a volitional test could be upheld if it were narrowly proscribed so as to "excuse only those who were utterly overwhelmed by their impulses." Again, while the Act overrides the A.L.I.'s provision for exculpation based on "substantial" incapacitation by requiring total impairment, it is readily apparent that avenues existed by which perceived abuses could be minimized, while still perpetuating a federal insanity test based on defects of control.

An intermediate position was also proposed by the Pennsylvania Supreme Court in the 1846 decision of *Commonwealth v Mosler*. In Mosler, a control test was upheld subject to express conditions that the offender's alleged volitional impairment must clearly exist and have evidenced itself on more than the occasion for which the volitional insanity plea was interposed.

Conclusion

Congress' decision to jettison all provisions for volitional exculpation from the federal insanity formulation is contrary to historical precedent, constitutionally infirm, and impeachable from a policy perspective. The Act denies mentally impaired offenders the right to be held blameless for conduct that is beyond their power to control and leaves them defenseless against criminal accusations. A law with such grim consequences for the truly mentally impaired offender should not be sustained.

APPENDIX A: SECTION 22

Disability Excuses

DISCUSSION MATERIALS
Issue: Should the Criminal Law Recognize an Excuse Defense for a Person Who Commits an Offense Because Coercively Indoctrinated with Values and Beliefs that Make the Person Want to Do So?
    Paul H. Robinson, Are We Responsible for Who We Are? The Case of Richard R. Tenneson
    Richard Delgado, Ascription of Criminal States of Mind: Toward a Defense Theory for the Coercively Persuaded ("Brainwashed") Defendant
    Joshua Dressler, Professor Delgado's "Brainwashing" Defense: Courting a Determinist Legal System

---

✳ DISCUSSION MATERIALS

Issue: Should the Criminal Law Recognize an Excuse Defense for a Person Who Commits an Offense Because Coercively Indoctrinated with Values and Beliefs that Make the Person Want to Do So?

The brief Robinson excerpt gives some background on the various indoctrination techniques employed by the Communist Chinese during the Korean War and their sometimes powerful effects. The next two articles provide a dialogue of sorts between Richard Delgado and Joshua Dressler, arguing, respectively, for and against a defense for the coercively persuaded defendant, comparing and contrasting it with the excuse defenses of insanity and duress.

Paul H. Robinson, Are We Responsible for Who We Are? The Case of Richard R. Tenneson
Criminal Law Case Studies 124, 125-126 (2d ed. 2002)

In the aftermath of the revolution in China, the Communists developed considerable expertise in what is now called "coercive indoctrination." Their methods have been studied by Westerners and their effectiveness proven. In fact, after the experience in Korea, the United States military changed its policy to no longer expect POWs to give only name, rank, and serial number, as the Geneva convention provides. The human psyche is too vulnerable, they concluded, to resist indoctrination by an experienced captor. The military services began giving special training to those in danger of capture to help them resist indoctrination. But early forms of the training, which give trainees a brief taste of the Communist Chinese methods, are discontinued when it becomes apparent they are counter-productive, causing trainees to fear the power and inevitability of the indoctrina-tion process.

The Communist Chinese coercive indoctrination techniques do not rely on physical beatings or torture. Such methods were used crudely by the Viet Cong against some POWs in Vietnam, but are judged counterproductive to effective coercive indoctrination because they trigger undesirable resistance by the subject. Nor does effective coercive indoctrination use drugs or hypnosis, as a popular 1962 American movie, *The Manchurian Candidate*, suggests. Torture or drugs may be used to obtain a confession or some other single propaganda perfor-mance, but to produce a fully indoctrinated true believer requires a more subtle process of several stages.

The indoctrinator first must establish isolation and control of the subject—isolation from other persons and information, and control over the prisoner's body and environment. These conditions then allow implementation of the two-stage program: destruction of the previously existing self, and construction of a new self with new beliefs and values.

The destruction stage follows several avenues: (a) systematic physiological debilitation, commonly by means of inadequate diet, insufficient sleep, and poor sanitation; (b) creation of constant background anxiety, including implied threats of injury or death by a seemingly all-powerful captor (often with occasional peri-ods of leniency, to create expectations that can be dashed, thereby reinforcing the subject's helplessness and the captor's power); (c) degradation of the sub-ject's pre-existing self, including at later stages the use of peer pressure among indoctrinees, often applied through ritual "struggle" sessions; and (d) required performance of symbolic acts of self-betrayal, betrayal of group norms, and public confession.

The construction stage is more prosaic. Once the subject is psychologically broken, he is built up again in the form that the captor desires through the allevia-tion of physical stress and deprivation and offerings of emotional support tied to the subject's appreciation of the rightness of the indoctrinator's views. The result is a true believer. While physical or psychological duress may be used during the indoctrination process, once the process is complete, the subject has internalized the captor's values and beliefs. His statements and conduct thereafter are guided by the coercively induced beliefs and values, but are not themselves coerced. Focusing only on the present, one would say that the "brainwashed" subject's beliefs and values are as much his own as our beliefs and values are our own.

In milder form, the techniques of coercive indoctrination are used in cults, which even in their less coercive form have the power to take over lives and even produce mass suicides, for example, Jonestown and Heaven's Gate. One may have thought it peculiar for a leader to move an entire cult from San Francisco to Guyana, but shifting members to a faraway jungle is an ingenious means for inexpensive complete isolation and dependency.

The psychological dynamics behind the indoctrination power of the captor is sufficiently great that a captor can have an effect almost without effort or intention. The "Stockholm Syndrome" is named for a 1973 episode in which four hostages of bank robbers bonded with their captives during six days in captivity, coming to conclude that the captors actually were protecting them from the police. A 1982 study reports that Stockholm Syndrome develops in half of all victims of hostage cases, even though captors rarely plan such an effect.

Richard Delgado, Ascription of Criminal States of Mind: Toward a Defense Theory for the Coercively Persuaded ("Brainwashed") Defendant
63 Minnesota Law Review 1, 1-11 (1978)

[C]ommentators who have considered the problem of the coercively persuaded defendant have concluded, largely on an analysis of the Patricia Hearst case, that no legal defense is available to such an individual. If they are correct, their conclusion is a troubling one, for it means denying a defense to a class of defendants who are, by ordinary moral intuitions, often more victims than perpetrators.

Consider a hypothetical individual captured by an outlaw gang and subjected to lengthy thought reform techniques, beginning with threats and terror, and continuing with isolation, starvation, sleep deprivation, and guilt manipulation carried out by seemingly all-powerful captors. At various intervals in the process, that individual's captors demand that he perform criminal acts for their benefit. Under traditional criminal defense theories, exculpation would be available for those crimes the victim commits during the initial stages of captivity, when classic duress and coercion exist, but not during the latter stages, when such overt coercion no longer is necessary for the captors to maintain control. Such a result is surely wrong. The breakdown of the victim's identity and will in the latter stages of the coercive persuasion process destroys the very mechanisms by which he might have offered resistance. Thus, acquiescence is rendered more certain than in the early stages when simple duress is applied. A person under direct threats of death will rarely cling to even deeply held beliefs. Rarer still is the individual who can resist protracted, unremitting, coercive thought reform techniques.

Consideration of theories traditionally believed to justify punishment also suggests that coercive persuasion should be taken into account in assessing a defendant's criminal guilt. . . .

Past experience demonstrates that most such victims, once removed from the coercive environment, soon lose their inculcated responses and return to their former modes of thinking and acting. This return often is accompanied by expressions of anger, in which the former captive accuses his captors of the "rape" of his mind and personality. Punishment of such individuals does little to promote the rationales of the criminal justice system.

If punishment of the coercively persuaded defendant conflicts with both basic intuitions and the justifications advanced for invocation of criminal punishment, yet cannot be avoided under any existing defense theory, it becomes necessary to fashion a new theory of defense. Occam's razor[1] dictates that any such new defense should constitute, insofar as is possible, a logical extension of existing concepts of act, intent, and blame. The actus reus of defendants who have undergone coercive persuasion is undisputed, they apparently are neither insane, coerced, nor acting under diminished capacity, and yet they seem less than fully responsible for their acts. This is so because the coercively persuaded defendant's choice to act criminally was not freely made and, indeed, appears to be not his choice at all. Traditional mens rea analysis has inquired only whether a defendant who committed an allegedly criminal act possessed the requisite state of criminal mind at the time of the act. In the case of the coercively persuaded defendant, it is appropriate to ask also whether the intent the actor possessed can properly be said to be his own.

The victim of thought reform typically commits criminal acts fully aware of their wrongfulness. He acts consciously, even enthusiastically, and without overt coercion. Yet, in an important sense, the guilty mind with which he acts is not his own. Rather, his mental state is more appropriately ascribed to the captors who instilled it in him for their own purposes.

[While a coercive indoctrination defense] is difficult to reduce to a precise set of necessary and sufficient conditions, there are factors which, in combination, warrant its application. These include:

a. *The defendant's mental state results from unusual or abnormal influences,* including drugs, hypnosis, prolonged confinement, physiological depletion, and deliberate manipulation of guilt, terror, and anxiety. These are not the mechanisms of ordinary attitudinal change, and a finding that they were instrumental in bringing about the criminal act suggests that the mens rea with which the victim acted was not his own.

b. *The induced mental state represents a sharp departure from the individual's ordinary mode of thinking.* The more gradual the change, the more likely it is to be found to be the product of education, maturation, or other ordinary processes which do not call for exculpation. In some instances, the changes induced may be so great as to suggest that the individual has undergone a change of identity. A defense based on ownership and ascription of mens rea does not require that a defendant be so transformed, however. Rather, exculpation from criminal liability is appropriate whenever a defendant's state of mind with reference to a particular criminal act is found to be implanted, inauthentic, and not of his own choosing.

c. *The state is one that is imposed on the subject,* rather than self-induced or consciously selected. Most victims of coercive persuasion, like Cardinal Mindszenty or the American prisoners of war, will be found to have resisted the process, at least initially. In other cases, for example those involving religious cults, the voluntary quality of the joining process may be placed in question by the employment of deception in luring potential converts to initial meetings, after which thought reform techniques are brought to bear. Resistance or deception suggest that the resulting condition of psychological servitude was not freely chosen by the victim. The Manson women, by contrast, appeared to have elected to voluntarily

---

1. Attributed to William of Occam, the principle—that entities should not be multiplied beyond necessity—urges that the simplest possible rule or theory be adopted that is consistent with the facts or phenomena to be explained. See, e.g., B. Russell, A History of Western Philosophy 472 (Essandess paperback ed. 1945).

become members of the group, and to undergo a lengthy process of initiation and indoctrination without protest. In such a case, a legal defense based on transferred mens rea should not be available. By analogy to voluntary intoxication, the victim can be blamed for his own condition. If his mental processes have been altered in such a way as to make it more likely that he will commit crimes, his initial choice to undergo such changes was made with a free will. This choice is itself blameworthy, rendering the actor an appropriate object of punishment.

d. *The criminal acts benefit the captors.* Since ordinary human motivation is self-seeking, a showing that an individual engaged in behavior that could only benefit another suggests the presence of abnormal influence. This is particularly true when the actions induced are dangerous and are ones the individual showed no interest in performing before falling under the control of the captors.

e. *The actor, when apprised of the manner in which he came to hold his beliefs, rejects them and sees them as inauthentic or foreign.* If, after having been acquainted with the details of his own treatment by the captors, including their motivation in subjecting him to it, he rejects his affiliation with them (and does so genuinely, and not simply to escape punishment), it seems reasonable to conclude that the mental state was not his own, but wrongfully implanted or superimposed.

f. *The actor evidences symptoms typical of the coercively persuaded personality,* including flattened affect, reduced cognitive flexibility, drastic alteration of values, and extreme dissociation.

Where all or many of these factors are present, a defense should lie; where few are present, it may properly be denied. Even with these criteria, some cases will be difficult. Nevertheless, as in cases involving duress, insanity, or diminished capacity, final judgment should be entrusted to the collective moral sense of the jury. In coercive persuasion, a number of symptoms and causes must be weighed. Just as no clear lines separate those who are sane from those who are not, so here the jury must decide where on a continuum of responsibility a particular defendant lies. But this is scarcely a new problem. Innumerable situations require that the jury members evaluate the evidence before them and apply a general standard to the case at hand.

Joshua Dressler, Professor Delgado's "Brainwashing" Defense: Courting a Determinist Legal System
63 Minnesota Law Review 335, 335-336, 339-340, 351-360 (1979)

Introduction

In 1951, journalist Edward Hunter wrote a book describing "brainwashing," a process of abrupt attitudinal change that was used in the People's Republic of China. At that time, the United States was involved in a "hot" war with the Communist government of North Korea and "cold" war with the ideology of Marxism. This situation caused both the unfamiliar term and the concept underlying it—that people can have their life-long values involuntarily and suddenly change—to become the subjects of widespread general interest and copious scientific literature. Except for some interest engendered by military court martial proceedings against American prisoners of war, however, brainwashing was largely ignored in legal circles until recently, when kidnaping victim Patricia Hearst was prosecuted for joining her captors in a bank robbery.

The absence of debate within the legal community is unfortunate, because the subject of coercive persuasion raises more than esoteric questions. Its consideration leads to fundamental philosophical quandaries concerning the continued viability of the concept of free will, one of the basic premises of our substantive criminal justice system.

Nor can it any longer be said that the issue of coercive persuasion, and the related debate regarding free will, are of mere academic interest. The likelihood that a defense based on coercive persuasion will be raised in the future is great. Prosecution following "terrorist" kidnaping is but one situation raising the issue. Another is in connection with certain religious cults that allegedly not only coercively indoctrinate new members to their religious views but also indoctrinate them to commit fraudulent acts. In response to the conversion techniques adopted by the cults, parents and professional deprogrammers have imprisoned cultists in order to reverse this influence. The propriety of both the original coercive persuasion and subsequent deprogramming has already been litigated in criminal cases, actions in intentional tort, civil rights actions, and competency and conservatorship hearings. Arguments based loosely on coercive persuasion have also been made in trials that did not involve cultists. . . .

Criticism of Delgado's

Thesis Professor Delgado presents a case that, on first view, is appealing. He provides a defense for people with whom he, and many others, obviously sympathize. At the same time, he assures us that such a result can be reached without radical changes in criminal law doctrine. Thus, reformers can appear humane while causing ripples, not waves, in the criminal law system.

Unfortunately, a careful review of substantive criminal law and current jurisprudential doctrine demonstrates that Delgado's claim is not on solid ground. A fundamental premise of the criminal law, and that which distinguishes the criminal sanction from the civil, is that societal condemnation of the violator of societal norms, or at least of his actions, is a necessary, although not sufficient, condition to punishing the offender. The criminal sanction is applied only when the actor is deserving of punishment. Delgado's defense, however, fails to properly identify those people whom society currently believes are blameworthy (deserving of condemnation) and those who are not. Second, because he fails to frame a defense that has sufficiently clear and just limits to make it susceptible of administration, his defense necessitates embracing a determinist view of society.

Excuses

[Two] societal standards of blameworthiness against which Delgado's coercive persuasion defense may be measured are the currently recognized excuses of insanity and duress. As with the mens rea and actus reus requirements, these excuses condition criminal responsibility on the presence or absence of meaningful choice. Insanity involves an internal circumstance—disease of the mind—that substantially or totally impairs the actor's cognitive capability. He must either be unaware of what he has done, or unaware of the wrongfulness of his conduct; alternatively, the disease must substantially impair his volitional capabilities, so that he cannot effectively control his conduct. Under these circumstances, talk of choice is meaningless. A person has no choice when disease causes him to lose all touch with reality or to be unable to conform to reality. Thus, blameworthiness is absent when insanity is proven.

Duress involves an external circumstance—an imminent threat of death or great bodily harm to the individual or a family member—that severely limits the actor's choice. Choice is greater in a case of duress than in a case of insanity, because the actor comprehends the alternatives and has the ability to not respond illegally. Nonetheless, practical choice is eliminated by the deadly threat. Again, the actor is blameless.

The case for exculpating the coercively persuaded defendant in the manner suggested by Delgado is far less compelling. First, he goes so far as to permit the defense not only in cases in which the person is indoctrinated to commit crimes but also in cases in which the defendant is the victim solely of attitudinal indoctrination and is free to choose the means by which to further his new ideology. As a result, Delgado would exculpate obviously morally blameworthy persons.

The only way, then, in which Delgado's defense could be framed so as to avoid exculpating morally blameworthy actors is if it applies only to cases involving crime indoctrination. Even so narrowed, the case for those coercively persuaded to commit crimes is less compelling than for those entitled to current excuses. Compared to the insane individual, the coercively persuaded actor's choices are far more substantial, and hence his blameworthiness commensurately greater. Since, as Delgado concedes, the coercively persuaded actor is aware of the wrongfulness of his action, choice is cognitively present. Delgado does not suggest that the actor is volitionally incapable of conforming his conduct to the law.

The case for the coercively persuaded defendant is also weaker than that of one acting under duress. A loaded and cocked gun pressed to one's head presents more substantial loss of choice, and a clearer example of blamelessness, than do the conditions undergone by religious cultists or Patricia Hearst. In the latter type of case, the person may experience a harsh environment, and thus have limited choice, but the residual options cannot be equated to the alternatives available to an actor under threat of immediate death.

Adequate Limitations

Even if Delgado could show that some coercively persuaded actors should be considered blameless, his defense would still be open to challenge on the ground that it does not impose clear and just limitations on the excuse's applicability. This failure forces society to choose between two alternatives, both of which are antithetical to current concepts of criminal responsibility. It must either allow some morally blameworthy actors to be excused, while not excusing some morally blameless actors, or accept a theory of criminal responsibility that embraces a determinist view of society.

Existing excuses are framed in a narrow and a relatively clear fashion so as to enable the trier of fact to make an uncomplicated moral judgment.

Delgado argues, however, that suitable line drawing is possible with his defense. He notes that there are certain external manifestations of coercive persuasion that will aid in identifying when it is appropriate to apply the defense.

First, coercively persuaded individuals exhibit dissociation, memory loss, confusion, and the like; second, there will be external evidence of imprisonment, isolation, sensory deprivation, interrogation, physiological depletion, and terror. The defense can be limited, Delgado claims, to cases involving such evidence.

Not even these external manifestations provide assurance that only blameless actors will be excused, however. One can easily envision a not-so-unlikely hypothetical situation that exemplifies the problem: A prison inmate is put in solitary confinement in a small dank, dark cell and fed little or nothing for an extended period of time. Upon his release from solitary confinement, he immediately comes under the influence of a fellow prisoner who speaks to him about a prison "religion" calling for the murder of guards. Would Delgado, or society, permit a coercive persuasion defense if the prisoner kills a guard? Although the factors for the defense arguably are present, it is unlikely that society would permit the prisoner's acquittal.

If Delgado requires that these external manifestations be present before applying the defense, his proposal may be criticized for an entirely different reason. It seems morally unexceptionable that excuses should be framed so that equal cases are treated equally. Indeed, Delgado asserts that a defense should not sacrifice individuals "for the sake of preserving an artificial conceptual simplicity." His defense, however, is far guiltier of artificial simplicity than is present law, because it fails to treat morally equal cases equally.

As discussed earlier, duress and insanity are limited to cases of substantial choice reduction. Society excuses the actor when substantial choice reduction is caused by a disease or defect, or by a lethal threat. No doubt certain mental conditions less substantial than disease and certain nonlethal threats also cause diminution, albeit of lesser degree, of the actor's available choices. Society has chosen, however, to limit the excuses to the more severe situations in the belief that extension to other cases might make the excuses limitless. A line has therefore been drawn: exculpation is permitted only for "diseases" and "imminent lethal threats" because society has found that choice is substantially limited in such cases, and not so in lesser situations. Such line drawing, while somewhat artificial, is at least fair because it separates the strong cases from the weak.

Delgado replaces this scheme with an artificiality far worse. He separates potentially *equal* cases from one another, so that defendants with arguably similar moral claims are treated unequally. He would excuse a defendant who is the victim of "abnormal influences," such as physical depletion, prolonged isolation, and interrogation, but would deny the defense to a person who presents some of the same symptoms of choice reduction, but whose symptoms are not the result of abnormal influences. Conditions such as life-long poverty, drug addiction, a broken home, peer group pressure, and lowered self-esteem might demonstrate that a ghetto inhabitant's choice in committing a criminal act was also substantially reduced, yet Delgado's defense would not apply.

Delgado offers no cogent explanation why one should prefer the artificial simplicity of his proposal over the present law of excuses. The morally relevant factor is choice reduction, not exposure to "abnormal influences." If one draws the line as he does, exculpating one form of choice reduction and ignoring others, one is obliged to explain why cases potentially equal on their face receive unequal treatment.

Delgado's defense, then, not only exculpates those who are blameworthy according to current standards and creates a test that is vague and difficult to apply, it also advocates the drawing of a new, morally doubtful line between criminal responsibility and blamelessness. There are only two ways to avoid such an unfair result: either reaffirm current law, which is strict but clear, or enlarge the coercive persuasion defense to include within its possible reach the full panoply of environmental influences. Such a defense would apply whenever the *conditions*, not merely threats or abnormal influences, affecting the actor were so great that a person of ordinary firmness in the actor's situation would have committed the crime. With the adoption of this test, however, determinists virtually win their case. Abundant scientific evidence demonstrates that the ordinary person will reject his preexisting moral values to obey antisocial orders even under comparatively noncoercive circumstances. The person of "ordinary firmness" is not very firm. Likewise, credible evidence shows that factors external to the actor serve as powerful influences, if not determinants, in a person's behavior. For example, parents who batter their children usually were battered in their youth; children of alcoholics are significantly more likely to have serious social problems than are those of nonalcoholic parents; juvenile prostitutes often are victims of physical and sexual abuse at home; some children can be made more susceptible to committing violent acts by the media; and, of course, the bitterness and conditions of ghetto life are conducive to crime. In short, if a defense based on reduced choice is to be created that treats equal cases equally, it must permit persons to present their entire life histories as part of a "blamelessness" defense to a crime.

Thus, we face a quandary: either we leave the law as it is, or we permit a defense which, if applied to all equal cases, would allow "morally blameless" but possibly dangerous persons back into society. If the latter path is followed, of course, society would have little choice but to throw away current jurisprudential underpinnings and incarcerate people on solely utilitarian grounds. Such a result may appear to some to be logical, even appropriate, but it is certainly revolutionary. Delgado, and other advocates of a coercive persuasion defense, should acknowledge that this is the real choice.

APPENDIX A: SECTION 23

Nonexculpatory Defenses

DISCUSSION MATERIALS

✳ DISCUSSION MATERIALS

Issue: *Should the Double Jeopardy Rule Be Modified to Provide Fewer Acquittals of Blameworthy Offenders?*

The Criminal Justice Act 2003, excerpted below, transformed the U.K. system of double jeopardy by allowing the retrial of qualifying offenses—namely serious offenses like murder, manslaughter and rape—upon the discovery of new and compelling evidence of the acquitted person's guilt. David S. Rudstein evaluates double jeopardy and the potential drawbacks of the U.K.'s new exceptions to the long-accepted rule. Levmore and Porat, on the other hand, present an argument for permitting defendants to bargain away their right against double jeopardy. This interesting view of the subject considers the merits of potentially removing double jeopardy protection as well as the economics of crime and law enforcement.

The Criminal Justice Act 2003
(United Kingdom)

Part 10. Retrial for Serious Offences

75. Cases that may be retried

(1) This Part applies where a person has been acquitted of a qualifying offence in proceedings—
　　　(a) on indictment in England and Wales,
　　　(b) on appeal against a conviction, verdict or finding in proceedings on indictment in England and Wales, or
　　　(c) on appeal from a decision on such an appeal. . . .

76. Application to Court of Appeal

(1) A prosecutor may apply to the Court of Appeal for an order—
　　　(a) quashing a person's acquittal in proceedings within section 75(1), and
　　　(b) ordering him to be retried for the qualifying offence. . . .

77. Determination by Court of Appeal

(1) On an application under section 76(1), the Court of Appeal—
　　　(a) if satisfied that the requirements of sections 78 and 79 are met, must make the order applied for;
　　　(b) otherwise, must dismiss the application. . . .

78. New and compelling evidence

(1) The requirements of this section are met if there is new and compelling evidence against the acquitted person in relation to the qualifying offence.
(2) Evidence is new if it was not adduced in the proceedings in which the person was acquitted (nor, if those were appeal proceedings, in earlier proceedings to which the appeal related).
(3) Evidence is compelling if—
　　　(a) it is reliable,
　　　(b) it is substantial, and
　　　(c) in the context of the outstanding issues, it appears highly probative of the case against the acquitted person.
(4) The outstanding issues are the issues in dispute in the proceedings in which the person was acquitted and, if those were appeal proceedings, any other issues remaining in dispute from earlier proceedings to which the appeal related.

79. Interests of Justice

(1) The requirements of this section are met if in all the circumstances it is in the interests of justice for the court to make the order under section 77.

(2) That question is to be determined having regard in particular to—

(a) whether existing circumstances make a fair trial unlikely;

(b) for the purposes of that question and otherwise, the length of time since the qualifying offence was allegedly committed;

(c) whether it is likely that the new evidence would have been adduced in the earlier proceedings against the acquitted person but for a failure by an officer or by a prosecutor to act with due diligence or expedition;

(d) whether, since those proceedings or, if later, since the commencement of this Part, any officer or prosecutor has failed to act with due diligence or expedition. . . .

Legislative Notes to Part 10—Retrial for Serious Offences

This Part of the Act reforms the law relating to double jeopardy, by permitting retrials in respect of a number of very serious offences, where new and compelling evidence has come to light. At present the law does not permit a person who has been acquitted or convicted of an offence to be retried for that same offence—this risk of retrial is known as "double jeopardy." There are two principles arising from the common law which prevent this. The first is known by the legal terms *autrefois acquit* and *autrefois convict*. These principles provide a bar to the trial, in respect of the same offence, of a person who has previously been either acquitted or convicted of that offence. In addition, the courts may consider it an abuse of process for additional charges to be brought, following an acquittal or conviction, for different offences which arose from the same behaviour or facts. There are certain exceptions to this rule.

The Government considers that the law should be reformed to permit a re-trial in cases of serious offences where there has been an acquittal in court, but compelling new evidence subsequently comes to light against the acquitted person. . . . Examples of new evidence might include DNA or fingerprint tests, or new witnesses to the offence coming forward. The measures amend the law to permit the police to re-investigate a person acquitted of serious offences in these circumstances, to enable the prosecuting authorities to apply to the Court of Appeal for an acquittal to be quashed, and for a re-trial to take place where the Court of Appeal is satisfied that the new evidence is highly probative of the case against the acquitted person. The measures provide safeguards aimed at preventing the possible harassment of acquitted persons in cases where there is not a genuine question of new and compelling evidence, by requiring the personal consent of the Director of Public Prosecutions (DPP) both to the taking of significant steps in the re-opening of investigations—except in urgent cases—and to the making of an application to the Court of Appeal. The DPP will take into account both the strength of the evidence and the public interest in determining whether a reinvestigation or application to the Court is appropriate.

The new arrangements will apply only in respect of serious offences. These are offences which carry a maximum sentence of life imprisonment, and for which the consequences for victims or for society as a whole are particularly serious. The offences are listed in Schedule 5 to the Act and include, for example, murder, manslaughter and rape. They do not include all offences for which life imprisonment is the maximum punishment, because this would catch a number of common law offences which may not have such serious consequences, and for which a life sentence would rarely be imposed.

Where the Court of Appeal quashes an acquittal, a new indictment for the same offence may then be preferred by the prosecuting authorities, and a retrial will follow. The retrial will take account of all the evidence available in the case. The Court of Appeal may refuse to quash an acquittal in cases where the evidence is not new and compelling, or where it is not considered in the interests of justice to proceed with a retrial.

David S. Rudstein, Retrying the Acquitted in England, Part I: The Exception to the Rule Against Double Jeopardy for "New and Compelling Evidence"

8 San Diego Int'l L.J. 387, 399-400, 403, 424-425, 456-457 (2007)

The principle that a person should not be tried twice for the same offense, commonly called the protection against "double jeopardy" in Anglo-American legal systems, is widely accepted throughout the world. . . . In the United States, the Fifth Amendment to the Constitution provides that "[n]o person shall . . . be subject for the same offence to be twice put in jeopardy of life or limb."

Prohibiting the government from reprosecuting an individual for the same offense following his trial and acquittal serves a number of related and often overlapping interests, both of the individual and of society as a whole. First, it "preserve[s] the finality of judgments." Second, it minimizes the "'heavy personal strain'" caused by a trial. Third, it reduces the risk of erroneously convicting an innocent person. Fourth, it protects the power (or perhaps the right) of the jury, acting as representatives of the community, to acquit an individual despite sufficient evidence establishing his guilt. Fifth, it "encourage[s] efficient investigation" and prosecution. Sixth, it helps to conserve scarce prosecutorial and judicial resources. Seventh, it helps to prevent prosecutors from using the criminal process to harass an individual who has been tried and acquitted. Finally, it helps to ensure that the legal system commands the respect and confidence of the public.

In the United States, there is no doubt that the Double Jeopardy Clause would . . . bar the retrial of any acquitted defendant in any situation when the government relies solely upon the discovery of new evidence. Over the years, the Supreme Court has made it clear that the constitutional guarantee against double jeopardy accords absolute finality to an acquittal and forbids "retrial once the defendant has been acquitted, no matter how egregiously erroneous the legal rulings leading to that judgment might be."

In England, until recently, the plea of *autrefois acquit* would have been available to . . . defendants in . . . cases involving newly discovered inculpatory evidence. With the enactment of the Criminal Procedure Act of 2003, however, Parliament created an exception to the principle against double jeopardy under which the government can, in limited circumstances, prosecute an acquitted individual a second time for the same offense on the basis of "new and compelling evidence."

Tinkering with the protections of the rule against double jeopardy by creating an exception for those rare situations in which the government discovers "new and compelling" evidence of an acquitted person's guilt of a qualifying offense hardly seems worth the cost. Not only will it require some individuals to undergo additional personal strain and expense, but it will also divert scarce prosecutorial and judicial resources, and, in some cases, will undermine a jury's power to nullify the law. It also could lead the police initially to investigate cases less diligently, and prosecutors initially to prosecute cases less vigorously, than they otherwise might, and to harass individuals whom they believe were wrongly acquitted in their first trial. The exception might also produce a loss of respect for, and confidence in, the criminal justice system. More importantly, though, it opens every judgment of acquittal for a "qualifying offence" to re-examination, and in addition to requiring significant numbers of acquitted individuals to "live in a continuing state of anxiety," it is likely to result in some innocent individuals being erroneously convicted and punished of a serious offense. Preserving the finality of all untainted judgments of acquittal, and allowing a few guilty individuals to avoid conviction, seems preferable.

Saul Levmore & Ariel Porat, Bargaining with Double Jeopardy

Journal of Legal Studies (forthcoming 2011)

In criminal law, where a prosecutor might be required to prove guilt beyond a reasonable doubt, the prosecutor is prevented from repeatedly drawing from the urn, as it were, by the familiar and nearly universal rule of double jeopardy. Everywhere, even in the least protective jurisdictions, the rule prevents the government from relitigating a case where a defendant was acquitted and where no new evidence (of the original crime or of a "tainted" first trial by virtue of perjury or corruption) has materialized. Without the double jeopardy rule, the government might bring charges over and over again until it won. "Beyond a reasonable doubt" would have a very different meaning, in both probabilistic and deontological terms, if the government could try again even when a unanimous jury found that the government failed in its first attempt to meet its burden of proof. Less robust forms of the double jeopardy protection are widespread, but in all such jurisdictions the idea of preventing repeated draws from the urn retains its force. Where the protection is stronger, as where the government may not relitigate even when significant new evidence of guilt materializes, the "repeated draw" idea is yet clearer. . . .

Overinvestment with a Double Jeopardy Rule

In the criminal law, we can think of the double jeopardy protection as a restriction on the prosecution. . . .

. . . [W]e advance the counterintuitive idea that both sides might at times benefit if the prosecutor has a "second chance." The key step in the argument is that when the prosecutor is limited to a single chance, the prosecutor has an incentive to invest more in the first and only trial. . . . A prosecutor who knows she has two chances, and has limited resources, will often invest less in the first trial than would one who has but a single chance. In turn, this produces a social benefit and even a benefit to some or most defendants.

One way to think about this idea is to refer . . . to conventional testing, or licensing. If applicants were limited to one driving test or one bar exam, it is easy to imagine much greater investments in test preparation. It is difficult to prove that such preparation is inefficient, but we rely on readers to share the intuition that such is the case, and perhaps similarly so for criminal defendants. Similarly, the prosecutor may overinvest in a world with the double jeopardy protection. If the defendant could also try again when disappointed with the first draw, both parties might invest less in the first round, or settle. But the double jeopardy rule is more interesting where it interacts with an asymmetric standard of proof, as it does in criminal law.

Alternatives to Double Jeopardy

. . . We do not advocate any direct weakening of the double jeopardy protection in order to reduce overinvestment in the first trial, but rather contemplate a rule under which prosecutors can choose when to offer defendants the "right" to waive the double jeopardy protection and thus provide the prosecution with the option of a second chance. Defendants might do this when they think that the prosecutor will then invest less in the first trial and—if that trial ends in acquittal—choose not to proceed to a second trial, perhaps because the defendant now appears more likely to be innocent. Defendants might waive the familiar protection more often if the prosecutor offered or was required to pay something for the option, perhaps in the form of a higher standard for conviction in either or both trials, or a lesser punishment in the event of conviction, or even a monetary payment to cover the defendant's costs in the event of a second trial. Alternatively, the rule might be that the defendant can agree that the prosecutor can try again after acquittal only if a magistrate or other decision maker certifies that there is new evidence that was not presented at the first trial. Of course, the less the prosecutor invests in the first trial, the more likely it is that there will be such new evidence for a second. Finally, we might also imagine a scheme in which the prosecutor has no choice but the defendant can always relinquish his protection and thus "impose" a second chance regime on the government. . . .

The Benefit of Relaxing the Double Jeopardy Rule

. . . Imagine then a world where the double jeopardy protection can be waived, or simply where there is no such protection, and where the prosecutor has a fixed $1 million budget. If many defendants have waived the protection (or if there is none), a prosecutor who might have invested $10,000 in each of 100 cases with double jeopardy protection, might now invest $7,000 per case, bring ten more cases (we can imagine a supply curve of increasingly difficult cases but there is no need for that here) and reserve $230,000 for second trials deemed worth bringing. Perhaps the prosecutor now loses 30 out of 110 cases, and under the single-trial rule would have lost 15 of 100. The lower success rate reflects not the greater number of trials but the smaller investments in first trials. The prosecutor might now choose to try again in one-half the lost cases, and she can afford $15,000 for each of those second trials. If she wins 10 of these 15, or two-thirds of the second trials (a rate which might reflect learning from the first trial plus the much greater investment in the second trials pursued), she emerges with 90 convictions (80+10) in this second-chance regime, instead of 85 under the single-chance rule. Of course, the prosecutor need not invest equally in all of the cases pursued in each round. The point is simply that each second-chance agreement allows the prosecutor to invest less in first trials, and then to choose how to allocate the savings between new cases and heavier expenditures in some seconds.

These numbers are, of course, illustrative. The conclusion, however, depends on the notions that the prosecutor's expected success in first trials is a function of her investment in those trials and, indeed, we assume that the prosecutor gains convictions with increasing investment, that there is some chance of new evidence, and that investment in some second trials will bring about convictions even where the first trial ended in acquittal. There is room for surprise. Perhaps the first acquittal should or would be known to the second jury—after all, witnesses might have a hard time playing along with a rule to the contrary, and both sides might want to grill a witness about any inconsistency between his or her testimony at the two trials. It seems both inevitable if not desirable for the second jury to know that the first trial ended in acquittal (or in a mistrial), and therefore it may turn out to be difficult to secure a conviction with the second chance. If so, the prosecutor will rarely attempt a second trial, and the defendant will exact only a very small payment for waiving his double jeopardy protection. On the other hand, the prosecutor might learn a good deal at the first trial. It might redirect her efforts in preparing for a second trial or it might show the prosecutor that her resources are better spent on other matters. She might even be convinced of the defendant's innocence, and then be pleased by the cost savings. . . .

Sorting Innocent and Guilty Defendants

. . . The argument thus far might be sufficient to convince most thoughtful citizens to rethink double jeopardy, and perhaps to support the idea that the protection is one that ought to be waivable, much as one who pleas can trade away the right to a trial. . . . [H]owever, we add to the case for a second-chance option by developing the possibility that the option would benefit innocent defendants and disadvantage guilty defendants. Indeed, even if there were somehow a requirement to maintain the expected level of punishment, a system can be made more efficient by sorting defendants according to their guilt.

Imagine first that the burden of proof does not change when a second-chance rule has been agreed upon. A second-chance agreement is often unattractive to defendants who know they are guilty because they run the risk that the prosecution will come across new evidence or simply choose to draw again from the urn. A second trial, therefore, may well increase the overall chance of conviction; it also increases pretrial and trial costs for many defendants. Moreover, to the extent that a guilty defendant can win at trial by surprising the prosecution—in a way that the latter cannot surprise the former because of the stricter requirement of revealing witnesses and strategies before trial . . . —the guilty defendant loses much of this advantage when agreeing to the possibility of a second trial. No doubt, some guilty persons would benefit because they would be acquitted as a result of the prosecution's smaller investments in their first trials followed by decisions not to proceed with second trials. Moreover, the prosecutor's reduced investment in a single trial will often translate into lower pretrial and trial costs for the accused as well. Sill, inasmuch as the guilty defendants will be subject to a higher risk of conviction than under the double jeopardy rule because of the relatively high likelihood of second trials, it is most plausible that guilty defendants would prefer not to be subject to a second-chance regime.

We turn then to defendants who know they are innocent. Such a defendant has less to fear from a second trial because there is less reason to expect that further effort by the prosecution will generate incriminating evidence. The typical innocent defendant is less likely than his guilty counterpart to face a second trial, to benefit from surprising the prosecution, and to lose in a second trial. And yet the prosecutor's ability to draw again from the urn lowers the effective burden of proof. Thus, assuming no implicit or explicit change in the burden of proof, it is hard to say whether any or many innocents will find it attractive to waive the double jeopardy protection. The chance of conviction at the first trial drops, because the prosecutor will invest less in the first trial. But the possibility of a second trial leaves the situation unclear. There is a greater chance of (false) conviction at the second trial and a lower chance of (false) conviction in the first.

In sum, and following our illustration, a switch from a double jeopardy rule to a second-chance rule likely increases the number of convictions. Moreover, the set of convicted persons contains a higher percentage of guilty persons than with an unalterable double jeopardy rule. The illustration and underlying intuitions suggest that innocent defendants will be more likely to waive the protection than will guilty defendants. . . .

Conclusion

We have suggested that single-chance tests are limited to high-cost, backward-looking inquiries, like trials. Where there is but a single chance, however, there is the problem of overpreparation, or overinvestment. In the criminal law context, this overinvestment gives room for the prosecutor and defendant to bargain for a waiver of the traditional double jeopardy protection in order to allow the possibility of a second trial, and thus the elimination of the incentive to overinvest. Defendants might give up their protection, if permitted to do so, knowing that on average the prosecutor would then invest less in the first trial. It is even possible that innocent defendants might be especially inclined to make the bargain.

Issue: Should the Statute of Limitations Be Lengthened or Eliminated to Provide Fewer Acquittals of Blameworthy Offenders?

The Model Penal Code commentary explains the purpose of having a statute of limitations at criminal law. Then the sample of various states' statutes of limitations, or lack thereof, shows the large variance of statutes of limitations based on severity of crime and on the jurisdiction where on commits a crime. Alan L. Adlestien's article argues against a strict written rule for statute of limitations and instead for a duty to prosecute a case in a timely fashion in order to achieve the aim of insuring fair, unbiased trials.

Model Penal Code Section 1.06 Commentary
Statute of Limitations
Official Draft and Revised Comments 85-86 (1985)

Statutes of limitations have been part of Anglo-American law for some three hundred fifty years; at the time of the drafting of the Model Penal Code only two states, South Carolina and Wyoming, imposed no limitations. Nevertheless, little attention has been directed toward the evaluation of the objectives of limitation provisions, despite their inevitable effect of allowing guilty persons to escape prosecution in some cases. There are several reasons for the imposition of time limitations: First, and foremost, is the desirability that prosecutions be based upon reasonably fresh evidence. With the passage of time memories fade, witnesses die or leave the area, and physical evidence becomes more difficult to obtain, identify, or preserve. In short, possibility of erroneous conviction is minimalized when prosecution is prompt. Second, if the actor long refrains from further criminal activity, the likelihood increases that he has reformed, diminishing the necessity for imposition of the criminal sanction. If he has repeated his criminal behavior, he can be prosecuted for recent offenses committed within the period of limitation. Hence, the need for protecting society against the perpetrator of a particular offense becomes less compelling as the years pass. Third, after a protracted period the retributive impulse which may have existed in the community is likely to yield to a sense of compassion aroused by the prosecution for an offense long forgotten. Fourth, it is desirable to reduce the possibility of blackmail based on threat to prosecute or to disclose evidence to enforcement officials. Finally, statutes of limitations "promote repose by giving security and stability to human affairs."[1]

SAMPLING OF STATUTES OF LIMITATIONS

Baldwin's Kentucky Revised Statutes Annotated
(2008)

Title L. Kentucky Penal Code

Chapter 500. General Provisions

Section 500.050 Time limitations

(1) Except as otherwise expressly provided, the prosecution of a felony is not subject to a period of limitation and may be commenced at any time.

(2) Except as otherwise expressly provided, the prosecution of an offense other than a felony must be commenced within one year after it is committed.

(3) For purposes of this section, an offense is committed either when every element occurs, or if a legislative purpose to prohibit a continuing course of conduct plainly appears, at the time when the course of conduct or the defendant's complicity therein is terminated.

---

1. Wood v Carpenter, 101 U.S. 135, 139 (1879) (Swayne, J.).

(4) No offense in KRS Chapter 510 involving deviate sexual intercourse or sexual intercourse by the other spouse shall be prosecuted unless formally reported to the police within one (1) year after the commission of the offense. The report shall be signed by the victim of the offense.

Code of Alabama

Title 15. Criminal Procedure

Chapter 3. Limitations on Prosecution

Section 15-3-1. Felonies Generally

The prosecution of all felonies, except those specified in Sections 15-3-3 and 15-3-5, must be commenced within three years after the commission of the offense.

Section 15-3-2. Misdemeanors

Unless otherwise provided, the prosecution of all misdemeanors before a circuit or district court must be commenced within 12 months after the commission of the offense.

West's Tennessee Code Annotated
(2007)

Title 40 Criminal Procedure

Chapter 2 Limitation of Prosecutions

Section 40-2-101 Felonies.

(a) A person may be prosecuted, tried and punished for an offense punishable with death or by imprisonment in the penitentiary during life, at any time after the offense is committed.

(b) Prosecution for a felony offense shall begin within:

    (1) Fifteen (15) years for a Class A felony;

    (2) Eight (8) years for a Class B felony;

    (3) Four (4) years for a Class C or Class D felony; and

    (4) Two (2) years for a Class E felony.

(c) Notwithstanding subsections (a) and (b), offenses arising under the revenue laws of the state shall be commenced within three (3) years next after the commission of the offense, except that the period of limitation of prosecution shall be six (6) years in the following instances:

    (1) Offenses involving the defrauding or attempting to defraud the state of Tennessee or any agency thereof, whether by conspiracy or not, and in any manner;

(2) The offense of willfully attempting in any manner to evade or defeat any tax or the payment thereof;

(3) The offense of willfully aiding or abetting, or procuring, counseling or advising, the preparation or presentation under, or in connection with, any matter arising under the revenue laws of the state, or a false or fraudulent return, affidavit, claim or document (whether or not such falsity or fraud is with the knowledge or consent of the person authorized or required to present such return, affidavit, claim or document);

(4) The offense of willfully failing to pay any tax, or make any return at the time or times required by law or regulation; and

(5) Notwithstanding the provisions of subdivision (b)(3) to the contrary, prosecution for the offense of arson as prohibited by § 39-14-301 shall commence within eight (8) years from the date the offense occurs.

(d) Prosecutions for any offense committed against a child prior to July 1, 1997 . . . shall commence no later than the date the child attains the age of majority or within four (4) years next after the commission of the offense, whichever occurs later; provided, that pursuant to subsection (a), an offense punishable by life imprisonment may be prosecuted at any time after the offense shall have been committed.

(e) For offenses committed prior to November 1, 1989, the limitation of prosecution in effect at that time shall govern.

(f) Prosecutions for any offense committed against a child on or after July 1, 1997 . . . shall commence no later than the date the child reaches twenty-one (21) years of age; provided, that if the provisions of subsection (a) or (b) provide a longer period of time within which prosecution may be brought than this subsection, the applicable provision of subsection (a) or (b) shall prevail.

Alan L. Adlestein, Conflict of the Criminal Statute of Limitations with Lesser Offenses at Trial
37 Wm. & Mary L. Rev. 199, 200, 261-262, 264, 269 (1995)

Criminal statutes of limitations have long been a familiar part of the American legal landscape. They are legislative devices to protect a defendant from the risk of erroneous conviction due to stale evidence. They are also perceived as protecting society from crime by promoting accurate results at trial and efficient use of the prosecutor's resources. In addition, such statutes imply that a lengthy passage of time after the commitment of a crime makes punishment unfair to the perpetrator and unproductive for society. . . . The Supreme Court's rationale for criminal statutes of limitations involves both the protection of the individual defendant from a potentially unfair trial and a now perhaps undeserved punishment, and the protection of society from unprosecuted offenders, by using the sanction of preclusion to encourage law enforcement officials to promptly investigate and prosecute crime. . . .

As part of the extensive study and debate that led to the adoption of the Model Penal Code, the American Law Institute considered the policy reasons for its proposed limitations section. The Commentary to the limitations section discusses five justifications for time limits in criminal prosecutions. First, and foremost, prosecutions should proceed with fresh evidence. Second, as time increases, the likelihood that the offender has reformed also increases, and the necessity for punishment diminishes (or the likelihood increases that the criminally inclined will be prosecuted for a more recent offense). Third, after a long period of time has passed, society's "retributive impulse" is likely to be replaced by sympathy for a defendant prosecuted for a long-forgotten offense. Fourth, reduction of the time of possible prosecution cuts off the ever-present potential for blackmail by one who is aware of the offense. Finally, criminal limitations statutes "promote repose by giving security and stability to human affairs."

. . . [T]he rationale of the Commentary is subject to serious question. The criminal trial process is specifically designed by its rules of evidence, by its strong commitment to the power of cross examination, and, most importantly, by its requirement of proof beyond a reasonable doubt, to exclude or discredit unreliable evidence. The argument based on the offender's reformation over time disregards both the general deterrence and retributive purposes of criminal punishment. . . . Although in some cases a community's impulse for the moral balance of retribution may weaken with the running of the limitations period, in many others, particularly those involving homicide or lasting physical or psychological damage, no such weakening occurs. Finally, there is the social stability argument. In the criminal context, this rationale must be different than that for civil statutes of limitations. In the civil context, the concern is for stabilizing commercial enterprise and preventing disruption to the market system that flows from the uncapped risk of plaintiffs seeking recourse in an untimely fashion.

In support of criminal limitations statutes, there seems to be some merit to the position that if a long time goes by, the expenditure of society's resources in criminal prosecution—in terms of the costs of the investigation, trial, and (if the burden of proof at trial is met) punishment—and the costs to the community that follow from removing a now productive member from its midst are not warranted. The rebuttal to this argument, however, is significant. The problem with statutes of limitations in general, and criminal statutes of limitations in particular, is that they paint with the broad brush of an inflexible general rule. No room remains for prosecutorial evaluation of the particular offense or offender or, as in the English system today, for a judicial consideration of a laches-like defense based on the facts of a particular case. Restricted by the Supreme Court's very narrow definition of due process in the context of pre-charge delay, the American defendant asserting an untimeliness defense must rely on the statute of limitations, if applicable, or, to obtain constitutional relief, prove that intentional and improperly motivated delay in either the investigation or initiation of the prosecution has caused actual prejudice. Perhaps neither the statutory nor the due process alternative serves the necessary social purposes as effectively as would a flexible, nonconstitutional approach that permits the court to weigh the actual prejudice caused by unjustifiable delay against the reasons for such delay. More importantly, criminal statutes of limitations using an all-or-nothing approach interfere with the prosecutor's discretion in a way that contradicts the efficient operation of the current system. The prosecutor is an executive officer who must exercise judgment as to whether it is appropriate to proceed with a particular prosecution or even to continue with a particular investigation. The factors considered in the exercise of this discretionary decision are myriad and include the seriousness of the offense, the personal circumstances of the defendant, the strength of the available evidence, and the significance of the prosecution in all its aspects measured against the limited resources of every prosecutor's office. The time that has passed since the commission of a particular offense may also be a factor, as well as the offender's demonstrated rehabilitation and the victim's call for retribution. . . .

Legislatures will likely continue to lengthen the periods of criminal statutes of limitations for particular offenses as the then-current "crime problem" warrants. Perhaps they will lengthen limitations periods in general or eliminate those periods entirely for certain serious offenses. . . .

Issue: Should the Exclusionary Rule Be Modified to Provide Fewer Acquittals of Blameworthy Offenders?

Akhil Reed Amar argues against the current American exclusionary rules by rebutting the current arguments in favor of them. He then gives recommendations for ways to change the current criminal law systems while still achieving the aims of the exclusionary rules. Carol S. Steiker rejects Professor Amar's argument on the grounds that it advocates a huge overhaul of the current interpretation of the Fourth Amendment that Steiker sees as unnecessary and unrealistic.

Akhil Reed Amar, Fourth Amendment First Principles

107 Harvard Law Review 757, 757-758, 791-794, 796, 797, 799-800, 811-816, 819 (1994)

The Fourth Amendment today is an embarrassment. Much of what the Supreme Court has said in the last half century—that the Amendment generally calls for warrants and probable cause for all searches and seizures, and exclusion of illegally obtained evidence—is initially plausible but ultimately misguided. As a matter of text, history, and plain old common sense, these three pillars of modern Fourth Amendment caselaw are hard to support; in fact, today's Supreme Court does not really support them. Except when it does. Warrants are not required—unless they are. All searches and seizures must be grounded in probable cause—but not on Tuesdays. And unlawfully seized evidence must be excluded whenever five votes say so. . . . The result is a vast jumble of judicial pronouncements that is not merely complex and contradictory, but often perverse. Criminals go free, while honest citizens are intruded upon in outrageous ways with little or no real remedy. If there are good reasons for these and countless other odd results, the Court has not provided them. . . .

[To justify the odd results created by the exclusionary rule, there exist] a variety of slogans wholly inadequate to the task at hand. These slogans—"judicial integrity and fairness," "preventing government from profiting from its own wrong," and "deterrence"—cannot explain the doctrine. They cannot explain where this nontextual and unprecedented remedy comes from. They cannot explain why it applies only in criminal and not civil cases. . . . In short, they prove too much—and also too little, for each slogan sits atop a pile of dubious assumptions and inferences.

Consider first "judicial integrity and fairness." Do courts in England—and many other countries, for that matter—lack integrity and fairness because they generally allow material and relevant evidence of criminal guilt? Surely the practices of other civilized and respected judicial systems should give pause to those who claim exclusion is mandated by basic notions of fair play. Do all American courts lack integrity and fairness in civil cases brought by the government as plaintiff? Given that civil exclusion is not the rule, never has been the rule, and shows little sign of becoming the rule, it seems that the near unanimous verdict of the American bench is that integrity does not invariably require exclusion. . . . More generally, we must remember that integrity and fairness are also threatened by excluding evidence that will help the justice system to reach a true verdict. Thus, the courts best affirm their integrity and fairness not by closing their eyes to truthful evidence, but by opening their doors to any civil suit brought against wayward government officials, even one brought by a convict.

Consider next the nice-sounding idea that government should not profit from its own wrongdoing. Our society, however, also cherishes the notion that cheaters—or murderers, or rapists, for that matter—should not prosper. When the murderer's bloody knife is introduced, it is not only the government that profits; the people also profit when those who truly do commit crimes against person and property are duly convicted on the basis of reliable evidence. When rapists, burglars, and murderers are convicted, are not the people often more "secure in their persons, houses, papers, and effects?"

The classic response is that setting criminals free is a cost of the Fourth Amendment itself, and not of the much-maligned exclusionary rule. If the government had simply obeyed the Fourth Amendment, it would never have found the bloody knife. Thus, excluding the knife simply restores the status quo ante and confers no benefit on the murderer. The classic response is too quick.

In many situations, it is far from clear that the illegality of a search is indeed a but-for cause of the later introduction into evidence of an item found in the search. Suppose the police could easily get a warrant, but fail to do so because they think the case at hand falls into a judicially recognized exception to the so-called warrant requirement. A court later disagrees—and so, under current doctrine, the search was unconstitutional. But if the court goes on to exclude the bloody knife, it does indeed confer a huge benefit on the murderer. The police could easily have obtained a warrant before the search, so the illegality is not a but-for cause of the introduction of the knife into evidence. . . . [E]xclusion makes the criminal better off. . . .

This brings us, finally, to deterrence. Government must be deterred from violating the people's Fourth Amendment rights. But the exclusionary rule is a bad way to go about this. For starters, note that, unlike "integrity and fairness," or the "nonprofit" principle, deterrence does not posit some inherent right in the criminal defendant. Deterrence is concerned with the government; it is concerned with systematic impact. It treats the criminal defendant merely as a surrogate for the larger public interest in restraining the government. The criminal defendant is a kind of private attorney general.

But the worst kind. He is self-selected and self-serving. He is often unrepresentative of the larger class of law-abiding citizens, and his interests regularly conflict with theirs. Indeed, he is often despised by the public, the class he implicitly is supposed to represent. He will litigate on the worst set of facts, heedless that the result will be a bad precedent for the Fourth Amendment generally. He cares only about the case at hand—his case—and has no long view. He is not a sophisticated repeat player. He rarely hires the best lawyer. He cares only about exclusion—and can get only exclusion—even if other remedies (damages or injunctions) would better prevent future violations. . . . He is, in short, an awkward champion of the Fourth Amendment. . . .

Put differently, if deterrence is the key, the idea is to make the government pay, in some way, for its past misdeeds, in order to discourage future ones. But why should that payment flow to the guilty? Under the exclusionary rule, the more guilty you are, the more you benefit. And when we think about this clearly, our minds balk. . . . [W]hen it comes to private attorneys general, the exclusionary rule's deterrence rationale looks in the wrong place—to paradigmatically guilty criminal defendants rather than to prototypically law-abiding civil plaintiffs. . . .

The exclusionary rule renders the Fourth Amendment contemptible in the eyes of judges and citizens. Judges do not like excluding bloody knives, so they distort doctrine, claiming the Fourth Amendment was not really violated. In the popular mind, the Amendment has lost its luster and become associated with grinning criminals getting off on crummy technicalities. When rapists are freed, the people are less secure in their houses and persons—and they lose respect for the Fourth Amendment. If exclusion is the remedy, all too often ordinary people will want to say that the right was not really violated. At first they will say it with a wink; later, with a frown; and one day, they will come to believe it. . . .

Thus, even if exclusion achieves short-term deterrence, it creates long-term instability, driving a wedge between We the People and Our Constitution. We have never enshrined Fourth Amendment exclusion in Our Constitution, nor sanctioned its root norm that the guilty should benefit more than the innocent. In the long run, popular sentiment will (quite literally) have its day in court, for the people elect Presidents, who in turn appoint federal judges. Judges who value long-run stability and sustainability should prefer institutions that connect the People to Our Constitution, rather than ones that alienate Us from it. . . .

Fixated on the exclusionary rule, the twentieth-century Supreme Court has betrayed the traditional civil-enforcement model, through acts of omission and commission. What follows are illustrative but not exhaustive suggestions for refurbishing the traditional civil-enforcement model.

1. Entity Liability and Abolition of Immunity. — . . . In our century . . . judges for the first time have created wide zones of individual officer immunity for constitutional torts. Within these zones, the innocent citizen victim is in effect "held liable" and left to pay for the government's constitutional wrong. The Framers would have found the current remedial regime, in which a victim of constitutional tort can in many cases recover from neither the officer nor the government, a shocking violation of first principles, trumpeted in *Marbury v. Madison*, that for every right there must be a remedy.

The best way to close this shocking remedial gap today would be to recognize direct liability of the government entity. . . . If the search or seizure is ultimately deemed unreasonable, the government entity should pay. And the damages assessed will be a visible sign to legislators and the general public of the true costs of unreasonable government conduct. . . .

2. Punitive Damages. — Because only a fraction of unconstitutional searches and seizures will ever come to light for judicial resolution, merely compensatory damages in the litigated cases would generate systematic underdeterrence. The problem is hardly unique to the Fourth Amendment, and a widespread technique today is to use multipliers and punitive damages. . . . And in keeping with that spirit of modest remedial creativity, we should note an insight of modern tort theory: Deterrence requires that the defendant must pay more than the plaintiff suffered, but not all this amount need go directly to the plaintiff. . . . Perhaps some portion of punitive damages could flow to a "Fourth Amendment Fund" to educate Americans about the Amendment and comfort victims of crime and police brutality, and thereby promote long-term deterrence, compensation, and "security."

3. Class Actions, Presumed Damages, and Attorney's Fees. — Large categories of unreasonable searches and seizures—street harassment, for example—will affect many persons, but each only a little. The offenses may be largely dignitary, and the citizen's out-of-pocket losses may be small or nonexistent. Here too, the problem is hardly unique to the Fourth Amendment, and modern law has developed general tools to address it. Class action aggregation techniques and minimum presumed damages are often the answer. . . .

In an isolated Fourth Amendment wrong involving a small dollar amount but large dignitary concerns, any plaintiff who proves a violation should receive reasonable attorney's fees, even if the fees bulk larger than the plaintiff's out-of-pocket damages, unless the government was willing to concede that a Fourth Amendment violation had indeed occurred.

4. Injunctive Relief. — Early prevention is often better than after-the-fact remedy. The Fourth Amendment says its right "shall not be violated." When judges can prevent violations before they occur, they should do so—especially if after-the-fact damages could never truly make amends. . . .

5. Administrative Relief. — The traditional judicial system is slow and cumbersome. Executive departments are typically the source of unconstitutional searches and seizures; is it too much to expect them to establish internal mechanisms to process citizen complaints quickly? Citizen review panels could serve a function akin to a traditional jury, and in many cases, victims of government unreasonableness might willingly forego a judicial lawsuit in favor of a cheaper, less adversarial, quicker administrative solution that would vindicate their dignitary claims. . . .

And this seems a good note on which to end. For I hope it is not too late to remember that the Fourth Amendment boldly proclaims a right of "the people." What better body than a jury of "the people"—a jury that truly looks like America—to cherish and protect this precious right?

Carol S. Steiker, Second Thoughts about First Principles
107 Harvard Law Review 820, 848-852, 856 (1994)

Despite its many flaws, the exclusionary rule is, I am convinced, the best we can realistically do. It is possible that the complete spectrum of civil remedies touted by Professor Amar would be, as he claims, superior to evidentiary exclusion as a system for deterring governmental misconduct. Yet Professor Amar crucially neglects to acknowledge that, when he proposes a system of civil remedies, he moves beyond construing the Fourth Amendment to suggesting significant legislative reform. In evaluating Professor Amar's Fourth Amendment package as a whole, we must therefore consider the plausibility in political terms of the legislative part of the package. Will legislatures be willing to create such a comprehensive remedial scheme for Fourth Amendment violations? Moreover, we must consider how such a package would work if passed. Even if legislatures enacted the kind of comprehensive remedial scheme proposed by Professor Amar, the ultimate distribution of such remedies would lie largely in the hands of juries. Can we be confident that juries would award Fourth Amendment remedies sufficient to create litigation incentives and thus to promote adequate deterrence?

The history of attempts to regulate police practices should make us extremely doubtful about reliance on legislatures to create effective remedial structures. Virtually since their inception, modern police forces have been the focus of calls for reform. But as we have seen, local politicians have been notoriously complicit in the corruption of police departments. Furthermore, state and federal legislators, although not dependent in precisely the same way upon local police forces, have consistently responded to public fears about crime by abdicating responsibility for controlling police misconduct, resulting in what Professor Anthony Amsterdam has aptly termed "wholesale 'legislative default.'"

. . . [S]ignificantly, almost half a century passed between the recognition of the exclusionary rule in federal prosecutions and the application of the exclusionary rule to the states. During that forty-seven-year period, not one of the majority of states that permitted the evidentiary use of illegally seized evidence managed to create an effective scheme of civil remedies for police misconduct. Indeed, the Supreme Court relied on just this failure when it extended the exclusionary rule to the states in *Mapp v. Ohio*: after noting that California adopted the exclusionary rule on its own because of the failure of other remedies, the Court observed that the "experience of California that such other remedies have been worthless and futile is buttressed by the experience of other States." There is no reason to think that the pre-*Mapp* political impediments to the creation of effective alternative remedies have miraculously disappeared. If anything, the escalating public hysteria over violent crime from the 1960s through the present makes it is even more "politically suicidal" today to support restrictions on police behavior than it was before 1961.

The problem of racial discrimination in law enforcement helps explain why there is so little public enthusiasm for policing the police. It is simply not the case that the risks of being victimized by malicious or merely overzealous police misconduct fall evenly across the population. As we have seen, the police frequently use race and class as means of targeting individuals for investigation and often subject predominantly minority neighborhoods to particularly intrusive law enforcement techniques. The "average" (meaning not impoverished and not minority) citizen is probably more likely to be a victim of crime than a victim of police overreaching—hence, the willingness of "average" citizens everywhere to give the police a free hand.

This widespread public support for unrestrained police power not only makes the passage of remedial legislation extremely unlikely, it also suggests that, even if such legislation were to be passed, popular juries would be unwilling to find much police conduct "unreasonable." Professor Amar suggests that this is not necessarily a bad thing: "the jury is perfectly placed to decide, in any given situation, whom it fears more, the cops or the robbers." But that is exactly my point: juries will almost always fear the robbers more than the cops, but this fact does not necessarily mean that everything the cops do is "reasonable." Juries will often fear the robbers more than the cops because the robbers tend to be mostly poor and/or members of minority groups and because the cops tend to focus their attentions on just such disfavored groups. . . . For the same reasons that we have turned to judges to enforce the anti-majoritarian provisions of the First and Fourteenth Amendments, we must rely upon the judge-made exclusionary rule as the device by which the Fourth Amendment should be enforced. Like it or not, the exclusionary rule, with all of its limitations, is in very real terms "the only game in town." . . .

Some argue that the complex body of law that the Supreme Court and other federal and state courts have constructed around the Fourth Amendment may not, when all is said and done, have much of a deterrent effect on police misconduct. Many respond to such claims by challenging the underlying empirical assertion. Another common response is that such observations miss the point because the exclusionary rule operates not so much to penalize violations of the Fourth Amendment as to remove the most common incentive for such violations—the discovery of evidence to be used to convict a criminal defendant. Yet the debate about deterrent effects may miss the point in a much more profound way: the body of constitutional law developed by exclusionary rule litigation may be important not so much for the fear that it inspires in the "bad cop," but rather in the way that it creates an alternative vision of the "good cop." Our modern police forces have developed a separate culture that rewards highly aggressive attitudes and behavior patterns, a culture that has proven largely impervious to outside influence. The development of an alternative vision of "good police work" founded on such a fundamental text as the Constitution offers "good cops" guidance in defining their mission and thus provides an aspirational counterpart to the internal ethos of local police departments.

Professor Amar's Fourth Amendment First Principles has the allure of every resort to "first principles"—the attraction of building an edifice that is wholly internally consistent. Although Professor Amar's proposals have the beauty of coherence and the power of simplicity, they simply do not reflect the realities of the world in which we have come to live. [E]videntiary exclusion [has] been pressed into service by twentieth-century judges in an effort to respond to seemingly intractable problems of police overreaching and racial discrimination. However inflexible [this] modern construction may be, [it is] responsive to the central realities of our times. . . .

✳ ADVANCED MATERIALS

Notes on Limiting the Detrimental Effects of Nonexculpatory Defenses

Reforms, such as special verdict
Less strict adherence to legality principle
Mistake as to nonexculpatory defense
Resisting aggressor with nonexculpatory defense
Collateral consequences of conviction
    Retaining collateral consequences of nonexculpatory acquittal
    Striking balance between competing interests
Need to distinguish nonexculpatory dismissals from standard acquittals

Reforms, such as special verdict Even while recognizing the need to allow nonexculpatory defenses, the current system could adopt certain reforms to reduce their negative side effects. While permitting an acquittal, for example, the system could nonetheless make clear its condemnation of the conduct and the actor. A special verdict of "guilty but not punishable" might accomplish this. The general "not guilty" verdict, today's common practice, exacerbates the detrimental effects of nonexculpatory acquittals, for it may mislead some into thinking that no crime was committed. Minimizing the detrimental effects of nonexculpatory defenses depends in part on public awareness of their special nature; yet at present there seems little public awareness of which defenses fall into this category, or even public appreciation that these defenses are different.

Less strict adherence to legality principle The special nature of nonexculpatory defenses also suggests that, in defining the scope of these defenses, less strict adherence to the legality principle might be in order. Recall that the legality principle is meant to assure, among other things, that an actor has the opportunity for notice of the rules governing liability. Such potential for notice is desirable because an actor cannot comply with the law's rules if those rules are not available to him. But in the case of nonexculpatory defenses, ambiguity in the scope of the defenses is less of a concern. There is little value in telling potential offenders precisely how much harmful or evil conduct they can engage in, and in what circumstances they can do it, while still avoiding liability. Indeed, some vagueness in the definition of a nonexculpatory defense may on occasion serve the useful purpose of deterring undesirable conduct by making would-be criminals unsure whether the nonexculpatory defense will apply to acquit them. This deterrence must be distinguished from the undesirable "chilling effect" of vague offense definitions. The prohibited conduct must always be clearly defined; only the limits of the nonexculpatory defense may tolerably be unclear. Thus, the immune foreign-embassy attaché may behave himself if he is unsure whether he is covered by diplomatic immunity for a contemplated offense. The corrupt congressman may decline to exercise improper influence if he is unsure whether his legislative immunity extends to such impropriety. Such offenders have little grounds to complain of the ambiguity of the defense, or to insist on a favorable construction, for they have notice that their conduct is prohibited and choose to engage in the conduct nonetheless.

Mistake as to nonexculpatory defense For these same reasons, there seems little reason to provide a defense to an actor who seeks to take advantage of a nonexculpatory defense, but is mistaken, even reasonably mistaken, as to the conditions of the defense. The better rule provides that an actor who believes she will be protected by a nonexculpatory defense acts at her own peril. If the requirements for the defense are not, in fact, satisfied—the attaché is not immune, legislative immunity does not extend to the contemplated crime—then the policy interests supporting the defense are not served, and no defense ought to be permitted.

Resisting aggressor with nonexculpatory defense Another important practical implication of a defense being nonexculpatory is found in situations of defensive force. Defensive force justifications generally give a right to resist physical aggression against oneself, one's property, or another person. But, in current law, this right should, and commonly does, depend on whether the aggressor's conduct is unlawful. If the aggression is not "unlawful," as with an officer making a lawful arrest, generally there is no right to resist or interfere. But when the aggressor has a nonexculpatory defense, resistance and interference should be permitted, even encouraged. Though protected from criminal liability by the defense, the aggressive conduct should still be viewed as "unlawful." The immune diplomat may escape conviction for an unjustified attack, but it hardly follows that the victim is bound to submit to it, or the observer to acquiesce in it. An arresting officer's justified force is consistent with the rules of conduct; society approves the use of such force in such situations, and would want it repeated in the future. The diplomat's attack, in contrast, avoids punishment only because of reasons external to the offense. Society disapproves of such conduct in such situations and wants it to be avoided in the future—and also prevented in the present, if possible. Many codes would reach this result, though existing formulations of justification rules are not always clear on the matter.

Collateral consequences of conviction An additional reform would be to allow some of the collateral consequences of conviction to attach for nonexculpatory acquittals. Conviction for a criminal offense typically carries with it not only punishment, as through imprisonment, fine, or probation, but also a host of other civil disabilities. An offender may lose many basic rights and privileges: citizenship; the rights to vote, hold public office, or carry a firearm; employment opportunities in licensed and unlicensed occupations; the capacity to litigate, to testify, and to serve as a juror or as a court-appointed fiduciary; parental, marital, and inheritance rights; and access to insurance, pension, and workmen's compensation benefits.[2] Conviction may increase the chances that an offender will suffer civil forfeiture, civil restraint or injunction, civil liability, and civil commitment.[3] Further, the conviction may be used to impeach an offender in a subsequent trial where the offender

---

2. See, e.g., Schanuel v. Anderson, 708 F.2d 316 (7th Cir. 1983) (statute prohibiting ex-felon from obtaining employment as detective held constitutional).

3. See, e.g., N.J. Stat. Ann. § 2C:13-12.1; N.D. Cent. Code § 12.1-33-01 to 12.1-33-02.1.

is a witness or a defendant-witness,[4] or to aggravate the sentence for a subsequent offense.[5]

Retaining collateral consequences of nonexculpatory acquittal Given the disfavored nature of nonexculpatory defenses, some of these collateral consequences might appropriately be retained if a defendant is acquitted only by virtue of the defenses. Some precedent exists for this: The criminal diplomat can be expelled from the country; the incompetent defendant can be incarcerated until trial is possible; collateral consequences may be retained where an offender is pardoned.[6] Under present practice, however, offenders acquitted under a nonexculpatory defense commonly escape all penalties and disabilities as if they were exculpated. Assume a guilty defendant's case is dismissed because of police or prosecutorial misconduct. Allowing such an offender to escape the primary consequences of conviction—condemnation and punishment—may be an acceptable, or necessary, cost of furthering the important societal interest of deterring such official misconduct. It does not follow, however, that societal interests also demand sacrificing the collateral consequences that would attach to such a violation. It does not seem necessary or desirable to allow the corrupt official to keep his public office; or to allow a rapist to escape sentencing as a repeat offender after a subsequent rape, merely because a nonexculpatory defense barred conviction for the earlier one; or to allow a school bus driver's license to the pedophile released because of the exclusionary rule.

Striking balance between competing interests Nonexculpatory defenses may be sensible or even necessary to advance a societal interest, even though they run counter to the usual interests of the criminal law. But it may also make sense to modify or limit a nonexculpatory defense, or its consequences, in order to strike a proper balance between those competing interests. Thus, a societal interest might justify exemption from custodial or supervisory sanctions, yet not justify exemption from all restrictions that might be imposed as a collateral consequence of conviction. Such restrictions often can provide critical protections for society, sometimes with modest infringement of an offender's interests.

Need to distinguish nonexculpatory dismissals from standard acquittals The greatest practical hurdle to imposing such collateral consequences is in identifying cases of nonexculpatory acquittal of blameworthy offenders. Many nonexculpatory defenses bar not only conviction, but prosecution, meaning that no authoritative determination of blameworthiness is readily available. Double jeopardy, diplomatic immunity, and incompetency, by their terms, bar trial of the defendant. Other nonexculpatory defenses, such as the statute of limitation and many immunities (judicial, legislative, executive, testimonial, and plea bargaining) often are litigated before trial, leading to dismissal if the defense claim succeeds. The difficulty can be resolved through a change in procedural rules. If the prosecution intends to seek the imposition of some of the collateral consequences of

---

4. See, e.g., Fed. R. Evid. 404, 609. See United States v. Keller, 624 F.2d 1154 (3d Cir. 1980) (government sought to introduce evidence of prior prosecution for drug dealing that resulted in acquittal on basis of entrapment; entrapment was defense in instant case; evidence held inadmissible).

5. Many States have enacted habitual or persistent offender statutes. See, e.g., Conn. Gen. Stat. Ann. § 53a-40.

6. See, e.g., Fed. R. Evid. 609 (impeachment by prior conviction permitted even though defendant subsequently pardoned).

conviction despite a nonexculpatory dismissal, determination of the nonexculpatory defense could be delayed until after a determination of guilt. Alternatively,
the issues of blameworthiness could be litigated at a separate hearing on the
imposition of the collateral consequences. Whether the additional expenditure of
resources would be worth the effort may depend on the extent of the harm or evil
threatened if no collateral consequences are imposed. Whatever the procedure,
if imposition of collateral consequences is contemplated after a nonexculpatory
defense, an actor must, of course, be given the opportunity to rely instead on an
exculpatory defense.

APPENDIX A: SECTION 24

Entrapment

DISCUSSION MATERIALS
Issue: Should the Criminal Law Recognize an Entrapment Defense?
    Model Penal Code Section 2.13 Commentary, Entrapment
    Louis Michael Seidman, The Supreme Court, Entrapment, and Our Criminal
        Justice Dilemma
    Andrew J. Ashworth, Defences of General Application: The Law Commission's
        Report No. 83: (3) Entrapment

✴ DISCUSSION MATERIALS

Issue: Should the Criminal Law Recognize an Entrapment Defense?

The Model Penal Code Commentary at the beginning of these materials provides the rationale for recognizing an objective formulation of the entrapment defense and reviews how the defense is formulated in various jurisdictions. In contrast, Louis Seidman offers a methodical counter-argument to each justification offered for the defense and calls into question the logic and necessity of the doctrine in the American criminal law system. Finally, Andrew Ashworth reviews a British proposal favoring the creation of an entrapment *offense*, comparing this with alternative methods of controlling undesirable law enforcement conduct—such as exclusion of evidence, mitigation of sentence, and an entrapment defense—and explains why each of these were rejected by the Royal Commission.

Model Penal Code Section 2.13 Commentary
Entrapment
Official Draft and Revised Comments 406-408, 411-415 (1985)

Rationale for Defense.   The defense of entrapment presents a fundamental policy choice of difficult dimensions. On the one hand, the defendant whose crime results from an entrapment is neither less reprehensible or dangerous, nor more reformable or deterrable, than other defendants who are properly convicted. Defendants who are aided, solicited, deceived or persuaded by police officials stand in the same moral position as those who are aided, solicited, deceived or persuaded by other persons; yet no one suggests a general defense for the latter. Thus, there is substantial reason to record convictions and take normal correctional measures in cases of defendants whose crimes are included by the police.

On the other hand, the harm done by increasing the risk of offending on the part of the innocent is great. Some persons will thus turn to crime and risk the pain of punishment in response to the call of law enforcement. Moreover, when officers are engaged in persuading citizens to commit criminal acts, they are absent from their proper task of apprehending those offenders who act without such encouragement. Such tactics spread suspicion in the community and can easily be employed as the expression of personal malice on the part of a police officer. Perhaps most important of all, however, is the injury to the reputation of law enforcement institutions that follows the employment of methods shocking to the moral standards of the community.

It is therefore the attempt to deter wrongful conduct on the part of the government that provides the justification for the defense of entrapment, not the innocence of the defendant. The extraordinary measure of freeing a defendant to deter the police is taken for several reasons. No other effective remedy to discourage the police is available as a practical matter; the ordinary civil or criminal sanctions are inadequate to prevent overreaching in the use of police instigation, persuasion or deceit. . . . Furthermore, the chief aims of the criminal law are to prevent people from engaging in socially harmful conduct and to instruct them in the basic requirements of good citizenship. It is consistent with these purposes to recognize a defense based upon those unsavory police methods that have the effect of fostering criminality.

This section is therefore concerned with those cases in which a crime has been committed but its commission has been induced by overzealous law enforcement. In such situations, the defense of entrapment has been almost universally recognized in the United States, though statements denying that it is recognized have occasionally been made. The defense has commonly been the product of judicial decision rather than statute. . . .

The Code's Standard. The original draft of the Code's entrapment defense presented alternatives designed to conform to . . . two positions. . . . The formulation that was adopted represents an objective standard. . . . The main criterion for evaluating the propriety of police methods is, therefore, the likely effect of such methods on law-abiding persons, and the propensities of the particular defendant are irrelevant.

Subsection (1)(a) makes the defense applicable whenever the government agents have knowingly made false representations designed to induce the belief that defendant's conduct was not prohibited. (This defense is supplemental to whatever defense may be available under Section 2.04.) The subsection represents a judgment both that this kind of police conduct is not appropriate, and that it is generally likely to induce persons to commit crimes when they would not otherwise do so. Thus, no evaluation of this kind of technique is required in particular cases.

The Institute was persuaded to adopt the "objective" approach of Subsection (1)(b) in preference to the "subjective" approach of *Sorrells* and *Sherman* for a number of reasons. First, if the defense is available only to those who are "innocent," its full deterrent effect is undermined. Police conduct toward a particular defendant may be seriously objectionable even though he entertained a purpose to commit crime prior to any inducement by officials. Law enforcement officers may feel free to employ forbidden methods if the "innocent" are to be freed but the habitual offenders, in whom they have greater interest, will nevertheless be punished.

Second, the very notion that certain police conduct may be improper in relation to the "innocent" (nonpredisposed), but acceptable when addressed to the "guilty" (predisposed), seems incompatible with the ideal of equality before the law. . . . Furthermore, to permit the use against a previously convicted person of police measures not permitted against the rest of society is to fix a permanent status of criminality on these persons against the hopes of enlightened penology.

Finally, the practical effect of the subjective approach is to lose sight in litigation of the main issue that should be before the court. The primary justification for the defense, as noted above, is to discourage unsavory police tactics; the defendant is just as guilty, with or without the entrapment. Yet as the defense has been actually litigated in many cases using the majority position of *Sorrells* and *Sherman*, investigation into the character of the defendant has often obscured the important task of judging the quality of the police behavior. The emphasis of courtroom inquiry is thus turned from the character of police conduct to the history of the accused and his immediate reaction to the enticement.

Those in the Institute who supported the alternative subjective approach did so mainly on two grounds. In their judgment, the greatest vice in entrapment cases inheres in police behavior that leads the previously innocent to crime. It is therefore a sensible judgment to limit the defense to that situation. Moreover, defendants who are predisposed to commit crime are largely the professionals, who constitute the greatest crime problem. Freeing them in order to discipline the police was thought too great a price. When officers deal with the criminally disposed, they may find it necessary to employ methods that would be quite out of place if directed to the "innocent." Thus, it was believed, they should be entitled to do.

Developments Since Promulgation of the Code. . . .

Some jurisdictions have followed the Model Code in making entrapment a matter of statutory formulation, but others have left the matter to judicial decision. The recently enacted and proposed codes that deal with entrapment are about equally divided between those that adopt the subjective approach of *Sorrells* and *Sherman* and those that follow the Model Code's objective approach and designated as the crucial consideration whether the police methods used would be likely to induce law-abiding persons to engage in criminal activity. A few also indicate specifically that the defense may be successfully invoked whenever government agents knowingly falsely represent that illegal behavior is lawful. In states where the law of entrapment is still governed exclusively by judicial decision, the courts remain divided between the subjective and objective approaches.

Louis Michael Seidman, The Supreme Court, Entrapment, and Our Criminal Justice Dilemma
5 The Supreme Court Review 111, 127-133, 135-137, 139-142, 145-146 (1981)

Rationales for the Entrapment Defense

. . . Sometimes, the Justices suggest that the defense is necessary because the entrapped defendant is in some sense "innocent" and unworthy of punishment. At other times, the Court suggests that the defense is unrelated to the defendant's guilt, but is instead necessary either to deter the police from engaging in objectionable behavior or to preserve the integrity of the courts. In fact, as others have demonstrated, the version of the defense actually fashioned by the Court is supported by neither of these arguments. It can hardly be maintained that entrapment doctrine is necessary to vindicate the innocent, so long as we continue to treat as guilty nondisposed defendants induced to commit crime by private, rather than by governmental, temptors. Because governmental conduct is a necessary predicate for the defense, it might therefore be thought that we allow a defendant to raise it in order to deter such conduct. But the defense is also inconsistent with this goal, since its success is unrelated to the wrongfulness of the government's actions.

Entrapment doctrine thus represents neither a consistent judgment as to the culpability of entrapped defendants nor an effective strategy for deterring unwanted police behavior. Although this simple observation has dominated academic discussion of the defense, the point should not be overstated. If that were all there were to the matter, entrapment would be no different from a score of other uneasy compromises in the law. The fact that such a compromise is not fully justified by any of the competing theories motivating it should neither surprise nor puzzle us.

But that is far from all there is to the matter. What should surprise and puzzle us is that each of these competing theories is itself incoherent. Moreover, while some anomalies result from the way the Court has defined predisposition and the special version of the entrapment defense it has thereby created, the problems are mostly intrinsic to the defense and cannot be remedied however it is reformulated.

A. The Culpability Theory

. . . [I]f a nondisposed defendant induced to commit a crime by another is "innocent," he should not be punished. But why should such a defendant be viewed as innocent? Ordinarily, one would expect to look to the statutory definition of a particular crime to discover the boundaries between guilt and innocence. Perhaps in response to this expectation, the Supreme Court has always treated the entrapment defense as somehow implicit in federal statutory law. But it is painfully obvious that the statutory basis for the defense is wholly fictional. An entrapped defendant has, by definition, committed an act made criminal by positive law, and he has done so with the requisite state of mind. One looks in vain through the United States Code for any indication that Congress meant to condition culpability on the defendant's predisposition, however that term is defined.

Indeed, Congress has consistently declined to codify any of the versions of the entrapment defense presented to it.

It is, of course, true that the criminal law has traditionally recognized a series of defenses to what would otherwise be criminal acts, and that not all of these have been codified. In general, such defenses fall into two categories: claims such as duress, necessity, and self-defense, relating to external pressures brought to bear on the defendant; and claims such as insanity, infancy, and mistake, relating to the defendant's internal thought processes. Regardless of the categorization, each defense proceeds from the premise that a defendant should not be blamed for an act when he has done what we want him to do under the circumstances, in which case we say that he is justified, or when he lacked meaningful freedom to act differently, in which case we say that he is excused.

Superficially, the entrapment defense might be thought quite consistent with these firmly established limits on culpability. Indeed, the doctrine seems to fit comfortably in both the external and internal categories: it looks, on the one hand, to external pressure which in some sense explains or mitigates the defendant's conduct, and, on the other, to the defendant's innocent state of mind prior to committing the offense. Upon closer analysis, however, entrapment doctrine is consistent with neither type of defense.

1. External Pressure. The Court has occasionally suggested that we have an entrapment defense to prevent the punishment of a person whose conduct is the product of external forces. When the defendant is not predisposed, the argument goes, the government inducement in effect creates a crime in order to punish it. In the words of Justice Hughes, it is improper for the government "to punish [a person otherwise innocent] for an alleged offense which is the product of the creative activity of its own officials."

It is true, of course, that when a government agent entraps a defendant, the agent may cause a crime to be committed in the "but for" sense. Depending on the facts, it may be unwise on policy grounds for the government to pursue this course. But it is far from clear why this type of government causation should be thought to bear on culpability. As noted above, entrapment doctrine presently requires the acquittal of a nondisposed defendant regardless of the attractiveness of the inducement. Thus, the doctrine exculpates a defendant who succumbs to a temptation that a person of reasonable moral fortitude would easily spurn. It is hard to imagine a culpability principle which requires the acquittal of such a defendant. . . .

2. Internal Behavior Controls. If one could show that nondisposed defendants were somehow congenitally less capable of resisting criminal offers, this might be a basis for exculpating them, since it would be unfair to hold such defendants to a standard devised for those better equipped to resist pressure. The Supreme Court's repeated references to victims of entrapment as "innocent" might be read as endorsing such a view.

But this defense of entrapment doctrine . . . founders on the Court's definition of "predisposition." There is no reason to suppose that a person lacking a criminal disposition or character is less able to control his behavior and, therefore, is less culpable. Indeed, from a culpability perspective, the predisposition requirement is perverse. An individual with an ordinary, "upstanding" life-style has presumably been thoroughly socialized to resist deviant behavior. The very reason we are surprised when such an individual commits a crime is because we "expect more" of him than of a person leading a dissolute life.

The argument cannot be salvaged by redefining "predisposed" to focus on the danger posed by the defendant. There is no culpability reason to acquit a defendant simply because he responded to an inducement unlikely to be replicated and therefore posed little danger. The culpability question is not *whether* the defendant is likely to commit a crime, but *why* he is likely to commit it. A defendant likely to respond to a small inducement may be disposed toward crime precisely because of a weakness in his behavior controls which reduces his culpability. Conversely, a defendant responding to only very large inducements may be able to resist smaller ones because of behavior controls which make him fully responsible for his conduct.

B. The Government Deterrence Theory

The inability to formulate a convincing argument that an entrapped defendant should be considered "innocent" strongly suggests that the defense does not in fact exist for his protection. If entrapment doctrine results in the release of culpable defendants, this must be because this cost is thought worth bearing to mold government conduct in desirable ways. . . .

[T]his view of entrapment is not easy to square with the actual defense, because the ability of the prosecution to convict the defendant does not depend on the wrongfulness *vel non*[1] of its conduct. But even if the defense were reformulated so as to meet this objection, its proponents would still have the burden of demonstrating why the government conduct should be deemed wrongful.

Several arguments can be quickly dismissed. First, it might be asserted that the offering of inducements by government agents is undesirable because such conduct creates the risk that innocent people will be corrupted. But this argument obviously depends upon the characterization of those responding to the inducements as innocent—a characterization which is untenable. . . .

A more troubling argument against pursuit of an entrapment strategy is that it stimulates antisocial conduct that would not otherwise occur and, therefore, serves no legitimate end. . . .

The observation that entrapment creates crime hardly ends the analysis, however. It is also true that we would have no prison breaks if we tore down penitentiaries, and that assaults on policemen would decline dramatically if officers were kept off the streets. Obviously, the question is not whether a particular law enforcement strategy creates crime, but whether it creates more crime than it prevents. The question is hard with respect to entrapment, because, while the strategy unquestionably creates crime, it may also be an effective tool for stopping it.

Entrapment may reduce crime in two ways. First, it serves as a means of identifying and incapacitating dangerous individuals likely to commit crime in the future if not apprehended. Indeed, in the case of "victimless" crime, where the technique is most often utilized, entrapment may be the only effective means of apprehending law violators. . . .

---

1. Editor's Note. —"or not."

Second, even if the entrapped defendant is not dangerous, his incarceration may nonetheless reduce crime by deterring others. Potential criminals who know that police are utilizing an entrapment policy will realize that there is greater risk that they will be apprehended and so will be less tempted to commit crime. Put in concrete terms, the few well-publicized cases of Arab sheikhs who turned out to be F.B.I. agents are likely to make members of Congress think twice before accepting a bribe.

Unfortunately, these observations leave us with an uncomfortable sense of indeterminacy as to the utility of the entrapment strategy. About all that can be said is that the strategy creates some crime, stops other crime, and that it is hard to generalize about which effect is predominant. To be sure, there may be certain forms of entrapment that are likely to be inefficient. For example, when government agents engage in very harmful conduct to detect very minor offenses, the strategy is difficult to defend. Most of us would agree that narcotics agents should not commit murders to preserve their cover when investigating marijuana offenses. This observation explains the dicta, now supported by a majority of the Court, establishing due process limits on the extent to which government agents can engage in antisocial conduct in order to fight crime. . . . But the existence of these constitutional limits does not explain the need for an additional entrapment defense in situations where government agents have not imposed severe social costs. . . .

There is . . . one distinction between an entrapment strategy and other uses of law enforcement resources. Entrapment might be thought especially dangerous, because it places in the hands of the executive power to make criminals. If the government can offer inducements that no one would refuse, it can pick and choose the persons who will obey the law. The risk that this power might be used to punish disfavored groups is obvious.

I suspect that this fear of the government's power to create criminals provides the ultimate answer to the entrapment puzzle. It is not an obvious answer, however. It will not do to claim that entrapment is necessary to prevent the executive from engaging in selective application of the criminal sanction, because within broad limits, we tolerate precisely this risk when the universe of potential criminals consists solely of persons acting without government inducement. When the government chooses which shoplifters, pickpockets, and drug users to prosecute and to jail, we regularly rely upon political checks to guard against abuse. Why do these checks become suddenly inadequate when the class of potential criminals is broader?

Andrew J. Ashworth, Defences of General Application: The Law Commission's Report No. 83: (3) Entrapment
[1978] Criminal Law Review 137-138

In this section of their Report the Law Commission might have been expected to examine the arguments for and against a defence of entrapment. Instead, they focus on the different issue of *controlling* undesirable practices in law enforcement, and conclude by proposing the creation of a new offence of entrapping someone into committing a crime. Thus the Law Commission begin by setting themselves the question, "can entrapment be controlled satisfactorily at the trial stage?" and they discuss the exclusionary discretion, the defence of entrapment and mitigation of sentence in terms of their effectiveness in controlling objectionable practices.

The judicial discretion to exclude unfairly obtained evidence is regarded as neither effective (since the discretionary element might lead to uncertainty and inconsistency) nor appropriate (the Law Commission argue that there is a distinction between unfairness in obtaining evidence of a crime which has already been committed and unfairness in contributing to the actual commission of a crime, and that the exclusionary discretion properly applies only to the former). Mitigation of sentence is likewise dismissed as "no sufficient disincentive to the continuance of objectionable practices," and is inappropriate since it does not strike at the errant trapper. The Commission also doubt whether a defence of entrapment could be an effective control on undesirable practices, since it would succeed only rarely, and they add that the drafting of a satisfactory defence would present great difficulty.

Having concluded that entrapment cannot be satisfactorily controlled at the trial stage, the Commission go on to consider and to dismiss administrative control by regulations and disciplinary proceedings for breach, and the prosecution of trappers as secondary parties to the crimes they incite. They argue that the most appropriate method of control might be a special offence of entrapment, with proceedings instituted only with the consent of the Director of Public Prosecutions. The provision should "in essence make it an offence to take the initiative in inciting or persuading someone into committing or attempting to commit a crime even though it was intended that the completion of the offence should be prevented or that its effect should be nullified." The definition of such an offence would depend on the types of practice agreed to be undesirable, and the Law Commission propose to hold further consultations on the matter. . . .

. . . We have noted the Commission's argument that a defence would be ineffective in preventing entrapment, but general defences are usually justified in terms of the defendant's culpability or "responsibility." Only one paragraph of the report is addressed to the question whether entrapment may so affect an accused's culpability as to justify a complete defence to criminal liability, and the Commission's negative conclusion is supported by three reasons: (i) entrapment does not affect either the *actus reus* or the *mens rea* of the crime committed; (ii) defendants are sometimes induced by "fellow criminals" to commit crimes, and the fact that the inducement comes from an *agent provocateur* "corresponds with no moral distinction in [the defendant's] behaviour"; and (iii) where there is an element of entrapment, its effect on culpability can adequately be taken into account by the court when sentencing.[2]

---

2. Editor's Note. —Subsequent to this article, the United Kingdom enacted two important pieces of legislation: the Police and Criminal Evidence Act 1984 and the Human Rights Act 1998. In *Regina v. Looseley*, the House of Lords reviewed the doctrine of entrapment, relying in large part on these statutes. Lord Nicholls concluded, "although entrapment is not a substantive defense, English law has now developed remedies in respect to entrapment: the court may stay the relevant criminal proceedings [where needed to insure a defendant the right to a fair trial embodied in Article 6 of the Human Rights Act], and the court may exclude evidence pursuant to section 78 [of the Police and Criminal Evidence Act, which authorizes exclusion when "the admission of the evidence would have such an adverse effect on the fairness of the proceedings that the court ought not to admit it"]. . . . Of these two remedies the grant of a stay, rather than the exclusion of evidence at the trial, should normally be regarded as the appropriate response in a case of entrapment." [2002] 1 Cr. App. R. 29.

APPENDIX A: SECTION 25

Rape

DISCUSSION MATERIALS
Issue: Should Rape Liability Be Allowed in the Absence of Force or Threat of Force? Should It Be Allowed upon Use of Nonphysical Coercion to Gain Acquiescence?
Susan Ager, The Incident
Stephen J. Schulhofer, Rape: Legal Aspects
David P. Bryden, Redefining Rape
Wisconsin Statutes (2006)
Catharine MacKinnon, A Rally Against Rape

✳ DISCUSSION MATERIALS

Issue: Should Rape Liability Be Allowed in the Absence of Force or Threat of Force? Should It Be Allowed upon Use of Nonphysical Coercion to Gain Acquiescence?

The materials begin with a stirring article by Susan Ager exploring the gray line between rape and defeated submission, and describing some of the traditional reasons why people submit to sex even when they would prefer not. The article serves as the basis for Problem Case #121 in this Section. Stephen Schulhofer traces the development of the force requirement, its construction and evidentiary requirement, and the trends that are emerging today in many jurisdictions that relax or eliminate the requirement. David Bryden argues the benefits of the "force and resistance requirement," noting the various functions it performs, its similarity to other criminal law requirements, and the problems with looking only to consent given the unique character of sex as a criminal offense. The Wisconsin statute provides an illustration of such an unconsented-to intercourse offense. Finally, the excerpt from Catharine MacKinnon's campus rally speech puts the case for aggressive criminalization and urges a view of rape based on the victim's sense of violation rather than the aggressor's use of force.

In addition to the materials below, recall the Discussion Materials in Section 5 (Culpability and Mistake) concerning the kind of mistake as to consent, if any, that should be permitted as a defense to rape.

Susan Ager, The Incident
Detroit Free Press Magazine 17 (March 22, 1992)

We were alone beneath the stars, high in the mountains, miles from the nearest light, our sleeping bags unrolled on the ground, weary from a long drive and anticipating sleep. Or so I thought.

We were not lovers, merely acquaintances. We worked together. We respected each other. He owned a few acres in the mountains, and I admired that back-to-the-land streak in anyone. So we agreed to make this weekend camping trip together to his patch of earth.

A few days earlier, oh so briefly, I thought about saying something. Issuing a "don't-get-any-ideas" warning. But I didn't. I thought he'd feel insulted.

He did not worry so much about my feelings.

For hours on that starlit night he pestered me. Stroked me. Whispered to me first, then argues, then whines: "Oh, come on. You'll love it. Why'd you come up here with me then? Just once. It's such a beautiful night. You'll enjoy it, really. Come on. Please?"

I didn't scream, because there was no one to hear. I didn't fight, because there was nowhere to run. It was his car, and he had the keys. Instead, I curled up. I buried my head against my chest while he touched me. I slapped blindly at his touches, as if I were batting away mosquitos.

Because this happened more than a decade ago, I can't remember with precision how long he continued. I wore no watch that night.

All I know is that he went on forever. Unrelenting.

Finally, weary and weepy, I gave up. I remember the sting of my tears rolling down my cheeks and into my ears as I lay on my back and he moaned.

Then, I fell instantly into sleep, as if from the top of a mountain.

Our weekend ended early, because I was sullen and that made him angry. There was nothing to say on the long ride home.

I never called what happened that night "rape." I still don't.

But it wasn't bliss, either.

I wonder why it has no names. Because it happens all the time: Men push. We submit.

No violence, no shouting, no cries of "rape" afterwards. Just sadness and defeat.

How many of us women have watched this sort of thing happen to us, as if we were outside our bodies, in the 30 years since a confluence of factors made sexual interaction easier, at least practically speaking?

That night in the mountains I surrendered for one reason: I was tired and wanted to escape.

But we surrender for reasons besides fatigue.

- Duty: Some women may feel an obligation to reward men who've been particularly kind, or patient, or ardent. Other women may feel an obligation to be a good-and-ready wife.

- Ambiguity: Part of us wants sex, and the other part is wary. And as the train is moving toward the station, so to speak, we're still not sure. We may surrender at the same moment that we conclude, "No, this is stupid."
- Some men claim not to understand this. But most women know there is a vast geography of shifting sentiment between Yes and No.
- Hope: Sometimes we surrender because our disinterest might turn into delight. A friend calls this the "No-but-I-could-be-convinced" approach. Sometimes it works. Often it doesn't, and we wonder why we gave in.

We make these excuses for our surrenders, but that's no consolation for the vanquished.

Years after that night in the mountains, I'm surprised to find how angry I am about it. Angrier than I was then. At both him and me, and the games people play.

Now, wiser and less polite, I would not whimper but shout! Not for help, but for my own integrity—to let him know how I felt about his boorish presumptions.

I would surrender only if he held me down and forced me to. And then I could call it rape.

Stephen J. Schulhofer, Rape: Legal Aspects
Encyclopedia of Crime and Justice 1306-1309 (2d ed. 2002)

Force and resistance. Under the traditional definition, a rape conviction requires proof that the sexual act was committed "forcibly and against [the victim's] will". Thus, there must be *both* force and lack of consent.

The rationale for requiring proof of force is not self-evident, since many think that intercourse without consent should be an offense whether or not force was used. One rationale for the force requirement is that rape is considered a crime of violence, and penalties are severe. But this explanation implies that non-consensual intercourse should qualify as a lesser offense, just as it is a crime to take property without consent by force (robbery) or without force (theft). But non-consensual intercourse without force traditionally was not an offense at all, and this is still true in most states. Legally, force remains essential to distinguish criminal misconduct from permissible behavior.

The need for proof of force is sometimes explained on the ground that consent is too amorphous in sexual matters; it is argued that in the absence of force, genuine non-consent is difficult to distinguish from "reluctant submission" or even from coy but voluntary participation. Others, however, argue that "reluctant submission" involves a harm the law should not ignore and that consent to sex is no more difficult to determine than consent in other important matters. Most fundamentally, critics of the force requirement argue that the law should protect not only physical safety but also sexual autonomy—the right to choose whether and when to be sexually intimate with another person. That right is denied not only by physical force but also by nonviolent actions that interfere with freely given consent.

These arguments for abolishing the force requirement have begun to make headway. Several states now punish all cases of intercourse without consent and treat force merely as a factor that aggravates the severity of the offense. But this remains a minority view, accepted in less than a dozen states. In most states force remains an essential element of the offense.

As traditionally interpreted, the force requirement could be met only by acts or threats of physical violence. In addition, as a corollary of the force requirement, the prosecution had to prove that the victim resisted. Absent resistance, courts assumed that the victim freely chose to acquiesce. One court, reflecting the view of early-twentieth-century judges, stated, a woman "is equipped to interpose most effective obstacles by means of hands and limbs and pelvic muscles. Indeed, medical writers insist that these obstacles are practically insuperable in the absence of more than the usual relative disproportion of age and strength between man and woman."

Under the traditional resistance standard, courts required that the victim resist "to the utmost." Convictions were therefore difficult to obtain even in cases of extreme abuse. In addition, the resistance rule in effect required the victim to fight her aggressor, even when that response could expose her to great danger.

Beginning in the 1950s courts and legislatures began to relax the resistance requirement, recognizing that resistance should not be required where it would be dangerous or futile. Today, most states still require resistance, but the requirement is less rigid than in the past. Courts require "reasonable" resistance, sometimes described as "resistance of a type reasonably to be expected from a person who genuinely refuses to participate in sexual intercourse" or as "a genuine physical effort to resist as judged by the circumstances."

Many states, taking the next step, have in theory abolished the resistance requirement. In these jurisdictions, however, the prosecution still must prove actual or threatened force. As a result, the resistance requirement often resurfaces in practice, because it is difficult to show that a defendant compelled submission by force, unless there is evidence that the victim physically resisted his advances. Evidence of resistance also remains important because some jurors still believe that a woman who only protests verbally, not physically, is not really unwilling.

With or without a resistance requirement, nearly all states require proof of "force," understood to mean that the defendant compelled submission by physically overpowering the victim or by threatening to inflict bodily injury. Current interpretations of the force requirement are more flexible than in the past. Courts once insisted, in most cases, on proof of extreme brutality or an explicit threat of physical harm. Today, courts are more willing to find implicit threats sufficient. And even without an implicit threat, a complainant's fear can satisfy the force requirement, provided the fear is "reasonably grounded."

But nearly all courts insist that the injury feared must involve bodily harm; coercion by threats to inflict nonphysical injury is generally considered insufficient. In *State v. Thomson*, 792 P.2d 1103 (Mont. 1990), a high school principal allegedly compelled a student to submit to intercourse by threatening to prevent her from graduating. The court held that this threat, though clearly coercive, did not make the principal guilty of rape because he had not threatened any *physical* harm.

A few states have modified the strict rule that force must involve physical violence. The Pennsylvania Supreme Court has held that force includes "[any] superior force—physical, moral, psychological, or intellectual—[used] to compel a person to do a thing against that person's volition." This approach avoids the narrow strictures of the physical force requirement. But as it leaves unclear the line between compulsion and legitimate persuasion, there is concern about its potential vagueness. The Model Penal Code expands the concept of force in a less amorphous manner, permitting a conviction for "gross sexual imposition" when a man compels a woman to submit "by any threat that would prevent resistance by a woman of ordinary resolution" (Model Penal Code §213.1(2)(a)).

The New Jersey Supreme Court has held that the force requirement can be met by the physical actions intrinsic to intercourse, whenever the complainant does not consent (*In re M.T.S.*, 609 A.2d 1266 (N.J. 1992)). This approach in effect eliminates force altogether and makes nonconsent sufficient to establish the offense. As a matter of statutory interpretation, this outcome is awkward because it equates violent and nonviolent rape for grading purposes and has the effect of imposing a high mandatory minimum sentence for both. Grading problems aside, *M.T.S.* achieves a significant result by criminalizing all intercourse without consent. Several states arrive at a similar outcome, with more tailored grading of penalties, through statutory reforms that require force for the most serious form of rape but create a lesser offense for nonconsensual intercourse without force.

To the extent that the criminal law should protect women and men not only from physical abuse but from all interference with sexual autonomy, this last approach seems best suited to a modern law of rape. Critics of this approach argue that nonviolent interference with autonomy is not sufficiently serious to warrant criminal sanctions, or that there is excessive danger of erroneous results when nonconsent alone is sufficient for conviction. Current law is far from static, with a slow but steady evolution in the direction of relaxing or eliminating the requirement of physical force.

David P. Bryden, Redefining Rape
3 Buffalo Criminal Law Review 317, 373-385 (2000)

Legitimate Functions of the Requirement

The Equal Treatment Function

To the extent that it reflects the average jury's attitude, the FRR [Force and Resistance Requirement] helps to assure equal treatment of similar defendants. If juries usually acquit defendants in a given set of circumstances, a legal rule that requires them to do so at least has the virtue of promoting equal treatment of defendants by controlling aberrant juries, however unwise the rule may be in other respects.

There is overwhelming evidence that, at least until recently, juries have often been highly lenient toward men accused of acquaintance rape, even in cases in which the victim claimed to have resisted strenuously. Although we lack empirical studies of the issue, perhaps juries will only rarely convict without evidence of force, even in jurisdictions that have abolished the FRR. On that admittedly speculative assumption, to allow conviction of a man who did not employ force, as that term has been defined in rape law, might in practice serve only to legitimize discrimination against an occasional unlucky defendant—perhaps a member of a minority group accused of raping a white woman, or someone who "looks like a rapist," or who has an incompetent lawyer, or an atypically pro-feminist jury.

Admittedly, even without the FRR courts would still reverse convictions when they thought that the evidence of nonconsent was too skimpy. But what if the evidence of subjective nonconsent (and mens rea) is legally adequate, yet the appellate court knows that the great majority of juries would have acquitted the defendant?

Even if jurors harbor no improper prejudices, a subjective consent test would be an invitation to inconsistent verdicts. To one jury, the woman's failure to offer physical resistance might be indicative of consent. To another jury, her verbal resistance or equivocation might suffice to demonstrate nonconsent. Whether juries would in fact behave less consistently under a subjective standard is uncertain, but it is at least a danger.

Standing alone, these problems may not be a sufficient justification for the FRR, especially now that evolving public attitudes apparently have reduced jurors' anti-victim biases. But equal treatment is only one of several functions of the FRR.

The Grading Function

In addition to drawing lines between lawful and unlawful conduct, the definitions of crimes determine the maximum penalty for which each convicted criminal is eligible. Although it is now unconstitutional to execute rapists, rape is still one of the most heinous and severely punished offenses. This is partly because it is a crime of violence: No nonviolent crime is punished as severely on average as forcible rape. Assuming that some new types of nonforcible sexual offenses should be established, the maximum penalty for these offenses should be lower than for forcible rape.

If the criminal code contains modern provisions establishing degrees of rape, nonforcible rapists can be convicted of a lesser offense, with a lighter maximum penalty. In defining such a crime, a court or legislature could abolish the FRR without creating a risk of excessive penalties. But in some states there are no degrees of rape. In those states, abolition of the FRR would lump together forcible and nonforcible offenders. Without corresponding changes in the sentencing structure, which of course are beyond the power of a court, this would create the possibility of excessive sentences for the nonforcible rapes. Admittedly, this problem is not novel. Moreover, it is not a reason for permanent retention of the FRR. But it is a reason, in some states, for dealing with the problem by comprehensive legislation, rather than by a premature judicial decision abolishing the FRR.

The Bright Line Function

Citizens need to know, approximately, the boundary between lawful and unlawful conduct. This is especially true of a serious crime like rape. Physical force marks the well-known bright line between seduction and rape. That purpose would be defeated if the only force required by the courts were the "force" that is inherent in intercourse. It would also be defeated by a wholly subjective definition of nonconsent. Courts could say, of course, that the man is guilty if the woman did not consent and he knew it. This would create a bright line of sorts, but the question would remain: When is he supposed to know it? Without an answer to that question, the line between lawful and unlawful behavior would be obscure and subject to the vagaries of aberrant juries.

The Corroborative Function

Another function of the FRR is to corroborate other evidence that the victim did not consent, and that the perpetrator had a culpable mens rea. Of course, we are not speaking here of the notorious "corroboration rule," a discarded evidentiary rule that required corroboration that the putative victim had been raped. Instead, we are dealing with a substantive rule (the FRR) that was shaped, like many rules (substantive as well as evidentiary, criminal as well as civil) by a judicial desire to control juries. If rape were defined simply as nonconsensual intercourse, then the physical act of rape would be indistinguishable from ordinary intercourse; criminality would turn on the parties' subjective states of mind. Interpreted subjectively, the concepts of consent to sex, and of intentional (or reckless) rape, are loaded with ambiguities and fact-finding difficulties. Whatever its other vices, the FRR has reduced the danger of erroneous convictions by requiring objective evidence of the victim's nonconsent and the perpetrator's intention to have nonconsensual intercourse. (Whether this benefit has come at too high a price is another question.)

If the rule is to perform this corroborative function, courts must require more force than is customary in consensual sex:

> Rape is the only form of violent criminal assault in which the physical act accomplished by the offender . . . is an act which may, under other circumstances, be desirable to the victim. This unique feature of the offense necessitates the drawing of a line between forcible rape on the one hand and reluctant submission on the other, between true aggression and desired intimacy. The difficulty of drawing this line is compounded by the fact that there often will be no witness to the event other than the participants and that their perceptions may change over time. The trial may turn as much on an assessment of the motives of the victim as of the actor.

To speak of a need for corroboration is to imply that some rape complainants are untrustworthy. Feminists are understandably suspicious of any such implication. The conventional scholarly wisdom today is that false reports of rape are no more common than for any other crime. But even on that assumption, it is difficult to tell whether, as some allege, the FRR reflects an inordinate and discriminatory suspicion of acquaintance rape accusations. Rules with a corroborative function are common in the criminal law. Some corroborative rules restrict defenses; others require extra proof of guilt. The common thread running through all these corroborative rules is not so much distrust of crime victims as distrust of the abilities of jurors to resolve certain types of issues.

For example, in the law of criminal attempts, some courts are reluctant to uphold convictions without objective evidence that corroborates the defendant's criminal intent. . . . The Model Penal Code requires that the "substantial step" toward commission of a crime, which is the act element of a criminal attempt, be corroborative of the actor's criminal intention. Without such corroboration, one cannot be convicted of a criminal attempt under the Code, even if there is proof beyond a reasonable doubt both that the defendant had a criminal purpose and that he engaged in seemingly innocent acts that were a substantial step in the execution of that purpose.

The same corroboration problem occurs in cases where the defendant is charged as an accessory in a crime committed by another. Some authorities indicate that knowing assistance to a criminal suffices to establish accessorial liability; others require a "purpose" to assist the principal. Where the alleged accessory is a supplier of goods, courts sometimes resolve the purpose issue by focusing on whether the goods can be used for lawful as well as unlawful purposes. In principle, this inquiry is irrelevant: If his purpose was to assist a crime, the defendant's culpability is not diminished by the fact that the goods have some lawful uses. But the lack of lawful uses for the goods is corroborative evidence that the accused indeed had a criminal purpose. . . .

Another example is the duress defense. Although the precise limits of freedom of the will are unknown, no one claims that effective coercion necessarily requires a threat that would cause a reasonable person to fear physical harm. Yet most courts limit the duress defense to such threats. In part, this limitation reflects a reluctance to excuse crime. But a corroborative rationale is also plausible: The universal fear of bodily injury corroborates the defendant's claim of duress, obviating the need for difficult subjective appraisals.

A similar motivation is at least one of the reasons for judicial rejection of broad definitions of insanity, in favor of narrower tests such as the M'Naghten rule. Ultimately, the rationale of the insanity defense is that the defendant lacked freedom of will, yet in all states the legal standard is at least somewhat narrower than that. In other words, courts do not allow juries to determine the ultimate question directly. In this respect, insanity rules are analogous to the FRR, which also (in effect) prevents juries from directly resolving the consent issue.

As these examples illustrate, corroborative rules are ad hoc efforts to remedy real or imagined weaknesses in the fact-finding process. They exist because judges sometimes do not trust juries to resolve a question that is in principle critical to a defendant's guilt, without the assistance of the corroborative evidence required by the rule. The reasons for this mistrust are speculative and perhaps various. In any event, the point is not that all corroborative rules are wise, but rather that the judicial desire for corroborative evidence is evident in many contexts, not just rape.

To the extent that a rule's justifications are corroborative, principled objections miss the point. Corroborative rules are not dictated by general jurisprudential principles; on the contrary, one sign that a rule's purpose may be corroborative is its inconsistency with, or apparent superfluity in light of, some substantive principle. That is the price of any corroborative rule.

In general, courts trust juries to decide the facts; as exceptions to this practice, all corroborative rules, even when weighed on their own terms, are at best debatable. The same commonsensical arguments that may seem to justify a corroborative rule can be turned against it: Aren't juries able to recognize such obvious realities as the evidentiary value of force? Why tie their hands in the cases, perhaps rare, where force is absent but they are certain beyond a reasonable doubt both that the woman did not consent and that the man knew it? Although this argument is plausible, few legal scholars consistently disapprove of corroborative rules.

Given the role of force in corroborating the man's intentions, the FRR and the mens rea of rape should be evaluated together. If the defendant used considerable force, his claim of a mistake will almost always be implausible. Consequently, in jurisdictions with a FRR it probably makes little practical difference whether courts treat rape as an intentional crime or, at the other extreme, a strict liability crime. But if the FRR is abolished, the physical act of rape will not necessarily differ from ordinary sex; the proper characterization will turn on the parties' intentions. Claims of mistake will be more plausible, and courts may become more receptive to those claims. Intentionally or not, a severe approach toward one element of the crime may beget a lenient approach toward another element.

The Rubicon Function

In legal discourse, one either consents or doesn't consent; equivocation is not a legal category. But consent, as a legal construct, is not synonymous with subjective desire, which is often equivocal. One may desire something in one sense but not in another. For example, one with no physical desire for sex may nevertheless accede to a companion's wishes in order to preserve a relationship, to make a loved one happy, to avoid a scene, or because one is weary of the ordeal of refusal and recrimination. On any given occasion, some combination of these ulterior motives may or may not outweigh one's purely sexual feelings, which of course may also be mixed. Conversely, one's affirmative sexual feelings may be outweighed by negative, ulterior feelings ("he's married," "it's too soon," etc.). Frequently, the affirmative and negative feelings are, for a time, in equipoise, or in flux.

Given the many possible combinations of mixed desires, the law's yes/no answer to the question, "Did she consent to have sex?" is, as a description of subjective desire, grossly simplistic: Yes/no answers do not take account of mixed or half-conscious feelings. No purely subjective approach to consent can solve this problem.

In everyday life, we recognize that "actions speak louder than words." When we act, or fail to act, our shadowy and conflicting feelings coalesce into meaningful intentions. Knutson wants to lose weight, but feels tired at the end of the day. Does he want to exercise? He may think he knows the answer to that question, but on many evenings not even he can be certain until he either steps on the treadmill or goes to bed.

Partly in recognition of this psychological reality, courts have created various behavioral gauges of desire. For example, to make a legally effective gift of personal property, the actor's donative intent does not suffice. Absent a deed of gift, the donor must deliver the property to the donee. As circumstantial evidence of intent, delivery has a corroborative function. But the delivery requirement is also based on a psychological insight: Sometimes, at least, one does not truly know one's intentions until the time comes to cross the Rubicon. Action is the crucible of intention.

In some types of situations, there is not even a scintilla juris[1] during which the actor has a subjective intention. A batter swings at a low, inside pitch. One can imagine a robotic jurisprudent trying to figure out the batter's intentions. Did he think that the ball was in the strike zone? Or did he realize it was not, but think that he could hit it anyway? Did he apprehend the risk that he had misjudged the pitch? These questions are, of course, ridiculous. As the ball approaches the plate, a batter isn't thinking, at least not in the same sense as one thinks about whether to go to the store; he reacts instinctively. A batter's behavior is not just more

---

1. Editor's Note—In property law, "a spark of right or interest."

important than his subjective intent, and not just easier to ascertain. Sometimes behavior is all there is.

The same is often true of consent to sex. Ambivalence, sudden decisions, and changes of mind are all extremely common. Even at the moment of decision, one's feelings may be conflicted. One sometimes responds impulsively, rather than by forming a conscious intention and then carrying it out. In some cases, even an omniscient fact-finder could not describe the woman's subjective state of mind as either "consent" or "nonconsent." Even if the law does not prescribe it, the fact finder must rely on some sort of external standard.

An external standard is also valuable in ascertaining the man's intentions. No doubt some men consciously decide to overpower their unwilling partners; others consciously try to avoid compulsion. But surely there are some acquaintance rapists—perhaps many—whose mental states do not correspond to a simple dichotomy between intentional and unintentional sexual compulsion. They are pursuing their sexual objectives, not (or at least not necessarily) deliberating about the degree to which, or the sense in which, their companions voluntarily consent—indeed, that lack of reflection may be part of the problem. For such men, intention and action are one: When the woman resists, they either overpower her and at that moment become "intentional" rapists, or they desist.

The legitimate functions of the FRR suffice, at least, to distinguish acquaintance rape from other crimes to which consent is a defense. For example, none of the purposes of the FRR would be substantially served by a similar requirement in the law of nonsexual assault and battery. (If Jones is beating up Smith, Smith's failure to resist is not suggestive of possible consent.) Likewise, in the classic types of theft cases a FRR would be pointless. The perpetrator usually is either armed (like many stranger rapists), or takes the property by stealth, when the owner is absent or sleeping. The act of theft, unlike the act of intercourse, usually bespeaks criminality; we would laugh if a robber or a burglar said that he thought his victim was consenting. It would be less laughable, but still usually implausible, if a man claimed that his acquaintance had given him his wallet full of cash, identification, and credit cards. In contrast, the mere act of intercourse is as consistent with consensual as with non-consensual sex. Indeed, since women usually resist unwanted advances, one normally assumes that intercourse is consensual unless the woman is offering at least verbal resistance. In short, the difficulties of drawing a boundary between consensual and nonconsensual events, and of ascertaining whether the defendant deliberately or negligently crossed that boundary, are far greater in the context of sex with an acquaintance than in such fields as transfers of property, stranger rapes, and nonsexual assaults.

Wisconsin Statutes
(2006)

Section 940.225. Sexual Assault

(1) First Degree Sexual Assault. Whoever does any of the following is guilty of a Class B felony:

(a) Has sexual contact or sexual intercourse with another person without consent of that person and causes pregnancy or great bodily harm to that person.

(b) Has sexual contact or sexual intercourse with another person without consent of that person by use or threat of use of a dangerous weapon or any article used or fashioned in a manner to lead the victim reasonably to believe it to be a dangerous weapon.

(c) Is aided or abetted by one or more other persons and has sexual contact or sexual intercourse with another person without consent of that person by use or threat of force or violence.

(2) Second Degree Sexual Assault. Whoever does any of the following is guilty of a Class C felony:

(a) Has sexual contact or sexual intercourse with another person without consent of that person by use or threat of force or violence.

(b) Has sexual contact or sexual intercourse with another person without consent of that person and causes injury, illness, disease or impairment of a sexual or reproductive organ, or mental anguish requiring psychiatric care for the victim.

(c) Has sexual contact or sexual intercourse with a person who suffers from a mental illness or deficiency which renders that person temporarily or permanently incapable of appraising the persons conduct, and the defendant knows of such condition.

(cm) Has sexual contact or sexual intercourse with a person who is under the influence of an intoxicant to a degree which renders that person incapable of appraising the person's conduct, and the defendant knows of such condition.

(d) Has sexual contact or sexual intercourse with a person who the defendant knows is unconscious.

(f) Is aided or abetted by one or more other persons and has sexual contact or sexual intercourse with another person without the consent of that person.

(g) Is an employee of a facility or program under §940.295(2)(b), (c), (h) or (k) and has sexual contact or sexual intercourse with a person who is a patient or resident of the facility or program.

(3) Third Degree Sexual Assault. Whoever has sexual intercourse with a person without the consent of that person is guilty of a Class G felony.[2] Whoever has sexual contact in the manner described in sub. (5)(b)2 with a person without the consent of that person is guilty of a Class G felony.

---

2. Editor's Note.—In *State v. Seeley*, 295 N.W.2d 226 (Table), 97 Wis. 2d 755, 1980 WL 99222 (Wis. App. 1980) (unpublished), in affirming a conviction for third-degree sexual assault, the court, citing Gates v. State, 91 Wis. 2d 512, 283 N.W.2d 474 (Ct. App. 1979), rejects the defendant's objection to the following jury instruction:

The second element requires that . . . [the prosecutrix] did not consent to the sexual intercourse. Consent means words or overt actions by a person indicating a freely given agreement to have sexual intercourse.

If you find beyond a reasonable doubt that the defendant had sexual intercourse with . . . [the prosecutrix] without consent as consent has been defined for you, then knowledge by the defendant of the lack of consent is not material, and the mistake regarding consent is not a defense.

(3m) Fourth Degree Sexual Assault. Except as provided in sub. (3), whoever has sexual contact with a person without the consent of that person is guilty of a Class A misdemeanor.

(4) Consent. "Consent", as used in this section, means words or overt actions by a person who is competent to give informed consent indicating a freely given agreement to have sexual intercourse or sexual contact. Consent is not an issue in alleged violations of sub. (2)(c), (cm), (d), (g). The following persons are presumed incapable of consent but the presumption may be rebutted by competent evidence, subject to the provisions of § 972.11(2):

(a) . . .

(b) A person suffering from a mental illness or defect which impairs capacity to appraise personal conduct.

(c) A person who is unconscious or for any other reason is physically unable to communicate unwillingness to an act.

(5) Definitions. In this section:

(ab) "Correctional institution" means a jail or correctional facility, as defined in §961.01 (12m), a secured correctional facility, as defined in §938.02 (15m), or a secure detention facility, as defined in §938.02 (16).

(ad) "Correctional staff member" means an individual who works at a correctional institution, including a volunteer.

(ag) "Inpatient facility" has the meaning designated in §51.01(10)

(ai) "Intoxicant" means any controlled substance, controlled substance analog or other drug, any combination of a controlled substance, controlled substance analog or other drug or any combination of an alcohol beverage and a controlled substance, controlled substance analog or other drug. "Intoxicant" does not include any alcohol beverage.

(am) "Patient" means any person who does any of the following:

1. Receives care or treatment from a facility or program under §940.295(2)(b), (c), (h) or (k), from an employee of a facility or program or from a person providing services under contract with a facility or program.

2. Arrives at a facility or program under §940.295(2)(b), (c), (h) or (k) for the purpose of receiving care or treatment from a facility or program under §940.295(2)(b), (c), (h) or (k), from an employee of a facility or program under §940.295(2)(b), (c), (h) or (k), or from a person providing services under contract with a facility or program under §940.295(2)(b), (c), (h) or (k)

(ar) "Resident" means any person who resides in a facility under §940.295(2) (b), (c), (h) or (k).

(b) "Sexual contact" means any of the following:

1. Intentional touching by the complainant or defendant, either directly or through clothing by the use of any body part or object, of the complainant's or defendant's intimate parts if that intentional touching is either for the purpose of sexually degrading; or for the purpose of sexually humiliating the complainant or sexually arousing or gratifying the defendant or if the touching contains the elements of actual or attempted battery under §940.19(1).

2. Intentional penile ejaculation of ejaculate or intentional emission of urine or feces by the defendant upon any part of the body clothed or unclothed of the complainant if that ejaculation or emission is either for the purpose of sexually degrading or sexually humiliating the complainant or for the purpose of sexually arousing or gratifying the defendant.

(c) "Sexual intercourse" includes the meaning assigned under §939.22(36) as well as cunnilingus, fellatio or anal intercourse between persons or any other intrusion, however slight, of any part of a person's body or of any object into the genital or anal opening either by the defendant or upon the defendant's instruction. The emission of semen is not required.

(d) "State treatment facility" has the meaning designated in §51.01(15).

(6) Marriage Not a Bar to Prosecution. A defendant shall not be presumed to be incapable of violating this section because of marriage to the complainant.

(7) Death of Victim. This section applies whether a victim is dead or alive at the time of the sexual contact or sexual intercourse.

Section 939.22. Words and Phrases Defined

(48) "Without consent" means no consent in fact or that consent is given for one of the following reasons:

(a) Because the actor put the victim in fear by the use or threat of imminent use of physical violence on the victim, or on a person in the victim's presence, or on a member of the victim's immediate family; or

(b) Because the actor purports to be acting under legal authority; or

(c) Because the victim does not understand the nature of the thing to which the victim consents, either by reason of ignorance or mistake of fact or of law other than criminal law or by reason of youth or defective mental condition, whether permanent or temporary.

Section 939.43. Mistake

(1) An honest error, whether of fact or of law other than criminal law, is a defense if it negatives the existence of a state of mind essential to the crime.

(2) A mistake as to the age of a minor or as to the existence or constitutionality of the section under which the actor is prosecuted or the scope or meaning of the terms used in that section is not a defense.

Catharine MacKinnon, A Rally Against Rape
Feminism Unmodified 81-83 (1987)

[This talk was given at White Plaza, Stanford University, Stanford, California, November 16, 1981, where several hundred students gathered to grieve and protest a series of rapes reported on campus.]

. . . Politically, I call it rape whenever a woman has sex and feels violated. You might think that's too broad. I'm not talking about sending all of you men to jail for that. I'm talking about attempting to change the nature of the relations between women and men by having women ask ourselves, "Did I feel violated?" To me, part of the culture of sexual inequality that makes women not report rape is that the definition of rape is not based on our sense of our violation.

I think it's fairly common, and is increasingly known to be common, for men to seek sexual access to women in ways that we find coercive and unwanted. On those occasions the amount and kind of force are only matters of degree. The problem is that rapes do not tend to be reported or prosecuted or sanctioned based on the force that was used; not based on how coercive it was and not based on how violated the woman feels; instead they are based on how intimate she is with the person who did it. This is why most women think we won't be believed in reporting the most common rapes, that is, rapes by people we know. As a result, I agree with what people have been saying, that rape is everyone's problem. But that doesn't mean that it's men's problem and women's problem in the same way.

To men I want to say: Have you ever had sex with a woman when she didn't want it? Were you and are you really careful to find out? Is it enough that you say to yourself now, "I don't know?" Are you really afraid that nothing will happen between you and a woman if you don't make it happen? Are you afraid of our rage today? That we will turn it against you? Is there perhaps a reason for your fear? I think you need to remember that we love you. And that as a result it's often very unclear to us why you are so urgent. It's unclear to us why you are so pressured in seeking sexual access to us. We want you not to denigrate us if we refuse. We want you to support us, to listen to us, and to back off a little. Maybe to back off a lot. And we also want you to realize that supporting us is not the same as taking over either our injuries or our pleasure.

To women I want to say: What do you really want? Do you feel that you have the conditions under which you can ask yourself that question? If you feel that you are going to be raped when you say no, how do you know that you really want sex when you say yes? Do you feel responsible for men's sexual feelings about you? What about their responsibility for yours, including your lack of them? I also want to say that women need self-protection; we do not need more paranoia. The Stanford police tell us, "A little fear is a good thing right now." I think we do not need more fear. We need to make fear unnecessary. . . .

APPENDIX A: SECTION 26

Hate Crimes

DISCUSSION MATERIALS
*Issue: Should the Criminal Law Impose Additional Liability and Punishment for an
Offense that Is Motivated by Hatred Toward an Identifiable Group?*
Frederick M. Lawrence, Punishing Hate: Bias Crimes Under American Law
Susan Gellman, Hate Crime Laws Are Thought Crime Laws

✳ DISCUSSION MATERIALS

Issue: Should the Criminal Law Impose Additional Liability and Punishment for an Offense that Is Motivated by Hatred Toward an Identifiable Group?

The Lawrence excerpt sets out the consequentialist and non-consequentialist justifications for adopting hate crime laws and argues that increased punishment is an appropriate response. In contrast, Susan Gellman's article questions the constitutionality of laws like those upheld in the *Mitchell* case, the principal case of the Section, and claims that these laws infringe on first amendment rights and fail to meet their intended goals. She offers alternative formulations and norm-changing proposals that purport to better serve the objective.

Frederick M. Lawrence, Punishing Hate: Bias Crimes Under American Law
58-63, 161-163, 167-169 (1999)

The Relative Seriousness of Bias Crimes

Reconsideration of the Unique Harm Caused by Bias Crimes

The seriousness of a crime . . . is a function of the offender's culpability and the harm caused. It follows, therefore, that the relative seriousness of bias crimes and parallel crimes will also turn on the culpability and harm associated with each. . . .

. . . To establish a bias crime, the prosecution must prove that the accused was motivated by bias in the commission of the parallel crime. Under both federal and state law, the burden is on the prosecution to show motivation. This proof would be necessary whether we are applying the racial animus model or the discriminatory selection model of bias crimes. Under the racial animus model, the offender must have purposefully acted in furtherance of his hostility toward the target group. Under the discriminatory selection model, the offender must have purposefully selected the victim on the basis of his perceived membership in the target group. Under either model, nothing short of this *mens rea* of *purpose* will constitute the requisite culpability for the second tier of a bias crime. Unless the perpetrator was motivated to cause harm to another because of the victim's race, the crime is clearly not a bias crime.

The culpability associated with the commission of parallel crimes and bias crimes is thus identical in terms of *what* the offender did and differs only in respect to *why* the offender did so. The relevance of this difference to the calculation of crime seriousness depends upon the reason that the culpability itself is relevant to crime seriousness.

Why is it that intentional murder ought to be punished more severely than the negligent killer? The result of the conduct of each is the death of the victim; they differ only as to their culpability. To the consequentialist, the murderer is punished more because he was more likely to cause death than was the negligent killer, or because the social value of his activity resulting in death was less relative to the chance of death. If this is the role of culpability in the calculation of crime seriousness, then the culpability associated with bias crimes makes these crimes more severe than parallel crimes. Bias crime offenders are more likely to cause harm than are those who commit the same crimes without bias motivation. [B]ias crimes generally are not more likely to be assaults than are parallel crimes, and bias-motivated assaults are far more likely to be brutal. Moreover, the social value of activity resulting in bias crimes is far less than even the antisocial behavior that results in the parallel crime.

An alternative explanation for punishing the murderer more severely than the negligent killer is that his act of intentionally killing is more blameworthy. If culpability is relevant to crime seriousness because it bears on blameworthiness, then the argument that the culpability associated with bias crimes makes these crimes more serious than parallel crimes is as compelling as it was for the consequentialist. The motivation of the bias crime offender violates the equality principle, one of the most deeply held tenets in our legal system and our culture. To the extent that crime seriousness is designed to capture a deontological concept of blameworthiness, bias crimes are more serious than other crimes. The rhetoric surrounding the enactment of bias crime laws suggests that most supporters of such legislation espouse a thoroughly deontological justification for the punishment of racially motivated violence.

This trend is well illustrated by an unusual punishment for bias crimes proposed in Marlborough, Massachusetts. The Marlborough city council unanimously approved an ordinance that would deny public services, such as local licenses, library cards, or even trash removal, to those convicted of bias crimes. Supporters of the ordinance drew upon the community's disdain for the racial prejudice demonstrated by the bias criminal rather than the harm caused by the criminal's conduct.

Culpability analysis, therefore, advances the argument for the relatively greater seriousness of bias crimes. The argument is equally supported by culpability theory based upon consequentialist and nonconsequentialist justifications for punishment.

A harms-based analysis also demonstrates that bias crimes are more serious than parallel crimes, regardless of the theory of punishment we assume. Under an ex ante analysis, the question is whether the rational person would risk a parallel crime before he would risk a bias crime. For several reasons, the answer is almost certainly yes. Consider first the context of vandalism. The parallel crime arising out of the defacement of a building or home is primarily a nuisance to the victim. The loss is insurable and, if not insured, is suffered in terms of time or money or both. However, if that vandalism is bias motivated, the defacement might take the form of swastikas on the home of a Jewish family or racist graffiti on the home of an African-American family. The harm here is not a mere nuisance. The potential for deep psychological harm, and the feelings of threat discussed earlier, exceed the harm ordinarily experienced by vandalism victims. No one can buy insurance to cover these additional harms.

The case of an electrical fire that destroyed a Boston-area synagogue provides the framework for a useful hypothetical example of the rational person's relative willingness to bear the risk of parallel vandalism versus bias-motivated vandalism. In the short period immediately after the fire, prior to the determination of the cause, there was widespread concern that the fire was the result of bias-motivated arson. The news that it was not was met with great relief. Part of this relief may be attributed to the fact that the fire had occurred accidentally and was not the result of arson, bias motivated or otherwise. But this explanation does not capture the entire reaction, part of which is attributable to the fact that anti-Semitism was ruled out as a cause. Had the fire been caused by foul play without bias motivation—for example, by pecuniarily motivated arson without any trace of anti-Semitism—surely the reaction of both victims and the general community would have exceeded the reaction that would have followed an accidental fire, but would not have been as great as if the cause were determined to have been religiously motivated. Faced with the choice between racist and nonracist vandalism, the rational person would risk the parallel crime before risking the more personally threatening bias crime with its longer-lasting effects.

This analysis applies to attacks against persons just as it does to those against property. In the parallel crime of assault, the perpetrator generally selects the victim (1) randomly or for no particularly conscious reason, (2) for a reason that has nothing to do with the victim's personal identity, such as the perpetrator's perceiving that the victim is carrying money, or (3) for a reason relating to personal animosity between the perpetrator and the victim. A random assault or mugging leaves a victim with, at least, a sense of being unfortunate and, at most, a sense of heightened vulnerability. An assault as a result of personal animosity causes, at most, a focused fear or anger directed at the perpetrator. Unlike a parallel assault, a bias-motivated assault is neither random nor directed at the victim as an individual, and this selection and the message it carries cause all the harms discussed earlier. The perpetrator selects the victim because of some immutable characteristic, actual or perceived. As unpleasant as a parallel assault is, the rational person would still risk being victimized in that manner before he would risk the unique humiliation of a bias-motivated assault.

An ex post analysis provides further clarity and support for this conclusion. A living standard analysis focuses on depth of injury caused by a crime to interests of physical safety, material possessions, personal dignity, and autonomy. Recall that when we compare a parallel crime with a bias crime, we are comparing the same crime with the addition of the perpetrator's bias motivation. The parallel assault crime and the bias assault crime will cause roughly similar injuries to the physical safety and material possessions of the victim. But the bias crime victim's injury to autonomy—in terms of his sense of control over his life—and to his personal dignity will exceed that inflicted upon the parallel assault victim. This is clear from the far greater occurrence of depression, withdrawal, anxiety, and feelings of helplessness and isolation among bias crime victims than is ordinarily experienced by assault victims.

Moreover, in order to assess completely the impact of bias crimes on living standards, we must look beyond the individual victims of these crimes. Here, too, we see a far greater societal injury caused by bias crimes than by parallel crimes. A parallel crime may cause concern or even sorrow among certain members of the victim's community, but it would be unusual for that impact to reach a level at which it would negatively affect their living standard. By contrast, bias crimes spread fear and intimidation beyond the immediate victims to those who share only racial characteristics with the victims. Members of the target group suffer injuries similar to those felt by the direct victim of the actual crime. Unlike the sympathetic nonvictims of a parallel crime, members of the target community will suffer a living standard loss in terms of a threat to dignity and autonomy and a perceived threat to physical safety. Bias crimes, therefore, cause a greater harm to a society's collective living standard than do parallel crimes.

A bias crime, as a matter of culpability or harm—and whether analyzed under retributive or consequentialist justifications for punishment—is more serious than the relevant parallel crime. Bias crimes thus warrant enhanced criminal punishment. . . .

Why Punish Hate?

> Let us dedicate ourselves to what the Greeks wrote so many years ago: to tame the savageness of man and to make gentle the life of this world. Let us dedicate ourselves to that, and say a prayer for our country and for our people.

Robert F. Kennedy, April 4, 1968

The last several decades have seen a dramatic increase in the awareness of bias crimes—both by the public generally and by the legal culture in particular—and the need for a legal response. We need look no further than the marked rise in the number of bias crime laws.

These developments, however, can obscure the controversy that often surrounds the debate over the enactment of a bias crime law. For example, during the debate over Arizona's bias crime law, enacted in 1997, one legislator objected on the grounds that "I still don't believe that a crime against one person is any more heinous than the same crime against someone else." Another put the matter more bluntly: "a few Jews" in the legislature were making the issue "emotional and divisive." Acrimony has surrounded the debate over many state laws. Is it really worth it?

This question is not entirely rhetorical. Obviously, the entire thrust of the preceding chapters argues that bias crime laws are justifiable and constitutional. But to a large extent, I have assumed the need to punish hate as my starting point. The implicit premise of the task has been to provide justifications for the punishment of racially motivated violence in criminal law doctrine, and to square this punishment with free expression doctrine.

Before concluding, it is wise to step back from this assumption, to ask not merely whether it is justified to punish hate, but whether it is *necessary* to punish hate. A state may do so—but should it?

The answer is that it is well worthwhile to have laws that expressly punish racially motivated violence. In order to see why, we must return to the general justifications for punishment, and now augment that discussion with a consideration of the expressive value of punishment, or what is sometimes known as the denunciation theory of punishment. The expressive value of punishment allows us to say not only that bias crime laws are warranted, but they are essential.

The Expressive Value of Punishing Bias Crimes

. . . What happens when proposed bias crime legislation becomes law? This act of lawmaking constitutes a societal condemnation of racism, religious intolerance, and other forms of bigotry that are covered by that law. Moreover, every act of condemnation is dialectically twinning with an act of expression of values—in Durkheim's terms, social cohesion. Punishment not only signals the border between that which is permitted and that which is proscribed, but also denounces that which is rejected and announces that which is embraced. Because racial harmony and equality are among the highest values held in our society, crimes that violate these values should be punished and must be punished specifically as bias crimes. Similarly, bias crimes must be punished more harshly than crimes that, although otherwise similar, do not violate these values. Moreover, racial harmony and equality are not values that exist only, or even primarily, in an abstract sense. The particular biases that are implicated by bias crimes are connected with a real, extended history of grave injustices to the victim groups, resulting in enormous suffering and loss. In many ways these injustices, and their legacies, persist.

What happens if bias crimes are not expressly punished in a criminal justice system, or, if expressly punished, are not punished more harshly than parallel crimes? Here, too, a message is expressed by the legislation, a message that racial harmony and equality are not among the highest values held by the community. Put differently, it is impossible for the punishment choices made by the society *not* to express societal values. There is no neutral position, no middle ground. The only question is the content of that expression and the resulting statement of those values.

Two cases, one of which involves the debate over a bias crime law, illustrate the point. Consider first the case of the creation of a legal holiday to commemorate the birth of Dr. Martin Luther King, Jr. Once the idea of such a holiday gained widespread attention, the federal government and most states created Martin Luther King Day within a relatively short period of time. It was impossible, however, for a state to take "no position" on the holiday. Several states, including South Carolina, Arizona, New Hampshire, North Carolina, and Texas, did not immediately adopt the holiday. These states were perceived as rejecting the values associated with Dr. King, which were to be commemorated by the holiday marking his birthday. Civil rights groups brought pressure against these states with economic boycotts and the like. Once ignited, the debate over Martin Luther King Day thus became one in which there was no neutral position. The lack of legislation was a rejection of the holiday and the values with which it was associated.

The second case concerns the debate in 1997 over a bias crime law in Georgia, the site of one of the most acrimonious legislative battles over such legislation. The tension surrounding the debate was heightened by the bombing that year of a lesbian nightclub in Atlanta. Ultimately, the legislation failed to reach the floor of the Georgia legislature for a vote. As with Martin Luther King Day, there was no middle position for Georgia to adopt. Either a bias crime law would be established, with the attending expression of certain values, or it would not, with a rejection of these values and an expression of other, antithetical values. The values expressed by the rejection of the law are aptly caught by the unusually blunt view of one Georgia legislator: "What's the big deal about a few swastikas on a synagogue?" Others derided the legislation as the "Queer Bill."

Thus far we have considered the enactment of a bias crime law to be a simply binary choice: a legislature enacts a bias crime law or it does not. To do so denounces racial hatred, and to fail to do so gives comfort to the racist. We can make a similar observation in the more subtle context of establishing grades of crimes and levels of criminal punishment. [Above] we discussed the ways in which both retributive and consequentialist theories of punishment embraced a concept of proportionality. Now we can see that expressive punishment theory does as well. Conduct that is more offensive to society should receive relatively greater punishment than that which is less offensive. We would be shocked if a legislature punished shoplifting equally with aggravated assault. We might disagree as to whether one was punished excessively or the other insufficiently, but we would agree that these crimes ought not to be treated identically. Society's most cherished values will be reflected in the criminal law by applying the harshest penalties to those crimes that violate these values. There will certainly be lesser penalties for those crimes that in some respects are similar but do not violate these values. The hierarchy of societal values involved in criminal conduct will thus be reflected by the lesser crime's status as a lesser offense included within the more serious crime.

The enshrinement of racial harmony and equality among our highest values not only calls for independent punishment of racially motivated violence as a bias crime and not merely as a parallel crime; it also calls for enhanced punishment of bias crimes over parallel crimes. If bias crimes are not punished more harshly than parallel crimes, the implicit message expressed by the criminal justice system is that racial harmony and equality are not among the highest values in our society. If a racially motivated assault is punished identically to a parallel assault, the racial motivation of the bias crime is rendered largely irrelevant and thus not part of that which is condemned. The individual victim, the target community, and indeed the society at large thus suffer the twin insults akin to those suffered by the narrator of Ralph Ellison's *Invisible Man*. Not only has the crime itself occurred, but the underlying hatred of the crime is invisible to the eyes of the legal system. The punishment of bias crimes as argued for in this book, therefore, is necessary for the full expression of commitment to American values of equality of treatment and opportunity.

Susan Gellman, Hate Crime Laws Are Thought Crime Laws

1992/1993 Annual Survey of American Law 509, 509-513, 518-520, 528-531

Introduction

"Hate crime" laws are a response to the demand that government "Do Something!" about bigotry generally and bias crime specifically. This is a commendable goal, and one that ought to generate creative, constitutional, and effective ideas. Unfortunately, the penalty-enhancement hate crime laws some jurisdictions have adopted are "all sizzle and no steak." They simply do not accomplish their objectives, and succeed only in creating additional problems. Furthermore, even when they are upheld as constitutional, they are damaging to constitutional values.

This is why it is so distressing to see organizations and individuals who are knowledgeable and concerned about the First Amendment willing to accept the narrow interpretation of the First Amendment that is necessary to defend these hate crime laws. Practitioners must acknowledge and accept the Supreme Court's decision in *State v. Mitchell* finding Wisconsin's hate crime law constitutional. Nevertheless, we may well question the soundness of the Court's reasoning.

The *Mitchell* statute was upheld as constitutional; it is well-intentioned and is better than most in some ways. But the most that can be said about even the law upheld in *Mitchell*—certainly one of the best of its type—is that it is just barely constitutional. The *Mitchell* decision is no shining moment in First Amendment law; in fact, the statute was a successful attempt to circumvent the First Amendment to reach a desired result, not an attempt to strengthen it. It is worrisome that those who are ordinarily so protective of the First Amendment are satisfied with *minimal* constitutional compliance, instead of insisting on approaches that afford *maximum* protection to First Amendment values. Certainly, the goals of these laws are appealing. But it ill becomes those concerned with civil liberties and civil rights to be enthusiastic about what amounts to an end run around First Amendment values. Furthermore, as Professor Jacobs points out, the laws do little, if anything, to accomplish these goals. There are numerous alternative approaches that do not focus on motives, and that would also serve these goals better than enhancement or bump-up type hate crimes laws. . . .

I. *What* Mitchell *Doesn't Say*

A. *There's More Than One Way to Skin This Cat: Alternatives to Hate Crime Enhancement Laws*

Discussion of hate crime laws often assumes that these laws are urgently needed because they are the only way to serve important social goals. In fact, not only are they not the only way, they are far from the best way. To begin with, noncriminal approaches are more likely to serve those goals than the punishment of selected motives. Realistically, only a major commitment to education and social and economic programs, which can alleviate the conditions of ignorance, frustration and despair that breed bias and crime, can be expected to make any significant progress toward discouraging bias crimes. Short of that, bias-crime-conscious victim assistance, police awareness training, and preventive measures such as community education and conscientious allocation of police protection are more likely to have measurable effects than hate crime laws. The reporting and statistical requirements adopted by many jurisdictions may or may not be useful. Even the symbolic function of hate crime laws is better achieved by other forms of governmental action, such as incentives for, recognition of, and the official practice of tolerance and pluralism. It is both futile and cynical for government to try to make a symbolic statement by punishing private persons' homophobic motives, while at the same time making the opposite statement by having sodomy laws, or by refusing to consider sexual orientation a "suspect classification" for equal protection purposes.

Even if a legislature determines that only some sort of penalty enhancement will do, the content- and viewpoint-specific approach is unnecessary, because many neutral enhancement factors would serve the same interests. For example, penalties could be enhanced where:

1. The offender acted with the specific intent to create (or with knowledge that he was likely to create) terror within a definable community.
2. The offender acted with specific intent to create (or with knowledge that he was likely to create) a threat of further crime.
3. The offender knew or should have known that a victim was particularly susceptible to the criminal conduct.
4. The offender, in the commission of the offense, intended to inflict serious emotional distress.
5. The commission of the offense created serious psychological harm (comparable to "serious physical harm" specifications that enhance penalties).
6. The offender acted with specific intent to interfere with another's exercise of constitutional or statutory rights, or another's enjoyment of or access to public facilities, or another's enjoyment of equal opportunity.

Each of these formulas is content- and viewpoint-neutral, and each alone or in conjunction with others would reach all the conduct contemplated by hate crimes laws. In fact, the federal sentencing guidelines upon which the third example above is based have already been used to enhance penalties for cross-burning offenses.

Indeed, these effects-centered approaches are better tailored to serve the government's asserted interest (which, after all, is claimed to focus on effects, not motives). The Wisconsin statute upheld in *Mitchell*, for example, was defended as punishing not bigotry, but the special harms to the victim and others created by "intentional selection of the victim" because of ethnicity. It therefore would apply where a victim is selected because of race, in a situation that has nothing to do with bigotry and creates no risk of the special harms which are said to justify the extra punishment. For example, A goes to her car and sees that the windshield has been smashed. A bystander tells her that the deed was done just a few seconds ago, by an Asian, B, whom she then assaults. A's selection of B was based upon his ethnicity, although it was significant only for identification, not for bias. Nevertheless, the law applies even though none of its purposes are implicated. If it doesn't, then the law demonstrably *is* punishing bigotry, not "intentional selection." At the same time, suppose C, motivated purely by bigotry and with specific intent to create fear and terror in the African-American community, assaults D, a white civil rights activist. C is not guilty under the Wisconsin statute, because D was not selected because of his race, but because of his identification with the civil rights movement.

These results do not make sense. C's actions were intentionally likely to create the racist shock waves the law seeks to prevent and punish; A's were not. The government's interest in preventing and punishing the specific harms and effects associated with hate crimes is not served by exposing A to an extra five years imprisonment, while not reaching C at all.

So why would a legislature insist on a motive-specific, "bump-up" type hate crime law? They do have some advantages over other approaches—for the legislature, anyway. They are quick, they are easy, they get great media coverage, they offend no important constituencies, and they cost nothing. They also punish bigotry, a purpose their proponents deny but which explains why none of the neutral alternatives is satisfactory.

B. Now You See It, Now You Don't: Are Hate Crime Laws About Punishing Bigotry?

Proponents of hate crime laws are hard to pin down on whether the state's interest underlying those laws has anything to do with bigotry. They deny (as they must, to avoid running afoul of the First Amendment) that the government interest underlying these laws has anything to do with suppression of bigotry itself, or of bigoted thought, opinion, or messages. In support of this defense, they assert that these laws do not actually require proof of a *negative* race-related motive. A positive or neutral race-related motive (whatever that could be) will also trigger the statute.

However, when stating the government interest that justifies these laws, proponents assert that bias-motivated crime creates different and worse effects than other crime, has an impact on the victim's entire group, and sends a message of hatred. It is hard to imagine that these are the results of any race-related motive other than bigotry. Moreover, when opponents point out that neutral laws would address these effects even better, the response is that neutral laws fail to send a message of governmental disapproval of bigotry.

It is inconsistent to argue that hate crime laws are not directed at bigotry in one step of the strict scrutiny analysis (assertion of a legitimate and compelling state interest), and then to argue that these laws are directed specifically at bigotry at another step (wherein the state must show that neutral alternatives would not adequately serve the state's interest). But proponents of hate crime laws are forced into playing this shell game, with bigotry as the "pea," because a law specifically punishing bigotry is unconstitutional, and a law punishing all crimes with an ethnic element (even where none of the effects caused by a bias element occurs, is intended, or is foreseeable) is pointless.

The *Mitchell* Court said that "the Wisconsin statute singles out for enhancement bias-inspired conduct because this conduct is thought to inflict greater individual and societal harm. For example, according to the State and its amici, bias-motivated crimes are more likely to provoke retaliatory crimes, inflict distinct emotional harms on their victims, and incite community unrest." However, fears of responsive violence do not justify content- and viewpoint-based restrictions. Motives, like all First Amendment activity, cannot be regulated on the basis of conclusory and speculative assertions of possible future harm. Even statistical evidence of the likelihood of that harm actually occurring would not permit regulation on the basis of content: pornography and even the Super Bowl have been statistically linked to increases in violence against women, but that does not justify their prohibition or punishment.

Moreover, even if it could be reasonably assumed that crimes motivated by bias are more provocative than crimes motivated by greed or need, it cannot similarly be assumed that crimes motivated by one of the subjects enumerated in hate crime laws are more provocative of retaliation or imitation than crimes motivated by politics, gender, abortion, or antiwar sentiment. Nor is there any reason to believe that offenders motivated by ethnic bias are more likely to repeat than offenders who selected their victims "because of" other reasons such as politics or abortion or, for that matter, greed. It is reasonable to assume, in fact, that the defendants in *United States v. O'Brien, Texas v. Johnson, United States v. Eichman*, and *Bray v. Alexandria Women's Health Clinic*, all of whom deliberately acted to make public statements, would be at least as likely as Todd Mitchell, who acted spontaneously, to engage in similar conduct again and to feel no remorse for their actions.

As for the "distinct emotional harms" cause by bias-motivated crimes, the Court in *R.A.V.* stated that these consist of the impact of the defendant's beliefs and the offensiveness of their communication. This harm may well be both real and significant, but in *R.A.V.* the Court had acknowledged that the beliefs and their communications are still squarely within the protection of the First Amendment:

> What makes the anger, fear, sense of dishonor, etc. produced by the violation of this ordinance distinct from the anger, fear, sense of dishonor, etc. produced by other fighting words is nothing other than the fact that it is caused by a distinctive idea, conveyed by a distinctive message. The First Amendment cannot be evaded that easily.

Thus, even if the injuries suffered by the victim or others from hate crimes are "distinct" from the injuries caused by crimes with other motives, the essence of that distinction is something that the government has no power to punish.

Indeed, if government can point to the harmful effects of "a distinctive idea" as a compelling state interest justifying punishment of motives, there is no reason it could not point to those same harmful effects to justify punishing bigoted books, marches, speeches, and associations as well. Nazi demonstrations in Skokie or distribution of *Mein Kampf* would have effects at least as terrifying and widespread as would a battery in which the victim was selected "because of" her being Jewish.

The Satanic Verses causes "special harms" that *A Child's Garden of Verses* does not; *The Last Temptation of Christ* spread resentment that *E.T.* did not; Robert Mapplethorpe's art is more upsetting than Norman Rockwell's; a speech by Louis Farrakhan is more likely to provoke retaliation than a speech by Bill Cosby. Government has the same compelling interest in redressing the same "special harm" irrespective of how it is caused. A state may not constitutionally enact a law stating that "No person shall publish a book that he knows or should know is likely to create the same types of harms as are created by a violation of the statute upheld in *Mitchell*," although its interest would be identical by definition. Understandable and even commendable as this interest may be, it cannot justify a law treating bigoted books differently from other books because the former create special harms. For the same reason, it does not justify hate crime laws, which treat bigoted crimes differently from other crimes because they do exactly the same thing.

III. *What* Mitchell *Could Not Reach: Policy Concerns*

A. *Encouragement of Other Bad Legislation*

Punishment of thought may not seem too terrible when the thought punished is as widely abhorred as bigotry. But proponents of hate crime laws cannot build fail-safe laws that grant government the power to punish motives only when the motives relate to bigotry. Power to punish some motives is power to punish all motives.

If it is constitutional for the government to add penalties for motives related to race and religion, then it is constitutional for government to add penalties for motives relating to Communism, environmental concerns, labor, or anything else. A legislature in a pro-choice jurisdiction might upgrade offenses committed with an *anti*-abortion motive ("by reason of protection of the unborn").

Unfortunately, this is no fanciful hypothetical. In the wake of the recent shootings of abortionists in Pensacola, Mobile, and Wichita, activists on both sides of the abortion debate have been calling for the law to recognize the offenders' anti-abortion motives. Some pro-choice advocates have demanded the enactment of a special trespass offense for abortion clinics, and some pro-life advocates have called for a "justifiable homicide" defense for those motivated by the defense of "innocent boys and girls."

It can get even worse. If the government has the power to *increase* penalties for motives it *does not* like, it also has the power to *decrease* or even eliminate penalties for motives it *does* like. A homophobic legislature could take an offense for which the penalty is three years, upgrade it to eight years if the offender was motivated by race, and *downgrade* it to six months (or even zero) if the offender was motivated by sexual orientation. Preposterous? Sure—but again, quite possible. A bill passed by a broad margin in the Louisiana House of Representatives that would have reduced penalties for battery from six months prison time and a fine of $500, to no prison time and only a $25 fine, *if* the battery was motivated by the victim's having burned an American flag.

Our criminal laws and social policies should not be dictated by which side of a controversy has more clout nor the imminency of the next election. In the case of hate crime laws, the obvious and widespread appeal of the proponents' views makes it seem harmless to punish bigotry-related motives. Unfortunately, viewpoints are more likely to be written into law for the number of votes they represent than for their merit or fairness. In the case of bigotry we may feel popularity and merit coincide; in other areas they will not, but popularity will still carry the day if permitted. That is why we have the Bill of Rights: to protect the individual from the overbearing will—well-intentioned or not—of the majority. Carving out exceptions to please the majority defeats the purpose.

B. Discouragement of Good Legislation

Criminal statutes are poorly suited as tools for creating a tolerant society. Anti-social behavior (criminal or not) seems to thrive in communities where it is tolerated—not in the sense that it is condoned, but where it has become so commonplace that it has lost its power to shock. This seems to be true of many kinds of behaviors, including littering, substance abuse, domestic violence, and owning assault weapons. These things are illegal in all communities, and they also may be equally disapproved of by the majority in all communities. But in some communities these things are still shocking; in others, they are not. People still disapprove, but they have learned to accept the behavior as a fact of life; wrong but not a taboo.

Community taboos prevent anti-social behavior better than criminal penalties do. All the "anti-hate" laws in the world won't stop people from believing and expressing bigoted views as well as would a general understanding that their own communities reject bigotry and reject the bigots themselves. The law cannot make hatred shocking nor bigots pariahs; only the community, over time, can do that. Perhaps this is an endorsement of pressure to conform to political correctness. Still, there is a world of difference between social pressure and government force for the same ends.

C. Disproportionate Enforcement Against Minorities

Hate crime laws invite disproportionate enforcement against minority group members. In December 1993, Klanwatch, a project of the Southern Poverty Law Center whose hate crime data tracking system is considered one of the most reliable available, reported that "[h]ate violence committed by blacks in the United States is 'escalating at an alarming rate.'" Forty-one percent of all racially motivated murders so far that year had been committed by blacks, or blacks had been arrested as suspects. The figure was 46% for 1991-1993, although Klanwatch had documented only one racially motivated murder committed by a black in 1990 and none in 1989.

F.B.I. statistics showed the same trend. Pursuant to the Hate Crime Statistics Act of 1990, the F.B.I. released statistics for the first time in February 1993. The data, supplied by 2,771 law enforcement agencies in 32 states, disclosed that members of minority groups are being charged with "hate crimes" in numbers far in excess of their proportion to the population.

Conclusion

Proponents of hate crime laws surely have the finest of intentions. People of good will everywhere share the vision of a society free from the curses of bigotry, hate, and violence. However, an incursion into liberty is no less prohibited when employed in the name of good than when employed in the name of evil, and is no less dangerous.

One generation's faith in its own good intentions and judgment must not blind it to the reality that the license it grants to itself today will someday be inherited by others, perhaps less committed to the ideas of brotherhood and tolerance. Had a hate crime law been in force in Alabama in 1964 when Dr. Martin Luther King, Jr. held a civil rights demonstration without complying with a permit law, he could have been subject to drastically greater penalties.

Moreover, if our ultimate goal is not just to redress the criminal fruits of intolerance, but to eliminate intolerance altogether, our best hope lies outside of laws like these. In *Texas v. Johnson* the Supreme Court said: "We do not consecrate the flag by punishing its desecration, for in doing so we dilute the freedom that this cherished emblem represents." So it is with hate crime laws: we will not cure bigotry by punishing it, nor teach tolerance by being intolerant. Locking up or silencing the bigots among us will bring only the illusion of mutual acceptance and respect.

Fortunately, government need not choose between punishing thought of which it disapproves on the one hand, and standing silently by while people suffer on the other. Government is free to espouse the ideals of mutual tolerance and even to punish those who, in rejecting those ideals, hurt others. It must simply do so in a way that is as faithful to our commitment to liberty as it is to our aspirations to equality.

APPENDIX A: SECTION 27

Corporate Criminality

DISCUSSION MATERIALS
Issue: Should Criminal Liability Be Imposed upon a Legal Fiction, Such as a Corporation?
    John Coffee, Corporate Criminal Responsibility
    Daniel R. Fischel & Alan O. Sykes, Corporate Crime
    Lawrence Friedman, In Defense of Corporate Criminal Liability
    Andrew Ashworth, A New Form of Corporate Liability?
ADVANCED MATERIALS
    Hypothetical: Collapse at Kalahoo No. 3
    Notes on Vicarious Liability, Including Liability of Corporate Officials

✴ DISCUSSION MATERIALS

Issue: Should Criminal Liability Be Imposed upon a Legal Fiction, Such as a Corporation?

John Coffee proposes various utilitarian arguments in favor of imposing corporate criminal liability but also points to the potential efficacy of using the civil justice system instead. Fischel and Sykes criticize corporate criminal liability as it leads to overdeterrence and excessive investment of resources in litigation. Lawrence Friedman presents an argument in favor of corporate criminality for its ability to provide retributive justice. Finally, Andrew Ashworth evaluates an alternative, prevention-seeking approach to corporate criminal liability, proposed by Fisse and Braithwaite, which would impose requirements on corporations that maintain the criminal label but are distinct from that which is required of individuals.

John Coffee, Corporate Criminal Responsibility
1 Encyclopedia of Crime and Justice 253, 256-261 (S. Kadish ed., 1983)

A Policy Appraisal: Is Corporate Criminal Liability Useful? "Corporations don't commit crimes; people do." This theme (borrowed, of course, from the opponents of gun control) has been implicit in a substantial body of legal commentary that has criticized the idea of corporate criminal liability. The criticism has had two quite different focal points: (1) the asserted injustice of vicarious criminal liability; and the alleged inefficiency of corporate liability. The following critiques have been repeatedly made. First, with respect to the rationale underlying corporate liability, it has been claimed that:

1. Vicarious liability is appropriate only as a principle of tort law since its justification lies in its allocation of the loss to the party more able to bear it (or at least more deserving of the burden), but it is unrelated to the purposes of retribution, deterrence, prevention, and rehabilitation that underlie the criminal law. . . .
2. Vicarious liability is unjust because its burden falls on the innocent rather than the guilty—that is, the penalty is borne by stockholders and others having an interest in the corporation, rather than by the guilty individual. . . .
3. Vicarious liability results in a disparity between businesses conducted in the corporate form and those run as a proprietorship, since the individual proprietor will not be criminally liable for the independent acts of his employees. . . .
4. Vicarious liability for the corporation may in the future open the door to expanded vicarious criminal liability for individuals as well.

Second, a number of arguments have been advanced to claim that corporate punishment is inefficient or even counterproductive [detailed below]:

1. Corporations are largely undeterrable; fines are ineffective, and only the imprisonment of guilty individuals achieves real deterrence. . . .
2. Prosecution of the corporation may lead courts, juries, and prosecutors to acquit or dismiss charges against individual defendants, and thus corporate liability serves as a shield behind which the truly guilty can hide. . . .
3. Civil remedies are more flexible and potentially severe, and they also avoid the constitutional restrictions associated with a criminal prosecution. . . .

Although none of these arguments is frivolous, each on closer examination seems seriously overbroad or at least unconfirmed by the relatively slim empirical evidence available. . . .

The Utility of Corporate Punishment   Some critics of corporate liability have doubted whether the corporation itself can be deterred. Such an evaluation seems premature, however, given another conclusion which virtually every commentator on the subject has reached: that corporations tend to receive very small fines in relation to their size, their earnings, or even their expected gain from the criminal transaction. . . . Thus, it is logically difficult to assert simultaneously that corporations are not punished and that they are not deterrable.

But here a problem noted earlier resurfaces: corporate punishment tends to fall on the innocent—not only on stockholders but also on employees (who may be laid off), creditors, the surrounding community, and, of course, the consumer, who may in effect indemnify the corporation if the fine can be passed on as a cost of doing business. Thus, an apparent paradox is reached: the economist's model asserts that only the imposition of severe fines in an amount well in excess of the expected gain will generate adequate deterrence, since it is necessary to compensate for a risk-of-apprehension factor that invariably falls well below 100 percent. But if corporate penalties are escalated in this fashion, the remedy may be worse than the disease, because layoffs, plant closings, and the threatened insolvency of major corporate institutions may be a more adverse result than the financial loss suffered by consumers or the government as a result of price-fixing or tax fraud. . . .

This problem suggests the desirability of corporate penalties that minimize "overspill." . . .

An argument frequently made against corporate liability is that it may interfere with the assignment of individual liability. Here, anecdotal evidence does suggest that juries have sometimes compromised, acquitting all individual defendants while convicting the corporation. . . . The pervasiveness of this pattern cannot be estimated. Still, public-opinion surveys suggest that many white-collar crimes are no longer viewed as mere "regulatory" or technical violations but are ranked relatively high on a scale of seriousness, and consequently this pattern of jury reluctance to convict individual defendants for white-collar crimes may be a declining phenomenon. In any event, the prosecution always has the option of not prosecuting the corporation—or, at least, of not doing so in the same proceeding. . . .

Still another perspective on the potential utility of corporate criminal liability begins from the much repeated observation that it is frequently difficult to identify the "true" culprit within a firm. Although the point is undoubtedly correct, its truth may lie less in the ability of the "true" culprit to hide his identity than in the absence of any such "true" offender in a broad range of cases. From a social-science perspective, it is virtually a truism that knowledge may exist collectively within an organization, even though it is not localized within any one individual. . . . [I]t is likely that information will exist at one level of an organization that would alter decisions at another, but no mechanism will necessarily force the transmission of this information to where it is needed. Some federal decisions appear to have responded already to such considerations by recognizing a "collective knowledge" doctrine, under which the corporation may be held liable even though no single individual had the requisite information. . . .

These problems indicate one inadequacy of an exclusive focus on the individual decision maker: recurrently, it is unlikely that any single individual within the corporate hierarchy will have the requisite intent, and yet the firm as an entity may have knowledge of an unsafe design, a carcinogenic risk, or a dangerous side effect that its products can cause. In this light, the argument for corporate liability rests not only on the evidentiary problems of identifying the "true" culprit but on the organizational reality that there may be no actual individual culprit at all, because of the diffusion of responsibility within the corporate hierarchy. Moreover, an insistence on finding a responsible individual decision maker might produce a scapegoat system of criminal justice, in which lower-echelon operating officials would probably bear the primary responsibility and risk exposure.

The forgoing arguments focus on the problem of cognitive failures within the corporation's internal information processing as a justification for corporate liability. An alternative justification proceeds from the motivational failures that also accompany the corporate form. Almost inevitably, there is an incongruence between the interests of the manager and those of the firm as an entity: criminal behavior may be attractive to the pressured or ambitious manager, even if it is not to the corporation. Compounding this problem is the tendency for conflicting

signals to issue from the senior levels of the corporate hierarchy to the middle ech-
elons, which tend to be the locus of criminal behavior. Such signals may formally
require obedience to law, but they also demand and reward short-term profit
maximization. The implicit signal may thus be read by middle-level managers as
meaning only "don't get caught." Of course, individual criminal liability may partially countervail this pressure on the middle manager. But even if the severity of
the criminal sanction vastly exceeds that of the counterthreats the corporation can
make, such as dismissal, demotion, or forgone promotion, the absolute severity of
the sanction must be discounted by its probability of imposition. . . . This means
that the discounted threat of apprehension and conviction by the state for a criminal offense may be less than that of the strong likelihood of internal discipline or
dismissal by the corporation for failure to maximize profits. Thus, the manager
faces both public and private sanction, and the latter, although lesser in gravity,
tend[s] to be higher in probability, making the outcome uncertain and possibly
dependent on the level of risk-aversion of the individual manager.

   The Alternative of Civil Remedies   Corporate sanctions may be necessary,
but it's far from clear that such sanctions must be criminal in nature. Civil penalties are now utilized by many, if not most, administrative agencies. Moreover, a
system of civil penalties offers some obvious advantages to the prosecutor. First,
the corporation could not claim the protection of constitutional rights, such as the
"reasonable doubt" standard or double jeopardy, that are applicable only to criminal proceedings. Second, the possibility of judicial or jury nullification is reduced
because of the lesser stigma. Third, courts of equity traditionally have been more
able than criminal courts to fashion flexible and novel forms of relief. Thus, from
the standpoint of specific deterrence and incapacitation, some have concluded the
civil penalties offer significant advantages over criminal law enforcement in the
case of the corporation. . . .

   In this light, what arguments remain for the use of the criminal law as a
preferred legislative strategy? Little agreement exists here, but the following
arguments deserve consideration. First, the criminal law has long been thought
uniquely capable of performing an educative role in defining and reinforcing the
boundaries of acceptable conduct. The civil law's quieter, less theatrical character
limits its ability to perform this socializing function. Closely allied to this point
is the criminal law's ability to stigmatize and employ publicity as a sanction. The
highly publicized prosecution of the Ford Motor Company in 1979 for the allegedly unsafe design of the Pinto illustrates this capacity of the criminal process.
Second, the criminal law characteristically moves at a faster pace than the civil law.
Thus, to the extent that restitution is an authorized sentence, the criminal law
can serve as the engine by which to obtain victim compensation more quickly.
In addition, because the double jeopardy clause does not preclude a successive
civil prosecution after an acquittal in a criminal trial, the prosecutor can in effect
obtain a second chance by proceeding first criminally and then civilly.

   Third, courts of equity have traditionally been barred from imposing penalties, and although this does not amount to a constitutional barrier, there may
linger a reluctance on the part of courts when operating in a civil mode to pursue
deterrent objectives. The basic format of the civil enforcement proceeding also
has yet to be resolved, and the fairness and reliability of administratively determined civil penalties is a matter of serious dispute.

Finally, joint prosecutions of the corporation and its agents require a criminal forum if the threat of incarceration is to be used to deter individuals. From a law enforcement perspective, such joint trials are desirable both because they are less costly than separate prosecutions and because they permit one prosecutor to pursue the case in an integrated fashion; a separate persecution, particularly if pursued in a different forum, might require a different prosecutor.

At most, these arguments suggest that corporate prosecutions for truly significant violations might best remain in a criminal courtroom, but they do not deny that corporate prosecutions for many regulatory and strict liability offenses, which today fit awkwardly at best within the criminal process, could be safely transferred to the civil process.

Daniel R. Fischel & Alan O. Sykes, Corporate Crime
25 Journal of Legal Studies 320 (1996)

. . . As accepted as it is today, this doctrine of corporate criminal liability is a relatively modern innovation in American law. Corporations are legal fictions, and legal fictions cannot commit criminal acts. Nor can they possess mens rea, a guilty state of mind. Only people can act and only people can have a guilty state of mind. For these reasons, it was accepted at common law and until the early 1900s in the United States that only people could commit crimes. Corporations might bear civil liability for crimes committed by agents acting within the scope of employment, but corporate criminal liability did not exist.

. . . The doctrine of corporate criminal liability has developed, however, without any theoretical justification. The law and economics literature, for example, is largely devoid of any discussion of vicarious criminal liability.

Our argument focuses on the obvious fact that corporations cannot be imprisoned; they can only be forced to pay money damages. The essential question, then, is whether the criminal law has any useful role to play in setting the damages that firms must pay for the wrongful acts of their agents. This in turn is really two questions: (1) when should the government rather than private parties sue for damages, and (2) in those cases where the government is the preferred plaintiff, when should the action be criminal rather than civil? The answers to these two questions are, respectively, sometimes and never. Although there are cases where government fines and penalties make sense, the civil liability system is better suited to calculate appropriate fines and penalties for organizational defendants. At best, the case for corporate criminal liability must rest on the need to correct some deficiency in the system of civil liability. But a close look at the cases reveals no such deficiency most of the time. Instead, corporate criminal liability is often heaped on top of substantial civil liability in circumstances where there is no reason to believe that civil liability alone would not produce appropriate deterrence. The result is overdeterrence ex ante, and an excessive investment of resources in litigation ex post. . . .

Individual Crime, Corporate Crime, and Optimal Internal Monitoring

If the wisdom of corporate criminal liability is in doubt, what distinguishes it from criminal liability for individuals, which has long been accepted as necessary and desirable? We begin with this most obvious of questions.

First, individual criminal liability can be useful when individuals lack assets to pay monetary judgments against them. Indeed, it is a lack of resources on the part of individuals that motivates many crimes. Monetary penalties are an ineffective deterrent to the extent that they cannot be paid, and the state can employ incarceration and related measures as a substitute against individual criminals. Of course, corporations may also lack the resources to pay monetary penalties against them, but the alternative of incarceration is not available for them.

Second, criminal penalties against individuals may in many instances be justified on grounds of incapacitation. Individuals who are incarcerated are largely disabled from committing additional crimes. But again, even if certain corporations employ agents with a propensity for further criminal activity, criminal penalties against the corporation do nothing to incapacitate them—personal criminal liability is the needed response.

Third, and more often misunderstood, the criminal justice system rarely makes any attempt to set the penalty equal to the social harm caused by the crime, a policy that *may* make sense in setting the level of sanctions against individual criminals. But sanctions uncalibrated to the level of harm can have quite a pernicious effect when the target of a sanction is a corporation. Because this point is so important, we will elaborate at some length.

Any legal system must decide whether to sanction particular types of activity, and if so by how much. As a broad generalization, activities that create no harm or create no increased risk of harm are not subject to sanctions. The law need not deter this type of conduct. And when the law does penalize conduct when the harm to third parties is not obvious (criminal penalties for prostitution being a prominent example), the resulting legal rules and expenditures on enforcement are inevitably controversial.

Other activities may impose harm on third parties but also may create benefits. The decision to breach a contract, for example, may harm the nonbreaching party but still may be beneficial if any loss is less than the resulting gains to the breaching party. Similarly, a decision not to invest resources to prevent an accident may result in harm to a third party if an accident occurs, but this loss must be balanced against the resources saved. The goal of legal rules in these examples and countless others where conduct creates gains and losses is conditional deterrence—to deter conduct only when the losses to third parties outweigh the gains.

Still other activities impose harm on third parties with little or no prospect of any offsetting benefits. Intentional harms such as murder and theft, for example, are presumptively undesirable in virtually all cases. Punitive damages in excess of actual harm caused and stiff criminal penalties *may* make sense for this type of conduct because overdeterrence is not a concern—any objection to penalties in excess of the harm caused must relate instead to an attendant increase in administrative costs, an increase that may be offset by the avoidance of the cost of calculating the harm caused.

But when penalties are levied at the corporate level, the analysis changes. Corporations are webs of contractual relationships consisting of individuals who band together for their mutual economic benefit. Except in the case of very small corporate entities, offenses that are labeled "corporate crimes" inevitably involve harmful actions by some corporate actors without the knowledge or consent of other contracting parties within the firm. The question in designing the appropriate legal rule, therefore, is what penalty should nonparticipants face for the harmful acts of the participants—put differently, what is the proper level of "vicarious" liability? This in turn depends primarily on the question of how much monitoring nonparticipants should engage in to prevent participants from committing crimes.

It is plainly undesirable for firms to invest infinite resources to prevent their agents' parties from committing crimes, even if those crimes themselves are clearly unproductive. Rather, monitoring is desirable, as first approximation, up to the point at which its marginal cost would exceed the marginal social gain in the form of reduced social harm from criminal activity. The task of the law, then, is to create an incentive for firms to engage in this level of monitoring.

Subject to some caveats that we discuss below in Section *B*, a penalty equal to the social harm caused by the crimes of corporate agents, adjusted if necessary for the probability that such crimes will escape detection, will achieve this objective. Ex ante, firms will then anticipate a penalty equal to the social cost of their agents' crimes, so that the private gains from monitoring and the social gains will converge.

Likewise, a penalty in excess of the social cost of the crime (adjusted for the probability of nondetection) will cause the private gains from monitoring to exceed the social gains. The result will be an inefficiently high level of investment in monitoring. And, because the costs of excessive monitoring must be recovered through prices, improperly high penalties create additional inefficiencies because the price of goods or services produced by corporations will exceed their social costs. Finally, higher penalties raise the stakes in litigation and tend to produce socially unproductive litigation costs.

This overdeterrence problem is most obvious when a lower level corporate agent commits a harm without the knowledge, approval, or consent of the board of directors. Excessive levels of damages will lead managers to invest too much in the avoidance of future liability by such agents. But what about the case where the entire board of directors approves an illegal act? To be sure, this conduct is unlikely to occur very often in practice. Corporate agents have weaker incentives to commit crimes than do individuals who are not agents because they must share the gains from the offense with the firm while bearing the full risk of punishment by the state. Involvement of others—the full board of directors—only increases the probability of detection. When these factors are combined with the fact that corporate executives are presumptively risk averse and will face additional penalties if caught in the form of damage to reputation and future earning capacity, this example is probably not very realistic.

But suppose it is, at least some of the time. Does the involvement of board members or top managers affect the analysis? The answer is no—it remains the case that the corporation should bear no more than the social cost of harm caused by crime, adjusted for the chance of nondetection, and the reason is once again in part the problem of excessive monitoring. Whatever the level of authority at which a decision is taken, there will always be opportunities for shareholders to utilize additional auditors, independent directors, consultants, and the like to economize on any attendant liability. If the expected cost of crime to the corporation exceeds its social cost, the incentive to utilize such measures will be excessive. Moreover, when the penalty exceeds the social harm, the problem of socially excessive product prices and litigation costs again arises.

Lawrence Friedman, In Defense of Corporate Criminal Liability

23 Harvard Journal of Law & Public Policy 833 (1999-2000)

The critics of corporate criminal liability assume that deterrence of unlawful conduct is the exclusive aim of corporate liability regimes. Deterrence traditionally has been viewed as a central justification for criminal liability generally, in conjunction with rehabilitation and incapacitation.[1] Deterrence offers a consequentialist rationale for criminal liability, in the sense that deterrence is concerned with promoting "certain socially desirable consequences," or "good" ends. The potential imposition of punishment for wrongdoing accordingly serves to encourage lawful behavior by creating incentives to engage in responsible conduct. Optimal deterrence of misconduct in the corporate context requires that the law offer such incentives up to "the point at which . . . marginal cost would exceed the marginal social gain in the form of reduced social harm" from unlawful activity. As . . . Fischel and Sykes demonstrate, economic analysis indicates that on the whole, civil liability regimes may deter unlawful conduct in the corporate context more efficiently than criminal liability regimes.

But deterrence has never been regarded as the sole justification for criminal liability. Retribution, too, has long been seen as providing normative support for criminal liability regimes. Oliver Wendell Holmes, Jr., in 1881 acknowledged the view that "the fitness of punishment following wrong-doing" could be regarded as "axiomatic."[2] Holmes was referring to principles whose origins may be traced to the classical, retributive framework of Immanuel Kant. Under Kant's theory, individuals in civil society have an intrinsic human dignity that is denied them when the state seeks to employ the criminal justice system to serve consequentialist ends, such as deterrence. To accord an individual's inherent dignity the appropriate respect, the state must punish individuals who violate the law because they have violated the law and only because they have violated the law—without regard, that is, for the consequences that might flow from the imposition of punishment.

To illustrate this theory of retribution, Kant explained:

> Even if a civil society were to dissolve itself by common agreement of all its members (for example, if the people inhabiting an island decided to separate and disperse themselves around the world), the last murderer remaining in prison must first be executed, so that everyone will duly receive what his actions are worth and so that the bloodguilt thereof will not be fixed on the people because they failed to insist on carrying out the punishment. . . . [3]

While this illustration, as H. L. A. Hart remarked, "may well be a parody of modern retributivism,"[4] the pure Kantian theory nonetheless remains a benchmark in discussing retributive theories of punishment in the criminal justice context.

---

1. See *Developments in the Law—Corporate Crime: Regulating Corporate Behavior Through Criminal Sanctions*, 92 Harv. L. Rev. 1227, 1231 (1979) [hereinafter *Developments*].

2. Oliver Wendell Holmes, Jr., The Common Law 42, 45 (Little, Brown 1923) (1881).

3. See Immanuel Kant, Metaphysical Elements of Justice 140 (John Ladd trans., Hackett Pub. Co. 1999) (1797).

4. H. L. A. Hart, Punishment and Responsibility: Essays in the Philosophy of Law 232 (1968).

Expressive theory offers an alternative and, perhaps, more palatable, retributive rationale for criminal liability. This approach reflects the sense that the commission of an act the community, through its laws, deems wrong should be met with disapprobation for the sake of the victim and the sake of the community. The expressive view posits:

> Social norms enable rational behavior by defining how persons (or communities) who value particular goods—whether the welfare of other persons, their own honor or dignity, or the beauty of the natural environment—should behave. Actions that conform to, or defy, these norms thus express a person's (or a community's) attitude toward these goods.[5]

On this view, conduct that evinces disrespect for established valuations of persons and goods is regarded as criminal. For example,

> [a]long one dimension—say, personal wealth—theft might hurt a person as much as being outperformed by a business competitor. The reason that theft but not competition is a crime . . . is that against the background of social norms theft expresses disrespect for the injured party's worth, whereas competition (at least ordinarily) does not.[6]

Criminal liability in turn expresses the community's condemnation of the wrongdoer's conduct by emphasizing the standards for appropriate behavior—that is, the standards by which persons and goods properly should be valued.

The expressive retributivist's commitment is "to assert[] moral truth in the face of its denial."[7] Criminal liability asserts this truth by countering "the appearance of the wrongdoer's superiority and thus affirm[ing] the victim's real value." The expressive rationale, like deterrence theory, is instrumental: There is, as Jean Hampton maintains, a telos to the expressive design. The expressive goal is "to establish goodness" by reinforcing the understanding among community members that persons and goods should be valued in certain ways. Contrary to a pure, Kantian view of retribution, then, the expressive approach can be regarded as consequentialist, a means to an end.

Notwithstanding the frequent invocation of deterrence to justify criminal justice regimes, retributive theories continue to provide viable rationales for the criminal law. . . .

[D]eterrence and efficiency are not the only interests in play. There is also the interest in expressive retribution, which provides reason enough not to dispense entirely with corporate criminal liability. Absent the possibility of criminal liability, corporations would escape moral condemnation for wrongdoing, and the retributive import of criminal liability to the community would be lost. For under a civil liability regime for the corporation qua corporation, there would be no moral condemnation equivalent to a criminal conviction: if found civilly liable, a corporation might be deemed negligent, or perhaps reckless, but no statement, in the form of a conviction, would attest to the proper valuation of the persons

---

5. See Dan M. Kahan & Martha C. Nussbaum, *Two Conceptions of Emotion in Criminal Law*, 96 COLUM. L. REV. 269, 351 (1996).

6. Dan M. Kahan, *What Do Alternative Sanctions Mean?*, 63 U. CHI. L. REV. 591, 597-98 (1996).

7. Jean Hampton, The Retributive Idea, in Jeffrie G. Murphy & Jean Hampton, Forgiveness and Mercy 111, 125 (1988); see also Kahan, supra note 48, at 598 (noting that by imposing criminal liability, "society says, in effect, that the offender's assessment of whose interests count is wrong").

or goods at issue. In the end, the financial liability imposed would come to be viewed, by both the corporation and the community, merely as a cost of doing business.

In effect, then, a corporate civil liability regime that paralleled ordinary criminal liability for individuals charged with the same wrongdoing would allow the corporation qua corporation to purchase exemption from moral condemnation. Such exemption would affect the expressive significance of criminal liability, as the vindication of the proper valuations of persons and goods would vary not with the conduct alleged—a distinction that rightly could affect the evaluative standard employed—but, rather, with the identity of the offender. The value of human health and safety, for example, would be regarded as less sacrosanct when denied by corporations as opposed to individuals. Thus corporate exemption from criminal liability would tend to undermine the condemnatory effect of criminal liability on individuals in respect to similar conduct—and, ultimately, to diminish the moral authority of the criminal law as a guide to rational behavior.

Andrew Ashworth, A New Form of Corporate Liability?
Principles of Criminal Law 86-88 (1991)

The theoretical arguments in favor of corporate criminal liability seem strong, but developments at common law have made [such liability] possible only to a limited extent [in England]. An alternative strategy of placing the emphasis on individual liability would be unlikely to work. Any particular individual might be dispensable within a corporation (e.g. the "Company Vice-President responsible for going to [jail]"), allowing the company [to] continue on its course with minimal disruption; or it might be difficult to identify the individual responsible, not least because companies sometimes have convoluted lines of accountability. A further alternative strategy would be to rely even more on new offenses of strict liability to punish corporate harm-doing, but this might not be a sufficient response to some [disasters], or to other harm-doing on a broad scale.

Reasoning of this kind has led to Fisse and Braithwaite's entirely new approach to corporate criminal liability, using concepts not applicable to individuals.[8] Their strategy rests on three key elements: "enforced accountability"; a new concept of corporate fault; and a fresh approach to sanctions. The idea of "enforced accountability" is that the law should recognize the complexity of lines of accountability in some corporations, and, rather than expending prosecutorial energy and court time trying to disentangle them, should require a company which has caused or threatened a proscribed harm to take its own disciplinary and rectificatory measures. The State should order the company to activate its own private justice system, and a court should then assess the adequacy of the measures taken. As this suggests, the concept of fault would then become a *post hoc* phenomenon. Rather than struggling to establish some antecedent fault within the

---

8. B. Fisse and J. Braithwaite, T*he Allocation of Responsibility for Corporate Crime: Individualism, Collectivism and Accountability* (1988) 11 SYDNEY L. R. 468; see also L. H. Leight, *The Criminal Liability of Corporations and Other Groups* (1977) 9 OTTAWA L. R. 247; and J. Braithwaite, Corporate Crime in the Pharmaceutical Industry (1984).

corporation, the prosecution would invite the court to infer fault from the nature and effectiveness of the company's remedial measures after it had been established that it was the author of a harm-causing or harm-threatening act or omission. The court would not find fault if it was persuaded that the company had taken realistic measures to prevent a recurrence, had ensured compensation to any victims, and had taken the event seriously in other respects. This "reactive corporate fault" is a far cry from the notions of *mens rea* and prior fault which dominate criminal-law doctrine. The third element in the scheme is that the courts should be able to impose new penalties, specially designed for application to companies. Under the present system, a company can hardly be imprisoned, moderate fines can be swallowed up as business overheads, and swinging fines might have such drastic side-effects on the employment and livelihoods of innocent employees as to render them inappropriate. The proposal is for a range of special penalties, some of which are rehabilitative (putting corporations on probation to supervise their compliance with the law), some of which are deterrent (punitive injunctions to require resources to be devoted to the development of new preventive measures), and others of which have mixed aims (e.g. community service by companies).

Fisse and Braithwaite's proposals for a radically new legal regime for corporate crime are grounded in arguments of prevention. They emphasize the enormity of the harms which corporations both cause and risk causing, and contend that the primary search should be for a regime which ensures maximum prevention. This is inconsistent with an approach to liability and punishment based on "just deserts": the authors explicitly reject the idea of holding corporations criminally liable according to their culpability in causing the harms, not merely because it is difficult in practice to make such enquiries, but also because they believe that the prevention of future harm is of greater social importance in this sphere than any abstract notion of "justice" based on past events.[9] "Desert" theory would, however, make a clearer distinction between preventive measures and conviction and sentence. In principle, punishment for corporations, no less than for individuals, should be proportioned to culpability: if that proves impossible in practice, for the reasons given by Fisse and Braithwaite, then that is an argument for legal presumptions or other special doctrines, but not for abandoning the distinctive aims of the criminal law and punishment. Broader preventive measures, perhaps through regulatory mechanisms, should be put in hand in order to reduce the risk of further harms from similar sources.

✳ ADVANCED MATERIALS

Hypothetical: Collapse at Kalahoo No. 3

Curt Calomen is operator of Kalahoo Mine, a small incorporated mining operation. Earl Single is his foreman. Mine inspectors frequently cite Kalahoo for

---

9. See further John Braithwaite, *Challenging Just Deserts: Punishing White Collar Criminals* (1982) 73 J. CRIM. LAW & CRIMINOLOGY 723, and the reply by Andrew von Hirsch, *Desert and White Collar Criminality: A Reply to Dr. Braithwaite*, id. at 1164.

safety violations, but none are serious enough to lead the inspectors to close the mine.

One day, Single, who is paid under a bonus system based on tonnage mined, insists on skipping the normal shoring procedures to meet his monthly bonus quota. Some miners object, but they are threatened with dismissal if they refuse to go along. Several hours later, an unshored section of Tunnel No. 3 collapses. Seven miners are hurt in the collapse; two are killed, including foreman Single.

Calomen is charged with two counts of manslaughter for failing to ensure compliance with mining safety rules while knowing that such failure created a risk of cave-in causing serious injury or death. Calomen argues that he always instructed Single to comply with mining safety rules and, beyond that, he left mine operations to Single. Like most owner-operators, he rarely visits the mining operations himself. He points out that Single was fully qualified and certified for the position he held.

Is Calomen liable for two counts of manslaughter?

Notes on Vicarious Liability, Including Liability of Corporate Officials

Disfavor of vicarious criminal liability
Limitations on vicarious liability
Situations where vicarious liability has been allowed
Arguments in favor of vicarious liability
    Similarity to arguments in favor of strict liability
MPC rejects vicarious liability, but allows corporate officer liability
    Example: How MPC would treat *Park* case
Analysis of "Collapse" hypothetical under MPC
Analysis of "Collapse" hypothetical under *Park*

Disfavor of vicarious criminal liability The standard requirements of complicity are sometimes abandoned when the law imposes what is often called *vicarious liability*. Like complicity, vicarious liability holds an actor liable for another's conduct. Vicarious liability, however, permits imputation of another's conduct without proof of the significant culpability that complicity provisions normally require, and sometimes without proof of aid or assistance to the perpetrator. The modest requirements for imposition of vicarious liability are often criticized as insufficient to support criminal liability.

Limitations on vicarious liability While a host of criminal statutes purport to authorize vicarious liability, courts have interpreted federal and state constitutional provisions to limit its use. In *State v. Akers*, for example, the New Hampshire Supreme Court barred the vicarious liability of parents, based solely upon the parent-child relationship and no other ground of accountability, for criminal acts of their children.[10] The defendant fathers' criminal liability for the unlawful snowmobiling of their minor sons was overturned as a violation of the state constitution's due process clause. In *Davis v. City of Peachtree City*, the Supreme Court of Georgia invalidated ordinances subjecting employer tavern-owners to

---

10. 400 A.2d 38 (N.H. 1979) (imposing criminal liability vicariously because of parental status, without more, would violate due process).

criminal liability for employee actions taken without the employer's knowledge, consent, or authorization, holding that such laws violated the due process clauses of the constitutions of both Georgia and the United States. According to the Court, such criminal liability is justified only upon proof of some culpability on the employer's part.[11]

Situations where vicarious liability has been allowed   On the other hand, in *Taylor v. Superior Court*, the defendant was held liable for the killing of his accomplice by a store owner whom he and his accomplice were in the process of robbing. The California Supreme Court upheld his conviction for murder even though no proof was required that he was culpable as to the death of his accomplice.[12] In *United States v. Park*, the defendant—the executive officer of Acme Markets, Inc., a corporation with 36,000 employees—appealed his conviction for health and safety violations arising from unsanitary conditions at the firm's Baltimore warehouse.[13] The United States Supreme Court concluded that the Constitution allows imposition of vicarious liability on a corporate official for the conduct or omissions of corporate agents or employees when the official, by virtue of his relationship to the corporation, has the power to prevent the violation.

Arguments in favor of vicarious liability   Supporters of vicarious liability have sought to justify it on several grounds. In *Park*, for example, the Court reasons that vicarious liability will make food distributors more careful. It also suggests that, in fact, defendant Park does bear some personal blameworthiness, because a high duty of care has been imposed on him and he has failed to meet that duty. Liability is not being imposed on the defendant only because of his "status," but rather because he had the power to avoid the violation and failed to do so. The *Park* opinion requires a defense for an official who is "powerless to prevent" the violation. But, apparently, it is not enough for Park to show that he was non-negligent and acted reasonably based on what he knew, because lacking awareness of violations is not the same as lacking the "power" to prevent them.

Similarity to arguments in favor of strict liability   The arguments in support of, and opposing, vicarious liability are analogous to those offered in the context of strict liability. Specifically, strict liability is said to be useful in limited applications because it stimulates caution and imposes only civil-like penalties; therefore, no serious injustice is committed. Yet by the same token, the arguments *against* strict liability can also be made in relation to vicarious liability. Strict liability is considered unjust because it can impose punishment where an actor could not have been expected to avoid the violation and, indeed, where a reasonable person in the actor's situation would not have avoided the violation. If the criminal law's objective is to demand reasonable conduct and to punish as blameworthy those who act unreasonably, then that purpose is served by punishing negligence, but not by imposing strict liability. The *Park* form of vicarious liability may be consistent with a distributive principle that looks only toward maximizing deterrence, but is difficult to justify under a distributive principle that looks to the offender's desert. Some courts, persuaded by these kinds of criticisms of *Park*, have limited its application to impose vicarious liability only for offenses that already allow

---

11. 304 S.E.2d 701 (Ga. 1983).
12. 477 P.2d 131 (Cal. 1970).
13. 421 U.S. 658 (1975).

strict liability. Thus, the conditions for vicarious liability approved in *Park* would be inadequate for an offense requiring a culpable state of mind.[14]

MPC rejects vicarious liability, but allows corporate officer liability The Model Penal Code does not authorize vicarious liability. Conduct of another may be imputed to an actor only as permitted in the Code's complicity provision, section 2.06. Several sections of the Code, however, do make it easier to prosecute a corporate official for the criminal acts of employees and agents of the corporation. Model Penal Code section 2.07(6)(a), for example, makes clear that a corporate official cannot use the corporation as a liability shield for criminal conduct that the official causes others to undertake, even if the official causes that conduct in the name of the corporation. Even more important, section 2.07(6) (b) provides that any legal duty imposed on a corporation is imposed as well on the corporate officials with "primary responsibility for the discharge of the duty." Such officials, like Park, can thus be held personally liable for a "reckless omission" to perform the duty. Neither of these special rules creates vicarious liability in corporate officials, but both may have the effect of broadening the liability of corporate officers for the conduct of agents and employees of the corporation.

Example: How MPC would treat Park case Recall the *Park* case, where the Supreme Court allowed vicarious liability for executive Park based on legal violations at a warehouse. Park might be liable under the Model Penal Code provisions, depending on what conduct he caused to be done, and on whether he satisfied the legal duties imposed on him as representative of the corporation. Park can argue that he did not have primary responsibility to discharge the corporation's duty to keep its warehouses clean. And, even if he did have this duty, a jury might conclude that Park was not reckless in failing to have the warehouses kept clean, as the Code provisions would require. The *Park* decision, in contrast, requires only that Park have a "responsible relation to the situation" and not be "powerless to prevent" the violation.

Analysis of "Collapse" hypothetical under MPC Under the Model Penal Code, operator Calomen in the "Collapse" hypothetical above is accountable for any conduct he performs, or causes another to perform, in the name of the company. Nothing in the facts, though, suggests that he caused Single to violate the safety rules governing shoring. Also, under the Code, Calomen may be personally accountable for performing certain legal duties imposed upon the corporation, such as the duty to shore up as required by safety regulations. Thus, he might be liable for a reckless omission to perform those duties, although he can argue that it was Single, rather than he, who was the officer with "primary responsibility for the discharge of the duty." Even if this were shown, however, it would only establish Calomen's liability for the safety violation. Liability for manslaughter would demand, in addition, that Calomen's breach of duty caused the deaths and that he was reckless as to causing the deaths at the time he failed to perform his legal duty—in other words, the normal requirements of manslaughter. As they are given, the facts of the case do not suggest recklessness as to

---

14. See, e.g., United States v. MacDonald & Watson Waste Oil Co., 933 F.2d 35 (1st Cir. 1991) (conviction of company president for violation of hazardous waste dumping reversed because of erroneous jury instruction that allowed employees' knowledge of improper dumping to be imputed to president, where offense expressly required proof of such knowledge by defendant).

causing death, but one can easily imagine a case in which such recklessness on the owner-operator's part could exist.

Analysis of "Collapse" hypothetical under *Park* *Park*, in contrast, would seem to allow liability for Calomen based on his status as executive officer of the company, which makes him responsible for the conduct of his foreman Single. As to whether Calomen was "powerless to prevent" the violation, one can argue that, while Calomen might not have been physically able to stop Single on the occasion at hand—because he was not present—he (Calomen) did have the authority to set conditions that would have avoided a situation like this occurring. It seems unlikely, however, that the Supreme Court would be as tolerant of strict and vicarious liability where, as here, a substantial penalty—manslaughter liability—is to be imposed, rather than simply the fine at stake in *Park*.

MODEL PENAL CODE SELECTED PROVISIONS

TABLE OF CONTENTS

Part I. General Provisions

Article 1. Preliminary

Article 2. General Principles of Liability

Article 3. General Principles of Justification

Article 4. Responsibility

Part II. Definition of Specific Crimes

Offenses Involving Danger to the Person

Article 210. Criminal Homicide

Article 211. Assault; Reckless Endangering; Threats

Article 212. Kidnapping and Related Offenses; Coercion

Article 213. Sexual Offenses

Offenses Against the Family

Article 230. Offenses Against the Family

Offenses Against Public Administration

Article 240. Bribery and Corrupt Influence

Article 241. Perjury and Other Falsification in Official Matters

Article 242. Obstructing Governmental Operations; Escapes

Article 243. Abuse of Office

Offenses Against Public Order and Decency

Article 250. Riot, Disorderly Conduct, and Related Offenses

Article 251. Public Indecency

Model Penal Code Selected Provisions
[Copyright 1962, 2007 by The American Law Institute]

Part I. General Provisions

Article 1. Preliminary

Section 1.01. Title and Effective Date.

(1) This Act is called the Penal and Correctional Code and may be cited as P.C.C. It shall become effective on

(2) Except as provided in Subsections (3) and (4) of this Section, the Code does not apply to offenses committed prior to its effective date and prosecutions for such offenses shall be governed by the prior law, which is continued in effect for that purpose, as if this Code were not in force. For the purposes of this Section, an offense was committed prior to the effective date of the Code if any of the elements of the offense occurred prior thereto.

(3) In any case pending on or after the effective date of the Code, involving an offense committed prior to such date:

(a) procedural provisions of the Code shall govern, insofar as they are justly applicable and their application does not introduce confusion or delay;

(b) provisions of the Code according a defense or mitigation shall apply, with the consent of the defendant;

(c) the Court, with the consent of the defendant, may impose sentence under the provisions of the Code applicable to the offense and the offender.

(4) Provisions of the Code governing the treatment and the release or discharge of prisoners, probationers and parolees shall apply to persons under sentence for offenses committed prior to the effective date of the Code, except that the minimum or maximum period of their detention or supervision shall in no case be increased.

Section 1.02(2). Purposes; Principles of Construction.

. . .

(2) The general purposes of the provisions governing sentencing and corrections, to be discharged by the many official actors within the sentencing and corrections system, are:

(a) in decisions affecting the sentencing and correction of individual offenders:

(i) to render punishment within a range of severity proportionate to the gravity of offenses, the harms done to crime victims, and the blameworthiness of offenders;

(ii) when possible with realistic prospect of success, to serve goals of offender rehabilitation, general deterrence, incapacitation of dangerous offenders, and restoration of crime victims and communities, provided that these goals are pursued within the boundaries of sentence severity permitted in subsection (a)(i); and

(iii) to render sentences no more severe than necessary to achieve the applicable purposes from subsections (a)(i) and (ii);

(b) in matters affecting the administration and evaluation of the sentencing and corrections system:

(i) to preserve substantial judicial discretion to individualize sentences within a framework of law;

(ii) to produce sentences that are uniform in their neutral application of the purposes in subsection (a);

(iii) to eliminate discrimination and inequities in punishment across population groups;

(iv) to ensure that steps are taken to forecast and prevent unjustified overrepresentations of racial and ethnic minorities in sentenced populations when laws and guidelines affecting sentencing are proposed, revised, or enacted;

(v) to encourage the use of intermediate punishments;

(vi) to ensure that adequate resources and facilities are available for carrying out sentences imposed on offenders and that rational priorities are established for the use of those resources;

(vii) to ensure that all criminal sanctions are administered in a humane fashion and that incarcerated offenders are provided reasonable benefits of subsistence, personal safety, medical and mental health care, and opportunities to rehabilitate themselves and improve their life chances following release;

(viii) to promote research on sentencing policy and practices, including assessments of the effectiveness of criminal sanctions as measured against their purposes, and the effects of criminal sanctions upon families and communities; and

(ix) to increase the transparency of the sentencing and corrections system, its accountability to the public, and the legitimacy of its operations as perceived by all affected communities.

Section 1.03. Territorial Applicability.

(1) Except as otherwise provided in this Section, a person may be convicted under the law of this State of an offense committed by his own conduct or the conduct of another for which he is legally accountable if:

(a) either the conduct which is an element of the offense or the result which is such an element occurs within this State; or

(b) conduct occurring outside the State is sufficient under the law of this State to constitute an attempt to commit an offense within the State; or

(c) conduct occurring outside the State is sufficient under the law of this State to constitute a conspiracy to commit an offense within the State and an overt act in furtherance of such conspiracy occurs within the State; or

(d) conduct occurring within the State establishes complicity in the commission of, or an attempt, solicitation or conspiracy to commit, an offense in another jurisdiction which also is an offense under the law of this State; or

(e) the offense consists of the omission to perform a legal duty imposed by the law of the State with respect to domicile, residence or a relationship to a person, thing or transaction in the State; or

(f) the offense is based on a statute of this State which expressly prohibits conduct outside the State, when the conduct bears a reasonable relation to a legitimate interest of this State and the actor knows or should know that his conduct is likely to affect that interest.

(2) Subsection (1)(a) does not apply when either causing a specified result or a purpose to cause or danger of causing such a result is an element of an offense and the result occurs or is designed or likely to occur only in another jurisdiction where the conduct charged would not constitute an offense, unless a legislative purpose plainly appears to declare the conduct criminal regardless of the place of the result.

(3) Subsection (1)(a) does not apply when causing a particular result is an element of an offense and the result is caused by conduct occurring outside the State which would not constitute an offense if the result had occurred there, unless the actor purposely or knowingly caused the result within the State.

(4) When the offense is homicide, either the death of the victim or the bodily impact causing death constitutes a "result," within the meaning of Subsection (1)(a) and if the body of a homicide victim is found within the State, it is presumed that such result occurred within the State.

(5) This State includes the land and water and the air space above such land and water with respect to which the State has legislative jurisdiction.

Section 1.04. Classes of Crimes; Violations.

(1) An offense defined by this Code or by any other statute of this State, for which a sentence of [death or of] imprisonment is authorized, constitutes a crime. Crimes are classified as felonies, misdemeanors or petty misdemeanors.

(2) A crime is a felony if it is so designated in this Code or if persons convicted thereof may be sentenced [to death or] to imprisonment for a term which, apart from an extended term, is in excess of one year.

(3) A crime is a misdemeanor if it is so designated in this Code or in a statute other than this Code enacted subsequent thereto.

(4) A crime is a petty misdemeanor if it is so designated in this Code or in a statute other than this Code enacted subsequent thereto or if it is defined by a statute other than this Code which now provides that persons convicted thereof may be sentenced to imprisonment for a term of which the maximum is less than one year.

(5) An offense defined by this Code or by any other statute of this State constitutes a violation if it is so designated in this Code or in the law defining the offense or if no other sentence than a fine, or fine and forfeiture or other civil penalty is authorized upon conviction or if it is defined by a statute other than this Code which now provides that the offense shall not constitute a crime. A violation does not constitute a crime and conviction of a violation shall not give rise to any disability or legal disadvantage based on conviction of a criminal offense.

(6) Any offense declared by law to constitute a crime, without specification of the grade thereof or of the sentence authorized upon conviction, is a misdemeanor.

(7) An offense defined by any statute of this State other than this Code shall be classified as provided in this Section and the sentence that may be imposed upon conviction thereof shall hereafter be governed by this Code.

Section 1.05. All Offenses Defined by Statute; Application of General Provisions of the Code.

(1) No conduct constitutes an offense unless it is a crime or violation under this Code or another statute of this State.

(2) The provisions of Part I of the Code are applicable to offenses defined by other statutes, unless the Code otherwise provides.

(3) This Section does not affect the power of a court to punish for contempt or to employ any sanction authorized by law for the enforcement of an order or a civil judgment or decree.

Section 1.06. Time Limitations.

(1) A prosecution for murder may be commenced at any time.

(2) Except as otherwise provided in this Section, prosecutions for other offenses are subject to the following periods of limitation:

(a) a prosecution for a felony of the first degree must be commenced within six years after it is committed;

(b) a prosecution for any other felony must be commenced within three years after it is committed;

(c) a prosecution for a misdemeanor must be commenced within two years after it is committed;

(d) a prosecution for a petty misdemeanor or a violation must be commenced within six months after it is committed.

(3) If the period prescribed in Subsection (2) has expired, a prosecution may nevertheless be commenced for:

(a) any offense a material element of which is either fraud or a breach of fiduciary obligation within one year after discovery of the offense by an aggrieved party or by a person who has a legal duty to represent an aggrieved party and who is himself not a party to the offense, but in no case shall this provision extend the period of limitation otherwise applicable by more than three years; and

(b) any offense based upon misconduct in office by a public officer or employee at any time when the defendant is in public office or employment or within two years thereafter, but in no case shall this provision extend the period of limitation otherwise applicable by more than three years.

(4) An offense is committed either when every element occurs, or, if a legislative purpose to prohibit a continuing course of conduct plainly appears, at the time when the course of conduct or the defendant's complicity therein is terminated. Time starts to run on the day after the offense is committed.

(5) A prosecution is commenced either when an indictment is found [or an information filed] or when a warrant or other process is issued, provided that such warrant or process is executed without unreasonable delay.

(6) The period of limitation does not run:

(a) during any time when the accused is continuously absent from the State or has no reasonably ascertainable place of abode or work within the State, but in no case shall this provision extend the period of limitation otherwise applicable by more than three years; or

(b) during any time when a prosecution against the accused for the same conduct is pending in this State.

Section 1.07. Method of Prosecution When Conduct Constitutes More Than One Offense.

(1) Prosecution for Multiple Offenses; Limitation on Convictions. When the same conduct of a defendant may establish the commission of more than one offense, the defendant may be prosecuted for each such offense. He may not, however, be convicted of more than one offense if:

(a) one offense is included in the other, as defined in Subsection (4) of this Section; or

(b) one offense consists only of a conspiracy or other form of preparation to commit the other; or

(c) inconsistent findings of fact are required to establish the commission of the offenses; or

(d) the offenses differ only in that one is defined to prohibit a designated kind of conduct generally and the other to prohibit a specific instance of such conduct; or

(e) the offense is defined as a continuing course of conduct and the defendant's course of conduct was uninterrupted, unless the law provides that specific periods of such conduct constitute separate offenses.

(2) Limitation on Separate Trials for Multiple Offenses. Except as provided in Subsection (3) of this Section, a defendant shall not be subject to separate trials for multiple offenses based on the same conduct or arising from the same criminal episode, if such offenses are known to the appropriate prosecuting officer at the time of the commencement of the first trial and are within the jurisdiction of a single court.

(3) Authority of Court to Order Separate Trials. When a defendant is charged with two or more offenses based on the same conduct or arising from the same criminal episode, the Court, on application of the prosecuting attorney or of the defendant, may order any such charge to be tried separately, if it is satisfied that justice so requires.

(4) Conviction of Included Offense Permitted. A defendant may be convicted of an offense included in an offense charged in the indictment [or the information]. An offense is so included when:

(a) it is established by proof of the same or less than all the facts required to establish the commission of the offense charged; or

(b) it consists of an attempt or solicitation to commit the offense charged or to commit an offense otherwise included therein; or

(c) it differs from the offense charged only in the respect that a less serious injury or risk of injury to the same person, property or public interest or a lesser kind of culpability suffices to establish its commission.

(5) Submission of Included Offense to Jury. The Court shall not be obligated to charge the jury with respect to an included offense unless there is a rational basis for a verdict acquitting the defendant of the offense charged and convicting him of the included offense.

Section 1.08. When Prosecution Barred by Former Prosecution for the Same Offense.

When a prosecution is for a violation of the same provision of the statutes and is based upon the same facts as a former prosecution, it is barred by such former prosecution under the following circumstances:

(1) The former prosecution resulted in an acquittal. There is an acquittal if the prosecution resulted in a finding of not guilty by the trier of fact or in a determination that there was insufficient evidence to warrant a conviction. A finding of guilty of a lesser included offense is an acquittal of the greater inclusive offense, although the conviction is subsequently set aside.

(2) The former prosecution was terminated, after the information had been filed or the indictment found, by a final order or judgment for the defendant, which has not been set aside, reversed, or vacated and which necessarily required a determination inconsistent with a fact or a legal proposition that must be established for conviction of the offense.

(3) The former prosecution resulted in a conviction. There is a conviction if the prosecution resulted in a judgment of conviction which has not been reversed or vacated, a verdict of guilty which has not been set aside and which is capable of supporting a judgment, or a plea of guilty accepted by the Court. In the latter two cases failure to enter judgment must be for a reason other than a motion of the defendant.

(4) The former prosecution was improperly terminated. Except as provided in this Subsection, there is an improper termination of a prosecution if the termination is for reasons not amounting to an acquittal, and it takes place after the first witness is sworn but before verdict. Termination under any of the following circumstances is not improper:

(a) The defendant consents to the termination or waives, by motion to dismiss or otherwise, his right to object to the termination.

(b) The trial court finds that the termination is necessary because:

(1) it is physically impossible to proceed with the trial in conformity with law; or

(2) there is a legal defect in the proceedings which would make any judgment entered upon a verdict reversible as a matter of law; or

(3) prejudicial conduct, in or outside the courtroom, makes it impossible to proceed with the trial without injustice to either the defendant or the State; or

(4) the jury is unable to agree upon a verdict; or

(5) false statements of a juror on voir dire prevent a fair trial.

Section 1.09. When Prosecution Barred by Former Prosecution for Different Offense.

Although a prosecution is for a violation of a different provision of the statutes than a former prosecution or is based on different facts, it is barred by such former prosecution under the following circumstances:

(1) The former prosecution resulted in an acquittal or in a conviction as defined in Section 1.08 and the subsequent prosecution is for:

(a) any offense of which the defendant could have been convicted on the first prosecution; or

(b) any offense for which the defendant should have been tried on the first prosecution under Section 1.07, unless the Court ordered a separate trial of the charge of such offense; or

(c) the same conduct, unless (i) the offense of which the defendant was formerly convicted or acquitted and the offense for which he is subsequently prosecuted each requires proof of a fact not required by the other and the law defining each of such offenses is intended to prevent a substantially different harm or evil, or (ii) the second offense was not consummated when the former trial began.

(2) The former prosecution was terminated, after the information was filed or the indictment found, by an acquittal or by a final order or judgment for the defendant which has not been set aside, reversed or vacated and which acquittal, final order or judgment necessarily required a determination inconsistent with a fact which must be established for conviction of the second offense.

(3) The former prosecution was improperly terminated, as improper termination is defined in Section 1.08, and the subsequent prosecution is for an offense of which the defendant could have been convicted had the former prosecution not been improperly terminated.

Section 1.10. Former Prosecution in Another Jurisdiction: When a Bar.

When conduct constitutes an offense within the concurrent jurisdiction of this State and of the United States or another State, a prosecution in any such other jurisdiction is a bar to a subsequent prosecution in this State under the following circumstances:

(1) The first prosecution resulted in an acquittal or in a conviction as defined in Section 1.08 and the subsequent prosecution is based on the same conduct, unless (a) the offense of which the defendant was formerly convicted or acquitted and the offense for which he is subsequently prosecuted each requires proof of a fact not required by the other and the law defining each of such offenses is intended to prevent a substantially different harm or evil or (b) the second offense was not consummated when the former trial began; or

(2) The former prosecution was terminated, after the information was filed or the indictment found, by an acquittal or by a final order or judgment for the defendant which has not been set aside, reversed or vacated and which acquittal, final order or judgment necessarily required a determination inconsistent with a fact which must be established for conviction of the offense of which the defendant is subsequently prosecuted.

Section 1.11. Former Prosecution Before Court Lacking Jurisdiction or When Fraudulently Procured by the Defendant.

A prosecution is not a bar within the meaning of Sections 1.08, 1.09 and 1.10 under any of the following circumstances:

(1) The former prosecution was before a court which lacked jurisdiction over the defendant or the offense; or

(2) The former prosecution was procured by the defendant without the knowledge of the appropriate prosecuting officer and with the purpose of avoiding the sentence which might otherwise be imposed; or

(3) The former prosecution resulted in a judgment of conviction which was held invalid in a subsequent proceeding on a writ of habeas corpus, coram nobis or similar process.

Section 1.12. Proof Beyond a Reasonable Doubt; Affirmative Defenses; Burden of Proving Fact When Not an Element of an Offense; Presumptions.

(1) No person may be convicted of an offense unless each element of such offense is proved beyond a reasonable doubt. In the absence of such proof, the innocence of the defendant is assumed.

(2) Subsection (1) of this Section does not:

(a) require the disproof of an affirmative defense unless and until there is evidence supporting such defense; or

(b) apply to any defense which the Code or another statute plainly requires the defendant to prove by a preponderance of evidence.

(3) A ground of defense is affirmative, within the meaning of Subsection (2)(a) of this Section, when:

(a) it arises under a section of the Code which so provides; or

(b) it relates to an offense defined by a statute other than the Code and such statute so provides; or

(c) it involves a matter of excuse or justification peculiarly within the knowledge of the defendant on which he can fairly be required to adduce supporting evidence.

(4) When the application of the Code depends upon the finding of a fact which is not an element of an offense, unless the Code otherwise provides:

(a) the burden of proving the fact is on the prosecution or defendant, depending on whose interest or contention will be furthered if the finding should be made; and

(b) the fact must be proved to the satisfaction of the Court or jury, as the case may be.

(5) When the Code establishes a presumption with respect to any fact which is an element of an offense, it has the following consequences:

(a) when there is evidence of the facts which give rise to the presumption, the issue of the existence of the presumed fact must be submitted to the jury, unless the Court is satisfied that the evidence as a whole clearly negatives the presumed fact; and

(b) when the issue of the existence of the presumed fact is submitted to the jury, the Court shall charge that while the presumed fact must, on all the evidence, be proved beyond a reasonable doubt, the law declares that the jury may regard the facts giving rise to the presumption as sufficient evidence of the presumed fact.

(6) A presumption not established by the Code or inconsistent with it has the consequences otherwise accorded it by law.

Section 1.13. General Definitions.

In this Code, unless a different meaning plainly is required:

(1) "statute" includes the Constitution and a local law or ordinance of a political subdivision of the State;

(2) "act" or "action" means a bodily movement whether voluntary or involuntary;

(3) "voluntary" has the meaning specified in Section 2.01;

(4) "omission" means a failure to act;

(5) "conduct" means an action or omission and its accompanying state of mind, or, where relevant, a series of acts and omissions;

(6) "actor" includes, where relevant, a person guilty of an omission;

(7) "acted" includes, where relevant, "omitted to act";

(8) "person," "he" and "actor" include any natural person and, where relevant, a corporation or an unincorporated association;

(9) "element of an offense" means (i) such conduct or (ii) such attendant circumstances or (iii) such a result of conduct as

    (a) is included in the description of the forbidden conduct in the definition of the offense; or

    (b) establishes the required kind of culpability; or

    (c) negatives an excuse or justification for such conduct; or

    (d) negatives a defense under the statute of limitations; or

    (e) establishes jurisdiction or venue;

(10) "material element of an offense" means an element that does not relate exclusively to the statute of limitations, jurisdiction, venue or to any other matter similarly unconnected with (i) the harm or evil, incident to conduct, sought to be prevented by the law defining the offense, or (ii) the existence of a justification or excuse for such conduct;

(11) "purposely" has the meaning specified in Section 2.02 and equivalent terms such as "with purpose," "designed" or "with design" have the same meaning;

(12) "intentionally" or "with intent" means purposely;

(13) "knowingly" has the meaning specified in Section 2.02 and equivalent terms such as "knowing" or "with knowledge" have the same meaning;

(14) "recklessly" has the meaning specified in Section 2.02 and equivalent terms such as "recklessness" or "with recklessness" have the same meaning;

(15) "negligently" has the meaning specified in Section 2.02 and equivalent terms such as "negligence" or "with negligence" have the same meaning;

(16) "reasonably believes" or "reasonable belief" designates a belief which the actor is not reckless or negligent in holding.

Article 2. General Principals of Liability.

Section 2.01. Requirement of Voluntary Act; Omission as Basis of Liability; Possession as an Act.

(1) A person is not guilty of an offense unless his liability is based on conduct which includes a voluntary act or the omission to perform an act of which he is physically capable.

(2) The following are not voluntary acts within the meaning of this Section:

(a) a reflex or convulsion;

(b) a bodily movement during unconsciousness or sleep;

(c) conduct during hypnosis or resulting from hypnotic suggestion;

(d) a bodily movement that otherwise is not a product of the effort or determination of the actor, either conscious or habitual.

(3) Liability for the commission of an offense may not be based on an omission unaccompanied by action unless:

(a) the omission is expressly made sufficient by the law defining the offense; or

(b) a duty to perform the omitted act is otherwise imposed by law.

(4) Possession is an act, within the meaning of this Section, if the possessor knowingly procured or received the thing possessed or was aware of his control thereof for a sufficient period to have been able to terminate his possession.

Section 2.02. General Requirements of Culpability.

(1) Minimum Requirements of Culpability. Except as provided in Section 2.05, a person is not guilty of an offense unless he acted purposely, knowingly, recklessly or negligently, as the law may require, with respect to each material element of the offense.

(2) Kinds of Culpability Defined.

(a) Purposely. A person acts purposely with respect to a material element of an offense when:

(i) if the element involves the nature of his conduct or a result thereof, it is his conscious object to engage in conduct of that nature or to cause such a result; and

(ii) if the element involves the attendant circumstances, he is aware of the existence of such circumstances or he believes or hopes that they exist.

(b) Knowingly. A person acts knowingly with respect to a material element of an offense when:

(i) if the element involves the nature of his conduct or the attendant circumstances, he is aware that his conduct is of that nature or that such circumstances exist; and

(ii) if the element involves a result of his conduct, he is aware that it is practically certain that his conduct will cause such a result.

(c) Recklessly. A person acts recklessly with respect to a material element of an offense when he consciously disregards a substantial and unjustifiable risk that the material element exists or will result from his conduct. The risk must be of such a nature and degree that, considering the nature and purpose of the actor's conduct and the circumstances known to him, its disregard involves a gross deviation from the standard of conduct that a law-abiding person would observe in the actor's situation.

(d) Negligently. A person acts negligently with respect to a material element of an offense when he should be aware of a substantial and unjustifiable risk that the material element exists or will result from his conduct. The risk must be of such a nature and degree that the actor's failure to perceive it, considering the nature and purpose of his conduct and the circumstances known to him, involves a gross deviation from the standard of care that a reasonable person would observe in the actor's situation.

(3) Culpability Required Unless Otherwise Provided. When the culpability sufficient to establish a material element of an offense is not prescribed by law, such element is established if a person acts purposely, knowingly or recklessly with respect thereto.

(4) Prescribed Culpability Requirement Applies to All Material Elements. When the law defining an offense prescribes the kind of culpability that is sufficient for the commission of an offense, without distinguishing among the material elements thereof, such provision shall apply to all the material elements of the offense, unless a contrary purpose plainly appears.

(5) Substitutes for Negligence, Recklessness and Knowledge. When the law provides that negligence suffices to establish an element of an offense, such element also is established if a person acts purposely, knowingly or recklessly. When recklessness suffices to establish an element, such element also is established if a person acts purposely or knowingly. When acting knowingly suffices to establish an element, such element also is established if a person acts purposely.

(6) Requirement of Purpose Satisfied if Purpose Is Conditional. When a particular purpose is an element of an offense, the element is established although such purpose is conditional, unless the condition negatives the harm or evil sought to be prevented by the law defining the offense.

(7) Requirement of Knowledge Satisfied by Knowledge of High Probability. When knowledge of the existence of a particular fact is an element of an offense, such knowledge is established if a person is aware of a high probability of its existence, unless he actually believes that it does not exist.

(8) Requirement of Wilfulness Satisfied by Acting Knowingly. A requirement that an offense be committed wilfully is satisfied if a person acts knowingly with respect to the material elements of the offense, unless a purpose to impose further requirements appears.

(9) Culpability as to Illegality of Conduct. Neither knowledge nor recklessness or negligence as to whether conduct constitutes an offense or as to the existence, meaning or application of the law determining the elements of an offense is an element of such offense, unless the definition of the offense or the Code so provides.

(10) Culpability as Determinant of Grade of Offense. When the grade or degree of an offense depends on whether the offense is committed purposely, knowingly, recklessly or negligently, its grade or degree shall be the lowest for which the determinative kind of culpability is established with respect to any material element of the offense.

Section 2.03. Causal Relationship Between Conduct and Result; Divergence Between Result Designed or Contemplated and Actual Result or Between Probable and Actual Result.

(1) Conduct is the cause of a result when:

(a) it is an antecedent but for which the result in question would not have occurred; and

(b) the relationship between the conduct and result satisfies any additional causal requirements imposed by the Code or by the law defining the offense.

(2) When purposely or knowingly causing a particular result is an element of an offense, the element is not established if the actual result is not within the purpose or the contemplation of the actor unless:

(a) the actual result differs from that designed or contemplated, as the case may be, only in the respect that a different person or different property is injured or affected or that the injury or harm designed or contemplated would have been more serious or more extensive than that caused; or

(b) the actual result involves the same kind of injury or harm as that designed or contemplated and is not too remote or accidental in its occurrence to have a [just] bearing on the actor's liability or on the gravity of his offense.

(3) When recklessly or negligently causing a particular result is an element of an offense, the element is not established if the actual result is not within the risk of which the actor is aware or, in the case of negligence, of which he should be aware unless:

(a) the actual result differs from the probable result only in the respect that a different person or different property is injured or affected or that the probable injury or harm would have been more serious or more extensive than that caused; or

(b) the actual result involves the same kind of injury or harm as the probable result and is not too remote or accidental in its occurrence to have a [just] bearing on the actor's liability or on the gravity of his offense.

(4) When causing a particular result is a material element of an offense for which absolute liability is imposed by law, the element is not established unless the actual result is a probable consequence of the actor's conduct.

Section 2.04. Ignorance or Mistake.

(1) Ignorance or mistake as to a matter of fact or law is a defense if:

(a) the ignorance or mistake negatives the purpose, knowledge, belief, recklessness or negligence required to establish a material element of the offense; or

(b) the law provides that the state of mind established by such ignorance or mistake constitutes a defense.

(2) Although ignorance or mistake would otherwise afford a defense to the offense charged, the defense is not available if the defendant would be guilty of another offense had the situation been as he supposed. In such case, however, the ignorance or mistake of the defendant shall reduce the grade and degree of the offense of which he may be convicted to those of the offense of which he would be guilty had the situation been as he supposed.

(3) A belief that conduct does not legally constitute an offense is a defense to a prosecution for that offense based upon such conduct when:

(a) the statute or other enactment defining the offense is not known to the actor and has not been published or otherwise reasonably made available prior to the conduct alleged; or

[Handwritten margin notes:]

Relationship between contemplated result and actual result

Causation in terms of Remoteness NOT foreseeability

Strict liability

eg selling sugar but thinks bag of coke → no intent to sell not culpable

selling coke but finding heroin → culpable, action still illegal

(b) he acts in reasonable reliance upon an official statement of the law, afterward determined to be invalid or erroneous, contained in (i) a statute or other enactment; (ii) a judicial decision, opinion or judgment; (iii) an administrative order or grant of permission; or (iv) an official interpretation of the public officer or body charged by law with responsibility for the interpretation, administration or enforcement of the law defining the offense.

(4) The defendant must prove a defense arising under Subsection (3) of this Section by a preponderance of evidence.

Section 2.05. When Culpability Requirements Are Inapplicable to Violations and to Offenses Defined by Other Statutes; Effect of Absolute Liability in Reducing Grade of Offense to Violation.

(1) The requirements of culpability prescribed by Sections 2.01 and 2.02 do not apply to:

(a) offenses which constitute violations, unless the requirement involved is included in the definition of the offense or the Court determines that its application is consistent with effective enforcement of the law defining the offense; or

(b) offenses defined by statutes other than the Code, insofar as a legislative purpose to impose absolute liability for such offenses or with respect to any material element thereof plainly appears.

(2) Notwithstanding any other provision of existing law and unless a subsequent statute otherwise provides:

(a) when absolute liability is imposed with respect to any material element of an offense defined by a statute other than the Code and a conviction is based upon such liability, the offense constitutes a violation; and

(b) although absolute liability is imposed by law with respect to one or more of the material elements of an offense defined by a statute other than the Code, the culpable commission of the offense may be charged and proved, in which event negligence with respect to such elements constitutes sufficient culpability and the classification of the offense and the sentence that may be imposed therefor upon conviction are determined by Section 1.04 and Article 6 of the Code.

Section 2.06. Liability for Conduct of Another; Complicity.

(1) A person is guilty of an offense if it is committed by his own conduct or by the conduct of another person for which he is legally accountable, or both.

(2) A person is legally accountable for the conduct of another person when:

(a) acting with the kind of culpability that is sufficient for the commission of the offense, he causes an innocent or irresponsible person to engage in such conduct; or

(b) he is made accountable for the conduct of such other person by the Code or by the law defining the offense; or

(c) he is an accomplice of such other person in the commission of the offense.

(3) A person is an accomplice of another person in the commission of an offense if:

(a) with the purpose of promoting or facilitating the commission of the offense, he

(i) solicits such other person to commit it; or

(ii) aids or agrees or attempts to aid such other person in planning or committing it; or

(iii) having a legal duty to prevent the commission of the offense, fails to make proper effort so to do; or

(b) his conduct is expressly declared by law to establish his complicity.

(4) When causing a particular result is an element of an offense, an accomplice in the conduct causing such result is an accomplice in the commission of that offense, if he acts with the kind of culpability, if any, with respect to that result that is sufficient for the commission of the offense.

(5) A person who is legally incapable of committing a particular offense himself may be guilty thereof if it is committed by the conduct of another person for which he is legally accountable, unless such liability is inconsistent with the purpose of the provision establishing his incapacity.

(6) Unless otherwise provided by the Code or by the law defining the offense, a person is not an accomplice in an offense committed by another person if:

(a) he is a victim of that offense; or

(b) the offense is so defined that his conduct is inevitably incident to its commission; or

(c) he terminates his complicity prior to the commission of the offense and

(i) wholly deprives it of effectiveness in the commission of the offense; or

(ii) gives timely warning to the law enforcement authorities or otherwise makes proper effort to prevent the commission of the offense.

(7) An accomplice may be convicted on proof of the commission of the offense and of his complicity therein, though the person claimed to have committed the offense has not been prosecuted or convicted or has been convicted of a different offense or degree of offense or has an immunity to prosecution or conviction or has been acquitted.

Section 2.07. Liability of Corporations, Unincorporated Associations and Persons Acting, or Under a Duty to Act, in Their Behalf.

(1) A corporation may be convicted of the commission of an offense if:

(a) the offense is a violation or the offense is defined by a statute other than the Code in which a legislative purpose to impose liability on corporations plainly appears and the conduct is performed by an agent of the corporation acting in behalf of the corporation within the scope of his office or employment, except that if the law defining the offense designates the agents for whose conduct the corporation is accountable or the circumstances under which it is accountable, such provisions shall apply; or

(b) the offense consists of an omission to discharge a specific duty of affirmative performance imposed on corporations by law; or

(c) the commission of the offense was authorized, requested, commanded, performed or recklessly tolerated by the board of directors or by a high managerial agent acting in behalf of the corporation within the scope of his office or employment.

(2) When absolute liability is imposed for the commission of an offense, a legislative purpose to impose liability on a corporation shall be assumed, unless the contrary plainly appears.

(3) An unincorporated association may be convicted of the commission of an offense if:

(a) the offense is defined by a statute other than the Code which expressly provides for the liability of such an association and the conduct is performed by an agent of the association acting in behalf of the association within the scope of his office or employment, except that if the law defining the offense designates the agents for whose conduct the association is accountable or the circumstances under which it is accountable, such provisions shall apply; or

(b) the offense consists of an omission to discharge a specific duty of affirmative performance imposed on associations by law.

(4) As used in this Section:

(a) "corporation" does not include an entity organized as or by a governmental agency for the execution of a governmental program;

(b) "agent" means any director, officer, servant, employee or other person authorized to act in behalf of the corporation or association and, in the case of an unincorporated association, a member of such association;

(c) "high managerial agent" means an officer of a corporation or an unincorporated association, or, in the case of a partnership, a partner, or any other agent of a corporation or association having duties of such responsibility that his conduct may fairly be assumed to represent the policy of the corporation or association.

(5) In any prosecution of a corporation or an unincorporated association for the commission of an offense included within the terms of Subsection (1)(a) or Subsection (3)(a) of this Section, other than an offense for which absolute liability has been imposed, it shall be a defense if the defendant proves by a preponderance of evidence that the high managerial agent having supervisory responsibility over the subject matter of the offense employed due diligence to prevent its commission. This paragraph shall not apply if it is plainly inconsistent with the legislative purpose in defining the particular offense.

(6)(a) A person is legally accountable for any conduct he performs or causes to be performed in the name of the corporation or an unincorporated association or in its behalf to the same extent as if it were performed in his own name or behalf.

(b) Whenever a duty to act is imposed by law upon a corporation or an unincorporated association, any agent of the corporation or association having primary responsibility for the discharge of the duty is legally accountable for a reckless omission to perform the required act to the same extent as if the duty were imposed by law directly upon himself.

(c) When a person is convicted of an offense by reason of his legal accountability for the conduct of a corporation or an unincorporated association, he is subject to the sentence authorized by law when a natural person is convicted of an offense of the grade and the degree involved.

Section 2.08. Intoxication.

(1) Except as provided in Subsection (4) of this Section, intoxication of the actor is not a defense unless it negatives an element of the offense.

(2) When recklessness establishes an element of the offense, if the actor, due to self-induced intoxication, is unaware of a risk of which he would have been aware had he been sober, such unawareness is immaterial.

(3) Intoxication does not, in itself, constitute mental disease within the meaning of Section 4.01.

(4) Intoxication which (a) is not self-induced or (b) is pathological is an affirmative defense if by reason of such intoxication the actor at the time of his conduct lacks substantial capacity either to appreciate its criminality [wrongfulness] or to conform his conduct to the requirements of law.

(5) Definitions. In this Section unless a different meaning plainly is required:

(a) "intoxication" means a disturbance of mental or physical capacities resulting from the introduction of substances into the body;

(b) "self-induced intoxication" means intoxication caused by substances which the actor knowingly introduces into his body, the tendency of which to cause intoxication he knows or ought to know, unless he introduces them pursuant to medical advice or under such circumstances as would afford a defense to a charge of crime;

(c) "pathological intoxication" means intoxication grossly excessive in degree, given the amount of the intoxicant, to which the actor does not know he is susceptible.

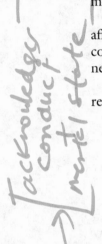

Section 2.09. Duress.

(1) It is an affirmative defense that the actor engaged in the conduct charged to constitute an offense because he was coerced to do so by the use of, or a threat to use, unlawful force against his person or the person of another, which a person of reasonable firmness in his situation would have been unable to resist.

(2) The defense provided by this Section is unavailable if the actor recklessly placed himself in a situation in which it was probable that he would be subjected to duress. The defense is also unavailable if he was negligent in placing himself in such a situation, whenever negligence suffices to establish culpability for the offense charged.

(3) It is not a defense that a woman acted on the command of her husband, unless she acted under such coercion as would establish a defense under this Section. [The presumption that a woman, acting in the presence of her husband, is coerced is abolished.]

(4) When the conduct of the actor would otherwise be justifiable under Section 3.02, this Section does not preclude such defense.

Section 2.10. Military Orders.

It is an affirmative defense that the actor, in engaging in the conduct charged to constitute an offense, does no more than execute an order of his superior in the armed services which he does not know to be unlawful.

Section 2.11. Consent.

(1) In General. The consent of the victim to conduct charged to constitute an offense or to the result thereof is a defense if such consent negatives an element of the offense or precludes the infliction of the harm or evil sought to be prevented by the law defining the offense.

(2) Consent to Bodily Injury. When conduct is charged to constitute an offense because it causes or threatens bodily injury, consent to such conduct or to the infliction of such injury is a defense if:

(a) the bodily injury consented to or threatened by the conduct consented to is not serious; or

(b) the conduct and the injury are reasonably foreseeable hazards of joint participation in a lawful athletic contest or competitive sport or other concerted activity not forbidden by law; or

(c) the consent establishes a justification for the conduct under Article 3 of the Code.

(3) Ineffective Consent. Unless otherwise provided by the Code or by the law defining the offense, assent does not constitute consent if:

(a) it is given by a person who is legally incompetent to authorize the conduct charged to constitute the offense; or

(b) it is given by a person who by reason of youth, mental disease or defect or intoxication is manifestly unable or known by the actor to be unable to make a reasonable judgment as to the nature or harmfulness of the conduct charged to constitute the offense; or

(c) it is given by a person whose improvident consent is sought to be prevented by the law defining the offense; or

(d) it is induced by force, duress or deception of a kind sought to be prevented by the law defining the offense.

Section 2.12. De Minimis Infractions.

The Court shall dismiss a prosecution if, having regard to the nature of the conduct charged to constitute an offense and the nature of the attendant circumstances, it finds that the defendant's conduct:

(1) was within a customary license or tolerance, neither expressly negatived by the person whose interest was infringed nor inconsistent with the purpose of the law defining the offense; or

(2) did not actually cause or threaten the harm or evil sought to be prevented by the law defining the offense or did so only to an extent too trivial to warrant the condemnation of conviction; or

(3) presents such other extenuations that it cannot reasonably be regarded as envisaged by the legislature in forbidding the offense. The Court shall not

dismiss a prosecution under Subsection (3) of this Section without filing a written statement of its reasons.

Section 2.13. Entrapment.

(1) A public law enforcement official or a person acting in cooperation with such an official perpetrates an entrapment if for the purpose of obtaining evidence of the commission of an offense, he induces or encourages another person to engage in conduct constituting such offense by either:

(a) making knowingly false representations designed to induce the belief that such conduct is not prohibited; or

(b) employing methods of persuasion or inducement which create a substantial risk that such an offense will be committed by persons other than those who are ready to commit it.

(2) Except as provided in Subsection (3) of this Section, a person prosecuted for an offense shall be acquitted if he proves by a preponderance of evidence that his conduct occurred in response to an entrapment. The issue of entrapment shall be tried by the Court in the absence of the jury.

(3) The defense afforded by this Section is unavailable when causing or threatening bodily injury is an element of the offense charged and the prosecution is based on conduct causing or threatening such injury to a person other than the person perpetrating the entrapment.

Article 3. General Principles of Justification.

Section 3.01. Justification an Affirmative Defense; Civil Remedies Unaffected.

(1) In any prosecution based on conduct which is justifiable under this Article, justification is an affirmative defense.

(2) The fact that conduct is justifiable under this Article does not abolish or impair any remedy for such conduct which is available in any civil action.

Section 3.02. Justification Generally: Choice of Evils.

(1) Conduct which the actor believes to be necessary to avoid a harm or evil to himself or to another is justifiable, provided that:

(a) the harm or evil sought to be avoided by such conduct is greater than that sought to be prevented by the law defining the offense charged; and

(b) neither the Code nor other law defining the offense provides exceptions or defenses dealing with the specific situation involved; and

(c) a legislative purpose to exclude the justification claimed does not otherwise plainly appear.

(2) When the actor was reckless or negligent in bringing about the situation requiring a choice of harms or evils or in appraising the necessity for his conduct, the justification afforded by this Section is unavailable in a prosecution for any offense for which recklessness or negligence, as the case may be, suffices to establish culpability.

Section 3.03. Execution of Public Duty.

(1) Except as provided in Subsection (2) of this Section, conduct is justifiable when it is required or authorized by:

(a) the law defining the duties or functions of a public officer or the assistance to be rendered to such officer in the performance of his duties; or

(b) the law governing the execution of legal process; or

(c) the judgment or order of a competent court or tribunal; or

(d) the law governing the armed services or the lawful conduct of war; or

(e) any other provision of law imposing a public duty.

(2) The other sections of this Article apply to:

(a) the use of force upon or toward the person of another for any of the purposes dealt with in such sections; and

(b) the use of deadly force for any purpose, unless the use of such force is otherwise expressly authorized by law or occurs in the lawful conduct of war.

(3) The justification afforded by Subsection (1) of this Section applies:

(a) when the actor believes his conduct to be required or authorized by the judgment or direction of a competent court or tribunal or in the lawful execution of legal process, notwithstanding lack of jurisdiction of the court or defect in the legal process; and

(b) when the actor believes his conduct to be required or authorized to assist a public officer in the performance of his duties, notwithstanding that the officer exceeded his legal authority.

Section 3.04. Use of Force in Self-Protection.

(1) Use of Force Justifiable for Protection of the Person. Subject to the provisions of this Section and of Section 3.09, the use of force upon or toward another person is justifiable when the actor believes that such force is immediately necessary for the purpose of protecting himself against the use of unlawful force by such other person on the present occasion.

(2) Limitations on Justifying Necessity for Use of Force.

(a) The use of force is not justifiable under this Section:

(i) to resist an arrest which the actor knows is being made by a peace officer, although the arrest is unlawful; or

(ii) to resist force used by the occupier or possessor of property or by another person on his behalf, where the actor knows that the person using the force is doing so under a claim of right to protect the property, except that this limitation shall not apply if:

(1) the actor is a public officer acting in the performance of his duties or a person lawfully assisting him therein or a person making or assisting in a lawful arrest; or

(2) the actor has been unlawfully dispossessed of the property and is making a re-entry or recaption justified by Section 3.06; or

(3) the actor believes that such force is necessary to protect himself against death or serious bodily harm.

(b) The use of deadly force is not justifiable under this Section unless the actor believes that such force is necessary to protect himself against death, serious bodily harm, kidnapping or sexual intercourse compelled by force or threat; nor is it justifiable if:

(i) the actor, with the purpose of causing death or serious bodily harm, provoked the use of force against himself in the same encounter; or

(ii) the actor knows that he can avoid the necessity of using such force with complete safety by retreating or by surrendering possession of a thing to a person asserting a claim of right thereto or by complying with a demand that he abstain from any action which he has no duty to take, except that:

(1) the actor is not obliged to retreat from his dwelling or place of work, unless he was the initial aggressor or is assailed in his place of work by another person whose place of work the actor knows it to be; and

(2) a public officer justified in using force in the performance of his duties or a person justified in using force in his assistance or a person justified in using force in making an arrest or preventing an escape is not obliged to desist from efforts to perform such duty, effect such arrest or prevent such escape because of resistance or threatened resistance by or on behalf of the person against whom such action is directed.

(c) Except as required by paragraphs (a) and (b) of this Subsection, a person employing protective force may estimate the necessity thereof under the circumstances as he believes them to be when the force is used, without retreating, surrendering possession, doing any other act which he has no legal duty to do or abstaining from any lawful action.

(3) Use of Confinement as Protective Force. The justification afforded by this Section extends to the use of confinement as protective force only if the actor takes all reasonable measures to terminate the confinement as soon as he knows that he safely can, unless the person confined has been arrested on a charge of crime.

Section 3.05. Use of Force for the Protection of Other Persons.

(1) Subject to the provisions of this Section and of Section 3.09, the use of force upon or toward the person of another is justifiable to protect a third person when:

(a) the actor would be justified under Section 3.04 in using such force to protect himself against the injury he believes to be threatened to the person whom he seeks to protect; and

(b) under the circumstances as the actor believes them to be, the person whom he seeks to protect would be justified in using such protective force; and

(c) the actor believes that his intervention is necessary for the protection of such other person.

(2) Notwithstanding Subsection (1) of this Section:

(a) when the actor would be obliged under Section 3.04 to retreat, to surrender the possession of a thing or to comply with a demand before using force in self-protection, he is not obliged to do so before using force for the protection of another person, unless he knows that he can thereby secure the complete safety of such other person; and

(b) when the person whom the actor seeks to protect would be obliged under Section 3.04 to retreat, to surrender the possession of a thing or to comply with a demand if he knew that he could obtain complete safety by so doing, the actor is obliged to try to cause him to do so before using force in his protection if the actor knows that he can obtain complete safety in that way; and

(c) neither the actor nor the person whom he seeks to protect is obliged to retreat when in the other's dwelling or place of work to any greater extent than in his own.

Section 3.06. Use of Force for the Protection of Property.

(1) Use of Force Justifiable for Protection of Property. Subject to the provisions of this Section and of Section 3.09, the use of force upon or toward the person of another is justifiable when the actor believes that such force is immediately necessary:

(a) to prevent or terminate an unlawful entry or other trespass upon land or a trespass against or the unlawful carrying away of tangible, movable property, provided that such land or movable property is, or is believed by the actor to be, in his possession or in the possession of another person for whose protection he acts; or

(b) to effect an entry or re-entry upon land or to retake tangible movable property, provided that the actor believes that he or the person by whose authority he acts or a person from whom he or such other person derives title was unlawfully dispossessed of such land or movable property and is entitled to possession, and provided, further, that:

(i) the force is used immediately or on fresh pursuit after such dispossession; or

(ii) the actor believes that the person against whom he uses force has no claim of right to the possession of the property and, in the case of land, the circumstances, as the actor believes them to be, are of such urgency that it would be an exceptional hardship to postpone the entry or re-entry until a court order is obtained.

(2) Meaning of Possession. For the purposes of Subsection (1) of this Section:

(a) a person who has parted with the custody of property to another who refuses to restore it to him is no longer in possession, unless the property is movable and was and still is located on land in his possession;

(b) a person who has been dispossessed of land does not regain possession thereof merely by setting foot thereon;

(c) a person who has a license to use or occupy real property is deemed to be in possession thereof except against the licensor acting under claim of right.

(3) Limitations on Justifiable Use of Force.

(a) Request to Desist. The use of force is justifiable under this Section only if the actor first requests the person against whom such force is used to desist from his interference with the property, unless the actor believes that:

(i) such request would be useless; or

(ii) it would be dangerous to himself or another person to make the request; or

(iii) substantial harm will be done to the physical condition of the property which is sought to be protected before the request can effectively be made.

(b) Exclusion of Trespasser. The use of force to prevent or terminate a trespass is not justifiable under this Section if the actor knows that the exclusion of the trespasser will expose him to substantial danger of serious bodily harm.

(c) Resistance of Lawful Re-entry or Recaption. The use of force to prevent an entry or re-entry upon land or the recaption of movable property is not justifiable under this Section, although the actor believes that such re-entry or recaption is unlawful, if:

(i) the re-entry or recaption is made by or on behalf of a person who was actually dispossessed of the property; and

(ii) it is otherwise justifiable under paragraph (1)(b) of this Section.

(d) Use of Deadly Force. The use of deadly force is not justifiable under this Section unless the actor believes that:

(i) the person against whom the force is used is attempting to dispossess him of his dwelling otherwise than under a claim of right to its possession; or

(ii) the person against whom the force is used is attempting to commit or consummate arson, burglary, robbery or other felonious theft or property destruction and either:

(1) has employed or threatened deadly force against or in the presence of the actor; or

(2) the use of force other than deadly force to prevent the commission or the consummation of the crime would expose the actor or another in his presence to substantial danger of serious bodily harm.

(4) Use of Confinement as Protective Force. The justification afforded by this Section extends to the use of confinement as protective force only if the actor takes all reasonable measures to terminate the confinement as soon as he knows that he can do so with safety to the property, unless the person confined has been arrested on a charge of crime.

(5) Use of Device to Protect Property. The justification afforded by this Section extends to the use of a device for the purpose of protecting property only if:

(a) the device is not designed to cause or known to create a substantial risk of causing death or serious bodily harm; and

(b) the use of the particular device to protect the property from entry or trespass is reasonable under the circumstances, as the actor believes them to be; and

 (c) the device is one customarily used for such a purpose or reasonable care is taken to make known to probable intruders the fact that it is used.

 (6) Use of Force to Pass Wrongful Obstructor. The use of force to pass a person whom the actor believes to be purposely or knowingly and unjustifiably obstructing the actor from going to a place to which he may lawfully go is justifiable, provided that:

 (a) the actor believes that the person against whom he uses force has no claim of right to obstruct the actor; and

 (b) the actor is not being obstructed from entry or movement on land which he knows to be in the possession or custody of the person obstructing him, or in the possession or custody of another person by whose authority the obstructor acts, unless the circumstances, as the actor believes them to be, are of such urgency that it would not be reasonable to postpone the entry or movement on such land until a court order is obtained; and

 (c) the force used is not greater than would be justifiable if the person obstructing the actor were using force against him to prevent his passage.

Section 3.07. Use of Force in Law Enforcement.

 (1) Use of Force Justifiable to Effect an Arrest. Subject to the provisions of this Section and of Section 3.09, the use of force upon or toward the person of another is justifiable when the actor is making or assisting in making an arrest and the actor believes that such force is immediately necessary to effect a lawful arrest.

 (2) Limitations on the Use of Force.

 (a) The use of force is not justifiable under this Section unless:

  (i) the actor makes known the purpose of the arrest or believes that it is otherwise known by or cannot reasonably be made known to the person to be arrested; and

  (ii) when the arrest is made under a warrant, the warrant is valid or believed by the actor to be valid.

 (b) The use of deadly force is not justifiable under this Section unless:

  (i) the arrest is for a felony; and

  (ii) the person effecting the arrest is authorized to act as a peace officer or is assisting a person whom he believes to be authorized to act as a peace officer; and

  (iii) the actor believes that the force employed creates no substantial risk of injury to innocent persons; and

  (iv) the actor believes that:

   (1) the crime for which the arrest is made involved conduct including the use or threatened use of deadly force; or

   (2) there is a substantial risk that the person to be arrested will cause death or serious bodily harm if his apprehension is delayed.

 (3) Use of Force to Prevent Escape from Custody. The use of force to prevent the escape of an arrested person from custody is justifiable when the force could justifiably have been employed to effect the arrest under which the person is in custody, except that a guard or other person authorized to act as a peace officer is

justified in using any force, including deadly force, which he believes to be immediately necessary to prevent the escape of a person from a jail, prison, or other institution for the detention of persons charged with or convicted of a crime.

(4) Use of Force by Private Person Assisting an Unlawful Arrest.

(a) A private person who is summoned by a peace officer to assist in effecting an unlawful arrest, is justified in using any force which he would be justified in using if the arrest were lawful, provided that he does not believe the arrest is unlawful.

(b) A private person who assists another private person in effecting an unlawful arrest, or who, not being summoned, assists a peace officer in effecting an unlawful arrest, is justified in using any force which he would be justified in using if the arrest were lawful, provided that (i) he believes the arrest is lawful, and (ii) the arrest would be lawful if the facts were as he believes them to be.

(5) Use of Force to Prevent Suicide or the Commission of a Crime.

(a) The use of force upon or toward the person of another is justifiable when the actor believes that such force is immediately necessary to prevent such other person from committing suicide, inflicting serious bodily harm upon himself, committing or consummating the commission of a crime involving or threatening bodily harm, damage to or loss of property or a breach of the peace, except that:

(i) any limitations imposed by the other provisions of this Article on the justifiable use of force in self-protection, for the protection of others, the protection of property, the effectuation of an arrest or the prevention of an escape from custody shall apply notwithstanding the criminality of the conduct against which such force is used; and

(ii) the use of deadly force is not in any event justifiable under this Subsection unless:

(1) the actor believes that there is a substantial risk that the person whom he seeks to prevent from committing a crime will cause death or serious bodily harm to another unless the commission or the consummation of the crime is prevented and that the use of such force presents no substantial risk of injury to innocent persons; or

(2) the actor believes that the use of such force is necessary to suppress a riot or mutiny after the rioters or mutineers have been ordered to disperse and warned, in any particular manner that the law may require, that such force will be used if they do not obey.

(b) The justification afforded by this Subsection extends to the use of confinement as preventive force only if the actor takes all reasonable measures to terminate the confinement as soon as he knows that he safely can, unless the person confined has been arrested on a charge of crime.

Section 3.08. Use of Force by Persons with Special Responsibility for Care, Discipline or Safety of Others.

The use of force upon or toward the person of another is justifiable if:

(1) the actor is the parent or guardian or other person similarly responsible for the general care and supervision of a minor or a person acting at the request of such parent, guardian or other responsible person and:

(a) the force is used for the purpose of safeguarding or promoting the welfare of the minor, including the prevention or punishment of his misconduct; and

(b) the force used is not designed to cause or known to create a substantial risk of causing death, serious bodily harm, disfigurement, extreme pain or mental distress or gross degradation; or

(2) the actor is a teacher or a person otherwise entrusted with the care or supervision for a special purpose of a minor and:

(a) the actor believes that the force used is necessary to further such special purpose, including the maintenance of reasonable discipline in a school, class or other group, and that the use of such force is consistent with the welfare of the minor; and

(b) the degree of force, if it had been used by the parent or guardian of the minor, would not be unjustifiable under Subsection (1)(b) of this Section; or

(3) the actor is the guardian or other person similarly responsible for the general care and supervision of an incompetent person; and:

(a) the force is used for the purpose of safeguarding or promoting the welfare of the incompetent person, including the prevention of his misconduct, or, when such incompetent person is in a hospital or other institution for his care and custody, for the maintenance of reasonable discipline in such institution; and

(b) the force used is not designed to cause or known to create a substantial risk of causing death, serious bodily harm, disfigurement, extreme or unnecessary pain, mental distress, or humiliation; or

(4) the actor is a doctor or other therapist or a person assisting him at his direction, and:

(a) the force is used for the purpose of administering a recognized form of treatment which the actor believes to be adapted to promoting the physical or mental health of the patient; and

(b) the treatment is administered with the consent of the patient or, if the patient is a minor or an incompetent person, with the consent of his parent or guardian or other person legally competent to consent in his behalf, or the treatment is administered in an emergency when the actor believes that no one competent to consent can be consulted and that a reasonable person, wishing to safeguard the welfare of the patient, would consent; or

(5) the actor is a warden or other authorized official of a correctional institution, and:

(a) he believes that the force used is necessary for the purpose of enforcing the lawful rules or procedures of the institution, unless his belief in the lawfulness of the rule or procedure sought to be enforced is erroneous and his error is due to ignorance or mistake as to the provisions of the Code, any other provision of the criminal law or the law governing the administration of the institution; and

(b) the nature or degree of force used is not forbidden by Article 303 or 304 of the Code; and

(c) if deadly force is used, its use is otherwise justifiable under this Article; or

(6) the actor is a person responsible for the safety of a vessel or an aircraft or a person acting at his direction, and

(a) he believes that the force used is necessary to prevent interference with the operation of the vessel or aircraft or obstruction of the execution of a lawful order, unless his belief in the lawfulness of the order is erroneous and his error is due to ignorance or mistake as to the law defining his authority; and

(b) if deadly force is used, its use is otherwise justifiable under this Article; or

(7) the actor is a person who is authorized or required by law to maintain order or decorum in a vehicle, train or other carrier or in a place where others are assembled, and:

(a) he believes that the force used is necessary for such purpose; and

(b) the force used is not designed to cause or known to create a substantial risk of causing death, bodily harm, or extreme mental distress.

Section 3.09. Mistake of Law as to Unlawfulness of Force or Legality of Arrest; Reckless or Negligent Use of Otherwise Justifiable Force; Reckless or Negligent Injury or Risk of Injury to Innocent Persons.

(1) The justification afforded by Sections 3.04 to 3.07, inclusive, is unavailable when:

(a) the actor's belief in the unlawfulness of the force or conduct against which he employs protective force or his belief in the lawfulness of an arrest which he endeavors to effect by force is erroneous; and

(b) his error is due to ignorance or mistake as to the provisions of the Code, any other provision of the criminal law or the law governing the legality of an arrest or search.

(2) When the actor believes that the use of force upon or toward the person of another is necessary for any of the purposes for which such belief would establish a justification under Sections 3.03 to 3.08 but the actor is reckless or negligent in having such belief or in acquiring or failing to acquire any knowledge or belief which is material to the justiciability of his use of force, the justification afforded by those Sections is unavailable in a prosecution for an offense for which recklessness or negligence, as the case may be, suffices to establish culpability.

(3) When the actor is justified under Sections 3.03 to 3.08 in using force upon or toward the person of another but he recklessly or negligently injures or creates a risk of injury to innocent persons, the justification afforded by those Sections is unavailable in a prosecution for such recklessness or negligence towards innocent persons.

Section 3.10. Justification in Property Crimes.

Conduct involving the appropriation, seizure or destruction of, damage to, intrusion on or interference with property is justifiable under circumstances which would establish a defense of privilege in a civil action based thereon, unless:

(1) the Code or the law defining the offense deals with the specific situation involved; or

(2) a legislative purpose to exclude the justification claimed otherwise plainly appears.

Section 3.11. Definitions.

In this Article, unless a different meaning plainly is required:

(1) "unlawful force" means force, including confinement, which is employed without the consent of the person against whom it is directed and the employment of which constitutes an offense or actionable tort or would constitute such offense or tort except for a defense (such as the absence of intent, negligence, or mental capacity; duress; youth; or diplomatic status) not amounting to a privilege to use the force. Assent constitutes consent, within the meaning of this Section, whether or not it otherwise is legally effective, except assent to the infliction of death or serious bodily harm.

(2) "deadly force" means force which the actor uses with the purpose of causing or which he knows to create a substantial risk of causing death or serious bodily harm. Purposely firing a firearm in the direction of another person or at a vehicle in which another person is believed to be constitutes deadly force. A threat to cause death or serious bodily harm, by the production of a weapon or otherwise, so long as the actor's purpose is limited to creating an apprehension that he will use deadly force if necessary, does not constitute deadly force;

(3) "dwelling" means any building or structure, though movable or temporary, or a portion thereof, which is for the time being the actor's home or place of lodging.

Article 4. Responsibility.

Section 4.01. Mental Disease or Defect Excluding Responsibility.

(1) A person is not responsible for criminal conduct if at the time of such conduct as a result of mental disease or defect he lacks substantial capacity either to appreciate the criminality [wrongfulness] of his conduct or to conform his conduct to the requirements of law.

(2) As used in this Article, the terms "mental disease or defect" do not include an abnormality manifested only by repeated criminal or otherwise antisocial conduct.

Section 4.02. Evidence of Mental Disease or Defect Admissible When Relevant to Element of the Offense; [Mental Disease or Defect Impairing Capacity as Ground for Mitigation of Punishment in Capital Cases].

(1) Evidence that the defendant suffered from a mental disease or defect is admissible whenever it is relevant to prove that the defendant did or did not have a state of mind which is an element of the offense.

[(2) Whenever the jury or the Court is authorized to determine or to recommend whether or not the defendant shall be sentenced to death or imprisonment upon conviction, evidence that the capacity of the defendant to appreciate the criminality [wrongfulness] of his conduct or to conform his conduct to the requirements of law was impaired as a result of mental disease or defect is admissible in favor of sentence of imprisonment.]

Section 4.03. Mental Disease or Defect Excluding Responsibility Is Affirmative Defense; Requirement of Notice; Form of Verdict and Judgment When Finding of Irresponsibility Is Made.

(1) Mental disease or defect excluding responsibility is an affirmative defense.

(2) Evidence of mental disease or defect excluding responsibility is not admissible unless the defendant, at the time of entering his plea of not guilty or within ten days thereafter or at such later time as the Court may for good cause permit, files a written notice of his purpose to rely on such defense.

(3) When the defendant is acquitted on the ground of mental disease or defect excluding responsibility, the verdict and the judgment shall so state.

Section 4.04. Mental Disease or Defect Excluding Fitness to Proceed.

No person who as a result of mental disease or defect lacks capacity to understand the proceedings against him or to assist in his own defense shall be tried, convicted or sentenced for the commission of an offense so long as such incapacity endures.

Section 4.05. Psychiatric Examination of Defendant with Respect to Mental Disease or Defect.

(1) Whenever the defendant has filed a notice of intention to rely on the defense of mental disease or defect excluding responsibility, or there is reason to doubt his fitness to proceed, or reason to believe that mental disease or defect of the defendant will otherwise become an issue in the cause, the Court shall appoint at least one qualified psychiatrist or shall request the Superintendent of the Hospital to designate at least one qualified psychiatrist, which designation may be or include himself, to examine and report upon the mental condition of the defendant. The Court may order the defendant to be committed to a hospital or other suitable facility for the purpose of the examination for a period of not exceeding sixty days or such longer period as the Court determines to be necessary for the purpose and may direct that a qualified psychiatrist retained by the defendant be permitted to witness and participate in the examination.

(2) In such examination any method may be employed which is accepted by the medical profession for the examination of those alleged to be suffering from mental disease or defect.

(3) The report of the examination shall include the following: (a) a description of the nature of the examination; (b) a diagnosis of the mental condition of the defendant; (c) if the defendant suffers from a mental disease or defect, an opinion as to his capacity to understand the proceedings against him and to assist in his own defense; (d) when a notice of intention to rely on the defense of irresponsibility has been filed, an opinion as to the extent, if any, to which the capacity of the defendant to appreciate the criminality [wrongfulness] of his conduct or to conform his conduct to the requirements of law was impaired at the time of the criminal conduct charged; and (e) when directed by the Court, an opinion

as to the capacity of the defendant to have a particular state of mind which is an element of the offense charged.

If the examination cannot be conducted by reason of the unwillingness of the defendant to participate therein, the report shall so state and shall include, if possible, an opinion as to whether such unwillingness of the defendant was the result of mental disease or defect.

The report of the examination shall be filed [in triplicate] with the clerk of the Court, who shall cause copies to be delivered to the district attorney and to counsel for the defendant.

Section 4.06. Determination of Fitness to Proceed; Effect of Finding of Unfitness; Proceedings if Fitness Is Regained; [Post-Commitment Hearing].

(1) When the defendant's fitness to proceed is drawn in question, the issue shall be determined by the Court. If neither the prosecuting attorney nor counsel for the defendant contests the finding of the report filed pursuant to Section 4.05, the Court may make the determination on the basis of such report. If the finding is contested, the Court shall hold a hearing on the issue. If the report is received in evidence upon such hearing, the party who contests the finding thereof shall have the right to summon and to cross-examine the psychiatrists who joined in the report and to offer evidence upon the issue.

(2) If the Court determines that the defendant lacks fitness to proceed, the proceeding against him shall be suspended, except as provided in Subsection (3) [Subsections (3) and (4)] of this Section, and the Court shall commit him to the custody of the Commissioner of Mental Hygiene [Public Health or Correction] to be placed in an appropriate institution of the Department of Mental Hygiene [Public Health or Correction] for so long as such unfitness shall endure. When the Court, on its own motion or upon the application of the Commissioner of Mental Hygiene [Public Health or Correction] or the prosecuting attorney, determines, after a hearing if a hearing is requested, that the defendant has regained fitness to proceed, the proceeding shall be resumed. If, however, the Court is of the view that so much time has elapsed since the commitment of the defendant that it would be unjust to resume the criminal proceeding, the Court may dismiss the charge and may order the defendant to be discharged or, subject to the law governing the civil commitment of persons suffering from mental disease or defect, order the defendant to be committed to an appropriate institution of the Department of Mental Hygiene [Public Health].

(3) The fact that the defendant's unfit to proceed does not preclude any legal objection to the prosecution which is susceptible of fair determination prior to trial and without the personal participation of the defendant. [Alternative: (3) At any time within ninety days after commitment as provided in Subsection (2) of this Section, or at any later time with permission of the Court granted for good cause, the defendant or his counsel or the Commissioner of Mental Hygiene [Public Health or Correction] may apply for a special post-commitment hearing. If the application is made by or on behalf of a defendant not represented by counsel, he shall be afforded a reasonable opportunity to obtain counsel, and if he

lacks funds to do so, counsel shall be assigned by the Court. The application shall be granted only if the counsel for the defendant satisfies the Court by affidavit or otherwise that as an attorney he has reasonable grounds for a good faith belief that his client has, on the facts and the law, a defense to the charge other than mental disease or defect excluding responsibility.]

[(4) If the motion for a special post-commitment hearing is granted, the hearing shall be by the Court without a jury. No evidence shall be offered at the hearing by either party on the issue of mental disease or defect as a defense to, or in mitigation of, the crime charged. After hearing, the Court may in an appropriate case quash the indictment or other charge, or find it to be defective or insufficient, or determine that it is not proved beyond a reasonable doubt by the evidence, or otherwise terminate the proceedings on the evidence or the law. In any such case, unless all defects in the proceedings are promptly cured, the Court shall terminate the commitment ordered under Subsection (2) of this Section and order the defendant to be discharged or, subject to the law governing the civil commitment of persons suffering from mental disease or defect, order the defendant to be committed to an appropriate institution of the Department of Mental Hygiene [Public Health].]

Section 4.07. Determination of Irresponsibility on Basis of Report; Access to Defendant by Psychiatrist of His Own Choice; Form of Expert Testimony When Issue of Responsibility Is Tried.

(1) If the report filed pursuant to Section 4.05 finds that the defendant at the time of the criminal conduct charged suffered from a mental disease or defect which substantially impaired his capacity to appreciate the criminality [wrongfulness] of his conduct or to conform his conduct to the requirements of law, and the Court, after a hearing if a hearing is requested by the prosecuting attorney or the defendant, is satisfied that such impairment was sufficient to exclude responsibility, the Court on motion of the defendant shall enter judgment of acquittal on the ground of mental disease or defect excluding responsibility.

(2) When, notwithstanding the report filed pursuant to Section 4.05, the defendant wishes to be examined by a qualified psychiatrist or other expert of his own choice, such examiner shall be permitted to have reasonable access to the defendant for the purposes of such examination.

(3) Upon the trial, the psychiatrists who reported pursuant to Section 4.05 may be called as witnesses by the prosecution, the defendant or the Court. If the issue is being tried before a jury, the jury may be informed that the psychiatrists were designated by the Court or by the Superintendent of the _____ Hospital at the request of the Court, as the case may be. If called by the Court, the witness shall be subject to cross-examination by the prosecution and by the defendant. Both the prosecution and the defendant may summon any other qualified psychiatrist or other expert to testify, but no one who has not examined the defendant shall be competent to testify to an expert opinion with respect to the mental condition or responsibility of the defendant, as distinguished from the validity of the procedure followed by, or the general scientific propositions stated by, another witness.

(4) When a psychiatrist or other expert who has examined the defendant testifies concerning his mental condition, he shall be permitted to make a statement as to the nature of his examination, his diagnosis of the mental condition of the defendant at the time of the commission of the offense charged and his opinion as to the extent, if any, to which the capacity of the defendant to appreciate the criminality [wrongfulness] of his conduct or to conform his conduct to the requirements of law or to have a particular state of mind which is an element of the offense charged was impaired as a result of mental disease or defect at that time. He shall be permitted to make any explanation reasonably serving to clarify his diagnosis and opinion and may be cross-examined as to any matter bearing on his competency or credibility or the validity of his diagnosis or opinion.

Section 4.08. Legal Effect of Acquittal on the Ground of Mental Disease or Defect Excluding Responsibility; Commitment; Release or Discharge.

(1) When a defendant is acquitted on the ground of mental disease or defect excluding responsibility, the Court shall order him to be committed to the custody of the Commissioner of Mental Hygiene [Public Health] to be placed in an appropriate institution for custody, care and treatment.

(2) If the Commissioner of Mental Hygiene [Public Health] is of the view that a person committed to his custody, pursuant to paragraph (1) of this Section, may be discharged or released on condition without danger to himself or to others, he shall make application for the discharge or release of such person in a report to the Court by which such person was committed and shall transmit a copy of such application and report to the prosecuting attorney of the county [parish] from which the defendant was committed. The Court shall thereupon appoint at least two qualified psychiatrists to examine such person and to report within sixty days, or such longer period as the Court determines to be necessary for the purpose, their opinion as to his mental condition. To facilitate such examination and the proceedings thereon, the Court may cause such person to be confined in any institution located near the place where the Court sits, which may hereafter be designated by the Commissioner of Mental Hygiene [Public Health] as suitable for the temporary detention of irresponsible persons.

(3) If the Court is satisfied by the report filed pursuant to paragraph (2) of this Section and such testimony of the reporting psychiatrists as the Court deems necessary that the committed person may be discharged or released on condition without danger to himself or others, the Court shall order his discharge or his release on such conditions as the Court determines to be necessary. If the Court is not so satisfied, it shall promptly order a hearing to determine whether such person may safely be discharged or released. Any such hearing shall be deemed a civil proceeding and the burden shall be upon the committed person to prove that he may safely be discharged or released. According to the determination of the Court upon the hearing, the committed person shall thereupon be discharged or released on such conditions as the Court determines to be necessary, or shall be recommitted to the custody of the Commissioner of Mental Hygiene [Public Health], subject to discharge or release only in accordance with the procedure prescribed above for a first hearing.

(4) If, within [five] years after the conditional release of a committed person, the Court shall determine, after hearing evidence, that the conditions of release have not been fulfilled and that for the safety of such person or for the safety of others his conditional release should be revoked, the Court shall forthwith order him to be recommitted to the Commissioner of Mental Hygiene [Public Health], subject to discharge or release only in accordance with the procedure prescribed above for a first hearing.

(5) A committed person may make application for his discharge or release to the Court by which he was committed, and the procedure to be followed upon such application shall be the same as that prescribed above in the case of an application by the Commissioner of Mental Hygiene [Public Health]. However, no such application by a committed person need be considered until he has been confined for a period of not less than [six months] from the date of the order of commitment, and if the determination of the Court be adverse to the application, such person shall not be permitted to file a further application until [one year] has elapsed from the date of any preceding hearing on an application for his release or discharge.

Section 4.09. Statements for Purposes of Examination or Treatment Inadmissible Except on Issue of Mental Condition.

A statement made by a person subjected to psychiatric examination or treatment pursuant to Sections 4.05, 4.06 or 4.08 for the purposes of such examination or treatment shall not be admissible in evidence against him in any criminal proceeding on any issue other than that of his mental condition but it shall be admissible upon that issue, whether or not it would otherwise be deemed a privileged communication [, unless such statement constitutes an admission of guilt of the crime charged].

Section 4.10. Immaturity Excluding Criminal Convictions; Transfer of Proceedings to Juvenile Court.

(1) A person shall not be tried for or convicted of an offense if:
   (a) at the time of the conduct charged to constitute the offense he was less than sixteen years of age [, in which case the Juvenile Court shall have exclusive jurisdiction*]; or
   (b) at the time of the conduct charged to constitute the offense he was sixteen or seventeen years of age, unless:
      (i) the Juvenile Court has no jurisdiction over him, or,
      (ii) the Juvenile Court has entered an order waiving jurisdiction and consenting to the institution of criminal proceedings against him.
(2) No court shall have jurisdiction to try or convict a person of an offense if criminal proceedings against him are barred by Subsection (1) of this Section. When it appears that a person charged with the commission of an offense may be of such an age that criminal proceedings may be barred under Subsection (1)

*The bracketed words are unnecessary if the Juvenile Court Act so provides or is amended accordingly.

of this Section, the Court shall hold a hearing thereon, and the burden shall be on the prosecution to establish to the satisfaction of the Court that the criminal proceeding is not barred upon such grounds. If the Court determines that the proceeding is barred, custody of the person charged shall be surrendered to the Juvenile Court, and the case, including all papers and processes relating thereto, shall be transferred.

Article 5. Inchoate Crimes.

Section 5.01. Criminal Attempt.

(1) Definition of Attempt. A person is guilty of an attempt to commit a crime if, acting with the kind of culpability otherwise required for commission of the crime, he:

(a) purposely engages in conduct which would constitute the crime if the attendant circumstances were as he believes them to be; or

(b) when causing a particular result is an element of the crime, does or omits to do anything with the purpose of causing or with the belief that it will cause such result without further conduct on his part; or

(c) purposely does or omits to do anything which, under the circumstances as he believes them to be, is an act or omission constituting a substantial step in a course of conduct planned to culminate in his commission of the crime.

(2) Conduct Which May Be Held Substantial Step Under Subsection (1)(c). Conduct shall not be held to constitute a substantial step under Subsection (1)(c) of this Section unless it is strongly corroborative of the actor's criminal purpose. Without negativing the sufficiency of other conduct, the following, if strongly corroborative of the actor's criminal purpose, shall not be held insufficient as a matter of law:

(a) lying in wait, searching for or following the contemplated victim of the crime;

(b) enticing or seeking to entice the contemplated victim of the crime to go to the place contemplated for its commission;

(c) reconnoitering the place contemplated for the commission of the crime;

(d) unlawful entry of a structure, vehicle or enclosure in which it is contemplated that the crime will be committed;

(e) possession of materials to be employed in the commission of the crime, which are specially designed for such unlawful use or which can serve no lawful purpose of the actor under the circumstances;

(f) possession, collection or fabrication of materials to be employed in the commission of the crime, at or near the place contemplated for its commission, where such possession, collection or fabrication serves no lawful purpose of the actor under the circumstances;

(g) soliciting an innocent agent to engage in conduct constituting an element of the crime.

(3) Conduct Designed to Aid Another in Commission of a Crime. A person who engages in conduct designed to aid another to commit a crime which would

establish his complicity under Section 2.06 if the crime were committed by such other person, is guilty of an attempt to commit the crime, although the crime is not committed or attempted by such other person.

(4) Renunciation of Criminal Purpose. When the actor's conduct would otherwise constitute an attempt under Subsection (1)(b) or (1)(c) of this Section, it is an affirmative defense that he abandoned his effort to commit the crime or otherwise prevented its commission, under circumstances manifesting a complete and voluntary renunciation of his criminal purpose. The establishment of such defense does not, however, affect the liability of an accomplice who did not join in such abandonment or prevention. Within the meaning of this Article, renunciation of criminal purpose is not voluntary if it is motivated, in whole or in part, by circumstances, not present or apparent at the inception of the actor's course of conduct, which increase the probability of detection or apprehension or which make more difficult the accomplishment of the criminal purpose. Renunciation is not complete if it is motivated by a decision to postpone the criminal conduct until a more advantageous time or to transfer the criminal effort to another but similar objective or victim.

Section 5.02. Criminal Solicitation.

(1) Definition of Solicitation. A person is guilty of solicitation to commit a crime if with the purpose of promoting or facilitating its commission he commands, encourages or requests another person to engage in specific conduct which would constitute such crime or an attempt to commit such crime or which would establish his complicity in its commission or attempted commission.

(2) Uncommunicated Solicitation. It is immaterial under Subsection (1) of this Section that the actor fails to communicate with the person he solicits to commit a crime if his conduct was designed to effect such communication.

(3) Renunciation of Criminal Purpose. It is an affirmative defense that the actor, after soliciting another person to commit a crime, persuaded him not to do so or otherwise prevented the commission of the crime, under circumstances manifesting a complete and voluntary renunciation of his criminal purpose.

Section 5.03. Criminal Conspiracy.

(1) Definition of Conspiracy. A person is guilty of conspiracy with another person or persons to commit a crime if with the purpose of promoting or facilitating its commission he:

(a) agrees with such other person or persons that they or one or more of them will engage in conduct which constitutes such crime or an attempt or solicitation to commit such crime; or

(b) agrees to aid such other person or persons in the planning or commission of such crime or of an attempt or solicitation to commit such crime.

(2) Scope of Conspiratorial Relationship. If a person guilty of conspiracy, as defined by Subsection (1) of this Section, knows that a person with whom he conspires to commit a crime has conspired with another person or persons to com-

mit the same crime, he is guilty of conspiring with such other person or persons, whether or not he knows their identity, to commit such crime.

(3) Conspiracy With Multiple Criminal Objectives. If a person conspires to commit a number of crimes, he is guilty of only one conspiracy so long as such multiple crimes are the object of the same agreement or continuous conspiratorial relationship.

(4) Joinder and Venue in Conspiracy Prosecutions.

(a) Subject to the provisions of paragraph (b) of this Subsection, two or more persons charged with criminal conspiracy may be prosecuted jointly if:

(i) they are charged with conspiring with one another; or

(ii) the conspiracies alleged, whether they have the same or different parties, are so related that they constitute different aspects of a scheme of organized criminal conduct.

(b) In any joint prosecution under paragraph (a) of this Subsection:

(i) no defendant shall be charged with a conspiracy in any county [parish or district] other than one in which he entered into such conspiracy or in which an overt act pursuant to such conspiracy was done by him or by a person with whom he conspired; and

(ii) neither the liability of any defendant nor the admissibility against him of evidence of acts or declarations of another shall be enlarged by such joinder; and

(iii) the Court shall order a severance or take a special verdict as to any defendant who so requests, if it deems it necessary or appropriate to promote the fair determination of his guilt or innocence, and shall take any other proper measures to protect the fairness of the trial.

(5) Overt Act. No person may be convicted of conspiracy to commit a crime, other than a felony of the first or second degree, unless an overt act in pursuance of such conspiracy is alleged and proved to have been done by him or by a person with whom he conspired.

(6) Renunciation of Criminal Purpose. It is an affirmative defense that the actor, after conspiring to commit a crime, thwarted the success of the conspiracy, under circumstances manifesting a complete and voluntary renunciation of his criminal purpose.

(7) Duration of Conspiracy. For purposes of Section 1.06(4):

(a) conspiracy is a continuing course of conduct which terminates when the crime or crimes which are its object are committed or the agreement that they be committed is abandoned by the defendant and by those with whom he conspired; and

(b) such abandonment is presumed if neither the defendant nor anyone with whom he conspired does any overt act in pursuance of the conspiracy during the applicable period of limitation; and

(c) if an individual abandons the agreement, the conspiracy is terminated as to him only if and when he advises those with whom he conspired of his abandonment or he informs the law enforcement authorities of the existence of the conspiracy and of his participation therein.

Section 5.04. Incapacity, Irresponsibility or Immunity of Party to Solicitation or Conspiracy.

(1) Except as provided in Subsection (2) of this Section, it is immaterial to the liability of a person who solicits or conspires with another to commit a crime that:

> (a) he or the person whom he solicits or with whom he conspires does not occupy a particular position or have a particular characteristic which is an element of such crime, if he believes that one of them does; or
>
> (b) the person whom he solicits or with whom he conspires is irresponsible or has an immunity to prosecution or conviction for the commission of the crime.

(2) It is a defense to a charge of solicitation or conspiracy to commit a crime that if the criminal object were achieved, the actor would not be guilty of a crime under the law defining the offense or as an accomplice under Section 2.06(5) or 2.06(6)(a) or (b).

Section 5.05. Grading of Criminal Attempt, Solicitation and Conspiracy; Mitigation in Cases of Lesser Danger; Multiple Convictions Barred.

(1) Grading. Except as otherwise provided in this Section, attempt, solicitation and conspiracy are crimes of the same grade and degree as the most serious offense which is attempted or solicited or is an object of the conspiracy. An attempt, solicitation or conspiracy to commit a [capital crime or a] felony of the first degree is a felony of the second degree.

(2) Mitigation. If the particular conduct charged to constitute a criminal attempt, solicitation or conspiracy is so inherently unlikely to result or culminate in the commission of a crime that neither such conduct nor the actor presents a public danger warranting the grading of such offense under this Section, the Court shall exercise its power under Section 6.12 to enter judgment and impose sentence for a crime of lower grade or degree or, in extreme cases, may dismiss the prosecution.

(3) Multiple Convictions. A person may not be convicted of more than one offense defined by this Article for conduct designed to commit or to culminate in the commission of the same crime.

Section 5.06. Possessing Instruments of Crime; Weapons.

(1) Criminal Instruments Generally. A person commits a misdemeanor if he possesses any instrument of crime with purpose to employ it criminally. "Instrument of crime" means:

> (a) anything specially made or specially adapted for criminal use; or
>
> (b) anything commonly used for criminal purposes and possessed by the actor under circumstances which do not negative unlawful purpose.

(2) Presumption of Criminal Purpose from Possession of Weapon. If a person possesses a firearm or other weapon on or about his person, in a vehicle occupied by him, or otherwise readily available for use, it is presumed that he had the purpose to employ it criminally, unless:

(a) the weapon is possessed in the actor's home or place of business;

(b) the actor is licensed or otherwise authorized by law to possess such weapon; or

(c) the weapon is of a type commonly used in lawful sport.

"Weapon" means anything readily capable of lethal use and possessed under circumstances not manifestly appropriate for lawful uses which it may have; the term includes a firearm which is not loaded or lacks a clip or other component to render it immediately operable, and components which can readily be assembled into a weapon.

(3) Presumptions as to Possession of Criminal Instruments in Automobiles. Where a weapon or other instrument of crime is found in an automobile, it shall be presumed to be in the possession of the occupant if there is but one. If there is more than one occupant, it shall be presumed to be in the possession of all, except under the following circumstances:

(a) where it is found upon the person of one of the occupants;

(b) where the automobile is not a stolen one and the weapon or instrument is found out of view in a glove compartment, car trunk, or other enclosed customary depository, in which case it shall be presumed to be in the possession of the occupant or occupants who own or have authority to operate the automobile;

(c) in the case of a taxicab, a weapon or instrument found in the passengers' portion of the vehicle shall be presumed to be in the possession of all the passengers, if there are any, and, if not, in the possession of the driver.

Section 5.07. Prohibited Offensive Weapons.

A person commits a misdemeanor if, except as authorized by law, he makes, repairs, sells, or otherwise deals in, uses, or possesses any offensive weapon. "Offensive weapon" means any bomb, machine gun, sawed-off shotgun, firearm specially made or specially adapted for concealment or silent discharge, any blackjack, sandbag, metal knuckles, dagger, or other implement for the infliction of serious bodily injury which serves no common lawful purpose. It is a defense under this Section for the defendant to prove by a preponderance of evidence that he possessed or dealt with the weapon solely as a curio or in a dramatic performance, or that he possessed it briefly in consequence of having found it or taken it from an aggressor, or under circumstances similarly negativing any purpose or likelihood that the weapon would be used unlawfully. The presumptions provided in Section 5.06(3) are applicable to prosecutions under this Section.

Article 6. Authorized Disposition of Offenders.

Section 6.01. Degrees of Felonies.

(1) Felonies defined by this Code are classified, for the purpose of sentence, into three degrees, as follows:

(a) felonies of the first degree;

(b) felonies of the second degree;

(c) felonies of the third degree. A felony is of the first or second degree when it is so designated by the Code. A crime declared to be a felony, without specification of degree, is of the third degree.

(2) Notwithstanding any other provision of law, a felony defined by any statute of this State other than this Code shall constitute for the purpose of sentence a felony of the third degree.

Section 6.02. Sentence in Accordance with Code; Authorized Dispositions.

(1) No person convicted of an offense shall be sentenced otherwise than in accordance with this Article.

[(2) The Court shall sentence a person who has been convicted of murder to death or imprisonment, in accordance with Section 210.6.]

(3) Except as provided in Subsection (2) of this Section and subject to the applicable provisions of the Code, the Court may suspend the imposition of sentence on a person who has been convicted of a crime, may order him to be committed in lieu of sentence, in accordance with Section 6.13, or may sentence him as follows:

(a) to pay a fine authorized by Section 6.03; or

(b) to be placed on probation [, and, in the case of a person convicted of a felony or misdemeanor to imprisonment for a term fixed by the Court not exceeding thirty days to be served as a condition of probation]; or

(c) to imprisonment for a term authorized by Sections 6.05, 6.06, 6.07, 6.08, 6.09, or 7.06; or

(d) to fine and probation or fine and imprisonment, but not to probation and imprisonment [, except as authorized in paragraph (b) of this Subsection].

(4) The Court may suspend the imposition of sentence on a person who has been convicted of a violation or may sentence him to pay a fine authorized by Section 6.03.

(5) This Article does not deprive the Court of any authority conferred by law to decree a forfeiture of property, suspend or cancel a license, remove a person from office, or impose any other civil penalty. Such a judgment or order may be included in the sentence.

Section 6.03. Fines.

A person who has been convicted of an offense may be sentenced to pay a fine not exceeding:

(1) $10,000, when the conviction is of a felony of the first or second degree;

(2) $5,000, when the conviction is of a felony of the third degree;

(3) $1,000, when the conviction is of a misdemeanor;

(4) $500, when the conviction is of a petty misdemeanor or a violation;

(5) any higher amount equal to double the pecuniary gain derived from the offense by the offender;

(6) any higher amount specifically authorized by statute.

Section 6.04. Penalties Against Corporations and Unincorporated Association; Forfeiture of Corporate Charter or Revocation of Certificate Authorizing Foreign Corporation to Do Business in the State.

(1) The Court may suspend the sentence of a corporation or an unincorporated association which has been convicted of an offense or may sentence it to pay a fine authorized by Section 6.03.

(2) (a) The [prosecuting attorney] is authorized to institute civil proceedings in the appropriate court of general jurisdiction to forfeit the charter of a corporation organized under the laws of this State or to revoke the certificate authorizing a foreign corporation to conduct business in this State. The Court may order the charter forfeited or the certificate revoked upon finding (i) that the board of directors or a high managerial agent acting in behalf of the corporation has, in conducting the corporation's affairs, purposely engaged in a persistent course of criminal conduct and (ii) that for the prevention of future criminal conduct of the same character, the public interest requires the charter of the corporation to be forfeited and the corporation to be dissolved or the certificate to be revoked.

(b) When a corporation is convicted of a crime or a high managerial agent of a corporation, as defined in Section 2.07, is convicted of a crime committed in the conduct of the affairs of the corporation, the Court, in sentencing the corporation or the agent, may direct the [prosecuting attorney] to institute proceedings authorized by paragraph (a) of this Subsection.

(c) The proceedings authorized by paragraph (a) of this Subsection shall be conducted in accordance with the procedures authorized by law for the involuntary dissolution of a corporation or the revocation of the certificate authorizing a foreign corporation to conduct business in this State. Such proceedings shall be deemed additional to any other proceedings authorized by law for the purpose of forfeiting the charter of a corporation or revoking the certificate of a foreign corporation.

Section 6.05. Young Adult Offenders.

(1) Specialized Correctional Treatment. A young adult offender is a person convicted of a crime who, at the time of sentencing, is sixteen but less than twenty-two years of age. A young adult offender who is sentenced to a term of imprisonment which may exceed thirty days [alternatives: (1) ninety days; (2) one year] shall be committed to the custody of the Division of Young Adult Correction of the Department of Correction, and shall receive, as far as practicable, such special and individualized correctional and rehabilitative treatment as may be appropriate to his needs.

(2) Special Term. A young adult offender convicted of a felony may, in lieu of any other sentence of imprisonment authorized by this Article, be sentenced to a special term of imprisonment without a minimum and with a maximum of four years, regardless of the degree of the felony involved, if the Court is of the opinion that such special term is adequate for his correction and rehabilitation and will not jeopardize the protection of the public. [(3) Removal of Disabilities; Vacation of Conviction.

(a) In sentencing a young adult offender to the special term provided by this Section or to any sentence other than one of imprisonment, the Court may order that so long as he is not convicted of another felony, the judgment shall not constitute a conviction for the purposes of any disqualification or disability imposed by law upon conviction of a crime.

(b) When any young adult offender is unconditionally discharged from probation or parole before the expiration of the maximum term thereof, the Court may enter an order vacating the judgment of conviction.] [(4) Commitment for Observation. If, after pre-sentence investigation, the Court desires additional information concerning a young adult offender before imposing sentence, it may order that he be committed, for a period not exceeding ninety days, to the custody of the Division of Young Adult Correction of the Department of Correction for observation and study at an appropriate reception or classification center. Such Division of the Department of Correction and the [Young Adult Division of the] Board of Parole shall advise the Court of their findings and recommendations on or before the expiration of such ninety-day period.]

Section 6.06. Sentence of Imprisonment for Felony; Ordinary Terms.

A person who has been convicted of a felony may be sentenced to imprisonment, as follows:

(1) in the case of a felony of the first degree, for a term the minimum of which shall be fixed by the Court at not less than one year nor more than ten years, and the maximum of which shall be life imprisonment;

(2) in the case of a felony of the second degree, for a term the minimum of which shall be fixed by the Court at not less than one year nor more than three years, and the maximum of which shall be ten years;

(3) in the case of a felony of the third degree, for a term the minimum of which shall be fixed by the Court at not less than one year nor more than two years, and the maximum of which shall be five years.

Alternate Section 6.06. Sentence of Imprisonment for Felony; Ordinary Terms.

A person who has been convicted of a felony may be sentenced to imprisonment, as follows:

(1) in the case of a felony of the first degree, for a term the minimum of which shall be fixed by the Court at not less than one year nor more than ten years, and the maximum at not more than twenty years or at life imprisonment;

(2) in the case of a felony of the second degree, for a term the minimum of which shall be fixed by the Court at not less than one year nor more than three years, and the maximum at not more than ten years;

(3) in the case of a felony of the third degree, for a term the minimum of which shall be fixed by the Court at not less than one year nor more than two years, and the maximum at not more than five years. No sentence shall be imposed under this Section of which the minimum is longer than one-half the maximum, or, when the maximum is life imprisonment, longer than ten years.

Section 6.07. Sentence of Imprisonment for Felony; Extended Terms.

In the cases designated in Section 7.03, a person who has been convicted of a felony may be sentenced to an extended term of imprisonment, as follows:

(1) in the case of a felony of the first degree, for a term the minimum of which shall be fixed by the Court at not less than five years nor more than ten years, and the maximum of which shall be life imprisonment;

(2) in the case of a felony of the second degree, for a term the minimum of which shall be fixed by the Court at not less than one year nor more than five years, and the maximum of which shall be fixed by the Court at not less than ten years nor more than twenty years;

(3) in the case of a felony of the third degree, for a term the minimum of which shall be fixed by the Court at not less than one year nor more than three years, and the maximum of which shall be fixed by the Court at not less than five years nor more than ten years.

Section 6.08. Sentence of Imprisonment for Misdemeanors and Petty Misdemeanors; Ordinary Terms.

A person who has been convicted of a misdemeanor or a petty misdemeanor may be sentenced to imprisonment for a definite term which shall be fixed by the Court and shall not exceed one year in the case of a misdemeanor or thirty days in the case of a petty misdemeanor.

Section 6.09. Sentence of Imprisonment for Misdemeanors and Petty Misdemeanors; Extended Terms.

(1) In the cases designated in Section 7.04, a person who has been convicted of a misdemeanor or a petty misdemeanor may be sentenced to an extended term of imprisonment, as follows:

(a) in the case of a misdemeanor, for a term the minimum of which shall be fixed by the Court at not more than one year and the maximum of which shall be three years;

(b) in the case of a petty misdemeanor, for a term the minimum of which shall be fixed by the Court at not more than six months and the maximum of which shall be two years.

(2) No such sentence for an extended term shall be imposed unless:

(a) the Director of Correction has certified that there is an institution in the Department of Correction, or in a county, city [or other appropriate political subdivision of the State] which is appropriate for the detention and correctional treatment of such misdemeanants or petty misdemeanants, and that such institution is available to receive such commitments; and

(b) the [Board of Parole] [Parole Administrator] has certified that the Board of Parole is able to visit such institution and to assume responsibility for the release of such prisoners on parole and for their parole supervision.

Section 6.10. First Release of All Offenders on Parole; Sentence of Imprisonment Includes Separate Parole Term; Length of Parole Term; Length of Recommitment and Reparole After Revocation of Parole; Final Unconditional Release.

(1) First Release of All Offenders on Parole. An offender sentenced to an indefinite term of imprisonment in excess of one year under Section 6.05, 6.06, 6.07, 6.09 or 7.06 shall be released conditionally on parole at or before the expiration of the maximum of such term, in accordance with Article 305.

(2) Sentence of Imprisonment Includes Separate Parole Term; Length of Parole Term. A sentence to an indefinite term of imprisonment in excess of one year under Section 6.05, 6.06, 6.07, 6.09 or 7.06 includes as a separate portion of the sentence a term of parole or of recommitment for violation of the conditions of parole which governs the duration of parole or recommitment after the offender's first conditional release on parole. The minimum of such term is one year and the maximum is five years, unless the sentence was imposed under Section 6.05(2) or Section 6.09, in which case the maximum is two years.

(3) Length of Recommitment and Re-parole After Revocation of Parole. If an offender is recommitted upon revocation of his parole, the term of further imprisonment upon such recommitment and of any subsequent re-parole or recommitment under the same sentence shall be fixed by the Board of Parole but shall not exceed in aggregate length the unserved balance of the maximum parole term provided by Subsection (2) of this Section.

(4) Final Unconditional Release. When the maximum of his parole term has expired or he has been sooner discharged from parole under Section 305.12, an offender shall be deemed to have served his sentence and shall be released unconditionally.

Section 6.11. Place of Imprisonment.

(1) When a person is sentenced to imprisonment for an indefinite term with a maximum in excess of one year, the Court shall commit him to the custody of the Department of Correction [or other single department or agency] for the term of his sentence and until release in accordance with law.

(2) When a person is sentenced to imprisonment for a definite term, the Court shall designate the institution or agency to which he is committed for the term of his sentence and until released in accordance with law.

Section 6.12. Reduction of Conviction by Court to Lesser Degree of Felony or to Misdemeanor.

If, when a person has been convicted of a felony, the Court, having regard to the nature and circumstances of the crime and to the history and character of the defendant, is of the view that it would be unduly harsh to sentence the offender in accordance with the Code, the Court may enter judgment of conviction for a lesser degree of felony or for a misdemeanor and impose sentence accordingly.

Section 6.13. Civil Commitment in Lieu of Prosecution or of Sentence.

(1) When a person prosecuted for a [felony of the third degree,] misdemeanor or petty misdemeanor is a chronic alcoholic, narcotic addict [or prostitute] or person suffering from mental abnormality and the Court is authorized by law to order the civil commitment of such person to a hospital or other institution for medical, psychiatric or other rehabilitative treatment, the Court may order such commitment and dismiss the prosecution.

The order of commitment may be made after conviction, in which event the Court may set aside the verdict or judgment of conviction and dismiss the prosecution.

(2) The Court shall not make an order under Subsection (1) of this Section unless it is of the view that it will substantially further the rehabilitation of the defendant and will not jeopardize the protection of the public.

Article 7. Authority of Court in Sentencing.

Section 7.01. Criteria for Withholding Sentence of Imprisonment and for Placing Defendant on Probation.

(1) The Court shall deal with a person who has been convicted of a crime without imposing sentence of imprisonment unless, having regard to the nature and circumstances of the crime and the history, character and condition of the defendant, it is of the opinion that his imprisonment is necessary for protection of the public because:

(a) there is undue risk that during the period of a suspended sentence or probation the defendant will commit another crime; or

(b) the defendant is in need of correctional treatment that can be provided most effectively by his commitment to an institution; or

(c) a lesser sentence will depreciate the seriousness of the defendant's crime.

(2) The following grounds, while not controlling the discretion of the Court, shall be accorded weight in favor of withholding sentence of imprisonment:

(a) the defendant's criminal conduct neither caused nor threatened serious harm;

(b) the defendant did not contemplate that his criminal conduct would cause or threaten serious harm;

(c) the defendant acted under a strong provocation;

(d) there were substantial grounds tending to excuse or justify the defendant's criminal conduct, though failing to establish a defense;

(e) the victim of the defendant's criminal conduct induced or facilitated its commission;

(f) the defendant has compensated or will compensate the victim of his criminal conduct for the damage or injury that he sustained;

(g) the defendant has no history of prior delinquency or criminal activity or has led a law-abiding life for a substantial period of time before the commission of the present crime;

(h) the defendant's criminal conduct was the result of circumstances unlikely to recur;

(i) the character and attitudes of the defendant indicate that he is unlikely to commit another crime;

(j) the defendant is particularly likely to respond affirmatively to probationary treatment;

(k) the imprisonment of the defendant would entail excessive hardship to himself or his dependents.

(3) When a person who has been convicted of a crime is not sentenced to imprisonment, the Court shall place him on probation if he is in need of the supervision, guidance, assistance or direction that the probation service can provide.

Section 7.02. Criteria for Imposing Fines.

(1) The Court shall not sentence a defendant only to pay a fine, when any other disposition is authorized by law, unless having regard to the nature and circumstances of the crime and to the history and character of the defendant, it is of the opinion that the fine alone suffices for protection of the public.

(2) The Court shall not sentence a defendant to pay a fine in addition to a sentence of imprisonment or probation unless:

(a) the defendant has derived a pecuniary gain from the crime; or

(b) the Court is of opinion that a fine is specially adapted to deterrence of the crime involved or to the correction of the offender.

(3) The Court shall not sentence a defendant to pay a fine unless:

(a) the defendant is or will be able to pay the fine; and

(b) the fine will not prevent the defendant from making restitution or reparation to the victim of the crime.

(4) In determining the amount and method of payment of a fine, the Court shall take into account the financial resources of the defendant and the nature of the burden that its payment will impose.

Section 7.03. Criteria for Sentence of Extended Term of Imprisonment; Felonies.

The Court may sentence a person who has been convicted of a felony to an extended term of imprisonment if it finds one or more of the grounds specified in this Section. The finding of the Court shall be incorporated in the record.

(1) The defendant is a persistent offender whose commitment for an extended term is necessary for protection of the public. The Court shall not make such a finding unless the defendant is over twenty-one years of age and has previously been convicted of two felonies or of one felony and two misdemeanors, committed at different times when he was over [insert Juvenile Court age] years of age.

2) The defendant is a professional criminal whose commitment for an ied term is necessary for protection of the public. The Court shall not make finding unless the defendant is over twenty-one years of age and:

(a) the circumstances of the crime show that the defendant has knowingly devoted himself to criminal activity as a major source of livelihood; or

(b) the defendant has substantial income or resources not explained to be derived from a source other than criminal activity.

(3) The defendant is a dangerous, mentally abnormal person whose commitment for an extended term is necessary for protection of the public. The Court shall not make such a finding unless the defendant has been subjected to a psychiatric examination resulting in the conclusions that his mental condition is gravely abnormal; that his criminal conduct has been characterized by a pattern of repetitive or compulsive behavior or by persistent aggressive behavior with heedless indifference to consequences; and that such condition makes him a serious danger to others.

(4) The defendant is a multiple offender whose criminality was so extensive that a sentence of imprisonment for an extended term is warranted. The Court shall not make such a finding unless:

(a) the defendant is being sentenced for two or more felonies, or is already under sentence of imprisonment for felony, and the sentences of imprisonment involved will run concurrently under Section 7.06; or

(b) the defendant admits in open court the commission of one or more other felonies and asks that they be taken into account when he is sentenced; and

(c) the longest sentences of imprisonment authorized for each of the defendant's crimes, including admitted crimes taken into account, if made to run consecutively would exceed in length the minimum and maximum of the extended term imposed.

Section 7.04. Criteria for Sentence of Extended Term of Imprisonment; Misdemeanors and Petty Misdemeanors.

The Court may sentence a person who has been convicted of a misdemeanor or petty misdemeanor to an extended term of imprisonment if it finds one or more of the grounds specified in this Section. The finding of the Court shall be incorporated in the record.

(1) The defendant is a persistent offender whose commitment for an extended term is necessary for protection of the public. The Court shall not make such a finding unless the defendant has previously been convicted of two crimes, committed at different times when he was over [insert Juvenile Court age] years of age.

(2) The defendant is a professional criminal whose commitment for an extended term is necessary for protection of the public. The Court shall not make such a finding unless:

(a) the circumstances of the crime show that the defendant has knowingly devoted himself to criminal activity as a major source of livelihood; or

(b) the defendant has substantial income or resources not explained to be derived from a source other than criminal activity.

(3) The defendant is a chronic alcoholic, narcotic addict, prostitute or person of abnormal mental condition who requires rehabilitative treatment for a substantial period of time. The Court shall not make such a finding unless, with respect to the particular category to which the defendant belongs, the Director of Correction has certified that there is a specialized institution or facility which is

satisfactory for the rehabilitative treatment of such persons and which otherwise meets the requirements of Section 6.09, Subsection (2).

(4) The defendant is a multiple offender whose criminality was so extensive that a sentence of imprisonment for an extended term is warranted. The Court shall not make such a finding unless:

(a) the defendant is being sentenced for a number of misdemeanors or petty misdemeanors or is already under sentence of imprisonment for crimes of such grades, or admits in open court the commission of one or more such crimes and asks that they be taken into account when he is sentenced; and

(b) maximum fixed sentences of imprisonment for each of the defendant's crimes, including admitted crimes taken into account, if made to run consecutively, would exceed in length the maximum period of the extended term imposed.

Section 7.05. Former Conviction in Another Jurisdiction; Definition and Proof of Conviction; Sentence Taking Into Account Admitted Crimes Bars Subsequent Conviction for Such Crimes.

(1) For purposes of paragraph (1) of Section 7.03 or 7.04, a conviction of the commission of a crime in another jurisdiction shall constitute a previous conviction. Such conviction shall be deemed to have been of a felony if sentence of death or of imprisonment in excess of one year was authorized under the law of such other jurisdiction, of a misdemeanor if sentence of imprisonment in excess of thirty days but not in excess of a year was authorized and of a petty misdemeanor if sentence of imprisonment for not more than thirty days was authorized.

(2) An adjudication by a court of competent jurisdiction that the defendant committed a crime constitutes a conviction for purposes of Sections 7.03 to 7.05 inclusive, although sentence or the execution thereof was suspended, provided that the time to appeal has expired and that the defendant was not pardoned on the ground of innocence.

(3) Prior conviction may be proved by any evidence, including fingerprint records made in connection with arrest, conviction or imprisonment, that reasonably satisfies the Court that the defendant was convicted.

(4) When the defendant has asked that other crimes admitted in open court be taken into account when he is sentenced and the Court has not rejected such request, the sentence shall bar the prosecution or conviction of the defendant in this State for any such admitted crime.

Section 7.06. Multiple Sentences; Concurrent and Consecutive Terms.

(1) Sentences of Imprisonment for More Than One Crime. When multiple sentences of imprisonment are imposed on a defendant for more than one crime, including a crime for which a previous suspended sentence or sentence of probation has been revoked, such multiple sentences shall run concurrently or consecutively as the Court determines at the time of sentence, except that:

(a) a definite and an indefinite term shall run concurrently and both sentences shall be satisfied by service of the indefinite term; and

(b) the aggregate of consecutive definite terms shall not exceed one year; and

(c) the aggregate of consecutive indefinite terms shall not exceed in minimum or maximum length the longest extended term authorized for the highest grade and degree of crime for which any of the sentences was imposed; and

(d) not more than one sentence for an extended term shall be imposed.

(2) Sentences of Imprisonment Imposed at Different Times. When a defendant who has previously been sentenced to imprisonment is subsequently sentenced to another term for a crime committed prior to the former sentence, other than a crime committed while in custody:

(a) the multiple sentences imposed shall so far as possible conform to Subsection (1) of this Section; and

(b) whether the Court determines that the terms shall run concurrently or consecutively, the defendant shall be credited with time served in imprisonment on the prior sentence in determining the permissible aggregate length of the term or terms remaining to be served; and

(c) when a new sentence is imposed on a prisoner who is on parole, the balance of the parole term on the former sentence shall be deemed to run during the period of the new imprisonment.

(3) Sentence of Imprisonment for Crime Committed While on Parole. When a defendant is sentenced to imprisonment for a crime committed while on parole in this State, such term of imprisonment and any period of re-imprisonment that the Board of Parole may require the defendant to serve upon the revocation of his parole shall run concurrently, unless the Court orders them to run consecutively.

(4) Multiple Sentences of Imprisonment in Other Cases. Except as otherwise provided in this Section, multiple terms of imprisonment shall run concurrently or consecutively as the Court determines when the second or subsequent sentence is imposed.

(5) Calculation of Concurrent and Consecutive Terms of Imprisonment.

(a) When indefinite terms run concurrently, the shorter minimum terms merge in and are satisfied by serving the longest minimum term and the shorter maximum terms merge in and are satisfied by discharge of the longest maximum term.

(b) When indefinite terms run consecutively, the minimum terms are added to arrive at an aggregate minimum to be served equal to the sum of all minimum terms and the maximum terms are added to arrive at an aggregate maximum equal to the sum of all maximum terms.

(c) When a definite and an indefinite term run consecutively, the period of the definite term is added to both the minimum and maximum of the indefinite term and both sentences are satisfied by serving the indefinite term.

(6) Suspension of Sentence or Probation and Imprisonment; Multiple Terms of Suspension and Probation. When a defendant is sentenced for more than one offense or a defendant already under sentence is sentenced for another offense committed prior to the former sentence:

(a) the Court shall not sentence to probation a defendant who is under sentence of imprisonment [with more than thirty days to run] or impose a sentence of probation and a sentence of imprisonment [, except as authorized by Section 6.02(3)(b)]; and

(b) multiple periods of suspension or probation shall run concurrently from the date of the first such disposition; and

(c) when a sentence of imprisonment is imposed for an indefinite term, the service of such sentence shall satisfy a suspended sentence on another count or a prior suspended sentence or sentence to probation; and

(d) when a sentence of imprisonment is imposed for a definite term, the period of a suspended sentence on another count or a prior suspended sentence or sentence to probation shall run during the period of such imprisonment.

(7) Offense Committed While Under Suspension of Sentence or Probation. When a defendant is convicted of an offense committed while under suspension of sentence or on probation and such suspension or probation is not revoked:

(a) if the defendant is sentenced to imprisonment for an indefinite term, the service of such sentence shall satisfy the prior suspended sentence or sentence to probation; and

(b) if the defendant is sentenced to imprisonment for a definite term, the period of the suspension or probation shall not run during the period of such imprisonment; and

(c) if sentence is suspended or the defendant is sentenced to probation, the period of such suspension or probation shall run concurrently with or consecutively to the remainder of the prior periods, as the Court determines at the time of sentence.

Section 7.07. Procedure on Sentence; Pre-sentence Investigation and Report; Remand for Psychiatric Examination; Transmission of Records to Department of Correction.

(1) The Court shall not impose sentence without first ordering a pre-sentence investigation of the defendant and according due consideration to a written report of such investigation where:

(a) the defendant has been convicted of a felony; or

(b) the defendant is less than twenty-two years of age and has been convicted of a crime; or

(c) the defendant will be [placed on probation or] sentenced to imprisonment for an extended term.

(2) The Court may order a pre-sentence investigation in any other case.

(3) The pre-sentence investigation shall include an analysis of the circumstances attending the commission of the crime, the defendant's history of delinquency or criminality, physical and mental condition, family situation and background, economic status, education, occupation and personal habits and any other matters that the probation officer deems relevant or the Court directs to be included.

(4) Before imposing sentence, the Court may order the defendant to submit to psychiatric observation and examination for a period of not exceeding

sixty days or such longer period as the Court determines to be necessary for the purpose. The defendant may be remanded for this purpose to any available clinic or mental hospital or the Court may appoint a qualified psychiatrist to make the examination. The report of the examination shall be submitted to the Court.

(5) Before imposing sentence, the Court shall advise the defendant or his counsel of the factual contents and the conclusions of any pre-sentence investigation or psychiatric examination and afford fair opportunity, if the defendant so requests, to controvert them. The sources of confidential information need not, however, be disclosed.

(6) The Court shall not impose a sentence of imprisonment for an extended term unless the ground therefor has been established at a hearing after the conviction of the defendant and on written notice to him of the ground proposed. Subject to the limitation of Subsection (5) of this Section, the defendant shall have the right to hear and controvert the evidence against him and to offer evidence upon the issue.

(7) If the defendant is sentenced to imprisonment, a copy of the report of any pre-sentence investigation or psychiatric examination shall be transmitted forthwith to the Department of Correction [or other state department or agency] or, when the defendant is committed to the custody of specific institution, to such institution.

Section 7.08. Commitment for Observation; Sentence of Imprisonment for Felony Deemed Tentative for Period of One Year; Re-sentence on Petition of Commissioner of Correction.

(1) If, after pre-sentence investigation, the Court desires additional information concerning an offender convicted of a felony or misdemeanor before imposing sentence, it may order that he be committed, for a period not exceeding ninety days, to the custody of the Department of Correction, or, in the case of a young adult offender, to the custody of the Division of Young Adult Correction, for observation and study at an appropriate reception or classification center. The Department and the Board of Parole, or the Young Adult Divisions thereof, shall advise the Court of their findings and recommendations on or before the expiration of such ninety-day period. If the offender is thereafter sentenced to imprisonment, the period of such commitment for observation shall be deducted from the maximum term and from the minimum, if any, of such sentence.

(2) When a person has been sentenced to imprisonment upon conviction of a felony, whether for an ordinary or extended term, the sentence shall be deemed tentative, to the extent provided in this Section, for the period of one year following the date when the offender is received in custody by the Department of Correction [or other state department or agency].

(3) If, as a result of the examination and classification by the Department of Correction [or other state department or agency] of a person under sentence of imprisonment upon conviction of a felony, the Commissioner of Correction [or other department head] is satisfied that the sentence of the Court may have been based upon a misapprehension as to the history, character or physical or mental condition of the offender, the Commissioner, during the period when the offender's sentence is deemed tentative under Subsection (2) of this Section shall file in

the sentencing Court a petition to re-sentence the offender. The petition shall set forth the information as to the offender that is deemed to warrant his re-sentence and may include a recommendation as to the sentence to be imposed.

(4) The Court may dismiss a petition filed under Subsection (3) of this Section without a hearing if it deems the information set forth insufficient to warrant reconsideration of the sentence. If the Court is of the view that the petition warrants such reconsideration, a copy of the petition shall be served on the offender, who shall have the right to be heard on the issue and to be represented by counsel.

(5) When the Court grants a petition filed under Subsection (3) of this Section, it shall re-sentence the offender and may impose any sentence that might have been imposed originally for the felony of which the defendant was convicted. The period of his imprisonment prior to re-sentence and any reduction for good behavior to which he is entitled shall be applied in satisfaction of the final sentence.

(6) For all purposes other than this Section, a sentence of imprisonment has the same finality when it is imposed that it would have if this Section were not in force.

(7) Nothing in this Section shall alter the remedies provided by law for vacating or correcting an illegal sentence.

Section 7.09. Credit for Time of Detention Prior to Sentence; Credit for Imprisonment Under Earlier Sentence for the Same Crime.

(1) When a defendant who is sentenced to imprisonment has previously been detained in any state or local correctional or other institution following his [conviction of] [arrest for] the crime for which such sentence is imposed, such period of detention following his [conviction] [arrest] shall be deducted from the maximum term, and from the minimum, if any, of such sentence. The officer having custody of the defendant shall furnish a certificate to the Court at the time of sentence, showing the length of such detention of the defendant prior to sentence in any state or local correctional or other institution, and the certificate shall be annexed to the official records of the defendant's commitment.

(2) When a judgment of conviction is vacated and a new sentence is thereafter imposed upon the defendant for the same crime, the period of detention and imprisonment theretofore served shall be deducted from the maximum term, and from the minimum, if any, of the new sentence. The officer having custody of the defendant shall furnish a certificate to the Court at the time of sentence, showing the period of imprisonment served under the original sentence, and the certificate shall be annexed to the official records of the defendant's new commitment.

Part II. Definition of Specific Crimes Offenses Involving Danger to the Person

Article 210. Criminal Homicide

Section 210.0. Definitions.

In Articles 210–213, unless a different meaning plainly is required:
(1) "human being" means a person who has been born and is alive;
(2) "bodily injury" means physical pain, illness or any impairment of physical condition;

(3) "serious bodily injury" means bodily injury which creates a substantial risk of death or which causes serious, permanent disfigurement, or protracted loss or impairment of the function of any bodily member or organ;

(4) "deadly weapon" means any firearm, or other weapon, device, instrument, material or substance, whether animate or inanimate, which in the manner it is used or is intended to be used is known to be capable of producing death or serious bodily injury.

Section 210.1. Criminal Homicide.

(1) A person is guilty of criminal homicide if he purposely, knowingly, recklessly or negligently causes the death of another human being.

(2) Criminal homicide is murder, manslaughter or negligent homicide.

Section 210.2. Murder.

(1) Except as provided in Section 210.3(1)(b), criminal homicide constitutes murder when:

(a) it is committed purposely or knowingly; or

(b) it is committed recklessly under circumstances manifesting extreme indifference to the value of human life. Such recklessness and indifference are presumed if the actor is engaged or is an accomplice in the commission of, or an attempt to commit, or flight after committing or attempting to commit robbery, rape or deviate sexual intercourse by force or threat of force, arson, burglary, kidnapping or felonious escape.

(2) Murder is a felony of the first degree [but a person convicted of murder may be sentenced to death, as provided in Section 210.6].

Section 210.3. Manslaughter.

(1) Criminal homicide constitutes manslaughter when:

(a) it is committed recklessly; or

(b) a homicide which would otherwise be murder is committed under the influence of extreme mental or emotional disturbance for which there is reasonable explanation or excuse. The reasonableness of such explanation or excuse shall be determined from the viewpoint of a person in the actor's situation under the circumstances as he believes them to be.

(2) Manslaughter is a felony of the second degree.

Section 210.4. Negligent Homicide.

(1) Criminal homicide constitutes negligent homicide when it is committed negligently.

(2) Negligent homicide is a felony of the third degree.

Section 210.5. Causing or Aiding Suicide.

(1) Causing Suicide as Criminal Homicide. A person may be convicted of criminal homicide for causing another to commit suicide only if he purposely causes such suicide by force, duress or deception.

(2) Aiding or Soliciting Suicide as an Independent Offense. A person who purposely aids or solicits another to commit suicide is guilty of a felony of the second degree if his conduct causes such suicide or an attempted suicide, and otherwise of a misdemeanor.

[Section 210.6. Sentence of Death for Murder; Further Proceedings to Determine Sentence.]

(1) Death Sentence Excluded. When a defendant is found guilty of murder, the Court shall impose sentence for a felony of the first degree if it is satisfied that:

(a) none of the aggravating circumstances enumerated in Subsection (3) of this Section was established by the evidence at the trial or will be established if further proceedings are initiated under Subsection (2) of this Section; or

(b) substantial mitigating circumstances, established by the evidence at the trial, call for leniency; or

(c) the defendant, with the consent of the prosecuting attorney and the approval of the Court, pleaded guilty to murder as a felony of the first degree; or

(d) the defendant was under 18 years of age at the time of the commission of the crime; or

(e) the defendant's physical or mental condition calls for leniency; or

(f) although the evidence suffices to sustain the verdict, it does not foreclose all doubt respecting the defendant's guilt.

(2) Determination by Court or by Court and Jury. Unless the Court imposes sentence under Subsection (1) of this Section, it shall conduct a separate proceeding to determine whether the defendant should be sentenced for a felony of the first degree or sentenced to death. The proceeding shall be conducted before the Court alone if the defendant was convicted by a Court sitting without a jury or upon his plea of guilty or if the prosecuting attorney and the defendant waive a jury with respect to sentence. In other cases it shall be conducted before the Court sitting with the jury which determined the defendant's guilt or, if the Court for good cause shown discharges that jury, with a new jury empaneled for the purpose.

In the proceeding, evidence may be presented as to any matter that the Court deems relevant to sentence, including but not limited to the nature and circumstances of the crime, the defendant's character, background, history, mental and physical condition and any of the aggravating or mitigating circumstances enumerated in Subsections (3) and (4) of this Section. Any such evidence, not legally privileged, which the Court deems to have probative force, may be received, regardless of its admissibility under the exclusionary rules of evidence, provided that the defendant's counsel is accorded a fair opportunity to rebut such evidence. The prosecuting attorney and the defendant or his counsel shall be permitted to present argument for or against sentence of death.

The determination whether sentence of death shall be imposed shall be in the discretion of the Court, except that when the proceeding is conducted before the Court sitting with a jury, the Court shall not impose sentence of death unless it submits to the jury the issue whether the defendant should be sentenced to death or to imprisonment and the jury returns a verdict that the sentence should be death. If the jury is unable to reach a unanimous verdict, the Court shall dismiss the jury and impose sentence for a felony of the first degree.

The Court, in exercising its discretion as to sentence, and the jury, in determining upon its verdict, shall take into account the aggravating and mitigating circumstances enumerated in Subsections (3) and (4) and any other facts that it deems relevant, but it shall not impose or recommend sentence of death unless it finds one of the aggravating circumstances enumerated in Subsection (3) and further finds that there are no mitigating circumstances sufficiently substantial to call for leniency. When the issue is submitted to the jury, the Court shall so instruct and also shall inform the jury of the nature of the sentence of imprisonment that may be imposed, including its implication with respect to possible release upon parole, if the jury verdict is against sentence of death.

Alternative formulation of Subsection (2):

(2) Determination by Court. Unless the Court imposes sentence under Subsection (1) of this Section, it shall conduct a separate proceeding to determine whether the defendant should be sentenced for a felony of the first degree or sentenced to death. In the proceeding, the Court, in accordance with Section 7.07, shall consider the report of the pre-sentence investigation and, if a psychiatric examination has been ordered, the report of such examination. In addition, evidence may be presented as to any matter that the Court deems relevant to sentence, including but not limited to the nature and circumstances of the crime, the defendant's character, background, history, mental and physical condition and any of the aggravating or mitigating circumstances enumerated in Subsections (3) and (4) of this Section. Any such evidence, not legally privileged, which the Court deems to have probative force, may be received, regardless of its admissibility under the exclusionary rules of evidence, provided that the defendant's counsel is accorded a fair opportunity to rebut such evidence. The prosecuting attorney and the defendant or his counsel shall be permitted to present argument for or against sentence of death.

The determination whether sentence of death shall be imposed shall be in the discretion of the Court. In exercising such discretion, the Court shall take into account the aggravating and mitigating circumstances enumerated in Subsections (3) and (4) and any other facts that it deems relevant but shall not impose sentence of death unless it finds one of the aggravating circumstances enumerated in Subsection (3) and further finds that there are no mitigating circumstances sufficiently substantial to call for leniency.

(3) Aggravating Circumstances.

(a) The murder was committed by a convict under sentence of imprisonment.

(b) The defendant was previously convicted of another murder or of a felony involving the use or threat of violence to the person.

(c) At the time the murder was committed the defendant also committed another murder.

(d) The defendant knowingly created a great risk of death to many persons.

(e) The murder was committed while the defendant was engaged or was an accomplice in the commission of, or an attempt to commit, or flight after committing or attempting to commit robbery, rape or deviate sexual intercourse by force or threat of force, arson, burglary or kidnapping.

(f) The murder was committed for the purpose of avoiding or preventing a lawful arrest or effecting an escape from lawful custody.

(g) The murder was committed for pecuniary gain.

(h) The murder was especially heinous, atrocious or cruel, manifesting exceptional depravity.

(4) Mitigating Circumstances.

(a) The defendant has no significant history of prior criminal activity.

(b) The murder was committed while the defendant was under the influence of extreme mental or emotional disturbance.

(c) The victim was a participant in the defendant's homicidal conduct or consented to the homicidal act.

(d) The murder was committed under circumstances which the defendant believed to provide a moral justification or extenuation for his conduct.

(e) The defendant was an accomplice in a murder committed by another person and his participation in the homicidal act was relatively minor.

(f) The defendant acted under duress or under the domination of another person.

(g) At the time of the murder, the capacity of the defendant to appreciate the criminality [wrongfulness] of his conduct or to conform his conduct to the requirements of law was impaired as a result of mental disease or defect or intoxication.

(h) The youth of the defendant at the time of the crime.

Article 211. Assault; Reckless Endangering; Threats

Section 211.0. Definitions.

In this Article, the definitions given in Section 210.0 apply unless a different meaning plainly is required.

Section 211.1. Assault.

(1) Simple Assault. A person is guilty of assault if he:

(a) attempts to cause or purposely, knowingly or recklessly causes bodily injury to another; or

(b) negligently causes bodily injury to another with a deadly weapon; or

(c) attempts by physical menace to put another in fear of imminent serious bodily injury. Simple assault is a misdemeanor unless committed in a fight or scuffle entered into by mutual consent, in which case it is a petty misdemeanor.

(2) Aggravated Assault. A person is guilty of aggravated assault if he:

(a) attempts to cause serious bodily injury to another, or causes such injury purposely, knowingly or recklessly under circumstances manifesting extreme indifference to the value of human life; or

(b) attempts to cause or purposely or knowingly causes bodily injury to another with a deadly weapon. Aggravated assault under paragraph (a) is a felony of the second degree; aggravated assault under paragraph (b) is a felony of the third degree.

Section 211.2. Recklessly Endangering Another Person.

A person commits a misdemeanor if he recklessly engages in conduct which places or may place another person in danger of death or serious bodily injury. Recklessness and danger shall be presumed where a person knowingly points a firearm at or in the direction of another, whether or not the actor believed the firearm to be loaded.

Section 211.3. Terroristic Threats.

A person is guilty of a felony of the third degree if he threatens to commit any crime of violence with purpose to terrorize another or to cause evacuation of a building, place of assembly, or facility of public transportation, or otherwise to cause serious public inconvenience, or in reckless disregard of the risk of causing such terror or inconvenience.

Article 212. Kidnapping and Related Offenses; Coercion.

Section 212.0. Definitions.

In this Article, the definitions given in Section 210.0 apply unless a different meaning plainly is required.

Section 212.1. Kidnapping.

A person is guilty of kidnapping if he unlawfully removes another from his place of residence or business, or a substantial distance from the vicinity where he is found, or if he unlawfully confines another for a substantial period in a place of isolation, with any of the following purposes:

(a) to hold for ransom or reward, or as a shield or hostage; or

(b) to facilitate commission of any felony or flight thereafter; or

(c) to inflict bodily injury on or to terrorize the victim or another; or

(d) to interfere with the performance of any governmental or political function.

Kidnapping is a felony of the first degree unless the actor voluntarily releases the victim alive and in a safe place prior to trial, in which case it is a felony of the second degree. A removal or confinement is unlawful within the meaning of this Section if it is accomplished by force, threat or deception, or, in the case of a person who is under the age of 14 or incompetent, if it is accomplished without the consent of a parent, guardian or other person responsible for general supervision of his welfare.

Section 212.2. Felonious Restraint.

A person commits a felony of the third degree if he knowingly:

(a) restrains another unlawfully in circumstances exposing him to risk of serious bodily injury; or

(b) holds another in a condition of involuntary servitude.

Section 212.3. False Imprisonment.

A person commits a misdemeanor if he knowingly restrains another unlawfully so as to interfere substantially with his liberty.

Section 212.4. Interference with Custody.

(1) Custody of Children. A person commits an offense if he knowingly or recklessly takes or entices any child under the age of 18 from the custody of its parent, guardian or other lawful custodian, when he has no privilege to do so. It is an affirmative defense that:

(a) the actor believed that his action was necessary to preserve the child from danger to its welfare; or

(b) the child, being at the time not less than 14 years old, as taken away at its own instigation without enticement and without purpose to commit a criminal offense with or against the child. Proof that the child was below the critical age gives rise to a presumption that the actor knew the child's age or acted in reckless disregard thereof.

The offense is a misdemeanor unless the actor, not being a parent or person in equivalent relation to the child, acted with knowledge that his conduct would cause serious alarm for the child's safety, or in reckless disregard of a likelihood of causing such alarm, in which case the offense is a felony of the third degree.

(2) Custody of Committed Persons. A person is guilty of a misdemeanor if he knowingly or recklessly takes or entices any committed person away from lawful custody when he is not privileged to do so. "Committed person" means, in addition to anyone committed under judicial warrant, any orphan, neglected or delinquent child, mentally defective or insane person, or other dependent or incompetent person entrusted to another's custody by or through a recognized social agency or otherwise by authority of law.

Section 212.5. Criminal Coercion.

(1) Offense Defined. A person is guilty of criminal coercion if, with purpose unlawfully to restrict another's freedom of action to his detriment, he threatens to:

(a) commit any criminal offense; or

(b) accuse anyone of a criminal offense; or

(c) expose any secret tending to subject any person to hatred, contempt or ridicule, or to impair his credit or business repute; or

(d) take or withhold action as an official, or cause an official to take or withhold action.

It is an affirmative defense to prosecution based on paragraphs (b), (c) or (d) that the actor believed the accusation or secret to be true or the proposed official action justified and that his purpose was limited to compelling the other to behave in a way reasonably related to the circumstances which were the subject of the accusation, exposure or proposed official action, as by desisting from further misbehavior, making good a wrong done, refraining from taking any action or responsibility for which the actor believes the other disqualified.

(2) Grading. Criminal coercion is a misdemeanor unless the threat is to commit a felony or the actor's purpose is felonious, in which cases the offense is a felony of the third degree.

Article 213. Sexual Offenses

Section 213.0. Definitions.

In this Article, unless a different meaning plainly is required:

(1) the definitions given in Section 210.0 apply;

(2) "Sexual intercourse" includes intercourse per os or per anum, with some penetration however slight; emission is not required;

(3) "Deviate sexual intercourse" means sexual intercourse per os or per anum between human beings who are not husband and wife, and any form of sexual intercourse with an animal.

Section 213.1. Rape and Related Offenses.

(1) Rape. A male who has sexual intercourse with a female not his wife is guilty of rape if:

(a) he compels her to submit by force or by threat of imminent death, serious bodily injury, extreme pain or kidnapping, to be inflicted on anyone; or

(b) he has substantially impaired her power to appraise or control her conduct by administering or employing without her knowledge drugs, intoxicants or other means for the purpose of preventing resistance; or

(c) the female is unconscious; or

(d) the female is less than 10 years old. Rape is a felony of the second degree unless (i) in the course thereof the actor inflicts serious bodily injury upon anyone, or (ii) the victim was not a voluntary social companion of the actor upon the occasion of the crime and had not previously permitted him sexual liberties, in which cases the offense is a felony of the first degree.

(2) Gross Sexual Imposition. A male who has sexual intercourse with a female not his wife commits a felony of the third degree if:

(a) he compels her to submit by any threat that would prevent resistance by a woman of ordinary resolution; or

(b) he knows that she suffers from a mental disease or defect which renders her incapable of appraising the nature of her conduct; or

(c) he knows that she is unaware that a sexual act is being committed upon her or that she submits because she mistakenly supposes that he is her husband.

Section 213.2. Deviate Sexual Intercourse by Force or Imposition.

(1) **By Force or Its Equivalent.** A person who engages in deviate sexual intercourse with another person, or who causes another to engage in deviate sexual intercourse, commits a felony of the second degree if:

(a) he compels the other person to participate by force or by threat of imminent death, serious bodily injury, extreme pain or kidnapping, to be inflicted on anyone; or

(b) he has substantially impaired the other person's power to appraise or control his conduct, by administering or employing without the knowledge of the other person drugs, intoxicants or other means for the purpose of preventing resistance; or

(c) the other person is unconscious; or

(d) the other person is less than 10 years old.

(2) **By Other Imposition.** A person who engages in deviate sexual intercourse with another person, or who causes another to engage in deviate sexual intercourse, commits a felony of the third degree if:

(a) he compels the other person to participate by any threat that would prevent resistance by a person of ordinary resolution; or

(b) he knows that the other person suffers from a mental disease or defect which renders him incapable of appraising the nature of his conduct; or

(c) he knows that the other person submits because he is unaware that a sexual act is being committed upon him.

Section 213.3. Corruption of Minors and Seduction.

(1) **Offense Defined.** A male who has sexual intercourse with a female not his wife, or any person who engages in deviate sexual intercourse or causes another to engage in deviate sexual intercourse, is guilty of an offense if:

(a) the other person is less than [16] years old and the actor is at least [4] years older than the other person; or

(b) the other person is less than 21 years old and the actor is his guardian or otherwise responsible for general supervision of his welfare; or

(c) the other person is in custody of law or detained in a hospital or other institution and the actor has supervisory or disciplinary authority over him; or

(d) the other person is a female who is induced to participate by a promise of marriage which the actor does not mean to perform.

(2) **Grading.** An offense under paragraph (a) of Subsection (1) is a felony of the third degree. Otherwise an offense under this section is a misdemeanor.

Section 213.4. Sexual Assault.

A person who has sexual contact with another not his spouse, or causes such other to have sexual contact with him, is guilty of sexual assault, a misdemeanor, if:

(1) he knows that the contact is offensive to the other person; or

(2) he knows that the other person suffers from a mental disease or defect which renders him or her incapable of appraising the nature of his or her conduct; or

(3) he knows that the other person is unaware that a sexual act is being committed; or

(4) the other person is less than 10 years old; or

(5) he has substantially impaired the other person's power to appraise or control his or her conduct, by administering or employing without the other's knowledge drugs, intoxicants or other means for the purpose of preventing resistance; or

(6) the other person is less than [16] years old and the actor is at least [4] years older than the other person; or

(7) the other person is less than 21 years old and the actor is his guardian or otherwise responsible for general supervision of his welfare; or

(8) the other person is in custody of law or detained in a hospital or other institution and the actor has supervisory or disciplinary authority over him.

Sexual contact is any touching of the sexual or other intimate parts of the person for the purpose of arousing or gratifying sexual desire.

Section 213.5. Indecent Exposure.

A person commits a misdemeanor if, for the purpose of arousing or gratifying sexual desire of himself or of any person other than his spouse, he exposes his genitals under circumstances in which he knows his conduct is likely to cause affront or alarm.

Section 213.6. Provisions Generally Applicable to Article 213.

(1) Mistake as to Age. Whenever in this Article the criminality of conduct depends on a child's being below the age of 10, it is no defense that the actor did not know the child's age, or reasonably believed the child to be older than 10. When criminality depends on the child's being below a critical age other than 10, it is a defense for the actor to prove by a preponderance of the evidence that he reasonably believed the child to be above the critical age.

(2) Spouse Relationships. Whenever in this Article the definition of an offense excludes conduct with a spouse, the exclusion shall be deemed to extend to persons living as man and wife, regardless of the legal status of their relationship. The exclusion shall be inoperative as respects spouses living apart under a decree of judicial separation. Where the definition of an offense excludes conduct with a spouse or conduct by a woman, this shall not preclude conviction of a spouse or woman as accomplice in a sexual act which he or she causes another person, not within the exclusion, to perform.

(3) Sexually Promiscuous Complainants. It is a defense to prosecution under Section 213.3 and paragraphs (6), (7) and (8) of Section 213.4 for the actor to prove by a preponderance of the evidence that the alleged victim had, prior to the time of the offense charged, engaged promiscuously in sexual relations with others.

(4) Prompt Complaint. No prosecution may be instituted or maintained under this Article unless the alleged offense was brought to the notice of public authority within [3] months of its occurrence or, where the alleged victim was less than [16] years old or otherwise incompetent to make complaint, within [3] months after a parent, guardian or other competent person specially interested in the victim learns of the offense.

(5) Testimony of Complainants. No person shall be convicted of any felony under this Article upon the uncorroborated testimony of the alleged victim. Corroboration may be circumstantial. In any prosecution before a jury for an offense under this Article, the jury shall be instructed to evaluate the testimony of a victim or complaining witness with special care in view of the emotional involvement of the witness and the difficulty of determining the truth with respect to alleged sexual activities carried out in private.

Offenses Against Property.

Article 220. Arson, Criminal Mischief, and Other Property Destruction.

Section 220.1. Arson and Related Offenses.

(1) Arson. A person is guilty of arson, a felony of the second degree, if he starts a fire or causes an explosion with the purpose of:

    (a) destroying a building or occupied structure of another; or

    (b) destroying or damaging any property, whether his own or another's, to collect insurance for such loss. It shall be an affirmative defense to prosecution under this paragraph that the actor's conduct did not recklessly endanger any building or occupied structure of another or place any other person in danger of death or bodily injury.

(2) Reckless Burning or Exploding. A person commits a felony of the third degree if he purposely starts a fire or causes an explosion, whether on his own property or another's, and thereby recklessly:

    (a) places another person in danger of death or bodily injury; or

    (b) places a building or occupied structure of another in danger of damage or destruction.

(3) Failure to Control or Report Dangerous Fire. A person who knows that a fire is endangering life or a substantial amount of property of another and fails to take reasonable measures to put out or control the fire, when he can do so without substantial risk to himself, or to give a prompt fire alarm, commits a misdemeanor if:

    (a) he knows that he is under an official, contractual, or other legal duty to prevent or combat the fire; or

    (b) the fire was started, albeit lawfully, by him or with his assent, or on property in his custody or control.

(4) Definitions. "Occupied structure" means any structure, vehicle or place adapted for overnight accommodation of persons, or for carrying on business therein, whether or not a person is actually present. Property is that of another, for the purposes of this section, if anyone other than the actor has a possessory or proprietary interest therein. If a building or structure is divided into separately occupied units, any unit not occupied by the actor is an occupied structure of another.

Section 220.2. Causing or Risking Catastrophe.

(1) Causing Catastrophe. A person who causes a catastrophe by explosion, fire, flood, avalanche, collapse of building, release of poison gas, radioactive material or other harmful or destructive force or substance, or by any other means of

causing potentially widespread injury or damage, commits a felony of the second degree if he does so purposely or knowingly, or a felony of the third degree if he does so recklessly.

(2) Risking Catastrophe. A person is guilty of a misdemeanor if he recklessly creates a risk of catastrophe in the employment of fire, explosives or other dangerous means listed in Subsection (1).

(3) Failure to Prevent Catastrophe. A person who knowingly or recklessly fails to take reasonable measures to prevent or mitigate a catastrophe commits a misdemeanor if:

> (a) he knows that he is under an official, contractual or other legal duty to take such measures; or

> (b) he did or assented to the act causing or threatening the catastrophe.

Section 220.3. Criminal Mischief.

(1) Offense Defined. A person is guilty of criminal mischief if he:

> (a) damages tangible property of another purposely, recklessly, or by negligence in the employment of fire, explosives, or other dangerous means listed in Section 220.2(1); or

> (b) purposely or recklessly tampers with tangible property of another so as to endanger person or property; or

> (c) purposely or recklessly causes another to suffer pecuniary loss by deception or threat.

(2) Grading. Criminal mischief is a felony of the third degree if the actor purposely causes pecuniary loss in excess of $5,000, or a substantial interruption or impairment of public communication, transportation, supply of water, gas or power, or other public service. It is a misdemeanor if the actor purposely causes pecuniary loss in excess of $100, or a petty misdemeanor if he purposely or recklessly causes pecuniary loss in excess of $25. Otherwise criminal mischief is a violation.

Article 221. Burglary and Other Criminal Intrusion.

Section 221.0. Definitions.

In this Article, unless a different meaning plainly is required:

(1) "occupied structure" means any structure, vehicle or place adapted for overnight accommodation of persons, or for carrying on business therein, whether or not a person is actually present.

(2) "night" means the period between thirty minutes past sunset and thirty minutes before sunrise.

Section 221.1. Burglary.

(1) Burglary Defined. A person is guilty of burglary if he enters a building or occupied structure, or separately secured or occupied portion thereof, with purpose to commit a crime therein, unless the premises are at the time open to the public or the actor is licensed or privileged to enter. It is an affirmative defense to prosecution for burglary that the building or structure was abandoned.

(2) Grading. Burglary is a felony of the second degree if it is perpetrated in the dwelling of another at night, or if, in the course of committing the offense, the actor:

(a) purposely, knowingly or recklessly inflicts or attempts to inflict bodily injury on anyone; or

(b) is armed with explosives or a deadly weapon.

Otherwise, burglary is a felony of the third degree.

An act shall be deemed "in the course of committing" an offense if it occurs in an attempt to commit the offense or in flight after the attempt or commission.

(3) Multiple Convictions. A person may not be convicted both for burglary and for the offense which it was his purpose to commit after the burglarious entry or for an attempt to commit that offense, unless the additional offense constitutes a felony of the first or second degree.

Section 221.2. Criminal Trespass.

(1) Buildings and Occupied Structures. A person commits an offense if, knowing that he is not licensed or privileged to do so, he enters or surreptitiously remains in any building or occupied structure, or separately secured or occupied portion thereof. An offense under this Subsection is a misdemeanor if it is committed in a dwelling at night. Otherwise it is a petty misdemeanor.

(2) Defiant Trespasser. A person commits an offense if, knowing that he is not licensed or privileged to do so, he enters or remains in any place as to which notice against trespass is given by:

(a) actual communication to the actor; or

(b) posting in a manner prescribed by law or reasonably likely to come to the attention of intruders; or

(c) fencing or other enclosure manifestly designed to exclude intruders. An offense under this Subsection constitutes a petty misdemeanor if the offender defies an order to leave personally communicated to him by the owner of the premises or other authorized person. Otherwise it is a violation.

(3) Defenses. It is an affirmative defense to prosecution under this Section that:

(a) a building or occupied structure involved in an offense under Subsection (1) was abandoned; or

(b) the premises were at the time open to members of the public and the actor complied with all lawful conditions imposed on access to or remaining in the premises; or

(c) the actor reasonably believed that the owner of the premises, or other person empowered to license access thereto, would have licensed him to enter or remain.

Article 222. Robbery.

Section 222.1. Robbery.

(1) Robbery Defined. A person is guilty of robbery if, in the course of committing a theft, he:

(a) inflicts serious bodily injury upon another; or

(b) threatens another with or purposely puts him in fear of immediate serious bodily injury; or

(c) commits or threatens immediately to commit any felony of the first or second degree. An act shall be deemed "in the course of committing a theft" if it occurs in an attempt to commit theft or in flight after the attempt or commission.

(2) Grading. Robbery is a felony of the second degree, except that it is a felony of the first degree if in the course of committing the theft the actor attempts to kill anyone, or purposely inflicts or attempts to inflict serious bodily injury.

Article 223. Theft and Related Offenses.

Section 223.0. Definitions.

In this Article, unless a different meaning plainly is required:

(1) "deprive" means:

(a) to withhold property of another permanently or for so extended a period as to appropriate a major portion of its economic value, or with intent to restore only upon payment of reward or other compensation; or

(b) to dispose of the property so as to make it unlikely that the owner will recover it.

(2) "financial institution" means a bank, insurance company, credit union, building and loan association, investment trust or other organization held out to the public as a place of deposit of funds or medium of savings or collective investment.

(3) "government" means the United States, any State, county, municipality, or other political unit, or any department, agency or subdivision of any of the foregoing, or any corporation or other association carrying out the functions of government.

(4) "movable property" means property the location of which can be changed, including things growing on, affixed to, or found in land, and documents although the rights represented thereby have no physical location. "Immovable property" is all other property.

(5) "obtain" means:

(a) in relation to property, to bring about a transfer or purported transfer of a legal interest in the property, whether to the obtainer or another; or

(b) in relation to labor or service, to secure performance thereof.

(6) "property" means anything of value, including real estate, tangible and intangible personal property, contract rights, chooses-in-action and other interests in or claims to wealth, admission or transportation tickets, captured or domestic animals, food and drink, electric or other power.

(7) "property of another" includes property in which any person oth the actor has an interest which the actor is not privileged to infringe, reg of the fact that the actor also has an interest in the property and regar the fact that the other person might be precluded from civil recovery the property was used in an unlawful transaction or was subject to forfe contraband. Property in possession of the actor shall not be deemed prop

another who has only a security interest therein, even if legal title is in the creditor pursuant to a conditional sales contract or other security agreement.

Section 223.1. Consolidation of Theft Offenses; Grading; Provisions Applicable to Theft Generally.

(1) Consolidation of Theft Offenses. Conduct denominated theft in this Article constitutes a single offense. An accusation of theft may be supported by evidence that it was committed in any manner that would be theft under this Article, notwithstanding the specification of a different manner in the indictment or information, subject only to the power of the Court to ensure fair trial by granting a continuance or other appropriate relief where the conduct of the defense would be prejudiced by lack of fair notice or by surprise.

(2) Grading of Theft Offenses.

(a) Theft constitutes a felony of the third degree if the amount involved exceeds $500, or if the property stolen is a firearm, automobile, airplane, motorcycle, motorboat, or other motor-propelled vehicle, or in the case of theft by receiving stolen property, if the receiver is in the business of buying or selling stolen property.

(b) Theft not within the preceding paragraph constitutes a misdemeanor, except that if the property was not taken from the person or by threat, or in breach of a fiduciary obligation, and the actor proves by a preponderance of the evidence that the amount involved was less than $50, the offense constitutes a petty misdemeanor.

(c) The amount involved in a theft shall be deemed to be the highest value, by any reasonable standard, of the property or services which the actor stole or attempted to steal. Amounts involved in thefts committed pursuant to one scheme or course of conduct, whether from the same person or several persons, may be aggregated in determining the grade of the offense.

(3) Claim of Right. It is an affirmative defense to prosecution for theft that the actor:

(a) was unaware that the property or service was that of another; or

(b) acted under an honest claim of right to the property or service involved or that he had a right to acquire or dispose of it as he did; or

(c) took property exposed for sale, intending to purchase and pay for it promptly, or reasonably believing that the owner, if present, would have consented.

(4) Theft from Spouse. It is no defense that theft was from the actor's spouse, except that misappropriation of household and personal effects, or other property normally accessible to both spouses, is theft only if it occurs after the parties have ceased living together.

Section 223.2. Theft by Unlawful Taking or Disposition.

(1) Movable Property. A person is guilty of theft if he unlawfully takes, or exercises unlawful control over, movable property of another with purpose to deprive him thereof.

(2) Immovable Property. A person is guilty of theft if he unlawfully transfers immovable property of another or any interest therein with purpose to benefit himself or another not entitled thereto.

Section 223.3. Theft by Deception.

A person is guilty of theft if he purposely obtains property of another by deception. A person deceives if he purposely:

(1) creates or reinforces a false impression, including false impressions as to law, value, intention or other state of mind; but deception as to a person's intention to perform a promise shall not be inferred from the fact alone that he did not subsequently perform the promise; or

(2) prevents another from acquiring information which would affect his judgment of a transaction; or

(3) fails to correct a false impression which the deceiver previously created or reinforced, or which the deceiver knows to be influencing another to whom he stands in a fiduciary or confidential relationship; or

(4) fails to disclose a known lien, adverse claim or other legal impediment to the enjoyment of property which he transfers or encumbers in consideration for the property obtained, whether such impediment is or is not valid, or is or is not a matter of official record.

The term "deceive" does not, however, include falsity as to matters having no pecuniary significance, or puffing by statements unlikely to deceive ordinary persons in the group addressed.

Section 223.4. Theft by Extortion.

A person is guilty of theft if he purposely obtains property of another by threatening to:

(1) inflict bodily injury on anyone or commit any other criminal offense; or

(2) accuse anyone of a criminal offense; or

(3) expose any secret tending to subject any person to hatred, contempt or ridicule, or to impair his credit or business repute; or

(4) take or withhold action as an official, or cause an official to take or withhold action; or

(5) bring about or continue a strike, boycott or other collective unofficial action, if the property is not demanded or received for the benefit of the group in whose interest the actor purports to act; or

(6) testify or provide information or withhold testimony or information with respect to another's legal claim or defense; or

(7) inflict any other harm which would not benefit the actor. It is an affirmative defense to prosecution based on paragraphs (2), (3) or (4) that the property obtained by threat of accusation, exposure, lawsuit or other invocation of official action was honestly claimed as restitution or indemnification for harm done in circumstances to which such accusation, exposure, lawsuit or other official action relates, or as compensation for property or lawful services.

Section 223.5. Theft of Property Lost, Mislaid, or Delivered by Mistake.

A person who comes into control of property of another that he knows to have been lost, mislaid, or delivered under a mistake as to the nature or amount of the property or the identity of the recipient is guilty of theft if, with purpose to deprive the owner thereof, he fails to take reasonable measures to restore the property to a person entitled to have it.

Section 223.6. Receiving Stolen Property.

(1) Receiving. A person is guilty of theft if he purposely receives, retains, or disposes of movable property of another knowing that it has been stolen, or believing that it has probably been stolen, unless the property is received, retained, or disposed with purpose to restore it to the owner. "Receiving" means acquiring possession, control or title, or lending on the security of the property.

(2) Presumption of Knowledge. The requisite knowledge or belief is presumed in the case of a dealer who:

(a) is found in possession or control of property stolen from two or more persons on separate occasions; or

(b) has received stolen property in another transaction within the year preceding the transaction charged; or

(c) being a dealer in property of the sort received, acquires it for a consideration which he knows is far below its reasonable value.

"Dealer" means a person in the business of buying or selling goods including a pawnbroker.

Section 223.7. Theft of Services.

(1) A person is guilty of theft is he purposely obtains services which he knows are available only for compensation, by deception or threat, or by false token or other means to avoid payment for the service. "Services" includes labor, professional service, transportation, telephone or other public service, accommodation in hotels, restaurants or elsewhere, admission to exhibitions, use of vehicles or other movable property. Where compensation for service is ordinarily paid immediately upon the rendering of such service, as in the case of hotels and restaurants, refusal to pay or absconding without payment or offer to pay gives rise to a presumption that the service was obtained by deception as to intention to pay.

(2) A person commits theft if, having control over the disposition of services of others, to which he is not entitled, he knowingly diverts such services to his own benefit or to the benefit of another not entitled thereto.

Section 223.8. Theft by Failure to Make Required Disposition of Funds Received.

A person who purposely obtains property upon agreement, or subject to a known legal obligation, to make specified payment or other disposition, whether from such property or its proceeds or from his own property to be reserved in equivalent amount, is guilty of theft if he deals with the property obtained as his own and fails to make the required payment or disposition. The foregoing applies notwithstanding that it may be impossible to identify particular property as belonging to the victim at the time of the actor's failure to make the required payment or disposition. An officer or employee of the government or of a financial institution is presumed: (i) to know any legal obligation relevant to his criminal liability under this Section, and (ii) to have dealt with the property as his own if he fails to pay or account upon lawful demand, or if an audit reveals a shortage or falsification of accounts.

Section 223.9. Unauthorized Use of Automobiles and Other Vehicles.

A person commits a misdemeanor if he operates another's automobile, airplane, motorcycle, motorboat, or other motor-propelled vehicle without consent of the owner. It is an affirmative defense to prosecution under this Section that the actor reasonably believed that the owner would have consented to the operation had he known of it.

Article 224. Forgery and Fraudulent Practices.

Section 224.0. Definitions.

In this Article, the definitions given in Section 223.0 apply unless a different meaning plainly is required.

Section 224.1. Forgery.

(1) Definition. A person is guilty of forgery if, with purpose to defraud or injure anyone, or with knowledge that he is facilitating a fraud or injury to be perpetrated by anyone, the actor:

    (a) alters any writing of another without his authority; or

    (b) makes, completes, executes, authenticates, issues or transfers any writing so that it purports to be the act of another who did not authorize that act, or to have been executed at a time or place or in a numbered sequence other than was in fact the case, or to be a copy of an original when no such original existed; or

    (c) utters any writing which he knows to be forged in a manner specified in paragraphs (a) or (b). "Writing" includes printing or any other method of recording information, money, coins, tokens, stamps, seals, credit cards, badges, trade-marks, and other symbols of value, right, privilege, or identification.

(2) Grading. Forgery is a felony of the second degree if the writing is or purports to be part of an issue of money, securities, postage or revenue stamps, or other instruments issued by the government, or part of an issue of stock, bonds or other instruments representing interests in or claims against any property or enterprise. Forgery is a felony of the third degree if the writing is or purports to be a will, deed, contract, release, commercial instrument, or other document evidencing, creating, transferring, altering, terminating, or otherwise affecting legal relations. Otherwise forgery is a misdemeanor.

Section 224.2. Simulating Objects of Antiquity, Rarity, Etc.

A person commits a misdemeanor if, with purpose to defraud anyone or with knowledge that he is facilitating a fraud to be perpetrated by anyone, he makes, alters or utters any object so that it appears to have value because of antiquity, rarity, source, or authorship which it does not possess.

Section 224.3. Fraudulent Destruction, Removal or Concealment of Recordable Instruments.

A person commits a felony of the third degree if, with purpose to deceive or injure anyone, he destroys, removes or conceals any will, deed, mortgage, security instrument or other writing for which the law provides public recording.

Section 224.4. Tampering with Records.

A person commits a misdemeanor if, knowing that he has no privilege to do so, he falsifies, destroys, removes or conceals any writing or record, with purpose to deceive or injure anyone or to conceal any wrongdoing.

Section 224.5. Bad Checks.

A person who issues or passes a check or similar sight order for the payment of money, knowing that it will not be honored by the drawee, commits a misdemeanor. For the purposes of this Section as well as in any prosecution for theft committed by means of a bad check, an issuer is presumed to know that the check or order (other than a postdated check or order) would not be paid, if:

    (1) the issuer had no account with the drawee at the time the check or order was issued; or

    (2) payment was refused by the drawee for lack of funds, upon presentation within 30 days after issue, and the issuer failed to make good within 10 days after receiving notice of that refusal.

Section 224.6. Credit Cards.

A person commits an offense if he uses a credit card for the purpose of obtaining property or services with knowledge that:

    (1) the card is stolen or forged; or

    (2) the card has been revoked or cancelled; or

    (3) for any other reason his use of the card is unauthorized by the issuer.

It is an affirmative defense to prosecution under paragraph (3) if the actor proves by a preponderance of the evidence that he had the purpose and ability to meet all obligations to the issuer arising out of his use of the card. "Credit card" means a writing or other evidence of an undertaking to pay for property or services delivered or rendered to or upon the order of a designated person or bearer. An offense under this Section is a felony of the third degree if the value of the property or services secured or sought to be secured by means of the credit card exceeds $500; otherwise it is a misdemeanor.

Section 224.7. Deceptive Business Practices.

A person commits a misdemeanor if in the course of business he:

(1) uses or possesses for use a false weight or measure, or any other device for falsely determining or recording any quality or quantity; or

(2) sells, offers or exposes for sale, or delivers less than the represented quantity of any commodity or service; or

(3) takes or attempts to take more than the represented quantity of any commodity or service when as buyer he furnishes the weight or measure; or

(4) sells, offers or exposes for sale adulterated or mislabeled commodities. "Adulterated" means varying from the standard of composition or quality prescribed by or pursuant to any statute providing criminal penalties for such variance, or set by established commercial usage. "Mislabeled" means varying from the standard of truth or disclosure in labeling prescribed by or pursuant to any statute providing criminal penalties for such variance, or set by established commercial usage; or

(5) makes a false or misleading statement in any advertisement addressed to the public or to a substantial segment thereof for the purpose of promoting the purchase or sale of property or services; or

(6) makes a false or misleading written statement for the purpose of obtaining property or credit; or

(7) makes a false or misleading written statement for the purpose of promoting the sale of securities, or omits information required by law to be disclosed in written documents relating to securities. It is an affirmative defense to prosecution under this Section if the defendant proves by a preponderance of the evidence that his conduct was not knowingly or recklessly deceptive.

Section 224.8. Commercial Bribery and Breach of Duty to Act Disinterestedly.

(1) A person commits a misdemeanor if he solicits, accepts or agrees to accept any benefit as consideration for knowingly violating or agreeing to violate a duty of fidelity to which he is subject as:

(a) partner, agent or employee of another;

(b) trustee, guardian, or other fiduciary;

(c) lawyer, physician, accountant, appraiser, or other professional adviser or informant;

(d) officer, director, manager or other participant in the direction of the affairs of an incorporated or unincorporated association; or

(e) arbitrator or other purportedly disinterested adjudicator or referee.

(2) A person who holds himself out to the public as being engaged in the business of making disinterested selection, appraisal, or criticism of commodities or services commits a misdemeanor if he solicits, accepts or agrees to accept any benefit to influence his selection, appraisal or criticism.

(3) A person commits a misdemeanor if he confers, or offers or agrees to confer, any benefit the acceptance of which would be criminal under this Section.

Section 224.9. Rigging Publicly Exhibited Contest.

(1) A person commits a misdemeanor if, with purpose to prevent a publicly exhibited contest from being conducted in accordance with the rules and usages purporting to govern it, he:

    (a) confers or offers or agrees to confer any benefit upon, or threatens any injury to a participant, official or other person associated with the contest or exhibition; or

    (b) tampers with any person, animal or thing.

(2) *Soliciting or Accepting Benefit for Rigging.* A person commits a misdemeanor if he knowingly solicits, accepts or agrees to accept any benefit the giving of which would be criminal under Subsection (1).

(3) *Participation in Rigged Contest.* A person commits a misdemeanor if he knowingly engages in, sponsors, produces, judges, or otherwise participates in a publicly exhibited contest knowing that the contest is not being conducted in compliance with the rules and usages purporting to govern it, by reason of conduct which would be criminal under this Section.

Section 224.10. Defrauding Secured Creditors.

A person commits a misdemeanor if he destroys, removes, conceals, encumbers, transfers or otherwise deals with property subject to a security interest with purpose to hinder enforcement of that interest.

Section 224.11. Fraud in Insolvency.

A person commits a misdemeanor if, knowing that proceedings have been or are about to be instituted for the appointment of a receiver or other person entitled to administer property for the benefit of creditors, or that any other composition or liquidation for the benefit of creditors has been or is about to made, he:

(1) destroys, removes, conceals, encumbers, transfers, or otherwise deals with any property with purpose to defeat or obstruct the claim of any creditor, or otherwise to obstruct the operation of any law relating to administration of property for the benefit of creditors; or

(2) knowingly falsifies any writing or record relating to the property; or

(3) knowingly misrepresents or refuses to disclose to a receiver or other person entitled to administer property for the benefit of creditors, the existence, amount or location of the property, or any other information which the actor could be legally required to furnish in relation to such administration.

Section 224.12. Receiving Deposits in a Failing Financial Institution.

An officer, manager or other person directing or participating in the direction of a financial institution commits a misdemeanor if he receives or permits the receipt of a deposit, premium payment or other investment in the institution knowing that:

(1) due to financial difficulties the institution is about to suspend operations or go into receivership or reorganization; and

(2) the person making the deposit or other payment is unaware of the precarious situation of the institution.

Section 224.13. Misapplication of Entrusted Property and Property of Government or Financial Institution.

A person commits an offense if he applies or disposes of property that has been entrusted to him as a fiduciary, or property of the government or of a financial institution, in a manner which he knows is unlawful and involves substantial risk of loss or detriment to the owner of the property or to a person for whose benefit the property was entrusted. The offense is a misdemeanor if the amount involved exceeds $50; otherwise it is a petty misdemeanor. "Fiduciary" includes trustee, guardian, executor, administrator, receiver and any person carrying on fiduciary functions on behalf of a corporation or other organization which is a fiduciary.

Section 224.14. Securing Execution of Documents by Deception.

A person commits a misdemeanor if by deception he causes another to execute any instrument affecting or purporting to affect or likely to affect the pecuniary interest of any person.

Offenses Against the Family.

Article 230. Offenses Against the Family.

Section 230.1. Bigamy and Polygamy.

(1) Bigamy. A married person is guilty of bigamy, a misdemeanor, if he contracts or purports to contract another marriage, unless at the time of the subsequent marriage:

(a) the actor believes that the prior spouse is dead; or

(b) the actor and the prior spouse have been living apart for five consecutive years throughout which the prior spouse was not known by the actor to be alive; or

(c) a Court has entered a judgment purporting to terminate or annul any prior disqualifying marriage, and the actor does not know that judgment to be invalid; or

(d) the actor reasonably believes that he is legally eligible to remarry.

(2) Polygamy. A person is guilty of polygamy, a felony of the third degree, if he marries or cohabits with more than one spouse at a time in purported exercise of the right of plural marriage. The offense is a continuing one until all cohabitation and claim of marriage with more than one spouse terminates. This section does not apply to parties to a polygamous marriage, lawful in the country of which they are residents or nationals, while they are in transit through or temporarily visiting this State.

(3) Other Party to Bigamous or Polygamous Marriage. A person is guilty of bigamy or polygamy, as the case may be, if he contracts or purports to contract marriage with another knowing that the other is thereby committing bigamy or polygamy.

Section 230.2. Incest.

A person is guilty of incest, a felony of the third degree, if he knowingly marries or cohabits or has sexual intercourse with an ancestor or descendant, a brother or sister of the whole or half blood [or an uncle, aunt, nephew or niece of the whole blood]. "Cohabit" means to live together under the representation or appearance of being married. The relationships referred to herein include blood relationships without regard to legitimacy, and relationship of parent and child by adoption.

Section 230.3. Abortion.

(1) Unjustified Abortion. A person who purposely and unjustifiably terminates the pregnancy of another otherwise than by a live birth commits a felony of the third degree or, where the pregnancy has continued beyond the twenty-sixth week, a felony of the second degree.

(2) Justifiable Abortion. A licensed physician is justified in terminating a pregnancy if he believes there is substantial risk that continuance of the pregnancy would gravely impair the physical or mental health of the mother or that the child would be born with grave physical or mental defect, or that the pregnancy resulted from rape, incest, or other felonious intercourse. All illicit intercourse with a girl below the age of 16 shall be deemed felonious for purposes of this subsection. Justifiable abortions shall be performed only in a licensed hospital except in case of emergency when hospital facilities are unavailable. [Additional exceptions from the requirement of hospitalization may be incorporated here to take account of situations in sparsely settled areas where hospitals are not generally accessible.]

(3) Physicians' Certificates; Presumption from Non-Compliance. No abortion shall be performed unless two physicians, one of whom may be the person performing the abortion, shall have certified in writing the circumstances which they believe to justify the abortion. Such certificate shall be submitted before the abortion to the hospital where it is to be performed and, in the case of abortion following felonious intercourse, to the prosecuting attorney or the police. Failure to comply with any of the requirements of this Subsection gives rise to a presumption that the abortion was unjustified.

(4) Self-Abortion. A woman whose pregnancy has continued beyond the twenty-sixth week commits a felony of the third degree if she purposely terminates her own pregnancy otherwise than by a live birth, or if she uses instruments, drugs or violence upon herself for that purpose. Except as justified under Subsection (2), a person who induces or knowingly aids a woman to use instruments, drugs or violence upon herself for the purpose of terminating her pregnancy otherwise than by a live birth commits a felony of the third degree whether or not the pregnancy has continued beyond the twenty-sixth week.

(5) Pretended Abortion. A person commits a felony of the third degree if, representing that it is his purpose to perform an abortion, he does an act adapted to cause abortion in a pregnant woman although the woman is in fact not pregnant, or the actor does not believe she is. A person charged with unjustified abortion under Subsection (1) or an attempt to commit that offense may be convicted thereof upon proof of conduct prohibited by this Subsection.

(6) Distribution of Abortifacients. A person who sells, offers to sell, possesses with intent to sell, advertises, or displays for sale anything specially designed to terminate a pregnancy, or held out by the actor as useful for that purpose, commits a misdemeanor, unless:

>   (a) the sale, offer or display is to a physician or druggist or to an intermediary in a chain of distribution to physicians or druggists; or

>   (b) the sale is made upon prescription or order of a physician; or

>   (c) the possession is with intent to sell as authorized in paragraphs (a) and (b); or

>   (d) the advertising is addressed to persons named in paragraph (a) and confined to trade or professional channels not likely to reach the general public.

(7) Section Inapplicable to Prevention of Pregnancy. Nothing in this Section shall be deemed applicable to the prescription, administration or distribution of drugs or other substances for avoiding pregnancy, whether by preventing implantation of a fertilized ovum or by any other method that operates before, at or immediately after fertilization.

Section 230.4. Endangering Welfare of Children.

A parent, guardian, or other person supervising the welfare of a child under 18 commits a misdemeanor if he knowingly endangers the child's welfare by violating a duty of care, protection or support.

Section 230.5. Persistent Non-Support.

A person commits a misdemeanor if he persistently fails to provide support which he can provide and which he knows he is legally obliged to provide to a spouse, child or other dependent.

Offenses Against Public Administration.

Article 240. Bribery and Corrupt Influence.

Section 240.0. Definitions.

In Articles 240–243, unless a different meaning plainly is required:

(1) "benefit" means gain or advantage, or anything regarded by the beneficiary as gain or advantage, including benefit to any other person or entity in whose welfare he is interested, but not an advantage promised generally to a group or class of voters as a consequence of public measures which a candidate engages to support or oppose;

(2) "government" includes any branch, subdivision or agency of the government of the State or any locality within it;

(3) "harm" means loss, disadvantage or injury, or anything so regarded by the person affected, including loss, disadvantage or injury to any other person or entity in whose welfare he is interested;

(4) "official proceeding" means a proceeding heard or which may be heard before any legislative, judicial, administrative or other governmental agency or official authorized to take evidence under oath, including any referee, hearing examiner, commissioner, notary or other person taking testimony or deposition in connection with any such proceeding;

(5) "party official" means a person who holds an elective or appointive post in a political party in the United States by virtue of which he directs or conducts, or participates in directing or conducting party affairs at any level of responsibility;

(6) "pecuniary benefit" is benefit in the form of money, property, commercial interests or anything else the primary significance of which is economic gain;

(7) "public servant" means any officer or employee of government, including legislators and judges, and any person participating as juror, advisor, consultant or otherwise, in performing a governmental function; but the term does not include witnesses;

(8) "administrative proceeding" means any proceeding, other than a judicial proceeding, the outcome of which is required to be based on a record or documentation prescribed by law, or in which law or regulation is particularized in application to individuals.

Section 240.1. Bribery in Official and Political Matters.

A person is guilty of bribery, a felony of the third degree, if he offers, confers or agrees to confer upon another, or solicits, accepts or agrees to accept from another:

(1) any pecuniary benefit as consideration for the recipient's decision, opinion, recommendation, vote or other exercise of discretion as a public servant, party official or voter; or

(2) any benefit as consideration for the recipient's decision, vote, recommendation or other exercise of official discretion in a judicial or administrative proceeding; or

(3) any benefit as consideration for a violation of a known legal duty as public servant or party official. It is no defense to prosecution under this section that a person whom the actor sought to influence was not qualified to act in the desired way whether because he had not yet assumed office, or lacked jurisdiction, or for any other reason.

Section 240.2. Threats and Other Improper Influence in Official and Political Matters.

(1) Offenses Defined. A person commits an offense if he:

(a) threatens unlawful harm to any person with purpose to influence his decision, opinion, recommendation, vote or other exercise of discretion as a public servant, party official or voter; or

(b) threatens harm to any public servant with purpose to influence his decision, opinion, recommendation, vote or other exercise of discretion in a judicial or administrative proceeding; or

(c) threatens harm to any public servant or party official with purpose to influence him to violate his known legal duty; or

(d) privately addresses to any public servant who has or will have an official discretion in a judicial or administrative proceeding any representation, entreaty, argument or other communication with purpose to influence the outcome on the basis of considerations other than those authorized by law. It is no defense to prosecution under this Section that a person whom the actor sought to influence was not qualified to act in the desired way, whether because he had not yet assumed office, or lacked jurisdiction, or for any other reason.

(2) Grading. An offense under this Section is a misdemeanor unless the actor threatened to commit a crime or made a threat with purpose to influence a judicial or administrative proceeding, in which cases the offense is a felony of the third degree.

Section 240.3. Compensation for Past Official Action.

A person commits a misdemeanor if he solicits, accepts or agrees to accept any pecuniary benefit as compensation for having, as public servant, given a decision, opinion, recommendation or vote favorable to another, or for having otherwise exercised a discretion in his favor, or for having violated his duty. A person commits a misdemeanor if he offers, confers or agrees to confer compensation acceptance of which is prohibited by this Section.

Section 240.4. Retaliation for Past Official Action.

A person commits a misdemeanor if he harms another by any unlawful act in retaliation for anything lawfully done by the latter in the capacity of public servant.

Section 240.5. Gifts to Public Servants by Persons Subject to Their Jurisdiction.

(1) Regulatory and Law Enforcement Officials. No public servant in any department or agency exercising regulatory functions, or conducting inspections or investigations, or carrying on civil or criminal litigation on behalf of the government, or having custody of prisoners, shall solicit, accept or agree to accept any pecuniary benefit from a person known to be subject to such regulation, inspection, investigation or custody, or against whom such litigation is known to be pending or contemplated.

(2) Officials Concerned with Government Contracts and Pecuniary Transactions. No public servant having any discretionary function to perform in connection with contracts, purchases, payments, claims or other pecuniary transactions of the government shall solicit, accept or agree to accept any pecuniary benefit from any person known to be interested in or likely to become interested in any such contract, purchase, payment, claim or transaction.

(3) Judicial and Administrative Officials. No public servant having judicial or administrative authority and no public servant employed by or in a court or other tribunal having such authority, or participating in the enforcement of its decisions, shall solicit, accept or agree to accept any pecuniary benefit from a person known to be interested in or likely to become interested in any matter before such public servant or a tribunal with which he is associated.

(4) Legislative Officials. No legislator or public servant employed by the legislature or by any committee or agency thereof shall solicit, accept or agree to accept any pecuniary benefit from any person known to be interested in a bill, transaction or proceeding, pending or contemplated, before the legislature or any committee or agency thereof.

(5) Exceptions. This Section shall not apply to:

(a) fees prescribed by law to be received by a public servant, or any other benefit for which the recipient gives legitimate consideration or to which he is otherwise legally entitled; or

(b) gifts or other benefits conferred on account of kinship or other personal, professional or business relationship independent of the official status of the receiver; or

(c) trivial benefits incidental to personal, professional or business contacts and involving no substantial risk of undermining official impartiality.

(6) Offering Benefits Prohibited. No person shall knowingly confer, or offer or agree to confer, any benefit prohibited by the foregoing Subsections.

(7) Grade of Offense. An offense under this Section is a misdemeanor.

Section 240.6. Compensating Public Servant for Assisting Private Interests in Relation to Matters Before Him.

(1) Receiving Compensation. A public servant commits a misdemeanor if he solicits, accepts or agrees to accept compensation for advice or other assistance in preparing or promoting a bill, contract, claim, or other transaction or proposal as to which he knows that he has or is likely to have an official discretion to exercise.

(2) Paying Compensation. A person commits a misdemeanor if he pays or offers or agrees to pay compensation to a public servant with knowledge that acceptance by the public servant is unlawful.

Section 240.7. Selling Political Endorsement; Special Influence.

(1) Selling Political Endorsement. A person commits a misdemeanor if he solicits, receives, agrees to receive, or agrees that any political party or other person shall receive, any pecuniary benefit as consideration for approval or disapproval of an appointment or advancement in public service, or for approval or disapproval of any person or transaction for any benefit conferred by an official or agency of government. "Approval" includes recommendation, failure to disapprove, or any other manifestation of favor or acquiescence. "Disapproval" includes failure to approve, or any other manifestation of disfavor or nonacquiescence.

(2) Other Trading in Special Influence. A person commits a misdemeanor if he solicits, receives or agrees to receive any pecuniary benefit as consideration

for exerting special influence upon a public servant or procuring another to do so. "Special influence" means power to influence through kinship, friendship or other relationship, apart from the merits of the transaction.

(3) Paying for Endorsement or Special Influence. A person commits a misdemeanor if he offers, confers or agrees to confer any pecuniary benefit receipt of which is prohibited by this Section.

Article 241. Perjury and Other Falsification in Official Matters.

Section 241.0. Definitions.

In this Article, unless a different meaning plainly is required:

(1) the definitions given in Section 240.0 apply; and

(2) "statement" means any representation, but includes a representation of opinion, belief or other state of mind only if the representation clearly relates to state of mind apart from or in addition to any facts which are the subject of the representation.

Section 241.1. Perjury.

(1) Offense Defined. A person is guilty of perjury, a felony of the third degree, if in any official proceeding he makes a false statement under oath or equivalent affirmation, or swears or affirms the truth of a statement previously made, when the statement is material and he does not believe it to be true.

(2) Materiality. Falsification is material, regardless of the admissibility of the statement under rules of evidence, if it could have affected the course or outcome of the proceeding. It is no defense that the declarant mistakenly believed the falsification to be immaterial. Whether a falsification is material in a given factual situation is a question of law.

(3) Irregularities No Defense. It is not a defense to prosecution under this Section that the oath or affirmation was administered or taken in an irregular manner or that the declarant was not competent to make the statement. A document purporting to be made upon oath or affirmation at any time when the actor presents it as being so verified shall be deemed to have been duly sworn or affirmed.

(4) Retraction. No person shall be guilty of an offense under this Section if he retracted the falsification in the course of the proceeding in which it was made before it became manifest that the falsification was or would be exposed and before the falsification substantially affected the proceeding.

(5) Inconsistent Statements. Where the defendant made inconsistent statements under oath or equivalent affirmation, both having been made within the period of the statute of limitations, the prosecution may proceed by setting forth the inconsistent statements in a single count alleging in the alternative that one or the other was false and not believed by the defendant. In such case it shall not be necessary for the prosecution to prove which statement was false but only that one or the other was false and not believed by the defendant to be true.

(6) Corroboration. No person shall be convicted of an offense under this Section where proof of falsity rests solely upon contradiction by testimony of a single person other than the defendant.

Section 241.2. False Swearing.

(1) False Swearing in Official Matters. A person who makes a false statement under oath or equivalent affirmation, or swears or affirms the truth of such a statement previously made, when he does not believe the statement to be true, is guilty of a misdemeanor if:

(a) the falsification occurs in an official proceeding; or

(b) the falsification is intended to mislead a public servant in performing his official function.

(2) Other False Swearing. A person who makes a false statement under oath or equivalent affirmation, or swears or affirms the truth of such a statement previously made, when he does not believe the statement to be true, is guilty of a petty misdemeanor, if the statement is one which is required by law to be sworn or affirmed before a notary or other person authorized to administer oaths.

(3) Perjury Provisions Applicable. Subsections (3) to (6) of Section 241.1 apply to the present Section.

Section 241.3. Unsworn Falsification to Authorities.

(1) In General. A person commits a misdemeanor if, with purpose to mislead a public servant in performing his official function, he:

(a) makes any written false statement which he does not believe to be true; or

(b) purposely creates a false impression in a written application for any pecuniary or other benefit, by omitting information necessary to prevent statements therein from being misleading; or

(c) submits or invites reliance on any writing which he knows to be forged, altered or otherwise lacking in authenticity; or

(d) submits or invites reliance on any sample, specimen, map, boundary-mark, or other object which he knows to be false.

(2) Statements "Under Penalty." A person commits a petty misdemeanor if he makes a written false statement which he does not believe to be true, on or pursuant to a form bearing notice, authorized by law, to the effect that false statements made therein are punishable.

(3) Perjury Provisions Applicable. Subsections (3) to (6) of Section 241.1 apply to the present section.

Section 241.4. False Alarms to Agencies of Public Safety.

A person who knowingly causes a false alarm of fire or other emergency to be transmitted to or within any organization, official or volunteer, for dealing with emergencies involving danger to life or property commits a misdemeanor.

Section 241.5. False Reports to Law Enforcement Authorities.

(1) Falsely Incriminating Another. A person who knowingly gives false information to any law enforcement officer with purpose to implicate another commits a misdemeanor.

(2) Fictitious Reports. A person commits a petty misdemeanor if he:

(a) reports to law enforcement authorities an offense or other incident within their concern knowing that it did not occur; or

(b) pretends to furnish such authorities with information relating to an offense or incident when he knows he has no information relating to such offense or incident.

Section 241.6. Tampering with Witnesses and Informants; Retaliation Against Them.

(1) Tampering. A person commits an offense if, believing that an official proceeding or investigation is pending or about to be instituted, he attempts to induce or otherwise cause a witness or informant to:

(a) testify or inform falsely; or

(b) withhold any testimony, information, document or thing; or

(c) elude legal process summoning him to testify or supply evidence; or

(d) absent himself from any proceeding or investigation to which he has been legally summoned. The offense is a felony of the third degree if the actor employs force, deception, threat or offer of pecuniary benefit. Otherwise it is a misdemeanor.

(2) Retaliation Against Witness or Informant. A person commits a misdemeanor if he harms another by any unlawful act in retaliation for anything lawfully done in the capacity of witness or informant.

(3) Witness or Informant Taking Bribe. A person commits a felony of the third degree if he solicits, accepts or agrees to accept any benefit in consideration of his doing any of the things specified in clauses (a) to (d) of Subsection (1).

Section 241.7. Tampering with or Fabricating Physical Evidence.

A person commits a misdemeanor if, believing that an official proceeding or investigation is pending or about to be instituted, he:

(1) alters, destroys, conceals or removes any record, document or thing with purpose to impair its verity or availability in such proceeding or investigation; or

(2) makes, presents or uses any record, document or thing knowing it to be false and with purpose to mislead a public servant who is or may be engaged in such proceeding or investigation.

Section 241.8. Tampering with Public Records or Information.

(1) Offense Defined. A person commits an offense if he:

(a) knowingly makes a false entry in, or false alteration of, any record, document or thing belonging to, or received or kept by, the government for information or record, or required by law to be kept by others for information of the government; or

(b) makes, presents or uses any record, document or thing knowing it to be false, and with purpose that it be taken as a genuine part of information or records referred to in paragraph (a); or

(c) purposely and unlawfully destroys, conceals, removes or otherwise impairs the verity or availability of any such record, document or thing.

(2) Grading. An offense under this Section is a misdemeanor unless the actor's purpose is to defraud or injure anyone, in which case the offense is a felony of the third degree.

Section 241.9. Impersonating a Public Servant.

A person commits a misdemeanor if he falsely pretends to hold a position in the public service with purpose to induce another to submit to such pretended official authority or otherwise to act in reliance upon that pretense to his prejudice.

Article 242. Obstructing Government Operations; Escapes.

Section 242.0. Definitions.

In this Article, unless another meaning plainly is required, the definitions given in Section 240.0 apply.

Section 242.1. Obstructing Administration of Law or Other Governmental Function.

A person commits a misdemeanor if he purposely obstructs, impairs or perverts the administration of law or other governmental function by force, violence, physical interference or obstacle, breach of official duty, or any other unlawful act, except that this Section does not apply to flight by a person charged with crime, refusal to submit to arrest, failure to perform a legal duty other than an official duty, or any other means of avoiding compliance with law without affirmative interference with governmental functions.

Section 242.2. Resisting Arrest or Other Law Enforcement.

A person commits a misdemeanor if, for the purpose of preventing a public servant from effecting a lawful arrest or discharging any other duty, the person creates a substantial risk of bodily injury to the public servant or anyone else, or employs means justifying or requiring substantial force to overcome the resistance.

Section 242.3. Hindering Apprehension or Prosecution.

A person commits an offense if, with purpose to hinder the apprehension, prosecution, conviction or punishment of another for crime, he:

(1) harbors or conceals the other; or

(2) provides or aids in providing a weapon, transportation, disguise or other means of avoiding apprehension or effecting escape; or

(3) conceals or destroys evidence of the crime, or tampers with a witness, informant, document or other source of information, regardless of its admissibility in evidence; or

(4) warns the other of impending discovery or apprehension, except that this paragraph does not apply to a warning given in connection with an effort to bring another into compliance with law; or

(5) volunteers false information to a law enforcement officer. The offense is a felony of the third degree if the conduct which the actor knows has been charged or is liable to be charged against the person aided would constitute a felony of the first or second degree. Otherwise it is a misdemeanor.

Section 242.4. Aiding Consummation of Crime.

A person commits an offense if he purposely aids another to accomplish an unlawful object of a crime, as by safeguarding the proceeds thereof or converting the proceeds into negotiable funds. The offense is a felony of the third degree if the principal offense was a felony of the first or second degree. Otherwise it is a misdemeanor.

Section 242.5. Compounding.

A person commits a misdemeanor if he accepts or agrees to accept any pecuniary benefit in consideration of refraining from reporting to law enforcement authorities the commission or suspected commission of any offense or information relating to an offense. It is an affirmative defense to prosecution under this Section that the pecuniary benefit did not exceed an amount which the actor believed to be due as restitution or indemnification for harm caused by the offense.

Section 242.6. Escape.

(1) Escape. A person commits an offense if he unlawfully removes himself from official detention or fails to return to official detention following temporary leave granted for a specific purpose or limited period. "Official detention" means arrest, detention in any facility for custody of persons under charge or conviction of crime or alleged or found to be delinquent, detention for extradition or deportation, or any other detention for law enforcement purposes; but "official detention" does not include supervision of probation or parole, or constraint incidental to release on bail.

(2) Permitting or Facilitating Escape. A public servant concerned in detention commits an offense if he knowingly or recklessly permits an escape. Any person who knowingly causes or facilitates an escape commits an offense.

(3) Effect of Legal Irregularity in Detention. Irregularity in bringing about or maintaining detention, or lack of jurisdiction of the committing or detaining authority, shall not be a defense to prosecution under this Section if the escape is from a prison or other custodial facility or from detention pursuant to commitment by official proceedings. In the case of other detentions, irregularity or lack of jurisdiction shall be a defense only if:

(a) the escape involved no substantial risk of harm to the person or property of anyone other than the detainee; or

(b) the detaining authority did not act in good faith under color of law.

[handwritten marginal note: Definition refers to post-detention escape.]

(4) Grading of Offenses. An offense under this Section is a felony of the third degree where:

    (a) the actor was under arrest for or detained on a charge of felony or following conviction of crime; or

    (b) the actor employs force, threat, deadly weapon or other dangerous instrumentality to effect the escape; or

    (c) a public servant concerned in detention of persons convicted of crime purposely facilitates or permits an escape from a detention facility. Otherwise an offense under this section is a misdemeanor.

Section 242.7. Implements for Escape; Other Contraband.

(1) Escape Implements. A person commits a misdemeanor if he unlawfully introduces within a detention facility, or unlawfully provides an inmate with, any weapon, tool or other thing which may be useful for escape. An inmate commits a misdemeanor if he unlawfully procures, makes, or otherwise provides himself with, or has in his possession, any such implement of escape. "Unlawfully" means surreptitiously or contrary to law, regulation or order of the detaining authority.

(2) Other Contraband. A person commits a petty misdemeanor if he provides an inmate with anything which the actor knows it is unlawful for the inmate to possess.

Section 242.8. Bail Jumping; Default in Required Appearance.

A person set at liberty by court order, with or without bail, upon condition that he will subsequently appear at a specified time and place, commits a misdemeanor if, without lawful excuse, he fails to appear at that time and place. The offense constitutes a felony of the third degree where the required appearance was to answer to a charge of felony, or for disposition of any such charge, and the actor took flight or went into hiding to avoid apprehension, trial or punishment. This Section does not apply to obligations to appear incident to release under suspended sentence or on probation or parole.

Article 243. Abuse of Office.

Section 243.0. Definitions.

In this Article, unless a different meaning plainly is required, the definitions given in Section 240.0 apply.

Section 243.1. Official Oppression.

A person acting or purporting to act in an official capacity or taking advantage of such actual or purported capacity commits a misdemeanor if, knowing that his conduct is illegal, he:

    (1) subjects another to arrest, detention, search, seizure, mistreatment, dispossession, assessment, lien or other infringement of personal or property rights; or

(2) denies or impedes another in the exercise or enjoyment of any right, privilege, power or immunity.

Section 243.2. Speculating or Wagering on Official Action or Information.

A public servant commits a misdemeanor if, in contemplation of official action by himself or by a governmental unit with which he is associated, or in reliance on information to which he has access in his official capacity and which has not been made public, he:

(1) acquires a pecuniary interest in any property, transaction or enterprise which may be affected by such information or official action; or

(2) speculates or wagers on the basis of such information or official action; or

(3) aids another to do any of the foregoing.

Offenses Against Public Order and Decency.

Article 250. Riot, Disorderly Conduct, and Related Offenses.

Section 250.1. Riot; Failure to Disperse.

(1) Riot. A person is guilty of riot, a felony of the third degree, if he participates with [two] or more others in a course of disorderly conduct:

(a) with purpose to commit or facilitate the commission of a felony or misdemeanor;

(b) with purpose to prevent or coerce official action; or

(c) when the actor or any other participant to the knowledge of the actor uses or plans to use a firearm or other deadly weapon.

(2) Failure of Disorderly Persons to Disperse Upon Official Order. Where [three] or more persons are participating in a course of disorderly conduct likely to cause substantial harm or serious inconvenience, annoyance or alarm, a peace officer or other public servant engaged in executing or enforcing the law may order the participants and others in the immediate vicinity to disperse. A person who refuses or knowingly fails to obey such an order commits a misdemeanor.

Section 250.2. Disorderly Conduct.

(1) Offense Defined. A person is guilty of disorderly conduct if, with purpose to cause public inconvenience, annoyance or alarm, or recklessly creating a risk thereof, he:

(a) engages in fighting or threatening, or in violent or tumultuous behavior; or

(b) makes unreasonable noise or offensively coarse utterance ~~ or display, or addresses abusive language to any person present; or

(c) creates a hazardous or physically offensive condition by which serves no legitimate purpose of the actor.

"Public" means affecting or likely to affect persons in a place to wh public or a substantial group has access; among the places included are hig transport facilities, schools, prisons, apartment houses, places of business or amusement, or any neighborhood.

(2) Grading. An offense under this section is a petty misdemeanor if the actor's purpose is to cause substantial harm or serious inconvenience, or if he persists in disorderly conduct after reasonable warning or request to desist. Otherwise disorderly conduct is a violation.

Section 250.3. False Public Alarms.

A person is guilty of a misdemeanor if he initiates or circulates a report or warning of an impending bombing or other crime or catastrophe, knowing that the report or warning is false or baseless and that it is likely to cause evacuation of a building, place of assembly, or facility of public transport, or to cause public inconvenience or alarm.

Section 250.4. Harassment.

A person commits a petty misdemeanor if, with purpose to harass another, he:

(1) makes a telephone call without purpose of legitimate communication; or

(2) insults, taunts or challenges another in a manner likely to provoke violent or disorderly response; or

(3) makes repeated communications anonymously or at extremely inconvenient hours, or in offensively coarse language; or

(4) subjects another to an offensive touching; or

(5) engages in any other course of alarming conduct serving no legitimate purpose of the actor.

Section 250.5. Public Drunkenness; Drug Incapacitation.

A person is guilty of an offense if he appears in any public place manifestly under the influence of alcohol, narcotics or other drug, not therapeutically administered, to the degree that he may endanger himself or other persons or property, or annoy persons in his vicinity. An offense under this Section constitutes a petty misdemeanor if the actor has been convicted hereunder twice before within a period of one year. Otherwise the offense constitutes a violation.

Section 250.6. Loitering or Prowling.

A person commits a violation if he loiters or prowls in a place, at a time, or in a manner not usual for law-abiding individuals under circumstances that warrant alarm for the safety of persons or property in the vicinity. Among the circumstances which may be considered in determining whether such alarm is warranted is the fact that the actor takes flight upon appearance of a peace officer, refuses to identify himself, or manifestly endeavors to conceal himself or any object. Unless flight by the actor or other circumstance makes it impracticable, a peace officer shall prior to any arrest for an offense under this section afford the actor an opportunity to dispel any alarm which would otherwise be warranted, by requesting him to identify himself and explain his presence and conduct. No person shall be convicted of an offense under this Section if the peace officer did not comply with the preceding sentence, or if it appears at trial that the explanation given by the actor was true and, if believed by the peace officer at the time, would have dispelled the alarm.

Section 250.7. Obstructing Highways and Other Public Passages.

(1) A person, who, having no legal privilege to do so, purposely or recklessly obstructs any highway or other public passage, whether alone or with others, commits a violation, or, in case he persists after warning by a law officer, a petty misdemeanor. "Obstructs" means renders impassable without unreasonable inconvenience or hazard. No person shall be deemed guilty of recklessly obstructing in violation of this Subsection solely because of a gathering of persons to hear him speak or otherwise communicate, or solely because of being a member of such a gathering.

(2) A person in a gathering commits a violation if he refuses to obey a reasonable official request or order to move:

(a) to prevent obstruction of a highway or other public passage; or

(b) to maintain public safety by dispersing those gathered in dangerous proximity to a fire or other hazard.

An order to move, addressed to a person whose speech or other lawful behavior attracts an obstructing audience, shall not be deemed reasonable if the obstruction can be readily remedied by police control of the size or location of the gathering.

Section 250.8. Disrupting Meetings and Processions.

A person commits a misdemeanor if, with purpose to prevent or disrupt a lawful meeting, procession or gathering, he does any act tending to obstruct or interfere with it physically, or makes any utterance, gesture or display designed to outrage the sensibilities of the group.

Section 250.9. Desecration of Venerated Objects.

A person commits a misdemeanor if he purposely desecrates any public monument or structure, or place of worship or burial, or if he purposely desecrates the national flag or any other object of veneration by the public or a substantial segment thereof in any public place. "Desecrate" means defacing, damaging, polluting or otherwise physically mistreating in a way that the actor knows will outrage the sensibilities of persons likely to observe or discover his action.

Section 250.10. Abuse of Corpse.

Except as authorized by law, a person who treats a corpse in a way th[at he] knows would outrage ordinary family sensibilities commits a misdemeanor.

Section 250.11. Cruelty to Animals.

A person commits a misdemeanor if he purposely or recklessly:

(1) subjects any animal to cruel mistreatment; or

(2) subjects any animal in his custody to cruel neglect; or

(3) kills or injures any animal belonging to another without legal privilege or consent of the owner.

Subsections (1) and (2) shall not be deemed applicable to accepted veterinary practices and activities carried on for scientific research.

Section 250.12. Violation of Privacy.

(1) Unlawful Eavesdropping or Surveillance. A person commits a misdemeanor if, except as authorized by law, he:

(a) trespasses on property with purpose to subject anyone to eavesdropping or other surveillance in a private place; or

(b) installs in any private place, without the consent of the person or persons entitled to privacy there, any device for observing, photographing, recording, amplifying or broadcasting sounds or events in such place, or uses any such unauthorized installation; or

(c) installs or uses outside a private place any device for hearing, recording, amplifying or broadcasting sounds originating in such place which would not ordinarily be audible or comprehensible outside, without the consent of the person or persons entitled to privacy there.

"Private place" means a place where one may reasonably expect to be safe from casual or hostile intrusion or surveillance, but does not include a place to which the public or a substantial group thereof has access.

(2) Other Breach of Privacy of Messages. A person commits a misdemeanor if, except as authorized by law, he:

(a) intercepts without the consent of the sender or receiver a message by telephone, telegraph, letter or other means of communicating privately; but this paragraph does not extend to (i) overhearing of messages through a regularly installed instrument on a telephone party line or on an extension, or (ii) interception by the telephone company or subscriber incident to enforcement of regulations limiting use of the facilities or incident to other normal operation and use; or

(b) divulges without the consent of the sender or receiver the existence or contents of any such message if the actor knows that the message was illegally intercepted, or if he learned of the message in the course of employment with an agency engaged in transmitting it.

Article 251. Public Indecency.

Section 251.1. Open Lewdness.

A person commits a petty misdemeanor if he does any lewd act which he knows is likely to be observed by others who would be affronted or alarmed.

Section 251.2. Prostitution and Related Offenses.

(1) Prostitution. A person is guilty of prostitution, a petty misdemeanor, if he or she:

(a) is an inmate of a house of prostitution or otherwise engages in sexual activity as a business; or

(b) loiters in or within view of any public place for the purpose of being hired to engage in sexual activity.

"Sexual activity" includes homosexual and other deviate sexual relations. A "house of prostitution" is any place where prostitution or promotion of prostitution is regularly carried on by one person under the control, management or supervision of another. An "inmate" is a person who engages in prostitution in or through the agency of a house of prostitution. "Public place" means any place to which the public or any substantial group thereof has access.

(2) Promoting Prostitution. A person who knowingly promotes prostitution of another commits a misdemeanor or felony as provided in Subsection (3). The following acts shall, without limitation of the foregoing, constitute promoting prostitution:

(a) owning, controlling, managing, supervising or otherwise keeping, alone or in association with others, a house of prostitution or a prostitution business; or

(b) procuring an inmate for a house of prostitution or a place in a house of prostitution for one who would be an inmate; or

(c) encouraging, inducing, or otherwise purposely causing another to become or remain a prostitute; or

(d) soliciting a person to patronize a prostitute; or

(e) procuring a prostitute for a patron; or

(f) transporting a person into or within this state with purpose to promote that person's engaging in prostitution, or procuring or paying for transportation with that purpose; or

(g) leasing or otherwise permitting a place controlled by the actor, alone or in association with others, to be regularly used for prostitution or the promotion of prostitution, or failure to make reasonable effort to abate such use by ejecting the tenant, notifying law enforcement authorities, or other legally available means; or

(h) soliciting, receiving, or agreeing to receive any benefit for doing or agreeing to do anything forbidden by this Subsection.

(3) Grading of Offenses Under Subsection (2). An offense under Subsection (2) constitutes a felony of the third degree if:

(a) the offense falls within paragraph (a), (b) or (c) of Subsection (2); or

(b) the actor compels another to engage in or promote prostitution; or

(c) the actor promotes prostitution of a child under 16, whether or not he is aware of the child's age; or

(d) the actor promotes prostitution of his wife, child, ward or any person for whose care, protection or support he is responsible. Otherwise the offense is a misdemeanor.

(4) *Presumption from Living off Prostitutes.* A person, other than the prostitute or the prostitute's minor child or other legal dependent incapable of self-support, who is supported in whole or substantial part by the proceeds of prostitution is presumed to be knowingly promoting prostitution in violation of Subsection (2).

(5) *Patronizing Prostitutes.* A person commits a violation if he hires a prostitute to engage in sexual activity with him, or if he enters or remains in a house of prostitution for the purpose of engaging in sexual activity.

(6) *Evidence.* On the issue whether a place is a house of prostitution the following shall be admissible evidence: its general repute; the repute of the persons who reside in or frequent the place; the frequency, timing and duration of visits by non-residents. Testimony of a person against his spouse shall be admissible to prove offenses under this Section.

Section 251.3. Loitering to Solicit Deviate Sexual Relations.

A person is guilty of a petty misdemeanor if he loiters in or near any public place for the purpose of soliciting or being solicited to engage in deviate sexual relations.

Section 251.4. Obscenity.

(1) *Obscene Defined.* Material is obscene if, considered as a whole, its predominant appeal is to prurient interest, that is, a shameful or morbid interest, in nudity, sex or excretion, and if in addition it goes substantially beyond customary limits of candor in describing or representing such matters. Predominant appeal shall be judged with reference to ordinary adults unless it appears from the character of the material or the circumstances of its dissemination to be designed for children or other specially susceptible audience. Undeveloped photographs, molds, printing plates, and the like, shall be deemed obscene notwithstanding that processing or other acts may be required to make the obscenity patent or to disseminate it.

(2) *Offenses.* Subject to the affirmative defense provided in Subsection (3), a person commits a misdemeanor if he knowingly or recklessly:

(a) sells, delivers or provides, or offers or agrees to sell, deliver or provide, any obscene writing, picture, record or other representation or embodiment of the obscene; or

(b) presents or directs an obscene play, dance or performance, or participates in that portion thereof which makes it obscene; or

(c) publishes, exhibits or otherwise makes available any obscene material; or

(d) possesses any obscene material for purposes of sale or other commercial dissemination; or

(e) sells, advertises or otherwise commercially disseminates material, whether or not obscene, by representing or suggesting that it is obscene. A person who disseminates or possesses obscene material in the course of his business is presumed to do so knowingly or recklessly.

(3) Justifiable and Non-Commercial Private Dissemination. It is an affirmative defense to prosecution under this Section that dissemination was restricted to:

(a) institutions or persons having scientific, educational, governmental or other similar justification for possessing obscene material; or

(b) non-commercial dissemination to personal associates of the actor.

(4) Evidence; Adjudication of Obscenity. In any prosecution under this Section evidence shall be admissible to show:

(a) the character of the audience for which the material was designed or to which it was directed;

(b) what the predominant appeal of the material would be for ordinary adults or any special audience to which it was directed, and what effect, if any, it would probably have on conduct of such people;

(c) artistic, literary, scientific, educational or other merits of the material;

(d) the degree of public acceptance of the material in the United States;

(e) appeal to prurient interest, or absence thereof, in advertising or other promotion of the material; and

(f) the good repute of the author, creator, publisher or other person from whom the material originated.

Expert testimony and testimony of the author, creator, publisher or other person from whom the material originated, relating to factors entering into the determination of the issue of obscenity, shall be admissible. The Court shall dismiss a prosecution for obscenity if it is satisfied that the material is not obscene.

Table of Cases

Table of Model Penal Code References

Index